# League Express

LEAGUE
Publications Ltd

# RUGBY LEAGUE
# 2019-2020
## *New beginnings*

---

League Publications Ltd

First published in Great Britain in 2019 by
League Publications Ltd, Wellington House, Briggate, Brighouse, West Yorkshire HD6 1DN

Copyright © League Publications Ltd

A CIP catalogue record for this book is available from the British Library
ISBN 978-1-901347-38-8

Designed and Typeset by League Publications Limited
Printed by H Charlesworth & Co Ltd, Wakefield

**Contributing Editor**
Tim Butcher

**Statistics, production and design**
Daniel Spencer

**Contributors**
Thomas Alderson
Robbie Andrews
Andrew Belt
Peter Bird
Ryan Booth
Aaron Bower
Steve Brady
Michael Burgess
Phil Caplan
Josh Chapman
Joseph Crabtree
Alex Davis
Joseph Eltringham
Daniel Fowler
Michael Gledhill
Ian Golden
Ryan Gould
Michael Hale
Sean Hayes
Phil Hodgson
Ash Hope
Mike Hyde
Stephen Ibbetson
Andrew Jackson
Chris Jackson
Steve Kilmartin
David Kuzio
Lorraine Marsden
Bryn May
Keith McGhie

Dave Musson
Michael Park
Dave Parkinson
Benedict Rhodes
Huw Richards
Ian Rigg
Andrew Robson
Martyn Sadler
Matthew Shaw
Steve Slater
Tom Smith
Joe Smith
Sebastian Sternik
James Stott
Harry Talbot
Doug Thomson
James Vukmirovic
Callum Walker
Gareth Walker
John Walsh
Jordan Weir
Adam Whiteside
Gavin Wilson
Ian Wilson
Peter Wilson

**Pictures**
Steve Gaunt
Magi Haroun
Richard Long
SWPix
Matthew Merrick
NRL Imagery
Craig Milner
Dean Williams
Mark Cosgrove
Craig Cresswell
Steve Jones/RLPix
David Greaves
Simon Hall
Craig Hawkhead
Paul Clayton
Prime Images
Richard Land
Catalans Dragons
Dave Jessop
Mal Walker
Melanie Allatt
Alex Coleman
Brian King
Steve McCormick
Steve Miller
Tom Pearson
Bernard Platt
Bernard Rieu
John Rushworth
Pete Smith
Ken Sparks
Craig Thomas

**Main cover picture**
SWPix

# CONTENTS

# ACKNOWLEDGEMENTS

The *League Express Yearbook 2019-2020* is the 24th of League Publications Ltd's annual series of Rugby League Yearbooks, which began in the first year of Super League in 1996.

This historical record of the Rugby League year would not be possible without the hard work and dedication of all the contributors to *Rugby Leaguer & Rugby League Express, Rugby League World* magazine and the totalrl.com website.

We are able to include some wonderful action photography provided by, in particular Steve Gaunt, Magi Haroun, Richard Long, SWPix, Matthew Merrick, NRL Imagery, Craig Milner, Dean Williams, Mark Cosgrove, Craig Cresswell and Steve Jones at RLPix.

Thanks to the Rugby Football League for their help during the year and to the historians and statisticians at clubs who help us resolve any anomalies.

Acknowledgement also to the *Rothmans Yearbook 1999*, compiled by our late friend Ray Fletcher, the *British Rugby Records Book* from London Publications and to the club officials, and some supporters, who helped us verify records.

Thanks also to Opta Sportdata, who compile the Opta Index Analysis in our statistical section.

Special thanks to Matthew Shaw, Lorraine Marsden and Alex Davis, who respectively wrote the Championship, League 1 and NRL sections.

The comprehensive statistical review is once again magnificent, compiled, as always, by Daniel Spencer, who also designed the book.

**TIM BUTCHER**
**Contributing Editor**

# INTRODUCTION

How will the Rugby League year of 2019 be remembered?

It was the year of league games being decided by golden-point extra-time. For the first time, we didn't have any draws, all season, with seven games decided by extra-time field goals. We also had the shot clock for the formation of scrums and goal-line drop-outs, with a noticeable speeding up of the game. Structure-wise, the middle-eights system was ditched after three years, with one up-one down back in, along with top-five play-offs.

We had four-time Super League champions Bradford Bulls, now in the Championship, performing a giant-killing act over Leeds Rhinos in the Challenge Cup before imploding financially once again and moving out of their famous Odsal home ground.

We saw Toronto Wolfpack earn the right to play in Super League after an all-conquering season in the Championship.

And despite a lacklustre tour by Great Britain at the end of the season, we marvelled at the emergence of Tonga into the top tier of international Rugby League in the context of a new Oceania Cup designed to aid the progression of Pacific Island nations.

Of course, there was as always political problems. Tonga's players fell out with their governing body and had to call themselves Tongan Invitational XIII. Lebanon's players threatened a boycott after a similar disagreement. France was in a similar quandary in the autumn.

And the year opened with the possibility that Catalans Dragons would not defend their Challenge Cup because the Rugby Football League was demanding a half-million pound bond from overseas teams. Thankfully a compromise was reached, though Toulouse and Toronto were not in the 2019 competition.

One change welcomed by most people was to see the last of the energy-sapping two-round Easter schedule.

We also saw the last seasons of some Super League stalwarts. Leeds fans said goodbye to Jamie-Jones Buchanan and Carl Ablett. Warrington's Ben Westwood also called it quits.

Another Leeds great, Danny McGuire also called time on a glorious playing career after two seasons at Hull KR. His generalship of Rovers' 32-16 victory at Headingley in Round 22, on his 400th Super League appearance, was one of the memorable moments of the year.

The Magic Weekend was switched to Anfield in Liverpool but the turnout wasn't great and was due to head back to Newcastle in 2020.

People will remember 2019 in different ways of course. It will be recalled fondly by St Helens supporters for sure. In 2018 they had seen their team dominate the league season and win the League Leaders Shield, only to fall at the penultimate games in both the Super League and the Challenge Cup.

Despite the disappointment of losing the Wembley final to arch-rivals Warrington, in 2019 that proved to be only a stutter for a multi-talented side steered brilliantly by coach Justin Holbrook. The performance in their Qualification Semi-final win over Wigan to reach the Grand Final was immense and they went on, two weeks later, to win the ultimate prize.

Unsurprisingly, Saints cleaned up the end-of-season awards, with Jonny Lomax winning the Albert Goldthorpe Medal; Matty Lees the Super League young player of the year, Holbrook the coach of the year and Tommy Makinson finishing as top try-scorer. They had five players in the Super League Dream Team.

Holbrook decided to take up the massive challenge at Gold Coast Titans for 2020 and he will be revered in the town of St Helens for many years to come.

The one big individual prize that St Helens didn't win was the Steve Prescott Man of Steel, which was picked up by Salford Red Devils halfback Jackson Hastings. That award, decided on a points-per-match basis for the first time, following the lead of the Albert Goldthorpe award, showed just how perceptive Rugby League supporters are, Hastings being voted the best newcomer in the League Express readers poll at the end of 2018, despite playing only six games for Salford.

Hastings was the leading player in 2019's biggest fairytale, the story of Salford's march to the Grand Final. They found Saints too good for them on the big night but there could be no taking away from the Red Devils' achievement, after they started the season among the also-rans. Even when they began to show some real form, they lost star turn Robert Lui in a mid-season transfer to Leeds, as well as knowing a raft of their players, including Hastings, would be leaving at the end of the season. Coached expertly by Ian Watson, they hardly missed a beat from then on in.

Warrington couldn't kick on from their magnificent 18-4 Challenge Cup Final win over St Helens, losing seven out of their last eight league games around the Wembley showcase before being edged by Castleford in the Elimination Play-off. But their day of glory at Wembley, with Daryl Clark winning the Lance Todd Trophy, was one to savour.

Wigan's season was a testament to the resilience of the club amongst some trying circumstances. Big names Sam Tomkins, John Bateman and Ryan Sutton were gone from the 2018 Championship-winning team. Some supporters were demanding the sacking of coach Adrian Lam following nine losses from their opening 12 games, including a 20-8 home defeat by the Sydney Roosters in the World Club Challenge.

Around then, Wigan fans learned that Shaun Edwards would not be coming to be head coach in 2020 and the contracts of overseas props Gabe Hamlin and Taulima Tautai were both terminated mid-season.

Credit to Lam. Up stepped a raft of junior products, with three of them - Albert Goldthorpe Rookie of the Year Morgan Smithies, Oliver Partington and Liam Byrne - not only cementing first team spots in the pack, but regularly getting the better of more experienced opponents. A run of just one loss in 13 games saw Wigan soar up the table and take almost everyone but themselves by surprise, removing Warrington from the second spot they had occupied for most of the season.

Castleford also had a tricky 2019. The season-ending Achilles injury to Luke Gale in pre-season had them on the back foot from the off, though the progression of Jake Trueman in an often injury-hit side persuaded the Tigers to let Gale go to Leeds for 2020. A superb 14-12 victory over Warrington at the Halliwell Jones Stadium in the Elimination Play-off set up an Elimination semi-final at Salford, where a 22-0 defeat ended their season.

Hull FC only dropped out of the play-offs in their second-to-last game, following their defeat by fellow challengers Castleford. Their season had begun with a bang as, after losing their first two games, the Airlie Birds registered seven victories in nine games to consolidate their position in the top five. From then, they were brilliant one week and dreadful the next. A 63-12 home hammering by Warrington was followed by a 23-16 victory over Salford, whilst a 55-2 thrashing by Huddersfield at the Magic Weekend was followed by a 51-8 triumph against Catalans.

Rugby League gained new ground in May with then high-flying Catalans Dragons'

## Introduction

33-16 victory over Wigan at Barcelona's Camp Nou in front of a record regular-season Super League crowd of 31,555. But the Dragons then suffered a slide, with just four victories in their last 15 games sending them hurtling down the table.

Leeds had high hopes going into the 2019 season following the capture of marquee signings Trent Merrin and Konrad Hurrell and Tongan playmaker Tui Lolohea. But coach David Furner, with only four victories under his belt in 14 league games, was shown the door in May. His assistant Richard Agar took over as interim coach with the Rhinos third-from-bottom and in real danger of slipping out of the top-flight for the first time. Agar helped steady it with eight victories in 15 games steering Leeds into eighth position and got the gig permanently.

The relegation battle provided a thrilling denouement on the last Friday of the regular season, with four clubs on 20 points in the mix to be relegated. By the end of the night, London Broncos went back down after a one-season spell in Super League after a 19-10 defeat at Wakefield, who they had beaten twice at home in 2019. Hull KR were thankful of that as they stayed up only on points difference after a golden-point defeat at Salford. The fourth side involved, Huddersfield Giants, just edged a home game with Catalans to secure their place in the top flight.

Danny Ward-coached London had been given hardly a chance by pundits and fans alike as they went into their first Super League season since 2014. But the 20 points they managed to accumulate in 2019 was their greatest haul at the top level since 2009.

Hull KR coach Tim Sheens was replaced by two-time Grand Final and three-time Challenge Cup winner Tony Smith in early June. With five wins from his last 12 games, Smith just managed to steer the Robins clear of the relegation trapdoor.

Huddersfield and Wakefield went backwards. The Giants' fifth-placed finish of 2018 had promised much and Trinity were tipped as play-off contenders in 2019. Both had more than their share of injuries, with Trinity losing 2018 Dream Team members Tom Johnstone, Bill Tupou and Matty Ashurst to long-term injury.

The full details of the 2019 Rugby League season are contained in the next 300 or so pages. Read on.

**TIM BUTCHER**
**Contributing Editor**

*The 24th League Express Yearbook contains the full story of the domestic year, the Australian season and match facts for all Super League, Challenge Cup games involving professional teams, Championship and League 1 games. Every player who has played Super League is also listed along with those players to have made their debuts this year. We have also selected five individuals who we judge to have made the biggest impact on Rugby League in 2019. There are scoring and attendance records for every club as well as League wide records. A full record of the 2019 Great Britain tour is also detailed.*

*League Publications publishes the weekly newspaper Rugby Leaguer & Rugby League Express, as well as the monthly glossy magazine Rugby League World and the UK's most popular League website 'totalrl.com'.*

# 1
# THE 2019 SEASON

# DECEMBER 2018
## *Tommy who?*

---

England's series win over New Zealand led to an off-season of relative, if not total, calm and great anticipation ahead of the 24th season of Super League.

England's reputation had risen, as had those of many homegrown players, none more so than St Helens' winger Tommy Makinson who, on the back of three superb performances in the white shirt, had been awarded the Golden Boot by the Rugby League International Federation (RLIF).

The selection caused a bit of a stir down under, sparking the likes of Brad Fittler into public comment, with the former Kangaroos stand-off claiming he hadn't even heard of the St Helens winger.

The controversy arose because the award's criteria had been changed, by the RLIF. From 1984 to 2016, the Golden Boot, inaugurated by Open Rugby magazine, which changed its name to Rugby League World in 1998, crowned a player as the best in the world based on both club and representative performances. The RLIF purchased the Boot in 2017 from League Publications Limited and it was now awarded to the best performer in international matches only.

The award took into consideration all Test matches from the 2017 World Cup Final to the second Test between England and New Zealand in 2018. The third Test was to be counted towards the 2019 award. Under that criterion, Makinson was a clear winner.

England's international upward curve was confirmed in early December when the England Academy, captained by Hull FC centre Cameron Scott, beat the once-all-conquering Australian Combined High Schools in both Tests, winning at Leigh Sports Village 14-8 before, a week later, emerging 18-6 winners at Headingley.

A row broke out after the Rugby Football League (RFL) demanded a bond in the region of £750,000 to accept Toronto or Toulouse's entry into the Challenge Cup. RFL officials decided to take action after suffering a significant financial blow as a result of the low attendance at the 2018 final between Catalans and Warrington. While the event didn't record a loss, the attendance, the lowest for a Cup final since 1945, did see the governing body miss out on significant projected income.

But the decision was met with anger from many people within the game, including Toronto director of rugby Brian Noble. 'I'm disappointed for our players who want to be in the Challenge Cup and our fans, who would like us to compete against the best,' he said. 'I'm gutted not to be in the Cup.'

Under the proposal, Toronto and Toulouse would have forfeited the bond if they made the final but would have received part of that figure back in accordance with the number of tickets they sold for the event.

The RFL issued a statement in which they admitted the absence of the two clubs was a 'significant source of regret' but necessary.

There was also much confusion over the formation of a reserve competition. It was reported that all 14 Super League clubs attended a meeting where all-but one - Leeds Rhinos, who were happy that the dual-registration/partnership was the best player-development vehicle - supported reserve grade. Ten of those teams were understood to have backed the launch of a formal competition in 2019, before reserve teams were made mandatory again in 2020.

But by the end of the year most of them had performed a U-turn. Hull FC and Wakefield were the only Super League teams that would run reserve sides in 2019, along with a handful of Championship sides. Hull chief executive James Clark argued in vain that clubs should only be allowed to sign high-earning overseas players if they ticked several other boxes, including running a reserve side.

Former Man of Steel Zak Hardaker, signed by Wigan while in the middle of a ban for cocaine use whilst at Castleford, received a drink-driving ban in October, two days before the 2018 Grand Final.

Hardaker continued to have the Wigan club's full support, according to new coach Adrian Lam, who believed it was his and the Warriors' responsibility to ensure the controversial fullback could finally banish his demons. Hardaker was admitted to the Sporting Chance rehabilitation clinic and was expected to commence training with the Warriors at the beginning of December.

Wigan Rugby Director Kris Radlinski confirmed the club didn't have plans for another overseas trip in 2019 (Wigan played Hull FC in Wollongong and South Sydney at the ANZ Stadium in 2018) although they had been approached by a number of cities.

However, on the back of Catalans' Challenge Cup win it was announced that the Dragons would play their Super League fixture against Wigan in May at Camp Nou, Barcelona FC's 100,000 capacity stadium, one of the most famous arenas in world sport, the first ever Rugby League game at the venue.

One of the Warriors' out-and-out stars of 2018, John Bateman, headed Down Under knowing he was a hit with League Express readers. The England forward, who joined Canberra Raiders, was named Player of the Year in the newspaper's annual Readers' Poll.

Wigan weren't too active on the player recruitment front, their one notable signing being the much-travelled Jarrod Sammut. The former London halfback completed a shock move to the defending Super League champions, signing a two-year deal. Sammut had played a huge part in the Broncos' promotion from the Championship but had to leave the club for personal reasons and re-locate to the north of England.

The Broncos were, for obvious reasons, in the market to strengthen their squad, signing centre Ryan Morgan from St Helens on loan for the entire 2019 season, along with Sheffield Eagles' Matty Fozard, prop from Leigh Greg Richards, both products of the St Helens Academy, and prop Nathan Mason, released by Huddersfield Giants.

They also snared Hull FC stand-off Jordan Abdull on a one-year contract, after the utility handed in a transfer request at the KCOM Stadium.

Salford coach Ian Watson labelled Australian winger Ken Sio an 'outstanding' signing. The 28-year-old former Hull KR player penned a three-year contract after spending the last two seasons in the NRL with Newcastle Knights. Sio scored 26 tries for Rovers over the 2015 and 2016 Super League campaigns and had crossed 17 times in 41 games for the Knights.

Adam Walker and Gil Dudson would also be Salford Red Devils players in 2019. The props both agreed deals in the wake of Craig Kopczak's departure to Wakefield. Fellow prop Lama Tasi also departed, with Salford receiving fees from both Trinity and Warrington respectively.

Walker was currently serving a drugs ban. He had been suspended in 2017 after making just seven appearances for Wakefield, who were interested in re-signing him before turning their attention solely to Kopczak. Walker was given a 20-month suspension from all sport for testing positive for cocaine after a Super League game against Widnes, backdated to 14th July 2017, the date of the test, meaning Walker could return to action on 13th March 2019.

The Red Devils had also managed to keep hold of halfback Jackson Hastings, for at least another year. Hastings was named the best overseas newcomer in the end-of-year

League Express Readers' Poll, despite only playing six games at the end of the season.

Wakefield's biggest move of the off-season saw the return of 35-year-old halfback Danny Brough, in a swap with Trinity fullback Scott Grix. Grix was set for a second stint with the Giants after Huddersfield contacted Wakefield about his availability, with a view to him joining their coaching staff, though it was unclear whether the Ireland international would continue to play on.

Trinity coach Chris Chester said he was happy and settled after signing a new three-year contract with Wakefield.

The Giants replaced Brough with Canterbury Bulldogs' 23-year-old halfback Matt Frawley on a two-year deal and also signed flying Fiji international winger Akuila Uate as they promised to build on their excellent late-season form in 2018 under coach Simon Woolford.

Catalans Dragons were another side aiming higher and confirmed Widnes back-rower Matt Whitley as their latest signing. The highly-rated 22-year-old, who toured with England Knights, signed a two-year contract with the Perpignan club after the relegation of the Vikings.

Wigan fullback Sam Tomkins and St Helens scrum-half Matty Smith had also been recruited for 2019.

Warrington finished runners-up in 2018 and were expected to be even stronger in 2019. The Wolves had brought in NRL stars Blake Austin, the Canberra halfback, and South Sydney forward Jason Clark, Kiwi forward Lama Tasi from Salford and back-rower Matt Davis from London Broncos. And they added Widnes's 19-year-old hooker Danny Walker, who was born in Warrington and came through the Widnes development system.

Ben Westwood would continue to be the oldest player in Super League for at least one more season after signing a new one-year contract for the 2019 season.

Former England captain Jamie Peacock departed his position as Hull KR's head of rugby after three years, heading back to Headingley to join the commercial department. The 40-year-old former Bradford and Leeds forward's role became part-time following the arrival two years before of head coach Tim Sheens, under whom Rovers returned to Super League in 2017 and maintained their top-flight status in 2018.

New Hull KR halfback Josh Drinkwater said the chance to work under Sheens helped lure him to Humberside. The 26-year-old Australian spent the bulk of the previous season at Catalans Dragons, kicking four goals to help them beat Warrington 20-14 to lift the Challenge Cup at Wembley. Drinkwater signed a one-year contract, which was made possible by the Rovers Supporters Group. Drinkwater was to be joined at KCOM Craven Park by Leeds prop Mitch Garbutt.

Meanwhile the Robins were hoping to be able to move back into the KCOM Craven Park early in the New Year after the collapse of a floodlighting pylon in high winds.

Castleford starlet Jake Trueman told League Express that the Jungle was the only place in which he saw his long-term future after agreeing a bumper new deal with the club. The highly-rated 19-year-old, who was named Super League's Young Player of the Year and Albert Goldthorpe Rookie of the Year in 2018, signed a new four-year extension with the Tigers to the end of the 2022 campaign.

Leeds Rhinos were also out to improve on their ninth-placed finish, signing two marquee players in Tongan centre Konrad Hurrell on a three-year deal and Australian international prop Trent Merrin, who penned a four-year contract.

The Rhinos had also signed former Kiwi international Tui Lolohea from Wests Tigers and he shone in the annual Boxing Day game against Wakefield, back at Headingley in front of the fully opened new South Stand, which was packed to the rafters.

Leeds won 10-4 as Lolohea masterminded a last-quarter revival, his wicked, bouncing kick eluding Lee Kershaw for Tom Briscoe to pounce, before his silky hands released Ash Handley on the left for the winning try.

In other Boxing Day games, a youthful Castleford side hammered neighbours Featherstone Rovers 56-0 and Batley won the Heavy Woollen derby 16-10.

# JANUARY
## *Cup confusion*

The year 2019 opened with the news that Catalans Dragons, who had made history the August before at Wembley by winning the Challenge Cup, were set to pull out of the competition, after they refused to pay a deposit of £500,000 demanded by the Rugby Football League to participate.

Toronto Wolfpack and Toulouse Olympique had already withdrawn from the 2019 competition when hit with the deposit request in November. The RFL claimed Catalans initially agreed to pay up, only to make a U-turn in December.

Wigan rugby director Kris Radlinski was one of many to voice his dismay. The Warriors were due to benefit directly from the Dragons' Challenge Cup win the previous year, having been invited to play at the iconic Nou Camp after Catalans were offered the chance to take a game to Barcelona following their victory at Wembley. 'I find it absolutely staggering, if I'm honest,' Radlinski told League Express.

The £500,000 deposit for non-English teams to take part would only be retained by the RFL were any team lodging it to reach the final. Catalans became the first club from outside England to win the sport's oldest trophy when they beat Warrington in the 2018 final. But the 50,672 crowd was Wembley's lowest for a Challenge Cup final since the second world war, with only around 1,800 tickets having been sold in France.

Before the end of the month the two parties reached a compromise. The Dragons would still lodge a bond with the RFL, significantly reduced from the amount the governing body had demanded.

**CORAL CHALLENGE CUP - ROUND 1**

*Saturday 26th January 2019*
Bentley 18 The Army 16
Bradford Dudley Hill 0 Milford Marlins 16
Clock Face Miners 0 Siddal 24
Dewsbury Moor 24 Skirlaugh 10
Distington 48 Torfaen Tigers 0
Drighlington 32 Gloucestershire All Golds 4
East Leeds 24 Batley Boys 10
Hunslet Club Parkside 16 Thornhill Trojans 30
Hunslet Warriors 16 Featherstone Lions 28
Kells 4 Rochdale Mayfield 14
Leigh East 12 Wigan St Patricks 24
Leigh Miners Rangers 22 Oulton Raiders 10
London Chargers 6 Wath Brow Hornets 34
Normanton Knights 50 Edinburgh Eagles 16
Orrell St James 12 Underbank Rangers 30
Ovenden 22 Woolston Rovers 20
Royal Navy 12 West Hull 42
Shaw Cross Sharks 18 Haydock 28
Thatto Heath Crusaders 32 Stanningley 6
Wallsend Eagles 18 Great Britain Police 44
West Bowling 42 Hammersmith Hills Hoists 12
Wigan St Judes 15 Crosfields 14
York Acorn 42 Beverley 4

*Sunday 27th January 2019*
Lock Lane 16 Longhorns 10
Millom 38 Red Star Belgrade 10
North Herts Crusaders 6 Royal Air Force 22

**CORAL CHALLENGE CUP - ROUND 2**

*Saturday 9th February 2019*
Distington 14 Royal Air Force 6
Drighlington 16 Wigan St Judes 20
East Leeds 16 Dewsbury Moor 20
Milford Marlins 22 Lock Lane 28
Millom 0 Siddal 26
Normanton Knights 22 Haydock 32
Ovenden 18 West Bowling 38
Thatto Heath Crusaders 36 Leigh Miners Rangers 6
Thornhill Trojans 20 Rochdale Mayfield 30
Underbank Rangers 26 Featherstone Lions 30
Wath Brow Hornets 8 York Acorn 9
West Hull 36 Bentley 0

*Sunday 10th February 2019*
Wigan St Patricks 28 Great Britain Police 20

That was just in time for the RFL to announce a new two-year, seven-figure sponsorship deal for the Challenge Cup and the Women's Challenge Cup with bookmakers Coral. The competition began on the last weekend of January, with 26 first-round ties. Red Star Belgrade, who didn't have to lodge a bond, entered the competition for the first time. They were eliminated at the first stage by Cumbrian amateurs Millom.

Super League boss Robert Elstone revealed that the body was considering

15

Zak Hardaker takes on Ben Nakubuwai during Wigan's pre-season clash with Salford

increasing the number of marquee players from two per club to three, although he reflected that might affect the openness of the competition, which in 2019 was shaping up to be highly unpredictable.

Warrington Wolves chief executive Karl Fitzpatrick said he would like to see more clubs use the marquee player provisions before an increase in the allowance was considered. The Wolves only had one marquee player in former Canberra stand-off Blake Austin. But they were to add another for 2020 in England stand-off Gareth Widdop, who Fitzpatrick hailed as the club's biggest-ever signing.

The Wolves won the race to sign the St George-Illawarra stand-off for the next season, agreeing a three-year deal with Widdop after he expressed his desire to test himself in Super League before the end of his career.

Austin played his first game in Warrington colours in Ryan Atkins' testimonial and was hugely influential in helping his side to a 38-12 win over Widnes, in which he scored a try and set up a number of others. He was already favourite to lift the Man of Steel award at the end of the season.

A former Man of Steel, Castleford halfback Luke Gale, was ruled out for the season after rupturing his Achilles tendon in training. Gale suffered a fractured kneecap early in 2018 which, although he briefly returned midway through the year, ruined his season.

It was a major blow for the Tigers, who were granted salary cap relief in order to sign a replacement for their star man. In 2015, clubs agreed that exemptions to the salary cap could be made if a player suffered a season-ending injury prior to the start of the season.

Castleford were in no rush to sign a big-money replacement and instead completed a transfer deal with Huddersfield. The Giants' utility back Jordan Rankin swapped clubs with Tigers forward Joe Wardle on an initial loan arrangement.

Three weeks later, Warrington vice-captain Kevin Brown suffered the same injury on the training ground. The 34-year-old former England halfback was also expected to out for the season.

Another Warrington halfback, youngster Morgan Smith, signed for London Broncos in the search for first-team rugby. The 20-year-old signed a one-year deal with Danny Ward's side.

St Helens were one of the pre-season favourites and were boosted by the return of prop Alex Walmsley, who had been out of the game for ten months with a neck injury. Saints also agreed new contracts with two other props in Matty Lees and Louie McCarthy-Scarsbrook. Rochdale Mayfield product Lees enjoyed a breakout season in 2018, making 19 appearances for his club before shining on the England Knights' tour of Papua New Guinea.

Zak Hardaker warned he was a long way from returning to the top of his game after making his Rugby League comeback. The controversial fullback made his first appearance in the game for 16 months, marking the occasion with a try and four goals as the reigning Super League Champions beat Salford 28-18 in a friendly at the AJ Bell Stadium. Hardaker said it might take years for the Rugby League public to ever believe he was a reformed character after his struggles with cocaine and alcohol and attention deficit hyperactivity disorder (ADHD).

Kallum Watkins also made his return from almost eight months out with a serious knee injury, scoring a try in his testimonial game, the Rhinos' pre-season match against Castleford at Headingley. The Tigers edged the game 26-24.

The Rhinos handed a one-year contract to forward James Donaldson who had impressed on a month's trial at Leeds after having been released by Hull KR.

The Robins named former Wigan forward Joel Tomkins as the club's new captain, with the playing future of Shaun Lunt still uncertain. At the end of 2018, the club skipper faced the toughest battle of his life after he contracted bacterial meningitis, and was still on the road to recovery.

*A raft of law changes were made for the 2019 season, copying successful innovations in the NRL.*

**SHOT CLOCK**
- Teams would have 35 seconds to form a scrum and 30 seconds to take goal-line drop-outs.
- Kickers had 80 seconds to kick goals, any penalty for a breach would be post-match.

**GOLDEN POINT**
- If scores were level at end of 80 minutes, five minutes each way of extra-time, ended by first score.

**INTERCHANGE**
- Reduced from ten to eight from four substitutes.

**LAST FIVE MINUTES**
- Referee to call 'time off' after conversion or when ball went out of play after a penalty or field-goal attempt.

**FREE PLAY**
- Ditched. Referee to decide if team had gained an advantage from a handling error.

# FEBRUARY
## *Golden-point history*

---

**Round 1**

Super League XXIV kicked off on the first weekend of February, although the first game of the opening round came on the last day of the previous month as St Helens hosted reigning champions Wigan on a freezing cold night in south Lancashire.

The weather played no part as the two great rivals produced a rip-roaring game that St Helens deserved to win, eventually by 22-12. Wigan staged an impressive first-half fightback, coming from 12-0 down to draw level at the break. But they were unable to get the decisive breakthrough in the second half, thanks to some magnificent defence from Saints.

St Helens had three former NRL debutants, with centre Kevin Naiqama making his mark with a try within two minutes, alongside Lachlan Coote and Joseph Paulo. And prop Alex Walmsley was huge after missing the bulk of 2018 with a neck injury. Coach Justin Holbrook picked Theo Fages in preference to 2018 ever-present Danny Richardson and the French international played a starring role.

Wigan handed two debuts of their own, with Zak Hardaker making a solid first Super League appearance in over 16 months. And he was joined by arguably the story of the night, with former Barrow prop Joe Bullock turning in a huge display off the bench for the Warriors after they lost Tony Clubb to concussion in the first half.

Played at a notably higher speed with the shot clock in operation for the first time, the action was relentless, with significantly fewer stoppages. Fiji international Naiqama brushed off Dan Sarginson one-on-one to give Saints the lead and they extended their lead through a well-worked try to Jonny Lomax 13 minutes later. A break through the middle from Dominique Peyroux on halfway found the England international in support and Lomax stepped the cover to score to the left of the posts.

But there was no doubting that Wigan's resilience of past seasons would continue under new coach Adrian Lam as they levelled by half-time. Ben Flower latched onto a flat pass to drive over next to the posts before, four minutes out from the break, Liam Marshall intercepted a rushed pass from Coote and raced the length of the field to lock things up.

After such a high quality first half, the second started in exceptional fashion as Regan Grace produced a diving, one-handed finish in the left corner, the try awarded by the video referee, to edge Saints back in front.

With the contest delicately poised entering the final ten minutes, it needed a gamebreaking moment to determine the victor and it came from Saints skipper James Roby.

Fresh from announcing a new three-year deal with the club, the England international spotted the slightest of chinks in the Wigan defence and burrowed over the line from dummy-half with five minutes to go.

The following night's TV game was played out in front of a record crowd at KCOM Craven Park and the finish couldn't have been closer as Jimmy Keinhorst marked his

Robins debut in perfect fashion, scoring a last-minute try to ensure Tim Sheens' side registered an 18-16 victory over cross-city rivals Hull FC.

Keinhorst's try came from a desperate Josh Drinkwater bomb on the last play of the game that was palmed back by Ben Crooks to Danny Addy, who fed Danny McGuire, for him to give the scoring pass to Keinhorst. The video referee confirmed the former Leeds man had got the ball down just before his foot drifted into touch in Bureta Faraimo's desperate tackle.

After a tight second half, Faraimo's bulldozing finish edged his side into a slender lead with just under 13 minutes to play and it looked as though it would be the Black and White side of the city celebrating the early bragging rights.

But Hull KR, with Keinhorst, Josh Drinkwater, Kane Linnett, Weller Hauraki and the outstanding Mitch Garbutt on debut showed great resilience, epitomised by Crooks, who dragged Josh Griffin back from the line four minutes from time to keep Rovers in the game.

Hull FC had shot into a 12-0 lead after 18 minutes through tries to Sika Manu and debutant Matty Dawson-Jones. Marc Sneyd converted both tries but missed a penalty before Rovers came back with Joel Tomkins and Garbutt tries converted by Drinkwater, who edged them in front by half-time with a penalty goal.

But without injured Albert Kelly and Jake Connor, suspended for one game for dissent in the pre-season game at St Helens, they couldn't find a creative spark until Fairamo was given half a chance down the left.

There was another bumper crowd the following evening as Warrington beat Leeds comfortably, by 26-6, at the Halliwell Jones Stadium.

Declan Patton featured alongside marquee signing Blake Austin in the halves after Kevin Brown's season-ending training injury, with former South Sydney forward Jason Clark and Widnes youngster Danny Walker also making Wolves debuts.

The Rhinos fielded marquee players Konrad Hurrell and Trent Merrin, with Tuimoala Lolohea and James Donaldson also making debuts. But they were well beaten by a Wolves side who won just about every contact and off-loaded with abandon. The sin-binnings of Jack Hughes and Toby King probably kept the score respectable for Leeds.

Austin produced an eye-catching debut that culminated in a smart second-half try after an interchange of passes with King, playing in the second row with great effect. That gave new life to Stefan Ratchford. Both he and non-stop hooker Daryl Clark also scored tries, Josh Charnley getting another, while out wide, Bryson Goodwin was by some distance the best centre on display, regularly swatting defenders off.

The Rhinos eventually did grab a consolation score when Stevie Ward forced his way over, with Lolohea adding the conversion.

King took a one-match penalty notice for his spear tackle on Stevie Ward, while Ben Westwood got two matches after the Match Review Panel judged he had made dangerous contact in an early tackle on Hurrell.

On the Friday night, Paul McShane guided Castleford to a hard-earned 20-4 home win over Catalans.

The Tigers, without scrum-half Luke Gale for the season with an Achilles tendon injury, had on-loan Jordan Rankin on debut in his place, and mercurial youngster Jake Trueman at stand-off.

Most interest in the Dragons centred on the debuts of Sam Tomkins, Matty Smith and Matt Whitley. Tomkins, the marquee signing from Wigan, operated at fullback but spent much of a bitterly cold evening, which was flavoured with flurries of snow, seeking to unlock a Castleford defence that was resolute throughout.

Tony Gigot, selected at stand-off by Catalans coach Steve McNamara, was the key danger-man for the Dragons in a game in which the Tigers prevailed because of a monumental defensive effort midway through the first half. The Catalans, who badly missed the injured Greg Bird and Michael McIlorum, were kept at bay despite enjoying sustained pressure through three successive penalties - all for holding down - three goal-line drop-outs and Gigot's 40/20. But Castleford, regardless, somehow carved out a 12-0 interval lead, which, in conditions that had put the fixture under threat, always looked like being enough to deny the Dragons.

McShane got the first try and Greg Eden the other, with McShane kicking both goals and then potting a penalty seven minutes after the break. A well-worked Lewis Tierney try 15 minutes from time gave the Dragons hope but Eden's dive into the left corner with four minutes left on the clock sealed the home win.

Salford were one of the unfancied teams going into the new season but they turned a few heads with a convincing 34-14 win at Huddersfield on the same night.

A hat-trick of tries and an assist saw Niall Evalds rightly claim the individual accolades but it was much more than a one-man show. Props Lee Mossop, who played over an hour in the front row, and Gil Dudson, one of two debutants alongside double-try-scorer Ken Sio, both impressed.

Huddersfield's two NRL signings, Matt Frawley and Akuila Uate didn't shine, though Uate's try converted by Izaac Farrell brought the scores level at 8-8 four minutes after the break. But after that it was all Salford amid some slick handling, with halfback Jackson Hastings playing a key role.

In mitigation, the Giants were missing Jermaine McGillvary, Leroy Cudjoe, Lee Gaskell, Paul Clough, Aaron Murphy, Dale Ferguson, Tom Holmes, Colton Roche and Jake Wardle through injury, with Ukuma Ta'ai unavailable because of a visa mix-up.

Only one club's chances had been rated lower than the Red Devils pre season and that was London Broncos, whose promotion in 2018 had taken the game by surprise. But they astounded just about everybody when they overturned Wakefield Trinity in Ealing on the Sunday afternoon. Their 42-24 win was all the more eye-popping after they trailed 12-0 and then 18-6 after 25 minutes.

Former Hull FC young gun Jordan Abdull excelled on debut at stand-off, while captain Jay Pitts was imperious on the edges. But London's star was former Sheffield Eagles forward Eddie Battye, who scored two tries and was a destructive influence all afternoon.

In the 15 minutes before half-time the Broncos scored four tries through Rhys Williams, Kieran Dixon, Battye and Matty Fozard to lead 26-18.

When Kyle Wood forced his way over and Danny Brough goaled on 53 minutes Trinity were expected to go on and win it. But the Broncos were having none of it as Williams and Battye grabbed their braces and Elliot Kear finished it off with three minutes to go. By then Brough was in the sin bin after questioning a decision.

After the first round, Super League sponsor Betfred had St Helens at 11/4 favourites to win the Grand Final at Old Trafford on October 12th with the Wolves second favourites at 7/2 and Wigan moving out to 11/2. The Rhinos went out to 6/1, with Castleford on their heels at 7/1.

**Round 2**

Competition favourites St Helens were made to work hard for a 24-18 win at Wakefield on the Sunday afternoon of round two, with Louie McCarthy-Scarsbrook's try two minutes from time eventually proving to be the difference between the two sides.

Trinity responded from their humbling at London the week before with a performance full of desire, effort and endeavour, despite losing prop Craig Huby on the stroke of half-time and Danny Kirmond soon after the restart with injury.

Saints took the lead, after Mark Percival's early try was ruled out for a double movement, when Morgan Knowles crashed over on the angle. Wakefield were under the cosh when Danny Brough was sin-binned eight minutes later for dissent - for the second successive game. But by the time he returned on 27 minutes, Trinity had reduced the deficit after Ryan Hampshire's fine pass sent Tom Johnstone over for a diving finish, though fullback Hampshire couldn't convert.

The battle between wingers Johnstone and Tommy Makinson was outstanding with Saints' Golden Boot winner Makinson getting the next try off a perfect Lachlan Coote pass before Johnstone was on the end of a superb piece of interpassing from Jacob Miller and Matty Ashurst to level the scores at 10-10 at half-time.

Five minutes after the restart, a Brough penalty made it 12-10. Three minutes later, the see-saw nature of the game continued when Coote's pass sent Regan Grace over to put the Saints back ahead. But after that the momentum was with Wakefield until, in a rare attack downfield, an inch-perfect pass from Jonny Lomax found its way to Makinson, though for the third time, Percival was off target, leaving the gap at just six points.

Five minutes later, Trinity made Percival pay for his waywardness as Brough combined with Hampshire to send Bill Tupou over, with the scrum-half converting to level the scores at 18-18.

From the resulting kick-off, Coote kicked out on the full - and Trinity opted to go for goal from halfway. For the first time in the afternoon, Brough was off-target from the tee. And while there were further chances for both teams, with two minutes left, Lomax struck the decisive pass to find McCarthy-Scarsbrook

Warrington had already made it a two-from-two start to the season the day before with a 28-14 home win over Hull KR.

Rovers started the brighter of the two sides, scoring inside ten minutes through Ben Crooks, who touched down Chris Atkin's kick. Josh Drinkwater missed the conversion, so when Declan Patton put Harvey Livett through a huge gap on the left, Stefan Ratchford's conversion gave the Wolves the lead.

Blake Austin was sin-binned shortly after for a hit on Joel Tomkins, which resulted in the Robins' skipper going to hospital with severe concussion, although Austin was found not guilty of foul play the following week. The Robins wasted no time in exploiting the man advantage as Craig Hall took a lovely cutout pass from Atkin to score out wide to see the lead change once again.

But, in the final minute of the half and on the back of poor discipline from Rovers, Warrington went left, with a long ball from Austin giving Bryson Goodwin space to tip on to Tom Lineham, who produced another miraculously acrobatic finish in the corner to give Warrington an unlikely half-time lead.

It took an error from Rovers to break the game open, as the Wolves opened a two-score lead. An innocuous set ended with Atkin spilling a high kick from Austin and Livett was on hand to stroll in for his second. Josh Charnley then popped up to take the game away from Rovers, with the former Wigan winger picking off Atkin's looping pass to race the length of the field to score, before Jimmy Keinhorst and Mike Cooper swapped tries in the last ten minutes.

Castleford also made it two from two with a 26-18 win at Hull FC in the Thursday-night TV game as Michael Shenton scored two tries to help inflict a 13th Super League defeat in a row on Hull FC.

Despite being only the second game of the season, both teams served up a showcase of entertaining free-flowing rugby, which could have gone either way right until the closing stages. The Tigers' slickness and at times patience near the line proved crucial, as they outscored the hosts five tries to three. But they had to show some real character without the ball, particularly near their own line, as Hull looked rejuvenated in attack with the return from suspension of Jake Connor.

Shenton and Jesse Sene-Lefao crossed early for the Paul McShane-inspired Tigers but tries from the returning Joe Westerman and Connor moved Hull 12-10 ahead. A second for Shenton just before the hooter gave Cas a half-time lead, with James Clare and Junior Moors scoring to put them 12 points up 14 minutes after the turnaround.

Within three minutes, Jamie Shaul's electric break and pass sent Jordan Lane over

21

for Hull with 20 minutes left as the game continued to see-saw and when Jordan Rankin nudged a penalty goal over from out wide on the back of a ball steal, Castleford extended their advantage to two scores for the second time. Connor had a try ruled out as he failed to ground the ball thanks to scrambling Tigers defence - he'd already had one chalked off earlier in the second half for obstruction by a lead runner - as the Tigers held on.

After the match Hull boss Lee Radford confirmed winger Matty Dawson-Jones, who had scored on debut in the defeat at Hull KR, was to miss the rest of the season after suffering a cruciate knee injury in training the previous Wednesday.

Wigan made up their two-point league deduction as George Williams stood out in their 34-16 home win over Leeds on the Friday night.

With Wigan twice falling behind inside the opening quarter, Williams was involved in each of the three tries that put the Warriors in command by half-time, the home side establishing a 22-12 lead against a Leeds team whose defensive capabilities, particularly when dealing with Williams' kicking game, deserted them.

Wigan could have easily killed the game off far sooner than Williams' 68th-minute try, which ensured there would be no way back for Leeds.

The Rhinos looked good early on, leading 12-6 through tries to Ash Handley and Brett Ferres, with one from Dan Sarginson in between, but fell apart before half-time.

First, Ben Flower grounded Tommy Leuluai's kick, although Leeds were unfortunate that all the officials missed an obvious knock-on from Liam Farrell in the build-up. Then Wigan were ahead for the first time as a Williams kick was claimed by Joe Greenwood, before Williams was again involved, this time as the impressive Joe Bullock rampaged his way to the line through Trent Merrin and over the top of Jack Walker to make it 22-12.

Just before half-time Wigan hooker Sam Powell reported an alleged biting incident to Ben Thaler that appeared to arise from a tackle involving Mikolaj Oledzki and the incident was placed on report. No charge was brought on the young Leeds prop.

After Williams' try Leeds briefly threatened a comeback when Tui Lolohea's pass sent Rhinos captain Kallum Watkins over. But any serious chance of overturning the deficit was killed by more handling errors and, in the final moments, a magnificent Zak Hardaker break was well supported by Farrell, who dived over to ensure Wigan's first win of the season.

Catalans Dragons got off the mark on the Saturday with a 27-10 home win over Huddersfield, Sam Tomkins and Matt Whitley, both on home debut, standing out in a see-saw game.

The Dragons were missing Greg Bird, Ben Garcia and David Mead, who had been allowed to go home to Papua New Guinea for a family matter, but the return of Michael McIlorum from injury stabilised the team.

The first 15 minutes were all Huddersfield though, with halfbacks Izaac Farrell and Matt Frawley dictating play from the start. Frawley was the first to score with an elusive skip through the Dragons' defence.

The Giants continued to dominate but, against the run of play, Dragons winger Brayden Wiliame collected McIlorum's kick to the in-goal area and touched down. Tomkins added the conversion to level the scores in the 16th minute. Wiliame then doubled his tally four minutes later after Whitley showed great strength to steal the ball from Joe Wardle and pass to Tony Gigot, who found the Fijian on the wing with an overlap for a simple run-in.

The Dragons took full control of the game three minutes before the interval when Matty Smith and Tomkins combined to put winger Lewis Tierney over in the right corner. Tomkins added two more points with a penalty two minutes after the break and after 25 minutes of impasse mopped up a loose ball in the 67th minute to score his first try for his new club, adding the conversion.

Oliver Roberts grounded Frawley's kick to in-goal to make the scoreline a more respectable 26-10 in the 72nd minute. And as the hooter sounded, Smith landed a field goal to put the seal on another solid home debut.

Salford moved to the top of the early Super League table as Jackson Hastings created two tries and scored another in their second straight win, this time a 24-0 home victory over London Broncos on the Sunday afternoon.

The Red Devils never looked in danger of losing and they move ahead of Warrington on points difference, having conceded just two tries in two games, as the Broncos couldn't find the attacking fluency that had shocked Wakefield seven days before.

Winger Ken Sio was another to stand out, both in attack and defence, while for the visitors, fullback Alex Walker again impressed, dealing with a host of varied kicks throughout, and Jay Pitts never stopped trying to drag his side back into the game.

The only score of the first half came after one of four goal-line drop-outs forced by the home side, and it saw Josh Jones' floated long pass picked up by Sio, who cut inside to score. Sio was denied a second try for a forward pass but the Broncos defence, which was so impressive under pressure in the first half, was breached within three minutes of the restart.

Niall Evalds' grubber struck an upright and Hastings was on hand to pounce under the posts. The scrum-half added the conversion and a penalty awarded for holding down George Griffin, while a rare Broncos attack ended with debutant Ryan Morgan's pass to Kieran Dixon finding only the touchline.

Hastings then returned Evalds' earlier favour with another smart kick for the third Salford try and, despite the loss of Lee Mossop to the sin bin following a brief altercation, the Red Devils completed the scoring when Jones crashed over from a Hastings pass.

## World Club Challenge

Super League Champions Wigan failed in their attempt to win a record fifth World Club Challenge as they were beaten 20-8 by NRL Premiers Sydney Roosters at the DW Stadium.

The Roosters' star player was Brett Morris, who scored three brilliant first-half tries. Wigan fought back, particularly in the second half, but were never able to get back on level terms.

The Warriors' chances were virtually ended as they trailed 10-0 after only nine minutes of the game, with the Roosters looking likely to repeat the scale of their 38-0 victory over St Helens at Bolton in 2003.

Morris went in for his first try after four minutes. The 32-year-old, debuting following his move from Canterbury, appeared to have been wrapped up. But he slipped out of Oliver Gildart's grasp and made his way over for the first score.

Within minutes Morris was in again in the same left corner as he crawled and wrestled his way to the line. Four Wigan defenders put him on his back but he unfathomably managed to free his arm and nonchalantly grab his second. Sio Siua Taukeiaho had missed the first conversion but nailed the second and, in the blink of an eye, Wigan were ten points behind.

Tom Davies got a reply on 20 minutes after smart passing from George Williams and Gildart but there was no panic from the Roosters. Eight minutes before the break,

### BETFRED WORLD CLUB CHALLENGE

*Sunday 17th February 2019*

**WIGAN WARRIORS 8 SYDNEY ROOSTERS 20**

**WARRIORS:** 20 Zak Hardaker; 2 Tom Davies; 4 Oliver Gildart; 3 Dan Sarginson; 17 Liam Marshall; 6 George Williams; 7 Thomas Leuluai; 8 Tony Clubb; 9 Sam Powell; 10 Ben Flower; 11 Joe Greenwood; 12 Liam Farrell; 13 Sean O'Loughlin (C). Subs (all used): 14 Romain Navarrete; 15 Willie Isa; 16 Gabe Hamlin; 22 Joe Bullock.
**Tries:** Davies (20), Marshall (65); **Goals:** Hardaker 0/2.
**ROOSTERS:** 1 James Tedesco; 2 Daniel Tupou; 4 Joseph Manu; 5 Brett Morris; 20 Matt Ikuvalu; 6 Luke Keary; 7 Cooper Cronk; 8 Jared Waerea-Hargreaves; 9 Jake Friend; 10 Sio Siua Taukeiaho; 11 Boyd Cordner (C); 3 Mitchell Aubusson; 13 Victor Radley. Subs (all used): 14 Isaac Liu; 15 Zane Tetevano; 16 Lindsay Collins; 17 Nat Butcher.
**Tries:** Morris (4, 9, 32), Tupou (78); **Goals:** Taukeiaho 2/5.
**Rugby Leaguer & League Express Men of the Match:**
*Warriors:* Thomas Leuluai; *Roosters:* Brett Morris.
**Penalty count:** 7-7; **Half-time:** 4-14;
**Referee:** Robert Hicks; **Attendance:** 21,331 *(at DW Stadium).*

Tom Davies claims a high ball during Wigan's World Club Challenge defeat to Sydney Roosters

they regained their ten-point advantage. Morris was the scorer again, collecting the ball in space and charging to the line.

After the break, the Warriors became more adventurous with the ball and enjoyed some success. Dan Sarginson went on a marauding run after intercepting a pass, Joe Greenwood nearly provided an offload to put Sarginson over and Tommy Leuluai was ankle-tapped after skipping out of a tackle.

Five minutes after Taukeiaho landed a penalty goal just after the hourmark, Wigan came up trumps. Williams provided a long, looping pass towards Liam Marshall on the left wing. Although he couldn't claim it, the winger poked it forward, calmly picked it up and dived in to score at the corner.

But the Roosters eventually secured the trophy in the 78th minute as the rangy Daniel Tupou leapt above Davies and claimed Luke Keary's kick to the corner.

**Round 10**

There were two games on the Sunday afternoon, brought forward to allow the previous season's bottom four teams to enter the Challenge Cup at the fifth round stage.

Leeds coach David Furner watched his side roar to their first win of his reign as the Rhinos blew away previously unbeaten Salford Red Devils at the AJ Bell Stadium, winning 46-14.

The Rhinos won the game with two scoring blasts, one in each half, after Salford had led early when Joey Lussick barged his way over from close range. The Red Devils were looking menacing in the opening exchanges but the momentum of the first half shifted when Kris Welham's pass was ruled forward as the hosts pushed for a second try. From there, Salford wouldn't touch the ball again until they were 12 points behind.

A six-minute purple patch yielded 18-unanswered points for the Rhinos; first, Trent Merrin's magnificent offload found Adam Cuthbertson, before Kallum Watkins' break downfield was ably supported by Jack Walker for back-to-back Leeds tries.

Three minutes after Walker's try, Konrad Hurrell claimed his first try in blue and amber after grounding Tui Lolohea's kick, with the stand-off converting all three scores to make it 18-6.

After the break, Josh Jones got a try back for Salford but, after Jansin Turgut was sin-binned for running in, Leeds scored five tries in the last 20 minutes.

Imports Trent Merrin, Hurrell - who finished with two tries - and Lolohea were all excellent but the pick of the bunch was 19-year-old Walker, who claimed a superb hat-trick of tries and was equally as impressive in broken play and defence.

Hull KR got their second win as the on-form Mitch Garbutt's two tries clinched a 22-12 home success over London Broncos. The former Leeds prop was in outstanding form at the start of the season and he continued to impress at a blustery KCOM Craven Park.

With the home side struggling for cohesion and making basic errors in the first 40 minutes, the Broncos enjoyed the better of the first period but went into the break just 6-4 ahead after spurning several golden opportunities.

That wastefulness came back to haunt them after the break, as the Robins raced out of the blocks after half-time, posting 18 points in 13 minutes – including Garbutt's double – to take a stranglehold on the contest.

**Round 3**

The last Sunday of February was historic for Super League as golden-point time decided a match for the first time. Hull FC were the beneficiaries as Marc Sneyd's extra-time field goal sealed a dramatic 23-22 win at Wigan. It was Hull's first win of the new season and ended a run of 13 consecutive losses stretching back to the previous June.

Hull's destiny rested firmly in the balance when Zak Hardaker lined up the 80th-minute conversion to Oliver Gildart's equalising try that would have ensured victory for Wigan. The Airlie Birds had led from the 20th minute until that point, with British Army winger Ratu Naulago scoring two tries on debut. But Wigan went into extra time as favourites, with Hull having no fit substitutes and having called 37-year-old Gareth Ellis out of his 18-month retirement amid a pre-match injury crisis.

But within seconds of the restart, Wigan had conceded a crucial penalty to spring Hull into field position and the chance to strike first. Field-goal expert Sneyd was on hand to provide the coup de grace.

Wigan could be forgiven if they had a World Club Challenge hangover and had lost Liam Farrell with a long-term pectoral injury suffered in the defeat to the Roosters. Jarrod Sammut made his debut along with young prop Liam Byrne, who marked his with a first-half try

The best game of the weekend was a Friday-night thriller at the Totally Wicked

Stadium as St Helens kept their hundred per cent record, being pushed all the way before ending 27-22 victors over Leeds.

At half-time a second consecutive win for the Rhinos looked likely. They had recovered from an early 10-0 deficit to post four tries in the first half, with Konrad Hurrell especially prominent, crossing for one himself, creating one for his winger Ash Handley and having one ruled out for a marginal forward pass.

The momentum was with the Rhinos. But as it turned out they were not to register another score in the second half, although they were desperately unlucky not to do so after Alex Walmsley and Luke Thompson had scored three tries between them to grab a 26-22 lead after 62 minutes.

The final 18 minutes combined tension with thrills and spills as the Rhinos tried to get back their advantage and they had tries by Adam Cuthbertson and Tui Lolohea disallowed, both of which might conceivably have been given by a referee in a non-televised game.

Saints then had a Jonny Lomax try disallowed for obstruction before the Rhinos had a genuine complaint at the other end of the field, when the referee failed to spot a Morgan Knowles knock-on that came from a Trent Merrin offload With four minutes to go that should have given the Rhinos a scrum close to the home line. Instead referee Robert Hicks awarded a scrum to St Helens.

The outstanding James Roby finally sealed victory with the first field goal of his career.

On the same night Warrington made it three wins from three with a 32-20 win at win-less Huddersfield.

Jermaine McGillvary, Lee Gaskell and Ukuma Ta'ai all played their first games of the season for the Giants but the Wolves didn't have to hit their best to get the win. Blake Austin produced another fine performance, scoring one of his side's six tries and having a hand in most of the others. And in the week when he discovered he would from July face new competition for a centre berth from incoming England rugby union international Luther Burrell, Warrington stalwart Ryan Atkins continued his good form by touching down twice.

The Wolves led 16-0 until three minutes before the break through Atkins' first and two tries from Josh Charnley. And just when Huddersfield looked like they might get back into it, having closed the Wolves' lead to six points with scores by McGillvary and Matty English either side of half-time, Adam Walne was sin-binned for a high tackle on Chris Hill.

Momentum was lost, and the Wolves were able to regain control, with two late home tries by Jordan Turner and Akuila Uate giving a final scoreline that made the game look closer than it was.

McGillvary was able to play without painkillers for the first time in years. He missed the opening two games of the season with a hamstring injury but returned for his first competitive appearance since double ankle surgery in the off-season, which helped clear a long-standing injury.

The Giants were missing scrum-half Danny Brough, who had gone to Wakefield in pre-season in a swap seal with Scott Grix. Brough played his 500th game the night before in the TV game and he was pivotal in Trinity's 22-12 home win over Catalans.

Brough put on a halfback clinic, kicking five goals, creating a try and terrorising the Dragons with his mischievous left foot.

With Tom Johnstone producing his trademark flying finish for the game's opening try and the outstanding David Fifita leading up front, Trinity had too much for a Catalans side that again flattered to deceive on the road.

The Dragons also lost star centre David Mead, who created their only first-half try, to an adductor injury and that weekend winger Jodie Broughton suffered a biceps tendon rupture in a reserve game at Albi as he started his comeback from an an ACL injury. But they did re-sign winger Fouad Yaha on a two-year contract after his five-game spell with

Agen rugby union club. Hooker Michael McIlorum also signed a new two-year deal after a superb first season in Perpignan.

Salford bounced back from their hammering by Leeds with a sensational 24-22 comeback win at Hull KR.

The Robins led 22-8 until just before the hour mark. Three tries in eight minutes before half-time from Craig Hall, George Lawler and Jimmy Keinhorst looked to have put the home side in the box seat. But the Red Devils came out refocused for the second half and, on the back of a dominant display from his forward pack, halfback Jackson Hastings pulled the Robins apart.

Derrell Olpherts went over to reduce the deficit, before the key moment of the game saw Rovers skipper Joel Tomkins denied a try at one end for a knock-on. Barely 60 seconds later former Robin Ken Sio dived in at the corner for a ten-point swing that proved decisive, as nine minutes from time Joey Lussick powered over from dummy-half by the posts and Sio won the game with the conversion.

Tomkins was charged with 'questioning integrity of a match official' and was banned for only two matches 'because of his good record and admittance of guilt'.

Castleford finished the month on top of Super League on points difference after claiming a comfortable 40-6 victory over London Broncos on the Saturday night.

Liam Watts led from the front as the Tigers overpowered their hosts, with Jake Trueman pulling the strings at stand-off. Jesse Sene-Lefao was a dangerous presence on the left edge for the Tigers and Paul McShane, Grant Millington and Nathan Massey were also standout performers

The Tigers, with eight players on the treatment table, made three changes to the 17 who won at Hull FC, with debutant Chris Clarkson and former Broncos Matt Cook and Tuoyo Egodo coming in for injured trio, Alex Foster, Mitch Clark and Ben Roberts.

The game was up for London when Watts bagged his first ever Castleford try in the 44th minute to extend the Tigers' lead to 22 points.

**BETFRED SUPER LEAGUE**
*Sunday 24th February*

| | P | W | D | L | F | A | D | Pts |
|---|---|---|---|---|---|---|---|---|
| Castleford Tigers | 3 | 3 | 0 | 0 | 86 | 28 | 58 | 6 |
| Warrington Wolves | 3 | 3 | 0 | 0 | 86 | 40 | 46 | 6 |
| St Helens | 3 | 3 | 0 | 0 | 73 | 52 | 21 | 6 |
| Salford Red Devils | 4 | 3 | 0 | 1 | 96 | 82 | 14 | 6 |
| Hull Kingston Rovers | 4 | 2 | 0 | 2 | 76 | 80 | -4 | 4 |
| Hull FC | 3 | 1 | 0 | 2 | 57 | 66 | -9 | 2 |
| Catalans Dragons | 3 | 1 | 0 | 2 | 43 | 52 | -9 | 2 |
| Leeds Rhinos | 4 | 1 | 0 | 3 | 90 | 101 | -11 | 2 |
| Wakefield Trinity | 3 | 1 | 0 | 2 | 64 | 78 | -14 | 2 |
| London Broncos | 4 | 1 | 0 | 3 | 60 | 110 | -50 | 2 |
| Wigan Warriors * | 3 | 1 | 0 | 2 | 68 | 61 | 7 | 0 |
| Huddersfield Giants | 3 | 0 | 0 | 3 | 44 | 93 | -49 | 0 |

*\* Denotes two points deducted for 2017 salary cap breach*

*\* The Sunday Championship fixture between Widnes and Sheffield was postponed after the Vikings, relegated in 2018, went into financial administration. The former World Club Champion club was threatened with liquidation if they could not raise in the region of £250,000 by the end of the following week.*

# MARCH
## *Unbeatable Saints*

**Round 4**

St Helens and Castleford remained joint top of the early Super League table after maintaining their winning starts.

Saints came away from Salford with a 26-4 win on a wet and murky Thursday night. Captain James Roby was magnificent, finishing with two tries, including one in the closing stages when he supported an 80-metre raid downfield to crash over on the following play. And Theo Fages, still keeping Danny Richardson out of the side, produced two first-half assists, a controlled performance with the ball and steel in defence, while others to impress included Jonny Lomax and Lachlan Coote.

Mark Percival, catching a Fages bomb on the run, Lomax and Roby scored tries as St Helens led 16-0 at half-time. Regan Grace added a fourth try as the Red Devils improved after the break and were rewarded when Derrell Olpherts caught Robert Lui's kick and went over.

But Saints had the final say, as Roby crashed over for his second of the night, after Tommy Makinson's long break had been ended by a superb chase-down from Olpherts and Niall Evalds.

The Tigers had to go through 80 feisty minutes the night after before emerging 32-16 home winners over Hull KR. Greg Eden scored twice as Castleford kept up their winning record with referee Gareth Hewer sending four players to the sin bin in the final ten minutes.

Adam Milner dropped out of the Castleford squad after suffering an injury in the Tigers' victory over London, whilst Hull KR's Joel Tomkins sat out the game pending his charge for questioning an official's integrity in the loss against Salford.

The Tigers, still without the likes of Luke Gale, Ben Roberts, Jamie Ellis, Oliver Holmes, Mike McMeeken and Alex Foster, handed a debut to youngster Jacques O'Neill, with James Greenwood returning for the Robins.

Rovers took an early lead through a barging Mose Masoe effort but it lasted only six minutes. The Tigers responded with three first-half tries through Jordan Rankin, gamestar Liam Watts and Eden. James Clare went over shortly after the break and at 20-6 it was as good as over as a contest.

Masoe pulled one back and was agonisingly close to getting his hat-trick as Eden got his second and Chris Clarkson another. Chris Atkin got the last try of the game with the Robins down to ten men and the Tigers twelve. Greenwood and Grant Millington went first after a set-to at the play the ball; Weller Hauraki followed for messing in the ruck with Rovers on a team warning and his captain Danny McGuire was yellow-carded for showing dissent.

Millington got a two-match penalty notice the following week.

Rovers were trying to find the identity of a fan of the club who struck their prop forward Robbie Mulhern with a thrown bottle after the defeat.

On the Saturday night, Warrington had their winning start to the season ended in Perpignan as, five minutes from time, Sam Tomkins kicked a 45-metre penalty goal to secure a 23-22 Dragons win. The Wolves were one point ahead in the 75th minute when scrum-half Declan Patton was penalised for getting in the way at the back of a play-the-ball.

Catalans, with winger Fouad Yaha on his second debut, shot into a 14-0 lead with tries from Brayden Wiliame and Kenny Edwards and two conversions and a penalty from Tomkins. Stefan Ratchford pegged a try back before Tony Gigot landed a field goal just before half-time to put his side 15-6 ahead.

Any hopes of a downhill run for the Dragons in the second half were soon dispelled when Daryl Clark sneaked over from dummy-half in the 45th minute. And 13 minutes later Ryan Atkins put his side ahead when he gathered a perfectly placed Patton kick and forced his way over the line. Ratchford failed to land the conversion but, at 15-16, the momentum was all Warrington's.

But back came the Dragons through Rémi Casty who took a clever pass from Michael McIlorum before forcing his way over the line near the posts. Tomkins added the conversion to make it 21-16. Then, minutes later, Wolves captain Chris Hill was sent clear by Mike Cooper, slipping an audacious reverse pass to the supporting Patton, which had both sets of fans applauding when replayed on the TV screen at the stadium.

Ratchford added the conversion from in front of the sticks and Warrington were ahead once more at 22-21 with the clock ticking and the game seemingly heading their way, until the whistle blew for the deciding penalty on 75 minutes.

The night before, Wakefield recorded their second victory of the season with a 35-18 win at Leeds. It was the Rhinos' first home game, with Headingley's North Stand redevelopment still ongoing and the new South Stand opened for the first time for Super League.

Trinity spoilt the party big-time though as the Rhinos' big win at Salford and good showing in defeat at St Helens was patently not the start of big things to come. They were thoroughly outplayed by their neighbours and that after opening the scoring with an excellently worked try from Ash Handley on the left wing.

Jack Walker failed a fitness test and Tui Lolohea dropped back to fullback, with forward Cameron Smith playing stand-off. By half-time the Rhinos were 22-10 down, with Tom Johnstone scoring an eleven-minute hat-trick, one of the tries another one-handed spectacular, and hooker Kyle Wood bagging the fourth try, Tom Briscoe getting one back for Leeds.

But by the 70th minute Trinity led 35-10, Jacob Miller and Danny Brough grabbing tries, the latter on the end of a Ben Jones-Bishop break that Brough himself launched. The effervescent Brough also kicked a penalty and a field goal for good measure. Two Leeds scores in the last ten minutes, with Trent Merrin in the sin bin for dissent, made the score less embarrassing, Handley's second a dive to rival Johnstone's first-half effort.

Trinity were good throughout the team but centre Bill Tupou stood out, making a remarkable 270 metres.

On the Sunday, Joe Westerman, on his 300th career appearance, and Josh Griffin both crossed twice as Hull FC stepped on the gas in the second half to condemn the Giants to a fourth defeat in as many matches, this time by 28-8.

Hull had Australian halfback Albert Kelly in their team for the first time since picking up a shoulder injury during pre-season and, after Jamie Shaul failed to pass a fitness test following a knock to the head against Wigan, former Huddersfield man Jake Connor switched from stand-off to fullback.

Westerman scored the first try of the game, kicking on after a fumble, but the Giants led 8-6 at the break with Darnell McIntosh's try and two Oliver Russell goals.

A second Westerman try four minutes into the second half restored the Hull lead and they then took control. Ratu Naulago went over in the corner and Josh Griffin wrapped up victory with his double.

## March

That Sunday afternoon provided a big shock as Wigan fell to an 18-16 defeat at London Broncos.

The Warriors looked on track to make it two wins from four as they led 10-0 after half an hour through tries from Liam Paisley and Willie Isa. But Eddie Battye and Matty Gee tries, Kieran Dixon converting both, gave the Broncos a 12-10 advantage at the break.

Within four minutes of the restart, a Wigan try looked likely when, with a huge overlap, George Williams threw a pass to Morgan Escaré on the left. But he failed to gather and London's Kieran Dixon snaffled the ball and streaked down the right for his fifth try of the season. Dixon couldn't convert but made up for the miss only a few minutes later, landing a penalty goal from 30 metres to take London into a two-score lead.

Wigan set the scene for a hugely tense final quarter close to the hour when Londoner Tony Clubb went over and Zak Hardaker converted. And they pressed hard after that, with Jarrod Sammut launching a succession of bombs. But the Broncos old boy found former team-mate Alex Walker – whom he had clattered in the first minute while pursuing a kick - in superb form, with a succession of takes under pressure

*\* Widnes, relegated from Super League in 2018, were within 24 hours of going out of existence before a takeover by a local consortium was finalised and on the Sunday the Vikings drew a crowd of 5,786 to witness a stunning 44-22 victory over Featherstone at the Halton Stadium.*

## Round 5

Huddersfield got their first win of the season at the fifth attempt and they took a notable scalp with a 14-6 Friday-night win at Wigan.

The defending champions were outplayed by the Giants and they looked more-than out of sorts, missing tackles and appearing aimless in attack. Wigan coach Adrian Lam had aimed the blame at his senior players for not stepping up in the defeat at London in the previous round and he cut a disconsolate figure after his side was booed off the DW Stadium pitch.

Huddersfield outplayed the Warriors in the first half as Kruise Leeming's try separated the two sides at the break. The Giants should have extended their lead before the break as Jermaine McGillvary headed for the line, only to be brought down by a great double cover tackle from Zak Hardaker and Oliver Gildart, while video referee James Child judged that Suaia Matagi had lost control of the ball as he attempted to score.

Wigan managed to hit back in the second half with a try from Morgan Escaré 13 minutes after the restart but they were unable to kick on and Joe Wardle ensured the points went back to Yorkshire with a try on 65 minutes.

Dom Manfredi was named in the Wigan starting line-up for the first time in 2019 but had to leave the field just before half-time with a mouth injury, while the Warriors lost Liam Marshall to a knee injury midway through the second half.

Taulima Tautai was sin-binned in the second half for kicking out while tackled on the floor and was subsequently banned for three matches.

The Giants lost Aaron Murphy, who along with Leeming was their best, his transformation from winger to backrower now seemingly permanent, with a medial knee injury.

Despite the defeat the Warriors ended the weekend on two points, as that week they had their two points deduction for historical salary cap breaches suspended by a Sports Resolution tribunal. Despite still being found guilty of breaching the cap, the penalty was relaxed, with the Warriors still to pay a fine but their points deduction suspended until the end of 2020.

The restoration of the two league point meant they were in tenth spot, a place above Leeds on points difference. The Rhinos' confidence looked shot to pieces as they saw a 10-point lead at Hull FC disappear, with the Airlie Birds running away to a 34-10 win, their third in a row.

A ruthless attacking display in the second quarter saw Hull score five tries in a blistering 16-minute spell.

Leeds led 10-0 after teenager Harry Newman and former Hull wing Tom Briscoe crossed early on. But after Ratu Naulago got the home side started they tore through the visitors - adding 30 points in 17 minutes. The pick of the tries came on 27 minutes. Marc Sneyd started and finished a sublime move down the left, creating a break for Mark Minichiello before backing up through the middle as Hull scored from 60 metres out.

Sika Manu was outstanding on the right edge. Causing chaos in the Leeds defence, the backrower repeatedly broke the line and offloaded at will in a dominant 80-minute display.

The Rhinos also had the blow of seeing Carl Ablett injured in the warm-up as he prepared to play his first game of the season.

That week Hull FC announced they had won the race to sign in-demand Brisbane forward Andre Savelio. The ex-St Helens, Castleford and Warrington star and former Albert Goldthorpe Rookie of the Year had been offered to Super League clubs after injury had wiped out his 2018 season.

At the top end of the table, Warrington had pegged back previously unbeaten Castleford Tigers on the Thursday night with a convincing 24-10 home win.

Former Tiger Daryl Clark was typically dangerous around the play-the-balls, aided by the emergence off the bench of Joe Philbin and Ben Murdoch-Masila midway through the first half, which helped end a promising start to the game by the Tigers. They led 4-0 early on through Greg Eden's try and could have doubled that lead, before the Wolves took a firm grip on proceedings.

Jake Mamo, on his home debut, was the main beneficiary, providing two smart finishes and creating another try as the Wolves established a match-winning 16-4 interval lead on the back of a 100 per cent first-half completion rate.

They then closed victory out after the restart, with Murdoch-Masila scoring a trademark rampaging second-half try. Ben Currie made an impressive comeback from a second serious knee injury, ending an 11-month absence following a second ACL injury suffered in the Challenge Cup clash against Bradford the previous season.

The Tigers' defeat left St Helens as the only 100 per cent side after their wet and windy Friday-night 26-0 home win over London Broncos.

Saints captain James Roby was rested with an injury niggle with 22-year-old Aaron Smith filling in dynamically at dummy half. Halfback Theo Fages had a hand in all five Saints tries, with fullback Lachlan Coote looking more composed and influential with every game

The tone was set from the opening whistle, when the Broncos conceded a penalty after Jordan Abdull's short kick-off failed to travel ten metres. Saints capitalised with their first set of six, as Dominique Peyroux tore a hole in the London defence to open the scoring inside 70 seconds.

The Broncos showed they were no pushovers but by the time Kevin Naiqama scored St Helens' fifth try on 76 minutes they were well beaten.

On the Saturday, Salford Red Devils produced a slick eight-try show in Perpignan to defeat Catalans Dragons 46-0 and stay fourth in the table. It was the biggest home defeat in the Dragons' history. Coach Steve McNamara described the defeat as: 'embarrassing and humiliating' at the end of a week in which the Dragons signed Melbourne Storm prop forward Sam Kasiano.

After the win Jackson Hastings was mobbed by supporters on a lap of honour more akin to a Cup Final victory than a round-five Super League clash. Hastings was outstanding throughout but was pushed close for the man-of-the-match award by Jake Bibby, who had been selected for the first time this season because of the absence of

## March

Junior Sa'u.

The young centre was sensational from start to finish and at the heart of almost every point scored by Salford. His double strike in the 40th and 41st minute - separated by the half-time break - was the killer blow to a Catalans side that had been expected to stroll to victory.

In the only Sunday game, Hull KR pulled off a shock win, by 10-6, at Wakefield. On a muddy, rainy and windy Sunday afternoon, for large periods it looked as though Trinity and Rovers would cancel out each other's respective defensive efforts to such an extent that penalties would prove to be the only scoring of the afternoon.

Going into the final ten minutes, Rovers were trailing by two points after three penalties from the boot of Danny Brough, with Craig Hall replying with two of his own for the Robins to make it 6-4 in the hosts' favour.

At that stage, it looked like Wakefield's recent upturn in form - as well as Hull KR's losing run - would continue, before Danny McGuire's try from a high Josh Drinkwater kick - with a hint of a knock-on in the build-up - won it for the spirited Rovers, who suffered another injury blow, with forward James Greenwood leaving the field with an ACL injury that ended his season.

### Round 6

London Broncos' pre-season tag as Super League write-offs was well and truly dispelled on the Friday night of round six when they produced an astounding 18-16 win at Leeds.

The success was all the more amazing, as they trailed 16-8 as the game entered its final five minutes. Danny Ward's men, seemingly down and out, found what it needed to come up with one of their most memorable away wins, not least thanks to his judicious reintroductions of form prop Eddie Battye, the indefatigable Eloi Pelissier and workhorse Matt Davis, back on loan from Warrington, to turn a second-half tide that looked as though it would swamp them.

The Broncos were 8-0 ahead at half-time courtesy of Kieran Dixon's goal and Jay Pitts' converted try. But the Rhinos turned the game around through Richie Myler and Trent Merrin before Tom Briscoe crossed on 60 minutes to extend their advantage to 16-8.

Thrown a late lifeline with seemingly little on, Pelissier, who had dominated the middle, switched play on the last tackle and Matty Fozard grubbered for himself and just exerted enough downward pressure as the Leeds defence failed to react quickly enough.

Then Battye led what turned out to be an 80-metre charge. Pelissier again made easy metres up the middle, releasing the ball for the elusive Alex Walker to gather in midfield. Jordan Abdull shipped on to Jay Pitts and another of Elliot Kear's piercing runs on the fifth tackle established territorial sovereignty.

On the last, with another pre-planned Abdull kick that landed on a sixpence, the ball was contested by two London players, including Fozard, ahead of the Leeds defenders. It rolled backwards and Will Lovell was on hand to gather and cross for Dixon to land the match-winning goal.

Only Huddersfield remained below the Rhinos in the table after their 40-12, Thursday-night home defeat to leaders St Helens. Saints weren't great in the first half and were held at 12-all late in the first half. But a Mark Percival try a couple of minutes before the break triggered a near faultless second stanza from the league leaders.

The Giants were good in the first half, buoyed by their first win of the season at Wigan the previous week, and tries from Jermaine McGillvary and Jordan Turner cancelled out Luke Thompson and Morgan Knowles six-pointers before Percival's effort.

Percival got another after the break and finely worked tries from Regan Grace, in a week when he signed an extended contract with the club, in-form Dominique Peyroux and Jonny Lomax saw St Helens stretch away, meaning six wins from six games, one better than their start to 2018. Their combination between fullback Lachlan Coote, still settling in after replacing Ben Barba, Jonny Lomax and Theo Fages was looking increasingly impressive.

On the Friday, Warrington maintained their strong start to the season and condemned Wigan to a fifth straight defeat with a 25-12 win at the Halliwell Jones Stadium.

Trailing 18-0 early in the second half and with Dan Sarginson in the sin bin, the Warriors looked set for a slaughtering against a Wolves team that had been clinical and composed. But the champions dug in, closing the gap to six points at one stage before Steve Price's men regained control to see the game out.

The game finished with two more yellow cards and a red for Ben Westwood, underlining the feeling between the two clubs, with the game having been promoted under the banner 'Bad Blood'.

The Wolves' early-season success had been built on the consistency of key men Stefan Ratchford and Daryl Clark and they again rose to the challenge in an impressive all-round team display.

Warrington opened the scoring in the seventh minute with a try straight off the training ground. Forwards Chris Hill and Westwood shifted the ball left from the ruck, where halfbacks Declan Patton and Blake Austin created the space for Jake Mamo to produce a spectacular diving finish in the corner.

It was 20 minutes before the next clear scoring opportunity as the sides jostled for field position with minimal mistakes and penalties. When it came, it produced the best defensive play of the match. Austin released Ben Currie down the left again and the backrower looked a certain scorer until Zak Hardaker somehow got himself underneath the ball, for a close call determined by the video referee.

But moments later the Wolves were over for a second try. After Daryl Clark earned a penalty by catching the Wigan markers out of position, Currie produced a flat pass from the tap that found Ratchford running an outstanding line. He touched down unopposed and converted himself.

Within six minutes of the second half the game looked over. Josh Charnley was on the spot when Wigan failed to deal with a spiralling Austin kick and produced a finish every bit as good as Mamo's opener. Ratchford rubbed salt in the Warriors' wound with a towering touchline conversion.

But after Sarginson was yellow-carded when spotted on camera during a stoppage in play whacking Ryan Atkins on the nose in a tackle, Wigan responded superbly as Jarrod Sammut's pass allowed Jake Shorrocks, playing his first Super League game for two years because of injury, to show terrific skill to kick for Tom Davies to finish out wide. Zak Hardaker's conversion from out wide made it 18-6.

The gap was just six points four minutes later as George Williams, who had been well contained up until that point, evaded six defenders in drifting across the defensive line and hit Willie Isa with a perfect flat pass.

But Declan Patton eased any home nerves with a coolly taken field goal and, although Wigan responded again, the late fracas between the teams and the resulting penalty to the Wolves ended their hopes.

Lam defended Isa's initial challenge on Toby King that sparked the melee, which resulted in yellow cards for Isa and Patton and a red for Westwood, who was seen to have head-butted Morgan Escaré on the big-screen replays.

Jack Hughes then capped his own strong performance by forcing his way over from close range in the closing stages, bringing the curtain down on an eventful night.

Westwood got a four-game ban.

On the same night Wakefield ended Hull's three-match unbeaten run with a 32-12 win at KCOM Stadium.

Ryan Hampshire and Bill Tupou tries, plus three Danny Brough goals, had given Trinity a 14-0 lead but Danny Houghton and Bureta Faraimo hit back for the hosts shortly before the break to make it 14-12. However, Tupou dived over in the corner for his second, before Pauli Pauli and Reece Lyne scores made the win safe.

Led by a fearsome display from prop David Fifita, Wakefield had to respond to adversity, losing two key men to injury and having two men sin-binned in a game featuring four yellow cards. Tom Johnstone and Tupou left the field in the first and second half respectively with knee problems, with winger Johnstone out for the season with an ACL injury.

Trinity back-rower Danny Kirmond got a two-match ban for his late tackle on Marc Sneyd.

On the Sunday, Lewis Tierney's late try converted by Sam Tomkins finally sealed an 18-16 victory for the Catalans Dragons in a brutal contest at Hull KR.

There hadn't been much between the sides for the bulk of the game, with Craig Hall and Tomkins exchanging penalty goals early on before back-to-back tries from Weller Hauraki and Joel Tomkins gave the Robins the advantage.

Brayden Wiliame and Lucas Albert touched down to tie the scores but a Craig Hall interception looked to have swung the momentum back in Rovers' favour, only for the Dragons to snatch it at the death when Tierney pounced on a Samisoni Langi kick.

Castleford put two points between them and fourth placed Salford with a 24-20 home win, in a game which saw former Tigers junior Adam Walker make his Red Devils debut after his ban for cocaine use.

Walker, back after 20 months out, came off the bench in the 26th minute and was involved in an incident which saw Paul McShane sin-binned. Before McShane went off, Jake Bibby ran in Salford's only first-half try after Nathan Massey and Jordan Rankin scores.

Greg Eden's dive into the corner for his seventh try in six games helped put the hosts 18-4 up after 47 minutes but two tries in four minutes from Jansin Turgut and Joey Lussick, gave Salford renewed hope.

Jesse Sene-Lefao bust through the line to edge the Tigers further ahead, with Rankin converting and adding a penalty for a two-score lead before Bibby set up a tense finish with the second of his tries.

**Round 7**

There was little doubt which was the team to beat after the Friday night of round seven as the highly anticipated clash between unbeaten St Helens and five-wins-out-of-six Castleford.

The match at the Jungle turned out to be one-sided, with Saints thrashing the Tigers 42-12.

Right-edge backrower Dominique Peyroux led the way with two tries, while Lachlan Coote had his best performance in a St Helens shirt yet, defending brilliantly and causing endless problems for the Tigers' defence. Coote opened the try-scoring after four minutes and from then on the Tigers went into panic mode.

Coote also kicked five goals, as Regan Grace, Zeb Taia, Louie McCarthy-Scarsbrook, Mark Percival and Jonny Lomax all crossed. Taia's try two minutes after the break to make it 24-0 ended any realistic hopes of a Castleford fightback.

They finally got on the board with tries from centre Michael Shenton and halfback Jake Trueman. Shenton got away with what should have been an an offside decision to go the length of the field for an interception try against his old club. Cas winger Greg Eden, was substituted in the second half after a string of bloopers.

The Tigers, already missing Luke Gale, said they were in no rush to sign a replacement for Ben Roberts, who left the club the previous week after struggling with injury.

Warrington were the only team at this stage of the season who could match Saints and the night before had looked like potential champions, for 55 minutes at least, when they led 28-6 at Wakefield.

But by the final whistle they were left hanging on, with Danny Brough's late conversion attempt to Joe Arundel's try to tie the scores at 34-all brushing the wrong side of the upright. Trinity had trailed 34-12 with just 16 minutes left before Kyle Wood and David Fifita inspired a spell of four quick tries to pull them to within two points.

The Wolves looked to be coasting to victory before the late drama, with Blake Austin catching the eye in an impressive performance.

Wakefield coach Chris Chester was forced into a host of switches, with his potent left-edge of Tom Johnstone, Bill Tupou and Matty Ashurst all missing through injury, while Danny Kirmond was suspended. The Trinity coach brought Joe Arundel and Max Jowitt into the threequarters and started with Pauli Pauli and Justin Horo in the back row.

Warrington ruthlessly exploited Wakefield's unfamiliarity on that side, scoring twice there in the opening nine minutes. A pinpoint Declan Patton kick was superbly taken by Toby King for the first, before the centre provided the last pass in a crisp handling move that was finished by Josh Charnley in the corner.

Wakefield barely touched the ball in the opening stages and when they did they came up with mistakes. Jowitt lost the ball in Charnley's tackle and moments later Chris Hill barged his way over to make it 18-0 after just 13 minutes.

Ryan Hampshire pulled a try back but it was a blip. An offload from the ever industrious Mike Cooper sparked a quick-fire move that ended with Ben Currie's inside pass allowing Austin to race through a big hole and under the posts. Stefan Ratchford added a fourth straight conversion and a penalty either side of the hooter to make it 28-6. Fifita and Charnley, the score made by a brilliant Austin dummy and break, exchanged tries before the breathless last 15 minutes.

Trinity confirmed that week they had secured a £3.15 million loan from Wakefield Council to buy the freehold of Belle Vue stadium and the surrounding land, with a view to redeveloping the stadium into a '10,000-plus facility'. Work was expected to begin that year.

Wigan got their second win of the season with a 30-22 success at Salford on the Sunday. Uncertainty about George Williams' future was rumoured to be a factor in Wigan's early season form, the stand-off seemingly destined for a deal in the NRL with Canberra at the end of the season. But his try hat-trick, his first for five years, proved to be the difference at the AJ Bell Stadium. His two second-half scores were set up by winger Joe Burgess, who was back in action after 11 months out injured.

Salford looked set to extend Wigan's poor run when Josh Jones grounded Robert Lui's kick for the first try of the game. Wigan responded with scores from Williams, Thomas Leuluai and Joe Greenwood but the Red Devils replied with three unanswered tries of their own to turn an 18-6 deficit into a four-point lead. Derrell Olpherts, Niall Evalds and Adam Walker all touched down either side of half-time for the hosts, who would have gone third with a victory, before Williams won it with two further tries to complete his hat-trick.

That weekend it became apparent that Shaun Edwards' arrival as head coach at Wigan was far from being a done deal. Chairman Ian Lenagan admitted that the press release the club put out the previous July, which suggested Edwards had signed a contract to take over from Adrian Lam for 2020, was misleading. A joint statement with Edwards officially released him from any obligation to coach the club next season.

Meanwhile the Red Devils confirmed that they were now able to register former Widnes forward Adam Lawton who had won a legal battle against his former Australian club Redcliffe Dolphins. A Rugby League International Federation tribunal determined Redcliffe had no right to hold Lawton's player registration after a contractual dispute over a signing-on fee.

Also on the Sunday, Hull FC held off a late London Broncos surge to move back into the top half of the Super League table, emerging 28-24 winners in Ealing.

The Broncos had led 14-10 at half-time, on course for their fourth win in eight games since their return to the top flight, thanks to tries from Elliot Kear and Eloi Pelissier and three Kieran Dixon goals against two tries from Josh Griffin.

After the break Hull added 18 points without reply, with Carlos Tuimavave, Jordan Thompson, Albert Kelly and Bureta Faraimo their second-half try-scorers. But Jordan Abdull and Rhys Williams got London back to within four points and it took a superb tackle from Hull winger Ratu Naulago, stopping centre Kear in his tracks, to keep the visitors ahead at the end. Even then, they had to scramble desperately post-hooter as London wing Rhys Williams pursued a cross-kick.

Bottom side Huddersfield finally hit their straps on the Friday night with a 42-8 home win over injury-hit Hull KR.

Shaun Lunt was making his first appearance in six months after being diagnosed with sepsis in September, which had threatened to cut his career short. However it was another hooker, Kruise Leeming who controlled the game from the moment Lee Gaskell kicked Huddersfield's first points until the final hooter. Leeming and wing Jermaine McGillvary both scored two tries each. Oliver Roberts, fullback Darnell McIntosh and prop Suaia Matagi got the Giants' other three tries, while Lee Gaskell landed six conversions and a penalty for a 14-point haul.

Second-row forward Weller Hauraki scored Rovers' only try, converted by Ryan Shaw, who kicked an early penalty.

The Giants' win meant that Leeds had to win at Catalans the next evening to stay off the foot of the table. They didn't, Fouad Yaha's fourth try, in the 72nd minute, edging a tight game 26-22.

A swashbuckling hat-trick for left winger Ash Handley gave the Rhinos some hope. But once again they couldn't sustain their advantage to press home for victory. Leading 16-6 the Rhinos were full value after half an hour but the emergence of Sam Kasiano for his Super League debut seemed to turn the tide.

Rhinos coach David Furner made a tactical choice to drop NRL recruit Tui Lolohea and play Liam Sutcliffe at stand-off in France.

## Round 8

Wigan chairman Ian Lenagan admitted the Warriors could improve communication with its supporters after embarrassment over whether Wigan icon Shaun Edwards would be the club's coach in 2020. The resulting impasse between the club and Edwards appeared to be affecting the morale of Wigan supporters,.

However, the mood at the DW Stadium lifted considerably on the last Sunday of March, with the Warriors hammering Catalans at home by 42-0, a victory that took them into eighth place in the Super League table. Winger Joe Burgess, who failed to make the England Elite Performance squad that was announced that week, scored three tries and fullback Zak Hardaker, another exclusion, also shone.

A Wigan team with no fewer than ten Academy products - including four forwards with only 15 first-team appearances between them - dismantled a far more experienced, established Catalans side.

Sam Tomkins was booed upon his every touch in the early moments but by the end the spotlight had rightly fallen on his successor in Hardaker, who claimed his first try for the Warriors in poetic fashion, rounding his predecessor to bring about the loudest cheer of the afternoon.

The first half was a tight, error-strewn affair, with only one try scored. It came from Burgess after 21 minutes, as the winger claimed a George Williams kick ahead of another ex-Wiganer in Lewis Tierney, to break the deadlock. Burgess's second ten minutes after the break may only have made it 12-0 but Catalans were playing poorly and there was no

Leeds' golden point hero Brad Dwyer looks for a way past Castleford's Adam Milner

way back.

Leeds were back on the winning trail but in much more dramatic circumstances as they beat local rivals Castleford in the Thursday-night TV game at Headingley.

With the scores locked at 20-all at the end of normal time, Brad Dwyer's 40-metre, 81st minute field goal, the first of his career, elicited scenes of wild euphoria for the hosts.

Going into the final set in normal time of a topsy-turvy encounter, Castleford had the upper hand after five minutes of gripping drama. Alex Foster's never-say-die chase of Peter Mata'utia's kick brought the scores level but Calum Turner's conversion drifted wide. Foster had been a late inclusion after Jordan Rankin's withdrawal with a hamstring injury.

Then Konrad Hurrell knocked on, establishing the position for Jake Trueman to slot over a one-pointer. But the referee ruled Liam Watts had baulked the chaser, Dwyer, and it was chalked off, a harsh call on replay.

Leeds failed to find touch from the resulting penalty but Trueman was wayward with another field-goal attempt at the end of the set, while Liam Sutcliffe did likewise, leaving Castleford to capitalise on a penalty with the final possession of normal time.

Adam Milner put them in the right part of the field, Trueman remained in the pocket ready for the potentially match-defining kick but, on the last, with the clock above him on the big screen signalling the game's finale, Paul McShane chose to run. Jack Walker, who had been magnificent throughout in all facets of the game, read the deception and made the match-saving tackle to set up Dwyer's astonishing party piece.

McShane that week copped a three-match ban for an elbow on Richie Myler.

On the Friday, a classy comeback by league leaders St Helens secured a 36-24 home win over Hull KR and preserved their 100 per cent record in 2019.

Key men James Roby, Mark Percival, Alex Walmsley and Zeb Taia were all missing from the Saints team sheet, while halfback Theo Fages limped off with a hip injury after 20 minutes.

Rovers themselves had massive injury woes but deserved their 24-18 lead 15 minutes into the second half. They welcomed back Ben Crooks (back), Kane Linnett (pectoral) and Mitch Garbutt (concussion) but were still huge underdogs going into the game, missing Danny McGuire, Robbie Mulhern, Adam Quinlan, James Greenwood, Lee Jewitt, Ryan Lannon, Will Dagger and Nick Scruton.

Lachlan Coote produced another dominant performance at fullback as Regan Grace's 72nd-minute four-pointer put the game beyond Rovers' reach.

Former Albert Goldthorpe Rookie of the Year Andre Savelio's return to Super League was more bitter than sweet on the Friday night as his new club Hull FC were hammered 63-12 at home by his former club Warrington.

Savelio was a late inclusion to the Black and Whites line-up on the bench and made a cameo 20-minute appearance, his first competitive game in a year and a half since rupturing his ACL whilst at Brisbane Broncos.

Fifth v second was not reflected, with Blake Austin finishing with four nonchalant tries, adding a cheeky field goal a minute from time. Warrington scored five tries in a six-set period in the opening 21 minutes of the game to end the contest and start a long night for Hull.

It was no way for Hull skipper Danny Houghton to make his 300th Super League appearance.

London Broncos coach Danny Ward bemoaned another slow start as the Broncos fell to home defeat against Huddersfield. The Broncos conceded 16 points in the opening 13 minutes of their 38-26 reverse, with Lee Gaskell in tactical control throughout and Akuila Uate scoring a try double.

Also on the Sunday afternoon, Wakefield just about outmuscled Salford at home, a 33-22 win leapfrogging the Red Devils in the Super League table and into fourth spot.

Pauli Pauli bulldozed his way through the Salford defence on numerous occasions, causing endless problems for the Red Devils as two Wakefield tries in six first-half minutes opened up an 18-6 lead from which Salford failed to recover.

The Red Devils' new signing Krisnan Inu admitted he was relieved to get minutes under his belt despite the loss. Inu was one of three players – along with Adam Tangata and Wellington Albert – released from their contracts following Widnes' financial downfall.

But there was bad news for Trinity, with Bill Tupou, ruled out for three months with a serious groin injury.

**BETFRED SUPER LEAGUE**
*Sunday 31st March*

| | P | W | D | L | F | A | D | Pts |
|---|---|---|---|---|---|---|---|---|
| St Helens | 8 | 8 | 0 | 0 | 243 | 104 | 139 | 16 |
| Warrington Wolves | 8 | 7 | 0 | 1 | 254 | 129 | 125 | 14 |
| Castleford Tigers | 8 | 5 | 0 | 3 | 184 | 151 | 33 | 10 |
| Wakefield Trinity | 8 | 4 | 0 | 4 | 202 | 174 | 28 | 8 |
| Salford Red Devils | 9 | 4 | 0 | 5 | 210 | 195 | 15 | 8 |
| | | | | | | | | |
| Hull FC | 8 | 4 | 0 | 4 | 171 | 203 | -32 | 8 |
| Catalans Dragons | 8 | 4 | 0 | 4 | 110 | 200 | -90 | 8 |
| Wigan Warriors | 8 | 3 | 0 | 5 | 174 | 140 | 34 | 6 |
| Huddersfield Giants | 8 | 3 | 0 | 5 | 158 | 201 | -43 | 6 |
| Hull Kingston Rovers | 9 | 3 | 0 | 6 | 150 | 214 | -64 | 6 |
| London Broncos | 9 | 3 | 0 | 6 | 146 | 234 | -88 | 6 |
| Leeds Rhinos | 9 | 2 | 0 | 7 | 177 | 234 | -57 | 4 |

*\* Thatto Heath Crusaders were the sole surviving community club in the Coral Challenge Cup after registering a 16-14 home victory against League 1 side North Wales Crusaders.*

# APRIL
## *Easter burn-out*

---

**Round 9**

Catalans Dragons ended St Helens' 100 per cent start to the season with a second-half defensive masterclass to win 18-10 in Perpignan on the first Saturday of April. Torrential rain in the first half turned the Gilbert Brutus pitch into a slippery quagmire but the second half saw blue skies and sunshine illuminate an eventful evening.

Saints were missing Jonny Lomax thanks to a stomach ailment and drafted in Danny Richardson at scrum-half for his first game of the season to replace the injured Theo Fages.

The sides traded tries in an error-strewn first half, Dominique Peyroux's early effort cancelled out by Fouad Yaha and then Tommy Makinson and Sam Tomkins scores making it 10-10 at the break.

Tomkins kicked a penalty in the 43rd minute but there were no further points until five minutes from the end as the game settled into a war of attrition.

Saints skipper James Roby, with blood pouring from his nose, battled ferociously to win the arm-wrestle. Alex Walmsley and Luke Thompson were full of vigour but they couldn't find a way through the Catalans' line. Dragons' second row Matt Whitley earned the sponsors' man-of-the-match award with an incredible effort in defence and Samisoni Langi, Greg Bird and Brayden Wiliame resisted all Saints' attacking efforts.

The game was in the balance at 12-10 until the 74th minute when substitute Lucas Albert slipped a grubber kick through the Saints line and Tony Gigot pounced for the matchwinner. Tomkins added the conversion and it remained 18-10 until the hooter and scenes of delirium in the Guasch Stand.

Saints' defeat meant that Warrington went top on points difference as they had beaten London Broncos at home the night before by 48-12.

The Broncos could feel unfortunate to have lost by such a margin. They matched Warrington for the majority of the first half but two tries in the final five minutes took the home side's lead to 20-0 and they were always likely to see the game out comfortably from there. Tom Lineham finished with a hat-trick.

Castleford kept the top two in sight, even if the margin was four league points, with an amazing 38-28 win over Wigan, their first win in three games.

It seemed unlikely. When Joe Burgess went in for Wigan's fourth try, the Warriors led 20-0 after only 22 minutes. Even after the loss of Jarrod Sammut with a knee injury, they still looked comfortable at 24-8.

But the Tigers took a 26-24 lead early in the second half after three tries in just six minutes through Mitch Clark, back for his first game since round two, Matt Cook and Adam Milner.

Burgess's second try on 65 minutes snatched back the lead but Tuoyo Egodo's try and Peter Mata'utia's superb touchline conversion brought his side within touching distance of victory at 32-28. Then a dropped ball by George Williams near his own line with the hooter sounding was gleefully scooped up by Mata'utia. As referee Chris Kendall awarded the try, the Jungle erupted. Mata'utia added the conversion to make it 38-28 to round off an unbelievable game.

Wigan's defeat came at the end of a week in which prop Gabriel Hamlin had been suspended by the RFL after being charged with a UK Anti-Doping violation.

On the same Friday night, Wakefield kept in the race with a 17-16 home win over Huddersfield, Danny Brough kicking the winning field goal four minutes from time.

Reece Lyne's early score gave Trinity the perfect start but England winger Jermaine McGillvary crossed to level. The first of two Darnell McIntosh tries helped put Giants 10-4 ahead. David Fifita then added a barnstorming try before McIntosh went over, but Fifita powered through again and Brough's boot earned victory.

Hull FC recovered from their thrashing by Warrington with a tight 23-16 win at Salford on the Sunday afternoon, their fourth successive away win. Josh Griffin's hat-trick against his old club pushed Hull up to fifth in the table as they inflicted a fourth straight defeat on the Red Devils.

Griffin's first try was the difference between the sides in a tight opening period as Hull led 10-6 at the break. He scored twice more in the second half as Hull, aided by 11 points from the boot of Marc Sneyd, pulled away.

Tries from Josh Jones, Niall Evalds and Jackson Hastings ensured Salford stayed competitive but they dropped to joint seventh.

They were joined by Hull KR, who had beaten Leeds 45-26 at Craven Park on the Thursday night. Four tries from Konrad Hurrell weren't enough to save the Rhinos from slipping to a painful defeat.

The damage was done in a dazzling first-half display from the Robins that saw them post three tries in the opening 15 minutes, on their way to establishing a 31-10 half-time advantage over a flat Leeds side.

A brace of Hurrell touchdowns kept the Rhinos in the game at the break and, when a Brad Singleton try was quickly followed up by Hurrell's hat-trick effort, it looked as though Leeds could set up an unlikely grandstand finish. But a penalty goal from the outstanding Craig Hall, Josh Drinkwater's first try for Rovers and one from Ben Crooks saw the Robins home, despite Hurrell snatching his fourth late on.

## Round 10

A bumper Friday-night crowd packed into St Helens' Totally Wicked Stadium to witness a hotly anticipated clash between the top two sides.

A close encounter was expected but it was Saints that emerged clear winners with a 38-12 success, their front row of Alex Walmsley, James Roby and Luke Thompson dominating the Wolves' pack.

St Helens led only 8-6 when Wolves prop Mike Cooper's high tackle on Danny Richardson saw him sin-binned in the 28th minute. While he was off the field, Saints took a stranglehold on the game with converted tries to the energetic Louie McCarthy-Scarsbrook and Jonny Lomax.

Daryl Clark pulled a try back six minutes after half-time but young prop Matty Lees took a try under the sticks superbly on 50 minutes, charging onto a bouncing ball following a bomb from Lachlan Coote that landed between Stefan Ratchford and Tom Lineham.

The final Saints tries from their wingers were pearlers. Regan Grace scored from around 80 metres out - his rounding of Wolves fullback Stefan Ratchford was a magical piece of play. Lineham fouled him in the act of scoring, which earned Saints an extra two points.

Then Tommy Makinson rounded off a brilliant passing movement from left to right, with Kevin Naiqama half rounding his marker before giving an exquisite scoring pass. Coote finished with seven goals after another superlative display.

St Helens were now two points clear at the top but Castleford had already blown their chance of closing the four-point gap on second-placed Warrington after a 20-18 defeat at Huddersfield the night before. Giants second row Alex Mellor scored a hat-trick as the lead changed hands no less than six times.

The Tigers had injuries aplenty and were missing Paul McShane through suspension but Junior Moors, Greg Minikin and Mike McMeeken all returned to the squad, with the latter having missed every game since round one, whilst prop Daniel Smith made his debut against his former side. Jake and Joe Wardle as well as Aaron Murphy, after a month out, returned for Huddersfield.

Mellor's hat-trick try with ten minutes to go proved the difference, the second-rower getting on the end of a great break by Jermaine McGillvary. Though the Tigers banged hard on the Huddersfield door, the home side held on for a priceless victory. And, the frustration was evident in the Castleford ranks as Adam Milner was sin-binned for a headbutt on Adam O'Brien when the Tigers were camped on the Giants' line with two minutes to go.

Wakefield moved level on points with the Tigers with a 30-20 Friday-night home win over Wigan.

Trinity got the advantage after a crazy end to the first half saw them score three tries in four minutes, with prop David Fifita putting in an 80-minute stint.

But Danny Brough became Trinity's latest injury worry after suffering a break in his thumb. Anthony England, Jacob Miller, Kyle Wood and Reece Lyne all left the field with injuries which made the win the more memorable.

Wigan made five alterations with Morgan Escaré, Tom Davies, Liam Paisley, Sam Powell and Joe Shorrocks all coming into the side, with the latter making his senior debut. Zak Hardaker pulled out late on for family reasons.

It was tight fo the first 35 minutes, when Craig Kopczak gave Wakefield a 6-4 lead with a converted try under the posts ten minutes after Joe Burgess had opened the scoring.

That proved to be the catalyst for an astonishing end to the first half. Trinity extended their lead just two minutes later, with Joe Arundel ending an eye-catching team move that saw the ball move through the hands of Brough and Ryan Hampshire.

And just when you thought that was it for an otherwise quiet first half, Fifita broke at pace down the left wing before offloading for Max Jowitt to score after the hooter had sounded.

The half-time break did little to disturb Wakefield's momentum or Wigan's turmoil. George Williams knocked on directly from kick-off before Justin Horo put Ben Jones-Bishop in for his first try of the season.

Miller became the third Wakefield player to be forced from the field seven minutes after the restart with a leg injury but Wigan were playing catch-up after Jones-Bishop made it 30-8 with his second try.

On the Saturday night, Marc Sneyd produced his second golden-point field goal of the season as Hull FC registered a 31-30 win in Perpignan, despite being behind in the 79th minute.

The Dragons had the game won with a 79th-minute try by NRL recruit Sam Kasiano, only for them to throw it all away with two fatal errors.

Sneyd resumed play with a short kick-off, which was collected within ten metres by Dragons centre Brayden Wiliame, although through French eyes the ball had crossed the ten-metre line before curling back. Sneyd kicked the resulting penalty goal from half-way and then saw his extra-time kick-off allowed to bounce into touch. Hull regained possession and Sneyd was almost predictably the man on hand for the decider.

It was a great win for the injury-hit Hull side, with Levy Nzoungou and Jack Brown both making debuts off the bench, and they were now back in level third.

41

*April*

**Challenge Cup Round 5**

Championship Halifax caused the upset of the round as they dumped Super League London Broncos out with a 24-16 Thursday home win. It was the third time in four years that Halifax had made it to round six after first-half tries from Ed Barber and Ben Kaye, followed by further scores from Reece Chapman-Smith and Quentin Laulu Togaga'e, plus four out of four goals from stand-in captain Steve Tyrer.

Bradford Bulls edged into the last 16 of the Cup with a mesmerising 27-26 win over fellow Championship side Featherstone Rovers at a bitterly cold Odsal.

With nine minutes remaining, Bradford, with Challenge Cup specialist John Kear at the coaching helm, were beaten. Trailing by 18 points, they needed a miracle. Dalton Grant's 71st-minute try felt like nothing more than a consolation.

Even Jordan Lilley's try five minutes later seemed inconsequential - yet when the hosts charged downfield in the final seconds, desperate for one more try to salvage something, they came up trumps. Frantically, the ball was hurled from side-to-side and eventually, the chink in the Featherstone line opened up enough for David Foggin-Johnston to touch down in the corner.

But back-rower Elliot Minchella, who only took up the kicking duties a few weeks before and had converted Grant and Lilley's tries, still had to convert from the touchline to send it to extra-time. He did that with nerves of steel and, just a few minutes later, Lilley claimed the heroics with a stunning golden-point field goal to send Bradford through.

Craig Hall's late score saved Hull KR from a shock Cup exit at the hands of part-timers Leigh. The Centurions had led from the sixth minute at Craven Park, with a heroic defensive effort frustrating a disjointed Rovers side. But Ryan Shaw and Hall went over in consecutive sets late on to spare the Super League side's blushes with a 14-10 win.

The other two Super League sides who entered the Cup at this stage both progressed comfortably, Leeds thrashing League 1 Workington at home by 78-6, with a memorable four-try show for threequarter Harry Newman, alongside three 19-year-old debutants, prop Muizz Mustapha, second row Owen Trout and halfback Callum McLelland.

Salford recorded a 76-6 home win over Championship Rochdale Hornets, Niall Evalds finishing with four tries, although they lost Ed Chamberlain for the season after he suffered an anterior cruciate ligament injury.

Doncaster were the only League 1 team left in the Cup after a shock 16-10 home win over Batley; while amateurs Thatto Heath were knocked out by Dewsbury Rams.

**Round 11**

Super League fans turned out in huge numbers for the first round of the Easter programme to help set a new attendance record for the competition. The total attendance for the six games of 79,173 beat the previous record for a 12-team Super League of 78,917, set in Round 25 of the 2007 season.

The programme started on the Thursday night as home team Castleford held off a remarkable late surge from Wakefield to emerge 28-26 winners.

The Tigers were brilliant for an hour before tiring - they lost Oliver Holmes and Jesse Sene-Lefao in the opening 25 minutes - and almost surrendering a 20-point lead. Wakefield were injury hit too - they only had three of their first choice backline. The stack of injuries meant that Cory Aston and Ben Reynolds were handed debuts for the Tigers and Trinity respectively. Winger Mason Caton-Brown made his second Wakefield debut after an emergency re-signing.

James Clare's two tries and one from Sene-Lefao had the Tigers 16-0 up on 18 minutes. When Aston scored a debut try on 24 minutes, supporting Daniel Smith's break after he was put through a gap by a great Liam Watts pass, the score was 22-0 and Wakefield's depleted side looked beaten.

But they plugged away and Caton-Brown marked his return with a diving finish at the left corner from Max Jowitt's excellent cut-out pass. Ryan Hampshire couldn't convert and Peter Mata'utia missed two penalty goal attempts too, leaving the score 22-4 at the break.

When Greg Minikin extended the lead to 22 points shortly after the break, Wakefield looked to have no chance. But Caton-Brown leapt above Clare to claim a Hampshire kick. Joe Arundel was forced off with a torn pectoral muscle, suffering the injury as he scored a try on 62 minutes after Reynolds and Jowitt combined. Hampshire's kick cut the deficit to just 14 points.

The arrears were soon down to eight. Wakefield chanced their arm on halfway, Jowitt raced through a gap and Reynolds had the legs to race 25 metres to score on debut.

Wakefield were on a roll and Castleford looked shot when Tinirau Arona scored in the corner after Ben Jones-Bishop batted down a crossfield kick, with Hampshire's conversion cutting the lead to two.

But the Tigers just held on. An Aston kick inside his own half was charged down by Reynolds, who was tackled 20 metres out. Wakefield decided on the next play to go for glory in the right corner but Mata'utia made an incredible try-saving cover tackle on Ben Jones-Bishop to prevent Wakefield from taking the lead.

Some good news for Trinity was that David Fifita had signed a new three-year contract.

On the same night the Catalans were proving far too good for London Broncos in Ealing, heading back to France with a 39-6 win under their belts thanks to a Greg Bird masterclass.

The defeat meant the Broncos were on the bottom of the table after Good Friday, albeit on points difference, after Leeds got their third win of the season, beating Huddersfield at home by 38-18.

Led by effervescent hooker Brad Dwyer, who set up tries with hand and foot and scored one himself, Leeds showed increased resolve to survive a Giants comeback and two sin-binnings in the heat.

It was 30-0 by the break and all the damage was done in the opening 40 minutes as Leeds racked up virtually a point-a-minute. But they weren't entirely comfortable until Ash Handley's 70th-minute breakaway score.

Leeds, it emerged, were rebuffed by Hull FC after a half a million pound bid to sign utility back Jake Connor, who starred in the Hull derby. Over 20,000 fans attended the game at the KCOM Stadium - the biggest crowd for a Hull FC home game since 2015.

It had taken a last-second Rovers try to decide the meeting earlier in the season but the Black and Whites exacted revenge in the most comprehensive of fashions as they embarrassed their rivals in the second half to secure a record victory over Rovers, Jack Logan scoring a hat-trick in a 56-12 win.

Lee Radford's choice to rotate his halfbacks, with Albert Kelly coming off the bench, proved to be a stroke of genius.

After the outstanding Connor started in the halves, the introduction of Kelly at half-time saw the Australian and Marc Sneyd torment Rovers, who had no answer to the onslaught. Kelly's ability to collect a kick and race downfield before offloading to Carlos Tuimavave to put Connor Wynne over for the game's final try was special.

Salford snapped a four-game losing streak and handed Warrington their first home loss of the season, winning 36-12 on Good Friday, piling on more misery seven days after the Wolves' crushing derby defeat at the hands of St Helens.

In the energy-sapping Cheshire sunshine, Red Devils enforcers Gil Dudson, Adam Walker and Greg Burke, as well as dummy-half Joey Lussick, who picked up three Albert

Jack Logan shows his delight at scoring in the Hull derby on Good Friday

Goldthorpe Medal points, controlled the middle of the field with a commanding display that laid the foundations.

The Red Devils raced into an early lead through Kris Welham and Lussick tries before a brief response came when Blake Austin crossed for the Wire.

But Salford continued to dominate as Daniel Murray and Robert Lui touched down and Krisnan Inu kicked 12 points to put them 28-6 up at the break. Jake Bibby made absolutely sure by crossing just after half-time, Inu converting that and a later penalty before Bryson Goodwin grabbed a consolation try.

The clash between Wigan Warriors and St Helens attracted the biggest crowd over the two days with 22,050 at the DW Stadium to see Saints go four points clear of the chasing pack after a convincing 36-10 win.

Both sides lost players to injury in the first quarter, Mark Percival suffering a hamstring tear in the opening minutes and then Tom Davies breaking an ankle after 20 minutes.

Saints' pack laid the platform for victory, with the double-act of Luke Thompson and Alex Walmsley leading the way in the early stages. Zak Hardaker and George Williams tries had Wigan still in the fight, trailing by 18-10 at half-time, Regan Grace scoring the first two of his first ever Super League hat-trick.

But Saints added further second-half tries through Tommy Makinson, Grace's superb third and Lachlan Coote, who also finished with six goals.

**Round 12**

St Helens' dominance of SLXXIV continued with a 62-16 Easter-Monday win at home over Hull FC. Kevin Naiqama scored four tries and Adam Swift a hat-trick as Saints ran in 11 tries against a team that had scored 56 points in the Hull derby four days before.

Joe Westerman and Carlos Tuimavave tries gave Hull a 10-0 lead after 11 minutes but Saints raced back through two Jonny Lomax tries - on his 200th Saints appearance - and by half-time it was 30-10 as Naiqama, Swift and Lachlan Coote crossed before the break.

Jez Litten cut the deficit early in the second half but that was Hull's last salvo. Swift completed his hat-trick while Naiqama scored twice more either side of Jack Welsby's try

Warrington remained the only club in sight of Saints as they got back on track with a resounding 54-6 win at Hull KR. The Wolves scored 36 points without reply after half-time with Tom Lineham and Joe Philbin both crossing twice as the Wire racked up nine tries, with Stefan Ratchford kicking all nine conversions.

Ben Crooks and Blake Austin traded early tries before Lineham went over to edge Warrington ahead, with Ratchford converting superbly from near the touchline. Philbin then scrambled over to extend the visitors' lead with Ratchford converting to make it 18-6 at half-time.

Austin set up Josh Charnley to score in the corner just a minute into the second half and from then on it was one-way traffic. Rovers had conceded 110 points over the Easter period.

Prop Julian Bousquet scored two tries as Catalans Dragons eased to a 37-16 home victory against Castleford at a packed Stade Gilbert Brutus.

Bousquet and gamestar Tony Gigot crossed for the hosts but Greg Eden reduced the deficit to 12-4 before half-time. Greg Bird produced a killer play nine minutes after the break when he stole the ball from James Clare on a kick return and ran in the try, with Gigot potting a field goal ten minutes later before Bousquet scored his second soon after.

Castleford replied straight from the restart through Eden, while Cory Aston also crossed but Matt Whitley and Sam Tomkins wrapped up a victory that moved the Dragons to the edge of the play-off spots.

Castleford lost captain Michael Shenton to an ankle injury just before the hour mark but had already announced the signing of Melbourne centre Cheyse Blair on a contract to the end of the 2022 season. He was expected to arrive in the next fortnight.

Jermaine McGillvary grabbed a try-brace as Huddersfield Giants battled to a 24-19 home win over bottom-of-the-table London Broncos.

The Broncos raced into an 8-0 lead thanks to two goals from Kieran Dixon and a bustling Jay Pitts try but the Giants fought back before the break with tries from Alex Mellor and Scott Grix, a beauty after a break down the left by Innes Senior, to lead 12-8.

But five minutes after half-time Rhys Williams raced away after intercepting a Grix pass to put the Broncos back in front before McGillvary went over for the hosts. Ryan Morgan levelled and a Morgan Smith field goal gave London a 19-18 lead with seven minutes remaining.

A late second from McGillvary off a brilliant Darnell McIntosh long pass won it, although Alex Walker was convinced he'd scored a try at the death, referee Marcus Griffiths disagreeing.

A second defeat over the Easter period kept London at the foot of the Super League table.

Wigan moved two points clear of the bottom as they survived a scare to beat Salford Red Devils 30-26 at the AJ Bell Stadium, ending a three-game losing streak.

Joe Burgess opened the scoring for Wigan before Joe Bullock crossed for the visitors' second. With Zak Hardaker - playing at centre, with Morgan Escaré at fullback - converting both after kicking an early penalty, Wigan led 14-0.

But George Griffin and Niall Evalds tries either side of the break pulled Salford to within two points before Joey Lussick put the hosts 26-20 in front after Joe Greenwood and Adam Walker traded tries.

The game took another twist when Derrell Olpherts coughed up possession bringing back an early carry and, gifted the unexpected possession, Wigan made it count when Greenwood thundered over for his second try.

Hardaker had been impeccable with the boot but his conversion to level the scores rebounded off the upright, leaving Wigan trailing by two points. But with three minutes to go, George Williams kicked, challenged for the ball, regained possession, swung the ball right and Hardaker cut through for the winning try that he converted.

Sean O'Loughlin was a late withdrawal, providing the chance for another youngster - hooker Amir Bourouh - to make his Wigan debut.

Leeds remained level bottom with London Broncos as they were edged 26-24 at Wakefield, who moved back into third spot.

It was level at the break, with debutant Lee Kershaw and Reece Lyne going over for Trinity and Liam Sutcliffe and Brett Ferres both touching down for the visitors.

But Wakefield took the game away from the Rhinos in the opening 20 minutes of the second half with a pair of Ryan Hampshire penalties and converted scores from Ben Jones-Bishop and Max Jowitt that stretched their lead to 26-12. Matt Parcell's try reduced the arrears with 10 minutes to play and Tui Lolohea crossed for the Rhinos on the hooter. But it was all too late.

## Round 13

Leeds Rhinos pulled themselves two points clear of the relegation spot on the last Sunday afternoon of April after just holding off a Hull KR fightback at Headingley to emerge 28-24 victors.

The poor form that had plagued Leeds for most of the season seemed a distant memory when Matt Parcell's try six minutes after the break made it 28-0 in favour of the hosts. Two Ash Handley tries and scores from Tom Briscoe and Jack Walker had helped the Rhinos to a 22-0 half-time advantage.

But when Ben Crooks' two tries made it 28-12 with 15 minutes remaining, the nerves were almost palpable around Headingley. The Rhinos began to panic, wasting further chances to kill the Robins off. And they were almost made to pay in spectacular fashion.

First, Kane Linnett's try with six minutes remaining reduced the deficit further before, with 90 seconds remaining, former Leeds player Weller Hauraki touched down, with Danny McGuire kicking a drop-goal conversion and making it 28-24.

Suddenly, it was a thrilling finish to a game that, for the first 50 minutes, seemed a formality for the hosts, who did just about enough to hang on.

Leaders St Helens gained revenge for their only defeat of the season so far as they comfortably saw off Catalans Dragons at home by 50-14.

Saints went down 18-10 in Perpignan in early April but this time their youngsters ran in nine tries in a remarkable show of strength in depth. They were without key men James Roby, Lachlan Coote, Tommy Makinson, Jonny Lomax, Luke Thompson, Morgan Knowles, Mark Percival and Louie McCarthy-Scarsbrook. But Roby's heir apparent Aaron Smith, exciting centre Matty Costello - who scored a hat-trick - and 18-year-old prodigy Jack Welsby stood out in a dominant showing.

Warrington strengthened their hold on second spot with what ended up being a comfortable 50-19 home victory over Huddersfield, who played their part in an enthralling first half that saw them overturn a 12-point deficit into a 19-12 lead at the break.

The Giants, however, never looked the same once they lost both Joe Wardle and Matty English to head knocks within six minutes of the restart. It left them down on two interchanges for the rest of the match and, coupled with an improved Warrington effort, Simon Woolford's men had no response.

Warrington, though, showed their ability to close out a match in the second half as they punished any errors which came their way, with Blake Austin stepping up when needed by providing two fine tries to allow his side to ease home.

In the fourth game played on the Sunday - it was the round where dummy-halves deliberately throwing the ball at a grounded defender in order to win a penalty would be penalised themselves - Hull FC moved into third spot in the table, leapfrogging Wakefield by beating them 30-14 at the KCOM Stadium.

Hull scored early through Albert Kelly and survived an early Gareth Ellis yellow card for a high tackle on Mason Caton-Brown to reach half-time 14-10 ahead. Trinity had made the most of their man advantage when Max Jowitt touched down but when the numbers were evened up Connor Wynne's try and the boot of Marc Sneyd put the home side back ahead.

Justin Horo's score got the visitors into the contest before the break but Lee Radford's team had just too much after the restart as Wakefield's completion rate dropped from 88 per cent in the first half to 36 in the second period.

Joe Westerman scored two tries off Albert Kelly passes before fatigue from both sets of players was evident.

Horo produced a desperate charge down on a Sneyd field-goal attempt and Wakefield went up the other end. A trademark defence skittling run from Pauli Pauli put Jowitt into space to grab his second on the left edge, before Sneyd had the last say with his second penalty goal of the half.

The day before, on the Saturday, regular downpours blighted the match between Wigan and Castleford, with the Warriors emerging 6-4 winners

The Tigers went in 4-0 up at the break thanks to two penalties from Peter Mata'utia in a first half in which attacking rugby was at a premium, with the Warriors spending the majority of the opening 40 minutes defending in their own half.

The defensive masterclass from both Wigan and Castleford continued in the second half, with only one try being scored when Sam Powell forced his way over from close range on 53 minutes.

It looked like the defensive stint from the Warriors in the first half would hurt them towards the end of the game, as the Tigers mounted a late surge in search of the victory, but it wasn't to be as Wigan held on.

On the same day, Salford produced a highly professional display to come away from London with a 30-10 win.

Four converted tries without reply gave the Red Devils a 24-0 advantage at the break, Joey Lussick, Niall Evalds, Daniel Murray and Jackson Hastings getting the tries and Kristian Inu the goals.

The Broncos twice breached the visitors defence in the second half as Rhys Williams and Matty Fleming crossed either side of a try from Lee Mossop.

The Red Devils remained sixth, closing to within two points of the four teams above them on 14 points. In the week it had emerged they had suspended forward Jansin Turgut for 'breaching club protocol'.

**BETFRED SUPER LEAGUE**
**Sunday 28th April**

| | P | W | D | L | F | A | D | Pts |
|---|---|---|---|---|---|---|---|---|
| St Helens | 13 | 12 | 0 | 1 | 439 | 174 | 265 | 24 |
| Warrington Wolves | 13 | 10 | 0 | 3 | 430 | 240 | 190 | 20 |
| Hull FC | 13 | 8 | 0 | 5 | 327 | 337 | -10 | 16 |
| Wakefield Trinity | 13 | 7 | 0 | 6 | 315 | 292 | 23 | 14 |
| Castleford Tigers | 13 | 7 | 0 | 6 | 288 | 268 | 20 | 14 |
| Catalans Dragons | 13 | 7 | 0 | 6 | 248 | 313 | -65 | 14 |
| Salford Red Devils | 13 | 6 | 0 | 7 | 318 | 270 | 48 | 12 |
| Wigan Warriors | 13 | 5 | 0 | 8 | 268 | 274 | -6 | 10 |
| Huddersfield Giants | 13 | 5 | 0 | 8 | 255 | 343 | -88 | 10 |
| Leeds Rhinos | 13 | 4 | 0 | 9 | 293 | 347 | -54 | 8 |
| Hull Kingston Rovers | 13 | 4 | 0 | 9 | 237 | 378 | -141 | 8 |
| London Broncos | 13 | 3 | 0 | 10 | 193 | 375 | -182 | 6 |

* *With over 80 players estimated to be missing from the weekend's fixtures, with some clubs reporting injury lists running into double figures, Super League coaches were leading a growing clamour to reduce the Easter schedule imposed on top-flight players from as early as the next season.*

# MAY
# *From Spain to the Mersey*

---

**Round 14**

With St Helens way ahead of the pack, the battle for the other top-five play-off spots was full of twists and turns.

On the first weekend of May there was a big re-shuffle, with Wakefield going back into third, Catalans Dragons fourth, while Salford went above Castleford, who fell to seventh.

Warrington were still in second place after they powered past an understrength Castleford side on the Friday night at the Mend-a-Hose Jungle, emerging with a 26-14 win, with hooker Daryl Clark at the hub of most of their best work against his former club.

Alongside Clark and Blake Austin, there were big shifts from frontrowers Chris Hill and Mike Cooper, a return to the side for winger Jack Johnson after a year out with a broken leg and two tries to centre Toby King.

Although Cory Aston's early try put the Tigers ahead, first-half tries for Cooper and King saw Wire seize control. King got his second and Ben Currie added another as the visitors restarted dynamically, Stefan Ratchford taking his goal tally to five.

Tuoyo Egodo and Greg Minikin got two tries back but it was not enough for the Tigers, who gave Australian centre Cheyse Blair a debut following his midweek arrival from Melbourne Storm. The seventh-minute loss of influential hooker Paul McShane with a rib injury was a further blow.

Wakefield moved back into third as they snatched victory over Huddersfield by a single point for the second time in the season. Ryan Hampshire slotted a late penalty as Wakefield earned a dramatic 26-25 win at the John Smith's Stadium.

The Giants trailed 18-6 at the break, with Mason Caton-Brown's double and David Fifita's lovely kick and chase putting the visitors in control after Matt Frawley's try for the home team. But in the first ten minutes after the turnaround, Jermaine McGillvary twice went over in the corner to level at 18-18.

Adam O'Brien scored under the posts for the hosts not long after and it looked like the Giants were in control. But ten minutes after, Ben Jones-Bishop intercepted to scamper the length of the pitch and Hampshire's conversion squared it up again.

The Giants were rocked three minutes later as Ukuma Ta'ai was sin-binned for a high shot. But still they re-took the lead on 71 minutes, Oliver Russell's deflected field-goal attempt just having the legs to go over.

But Huddersfield couldn't hold on. After restricting Wakefield to a kick from their own half, Darnell McIntosh attempted to pick the ball up at his feet, rather than control it. He spilled it, Wakefield won a penalty a few plays later and Hampshire kicked what proved to be the winning points.

More bad news for Trinity was a season-ending knee injury for prop Tinirau Arona.

Catalans were well in the mix after they hammered Hull FC 37-6 at the KCOM Stadium. After an early Sam Tomkins penalty, Hull led with a converted try from Mickey Paea, before the Dragons responded through Fouad Yaha, Tony Gigot and Brayden Wiliame.

48

Arthur Romano, Matt Whitley and Samisoni Langi added three further tries after the break, with Tomkins slotting three kicks and Gigot a field goal that sealed the win.

Hull had young centre Kieran Buchanan on debut, while Marc Sneyd and halfback partner Albert Kelly were out injured. Jake Connor's sin-binning for dissent just before half-time didn't help their cause.

Salford moved into sixth, two points behind Hull, as a five-star performance against Leeds by stand-off Robert Lui and a rare two-try haul to bench prop Adam Walker snapped their five-game losing streak at home, by 28-16.

Tries from Lee Mossop and Walker earned the Red Devils a 12-0 lead before Mikolaj Oledzki pulled one back before half-time. Walker, Joey Lussick and Lui added three more Salford tries after the break.

And, although Harry Newman and Ash Handley replied in the last ten minutes with two more tries for the Rhinos, the 2017 Super League champions fell to a tenth defeat in 14 games, only two points off the bottom, trailing Huddersfield by two points and four behind reigning champions Wigan.

Wigan had secured two more points the night before in the Thursday TV match, an 18-8 home win over London making it three victories in a row.

The Broncos, who were looking to do the double over Wigan for the first time in 14 years, led 8-6 at the break thanks to two goals from Kieran Dixon and a Jay Pitts try, with Jake Shorrocks crossing for the home side.

The Warriors improved considerably after the break, in both attack and defence, and were rewarded with tries from Chris Hankinson and Morgan Escaré as they held on to secure the two competition points.

The Broncos certainly had their chances to come away with the win, with Dixon and Rhys Williams guilty of dropping the ball close to the line, while James Cunningham spilled the ball with no one in front of him following a break from Dixon.

On the Sunday, Kevin Naiqama and Tommy Makinson each bagged hat-tricks as St Helens survived a scare at Hull KR to win 42-26. The league leaders turned in a clinical display, with their right flank in sparkling form. But they were made to work hard by a Rovers side who put a torrid Easter period behind them to make Saints fight right to the end.

Rovers had gone 12-0 up with tries from Danny Addy and Ryan Shaw but Naiqama's double and Makinson's first put Saints four points ahead at the interval. Jimmy Keinhorst briefly gave Rovers the lead again after half-time. But Naiqama and Makinson completed trebles and Jonny Lomax and Regan Grace also crossed, with Will Oakes replying.

## Challenge Cup Round 6

Bradford Bulls produced one of the biggest cup shocks in recent years as they beat Leeds Rhinos at Odsal by 24-22, watched by a peak audience on BBC1 on over 1.1 million on the Saturday afternoon.

It was a huge win in particular for Bulls halfback Jordan Lilley, who was man of the match at the end of a week in which he was told by the Rhinos he would not be required at Headingley any more.

Leeds had that week also decided to terminate head coach David Furner's contract, with assistant coach Richard Agar taking interim control.

Championship Bradford led 22-14 at half-time thanks to tries from Dalton Grant, Jake Webster, Sam Hallas and Mikey Wood, although they twice fell behind, first to an early Tui Lolohea score and then when Callum McLelland responded to Grant's try. The Bulls defended for their lives after the break, although rising star Harry Newman got a try back on 49 minutes.

The Rhinos almost forced extra-time when Tom Briscoe crossed late on. But Liam Sutcliffe's conversion hit the post and the Bulls held out.

Bradford were rewarded with a mouthwatering all-Championship Challenge Cup quarter-final tie against their other local rivals, Halifax, who ran in six tries, including doubles for Chester Butler and James Saltonstall, in their 34-6 win at Dewsbury.

Catalans Dragons hooker Michael McIlorum returned to the side on the Saturday for the 62-6 home victory over Doncaster, with Brayden Wiliame scoring four tries against the League 1 side.

Three tries in the final six minutes gave Wakefield a hard-fought, rain-affected, 26-6 home victory over a stubborn Widnes side. Max Jowitt had a star game as Ben Jones-Bishop's try six minutes from the end to make it 16-6 ended any hopes for Widnes.

Hull KR coach Tim Sheens said he wasn't getting carried away after the Robins' stunning 32-18 win over Salford on the Saturday. The Robins racked up 26 points in a huge second-half comeback.

Salford led 16-6 shortly after half-time thanks to tries from Krisnan Inu, Niall Evalds and Kris Welham against a Kane Linnett try. But, after the break, Josh Drinkwater crossed and, after Inu kicked a penalty, Junior Vaivai scored and Ryan Shaw added the extras to draw Rovers level. Danny Addy's close-range score then put the visitors ahead before Weller Hauraki's late try sealed victory.

Hull FC kept on course for a third Wembley appearance in four years as they knocked out Castleford with a 28-12 win at the KCOM Stadium on the Friday night.

Jake Connor and Marc Sneyd were the architects, dictating the pace of the game, with Albert Kelly playing an impressive supporting role from fullback, to have Castleford chasing the game constantly after three first-half tries through Connor, Bureta Faraimo and Kelly.

James Clare pulled one back for Castleford before the break, followed by a fifth try late on for Cory Aston. By then a try for Mark Minichiello had already settled it for Hull.

St Helens didn't have it all their own way in the Sunday afternoon TV game but they dug deep for a 22-16 win at the John Smith's Stadium.

The 12-times winners edged a tight first half 12-10 with tries from Regan Grace and Theo Fages, as the Giants crossed through Joe Wardle and Aaron Murphy. Lachlan Coote's score early in the second half took them further clear but Wardle hit straight back for the hosts.

The game was decided by Theo Fages' high kick, tipped back by Tommy Makinson, which Kevin Naiqama touched down, the video referee giving the footage plenty of scrutiny before awarding the try. Saints then showed all of the steel that had taken them to the top of the league table by seeing out the final 20 minutes.

Earlier in the afternoon, Warrington survived an almighty effort from Wigan to secure a 26-24 home win.

A late penalty from the boot of Stefan Ratchford proved to be the difference in a thrilling encounter between two sides who had won Rugby League's most prestigious knockout competition 27 times between them.

Led by Daryl Clark at hooker and Ratchford at fullback, the hosts led on three separate occasions in the first half and looked well placed to push on and record a comfortable victory after Ryan Atkins' 47th-minute try, converted by Ratchford, made it 24-14.

However, Wigan fought back superbly, with two tries in four minutes levelling the scores and the fact that Ratchford's penalty goal which won the game was the only score in the final quarter underlined how closely matched the sides were.

**Round 15**

'Historique, fantastique, énorme,' Catalans Dragons president Bernard Guasch told League Express after witnessing his team's 33-16 victory over Wigan at Barcelona's Camp Nou in front of a record regular-season Super League crowd of 31,555.

Matt Whitley halted by Oliver Gildart and Joe Bullock during Catalans' win against Wigan in Barcelona

*May*

It was fine event and a fine win for the Dragons, who were missing Sam Tomkins with a back problem and lost stand-in halfback Greg Bird to a biceps injury after 15 minutes.

There were only two points in it at half-time, as winger Liam Marshall's late try in reply to Wigan old boy Michael McIlorum's score made it 8-6. However, Catalans then took control, David Mead claiming two tries, while the outstanding Samisoni Langi and Sam Kasiano also scored to help the Dragons go third in the table.

Oliver Gildart and Zak Hardaker's late tries were consolations for Wigan.

The night before, Hull made their way across the Pennines without ten first-team players, including captain Danny Houghton and frontline outside backs Bureta Faraimo and Carlos Tuimavave but they came back from Warrington with a 19-12 victory under their belts.

The Black and Whites scored 18-unanswered points in nine first-half minutes and some outstanding defensive rearguard action laid the platform for them to hold out Warrington time and time again to move up to fourth.

Jamie Shaul made an impeccable return from two months out after concussion problems as Marc Sneyd's field goal 12 minutes from time put the game beyond Warrington.

The defeat left the second-placed Wolves six points adrift of St Helens, who on the same night snatched a 32-30 home victory over Salford, substitute James Bentley barging over in the 79th minute to give fullback Lachlan Coote the chance to slot the winning conversion, after he himself had bagged a hat-trick of tries.

Video-referee James Child ruled there had been no double movement or knock-on by Bentley in the act of grounding the ball, although plenty of people disagreed.

St Helens shot into a 16-nil lead inside twelve minutes after Coote, twice, and Tommy Makinson crossed before Salford ran in 30-unanswered points to lead 30-16 on the hour mark. Converted tries from Gil Dudson, Niall Evalds and Derrell Olpherts gave the Red Devils a half-time lead and after the break Evalds' second and Rob Lui's try seemingly set Salford fair.

But Coote's third, Tommy Makinson's second and Bentley's winner, which was his first try in Saints colours in only his third appearance of the season, completed the breathtaking victory.

Kruise Leeming was the spark that produced Huddersfield's 30-22 home win over Hull KR, with the hooker scoring the match-sealing try five minutes from time.

Winger Jermaine McGillvary scored two of his side's six tries as Huddersfield came from 16-8 down at half-time. Junior Vaivai, Joel Tomkins and Craig Hall all scored first-half tries for Rovers but then came a turnaround. Leeming and the Wardle brothers, Joe and Jake, both crossed to add to Huddersfield's two first-half tries from McGillvary and Innes Senior.

Danny Addy got one back late on but too late to prevent a fifth straight loss for the Robins. The Giants' first win in three matches lifted them level on points with eighth-placed Wigan.

On the Saturday, London Broncos registered their second home win of the season over Wakefield by 42-34.

The Broncos were thankful for the points they'd scored earlier as what looked like a comfortable win became anything but after Ryan Hampshire sparked a wild Wakefield comeback that just fell short as time ran out.

A four-try show by man of the match Jordan Abdull helped the Broncos go 42-6 up and look comfortable but, after a David Fifita try woke Trinity up, they began exploiting holes in the Broncos' defence and scored 28 points in 13 minutes to draw within eight points of the hosts.

The round had opened on the Thursday night as Leeds opened their new North Stand, with Castleford happily playing the role of party poopers by hammering the Rhinos

52

30-8, halting a four-match losing run in the process.

Leeds enjoyed periods of possession but were wasteful in their execution - notably when Harry Newman and Kallum Watkins sliced the Tigers defence open but the final pass, with the line beckoning, went to ground.

The Rhinos went in front from the tee when Liam Sutcliffe knocked over a penalty but Jesse Sene-Lefao prised his way through from Paul McShane's dummy-half pass and, after Watkins was sin-binned for a spear tackle, Jake Trueman looped a peach of a pass wide to Greg Eden to set up the winger's 100th Super League try and a 12-2 half-time lead.

Sene-Lefao raced over again following the break, after Mike McMeeken's ball-steal on Newman created the position, but Matt Parcell's dive over narrowed the deficit.

It was only a temporary reprieve, as James Clare pounced on a spilled chip in-goal and Trueman scorched through the defence to dot down and blow out the score.

After the game, League Express revealed the Rhinos had tried and failed with a bid to bring Danny McGuire back from Hull KR for the final months of his playing career.

## Round 16

The Magic Weekend was moved from Newcastle to Liverpool's Anfield Stadium in 2019.

The aggregate attendance of 56,869 was below the 64,319 that watched the 2018 event in Newcastle but above the record low of 52,043 at Murrayfield in 2010.

The weekend kicked off with a thriller as Catalans edged Wakefield in the last five minutes of the game, finishing 25-18 winners. Tony Gigot potted a 40-metre field goal in the 76th minute with the scores at 18-all before Benjamin Garcia barged over for his second try to clinch the points.

Catalans were in cruise control in the opening 40 minutes of the game and deservedly led 12-0 at the break against a Wakefield side who, up until that point, had struggled to find any attacking fluidity. Fouad Yaha's early score broke the deadlock and, while there was an element of good fortune to their second try, as a suspiciously forward pass found its way to Yaha before Tony Gigot finished the move, Catalans were undeniably the better team in that first half.

By the 50th minute, Trinity's 12-0 deficit had become a 14-12 lead. First, a scintillating long-range move involving Mason Caton-Brown and Jacob Miller was finished expertly by Kyle Wood, before three minutes later, a deft Ryan Hampshire pass sent Danny Kirmond over on the angle.

Hampshire converted both before adding a penalty after 47 minutes to put Wakefield ahead for the first time. But when industrious forward Garcia crossed with the hour mark approaching, it put Catalans back in control.

After a period of prolonged pressure on the Dragons' line, Trinity got their reward with 12 minutes remaining. They shifted the ball one way and then the other and, with Max Jowitt expertly supporting from the back, the extra man proved telling as Ben Jones-Bishop had just enough space to squeeze over in the right corner. That made it 18-18 but Hampshire missed the crucial conversion attempt, meaning it was now a test of who would hold their nerve.

And crucially, it was Gigot and Catalans who answered that question before Garcia's late effort.

For Trinity fans there was the added worry of seeing star forward David Fifita hobbling off in the final moments of the game.

Huddersfield handed Hull FC an astounding a 55-2 hiding in game two. Giants fullback Darnell McIntosh lit up the stadium, with Jermaine McGillvary and Adam O'Brien both adding braces of their own as the Claret and Golds ran riot in a 10-try rout. Marc Sneyd got the Airlie Birds' only points with a penalty goal on the stroke of half-time.

Hull prop Josh Bowden made his first Super League appearance in 385 days, more than twelve months after rupturing the anterior cruciate ligament in his left knee against

*May*

Featherstone in the previous year's Challenge Cup.

In the finale to Saturday, Warrington beat Wigan for the second time in 13 days, this time by 26-14.

After Zak Hardaker kicked the Warriors ahead, Declan Patton converted his own try to put the Wire into the lead. Wigan broke back through Joe Burgess but Blake Austin re-established Warrington's six-point advantage after Hardaker had kicked Wigan level. Toby King crossed, running 65 metres to touch down following an interception to secure the win, before Willie Isa's late consolation.

In the first game of the Sunday, Ryan Shaw's nerveless 74th-minute penalty earned Hull KR a crucial 22-20 win over Salford as the pressure at the bottom of Super League heated up.

Shaw's kicking was ultimately the difference between the two sides, with the winger kicking five goals from as many attempts to secure the win, despite Salford scoring four tries to three.

Rovers were in a commanding 14-0 position after tries to Kane Linnett and Craig Hall, playing against twelve men near the end of the first half, with on-loan Pauli Pauli in the sin bin.

But the Red Devils mounted a thrilling comeback after Joey Lussick's try at the end of the first half, despite Hall's second try four minutes into the second half. Pauli scored a try, followed by Ken Sio's brace that drew them level before Shaw's late decider after Lussick was penalised for a high shot on Josh Drinkwater.

Jackson Hastings was wearing a tribute to former Salford player Jansin Turgut on his shirt and presented it to the girlfriend of his former teammate in a gesture of support for the former Red Devil. Doctors in Ibiza had told Turgut's family they hoped the former England Academy captain would make a full recovery following his fall from the third storey of an airport carpark the previous week.

Leeds edged a bottom-of-the-table four pointer with a 24-22 victory over London Broncos, a first win for interim coach Richard Agar.

The Rhinos raced ahead with tries from Liam Sutcliffe and Ash Handley. Ryan Morgan got London on the board and, after Jack Walker put Leeds further ahead, Jordan Abdull sent the Broncos into double figures. Harry Newman scored for Leeds against the run of play and gamestar Richie Myler put the Rhinos ahead 24-10 with 12 minutes remaining, before Abdull and Alex Walker tries set up a tense finale.

Later that week, Rhinos hooker Matt Parcell was suspended for two matches by the RFL for two separate incidents when he collided with referee James Child. The two incidents occurred in the 34th and 52 minutes of the game. On each occasion Parcell was rushing back in defence and accidentally knocked Child over, although fortunately the referee wasn't injured and he didn't take any action on the field. Nonetheless the incidents were picked up by the RFL Match Review Panel and they issued Parcell with a one-match suspension for each incident, which they described as 'reckless', to be served consecutively.

The weekend ended with league leaders St Helens looking unstoppable as they beat Castleford 36-16.

Saints quickly took control with first-half tries from Tommy Makinson, Regan Grace, Jonny Lomax and Theo Fages. Grant Millington scored for Cas, while Jack Ashworth went in under the sticks to extend Saints' lead after half-time.

Lachlan Coote and Kevin Naiqama also crossed for Saints, with Chris Clarkson and Greg Eden running in late replies.

**BETFRED SUPER LEAGUE**
*Sunday 26th May*

| | P | W | D | L | F | A | D | Pts |
|---|---|---|---|---|---|---|---|---|
| St Helens | 16 | 15 | 0 | 1 | 549 | 246 | 303 | 30 |
| Warrington Wolves | 16 | 12 | 0 | 4 | 494 | 287 | 207 | 24 |
| Catalans Dragons | 16 | 10 | 0 | 6 | 343 | 353 | -10 | 20 |
| Hull FC | 16 | 9 | 0 | 7 | 354 | 441 | -87 | 18 |
| Castleford Tigers | 16 | 8 | 0 | 8 | 348 | 338 | 10 | 16 |
| Wakefield Trinity | 16 | 8 | 0 | 8 | 393 | 384 | 9 | 16 |
| Salford Red Devils | 16 | 7 | 0 | 9 | 396 | 340 | 56 | 14 |
| Huddersfield Giants | 16 | 7 | 0 | 9 | 365 | 393 | -28 | 14 |
| Wigan Warriors | 16 | 6 | 0 | 10 | 316 | 341 | -25 | 12 |
| Leeds Rhinos | 16 | 5 | 0 | 11 | 341 | 427 | -86 | 10 |
| Hull Kingston Rovers | 16 | 5 | 0 | 11 | 307 | 470 | -163 | 10 |
| London Broncos | 16 | 4 | 0 | 12 | 265 | 451 | -186 | 8 |

# JUNE
## *Stick to the 'Fax*

**Challenge Cup Quarter-finals**

Halifax head coach Simon Grix called on his club's historic Challenge Cup semi-final appearance to be the catalyst for a new era at one of the sport's sleeping giants.

On the first Sunday of June the part-timers re-wrote history as a late James Woodburn-Hall try snatched a 20-16 victory over fierce rivals Bradford at Odsal, securing them a first semi-final appearance since 1988.

Former Warrington star Grix, who was born in and lived in the town throughout his life, was only three years old the last time Halifax reached the penultimate stage of the competition.

The 6,591 crowd was the biggest of the four ties, beating the three all-Super League showdowns and drawing a sizeable viewing figure on BBC TV as Fax became the first Championship side since 2006 to get to the semi-finals of the Challenge Cup.

On three separate occasions during a pulsating quarter-final, Halifax were forced to come from behind. They did so on each instance, with Woodburn-Hall's try six minutes from time proving to be the most decisive moment of all, putting Fax ahead for the third and final time. The London-product was the star, having played for League One Hunslet on dual-registration just seven days earlier.

The Bulls were unable to replicate their heroics from the previous round, when they defeated Leeds in an equally-thrilling tie, the loss of young halfback Rowan Milnes to a broken fibula midway through the first half a blow to them.

Milnes had opened the scoring in the eighth minute, supporting a fantastic break by David Foggin-Johnston down the left wing. A Jordan Lilley penalty goal made it 6-0 at half-time.

But, six minutes after the restart, Halifax were in front. Steve Tyrer claimed Scott Murrell's towering kick and was adjudged to have been fouled by Jake Webster in the act of scoring. Video referee Chris Kendall opted to award an eight-point try, with Tyrer converting both goals to put Fax ahead.

Five minutes later, Webster atoned for his error by dislodging the ball from Scott Grix as he took a kick and touching down, with Lilley converting to make it 12-8. Then back came Fax, this time when Woodburn-Hall, Quentin Laulu-Toga'gae and Grix combined to send the latter through and put the visitors in front once more.

However, four minutes after that, the topsy-turvy nature of the game continued when Matt Wildie pounced on a handling error from Kevin Larroyer in midfield, darting through to make it 16-14.

With six minutes left Woodburn-Hall danced his way through the line, before fooling Ethan Ryan with a huge dummy to put Halifax ahead for the final time.

Halifax's reward was a semi-final tie with St Helens who had beaten injury-shot Wakefield 48-10 in the Saturday quarter-final.

Four tries to one in both halves booked the Red Vee's semi-final ticket, steamrolling an injury-hit Trinity side. Lachlan Coote racked up 20 points from a try and eight goals, while backrower Zeb Taia and stand-off Jonny Lomax both produced stand-out performances.

Wakefield fans were buoyed by the return of Danny Brough from a broken thumb and by the debut of 19-year-old centre Jack Croft, who scored with his first touch of the ball at senior level.

The scoreline didn't reflect Trinity's effort. They leaked four tries in the final 20 minutes with Matty Ashurst (back), Danny Kirmond (concussion) and Tyler Randell (ankle) all confined to the bench.

Catalans Dragons' reign as Challenge Cup champions had come to an underwhelming end on the Thursday night as the current holders were thrashed 51-8 by previous holders Hull FC.

Five days after their Magic Weekend humbling by Huddersfield, the Black and Whites turned rocks to diamonds, producing a blistering second-half display that saw them rip Catalans apart, scoring six tries without reply.

Trailing only 12-8 at half-time, the French side were then opened up repeatedly by an attack led by the running of Albert Kelly and the kicking of Marc Sneyd.

Jake Connor and Bureta Faraimo's tries had Hull 12-0 up but two Lewis Tierney scores put Catalans within four points. But the hosts scored a remarkable 39-unanswered second-half points as they ran riot at the KCOM Stadium.

Tries from Sika Manu, Albert Kelly, Jamie Shaul, Danny Houghton and two from Ratu Naulago saw the five-time Cup winners ease into the last four.

On the Friday night, Warrington survived a stirring Hull KR comeback at KCOM Stadium to win 28-22.

They had looked home and hosed at 22-nil up early in the second half, despite having to play part of the first half with just eleven men after the double sin-binning of Tom Lineham and Declan Patton. Tries from Jake Mamo and Blake Austin put the Wire 12-0 up at the break. Lineham and Ben Murdoch-Masila both powered over to extend the lead to 22-0.

But Ben Crooks' 70-metre ball-steal and breakaway and a double from Josh Drinkwater plunged the tie back into the melting pot before Ben Currie's late score saw Warrington home, Craig Hall's brilliant solo score a late consolation for the Robins.

*\* The Challenge Cup semi-finals would have been switched to Bradford City's Valley Parade if the Rugby Football League had not been given assurances that Bolton would be capable of hosting the triple-header at the end of July. Bolton Wanderers soccer club were in administration, following long-standing financial troubles but the RFL eventually received the assurances they were looking for on safety certificates and the ability to host the major event.*

**Round 17**

Tim Sheens became the second coaching casualty of the Super League season when he was sacked by relegation-threatened Hull KR. The 68-year-old former Kangaroos coach was moved out with the Robins only two points above the relegation spot and was replaced by former Great Britain, Huddersfield, Leeds and Warrington coach Tony Smith on a deal to the end of the season.

Smith took charge of the club for the first time on the Sunday afternoon, as the Robins went down to an agonising 19-18 defeat at home to Wigan, Sam Powell deciding the game with a 78th minute field goal from 43 metres out. And London Broncos' astounding home win against leaders St Helens meant Rovers were now only off the foot of the table on points difference, with both sides on ten league points.

Smith's first selection as Rovers coach featured several changes, including the absence of Danny McGuire, who suffered a calf injury in the final session before the game. He was replaced by Will Dagger at halfback.

Morgan Smith mobbed by teammates after landing London's winning field goal against St Helens

Wigan welcomed back Liam Farrell from four months out injured but they were dealt a blow inside the opening ten minutes when prop Ben Flower limped off with a back injury. Still, they led 14-6 at half-time through George Williams, Dan Sarginson and Joe Burgess tries. After the break, Dagger and Ryan Lannon added scores to Jimmy Keinhorst's first-half try and, with Ryan Shaw's three conversions, Hull KR led 18-14 before Liam Marshall levelled on 66 minutes with a try that George Williams couldn't convert.

Now it was a case of who could hold their nerve. With news of London's win in Ealing filtering through, tension rose inside the stadium and, after both teams had tries disallowed, Chris Atkin's for Hull KR and Marshall's for Wigan, up stepped Powell with two minutes remaining.

There had been other explosive news that week when Leeds Rhinos announced they had come to an agreement with their captain Kallum Watkins that would see him leave at the end of the season, despite having two years left to run on his contract. It was believed the decision was made solely for salary cap purposes, with Watkins set to earn a marquee status salary the following year.

The England centre's form had been poor but he put in a fine display in the back row on the Friday night at a wet and murky Belle Vue as the Rhinos won a crucial derby 10-0. The only try of the game, in which Wakefield - missing David Fifita, Tom Johnstone, Bill Tupou and Mason Caton-Brown - had chances they couldn't finish off, came in the 54th minute when Trinity's recently imported forward Kelepi Tanginoa broke downfield and fed the ball straight into the hands of Tui Lolohea who raced the length of the field to touch down.

Leeds' defensive effort couldn't be faulted though as they moved two points clear of the bottom.

London Broncos produced the shock of the season, a Morgan Smith field goal a minute into extra time giving them a 23-22 home win over runaway leaders St Helens, after they trailed 12-0 after only ten minutes of the game. But by the 67th minute they were 22-16 ahead until Regan Grace's converted try a minute from time levelled.

*June*

And when St Helens won the toss to begin extra time it looked as though London's hopes might be dashed. But when Louie McCarthy-Scarsbrook lost the ball on Saints' third tackle only 20 metres out, the odds swung again, and Smith obliged.

Saints loanee Ryan Morgan had his best game for London, highlighted by two tries.

London's win was the second golden-point decider of the round. On the Friday night, Castleford were singing in the rain after a remarkable 27-26 victory over Huddersfield in horrendous conditions at the Jungle.

Peter Mata'utia was the hero for the Tigers, sending over an 87th minute field goal to hand Castleford only their second victory in seven games, while Huddersfield had won their last two. Mata'utia kicked seven goals as well as the field goal in a superb individual performance, with Giants stand-off Lee Gaskell scoring a hat-trick of tries in defeat.

Meanwhile, over in Hull, the rain couldn't spoil a great contest as FC just held off Salford 35-32 to move level third with Catalans.

Despite the rain teeming down hours before kick-off, conservative rugby went out of the window from the opening minutes, with both sides having the confidence to spread the ball wide, contributing to some thrilling tries in a game that had everything, with a late flurry of red and yellow cards seeing the clash finish with eleven men v twelve in Salford's favour.

Hull just couldn't kill the game off. After racing into an 18-0 lead early, they led by three scores on four occasions and had a 19-point lead late in the game, before having to scramble desperately to save the result. Ratu Naulago's length-of-the-field effort put Hull out to a 35-16 lead that Salford ultimately couldn't overcome, despite a late surge.

Josh Thewlis became the second youngest player in the history of the club at 17 years and 39 days in Warrington's comfortable 34-4 home win over Catalans Dragons on the Saturday. The youngster was selected at fullback after Jake Mamo picked up a one-match suspension for dangerous contact in the Cup win at Hull KR and he did not look out of place.

The Wolves were behind until the 32nd minute but ran in 34-unanswered points, starting with Daryl Clark's trademark break.

Thewlis was flawless on debut and Bryson Goodwin excelled in attack and defence and was rewarded with his 100th career try.

*\* Super League sponsor Betfred announced an extension of their existing three-year contract with the competition for a further two years, taking the sponsorship to the end of the 2021 season.*

**Round 18**

Hull FC moved clear into third in the ladder with a convincing 31-18 win at fifth-placed Castleford in the Thursday TV game.

Albert Kelly grabbed an opportunist hat-trick and winger Ratu Naulago a brace, while Marc Sneyd moved over the 1,000-point mark for Hull. But it was Jake Connor who proved the decisive factor in the battle between the sides starting fourth and fifth in the table. The livewire England centre was the innovative architect of the majority of the five tries that helped the East Yorkshire side come from 14-4 behind to ultimately see off a spirited Tigers' attempt to strengthen their own play-off claims.

The victory was Hull's fifth win in six games in all competitions, leaving tangible daylight between themselves and the play-off cut-off line.

Wigan were edging towards the play-off spots and they continued their progress with a 23-14 win at Leeds on the Friday night.

It was a game of fine margins, Leeds prop Ava Seumanufagai magnificently held up just after Wigan had retaken the lead on the hour by the outstanding young forward Morgan Smithies, aided by try-scorer from a minute before, Oliver Partington.

58

After a Leeds penalty, Oliver Gildart's stunning first-half try, three Chris Hankinson kicks and Sam Powell's field goal helped Wigan lead, only for Adam Cuthbertson to narrow the gap to 11-8.

Trent Merrin's converted try, improved by Liam Sutcliffe's second successful kick, put Leeds back in front. But Partington's try, his first for Wigan, was followed by Tony Clubb's clincher. TV evidence showed Clubb had lost control and it should actually have been chalked off, but it was not referred upstairs.

After the defeat, Kallum Watkins revealed he was to join Gold Coast Titans on 1st July on a two-a-half year contract.

On the same night, St Helens' key quartet of returning stars helped the table toppers make a rapid recovery from their defeat in London five days earlier with an accomplished 38-2 home win over Huddersfield.

Lachlan Coote, Tommy Makinson and Jonny Lomax all played integral roles in the backs, while Alex Walmsley was a tower of strength up front. Makinson finished with a hat-trick of tries, with Lomax getting a brace.

Wigan and Salford both leapfrogged Wakefield, who the Red Devils beat comprehensively at home on the Sunday, Niall Evalds finishing with a hat-trick in a 44-20 win.

Salford's halfback pairing of Robert Lui and Jackson Hastings looked untouchable at times as the Red Devils went from two points clear of the relegation zone to just two points off the play-offs within eighty minutes.

With five first-choice forwards missing through injury and the deadly strike duo of Bill Tupou and Tom Johnstone long term absentees, early season play-off hopefuls Trinity now looked a side ready for a battle against relegation.

By Saturday night, Leeds were back level on points with bottom sides Hull KR and London Broncos, who both recorded wins.

In east Hull, Adam Quinlan returned from a nine-month injury lay-off to help Hull KR stun Warrington, the Robins emerging 16-14 winners. The Australian fullback capped an excellent display with a try four minutes from time that tied the scores, giving Ryan Shaw the chance, which he took, to land the sideline conversion to seal victory.

Bryson Goodwin got the only try of a first half which saw the Wire 8-4 up. Mose Masoe's try put Hull KR ahead but a Josh Charnley score seemed to rescue the visitors, before Quinlan's effort gave coach Tony Smith a first win in charge.

Bottom side London Broncos made it back-to-back Super League victories with a superb 30-12 win over Catalans Dragons in Perpignan.

Fouad Yaha scored a hat-trick for the French hosts but they were unable to convert early second-half pressure. The Broncos led 12-8 at the break, Jordan Abdull and Rhys Williams going over. Elliot Kear scored against the run of play to put daylight between the two teams, with tries from Kieran Dixon and Williams giving the visitors breathing space.

Stand-off Jordan Abdull was once again the stand-out for the Broncos. The win nicely set up the following Thursday's showdown between the Broncos and Hull KR.

**Round 19**

The Thursday-night TV game turned out to be a belter, with home side London Broncos edging Hull KR 26-24 to lift themselves off the foot of the table.

The Broncos had led 8-0 just before the break, thanks to the accuracy of halfbacks Jordan Abdull and Morgan Smith in hoisting targets for Essex-born fullback Alex Walker.

London's first two scores came by this route. Kieran Dixon kicked a penalty after Walker was impeded in mid-air, then the fullback's deft catch and offload launched a handling move from which Dixon kicked quickly and precisely inside for Smith to gather and cross. Another Dixon goal, after a high tackle on the tireless Luke Yates, made it 8-0 shortly after the half-hour mark.

But Hull KR scored 18-unanswered points with three tries either side of half-time. On 35 minutes, London's favourite tactic rebounded on them. Abdull hoisted, Josh Drinkwater blocked Walker's chase, many thought illegally, and Rovers wing Ryan Shaw followed his catch with a weaving 75-metre run out of defence. Four tackles later Weller Hauraki reacted fastest to Tommy Lee's neat grubber to touch down and Shaw added the goal to cut London's interval lead to 8-6.

Within six minutes after the turnaround, converted tries from Adam Quinlan and Chris Atkin looked to have set the Robins on course for the win.

But Abdull rifled the only 40/20 of the match, left-footed, to within a few metres of the Rovers line. Two tackles later the elusive Smith shimmied to the right and, while his left arm was seized by Harvey Livett, he managed to slide a grubber for Walker to touch down. Dixon converted and the margin was back to four points.

London pressed again and were rewarded, somewhat contentiously, on the hour. Abdull chipped towards the Rovers line, where the chasing Dixon collided with Shaw. As the ball ran loose in goal, both Quinlan and Abdull plunged for it. With the match on television, referee Chris Kendall ruled no try but referred the decision to video-referee Ben Thaler. He decided that Dixon had not pushed Shaw and Abdull had at the very least touched down simultaneously with Quinlan.

Kieran Dixon's goal regained the lead and former Medway Dragon prop Rob Butler's score five minutes from time, his first for the club, proved decisive. Drinkwater pulled his side back to within two points in the last two minutes but it was in vain.

Rovers had three debutant loanees. Luis Johnson from Warrington started at loose forward, while clubmate Livett and Daniel Murray from Salford came off the bench. Kane Linnett also returned for Rovers after injury.

Leeds had a chance the following night at St Helens to leave the Robins stranded at the bottom of the table but they got off to a slow start before succumbing 36-10.

They were 12-0 down after four minutes. The opening set of the game saw fullback Jack Walker drop a towering kick, allowing Kevin Naiqama the opportunity to collect and go in under the posts. Lachlan Coote converted, as he would three minutes later when the hosts doubled their lead.

This time, some magnificent play from Jonny Lomax saw him ghost through the line, with Louie McCarthy-Scarsbrook on hand to support the England international and make it 12-0 in the blink of an eye.

At that stage, the evening of the Summer Solstice certainly looked as though it would be the longest day of the year for the Rhinos. But they were dogged, particularly in the second half, to make it a contest. Leeds' tries - one in each half - came from Brad Dwyer and Luke Briscoe.

For Saints, McCarthy-Scarsbrook crossed for another, with Lachlan Coote, Tommy Makinson - another spectacular one-handed mid-air finish - and James Bentley getting the other tries, Coote converting all six.

That weekend, St Helens Chairman Eamonn McManus slammed South Sydney, the club of England and Great Britain coach Wayne Bennett, for making an approach to boom Saints prop Luke Thompson.

Salford moved into the top five on the same night with a tight 26-16 home win over Castleford, who themselves dropped to seventh on points difference.

Just two points separated the teams after a ding-dong first 40 minutes, which featured fine solo tries for Jackson Hastings and Jordan Rankin. On the hour mark, Hastings offloaded to Derrell Olpherts to break a second-half stalemate, on the back of a dynamic bust by dummy-half Joey Lussick.

Inu's sideline conversion opened up an eight-point buffer at 24-16 that proved too great for Castleford to overcome, especially once Paul McShane limped off with a dead leg with 14 minutes left on the clock. The game was finally put to bed by Inu's penalty goal after the siren.

Wakefield were left two points adrift in eighth after their Friday-night 30-6 loss at Warrington.

Trinity got off to the perfect start when Ryan Hampshire went over in the first minute off David Fifita's break. But, with Declan Patton threatening throughout, Warrington hit back to lead 16-6 at the break with tries from Ben Currie, Josh Charnley and Mike Cooper. Blake Austin added a fourth try early in the second half before Jack Johnson went over with the game's final act.

Huddersfield were also in the relegation mix after their 38-22 defeat at home to Wigan, Warriors coach Adrian Lam opining that it was Wigan's 'best 70 minutes of the season'. It was a far cry from his more bewildered demeanour after the Warriors lost seven of their opening nine matches and looked more likely to be staving off relegation than fighting for honours.

Three tries in either half helped move the 2018 Champions up to sixth in the table, level on points with fifth-placed Salford, who they were due to host the following Friday.

And on the Saturday, Marc Sneyd stuck the boot into Catalans Dragons once again as Hull FC ran riot in a 50-10 win at Stade Gilbert Brutus.

The Airlie Birds' marksman, who killed off Catalans with a golden-point winner in Perpignan two months before, returned to strike nine perfect goals as Hull flattened their French hosts for the third time this season.

Catalans had no answer to a series of counter-attacks and long-range strikes from Albert Kelly, two-try Josh Griffin and Ratu Naulago. And Jake Connor was at his lethal best.

## Round 20

The last Friday of June provided a game of Grand Final quality as first took on second, with St Helens extending their lead at the top of the table to eight points with a 21-10 victory at their nearest rivals Warrington.

It was Rugby League at its best as, after a try-less opening hour and a frenetic final quarter - with the Wolves 6-0 ahead via penalty goals - Saints ground out the win. The pacesetters had been unable to break down their dogged opponents for over 60 minutes before Mark Percival's disputed opener - the pass from Theo Fages looked forward - which sparked a spell of four tries in 17 minutes as both teams looked to put down a marker for the remainder of the season.

As had so often been the case in 2019, when it mattered most, Jonny Lomax came up with big plays. His first was a clean break that led to Percival's try, before then chasing his own spiralling kick to force an error from Jake Mamo and send Luke Thompson on an eye-catching run to the line.

When Lachlan Coote's field goal then put Saints seven points ahead there looked no way back for the Wolves, only for Mamo to atone for his Lomax mistake to collect the short kick-off and race away down the left wing and set up a grandstand finale.

But Alex Walmsley's powerful effort soon afterwards eventually sealed matters.

Saints coped with significant adversity after young hooker Aaron Smith was stretchered from the field in a neck brace after less than three minutes, creating a discussion over the running style of Wolves prop Sitaleki Akauola.

Former Bradford forward James Bentley came on and played the whole game in the relatively unfamiliar position of hooker, contributing fully to his side's gutsy win.

The Wolves were rewarded for an imaginative marketing campaign with a bumper crowd. The week before they hired a plane with a streamer and the message 'The Wolves are Waiting' which flew round and round over the Totally Wicked Stadium while St Helens were beating Leeds Rhinos.

The night before, the third Hull derby went the way of the Robins, who beat Hull FC at home by 18-10 to lift themselves off the foot of the table, albeit on points difference.

## June

The win was sealed two minutes from time by a trademark try from Matt Parcell, on a brilliant debut after a midweek swap deal with Leeds that involved Shaun Lunt going to Headingley. But it was a fine team showing from Rovers, the highlight their first try, with Adam Quinlan combining with Ben Crooks in a showcase of speed and skill to open Hull up out wide. Crooks' one-handed take of Quinlan's kick was memorable.

After six games on the road, Wigan moved into the play-off spots with a 28-12 home win over Salford, who themselves slipped into seventh, despite the third-minute withdrawal of Sean O'Loughlin with an Achilles injury.

Midweek transfer dealings saw Tui Lolohea come into the Salford side in place of the departed Robert Lui, who swapped the AJ Bell Stadium for Emerald Headingley in a high-profile transfer.

After Krisnan Inu's early penalty goal was matched by Chris Hankinson, a Hankinson break enabled Liam Marshall to cross for the opening Wigan try before Joe Greenwood's score after a George Williams kick made it 10-2.

Derrell Olpherts scored in the corner for Salford on the stroke of half-time but Zak Hardaker went over after the break and Marshall finished another out wide. Although Kris Welham replied, Oliver Partington sealed victory late on.

Tyler Randell registered the first hat-trick of his career as Wakefield ended a run of six defeats with a 36-10 home win over Huddersfield, who at the end of the weekend were level on points with the three other clubs at the bottom of the table.

One plus point for the Giants was the return of captain Leroy Cudjoe, after ten months out following knee surgery. The former England centre made his 250th Super League appearance while, for Wakefield, Bill Tupou returned after a three-month absence, having signed a long-term deal at Trinity along with fellow centre Reece Lyne.

The two games on the Sunday had a bearing on the relegation dogfight which was building week by week.

London Broncos' three-match winning run came to a sudden end with a 42-10 defeat at Castleford, who re-found their mojo to move back into fourth spot.

A breathtaking 17-minute spell just after half-time in which they ran in five tries to utterly destroy their opponents saw the Tigers at their best. London old boy Mike McMeeken was sensational, scoring twice and causing the Broncos' defence issues all afternoon.

Leeds stayed level at the bottom on 14 points with a 31-12 home win over Catalans, themselves in the middle of their own form slump, although the game wasn't won for Leeds until 13 minutes from time, when the outstanding Konrad Hurrell charged over

Leeds' big gamble in the transfer market paid off. Shaun Lunt didn't make the 17 due to an ankle injury but fellow new signing Robert Lui managed to have an impact and his presence rubbed off on his halfback partner. Richie Myler had been playing without a recognised halfback alongside him for large periods and with Lui alongside him, he looked far more composed. And with Lui inside him, Hurrell was ferocious in attack, and outstanding defensively.

**BETFRED SUPER LEAGUE**
*Sunday 30th June*

| | P | W | D | L | F | A | D | Pts |
|---|---|---|---|---|---|---|---|---|
| St Helens | 20 | 18 | 0 | 2 | 666 | 291 | 375 | 36 |
| Warrington Wolves | 20 | 14 | 0 | 6 | 582 | 334 | 248 | 28 |
| Hull FC | 20 | 12 | 0 | 8 | 480 | 519 | -39 | 24 |
| Castleford Tigers | 20 | 10 | 0 | 10 | 451 | 431 | 20 | 20 |
| Wigan Warriors | 20 | 10 | 0 | 10 | 424 | 407 | 17 | 20 |
| Catalans Dragons | 20 | 10 | 0 | 10 | 381 | 498 | -117 | 20 |
| Salford Red Devils | 20 | 9 | 0 | 11 | 510 | 439 | 71 | 18 |
| Wakefield Trinity | 20 | 9 | 0 | 11 | 455 | 478 | -23 | 18 |
| Leeds Rhinos | 20 | 7 | 0 | 13 | 406 | 498 | -92 | 14 |
| Huddersfield Giants | 20 | 7 | 0 | 13 | 425 | 532 | -107 | 14 |
| Hull Kingston Rovers | 20 | 7 | 0 | 13 | 383 | 539 | -156 | 14 |
| London Broncos | 20 | 7 | 0 | 13 | 354 | 551 | -197 | 14 |

# JULY
## *O Danny Boy*

---

**Round 21**

Leeds Rhinos registered an 18-10 win at Castleford on the first Friday of July to move two points clear of the relegation zone, with the Tigers falling out of the top five.

The victory meant interim coach Richard Agar had led Leeds to six wins from eleven games in charge and it was clear from the Rhinos' conservative gameplan that a focus on tightening their defence was reaping dividends.

For 60 minutes local rivals Castleford failed to unlock a Rhinos rearguard that made a mockery of the criticism that had been so prevalent for much of a traumatic year for the Headingley side.

The Rhinos were on the receiving end of a heavily adverse penalty count and, at one stage, were forced to face five successive sets near their own line. Trent Merrin, who had taken over the captaincy after the departure of Kallum Watkins, led the effort from the front.

Agar's troops refused to wilt under the heavy fire and took their chances when they came to force the Tigers to play catch-up from midway through the first half, when the supporting Merrin took advantage of a wonderful Adam Cuthbertson offload to go under the posts.

Jack Walker helped double the Rhinos' advantage just after the break, before a moment of individual brilliance from recent signing Robert Lui stemmed a possible Castleford comeback that was triggered by a quick-fire James Clare brace.

The recruitment of Lui had proved shrewd business and another recent signing looked as likely to strengthen the Rhinos. As debuts go, especially after only one short, sharp captain's run – a misplaced kick apart – PNG international Rhyse Martin's bow for Leeds could hardly have gone much better. The 26-year-old former Canterbury backrower came off the bench in the 48th minute and helped ensure a Leeds win at the Mend-a-Hose Jungle for the first time since 2015.

For the Tigers there was some mitigation. They were forced to ring the changes again at halfback and also on the wing, after Jake Trueman, whose incisive bursts were sorely missed, and Tuoyo Egodo suffered head knocks in the Tigers' 42-10 defeat of London Broncos.

Still, the game was in the balance with the Rhinos leading 14-10 going into the last ten minutes. A thrilling Clare break, this time down centre field, took him within ten metres of his hat-trick before, at the other end, an outrageous Greg Eden panic pass across the field left Cheyse Blair stranded and forced to fumble as the Tigers tried to clear their line.

Shortly after the subsequent scrum, Lui stepped off of his left foot to score his first try for Leeds.

The night before, Huddersfield had also moved two points clear of the bottom spot with a 36-18 win at Salford.

It was a creditable and convincing performance by a Giants team that had eight players produced by their youth system and two players on debut in scrum-half Tom Holmes and teenage prop Oliver Wilson, recently signed from Bradford Bulls.

It was the introduction of Wilson and Matty English from the bench midway through the first half that gave the Giants momentum, while hooker Kruise Leeming was superb, having to play 70 unbroken minutes after an early concussion injury to Adam O'Brien. Jake Wardle's try with ten minutes left sealed the win for Huddersfield.

The off-colour Red Devils were now only four points clear of the relegation spot, with Hull KR and London Broncos both still on 14 points.

The Robins got a 52-10 hammering at Wigan on the Friday night, with the Warriors recording their fifth consecutive win, coach Adrian Lam again claiming their best performance of the season.

An entertaining opening 40 minutes saw the Warriors hold an 18-point lead after outscoring their opponents four tries to one. Liam Farrell opened the scoring inside five minutes, before Adam Quinlan got his side back in the game. Two quick tries from Liam Marshall ensured Wigan had some breathing space before Zak Hardaker went over before the half-time hooter.

Marshall completed his hat-trick after the break, while George Williams, Farrell, Oliver Gildart and Joe Burgess all crossed, Quinlan getting his second to end the scoring.

The Broncos copped a fair hiding too on the Saturday, by 36-6, at the hands of Warrington, thanks to the Wolves' hugely dominant first-half display at Ealing - it was 36-0 at half-time.

London were not overrun but steadily ground down. Warrington, with captain Chris Hill missing after collecting a two-match ban for dangerous contact in the defeat by St Helens, worked their way through their possessions, making steady progress downfield with second rowers Ben Currie and Jack Hughes consistently dangerous, before they then kicked deep into London territory, avoiding the rock-solid Alex Walker at fullback and targeting the wings.

London got the only score of the second half. Within two minutes of the restart Matty Fozard forced his way over from close range, with Jordan Abdull adding the conversion. That, essentially, was that.

Former rugby union international Luther Burrell featured for the Wolves in the latter stages of the game, his maiden outing as a League player following his cross-code switch from Northampton Saints.

On the Friday, St Helens put together another relentless performance to rip third-placed Hull FC apart by 40-12 at KCOM Stadium.

The fluency of the Saints' 'spine' was a joy to watch. The lack of a recognised hooker did little to slow them down as Theo Fages, Jonny Lomax and the exceptional Lachlan Coote, who scored two tries and kicked six goals, dazzled, scoring four of their team's seven tries between them, toying with the Hull defence at times. They scored four tries in ten minutes early in the second half to leave Hull playing for nothing but pride.

Catalans' five-game losing streak ended in emphatic style as Wakefield melted away in blistering conditions in Perpignan to crash to a 44-10 defeat.

The game had to pause regularly for water-breaks as players struggled to deal with 34-degree heat and humidity. But the Catalans, who dropped halfback Matty Smith, coped best and a hat-trick for Jodie Broughton and two tries for Tony Gigot were enough to burn the opposition.

The return from injury of Michael Mcllorum, Matt Whitley and Kenny Edwards had a major influence on the game, with Mcllorum in particular playing with such ferocity that Wakefield's huge pack were second best from start to finish.

David Fifita limped from the pitch with a foot injury, at the end of a week in which Matty Ashurst underwent surgery and joined Tom Johnstone and Tinirau Arona on Trinity's long-term injury list.

**Round 22**

Former Leeds halfback Danny McGuire steered Hull KR to a 32-16 victory in the Friday night TV game at Headingley to put the two sides level on 16 points, just above the relegation spot.

It was a great performance by McGuire in his last season as a player and on his 400th Super League appearance. All five former Leeds players played an important role in the Robins' victory, with prop Mitch Garbutt coming off the bench and making 192 metres

Hooker Matt Parcell, offloaded on loan by the Rhinos weeks before to make way for the signing of Robert Lui, was also prominent throughout and the Leeds supporters generously gave him a great ovation when he departed from the pitch six minutes before the end of the game.

The Robins' third try, in a start that put them 14-0 up after only 20 minutes, best summed up their approach, in a performance where speed of ball movement, especially when turning it back inside, bamboozled the Rhinos. On a power play close to the home line, McGuire decided to test the Leeds left, intricately linking with Adam Quinlan and Ben Crooks, taking the ball near the touchline and releasing a one-handed pass back on the inside to Jimmy Keinhorst, who sent Quinlan over the line.

Leeds scored eight points before the break but when Kane Linnett got his second try Rovers led 26-8. Parcell had opened the scoring against his parent club, while two-try Linnett, Quinlan, Harvey Livett and Craig Hall got the other tries.

Leeds Richie Myler was later banned for one game for a trip.

Speculation over the future of St Helens coach Justin Holbrook continued to grow. He had been offered a contract extension by the runaway Super League leaders but Gold Coast Titans' decision to part company with head coach Garth Brennan suggested Holbrook was holding off signing a new deal with Saints.

Saints supporters made their feelings known about wanting Holbrook to stay after Friday night's 32-10 home win over Wigan, which moved Saints to the brink of a second successive League Leaders' Shield.

With the midfield trio of Jonny Lomax, Theo Fages and Lachlan Coote again central to everything Saints did and with a dominant pack led by Alex Walmsley, Morgan Knowles and Dominique Peyroux, they had far too much for a Wigan side missing the bulk of their experienced forwards.

The Warriors competed fully in the first half despite rarely threatening but they saw the game go away from them in a dominant third quarter from the home side, who scored 18 points in 15 minutes.

Adrian Lam's side - the former Wigan halfback had committed his future to the club during the week - then regrouped and scored the only try of the final quarter through the non-stop Zak Hardaker. But they were clearly second best on the night.

At the end of Friday night, St Helens' lead at the top was ten points, with Jackson Hastings-inspired Salford Red Devils pulling off a huge 22-12 victory at second-placed Warrington.

Only four days after confirming his move to Wigan in 2020, Hastings' boot created two second-half tries for Krisnan Inu to seal the shock win. It was Salford's second boil-over at the Halliwell Jones Stadium this season, following their 36-12 triumph on Good Friday.

The Red Devils clawed their way to a two-point lead after a dour first half and moved away early in the second thanks to Inu's brace and a Kris Welham four-pointer, keeping Ian Watson's men only two points adrift of the fifth-placed Warriors

Despite the defeat, the Wolves looked bound for a second-placed finish, still four points clear of the chasing pack. Prop Sitaleki Akauola received a two-match ban after being sin-binned late on for a dangerous throw.

Salford coach Watson remained positive for the future but the feeling outside the club was that the Red Devils would fade in the season run-in.

Hull FC had confirmed their status as Super League's Jekyll and Hyde side on the Thursday night. They conceded 22 second-half points at home to London Broncos, with only a 72nd minute Marc Sneyd field goal in reply.

But they had led 34-0 at half-time and finished 35-22 winners.

Josh Griffin was was at the heart of everything Hull did well in the first half and his try made it 28-0 after just 22 minutes. Ratu Naulago's try four minutes before the break was spectacular. With London on the attack and desperately trying to keep the ball alive, the Fijian winger plucked a pass from midair on his own line. Around nine or ten seconds later, he was diving over to make it 32-0, with Sneyd's conversion extending the lead.

London remained bottom and one of the teams they were chasing, Huddersfield, remained only two points above them after a 32-28 home defeat to Catalans, who consequently moved above Wigan into fourth spot.

The Dragons, with Sam Tomkins scoring a first-half hat-trick of tries along with four successful kicks for a personal 20-point haul, almost managed to lose the match, after having established a 20-point lead with 17 minutes left. And the sin-binning, he got a one-match ban, of Kenny Edwards in the 74th minute for dissent didn't help.

Jodie Broughton's third-quarter try-double before he suffered knee damage made it 32-12. But three of the Giants' five tries came late on, for Darnell McIntosh, a brilliant Lee Gaskell solo and a second for Innes Senior, which meant that ultimately the Catalans had to survive a last-play scramble on their own try-line to win the match. It was a dramatic play that left both sets of players on the turf at the end.

Wakefield were also looking over their shoulder at the relegation battle after their 36-16 home defeat to Castleford, who moved level on points with fifth-placed Wigan.

Despite the 18-point margin, the contest could have gone either way until the Tigers, in a strong finish, posted three unanswered tries in the last ten minutes, with two going to hat-trick hero James Clare.

Trinity badly missed influential forward David Fifita, who was still unfit after injuring his foot in the heavy defeat the previous week against the Catalans, while the Tigers' young stand-off Jake Trueman helped create two super tries and was a threat to Wakefield throughout.

Danny Brough was Wakefield's best and moved into second place, overtaking Paul Deacon, in the list of Super League's all-time points scorers, with 2,423 Super League points, second only to Kevin Sinfield (3,443).

**Round 23**

London Broncos moved level on league points with Leeds and Hull KR after their 32-12, Sunday afternoon win over St Helens, their second home win over the leaders.

They remained bottom on points difference but with everything to play for heading into the final six rounds.

Saints coach Justin Holbrook was unrepentant amid criticism for resting most of his star players ahead of the following week's Challenge Cup semi-final against Halifax, giving Super League debuts to three bright young Academy players. The result did nothing to lessen the complaints emanating from Hull and Leeds but none of the trio – starting centre Josh Simm and replacements Callum Hazzard and Josh Eaves – let themselves or their teammates down.

Matty Fleming and Luke Yates ran in tries either side of Aaron Smith's effort for Saints to put the Jordan Abdull-led Broncos 14-6 up at the break. Danny Richardson's try got Saints to within two points before Alex Walker went over to extend London's lead. That changed the momentum back the Broncos way and a Matty Gee try and second from Fleming completed the shock victory.

On the same afternoon, Hull FC registered a 26-24 victory over Leeds to secure their first win at Headingley in over twelve years. The Black and Whites had surrendered a 20-6 lead in the second half. And when Rhyse Martin converted Tom Briscoe's second try on 74 minutes to make it 24-20, Headingley was rocking. But the Leeds supporters were silenced seconds later when the Rhinos failed to collect the kick-off, piling the pressure back on themselves once again.

And they lost the match when Ratu Naulago dived over to level it at 24-24 and Marc Sneyd nervelessly converted from the touchline. This time, there would be no way back for the Rhinos and, with London winning, it meant that yet again, with six games remaining, Leeds were joint-bottom of the table.

So were Hull KR, who weren't able to follow up their impressive win over relegation rivals Leeds with another victory against Huddersfield on the Friday, as the Giants ground out an 18-12 win at KCOM Craven Park to edge themselves further towards safety, Jermaine McGillvary scoring the sealing try two minutes from time.

Lee Gaskell gave a dominant performance for the Giants, with a superb kicking, passing and running game as the Giants' young middle once again excelled. Matty English got their only try of the first half, with Alex Mellor scoring just after the break to put them in the lead for the first time. Two Darnell McIntosh penalties edged them eight points in front until Craig Hall's self-converted try made for an exciting final five minutes.

The Robins looked a shadow of the side that tore the Rhinos apart seven days earlier. Having already lost hooker Matt Parcell to a potentially season-ending shoulder injury, Rovers then saw Warrington loanees Luis Johnson and Harvey Livett recalled by their parent club just 24 hours before kick-off, while in-form centre Kane Linnett was forced off after just 15 minutes with a calf problem.

St Helens were still ten points clear at the top of the table as Warrington fell short at Castleford on the Sunday, going down 27-18, the Tigers recording back-to-back victories for the first time since March.

A James Clare try and three Peter Mata'utia penalties put Castleford 12-8 up at the break, with Jake Mamo grabbing the Wolves' try and Declan Patton kicking two goals in response.

Tom Lineham's early second-half converted try gave Warrington a lead. But three tries in 14 minutes from Greg Minikin, Jake Trueman and Tuoyo Egodo ensured the Tigers victory, with a late Toby King score for Wolves of no bearing.

Trueman was in inspiring form, controlling the game and leaving opposite star halfback Blake Austin in the shadows. His 70-metre try after he pounced on a loose ball had the home supporters on their feet

The Tigers moved into Super League's top five after Catalans took a 40-14 hiding at Salford, the Red Devils showing little sign of fading after the departure of Robert Lui and Jackson Hastings' decision to leave at the end of the season.

Lining up for his 300th career appearance, former Hull KR stalwart Kris Welham scored two tries and laid on another two assists as Salford boosted their own top-five hopes. The Red Devils were just one win outside the top five with six rounds left.

Welham earned three Albert Goldthorpe Medal points in the pivotal victory, bagging two tries off Tui Lolohea kicks, plus setting up Derrell Olpherts and Lolohea for scores.

Wigan had already jumped into fourth spot after their Thursday-night 46-16 home win over down-at-heel Wakefield.

The game was over as a contest a lot earlier than many predicted with Wigan running in three tries inside the first 15

**BETFRED SUPER LEAGUE**

*Sunday 21st July*

| | P | W | D | L | F | A | D | Pts |
|---|---|---|---|---|---|---|---|---|
| St Helens | 23 | 20 | 0 | 3 | 750 | 345 | 405 | 40 |
| Warrington Wolves | 23 | 15 | 0 | 8 | 648 | 389 | 259 | 30 |
| Hull FC | 23 | 14 | 0 | 9 | 553 | 605 | -52 | 28 |
| Wigan Warriors | 23 | 12 | 0 | 11 | 532 | 465 | 67 | 24 |
| Castleford Tigers | 23 | 12 | 0 | 11 | 524 | 483 | 41 | 24 |
| Catalans Dragons | 23 | 12 | 0 | 11 | 471 | 576 | -105 | 24 |
| Salford Red Devils | 23 | 11 | 0 | 12 | 590 | 501 | 89 | 22 |
| Huddersfield Giants | 23 | 9 | 0 | 14 | 507 | 594 | -87 | 18 |
| Wakefield Trinity | 23 | 9 | 0 | 14 | 497 | 604 | -107 | 18 |
| Leeds Rhinos | 23 | 8 | 0 | 15 | 464 | 566 | -102 | 16 |
| Hull Kingston Rovers | 23 | 8 | 0 | 15 | 437 | 625 | -188 | 16 |
| London Broncos | 23 | 8 | 0 | 15 | 414 | 634 | -220 | 16 |

Joe Philbin races away to score Warrington's final try against Hull FC, as the Wolves earn their place at Wembley

minutes thanks to Liam Farrell, Zak Hardaker and Willie Isa.

Farrell added his second, Jake Shorrocks raced 60 metres to score and Jarrod Sammut got in on the act as the Warriors led 34-0 at half-time.

Ryan Hampshire scored twice for Wakefield either side of a length-of-the-field effort from Oliver Gildart, while the outstanding Farrell completed his hat-trick before Max Jowitt had the final say for Wakefield.

Wigan were starting to hit form at the right time, despite the presence of four forwards aged 20 or under. And that week the club completed a move for Parramatta utility back Bevan French, who was signed with immediate effect.

London Broncos also bolstered their squad with the signing of Sydney Roosters' former Newcastle Knights halfback Brock Lamb until the end of the campaign.

*\* West Wales Raiders scored their first win as a professional club with a 44-16 win over Coventry Bears, ending a run of 44 straight defeats since adopting the Raiders moniker at the start of 2018.*

**Challenge Cup Semi-finals**

Super League's top two sides won the right to meet in the Challenge Cup Final at Wembley after a double header of semis at the University of Bolton Stadium.

Warrington Wolves booked their third trip to Wembley in four years at the expense of Hull FC with a 22-14 victory in the first game.

The game was on a knife edge until the final minutes in what was a full blooded and pulsating encounter, despite being played in torrential rain throughout. Warrington's ability to produce the killer punch at crucial times was the ultimate difference between the sides.

The Wire dominated large parts of the game with territory and possession, on the back of a tremendous kicking game from Blake Austin and Declan Patton, which had Hull coming off their own tryline time and time again, as well as creating two of their four tries.

Alex Walmsley offloads as St Helens see off battling Halifax to reach the Challenge Cup Final

Hull battled hard and showed a never-say-die attitude to have every chance of snatching the game at the death. But they were left to rue their near-misses, having had two try claims correctly disallowed in the second half and having come up with a crucial error in an attacking position with minutes remaining.

Tries from Bryson Goodwin and Ben Currie saw the Wolves edge a tense first half, but Marc Sneyd's boot and Bureta Faraimo's try kept Hull in touch at 10-8. Toby King extended Warrington's lead on 49 minutes, only for Scott Taylor's reply for Hull to ensure a tense finale. There was little over a minute left when Joe Philbin went over to secure a second successive Wembley final.

St Helens progressed with a hard-won 26-2 success over Championship Halifax.

In the end, four tries from Justin Holbrook's side proved more than enough for Saints, but the fact that the expected barrage of points after each of those tries never materialised reflected how dogged Halifax were.

It was evident that Halifax would make a game of the semi-final from the opening tackle of the game. With everyone expecting Fax to send the kick-off long downfield and try and camp themselves in Saints territory, Scott Murrell instead went short and Shaun Robinson collected the ball at speed to put the Championship side immediately on the attack.

An engrossing, bruising opening half-hour yielded just four points, two for each team. By that stage, many had expected the game to be already over as a contest but Danny Richardson and Steve Tyrer penalties for their respective sides were the only acts of scoring. Had Halifax held out until the interval, who knows what could have happened after that.

But five minutes from half-time, Saints captain James Roby exploited a rare gap in the Fax defence to crash over. With Richardson converting to make it 8-2, it was a pivotal passage of play - and from there, Halifax never really threatened in attack again.

Three more tries after the break - from Dominique Peyroux, Jonny Lomax and Theo Fages - sealed it for St Helens.

# AUGUST
## *Wolves howl*

---

**Round 24**

St Helens won the League Leaders' Shield for the second season in succession and the eighth time in total after their 26-6 home win over Wakefield and Catalans' defeat of Warrington the next day.

It came at the end of a week in which the long-running saga with head coach Justin Holbrook came to an end when he was confirmed as the new Gold Coast Titans coach from the start of next season, with chief executive Mike Rush flying to Australia to identify a successor.

Holbrook's side kept their focus sufficiently to secure victory over Wakefield, putting themselves 12 points ahead of Warrington, with Trinity now truly involved in the relegation dogfight.

In an often flat contest, James Roby, on his 400th Super League appearance, and Luke Thompson were both excellent. Scrum-half Danny Richardson also showed some smart touches in the absence of Jonny Lomax and Lachlan Coote, particularly during a nine-minute first-half spell that effectively sealed the game.

Trinity were arguably the better side for the opening 25 minutes, after which the sides were locked together at 2-2. Chris Annakin produced two big stints in the pack and Danny Kirmond kept putting his hand up for his team before being forced off with a shoulder injury.

But three converted tries in that crucial second-quarter spell - from Richardson, Louie McCarthy-Scarsbrook and Tommy Makinson - took the game away from Trinity.

Bottom five Huddersfield, Wakefield, Leeds, Hull KR and London were all separated by just two points as the competition headed into the final furlong.

The Rhinos were the top of that group on points difference after a seismic Friday-night 44-0 victory over Huddersfield Giants at the John Smith's Stadium.

Tongan powerhouse Konrad Hurrell and flying winger Ash Handley, who was making his 100th career appearance, both registered doubles, whilst Brad Dwyer was a constant threat from dummy-half and Robert Lui outlined just why Leeds were desperate to sign him with a controlled display. The only downside for Leeds was the ACL injury suffered by winger Tom Briscoe.

On the Sunday, Hull KR kept themselves two points clear of bottom-placed London as Danny McGuire kicked a field goal in golden point extra-time to give them a crucial 27-26 win over Castleford, who sank to seventh spot.

Rovers raced into a 12-0 lead with tries from Daniel Murray and Adam Quinlan, both off McGuire grubbers. However, Castleford hit back to lead 26-14 with just over 20 minutes left through tries from Peter Mata'utia, Jordan Rankin, an eight-point James Clare try and, after the break, a breakaway from Greg Minikin. But two Ben Crooks tries levelled the scores to set up a breathless finish.

McGuire and Josh Drinkwater missed three field-goal attempts between them in the closing moments, affording Castleford a chance of their own. But Mata'utia pushed a penalty wide after a high tackle on Liam Watts. McGuire charged down Trueman's field-goal attempt before, with the Tigers well-placed again, Mata'utia somehow made a mess of a gilt-edged opportunity.

It was all decided in the opening set of extra time. Rovers battled their way downfield before, with nobody expecting it, McGuire nailed a sublime 40/20 to put Rovers in position and after the tap was thrown his way on the first tackle, he finally kicked the winning point to spark dramatic scenes.

The Tigers fielded Greg Eden on the wing, days after he appeared at Leeds Crown Court to face an initial hearing after being charged with an off-field ABH charge.

The Broncos remained two points adrift after a 58-28 home defeat to Salford on the Saturday, a third win in a row that moved the Red Devils to the verge of the top five. They were three tries up within 15 minutes, with Jackson Hastings threatening havoc and Josh Jones making ground pretty much every time he handled the ball.

Niall Evalds finished with a hat-trick after the Red Devils raced into a 36-6 half-time lead through two Krisnan Inu tries and scores for Mark Flanagan, Jones, Evalds and Tui Lolohea.

Evalds ran in two more after the break, while Kris Welham and Hastings also went over. Rhys Williams, Luke Yates, Matty Fleming, Sadiq Adebiyi and Rob Butler crossed for the well-beaten Broncos.

Wigan made it seven wins from eight, as Zak Hardaker's 76th-minute field goal ensured a 15-14 Thursday-night win at third-placed Hull FC, leaving them just two points behind the Black and Whites with a better points difference.

Wigan led for long periods of the game on the back of clinical attack and an outstanding desire without the ball. They restricted Hull to just one try before their never-say-die attitude got them in position to firstly prevent Marc Sneyd from landing the vital one-pointer, before getting Hardaker in range to hit the mark from 40 metres out. It was only the second field goal of the in-form fullback's career. Winger Liam Marshall scored both of Wigan's tries.

A major investigation was promised into shocking scenes of violence at the Stade Gilbert Brutus in Perpignan on the Saturday night, following the Catalans Dragons' 30-10 defeat of Warrington. Dozens of spectators were seen fighting in the Puig Aubert Stand following the final hooter in a bad-tempered game that had been littered with foul play and mass face-offs.

The violence reflected several on-field incidents that scarred a terrific contest and resulted in four yellow cards and two reds. Referee James Child had to be escorted from the pitch by security guards as both sets of supporters howled in protest at their perception that the game had been allowed to descend into chaos.

Sam Tomkins and Michael Mcllorum were both sent off following the final hooter as a huge brawl erupted involving all 26 players, mirroring terrible images that were developing in the away end of the stadium.

The first half had been a bitter battle with few points scored. But Catalans found their form after the interval to score 22 points and move back into Super League's top five, Matt Whitley's try eight minutes from the end settling it.

The fall-out hit the Dragons hard after a complicated series of disciplinary hearings and appeals. Sam Tomkins failed with his appeal and was banned for three matches. Mcllorum had a one-match ban increased to two games after appeal. Brayden Wiliame had a one-match ban downgraded to no suspension and Mikael Simon, originally suspended for one match for a head-butt was found not guilty on appeal. Kenny Edwards was found not guilty after being referred to a tribunal for 'other contrary behaviour'.

The only Wolves player suspended was Tom Lineham, who got one match for a shoulder charge. But a potentially bigger blow was the ankle sprain suffered by Blake Austin in the 25th minute of the game.

*August*
**Round 25**

St Helens proved they were the top dogs in Super League, one of many spectacular Tommy Makinson tries capping a 30-12 win at Warrington in the Thursday TV game.

The Wolves were missing ten first-choice players and Saints six and the teams that would run out for the Challenge Cup Final in two weeks time would look significantly different. But with a host of replacements putting their hands up on both sides, the teams played out a captivating clash that was only decided in the closing quarter.

Warrington hung in until then, despite losing four players to injury during the game in Ben Currie, Danny Walker, Luis Johnson and Ben Murdoch-Masila, hugely limiting their substitution options. But they succumbed to two tries in five minutes created by Saints' 18-year-old fullback Jack Welsby, who produced a mature display from fullback, creating three tries and stopping another.

The Wolves had two 17-year-olds in their starting line-up in threequarter Josh Thewlis and debutant stand-off Riley Dean. And on-loan halfback Matty Smith made a solid debut after one training session after his move from Catalans.

In the days after crowd trouble and violence on the pitch during the Dragons' victory over Warrington, RFL Match Officials Director Steve Ganson called on coaches and players to think hard about harassing referees, or risk some lengthy suspensions and punitive action from the RFL. The RFL had appointed a special investigator to report on the events at the Stade Gilbert Brutus.

The Dragons' morale looked shot to pieces the following Friday night at Headingley as Leeds scored a 40-plus point win for the second week running, emerging 48-8 victors, despite the sin-binning of Konrad Hurrell and then, on his return, the 51st-minute dismissal of prop Brad Singleton, for a high tackle on Sam Kasiano.

At that stage the Rhinos led 16-8 but within minutes Ash Handley's try began a points deluge that delighted the home fans.

A repeat clash from a month before - the 29-fixture season demanding six 'loop fixtures' brought blanket rain, thunder and lightning for the opening stages. But the gloom lifted, literally and metaphorically, as Leeds went in for their first try, dominated the opening quarter and produced a scintillating second half.

Mid-season capture Rhyse Martin had, along with Robert Lui, been a catalyst for the Rhinos' late-season revival and he claimed half his side's points with a majestic try and a perfect ten goals. Young boom centre Harry Newman was the match's leading metre-maker. Singleton copped a two-match ban.

The win meant the Rhinos were four points above the relegation spot with a handsome points difference also counting in their favour.

Wakefield were two behind, with only one win from their last twelve league games, after losing 26-16 at home to Hull FC on the Sunday.

Trinity, with on-loan Wigan fullback Morgan Escaré on debut, were left to rue an eleven-minute passage of play in the first half which saw a 6-0 lead - courtesy of a Ryan Hampshire try - transformed into a 20-6 deficit.

Marc Sneyd inspired the Hull comeback, kicking two first half 40/20s, Bureta Faraimo, Carlos Tuimavave, a long-range interception, Sneyd himself and Ratu Naulago all crossing for tries. Naulago touched down again after half-time from another mis-fired Trinity attack, before Joe Arundel and Jacob Miller scored consolations.

The win moved Hull level on points with Warrington in second. 'We're swinging,' coach Lee Radford said. 'Nobody is giving us a mention.'

The three clubs below Wakefield also lost that weekend. On the Friday night Hull KR had put up a much better show than they had in the same fixture four weeks before but they still went down 36-18 at Wigan, a Liam Farrell double and Joe Burgess's 100th try in the cherry-and-white securing the two points for the Warriors, who were now two points clear in fourth spot, just one win behind second-placed Warrington.

Tony Smith gave a debut to 18-year-old half Mikey Lewis, who was filling Danny McGuire's boots and provided several try assists despite an early defensive error that led to George Williams opening the scoring. Dewsbury recruit Kyle Trout also made his Rovers debut from the bench.

Rovers erased six-point deficits three times in the opening 50 minutes, until Tony Clubb's 68th-minute barge-over opened up an unassailable two-score advantage. Aussie flyer Bevan French made his Wigan debut off the bench.

On the Sunday, Castleford inflicted further wounds on bottom side London with a hard-fought, if less than impressive 20-6 home victory to keep their play-off hopes alive.

Jordan Rankin caused the London defence all sorts of problems with his elusive running game, with Tuoyo Egodo's second try on 63 minutes putting the game to bed on the back of Oliver Holmes and Jacques O'Neill tries. London coach Danny Ward was still talking up the Broncos' chances of survival after the game.

Salford coach Ian Watson was well aware their play-off future was in their own hands after seeing his side move into the top-five spots with a 32-12 home win over Huddersfield Giants on the same afternoon. 'We want to keep hold of fifth,' he said.

The Red Devils came from behind late in the second half to leapfrog the Tigers and the Dragons back into fifth place with just four league games remaining.

Salford dominated the opening 40 minutes but only held a four-point lead, thanks to six points from the boot of Krisnan Inu and a try from Logan Tomkins, while Darnell McIntosh replied for the Giants, with Oliver Russell adding a penalty.

The Giants looked a different side in the second half and took the lead for the first time on 50 minutes, with Russell going over. But a loss of personnel, with three players all having head knocks, saw them tire and Salford managed to hit back and grab the two points. Mark Flanagan and Tui Lolohea made the game safe before the outstanding Inu took his points tally to twenty.

## Round 26

London Broncos shook up the relegation dogfight once again after their 17-4 Saturday night win over Catalans in Perpignan, backing up their 30-12 win at Stade Gilbert Brutus in Round 18.

The match was not a classic, littered with handling errors and stoppages but the sheer effort and teamwork of the Broncos shone out, in stark contrast to the disjointed and disconnected Catalans, who now faced a massive challenge to reach the top five play-offs.

The Broncos remained bottom but their ninth win of the season lifted them level on 18 points with three clubs - Hull KR and Wakefield, due to meet the next day, and Huddersfield. Alex Walker and Kieran Dixon, who also kicked four goals, got the Broncos' tries. Walker struck the killer blow with his try in the 52nd minute and Brock Lamb's late field goal clinched it on a day of just one home score, from Brayden Wiliame just after half-time.

Huddersfield Giants were nilled at home for a second game running - suffering a ninth home defeat of the season - as they went down 24-0 to Castleford, a result that left them joint bottom. The Tigers' victory had them in sixth but just a win behind Challenge Cup finalists Warrington in second.

Castleford, with Jake Trueman the key at halfback, were far from perfect but were still too good for a Huddersfield side that looked broken.

James Clare's early try provided the only points in a tight first 40 minutes. The Giants had some chances to get on the scoreboard in the first half but never recovered once Adam Milner crashed over for Castleford's second score. Mike McMeeken and Jesse Sene-Lefao tries finished the contest off.

*August*

Wakefield ran away with the crucial four-pointer at Craven Park, beating Hull KR 38-10 and ending a run of five successive losses - and just one victory in their last eleven league games. They were still two points clear of now-bottom trio Huddersfield, Hull KR and London. But that was effectively three points due to a superior points difference, with just three games left.

Jacob Miller and Ryan Hampshire both scored doubles and Miller was part of a midfield triumvirate alongside Danny Brough and Kyle Wood that outplayed their opposite numbers, as error-ridden Rovers - slight favourites going into the match - looked a shadow of themselves from the off. They were chasing the game from the tenth minute when Miller got his first try and, a brief spell at the end of the first half apart, they never looked like winners.

Rovers managed just two tries, both late on in the first half from Ben Crooks and Mitch Garbutt as, despite a reshuffle following the loss of fullback Adam Quinlan to an adductor injury, the Robins came from 14-0 down after 19 minutes to trail just 14-10 at the break.

But Trinity ran in four more second-half tries and Bill Tupou's 64th-minute try ended Rovers' hopes.

Hull FC captain Danny Houghton urged his teammates to come back fighting after a 44-22 home defeat to Salford Red Devils dented their play-off campaign.

With Warrington having lost to Wigan on the Friday night, Lee Radford's side missed an opportunity to go second the day after, as Salford dominated the second half, Ken Sio, Lee Mossop and Kristian Inu all finishing with try-doubles. Two tries in four minutes via Jake Bibby and Mossop after the break handed the Red Devils the winning momentum.

Wigan's 20-6 win over Warrington was the Wolves' fifth league defeat in a row and saw the Warriors climb into joint second.

The Warriors dominated the first 40 minutes and went in at the break 18 points to the good, thanks to tries from new boy Bevan French, George Williams and Zak Hardaker, as they ripped the Wolves to pieces.

Wigan only added two more points after the break from Hardaker's boot and it could have been different had Declan Patton been awarded two scores at the start of the second half. But the Warriors deserved the victory. They were made to work hard in defence with the likes of Morgan Smithies, Oliver Partington and Liam Byrne growing in confidence with every game.

Wigan's third try, from Hardaker on 25 minutes, was crucial to the outcome of the game, putting Wigan 18 points ahead.

Warrington's opponents at Wembley the following weekend, St Helens, enjoyed a better evening on the Thursday as a second-half blast secured them a 36-20 win at resurgent Leeds, despite the absence of half-a-dozen stars. Three tries either side of half-time secured them the two points.

Saints also had the luxury, when they were 36-10 up, to withdraw Jonny Lomax after 68 minutes to save him for the big day. The stand-off was outstanding throughout, whether running with the ball and invariably beating the first line, or shipping it into space for his outside backs.

Mark Percival, who was almost unstoppable in the centre, wasn't far behind him, finishing with a game-high 155 metres, while co-centre Kevin Naiqama was the destroyer-in-chief with a wonderful hat-trick, showing strength, speed and poise to bamboozle the Leeds defence.

*\* Rugby League was in mourning after the sudden passing of Batley Bulldogs player Archie Bruce, aged 20. The youngster was found in his hotel room on Sunday morning, just twelve hours after making his professional debut for the Bulldogs at Toulouse Olympique.*

**Challenge Cup Final**

Warrington went into the 118th Challenge Cup Cup Final as underdogs against runaway League Leaders St Helens but came out as deserved 18-4 winners on an energy-sapping afternoon.

The Wolves' clinical and almost mistake-free display came without the player who gained so many of the plaudits during their early season successes after Blake Austin failed to recover from an ankle injury sustained at Catalans at the start of August.

Warrington's players and management made a pledge to each other, after they knew that their star man would be missing from their Wembley line-up, that only a supreme effort as a collective would bring them glory.

The fact that the voting for the man of the match saw only Warrington players included illustrated perfectly their work ethic.

As the papers were collected, Daryl Clark slipped over for the clinching try to cap a superb all-round performance that assured him over 60 per cent of the vote.

The match was still in the balance with the Wolves 12-4 ahead going into the final ten minutes when Clark, who had got his side upfield with a superb dart from dummy-half, sniped over from close range to seal the win.

In the Lance Todd voting, Clark was a comfortable winner with 21 of the 34 votes registered. Stefan Ratchford received seven votes; there were three for Ben Murdoch-Masila; and one each for Bryson Goodwin, Joe Philbin and Jack Hughes. Tom Lineham didn't get a vote but he had a fine industrious game.

However, had a key moment in the opening ten minutes gone Saints' way, who knows what could have followed. Having started the stronger of the two sides, Saints forward Morgan Knowles could be forgiven for feeling incensed that referee Robert Hicks didn't go to the video referee when he thought he'd grounded Theo Fages' grubber behind the posts.

**CORAL CHALLENGE CUP FINAL**

*Saturday 24th August 2019*

**ST HELENS 4 WARRINGTON WOLVES 18**

**SAINTS:** 23 Lachlan Coote; 2 Tommy Makinson; 3 Kevin Naiqama; 4 Mark Percival; 5 Regan Grace; 1 Jonny Lomax; 6 Theo Fages; 8 Alex Walmsley; 9 James Roby (C); 10 Luke Thompson; 11 Zeb Taia; 17 Dominique Peyroux; 15 Morgan Knowles. Subs (all used): 13 Louie McCarthy-Scarsbrook; 16 Kyle Amor; 20 Jack Ashworth; 12 Joseph Paulo.
**Try:** Fages (56); **Goals:** Coote 0/1.
**WOLVES:** 1 Stefan Ratchford; 2 Tom Lineham; 3 Bryson Goodwin; 18 Toby King; 5 Josh Charnley; 11 Ben Currie; 15 Declan Patton; 8 Chris Hill (C); 9 Daryl Clark; 10 Mike Cooper; 13 Ben Murdoch-Masila; 12 Jack Hughes (C); 14 Jason Clark. Subs (all used): 19 Sitaleki Akauola; 17 Joe Philbin; 23 Matt Davis; 22 Jake Mamo.
**Tries:** Philbin (26), Murdoch-Masila (33), D Clark (72);
**Goals:** Ratchford 2/2, Patton 1/1.
**Rugby Leaguer & League Express Men of the Match:**
*Saints:* Tommy Makinson; *Wolves:* Daryl Clark.
**Penalty count:** 4-2; **Half-time:** 0-12; **Referee:** Robert Hicks;
**Attendance:** 62,717 (at Wembley Stadium).

Replays appeared to show Knowles scoring. And while Saints coach Justin Holbrook wasn't keen to blame the officials for the result afterwards, it was clear he was frustrated by the decision not to refer the incident.

Having survived that early scare, the Wolves then avoided going behind again when Mark Percival's try was ruled out for a knock-on in the build-up on 24 minutes. Two minutes later, they pounced at the other end when boom forward Joe Philbin took the direct route to the line, crashing his way over from 20 metres out. It swung the momentum of the contest on its head.

Stefan Ratchford converted and, seven minutes later, he was on hand to double Warrington's lead to 12-0 following an uncharacteristic error from one of the Saints' best that season. Lachlan Coote's performance was perhaps symptomatic of the Saints' all-round display, with several key men struggling to exert the influence on a game they had enjoyed for most of this season.

Coote dropped a high ball to hand Warrington more field position and, from it, the Wolves held their nerve, shifting the ball right - through makeshift halfback Jack Hughes' hands - for Ben Murdoch-Masila to barge over.

*August*

In a Challenge Cup final played in energy-sapping heat, 12-0 at half-time was a huge advantage that, ultimately, the Saints were unable to overturn.

They had to score first after half-time to stand any chance. But even when they did, on 56 minutes, they were now in a race against both time and resolute Warrington defending to save the final.

Theo Fages stepped off his left foot and dived over the line to give Saints real hope. But inexplicably, Coote missed the goal from a position he would normally nail with ease.

Saints then enjoyed a period on Warrington's line. But Bryson Goodwin produced the tackle of the year, going straight for Tommy Makinson's arm rather than his body, resulting in the ball being dislodged as Makinson attempted to touch down in the corner.

Saints then spurned a number of subsequent sets, failing to kick on two consecutive occasions on the last tackle, instead turning the ball over.

And as the minutes ticked away and the pressure began to subside on Warrington, fittingly Clark, in his 150th Wolves appearance, was on hand to settle matters. He had enjoyed an absolutely outstanding afternoon, running his blood to water all game. And when he barged his way over in instinctive fashion from dummy-half with eight minutes remaining, Declan Patton's conversion to make it 18-4 sealed it.

Clark became the third hooker to win the Lance Todd since the award was instituted in 1946, following in the footsteps of fellow Wire Michael Monaghan (2009) and Hull's Tommy Harris, in defeat in 1960. The dummy-half's previous three visits, one for home-town Castleford and two with the Wolves, had ended in defeat.

The trophy was presented by the Duke of Sussex, the patron of the RFL, with chief executive Ralph Rimmer declaring himself happy with the event - which culminated with Sheffield beating Widnes 36-18 in the inaugural final of the 1895 Cup for Championship sides - despite the disappointing attendance of 62,717.

It was the last Cup Final to be played on the August Bank Holiday. The showpiece game was to be moved forward in the season to July from 2020.

**Round 27**

St Helens were presented with the League Leaders' Shield after a hard-fought 4-0 home victory over Castleford, after displaying some superb scrambling defence to protect the slender lead they earned through Regan Grace's 32nd-minute try.

The result equalled the lowest-scoring game in Super League history - Saints having beaten Celtic Crusaders by the same scoreline in 2009. The hosts should have at least doubled their score late on, when Jonny Lomax's match-sealing try was dubiously chalked off for obstruction. But they had to produce an inspiring defensive effort in the face of an avalanche of Tigers' attacks, particularly in the second half.

The loss extended Castleford's winless run at St Helens, which stretched all the way back to 1990 in the league and left their play-off hopes on a knife edge, one win off fifth with two matches to play.

Despite great celebrations after the game, there was controversy over an extraordinary tirade in St Helens chairman Eamonn McManus's programme notes at the officials in the Challenge Cup Final defeat to Warrington.

McManus slammed the 'publicity stunt' arranged by Cup-winners Warrington in the build-up to the decider, when Wolves CEO Karl Fitzpatrick organised a meeting between Wembley referee Robert Hicks and a Wire fan who had made a death threat via social media earlier in the season. The chairman also criticised Hicks' performance on the big day - particularly his refusal to refer Morgan Knowles' 'clear and legitimate opening try' to the video referee, followed by 'other highly questionable decisions. The perception of officiating impartiality was destroyed even before kick-off.' McManus copped a three thousand pounds fine after the end of the season.

Wigan coach Adrian Lam insisted he always believed his side could recover from a

The victorious Warrington side celebrate their Challenge Cup Final win against St Helens

St Helens captain James Roby lifts the League Leaders' Shield

horrendous start to 2019 to make the play-offs after they all-but secured a top-five place with a 24-16 success at Wakefield Trinity on the Sunday. The Warriors had won ten of their last eleven league games and were now outright second.

Wakefield had done well to battle back from 10-0 down to level at half-time before the 58th minute produced the game's crucial moment.

A Danny Brough bomb was defused well by Liam Marshall, who raced to the 20-metre line for a tap restart. However, he was several metres off the centre marking on the line where players were required to tap the ball. Scott Mikalauskas waved play-on and the Wigan winger raced upfield to complete his hat-trick and put the visitors ahead. Ben Jones-Bishop got a try back but Sam Powell's short-range try in the last seconds sealed it.

The result meant Trinity remained in the relegation battle and coach Chris Chester could not hide his disgust at the decision.

Wigan went two points clear of Warrington who couldn't replicate their Wembley effort on the Thursday night at Salford, the Red Devils winning 22-6, their sixth consecutive win that moved them level in third with the Wolves.

Expecting the Wolves to back up just five days after winning the Challenge Cup was a tall order. And so it proved.

Nevertheless Ken Sio's hat-trick contributed to another accomplished performance that convinced more people that Salford were serious contenders. They led 2-0 at the break after an arm-wrestle of a first half. The only points came when Krisnan Inu slotted a straight-forward penalty in the tenth minute after Danny Walker was caught offside.

A total of eleven penalties didn't help the flow of the game, with both sides guilty of committing foul play as well as handling errors in key areas.

The main moment of note came when Lama Tasi, one of four former Red Devils in the Wolves starting line-up, rushed out of the line to smash Tyrone McCarthy. The Salford man objected to being twisted in the tackle and his head driven towards the ground but his reaction meant it was Warrington who received the penalty.

The try-scoring deadlock was eventually broken nine minutes into the second half.

Tom Lineham, running backwards, spilled a spiralling Tui Lolohea kick and Sio was on hand to finish from close range. Inu's conversion attempt struck an upright and bounced out. Eight minutes later Sio was over again after a Jake Mamo error on his own line gifted them another attacking opportunity. The Red Devils took it gratefully, with superb hands from Kris Welham and Niall Evalds allowing Sio to step inside two defenders and touch down.

Salford touched down again in the next set, with Joey Lussick breaking from deep, Jackson Hastings supporting and Jake Bibby finishing off an excellent move. And Sio had his hat-trick when he scooped up a loose ball from Lineham's attempted grubber and raced 80 metres to score.

Hull FC dropped to fifth on points difference after a 22-12 home defeat to Huddersfield, who ended a horrendous form slump and boosted their hopes of staving off relegation. Australian scrum-half Matt Frawley returned to the fold to partner Lee Gaskell in the halves and was instrumental, scoring a crucial try from a kick with eight minutes to play.

Danny McGuire produced a virtuoso display that put Hull Kingston Rovers back on the winning track and ended the competitive season for Catalans Dragons. The Robins took over a thousand supporters to Perpignan to cheer them on to a 24-6 victory on the Saturday afternoon, at the end of a week in which coach Tony Smith signed a new three-year contract with the club.

McGuire was unstoppable from start to finish, with winger Ryan Shaw making a 20-point contribution with two tries and six goals.

Leeds were safe from relegation after a 36-10 win at London Broncos, their vastly superior points difference acting as insurance. London, two points adrift again and themselves handicapped on points difference, would be relegated if they lost the following Friday at Hull Kingston Rovers.

Three late tries - from Ash Handley, a second from gamestar Jack Walker and Brad Dwyer - exaggerated the Rhinos' superiority as London for once lost both shape and discipline, ending with eleven men as Kieran Dixon went to the sin bin for slowing a play the ball, Elliot Kear following for dissent.

**BETFRED SUPER LEAGUE**
*Sunday 1st September*

| | P | W | D | L | F | A | D | Pts |
|---|---|---|---|---|---|---|---|---|
| St Helens | 27 | 24 | 0 | 3 | 846 | 383 | 463 | 48 |
| Wigan Warriors | 27 | 16 | 0 | 11 | 627 | 519 | 108 | 32 |
| Warrington Wolves | 27 | 15 | 0 | 12 | 682 | 491 | 191 | 30 |
| Salford Red Devils | 27 | 15 | 0 | 12 | 746 | 569 | 177 | 30 |
| Hull FC | 27 | 15 | 0 | 12 | 627 | 702 | -75 | 30 |
| Castleford Tigers | 27 | 14 | 0 | 13 | 594 | 520 | 74 | 28 |
| Catalans Dragons | 27 | 13 | 0 | 14 | 519 | 675 | -156 | 26 |
| Leeds Rhinos | 27 | 11 | 0 | 16 | 612 | 620 | -8 | 22 |
| Wakefield Trinity | 27 | 10 | 0 | 17 | 573 | 690 | -117 | 20 |
| Huddersfield Giants | 27 | 10 | 0 | 17 | 541 | 706 | -165 | 20 |
| Hull Kingston Rovers | 27 | 10 | 0 | 17 | 516 | 731 | -215 | 20 |
| London Broncos | 27 | 9 | 0 | 18 | 475 | 752 | -277 | 18 |

*\* Over seven and a half thousand spectators witnessed Bradford Bulls' last match at Odsal - a 30-10 win over Sheffield Eagles on Sunday 1st September. The cost of renting and maintaining the famous stadium had become too great and the Bulls were to play home games at Dewsbury Rams' Tetley's Stadium in 2020.*

# SEPTEMBER
## *That old Red Devil...*

**Round 28**

Salford confirmed they would be in the play-offs with a seventh successive win - a 20-12 success at Leeds, only their second at Headingley in the summer era, ten years after their last and with their first seasonal double over Leeds since 1946.

From Krisnan Inu's four mesmeric offloads, to George Griffin's 55 tackles, Josh Jones's 138 metres and Jackson Hastings' all-round generalship, the Red Devils showed again that their elevated position was no fluke.

Early converted tries from Niall Evalds and Jake Bibby had the Red Devils in the ascendancy despite Richie Myler's try making it only 14-6 at half-time. Leeds hung in for most of a gripping second half and were arguably a Harry Newman fingertip away from wresting victory. His attempted interception, with eleven minutes to go and his side two points behind after Jamie Jones-Buchanan's try, just slipped out of his grasp.

Joey Lussick made the Rhinos pay with a try eight minutes from time.

The fifth play-off spot was still up for grabs going into the weekend and Castleford made themselves favourites with a 44-12 home victory over Hull FC, who themselves would have confirmed a top-five finish with a win.

But defeat meant the two were now level on points but with the Tigers on a far superior points difference. Hull were due to face St Helens on the final weekend.

The key man in Castleford's win was halfback Jake Trueman. After 42 minutes the young gun could have easily put his feet up, having scored a hat-trick and put his side 26-6 ahead against a team that didn't look likely to mount a comeback of that scale.

But Trueman kept displaying his artistry and kept the Tigers on top until the very final whistle, by which time they had run out commanding victors.

The Tigers raced into a 20-0 lead as Cheyse Blair crossed and Trueman scored twice before Masi Matongo replied for the visitors before the break. After it, Trueman completed his hat-trick before Jack Logan notched a breakaway try.

But the last ten minutes saw Castleford register three converted tries - with Jamie Ellis kicking eight goals from eight attempts - through James Clare, Jordan Rankin and Matt Cook. Cook's try came after Jake Connor had been sin-binned for disputing a decision as a scrum formed, with TV cameras picking up a verbal spat between Connor, whose form had dipped late in 2019, and retiring teammate Mark Minichiello.

As in many previous seasons the media spotlight was on the battle to avoid relegation, which involved four clubs on 20 points going into the last weekend.

London Broncos were still bottom but only on points difference after an astounding 20-16 win in a relegation four-pointer at Hull KR, Jay Pitts' dramatic 76th-minute try stealing the two points. Defeat would have meant the Broncos were relegated.

With the clock counting down towards a tense Hull KR victory that would confirm the Robins' safety, London were looking at an immediate return to the Championship, despite their heroics this season. But Ryan Morgan's break down the right laid the position and there was no stopping Pitts, the capital club's captain.

The Broncos had stormed into a 12-0 lead inside the first ten minutes of the game. Mid-season signing Brock Lamb was the key figure, scoring one try and making another. The former Newcastle Knights and Sydney Roosters halfback produced a moment of skill to pick a Jason Abdull pass off his bootlaces and pass to the on-rushing Matty Gee in the same motion for the opening try.

Then moments later Lamb took another ball from Abdull, stepped past Josh Drinkwater and dummied around Craig Hall for a brilliant solo effort that was converted off a post by Kieran Dixon.

But Rovers bounced back to trail only 14-12 through scores from Will Dagger and Chris Atkin. And Danny McGuire looked like he'd won it when he went over on 51 minutes.

Rovers seemed set for victory until Morgan broke down the right with the clock ticking down. Though Atkin produced an excellent cover tackle, there was no stopping Pitts when the ball went left, setting up one of the most dramatic finales in Super League history the following Friday.

Wakefield and Huddersfield would be the other two clubs involved, both losing on the same Friday night.

Warrington ended their losing run with a 23-16 home win over Wakefield on a night when Wolves fans paid an emotional tribute to Ben Westwood as he paraded around the pitch.

There was, however, no place in the matchday squad for Westwood as he watched Warrington run out winners over his boyhood club to end a six-game losing streak in the Super League. Josh Charnley's try to put the Wolves 16 points up before the break ensured the home side had enough of a buffer to keep a valiant Trinity side at bay.

Meanwhile Huddersfield took a 48-6 hammering at St Helens, boom prop Luke Thompson in unstoppable mood.

Jonny Lomax wasn't awarded any Albert Goldthorpe points but he was confirmed the 2019 winner with a full round of fixtures remaining, when Salford's Jackson Hastings, who was six points behind him going into Round 28, was only awarded one point for his efforts in the Red Devils' victory against Leeds.

Bevan French cemented himself as a Wigan fans' favourite as he crossed for a hat-trick of tries as the Warriors moved a step closer to securing second place on the ladder with a 46-12 home win over Catalans.

It was also a special night for young halfback Harry Smith, who marked his first-team debut with a try.

Wigan were second best for the opening stages of the first half but the Catalans' inability to break down Wigan's resolute defence proved to be their downfall. Two French tries and three Zak Hardaker goals made it 14-0 at half-time and French's hat-trick score just after the break halted any chance of the Dragons making a game of it.

There was no Tony Gigot in the Dragons line-up, with the unpredictable fullback rumoured to have signed for St George Illawarra for 2020.

## Round 29

It wasn't that straightforward going into the last round.

London Broncos could assure their top-flight status, at the end of a season in which they were widely expected to scrape a couple of wins at most, by winning at Wakefield. If they did, Wakefield had a much better points difference and could still survive if either Huddersfield lost at home to Catalans, or Hull KR lost at Salford, who had a mathematical chance of going into second going into the round and, after Wigan's defeat of Castleford on the Thursday night, a chance of finishing third. Castleford's defeat meant that Hull FC had the chance to leapfrog them into fifth, if they could beat League Leaders St Helens at home.

Wakefield's Ryan Hampshire beats London's Kieran Dixon to score

At the end of the evening of Friday 13th, it was the Broncos, despite collecting 20 league points with ten wins, who went back down into the Championship as Wakefield put in a near-perfect performance to thwart them.

London didn't even trouble the scorers until nine minutes from the end. But by the time Alex Walker's try against his future employers was given, Brock Lamb also scoring in the last minute, Wakefield had long since ensured that any final-night drama was out of the question. Led by Danny Brough's masterclass in kicking and some real leadership in the pack from mid-season recruit Kelepi Tanginoa, two tries from Ryan Hampshire and one from Reece Lyne had Trinity safe before Brough kicked a 68th-minute field goal to make it 19-0.

There was some relief then for Hull KR fans when the news of Wakefield's win came through to the AJ Bell Stadium as their side entered golden-point extra time, locked at 16-all with the Red Devils after Joey Lussick's last-minute try.

An uneventful first period of extra-time ended with a wild Craig Hall pot-shot at the sticks and Krisnan Inu unleashed a similarly speculative effort from the halfway line midway through the second. However, the resultant charge-down gave Salford a scrum inside Rovers' half and Inu's field goal from 20 metres out directly in front proved the difference off the next set.

It was a club-record eighth straight victory for Salford to leapfrog Warrington into third.

Retiring halfback Danny McGuire marked his final game with a vintage try assist and then a sin-binning, while opposite number Jackson Hastings produced a typically dominant display for the hosts. Rovers were without captain Joel Tomkins, who had a one-match ban for punching London prop Rob Butler the week before increased to two matches after an appeal, which the RFL Disciplinary considered 'frivolous'.

Winger Louis Senior's four tries secured a narrow 24-22 victory over Catalans to secure the Giants' Super League status.

Huddersfield's Louis Senior slides past Robin Brochon for one of his four tries against Catalans

Huddersfield scraped over the line. They were second best for the majority of the game and could have no complaints when they found themselves 12 points behind to a threadbare Dragons team.

They were still eight points down with ten minutes to go. But then followed a 90-second period in which Louis Senior galloped 80 metres to cut the deficit to two and Kruise Leeming nailed a majestic 40/20 to set up Jermaine McGillvary's winner.

Catalans absentee list meant that Arthur Mourgue, who impressed at halfback, and Robin Brochon made their first appearances of the season in what was Greg Bird's last game before retiring.

Jamie Jones-Buchanan landed his first goal on his final appearance to cap a glorious 20-year career in Leeds' 26-4 home win over Warrington.

Led by seemingly dinner-jacketed Robert Lui and supported by Rhyse Martin and backed up by the constantly probing Richie Myler, the Leeds midfield dominated their counterparts, setting the platform for victory in a game that initially was characterised by handling errors on both sides, despite the near-perfect conditions.

The Wire pulled it back, through a Josh Charnley try, to ten points behind with as many minutes to go but couldn't get past the first tackle of the re-start set and Adam Cuthbertson immediately made them pay.

Hull FC rounded off their season so near and yet so far, as their hugely improved display was not good enough to overhaul an impressive St Helens side, the League Leaders winning 22-6 at KCOM Stadium.

The cutting edge on show from St Helens was marvelled at by the large and vocal home crowd. They were deadly when close to the line and took their chances to the tune of five well-worked tries. Lachlan Coote marshalled his side brilliantly in defence and was relentless and composed with the ball, having a hand in several of his side's tries.

Hull KR's Danny McGuire leaves the field after his final game before retirement, a golden point defeat at Salford

That week Saints announced that Kristian Woolf, who had revolutionised the Tongan national team and also temporarily took charge of NRL side Newcastle Knights in recent weeks, was to be their new head coach from 2020.

Hull, after looking play-off certainties a month before, had missed their chance to make the play-offs. Instead, despite their 26-8 defeat at Wigan the previous evening, Castleford finished fifth.

Two tries in three minutes early in the second half from Zak Hardaker and Joe Greenwood put Wigan in the ascendency and from that moment they never looked like losing. And in the 66th minute the Tigers suffered another blow when Jesse Sene-Lefao was red carded for aiming his knees at tackled Oliver Partington's head. He was suspended for two games.

Once again the young Wigan forwards stood out and, the following Monday, League Express announced that

**BETFRED SUPER LEAGUE**
*Final table - Sunday 15th September*

| | P | W | D | L | F | A | D | Pts |
|---|---|---|---|---|---|---|---|---|
| St Helens | 29 | 26 | 0 | 3 | 916 | 395 | 521 | 52 |
| Wigan Warriors | 29 | 18 | 0 | 11 | 699 | 539 | 160 | 36 |
| Salford Red Devils | 29 | 17 | 0 | 12 | 783 | 597 | 186 | 34 |
| Warrington Wolves | 29 | 16 | 0 | 13 | 709 | 533 | 176 | 32 |
| Castleford Tigers | 29 | 15 | 0 | 14 | 646 | 558 | 88 | 30 |
| Hull FC | 29 | 15 | 0 | 14 | 645 | 768 | -123 | 30 |
| Catalans Dragons | 29 | 13 | 0 | 16 | 553 | 745 | -192 | 26 |
| Leeds Rhinos | 29 | 12 | 0 | 17 | 650 | 644 | 6 | 24 |
| Wakefield Trinity | 29 | 11 | 0 | 18 | 608 | 723 | -115 | 22 |
| Huddersfield Giants | 29 | 11 | 0 | 18 | 571 | 776 | -205 | 22 |
| Hull Kingston Rovers | 29 | 10 | 0 | 19 | 548 | 768 | -220 | 20 |
| London Broncos | 29 | 10 | 0 | 19 | 505 | 787 | -282 | 20 |

Morgan Smithies had won the Albert Goldthorpe Rookie of the Year award, beating off the challenge of five other nominees - Alex Walker of London Broncos, Ratu Naulago of Hull FC, Jack Welsby of St Helens, Joey Lussick of Salford Red Devils and Harry Newman of Leeds Rhinos. Siddal product Smithies, 18, made his debut off the bench for the Warriors in Round 8 against Catalans and he had been a virtual ever-present since then, making 21 Super League appearances in the regular season.

**Super League Play-offs - Week 1**

**Qualifying Play-off**

Second-placed Wigan edged out third-placed Salford 18-12 in a Friday-night thriller at the DW Stadium. Both defences were ferocious and each player ran his blood to water, with 18-year-old forward Morgan Smithies creating a new Super League record with 72 tackles.

Salford were the better team for the opening 20 minutes but they were unable to find a way through the Wigan defence - although Jake Bibby was only thwarted by an awkward bounce from Jackson Hastings' grubber - which allowed Wigan to finally adapt to the pace of the game and they took the lead. A mistake from Kristian Inu gave possession to Wigan, although replays suggested the ball was stolen in the tackle. The Warriors didn't argue and the soon broke the deadlock when George Williams took on the Salford line and sent a ball out for Oliver Gildart, who stepped Kris Welham to score. Zak Hardaker converted for a 6-0 lead.

The Red Devils deservedly went in level at the break as George Griffin powered over from close range just moments after Joey Lussick had been denied by the video referee.

After half-time, Ken Sio had a try denied by video for a foot in touch before two tries in three minutes from Thomas Leuluai and Williams, both converted by Hardaker, seemed to put the Warriors in the driving seat heading into the final quarter. But some individual magic from Hastings set up a tense last 17 minutes, as he evaded the clutches of Liam Farrell to go over under the posts. Inu converted to close the gap to just six points.

Salford threw everything at the Warriors in the final ten minutes but Wigan's defensive wall would not crumble and they could look forward to a crack at St Helens the following week.

*\* Morgan Smithies' tackle count put him three ahead of the previous record, 69 tackles made by Malcolm Alker for Salford against Castleford on 25th April 2010, a record equalled by Hull FC's current captain Danny Houghton for Hull against Widnes on 23rd March 2014.*

**Elimination Play-off**

Fifth beat fourth as Castleford edged Warrington on their own patch by 14-12 on the Thursday night.

Without eight frontline players due to injury and suspension, Castleford abandoned the flamboyant style that won them so many admirers in 2017. Instead, led from the front by Liam Watts and Grant Millington, Castleford's defensive grit made sure their season stayed alive for at least another week.

Warrington had finished the year with just one win from their last nine league games. They looked bereft of ideas in attack for most of the night, illustrated by Stefan Ratchford's decision to try and level the scores at 14-14 late on with a penalty from halfway. He missed it and it allowed Castleford to book their place in week two.

The Wolves' cause was not helped by the loss of marquee man Blake Austin. The Australian, who had returned from the ankle injury that ruled him out of Wembley, suffered two or three crunching hits throughout the course of the first half which left him heavily limping as the teams headed off for half-time.

The Tigers edged the first half. Adam Milner touched down a deft Paul McShane kick with the half-hour mark approaching, with Peter Mata'utia's goal making it 6-0.

When Austin didn't return after the break and Jake Mamo came on in his place, Warrington appeared more settled. That was proven when, 90 seconds after the restart, the Wolves levelled the game when Mamo touched down in the corner, with Ratchford converting superbly. But seven minutes later, Castleford went back ahead.

Some wonderful handling led to Jordan Rankin scything through to touch down, with Mata'utia converting for a six-point lead once again. And with 12 minutes left, back-to-back penalties enabled Mata'utia to make it 14-6 from the tee.

Warrington needed to score twice. And after they regained the short kick-off, captain Chris Hill touched down a smart Daryl Clark kick to make it 14-12, setting up a grandstand finish.

Then came the decisive moment. Watts was penalised on halfway and, after plenty of deliberation, the call came to go for goal, rather than run it to try to win the game.

Ratchford's kick didn't have the required length, allowing Rankin to take it and let Castleford hold on.

**Super League Play-offs - Week 2**

**Qualifying Semi-final**

St Helens - who had finished the regular season 16 points clear at the top of the table - blew arch-rivals Wigan away, a 40-10 home victory seeing them through to their first Grand Final since 2014.

In what was their most complete performance of the whole campaign, Saints brushed aside their local rivals with a display of pace, power and execution. Up against a Wigan team that had won eight in a row, they overwhelmed them from the start, running over the top and around their opponents at different stages. The inexperienced Warriors pack could not handle their counterparts, especially the outstanding Luke Thompson and Morgan Knowles.

Both made metres at will, with Thompson scoring a try in a superb 54-minute spell that laid the platform for victory.

Behind them, Jonny Lomax and Theo Fages linked as well as they had all season, while Lachlan Coote looked back to his pre-Wembley best.

Elsewhere, Tommy Makinson again got through huge levels of work, Louie McCarthy-Scarsbrook impressed off the bench and Mark Percival had one of his best games of 2019.

It could hardly have been a more comprehensive way to book a record eleventh Grand Final place.

Saints led 26-6 at half-time after tries from Fages, Kevin Naiqama, Thompson and Lomax with one in reply from Liam Marshall. Zeb Taia's try and a Percival double extended the lead before Bevan French's late consolation.

**Elimination Semi-final**

Salford ruthlessly ended Castleford's own tilt at the Grand Final to book their place in the Final Eliminator after a 22-0 home win on the Thursday night.

Defensively, it was almost perfect and the Red Devils' prowess was epitomised by one game-defining moment. As Salford led 12-0 early on thanks to well-taken tries for Tyrone McCarthy and Jake Bibby, a rare break from Castleford saw Jordan Rankin cut through the home defence and race downfield.

Rankin, to his credit, did everything right. He pinned his ears back and went for the corner. But he was not only halted by Niall Evalds, the fullback had the wherewithal to roll his opposite number over and bundle him into touch.

A 12-0 deficit could have become 12-6 and Castleford could have grown into the game. Instead, the Red Devils added a penalty from the boot of Krisnan Inu to make it 14-0 and, by half-time, the hosts had one foot in the next stage of the play-offs.

Castleford had started the game well, with Greg Eden, who was back in the side for

Salford's Niall Evalds completes a stunning tackle on Castleford's Jordan Rankin

Calum Turner, looking particularly threatening on one or two attacking kicks but it was the hosts who struck first. An inch-perfect kick from Tui Lolohea found in-form forward McCarthy, who beat a Castleford defender to the ball to touch down under the sticks.

Inu converted to make it 6-0 and he was on hand again three minutes later. Castleford thought they had done enough to force Bibby into touch when he went for the corner as Greg Minikin tackled him. Their players marched out to the 20-metre line when the decision was being replayed on the big screen and most inside the ground thought it would be no try.

But in the end, Ben Thaler's on-field call of try seemed decisive, as the score was awarded and Inu converted from the touchline to open up a 12-point lead in almost as many minutes.

After a hard battle in the second half Jackson Hastings was the man who settled the game when he ghosted through for a 72nd-minute try. Inu converted that and added a penalty to send Salford through.

# OCTOBER
## *Saints finish in style*

---

**Super League Play-offs - Week 3**

**Final Eliminator**

Salford Red Devils made the 2019 Betfred Super League Grand Final in stunning fashion, beating Wigan 28-4 at the DW Stadium, two weeks after an 18-12 defeat at the same venue in the opening week of the play-offs.

Salford responded to that defeat by holding out Castleford to zero points the following week and then they returned to the DW Stadium and not only defeated Wigan, but hammered them. It was a remarkable achievement for a club that had lost its millionaire benefactor in 2018 and in 2016 had been minutes away from being relegated in the 'Million Pound Game' at Hull KR.

The key statistic for Salford's win was that they only made two handling errors in the match, compared to Wigan's twelve. Admittedly the Warriors had a major problem as Thomas Leuluai was forced off with a head knock and eventually failed his concussion assessment. He was replaced by the elusive Bevan French, who scored their only try, a consolation eight minutes from time. By then the reigning champions were well beaten, Jackson Hastings scheming behind a dominant pack led by former Wigan prop Gil Dudson and backrower Josh Jones.

Salford dominated the opening 40 minutes and led 12-0 at the break, thanks to eight points from the boot of Krisnan Inu and a try from Dudson.

Wigan were slow out of the blocks and found themselves on the back foot. They did manage to enjoy a lot of possession but looked short of attacking ideas, aggression and energy against the inspired Red Devils.

The Warriors failed to improve after the break and Salford got better as Joey Lussick and Lee Mossop both scored close-range tries, while Inu continued his fine form with the boot with a further eight points.

The Red Devils had around 4,000 fans in the stand behind the goalposts and they all stayed long after the final whistle to celebrate a historic win.

*\* Toronto Wolfpack won promotion to Super League after three years of existence with a 24-6 Championship Grand Final win over Featherstone in front of a capacity crowd at Lamport Stadium.*

**Super League Grand Final**

St Helens won the 2019 Super League Grand Final, emerging 23-6 winners over Salford Red Devils at Old Trafford to confirm their status as the best team in the competition.

Having lost only three games and one Cup game all year, they had finished the regular season 16 points clear of Wigan at the top of the table and demolished the Warriors in the Qualifying Play-off semi-final.

Alex Walmsley and Lachlan Coote celebrate as Morgan Knowles scores the first try of the Super League Grand Final

It was coach Justin Holbrook's final game in charge of Saints before he left to take up the head coach's role at Gold Coast Titans.

Luke Thompson received the Harry Sunderland Trophy as man of the match amid an outstanding team performance, the first prop forward to win the award since Andy Platt for Wigan against St Helens in the old-style old Premiership final in 1992.

Thompson received eleven votes from the media for the trophy, while fullback Lachlan Coote got eight and fellow prop Alex Walmsley seven, with no other players receiving any votes. Thompson probably shaved the decision after playing almost all the game, a rare occurrence for the modern-day prop. Only when he suffered cramp with seven minutes to play did he finally leave the field.

The atmosphere was electric right from the kick-off and it took Salford most of the first half to adjust to the pace of a Grand Final.

The Red Devils were immediately pinned back when captain Lee Mossop spilled the ball in the second tackle of the match, after a shot from Kevin Naiqama put Saints on immediate attack.

Salford would stand firm - buoyed on by their noisy support cheering every single tackle made - and they kept up their defensive resilience for most of the opening 15 minutes.

Saints turned the ball over on Salford's line on several occasions, coming close to the opening score a couple of times - including when a half-break from Coote saw him try to flick a pass out to Regan Grace, only to find touch.

But the pressure and the amount of defending Salford were having to do was always going to force them to crack eventually. And it did on 15 minutes. Another Saints set started deep in Salford territory and Walmsley's inch-perfect short pass one off the ruck sent Morgan Knowles through a gap to touch down by the posts, with Coote making it 6-0.

Salford were struggling to deal with Saints' physicality and power, with a half-break from Grace being halted as he acrobatically tried to leap over Niall Evalds rather than go around him.

**BETFRED SUPER LEAGUE GRAND FINAL**

*Saturday 12th October 2019*

**SALFORD RED DEVILS 6 ST HELENS 23**

**RED DEVILS:** 1 Niall Evalds; 23 Ken Sio; 3 Kris Welham; 5 Jake Bibby; 26 Krisnan Inu; 30 Tuimoala Lolohea; 31 Jackson Hastings; 8 Lee Mossop (C); 19 Logan Tomkins; 10 Gil Dudson; 11 Josh Jones; 12 George Griffin; 17 Tyrone McCarthy. Subs (all used): 13 Mark Flanagan; 14 Joey Lussick; 15 Adam Walker; 16 Greg Burke.
**Try:** Bibby (32); **Goals:** Inu 1/1.
**SAINTS:** 23 Lachlan Coote; 2 Tommy Makinson; 3 Kevin Naiqama; 4 Mark Percival; 5 Regan Grace; 1 Jonny Lomax; 6 Theo Fages; 8 Alex Walmsley; 9 James Roby (C); 10 Luke Thompson; 11 Zeb Taia; 17 Dominique Peyroux; 15 Morgan Knowles. Subs (all used): 13 Louie McCarthy-Scarsbrook; 16 Kyle Amor; 20 Jack Ashworth; 21 Aaron Smith.
**Tries:** Knowles (16), Taia (24), Percival (50); **Goals:** Coote 5/5; **Field goal:** Makinson (78).
**Rugby Leaguer & League Express Men of the Match:**
*Red Devils:* Josh Jones; *Saints:* Luke Thompson.
**Penalty count:** 5-6; **Half-time:** 6-12; **Referee:** Chris Kendall; **Attendance:** 64,102 *(at Old Trafford, Manchester).*

But when a Ken Sio knock-on pilled the pressure on the Red Devils again, Saints took full advantage. An inspired short-side play directly from the scrum caught the Salford defence out, with James Roby's lovely reverse pass, as Theo Fages ran a sideways decoy, sending Zeb Taia over.

At 12-0, the writing looked well and truly on the wall for Salford. But they not only stemmed the flow, they finished the first half well on top.

Tui Lolohea's lovely stepping solo effort was ruled out by referee Chris Kendall for an apparent obstruction but, just a few minutes later, after earning a fresh set of six in St Helens territory, Salford struck.

Lolohea and Jackson Hastings combined to send Jake Bibby away down the left and he fooled Tommy Makinson with a wonderful dummy to slide over, with Kristian Inu converting from out wide. Suddenly, the gap was just six at half-time and it was game on once again.

The first try after half-time was always going to be decisive - and it was Saints who got it. With not much on as they attacked, Mark Percival cut back on the angle and slid a

St Helens players and fans show their delight at their Super League Grand Final success

grubber through the Salford defensive line. With the kick catching everyone cold, Percival seized the initiative, just beating teammate Kyle Amor and Hastings to touch down under the posts.

From there, Saints took control of proceedings again. A penalty from Coote on the hour mark opened up a three-score lead and Salford coach Ian Watson conceded post-match that the amount of energy-sapping defending the Red Devils had to do in the opening half-hour depleted them significantly. They were unable to provide any real telling moments in attack and when they did get near Saints' line, Gil Dudson was ruled to have knocked on playing the ball, when TV replays suggested he should have had a penalty. And by the time Coote added another penalty to make it 22-6, the Saints' celebrations had already begun.

There was still time for a party piece from Makinson, who had suffered a dislocated shoulder earlier in the half, as he slotted the first field goal of his career from 40 metres.

It was a champagne moment to crown a champagne year for a side that swept aside all before it in Super League in 2019.

# WOMEN'S LEAGUE
## *Double top for Rhinos*

Despite not retaining their League Leaders Shield trophy, **LEEDS RHINOS** were still celebrating after completing a League and Cup double.

Twelve-months on from losing out to Wigan Warriors in the 2018 Grand Final, Leeds were partying in front of the Sky TV cameras as the network broadcast their 20-12 win over **CASTLEFORD TIGERS**.

It was the first time Sky had shown a women's game live and it was a treat for everyone watching both at home and at the Totally Wicked Stadium.

The Rhinos had to fight back from 8-0 down after tries from Castleford's Maisie Lumb and Lacey Owen. Abby Eatock, who was playing only her fifth game for Leeds since signing from the Army, then went over the Rhinos to half the deficit and Leeds were starting to build their way into the game.

The Rhinos made the game their own in the second half and 16-year-old winger Fran Goldthorp bagged two tries before Elle Frain also crossed. Woman of Steel nominee Kelsey Gentles got a late consolation try for Castleford but it was Leeds who were left celebrating at the final hooter.

Castleford had hoped to take their revenge against the Rhinos in that game, after losing out in an even closer Challenge Cup Final at Bolton in July. The Tigers went into that clash unbeaten in all competitions and were the hot favourites to lift the trophy.

Again, the Tigers took an early lead - this time through Rhiannion Marshall - but were soon pegged bagged through Goldthorp. The sides traded further tries before half time, with Caitlin Beevers crossing for Leeds and Tamzin Renouf going in for the Tigers, leaving matters at 10-10 at the break.

The crucial moment came with 20 minutes left. A break and then pin-perfect pass by Dannielle Anderson found Women of Steel winner Courtney Hill to race in under the posts.

Despite their best efforts Castleford, who had handed a debut to Hollie Dodd the day after her 16th birthday, could not find another way through as Leeds retained the Challenge Cup.

The Rhinos' post-season celebrations will have been tempered however by the news that former captain, England international and Women's Rugby League trailblazer Lois Forsell had been forced into retirement due to the injury that had kept her out of action for over a year.

The two final defeats aside, 2019 was still hugely positive year for the Tigers.

A 44-0 victory over York City Knights on a Tuesday night at the Jungle saw Castleford claim the League Leaders Shield in emphatic style. Up until that point they were unbeaten in the league and had regularly steamrolled many sides to head the table. They lost to St Helens in the final league match but they won't let that put a dampener on their incredible campaign.

As well as getting on-field matters right on the majority of occasions, they were also leading the way off it. Superb social media work not only helped showcase the players and their talents but it also saw the club regularly attract four-figure crowds to their games.

## Women's League

**ST HELENS** were once again never far away from success, losing out to Leeds at the semi-final stage of both the Challenge Cup and the Play-offs.

Working under a new head coach in Derek Hardman, the club continued to make steady progress in their second season with the experience of Jodie Cunningham, Emily Rudge and Faye Gaskin proving crucial at key moments.

**WIGAN WARRIORS** went into the campaign as reigning Champions and were quickly given a lesson in how tough retaining the title would be after defeats to both St Helens and Castleford in the opening weeks. The Warriors won five out of their six games by scoring more than 40 points but couldn't get that potency as consistently as they would have liked. The main downside of the Warriors season was the fact they waved goodbye to coach Amanda Wilkinson, who was so influential in setting the club up. She was replaced by assistant Kris Ratcliffe.

Outside of the Play-offs **FEATHERSTONE ROVERS** had a positive end to the season with four consecutive wins that ultimately saw them miss out on the top four by a single point. In these results, plus their other two victories earlier in the campaign, they showed glimpses of returning to the force they once were in the Women's game.

**BRADFORD BULLS**, now under the stewardship of former England internationals Kirsty Moroney and Beth Sutcliffe, were very much enduring a rebuilding process from the glory season of 2017. The coaching duo has seen some success in their aim to develop a number of local youngsters into future Super League stars. The squad they worked with were young and enthusiastic but could not find the consistency needed to challenge for the play-offs.

**YORK CTY KNIGHTS** continued to find their feet at this level with visibly improved performances against some of the bigger teams in the league. They also had reason to celebrate when Rebecca Waterworth made her debut against Wakefield in August. She was the first player from the club's 'Foundation's Girls Excel' programme to be picked by the first team.

**WAKEFIELD TRINITY** found their first season at this level hard, with the transition from Championship winners to Super League competitors a tough one. Losing coach Wayne Hirst midway through the year and losing 100-0 in the Challenge Cup semi-final were particular low points but the fact they got that far in the cup competition should be applauded. As should the fact they never gave up in games - even when they were being blown away on the scoreboard.

Away from Super League, **WARRINGTON WOLVES** have earned a place in 2020's top flight after finishing up as League Leaders and then beating **BARROW** 40-4 in the Grand Final double-header at the Manchester Regional Arena.

In the other game that day, League 1 table-toppers **KEIGHLEY ALBION** beat **CUTSYKE RAIDETTES** 54-12.

**THE ARMY** upset the odds by beating York City Knights 40-4 in the Challenge Shield Final over the summer.

**HUDDERSFIELD GIANTS**, who finished fourth in the Championship, will also make the step up to Super League in 2020, making it a ten-team competition.

Leeds Rhinos - 2019 Super League Champions

## SUPER LEAGUE - FINAL TABLE

|  | P | W | D | L | F | A | D | Pts |
|---|---|---|---|---|---|---|---|---|
| Castleford Tigers | 14 | 13 | 0 | 1 | 625 | 160 | 465 | 26 |
| St Helens | 14 | 12 | 1 | 1 | 522 | 131 | 391 | 25 |
| Leeds Rhinos | 14 | 10 | 1 | 3 | 410 | 151 | 259 | 21 |
| Wigan Warriors | 14 | 6 | 1 | 7 | 328 | 224 | 104 | 13 |
| | | | | | | | | |
| Featherstone Rovers | 14 | 6 | 0 | 8 | 237 | 450 | -213 | 12 |
| Bradford Bulls | 13 | 4 | 1 | 8 | 300 | 282 | 18 | 9 |
| York City Knights | 13 | 1 | 0 | 12 | 68 | 522 | -454 | 2 |
| Wakefield Trinity | 14 | 1 | 0 | 13 | 64 | 634 | -570 | 2 |

*Bradford Bulls v York City Knights (29th September) not played due to weather conditions*

## SUPER LEAGUE GRAND FINAL

*Friday 11th October 2019*

### CASTLEFORD TIGERS 12 LEEDS RHINOS 20

**TIGERS:** 1 Tara Stanley; 16 Maisie Lumb; 24 Lucy Eastwood; 12 Lacey Owen; 4 Kelsey Gentles; 6 Georgia Roche; 33 Jasmine Cudjoe; 10 Grace Field; 9 Sinead Peach; 68 Shona Hoyle; 28 Hollie Dodd; 11 Tamzin Renouf; 13 Rhiannion Marshall. Subs (all used): 14 Sammy Watts; 8 Emma Lumley; 31 Frankie Townend; 44 Emma Slowe.
**Tries:** Lumb (2), Owen (6), Gentles (73); **Goals:** Stanley 0/3.
**RHINOS:** 1 Caitlin Beevers; 15 Sophie Nuttall; 30 Abby Eatock; 16 Chloe Kerrigan; 24 Fran Goldthorp; 6 Hanna Butcher; 7 Courtney Hill; 10 Dannielle Anderson; 14 Tasha Gaines; 13 Amy Johnson; 11 Aimee Staveley; 4 Charlotte Booth; 28 Paige Webster. Subs (all used): 27 Keara Bennett; 19 Elle Frain; 8 Danika Priim; 22 Ellie Oldroyd.
**Tries:** Eatock (12), Goldthorp (56, 64), Frain (68); **Goals:** Hill 2/4.
**Rugby Leaguer & League Express Women of the Match:**
*Tigers:* Rhiannion Marshall; *Rhinos:* Fran Goldthorp.
**Penalty count:** 5-6; **Half-time:** 8-4; **Referee:** Greg Dolan;
**Attendance:** 1,673 (at Totally Wicked Stadium, St Helens).

## SUPER LEAGUE SEMI-FINALS

*Sunday 6th October 2019*

Castleford Tigers 34.................................................. Wigan Warriors 4
St Helens 14 ..................................................................Leeds Rhinos 18

## CHALLENGE CUP FINAL

*Saturday 27th July 2019*

### CASTLEFORD TIGERS 10 LEEDS RHINOS 16

**TIGERS:** 1 Tara Stanley; 28 Hollie Dodd; 12 Lacey Owen; 15 Olivia Grace; 4 Kelsey Gentles; 6 Georgia Roche; 7 Claire Garner; 10 Grace Field; 9 Sinead Peach; 8 Emma Lumley; 11 Tamzin Renouf; 68 Shona Hoyle; 13 Rhiannion Marshall. Subs: 14 Sammy Watts; 17 Kirsty Higo (not used); 23 Esme Reynolds; 33 Jasmine Cudjoe.
**Tries:** Marshall (18), Renouf (30); **Goals:** Stanley 1/2.
**RHINOS:** 1 Caitlin Beevers; 15 Sophie Nuttall; 3 Sophie Robinson; 16 Chloe Kerrigan; 24 Fran Goldthorp; 6 Hanna Butcher; 7 Courtney Hill; 10 Dannielle Anderson; 14 Tasha Gaines; 13 Amy Johnson; 11 Aimee Staveley; 4 Charlotte Booth; 17 Shannon Lacey. Subs (all used): 8 Danika Priim; 27 Keara Bennett; 19 Elle Frain; 22 Ellie Oldroyd.
**Tries:** Goldthorp (20), Beevers (26), Hill (58); **Goals:** Hill 2/3.
**Rugby Leaguer & League Express Women of the Match:**
*Tigers:* Sinead Peach; *Rhinos:* Fran Goldthorp.
**Penalty count:** 2-1; **Half-time:** 10-10; **Referee:** Cameron Worsley.
*(at University of Bolton Stadium).*

## CHALLENGE CUP SEMI-FINALS

*Sunday 7th July 2019*

St Helens 10.................................................................Leeds Rhinos 16
Wakefield Trinity 0 ..............................................Castleford Tigers 100

Castleford's Tara Stanley tackled by Leeds' Amy Johnson during the Challenge Cup Final

# 2
# CHAMPIONSHIP
# & LEAGUE 1 2019

# CHAMPIONSHIP SEASON
## *Beware the Wolfpack*

---

After heartache in 2018, **TORONTO WOLFPACK** ensured there was no repeat as they famously earned promotion to Super League just three years after their inception.

Brian McDermott, Super League's most successful ever coach, arrived at the club alongside a number of signings headed by the marquee addition of centre Ricky Leutele from Cronulla and the experienced Jon Wilkin from St Helens.

The early stages of the season saw them stutter to wins over the likes of York, Leigh and Dewsbury. And eventually, they were picked off as Toulouse Olympique dismantled them in a 46-16 reverse.

However, that would be the Wolfpack's first and only defeat of the entire year. 21 straight victories saw them win the league by a mammoth 12-point margin.

In the play-offs, a strong performance against Toulouse saw them win 40-24, securing a Grand Final home fixture against Featherstone.

Despite falling behind and going into the final 20 minutes behind, Blake Wallace, a firm favourite at Lamport, saw him put Toronto ahead and further tries ensured the Wolfpack would be a Super League team in 2020 to the delight of their fanbase. The Grand Final attracted a crowd of 9,974.

Gareth O'Brien was named as the Championship's player of the year.

**TOULOUSE OLYMPIQUE's** fourth year in the Championship saw them record their highest ever league finish, ending the year second only to Toronto.

However, their wait for Super League continues, eventually losing to Featherstone in the play-off semi-final.

Sylvain Houles' side never looked like finishing anywhere but the top five, though they started the season with back-to-back defeats to Leigh and Widnes.

But they lost just five more games all season and took the scalp of Toronto in March, in front of more than 6,000 spectators at Stade Ernest Wallon, the ground they were due to share with Toulouse rugby union club from 2020.

With the second-best attack and second-best defence by the end of the season, they were being widely tipped as the team to bring down the Wolfpack.

Victory over York in the first week of the play-offs suggested that was possible, as they hammered the Knights 44-6.

But they were defeated by Toronto in Canada in the first play-off semi-final. Then, a week later, they were dumped out as in-form Featherstone defeated them 36-12.

Newly promoted **YORK CITY KNIGHTS** had one of the lowest budgets in the league.

Yet York defied all the odds as they secured an unexpected play-off place in their first year in the Championship.

An outstanding start to the season saw them lose just one of their first seven games, and they never gave up their place in the top five from there.

The impressive wins racked up quickly. By the end of the season, the only two sides York had failed to beat were Toronto and Toulouse.

Toronto Wolfpack suffered just one defeat all season as they stormed to the Championship title

Toulouse beat them three times, including once in the play-offs, before they were dumped out by Featherstone at Bootham Crescent.

James Ford's side never got going in the play-offs but it didn't overshadow their exploits, as Ford was named the Championship's coach of the year for 2019.

With a new stadium set in stone for 2020, things were looking up for the Knights.

**LEIGH CENTURIONS** came into the year happy to exist after a turbulent 2019 that saw the club on the brink after a disastrous first year back in the Championship.

Ultimately, the club managed to clear the decks and rebuild under John Duffy, who assembled a group of local players to steer the club through the year.

They started impressively, picking up eye-catching wins over Toulouse and Featherstone and pushing Toronto the distance.

But it wasn't until Easter that the Leythers truly got going.

Owner Derek Beaumont, enthused by their early promise, started investing money again and that coincided with a run of eight league wins in nine which propelled the Centurions into a top-five spot.

They ultimately finished in the top five comfortably, though two straight defeats at the end of the year saw them finish fourth.

But that was the end of the road, as they were dispatched in the first play-off eliminator by Featherstone.

In the 1895 Cup, they too came just short, losing at home to Widnes in the semi-final and missing out on Beaumont's dream to lead them out at Wembley.

Though a tinge of disappointment may have lingered come the end of the season, it was a good year all the same for Leigh.

## Championship Season

**FEATHERSTONE ROVERS** have never been in Super League but this is the closest they've ever come to reaching the Promised Land.

Rovers ultimately reached the Grand Final and for large parts were ahead, before eventually succumbing to heavy favourites Toronto in the final quarter.

It was a remarkable and unlikely story.

Previous head coach John Duffy had walked away from the club to join Leigh, leaving them coachless and without a full squad of players.

Unproven, unheard of Australian Ryan Carr took the job and arrived in January, only weeks before the season started.

Unsurprisingly, things started jittery, with Rovers winning just four of their opening nine league games.

But after Easter they kicked into gear. They won 13 of their final 18 league games, which included two heavy drubbings of York, most noticeably at the Summer Bash Weekend, and Bradford.

Dane Chisholm, a mid-season recruit from the Bulls, was instrumental in their rise up the league, alongside Australian hooker Cameron King.

Fev ultimately finished fifth, leaving them facing the unenviable task of four straight away games to earn promotion.

However, they stormed to victories over Leigh, York and Toulouse, leaving them one game away.

They ultimately fell at the final hurdle but it didn't detract from a fabulous season. Carr left at the end of the season to return to Australia.

You can guarantee one thing with **BRADFORD BULLS**, the season will never be uneventful.

That was the case in 2019 too as the club and the side went through highs and lows aplenty.

Things started well enough as they won eight of their opening 12 games, including wins over Featherstone, Leigh and Halifax.

But a slump in form thereafter saw them win just one of their next five Championship matches, putting them up against it with regards to a top-five finish.

However, in that time, the Bulls picked up one of their most famous victories, defeating fierce rivals Leeds Rhinos in the Challenge Cup in what was said by some to be a pivotal moment in the club's resurgence.

However, they were defeated in the next round by Halifax and talk of a departure from their historic Odsal ground began to surface.

That became a reality in September as the club confirmed it would leave its home of 85 years due to crippling costs.

Ultimately, they missed out on a play-off place by just one point, a decent return given it was their first year back in the Championship. Coupled with their Cup exploits, it was a good year on the field but, not for the first time, perhaps best remembered for what happened off it.

After several years of frustration, **SHEFFIELD EAGLES** came back with a bang in 2019 as Mark Aston's side enjoyed their best campaign for years.

A huge recruitment drive saw them attract some top players from several lower-end Championship sides and together they succeeded.

A superb start to the season saw them win six of their opening seven games, impressively despatching York at Bootham Crescent.

But a poor run of form in the middle of the season saw them picked off by stronger teams in the competition, with seven defeats in nine games seeing them lose pace with the play-off chasers.

However, the club would soon begin a marvellous 1895 Cup adventure. Victories

Dalton Grant, David Foggin-Johnston and Ross Oakes celebrate Bradford's Challenge Cup victory against Leeds

over Halifax, Doncaster and Batley saw them reach the inaugural final at Wembley. There, in just their second Wembley appearance and first since one of the biggest shocks the iconic stadium has ever seen, the Eagles won again, defeating Widnes 36-18 to re-write history and ensure Mark Aston became a Wembley-winning coach to go alongside his Lance Todd Trophy of 1998.

They ultimately finished the season seventh, four points shy of the top-five.
All in all, a fantastic season.

This was a year that **HALIFAX** will want to forget for many reasons, yet remember for others.

Their league form was dismal as they recorded their lowest league finish in 15 years.

A poor start to the season saw Richard Marshall, who had superbly guided them to three top-four finishes in the Super 8s era, depart, to the dismay of their fanbase.

Simon Grix came in and five wins in six games saw Halifax enjoy their best run of the season and Grix get the job permanently.

That spell saw them defeat their arch-nemesis, Bradford, at the Summer Bash, before James Woodburn-Hall's late magic saw them despatch the Bulls again in front of the BBC cameras to reach the Challenge Cup semi-finals for the first time since 1988.

While their performance in Bolton gained them many admirers as they performed valiantly against St Helens, their league form declined. They ended the year winning just two of their final 13 league games.

That saw them end the season in eighth place, 13 points adrift of the play-offs and nearer to relegation than the top five.

Ultimately, a disappointing year, salvaged by their memorable cup heroics, which saw them defeat Super League outfit London in the earlier rounds.

## Championship Season

When **SWINTON LIONS** lost their opening seven games of the season, you could understand the concern among the Lions faithful.

But Swinton stuck by their coach, Stuart Littler, and he put faith in his young squad to deliver the goods eventually.

Once they got on the board with a 33-26 win at Barrow, it was the catalyst for the Lions to roar, and roar they did.

By the time May arrived, Litter's young pride was finding its feet and five wins in seven games saw them ease away from relegation, and enjoy their rugby.

The main man in all that was youngster Matty Ashton, who had been recruited from amateur side Rochdale Mayfield in the off-season and ended the season as the Championship's try-scorer, scoring a phenomenal 30 tries in 25 games. That earned him a move to Warrington in 2020.

With the threat of relegation behind them, Swinton pitted their wits against some of the top teams. By the end of the year, they had picked up a fabulous win in Toulouse and comfortable victories over Halifax and Sheffield, while also drawing with Bradford at Odsal.

Sadly, the year ended on a sour note as the club's board of directors resigned following strong opposition to their plans to rebrand the club as Manchester Lions.

It was a year overshadowed by tragedy for **BATLEY BULLDOGS** as they sadly lost two members of their club.

In July, Beverley Nicholas, the wife of chairman, Kevin, sadly past away after a long battle with cancer.

Then, in August, the club endured the tragic death of Archie Bruce, the 20-year-old who had just hours earlier made his professional debut in defeat to Toulouse, before sadly being found dead in his hotel room the following morning.

The club wonderfully paid tribute to Beverley both off the pitch and on it, marking her passing with an excellent victory over Halifax in what was their best win of the season.

But they struggled to impress beyond that. They failed to beat any of the sides to finish in the top half of the competition and ended the season tenth in the league, just six points clear of relegation.

Matt Diskin stepped away from the club at the end of the season after three years at the helm.

It was supposed to be a season that saw **WIDNES VIKINGS** challenge for a return to Super League at the first time of asking.

By the end of it, Widnes' fans were happy to have a club to support.

Financial difficulties caught up with them and they were placed in administration in February, which saw them within hours of extinction.

Thankfully, they were saved by a local consortium but with a 12-point deduction, survival in the Championship was now the goal.

They did that comfortably in the end, with their re-enthused fanbase turning out in their thousands to see the club end the year five points clear of relegation and reach Wembley for the first time in 20 years.

They lost in the 1895 Cup Final to Sheffield, while in the league there were some bumps along the way.

However, despite losing key players as a result of their financial problems, without the points deduction, the Vikings would still have finished the season eighth, just six points away from the play-offs.

**DEWSBURY RAMS** ultimately succeeded in 2019 as they fulfilled their goal of retaining Championship status.

New head coach Lee Greenwood came in midway through the off-season and was forced to hurriedly assemble a squad ready for the start of the season.

Despite that, they started okay but ultimately should have done better after agonisingly surrendering leads against York, Barrow, Toronto and Sheffield, leaving them with just three points from their opening six games.

However, they picked up a superb result away at Featherstone in round eight, defeating the Grand Finalists 32-22.

Unfortunately, they managed just one victory in their next 11, though even that was an impressive one as Liam Finn's late field goal secured them a 25-24 win at Widnes.

A run of two wins and a draw in four games steered them clear of relegation and they ultimately stayed afloat by three points to ensure Greenwood's first year in charge was a success.

Second-season syndrome hit **BARROW RAIDERS** in full effect after they suffered relegation from the Championship.

Things started so well. They picked up an away win against Batley on the opening day, which equalled their number of away wins in 2018 at the first attempt.

But it took Paul Crarey's side three months to win in the league again. A 13-game losing streak saw them stuck at the bottom of the league, even after defeating Rochdale.

That triggered something within the Raiders, who then picked up stunning back-to-back wins over Halifax and Featherstone.

However, they couldn't kick on. Eight straight defeats culminated in their Championship status being lost, eventually going down after defeat to Toronto in the penultimate round of the season.

Despite ending on a high, defeating Batley 24-16, it was too little, too late for the Cumbrians.

They will look back on a bizarre injury to Gareth Hock, their star signing, suffering a shoulder injury in a pre-season charity boxing match, as a key blow, while another key forward, Josh Johnson, left for Salford midway through the year.

The less said about **ROCHDALE HORNETS'** 2019, the better. It was a disaster from start to finish.

A reduced budget left them up against it but even they couldn't have predicted what was to come.

Rochdale won two games all season and both came in March. They picked up their first and only league win of the season on March 5th against Barrow Raiders before coming from behind to defeat League 1 outfit Whitehaven in the Challenge Cup.

Head coach Carl Forster was sacked soon after and replaced by former Championship-winning coach Matt Calland.

But he couldn't change their fortunes as the Hornets lost 21 straight matches in all competitions, leaving them with one of the worst records ever seen in the second-tier.

They ended the league campaign having conceded a whopping 1,268 points, an average of almost 47 points per match, 12 points adrift of Dewsbury Rams in twelfth. A nightmare from start to finish.

**CHAMPIONSHIP AWARDS**

**PLAYER OF THE YEAR**
Gareth O'Brien
(Toronto Wolfpack)

**YOUNG PLAYER OF THE YEAR**
Matty Ashton (Swinton Lions)

**COACH OF THE YEAR**
James Ford (York City Knights)

Matty Ashton

## Championship Play-offs

Fifth-placed Featherstone Rovers were the form team going in to the play-offs and they went all the way to the Grand Final with three straight away victories.

In week one they stunned fourth-place Leigh in the Elimination Play-off at Leigh Sports Village thanks to a great performance from on-loan Leeds halfback Callum McLelland, who kicked superbly, scored a superb solo effort and had a hand in most of the other tries. There was a strong element of Rhinos loan and former players in the Rovers side all year.

The win meant Featherstone faced a trip to third-placed York, who had lost their Qualifying Play-off in Toulouse, rampant Olympique registering a 44-6 win, with two-try Mark Kheirallah on fire from fullback.

The York-Featherstone Elimination Semi-final was nicely poised at 8-4 in Rovers' favour at half-time in front of a bumper 3,000-plus crowd at Bootham Crescent. But McLelland was once again pivotal as two tries within three minutes in the second half through James Harrison and Brad Day gave Rovers the ascendancy, 30-4 the final scoreline.

On the same weekend Toronto Wolfpack burst the Toulouse bubble with a 40-24 home victory, with centre Ricky Leutele grabbing a hat-trick as the Wolfpack earned their place in the Grand Final. Kheirallah finished with a hat-trick for Olympique after a late flurry.

Featherstone booked their Grand Final spot - which was due to be played on the ground of the highest placed team - with a comprehensive 36-12 Final Eliminator win at Stade Ernest Argeles. Two-try prop John Davies was the stand-out in a great team performance.

## Championship Grand Final

Toronto Wolfpack's dream of getting into Super League became a reality at a packed Lamport Stadium, as they won the Championship Grand Final against a valiant Featherstone Rovers side, winning their 23rd match in a row.

The 24-6 win came 12 months after they were defeated by the London Broncos at the same stage in 2018.

Battling both the windy conditions and the cold temperature that had rolled into the city, for the first 25 minutes of the match it was hard to pick between the teams, as both were sensational defensively.

Rovers scored first, as Alex Sutcliffe ran onto a kick from Dane Chisholm that Toronto winger Liam Kay mis-read. Chisholm slotted the conversion and Featherstone were up 6-0.

Moments later, Wolfpack skipper Josh McCrone replied for the hosts, squeezing his way over the line in the 32nd minute. Gareth O'Brien missed the conversion however and Featherstone took a 6-4 lead into half-time.

The Wolfpack took their first lead of the match in the 57th minute. It was a

**BETFRED CHAMPIONSHIP GRAND FINAL**

*Saturday 5th October 2019*

**TORONTO WOLFPACK 24 FEATHERSTONE ROVERS 6**

**WOLFPACK:** 1 Gareth O'Brien; 5 Liam Kay; 3 Chase Stanley; 4 Ricky Leutele; 2 Matty Russell; 6 Joe Mellor; 7 Josh McCrone; 21 Anthony Mullally; 14 Andy Ackers; 10 Ashton Sims; 11 Andrew Dixon; 12 Bodene Thompson; 13 Jon Wilkin. Subs (all used): 17 Blake Wallace; 15 Darcy Lussick; 16 Tom Olbison; 18 Gadwin Springer.
**Tries:** McCrone (32), Wallace (57), Thompson (62), Mellor (70);
**Goals:** O'Brien 2/3, Wallace 2/2.
**ROVERS:** 33 Ashton Golding; 25 Jack Render; 4 Josh Hardcastle; 32 Alex Sutcliffe; 46 Jack Johnson; 38 Dane Chisholm; 37 Callum McLelland; 14 John Davies; 45 Connor Jones; 29 Jack Ormondroyd; 10 Jack Bussey; 17 James Harrison; 13 James Lockwood. Subs (all used): 42 Wellington Albert; 15 Luke Cooper; 23 Makahesi Makatoa; 9 Cameron King.
**Try:** Sutcliffe (28); **Goals:** Chisholm 1/1.
**Rugby Leaguer & League Express Men of the Match:**
*Wolfpack:* Jon Wilkin; *Rovers:* Ashton Golding.
**Penalty count:** 10-7; **Half-time:** 4-6;
**Referee:** Chris Kendall; **Attendance:** 9,974.

Ashton Sims looks for a way past Connor Jones during the Championship Grand Final

decisive moment as Blake Wallace, who had been with the Wolfpack since their inaugural season in 2017, steamrolled his way through the Rovers defence before reaching over the line for an excellent solo try. Gareth O'Brien was successful with the conversion this time, giving Toronto a four-point lead.

The game then opened up a bit and Bodene Thompson crossed the line five minutes later, extending the Wolfpack's lead to 10.

Featherstone threw everything they had at Toronto in one final push but Toronto stood strong, preventing the visitors from closing the gap.

Then, after taking a pass from Jon Wilkin, Joe Mellor confirmed victory for Toronto in the 70th minute. He danced around a defender and, when it looked as though he had been tackled a few metres out, he jumped up and carried the ball over the line. Wallace converted his first attempt of the day, giving Toronto a 22-6 advantage.

After ten minutes of ovations, including a loud roar for the retiring fan-favourite Ashton Sims - who came back off the bench for the last ten minutes - and a Wallace penalty goal with seconds remaining, the Wolfpack's first-ever sellout crowd started chanting 'Su-per League, Su-per League' and the party was underway at Lamport Stadium.

### 1895 Cup Final

Sheffield Eagles won the inaugural 1895 Cup, beating Widnes Vikings 36-18 in the Final played at Wembley directly after the Challenge Cup Final.

The 1895 Cup, sponsored by Leigh chairman Derek Beaumont's company AB Sundecks, was a seeded knockout competition for teams outside Super League involving eight League 1 and twelve Championship clubs.

Toronto and Toulouse from the Championship and Coventry Bears, London Skolars and North Wales Crusaders from League 1 decided against entering the competition for logistical reasons, with later rounds being played midweek.

The Eagles' win was largely down to centre Aaron Brown, who delivered on the biggest stage with a hat-trick. His second try put Sheffield ahead for the first time on 49 minutes and they never looked back from there as they raced in 24-unanswered second-half points.

Before that, Widnes had been a constant threat and had troubled the Eagles with their speed and guile of halfbacks Danny Craven and Tom Gilmore. They deservedly held an 18-12 lead at half-time.

But the Sheffield pack came to the fore after the break and out-powered Widnes' young side, whose frailties were ruthlessly exposed following the interval.

When Corey Makelim scored on 55 minutes to move the Eagles 16 ahead, Widnes were gone.

**AB SUNDECKS 1895 CUP FINAL**

*Saturday 24th August 2019*

**SHEFFIELD EAGLES 36 WIDNES VIKINGS 18**

**EAGLES:** 1 Josh Guzdek; 2 Ryan Millar; 29 Ben Hellewell; 13 Aaron Brown; 5 Ben Blackmore; 6 Pat Walker; 7 Anthony Thackeray; 17 Shaun Pick; 14 Greg Burns; 11 Brad Knowles; 15 Olly Davies; 12 Joel Farrell; 16 Corey Makelim. Subs (all used): 9 James Davey; 21 Blake Broadbent; 22 Paddy Burns; 31 Nathan Mason.
**Tries:** Brown (22, 49, 76), Thackeray (26), Farrell (42), Makelim (55); **Goals:** Walker 6/9.
**VIKINGS:** 5 Jack Owens; 29 Jayden Hatton; 4 Anthony Gelling; 24 Keanan Brand; 36 Patrick Ah Van; 6 Danny Craven; 7 Tom Gilmore; 18 Ted Chapelhow; 15 Jordan Johnstone; 13 Hep Cahill; 11 Harrison Hansen; 12 Chris Dean; 19 Brad Walker. Subs (all used): 8 Jay Chapelhow; 16 MacGraff Leuluai; 26 Dan Norman; 17 Sam Wilde.
**Tries:** Hansen (14), Dean (16), Gilmore (36); **Goals:** Owens 3/3.
**Rugby Leaguer & League Express Men of the Match:**
*Eagles:* Aaron Brown; *Vikings:* Harrison Hansen.
**Penalty count:** 7-6; **Half-time:** 12-18; **Referee:** Chris Kendall.
*(at Wembley Stadium).*

The victorious Sheffield Eagles team celebrate their 1895 Cup Final triumph

# LEAGUE 1 SEASON
## *Safe 'Haven*

**WHITEHAVEN** defied the odds to earn automatic promotion to the Championship for 2020 and did it with local pride to the fore.

Having narrowly avoided extinction at the end of the previous season, not that much was expected from a club that was very much in a rebuilding process. Even new coach Gary Charlton admitted at the end of the season that their main aim had simply been to make the play-offs.

But wins over Keighley Cougars and Doncaster in the opening three rounds showed Charlton had built a strong squad of locally-based players, proud to be pulling on the shirt every week. The loyal band of supporters who followed them across the country gained rich reward.

As the season progressed and the wins kept coming, belief was growing that Haven could really challenge for the top spot and automatic promotion. But with Oldham and Newcastle keeping up the chase it came down to the last match of the season before any celebrations could begin.

Haven went into the game at Coventry Bears on the last Saturday afternoon knowing that a win would be enough, no matter how other scores went the following day. It was a chance they weren't going to miss and were in control from the start. Fullback Jordan Burns was the star of the day, bagging four tries in the 72-0 win.

Having not won any major honours in his time as a player, Charlton delayed travel plans to attend the game and celebrate his first trophy win as a coach. He had been due

Whitehaven's Jake Moore makes a break against Coventry, with League 1 Player of the Year Dion Aiye in support

to fly to Mexico to celebrate a friend's son's wedding but hours before he should have left for the airport he decided to make the trip to the Midlands instead. He flew out a couple of days later however and made the wedding, so no friendships were ruined along the way.

There was plenty to celebrate on his return as well as the club enjoyed a clean sweep at the RFL End of Season Awards night. Charlton was named Coach of the Year, while Dion Aiye won Player of the Year and Andrew Bulman the Young Player of the Year. Marc Shackley also had an outstanding year and swept the board at the club's presentation night.

**OLDHAM** banished previous bad luck in play-off games to earn a second promotion in five years.

It was the perfect send-off for coach Scott Naylor, who announced in August he was to step down from his role after seven years and move onto a fresh challenge.

With many of the players who were relegated back to League 1 in 2017 still at the club, there was a strong determination to get the club back to the Championship.

With Naylor on the way out and some players set for pastures new, the squad went into that play-off final knowing it was the last time they would all be together as a group. And they wanted to make it count.

That they did, although they were made to work hard for it, with Newcastle Thunder pushing them all the way before the Roughyeds emerged with an 18-14 win.

Once again, Naylor had a small budget to work with but that couldn't stop the squad playing with more grit and determination as the season went on.

In the early stages of the year, close defeats to Workington, Newcastle and Hunslet frustrated Naylor as they just couldn't quite find an 80-minute performance.

But as the season progressed and confidence grew they found a way to come out of these tight games on the right side of the result and with 11 wins in the final 12 games - only losing to table-toppers Whitehaven - they definitely ended the year as one of the form teams. That run started after a 31-0 defeat to Doncaster that Naylor described as 'embarrassing'.

Within days of the season coming to an end, former Super League hooker Matt Diskin was named as Naylor's replacement following his departure from Batley Bulldogs.

**NEWCASTLE THUNDER** continue to be the epitome of what every club at this level, and higher, should be aiming for.

In what was their 20th year as a club, they were competitive on the pitch in every game, handed more debuts to Academy graduates and continued to support the vibrant, and ever-growing participation levels across the city at all age ranges.

But it wasn't the best of starts. After losing their opening two games to Doncaster and Coventry Bears, albeit by six points and four points respectively, the shock decision was made to remove Jason Payne from his role as head coach.

Assistant coach and former Oxford-man Tim Rumford and Academy Manager Michael Heap stepped into the role temporarily, with the club signalling their intent of a promotion push by bringing in former Wigan Warriors and Widnes Vikings coach Denis Betts as director of rugby.

Performances were definitely improving and they picked up two wins from three before ex-Super League player and Toronto assistant coach Simon Finnigan took the role of head coach.

Having played a major role in Toronto's successful opening two seasons, Finnigan's impact was almost immediate. And while there were a few blips along the way, they quickly became one of the form teams in the league.

Finnigan used his contacts across the game to bring in a number of key players in Samoan international Matthew Wright, Joel Edwards, Quentin Laulu-Togaga'e and Nick

Newman. They all had a significant impact, as did the young wing-centre partnership of Kieran Gill and Alex Clegg, who between them bagged 42 tries. Fullback Lewis Young chipped in with 16 touchdowns as well to give Thunder the most potent back line in the league.

As in the previous season, **DONCASTER** kept in the promotion race until the very last minute but a smaller squad then several of their main competitors made the task much harder.

While they were able to utilise the dual-registration deal with Super League side Hull FC - as well as handing a playing lifeline to Rangi Chase - it did at times lead to issues with continuity and consistency. This could be seen when their opening six-game run saw them win and lose on alternative weeks.

Down on numbers due to a number of impact injuries at the back end of the year, the final two play-off games against Oldham and Newcastle were a bridge too far for Richard Horne's men.

But they learnt a lot from the season and quickly made plans to recruit a bigger squad that could mount a serious challenge next time around.

As one of the youngest coaches in the league, Horne is still developing and the fact his team had the second-best defensive record in the league will be particularly pleasing for him.

In 20 league games they stopped the opposition from scoring on four occasions - against North Wales Crusaders, West Wales Raiders twice and, impressively, Oldham. They also kept opposing teams down to two scores or less in a further six matches.

This season signalled the end of an era for one regular Dons star, with Kyle Kesik moving on after 11 seasons with the club.

In the Challenge Cup, Doncaster went further than any other League 1 club in the competition, making it through to the sixth round, their run coming to an end in the South of France, where they went down 62-6 to Catalans Dragons.

Of all the teams that finished in the play-offs, **HUNSLET** will be the most disappointed with how their season ended.

After a great start which saw them win seven out of their opening ten games - including impressive away wins at Doncaster, Oldham and Newcastle - hopes were high they could genuinely make a challenge for the Championship, especially as the second half of the season included six games at the South Leeds Stadium. However, five defeats in those six games ultimately proved their undoing.

In defeat as well as victory, Hunslet showed many glimpses of the sort of rugby that would ordinarily see them promoted. There was entertaining, attacking rugby as well as solid defensive displays, however, they were often unable to maintain that for the full game, which cost them numerous points.

Injuries also hurt them, especially so in their knock-out play-off game against Workington. Knocks to captain Duane Straugheir, who had already missed part of the year with a broken hand and Ryan Wright meant players had to be moved around and they were left with no recognised hooker.

The biggest injury though came right at the start of the season when the vastly-experienced Richard Moore let the field during the season opener with a head injury. He failed to recover from it and later announced his retirement. His presence was definitely missed in the middle.

**WORKINGTON TOWN**, who were 80 minutes from promotion to the Championship last season, found the play-offs a step too far this time around.

A small squad and a coaching change early in the year caused some disruption, with the club unable to play the full complement of 17 players on a number of occasions.

Wins over Oldham, North Wales and Newcastle Thunder in the opening month of the season were offset with defeats to Doncaster, London Skolars and Whitehaven, with the latter proving to be coach Leon Pryce's last game in charge.

Pryce had helped turn the club into serious Championship contenders over the previous 18 months so the decision was met with questions from certain quarters. But the club felt they had made the right call. With former Super League player Oliver Wilkes taking charge temporarily, it wasn't long before the club brought in another former top-flight player to take charge in Chris Thorman.

Although his first game in charge ended in defeat to Coventry, it wasn't long before fortunes started to change. His fresh approach often saw him question the attitude and desire of his squad but the tough love brought the best out of his players. But injuries proved their undoing and when they were only able to send 14 fit players to their knock-out clash at Newcastle Thunder, the way their season was going to end was almost inevitable.

The very fact that **NORTH WALES CRUSADERS** finished the year disappointed to miss out on the play-offs shows just how far they have come under Anthony Murray, in his second spell at the club.

Having returned to the club in the early stages of the 2018 season, Murray and the Crusaders definitely benefitted from having a full pre-season together. While it took until round five for their first victory to come, they were never that far behind, losing three of the four opening fixtures by ten or fewer points.

As the season progressed after that first win, particularly impressive victories over Doncaster, Whitehaven and Workington followed as they fought right until the final weeks for a play-off spot.

They ultimately missed out by just three points.

The fact they had such a strong season without talismanic fullback Tommy Johnson makes their achievements even greater. He missed the full year with a knee injury but is back fit and ready to make an impression once again in 2020.

After a promising first half of the season, **LONDON SKOLARS** had a dramatic fall from grace and finished the year six-points adrift of a play-off spot.

Such a finish seemed unlikely when, after ten games, Skolars were third in the league and just four points behind leaders Whitehaven.

Wins over West Wales Raiders, Workington Town, Coventry Bears, Hunslet, North Wales Crusaders and Doncaster, plus a draw against Keighley Cougars had got the capital side into such a position. After a disappointing 2018 season, there was a real desire in the squad to put things right and, with coach Jermaine Coleman admitting to having a renewed vigour for the task in hand following his work with the Jamaica national squad, enthusiasm was never in doubt as the team chased a top-six finish.

However, some crucial injuries in key positions as the season wore on took their toll and a run of three defeats by less than four points each, when they couldn't quite close out games, proved their undoing.

**COVENTRY BEARS** certainly sprung a few surprises in 2019 and their results show they are definitely a success story as far as expansion is concerned.

It may be some time before they are genuinely pushing for the play-offs but picking up wins against promotion challengers Newcastle and Workington shows they have what it takes to be competitive. Now they just need to do it on a more consistent level.

A string of injuries and the transfer of Nick Newman to Newcastle did derail the Bears and they often lacked continuity in both performance and personnel.

Continuity wasn't helped either by the fact they only played three games at their Butts Park Arena home.

Work being carried out on that pitch, meant the Bears had to temporarily move out, playing three games at Broadstreet RFC and four at Rugby Lions' Webb Ellis Road.

The injury disruption also forced coach Tom Tsang to use the loan and dual registration system more than he has in the past. But there was still a lot of local talent given a shot. That included Midlands-born Jacob Jones, who joined the club from London Broncos Academy, after a previous spell on loan at the Bears.

His form saw him nominated for the Young Player of the Year prize at the official RFL End-of-Season Awards night.

A number of players that the club has helped develop over the last couple of years have been courted by other League 1 and Championship clubs, which just proves the Bears are making all the right moves off the field.

At the end of the season, it was announced Tsang was moving on to join London Broncos as their reserves team coach.

With a 12-point deduction before the season started for the transfer of club membership, **KEIGHLEY COUGARS** were always going to be up against it to make a push for the play-offs and promotion. Especially as they were only saved from extinction by Mick O'Neill and other former directors from the 'Cougarmania' days a matter of weeks before the opening game, giving little time for a structured pre-season.

The last couple of seasons had seen the Cougars start the year confident of pushing for a place in the Championship, yet this year they'll have just been aiming to wipe out the points deficit and avoid the League 1 wooden spoon.

Despite the tumultuous start to the season off-the-field, the Cougars started well enough on it, picking up five wins and a draw from their opening eight games - edging to within one point of wiping out the deduction. The decision therefore to part company with head coach Craig Lingard at that point was a strange one.

The club stated that 'the time had come to look elsewhere in order to take the club forward' and Lingard's assistant Rhys Lovegrove took the reins temporarily before later behind handed the role permanently.

The Cougars picked up just three further wins under the former Super League player but with Cougarmania returning to the club they will soon be on the rise again.

Saturday 20th July 2019 was a day everyone involved with **WEST WALES RAIDERS** will never forget. At the 45th time of asking, the club finally celebrated its first win. And it was certainly a memorable victory, beating Coventry Bears 44-16 in a game they dominated from the kick-off.

Many of the stars that day were local Welsh players, which made the result all the sweeter for coach Kim Williams and Chairman Andrew Thorne, who have long advocated the desire for the club to eventually be a real force in Welsh Rugby League.

While the rest of the season may not have allowed any more celebrations, Williams will have been able to take some positives out of their efforts. The Raiders' points-conceded average over the course of this season was less than 55 per game, down from 81 per game in 2018, while they were generally more competitive throughout.

Add to that, a number of players coming through the local college system into the first team and things were definitely looking brighter in Llanelli.

**LEAGUE 1 AWARDS**

**PLAYER OF THE YEAR**
Dion Aiye (Whitehaven)

**YOUNG PLAYER OF THE YEAR**
Andrew Bulman (Whitehaven)

**COACH OF THE YEAR**
Gary Charlton (Whitehaven)

Andrew Bulman

## League 1 Play-offs

Whitehaven won automatic promotion to the Championship by finishing top of the eleven-team table after 20 rounds. The teams finishing second to sixth then entered a top-five play-off-format system to decide the second promotion spot.

In the Elimination Play-off between fifth and sixth, Hunslet were 24-18 ahead at the break but were kept scoreless by Workington in the second period, Town emerging 32-24 winners at the South Leeds Stadium. Gamestar Sean Penkywicz's try on 71 minutes, coupled with Carl Forber's conversion, gave Town an unassailable eight-point cushion.

Fourth-placed Doncaster stunned Newcastle Thunder, who finished third, with a 20-6 win at Kingston Park. Frankie Mariano's try on 47 minutes was the killer blow as Thunder didn't get on the scoreboard until two minutes from time.

The win earned Doncaster a trip second placed Oldham the following week but the Roughyeds' defence proved too good in a 22-12 win, halfback Dave Hewitt the stand-out.

Newcastle earned another crack at Doncaster with a 38-18 win over depleted Workington the following week.

Injuries to Dec O'Donnell and Tom Curwen, alongside a suspension for Danny Tickle, meant Town were down on numbers and only fielded 14 players. Tongan prop Fuifui Moimoi played the full 80 minutes – just four days short of his 40th birthday!

Mid-season recruit from Coventry, Aussie halfback Nick Newman scored two well-taken tries and was influential throughout in a professional Thunder win.

The next week, a hat-trick from former Castleford Tigers centre Kieran Gill helped Newcastle book their place in the promotion play-off final after a commanding 34-4 victory over Doncaster at Kingston Park. Fullback Lewis Young also produced a standout performance in both and attack and defence.

In the play-off final, Oldham marked their return to the Championship in coach Scott Naylor's final game with an 18-14 home win over Newcastle.

The Roughyeds managed the majority of the game superbly, with Paul Crook and Dave Hewitt's kicking games decisive in not only putting them in front on several occasions but helping close out a tense final few minutes as Thunder pressed hard for victory.

On-loan Featherstone forward Jimmy Beckett's try 16 minutes from time ultimately secured promotion for Oldham.

### BETFRED LEAGUE 1 PLAY-OFF FINAL

*Sunday 6th October 2019*

#### OLDHAM 18 NEWCASTLE THUNDER 14

**OLDHAM:** 5 Ritchie Hawkyard; 55 Dec Kay; 3 Zack McComb; 29 Cameron Leeming; 1 Kyran Johnson; 6 Paul Crook; 7 Dave Hewitt; 8 Phil Joy; 9 Gareth Owen; 10 Scott Law; 25 Danny Bridge; 16 Danny Langtree; 24 Liam Bent. Subs (all used): 17 Jimmy Beckett; 12 Emmerson Whittel; 13 Jack Spencer; 20 Matty Wilkinson.
**Tries:** Langtree (14), McComb (52), Beckett (64); **Goals:** Crook 3/3.
**THUNDER:** 1 Lewis Young; 19 Misi Taulapapa; 2 Tyler Craig; 4 Kieran Gill; 5 Alex Clegg; 6 Quentin Laulu-Togaga'e; 7 Nick Newman; 8 Liam McAvoy; 9 Keal Carlile; 15 Sam Luckley; 18 Rhys Clarke; 10 Joel Edwards; 13 Harry Aldous. Subs (all used): 14 Evan Simons; 20 Jack Aldous; 16 Carne Doyle-Manga; 17 Conor Fitzsimmons.
**Tries:** Taulapapa (9, 56), Edwards (47); **Goals:** Clarke 1/3.
**Rugby Leaguer & League Express Men of the Match:**
*Oldham:* Dave Hewitt; *Thunder:* Sam Luckley.
**Penalty count:** 2-5; **Half-time:** 6-4;
**Referee:** Gareth Hewer; **Attendance:** 1,209.

Zack McComb wrapped up by Quentin Laulu-Togaga'e and Kieran Gill during the League 1 Play-off Final

# 3
# INTERNATIONAL YEAR

# GREAT BRITAIN TOUR
## *Lions wane*

Great Britain suffered a 4-0 whitewash on their comeback tour, their first since 2006, after an ebullient Papua New Guinea stunned the Lions in their final game.

The re-introduction of the Lions concept, the last incarnation of Great Britain had been for the 2007 home series against New Zealand and they had last travelled down under when they competed in the 2006 Tri Nations, was highly anticipated.

But the Lions suffered a 14-6 defeat in their first game against Tonga in Hamilton, New Zealand and never recovered, losing a two-match series against the Kiwis before falling to defeat in Port Moresby.

Wigan's Sean O'Loughlin was expected to lead the Lions but withdrew with injury. South Sydney's Sam Burgess announced his retirement from the game with a shoulder injury shortly before the tour. Four members of the St Helens Grand Final winning team - Morgan Knowles, James Roby, Tommy Makinson and Mark Percival - were also unavailable.

Coach Wayne Bennett came in for much criticism for selecting a squad light on threequarters and that was exacerbated with injuries to Ryan Hall, Zak Hardaker and Oliver Gildart. Leeds winger Ash Handley was flown out to add cover but he wasn't selected. Warrington stand-off Blake Austin played the final two games on the left wing. Bennett also stuck with Jackson Hastings and Gareth Widdop at halfback for all four Tests. Castleford young gun half Jake Trueman didn't play, while Wigan's George Williams played less than half a game against the Kumuls.

**GAME ONE**

The Lions tour got off to a torrid start when Tonga (who had to go by the name of Tonga Invitational XIII because of a player dispute with the official governing body) beat them fair and square at Waikato Stadium in Hamilton, New Zealand.

The final result of 14-6 was testament to the defensive resolve of the Lions who were under a barrage from start to finish.

GB coach Wayne Bennett had a squad that was short of centres and he addressed that problem by selecting Zak Hardaker at right centre to partner Oliver Gildart, leaving Jake Connor out of the side, while Lachlan Coote got the fullback berth. In the front row he selected Chris Hill and Luke Thompson, with captain James Graham at loose forward,

---

**TOUR SQUADS**

**GREAT BRITAIN:** Blake Austin (Warrington Wolves); John Bateman (Canberra Raiders); Tom Burgess (South Sydney Rabbitohs); Daryl Clark (Warrington Wolves); Jake Connor (Hull FC); Lachlan Coote (St Helens); Oliver Gildart (Wigan Warriors); James Graham (St George Illawarra Dragons) (C); Ryan Hall (Sydney Roosters); Zak Hardaker (Wigan Warriors); Jackson Hastings (Salford Red Devils); Chris Hill (Warrington Wolves); Josh Hodgson (Canberra Raiders); Jack Hughes (Warrington Wolves); Josh Jones (Salford Red Devils); Jonny Lomax (St Helens); Jermaine McGillvary (Huddersfield Giants); Joe Philbin (Warrington Wolves); Luke Thompson (St Helens); Jake Trueman (Castleford Tigers); Alex Walmsley (St Helens); Elliott Whitehead (Canberra Raiders); Gareth Widdop (St George Illawarra Dragons); George Williams (Wigan Warriors).

*Ash Handley (Leeds Rhinos) joined the squad after injuries.*

**ENGLAND 9s:** Tom Burgess (South Sydney Rabbitohs); Daryl Clark (Warrington Wolves); Jake Connor (Hull FC); James Graham (St George Illawarra Dragons) (C); Ryan Hall (Sydney Roosters); Ash Handley (Leeds Rhinos); Jack Hughes (Warrington Wolves); Reece Lyne (Wakefield Trinity); Jermaine McGillvary (Huddersfield Giants); Ryan Sutton (Canberra Raiders); Sam Tomkins (Catalans Dragons); Jake Trueman (Castleford Tigers); Liam Watts (Castleford Tigers); Elliott Whitehead (Canberra Raiders); Gareth Widdop (St George Illawarra Dragons); George Williams (Wigan Warriors).

Oliver Gildart and Elliott Whitehead combine to halt Konrad Hurrell

although he had to contend with Thompson leaving the field after only twelve minutes with a rib injury.

By the end of the game he had also lost Gildart to a dislocated shoulder.

Halfback Ata Hingano was a late withdrawal from the Tongan team and he was replaced by inexperienced youngster Fanitesi Niu, yet to make his NRL debut for Brisbane Broncos. Niu played the entire game at fullback and acquitted himself superbly.

Leeds Rhinos star Konrad Hurrell also replaced Kotoni Staggs at centre just before the game began. Hurrell was in tears when the Tongan National Anthem was sung, and his passion was shared by the Tongan team, spurred on, as in the 2018 World Cup, by their passionate supporters, although the match wasn't a sellout, with the Tonga Rugby League rumoured to have advised locals to boycott the match.

The Tongan pack was perhaps one of the best assembled in the modern era, with power, size and footwork. And they delivered on their potential.

The opening score came from a mistake after a clever kick from Sione Katoa on halfway caused confusion between Gareth Widdop and Coote. Tui Lolohea got hold of the ball and handed it on to John Asiata, who gave the scoring pass to Michael Jennings.

A superb Widdop tackle saw Manu Ma'u to lose the ball over the line but Tonga were rewarded for their dominance in the final play of the first half after an amazing period of hot potato football (encompassing 15 passes) ended with Katoa reaching Jennings' grubber, with the conversion by Sio Siua Taukeiaho doubling the Tongans' lead.

The Lions came back into the match in the third quarter but lacked creativity. Alex Walmsley was fortunate to avoid a sin-binning after taking out Niu as he chased a Lolohea grubber near the posts. The resulting penalty from Taukeiaho extended the lead to 14 points, before John Bateman's 69th minute try, when he skipped outside Will Hopoate, gave the Lions some hope.

GB's last two throws of the dice came with a fine run by Ryan Hall from a pass by debutant Jackson Hastings, only for him to lose the ball, while, with seconds remaining, Josh Hodgson's grubber to the line was dropped on by a Tongan defender for a welcome and deserved victory.

The result was put into context by Tonga's 16-12 victory over Australia in Auckland the following Saturday.

**GAME TWO**

Great Britain didn't abandon their conservative approach the following Saturday at Eden Park in Auckland and sank to a 12-8 defeat in the first of their two Tests against New Zealand.

It was the first time Great Britain had travelled to play the Kiwis since 2006 and it was an old-fashioned Test match, with few frills, but plenty of physicality and intent. 'We are not here to put on a spectacle, we are here to win,' said Kiwis captain Benji Marshall after the match, and his words rang true for both teams, who seemed reluctant to chance their arm too often, given what was at stake.

The only scores of the first half were a penalty each from Jamayne Isaako and Gareth Widdop as the sides went into the break level.

The Kiwis were more clinical in taking their chances, breaking the contest open with two tries early in the second half, while Great Britain couldn't make the most of their opportunities, despite having more possession and a superior completion rate.

There were three changes to Wayne Bennett's line-up from the defeat by Tonga, though two were injury enforced, with Oliver Gildart (shoulder) and Luke Thompson (rib) ruled out. Lachlan Coote was replaced by his St Helens teammate Jonny Lomax. Jake Connor came into the centres, having played all four games against the Kiwis in 2018, and Tom Burgess was promoted from the interchange bench. The Warrington Wolves duo of Joe Philbin and Daryl Clark came into the 17, with both of them on the bench.

The axing of Shaun Johnson was the big news around Michael Maguire's team selection. Since 2013 Johnson had played 30 of 34 possible Tests, only missing the 2015 tour to England with an ankle injury and the previous year's clash in Denver (hamstring). Kieran Foran, who was a mainstay of the side in the first half of this decade before off-field issues and a series of injury problems, replaced Johnson but he played only five minutes before dislocating his shoulder.

Roger Tuivasa-Sheck created the Kiwis' first try with a moment of individual brilliance when he rounded Alex Walmsley on halfway before flicking a reverse pass to Jamayne Isaako as he was tackled by Lomax.

Corey Harawira-Naera's try six minutes later was a soft one as as he managed to get the ball down in a gang tackle.

Then the Lions began to throw the ball around and got a reward. Walmsley was stopped a metre short but the ball came free and sub Daryl Clark scampered over. Widdop's conversion cut the margin to four points.

Jermaine McGillvary was desperately close to scoring with three minutes left to play. That would have given Widdop the chance to kick a match-winning conversion, albeit from the sideline, but a miraculous tackle by Kenny Bromwich jolted the ball out of McGillvary's grasp as he went over.

The result kept alive New Zealand's unbeaten record against Great Britain on home soil since 1992, while Adam Blair became just the second player, after Ruben Wiki, to make 50 Test appearances for the Kiwis.

**GAME THREE**

Great Britain fell to their third consecutive defeat when they went down 23-8 to New Zealand in Christchurch.

A Lions team that defended solidly for long spells was often toothless in attack, struggled to get momentum in the ruck, then lacked creativity and thrust when they had good ball in the opposition '20'. The kicking game of Gareth Widdop put little pressure on the Kiwis back-three, with fullback Roger Tuivasa-Sheck thriving in the space he was allowed.

Josh Jones wrapped up by Joseph Tapine during Great Britain's Second Test defeat to New Zealand

The second Test against the Kiwis looked over just after half-time, when they held an 18-point advantage after Ken Maumalo's try. At that stage the Lions could have thrown in the towel but they showed impressive resolve to come back into the contest. Josh Hodgson crossed in the 49th minute and the Lions then dominated most of the final half-hour without being able to score any more points.

Twice they had tries scratched by the video referee (correctly) and the Kiwis were hanging on grimly for long periods. If the tourists had crossed to bring the margin back to six points, it could have made for a nervous finish. But a combination of bad luck, poor execution and some impressive defending kept them out.

Going into the game, GB had lost Ryan Hall (knee), then Zak Hardaker during the captain's run. That meant Warrington second-rower Jack Hughes played at centre and Warrington stand-off Blake Austin filled in on the wing. St Helens' prop Luke Thompson was a late switch for Joe Philbin on the interchange bench.

After his axing the week before, Shaun Johnson returned for the Kiwis following Kieran Foran's injury and he played a blinder.

After an early penalty apiece, Joseph Manu and Johnson tries plus three Jamayne Isaako penalty goals and one conversion left the Lions staring at a 16-2 half-time deficit. Johnson's was a beauty as he stepped Elliott Whitehead and then Jonny Lomax in trademark fashion.

Maumalo finished off a wide move in spectacular style six minutes after the break, before Hodgson's score gave the tourists some belief. But Isaako's field goal and penalty late on saw the Kiwis home.

**GAME FOUR**

Great Britain failed to register a single second-half point as Papua New Guinea thrilled their home support with a 28-10 win over the Lions.

GB had shown an increased appetite from their previous three defeats to throw the ball around and that had paid dividends as they led 10-nil after 22 minutes. But a 60-metre, dummy-half, breakaway try from interchange hooker Edwin Ipape on the stroke of half-time, to reduce the deficit to four points, turned the game on its head.

Coach Wayne Bennett went with the same starting XIII that had lost to New Zealand the week before, though George Williams was on the bench for his first GB cap and Joe Philbin returned. Daryl Clark and Josh Jones dropped out.

GB suffered from the first minute when captain James Graham copped a game-ending head injury making the first tackle of the game on Kumul prop Luke Page. And they had to soak up some early pressure before taking the lead in the wake of some promising passages of attack.

Jermaine McGillvary made two exciting runs down the right and, after Tom Burgess went close, the ball was moved slickly to the left by Jackson Hastings, Gareth Widdop and Jake Connor for Blake Austin to go in at the left corner after 13 minutes, not long after he'd had a similar effort disallowed.

Nine minutes later, Josh Hodgson stepped through from close range, Widdop converted and the Lions looked comfortable.

But they were far from home and hosed and PNG winger Edene Gebbie was denied a sensational try in the left corner by the video referee.

Then on the last set of the half, Ipape scooted from dummy-half as Alex Walmsley appealed to the referee for a knock-on at the play-the-ball. Ipape didn't hang about and rounded fullback Jonny Lomax with an amazing turn of speed.

After the turnaround Britain gave the Kumuls possession at regular intervals as they looked disorganised, Hastings and Austin, twice, knocking on.

The pressure from then on was immense. The Kumuls ran with real intent and their enthusiasm in chasing kicks paid huge dividends as early as the 44th minute.

Doncaster's Watson Boas raced onto an impromptu kick to the in-goal from Gebbie, with Rhyse Martin's conversion edging the Kumuls ahead.

Justin Olam dropped on a deflected kick from stand-off Kyle Laybutt and Alex Johnston dived over on the left edge for a fourth Kumuls try, after Boas's grubber got a ricochet and the halfback picked up superbly to feed the South Sydney star.

With 14 minutes to go, Jonny Lomax, who had been one of GB's best, spilled Laybutt's bomb and Nixon Putt collected to race over and confirm PNG's win.

GB almost scored when Hodgson chased his own deflected grubber but the fact he was the only chaser reflected Britain's spirit at the end of a disappointing tour.

# GREAT BRITAIN TOUR

## GAME ONE

*Saturday 26th October 2019*

### TONGA INVITATIONAL 14 GREAT BRITAIN 6

**TONGA INVITATIONAL:** 20 Tesi Niu (Brisbane Broncos); 2 David Fusitu'a (New Zealand Warriors); 3 Michael Jennings (Parramatta Eels); 19 Konrad Hurrell (Leeds Rhinos); 5 Daniel Tupou (Sydney Roosters); 6 Tuimoala Lolohea (Salford Red Devils); 1 Will Hopoate (Canterbury Bulldogs); 15 Addin Fonua-Blake (Manly Sea Eagles); 9 Siliva Havili (Canberra Raiders); 10 Sio Siua Taukeiaho (Sydney Roosters) (C); 11 Ben Murdoch-Masila (Warrington Wolves); 12 Manu Ma'u (Parramatta Eels); 13 Jason Taumalolo (North Queensland Cowboys) (C). Subs (all used): 14 Sione Katoa (Cronulla Sharks); 8 Andrew Fifita (Cronulla Sharks); 16 John Asiata (North Queensland Cowboys); 17 Sitili Tupouniua (Sydney Roosters).
**Tries:** Jennings (29), Katoa (40); **Goals:** Taukeiaho 3/3.
**GREAT BRITAIN:** 1 Lachlan Coote (St Helens); 2 Jermaine McGillvary (Huddersfield Giants); 3 Zak Hardaker (Wigan Warriors); 4 Oliver Gildart (Wigan Warriors); 5 Ryan Hall (Sydney Roosters); 6 Gareth Widdop (St George Illawarra Dragons); 7 Jackson Hastings (Salford Red Devils); 8 Chris Hill (Warrington Wolves); 9 Josh Hodgson (Canberra Raiders); 10 Luke Thompson (St Helens); 11 John Bateman (Canberra Raiders); 12 Elliott Whitehead (Canberra Raiders) (C). Subs (all used): 14 Josh Jones (Salford Red Devils); 15 Tom Burgess (South Sydney Rabbitohs); 16 Jonny Lomax (St Helens); 17 Alex Walmsley (St Helens).
**Try:** Bateman (69); **Goals:** Widdop 1/1.
**Rugby Leaguer & League Express Men of the Match:**
*Tonga Invitational:* Sio Siua Taukeiaho; *Great Britain:* John Bateman.
**Penalty count:** 5-7; **Half-time:** 12-0; **Referee:** Chris Kendall (England); **Attendance:** 9,420 *(at Waikato Stadium, Hamilton)*.

## GAME TWO

*Saturday 2nd November 2019*

### NEW ZEALAND 12 GREAT BRITAIN 8

**NEW ZEALAND:** 1 Roger Tuivasa-Sheck (New Zealand Warriors); 2 Ken Maumalo (New Zealand Warriors); 3 Charnze Nicoll-Klokstad (Canberra Raiders); 4 Joseph Manu (Sydney Roosters); 5 Jamayne Isaako (Brisbane Broncos); 6 Kieran Foran (Canterbury Bulldogs); 7 Benji Marshall (Wests Tigers) (C); 8 Zane Tetevano (Sydney Roosters); 21 Kodi Nikorima (New Zealand Warriors); 10 Jared Waerea-Hargreaves (Sydney Roosters); 11 Briton Nikora (Cronulla Sharks); 12 Kenny Bromwich (Melbourne Storm); 13 Joseph Tapine (Canberra Raiders). Subs (all used): 14 Jahrome Hughes (Melbourne Storm); 15 Corey Harawira-Naera (Canterbury Bulldogs); 16 Leeson Ah Mau (New Zealand Warriors); 17 Adam Blair (New Zealand Warriors).
**Tries:** Isaako (48), Harawira-Naera (54); **Goals:** Isaako 2/3.
**GREAT BRITAIN:** 1 Jonny Lomax (St Helens); 2 Jermaine McGillvary (Huddersfield Giants); 3 Zak Hardaker (Wigan Warriors); 4 Jake Connor (Hull FC); 5 Ryan Hall (Sydney Roosters); 6 Gareth Widdop (St George Illawarra Dragons); 7 Jackson Hastings (Salford Red Devils); 8 Chris Hill (Warrington Wolves); 9 Josh Hodgson (Canberra Raiders); 10 Tom Burgess (South Sydney Rabbitohs); 11 John Bateman (Canberra Raiders); 12 Elliott Whitehead (Canberra Raiders); 13 James Graham (St George Illawarra Dragons) (C). Subs (all used): 14 Josh Jones (Salford Red Devils); 15 Joe Philbin (Warrington Wolves); 16 Daryl Clark (Warrington Wolves); 17 Alex Walmsley (St Helens).
**Try:** Clark (67); **Goals:** Widdop 2/2.
**Rugby Leaguer & League Express Men of the Match:**
*New Zealand:* Roger Tuivasa-Sheck; *Great Britain:* John Bateman.
**Penalty count:** 5-8; **Half-time:** 2-2; **Referee:** Chris Kendall (England); **Attendance:** 25,575 *(at Eden Park, Auckland)*
*(triple header with Fiji v Samoa & Australia v Tonga Invitational)*.

## GAME THREE

*Saturday 9th November 2019*

### NEW ZEALAND 23 GREAT BRITAIN 8

**NEW ZEALAND:** 1 Roger Tuivasa-Sheck (New Zealand Warriors); 2 Ken Maumalo (New Zealand Warriors); 3 Charnze Nicoll-Klokstad (Canberra Raiders); 4 Joseph Manu (Sydney Roosters); 5 Jamayne Isaako (Brisbane Broncos); 6 Shaun Johnson (Cronulla Sharks); 7 Benji Marshall (Wests Tigers) (C); 8 Zane Tetevano (Sydney Roosters); 9 Brandon Smith (Melbourne Storm); 10 Jared Waerea-Hargreaves (Sydney Roosters); 11 Briton Nikora (Cronulla Sharks); 15 Kevin Proctor (Gold Coast Titans); 13 Joseph Tapine (Canberra Raiders). Subs (all used): 12 Corey Harawira-Naera (Canterbury Bulldogs); 14 Kodi Nikorima (New Zealand Warriors); 16 Leeson Ah Mau (New Zealand Warriors); 17 Adam Blair (New Zealand Warriors).
**Tries:** Manu (13), Johnson (34), Maumalo (46); **Goals:** Isaako 5/7; **Field goal:** Isaako (75).
**GREAT BRITAIN:** 1 Jonny Lomax (St Helens); 2 Jermaine McGillvary (Huddersfield Giants); 3 Jack Hughes (Warrington Wolves); 4 Jake Connor (Hull FC); 18 Blake Austin (Warrington Wolves); 6 Gareth Widdop (St George Illawarra Dragons); 7 Jackson Hastings (Salford Red Devils); 8 Chris Hill (Warrington Wolves); 9 Josh Hodgson (Canberra Raiders); 10 Tom Burgess (South Sydney Rabbitohs); 11 John Bateman (Canberra Raiders); 12 Elliott Whitehead (Canberra Raiders); 13 James Graham (St George Illawarra Dragons) (C). Subs (all used): 14 Josh Jones (Salford Red Devils); 16 Daryl Clark (Warrington Wolves); 17 Alex Walmsley (St Helens); 20 Luke Thompson (St Helens).
**Try:** Hodgson (50); **Goals:** Widdop 2/2.
**On report:** Bateman (55) - alleged high tackle on Maumalo.
**Rugby Leaguer & League Express Men of the Match:**
*New Zealand:* Jared Waerea-Hargreaves; *Great Britain:* John Bateman.
**Penalty count:** 7-8; **Half-time:** 16-2; **Referee:** Gerard Sutton (Australia); **Attendance:** 8,875 *(at Orangetheory Stadium, Christchurch)*
*(double header with Fiji v Papua New Guinea)*.

## GAME FOUR

*Saturday 16th November 2019*

### PAPUA NEW GUINEA 28 GREAT BRITAIN 10

**PAPUA NEW GUINEA:** 1 Alex Johnston (South Sydney Rabbitohs); 2 Edene Gebbie (Wynnum Manly Seagulls); 3 David Mead (Catalans Dragons); 4 Justin Olam (Melbourne Storm); 5 Stargroth Amean (Barrow Raiders); 6 Kyle Laybutt (Townsville Blackhawks); 7 Watson Boas (Doncaster); 8 Wellington Albert (Leeds Rhinos); 9 Wartovo Puara (Barrow Raiders); 10 Luke Page (Burleigh Bears); 11 Nixon Putt (Norths Devils); 12 Dan Russell (North Queensland Cowboys); 13 Rhyse Martin (Leeds Rhinos) (C). Subs (all used): 14 Edwin Ipape (Wynnum Manly Seagulls); 15 Garry Lo (PNG Hunters); 16 Stanton Albert (PNG Hunters); 17 Moses Meninga (PNG Hunters).
**Tries:** Ipape (39), Boas (46), Olam (51), Johnston (56), Putt (65); **Goals:** Laybutt 1/1, Martin 3/4.
**GREAT BRITAIN:** 1 Jonny Lomax (St Helens); 2 Jermaine McGillvary (Huddersfield Giants); 3 Jack Hughes (Warrington Wolves); 4 Jake Connor (Hull FC); 5 Blake Austin (Warrington Wolves); 6 Gareth Widdop (St George Illawarra Dragons); 7 Jackson Hastings (Salford Red Devils); 8 Chris Hill (Warrington Wolves); 9 Josh Hodgson (Canberra Raiders); 10 Tom Burgess (South Sydney Rabbitohs); 11 John Bateman (Canberra Raiders); 12 Elliott Whitehead (Canberra Raiders); 13 James Graham (St George Illawarra Dragons) (C). Subs (all used): 15 Luke Thompson (St Helens); 17 Alex Walmsley (St Helens); 18 Joe Philbin (Warrington Wolves); 19 George Williams (Wigan Warriors).
**Tries:** Austin (14), Hodgson (20); **Goals:** Widdop 1/2.
**Rugby Leaguer & League Express Men of the Match:**
*Papua New Guinea:* Watson Boas; *Great Britain:* Tom Burgess.
**Penalty count:** 5-2; **Half-time:** 6-10; **Referee:** Grant Atkins (Australia); **Attendance:** 14,800 *(at PNG Football Stadium, Port Moresby)*.

# INTERNATIONALS
## *Young Lions shine*

### England Knights

England Knights played one game in 2019 when they beat Jamaica at Headingley by 38-6.

The young England side completely dominated the Reggae Warriors in the first half, going in at the break 28-0 in front, with Castleford's Greg Minikin getting all thee opening tries, with Warrington pair Tom Lineham and Toby King getting the others, Danny Richardson kicking four of the five conversions.

Jamaica came out after half-time with energy and determination and put the Knights on the back foot, Mason Caton-Brown scoring from what looked an impossible position. King was yellow carded for a professional foul and that helped Jamaica have more success, with Halifax's James Woodburn-Hall forcing three second-half drop-outs.

But impressively, England weathered the storm, and eventually worked try-scoring positions, leading to two further scores, one from Lineham and the last score from Wigan second-rower Joe Greenwood.

**REPRESENTATIVE MATCH**

*Sunday 20th October 2019*

**ENGLAND KNIGHTS 38 JAMAICA 6**

**ENGLAND KNIGHTS:** 1 Niall Evalds (Salford Red Devils); 2 Tom Lineham (Warrington Wolves); 3 Harry Newman (Leeds Rhinos); 4 Toby King (Warrington Wolves); 5 Greg Minikin (Castleford Tigers); 6 Harry Smith (Wigan Warriors); 7 Danny Richardson (St Helens); 8 Rob Butler (London Broncos); 9 Sam Powell (Wigan Warriors) (C); 10 Oliver Partington (Wigan Warriors); 11 Joe Greenwood (Wigan Warriors); 12 Cameron Smith (Leeds Rhinos); 13 Morgan Smithies (Wigan Warriors). Subs (all used): 14 Kruise Leeming (Huddersfield Giants); 15 Mikolaj Oledzki (Leeds Rhinos); 16 Matty English (Huddersfield Giants); 17 Jack Ashworth (St Helens).
**Tries:** Minikin (5, 17, 20), Lineham (34, 66), King (36), Greenwood (79);
**Goals:** Richardson 5/7.
**Sin bin:** King (55) - professional foul.
**JAMAICA:** 1 Ashton Golding (Leeds Rhinos); 2 Ben Jones-Bishop (Wakefield Trinity); 3 Joe Brown (Newcastle Thunder); 4 Mason Caton-Brown (unattached); 5 Greg Johnson (Salford Red Devils); 6 Jy-mel Coleman (London Skolars); 7 James Woodburn-Hall (Halifax); 8 Khamisi McKain (unattached); 9 Danny Thomas (unattached); 10 Jon Magrin (Bradford Bulls); 11 Keenen Tomlinson (Batley Bulldogs); 12 Joel Farrell (Sheffield Eagles); 13 Michael Lawrence (Huddersfield Giants) (C). Subs (all used): 14 Ross Peltier (Bradford Bulls); 15 Jordan Andrade (Hunslet); 16 Mo Agoro (Newcastle Thunder); 17 Jenson Morris (unattached).
**Try:** Caton-Brown (51); **Goals:** Woodburn-Hall 1/1.
**Rugby Leaguer & League Express Men of the Match:**
*England Knights:* Sam Powell; *Jamaica:* Khamisi McKain.
**Penalty count:** 8-12; **Half-time:** 28-0; **Referee:** Ben Thaler (England);
**Attendance:** 7,113 *(at Emerald Headingley, Leeds)*.

England Knights' Greg Minikin beats Jamaica's James Woodburn-Hall on the way to scoring

Australia's Damien Cook looks to escape from New Zealand's Jared Waerea-Hargreaves

## Anzac Test

Australia won the annual encounter, which this year doubled as an Oceania Cup game, at a canter in Wollongong as the Kiwis wilted after half-time, with Shaun Johnson taking the brunt of the blame.

Johnson's kicking game cost New Zealand several seven-tackle sets but there were errors aplenty throughout the rest of the team. Benji Marshall led the pre-match haka on his international return as captain.

Brisbane's 19-year-old forward Payne Haas was outstanding for the Aussies, coming off the bench to make 174 metres in a destructive 37-minute spell. There were also debuts for Canberra pair Jack Wighton and Nick Cotric, who operated on the right-hand side for Australia, as well as former Italy international Paul Vaughan, who had starred for New South Wales in the past two seasons.

Two quick tries for the Aussies in the second half through Damien Cook and James Tedesco killed off the Kiwis' challenge.

### ANZAC TEST

*Friday 25th October 2019*

**AUSTRALIA 26 NEW ZEALAND 4**

**AUSTRALIA:** 1 James Tedesco (Sydney Roosters); 2 Josh Addo-Carr (Melbourne Storm); 3 Latrell Mitchell (Sydney Roosters); 4 Jack Wighton (Canberra Raiders); 5 Nick Cotric (Canberra Raiders); 6 Cameron Munster (Melbourne Storm); 7 Daly Cherry-Evans (Manly Sea Eagles); 8 Josh Papalii (Canberra Raiders); 9 Damien Cook (South Sydney Rabbitohs); 10 David Klemmer (Newcastle Knights); 11 Boyd Cordner (Sydney Roosters) (C); 12 Tyson Frizell (St George Illawarra Dragons); 13 Jake Trbojevic (Manly Sea Eagles). Subs (all used): 14 Ben Hunt (St George Illawarra Dragons); 15 Payne Haas (Brisbane Broncos); 16 Paul Vaughan (St George Illawarra Dragons); 17 Wade Graham (Cronulla Sharks).
**Tries:** Addo-Carr (20), Frizell (27), Cook (53), Tedesco (58);
**Goals:** Mitchell 4/5, Cherry-Evans 1/1.
**NEW ZEALAND:** 1 Roger Tuivasa-Sheck (New Zealand Warriors); 2 Ken Maumalo (New Zealand Warriors); 3 Charnze Nicoll-Klokstad (Canberra Raiders); 4 Joseph Manu (Sydney Roosters); 5 Jamayne Isaako (Brisbane Broncos); 6 Shaun Johnson (Cronulla Sharks); 7 Benji Marshall (Wests Tigers) (C); 8 Leeson Ah Mau (New Zealand Warriors); 9 Brandon Smith (Melbourne Storm); 10 Jared Waerea-Hargreaves (Sydney Roosters); 11 Briton Nikora (Cronulla Sharks); 12 Kenny Bromwich (Melbourne Storm); 13 Adam Blair (New Zealand Warriors). Subs (all used): 14 Jahrome Hughes (Melbourne Storm); 15 Zane Tetevano (Sydney Roosters); 16 Braden Hamlin-Uele (Cronulla Sharks); 17 Corey Harawira-Naera (Canterbury Bulldogs).
**Try:** Nicoll-Klokstad (34); **Goals:** Johnson 0/1.
**Rugby Leaguer & League Express Men of the Match:**
*Australia:* Payne Haas; *New Zealand:* Charnze Nicoll-Klokstad.
**Penalty count:** 7-3; **Half-time:** 12-4; **Referee:** Gerard Sutton (Australia); **Attendance:** 18,104 *(at WIN Stadium, Wollongong).*

Australia's Kyle Feldt makes a break during the World Cup 9s Final

**WORLD CUP 9s**

**POOL A**
Papua New Guinea 27 USA 10
Australia 25 New Zealand 12
New Zealand 18 Papua New Guinea 17
Australia 41 USA 11
New Zealand 46 USA 0
Australia 26 Papua New Guinea 0

**POOL B**
England 25 Wales 4
Lebanon 12 France 8
France 23 Wales 6
Lebanon 16 England 13
Wales 25 Lebanon 14
England 38 France 4

**POOL C**
Samoa 32 Fiji 17
Cook Islands 30 Tonga Invitational 7
Samoa 17 Cook Islands 4
Tonga Invitational 21 Fiji 17
Cook Islands 12 Fiji 10
Samoa 24 Tonga Invitational 20

**SEMI-FINALS**
New Zealand 22 England 6
Australia 25 Samoa 8

**FINAL**
Australia 24 New Zealand 10

**WOMEN'S WORLD CUP 9s**

Australia 22 New Zealand 8
England 25 Papua New Guinea 4
New Zealand 24 Papua New Guinea 12
Australia 42 England 4
Australia 30 Papua New Guinea 6
New Zealand 33 England 4

**FINAL**
New Zealand 17 Australia 15

**Attendance:** Friday 12,528; Saturday 15,653

# World Cup 9s

Australia won the inaugural men's World Cup 9s (there had been Super League World 9s tournaments in 1996 and 1997) with New Zealand winning the women's competition.

Twelve nations contested the men's tournament and four the women's over the course of two days at the Bankwest Stadium, Parramatta, on Friday October 18th and Saturday, October 19th.

In the men's, Australia beat New Zealand in the final by 24-10 with Parramatta stand-off Mitchell Moses scoring a hat-trick. England qualified for the semi-finals despite losing their pool game to Lebanon but were eliminated by New Zealand in the semi-final.

The New Zealand Ferns just got over the Jillaroos in the women's final by 17-15.

**POOL A**

| | P | W | D | L | F | A | D | Pts |
|---|---|---|---|---|---|---|---|---|
| Australia | 3 | 3 | 0 | 0 | 92 | 23 | 69 | 6 |
| New Zealand | 3 | 2 | 0 | 1 | 76 | 42 | 34 | 4 |
| Papua New Guinea | 3 | 1 | 0 | 2 | 44 | 54 | -10 | 2 |
| USA | 3 | 0 | 0 | 3 | 21 | 114 | -93 | 0 |

**POOL B**

| | P | W | D | L | F | A | D | Pts |
|---|---|---|---|---|---|---|---|---|
| England | 3 | 2 | 0 | 1 | 76 | 24 | 52 | 4 |
| Lebanon | 3 | 2 | 0 | 1 | 42 | 46 | -4 | 4 |
| France | 3 | 1 | 0 | 2 | 35 | 56 | -21 | 2 |
| Wales | 3 | 1 | 0 | 2 | 35 | 62 | -27 | 2 |

**POOL C**

| | P | W | D | L | F | A | D | Pts |
|---|---|---|---|---|---|---|---|---|
| Samoa | 3 | 3 | 0 | 0 | 73 | 41 | 32 | 6 |
| Cook Islands | 3 | 2 | 0 | 1 | 46 | 34 | 12 | 4 |
| Tonga Invitational | 3 | 1 | 0 | 2 | 48 | 71 | -23 | 2 |
| Fiji | 3 | 0 | 0 | 3 | 44 | 65 | -21 | 0 |

**WOMEN**

| | P | W | D | L | F | A | D | Pts |
|---|---|---|---|---|---|---|---|---|
| Australia | 3 | 3 | 0 | 0 | 94 | 18 | 76 | 6 |
| New Zealand | 3 | 2 | 0 | 1 | 65 | 38 | 27 | 4 |
| England | 3 | 1 | 0 | 2 | 33 | 79 | -46 | 2 |
| Papua New Guinea | 3 | 0 | 0 | 3 | 22 | 79 | -57 | 0 |

## World Cup Qualifiers

The 16 teams to contest the 2021 World Cup to be held in England were finalised by the end of 2019.

The eight quarter-finalists of the 2017 tournament - England, Australia, Fiji, Tonga, New Zealand, Papua New Guinea, Samoa and Lebanon - earned automatic qualification.

In 2018, France qualified as European winners, Wales as runners-up, while Jamaica won the Americas tournament, from which runners-up USA entered a repechage with South Africa and Cook Islands.

In 2019, Cook Islands won that and qualified by beating South Africa and USA.

Six European teams competed at the end of 2019 for the four remaining places, with Scotland, Italy, Ireland and Greece qualifying, at the expense of Spain and Serbia, who had replaced Russia following their withdrawal in August.

### WORLD CUP QUALIFIERS - WINTER 2019

*Saturday 26th October 2019*

#### SCOTLAND 86 SERBIA 0

**SCOTLAND:** 1 Alex Walker (London Broncos); 2 Davey Dixon (Keighley Cougars); 3 Dave Scott (Batley Bulldogs); 4 Ben Hellewell (London Broncos); 5 Will Oakes (Hull Kingston Rovers); 6 Callum McLelland (Leeds Rhinos); 7 Ryan Brierley (Leigh Centurions); 8 Luke Douglas (Leigh Centurions); 9 Danny Addy (Hull Kingston Rovers); 10 Adam Walker (Salford Red Devils); 11 Nick Glohe (Lakes United Seagulls); 12 Ben Kavanagh (Halifax); 13 Dale Ferguson (unattached). Subs (all used): 20 Matt Hogg (Edinburgh Eagles); 15 Sam Luckley (Newcastle Thunder); 23 Dan Turland (Murwillumbah Mustangs); 17 Kieran Moran (Keighley Cougars).
**Tries:** Oakes (2, 6, 19), Walker (3, 47), Brierley (8, 33), Glohe (11), Scott (17, 21, 68), McLelland (30), Kavanagh (58), Hellewell (64), Turland (73); **Goals:** Brierley 13/15.
**Sin bin:** Addy (63) - fighting.
**SERBIA:** 1 Vojislav Dedic (Red Star Belgrade); 2 Zane Bijorac (South Sydney Rabbitohs); 3 Aleksandar Djordjevic (Red Star Belgrade); 4 James Mirceski (Asquith Cheetahs Magpies); 5 Dragan Jankovic (Partizan Belgrade); 6 Ben Stevanovic (Wests Tigers); 7 Daniel Marjanovic (Sydney University); 8 Vladica Nikolic (Villeneuve); 9 Rajko Jankovic (Wests Tigers); 10 Milos Calic (Villefranche); 11 Stefan Nedeljkovic (Red Star Belgrade); 12 Jason Muranka (Keighley Cougars); 13 Stevan Stevanovic (Tasmajdan Tigers). Subs (all used): 14 Lazar Zivkovic (Radniki Nis); 15 Vladimir Milutinovic (Villeneuve); 16 Ilija Radan (Narabeen Sharks); 17 Daniel Burke (Warilla Gorillas).
**Sin bin:** Mirceski (23) - high tackle; Radan (62) - shoulder charge; Jankovic (63) - fighting.
**Rugby Leaguer & League Express Men of the Match:**
*Scotland:* Callum McLelland; *Serbia:* Ben Stevanovic.
**Penalty count:** 14-5; **Half-time:** 56-0; **Referee:** Tom Grant (England); **Attendance:** 274 *(at Lochinch, Glasgow)*.

*Saturday 26th October 2019*

#### SPAIN 8 IRELAND 42

**SPAIN:** 1 Romain Franco (Catalans Dragons); 2 Alexis Escamilla (Carcassonne); 3 Antonio Puerta (Custodians Madrid); 4 Alex Doutres (Palau); 5 Daniel Garcia (Crosfields); 6 Luc Franco (Albi); 7 Romain Pallares (Carcassonne); 8 Gaetan Estruga (Albi); 9 Miguel Blanco (Seaton Rangers); 10 Maxime Garcia (Albi); 11 Emir-Walid Bouregba (Lezignan); 12 Anthony Delgado (Carcassonne); 13 Julien Agullo (Carcassonne). Subs (all used): 14 Kevin Aparicio (Rennes Etudiants); 15 Ludovic Renu (Villeghailhenc-Aragon); 16 Rafael Garcia (Custodians Madrid); 17 Simon Juarez (Albi).
**Try:** R Franco (53); **Goals:** Pallares 2/2.
**Sin bin:** Delgado (52) - fighting.
**IRELAND:** 1 Ethan Ryan (Bradford Bulls); 2 Matty Coade (Longhorns); 3 Frankie Halton (Swinton Lions); 4 James Bentley (St Helens); 5 Roland Podesta (Manly Sea Eagles); 6 Gregg McNally (Leigh Centurions); 7 Joe Keyes (Bradford Bulls); 8 Liam Byrne (Wigan Warriors); 9 Bob Beswick (Toronto Wolfpack); 10 Pat Moran (Warrington Wolves); 11 Oliver Roberts (Huddersfield Giants); 12 Tyrone McCarthy (Salford Red Devils); 13 George King (Wakefield Trinity). Subs (all used): 14 Dec O'Donnell (Leigh Centurions); 15 Ronan Michael (Huddersfield Giants); 16 Danny Bridge (Oldham); 17 Michael Ward (Batley Bulldogs).

**Tries:** McNally (18), Podesta (21), Ryan (43), McCarthy (70, 76), Bentley (73), Roberts (77); **Goals:** Podesta 7/7.
**Sin bin:** Keyes (52) - fighting.
**Rugby Leaguer & League Express Men of the Match:**
*Spain:* Luc Franco; *Ireland:* Roland Podesta.
**Penalty count:** 13-0; **Half-time:** 2-12; **Referee:** Geoffrey Poumes (France). *(at Polideportivo Municipal, Valencia)*.

*Friday 1st November 2019*

#### GREECE 24 SCOTLAND 42

**GREECE:** 1 Terry Constantinou (Sunbury); 2 John Mitsias (North Sydney); 3 Grigoris Koutsimporgiogos (Aris Sea Eagles); 4 Mitch Zampetides (Hills District); 5 Nick Mougios (South Sydney Rabbitohs); 6 Chaise Robinson (Sydney Roosters); 7 Jordan Meads (Beerwah); 8 Stefano Totidis (Belrose); 9 Peter Mamouzelelos (South Sydney Rabbitohs); 10 Robert Tuliatu (London Skolars); 11 Sebastian Sell (Mittagong); 12 Jake Kambos (Sydney Roosters); 13 Billy Magoulias (Cronulla Sharks). Subs (all used): 14 Kostas Katsidonis (Rhodes Knights); 15 Stefanos Bastas (Villeghailhenc-Aragon); 16 Jake Vrahnos (Salon); 17 Theodoros Nianiakas (Aris Sea Eagles).
**Tries:** Zampetides (24), Tuliatu (27), Mamouzelelos (40), Robinson (56); **Goals:** Meads 4/5.
**SCOTLAND:** 1 Alex Walker (London Broncos); 20 Matt Hogg (Edinburgh Eagles); 2 Davey Dixon (Keighley Cougars); 3 Dave Scott (Batley Bulldogs); 5 Will Oakes (Hull Kingston Rovers); 6 Callum McLelland (Leeds Rhinos); 7 Ryan Brierley (Leigh Centurions); 8 Luke Douglas (Leigh Centurions); 9 Oscar Thomas (Rochdale Hornets); 15 Sam Luckley (Newcastle Thunder); 11 Nick Glohe (Lakes United Seagulls); 12 Ben Kavanagh (Halifax); 13 Dale Ferguson (unattached). Subs (all used): 10 Dan Turland (Murwillumbah Mustangs); 16 Joe McClean (West Wales Raiders); 17 Kieran Moran (Keighley Cougars); 21 Liam Faughlin (Newcastle University).
**Tries:** Brierley (3), McLelland (10, 45), Kavanagh (17, 70), Scott (31), Oakes (67), Douglas (80); **Goals:** Brierley 2/5, Thomas 2/2, Douglas 1/1.
**Sin bin:** Moran (42) - high tackle.
**Rugby Leaguer & League Express Men of the Match:**
*Greece:* Jordan Meads; *Scotland:* Luke Douglas.
**Penalty count:** 7-10; **Half-time:** 16-18; **Referee:** James Child (England); **Attendance:** 500 *(at New River Stadium, London)*.

*Saturday 2nd November 2019*

#### ITALY 34 SPAIN 4

**ITALY:** 1 Samuel Doleres (Eastwood); 2 Emanuele Passera (Parma Cowboys); 3 Ethan Natoli (Coogee Randwick); 4 Ronny Palumbo (London Skolars); 5 Richard Lepori (Swinton Lions); 6 Gus Garzaniti (Western Suburbs Magpies); 7 Jack Campagnolo (Northern Pride); 8 Alec Susino (Barrow Raiders); 9 Joey Tramontana (Blacktown Workers); 10 Brenden Santi (Toulouse Olympique); 11 Ryan King (Mounties); 12 Alexander Myles (Penrith Panthers); 13 Gioele Celerino (West Wales Raiders). Subs (all used): 14 Daniel Petralia (Wentworthville Magpies); 15 Anton Ilaria (St Marys); 16 Rhys Sciglitano (Blacktown Workers); 17 John Trimboli (Penrith Panthers).
**Tries:** Santi (10), Campagnolo (26), Passera (46, 58), Tramontana (61), King (78); **Goals:** Campagnolo 5/7.
**Dismissal:** Natoli (43) - high tackle.
**Sin bin:** Passera (65) - high tackle.

# Internationals

**SPAIN:** 1 Romain Franco (Catalans Dragons); 2 Alexis Escamilla (Carcassonne); 3 Daniel Garcia (Crosfields); 4 Alex Doutres (Palau); 5 Ludovic Renu (Villeghailhenc-Aragon); 6 Luc Franco (Albi); 7 Romain Pallares (Carcassonne); 8 Gaetan Estruga (Albi); 9 Miguel Blanco (Seaton Rangers); 10 Kevin Aparicio (Rennes Etudiants); 11 Antonio Puerta (Custodians Madrid); 12 Rafael Garcia (Custodians Madrid); 13 Julien Agullo (Carcassonne). Subs (all used): 14 Miquel Tomas (Torrent Tigers); 15 Maxime Garcia (Albi); 16 Emir-Walid Bouregba (Lezignan); 17 Anthony Delgado (Carcassonne).
**Try:** L Franco (17); **Goals:** Pallares 0/1.
**Sin bin:** Agullo (45) - shoulder charge.
**Rugby Leaguer & League Express Men of the Match:**
*Italy:* Jack Campagnolo; *Spain:* Gaetan Estruga.
**Half-time:** 14-4; **Referee:** Benjamin Casty (France).
*(at Stadio Communale Teghil, Lignano).*

---

*Saturday 9th November 2019*

### SERBIA 6 GREECE 82

**SERBIA:** 1 Milos Zogovic (Red Star Belgrade); 2 Dragan Jankovic (Partizan Belgrade); 3 Zane Bijorac (South Sydney Rabbitohs); 4 Aleksandar Djordjevic (Red Star Belgrade); 5 Rajko Trifunovic (Red Star Belgrade); 7 Daniel Burke (Warilla Gorillas); 6 Vojislav Dedic (Red Star Belgrade); 8 Vladica Nikolic (Villeneuve); 9 Vladislav Dedic (Red Star Belgrade); 16 Milos Calic (Villefranche); 11 Jason Muranka (Keighley Cougars); 12 James Mirceski (Asquith Cheetahs Magpies); 13 Stevan Stevanovic (Tasmajdan Tigers). Subs (all used): 10 Vladimir Milutinovic (Villeneuve); 14 Ilija Radan (Narabeen Sharks); 15 Nikola Srbljanin (Partizan Belgrade); 17 Lazar Zivkovic (Radniki Nis).
**Try:** Mirceski (1); **Goals:** Zogovic 1/1.
**GREECE:** 6 Chaise Robinson (Sydney Roosters); 2 Nikolaos Bosmos (Rhodes Knights); 5 Nick Mougios (South Sydney Rabbitohs); 4 Terry Constantinou (Sunbury); 3 John Mitsias (North Sydney); 13 Billy Magoulias (Cronulla Sharks); 7 Jordan Meads (Beerwah); 8 Stefanos Bastas (Villeghailhenc-Aragon); 9 Peter Mamouzelelos (South Sydney Rabbitohs); 16 Vasili Tsikrikas (St Marys); 11 Jake Kambos (Sydney Roosters); 12 Sebastian Sell (Mittagong); 10 George Tsikrikas (St Marys). Subs (all used): 1 Adam Vrahnos (Sydney University); 15 Stefano Totidis (Belrose); 17 Robert Tuliatu (London Skolars); 18 Aris Dardamanis (Aris Sea Eagles).
**Tries:** Robinson (6, 16, 64), Mitsias (9, 67), G Tsikrikas (17), Constantinou (20), Kambos (24), Mamouzelelos (33), Meads (39, 78), Magoulias (42), Bosmos (47, 70), Mougios (60), Dardamanis (79);
**Goals:** Meads 9/16.
**Rugby Leaguer & League Express Men of the Match:**
*Serbia:* James Mirceski; *Greece:* Sebastian Sell.
**Half-time:** 6-46; **Referee:** Robert Hicks (England).
*(at Makis Stadium, Belgrade).*

---

*Saturday 9th November 2019*

### IRELAND 25 ITALY 4

**IRELAND:** 1 Ethan Ryan (Bradford Bulls); 2 Matty Coade (Longhorns); 3 Zack McComb (Oldham); 4 James Bentley (St Helens); 5 Roland Podesta (Manly Sea Eagles); 6 Gregg McNally (Leigh Centurions); 7 Joe Keyes (Bradford Bulls); 8 Liam Byrne (Wigan Warriors); 9 Bob Beswick (Toronto Wolfpack); 10 Pat Moran (Warrington Wolves); 11 Frankie Halton (Swinton Lions); 12 Tyrone McCarthy (Salford Red Devils); 13 George King (Wakefield Trinity). Subs (all used): 14 James Mulvaney (Longhorns); 15 Ronan Michael (Huddersfield Giants); 16 Danny Bridge (Oldham); 17 Michael Ward (Batley Bulldogs).
**Tries:** Moran (3, 15), King (11), McNally (74); **Goals:** Podesta 4/4;
**Field goal:** Keyes (78).
**ITALY:** 1 Samuel Doleres (Eastwood); 2 Emanuele Passera (Parma Cowboys); 3 Ethan Natoli (Coogee Randwick); 4 Ronny Palumbo (London Skolars); 5 Richard Lepori (Swinton Lions); 6 Gus Garzaniti (Western Suburbs Magpies); 7 Jack Campagnolo (Northern Pride); 8 Alec Susino (Barrow Raiders); 9 Joey Tramontana (Blacktown Workers); 10 Brenden Santi (Toulouse Olympique); 11 Ryan King (Mounties); 12 Alexander Myles (Penrith Panthers); 13 Gioele Celerino (West Wales Raiders). Subs (all used): 14 Daniel Petralia (Wentworthville Magpies); 15 Anton Ilaria (St Marys); 16 Rhys Sciglitano (Blacktown Workers); 17 John Trimboli (Penrith Panthers).
**Try:** Tramontana (7); **Goals:** Campagnolo 0/1.
**Sin bin:** Santi (52) - dissent.
**Rugby Leaguer & League Express Men of the Match:**
*Ireland:* Bob Beswick; *Italy:* Joey Tramontana.
**Half time:** 18-4; **Referee:** Liam Moore (England).
*(at Morton Stadium, Santry).*

**Greece celebrate qualification after defeating Serbia**

*Saturday 16th November 2019*

### USA 16 COOK ISLANDS 38

**USA:** 1 Corey Makelim (Sheffield Eagles); 2 Ryan Burroughs (NOVA Eagles); 3 Bureta Faraimo (Hull FC); 4 Elijah Ieriko (Cronulla Sharks); 5 Jamil Robinson (Brooklyn Kings); 6 Rory Humphreys (Ipswich Jets); 7 Connor Donehue (Brooklyn Kings); 14 Mark Offerdahl (Goondiwindi Boars); 9 Kristian Freed (Wests Mitchelton); 15 Sonny Pettybourne (Burleigh Bears); 11 Matt Shipway (Port Macquarie Sharks); 12 Danny Howard (Wentworthville Magpies); 13 Eddy Pettybourne (Central Queensland Capras). Subs (all used): 10 Tim Stubbs (Brooklyn Kings); 19 Kevin Reed (Brooklyn Kings); 18 Charlie Jones (Jacksonville Axemen); 17 Joseph Eichner (Northern Pride).
**Tries:** Shipway (29), Faraimo (42), Howard (68); **Goals:** Faraimo 2/3.
**COOK ISLANDS:** 1 Kayal Iro (Newcastle Knights); 2 Paul Ulberg (Norths Devils); 3 Reuben Rennie (Mounties); 4 Anthony Gelling (Widnes Vikings); 5 Steven Marsters (South Sydney Rabbitohs); 6 Brad Takairangi (Parramatta Eels); 7 Troy Dargan (South Sydney Rabbitohs); 8 Sam Mataora (Belconnen); 9 Aaron Teroi (Central Queensland Capras); 10 Vincent Rennie (Mounties); 11 Alex Glenn (Brisbane Broncos); 12 Marata Niukore (Parramatta Eels); 13 Dominique Peyroux (St Helens). Subs (all used): 15 Moses Nooao-McGreal (Norths Devils); 16 Adam Tangata (Wakefield Trinity); 18 Uiti Baker (Newcastle Knights); 19 Tevin Arona (Canterbury Bulldogs).
**Tries:** Dargan (8, 72), Gelling (10), Glenn (56), V Rennie (64), R Rennie (77), Arona (79); **Goals:** Marsters 5/7.
**Sin bin:** Peyroux (53) - dangerous challenge.
**Rugby Leaguer & League Express Men of the Match:**
*USA:* Bureta Faraimo; *Cook Islands:* Troy Dargan.
**Half-time:** 6-12; **Referee:** Scott Mikalauskas (England);
**Attendance:** 200 *(at University of North Florida, Jacksonville).*

## WORLD CUP QUALIFIERS - WINTER 2018/SUMMER 2019

**Americas Cup** *(all played at Hodges Stadium, Jacksonville)*
*Tuesday 13th November 2018*
USA 64 Chile 0
Canada 8 Jamaica 38
*Saturday 17th November 2018*
Canada 62 Chile 6
USA 10 Jamaica 16

**Europe Pool C - Play-off**
*Saturday 18th May 2019*
Greece 56 Norway 26 *(at New River Stadium, London)*

*Friday 21st June 2019*
Cook Islands 66 South Africa 6 *(at Ringrose Park, Wentworthville)*

## WORLD CUP QUALIFIERS - EUROPE

**POOL A**

| | P | W | D | L | F | A | D | Pts |
|---|---|---|---|---|---|---|---|---|
| Ireland | 2 | 2 | 0 | 0 | 67 | 12 | +55 | 4 |
| Italy | 2 | 1 | 0 | 1 | 38 | 29 | +9 | 2 |
| Spain | 2 | 0 | 0 | 2 | 12 | 76 | -64 | 0 |

**POOL B**

| | P | W | D | L | F | A | D | Pts |
|---|---|---|---|---|---|---|---|---|
| Scotland | 2 | 2 | 0 | 0 | 128 | 24 | +104 | 4 |
| Greece | 2 | 1 | 0 | 1 | 106 | 48 | +58 | 2 |
| Serbia | 2 | 0 | 0 | 2 | 6 | 168 | -162 | 0 |

## Oceania Cup

Australia won the inaugural Oceania Cup on points difference, with Fiji winning the second tier Oceania Shield.

The new tournament was designed to establish a regular, meaningful programme of fixtures to consolidate the growth of Rugby League in the south Pacific.

The tournament was played in two pools; Pool A comprising New Zealand, Australia and Tonga, and Pool B, Samoa, Fiji and Papua New Guinea. Fiji, as winner of Pool B, were to be promoted to Pool A in 2020, in the place of Australia, who were due to travel to Europe for their first Kangaroos tour since 2003.

New Zealand, Australia and Tonga finished with one win each, Tonga stunning Australia in Auckland in the final game of Pool A. Fiji edged their deciding game against Papua New Guinea the following weekend in Christchurch to win Pool B.

### OCEANIA CUP

*Saturday 22nd June 2019*

#### NEW ZEALAND 34 TONGA 14

**NEW ZEALAND:** 1 Roger Tuivasa-Sheck (New Zealand Warriors); 2 Ken Maumalo (New Zealand Warriors); 3 Esan Marsters (Wests Tigers); 4 Joseph Manu (Sydney Roosters); 5 Dallin Watene-Zelezniak (Canterbury Bulldogs); 6 Shaun Johnson (Cronulla Sharks); 7 Benji Marshall (Wests Tigers) (C); 8 Jesse Bromwich (Melbourne Storm); 9 Brandon Smith (Melbourne Storm); 10 Jared Waerea-Hargreaves (Sydney Roosters); 11 Briton Nikora (Cronulla Sharks); 12 Kenny Bromwich (Melbourne Storm); 13 Isaac Liu (Sydney Roosters). Subs (all used): 14 Jahrome Hughes (Melbourne Storm); 15 Leeson Ah Mau (New Zealand Warriors); 16 Nelson Asofa-Solomona (Melbourne Storm); 17 James Fisher-Harris (Penrith Panthers).
**Tries:** Smith (11), Johnson (29, 39), Tuivasa-Sheck (43), Hughes (60), Manu (67); **Goals:** Marsters 5/6.
**TONGA:** 1 Will Hopoate (Canterbury Bulldogs); 2 Daniel Tupou (Sydney Roosters); 3 Kotoni Staggs (Brisbane Broncos); 4 Solomone Kata (New Zealand Warriors); 5 David Fusitu'a (New Zealand Warriors); 6 John Asiata (North Queensland Cowboys); 7 Tuimoala Lolohea (Leeds Rhinos); 15 Addin Fonua-Blake (Manly Sea Eagles); 9 Siliva Havili (Canberra Raiders); 10 Sio Siua Taukeiaho (Sydney Roosters) (C); 11 Tevita Pangai Jnr (Brisbane Broncos); 12 Manu Ma'u (Parramatta Eels); 13 Jason Taumalolo (North Queensland Cowboys) (C). Subs (all used): 14 Manase Fainu (Manly Sea Eagles); 16 Peni Terepo (Parramatta Eels); 17 Sitili Tupouniua (Sydney Roosters); 19 Tevita Tatola (South Sydney Rabbitohs).
**Tries:** Kata (21), Taukeiaho (72), Tupou (76); **Goals:** Taukeiaho 1/3.
**Rugby Leaguer & League Express Men of the Match:**
*New Zealand:* Brandon Smith; *Tonga:* Sio Siua Taukeiaho.
**Penalty count:** 1-8; **Half-time:** 16-4; **Referee:** Ben Cummins (Australia);
**Attendance:** 23,624 *(at Mt Smart Stadium, Auckland).*

*Saturday 22nd June 2019*

#### PAPUA NEW GUINEA 6 SAMOA 24

**PAPUA NEW GUINEA:** 1 Edene Gebbie (Wynnum Manly Seagulls); 2 Junior Rau (PNG Hunters); 3 Brandon Nima (PNG Hunters); 4 Xavier Coates (Brisbane Broncos); 5 Terry Wapi (PNG Hunters); 6 Edwin Ipape (Wynnum Manly Seagulls); 7 Kyle Laybutt (Townsville Blackhawks); 8 Enock Maki (PNG Hunters); 9 James Segeyaro (Brisbane Broncos); 10 Luke Page (Burleigh Bears); 11 Rhyse Martin (Canterbury Bulldogs) (C); 12 Nixon Putt (Norths Devils); 13 Moses Meninga (PNG Hunters). Subs (all used): 14 Kurt Baptiste (North Queensland Cowboys); 15 Zev John (Redcliffe Dolphins); 16 Radley Brawa (Wynnum Manly Seagulls); 17 Stanton Albert (PNG Hunters).
**Try:** Wapi (30); **Goals:** Martin 1/1.
**SAMOA:** 1 Jamayne Isaako (Brisbane Broncos); 2 Jorge Taufua (Manly Sea Eagles); 4 Hymel Hunt (Newcastle Knights); 4 Marion Seve (Melbourne Storm); 5 David Nofoaluma (Wests Tigers); 6 Chanel Harris-Tavita (New Zealand Warriors); 7 Anthony Milford (Brisbane Broncos) (C); 8 Junior Paulo (Parramatta Eels); 9 Jarome Luai (Penrith Panthers); 17 Josh Aloiai (Wests Tigers); 11 Raymond Faitala-Mariner (Canterbury Bulldogs); 12 Jaydn Su'a (Brisbane Broncos); 13 Martin Taupau (Manly Sea Eagles). Subs (all used): 10 James Gavet (Newcastle Knights); 14 Mason Lino (Newcastle Knights); 15 Michael Chee-Kam (Wests Tigers); 16 Herman Ese'ese (Newcastle Knights).
**Tries:** Luai (5), Aloiai (21), Paulo (66), Harris-Tavita (76); **Goals:** Isaako 4/4.
**On report:** Lino (35) - alleged use of the knees.

**Rugby Leaguer & League Express Men of the Match:**
*Papua New Guinea:* Terry Wapi; *Samoa:* Martin Taupau.
**Half-time:** 6-12; **Referees:** Adam Gee & Dave Munro (Australia);
**Attendance:** 8,408 *(at Leichhardt Oval, Sydney).*

*Friday 25th October 2019*

#### AUSTRALIA 26 NEW ZEALAND 4 *(at WIN Stadium, Wollongong)*
*(for full details, see Anzac Test, page 125)*

*(for full details, see Anzac Test, page 125)*

*Saturday 2nd November 2019*

#### FIJI 44 SAMOA 18

**FIJI:** 1 Siti Moceidreke (Sunshine Coast Falcons); 2 Isaac Lumelume (Melbourne Storm); 3 Taane Milne (New Zealand Warriors); 4 Brayden Wiliame (Catalans Dragons); 5 Suliasi Vunivalu (Melbourne Storm); 6 Kevin Naiqama (St Helens) (C); 7 Brandon Wakeham (Canterbury Bulldogs); 8 Kane Evans (Parramatta Eels); 9 Joe Lovodua (St George Illawarra Dragons); 10 Tui Kamikamica (Melbourne Storm); 11 Viliame Kikau (Penrith Panthers); 12 Ben Nakubuwai (Salford Red Devils); 13 D'Rhys Miller (Wentworthville Magpies). Subs (all used): 14 Lamar Liolevave (Tweed Seagulls); 15 Joseph Ratuvakacereivalu (Western Suburbs Magpies); 18 King Vuniyayawa (New Zealand Warriors); 19 Penioni Tagituimua (Nadera Panthers).
**Tries:** Lovodua (6), Miller (9), Kikau (15, 37), Ratuvakacereivalu (24), Lumelume (53), Wiliame (63), Naiqama (67);
**Goals:** Wakeham 5/6, Moceidreke 1/2.
**SAMOA:** 1 Ronaldo Mulitalo (Cronulla Sharks); 2 Jorge Taufua (Manly Sea Eagles); 3 Tim Lafai (St George Illawarra Dragons); 4 Joey Leilua (Canberra Raiders) (C); 5 Brian To'o (Penrith Panthers); 6 Marion Seve (Melbourne Storm); 7 Jarome Luai (Penrith Panthers); 8 Junior Paulo (Parramatta Eels); 9 Danny Levi (Newcastle Knights); 10 Martin Taupau (Manly Sea Eagles); 11 Tino Fa'asuamaleaui (Melbourne Storm); 12 Michael Chee-Kam (Wests Tigers); 14 Dunamis Lui (Canberra Raiders). Subs (all used): 13 Bunty Afoa (New Zealand Warriors); 15 Moses Leota (Penrith Panthers); 16 Luciano Leilua (St George Illawarra Dragons); 17 James Gavet (Newcastle Knights).
**Tries:** Lafai (27), Taufua (51, 78), Mulitalo (80); **Goals:** Lafai 1/4.
**Rugby Leaguer & League Express Men of the Match:**
*Fiji:* Brandon Wakeham; *Samoa:* Tim Lafai.
**Penalty count:** 3-4; **Half-time:** 30-6; **Referee:** Grant Atkins (Australia);
**Attendance:** 25,575 *(at Eden Park, Auckland) (triple header with Australia v Tonga Invitational & New Zealand v Great Britain).*

*Saturday 2nd November 2019*

#### AUSTRALIA 12 TONGA INVITATIONAL 16

**AUSTRALIA:** 1 James Tedesco (Sydney Roosters); 2 Josh Addo-Carr (Melbourne Storm); 3 Latrell Mitchell (Sydney Roosters); 4 Jack Wighton (Canberra Raiders); 5 Nick Cotric (Canberra Raiders); 6 Cameron Munster (Melbourne Storm); 7 Daly Cherry-Evans (Manly Sea Eagles); 8 Josh Papalii (Canberra Raiders); 9 Damien Cook (South Sydney Rabbitohs); 10 David Klemmer (Newcastle Knights); 11 Boyd Cordner (Sydney Roosters) (C); 12 Tyson Frizell (St George Illawarra Dragons); 13 Jake Trbojevic (Manly Sea Eagles). Subs (all used): 14 Cameron Murray (South Sydney Rabbitohs); 15 Payne Haas (Brisbane Broncos); 16 Paul Vaughan (St George Illawarra Dragons); 17 Wade Graham (Cronulla Sharks).
**Tries:** Wighton (27), Vaughan (31); **Goals:** Mitchell 2/2.

129

# Internationals

**TONGA INVITATIONAL:** 1 Will Hopoate (Canterbury Bulldogs); 2 David Fusitu'a (New Zealand Warriors); 3 Michael Jennings (Parramatta Eels); 4 Konrad Hurrell (Leeds Rhinos); 5 Daniel Tupou (Sydney Roosters); 6 Tuimoala Lolohea (Salford Red Devils); 21 Kotoni Staggs (Brisbane Broncos); 15 Addin Fonua-Blake (Manly Sea Eagles); 9 Siliva Havili (Canberra Raiders); 10 Sio Siua Taukeiaho (Sydney Roosters) (C); 11 Ben Murdoch-Masila (Warrington Wolves); 12 Manu Ma'u (Parramatta Eels); 13 Jason Taumalolo (North Queensland Cowboys) (C). Subs (all used): 8 Andrew Fifita (Cronulla Sharks); 14 Sione Katoa (Cronulla Sharks); 19 Tevita Pangai Jnr (Brisbane Broncos); 20 Joe Ofahengaue (Brisbane Broncos).
**Tries:** Hopoate (21), Jennings (46), Pangai Jnr (54); **Goals:** Staggs 2/3.
**Rugby Leaguer & League Express Men of the Match:**
*Australia:* Payne Haas; *Tonga Invitational:* Tuimoala Lolohea.
**Penalty count:** 4-7; **Half-time:** 12-6; **Referee:** Gerard Sutton (Australia); **Attendance:** 25,575 *(at Eden Park, Auckland) (triple header with Fiji v Samoa & New Zealand v Great Britain).*

*Saturday 9th November 2019*

### FIJI 22 PAPUA NEW GUINEA 20

**FIJI:** 1 Siti Moceidreke (Sunshine Coast Falcons); 2 Maika Sivo (Parramatta Eels); 3 Taane Milne (New Zealand Warriors); 4 Brayden Wiliame (Catalans Dragons); 5 Suliasi Vunivalu (Melbourne Storm); 6 Kevin Naiqama (St Helens) (C); 7 Brandon Wakeham (Canterbury Bulldogs); 8 Kane Evans (Parramatta Eels); 9 Joe Lovodua (St George Illawarra Dragons); 10 Tui Kamikamica (Melbourne Storm); 11 Viliame Kikau (Penrith Panthers); 12 Ben Nakubuwai (Salford Red Devils); 13 D'Rhys Miller (Wentworthville Magpies). Subs (all used): 14 Lamar Liolevave (Tweed Seagulls); 15 Joseph Ratuvakacereivalu (Western Suburbs Magpies); 16 King Vuniyayawa (New Zealand Warriors); 17 Penioni Tagituimua (Nadera Panthers).
**Tries:** Kamikamica (22), Wiliame (32), Kikau (43), Nakubuwai (52);
**Goals:** Wakeham 3/4.
**PAPUA NEW GUINEA:** 1 Alex Johnston (South Sydney Rabbitohs); 2 Edene Gebbie (Wynnum Manly Seagulls); 3 Dan Russell (North Queensland Cowboys); 4 Justin Olam (Melbourne Storm); 5 Terry Wapi (PNG Hunters); 6 Kyle Laybutt (Townsville Blackhawks); 7 Watson Boas (Doncaster); 8 Wellington Albert (Leeds Rhinos); 9 Wartovo Puara (Barrow Raiders); 10 Luke Page (Burleigh Bears); 11 Nixon Putt (Norths Devils); 12 Rhyse Martin (Leeds Rhinos) (C); 13 Moses Meninga (PNG Hunters). Subs (all used): 14 Edwin Ipape (Wynnum Manly Seagulls); 15 Stanton Albert (PNG Hunters); 16 Enock Maki (PNG Hunters); 17 Stargroth Amean (Barrow Raiders).
**Tries:** Martin (26), Boas (34), Gebbie (47); **Goals:** Martin 4/4.
**Rugby Leaguer & League Express Men of the Match:**
*Fiji:* Maika Sivo; *Papua New Guinea:* Edene Gebbie.
**Half-time:** 12-14; **Referee:** Chris Kendall (England); **Attendance:** 8,875 *(at Orangetheory Stadium, Christchurch) (double header with New Zealand v Great Britain).*

Tevita Pangai Jnr is mobbed by Tonga teammates after scoring against Australia

---

**OTHER INTERNATIONALS**

*Saturday 22nd June 2019*
Fiji 58 Lebanon 14
*(at Leichhardt Oval, Sydney)*

**Kingston International Test Match**
*Saturday 22nd June 2019*
Jamaica 26 United States 24
*(at UWI Mona Bowl, Kingston)*

*Saturday 28th September 2019*
Poland 34 Czech Republic 18
*(at Stadium KS Budowlani, Lodz)*
*Saturday 12th October 2019*
Poland 16 Sweden 50
*(at Stadium KS Budowlani, Lodz)*
Malta 23 Italy 20
*(at Harvey Shepherd Oval, Kirkham Park, Sydney)*
*Saturday 19th October 2019*
Poland 0 Norway 68
*(at Stadium KS Budowlani, Lodz)*

**MEA Championship**
*(all played at Teslim Balogun Stadium, Lagos)*
*Tuesday 1st October 2019*
Nigeria 23 Ghana 12
Cameroon 4 Morocco 8
*Saturday 5th October 2019*
Nigeria 38 Morocco 10
Cameroon 4 Ghana 10

**REPRESENTATIVE MATCHES**

*Saturday 11th October 2019*
Australian Prime Minister's XIII 52 Fiji 10
*(played in Suva)*
*Saturday 25th October 2019*
Junior Kangaroos (under-23s) 62 France 4
*(played in Wollongong)*

**WOMEN'S INTERNATIONALS**

*Saturday 18th May 2019*
Turkey 18 Italy 14
*(at Beylerbeyi Stadium, Istanbul)*
*Saturday 22nd June 2019*
Fiji 28 Papua New Guinea 0
*(at Leichhardt Oval, Sydney)*
Italy 26 Serbia 0
*(at Bella Italia EFA Village, Lignano)*
New Zealand 46 Samoa 8
*(at Mt Smart Stadium, Auckland)*
*Saturday 14th September 2019*
Turkey 40 Greece 4
*(in Edrine)*
Serbia 6 Canada 34
*(at Makis Stadium, Belgrade)*
*Saturday 21st September 2019*
Serbia 4 Canada 26
*(at Makis Stadium, Belgrade)*
*Saturday 28th September 2019*
Turkey 0 France 54
*(at Beylerbeyi Stadium, Istanbul)*

*Friday 25th October 2019*
Australia 28 New Zealand 8
*(in Wollongong)*
*Saturday 9th November 2019*
Papua New Guinea 10 England 24
*(in Goroka)*
*Saturday 16th November 2019*
Papua New Guinea 20 England 16
*(in Port Moresby)*

**WHEELCHAIR INTERNATIONALS**

*Friday 21st June 2019*
France 25 England 31
*(in Apt, France)*
*Sunday 23rd June 2019*
France 50 England 46
*(at Toulon Sports Palace)*
*Saturday 28th September 2019*
*(all played at Plas Madoc Leisure Centre, Wrexham)*
Wales 90 Scotland 12
England 24 Wales 48
Scotland 1 England 136
*Sunday 29th September 2019*
Wales 40 England 54
*(at Plas Madoc Leisure Centre, Wrexham)*
*Monday 21st October 2019*
Australia 28 England 84
*(at Whitlam Centre Liverpool, Sydney)*
*Thursday 24th October 2019*
Australia 20 England 58
*(at University of Wollongong)*

# 4
# SEASON DOWN UNDER

# NRL
# *Roosters cock-a-hoop*

For the first time in 26 years, the NRL Premiership was retained. Sydney Roosters once again came out on top in the Grand Final, this time against Canberra Raiders who were in their first Final for a quarter of a century.

It was a special climax to the season for those in the northern hemisphere, as three Englishmen featured in the Raiders' starting XIII.

Alas, at the end of the game, most weren't talking of the incredible achievements of both teams but about one particular refereeing decision. Main referee Ben Cummins appeared to change his mind on a key piece of play. After signalling for six again from a rebounded Raiders kick, he then stuck his hand up to indicate the last tackle. Jack Wighton, only seeing his original signal, took a tackle and was forced to hand the ball over. With the scores level at that point, the Roosters went up field and scored the winning try through James Tedesco.

It was a great shame that such an incident detracted from what was a thrilling Final in front of an excellent crowd of almost 83,000 intrigued spectators.

The Roosters were the favourites heading into the game. They'd finished four points ahead of their opponents and boasted a huge amount of Grand Final experience within their ranks, having triumphed the year before. But it was one of the few players in their squad without a Grand Final ring who struck the first blow in the seventh minute as 20-year-old hooker Sam Verrills - in his rookie year - jumped out of dummy half to register the first points.

There had been controversy before that when a charged down Luke Keary kick hit the Roosters trainer on the head and under the rules the Roosters got the feed at the scrum.

Latrell Mitchell converted the try and added a penalty for Joseph Tapine's high shot on Victor Radley, in a first half that was keenly contested.

The Raiders responded before the half was up when Clive Churchill Medal winner Wighton dummied and stepped his way over for a try which was converted by Jarrod Croker.

Canberra captain Croker levelled the scores with a penalty after 50 minutes. The Raiders piled on the pressure to take the lead but they were unable to do so, even when Cooper Cronk - in his last NRL game and his ninth Grand Final - was sin-binned on 50 minutes for a professional foul, tackling Josh Papalii without the ball under his own sticks.

With seven minutes to go, a superb long-range break down the left created by Keary, Mitchell and Daniel Tupou saw Tedesco cross, Mitchell convert and the trophy stayed in Bondi for another year at least.

The Raiders brought plenty to the party at ANZ Stadium, including their incredible pre-match Viking clap, led by current Australia head coach and Raiders legend Mal Meninga.

Just like the regular season, the Grand Final was full of quality, surprises, and controversy. Here's how the 16 teams all fared throughout a turbulent season down under.

Sydney Roosters captain Boyd Cordner and coach Trent Robinson show off the NRL Premiership trophy

### SYDNEY ROOSTERS (Premiers/2nd in the table)
*Top pointscorer: Latrell Mitchell (273); Top tryscorer: Latrell Mitchell (19)*

Sydney Roosters once again ruled the roost in 2019.

They had been the best team, hands down, in 2018 and whilst they weren't able to land the Minor Premiership in 2019, they looked formidable throughout the play-offs. They saw off Melbourne Storm in the Preliminary Final before dispensing with Canberra Raiders in the Grand Final.

The year 2019 proved to be the last season for one of the game's all-time greats in Cooper Cronk. The halfback ended his career with three straight Premiership wins, an incredible feat along with his other wins, two of which were stripped at a later date as a result of salary cap infringements by Melbourne Storm.

The scary thing for the other teams around the Roosters is that they can probably continue to improve, even without Cronk.

Star centre Latrell Mitchell had an up and down season but still finished as the club's top tryscorer and pointscorer with 19 tries and 273 points while James Tedesco has well and truly sealed the Kangaroos fullback spot after the retirement of Billy Slater.

Jake Friend's long-term injury saw the emergence of Sam Verrills at dummy-half and he scored one of the club's two tries in the Grand Final.

## CANBERRA RAIDERS (Runners-up/4th)
*Top pointscorer: Jarrod Croker (228); Top tryscorer: Jarrod Croker (13)*

Perhaps for those in the Australian capital, it was a surprise to see English forward John Bateman's incredible season that saw him named as the Dally M Backrower of the year. But it certainly wasn't for those who have watched him play in the Super League these past few years.

Bateman, alongside fellow Englishmen Elliott Whitehead, Josh Hodgson and Ryan Sutton, helped Canberra Raiders reach their first Grand Final in a quarter of a century, only to come unstuck against a formidable Sydney Roosters side. The Raiders beat Melbourne Storm and South Sydney Rabbitohs in the play-offs on their way to the Final.

Quite often, moving a fullback into the halves doesn't work out but Jack Wighton's move into the front line certainly did. Wighton was named as Clive Churchill Medal winner and has gained a place in the centres in the New South Wales and the Australian Test sides.

The man to replace Wighton at fullback holds a remarkable story as well. Not able to gain a place in New Zealand Warriors' starting side, Charnze Nicoll-Klokstad travelled to Canberra and, not only nailed down a spot in the Raiders' side but starred, making the New Zealand team in their Test Series against Great Britain.

## MELBOURNE STORM (Minor Premiers)
*Top pointscorer: Cameron Smith (216); Top tryscorer: Josh Addo-Carr (16)*

In many ways, Melbourne's season was one of huge disappointment. The first 28 games were great! They only lost four games, to Sydney Roosters, Cronulla Sharks, Manly Sea Eagles and Canberra Raiders, finishing as Minor Premiers by a clear six points over the Roosters. But when it came down to the key matches in the play-offs, they were found wanting.

They lost their opening Final against the Raiders before despatching Parramatta Eels at home to move through to the Preliminary Finals. But they again fell short against the Roosters who had beaten them 12 months before in the Grand Final.

The era of Cameron Smith, Billy Slater and Cooper Cronk is almost at an end for the Storm. Smith signed a new contract to go around again in 2020 way back in January 2019 but hints were dropped by the hooker after their defeat to the Roosters in the Finals that he could decide to hang up his boots for good before next season.

The Storm are ready for their skipper's retirement, however. They have a ready-made replacement in New Zealand international and Dally M Interchange of the Year Brandon Smith sitting on their bench while Cameron Munster, Jahrome Hughes and Ryan Papenhuyzen have the rest of the spine sorted alongside halfback Brodie Croft.

## SOUTH SYDNEY RABBITOHS (3rd)
*Top pointscorer: Adam Reynolds (207); Top tryscorer: Cody Walker (16)*

It was deja vu for the Rabbitohs in 2019. Their season was almost an exact replica of that in 2018. They managed to finish third in the table in the regular rounds before being knocked out of the competition in the Preliminary Final, except not by the Roosters this time, Canberra Raiders doing the deed.

They also had a different coach in charge. Over the off-season, the Rabbitohs and the Broncos swapped coaches with Anthony Seibold heading north to Brisbane and Wayne Bennett south to Sydney.

It's fair to say that in 2019, Bennett got the better of that deal, with Seibold struggling to get his charges into the Finals.

Bennett has been able to keep a close eye on his English NRL contingent whilst in charge of the Rabbitohs with the three Burgess brothers at the Bunnies.

But Sam Burgess was in and out of the side through both suspension and injury and has since called time on his career, while George also faced a nine-game suspension for an eye-gouging incident on former teammate Robbie Farah.

It also proved to be George's final season in the red and green. George will become the fourth Burgess brother to play in Super League, with Wigan Warriors in 2020 after his brothers Luke, Sam and Tom. Greg Inglis was also forced to retire due to injury, bringing an end to a glittering career with Melbourne, Souths, Queensland and Australia.

## PARRAMATTA EELS (5th)
*Top pointscorer: Mitchell Moses (201); Top tryscorer: Maika Sivo (22)*

After winning the wooden spoon in 2018, 2019 was a huge turnaround year for Parramatta Eels.

The year saw them open their new stadium, Bankwest, make it a fortress and comfortably make the Finals. Not only did they make the play-offs but they embarrassed big-hitters Brisbane Broncos in the opening round, by a whopping 58-0. However, they weren't able to replicate that form away from home, falling to a 32-0 defeat at AAMI Park in Melbourne which saw their season end.

Another success story for the Eels in 2019 was the emergence of Fijian winger Maika Sivo, who topped the try scoring charts with some fearsome running to thrill the fans.

Sivo was a complete unknown when the season began but he finished with a remarkable tally of 22, three clear of his closest challenger in the Roosters' Latrell Mitchell.

Sivo was aided brilliantly by Mitchell Moses, who earned international acclaim in the World Cup 9s, Manu Ma'u, who will be heading for Hull FC in 2020, and Blake Ferguson, an excellent signing for Parramatta. The winger's form earned him a recall for New South Wales under coach Brad Fittler in 2019.

## MANLY SEA EAGLES (6th)
*Top pointscorer: Reuben Garrick (194); Top tryscorer: Reuben Garrick (16)*

Manly Sea Eagles are another team that saw their fortunes greatly improve in 2019. The Sea Eagles finished next to bottom in 2018 but earned themselves a home semi-final in the play-offs. They were able to see off Cronulla Sharks in the opening round of the Finals but faced a strong South Sydney side in the second week and came up eight points short at ANZ Stadium.

Daly Cherry-Evans' stunning form for the Sea Eagles has seen him slide back into the Australian Test side, while another unknown winger in Reuben Garrick, shown the door by St George Illawarra Dragons after 2018, shone after making his NRL debut in round one. He finished with a total of 16 tries and played for the Australian PM's XIII in Fiji and the Junior Kangaroos in their win over France.

Des Hasler has to take a great amount of credit for the Sea Eagles' turnaround in fortunes. The club were in turmoil after the exit of Trent Barrett as head coach but Hasler returned to Lottoland and not only steadied the ship but turned them into a formidable team that more than earned their spot in the top eight.

## CRONULLA SHARKS (7th)
*Top pointscorer: Shaun Johnson (102); Top tryscorer: Josh Morris (15)*

2019 was an indifferent year for Cronulla Sharks. When you looked at their squad, there was a huge amount of talent. A seventh-placed finish didn't reflect that.

If they were able to progress well in the Finals, it would have made up for it. But as it was, the Sharks lost to Manly Sea Eagles in the first game of the play-offs.

The key signing for the Sharks ahead of 2019 was Shaun Johnson from New Zealand Warriors. Everyone within Rugby League knew exactly what the halfback could do but they also know that his injury record sometimes gets in the way of his huge talent and 2019 was a metaphor for that. Johnson wasn't able to play enough games to help his side climb the table.

Injuries were a general problem for the Sharks with Matt Moylan, Josh Dugan and Andrew Fifita, amongst others, suffering long-term injuries through the year.

The Sharks did see the emergence of a real star, however. Another complete unknown before the season began, Briton Nikora, played 24 games for Cronulla having made his debut in March. He was able to earn international honours with New Zealand off the back of his excellent form in the blue of Cronulla.

2019 also saw the end of Paul Gallen's career. Gallen was a one-club man, playing 349 times for the Sharks, 24 times for New South Wales and 32 games for Australia in a career that started way back in 2001.

## BRISBANE BRONCOS (8th)

*Top pointscorer: Jamayne Isaako (121); Top tryscorer: Corey Oates (13)*

With the appointment of Anthony Seibold at the beginning of 2019, expectations were high after he had led South Sydney admirably the year before. But the Broncos weren't able to live up to expectations.

They did manage to sneak into the top eight on the final day of the season but when it came to the play-offs, they came up badly short, suffering a humiliating 58-0 defeat to Parramatta Eels in the first round.

Brisbane have a unique combination of aging stars and incredibly young talent with not much in between. Darius Boyd comes in for a lot of criticism from the fans as he nears the end of his career while Matt Gillett has been forced to retire.

The young talent is the real positive for the Broncos. Their 19-year-old prop forward Payne Haas made his international debut for the Kangaroos at the end of the year and was, by far, their best player in 2019.

If they have more luck with injuries in 2020, they could begin to rise further into the top eight.

## WESTS TIGERS (9th)

*Top pointscorer: Esan Marsters (116); Top tryscorer: Esan Marsters, Corey Thompson (9)*

They continue to surprise.

Not many had the Tigers pushing for the top eight in 2019. They had lost their coach, Ivan Cleary to Penrith Panthers but made a shrewd appointment themselves in former Wigan team boss Michael Maguire.

The odds on the Tigers finishing above Cleary's Panthers were long for sure but they managed just that. They were even within a shout of a top eight spot up until the final day of the regular season but couldn't beat the Sharks in a winner-takes-all play-off qualifier.

Corey Thompson continues to inspire at fullback after his return to the competition from Widnes Vikings but joint top tryscorer Esan Marsters has left the club to join North Queensland Cowboys, which is a blow.

This season also saw the retirement of Ben Matulino, a great servant to the Tigers, New Zealand Warriors and the Kiwis.

## PENRITH PANTHERS (10th)
*Top pointscorer: Nathan Cleary (157); Top tryscorer: Nathan Cleary (10)*

2019 was a season of immense disappointment for the Panthers. They got their man in Ivan Cleary as their new Head Coach in the offseason. With his son Nathan in the halves, they looked like they had all the ingredients to make a challenge for the Premiership.

But that never looked likely from the get-go. A nightmare start had them joint bottom of the NRL after nine games. A pick up in fortune mid-way through the season brought hope to the fans at the foot of the mountains but they couldn't keep it up and ended up finishing comfortably outside the top-eight positions.

Top earner Reagan Campbell-Gillard's form suffered throughout the year, forcing him to leave for the Eels in search of his best Rugby League at the end of the year, while Phil Gould's long association with the club also ended in 2019. He is set to join St George Illawarra Dragons on a permanent basis in 2020.

## NEWCASTLE KNIGHTS (11th)
*Top pointscorer: Kalyn Ponga (140); Top tryscorer: Kalyn Ponga (11)*

They have promised so much in the last two years but have always come up just short.

Newcastle Knights were expected to be in and around the top eight picture in 2019 and while that was true for a good part of the campaign, they just weren't able to complete the job this year.

Nathan Brown, who left the club at the end of the year to be replaced by Adam O'Brien, experimented by moving Kalyn Ponga into the halves but that didn't work. While the young fullback was still in fine form for the Knights, he didn't kick on in the way that the Knights fans would have envisaged heading into the year.

But the reality is the Knights are still building after a nightmare few years earlier in the decade. Next year could be the year where they finally make the jump back into the play-off picture.

## CANTERBURY BULLDOGS (12th)
*Top pointscorer: Nick Meaney (88); Top tryscorer: Reimis Smith (12)*

Up until the last few weeks of the season, the Bulldogs were all set to finish the season well outside the top eight and were languishing second from bottom, above only Gold Coast Titans.

But the last month or so of the regular season saw the Bulldogs become a force with which to be reckoned. In their last six games, they lost only once, including beating both South Sydney and Parramatta away from home.

It means the Bulldogs fans, instead of feeling down about their season, are reasonably optimistic about their chances in 2020.

Their upturn in fortune coincided with the return into the halves of Lachlan Lewis from injury and the Bulldogs fans will be glad to see him staying at the club for at least another two years.

## NEW ZEALAND WARRIORS (13th)
*Top pointscorer: Ken Maumalo (68); Top tryscorer: Ken Maumalo (17)*

After 2018 saw the Warriors finally make the play-offs, 2019 was most definitely a step in the wrong direction for New Zealand.

Shaun Johnson's move away from the club was a bold one and they got themselves a good replacement in Kodi Nikorima from Brisbane. But the Warriors never looked likely to trouble the top-eight picture throughout the season.

David Fusitu'a was the star for the Warriors in 2018, scoring 23 tries but he only managed five in 2019 while the tries were gobbled up by Ken Maumalo on the other side of the field.

New Zealand are far too reliant on Roger Tuivasa-Sheck. He is comfortably their most consistent performer but for them to target a return to the play-offs in 2020, they need more from the players around their fullback, particularly through the middle third of the field.

## NORTH QUEENSLAND COWBOYS (14th)
*Top pointscorer: Jordan Kahu (86); Top tryscorer: Kyle Feldt (11)*

Another season of disappointment for the Cowboys.

They just don't seem to have been able to deal with the retirement of Johnathan Thurston. Michael Morgan hasn't been able to step up into the leadership role in the halves in the last few years as his seasons have been constantly hampered with injuries.

North Queensland have become increasingly reliant on young half Jake Clifford who has done an admirable job in Morgan's absence.

2019 was probably one of Jason Taumalolo's more quiet spells in the NRL as well. Normally such a destructive runner, always averaging above 200 metres per game, the big Tongan wasn't quite able to replicate the form which had earned him a ten-year contract with the club.

Exciting times are on the horizon for the club, however. They will move to their new stadium, the North Queensland stadium, in 2020 after playing their final game at 1300SMILES Stadium at the end of 2019.

## ST GEORGE ILLAWARRA DRAGONS (15th)
*Top pointscorer: Gareth Widdop (64); Top tryscorer: Mikaele Ravalawa (11)*

Gareth Widdop's final season with the Dragons didn't go to plan at all.

It was announced early in the season he would be linking up with Warrington Wolves in 2020 but his season in 2019 was almost utterly ruined by injury.

Yet another shoulder problem meant he was only able to play a handful of games for St George in 2019 but he was back and able to feature for Great Britain in their tour of New Zealand.

2019 was the year of the unknown Fijian winger and after Parramatta's Maika Sivo, St George had their own star. Mikaele Ravalawa came out of nowhere to top try score for the club.

With all their injury problems, 2019 was a damp squib for the Dragons all round.

## GOLD COAST TITANS (16th)
*Top pointscorer: Michael Gordon (66); Top tryscorer: Dale Copley (9)*

Gold Coast were comfortably the worst side in the competition.

They finished eight points adrift at the bottom of the division, winning only four games out of a possible 24.

Penrith, Newcastle, Manly and Brisbane were the unlucky quartet that suffered defeat at the hands of the bottom club. But the Titans still managed 11 straight defeats to end the campaign.

Their solution? St Helens' Justin Holbrook.

It's not a bad one. They've managed to snare the Super League champions' coach who is looking for a new challenge and boy, has he got one!

Kallum Watkins ended the season with the Titans after his move from Leeds Rhinos but failed to make any initial impact despite a string of appearances in the centres.

## NRL PREMIERSHIP FINALS SERIES

### QUALIFYING FINALS
*Friday 13th September 2019*

Sydney Roosters 30 ................................................South Sydney Rabbitohs 6

*Saturday 14th September 2019*

Melbourne Storm 10 ...............................................Canberra Raiders 12

### ELIMINATION FINALS
*Saturday 14th September 2019*

Manly Sea Eagles 28................................................Cronulla Sharks 16

*Sunday 15th September 2019*

Parramatta Eels 58.................................................Brisbane Broncos 0

### SEMI-FINALS
*Friday 20th September 2019*

South Sydney Rabbitohs 34 ..........................................Manly Sea Eagles 26

*Saturday 21st September 2019*

Melbourne Storm 32..................................................Parramatta Eels 0

### PRELIMINARY FINALS
*Friday 27th September 2019*

Canberra Raiders 16 .................................................South Sydney Rabbitohs 10

*Saturday 28th September 2019*

Sydney Roosters 14 ..................................................Melbourne Storm 6

## NRL GRAND FINAL

*Sunday 6th October 2019*

### CANBERRA RAIDERS 8 SYDNEY ROOSTERS 14

**RAIDERS:** 1 Charnze Nicoll-Klokstad; 2 Nick Cotric; 3 Jarrod Croker (C); 4 Joey Leilua; 5 Jordan Rapana; 6 Jack Wighton; 7 Aidan Sezer; 8 Josh Papalii; 9 Josh Hodgson; 10 Iosia Soliola; 11 John Bateman; 12 Elliott Whitehead; 13 Joseph Tapine. Subs (all used): 14 Bailey Simonsson; 15 Emre Guler; 16 Corey Horsburgh; 17 Dunamis Lui.
**Try:** Wighton (31); **Goals:** Croker 2/2.
**ROOSTERS:** 1 James Tedesco; 2 Daniel Tupou; 3 Latrell Mitchell; 4 Joseph Manu; 5 Brett Morris; 6 Luke Keary; 7 Cooper Cronk; 8 Jared Waerea-Hargreaves; 9 Sam Verrills; 10 Isaac Liu; 11 Boyd Cordner (C); 12 Mitchell Aubusson; 13 Victor Radley. Subs (all used): 14 Angus Crichton; 16 Nat Butcher; 17 Sio Siua Taukeiaho; 20 Jake Friend (C).
**Tries:** Verrills (7), Tedesco (73); **Goals:** Mitchell 3/5.
**Sin bin:** Cronk (50) - professional foul.
**Clive Churchill Medal:** Jack Wighton (Canberra Raiders).
**Rugby Leaguer & League Express Men of the Match:**
*Raiders:* Jack Wighton; *Roosters:* James Tedesco.
**Half-time:** 6-8; **Referees:** Ben Cummins & Gerard Sutton;
**Attendance:** 82,922 *(at ANZ Stadium, Sydney)*.

## NRL PREMIERSHIP - FINAL TABLE

| | P | W | D | L | B | F | A | D | Pts |
|---|---|---|---|---|---|---|---|---|---|
| Melbourne Storm | 24 | 20 | 0 | 4 | 1 | 631 | 300 | 331 | 42 |
| Sydney Roosters | 24 | 17 | 0 | 7 | 1 | 627 | 363 | 264 | 36 |
| South Sydney Rabbitohs | 24 | 16 | 0 | 8 | 1 | 521 | 417 | 104 | 34 |
| Canberra Raiders | 24 | 15 | 0 | 9 | 1 | 524 | 374 | 150 | 32 |
| Parramatta Eels | 24 | 14 | 0 | 10 | 1 | 533 | 473 | 60 | 30 |
| Manly Sea Eagles | 24 | 14 | 0 | 10 | 1 | 496 | 446 | 50 | 30 |
| Cronulla Sharks | 24 | 12 | 0 | 12 | 1 | 514 | 464 | 50 | 26 |
| Brisbane Broncos | 24 | 11 | 1 | 12 | 1 | 432 | 489 | -57 | 25 |
| Wests Tigers | 24 | 11 | 0 | 13 | 1 | 475 | 486 | -11 | 24 |
| Penrith Panthers | 24 | 11 | 0 | 13 | 1 | 413 | 474 | -61 | 24 |
| Newcastle Knights | 24 | 10 | 0 | 14 | 1 | 485 | 522 | -37 | 22 |
| Canterbury Bulldogs | 24 | 10 | 0 | 14 | 1 | 326 | 477 | -151 | 22 |
| New Zealand Warriors | 24 | 9 | 1 | 14 | 1 | 433 | 574 | -141 | 21 |
| North Queensland Cowboys | 24 | 9 | 0 | 15 | 1 | 378 | 500 | -122 | 20 |
| St George Illawarra Dragons | 24 | 8 | 0 | 16 | 1 | 427 | 575 | -148 | 18 |
| Gold Coast Titans | 24 | 4 | 0 | 20 | 1 | 370 | 651 | -281 | 10 |

### LEADING POINTSCORERS

| | | |
|---|---|---|
| Latrell Mitchell | Sydney Roosters | 273 |
| Jarrod Croker | Canberra Raiders | 228 |
| Cameron Smith | Melbourne Storm | 216 |
| Adam Reynolds | South Sydney Rabbitohs | 207 |
| Mitchell Moses | Parramatta Eels | 201 |

### TOP TRYSCORERS

| | | |
|---|---|---|
| Maika Sivo | Parramatta Eels | 22 |
| Latrell Mitchell | Sydney Roosters | 19 |
| James Tedesco | Sydney Roosters | 18 |
| Ken Maumalo | New Zealand Warriors | 17 |
| Josh Addo-Carr | Melbourne Storm | 16 |
| Reuben Garrick | Manly Sea Eagles | 16 |
| Cody Walker | South Sydney Rabbitohs | 16 |

### STATE CHAMPIONSHIP *(Winners of Queensland and NSW Cups)*
*Sunday 6th October 2019*

Burleigh Bears 16 ...............................................Newtown Jets 20

*(at ANZ Stadium, Sydney)*

### NRLW GRAND FINAL *(Women's Premiership)*
*Sunday 6th October 2019*

Brisbane Broncos 30.....................................St George Illawarra Dragons 6

*(at ANZ Stadium, Sydney)*

## DALLY M AWARDS

**Dally M Medal (Player of the Year):** James Tedesco (Sydney Roosters)
**Provan Summons Medal (People's Choice):**
Josh Jackson (Canterbury Bulldogs)
**Coach of the Year:** Craig Bellamy (Melbourne Storm)
**Captain of the Year:** Cameron Smith (Melbourne Storm)
**Rookie of the Year:** Payne Haas (Brisbane Broncos)
**Female Player of the Year:** Jess Sergis (St George Illawarra Dragons)

141

# STATE OF ORIGIN
## *Singing the Blues*

For the second year in a row, New South Wales won the State of Origin series but it wasn't as easy as some people thought it would be.

In fact, it went down to the very last second of a decider. Luckily for all the home fans packed into a sell-out ANZ Stadium in Sydney, Blake Ferguson managed to tiptoe his way down the sideline and set up James Tedesco for the winning try.

It was the first time in eight attempts that New South Wales had won a decider and it's not often that a side wins the series having lost the opener.

The Maroons of Queensland had taken the first game in Brisbane, 18-14, against most people's odds before the Blues levelled the series with a clinical performance in Perth. Tom Trbojevic's hat-trick from the centres saw New South Wales comfortably win, 38-6 despite a penalty try for Will Chambers.

**STATE OF ORIGIN - GAME I**

*Wednesday 5th June 2019*

**QUEENSLAND 18 NEW SOUTH WALES 14**

**QUEENSLAND:** 1 Kalyn Ponga (Newcastle Knights); 2 Corey Oates (Brisbane Broncos); 3 Michael Morgan (North Queensland Cowboys); 4 Will Chambers (Melbourne Storm); 5 Dane Gagai (South Sydney Rabbitohs); 6 Cameron Munster (Melbourne Storm); 7 Daly Cherry-Evans (Manly Sea Eagles) (C); 8 Jai Arrow (Gold Coast Titans); 9 Ben Hunt (St George Illawarra Dragons); 10 Josh Papalii (Canberra Raiders); 11 Felise Kaufusi (Melbourne Storm); 12 Matt Gillett (Brisbane Broncos); 13 Josh McGuire (North Queensland Cowboys). Subs (all used): 14 Moses Mbye (Wests Tigers); 15 Joe Ofahengaue (Brisbane Broncos); 16 Dylan Napa (Canterbury Bulldogs); 17 David Fifita (Brisbane Broncos).
**Tries:** Oates (53), Gagai (67, 71); **Goals:** Ponga 3/4.
**NEW SOUTH WALES:** 1 James Tedesco (Sydney Roosters); 2 Nick Cotric (Canberra Raiders); 3 Latrell Mitchell (Sydney Roosters); 4 Josh Morris (Cronulla Sharks); 5 Josh Addo-Carr (Melbourne Storm); 6 Cody Walker (South Sydney Rabbitohs); 7 Nathan Cleary (Penrith Panthers); 8 David Klemmer (Newcastle Knights); 9 Damien Cook (South Sydney Rabbitohs); 10 Paul Vaughan (St George Illawarra Dragons); 11 Boyd Cordner (Sydney Roosters) (C); 12 Tyson Frizell (St George Illawarra Dragons); 13 Jake Trbojevic (Manly Sea Eagles). Subs (all used): 14 Jack Wighton (Canberra Raiders); 15 Payne Haas (Brisbane Broncos); 16 Cameron Murray (South Sydney Rabbitohs); 17 Angus Crichton (Sydney Roosters).
**Tries:** Morris (20), J Trbojevic (75); **Goals:** Cleary 3/3.
**Sin bin:** Mitchell (58) - professional foul.
**Rugby Leaguer & League Express Men of the Match:**
*Queensland:* Dane Gagai; *New South Wales:* James Tedesco.
**Half-time:** 0-8; **Referees:** Ashley Klein & Gerard Sutton;
**Attendance:** 52,191 *(at Suncorp Stadium, Brisbane).*

That meant that the Blues could return home knowing a win would seal a second consecutive series. And so it proved.

Queensland know all too well how a State can dominate a generation of series so they will be anxious looking at New South Wales' squad and the potential therein.

In the Blues' deciding team, only the halves pairing of James Maloney and Mitchell Pearce are coming to the end of their careers. The vast majority of the rest could make up that team for many years to come.

Meanwhile, Queensland still haven't managed to get over losing the entirety of their spine in the last few years. Cameron Smith hasn't been replaced properly. So much so that there were rumours that the Storm hooker could return for the 2019 series. But the hooking role was left to Ben Hunt. Although he performed admirably, he's a halfback by trade.

Despite losing the series, Queensland head coach Kevin Walters will be pretty happy with his side's efforts over the three games. Not many gave the Maroons a chance but they were within a whisker of snatching the series. Queensland sides seem to have a grit and determination about them that won't go away and their fans will hope that trait continues.

As usual, the first game of the series brought with it plenty of debutants. New

New South Wales' Jake Trbojevic is collared by the Queensland defence during Origin II in Perth

South Wales had five: Nick Cotric and Cody Walker started the game while Jack Wighton, Cameron Murray and 19-year-old Payne Haas came off the bench. Meanwhile, the Maroons' bench featured three first timers in Moses Mbye, Joe Ofahengaue and young Brisbane backrower David Fifita.

The first half in Brisbane went to script with a spirited Queensland outfit pegged back by the Blues. It was an old timer in Josh Morris who got New South Wales' try in the first half which was added to by Nathan Cleary's conversion and penalty.

But 18 straight points for the home side in the second half swung the game. Corey Oates scored the first before a double for Dane Gagai helped seal the first game, though Jake Trbojevic scored a late try to bring New South Wales back to within four points. Kalyn Ponga kicked three of his four attempts at goal as it

### STATE OF ORIGIN - GAME II

*Sunday 23rd June 2019*

#### NEW SOUTH WALES 38 QUEENSLAND 6

**NEW SOUTH WALES:** 1 James Tedesco (Sydney Roosters); 2 Blake Ferguson (Parramatta Eels); 3 Tom Trbojevic (Manly Sea Eagles); 4 Jack Wighton (Canberra Raiders); 5 Josh Addo-Carr (Melbourne Storm); 6 James Maloney (Penrith Panthers); 7 Nathan Cleary (Penrith Panthers); 8 Daniel Saifiti (Newcastle Knights); 9 Damien Cook (South Sydney Rabbitohs); 13 Jake Trbojevic (Manly Sea Eagles); 11 Boyd Cordner (Sydney Roosters) (C); 12 Tyson Frizell (St George Illawarra Dragons); 14 Dale Finucane (Melbourne Storm). Subs (all used): 10 Paul Vaughan (St George Illawarra Dragons); 15 Tariq Sims (St George Illawarra Dragons); 16 Cameron Murray (South Sydney Rabbitohs); 17 Wade Graham (Cronulla Sharks).
**Tries:** T Trbojevic (8, 36, 54), Frizell (19), Addo-Carr (58, 75);
**Goals:** Cleary 2/2, Maloney 5/6.
**QUEENSLAND:** 1 Kalyn Ponga (Newcastle Knights); 2 Corey Oates (Brisbane Broncos); 3 Michael Morgan (North Queensland Cowboys); 4 Will Chambers (Melbourne Storm); 5 Dane Gagai (South Sydney Rabbitohs); 6 Cameron Munster (Melbourne Storm); 7 Daly Cherry-Evans (Manly Sea Eagles) (C); 8 Dylan Napa (Canterbury Bulldogs); 9 Ben Hunt (St George Illawarra Dragons); 10 Josh Papalii (Canberra Raiders); 11 Felise Kaufusi (Melbourne Storm); 12 Matt Gillett (Brisbane Broncos); 13 Josh McGuire (North Queensland Cowboys). Subs (all used): 14 Moses Mbye (Wests Tigers); 15 Jarrod Wallace (Gold Coast Titans); 16 Tim Glasby (Newcastle Knights); 17 David Fifita (Brisbane Broncos).
**Try:** Chambers (14, pen); **Goals:** Ponga 1/1.
**On report:** Wallace (50) - alleged late challenge.
**Rugby Leaguer & League Express Men of the Match:**
*New South Wales:* Tom Trbojevic; *Queensland:* Josh McGuire.
**Half-time:** 18-6; **Referees:** Ashley Klein & Gerard Sutton;
**Attendance:** 59,721 *(at Optus Stadium, Perth)*.

ended 18-14.

Latrell Mitchell had a poor game by his high standards culminating in his sin binning for a professional foul on Matt Gillett and his subsequent dropping for the second game of the series.

The Blues needed to bounce back to send the series to a decider and they did just that with a 38-6 win. It was the series' first foray into Western Australia as Perth's Optus Stadium played host to the showpiece.

Blues Head Coach Brad Fittler had to make some serious calls after a poor performance in the first game and so changes were widespread. There were debuts for Daniel Saifiti and Dale Finucane plus recalls for James Maloney, Wade Graham, Tom Trbojevic and Ferguson.

Meanwhile, Walters was forced into two changes of his own with Tim Glasby and Jarrod Wallace called up to replace injured duo Jai Arrow and Ofahengaue.

But it was a nightmare from the start for Queensland. They were only able to notch a penalty try for Chambers and Ponga's conversion in the first half. Tom Trbojevic's hat-trick laid the platform for the Blues and Tyson Frizell and Josh Addo-Carr both added to the scoreline with tries of their own. Nathan Cleary kicked two conversions and Maloney nailed five.

That led the series to a decider at ANZ Stadium and it was an absolute Origin classic. The scores were level at the break with Felise Kaufusi's try and Ethan Lowe's penalty for Queensland cancelled out by Paul Vaughan's four-pointer and Maloney's penalty for the home side.

New South Wales built up what seemed to be an unassailable lead in the third quarter with tries for Tedesco and Damien Cook but back came the visitors. Josh McGuire and Josh Papalii both crossed, with Lowe's conversions levelling the game, only for Tedesco to support Ferguson's last-second run up the right wing and keep the shield Blue for another year.

### STATE OF ORIGIN - GAME III

*Wednesday 10th July 2019*

#### NEW SOUTH WALES 26 QUEENSLAND 20

**NEW SOUTH WALES:** 1 James Tedesco (Sydney Roosters); 2 Blake Ferguson (Parramatta Eels); 3 Tom Trbojevic (Manly Sea Eagles); 4 Jack Wighton (Canberra Raiders); 5 Josh Addo-Carr (Melbourne Storm); 6 James Maloney (Penrith Panthers); 7 Mitchell Pearce (Newcastle Knights); 8 Daniel Saifiti (Newcastle Knights); 9 Damien Cook (South Sydney Rabbitohs); 15 David Klemmer (Newcastle Knights); 11 Boyd Cordner (Sydney Roosters) (C); 12 Tyson Frizell (St George Illawarra Dragons); 13 Jake Trbojevic (Manly Sea Eagles). Subs (all used): 10 Paul Vaughan (St George Illawarra Dragons); 14 Dale Finucane (Melbourne Storm); 16 Cameron Murray (South Sydney Rabbitohs); 17 Wade Graham (Cronulla Sharks). **Tries:** Vaughan (35), Tedesco (51, 80), Cook (60); **Goals:** Maloney 5/5.
**QUEENSLAND:** 1 Cameron Munster (Melbourne Storm); 2 Corey Oates (Brisbane Broncos); 14 Moses Mbye (Wests Tigers); 4 Will Chambers (Melbourne Storm); 5 Dane Gagai (South Sydney Rabbitohs); 6 Corey Norman (St George Illawarra Dragons); 7 Daly Cherry-Evans (Manly Sea Eagles) (C); 8 Joe Ofahengaue (Brisbane Broncos); 9 Ben Hunt (St George Illawarra Dragons); 10 Josh Papalii (Canberra Raiders); 11 Felise Kaufusi (Melbourne Storm); 18 Ethan Lowe (South Sydney Rabbitohs); 13 Josh McGuire (North Queensland Cowboys). Subs (all used): 3 Michael Morgan (North Queensland Cowboys); 15 Christian Welch (Melbourne Storm); 16 Tim Glasby (Newcastle Knights); 17 David Fifita (Brisbane Broncos). **Tries:** Kaufusi (15), McGuire (72), Papalii (78); **Goals:** Lowe 4/4.
**Rugby Leaguer & League Express Men of the Match:**
*New South Wales:* James Tedesco; *Queensland:* Ethan Lowe.
**Half-time:** 8-8; **Referees:** Ashley Klein & Gerard Sutton; **Attendance:** 82,565 *(at ANZ Stadium, Sydney)*.

**Wally Lewis Medal (Man of the Series):**
James Tedesco (New South Wales)

n Justin Holbrook arrived at St Helens in May of 2017,
e knew about him was that he'd worked as assistant to
er Catalans coach Trent Robinson at Sydney Roosters.

Saints chief executive Mike Rush had gone to Australia
d a successor to Keiron Cunningham, who had been
ed almost two months before after Saints had lost four
drawn one of their first eight games of the season. And
rook was selected as the club's favoured option among a
f some well-known names.

After Holbrook's arrival, things improved that season,
e point where Saints were just a whisker away from
ing the Grand Final, losing in dramatic circumstances to a
en-point field goal from Castleford's Luke Gale. The mid-
on recruitment of Ben Barba helped, even though he was
ended and didn't make his debut until August.

In 2018, with Barba a star turn, Saints topped the Super
ue table from start to finish, losing only four games and
nding the thrilling attacking play that had become their
nark. But still no silverware followed as they fell at the
-final stages of both Super League and the Challenge

Barba won the Man of Steel and went home as Holbrook
e two smart signings in Lachlan Coote and Kevin Naiqama.
2019 season was even better for Saints, as they recorded
three defeats in the league and finally fulfilled their
ny in the 23-6 Old Trafford win over Salford Red Devils.

It was coach Holbrook's last game in charge before
ft for Australia to take up the challenge at perennial
glers Gold Coast Titans. It was one heck of a
to say farewell.

## Justin Holbrook
### St Helens

## John Bateman
## Canberra & Great Britain

There is always an air of uncertainty when a star player from Super League heads to test himself in the National Rugby League down under. Joh Bateman had been a Man of St nominee and Grand Final winne with Wigan in 2018 before he le to take up a three-year contrac with Canberra Raiders.

Bateman probably heade to the best NRL club he could, v Englishmen Josh Hodgson and Elliott Whitehead having alrea established themselves as top players there.

From his first game, 26-ye old Bateman marked himself down as something special. He stunned Aussie commentators in the Raiders' 21-0 win over Go Coast, running 155 metres, mak 36 tackles, 19 runs and five tack breaks in an 80-minute debut. Coach Ricky Stuart labelled hin world-class backrower after the game.

It was no flash in the pan. One thing we all knew was that Bateman never stops and by the end of the season he was recognised as the best in his position after being named Dal M second-rower of the year.

And Bateman played a m role as Canberra made their firs Grand Final since 1994. It was a close and controversial defeat the Roosters too.

Bateman was highly soug after as the stand-out player o his generation when he played at Bradford Dudley Hill, opting to sign for hometown Bulls, and made his debut as a 17-year-old against Catalans Dragons in rai swept Perpignan. At the end of the next season he won the Alb Goldthorpe Rookie of the Year.

He was transferred to Wig at the end of the 2013 season, where he won two Grand Finals and earned a reputation as one of the toughest players in the competition. He made his Engla debut in 2015, as man of the match, and scored two tries in a 88-4 rout of France. He's been a first-pick international ever sin Pound for pound there can be n tougher player in the world.

DACIA MAGIC WEEKEND

**ABOVE: Warrington's Daryl Clark takes on Wigan's George Williams and Morgan Smithies**

**LEFT: Catalans' Tony Gigot touches down against Wakefield**

**ABOVE: Huddersfield's Adam O'Brien celebrates scoring against Hull FC**

**ABOVE: Hull KR's Kane Linnett collared by Salford's Robert Lui and Niall Evalds**

**ABOVE: Castleford's Jake Trueman closes down St Helens' Kevin Naiqama**

**ABOVE: Leeds' Kallum Watkins surrounded by the London defence**

## SUPER LEAGUE AWARDS

**STEVE PRESCOTT MBE MAN OF STEEL**
Jackson Hastings (Salford Red Devils)

**YOUNG PLAYER OF THE YEAR**
Matty Lees (St Helens)

**COACH OF THE YEAR**
Justin Holbrook (St Helens)

**TOP TRY SCORER**
Tommy Makinson (St Helens) (23)

**TOP METRE MAKER**
Tommy Makinson (St Helens) (3,803)

**TOP TACKLER**
Danny Houghton (Hull FC) (1259)

*(totals include regular season only)*

**SUPER LEAGUE DREAM TEAM**
*(previous selections in italics)*

1. Lachlan Coote (St Helens) *Debut*
2. Tommy Makinson (St Helens) *2014, 2018*
3. Kevin Naiqama (St Helens) *Debut*
4. Konrad Hurrell (Leeds) *Debut*
5. Ash Handley (Leeds) *Debut*
6. Blake Austin (Warrington) *Debut*
7. Jackson Hastings (Salford) *Debut*
8. Liam Watts (Castleford) *Debut*
9. Daryl Clark (Warrington) *2014*
10. Luke Thompson (St Helens) *2018*
11. Josh Jones (Salford) *Debut*
12. Liam Farrell (Wigan) *2015*
13. Morgan Knowles (St Helens) *Debut*

**ALBERT GOLDTHORPE MEDAL**
Jonny Lomax (St Helens)

**ALBERT GOLDTHORPE ROOKIE OF THE YEAR**
Morgan Smithies (Wigan Warriors)

ABOVE: Peter Mata'utia cha[rges]
past Joe Philbin as Castlefor[d]
eliminate Warrington

LEFT: Thomas L[e]
tackled by
Logan Tomkins a[s]
Wigan progress p[ast]
Salford

RIGHT: Alex Walm[sley]
meets Wigan's
Sean O'Loughlin [as]
Zak Hardaker hea[ds]
as St Helens adva[nce]
to Old Trafford

Matty Lees *(above, Super League Young Player of the Year)*, Courtney Hill *(right, Woman of Steel)* and Jackson Hastings *(far right, Man of Steel)* show off their awards

# BETFRED SUPER LEAGUE
# PLAY-OFFS

**ABOVE:** Jackson Hastings celebrates with Salford fans following the Red Devils' memorable victory at Wigan

**BELOW:** George Griffin takes on Paul McShane as Salford end Castleford's season

Semi-final action as St Helens' James Roby kicks through against Halifax *(left)* and Warrington's Bryson Goodwin celebrates scoring against Hull FC *(right)*

# CORAL
## CHALLENGE CUP

ABOVE: Chris Hill and Jack Hughes lift the Challenge Cup

## CORAL CHALLENGE CUP

RIGHT: The Challenge Cup Final's most controversial moment as Morgan Knowles has a try claim ruled out by referee Robert Hicks

BELOW: Ben Murdoch-Masila crashes past Jonny Lomax for a try

LEFT: Daryl Clark show off the Lance Todd Trop and Challenge Cup

BETFRED ⚡ SUPER LEAGUE
# GRAND FINAL

SALFORD RED DEVILS..........................6
ST HELENS.............................................23

**ABOVE:** Tommy Makinson, Mark Percival and Luke Thompson hold aloft the Super League trophy

**LEFT:** Lachlan Coote looks to get the ball away as Kris Welham and Ken Sio attempt to halt his progress

**BELOW:** Jake Bibby heads for the St Helens tryline to score

# NRL TELSTRA PREMIERSHIP
# GRAND FINAL
## SYDNEY 2019

LEFT: The ANZ Stadium crowd looks on a
Joey Leilua skips past Boyd Cordner

ABOVE: James Tedesco looks to break free from the
challenge of John Bateman

LEFT: Roosters coach Trent Robinson, flanked by
Daniel Tupou and Brett Morris, receives a Gatorade show

Holden
STATE OF
ORIGIN

LEFT: New South
Wales celebrate
Origin victory

RIGHT:
Cameron Murray
beats Corey Norman
in Origin III

# BETFRED CHAMPIONSHIP

**TOP:** The champagne flows as Toronto Wolfpack celebrate Championship Grand Final victory, and promotion to Super League

**ABOVE:** Gadwin Springer brought down by Cameron King and John Davies

**BELOW:** Anthony Thackeray takes the 1895 Cup to his teammates after Sheffield's Wembley win against Widnes

**LEFT:** Eagles winger Ryan Millar halted by the Vikings defence

**BETFRED CHAMPIONSHIP**

**TOP:** Jack Johnson dives over for a try during Featherstone's Elimination Semi-Final triumph at York

**ABOVE:** Callum McLelland shows his delight at scoring in Featherstone's Elimination Play-off victory at Leigh

**ABOVE RIGHT:** Leigh's Martyn Ridyard in action against Widnes at the Summer Bash in Blackpool

**ABOVE:** Oldham celebrate earning the second promotion spot to the Championship

**BETFRED LEAGUE**

**BETFRED LEAGUE 1 CHAMPIONS**

**ABOVE:** A jubilant Whitehaven side celebrates

GREAT BRITAIN
RUGBY LEAGUE

**ABOVE:** Shaun Johnson gets an offload away under pressure from Jackson Hastings and Elliott Whitehead in the Second Test between the Kiwis and the Lions

**RIGHT:** Jermaine McGillvary can't ground the ball under the challenge of Kenny Bromwich during Great Britain's First Test defeat to New Zealand

**ABOVE:** Sione Katoa *(centre)* mobbed by Tonga Invitational teammates after scoring against the Lions

**ABOVE:** No way through the Papua New Guinea defence for Tom Burgess

ABOVE: Leeds Rhinos - Challenge Cup winners

BELOW: Caitlin Beevers beats Castleford's Kelsey Gentles to score in the Final

ABOVE: Castleford Tigers - Super League Leaders' Shield winners

BELOW: Courtney Hill and Lois Forsell celebrate after Leeds' Grand Final win against Castleford

WOMEN'S SUPER LEAGUE

BELOW: Fran Goldthorp crashes over for a try in the Super League Grand Final

# 6
# STATISTICAL REVIEW

# SUPER LEAGUE PLAYERS
## *1996-2019*

## *Super League Players 1996-2019*

| PLAYER | CLUB | YEAR | APP | TRIES | GOALS | FG | PTS |
|---|---|---|---|---|---|---|---|
| Jordan Abdull | London | 2019 | 25(2) | 10 | 1 | 0 | 42 |
|  | Hull | 2014-16, 2018 | 32(20) | 9 | 7 | 0 | 50 |
| Carl Ablett | Leeds | 2004, 2006-18 | 238(37) | 63 | 0 | 0 | 252 |
|  | London | 2005 | 3(2) | 0 | 0 | 0 | 0 |
| Darren Abram | Oldham | 1996-97 | 25(2) | 11 | 0 | 0 | 44 |
| Mitch Achurch | Leeds | 2013-16 | 25(50) | 14 | 0 | 0 | 56 |
| Jamie Acton | Leigh | 2017 | 11(4) | 4 | 0 | 0 | 16 |
| Brad Adams | Bradford | 2014 | 1(1) | 0 | 0 | 0 | 0 |
| Darren Adams | Paris | 1996 | 9(1) | 1 | 0 | 0 | 4 |
| Guy Adams | Huddersfield | 1998 | 1(2) | 0 | 0 | 0 | 0 |
| Luke Adamson | Salford | 2006-07, 2009-12 | 73(39) | 11 | 1 | 0 | 46 |
| Matt Adamson | Leeds | 2002-04 | 54(8) | 9 | 0 | 0 | 36 |
| Phil Adamson | St Helens | 1999 | (1) | 0 | 0 | 0 | 0 |
| Toby Adamson | Salford | 2010 | (1) | 0 | 0 | 0 | 0 |
| Danny Addy | Hull KR | 2019 | 9(10) | 2 | 0 | 0 | 8 |
|  | Bradford | 2010-14 | 49(42) | 13 | 7 | 0 | 66 |
| Ade Adebisi | London | 2004 | (1) | 0 | 0 | 0 | 0 |
| Sadiq Adebiyi | London | 2019 | 6(7) | 3 | 0 | 0 | 12 |
| Patrick Ah Van | Widnes | 2012-18 | 99 | 73 | 56 | 0 | 404 |
|  | Bradford | 2011 | 26 | 9 | 87 | 0 | 210 |
| Jamie Ainscough | Wigan | 2002-03 | 30(2) | 18 | 0 | 0 | 72 |
| Shaun Ainscough | Bradford | 2011-12 | 27 | 15 | 0 | 0 | 60 |
|  | Wigan | 2009-10 | 12 | 13 | 0 | 0 | 52 |
|  | Castleford | 2010 | 7 | 4 | 0 | 0 | 16 |
| Glen Air | London | 1998-2001 | 57(13) | 27 | 0 | 1 | 109 |
| Paul Aiton | Catalans | 2016-18 | 30(11) | 3 | 0 | 0 | 12 |
|  | Leeds | 2014-15 | 36(6) | 2 | 0 | 0 | 8 |
|  | Wakefield | 2012-13 | 43(2) | 7 | 0 | 0 | 28 |
| Makali Aizue | Hull KR | 2007-09 | 18(32) | 4 | 0 | 0 | 16 |
| Sitaleki Akauola | Warrington | 2018-19 | 8(29) | 5 | 0 | 0 | 20 |
| Darren Albert | St Helens | 2002-05 | 105 | 77 | 0 | 0 | 308 |
| Lucas Albert | Catalans | 2015-19 | 34(10) | 7 | 23 | 0 | 74 |
| Wellington Albert | Leeds | 2019 | 2(2) | 0 | 0 | 0 | 0 |
|  | Widnes | 2018 | (11) | 2 | 0 | 0 | 8 |
| Paul Alcock | Widnes | 2003, 2005 | 1(7) | 1 | 0 | 0 | 4 |
| Neil Alexander | Salford | 1998 | (1) | 0 | 0 | 0 | 0 |
| Malcolm Alker | Salford | 1997-2002, 2004-07, 2009-10 | 271(2) | 40 | 0 | 1 | 161 |
| Danny Allan | Leeds | 2008-09 | 2(5) | 0 | 0 | 0 | 0 |
| Chris Allen | Castleford | 1996 | (1) | 0 | 0 | 0 | 0 |
| Dave Allen | Widnes | 2012-14 | 50(13) | 5 | 0 | 0 | 20 |
|  | Wigan | 2003, 2005 | 6(15) | 2 | 0 | 0 | 8 |
| Gavin Allen | London | 1996 | 10 | 0 | 0 | 0 | 0 |
| John Allen | Workington | 1996 | 20(1) | 6 | 0 | 0 | 24 |
| Ray Allen | London | 1996 | 5(3) | 3 | 0 | 0 | 12 |
| Mitch Allgood | Wakefield | 2017 | 6(2) | 0 | 0 | 0 | 0 |
|  | Hull KR | 2015-16 | 27(2) | 5 | 0 | 0 | 20 |
| Richard Allwood | Gateshead | 1999 | (4) | 0 | 0 | 0 | 0 |
| Sean Allwood | Gateshead | 1999 | 3(17) | 1 | 0 | 0 | 4 |
| David Alstead | Warrington | 2000-02 | 23(10) | 3 | 0 | 0 | 12 |
| Luke Ambler | Harlequins | 2011 | 5(17) | 1 | 0 | 0 | 4 |
|  | Leeds | 2010 | 1(8) | 1 | 0 | 0 | 4 |
| Asa Amone | Halifax | 1996-97 | 32(7) | 10 | 0 | 0 | 40 |
| Kyle Amor | St Helens | 2014-19 | 100(53) | 17 | 0 | 0 | 68 |
|  | Wakefield | 2011-13 | 51(23) | 9 | 0 | 0 | 36 |
|  | Leeds | 2010 | (3) | 0 | 0 | 0 | 0 |
| Thibaut Ancely | Catalans | 2011 | (2) | 0 | 0 | 0 | 0 |
| Grant Anderson | Castleford | 1996-97 | 15(6) | 3 | 0 | 0 | 12 |
| Louis Anderson | Catalans | 2012-18 | 86(41) | 32 | 0 | 0 | 128 |
|  | Warrington | 2008-11 | 92 | 18 | 0 | 0 | 72 |
| Paul Anderson | St Helens | 2005-06 | 48(5) | 7 | 1 | 0 | 30 |
|  | Bradford | 1997-2004 | 74(104) | 30 | 0 | 0 | 120 |
|  | Halifax | 1996 | 5(1) | 1 | 0 | 0 | 4 |
| Paul Anderson | Sheffield | 1999 | 3(7) | 1 | 0 | 0 | 4 |
|  | St Helens | 1996-98 | 2(28) | 4 | 1 | 0 | 18 |
| Scott Anderson | Wakefield | 2014-16 | 25(18) | 2 | 0 | 0 | 8 |
| Vinnie Anderson | Salford | 2011-12 | 33(3) | 14 | 0 | 0 | 56 |
|  | Warrington | 2007-10 | 57(19) | 22 | 0 | 0 | 88 |
|  | St Helens | 2005-06 | 28(14) | 17 | 0 | 0 | 68 |
| Phil Anderton | St Helens | 2004 | 1 | 0 | 0 | 0 | 0 |
| Chris Annakin | Wakefield | 2013-19 | 7(62) | 1 | 0 | 0 | 4 |
| Eric Anselme | Leeds | 2008 | 2(2) | 2 | 0 | 0 | 8 |
|  | Halifax | 1997 | (2) | 0 | 0 | 0 | 0 |
| Mark Applegarth | Wakefield | 2004-07 | 20(5) | 3 | 0 | 0 | 12 |
| Graham Appo | Warrington | 2002-05 | 60(13) | 35 | 80 | 0 | 300 |
|  | Huddersfield | 2001 | 7 | 4 | 0 | 0 | 16 |
| Guy Armitage | London | 2019 | (2) | 0 | 0 | 0 | 0 |
| Anthony Armour | London | 2005 | 11(7) | 1 | 0 | 0 | 4 |
| Colin Armstrong | Workington | 1996 | 11(2) | 1 | 0 | 0 | 4 |
| Tom Armstrong | Widnes | 2017 | 11 | 1 | 0 | 0 | 4 |
|  | St Helens | 2009-11 | 10(5) | 9 | 0 | 0 | 36 |
| Richard Armswood | Workington | 1996 | 5(1) | 1 | 0 | 0 | 4 |
| Danny Arnold | Salford | 2001-02 | 26(13) | 13 | 0 | 0 | 52 |
|  | Huddersfield | 1998-2000 | 55(7) | 26 | 0 | 0 | 104 |
|  | Castleford | 2000 | (4) | 0 | 0 | 0 | 0 |
|  | St Helens | 1996-97 | 40(1) | 33 | 0 | 0 | 132 |
| Tinirau Arona | Wakefield | 2016-19 | 63(36) | 5 | 0 | 0 | 20 |
| Joe Arundel | Wakefield | 2015-19 | 71(9) | 20 | 4 | 0 | 88 |
|  | Bradford | 2014 | 9(3) | 5 | 0 | 0 | 20 |
|  | Hull | 2013-14 | 16 | 7 | 1 | 0 | 30 |
|  | Castleford | 2008, 2010-12 | 35(4) | 14 | 2 | 0 | 60 |
| Craig Ashall | St Helens | 2006 | 1 | 1 | 0 | 0 | 4 |
| Olly Ashall-Bott | Widnes | 2018 | 5 | 1 | 0 | 0 | 4 |
| Nathan Ashe | St Helens | 2011-13 | 6(4) | 0 | 0 | 0 | 0 |
| Chris Ashton | Wigan | 2005-07 | 44(2) | 25 | 2 | 0 | 104 |
| Matty Ashurst | Wakefield | 2015-19 | 96(3) | 15 | 0 | 0 | 60 |
|  | Salford | 2012-14 | 65(7) | 11 | 0 | 0 | 44 |
|  | St Helens | 2009-11 | 12(39) | 8 | 0 | 0 | 32 |
| Jack Ashworth | St Helens | 2015-16, 2018-19 | 6(33) | 4 | 0 | 0 | 16 |
| Roy Asotasi | Warrington | 2014-15 | 16(37) | 5 | 1 | 0 | 22 |
| Peter Aspinall | Huddersfield | 2013 | 1(1) | 0 | 0 | 0 | 0 |
| Martin Aspinwall | Hull | 2012 | 12(15) | 0 | 0 | 0 | 0 |
|  | Castleford | 2011 | 12(6) | 2 | 0 | 0 | 8 |
|  | Huddersfield | 2006-10 | 72(8) | 22 | 0 | 0 | 88 |
|  | Wigan | 2001-05 | 85(13) | 27 | 0 | 0 | 108 |
| Cory Aston | Castleford | 2019 | 8 | 3 | 0 | 0 | 12 |
| Mark Aston | Sheffield | 1996-99 | 67(6) | 6 | 243 | 6 | 516 |
| Paul Atcheson | Widnes | 2002-04 | 16(35) | 4 | 0 | 0 | 16 |
|  | St Helens | 1998-2000 | 58(4) | 18 | 0 | 0 | 72 |
|  | Oldham | 1996-97 | 40 | 21 | 0 | 0 | 84 |
| Chris Atkin | Hull KR | 2018-19 | 28(20) | 7 | 1 | 3 | 33 |
| David Atkins | Huddersfield | 2001 | 26(1) | 4 | 0 | 0 | 16 |
| Jordan Atkins | London | 2014 | 13(1) | 4 | 0 | 0 | 16 |
| Ryan Atkins | Wakefield | 2006-09, 2019 | 87(2) | 45 | 0 | 0 | 180 |
|  | Warrington | 2010-19 | 235(2) | 139 | 0 | 0 | 556 |
| Josh Atkinson | Castleford | 2012 | 2 | 0 | 0 | 0 | 0 |
| Brad Attwood | Halifax | 2003 | (3) | 0 | 0 | 0 | 0 |
| Blake Austin | Warrington | 2019 | 27 | 18 | 0 | 1 | 73 |
| Warren Ayres | Salford | 1999 | 2(9) | 1 | 2 | 0 | 8 |
| Jerome Azema | Paris | 1997 | (1) | 0 | 0 | 0 | 0 |
| Marcus Bai | Bradford | 2006 | 24 | 9 | 0 | 0 | 36 |
|  | Leeds | 2004-05 | 57 | 42 | 0 | 0 | 168 |
| David Baildon | Hull | 1998-99 | 26(2) | 4 | 0 | 0 | 16 |
| Jean-Philippe Baile | Catalans | 2008-14 | 62(16) | 23 | 0 | 0 | 92 |
| Andy Bailey | Hull | 2004-05 | 2(8) | 1 | 0 | 0 | 4 |
| Chris Bailey | Huddersfield | 2014-15 | 17(17) | 5 | 0 | 0 | 20 |
|  | London | 2012-13 | 41 | 14 | 0 | 0 | 56 |
|  | Harlequins | 2011 | 24 | 3 | 0 | 0 | 12 |
| Julian Bailey | Huddersfield | 2003-04 | 47 | 13 | 0 | 0 | 52 |
| Phil Bailey | Wigan | 2007-10 | 84(4) | 13 | 0 | 0 | 52 |
| Ricky Bailey | St Helens | 2015, 2017 | 2 | 0 | 0 | 0 | 0 |
| Ryan Bailey | Warrington | 2016 | 1(11) | 0 | 0 | 0 | 0 |
|  | Castleford | 2015 | 3(2) | 0 | 0 | 0 | 0 |
|  | Hull KR | 2015 | (1) | 1 | 0 | 0 | 4 |
|  | Leeds | 2002-14 | 171(102) | 17 | 0 | 0 | 68 |
| Jason Baitieri | Catalans | 2011-19 | 135(65) | 19 | 0 | 0 | 76 |
| Simon Baldwin | Salford | 2004-09 | 20(29) | 3 | 0 | 0 | 12 |
|  | Sheffield | 1999 | 7(15) | 2 | 0 | 0 | 8 |
|  | Halifax | 1996-98 | 41(15) | 16 | 0 | 1 | 65 |
| Jordan Baldwinson | Wakefield | 2018 | (4) | 0 | 0 | 0 | 0 |
|  | Leeds | 2013, 2016-17 | 4(9) | 1 | 0 | 0 | 4 |
|  | Bradford | 2014 | 2(4) | 0 | 0 | 0 | 0 |
| Rob Ball | Wigan | 1998-2000 | 3(4) | 0 | 0 | 0 | 0 |
| Paul Ballard | Celtic | 2009 | 2 | 0 | 0 | 0 | 0 |
|  | Widnes | 2005 | 3(1) | 2 | 0 | 0 | 8 |
| Darren Bamford | Salford | 2005 | 2(1) | 0 | 0 | 0 | 0 |
| Michael Banks | Bradford | 1998 | (1) | 0 | 0 | 0 | 0 |
| Steve Bannister | Harlequins | 2007 | (6) | 0 | 0 | 0 | 0 |
|  | St Helens | 2006-07 | (3) | 0 | 0 | 0 | 0 |
| Frederic Banquet | Paris | 1996 | 16(2) | 7 | 4 | 0 | 36 |
| Ben Barba | St Helens | 2017-18 | 31 | 31 | 0 | 0 | 124 |
| Lee Bardauskas | Castleford | 1996-97 | (2) | 0 | 0 | 0 | 0 |
| Harry Bardle | Hull KR | 2019 | (1) | 0 | 0 | 0 | 0 |
| Craig Barker | Workington | 1996 | (2) | 0 | 0 | 0 | 0 |
| Dwayne Barker | Harlequins | 2008 | 5(5) | 1 | 0 | 0 | 4 |
|  | London | 2004 | 3 | 1 | 0 | 0 | 4 |
|  | Hull | 2003 | (1) | 0 | 0 | 0 | 0 |
| Mark Barlow | Wakefield | 2002 | (1) | 0 | 0 | 0 | 0 |
| Danny Barnes | Halifax | 1999 | 2 | 0 | 0 | 0 | 0 |
| Richie Barnett | Salford | 2007 | 7 | 4 | 0 | 0 | 16 |
|  | Warrington | 2006-07 | 26(10) | 15 | 0 | 0 | 60 |
|  | Hull | 2004-05 | 21(5) | 21 | 0 | 0 | 84 |
|  | Widnes | 2005 | 4 | 2 | 0 | 0 | 8 |
| Richie Barnett | Hull | 2003-04 | 31(1) | 17 | 0 | 0 | 68 |
|  | London | 2001-02 | 31(4) | 13 | 0 | 0 | 52 |

164

| PLAYER | CLUB | YEAR | APP | TRIES | GOALS | FG | PTS |
|---|---|---|---|---|---|---|---|
| David Barnhill | Leeds | 2000 | 20(8) | 5 | 0 | 0 | 20 |
| Trent Barrett | Wigan | 2007-08 | 53(1) | 22 | 0 | 4 | 92 |
| Paul Barrow | Warrington | 1996-97 | 1(10) | 1 | 0 | 0 | 4 |
| Scott Barrow | St Helens | 1997-2000 | 9(13) | 1 | 0 | 0 | 4 |
| Steve Barrow | London | 2000 | 2 | 0 | 0 | 0 | 0 |
|  | Hull | 1998-99 | 4(17) | 1 | 0 | 0 | 4 |
|  | Wigan | 1996 | (8) | 3 | 0 | 0 | 12 |
| William Barthau | Catalans | 2010, 2012-14 | 13(3) | 2 | 15 | 0 | 38 |
| Ben Barton | Huddersfield | 1998 | 1(6) | 1 | 0 | 0 | 4 |
| Danny Barton | Salford | 2001 | 1 | 0 | 0 | 0 | 0 |
| Wayne Bartrim | Castleford | 2002-03 | 41(2) | 9 | 157 | 0 | 350 |
| Greg Barwick | London | 1996-97 | 30(4) | 21 | 110 | 2 | 306 |
| David Bastian | Halifax | 1996 | (2) | 0 | 0 | 0 | 0 |
| James Batchelor | Wakefield | 2016-19 | 26(13) | 6 | 13 | 0 | 50 |
| Joe Batchelor | St Helens | 2019 | 2(2) | 0 | 0 | 0 | 0 |
| Ashley Bateman | Celtic | 2009 | 1 | 0 | 0 | 0 | 0 |
| John Bateman | Wigan | 2014-18 | 110(8) | 31 | 0 | 0 | 124 |
|  | Bradford | 2011-13 | 25(5) | 7 | 0 | 0 | 28 |
| David Bates | Castleford | 2001-02 | (4) | 0 | 0 | 0 | 0 |
|  | Warrington | 2001 | 1(2) | 0 | 0 | 0 | 0 |
| Sam Bates | Bradford | 2014 | (2) | 0 | 0 | 0 | 0 |
| Nathan Batty | Wakefield | 2001 | 1(1) | 0 | 0 | 0 | 0 |
| Eddie Battye | London | 2019 | 19(10) | 3 | 0 | 0 | 12 |
| Andreas Bauer | Hull KR | 2007 | 10(2) | 5 | 0 | 0 | 20 |
| Russell Bawden | London | 1996-97, 2002-04 | 50(49) | 15 | 0 | 0 | 60 |
| Neil Baxter | Salford | 2001 | 1 | 0 | 0 | 0 | 0 |
| Neil Baynes | Salford | 1999-2002, 2004 | 84(19) | 10 | 0 | 0 | 40 |
|  | Wigan | 1996-98 | (10) | 1 | 0 | 0 | 4 |
| Chris Beasley | Celtic | 2009 | 15(5) | 2 | 0 | 0 | 8 |
| Chris Beattie | Catalans | 2006 | 22(5) | 3 | 0 | 0 | 12 |
| Richard Beaumont | Hull KR | 2011-13 | 1(16) | 1 | 0 | 0 | 4 |
| Robbie Beazley | London | 1997-99 | 48(15) | 13 | 0 | 0 | 52 |
| Robbie Beckett | Halifax | 2002 | 27 | 15 | 0 | 0 | 60 |
| Matty Beharrell | Hull KR | 2013 | 1 | 0 | 0 | 0 | 0 |
| Dean Bell | Leeds | 1996 | 1 | 1 | 0 | 0 | 4 |
| Ian Bell | Hull | 2003 | (1) | 0 | 0 | 0 | 0 |
| Mark Bell | Wigan | 1998 | 22 | 12 | 0 | 0 | 48 |
| Paul Bell | Leeds | 2000 | 1 | 0 | 0 | 0 | 0 |
| Steven Bell | Catalans | 2009-10 | 43 | 14 | 0 | 0 | 56 |
| Troy Bellamy | Paris | 1997 | 5(10) | 0 | 0 | 0 | 0 |
| Adrian Belle | Huddersfield | 1998 | 10(2) | 0 | 0 | 0 | 0 |
|  | Oldham | 1996 | 19 | 8 | 0 | 0 | 32 |
| Lambert Belmas | Catalans | 2017-19 | 3(10) | 0 | 0 | 0 | 0 |
| Jamie Benn | Castleford | 1998, 2000 | 3(8) | 1 | 15 | 0 | 34 |
| Andy Bennett | Warrington | 1996 | 6(5) | 1 | 0 | 0 | 4 |
| Mike Bennett | St Helens | 2000-08 | 74(70) | 15 | 0 | 0 | 60 |
| Gavin Bennion | Salford | 2018 | 1(1) | 0 | 0 | 0 | 0 |
| Andrew Bentley | Catalans | 2007-10 | 9(15) | 1 | 0 | 0 | 4 |
| James Bentley | St Helens | 2018-19 | 7(12) | 2 | 0 | 0 | 8 |
| John Bentley | Huddersfield | 1999 | 13(4) | 3 | 0 | 0 | 12 |
|  | Halifax | 1996, 1998 | 22(3) | 24 | 0 | 0 | 96 |
| Kane Bentley | Catalans | 2007-10 | 11(19) | 5 | 0 | 0 | 20 |
| Phil Bergman | Paris | 1997 | 20(1) | 14 | 0 | 0 | 56 |
| Shaun Berrigan | Hull | 2008-10 | 60(8) | 12 | 0 | 0 | 48 |
| Joe Berry | Huddersfield | 1998-99 | 25(14) | 3 | 0 | 0 | 12 |
| David Berthezene | Salford | 2007 | 9(1) | 0 | 0 | 0 | 0 |
|  | Catalans | 2006-07 | 5(14) | 0 | 0 | 0 | 0 |
| Colin Best | Hull | 2003-04 | 57 | 34 | 0 | 0 | 136 |
| Roger Best | London | 1997-98 | 1(5) | 1 | 0 | 0 | 4 |
| Bob Beswick | Wigan | 2004-05 | 5(14) | 2 | 0 | 0 | 8 |
| Monty Betham | Wakefield | 2006 | 26 | 2 | 0 | 0 | 8 |
| Mike Bethwaite | Workington | 1996 | 17(3) | 1 | 0 | 0 | 4 |
| Denis Betts | Wigan | 1998-2001 | 82(24) | 33 | 0 | 0 | 132 |
| Cliff Beverley | Salford | 2004-05 | 47(1) | 14 | 0 | 0 | 56 |
| Kyle Bibb | Wakefield | 2008-10 | 1(24) | 0 | 0 | 0 | 0 |
|  | Harlequins | 2010 | (2) | 0 | 0 | 0 | 0 |
|  | Hull KR | 2009 | (2) | 0 | 0 | 0 | 0 |
| Jake Bibby | Salford | 2016-19 | 65(1) | 32 | 0 | 0 | 128 |
| Adam Bibey | Widnes | 2004 | (1) | 0 | 0 | 0 | 0 |
| Ricky Bibey | Wakefield | 2007-09 | 32(25) | 1 | 0 | 0 | 4 |
|  | St Helens | 2004 | 4(14) | 0 | 0 | 0 | 0 |
|  | Wigan | 2001-03 | 5(29) | 0 | 0 | 0 | 0 |
| Lewis Bienek | Hull | 2018 | (7) | 0 | 0 | 0 | 0 |
| Chris Birchall | Halifax | 2002-03 | 24(22) | 4 | 0 | 0 | 16 |
|  | Bradford | 2000 | (1) | 0 | 0 | 0 | 0 |
| Deon Bird | Castleford | 2006 | 17(6) | 5 | 0 | 0 | 20 |
|  | Widnes | 2003-04 | 39(6) | 9 | 0 | 0 | 36 |
|  | Wakefield | 2002 | 10(1) | 1 | 0 | 0 | 4 |
|  | Hull | 2000-02 | 37(22) | 20 | 0 | 0 | 80 |
|  | Gateshead | 1999 | 19(3) | 13 | 0 | 0 | 52 |
|  | Paris | 1996-97 | 30 | 12 | 2 | 0 | 52 |
| Greg Bird | Catalans | 2009, 2017-19 | 68(6) | 11 | 3 | 0 | 50 |
| Mike Bishay | London | 2013-14 | 7(11) | 2 | 2 | 0 | 12 |
| Nathan Blacklock | Hull | 2005-06 | 44(3) | 33 | 0 | 0 | 132 |
| Ben Blackmore | Huddersfield | 2013-14 | 3 | 4 | 0 | 0 | 16 |
|  | Castleford | 2012 | 1 | 0 | 0 | 0 | 0 |
| Richie Blackmore | Leeds | 1997-2000 | 63 | 25 | 0 | 0 | 100 |
| Anthony Blackwood |  |  |  |  |  |  |  |
|  | Crusaders | 2010 | 1 | 0 | 0 | 0 | 0 |
|  | Celtic | 2009 | 25 | 5 | 0 | 0 | 20 |
| Jack Blagbrough | Huddersfield | 2013 | (1) | 0 | 0 | 0 | 0 |
| Cheyse Blair | Castleford | 2019 | 17 | 2 | 0 | 0 | 8 |
| Maurice Blair | Hull KR | 2015-16, 2018 | 62(3) | 10 | 1 | 0 | 42 |
| Luke Blake | Wakefield | 2009 | (2) | 0 | 0 | 0 | 0 |
| Matthew Blake | Wakefield | 2003-04 | 1(5) | 0 | 0 | 0 | 0 |
| Steve Blakeley | Salford | 1997-2002 | 103(5) | 26 | 241 | 2 | 588 |
|  | Warrington | 2000 | 4(3) | 1 | 9 | 0 | 22 |
| Richard Blakeway | Castleford | 2002-04 | 1(14) | 0 | 0 | 0 | 0 |
| Damien Blanch | Catalans | 2011-13 | 70 | 42 | 0 | 0 | 168 |
|  | Wakefield | 2008-10 | 44(3) | 31 | 0 | 0 | 124 |
|  | Castleford | 2006 | 3(2) | 0 | 0 | 0 | 0 |
| Matt Blaymire | Wakefield | 2007-11 | 96(3) | 26 | 0 | 1 | 105 |
| Ian Blease | Salford | 1997 | (1) | 0 | 0 | 0 | 0 |
| Jamie Bloem | Huddersfield | 2003 | 18(4) | 3 | 11 | 0 | 34 |
|  | Halifax | 1998-2002 | 82(25) | 25 | 100 | 2 | 302 |
| Vea Bloomfield | Paris | 1996 | 4(15) | 3 | 0 | 0 | 12 |
| Matty Blythe | Warrington | 2007-12, 2017 | 30(28) | 12 | 0 | 0 | 48 |
|  | Bradford | 2013-14 | 24(6) | 8 | 0 | 0 | 32 |
| Ben Bolger | London | 2012 | 2(7) | 1 | 0 | 0 | 4 |
|  | Harlequins | 2010-11 | 4(15) | 0 | 0 | 0 | 0 |
| Pascal Bomati | Paris | 1996 | 17(1) | 10 | 0 | 0 | 40 |
| Simon Booth | Hull | 1998-99 | 15(9) | 2 | 0 | 0 | 8 |
|  | St Helens | 1996-97 | 10(4) | 1 | 0 | 0 | 4 |
| Steve Booth | Huddersfield | 1998-99 | 16(4) | 2 | 3 | 0 | 14 |
| Alan Boothroyd | Halifax | 1997 | 2(3) | 0 | 0 | 0 | 0 |
| Thomas Bosc | Catalans | 2006-17 | 199(21) | 48 | 483 | 12 | 1170 |
| John Boslem | Paris | 1996 | (5) | 0 | 0 | 0 | 0 |
| Liam Bostock | St Helens | 2004 | 1 | 0 | 0 | 0 | 0 |
| Liam Botham | Wigan | 2005 | 5 | 0 | 0 | 0 | 0 |
|  | Leeds | 2003-05 | 2(11) | 4 | 0 | 0 | 16 |
|  | London | 2004 | 6(2) | 3 | 7 | 0 | 26 |
| Frano Botica | Castleford | 1996 | 21 | 5 | 84 | 2 | 190 |
| Matthew Bottom | Leigh | 2005 | (1) | 0 | 0 | 0 | 0 |
| Hadj Boudebza | Paris | 1996 | (2) | 0 | 0 | 0 | 0 |
| John Boudebza | Hull KR | 2015-16 | 13(17) | 2 | 0 | 0 | 8 |
| David Boughton | Huddersfield | 1999 | 26(1) | 4 | 0 | 0 | 16 |
| Amir Bourouh | Wigan | 2019 | (2) | 0 | 0 | 0 | 0 |
| Julian Bousquet | Catalans | 2012-19 | 56(104) | 15 | 0 | 0 | 60 |
| David Bouveng | Halifax | 1997-99 | 66(2) | 19 | 0 | 0 | 76 |
| Josh Bowden | Hull | 2012-19 | 53(80) | 11 | 0 | 0 | 44 |
| Matt Bowen | Wigan | 2014-15 | 43 | 21 | 31 | 0 | 146 |
| Tony Bowes | Huddersfield | 1998 | 3(2) | 0 | 0 | 0 | 0 |
| Radney Bowker | London | 2004 | 3 | 1 | 0 | 0 | 4 |
|  | St Helens | 2001 | (1) | 0 | 0 | 0 | 0 |
| David Boyle | Bradford | 1999-2000 | 36(13) | 15 | 0 | 1 | 61 |
| Ryan Boyle | Castleford | 2006, 2008-09, 2013-16 | 12(60) | 5 | 0 | 0 | 20 |
|  | Salford | 2010-13 | 57(14) | 3 | 0 | 0 | 12 |
| Andy Bracek | Crusaders | 2011 | (2) | 0 | 0 | 0 | 0 |
|  | Warrington | 2005-08 | 7(49) | 7 | 0 | 0 | 28 |
|  | St Helens | 2004 | (2) | 0 | 0 | 0 | 0 |
| David Bradbury | Hudds-Sheff | 2000 | 2(2) | 1 | 0 | 0 | 4 |
|  | Salford | 1997-99 | 23(10) | 6 | 0 | 0 | 24 |
|  | Oldham | 1996-97 | 19(6) | 9 | 0 | 0 | 36 |
| John Braddish | St Helens | 2001-02 | 1(1) | 0 | 3 | 0 | 6 |
| Graeme Bradley | Bradford | 1996-98 | 62(1) | 29 | 0 | 0 | 116 |
| Nick Bradley-Qalilawa |  |  |  |  |  |  |  |
|  | Harlequins | 2006 | 27 | 6 | 0 | 0 | 24 |
|  | London | 2005 | 28 | 19 | 0 | 0 | 76 |
| Darren Bradstreet | London | 1999-2000 | 1(3) | 0 | 0 | 0 | 0 |
| Dom Brambani | Castleford | 2004 | 2(2) | 0 | 0 | 0 | 0 |
| Keanan Brand | Widnes | 2018 | 1 | 0 | 0 | 0 | 0 |
| Joe Bretherton | Wigan | 2016-17 | 2(13) | 1 | 0 | 0 | 0 |
| Liam Bretherton | Wigan | 1999 | (5) | 2 | 0 | 0 | 8 |
|  | Warrington | 1997 | (2) | 0 | 0 | 0 | 0 |
| Johnny Brewer | Halifax | 1996 | 4(2) | 2 | 0 | 0 | 8 |
| Chris Bridge | Widnes | 2016-17 | 28(1) | 4 | 11 | 0 | 38 |
|  | Warrington | 2005-15 | 186(17) | 89 | 248 | 1 | 853 |
|  | Bradford | 2003-04 | 2(14) | 4 | 6 | 0 | 28 |
| Danny Bridge | Bradford | 2014 | 4(4) | 0 | 0 | 0 | 0 |
|  | Warrington | 2013 | (2) | 0 | 0 | 0 | 0 |
| Ryan Brierley | Huddersfield | 2016-17 | 19(1) | 6 | 2 | 0 | 28 |
| Lee Briers | Warrington | 1997-2013 | 365(12) | 130 | 810 | 70 | 2210 |
|  | St Helens | 1997 | 3 | 0 | 11 | 0 | 22 |
| Carl Briggs | Salford | 1999 | 8(5) | 3 | 0 | 1 | 13 |
|  | Halifax | 1996 | 5(3) | 1 | 0 | 0 | 4 |
| Kyle Briggs | Bradford | 2011 | 6 | 4 | 0 | 0 | 16 |
|  | Harlequins | 2011 | 3 | 0 | 0 | 0 | 0 |

# Super League Players 1996-2019

| PLAYER | CLUB | YEAR | APP | TRIES | GOALS | FG | PTS |
|---|---|---|---|---|---|---|---|
| Mike Briggs | Widnes | 2002 | 1(2) | 1 | 0 | 0 | 4 |
| Kriss Brining | Salford | 2017 | 2(20) | 4 | 0 | 0 | 16 |
| Luke Briscoe | Leeds | 2014, 2016, 2018-19 | 15(4) | 8 | 0 | 0 | 32 |
| | Wakefield | 2014 | 2 | 0 | 0 | 0 | 0 |
| Shaun Briscoe | Widnes | 2012-13 | 11(2) | 4 | 0 | 0 | 16 |
| | Hull KR | 2008-11 | 92 | 27 | 0 | 0 | 108 |
| | Hull | 2004-07 | 83(9) | 50 | 0 | 0 | 200 |
| | Wigan | 2002-03 | 23(5) | 11 | 0 | 0 | 44 |
| Tom Briscoe | Leeds | 2014-19 | 124 | 53 | 0 | 0 | 212 |
| | Hull | 2008-13 | 131(3) | 83 | 0 | 0 | 332 |
| Darren Britt | St Helens | 2002-03 | 41 | 3 | 0 | 0 | 12 |
| Gary Broadbent | Salford | 1997-2002 | 117(2) | 22 | 0 | 0 | 88 |
| Paul Broadbent | Wakefield | 2002 | 16(5) | 0 | 0 | 0 | 0 |
| | Hull | 2000-01 | 40(9) | 3 | 0 | 0 | 12 |
| | Halifax | 1999 | 26(1) | 2 | 0 | 0 | 8 |
| | Sheffield | 1996-98 | 63(1) | 6 | 0 | 0 | 24 |
| Robin Brochon | Catalans | 2018-19 | 2 | 0 | 0 | 0 | 0 |
| Andrew Brocklehurst | | | | | | | |
| | Salford | 2004-07 | 34(23) | 5 | 0 | 0 | 20 |
| | London | 2004 | 12(6) | 2 | 0 | 0 | 8 |
| | Halifax | 2001-03 | 37(8) | 2 | 0 | 0 | 8 |
| Justin Brooker | Wakefield | 2001 | 25 | 9 | 0 | 0 | 36 |
| | Bradford | 2000 | 17(4) | 11 | 0 | 0 | 44 |
| Sam Brooks | Widnes | 2016-17 | 1(3) | 1 | 0 | 0 | 4 |
| Danny Brough | Wakefield | 2008-10, 2019 | 73(1) | 16 | 246 | 9 | 565 |
| | Huddersfield | 2010-18 | 220(4) | 45 | 721 | 20 | 1642 |
| | Castleford | 2006 | 10 | 1 | 31 | 2 | 68 |
| | Hull | 2005-06 | 25(12) | 3 | 85 | 1 | 183 |
| Jodie Broughton | Catalans | 2016-19 | 48 | 34 | 0 | 0 | 136 |
| | Huddersfield | 2014-15 | 30 | 16 | 0 | 0 | 64 |
| | Salford | 2010-13 | 93 | 53 | 0 | 0 | 212 |
| | Hull | 2008-09 | 9(3) | 6 | 0 | 0 | 24 |
| Alex Brown | Hull KR | 2013 | 16 | 9 | 0 | 0 | 36 |
| | Huddersfield | 2009 | 1 | 0 | 0 | 0 | 0 |
| Darren Brown | Salford | 1999-2001 | 47(9) | 11 | 6 | 0 | 56 |
| Gavin Brown | Leeds | 1996-97 | 5(2) | 1 | 2 | 0 | 8 |
| Jack Brown | Hull | 2019 | (2) | 1 | 0 | 0 | 4 |
| Kevin Brown | Warrington | 2017-18 | 41(1) | 9 | 0 | 0 | 36 |
| | Widnes | 2013-16 | 80 | 37 | 1 | 1 | 151 |
| | Huddersfield | 2006-12 | 156 | 43 | 0 | 1 | 173 |
| | Wigan | 2003-06 | 46(18) | 27 | 0 | 0 | 108 |
| Lee Brown | Hull | 1999 | (1) | 0 | 0 | 0 | 0 |
| Michael Brown | Huddersfield | 2008 | (1) | 0 | 0 | 0 | 0 |
| Michael Brown | London | 1996 | (2) | 0 | 0 | 0 | 0 |
| Mitch Brown | Warrington | 2018 | 10(1) | 2 | 0 | 0 | 8 |
| | Leigh | 2017 | 21 | 4 | 0 | 0 | 16 |
| Todd Brown | Paris | 1996 | 8(1) | 2 | 0 | 0 | 8 |
| Adrian Brunker | Wakefield | 1999 | 17 | 6 | 0 | 0 | 24 |
| Lamont Bryan | Harlequins | 2008-11 | 9(22) | 2 | 0 | 0 | 8 |
| Justin Bryant | Paris | 1996 | 4(1) | 0 | 0 | 0 | 0 |
| | London | 1996 | 7(8) | 1 | 0 | 0 | 4 |
| Mark Bryant | London | 2012-13 | 16(36) | 3 | 1 | 0 | 14 |
| | Crusaders | 2010-11 | 42(8) | 1 | 0 | 0 | 4 |
| | Celtic | 2009 | 23(3) | 0 | 0 | 0 | 0 |
| Austin Buchanan | Wakefield | 2005-06 | 6 | 2 | 0 | 0 | 8 |
| | London | 2003 | 3(1) | 2 | 0 | 0 | 8 |
| Jack Buchanan | Widnes | 2016-17 | 29(2) | 2 | 0 | 0 | 8 |
| Kieran Buchanan | Hull | 2019 | 6(1) | 1 | 0 | 0 | 4 |
| Owen Buckley | Widnes | 2018 | 4 | 3 | 0 | 0 | 12 |
| Danny Buderus | Leeds | 2009-11 | 57(14) | 14 | 0 | 0 | 56 |
| Neil Budworth | Celtic | 2009 | 8(19) | 0 | 0 | 0 | 0 |
| | Harlequins | 2006 | 2(19) | 0 | 0 | 0 | 0 |
| | London | 2002-05 | 59(11) | 4 | 1 | 0 | 18 |
| Joe Bullock | Wigan | 2019 | 9(12) | 2 | 0 | 0 | 8 |
| James Bunyan | Huddersfield | 1998-99 | 8(7) | 2 | 0 | 0 | 8 |
| Andy Burgess | Salford | 1997 | 3(12) | 0 | 0 | 0 | 0 |
| Joe Burgess | Wigan | 2013-15, 2017-19 | 104 | 85 | 0 | 0 | 340 |
| Luke Burgess | Salford | 2018 | 3(8) | 0 | 0 | 0 | 0 |
| | Catalans | 2017 | 3(2) | 0 | 0 | 0 | 0 |
| | Leeds | 2008-11 | 10(63) | 6 | 0 | 0 | 24 |
| | Harlequins | 2007 | (3) | 0 | 0 | 0 | 0 |
| Sam Burgess | Bradford | 2006-09 | 46(34) | 14 | 5 | 0 | 66 |
| Tom Burgess | Bradford | 2011-12 | 1(41) | 3 | 0 | 0 | 12 |
| Greg Burke | Salford | 2018-19 | 12(22) | 1 | 0 | 0 | 4 |
| | Widnes | 2016-18 | 21(12) | 1 | 0 | 0 | 4 |
| | Wigan | 2013-14, 2016 | 13(26) | 1 | 0 | 0 | 4 |
| | Hull KR | 2015 | 9(5) | 0 | 0 | 0 | 0 |
| | Bradford | 2014 | (1) | 0 | 0 | 0 | 0 |
| Joe Burke | Crusaders | 2011 | (1) | 0 | 0 | 0 | 0 |
| Mike Burnett | Harlequins | 2011 | 16(4) | 1 | 0 | 0 | 4 |
| | Hull | 2008-10 | 13(21) | 3 | 0 | 0 | 12 |
| Darren Burns | Warrington | 2002-04 | 66(6) | 19 | 0 | 0 | 76 |
| Gary Burns | Oldham | 1996 | 6 | 1 | 0 | 0 | 4 |
| Paul Burns | Workington | 1996 | 5(2) | 1 | 0 | 0 | 4 |
| Travis Burns | St Helens | 2015-16 | 27(2) | 4 | 28 | 0 | 72 |
| | Hull KR | 2013-14 | 46 | 8 | 81 | 2 | 196 |
| Lachlan Burr | Leigh | 2017 | 5(14) | 1 | 0 | 0 | 4 |
| Luther Burrell | Warrington | 2019 | 2(1) | 0 | 0 | 0 | 0 |
| Rob Burrow | Leeds | 2001-17 | 313(116) | 168 | 131 | 5 | 939 |
| Dean Busby | Warrington | 1999-2002 | 34(34) | 7 | 0 | 0 | 28 |
| | Hull | 1998 | 8(6) | 0 | 0 | 0 | 0 |
| | St Helens | 1996-98 | 1(7) | 0 | 0 | 0 | 0 |
| Tom Bush | Leeds | 2010 | 3(1) | 1 | 0 | 0 | 4 |
| Chester Butler | Huddersfield | 2019 | (1) | 0 | 0 | 0 | 0 |
| Rob Butler | London | 2019 | 17(7) | 2 | 0 | 0 | 8 |
| Ikram Butt | London | 1996 | 5(1) | 0 | 0 | 0 | 0 |
| Liam Byrne | Wigan | 2019 | 1(13) | 1 | 0 | 0 | 4 |
| Shane Byrne | Huddersfield | 1998-99 | 1(5) | 0 | 0 | 0 | 0 |
| Todd Byrne | Hull | 2008-09 | 20 | 4 | 0 | 0 | 16 |
| Didier Cabestany | Paris | 1996-97 | 20(6) | 2 | 0 | 0 | 8 |
| Hep Cahill | Widnes | 2012-18 | 106(13) | 4 | 0 | 0 | 16 |
| | Crusaders | 2011 | 16 | 2 | 0 | 0 | 8 |
| Joel Caine | Salford | 2004 | 24 | 8 | 13 | 0 | 58 |
| | London | 2003 | 6 | 4 | 1 | 0 | 18 |
| Mark Calderwood | Harlequins | 2011 | 13 | 2 | 0 | 0 | 8 |
| | Hull | 2009-10 | 23 | 6 | 0 | 0 | 24 |
| | Wigan | 2006-08 | 64 | 23 | 0 | 0 | 92 |
| | Leeds | 2001-05 | 117(9) | 88 | 0 | 0 | 352 |
| Mike Callan | Warrington | 2002 | (4) | 0 | 0 | 0 | 0 |
| Matt Calland | Huddersfield | 2003 | 2 | 0 | 0 | 0 | 0 |
| | Hull | 1999 | 1 | 0 | 0 | 0 | 0 |
| | Bradford | 1996-98 | 44(5) | 24 | 0 | 0 | 96 |
| Dean Callaway | London | 1999-2000 | 26(24) | 12 | 0 | 0 | 48 |
| Laurent Cambres | Paris | 1996 | (1) | 0 | 0 | 0 | 0 |
| Chris Campbell | Warrington | 2000 | 7(1) | 2 | 0 | 0 | 8 |
| Liam Campbell | Wakefield | 2005 | (1) | 0 | 0 | 0 | 0 |
| Logan Campbell | Hull | 1998-99, 2001 | 70(13) | 14 | 0 | 0 | 56 |
| | Castleford | 2000 | 14(2) | 3 | 0 | 0 | 12 |
| | Workington | 1996 | 7(1) | 1 | 0 | 0 | 4 |
| Terry Campese | Hull KR | 2015-16 | 19(1) | 2 | 4 | 0 | 16 |
| Blake Cannova | Widnes | 2002 | (1) | 0 | 0 | 0 | 0 |
| Phil Cantillon | Widnes | 2002-03 | 27(21) | 18 | 0 | 0 | 72 |
| | Leeds | 1997 | (1) | 0 | 0 | 0 | 0 |
| Liam Carberry | Widnes | 2014-15 | 2(5) | 0 | 0 | 0 | 0 |
| Damien Cardace | Catalans | 2012, 2014-15 | 23 | 14 | 0 | 0 | 56 |
| Daryl Cardiss | Warrington | 2003-04 | 23(2) | 3 | 4 | 0 | 20 |
| | Halifax | 1999-2003 | 91(8) | 39 | 4 | 0 | 164 |
| | Wigan | 1996-98 | 12(6) | 4 | 0 | 0 | 16 |
| Dale Cardoza | Warrington | 2002 | 5 | 1 | 0 | 0 | 4 |
| | Halifax | 2001 | 3 | 1 | 0 | 0 | 4 |
| | Huddersfield | 2000-01 | 20(9) | 11 | 0 | 0 | 44 |
| | Sheffield | 1998-99 | 11(7) | 3 | 0 | 0 | 12 |
| Paul Carige | Salford | 1999 | 24(1) | 7 | 0 | 0 | 28 |
| Dane Carlaw | Catalans | 2008-10 | 58(15) | 9 | 0 | 0 | 36 |
| Keal Carlile | Hull KR | 2012-15 | 6(28) | 1 | 0 | 0 | 4 |
| | Huddersfield | 2009, 2011 | 2(1) | 1 | 0 | 0 | 4 |
| | Bradford | 2008 | (1) | 0 | 0 | 0 | 0 |
| Jim Carlton | Huddersfield | 1999 | 3(11) | 2 | 0 | 0 | 8 |
| George Carmont | Wigan | 2008-12 | 136 | 71 | 0 | 0 | 284 |
| Brian Carney | Warrington | 2009 | 4 | 2 | 0 | 0 | 8 |
| | Wigan | 2001-05 | 91(10) | 42 | 1 | 0 | 170 |
| | Hull | 2000 | 13(3) | 7 | 0 | 0 | 28 |
| | Gateshead | 1999 | 3(2) | 2 | 0 | 0 | 8 |
| Justin Carney | Hull KR | 2018 | 14 | 3 | 0 | 0 | 12 |
| | Salford | 2016-17 | 28 | 12 | 0 | 0 | 48 |
| | Castleford | 2013-15 | 58 | 56 | 0 | 0 | 224 |
| Martin Carney | Warrington | 1997 | (1) | 0 | 0 | 0 | 0 |
| Todd Carney | Hull KR | 2018 | (1) | 0 | 0 | 0 | 0 |
| | Salford | 2017 | 9(5) | 0 | 7 | 0 | 14 |
| | Catalans | 2015-16 | 32 | 9 | 4 | 1 | 45 |
| Omari Caro | Hull KR | 2013-14 | 21 | 20 | 0 | 0 | 80 |
| | London | 2012 | 11 | 4 | 0 | 0 | 16 |
| Paul Carr | Sheffield | 1996-98 | 45(5) | 15 | 0 | 0 | 60 |
| Bernard Carroll | London | 1996 | 2(1) | 1 | 0 | 0 | 4 |
| Mark Carroll | London | 1998 | 15(3) | 1 | 0 | 0 | 4 |
| Tonie Carroll | Leeds | 2001-02 | 42(2) | 30 | 0 | 0 | 120 |
| Darren Carter | Workington | 1996 | 10(3) | 0 | 1 | 0 | 2 |
| Steve Carter | Widnes | 2002 | 14(7) | 4 | 0 | 0 | 16 |
| John Cartwright | Salford | 1997 | 9 | 0 | 0 | 0 | 0 |
| Garreth Carvell | Castleford | 2014 | 1(4) | 1 | 0 | 0 | 4 |
| | Hull | 2001-08, 2014 | 75(84) | 22 | 0 | 0 | 88 |
| | Warrington | 2009-13 | 77(40) | 13 | 0 | 0 | 52 |
| | Leeds | 1997-2000 | (4) | 0 | 0 | 0 | 0 |
| | Gateshead | 1999 | 4(4) | 1 | 0 | 0 | 4 |
| Garen Casey | Salford | 1999 | 13(5) | 3 | 23 | 0 | 58 |
| Ray Cashmere | Salford | 2009-11 | 63(3) | 5 | 0 | 0 | 20 |
| Mick Cassidy | Widnes | 2005 | 24 | 0 | 0 | 0 | 0 |
| | Wigan | 1996-2004 | 184(36) | 30 | 0 | 0 | 120 |

| PLAYER | CLUB | YEAR | APP | TRIES | GOALS | FG | PTS |
|---|---|---|---|---|---|---|---|
| Remi Casty | Catalans | 2006-13, | | | | | |
| | | 2015-19 | 193(96) | 26 | 0 | 0 | 104 |
| Ned Catic | Castleford | 2008 | 7(7) | 3 | 0 | 0 | 12 |
| | Wakefield | 2006-07 | 17(29) | 4 | 0 | 0 | 16 |
| Mason Caton-Brown | | | | | | | |
| | Wakefield | 2017-19 | 33 | 27 | 0 | 0 | 108 |
| | Salford | 2014-16 | 28 | 10 | 0 | 0 | 40 |
| | London | 2013-14 | 19 | 15 | 0 | 0 | 60 |
| Joe Cator | Hull KR | 2016, 2018 | 2(3) | 0 | 0 | 0 | 0 |
| Chris Causey | Warrington | 1997-99 | (18) | 1 | 0 | 0 | 4 |
| Jason Cayless | St Helens | 2006-09 | 62(9) | 7 | 0 | 0 | 28 |
| Arnaud Cervello | Paris | 1996 | 4 | 4 | 0 | 0 | 16 |
| Marshall Chalk | Celtic | 2009 | 13 | 4 | 0 | 0 | 16 |
| Ed Chamberlain | Salford | 2018-19 | 7(1) | 1 | 18 | 0 | 40 |
| | Widnes | 2016-18 | 15(1) | 2 | 7 | 0 | 22 |
| Gary Chambers | Warrington | 1996-2000 | 65(28) | 2 | 0 | 0 | 8 |
| Pierre Chamorin | Paris | 1996-97 | 27(3) | 8 | 3 | 0 | 38 |
| Alex Chan | Catalans | 2006-08 | 59(19) | 11 | 0 | 0 | 44 |
| Jason Chan | Hull KR | 2014 | 5(1) | 3 | 0 | 0 | 12 |
| | Huddersfield | 2012-14 | 46(12) | 9 | 0 | 0 | 36 |
| | Crusaders | 2010-11 | 48(1) | 10 | 0 | 0 | 40 |
| | Celtic | 2009 | 17(6) | 3 | 0 | 0 | 12 |
| Joe Chandler | Leeds | 2008 | (1) | 0 | 0 | 0 | 0 |
| Michael Channing | Castleford | 2013-15 | 27(2) | 8 | 0 | 0 | 32 |
| | London | 2012-13 | 15(3) | 2 | 0 | 0 | 8 |
| Jay Chapelhow | Widnes | 2016-18 | 23(15) | 4 | 0 | 0 | 16 |
| Ted Chapelhow | Widnes | 2016-18 | 7(13) | 0 | 0 | 0 | 0 |
| Chris Chapman | Leeds | 1999 | (1) | 0 | 0 | 0 | 0 |
| Damien Chapman | London | 1998 | 6(2) | 3 | 4 | 1 | 21 |
| David Chapman | Castleford | 1996-98 | 24(6) | 8 | 0 | 0 | 32 |
| Jaymes Chapman | Halifax | 2002-03 | 5(8) | 1 | 0 | 0 | 4 |
| Richard Chapman | Sheffield | 1996 | 1 | 2 | 0 | 0 | 8 |
| Chris Charles | Salford | 2004-06 | 59(16) | 6 | 140 | 0 | 304 |
| | Castleford | 2001 | 1(4) | 1 | 0 | 0 | 4 |
| Olivier Charles | Catalans | 2007 | 2 | 2 | 0 | 0 | 8 |
| Josh Charnley | Warrington | 2018-19 | 49 | 33 | 0 | 0 | 132 |
| | Wigan | 2010-16 | 151(2) | 141 | 77 | 0 | 718 |
| | Hull KR | 2010 | 5 | 5 | 0 | 0 | 20 |
| Lewis Charnock | St Helens | 2013, 2015 | 4(1) | 2 | 6 | 0 | 20 |
| Rangi Chase | Widnes | 2017 | 6 | 0 | 0 | 0 | 0 |
| | Castleford | 2009-13, | | | | | |
| | | 2016-17 | 122(12) | 39 | 0 | 3 | 159 |
| | Salford | 2014-15 | 37 | 10 | 13 | 2 | 68 |
| Andy Cheetham | Huddersfield | 1998-99 | 30 | 11 | 0 | 0 | 44 |
| Kris Chesney | London | 1998 | 1(2) | 0 | 0 | 0 | 0 |
| Chris Chester | Hull KR | 2007-08 | 28(6) | 4 | 0 | 0 | 16 |
| | Hull | 2002-06 | 67(25) | 13 | 0 | 0 | 52 |
| | Wigan | 1999-2001 | 21(22) | 5 | 0 | 0 | 20 |
| | Halifax | 1996-99 | 47(14) | 16 | 15 | 1 | 95 |
| Lee Chilton | Workington | 1996 | 10(3) | 6 | 0 | 0 | 24 |
| Dane Chisholm | Hull KR | 2015 | 1 | 0 | 0 | 0 | 0 |
| Gary Christie | Bradford | 1996-97 | 4(7) | 1 | 0 | 0 | 4 |
| James Clare | Castleford | 2012-15, | | | | | |
| | | 2018-19 | 79(1) | 44 | 0 | 0 | 176 |
| Daryl Clark | Warrington | 2015-19 | 123(10) | 30 | 0 | 0 | 120 |
| | Castleford | 2011-14 | 34(51) | 31 | 0 | 0 | 124 |
| Dean Clark | Leeds | 1996 | 11(2) | 3 | 0 | 0 | 12 |
| Des Clark | St Helens | 1999 | 4 | 0 | 0 | 0 | 0 |
| | Halifax | 1998-99 | 35(13) | 6 | 0 | 0 | 24 |
| Jason Clark | Warrington | 2019 | 7(21) | 2 | 0 | 0 | 8 |
| Mitch Clark | Castleford | 2018-19 | (24) | 3 | 0 | 0 | 12 |
| Greg Clarke | Halifax | 1997 | 1(1) | 0 | 0 | 0 | 0 |
| John Clarke | Oldham | 1996-97 | 27(4) | 5 | 0 | 0 | 20 |
| Jon Clarke | Widnes | 2012-14 | 59(1) | 5 | 0 | 0 | 20 |
| | Warrington | 2001-11 | 217(25) | 56 | 2 | 0 | 228 |
| | London | 2000-01 | 19(11) | 2 | 0 | 0 | 8 |
| | Wigan | 1997-99 | 13(10) | 3 | 0 | 0 | 12 |
| Chris Clarkson | Castleford | 2019 | 11(8) | 4 | 0 | 0 | 16 |
| | Hull KR | 2016, 2018 | 38(2) | 4 | 0 | 0 | 16 |
| | Widnes | 2015 | 17(1) | 4 | 0 | 0 | 16 |
| | Leeds | 2010-14 | 61(39) | 9 | 0 | 0 | 36 |
| Adam Clay | Salford | 2011 | 2 | 3 | 0 | 0 | 12 |
| Ryan Clayton | Castleford | 2004, | | | | | |
| | | 2008-10 | 36(24) | 5 | 0 | 0 | 20 |
| | Salford | 2006 | 3(8) | 2 | 0 | 0 | 8 |
| | Huddersfield | 2005 | 4(6) | 0 | 0 | 0 | 0 |
| | Halifax | 2000, | | | | | |
| | | 2002-03 | 28(12) | 6 | 0 | 0 | 24 |
| Gavin Clinch | Salford | 2004 | 21(1) | 1 | 0 | 1 | 5 |
| | Halifax | 1998-99, | | | | | |
| | | 2001-02 | 88(2) | 26 | 45 | 5 | 199 |
| | Hudds-Sheff | 2000 | 18(5) | 5 | 0 | 1 | 21 |
| | Wigan | 1999 | 10(2) | 4 | 12 | 0 | 40 |
| Joel Clinton | Hull KR | 2010-12 | 42(14) | 2 | 0 | 0 | 8 |
| John Clough | Salford | 2004-06 | 1(16) | 0 | 0 | 0 | 0 |

| PLAYER | CLUB | YEAR | APP | TRIES | GOALS | FG | PTS |
|---|---|---|---|---|---|---|---|
| Paul Clough | Huddersfield | 2017-19 | 34(39) | 2 | 0 | 0 | 8 |
| | Widnes | 2014 | 4(8) | 1 | 0 | 0 | 4 |
| | St Helens | 2005-13 | 53(113) | 16 | 0 | 0 | 64 |
| Tony Clubb | Wigan | 2014-19 | 67(66) | 20 | 0 | 0 | 80 |
| | London | 2012-13 | 24(8) | 7 | 0 | 0 | 28 |
| | Harlequins | 2006-11 | 100(11) | 29 | 0 | 0 | 116 |
| Bradley Clyde | Leeds | 2001 | 7(5) | 1 | 0 | 0 | 4 |
| Michael Coady | Leeds | 2010 | 1 | 0 | 0 | 0 | 0 |
| Evan Cochrane | London | 1996 | 5(1) | 1 | 0 | 0 | 4 |
| Ben Cockayne | Hull KR | 2007-11, | | | | | |
| | | 2014-16 | 125(30) | 38 | 18 | 0 | 188 |
| | Wakefield | 2012-13 | 54 | 28 | 2 | 0 | 116 |
| Liam Colbon | Hull | 2014 | 8 | 1 | 0 | 0 | 4 |
| | London | 2012-13 | 22 | 5 | 0 | 0 | 20 |
| | Hull KR | 2009-11 | 51 | 20 | 0 | 0 | 80 |
| | Wigan | 2004-05, | | | | | |
| | | 2007-08 | 37(14) | 15 | 0 | 0 | 60 |
| Anthony Colella | Huddersfield | 2003 | 5(1) | 2 | 0 | 0 | 8 |
| Liam Coleman | Leigh | 2005 | 1(4) | 0 | 0 | 0 | 0 |
| Andy Coley | Wigan | 2008-11 | 100(10) | 8 | 0 | 0 | 32 |
| | Salford | 2001-02, | | | | | |
| | | 2004-07 | 112(34) | 34 | 0 | 0 | 136 |
| Richard Colley | Bradford | 2004 | 1 | 0 | 0 | 0 | 0 |
| Steve Collins | Hull | 2000 | 28 | 17 | 0 | 0 | 68 |
| | Gateshead | 1999 | 20(4) | 13 | 0 | 0 | 52 |
| Wayne Collins | Leeds | 1997 | 21 | 3 | 0 | 0 | 12 |
| Dean Collis | Wakefield | 2012-15 | 64 | 28 | 0 | 0 | 112 |
| Aurelien Cologni | Catalans | 2006 | 4(1) | 3 | 0 | 0 | 12 |
| Gary Connolly | Widnes | 2005 | 20 | 4 | 1 | 0 | 18 |
| | Wigan | 1996-2002, | | | | | |
| | | 2004 | 168(10) | 70 | 5 | 0 | 290 |
| | Leeds | 2003-04 | 27 | 6 | 0 | 0 | 24 |
| Jake Connor | Hull | 2017-19 | 63(12) | 20 | 61 | 2 | 204 |
| | Huddersfield | 2013-16 | 47(1) | 21 | 2 | 0 | 88 |
| Nathan Conroy | Bradford | 2013-14 | (4) | 0 | 0 | 0 | 0 |
| Matt Cook | Castleford | 2008, | | | | | |
| | | 2015-19 | 22(86) | 13 | 0 | 0 | 52 |
| | London | 2012-14 | 50(7) | 8 | 0 | 0 | 32 |
| | Hull KR | 2010-11 | 9(16) | 7 | 0 | 0 | 28 |
| | Bradford | 2005-09 | 11(52) | 4 | 0 | 0 | 16 |
| Mick Cook | Sheffield | 1996 | 9(10) | 2 | 0 | 0 | 8 |
| Paul Cook | Huddersfield | 1998-99 | 11(6) | 2 | 13 | 0 | 34 |
| | Bradford | 1996-97 | 14(8) | 7 | 38 | 1 | 105 |
| Peter Cook | St Helens | 2004 | (1) | 0 | 0 | 0 | 0 |
| Paul Cooke | Wakefield | 2010 | 16(1) | 3 | 11 | 0 | 85 |
| | Hull KR | 2007-10 | 54(5) | 8 | 76 | 2 | 186 |
| | Hull | 1999-2007 | 177(27) | 32 | 333 | 4 | 798 |
| Ben Cooper | Leigh | 2005 | 25(1) | 5 | 0 | 0 | 20 |
| | Huddersfield | 2000-01, | | | | | |
| | | 2003-04 | 28(12) | 3 | 0 | 0 | 12 |
| Mike Cooper | Warrington | 2006-13, | | | | | |
| | | 2017-19 | 99(88) | 15 | 0 | 0 | 60 |
| | Castleford | 2010 | 1(5) | 2 | 0 | 0 | 8 |
| Lachlan Coote | St Helens | 2019 | 24 | 14 | 106 | 1 | 269 |
| Ged Corcoran | Halifax | 2003 | 1(11) | 0 | 0 | 0 | 0 |
| Wayne Corcoran | Halifax | 2003 | 4(2) | 0 | 0 | 0 | 0 |
| Jamie Cording | Huddersfield | 2011-13 | 4(21) | 5 | 0 | 0 | 20 |
| Josh Cordoba | Hull | 2009 | 8 | 1 | 0 | 0 | 4 |
| Mark Corvo | Salford | 2002 | 7(5) | 0 | 0 | 0 | 0 |
| Matthew Costello | St Helens | 2018-19 | 16(1) | 4 | 0 | 0 | 16 |
| Neville Costigan | Hull KR | 2014 | 24 | 3 | 0 | 0 | 12 |
| Brandon Costin | Huddersfield | 2001, | | | | | |
| | | 2003-04 | 69 | 42 | 93 | 3 | 357 |
| | Bradford | 2002 | 20(1) | 8 | 0 | 0 | 32 |
| Wes Cotton | London | 1997-98 | 12 | 3 | 0 | 0 | 12 |
| Phil Coussons | Salford | 1997 | 7(2) | 3 | 0 | 0 | 12 |
| Alex Couttet | Paris | 1997 | 1 | 0 | 0 | 0 | 0 |
| Nick Couttet | Paris | 1997 | 1 | 0 | 0 | 0 | 0 |
| Jamie Coventry | Castleford | 1996 | 1 | 0 | 0 | 0 | 0 |
| Jimmy Cowan | Oldham | 1996-97 | 2(8) | 0 | 0 | 0 | 0 |
| Will Cowell | Warrington | 1998-2000 | 6(8) | 1 | 0 | 0 | 4 |
| Neil Cowie | Wigan | 1996-2001 | 116(27) | 10 | 0 | 1 | 41 |
| Danny Cowling | Wakefield | 2012-13 | 2 | 0 | 0 | 0 | 0 |
| Jordan Cox | Warrington | 2016 | (16) | 0 | 0 | 0 | 0 |
| | Hull KR | 2011-15 | 17(44) | 4 | 0 | 0 | 16 |
| | Huddersfield | 2015 | (2) | 0 | 0 | 0 | 0 |
| Mark Cox | London | 2003 | (3) | 0 | 0 | 0 | 0 |
| James Coyle | Wigan | 2005 | 2(3) | 1 | 0 | 0 | 4 |
| Thomas Coyle | Wigan | 2008 | 2(1) | 0 | 0 | 0 | 0 |
| Eorl Crabtree | Huddersfield | 2001, | | | | | |
| | | 2003-16 | 180(167) | 52 | 0 | 0 | 208 |
| Andy Craig | Halifax | 1999 | 13(7) | 1 | 3 | 0 | 10 |
| | Wigan | 1996 | 5(5) | 2 | 0 | 0 | 8 |
| Owen Craigie | Widnes | 2005 | 15 | 7 | 0 | 2 | 30 |
| Scott Cram | London | 1999-2002 | 65(7) | 4 | 0 | 0 | 16 |

167

# Super League Players 1996-2019

| PLAYER | CLUB | YEAR | APP | TRIES | GOALS | FG | PTS |
|---|---|---|---|---|---|---|---|
| Danny Craven | Widnes | 2012-15, 2017-18 | 52(17) | 13 | 6 | 3 | 67 |
| Steve Craven | Hull | 1998-2003 | 53(42) | 4 | 0 | 0 | 16 |
| Nicky Crellin | Workington | 1996 | (2) | 0 | 0 | 0 | 0 |
| Jason Critchley | Wakefield | 2000 | 7(1) | 4 | 0 | 0 | 16 |
|  | Castleford | 1997-98 | 27(3) | 11 | 0 | 0 | 44 |
| Jack Croft | Wakefield | 2019 | 3 | 0 | 0 | 0 | 0 |
| Jason Croker | Catalans | 2007-09 | 56(2) | 11 | 0 | 1 | 45 |
| Martin Crompton | Salford | 1998-2000 | 30(6) | 11 | 6 | 2 | 58 |
|  | Oldham | 1996-97 | 36(1) | 16 | 0 | 3 | 67 |
| Paul Crook | Widnes | 2005 | 2(2) | 0 | 5 | 1 | 11 |
| Paul Crook | Oldham | 1996 | 4(9) | 0 | 3 | 0 | 6 |
| Jason Crookes | Hull | 2013-14 | 15(1) | 5 | 0 | 0 | 20 |
|  | Bradford | 2009-12 | 25(1) | 7 | 0 | 0 | 28 |
| Ben Crooks | Hull KR | 2018-19 | 25 | 10 | 0 | 0 | 40 |
|  | Leigh | 2017 | 19 | 6 | 0 | 0 | 24 |
|  | Castleford | 2016 | 24(2) | 5 | 1 | 0 | 22 |
|  | Hull | 2012-14 | 42(3) | 30 | 23 | 0 | 166 |
| Lee Crooks | Castleford | 1996-97 | 27(2) | 2 | 14 | 0 | 36 |
| Dominic Crosby | Leeds | 2018 | (2) | 0 | 0 | 0 | 0 |
|  | Warrington | 2017-18 | (16) | 0 | 0 | 0 | 0 |
|  | Wigan | 2012-16 | 57(35) | 6 | 0 | 0 | 24 |
| Alan Cross | St Helens | 1997 | (2) | 0 | 0 | 0 | 0 |
| Ben Cross | Widnes | 2012-13 | 27(1) | 2 | 0 | 0 | 8 |
|  | Wigan | 2011 | (4) | 0 | 0 | 0 | 0 |
|  | Leeds | 2011 | 1(9) | 0 | 0 | 0 | 0 |
| Steve Crossley | Castleford | 2015 | (6) | 0 | 0 | 0 | 0 |
|  | Bradford | 2010-11 | (9) | 1 | 0 | 0 | 4 |
| Garret Crossman | Hull KR | 2008 | 8(18) | 0 | 0 | 0 | 0 |
| Steve Crouch | Castleford | 2004 | 4(1) | 2 | 0 | 0 | 8 |
| Kevin Crouthers | Warrington | 2001-03 | 12(1) | 4 | 0 | 0 | 16 |
|  | London | 2000 | 6(4) | 1 | 0 | 0 | 4 |
|  | Wakefield | 1999 | 4(4) | 1 | 0 | 0 | 4 |
|  | Bradford | 1997-98 | 3(9) | 2 | 0 | 0 | 8 |
| Jordan Crowther | Wakefield | 2014-19 | 22(14) | 2 | 0 | 0 | 8 |
| Matt Crowther | Hull | 2001-03 | 48 | 20 | 166 | 0 | 412 |
|  | Hudds-Sheff | 2000 | 10(4) | 5 | 22 | 0 | 64 |
|  | Sheffield | 1996-99 | 43(4) | 22 | 10 | 0 | 108 |
| Heath Cruckshank | Halifax | 2003 | 19(1) | 0 | 0 | 0 | 0 |
|  | St Helens | 2001 | 1(12) | 0 | 0 | 0 | 0 |
| Leroy Cudjoe | Huddersfield | 2008-19 | 249(1) | 100 | 57 | 1 | 515 |
| Paul Cullen | Warrington | 1996 | 19 | 3 | 0 | 0 | 12 |
| Francis Cummins | Leeds | 1996-2005 | 217(13) | 120 | 26 | 2 | 534 |
| James Cunningham | London | 2014, 2019 | 34(8) | 3 | 0 | 0 | 12 |
|  | Hull | 2012, 2014-15 | (9) | 0 | 0 | 0 | 0 |
| Keiron Cunningham | St Helens | 1996-2010 | 357(24) | 138 | 0 | 0 | 552 |
| Liam Cunningham | Hull | 2010 | (1) | 0 | 0 | 0 | 0 |
| Ben Currie | Warrington | 2012-19 | 108(31) | 54 | 0 | 0 | 216 |
| Andy Currier | Warrington | 1996-97 | (2) | 1 | 0 | 0 | 4 |
| Peter Cusack | Hull | 2008-10 | 34(22) | 3 | 0 | 0 | 12 |
| Adam Cuthbertson | Leeds | 2015-19 | 87(30) | 29 | 0 | 0 | 116 |
| Alrix Da Costa | Catalans | 2016-19 | 22(30) | 2 | 0 | 0 | 8 |
| Will Dagger | Hull KR | 2018-19 | 14(2) | 2 | 0 | 0 | 8 |
|  | Warrington | 2017 | 3 | 0 | 0 | 0 | 0 |
| Joe Dakuitoga | Sheffield | 1996 | 6(3) | 1 | 0 | 0 | 4 |
| Matty Dale | Hull | 2006, 2008 | (7) | 1 | 0 | 0 | 4 |
|  | Wakefield | 2008 | 1(1) | 0 | 0 | 0 | 0 |
| Brett Dallas | Wigan | 2000-06 | 156 | 89 | 0 | 0 | 356 |
| Mark Dalle Cort | Celtic | 2009 | 23 | 4 | 0 | 0 | 16 |
| Paul Darbyshire | Warrington | 1997 | (6) | 0 | 0 | 0 | 0 |
| James Davey | Wakefield | 2009-11 | 3(14) | 1 | 0 | 0 | 4 |
| Maea David | Hull | 1998 | 1 | 0 | 0 | 0 | 0 |
| Alex Davidson | Salford | 2011, 2013 | (3) | 0 | 0 | 0 | 0 |
| Paul Davidson | Halifax | 2001-03 | 22(30) | 10 | 0 | 0 | 40 |
|  | London | 2000 | 6(10) | 4 | 0 | 0 | 16 |
|  | St Helens | 1998-99 | 27(16) | 7 | 0 | 0 | 28 |
|  | Oldham | 1996-97 | 17(18) | 14 | 0 | 1 | 57 |
| Ben Davies | Castleford | 2011, 2013 | 3(4) | 2 | 0 | 0 | 8 |
|  | Widnes | 2012-13 | 10(15) | 3 | 0 | 0 | 12 |
|  | Wigan | 2010 | (5) | 0 | 0 | 0 | 0 |
| Gareth Davies | Warrington | 1996-97 | 1(6) | 0 | 0 | 0 | 0 |
| Geraint Davies | Celtic | 2009 | (7) | 0 | 0 | 0 | 0 |
| John Davies | Castleford | 2010-12 | 1(6) | 1 | 0 | 0 | 4 |
| Jordan Davies | Salford | 2013 | 2(3) | 0 | 0 | 0 | 0 |
| Macauley Davies | Wigan | 2016 | (1) | 0 | 0 | 0 | 0 |
| Matthew Davies | London | 2019 | (1) | 0 | 0 | 0 | 0 |
| Olly Davies | St Helens | 2016 | (1) | 0 | 0 | 0 | 0 |
| Tom Davies | Wigan | 2017-19 | 57 | 27 | 0 | 0 | 108 |
| Wes Davies | Wigan | 1998-2001 | 22(22) | 11 | 0 | 0 | 44 |
| Brad Davis | Castleford | 1997-2000, 2004, 2006 | 102(3) | 31 | 43 | 10 | 220 |
|  | Wakefield | 2001-03 | 51(12) | 15 | 22 | 5 | 109 |
| Matt Davis | Warrington | 2019 | 4(11) | 1 | 0 | 0 | 4 |
|  | London | 2019 | 4 | 0 | 0 | 0 | 0 |
| Sam Davis | London | 2019 | 2(1) | 0 | 0 | 0 | 0 |
| Matty Dawson-Jones | Hull | 2019 | 1 | 1 | 0 | 0 | 4 |
|  | Leigh | 2017 | 23 | 12 | 0 | 0 | 48 |
|  | St Helens | 2014-16 | 46(1) | 15 | 0 | 0 | 60 |
|  | Huddersfield | 2012-13 | 4 | 0 | 0 | 0 | 0 |
| Brad Day | Castleford | 2014 | (1) | 0 | 0 | 0 | 0 |
| Matt Daylight | Hull | 2000 | 17(1) | 7 | 0 | 0 | 28 |
|  | Gateshead | 1999 | 30 | 25 | 0 | 0 | 100 |
| Michael De Vere | Huddersfield | 2005-06 | 36 | 6 | 74 | 0 | 172 |
| Paul Deacon | Wigan | 2010-11 | 32(11) | 4 | 14 | 0 | 44 |
|  | Bradford | 1998-2009 | 258(43) | 72 | 1029 | 23 | 2369 |
|  | Oldham | 1997 | (2) | 0 | 0 | 0 | 0 |
| Chris Dean | Widnes | 2012-18 | 114(6) | 23 | 0 | 0 | 92 |
|  | Wakefield | 2011 | 20 | 8 | 0 | 0 | 32 |
|  | St Helens | 2007-10 | 18(3) | 9 | 0 | 0 | 36 |
| Craig Dean | Halifax | 1996-97 | 25(11) | 12 | 1 | 1 | 51 |
| Gareth Dean | London | 2002 | (4) | 0 | 0 | 0 | 0 |
| Riley Dean | Warrington | 2019 | 1 | 0 | 0 | 0 | 0 |
| Yacine Dekkiche | Hudds-Sheff | 2000 | 11(3) | 3 | 0 | 0 | 12 |
| Brett Delaney | Leeds | 2010-18 | 151(30) | 23 | 0 | 0 | 92 |
| Jason Demetriou | Wakefield | 2004-10 | 174(3) | 50 | 2 | 0 | 204 |
|  | Widnes | 2002-03 | 47(1) | 15 | 1 | 0 | 62 |
| Martin Dermott | Warrington | 1997 | 1 | 0 | 0 | 0 | 0 |
| David Despin | Paris | 1996 | (1) | 0 | 0 | 0 | 0 |
| Fabien Devecchi | Paris | 1996-97 | 17(10) | 2 | 0 | 0 | 8 |
| Paul Devlin | Widnes | 2002-04 | 32 | 16 | 0 | 0 | 64 |
| Jordan Dezaria | Catalans | 2016-17 | 3(2) | 0 | 0 | 0 | 0 |
| Stuart Dickens | Salford | 2005 | 4(5) | 0 | 4 | 0 | 8 |
| Tyler Dickinson | Huddersfield | 2016-18 | (17) | 1 | 0 | 0 | 4 |
| Matt Diskin | Bradford | 2011-14 | 64(16) | 11 | 0 | 0 | 44 |
|  | Leeds | 2001-10 | 195(37) | 40 | 0 | 0 | 160 |
| Andrew Dixon | Salford | 2013-14 | 34(2) | 8 | 0 | 0 | 32 |
|  | St Helens | 2009-12 | 19(41) | 12 | 0 | 0 | 48 |
| Kieran Dixon | London | 2012-14, 2019 | 76(1) | 42 | 77 | 0 | 322 |
|  | Hull KR | 2015-16 | 23(4) | 21 | 9 | 0 | 102 |
| Kirk Dixon | Castleford | 2008-14 | 143(2) | 63 | 267 | 0 | 786 |
|  | Hull | 2004-06 | 13(4) | 7 | 4 | 0 | 36 |
| Paul Dixon | Sheffield | 1996-97 | 5(9) | 1 | 0 | 0 | 4 |
| Nabil Djalout | Catalans | 2017 | 1 | 0 | 0 | 0 | 0 |
| Gareth Dobson | Castleford | 1998-2000 | (10) | 0 | 0 | 0 | 0 |
| Michael Dobson | Salford | 2015-17 | 58(1) | 14 | 77 | 1 | 211 |
|  | Hull KR | 2008-13 | 142 | 51 | 500 | 11 | 1215 |
|  | Wigan | 2006 | 14 | 5 | 61 | 0 | 142 |
|  | Catalans | 2006 | 10 | 4 | 31 | 1 | 79 |
| Michael Docherty | Hull | 2000-01 | (6) | 0 | 0 | 0 | 0 |
| Mitchell Dodds | Warrington | 2016 | (2) | 0 | 0 | 0 | 0 |
| Erjon Dollapi | London | 2013-14 | (18) | 4 | 0 | 0 | 16 |
| Sid Domic | Hull | 2006-07 | 39(4) | 15 | 0 | 0 | 60 |
|  | Wakefield | 2004-05 | 48 | 30 | 0 | 0 | 120 |
|  | Warrington | 2002-03 | 41(4) | 17 | 0 | 0 | 68 |
| Scott Donald | Leeds | 2006-10 | 131 | 77 | 0 | 0 | 308 |
| James Donaldson | Leeds | 2019 | 2(22) | 1 | 0 | 0 | 4 |
|  | Hull KR | 2015-16, 2018 | 12(30) | 4 | 0 | 0 | 16 |
|  | Bradford | 2009-14 | 38(35) | 4 | 0 | 0 | 16 |
| Glen Donkin | Hull | 2002-03 | (10) | 1 | 0 | 0 | 4 |
| Stuart Donlan | Castleford | 2008 | 20 | 8 | 0 | 0 | 32 |
|  | Huddersfield | 2004-06 | 59(3) | 15 | 0 | 0 | 60 |
|  | Halifax | 2001-03 | 65(2) | 22 | 0 | 0 | 88 |
| Jason Donohue | Bradford | 1996 | (4) | 0 | 0 | 0 | 0 |
| Jeremy Donougher | Bradford | 1996-99 | 40(21) | 13 | 0 | 0 | 52 |
| Justin Dooley | London | 2000-01 | 37(18) | 2 | 0 | 0 | 8 |
| Dane Dorahy | Halifax | 2003 | 20 | 7 | 45 | 0 | 118 |
|  | Wakefield | 2000-01 | 16(2) | 4 | 19 | 1 | 55 |
| Jamie Doran | Wigan | 2014 | (2) | 0 | 0 | 0 | 0 |
| Luke Dorn | Castleford | 2008, 2014-16 | 78(2) | 60 | 0 | 0 | 240 |
|  | London | 2005, 2012-13 | 58(8) | 42 | 0 | 0 | 168 |
|  | Harlequins | 2006, 2009-11 | 83(1) | 57 | 0 | 0 | 228 |
|  | Salford | 2007 | 19(8) | 11 | 0 | 0 | 44 |
| Brandon Douglas | Castleford | 2016 | (1) | 0 | 0 | 0 | 0 |
| Luke Douglas | St Helens | 2017-18 | 23(32) | 5 | 0 | 0 | 20 |
| Ewan Dowes | Hull | 2003-11 | 169(51) | 10 | 0 | 0 | 40 |
|  | Leeds | 2001-03 | 1(9) | 0 | 0 | 0 | 0 |
| Jack Downs | Hull | 2015-18 | 5(15) | 1 | 0 | 0 | 4 |
| Adam Doyle | Warrington | 1998 | 9(3) | 4 | 0 | 0 | 16 |
| Rod Doyle | Sheffield | 1997-99 | 52(10) | 10 | 0 | 0 | 40 |
| Brad Drew | Huddersfield | 2005-07, 2010 | 78(13) | 18 | 13 | 1 | 99 |
|  | Wakefield | 2008-09 | 27(9) | 7 | 14 | 1 | 57 |
| Josh Drinkwater | Hull KR | 2019 | 29 | 4 | 6 | 0 | 28 |
|  | Catalans | 2018 | 17 | 7 | 53 | 0 | 134 |
|  | Leigh | 2017 | 19 | 1 | 12 | 1 | 29 |
|  | London | 2014 | 23(1) | 5 | 54 | 0 | 128 |
| Damien Driscoll | Salford | 2001 | 23(1) | 1 | 0 | 0 | 4 |

| PLAYER | CLUB | YEAR | APP | TRIES | GOALS | FG | PTS |
|---|---|---|---|---|---|---|---|
| James Duckworth | London | 2014 | 3 | 0 | 0 | 0 | 0 |
| | Leeds | 2013 | 2 | 1 | 0 | 0 | 4 |
| Gil Dudson | Salford | 2019 | 30 | 2 | 0 | 0 | 8 |
| | Widnes | 2015-18 | 57(11) | 1 | 0 | 0 | 4 |
| | Wigan | 2012-14 | 26(16) | 2 | 0 | 0 | 8 |
| | Crusaders | 2011 | 3(7) | 0 | 0 | 0 | 0 |
| | Celtic | 2009 | (1) | 0 | 0 | 0 | 0 |
| Jason Duffy | Leigh | 2005 | 3(1) | 0 | 0 | 0 | 0 |
| John Duffy | Leigh | 2005 | 21 | 6 | 0 | 0 | 24 |
| | Salford | 2000 | 3(11) | 0 | 1 | 1 | 3 |
| | Warrington | 1997-99 | 12(12) | 0 | 0 | 0 | 0 |
| Tony Duggan | Celtic | 2009 | 4 | 3 | 0 | 0 | 12 |
| Andrew Duncan | London | 1997 | 2(4) | 2 | 0 | 0 | 8 |
| | Warrington | 1997 | (1) | 0 | 0 | 0 | 0 |
| Andrew Dunemann | Salford | 2006 | 25 | 1 | 0 | 2 | 6 |
| | Leeds | 2003-05 | 76(4) | 11 | 0 | 2 | 46 |
| | Halifax | 1999-2002 | 68 | 19 | 0 | 1 | 77 |
| Matt Dunford | London | 1997-98 | 18(20) | 3 | 0 | 1 | 13 |
| Vincent Duport | Catalans | 2007-09, 2011-18 | 156(16) | 75 | 0 | 0 | 300 |
| Jamie Durbin | Widnes | 2005 | 1 | 0 | 0 | 0 | 0 |
| | Warrington | 2003 | (1) | 0 | 0 | 0 | 0 |
| Scott Dureau | Catalans | 2011-15 | 88(1) | 29 | 315 | 10 | 756 |
| James Durkin | Paris | 1997 | (5) | 0 | 0 | 0 | 0 |
| Bernard Dwyer | Bradford | 1996-2000 | 65(10) | 14 | 0 | 0 | 56 |
| Brad Dwyer | Leeds | 2018-19 | 25(16) | 9 | 0 | 1 | 37 |
| | Warrington | 2012-17 | 12(63) | 11 | 0 | 0 | 44 |
| | Huddersfield | 2013 | (6) | 0 | 0 | 0 | 0 |
| Luke Dyer | Crusaders | 2010 | 23(1) | 5 | 0 | 0 | 20 |
| | Celtic | 2009 | 21 | 6 | 0 | 0 | 24 |
| | Hull KR | 2007 | 26 | 13 | 0 | 0 | 52 |
| | Castleford | 2006 | 17(2) | 5 | 0 | 0 | 20 |
| Adam Dykes | Hull | 2008 | 12 | 1 | 0 | 2 | 6 |
| Jim Dymock | London | 2001-04 | 94(1) | 15 | 0 | 1 | 61 |
| Leo Dynevor | London | 1996 | 8(11) | 5 | 7 | 0 | 34 |
| Jason Eade | Paris | 1997 | 9 | 4 | 0 | 0 | 16 |
| Michael Eagar | Hull | 2004-05 | 12 | 4 | 0 | 0 | 16 |
| | Castleford | 1999-2003 | 130(2) | 60 | 0 | 0 | 240 |
| | Warrington | 1998 | 21 | 6 | 0 | 0 | 24 |
| Kyle Eastmond | St Helens | 2007-11 | 46(20) | 35 | 117 | 3 | 377 |
| Greg Eastwood | Leeds | 2010 | 5(12) | 1 | 0 | 0 | 4 |
| Barry Eaton | Widnes | 2002 | 25 | 2 | 49 | 4 | 110 |
| | Castleford | 2000 | 1(4) | 0 | 3 | 0 | 6 |
| Josh Eaves | St Helens | 2019 | (2) | 0 | 0 | 0 | 0 |
| Greg Ebrill | Salford | 2002 | 15(6) | 1 | 0 | 0 | 4 |
| Cliff Eccles | Salford | 1997-98 | 30(5) | 1 | 0 | 0 | 4 |
| Chris Eckersley | Warrington | 1996 | 1 | 0 | 0 | 0 | 0 |
| Greg Eden | Castleford | 2011, 2017-19 | 67 | 70 | 0 | 0 | 280 |
| | Hull KR | 2013-14 | 37 | 23 | 0 | 0 | 92 |
| | Salford | 2014 | 4 | 1 | 0 | 0 | 4 |
| | Huddersfield | 2012 | 24 | 8 | 0 | 0 | 32 |
| Steve Edmed | Sheffield | 1997 | 15(1) | 0 | 0 | 0 | 0 |
| Mark Edmondson | Salford | 2007 | 10(2) | 0 | 0 | 0 | 0 |
| | St Helens | 1999-2005 | 27(75) | 10 | 0 | 0 | 40 |
| Diccon Edwards | Castleford | 1996-97 | 10(5) | 1 | 0 | 0 | 4 |
| Grant Edwards | Castleford | 2006 | (2) | 0 | 0 | 0 | 0 |
| Kenny Edwards | Catalans | 2018-19 | 14(18) | 10 | 0 | 0 | 40 |
| Max Edwards | Harlequins | 2010 | 1 | 0 | 0 | 0 | 0 |
| Peter Edwards | Salford | 1997-98 | 35(2) | 4 | 0 | 0 | 16 |
| Shaun Edwards | London | 1997-2000 | 32(8) | 16 | 1 | 0 | 66 |
| | Bradford | 1998 | 8(2) | 4 | 0 | 0 | 16 |
| | Wigan | 1996 | 17(3) | 12 | 1 | 0 | 50 |
| Tuoyo Egodo | Castleford | 2017-19 | 10(4) | 11 | 0 | 0 | 44 |
| Danny Ekis | Halifax | 2001 | (1) | 0 | 0 | 0 | 0 |
| Abi Ekoku | Bradford | 1997-98 | 21(4) | 6 | 0 | 0 | 24 |
| | Halifax | 1996 | 15(1) | 5 | 0 | 0 | 20 |
| Shane Elford | Huddersfield | 2007-08 | 26(1) | 7 | 0 | 0 | 28 |
| Olivier Elima | Catalans | 2008-10, 2013-16 | 99(35) | 34 | 0 | 0 | 136 |
| | Bradford | 2011-12 | 37(3) | 12 | 0 | 0 | 48 |
| | Wakefield | 2003-07 | 40(47) | 13 | 0 | 0 | 52 |
| | Castleford | 2002 | (1) | 1 | 0 | 0 | 4 |
| Abderazak Elkhalouki | Paris | 1997 | (1) | 0 | 0 | 0 | 0 |
| George Elliott | Leeds | 2011 | 1 | 0 | 0 | 0 | 0 |
| Andy Ellis | Wakefield | 2012 | 10 | 0 | 0 | 0 | 0 |
| | Harlequins | 2010-11 | 26(11) | 8 | 0 | 0 | 32 |
| Gareth Ellis | Hull | 2013-17, 2019 | 91(14) | 19 | 0 | 0 | 76 |
| | Leeds | 2005-08 | 109 | 24 | 1 | 0 | 98 |
| | Wakefield | 1999-2004 | 86(17) | 21 | 2 | 0 | 88 |
| Jamie Ellis | Castleford | 2012-14, 2018-19 | 58(8) | 12 | 150 | 2 | 350 |
| | Huddersfield | 2015-16 | 37(3) | 14 | 31 | 3 | 121 |
| | Hull | 2012 | 4(5) | 1 | 0 | 0 | 4 |
| | St Helens | 2009 | 1(2) | 0 | 1 | 0 | 2 |
| Danny Ellison | Castleford | 1998-99 | 7(16) | 6 | 0 | 0 | 24 |
| | Wigan | 1996-97 | 15(1) | 13 | 0 | 0 | 52 |
| Andrew Emelio | Widnes | 2005 | 22(2) | 8 | 0 | 0 | 32 |
| Jake Emmitt | Salford | 2013 | 5(10) | 0 | 0 | 0 | 0 |
| | Castleford | 2011-13 | 32(17) | 0 | 0 | 0 | 0 |
| | St Helens | 2008-10 | 1(16) | 1 | 0 | 0 | 4 |
| Anthony England | Wakefield | 2016-19 | 67(11) | 2 | 0 | 0 | 8 |
| | Warrington | 2014-15 | 12(21) | 3 | 0 | 0 | 12 |
| Matty English | Huddersfield | 2017-19 | 15(19) | 3 | 0 | 0 | 12 |
| Patrick Entat | Paris | 1996 | 2 | 2 | 0 | 0 | 8 |
| Jason Erba | Sheffield | 1997 | 1(4) | 0 | 0 | 0 | 0 |
| Morgan Escare | Wakefield | 2019 | 5 | 1 | 0 | 0 | 4 |
| | Wigan | 2017-19 | 23(22) | 14 | 39 | 2 | 136 |
| | Catalans | 2013-16 | 83 | 58 | 1 | 2 | 236 |
| Ryan Esders | Harlequins | 2009-16 | 9(11) | 3 | 0 | 0 | 12 |
| | Hull KR | 2009 | (1) | 0 | 0 | 0 | 0 |
| Sonny Esslemont | Hull KR | 2014-15 | (5) | 0 | 0 | 0 | 0 |
| Niall Evalds | Salford | 2013-19 | 108(11) | 78 | 0 | 0 | 312 |
| Ben Evans | Warrington | 2014-15 | 3(16) | 2 | 0 | 0 | 8 |
| | Bradford | 2013 | 3(12) | 1 | 0 | 0 | 4 |
| James Evans | Castleford | 2009-10 | 26(1) | 13 | 0 | 0 | 52 |
| | Bradford | 2007-08 | 43(5) | 20 | 0 | 0 | 80 |
| | Wakefield | 2006 | 6 | 3 | 0 | 0 | 12 |
| | Huddersfield | 2004-06 | 51 | 22 | 0 | 0 | 88 |
| Paul Evans | Paris | 1997 | 18 | 8 | 0 | 0 | 32 |
| Rhys Evans | Warrington | 2010-17 | 87(7) | 37 | 0 | 0 | 148 |
| Wayne Evans | London | 2002 | 11(6) | 2 | 0 | 0 | 8 |
| Toby Everett | London | 2014 | (2) | 0 | 0 | 0 | 0 |
| Richie Eyres | Warrington | 1997 | 2(5) | 0 | 0 | 0 | 0 |
| | Sheffield | 1997 | 2(3) | 0 | 0 | 0 | 0 |
| Henry Fa'afili | Warrington | 2004-07 | 90(1) | 70 | 0 | 0 | 280 |
| David Fa'alogo | Huddersfield | 2010-12 | 38(16) | 13 | 0 | 0 | 52 |
| Sala Fa'alogo | Widnes | 2004-05 | 8(15) | 2 | 0 | 0 | 8 |
| Richard Fa'aoso | Castleford | 2006 | 10(15) | 5 | 0 | 0 | 20 |
| Maurie Fa'asavalu | St Helens | 2004-10 | 5(137) | 29 | 0 | 0 | 116 |
| Bolouagi Fagborun | Huddersfield | 2004-06 | 4(2) | 1 | 0 | 0 | 4 |
| Theo Fages | St Helens | 2016-19 | 73(25) | 28 | 0 | 0 | 112 |
| | Salford | 2013-15 | 57(5) | 18 | 4 | 0 | 80 |
| Esene Faimalo | Salford | 1997-99 | 23(25) | 2 | 0 | 0 | 8 |
| | Leeds | 1996 | 3(3) | 0 | 0 | 0 | 0 |
| Joe Faimalo | Salford | 1998-2000 | 23(47) | 7 | 0 | 0 | 28 |
| | Oldham | 1996-97 | 37(5) | 7 | 0 | 0 | 28 |
| Jacob Fairbank | Huddersfield | 2011-15 | 12(3) | 0 | 0 | 0 | 0 |
| | Wakefield | 2014 | 1(3) | 0 | 0 | 0 | 0 |
| | London | 2013 | 4(1) | 1 | 0 | 0 | 4 |
| | Bradford | 2013 | (2) | 0 | 0 | 0 | 0 |
| Karl Fairbank | Bradford | 1996 | 17(2) | 4 | 0 | 0 | 16 |
| David Fairleigh | St Helens | 2001 | 26(1) | 8 | 0 | 0 | 32 |
| David Faiumu | Huddersfield | 2008-14 | 38(108) | 13 | 0 | 0 | 52 |
| Jamal Fakir | Bradford | 2014 | 5(8) | 1 | 0 | 0 | 4 |
| | Catalans | 2006-14 | 55(100) | 13 | 0 | 0 | 52 |
| Jim Fallon | Leeds | 1996 | 10 | 5 | 0 | 0 | 20 |
| Beau Falloon | Leeds | 2016 | 8(2) | 0 | 0 | 0 | 0 |
| Bureta Faraimo | Hull | 2018-19 | 51 | 27 | 4 | 0 | 116 |
| Owen Farnworth | Widnes | 2017-18 | 1(4) | 0 | 0 | 0 | 0 |
| Ben Farrar | London | 2014 | 22 | 1 | 0 | 0 | 4 |
| | Catalans | 2011 | 13 | 3 | 0 | 0 | 12 |
| Danny Farrar | Warrington | 1998-2000 | 76 | 13 | 0 | 0 | 52 |
| Andy Farrell | Wigan | 1996-2004 | 230 | 77 | 1026 | 16 | 2376 |
| Anthony Farrell | Widnes | 2002-03 | 24(22) | 4 | 1 | 0 | 18 |
| | Leeds | 1997-2001 | 99(23) | 18 | 0 | 0 | 72 |
| | Sheffield | 1996 | 14(5) | 5 | 0 | 0 | 20 |
| Connor Farrell | Widnes | 2016 | 3(9) | 3 | 0 | 0 | 12 |
| | Wigan | 2014-15 | 1(8) | 1 | 0 | 0 | 4 |
| Craig Farrell | Hull | 2000-01 | 1(3) | 0 | 0 | 0 | 0 |
| Izaac Farrell | Huddersfield | 2019 | 2 | 0 | 4 | 0 | 8 |
| Liam Farrell | Wigan | 2010-19 | 170(50) | 85 | 0 | 0 | 340 |
| Brad Fash | Hull | 2015, 2017-19 | 2(62) | 2 | 0 | 0 | 8 |
| Abraham Fatnowna | London | 1997-98 | 7(2) | 2 | 0 | 0 | 8 |
| | Workington | 1996 | 5 | 2 | 0 | 0 | 8 |
| Sione Faumuina | Castleford | 2009 | 18 | 1 | 0 | 0 | 4 |
| | Hull | 2005 | 3 | 1 | 0 | 0 | 4 |
| Vince Fawcett | Wakefield | 1999 | 13(1) | 2 | 0 | 0 | 8 |
| | Warrington | 1998 | 4(7) | 1 | 0 | 0 | 4 |
| | Oldham | 1997 | 5 | 3 | 0 | 0 | 12 |
| Danny Fearon | Huddersfield | 2001 | (1) | 0 | 0 | 0 | 0 |
| | Halifax | 1999-2000 | 5(6) | 1 | 0 | 0 | 4 |
| Chris Feather | Castleford | 2009 | 1(23) | 0 | 0 | 0 | 0 |
| | Bradford | 2007-08 | 7(20) | 1 | 0 | 0 | 4 |
| | Leeds | 2003-04, 2006 | 16(35) | 6 | 0 | 0 | 24 |
| | Wakefield | 2001-02, 2004-05 | 29(32) | 9 | 0 | 0 | 36 |
| Dom Feaunati | Leigh | 2005 | 4 | 1 | 0 | 0 | 4 |
| | St Helens | 2004 | 10(7) | 7 | 0 | 0 | 28 |

# Super League Players 1996-2019

| PLAYER | CLUB | YEAR | APP | TRIES | GOALS | FG | PTS |
|---|---|---|---|---|---|---|---|
| Adel Fellous | Hull | 2008 | 1(2) | 0 | 0 | 0 | 0 |
|  | Catalans | 2006-07 | 16(22) | 4 | 0 | 0 | 16 |
| Luke Felsch | Hull | 2000-01 | 46(6) | 7 | 0 | 0 | 28 |
|  | Gateshead | 1999 | 28(1) | 2 | 0 | 0 | 8 |
| Leon Felton | Warrington | 2002 | 4(2) | 0 | 0 | 0 | 0 |
|  | St Helens | 2001 | 1(1) | 0 | 0 | 0 | 0 |
| Dale Ferguson | Huddersfield | 2011-13, 2017-19 | 61(23) | 16 | 0 | 0 | 64 |
|  | Bradford | 2014 | 3(3) | 0 | 0 | 0 | 0 |
|  | Hull KR | 2013 | 3(1) | 1 | 0 | 0 | 4 |
|  | Wakefield | 2007-11 | 40(14) | 12 | 0 | 0 | 48 |
| Brett Ferres | Leeds | 2016-19 | 50(14) | 11 | 0 | 0 | 44 |
|  | Huddersfield | 2012-15 | 72 | 27 | 0 | 0 | 108 |
|  | Castleford | 2009-12 | 78(5) | 26 | 0 | 0 | 104 |
|  | Wakefield | 2007-08 | 36(2) | 6 | 5 | 0 | 34 |
|  | Bradford | 2005-06 | 18(17) | 11 | 2 | 0 | 48 |
| David Ferriol | Catalans | 2007-12 | 72(55) | 8 | 0 | 0 | 32 |
| Jason Ferris | Leigh | 2005 | 4 | 1 | 0 | 0 | 4 |
| Callum Field | Wigan | 2017-18 | (8) | 0 | 0 | 0 | 0 |
| Jamie Field | Wakefield | 1999-2006 | 133(59) | 19 | 0 | 0 | 76 |
|  | Huddersfield | 1998 | 15(5) | 0 | 0 | 0 | 0 |
|  | Leeds | 1996-97 | 3(11) | 0 | 0 | 0 | 0 |
| Mark Field | Wakefield | 2003-07 | 28(7) | 3 | 0 | 0 | 12 |
| Jamie Fielden | London | 2003 | (1) | 0 | 0 | 0 | 0 |
|  | Huddersfield | 1998-2000 | 4(8) | 0 | 0 | 0 | 0 |
| Stuart Fielden | Huddersfield | 2013 | 8(1) | 0 | 0 | 0 | 0 |
|  | Wigan | 2006-12 | 105(24) | 2 | 0 | 0 | 8 |
|  | Bradford | 1998-2006 | 142(78) | 41 | 0 | 0 | 164 |
| David Fifita | Wakefield | 2016-19 | 49(31) | 15 | 0 | 0 | 60 |
| Lafaele Filipo | Workington | 1996 | 15(4) | 3 | 0 | 0 | 12 |
| Salesi Finau | Warrington | 1996-97 | 16(15) | 8 | 0 | 0 | 32 |
| Brett Finch | Wigan | 2011-12 | 49(3) | 16 | 0 | 0 | 64 |
| Vinny Finigan | Bradford | 2010 | 4(1) | 4 | 0 | 0 | 16 |
| Liam Finn | Widnes | 2018 | 1 | 0 | 0 | 0 | 0 |
|  | Wakefield | 2004, 2016-18 | 70(4) | 5 | 219 | 0 | 458 |
|  | Castleford | 2014-15 | 45(2) | 8 | 5 | 2 | 44 |
|  | Halifax | 2002-03 | 16(5) | 2 | 30 | 1 | 69 |
| Lee Finnerty | Halifax | 2003 | 18(2) | 5 | 2 | 0 | 24 |
| Phil Finney | Warrington | 1998 | 1 | 0 | 0 | 0 | 0 |
| Simon Finnigan | Widnes | 2003-05, 2012 | 56(24) | 21 | 0 | 0 | 84 |
|  | Huddersfield | 2009-10 | 22(5) | 6 | 0 | 0 | 24 |
|  | Bradford | 2008 | 14(13) | 8 | 0 | 0 | 32 |
|  | Salford | 2006-07 | 50 | 17 | 0 | 0 | 68 |
| Matt Firth | Halifax | 2000-01 | 12(2) | 0 | 0 | 0 | 0 |
| Andy Fisher | Wakefield | 1999-2000 | 31(8) | 4 | 0 | 0 | 16 |
| Ben Fisher | London | 2013 | 8(12) | 1 | 0 | 0 | 4 |
|  | Catalans | 2012 | 9(5) | 1 | 0 | 0 | 4 |
|  | Hull KR | 2007-11 | 78(46) | 18 | 0 | 0 | 72 |
| Craig Fitzgibbon | Hull | 2010-11 | 42(1) | 9 | 8 | 0 | 52 |
| Daniel Fitzhenry | Hull KR | 2008-09 | 36(11) | 14 | 0 | 0 | 56 |
| Karl Fitzpatrick | Salford | 2004-07, 2009-10 | 89(11) | 33 | 2 | 0 | 136 |
| Conor Fitzsimmons | Castleford | 2016 | (2) | 0 | 0 | 0 | 0 |
| Mark Flanagan | Salford | 2016-19 | 58(21) | 8 | 0 | 0 | 32 |
|  | St Helens | 2012-15 | 40(39) | 9 | 0 | 0 | 36 |
|  | Wigan | 2009 | 3(7) | 1 | 0 | 0 | 4 |
| Chris Flannery | St Helens | 2007-12 | 108(11) | 32 | 0 | 0 | 128 |
| Darren Fleary | Leigh | 2005 | 24 | 1 | 0 | 0 | 4 |
|  | Huddersfield | 2003-04 | 43(8) | 4 | 0 | 0 | 16 |
|  | Leeds | 1997-2002 | 98(9) | 3 | 0 | 0 | 12 |
| Daniel Fleming | Castleford | 2013-14 | (15) | 1 | 0 | 0 | 4 |
| Greg Fleming | London | 1999-2001 | 64(1) | 40 | 2 | 0 | 164 |
| Matty Fleming | London | 2019 | 12(1) | 6 | 0 | 0 | 24 |
|  | Leigh | 2017 | 5 | 1 | 0 | 0 | 4 |
|  | St Helens | 2015-17 | 17 | 7 | 0 | 0 | 28 |
| Adam Fletcher | Castleford | 2006, 2008 | 16(7) | 11 | 0 | 0 | 44 |
| Bryan Fletcher | Wigan | 2006-07 | 47(2) | 14 | 0 | 0 | 56 |
| Richard Fletcher | Castleford | 2006 | 13(5) | 3 | 4 | 0 | 20 |
|  | Hull | 1999-2004 | 11(56) | 5 | 0 | 0 | 20 |
| Greg Florimo | Halifax | 2000 | 26 | 6 | 4 | 0 | 32 |
|  | Wigan | 1999 | 18(2) | 7 | 1 | 0 | 30 |
| Ben Flower | Wigan | 2012-19 | 129(30) | 20 | 0 | 0 | 80 |
|  | Crusaders | 2010-11 | 10(23) | 2 | 0 | 0 | 8 |
|  | Celtic | 2009 | 2(15) | 0 | 0 | 0 | 0 |
| Jason Flowers | Salford | 2004 | 6(1) | 0 | 0 | 0 | 0 |
|  | Halifax | 2002 | 24(4) | 4 | 0 | 0 | 16 |
|  | Castleford | 1996-2001 | 119(19) | 33 | 0 | 1 | 133 |
| Stuart Flowers | Castleford | 1996 | (3) | 0 | 0 | 0 | 0 |
| Adrian Flynn | Castleford | 1996-97 | 19(2) | 10 | 0 | 0 | 40 |
| Paddy Flynn | Castleford | 2016 | 9(1) | 6 | 0 | 0 | 24 |
|  | Widnes | 2012-15 | 72 | 41 | 0 | 0 | 164 |
| Wayne Flynn | Sheffield | 1997 | 3(5) | 0 | 0 | 0 | 0 |
| Adam Fogerty | Warrington | 1998 | 4 | 0 | 0 | 0 | 0 |
|  | St Helens | 1996 | 13 | 1 | 0 | 0 | 4 |
| Mahe Fonua | Hull | 2016-17 | 50 | 25 | 0 | 0 | 100 |
| Liam Foran | Salford | 2013 | 10(3) | 1 | 0 | 0 | 4 |
| Carl Forber | Leigh | 2005 | 4 | 1 | 0 | 0 | 4 |
|  | St Helens | 2004 | 1(1) | 0 | 6 | 0 | 12 |
| Paul Forber | Salford | 1997-98 | 19(12) | 4 | 0 | 0 | 16 |
| Byron Ford | Hull KR | 2007 | 13 | 6 | 0 | 0 | 24 |
| James Ford | Castleford | 2009 | 3(5) | 1 | 0 | 0 | 4 |
| Mike Ford | Castleford | 1997-98 | 25(12) | 5 | 0 | 3 | 23 |
|  | Warrington | 1996 | 3 | 0 | 0 | 0 | 0 |
| Jim Forshaw | Salford | 1999 | (1) | 0 | 0 | 0 | 0 |
| Mike Forshaw | Warrington | 2004 | 20(1) | 5 | 0 | 0 | 20 |
|  | Bradford | 1997-2003 | 162(7) | 32 | 0 | 0 | 128 |
|  | Leeds | 1996 | 11(3) | 5 | 0 | 0 | 20 |
| Carl Forster | Salford | 2015-16 | 5(7) | 1 | 0 | 0 | 4 |
|  | St Helens | 2011-12, 2014 | (4) | 0 | 0 | 0 | 0 |
|  | London | 2014 | 2(3) | 0 | 0 | 0 | 0 |
| Mark Forster | Warrington | 1996-2000 | 102(1) | 40 | 0 | 0 | 160 |
| Liam Forsyth | Wigan | 2017-18 | 11(2) | 3 | 0 | 0 | 12 |
| Alex Foster | Castleford | 2017-19 | 28(11) | 8 | 0 | 0 | 32 |
|  | London | 2014 | 20 | 3 | 0 | 0 | 12 |
|  | Leeds | 2013 | (8) | 1 | 0 | 0 | 4 |
| David Foster | Halifax | 2000-01 | 4(9) | 0 | 0 | 0 | 0 |
| Jamie Foster | Huddersfield | 2016 | 3 | 2 | 5 | 0 | 18 |
|  | Bradford | 2013-14 | 32 | 12 | 111 | 0 | 270 |
|  | Hull | 2012 | 9 | 5 | 45 | 0 | 110 |
|  | St Helens | 2010-12 | 44(3) | 30 | 201 | 0 | 522 |
| Peter Fox | Wakefield | 2007, 2012-14 | 85 | 44 | 0 | 0 | 176 |
|  | Hull KR | 2008-11 | 95 | 52 | 0 | 0 | 208 |
| Matty Fozard | London | 2019 | 7(16) | 3 | 0 | 0 | 12 |
|  | St Helens | 2014 | 1 | 0 | 0 | 0 | 0 |
| Nick Fozzard | Castleford | 2011 | 7(10) | 0 | 0 | 0 | 0 |
|  | St Helens | 2004-08, 2010 | 100(25) | 7 | 0 | 0 | 28 |
|  | Hull KR | 2009 | 18(4) | 1 | 0 | 0 | 4 |
|  | Warrington | 2002-03 | 43(11) | 2 | 0 | 0 | 8 |
|  | Huddersfield | 1998-2000 | 24(8) | 2 | 0 | 0 | 8 |
|  | Leeds | 1996-97 | 6(16) | 3 | 0 | 0 | 12 |
| David Fraisse | Workington | 1996 | 8 | 0 | 0 | 0 | 0 |
| Daniel Frame | Widnes | 2002-05 | 100(6) | 24 | 0 | 0 | 96 |
| Paul Franze | Castleford | 2006 | 2(1) | 0 | 0 | 0 | 0 |
| Matt Frawley | Huddersfield | 2019 | 19(2) | 4 | 0 | 0 | 16 |
| Laurent Frayssinous | Catalans | 2006 | 14(2) | 3 | 32 | 0 | 76 |
| Bevan French | Wigan | 2019 | 3(5) | 6 | 0 | 0 | 24 |
| Andrew Frew | Halifax | 2003 | 17 | 5 | 0 | 0 | 20 |
|  | Wakefield | 2002 | 21 | 8 | 0 | 0 | 32 |
|  | Huddersfield | 2001 | 26 | 15 | 0 | 0 | 60 |
| Dale Fritz | Castleford | 1999-2003 | 120(4) | 9 | 0 | 0 | 36 |
| Gareth Frodsham | St Helens | 2008-09 | 1(9) | 0 | 0 | 0 | 0 |
| Liam Fulton | Huddersfield | 2009 | 12(3) | 4 | 0 | 0 | 16 |
| David Furner | Leeds | 2003-04 | 45 | 8 | 23 | 0 | 78 |
|  | Wigan | 2001-02 | 51(2) | 21 | 13 | 0 | 110 |
| David Furness | Castleford | 1996 | (1) | 0 | 0 | 0 | 0 |
| Matt Gafa | Harlequins | 2006-09 | 81 | 26 | 16 | 0 | 136 |
| Luke Gale | Castleford | 2015-18 | 100 | 32 | 402 | 15 | 947 |
|  | Bradford | 2012-14 | 56(3) | 13 | 108 | 4 | 272 |
|  | Harlequins | 2009-11 | 56(12) | 18 | 86 | 3 | 247 |
| Ben Galea | Hull | 2013 | 12(2) | 3 | 0 | 0 | 12 |
|  | Hull KR | 2008-12 | 115(2) | 33 | 0 | 0 | 132 |
| Danny Galea | Widnes | 2014-15 | 38(4) | 5 | 0 | 0 | 20 |
| Tommy Gallagher | Hull KR | 2007 | 1(7) | 0 | 0 | 0 | 0 |
|  | Widnes | 2004 | (6) | 0 | 0 | 0 | 0 |
|  | London | 2003 | 1(9) | 1 | 0 | 0 | 4 |
| Keith Galloway | Leeds | 2016-17 | 28(4) | 1 | 0 | 0 | 4 |
| Mark Gamson | Sheffield | 1996 | 3 | 0 | 0 | 0 | 0 |
| Jim Gannon | Hull KR | 2007 | 7(16) | 1 | 0 | 0 | 4 |
|  | Huddersfield | 2003-06 | 79(14) | 11 | 0 | 0 | 44 |
|  | Halifax | 1999-2002 | 83(4) | 14 | 0 | 0 | 56 |
| Josh Ganson | Wigan | 2017-18 | 1(6) | 2 | 0 | 0 | 8 |
| Mitch Garbutt | Hull KR | 2019 | 2(17) | 5 | 0 | 0 | 20 |
|  | Leeds | 2015-18 | 36(25) | 7 | 0 | 0 | 28 |
| Steve Garces | Salford | 2001 | (1) | 0 | 0 | 0 | 0 |
| Benjamin Garcia | Catalans | 2013-19 | 66(46) | 19 | 0 | 0 | 76 |
| Jean-Marc Garcia | Sheffield | 1996-97 | 35(3) | 22 | 0 | 0 | 88 |
| Ade Gardner | Hull KR | 2014 | 18 | 7 | 0 | 0 | 28 |
|  | St Helens | 2002-13 | 236(12) | 146 | 0 | 0 | 584 |
| Matt Gardner | Harlequins | 2009 | 6(3) | 2 | 0 | 0 | 8 |
|  | Huddersfield | 2006-07 | 22(3) | 7 | 0 | 0 | 28 |
|  | Castleford | 2004 | 1 | 1 | 0 | 0 | 4 |
| Steve Gartland | Oldham | 1996 | 1(1) | 0 | 0 | 1 | 2 |
| Daniel Gartner | Bradford | 2001-03 | 74(1) | 26 | 0 | 0 | 104 |
| Dean Gaskell | Warrington | 2002-05 | 58(1) | 10 | 0 | 0 | 40 |

| PLAYER | CLUB | YEAR | APP | TRIES | GOALS | FG | PTS |
|---|---|---|---|---|---|---|---|
| Lee Gaskell | Huddersfield | 2017-19 | 71 | 21 | 29 | 0 | 142 |
| | Bradford | 2014 | 21 | 5 | 0 | 0 | 20 |
| | Salford | 2013 | 17 | 8 | 2 | 0 | 36 |
| | St Helens | 2010-13 | 33(9) | 14 | 12 | 1 | 81 |
| George Gatis | Huddersfield | 2008 | 5(5) | 1 | 0 | 0 | 4 |
| Richard Gay | Castleford | 1996-2002 | 94(16) | 39 | 0 | 0 | 156 |
| Andrew Gee | Warrington | 2000-01 | 33(1) | 4 | 0 | 0 | 16 |
| Matty Gee | London | 2019 | 14(8) | 5 | 0 | 0 | 20 |
| | Salford | 2015 | (2) | 0 | 0 | 0 | 0 |
| Anthony Gelling | Wigan | 2012-17 | 101(1) | 52 | 0 | 0 | 208 |
| Stanley Gene | Hull KR | 2007-09 | 37(17) | 9 | 0 | 0 | 36 |
| | Bradford | 2006 | 5(16) | 8 | 0 | 0 | 32 |
| | Huddersfield | 2001, 2003-05 | 70(6) | 27 | 0 | 0 | 108 |
| | Hull | 2000-01 | 5(23) | 6 | 0 | 0 | 24 |
| Steve Georgallis | Warrington | 2001 | 5(1) | 2 | 0 | 0 | 8 |
| Luke George | Bradford | 2014 | 9(1) | 3 | 0 | 0 | 12 |
| | Huddersfield | 2012-13 | 28(2) | 18 | 0 | 0 | 72 |
| | Hull KR | 2013 | 4 | 2 | 0 | 0 | 8 |
| | Wakefield | 2007-11 | 38(3) | 24 | 0 | 0 | 96 |
| Shaun Geritas | Warrington | 1997 | (5) | 1 | 0 | 0 | 4 |
| Alex Gerrard | Widnes | 2012-18 | 48(40) | 4 | 0 | 0 | 16 |
| Anthony Gibbons | Leeds | 1996 | 9(4) | 2 | 0 | 1 | 9 |
| David Gibbons | Leeds | 1996 | 3(4) | 2 | 0 | 0 | 8 |
| Scott Gibbs | St Helens | 1996 | 9 | 3 | 0 | 0 | 12 |
| Ashley Gibson | Wakefield | 2016-17 | 9 | 4 | 0 | 0 | 16 |
| | Castleford | 2014-15 | 27 | 9 | 0 | 0 | 36 |
| | Salford | 2010-13 | 77(4) | 41 | 0 | 0 | 164 |
| | Leeds | 2005-09 | 25(7) | 13 | 9 | 0 | 70 |
| Damian Gibson | Castleford | 2003-04 | 40(3) | 5 | 0 | 0 | 20 |
| | Salford | 2002 | 28 | 3 | 0 | 0 | 12 |
| | Halifax | 1998-2001 | 104(1) | 39 | 0 | 0 | 156 |
| | Leeds | 1997 | 18 | 3 | 0 | 0 | 12 |
| Kurt Gidley | Warrington | 2016-17 | 44 | 11 | 97 | 0 | 238 |
| Matt Gidley | St Helens | 2007-10 | 105 | 40 | 6 | 0 | 172 |
| Tony Gigot | Catalans | 2010-11, 2015-19 | 117(13) | 43 | 51 | 12 | 286 |
| | London | 2014 | 2 | 0 | 4 | 0 | 8 |
| Ian Gildart | Oldham | 1996-97 | 31(7) | 0 | 0 | 0 | 0 |
| Oliver Gildart | Wigan | 2015-19 | 106(2) | 50 | 0 | 0 | 200 |
| | Salford | 2015 | 3 | 1 | 0 | 0 | 4 |
| Chris Giles | Widnes | 2003-04 | 35 | 12 | 0 | 0 | 48 |
| | St Helens | 2002 | (1) | 0 | 0 | 0 | 0 |
| Kieran Gill | Castleford | 2017-18 | 4 | 4 | 0 | 0 | 16 |
| Peter Gill | London | 1996-99 | 75(6) | 20 | 0 | 0 | 80 |
| Carl Gillespie | Halifax | 1996-99 | 47(36) | 13 | 0 | 0 | 52 |
| Michael Gillett | London | 2001-02 | 23(21) | 12 | 2 | 0 | 52 |
| Simon Gillies | Warrington | 1999 | 28 | 6 | 0 | 0 | 24 |
| Tom Gilmore | Widnes | 2012-18 | 38(1) | 11 | 51 | 3 | 149 |
| Lee Gilmour | Wakefield | 2014 | 10(3) | 2 | 0 | 0 | 8 |
| | Castleford | 2013 | 10(2) | 0 | 0 | 0 | 0 |
| | Huddersfield | 2010-12 | 71(1) | 17 | 0 | 0 | 68 |
| | St Helens | 2004-09 | 149(3) | 41 | 0 | 0 | 164 |
| | Bradford | 2001-03 | 44(31) | 20 | 0 | 0 | 80 |
| | Wigan | 1997-2000 | 44(39) | 22 | 0 | 0 | 88 |
| Marc Glanville | Leeds | 1998-99 | 43(3) | 5 | 0 | 0 | 20 |
| Eddie Glaze | Castleford | 1996 | 1 | 0 | 0 | 0 | 0 |
| Paul Gleadhill | Leeds | 1996 | 4 | 0 | 0 | 0 | 0 |
| Ben Gledhill | Salford | 2012-13 | 3(10) | 1 | 0 | 0 | 4 |
| | Wakefield | 2010-11 | (16) | 0 | 0 | 0 | 0 |
| Mark Gleeson | Warrington | 2000-08 | 38(102) | 12 | 0 | 0 | 48 |
| Martin Gleeson | Salford | 2013-14 | 26(1) | 4 | 0 | 0 | 16 |
| | Hull | 2011 | 6 | 4 | 0 | 0 | 16 |
| | Wigan | 2009-11 | 46(1) | 19 | 0 | 0 | 76 |
| | Warrington | 2005-09 | 110(1) | 44 | 0 | 0 | 176 |
| | St Helens | 2002-04 | 56(1) | 25 | 0 | 0 | 100 |
| | Huddersfield | 1999-2001 | 47(9) | 18 | 0 | 0 | 72 |
| Sean Gleeson | Hull KR | 2013 | 6 | 0 | 0 | 0 | 0 |
| | Salford | 2011-12 | 35 | 14 | 0 | 0 | 56 |
| | Wakefield | 2007-10 | 67(6) | 20 | 0 | 0 | 80 |
| | Wigan | 2005-06 | 3(3) | 0 | 0 | 0 | 0 |
| Jon Goddard | Hull KR | 2007 | 20 | 2 | 0 | 0 | 8 |
| | Castleford | 2000-01 | (2) | 0 | 0 | 0 | 0 |
| Richard Goddard | Castleford | 1996-97 | 11(3) | 2 | 10 | 0 | 28 |
| Brad Godden | Leeds | 1998-99 | 47 | 15 | 0 | 0 | 60 |
| Pita Godinet | Wakefield | 2014-15 | 18(19) | 10 | 0 | 0 | 40 |
| Wayne Godwin | Salford | 2011-13, 2015 | 43(8) | 6 | 0 | 0 | 24 |
| | Bradford | 2008-10 | 16(44) | 9 | 0 | 0 | 36 |
| | Hull | 2007 | 3(13) | 1 | 0 | 0 | 4 |
| | Wigan | 2005-06 | 9(38) | 6 | 0 | 0 | 24 |
| | Castleford | 2001-04 | 30(33) | 18 | 56 | 0 | 184 |
| Jason Golden | London | 2012 | 7(2) | 1 | 0 | 0 | 4 |
| | Harlequins | 2009-11 | 34(12) | 3 | 0 | 0 | 12 |
| | Wakefield | 2007-08 | 26(5) | 1 | 0 | 0 | 4 |
| Marvin Golden | Widnes | 2003 | 4 | 1 | 0 | 0 | 4 |
| | London | 2001 | 17(2) | 1 | 0 | 0 | 4 |
| | Halifax | 2000 | 20(2) | 5 | 0 | 0 | 20 |
| | Leeds | 1996-99 | 43(11) | 19 | 0 | 0 | 76 |
| Ashton Golding | Leeds | 2014-18 | 42(9) | 5 | 14 | 0 | 48 |
| Brett Goldspink | Halifax | 2000-02 | 64(5) | 2 | 0 | 0 | 8 |
| | Wigan | 1999 | 6(16) | 1 | 0 | 0 | 4 |
| | St Helens | 1998 | 19(4) | 2 | 0 | 0 | 8 |
| | Oldham | 1997 | 13(2) | 0 | 0 | 0 | 0 |
| Lee Gomersall | Hull KR | 2008 | 1 | 0 | 0 | 0 | 0 |
| Bryson Goodwin | Warrington | 2018-19 | 52 | 20 | 29 | 0 | 138 |
| Luke Goodwin | London | 1998 | 9(2) | 3 | 1 | 1 | 15 |
| | Oldham | 1997 | 16(4) | 10 | 17 | 2 | 76 |
| Grant Gore | Widnes | 2012-15 | 6(11) | 1 | 0 | 0 | 4 |
| Aaron Gorrell | Catalans | 2007-08 | 23 | 6 | 14 | 0 | 52 |
| Andy Gorski | Salford | 2001-02 | (2) | 0 | 0 | 0 | 0 |
| Cyrille Gossard | Catalans | 2006-12 | 54(30) | 5 | 0 | 0 | 20 |
| Mickael Goudemand | Catalans | 2018-19 | 7(22) | 1 | 0 | 0 | 4 |
| Bobbie Goulding | Salford | 2001-02 | 31(1) | 2 | 56 | 4 | 124 |
| | Wakefield | 2000 | 12 | 3 | 25 | 3 | 65 |
| | Huddersfield | 1998-99 | 27(1) | 3 | 65 | 4 | 146 |
| | St Helens | 1996-98 | 42(2) | 9 | 210 | 4 | 460 |
| Bobbie Goulding (Jnr) | Wakefield | 2013 | 1(2) | 0 | 1 | 0 | 2 |
| Darrell Goulding | Hull KR | 2015 | 8 | 1 | 0 | 0 | 4 |
| | Wigan | 2005-14 | 129(24) | 68 | 0 | 0 | 272 |
| | Salford | 2009 | 9 | 5 | 0 | 0 | 20 |
| Mick Govin | Leigh | 2005 | 5(6) | 4 | 0 | 0 | 16 |
| Craig Gower | London | 2012-13 | 40 | 7 | 24 | 0 | 76 |
| David Gower | Salford | 2006-07 | (16) | 0 | 0 | 0 | 0 |
| Regan Grace | St Helens | 2017-19 | 82 | 46 | 0 | 0 | 184 |
| Shane Grady | London | 2013 | 5(4) | 1 | 2 | 0 | 8 |
| James Graham | St Helens | 2003-11 | 132(63) | 47 | 0 | 0 | 188 |
| Nathan Graham | Bradford | 1996-98 | 17(28) | 4 | 0 | 1 | 17 |
| Nick Graham | Wigan | 2003 | 13(1) | 2 | 0 | 0 | 8 |
| Dalton Grant | Crusaders | 2011 | (1) | 0 | 0 | 0 | 0 |
| Jon Grayshon | Harlequins | 2007-09 | 10(32) | 4 | 0 | 0 | 16 |
| | Huddersfield | 2003-06 | 7(43) | 5 | 0 | 0 | 20 |
| Blake Green | Wigan | 2013-14 | 42(1) | 15 | 0 | 0 | 60 |
| | Hull KR | 2011-12 | 35 | 14 | 0 | 0 | 56 |
| Brett Green | Gateshead | 1999 | 10(2) | 0 | 0 | 0 | 0 |
| Chris Green | Wakefield | 2019 | (4) | 0 | 0 | 0 | 0 |
| | Hull | 2012-19 | 33(92) | 7 | 0 | 0 | 28 |
| James Green | Castleford | 2018 | 1(3) | 0 | 0 | 0 | 0 |
| | Leigh | 2017 | 4(5) | 0 | 0 | 0 | 0 |
| | Hull KR | 2012-16 | 8(64) | 3 | 0 | 0 | 12 |
| Toby Green | Huddersfield | 2001 | 3(1) | 1 | 0 | 0 | 4 |
| Craig Greenhill | Castleford | 2004 | 21(4) | 1 | 0 | 0 | 4 |
| | Hull | 2002-03 | 56 | 3 | 2 | 0 | 16 |
| Clint Greenshields | Catalans | 2007-12 | 137 | 81 | 0 | 0 | 324 |
| Brandon Greenwood | Halifax | 1996 | 1 | 0 | 0 | 0 | 0 |
| Gareth Greenwood | Huddersfield | 2003 | (1) | 0 | 0 | 0 | 0 |
| | Halifax | 2002 | 1 | 0 | 0 | 0 | 0 |
| James Greenwood | Hull KR | 2015-16, 2018-19 | 29(23) | 7 | 0 | 0 | 28 |
| | Salford | 2015 | 1(1) | 1 | 0 | 0 | 4 |
| | Wigan | 2013, 2015 | | | | | |
| | London | 2014 | 10(5) | 3 | 0 | 0 | 12 |
| Joe Greenwood | Wigan | 2018-19 | 21(10) | 11 | 0 | 0 | 44 |
| | St Helens | 2012-17 | 40(28) | 26 | 0 | 0 | 104 |
| Lee Greenwood | Huddersfield | 2005 | 7 | 3 | 0 | 0 | 12 |
| | London | 2004-05 | 30(2) | 19 | 0 | 0 | 76 |
| | Halifax | 2000-03 | 38(2) | 17 | 0 | 0 | 68 |
| | Sheffield | 1999 | 1(1) | 0 | 0 | 0 | 0 |
| Nick Gregson | Wigan | 2016-17 | 5(9) | 1 | 0 | 0 | 4 |
| James Grehan | Castleford | 2012 | 2(2) | 0 | 0 | 0 | 0 |
| Maxime Greseque | Wakefield | 2007 | 2(1) | 0 | 0 | 0 | 0 |
| Mathieu Griffi | Catalans | 2006-08 | 1(25) | 0 | 0 | 0 | 0 |
| Darrell Griffin | Salford | 2013-15 | 31(27) | 1 | 0 | 0 | 4 |
| | Leeds | 2012 | 8(19) | 2 | 0 | 0 | 8 |
| | Huddersfield | 2007-11 | 65(60) | 13 | 0 | 0 | 52 |
| | Wakefield | 2003-06 | 55(37) | 9 | 3 | 0 | 42 |
| George Griffin | Salford | 2015-19 | 69(22) | 16 | 0 | 0 | 64 |
| | Wakefield | 2015 | 5 | 0 | 0 | 0 | 0 |
| | London | 2014 | (19) | 1 | 0 | 0 | 4 |
| | Hull KR | 2012-13 | 11(7) | 0 | 0 | 0 | 0 |
| Josh Griffin | Hull | 2017-19 | 69(5) | 22 | 0 | 0 | 88 |
| | Salford | 2014-16 | 42 | 23 | 77 | 0 | 246 |
| | Castleford | 2012 | 20 | 13 | 1 | 0 | 54 |
| | Wakefield | 2011 | 17 | 5 | 21 | 0 | 62 |
| | Huddersfield | 2009 | 2 | 0 | 0 | 0 | 0 |
| Jonathan Griffiths | Paris | 1996 | (4) | 1 | 0 | 0 | 4 |
| Andrew Grima | Workington | 1996 | 2(9) | 2 | 0 | 0 | 8 |

171

# Super League Players 1996-2019

| PLAYER | CLUB | YEAR | APP | TRIES | GOALS | FG | PTS |
|---|---|---|---|---|---|---|---|
| Tony Grimaldi | Hull | 2000-01 | 56(1) | 14 | 0 | 0 | 56 |
| | Gateshead | 1999 | 27(2) | 10 | 0 | 0 | 40 |
| Danny Grimley | Sheffield | 1996 | 4(1) | 1 | 0 | 0 | 4 |
| Scott Grix | Huddersfield | 2010-16, 2019 | 141(11) | 53 | 32 | 0 | 276 |
| | Wakefield | 2008-09, 2017-18 | 80(3) | 32 | 0 | 0 | 128 |
| Simon Grix | Warrington | 2006-14 | 133(25) | 42 | 0 | 0 | 168 |
| | Halifax | 2003 | 2(4) | 0 | 0 | 0 | 0 |
| Brett Grogan | Gateshead | 1999 | 14(7) | 3 | 0 | 0 | 12 |
| Brent Grose | Warrington | 2003-07 | 134(1) | 55 | 0 | 0 | 220 |
| David Guasch | Catalans | 2010 | 1 | 0 | 0 | 0 | 0 |
| Joan Guasch | Catalans | 2014-15 | (6) | 0 | 0 | 0 | 0 |
| Renaud Guigue | Catalans | 2006 | 14(4) | 3 | 0 | 0 | 12 |
| Jerome Guisset | Catalans | 2006-10 | 102(23) | 9 | 0 | 0 | 36 |
| | Wigan | 2005 | 20(2) | 3 | 0 | 0 | 12 |
| | Warrington | 2000-04 | 59(65) | 21 | 0 | 0 | 84 |
| Awen Guttenbeil | Castleford | 2008 | 19 | 0 | 0 | 0 | 0 |
| Reece Guy | Oldham | 1996 | 3(4) | 0 | 0 | 0 | 0 |
| Josh Guzdek | Hull KR | 2013, 2015 | 2 | 1 | 0 | 0 | 4 |
| Titus Gwaze | Wakefield | 2019 | (4) | 0 | 0 | 0 | 0 |
| Tom Haberecht | Castleford | 2008 | 2(2) | 1 | 0 | 0 | 4 |
| Dean Hadley | Hull KR | 2019 | 5(1) | 0 | 0 | 0 | 0 |
| | Hull | 2013-16, 2018-19 | 55(26) | 10 | 0 | 0 | 40 |
| | Wakefield | 2017 | 14(7) | 2 | 0 | 0 | 8 |
| Gareth Haggerty | Harlequins | 2008-09 | 8(28) | 6 | 0 | 0 | 24 |
| | Salford | 2004-07 | 1(93) | 15 | 0 | 0 | 60 |
| | Widnes | 2002 | 1(2) | 1 | 0 | 0 | 4 |
| Kurt Haggerty | Widnes | 2012 | 6(8) | 2 | 0 | 0 | 8 |
| Andy Haigh | St Helens | 1996-98 | 20(16) | 11 | 0 | 0 | 44 |
| Scott Hale | St Helens | 2011 | (3) | 1 | 0 | 0 | 4 |
| Michael Haley | Leeds | 2008 | (1) | 0 | 0 | 0 | 0 |
| Carl Hall | Leeds | 1996 | 7(2) | 3 | 0 | 0 | 12 |
| Craig Hall | Hull KR | 2011-14, 2018-19 | 102(3) | 51 | 65 | 2 | 336 |
| | Wakefield | 2015-16 | 35 | 14 | 30 | 0 | 116 |
| | Hull | 2007-10 | 59(9) | 39 | 11 | 0 | 178 |
| Glenn Hall | Bradford | 2010 | 7(18) | 2 | 0 | 0 | 8 |
| Martin Hall | Halifax | 1998 | 2(10) | 0 | 0 | 0 | 0 |
| | Hull | 1999 | 7 | 0 | 0 | 0 | 0 |
| | Castleford | 1998 | 4 | 0 | 0 | 0 | 0 |
| | Wigan | 1996-97 | 31(5) | 7 | 6 | 0 | 40 |
| Ryan Hall | Leeds | 2007-18 | 278(3) | 196 | 0 | 0 | 784 |
| Steve Hall | Widnes | 2004 | 1 | 0 | 0 | 0 | 0 |
| | London | 2002-03 | 35(3) | 10 | 0 | 0 | 40 |
| | St Helens | 1999-2001 | 36(22) | 19 | 0 | 0 | 76 |
| Graeme Hallas | Huddersfield | 2001 | 1 | 0 | 0 | 0 | 0 |
| | Hull | 1998-99 | 30(10) | 6 | 39 | 1 | 103 |
| | Halifax | 1996 | 11(4) | 5 | 0 | 0 | 20 |
| Sam Hallas | Leeds | 2016 | (2) | 0 | 0 | 0 | 0 |
| Macauley Hallett | Hull KR | 2014 | 2 | 3 | 0 | 0 | 12 |
| Dave Halley | Bradford | 2007-10 | 63(12) | 20 | 0 | 0 | 80 |
| | Wakefield | 2009 | 5 | 4 | 0 | 0 | 16 |
| Danny Halliwell | Salford | 2007 | 2(3) | 0 | 0 | 0 | 0 |
| | Leigh | 2005 | 5 | 3 | 0 | 0 | 12 |
| | Halifax | 2000-03 | 17(8) | 4 | 0 | 0 | 16 |
| | Warrington | 2002 | 9(1) | 8 | 0 | 0 | 32 |
| | Wakefield | 2002 | 3 | 0 | 0 | 0 | 0 |
| Colum Halpenny | Wakefield | 2003-06 | 103(1) | 36 | 0 | 0 | 144 |
| | Halifax | 2002 | 22 | 12 | 0 | 0 | 48 |
| Jon Hamer | Bradford | 1996 | (1) | 0 | 0 | 0 | 0 |
| Andrew Hamilton | London | 1997, 2003 | 1(20) | 3 | 0 | 0 | 12 |
| John Hamilton | St Helens | 1998 | 3 | 0 | 0 | 0 | 0 |
| Gabe Hamlin | Wigan | 2018-19 | 6(18) | 3 | 0 | 0 | 12 |
| Karle Hammond | Halifax | 2002 | 10(2) | 2 | 14 | 0 | 36 |
| | Salford | 2001 | 2(3) | 1 | 0 | 0 | 4 |
| | London | 1999-2000 | 47 | 23 | 2 | 3 | 99 |
| | St Helens | 1996-98 | 58(8) | 28 | 0 | 4 | 116 |
| Ryan Hampshire | Wakefield | 2018-19 | 49(5) | 19 | 86 | 1 | 249 |
| | Leigh | 2017 | 12(1) | 3 | 0 | 0 | 12 |
| | Castleford | 2016 | 19(2) | 8 | 0 | 0 | 32 |
| | Wigan | 2013-15 | 20(5) | 8 | 24 | 0 | 80 |
| Rhys Hanbury | Widnes | 2012-18 | 152 | 71 | 99 | 1 | 483 |
| | Crusaders | 2010-11 | 26(1) | 14 | 0 | 0 | 56 |
| Anthony Hancock | Paris | 1997 | 8(6) | 1 | 0 | 0 | 4 |
| Michael Hancock | Salford | 2001-02 | 12(24) | 7 | 0 | 0 | 28 |
| Jordan Hand | Wakefield | 2015 | (2) | 0 | 0 | 0 | 0 |
| | St Helens | 2013-14 | (3) | 0 | 0 | 0 | 0 |
| Gareth Handford | Castleford | 2001 | 7(2) | 0 | 0 | 0 | 0 |
| | Bradford | 2000 | 1(1) | 0 | 0 | 0 | 0 |
| Paul Handforth | Castleford | 2006 | 2(15) | 2 | 1 | 0 | 10 |
| | Wakefield | 2000-04 | 17(44) | 10 | 13 | 0 | 66 |
| Ash Handley | Leeds | 2014-19 | 89(3) | 51 | 0 | 0 | 204 |
| Paddy Handley | Leeds | 1996 | 1(1) | 2 | 0 | 0 | 8 |
| Dean Hanger | Warrington | 1999 | 7(11) | 3 | 0 | 0 | 12 |
| | Huddersfield | 1998 | 20(1) | 5 | 0 | 0 | 20 |

| PLAYER | CLUB | YEAR | APP | TRIES | GOALS | FG | PTS |
|---|---|---|---|---|---|---|---|
| Chris Hankinson | Wigan | 2018-19 | 15(4) | 3 | 16 | 0 | 44 |
| Josh Hannay | Celtic | 2009 | 17 | 2 | 24 | 0 | 56 |
| Harrison Hansen | Widnes | 2018 | 1 | 1 | 0 | 0 | 4 |
| | Leigh | 2017 | 19(2) | 1 | 0 | 0 | 4 |
| | Salford | 2014-15 | 41(2) | 7 | 0 | 0 | 28 |
| | Wigan | 2004-13 | 155(62) | 39 | 0 | 0 | 156 |
| Lee Hansen | Wigan | 1997 | 10(5) | 0 | 0 | 0 | 0 |
| Shontayne Hape | Bradford | 2003-08 | 123(2) | 79 | 0 | 0 | 316 |
| Lionel Harbin | Wakefield | 2001 | (1) | 0 | 0 | 0 | 0 |
| Zak Hardaker | Wigan | 2019 | 30 | 11 | 93 | 1 | 231 |
| | Castleford | 2017 | 28 | 12 | 1 | 0 | 50 |
| | Leeds | 2011-16 | 135 | 57 | 43 | 1 | 315 |
| Ian Hardman | Hull KR | 2007 | 18 | 4 | 0 | 0 | 16 |
| | St Helens | 2003-07 | 32(11) | 9 | 5 | 0 | 46 |
| Jeff Hardy | Hudds-Sheff | 2000 | 20(5) | 6 | 0 | 1 | 25 |
| | Sheffield | 1999 | 22(4) | 7 | 0 | 0 | 28 |
| Spencer Hargrave | Castleford | 1996-99 | (6) | 0 | 0 | 0 | 0 |
| Bryn Hargreaves | Bradford | 2011-12 | 45(5) | 1 | 0 | 0 | 4 |
| | St Helens | 2007-10 | 53(44) | 7 | 0 | 0 | 28 |
| | Wigan | 2004-06 | 16(12) | 1 | 0 | 0 | 4 |
| Lee Harland | Castleford | 1996-2004 | 148(35) | 20 | 0 | 0 | 80 |
| Neil Harmon | Halifax | 2003 | 13(3) | 0 | 0 | 0 | 0 |
| | Salford | 2001 | 6(5) | 0 | 0 | 0 | 0 |
| | Bradford | 1998-2000 | 15(13) | 2 | 0 | 0 | 8 |
| | Huddersfield | 1998 | 12 | 1 | 0 | 0 | 4 |
| | Leeds | 1996 | 10 | 1 | 0 | 0 | 4 |
| Ben Harris | Bradford | 2005-07 | 70(4) | 24 | 0 | 0 | 96 |
| Iestyn Harris | Bradford | 2004-08 | 109(11) | 35 | 87 | 2 | 316 |
| | Leeds | 1997-2001 | 111(7) | 57 | 490 | 6 | 1214 |
| | Warrington | 1996 | 16 | 4 | 63 | 2 | 144 |
| Liam Harris | Hull | 2018 | 9(2) | 3 | 0 | 0 | 12 |
| Ben Harrison | Wakefield | 2016 | 3 | 0 | 0 | 0 | 0 |
| | Warrington | 2007-15 | 125(59) | 14 | 0 | 0 | 56 |
| Karl Harrison | Hull | 1999 | 26 | 2 | 0 | 0 | 8 |
| | Halifax | 1996-98 | 60(2) | 2 | 0 | 0 | 8 |
| Owen Harrison | Hull KR | 2019 | 2(4) | 0 | 0 | 0 | 0 |
| Andrew Hart | London | 2004 | 12(1) | 2 | 0 | 0 | 8 |
| Tim Hartley | Harlequins | 2006 | 2 | 1 | 0 | 0 | 4 |
| | Salford | 2004-05 | 6(7) | 5 | 0 | 0 | 20 |
| Carlos Hassan | Bradford | 1996 | 6(4) | 2 | 0 | 0 | 8 |
| Phil Hassan | Wakefield | 2002 | 9(1) | 0 | 0 | 0 | 0 |
| | Halifax | 2000-01 | 25(4) | 3 | 0 | 0 | 12 |
| | Salford | 1998 | 15 | 2 | 0 | 0 | 8 |
| | Leeds | 1996-97 | 38(4) | 12 | 0 | 0 | 48 |
| James Hasson | Wakefield | 2017 | (4) | 0 | 0 | 0 | 0 |
| | Salford | 2017 | 4(1) | 0 | 0 | 0 | 0 |
| Jackson Hastings | Salford | 2018-19 | 34 | 11 | 4 | 0 | 52 |
| Tom Haughey | Castleford | 2006 | 1(3) | 1 | 0 | 0 | 4 |
| | London | 2003-04 | 10(8) | 1 | 0 | 0 | 4 |
| | Wakefield | 2001-02 | 5(11) | 0 | 0 | 0 | 0 |
| Simon Haughton | Wigan | 1996-2002 | 63(46) | 32 | 0 | 0 | 128 |
| Solomon Haumono | | | | | | | |
| | Harlequins | 2006 | 10(9) | 6 | 0 | 0 | 24 |
| | London | 2005 | 24(5) | 8 | 0 | 0 | 32 |
| Weller Hauraki | Hull KR | 2019 | 25(4) | 5 | 0 | 0 | 20 |
| | Widnes | 2018 | 7 | 0 | 0 | 0 | 0 |
| | Salford | 2015-18 | 45(12) | 8 | 0 | 0 | 32 |
| | Castleford | 2013-14 | 50(2) | 9 | 0 | 0 | 36 |
| | Leeds | 2011-12 | 18(17) | 6 | 0 | 0 | 24 |
| | Crusaders | 2010 | 26(1) | 11 | 0 | 0 | 44 |
| Ethan Havard | Wigan | 2019 | (1) | 0 | 0 | 0 | 0 |
| Richie Hawkyard | Bradford | 2007 | 1(2) | 1 | 0 | 0 | 4 |
| Andy Hay | Widnes | 2003-04 | 50(2) | 7 | 0 | 0 | 28 |
| | Leeds | 1997-2002 | 112(27) | 43 | 0 | 0 | 172 |
| | Sheffield | 1996-97 | 17(3) | 5 | 0 | 0 | 20 |
| Adam Hayes | Hudds-Sheff | 2000 | 2(1) | 0 | 0 | 0 | 0 |
| Joey Hayes | Salford | 1999 | 9 | 2 | 0 | 0 | 8 |
| | St Helens | 1996-98 | 11(6) | 7 | 0 | 0 | 28 |
| James Haynes | Hull KR | 2009 | 1 | 0 | 0 | 0 | 0 |
| Callum Hazzard | St Helens | 2019 | (1) | 0 | 0 | 0 | 0 |
| Mathew Head | Hull | 2007 | 9(1) | 1 | 0 | 1 | 5 |
| Mitch Healey | Castleford | 2001-03 | 68(1) | 10 | 16 | 0 | 72 |
| Daniel Heckenberg | Harlequins | 2006-09 | 31(39) | 4 | 0 | 0 | 16 |
| Andrew Heffernan | Hull KR | 2018 | 7 | 2 | 0 | 0 | 8 |
| Chris Heil | Hull KR | 2012-13 | 4 | 2 | 0 | 0 | 8 |
| Ben Hellewell | London | 2019 | 2 | 0 | 0 | 0 | 0 |
| Ricky Helliwell | Salford | 1997-99 | (2) | 0 | 0 | 0 | 0 |
| Tom Hemingway | Huddersfield | 2005-09 | 7(7) | 1 | 17 | 0 | 38 |
| Bryan Henare | St Helens | 2000-01 | 4(12) | 1 | 0 | 0 | 4 |
| Richard Henare | Warrington | 1996-97 | 28(2) | 24 | 0 | 0 | 96 |
| Andrew Henderson | Castleford | 2006, 2008 | 44(11) | 4 | 0 | 0 | 16 |
| Ian Henderson | Catalans | 2011-15 | 118(9) | 12 | 0 | 0 | 48 |
| | Bradford | 2005-07 | 33(37) | 13 | 0 | 0 | 52 |
| Kevin Henderson | Wakefield | 2005-11 | 52(68) | 9 | 0 | 0 | 36 |
| | Leigh | 2005 | (1) | 0 | 0 | 0 | 0 |
| Adam Henry | Bradford | 2014 | 23(1) | 5 | 0 | 0 | 20 |

172

| PLAYER | CLUB | YEAR | APP | TRIES | GOALS | FG | PTS |
|---|---|---|---|---|---|---|---|
| Mark Henry | Salford | 2009-11 | 67 | 22 | 0 | 0 | 88 |
| Brad Hepi | Castleford | 1999, 2001 | 9(21) | 3 | 0 | 0 | 12 |
| | Salford | 2000 | 3(5) | 0 | 0 | 0 | 0 |
| | Hull | 1998 | 15(1) | 3 | 0 | 0 | 12 |
| Tyla Hepi | Hull KR | 2013 | (4) | 0 | 0 | 0 | 0 |
| Jon Hepworth | Castleford | 2003-04 | 19(23) | 7 | 8 | 0 | 44 |
| | Leeds | 2003 | (1) | 0 | 0 | 0 | 0 |
| | London | 2002 | (2) | 0 | 0 | 0 | 0 |
| Marc Herbert | Bradford | 2011 | 20 | 4 | 2 | 0 | 20 |
| Aaron Heremaia | Widnes | 2015-18 | 43(41) | 7 | 0 | 0 | 28 |
| | Hull | 2012-14 | 27(37) | 12 | 0 | 0 | 48 |
| Maxime Herold | London | 2014 | (2) | 0 | 0 | 0 | 0 |
| Ian Herron | Hull | 2000 | 9 | 1 | 17 | 0 | 38 |
| | Gateshead | 1999 | 25 | 4 | 105 | 0 | 226 |
| Jason Hetherington | London | 2001-02 | 37 | 9 | 0 | 0 | 36 |
| Gareth Hewitt | Salford | 1999 | 2(1) | 0 | 0 | 0 | 0 |
| Sam Hewitt | Huddersfield | 2018-19 | 5(8) | 1 | 0 | 0 | 4 |
| Andrew Hick | Hull | 2000 | 9(9) | 1 | 0 | 0 | 4 |
| | Gateshead | 1999 | 12(5) | 2 | 0 | 0 | 8 |
| Jarrad Hickey | Wakefield | 2011 | (8) | 2 | 0 | 0 | 8 |
| Chris Hicks | Warrington | 2008-10 | 72 | 56 | 119 | 0 | 462 |
| Paul Hicks | Wakefield | 1999 | (1) | 0 | 0 | 0 | 0 |
| Darren Higgins | London | 1998 | 5(6) | 2 | 0 | 0 | 8 |
| Iain Higgins | London | 1997-98 | 1(7) | 2 | 0 | 0 | 8 |
| Liam Higgins | Wakefield | 2011 | 4(12) | 0 | 0 | 0 | 0 |
| | Castleford | 2008-10 | 42(32) | 2 | 0 | 0 | 8 |
| | Hull | 2003-06 | 1(34) | 0 | 0 | 0 | 0 |
| Jack Higginson | Wigan | 2016 | 2(1) | 1 | 0 | 0 | 4 |
| Micky Higham | Leigh | 2017 | 11(1) | 2 | 0 | 0 | 8 |
| | Warrington | 2009-15 | 73(78) | 34 | 0 | 0 | 136 |
| | Wigan | 2006-08 | 61(28) | 13 | 0 | 0 | 52 |
| | St Helens | 2001-05 | 43(56) | 32 | 0 | 0 | 128 |
| Chris Highton | Warrington | 1997 | 1(1) | 0 | 0 | 0 | 0 |
| David Highton | London | 2004-05 | 21(24) | 2 | 0 | 0 | 8 |
| | Salford | 2002 | 4(5) | 2 | 0 | 0 | 8 |
| | Warrington | 1998-2001 | 18(14) | 2 | 0 | 0 | 8 |
| Paul Highton | Salford | 1998-2002, 2004-07 | 114(80) | 14 | 0 | 0 | 56 |
| | Halifax | 1996-97 | 12(18) | 2 | 0 | 0 | 8 |
| Adam Higson | Leigh | 2017 | 13 | 2 | 0 | 0 | 8 |
| Peta Hiku | Warrington | 2017 | 4 | 1 | 0 | 0 | 4 |
| Andy Hill | Huddersfield | 1999 | (4) | 0 | 0 | 0 | 0 |
| | Castleford | 1999 | 4(4) | 0 | 0 | 0 | 0 |
| Chris Hill | Warrington | 2012-19 | 212(10) | 25 | 0 | 0 | 100 |
| | Leigh | 2005 | (1) | 0 | 0 | 0 | 0 |
| Danny Hill | Wigan | 2006-07 | 1(10) | 0 | 0 | 0 | 0 |
| | Hull KR | 2007 | 2 | 0 | 0 | 0 | 0 |
| | Hull | 2004-06 | 4(6) | 0 | 0 | 0 | 0 |
| Howard Hill | Oldham | 1996-97 | 22(12) | 4 | 0 | 0 | 16 |
| John Hill | St Helens | 2003 | (1) | 0 | 0 | 0 | 0 |
| | Halifax | 2003 | 1(2) | 0 | 0 | 0 | 0 |
| | Warrington | 2001-02 | (4) | 0 | 0 | 0 | 0 |
| Scott Hill | Harlequins | 2007-08 | 41(2) | 13 | 0 | 0 | 52 |
| Mark Hilton | Warrington | 1996-2000, 2002-06 | 141(40) | 7 | 0 | 0 | 28 |
| Ryan Hinchcliffe | Huddersfield | 2016-18 | 70(11) | 11 | 0 | 0 | 44 |
| Daniel Hindmarsh | London | 2019 | (6) | 0 | 0 | 0 | 0 |
| Ian Hindmarsh | Catalans | 2006 | 25 | 3 | 0 | 0 | 12 |
| Keegan Hirst | Wakefield | 2017-19 | 17(44) | 1 | 0 | 0 | 4 |
| Jy Hitchcox | Castleford | 2016-18 | 25(1) | 21 | 0 | 0 | 84 |
| Brendan Hlad | Castleford | 2008 | (3) | 0 | 0 | 0 | 0 |
| Andy Hobson | Widnes | 2004 | 5(13) | 0 | 0 | 0 | 0 |
| | Halifax | 1998-2003 | 51(85) | 8 | 0 | 0 | 32 |
| Gareth Hock | Leigh | 2017 | 12(1) | 3 | 0 | 0 | 12 |
| | Salford | 2014-15 | 15(1) | 4 | 0 | 0 | 16 |
| | Widnes | 2013 | 15(2) | 9 | 1 | 0 | 38 |
| | Wigan | 2003-09, 2011-12 | 126(43) | 38 | 0 | 0 | 152 |
| Tommy Hodgkinson | St Helens | 2006 | (1) | 0 | 0 | 0 | 0 |
| Andy Hodgson | Wakefield | 1999 | 14(2) | 2 | 1 | 0 | 10 |
| | Bradford | 1997-98 | 8(2) | 4 | 0 | 0 | 16 |
| Brett Hodgson | Warrington | 2011-13 | 66 | 33 | 268 | 1 | 669 |
| | Huddersfield | 2009-10 | 45 | 13 | 166 | 0 | 384 |
| David Hodgson | Hull KR | 2012-14 | 51 | 31 | 0 | 0 | 124 |
| | Huddersfield | 2008-11 | 84 | 59 | 0 | 0 | 236 |
| | Salford | 2005-07 | 81 | 30 | 47 | 0 | 214 |
| | Wigan | 2000-04 | 90(19) | 43 | 0 | 0 | 172 |
| | Halifax | 1999 | 10(3) | 5 | 0 | 0 | 20 |
| Elliot Hodgson | Huddersfield | 2009 | 1 | 0 | 0 | 0 | 0 |
| Josh Hodgson | Hull KR | 2010-14 | 98(29) | 35 | 0 | 0 | 140 |
| | Hull | 2009 | (2) | 0 | 0 | 0 | 0 |
| Ryan Hoffman | Wigan | 2011 | 28(1) | 11 | 0 | 0 | 44 |
| Darren Hogg | London | 1996 | (1) | 0 | 0 | 0 | 0 |
| Michael Hogue | Paris | 1997 | 5(7) | 0 | 0 | 0 | 0 |
| Lance Hohaia | St Helens | 2012-15 | 67(9) | 21 | 0 | 1 | 85 |
| Chris Holden | Warrington | 1996-97 | 2(1) | 0 | 0 | 0 | 0 |
| Daniel Holdsworth | Hull | 2013 | 19 | 2 | 28 | 2 | 66 |
| | Salford | 2010-12 | 71 | 18 | 183 | 1 | 439 |
| Stephen Holgate | Halifax | 2000 | 1(10) | 0 | 0 | 0 | 0 |
| | Hull | 1999 | 1 | 0 | 0 | 0 | 0 |
| | Wigan | 1997-98 | 11(26) | 2 | 0 | 0 | 8 |
| | Workington | 1996 | 19 | 3 | 0 | 0 | 12 |
| Stephen Holker | Hull KR | 2015-16 | (4) | 0 | 0 | 0 | 0 |
| Martyn Holland | Wakefield | 2000-03 | 52(3) | 6 | 0 | 0 | 24 |
| Oliver Holmes | Castleford | 2010-19 | 151(33) | 35 | 0 | 0 | 140 |
| Tim Holmes | Widnes | 2004-05 | 15(4) | 0 | 0 | 0 | 0 |
| Tom Holmes | Huddersfield | 2019 | 6 | 0 | 0 | 0 | 0 |
| | Castleford | 2015-17 | 7(8) | 3 | 0 | 0 | 12 |
| Graham Holroyd | Huddersfield | 2003 | 3(5) | 0 | 0 | 0 | 0 |
| | Salford | 2000-02 | 40(11) | 8 | 75 | 5 | 187 |
| | Halifax | 1999 | 24(2) | 3 | 74 | 5 | 165 |
| | Leeds | 1996-98 | 40(26) | 22 | 101 | 8 | 298 |
| Tom Holroyd | Leeds | 2018-19 | (4) | 0 | 0 | 0 | 0 |
| Dallas Hood | Wakefield | 2003-04 | 18(9) | 1 | 0 | 0 | 4 |
| Liam Hood | Leigh | 2017 | 8(5) | 3 | 0 | 0 | 12 |
| | Salford | 2015 | 2(15) | 0 | 0 | 0 | 0 |
| | Leeds | 2012 | 1(4) | 3 | 0 | 0 | 12 |
| Jason Hooper | St Helens | 2003-07 | 89(6) | 35 | 30 | 0 | 200 |
| Will Hope | Salford | 2013 | 1(2) | 0 | 0 | 0 | 0 |
| Lee Hopkins | Harlequins | 2006-07 | 44(3) | 11 | 0 | 0 | 44 |
| | London | 2005 | 29 | 6 | 0 | 0 | 24 |
| Sam Hopkins | Leigh | 2017 | 3(17) | 6 | 0 | 0 | 24 |
| Sean Hoppe | St Helens | 1999-2002 | 69(16) | 32 | 0 | 0 | 128 |
| Graeme Horne | Hull KR | 2012-16 | 81(18) | 21 | 0 | 0 | 84 |
| | Huddersfield | 2010-11 | 23(17) | 11 | 0 | 0 | 44 |
| | Hull | 2003-09 | 49(74) | 24 | 0 | 0 | 96 |
| Richard Horne | Hull | 1999-2014 | 341(16) | 115 | 12 | 6 | 490 |
| Justin Horo | Wakefield | 2018-19 | 22(14) | 6 | 0 | 0 | 24 |
| | Catalans | 2016-17 | 34(1) | 12 | 0 | 0 | 48 |
| John Hough | Warrington | 1996-97 | 9 | 2 | 0 | 0 | 8 |
| Danny Houghton | Hull | 2007-19 | 271(47) | 39 | 0 | 0 | 156 |
| Sylvain Houles | Wakefield | 2003, 2005 | 8(1) | 1 | 0 | 0 | 4 |
| | London | 2001-02 | 17(10) | 11 | 0 | 0 | 44 |
| | Hudds-Sheff | 2000 | 5(2) | 1 | 0 | 0 | 4 |
| Chris Houston | Widnes | 2016-18 | 57(1) | 5 | 0 | 0 | 20 |
| Harvey Howard | Wigan | 2001-02 | 25(27) | 1 | 0 | 0 | 4 |
| | Bradford | 1998 | 4(2) | 1 | 0 | 0 | 4 |
| | Leeds | 1996 | 8 | 0 | 0 | 0 | 0 |
| Kim Howard | London | 1997 | 4(5) | 0 | 0 | 0 | 0 |
| Stuart Howarth | Wakefield | 2011, 2015-16 | 30(5) | 4 | 0 | 0 | 16 |
| | Hull | 2015 | 2(3) | 0 | 0 | 0 | 0 |
| | Salford | 2012-14 | 25(12) | 1 | 0 | 0 | 4 |
| | St Helens | 2013 | 14(1) | 0 | 0 | 0 | 0 |
| Stuart Howarth | Workington | 1996 | (2) | 0 | 0 | 0 | 0 |
| David Howell | London | 2012-13 | 24 | 5 | 0 | 0 | 20 |
| | Harlequins | 2008-11 | 76 | 26 | 0 | 0 | 104 |
| Phil Howlett | Bradford | 1999 | 5(1) | 2 | 0 | 0 | 8 |
| Craig Huby | Wakefield | 2017-19 | 24(26) | 3 | 0 | 0 | 12 |
| | Huddersfield | 2015-16 | 37(2) | 2 | 0 | 0 | 8 |
| | Castleford | 2003-04, 2006, 2008-14 | 130(57) | 27 | 41 | 0 | 190 |
| Ryan Hudson | Castleford | 2002-04, 2009-12 | 138(12) | 31 | 0 | 0 | 124 |
| | Huddersfield | 1998-99, 2007-08 | 51(22) | 10 | 0 | 0 | 40 |
| | Wakefield | 2000-01 | 42(9) | 11 | 0 | 1 | 45 |
| Adam Hughes | Widnes | 2002-03 | 89(2) | 45 | 51 | 0 | 282 |
| | Halifax | 2001 | 8(8) | 8 | 0 | 0 | 32 |
| | Wakefield | 1999-2000 | 43(3) | 21 | 34 | 0 | 152 |
| | Leeds | 1996-97 | 4(5) | 4 | 0 | 0 | 16 |
| Ian Hughes | Sheffield | 1996 | 9(8) | 4 | 0 | 0 | 16 |
| Jack Hughes | Warrington | 2016-19 | 106(1) | 18 | 0 | 0 | 72 |
| | Huddersfield | 2015 | 30(1) | 5 | 0 | 0 | 20 |
| | Wigan | 2011-14 | 31(33) | 9 | 0 | 0 | 36 |
| Mark Hughes | Catalans | 2006 | 23 | 9 | 0 | 0 | 36 |
| Steffan Hughes | London | 1999-2001 | 1(13) | 1 | 0 | 0 | 4 |
| David Hulme | Salford | 1997-99 | 53(1) | 5 | 0 | 0 | 20 |
| | Leeds | 1996 | 8(1) | 2 | 0 | 0 | 8 |
| Declan Hulme | Widnes | 2013-15 | 5 | 2 | 0 | 0 | 8 |
| Paul Hulme | Warrington | 1996-97 | 23(1) | 2 | 0 | 0 | 8 |
| Gary Hulse | Widnes | 2005 | 12(5) | 2 | 0 | 0 | 8 |
| | Warrington | 2001-04 | 20(28) | 8 | 0 | 1 | 33 |
| Alan Hunte | Salford | 2002 | 19(2) | 9 | 0 | 0 | 36 |
| | Warrington | 1999-2001 | 83 | 49 | 0 | 0 | 196 |
| | Hull | 1998 | 21 | 7 | 0 | 0 | 28 |
| | St Helens | 1996-97 | 30(2) | 28 | 0 | 0 | 112 |
| Konrad Hurrell | Leeds | 2019 | 24 | 14 | 0 | 0 | 56 |
| Alex Hurst | London | 2013 | 8(2) | 2 | 0 | 0 | 8 |
| Kieran Hyde | Wakefield | 2010-11 | 11 | 4 | 4 | 0 | 24 |

| PLAYER | CLUB | YEAR | APP | TRIES | GOALS | FG | PTS |
|---|---|---|---|---|---|---|---|
| Nick Hyde | Paris | 1997 | 5(5) | 1 | 0 | 0 | 4 |
| Chaz I'Anson | Hull KR | 2007-10 | 17(13) | 3 | 0 | 0 | 12 |
| Sebastine Ikahihifo | Huddersfield | 2016-19 | 45(23) | 1 | 0 | 0 | 4 |
| Ryan Ince | Widnes | 2016-18 | 19 | 11 | 0 | 0 | 44 |
| Krisnan Inu | Salford | 2019 | 24(1) | 7 | 93 | 1 | 215 |
|  | Widnes | 2018 | 13 | 6 | 21 | 0 | 66 |
|  | Catalans | 2015-17 | 39 | 11 | 3 | 0 | 50 |
| Mark Ioane | London | 2019 | 1(14) | 1 | 0 | 0 | 4 |
| Andy Ireland | Hull | 1998-99 | 22(15) | 0 | 0 | 0 | 0 |
|  | Bradford | 1996 | 1 | 0 | 0 | 0 | 0 |
| Kevin Iro | St Helens | 1999-2001 | 76 | 39 | 0 | 0 | 156 |
|  | Leeds | 1996 | 16 | 9 | 0 | 0 | 36 |
| Willie Isa | Wigan | 2016-19 | 96(19) | 10 | 0 | 0 | 40 |
|  | Widnes | 2012-15 | 44(33) | 3 | 0 | 0 | 12 |
|  | Castleford | 2011 | 7(2) | 6 | 0 | 0 | 24 |
| Andrew Isherwood | Wigan | 1998-99 | (5) | 0 | 0 | 0 | 0 |
| Olu Iwenofu | London | 2000-01 | 2(1) | 0 | 0 | 0 | 0 |
| Chico Jackson | Hull | 1999 | (4) | 0 | 0 | 0 | 0 |
| Lee Jackson | Hull | 2001-02 | 37(9) | 12 | 1 | 0 | 50 |
|  | Leeds | 1999-2000 | 28(24) | 7 | 0 | 0 | 28 |
| Michael Jackson | Sheffield | 1998-99 | 17(17) | 2 | 0 | 0 | 8 |
|  | Halifax | 1996-97 | 27(6) | 11 | 0 | 0 | 44 |
| Paul Jackson | Castleford | 2003-04, 2010-12 | 44(30) | 5 | 0 | 0 | 20 |
|  | Huddersfield | 1998, 2005-09 | 50(73) | 4 | 0 | 0 | 16 |
|  | Wakefield | 1999-2002 | 57(42) | 2 | 0 | 0 | 8 |
| Rob Jackson | Leigh | 2005 | 20(3) | 5 | 0 | 0 | 20 |
|  | London | 2002-04 | 26(14) | 9 | 0 | 0 | 36 |
| Wayne Jackson | Halifax | 1996-97 | 17(5) | 2 | 0 | 0 | 8 |
| Aled James | Crusaders | 2011 | 1 | 0 | 0 | 0 | 0 |
|  | Celtic | 2009 | 3(3) | 0 | 0 | 0 | 0 |
|  | Widnes | 2003 | 3 | 0 | 0 | 0 | 0 |
| Andy James | Halifax | 1996 | (4) | 0 | 0 | 0 | 0 |
| Jordan James | Wigan | 2006, 2014 | 3(18) | 4 | 0 | 0 | 16 |
|  | Salford | 2012-13 | 1(40) | 6 | 0 | 0 | 24 |
|  | Crusaders | 2010-11 | 5(24) | 3 | 0 | 0 | 12 |
|  | Celtic | 2009 | 17(4) | 1 | 0 | 0 | 4 |
| Matt James | Wakefield | 2012 | (4) | 0 | 0 | 0 | 0 |
|  | Harlequins | 2010 | (2) | 0 | 0 | 0 | 0 |
|  | Bradford | 2006-09 | 1(23) | 0 | 0 | 0 | 0 |
| Pascal Jampy | Catalans | 2006 | 4(7) | 0 | 0 | 0 | 0 |
|  | Paris | 1996-97 | 3(2) | 0 | 0 | 0 | 0 |
| Adam Janowski | Harlequins | 2008 | (1) | 0 | 0 | 0 | 0 |
| Ben Jeffries | Bradford | 2008-09, 2011-12 | 76(3) | 20 | 0 | 0 | 80 |
|  | Wakefield | 2003-07, 2010-11 | 151(10) | 70 | 20 | 6 | 326 |
| Mick Jenkins | Hull | 2000 | 24 | 2 | 0 | 0 | 8 |
|  | Gateshead | 1999 | 16 | 3 | 0 | 0 | 12 |
| Ed Jennings | London | 1998-99 | 1(2) | 0 | 0 | 0 | 0 |
| Rod Jensen | Huddersfield | 2007-08 | 26(3) | 13 | 0 | 0 | 52 |
| Anthony Jerram | Warrington | 2007 | (2) | 0 | 0 | 0 | 0 |
| Lee Jewitt | Hull KR | 2018-19 | 10(2) | 0 | 0 | 0 | 0 |
|  | Castleford | 2014-16 | 22(12) | 0 | 0 | 0 | 0 |
|  | Salford | 2007, 2009-13 | 32(62) | 4 | 0 | 0 | 16 |
|  | Wigan | 2005 | (2) | 0 | 0 | 0 | 0 |
| Isaac John | Wakefield | 2012 | 13 | 1 | 19 | 0 | 42 |
| Andrew Johns | Warrington | 2005 | 3 | 1 | 12 | 1 | 29 |
| Matthew Johns | Wigan | 2001 | 24 | 3 | 0 | 1 | 13 |
| Andy Johnson | Salford | 2004-05 | 8(26) | 7 | 0 | 0 | 28 |
|  | Castleford | 2002-03 | 32(16) | 11 | 0 | 0 | 44 |
|  | London | 2000-01 | 24(21) | 12 | 0 | 0 | 48 |
|  | Huddersfield | 1999 | 5 | 1 | 0 | 0 | 4 |
|  | Wigan | 1996-99 | 24(20) | 19 | 0 | 0 | 76 |
| Bruce Johnson | Widnes | 2004-05 | (4) | 0 | 0 | 0 | 0 |
| Corey Johnson | Leeds | 2019 | (1) | 0 | 0 | 0 | 0 |
| Dallas Johnson | Catalans | 2010 | 26 | 1 | 0 | 0 | 4 |
| Greg Johnson | Salford | 2014-19 | 86 | 36 | 1 | 0 | 146 |
|  | Wakefield | 2011 | 12 | 2 | 0 | 0 | 8 |
| Jack Johnson | Warrington | 2015-17, 2019 | 17 | 5 | 0 | 0 | 20 |
|  | Widnes | 2017 | 3 | 1 | 0 | 0 | 4 |
| Jason Johnson | St Helens | 1997-99 | 2 | 0 | 0 | 0 | 0 |
| Josh Johnson | Salford | 2019 | (7) | 1 | 0 | 0 | 4 |
|  | Hull KR | 2018 | 2(2) | 0 | 0 | 0 | 0 |
|  | Huddersfield | 2013-16 | 14(17) | 0 | 0 | 0 | 0 |
| Luis Johnson | Warrington | 2018-19 | (3) | 0 | 0 | 0 | 0 |
|  | Hull KR | 2019 | 4 | 0 | 0 | 0 | 0 |
| Mark Johnson | Salford | 1999-2000 | 22(9) | 16 | 0 | 0 | 64 |
|  | Hull | 1998 | 10(1) | 4 | 0 | 0 | 16 |
|  | Workington | 1996 | 12 | 4 | 0 | 0 | 16 |
| Nick Johnson | Hull KR | 2012 | 1 | 0 | 0 | 0 | 0 |
| Nick Johnson | London | 2003 | (1) | 0 | 0 | 0 | 0 |
| Paul Johnson | Crusaders | 2011 | 6(4) | 0 | 0 | 0 | 0 |
|  | Wakefield | 2010 | 12(3) | 4 | 0 | 0 | 16 |
|  | Warrington | 2007-09 | 37(9) | 17 | 0 | 0 | 68 |
|  | Bradford | 2004-06 | 46(8) | 19 | 0 | 0 | 76 |
|  | Wigan | 1996-2003 | 74(46) | 54 | 0 | 0 | 216 |
| Paul Johnson | Widnes | 2014 | 5(11) | 0 | 0 | 0 | 0 |
|  | Hull | 2013 | 3(16) | 0 | 0 | 0 | 0 |
|  | Wakefield | 2011-12 | 25(21) | 6 | 0 | 0 | 24 |
|  | St Helens | 2010 | (2) | 0 | 0 | 0 | 0 |
| Richard Johnson | Bradford | 2008 | (2) | 0 | 0 | 0 | 0 |
| Ben Johnston | Castleford | 2012 | 2 | 0 | 0 | 0 | 0 |
| Jordan Johnstone | Widnes | 2016-18 | 16(13) | 1 | 0 | 0 | 4 |
| Tom Johnstone | Wakefield | 2015-19 | 73 | 60 | 0 | 0 | 240 |
| Ben Jones | Harlequins | 2010 | (2) | 0 | 0 | 0 | 0 |
| Chris Jones | Leigh | 2005 | 1(1) | 0 | 0 | 0 | 0 |
| Danny Jones | Halifax | 2003 | 1 | 0 | 0 | 0 | 0 |
| David Jones | Oldham | 1997 | 14(1) | 5 | 0 | 0 | 20 |
| Josh Jones | Salford | 2016-19 | 92(4) | 17 | 0 | 0 | 68 |
|  | St Helens | 2012-15 | 88(9) | 22 | 0 | 0 | 88 |
| Mark Jones | Warrington | 1996 | 8(11) | 2 | 0 | 0 | 8 |
| Phil Jones | Leigh | 2005 | 16 | 8 | 31 | 0 | 94 |
|  | Wigan | 1999-2001 | 14(7) | 6 | 25 | 0 | 74 |
| Stacey Jones | Catalans | 2006-07 | 39 | 11 | 43 | 3 | 133 |
| Stephen Jones | Huddersfield | 2005 | (1) | 0 | 0 | 0 | 0 |
| Stuart Jones | Castleford | 2009-12 | 69(27) | 14 | 0 | 0 | 56 |
|  | Huddersfield | 2004-08 | 96(22) | 17 | 0 | 0 | 68 |
|  | St Helens | 2003 | (18) | 2 | 0 | 0 | 8 |
|  | Wigan | 2002 | 5(3) | 1 | 0 | 0 | 4 |
| Ben Jones-Bishop | Wakefield | 2016-19 | 102 | 58 | 0 | 0 | 232 |
|  | Salford | 2015 | 17 | 12 | 0 | 0 | 48 |
|  | Leeds | 2008-09, 2011-14 | 70(2) | 46 | 0 | 0 | 184 |
|  | Harlequins | 2010 | 17 | 10 | 0 | 0 | 40 |
| Jamie Jones-Buchanan | Leeds | 1999-2019 | 293(73) | 70 | 1 | 0 | 282 |
| Tim Jonkers | Wigan | 2006 | 3(1) | 0 | 0 | 0 | 0 |
|  | Salford | 2004-06 | 5(11) | 0 | 0 | 0 | 0 |
|  | St Helens | 1999-2004 | 41(64) | 12 | 0 | 0 | 48 |
| Darren Jordan | Wakefield | 2003 | (1) | 0 | 0 | 0 | 0 |
| Josh Jordan-Roberts | Leeds | 2017 | (1) | 0 | 0 | 0 | 0 |
| Phil Joseph | Salford | 2016 | (12) | 0 | 0 | 0 | 0 |
|  | Widnes | 2013-15 | 11(38) | 1 | 0 | 0 | 4 |
|  | Bradford | 2012 | (6) | 0 | 0 | 0 | 0 |
|  | Huddersfield | 2004 | 7(6) | 0 | 0 | 0 | 0 |
| Max Jowitt | Wakefield | 2014-19 | 48(2) | 14 | 0 | 0 | 56 |
| Warren Jowitt | Hull | 2003 | (2) | 0 | 0 | 0 | 0 |
|  | Salford | 2001-02 | 17(4) | 2 | 0 | 0 | 8 |
|  | Wakefield | 2000 | 19(3) | 8 | 0 | 0 | 32 |
|  | Bradford | 1996-99 | 13(25) | 5 | 0 | 0 | 20 |
| Chris Joynt | St Helens | 1996-2004 | 201(14) | 68 | 0 | 0 | 272 |
| Benjamin Jullien | Catalans | 2018-19 | 35(5) | 7 | 0 | 0 | 28 |
|  | Warrington | 2016-17 | 19(7) | 4 | 0 | 0 | 16 |
| Gregory Kacala | Paris | 1996 | 7 | 1 | 0 | 0 | 4 |
| Andy Kain | Castleford | 2004, 2006 | 9(7) | 3 | 10 | 0 | 32 |
| Sam Kasiano | Catalans | 2019 | 3(18) | 3 | 0 | 0 | 12 |
| Antonio Kaufusi | Huddersfield | 2014 | 15(2) | 1 | 0 | 0 | 4 |
|  | Bradford | 2014 | 4 | 0 | 0 | 0 | 0 |
|  | London | 2012-13 | 44(5) | 5 | 0 | 0 | 20 |
| Mal Kaufusi | London | 2004 | 1(3) | 0 | 0 | 0 | 0 |
| Ben Kavanagh | Hull KR | 2018 | 13(8) | 0 | 0 | 0 | 0 |
|  | Wakefield | 2015 | 6(3) | 0 | 0 | 0 | 0 |
|  | Widnes | 2012-15 | 18(33) | 0 | 0 | 0 | 0 |
| Liam Kay | Wakefield | 2012-13 | 4 | 4 | 0 | 0 | 16 |
| Ben Kaye | Harlequins | 2009-10 | 2(13) | 0 | 0 | 0 | 0 |
|  | Leeds | 2008 | 2(2) | 1 | 0 | 0 | 4 |
| Elliot Kear | London | 2019 | 26 | 3 | 0 | 0 | 12 |
|  | Bradford | 2012-14 | 53(2) | 17 | 0 | 0 | 68 |
|  | Crusaders | 2010-11 | 16(1) | 4 | 0 | 0 | 16 |
|  | Celtic | 2009 | 3 | 0 | 0 | 0 | 0 |
| Brett Kearney | Bradford | 2010-14 | 107 | 55 | 0 | 0 | 220 |
| Stephen Kearney | Hull | 2005 | 22(2) | 5 | 0 | 0 | 20 |
| Damon Keating | Wakefield | 2002 | 7(17) | 1 | 0 | 0 | 4 |
| Kris Keating | Hull KR | 2014 | 23 | 5 | 0 | 0 | 20 |
| Shaun Keating | London | 1996 | 1(3) | 0 | 0 | 0 | 0 |
| Mark Keenan | Workington | 1996 | 3(4) | 1 | 0 | 0 | 4 |
| Jimmy Keinhorst | Hull KR | 2019 | 22(3) | 6 | 0 | 0 | 24 |
|  | Leeds | 2012-18 | 46(23) | 25 | 0 | 0 | 100 |
|  | Widnes | 2018 | 3 | 1 | 0 | 0 | 4 |
|  | Wakefield | 2014 | 7 | 1 | 0 | 0 | 4 |
| Albert Kelly | Hull | 2017-19 | 56(2) | 36 | 0 | 1 | 145 |
|  | Hull KR | 2015-16 | 37 | 21 | 3 | 0 | 90 |
| Tony Kemp | Wakefield | 1999-2000 | 15(5) | 2 | 0 | 1 | 9 |
|  | Leeds | 1996-98 | 23(2) | 5 | 0 | 2 | 22 |
| Damien Kennedy | London | 2003 | 5(11) | 1 | 0 | 0 | 4 |
| Ian Kenny | St Helens | 2004 | (1) | 0 | 0 | 0 | 0 |

| PLAYER | CLUB | YEAR | APP | TRIES | GOALS | FG | PTS |
|---|---|---|---|---|---|---|---|
| Sean Kenny | Salford | 2016 | (4) | 0 | 0 | 0 | 0 |
| Jason Kent | Leigh | 2005 | 23 | 1 | 0 | 0 | 4 |
| Liam Kent | Hull | 2012-13 | 1(5) | 0 | 0 | 0 | 0 |
| Shane Kenward | Wakefield | 1999 | 28 | 6 | 0 | 0 | 24 |
|  | Salford | 1998 | 1 | 0 | 0 | 0 | 0 |
| Jason Keough | Paris | 1997 | 2 | 1 | 0 | 0 | 4 |
| Keiran Kerr | Widnes | 2005 | 6 | 2 | 0 | 0 | 8 |
| Lee Kershaw | Wakefield | 2019 | 4 | 1 | 0 | 0 | 4 |
| Martin Ketteridge | Halifax | 1996 | 7(5) | 0 | 0 | 0 | 0 |
| Ronnie Kettlewell | Warrington | 1996 | (1) | 0 | 0 | 0 | 0 |
| Joe Keyes | London | 2014 | 7 | 5 | 0 | 0 | 20 |
| Younes Khattabi | Catalans | 2006-08 | 24(4) | 10 | 0 | 0 | 40 |
| Samy Kibula | Wigan | 2018 | (1) | 0 | 0 | 0 | 0 |
| David Kidwell | Warrington | 2001-02 | 14(12) | 9 | 0 | 0 | 36 |
| Andrew King | London | 2003 | 23(1) | 15 | 0 | 0 | 60 |
| Dave King | Huddersfield | 1998-99 | 11(17) | 2 | 0 | 0 | 8 |
| George King | Wakefield | 2019 | 7(18) | 0 | 0 | 0 | 0 |
|  | Warrington | 2014-18 | 12(68) | 1 | 0 | 0 | 4 |
| James King | Leigh | 2005 | 5(7) | 0 | 0 | 0 | 0 |
| Kevin King | Wakefield | 2005 | 8(1) | 2 | 0 | 0 | 8 |
|  | Castleford | 2004 | (1) | 0 | 0 | 0 | 0 |
| Matt King | Warrington | 2008-11 | 91 | 58 | 0 | 0 | 232 |
| Paul King | Wakefield | 2010-11 | 10(19) | 0 | 0 | 1 | 1 |
|  | Hull | 1999-2009 | 136(93) | 20 | 0 | 1 | 81 |
| Toby King | Warrington | 2014-19 | 68(7) | 25 | 0 | 0 | 100 |
| Jon Luke Kirby | Huddersfield | 2019 | (3) | 0 | 0 | 0 | 0 |
| Andy Kirk | Wakefield | 2005 | 6(3) | 1 | 0 | 0 | 4 |
|  | Salford | 2004 | 20 | 5 | 0 | 0 | 20 |
|  | Leeds | 2001-02 | 4(4) | 0 | 0 | 0 | 0 |
| Ian Kirke | Wakefield | 2015 | 2(2) | 1 | 0 | 0 | 4 |
|  | Leeds | 2006-14 | 52(132) | 10 | 0 | 0 | 40 |
| John Kirkpatrick | London | 2004-05 | 18(1) | 5 | 0 | 0 | 20 |
|  | St Helens | 2001-03 | 10(11) | 10 | 0 | 0 | 40 |
|  | Halifax | 2003 | 4 | 1 | 0 | 0 | 4 |
| Danny Kirmond | Wakefield | 2010, 2012-19 | 146(12) | 42 | 0 | 0 | 168 |
|  | Huddersfield | 2008-11 | 18(31) | 9 | 0 | 0 | 36 |
| Wayne Kitchin | Workington | 1996 | 11(6) | 3 | 17 | 1 | 47 |
| Sione Kite | Widnes | 2012 | 6(8) | 1 | 0 | 0 | 4 |
| Ian Knott | Leigh | 2005 | 8(1) | 2 | 0 | 0 | 8 |
|  | Wakefield | 2002-03 | 34(5) | 7 | 79 | 0 | 186 |
|  | Warrington | 1996-2001 | 68(41) | 24 | 18 | 0 | 132 |
| Matt Knowles | Wigan | 1996 | (3) | 0 | 0 | 0 | 0 |
| Michael Knowles | Castleford | 2006 | (1) | 0 | 0 | 0 | 0 |
| Morgan Knowles | St Helens | 2016-19 | 56(48) | 17 | 0 | 0 | 68 |
| Phil Knowles | Salford | 1997 | 1 | 0 | 0 | 0 | 0 |
| Simon Knox | Halifax | 1999 | (6) | 0 | 0 | 0 | 0 |
|  | Salford | 1998 | 1(1) | 0 | 0 | 0 | 0 |
|  | Bradford | 1996-98 | 9(19) | 7 | 0 | 0 | 28 |
| Toa Kohe-Love | Warrington | 1996-2001, 2005-06 | 166(3) | 90 | 0 | 0 | 360 |
|  | Bradford | 2004 | 1(1) | 0 | 0 | 0 | 0 |
|  | Hull | 2002-03 | 42 | 19 | 0 | 0 | 76 |
| Paul Koloi | Wigan | 1997 | 1(2) | 1 | 0 | 0 | 4 |
| Craig Kopczak | Wakefield | 2019 | 13(14) | 2 | 0 | 0 | 8 |
|  | Salford | 2016-18 | 39(27) | 11 | 0 | 0 | 44 |
|  | Huddersfield | 2013-15 | 48(37) | 6 | 0 | 0 | 24 |
|  | Bradford | 2006-12 | 32(83) | 10 | 0 | 0 | 40 |
| Michael Korkidas | Wakefield | 2003-06, 2009-11 | 133(36) | 15 | 0 | 0 | 60 |
|  | Huddersfield | 2009 | 4(1) | 1 | 0 | 0 | 4 |
|  | Castleford | 2008 | 15(6) | 1 | 0 | 0 | 4 |
|  | Salford | 2007 | 26(1) | 1 | 0 | 0 | 4 |
| Nick Kouparitsas | Harlequins | 2011 | 2(13) | 1 | 0 | 0 | 4 |
| Olsi Krasniqi | London | 2012-14, 2019 | 36(35) | 3 | 0 | 0 | 12 |
|  | Salford | 2015-17 | 8(29) | 1 | 0 | 0 | 4 |
|  | Harlequins | 2010-11 | 3(20) | 1 | 0 | 0 | 4 |
| David Krause | London | 1996-97 | 22(1) | 7 | 0 | 0 | 28 |
| Ben Kusto | Huddersfield | 2001 | 21(4) | 9 | 0 | 1 | 37 |
| Anthony Laffranchi | St Helens | 2012-14 | 50(18) | 19 | 0 | 0 | 76 |
| James Laithwaite | Warrington | 2013-15 | 23(22) | 1 | 0 | 0 | 4 |
|  | Hull KR | 2012 | 1(2) | 1 | 0 | 0 | 4 |
| Adrian Lam | Wigan | 2001-04 | 105(2) | 40 | 1 | 9 | 171 |
| Brock Lamb | London | 2019 | 6 | 3 | 0 | 1 | 13 |
| Callum Lancaster | Hull | 2014-16 | 7 | 9 | 0 | 0 | 36 |
| Jordan Lane | Hull | 2018-19 | 12(19) | 4 | 0 | 0 | 16 |
| Mark Lane | Paris | 1996 | (2) | 0 | 0 | 0 | 0 |
| Allan Langer | Warrington | 2000-01 | 47 | 13 | 4 | 0 | 60 |
| Kevin Langer | London | 1996 | 12(4) | 2 | 0 | 0 | 8 |
| Junior Langi | Salford | 2005-06 | 27(7) | 7 | 0 | 0 | 28 |
| Samisoni Langi | Catalans | 2018-19 | 45 | 6 | 0 | 0 | 24 |
|  | Leigh | 2017 | 3 | 1 | 0 | 0 | 4 |
| Chris Langley | Huddersfield | 2000-01 | 18(1) | 3 | 0 | 0 | 12 |
| Gareth Langley | St Helens | 2006 | 1 | 1 | 3 | 0 | 10 |
| Jamie Langley | Hull KR | 2014 | 6(5) | 1 | 0 | 0 | 4 |
|  | Bradford | 2002-13 | 182(57) | 36 | 0 | 0 | 144 |
| Ryan Lannon | Salford | 2015-19 | 27(25) | 6 | 0 | 0 | 24 |
|  | Hull KR | 2019 | 1(5) | 1 | 0 | 0 | 4 |
| Kevin Larroyer | Castleford | 2017 | 2(4) | 0 | 0 | 0 | 0 |
|  | Hull KR | 2014-16 | 34(13) | 9 | 0 | 0 | 36 |
|  | Catalans | 2012-13 | 9(10) | 6 | 0 | 0 | 24 |
| Andy Last | Hull | 1999-2005 | 16(10) | 4 | 0 | 0 | 16 |
| Sam Latus | Hull KR | 2010-13 | 34(3) | 13 | 0 | 0 | 52 |
| Epalahame Lauaki | Wigan | 2012-13 | 14(16) | 2 | 0 | 0 | 8 |
|  | Hull | 2009-11 | 3(50) | 4 | 0 | 0 | 16 |
| Dale Laughton | Warrington | 2002 | 15(1) | 0 | 0 | 0 | 0 |
|  | Huddersfield | 2000-01 | 36(2) | 4 | 0 | 0 | 16 |
|  | Sheffield | 1996-99 | 48(22) | 5 | 0 | 0 | 20 |
| Ali Lauitiiti | Wakefield | 2012-15 | 46(31) | 16 | 0 | 0 | 64 |
|  | Leeds | 2004-11 | 64(117) | 58 | 0 | 0 | 232 |
| Quentin Laulu-Togaga'e | Castleford | 2018 | 8(1) | 6 | 0 | 0 | 24 |
| Jason Laurence | Salford | 1997 | 1 | 0 | 0 | 0 | 0 |
| Graham Law | Wakefield | 1999-2002 | 34(30) | 6 | 40 | 0 | 104 |
| Neil Law | Wakefield | 1999-2002 | 83 | 39 | 0 | 0 | 156 |
|  | Sheffield | 1998 | 1(1) | 1 | 0 | 0 | 4 |
| Dean Lawford | Widnes | 2003-04 | 17(1) | 5 | 2 | 4 | 28 |
|  | Halifax | 2001 | 1(1) | 0 | 0 | 0 | 0 |
|  | Leeds | 1997-2000 | 15(8) | 2 | 3 | 0 | 14 |
|  | Huddersfield | 1999 | 6(1) | 0 | 6 | 1 | 13 |
|  | Sheffield | 1996 | 9(5) | 2 | 1 | 1 | 11 |
| George Lawler | Hull KR | 2016, 2018-19 | 36(7) | 3 | 0 | 0 | 12 |
| Johnny Lawless | Halifax | 2001-03 | 73(1) | 10 | 0 | 0 | 40 |
|  | Hudds-Sheff | 2000 | 19(6) | 3 | 0 | 0 | 12 |
|  | Sheffield | 1996-99 | 76(4) | 11 | 0 | 0 | 44 |
| Michael Lawrence | Huddersfield | 2007-19 | 206(49) | 46 | 0 | 0 | 184 |
| Adam Lawton | Salford | 2019 | 1(1) | 0 | 0 | 0 | 0 |
|  | Widnes | 2013-14 | 2(10) | 5 | 0 | 0 | 20 |
| Charlie Leaeno | Wakefield | 2010 | 7(3) | 2 | 0 | 0 | 8 |
| Mark Leafa | Castleford | 2008 | 5(9) | 1 | 0 | 0 | 4 |
|  | Leigh | 2005 | 28 | 2 | 0 | 0 | 8 |
| Leroy Leapai | London | 1996 | 2 | 0 | 0 | 0 | 0 |
| Jim Leatham | Hull | 1998-99 | 20(18) | 4 | 0 | 0 | 16 |
|  | Leeds | 1997 | (1) | 0 | 0 | 0 | 0 |
| Andy Leathem | Warrington | 1999 | 2(8) | 0 | 0 | 0 | 0 |
|  | St Helens | 1996-98 | 20(1) | 1 | 0 | 0 | 4 |
| Danny Lee | Gateshead | 1999 | 16(2) | 0 | 0 | 0 | 0 |
| Jason Lee | Halifax | 2001 | 10(1) | 2 | 0 | 0 | 8 |
| Mark Lee | Salford | 1997-2000 | 25(11) | 1 | 0 | 4 | 8 |
| Robert Lee | Hull | 1999 | 4(3) | 0 | 0 | 0 | 0 |
| Tommy Lee | Hull KR | 2018-19 | 24(6) | 2 | 0 | 0 | 8 |
|  | St Helens | 2017 | 9(9) | 0 | 0 | 0 | 0 |
|  | Salford | 2014-16 | 37(5) | 4 | 0 | 0 | 16 |
|  | London | 2013 | 16(4) | 2 | 0 | 0 | 8 |
|  | Huddersfield | 2012 | 11(7) | 3 | 0 | 0 | 12 |
|  | Wakefield | 2011 | 25 | 6 | 0 | 0 | 24 |
|  | Crusaders | 2010 | 3(9) | 0 | 0 | 0 | 0 |
|  | Hull | 2005-09 | 44(27) | 6 | 0 | 0 | 24 |
| Kruise Leeming | Huddersfield | 2013-19 | 49(67) | 15 | 0 | 0 | 60 |
| Matty Lees | St Helens | 2017-19 | 14(29) | 2 | 0 | 0 | 8 |
| Matthew Leigh | Salford | 2000 | (6) | 0 | 0 | 0 | 0 |
| Chris Leikvoll | Warrington | 2004-07 | 72(18) | 4 | 0 | 0 | 16 |
| Jim Lenihan | Huddersfield | 1999 | 19(1) | 10 | 0 | 0 | 40 |
| Mark Lennon | Celtic | 2009 | 10(3) | 1 | 8 | 0 | 20 |
|  | Hull KR | 2007 | 11(4) | 5 | 7 | 0 | 34 |
|  | Castleford | 2001-03 | 30(21) | 10 | 21 | 0 | 82 |
| Tevita Leo-Latu | Wakefield | 2006-10 | 28(49) | 10 | 0 | 0 | 40 |
| Gary Lester | Hull | 1998-99 | 46 | 17 | 0 | 0 | 68 |
| Stuart Lester | Wigan | 1997 | 1(3) | 0 | 0 | 0 | 0 |
| Heath L'Estrange | Bradford | 2010-13 | 56(35) | 7 | 0 | 0 | 28 |
| Afi Leuila | Oldham | 1996-97 | 17(3) | 2 | 0 | 0 | 8 |
| Kylie Leuluai | Leeds | 2007-15 | 182(45) | 20 | 0 | 0 | 80 |
| Macgraff Leuluai | Widnes | 2012-18 | 52(64) | 5 | 0 | 0 | 20 |
| Phil Leuluai | Salford | 2007, 2009-10 | 7(47) | 3 | 0 | 0 | 12 |
| Thomas Leuluai | Wigan | 2007-12, 2017-19 | 252(2) | 62 | 0 | 1 | 249 |
|  | Harlequins | 2006 | 15(2) | 6 | 0 | 0 | 24 |
|  | London | 2005 | 20 | 13 | 0 | 0 | 52 |
| Mikey Lewis | Hull KR | 2019 | 1 | 0 | 0 | 0 | 0 |
| Simon Lewis | Castleford | 2001 | 4 | 3 | 0 | 0 | 12 |
| Paul Leyland | St Helens | 2006 | 1 | 0 | 0 | 0 | 0 |
| Jon Liddell | Leeds | 2001 | 1 | 0 | 0 | 0 | 0 |
| Jason Lidden | Castleford | 1997 | 15(1) | 7 | 0 | 0 | 28 |
| Jordan Lilley | Leeds | 2015-18 | 21(11) | 2 | 42 | 0 | 92 |
| Danny Lima | Wakefield | 2007 | (3) | 0 | 0 | 0 | 0 |
|  | Salford | 2006 | 7(2) | 0 | 0 | 0 | 0 |
|  | Warrington | 2004-06 | 15(47) | 9 | 0 | 0 | 36 |
| Jeff Lima | Catalans | 2014-15 | 37(7) | 3 | 1 | 0 | 14 |
|  | Wigan | 2011-12 | 24(29) | 4 | 0 | 0 | 16 |
| Tom Lineham | Warrington | 2016-19 | 90 | 60 | 0 | 0 | 240 |
|  | Hull | 2012-15 | 61(1) | 50 | 0 | 0 | 200 |

*Super League Players 1996-2019*

# Super League Players 1996-2019

| PLAYER | CLUB | YEAR | APP | TRIES | GOALS | FG | PTS |
|---|---|---|---|---|---|---|---|
| Kane Linnett | Hull KR | 2019 | 23(1) | 9 | 0 | 0 | 36 |
| Jez Litten | Hull KR | 2019 | (4) | 0 | 0 | 0 | 0 |
|  | Hull | 2017-19 | (17) | 1 | 0 | 0 | 4 |
| Harry Little | London | 2013 | 2 | 0 | 0 | 0 | 0 |
| Jack Littlejohn | Salford | 2018 | 15(3) | 3 | 1 | 0 | 14 |
| Craig Littler | St Helens | 2006 | 1 | 1 | 0 | 0 | 4 |
| Stuart Littler | Salford | 1998-2002, 2004-07, 2009-10 | 217(30) | 65 | 0 | 0 | 260 |
| Harvey Livett | Warrington | 2017-19 | 23(15) | 13 | 21 | 0 | 94 |
|  | Hull KR | 2019 | 1(3) | 1 | 0 | 0 | 4 |
| Peter Livett | Workington | 1996 | 3(1) | 0 | 0 | 0 | 0 |
| Rhodri Lloyd | Wigan | 2012-13, 2015 | 3(4) | 0 | 0 | 0 | 0 |
|  | Widnes | 2014 | (4) | 0 | 0 | 0 | 0 |
|  | London | 2013 | 2 | 0 | 0 | 0 | 0 |
| Garry Lo | Castleford | 2018 | 1 | 1 | 0 | 0 | 4 |
| Kevin Locke | Wakefield | 2015 | 3 | 0 | 0 | 0 | 0 |
|  | Salford | 2014-15 | 13 | 6 | 11 | 0 | 46 |
| Jack Logan | Hull | 2014-16, 2018-19 | 36(2) | 15 | 0 | 0 | 60 |
| Scott Logan | Wigan | 2006 | 10(11) | 0 | 0 | 0 | 0 |
|  | Hull | 2001-03 | 27(20) | 5 | 0 | 0 | 20 |
| Jamahl Lolesi | Huddersfield | 2007-10 | 75(9) | 27 | 0 | 0 | 108 |
| Filimone Lolohea | Harlequins | 2006 | 3(6) | 0 | 0 | 0 | 0 |
|  | London | 2005 | 8(15) | 0 | 0 | 0 | 0 |
| Tuimoala Lolohea | Salford | 2019 | 14 | 4 | 11 | 0 | 38 |
|  | Leeds | 2019 | 15 | 2 | 19 | 0 | 46 |
| David Lomax | Huddersfield | 2000-01 | 45(9) | 4 | 0 | 0 | 16 |
|  | Paris | 1997 | 19(2) | 1 | 0 | 0 | 4 |
| Jonny Lomax | St Helens | 2009-19 | 199(2) | 100 | 84 | 2 | 570 |
| Dave Long | London | 1999 | (1) | 0 | 0 | 0 | 0 |
| Karl Long | London | 2003 | (1) | 0 | 0 | 0 | 0 |
|  | Widnes | 2002 | 4 | 1 | 0 | 0 | 4 |
| Sean Long | Hull | 2010-11 | 22 | 6 | 0 | 0 | 24 |
|  | St Helens | 1997-2009 | 263(8) | 126 | 826 | 20 | 2176 |
|  | Wigan | 1996-97 | 1(5) | 0 | 0 | 0 | 0 |
| Davide Longo | Bradford | 1996 | 1(3) | 0 | 0 | 0 | 0 |
| Gary Lord | Oldham | 1996-97 | 28(12) | 3 | 0 | 0 | 12 |
| Paul Loughlin | Huddersfield | 1998-99 | 34(2) | 4 | 4 | 0 | 24 |
|  | Bradford | 1996-97 | 36(4) | 15 | 8 | 0 | 76 |
| Rhys Lovegrove | Hull KR | 2007-14 | 75(74) | 19 | 0 | 0 | 76 |
| Karl Lovell | Hudds-Sheff | 2000 | 14 | 5 | 0 | 0 | 20 |
|  | Sheffield | 1999 | 22(4) | 8 | 0 | 0 | 32 |
| Will Lovell | London | 2012-14, 2019 | 26(23) | 5 | 0 | 0 | 20 |
| James Lowes | Bradford | 1996-2003 | 205 | 84 | 2 | 2 | 342 |
| Laurent Lucchese | Paris | 1996 | 13(5) | 2 | 0 | 0 | 8 |
| Robert Lui | Leeds | 2019 | 10 | 3 | 0 | 0 | 12 |
|  | Salford | 2016-19 | 84(3) | 26 | 33 | 0 | 170 |
| Zebastian Luisi | Harlequins | 2006-07 | 23(2) | 4 | 0 | 0 | 16 |
|  | London | 2004-05 | 21(1) | 7 | 0 | 0 | 28 |
| Keith Lulia | Bradford | 2012-13 | 50 | 19 | 0 | 0 | 76 |
| Shaun Lunt | Leeds | 2012, 2019 | 15(10) | 7 | 0 | 0 | 28 |
|  | Hull KR | 2015-16, 2018-19 | 25(18) | 12 | 0 | 0 | 48 |
|  | Huddersfield | 2009-15 | 73(39) | 60 | 0 | 0 | 240 |
| Peter Lupton | Crusaders | 2010-11 | 37(9) | 10 | 0 | 0 | 40 |
|  | Celtic | 2009 | 16(4) | 4 | 0 | 0 | 16 |
|  | Castleford | 2006, 2008 | 40 | 11 | 0 | 0 | 44 |
|  | Hull | 2003-06 | 19(26) | 10 | 3 | 0 | 46 |
|  | London | 2000-02 | 10(15) | 2 | 2 | 0 | 12 |
| Joey Lussick | Salford | 2019 | 17(16) | 13 | 4 | 0 | 60 |
| Andy Lynch | Castleford | 1999-2004, 2014-17 | 157(54) | 17 | 0 | 0 | 68 |
|  | Hull | 2012-13 | 39(14) | 3 | 0 | 0 | 12 |
|  | Bradford | 2005-11 | 159(29) | 46 | 0 | 0 | 184 |
| Reece Lyne | Wakefield | 2013-19 | 150(1) | 50 | 0 | 0 | 200 |
|  | Hull | 2010-11 | 11(1) | 2 | 0 | 0 | 8 |
| Jamie Lyon | St Helens | 2005-06 | 54(1) | 39 | 172 | 0 | 500 |
| Iliess Macani | London | 2013-14 | 12(3) | 4 | 0 | 0 | 16 |
| Duncan MacGillivray |  |  |  |  |  |  |  |
|  | Wakefield | 2004-08 | 75(18) | 6 | 0 | 0 | 24 |
| Brad Mackay | Bradford | 2000 | 24(2) | 8 | 0 | 0 | 32 |
| Graham Mackay | Hull | 2002 | 27 | 18 | 24 | 0 | 120 |
|  | Bradford | 2001 | 16(3) | 12 | 1 | 0 | 50 |
|  | Leeds | 2000 | 12(8) | 10 | 2 | 0 | 44 |
| Keiron Maddocks | Leigh | 2005 | 1(3) | 0 | 0 | 0 | 0 |
| Steve Maden | Leigh | 2005 | 23 | 9 | 0 | 0 | 36 |
|  | Warrington | 2002 | 3 | 0 | 0 | 0 | 0 |
| Mateaki Mafi | Warrington | 1996-97 | 7(8) | 7 | 0 | 0 | 28 |
| Shaun Magennis | St Helens | 2010-12 | 7(19) | 3 | 0 | 0 | 12 |
| Brendan Magnus | London | 2000 | 3 | 1 | 0 | 0 | 4 |
| Mark Maguire | London | 1996-97 | 11(4) | 7 | 13 | 0 | 54 |
| Adam Maher | Hull | 2000-03 | 88(4) | 24 | 0 | 0 | 96 |
|  | Gateshead | 1999 | 21(5) | 3 | 0 | 0 | 12 |
| Lee Maher | Leeds | 1996 | 4(1) | 0 | 0 | 0 | 0 |
| Will Maher | Castleford | 2014-19 | 5(30) | 1 | 0 | 0 | 4 |

| PLAYER | CLUB | YEAR | APP | TRIES | GOALS | FG | PTS |
|---|---|---|---|---|---|---|---|
| Shaun Mahony | Paris | 1997 | 5 | 0 | 0 | 0 | 0 |
| Hutch Maiava | Hull | 2007 | (19) | 1 | 0 | 0 | 4 |
| David Maiden | Hull | 2000-01 | 32(10) | 11 | 0 | 0 | 44 |
|  | Gateshead | 1999 | 5(16) | 8 | 0 | 0 | 32 |
| Craig Makin | Salford | 1999-2001 | 24(20) | 2 | 0 | 0 | 8 |
| Tommy Makinson | St Helens | 2011-19 | 206(5) | 120 | 102 | 1 | 685 |
| Brady Malam | Wigan | 2000 | 5(20) | 1 | 0 | 0 | 4 |
| Dominic Maloney | Hull | 2009 | (7) | 0 | 0 | 0 | 0 |
| Francis Maloney | Castleford | 1998-99, 2003-04 | 71(7) | 24 | 33 | 3 | 165 |
|  | Salford | 2001-02 | 45(1) | 26 | 5 | 0 | 114 |
|  | Wakefield | 2000 | 11 | 1 | 1 | 0 | 6 |
|  | Oldham | 1996-97 | 39(2) | 12 | 91 | 2 | 232 |
| Jake Mamo | Warrington | 2019 | 15(4) | 9 | 0 | 0 | 36 |
|  | Huddersfield | 2017-18 | 23 | 17 | 0 | 0 | 68 |
| Dom Manfredi | Wigan | 2013-16, 2018-19 | 61 | 51 | 0 | 0 | 204 |
|  | Salford | 2014 | 1 | 2 | 0 | 0 | 8 |
| George Mann | Warrington | 1997 | 14(5) | 1 | 0 | 0 | 4 |
|  | Leeds | 1996 | 11(4) | 2 | 0 | 0 | 8 |
| Dane Manning | Leeds | 2009 | (1) | 0 | 0 | 0 | 0 |
| Josh Mantellato | Hull KR | 2015-16 | 26 | 16 | 88 | 0 | 240 |
| Misili Manu | Widnes | 2005 | 1 | 0 | 0 | 0 | 0 |
| Sika Manu | Hull | 2016-19 | 90(4) | 10 | 0 | 0 | 40 |
| Willie Manu | St Helens | 2013-14 | 35(11) | 9 | 0 | 0 | 36 |
|  | Hull | 2007-12 | 133(18) | 33 | 0 | 0 | 132 |
|  | Castleford | 2006 | 19(4) | 9 | 0 | 0 | 36 |
| Manase Manuokafoa |  |  |  |  |  |  |  |
|  | Widnes | 2015-17 | 3(54) | 3 | 0 | 0 | 12 |
|  | Bradford | 2012-14 | 49(21) | 3 | 0 | 0 | 12 |
| Darren Mapp | Celtic | 2009 | 9(2) | 1 | 0 | 0 | 4 |
| David March | Wakefield | 1999-2007 | 164(23) | 34 | 126 | 0 | 388 |
| Paul March | Wakefield | 1999-2001, 2007 | 42(31) | 17 | 23 | 0 | 114 |
|  | Huddersfield | 2003-06 | 71(19) | 17 | 36 | 1 | 141 |
| Nick Mardon | London | 1997-98 | 14 | 2 | 0 | 0 | 8 |
| Thibaut Margalet | Catalans | 2013-18 | 1(22) | 0 | 0 | 0 | 0 |
| Remy Marginet | Catalans | 2011 | 2 | 0 | 9 | 0 | 18 |
| Antoni Maria | Catalans | 2012-16, 2018-19 | 10(54) | 0 | 0 | 0 | 0 |
|  | Hull KR | 2019 | 2(3) | 0 | 0 | 0 | 0 |
|  | Leigh | 2017 | 2(6) | 0 | 0 | 0 | 0 |
| Frankie Mariano | Castleford | 2014-16 | 14(21) | 8 | 0 | 0 | 32 |
|  | Wakefield | 2011-13 | 41(12) | 20 | 0 | 0 | 80 |
|  | Hull KR | 2010 | 3 | 0 | 0 | 0 | 0 |
| Oliver Marns | Halifax | 1996-2002 | 54(19) | 23 | 0 | 0 | 92 |
| Paul Marquet | Warrington | 2002 | 23(2) | 0 | 0 | 0 | 0 |
| Callum Marriott | Salford | 2011 | (1) | 0 | 0 | 0 | 0 |
| Iain Marsh | Salford | 1998-2001 | 1(4) | 0 | 0 | 0 | 0 |
| Lee Marsh | Salford | 2001-02 | 3(4) | 0 | 0 | 0 | 0 |
| Matty Marsh | Hull KR | 2015-16, 2018 | 18(4) | 3 | 0 | 0 | 12 |
| Stefan Marsh | Widnes | 2012-18 | 121 | 56 | 21 | 0 | 266 |
|  | Wigan | 2010-11 | 12 | 3 | 0 | 0 | 12 |
| Liam Marshall | Wigan | 2017-19 | 63 | 53 | 5 | 0 | 222 |
| Richard Marshall | Leigh | 2005 | 4(16) | 0 | 0 | 0 | 0 |
|  | London | 2002-03 | 33(11) | 1 | 0 | 0 | 4 |
|  | Huddersfield | 2000-01 | 35(14) | 1 | 0 | 0 | 4 |
|  | Halifax | 1996-99 | 38(34) | 2 | 0 | 0 | 8 |
| Charlie Martin | Castleford | 2013 | (6) | 0 | 0 | 0 | 0 |
| Jason Martin | Paris | 1997 | 15(2) | 3 | 0 | 0 | 12 |
| Rhyse Martin | Leeds | 2019 | 8(1) | 2 | 34 | 0 | 76 |
| Scott Martin | Salford | 1997-99 | 32(18) | 8 | 0 | 0 | 32 |
| Tony Martin | Hull | 2012 | 10 | 1 | 0 | 0 | 4 |
|  | Crusaders | 2010-11 | 40(1) | 14 | 1 | 0 | 58 |
|  | Wakefield | 2008-09 | 33 | 10 | 33 | 0 | 106 |
|  | London | 1996-97, 2001-03 | 97(1) | 36 | 170 | 1 | 485 |
| Ugo Martin | Catalans | 2018 | 1 | 0 | 0 | 0 | 0 |
| Mick Martindale | Halifax | 1996 | (4) | 0 | 0 | 0 | 0 |
| Sebastien Martins | Catalans | 2006, 2009-11 | (21) | 2 | 0 | 0 | 8 |
| Tommy Martyn | St Helens | 1996-2003 | 125(20) | 87 | 63 | 12 | 486 |
| Dean Marwood | Workington | 1996 | 9(6) | 0 | 22 | 0 | 44 |
| Martin Masella | Warrington | 2001 | 10(14) | 5 | 0 | 0 | 20 |
|  | Wakefield | 2000 | 14(8) | 4 | 0 | 0 | 16 |
|  | Leeds | 1997-1999 | 59(5) | 1 | 0 | 0 | 4 |
| Colin Maskill | Castleford | 1996 | 8 | 1 | 1 | 0 | 6 |
| Mose Masoe | Hull KR | 2018-19 | 28(18) | 6 | 0 | 0 | 24 |
|  | St Helens | 2014-15 | 17(39) | 10 | 0 | 0 | 40 |
| Keith Mason | Castleford | 2006, 2013 | 11(6) | 0 | 0 | 0 | 0 |
|  | Huddersfield | 2006-12 | 118(14) | 4 | 0 | 0 | 16 |
|  | St Helens | 2003-05 | 33(23) | 4 | 0 | 0 | 16 |
|  | Wakefield | 2000-01 | 5(17) | 0 | 0 | 0 | 0 |
| Nathan Mason | London | 2019 | 5(10) | 1 | 0 | 0 | 4 |
|  | Huddersfield | 2013, 2015-17 | 3(26) | 3 | 0 | 0 | 12 |

| PLAYER | CLUB | YEAR | APP | TRIES | GOALS | FG | PTS |
|---|---|---|---|---|---|---|---|
| Willie Mason | Catalans | 2016 | 6(8) | 1 | 0 | 0 | 4 |
| | Hull KR | 2011 | 6 | 1 | 0 | 0 | 4 |
| Samy Masselot | Wakefield | 2011 | (1) | 0 | 0 | 0 | 0 |
| Nathan Massey | Castleford | 2008-19 | 148(64) | 9 | 0 | 0 | 36 |
| Suaia Matagi | Huddersfield | 2018-19 | 28(7) | 1 | 0 | 0 | 4 |
| Nesiasi Mataitonga | | | | | | | |
| | London | 2014 | 11(1) | 1 | 0 | 0 | 4 |
| Peter Mata'utia | Castleford | 2018-19 | 38 | 4 | 54 | 1 | 125 |
| Vila Matautia | St Helens | 1996-2001 | 31(68) | 9 | 0 | 0 | 36 |
| Feleti Mateo | London | 2005 | 4(10) | 1 | 0 | 0 | 4 |
| Barrie-Jon Mather | Castleford | 1998, | | | | | |
| | | 2000-02 | 50(12) | 21 | 0 | 0 | 84 |
| Richard Mathers | Wakefield | 2012-14 | 71 | 24 | 0 | 0 | 96 |
| | Castleford | 2011 | 21(1) | 7 | 0 | 0 | 28 |
| | Warrington | 2002, | | | | | |
| | | 2009-10 | 42(3) | 11 | 0 | 0 | 44 |
| | Wigan | 2008-09 | 23(1) | 2 | 0 | 0 | 8 |
| | Leeds | 2002-06 | 85(2) | 26 | 0 | 0 | 104 |
| Jamie Mathiou | Leeds | 1997-2001 | 31(82) | 3 | 0 | 0 | 12 |
| Masi Matongo | Hull | 2015, 2017-19 | 16(34) | 3 | 0 | 0 | 12 |
| Terry Matterson | London | 1996-98 | 46 | 15 | 90 | 6 | 246 |
| Vic Mauro | Salford | 2013 | 1(7) | 1 | 0 | 0 | 4 |
| Luke May | Harlequins | 2009-10 | (3) | 0 | 0 | 0 | 0 |
| Casey Mayberry | Halifax | 2000 | 1(1) | 0 | 0 | 0 | 0 |
| Chris Maye | Halifax | 2003 | 3(4) | 0 | 0 | 0 | 0 |
| Judah Mazive | Wakefield | 2016 | 2 | 1 | 0 | 0 | 4 |
| Joe Mbu | Harlequins | 2006-09 | 33(20) | 3 | 0 | 0 | 12 |
| | London | 2003-05 | 29(19) | 4 | 0 | 0 | 16 |
| Danny McAllister | Gateshead | 1999 | 3(3) | 1 | 0 | 0 | 4 |
| | Sheffield | 1996-97 | 33(7) | 10 | 0 | 0 | 40 |
| John McAtee | St Helens | 1996 | 2(1) | 0 | 0 | 0 | 0 |
| Nathan McAvoy | Bradford | 1998-2002, | | | | | |
| | | 2007 | 83(31) | 46 | 0 | 0 | 184 |
| | Wigan | 2006 | 15(2) | 5 | 0 | 0 | 20 |
| | Salford | 1997-98, | | | | | |
| | | 2004-05 | 57(4) | 18 | 0 | 0 | 72 |
| Tyrone McCarthy | Salford | 2017-19 | 29(17) | 7 | 2 | 0 | 32 |
| | Hull KR | 2015 | 20(1) | 4 | 0 | 0 | 16 |
| | Warrington | 2009-13 | 12(24) | 2 | 0 | 0 | 8 |
| | Wakefield | 2011 | 2(5) | 1 | 0 | 0 | 4 |
| Louie McCarthy-Scarsbrook | | | | | | | |
| | St Helens | 2011-19 | 129(123) | 51 | 0 | 0 | 204 |
| | Harlequins | 2006-10 | 41(50) | 17 | 0 | 0 | 68 |
| Dave McConnell | London | 2003 | (4) | 0 | 0 | 0 | 0 |
| | St Helens | 2001-02 | 3(2) | 4 | 0 | 0 | 16 |
| Robbie McCormack | | | | | | | |
| | Wigan | 1998 | 24 | 2 | 0 | 0 | 8 |
| Steve McCurrie | Leigh | 2005 | 7(3) | 1 | 0 | 0 | 4 |
| | Widnes | 2002-04 | 55(22) | 10 | 0 | 0 | 40 |
| | Warrington | 1998-2001 | 69(26) | 31 | 0 | 0 | 124 |
| Barrie McDermott | Leeds | 1996-2005 | 163(69) | 28 | 0 | 0 | 112 |
| Brian McDermott | Bradford | 1996-2002 | 138(32) | 33 | 0 | 0 | 132 |
| Ryan McDonald | Widnes | 2002-03 | 6(4) | 0 | 0 | 0 | 0 |
| Wayne McDonald | Huddersfield | 2005-06 | 11(23) | 1 | 0 | 0 | 4 |
| | Wigan | 2005 | (4) | 0 | 0 | 0 | 0 |
| | Leeds | 2002-05 | 34(47) | 14 | 0 | 0 | 56 |
| | St Helens | 2001 | 7(11) | 4 | 0 | 0 | 16 |
| | Hull | 2000 | 5(8) | 4 | 0 | 0 | 16 |
| | Wakefield | 1999 | 9(17) | 8 | 0 | 0 | 32 |
| Shannon McDonnell | | | | | | | |
| | St Helens | 2014-16 | 28 | 15 | 0 | 0 | 60 |
| | Hull | 2013 | 19 | 2 | 0 | 0 | 8 |
| | Hull KR | 2012 | 21 | 6 | 0 | 0 | 24 |
| Craig McDowell | Huddersfield | 2003 | (1) | 0 | 0 | 0 | 0 |
| | Warrington | 2002 | (1) | 0 | 0 | 0 | 0 |
| | Bradford | 2000 | (1) | 0 | 0 | 0 | 0 |
| Wes McGibbon | Halifax | 1999 | 1 | 0 | 0 | 0 | 0 |
| Jermaine McGillvary | | | | | | | |
| | Huddersfield | 2010-19 | 228 | 161 | 0 | 0 | 644 |
| Dean McGilvray | Salford | 2009-10 | 14 | 4 | 0 | 0 | 16 |
| | St Helens | 2006-08 | 5(1) | 1 | 0 | 0 | 4 |
| Billy McGinty | Workington | 1996 | 1 | 0 | 0 | 0 | 0 |
| Ryan McGoldrick | Salford | 2013 | 19(1) | 3 | 0 | 1 | 13 |
| | Hull | 2012 | 8 | 1 | 0 | 0 | 4 |
| | Castleford | 2006, | | | | | |
| | | 2008-12 | 129(5) | 24 | 11 | 0 | 118 |
| Kevin McGuinness | Salford | 2004-07 | 63(3) | 11 | 0 | 0 | 44 |
| Casey McGuire | Catalans | 2007-10 | 87(4) | 27 | 0 | 0 | 108 |
| Danny McGuire | Hull KR | 2018-19 | 36 | 9 | 1 | 3 | 41 |
| | Leeds | 2001-17 | 331(39) | 238 | 0 | 6 | 958 |
| Gary McGuirk | Workington | 1996 | (4) | 0 | 0 | 0 | 0 |
| Michael McIlorum | Catalans | 2018-19 | 37 | 4 | 0 | 0 | 16 |
| | Wigan | 2007-17 | 156(54) | 22 | 0 | 0 | 88 |
| Darnell McIntosh | Huddersfield | 2017-19 | 70(1) | 38 | 12 | 0 | 176 |
| Richard McKell | Castleford | 1997-98 | 22(7) | 2 | 0 | 0 | 8 |

| PLAYER | CLUB | YEAR | APP | TRIES | GOALS | FG | PTS |
|---|---|---|---|---|---|---|---|
| Chris McKenna | Bradford | 2006-07 | 40(7) | 7 | 0 | 0 | 28 |
| | Leeds | 2003-05 | 65(4) | 18 | 0 | 0 | 72 |
| Phil McKenzie | Workington | 1996 | 4 | 0 | 0 | 0 | 0 |
| Chris McKinney | Oldham | 1996-97 | 4(9) | 2 | 0 | 0 | 8 |
| Wade McKinnon | Hull | 2012 | 10 | 4 | 0 | 0 | 16 |
| Callum McLelland | Leeds | 2019 | 1 | 0 | 0 | 0 | 0 |
| Mark McLinden | Harlequins | 2006-08 | 46(1) | 20 | 0 | 1 | 81 |
| | London | 2005 | 22(3) | 8 | 0 | 0 | 32 |
| Mike McMeeken | Castleford | 2015-19 | 105(11) | 26 | 0 | 0 | 104 |
| | London | 2012-14 | 25(9) | 5 | 0 | 0 | 20 |
| Shayne McMenemy | | | | | | | |
| | Hull | 2003-07 | 80(8) | 12 | 0 | 0 | 48 |
| | Halifax | 2001-03 | 63 | 11 | 0 | 0 | 44 |
| Andy McNally | London | 2004 | 5(3) | 0 | 0 | 0 | 0 |
| | Castleford | 2001, 2003 | 2(5) | 1 | 0 | 0 | 4 |
| Gregg McNally | Leigh | 2017 | 9 | 3 | 0 | 0 | 12 |
| | Huddersfield | 2011 | 0 | 6 | 0 | 12 | |
| Steve McNamara | Huddersfield | 2001, 2003 | 41(9) | 3 | 134 | 1 | 281 |
| | Wakefield | 2000 | 15(2) | 2 | 32 | 0 | 72 |
| | Bradford | 1996-99 | 90(3) | 14 | 348 | 7 | 759 |
| Paul McNicholas | Hull | 2004-05 | 28(12) | 4 | 0 | 0 | 16 |
| Neil McPherson | Salford | 1997 | (1) | 0 | 0 | 0 | 0 |
| Shannan McPherson | | | | | | | |
| | Salford | 2012-14 | 20(11) | 0 | 0 | 0 | 0 |
| Duncan McRae | London | 1996 | 11(2) | 3 | 0 | 1 | 13 |
| Paul McShane | Castleford | 2015-19 | 102(22) | 18 | 39 | 0 | 150 |
| | Wakefield | 2014-15 | 39(9) | 5 | 0 | 0 | 20 |
| | Leeds | 2009-13 | 17(38) | 12 | 0 | 0 | 48 |
| | Widnes | 2012 | 6(5) | 3 | 4 | 0 | 20 |
| | Hull | 2010 | (4) | 0 | 0 | 0 | 0 |
| Derek McVey | St Helens | 1996-97 | 28(4) | 6 | 1 | 0 | 26 |
| Dallas Mead | Warrington | 1997 | 2 | 0 | 0 | 0 | 0 |
| David Mead | Catalans | 2018-19 | 44 | 19 | 0 | 0 | 76 |
| James Meadows | London | 2019 | 1 | 0 | 0 | 0 | 0 |
| Robbie Mears | Leigh | 2005 | 8(6) | 0 | 0 | 0 | 0 |
| | Leeds | 2001 | 23 | 6 | 0 | 0 | 24 |
| Paul Medley | Bradford | 1996-98 | 6(35) | 9 | 0 | 0 | 36 |
| Francis Meli | Salford | 2014 | 16 | 11 | 0 | 0 | 44 |
| | St Helens | 2006-13 | 194(1) | 122 | 0 | 0 | 488 |
| Vince Mellars | Wakefield | 2012-13 | 21(5) | 4 | 0 | 0 | 16 |
| | Crusaders | 2010-11 | 46 | 17 | 0 | 0 | 68 |
| Chris Melling | London | 2012-13 | 25(12) | 5 | 2 | 0 | 24 |
| | Harlequins | 2007-11 | 100(11) | 33 | 6 | 0 | 144 |
| | Wigan | 2004-05 | 8(2) | 1 | 3 | 0 | 10 |
| Alex Mellor | Huddersfield | 2017-19 | 65(10) | 19 | 0 | 0 | 76 |
| | Bradford | 2013-16 | (10) | 0 | 0 | 0 | 0 |
| Joe Mellor | Widnes | 2012-18 | 133(1) | 46 | 0 | 1 | 185 |
| | Wigan | 2012 | 1(1) | 1 | 0 | 0 | 4 |
| | Harlequins | 2011 | (1) | 0 | 0 | 0 | 0 |
| Paul Mellor | Castleford | 2003-04 | 36(3) | 18 | 0 | 0 | 72 |
| James Mendeika | London | 2013 | 4(2) | 2 | 0 | 0 | 8 |
| Craig Menkins | Paris | 1997 | 4(5) | 0 | 0 | 0 | 0 |
| Luke Menzies | Hull KR | 2008 | (1) | 0 | 0 | 0 | 0 |
| Steve Menzies | Catalans | 2011-13 | 61(6) | 30 | 0 | 0 | 120 |
| | Bradford | 2009-10 | 52(1) | 24 | 1 | 0 | 98 |
| Gary Mercer | Castleford | 2002 | (1) | 0 | 0 | 0 | 0 |
| | Leeds | 1996-97, 2001 | 40(2) | 9 | 0 | 0 | 36 |
| | Warrington | 2001 | 18 | 2 | 0 | 0 | 8 |
| | Halifax | 1998-2001 | 73(2) | 16 | 0 | 0 | 64 |
| Trent Merrin | Leeds | 2019 | 27 | 4 | 0 | 0 | 16 |
| Tony Mestrov | London | 1996-97, | | | | | |
| | | 2001 | 59(8) | 4 | 0 | 0 | 16 |
| | Wigan | 1998-2000 | 39(39) | 3 | 0 | 0 | 12 |
| Keiran Meyer | London | 1996 | 4 | 1 | 0 | 0 | 4 |
| Brad Meyers | Bradford | 2005-06 | 40(11) | 13 | 0 | 0 | 52 |
| Steve Michaels | Hull | 2015-17 | 68(1) | 26 | 0 | 0 | 104 |
| Gary Middlehurst | Widnes | 2004 | (2) | 0 | 0 | 0 | 0 |
| Simon Middleton | Castleford | 1996-97 | 19(3) | 8 | 0 | 0 | 32 |
| Constantine Mika | Hull KR | 2012-13 | 45(4) | 9 | 0 | 0 | 36 |
| Daryl Millard | Catalans | 2011-14 | 91 | 38 | 1 | 0 | 154 |
| | Wakefield | 2010-11 | 21(1) | 11 | 0 | 0 | 44 |
| Shane Millard | Wigan | 2007 | 19(6) | 3 | 0 | 0 | 12 |
| | Leeds | 2006 | 6(21) | 3 | 0 | 0 | 12 |
| | Widnes | 2003-05 | 69 | 23 | 0 | 0 | 92 |
| | London | 1998-2001 | 72(14) | 11 | 0 | 0 | 46 |
| Jack Miller | Huddersfield | 2013 | 1 | 0 | 0 | 0 | 2 |
| Jacob Miller | Wakefield | 2015-19 | 120(3) | 45 | 17 | 5 | 219 |
| | Hull | 2013-14 | 20 | 6 | 9 | 0 | 42 |
| Grant Millington | Castleford | 2012-19 | 141(63) | 28 | 0 | 0 | 112 |
| David Mills | Harlequins | 2006-07, | | | | | |
| | | 2010 | 25(32) | 2 | 0 | 0 | 8 |
| | Hull KR | 2008-09 | 20(11) | 1 | 0 | 0 | 4 |
| | Widnes | 2002-05 | 17(77) | 8 | 0 | 0 | 32 |
| Lewis Mills | Celtic | 2009 | (4) | 0 | 0 | 0 | 0 |
| Adam Milner | Castleford | 2010-19 | 149(79) | 34 | 1 | 0 | 138 |
| Lee Milner | Halifax | 1999 | (1) | 0 | 0 | 0 | 0 |

177

| PLAYER | CLUB | YEAR | APP | TRIES | GOALS | FG | PTS |
|---|---|---|---|---|---|---|---|
| Hakim Miloudi | Hull | 2018-19 | 13(2) | 5 | 1 | 0 | 22 |
| Elliot Minchella | Leeds | 2013-14 | (6) | 1 | 0 | 0 | 4 |
| Mark Minichiello | Hull | 2015-19 | 118(4) | 20 | 0 | 0 | 80 |
| Greg Minikin | Castleford | 2016-19 | 89(2) | 39 | 0 | 0 | 156 |
| Thomas Minns | Hull KR | 2016, 2018 | 24(1) | 14 | 0 | 0 | 56 |
|  | London | 2014 | 23 | 6 | 0 | 0 | 24 |
|  | Leeds | 2013 | 2(1) | 1 | 0 | 0 | 4 |
| John Minto | London | 1996 | 13 | 4 | 0 | 0 | 16 |
| Lee Mitchell | Castleford | 2012 | 13(10) | 2 | 0 | 0 | 8 |
|  | Warrington | 2007-11 | 8(27) | 4 | 0 | 0 | 16 |
|  | Harlequins | 2011 | 11(1) | 1 | 0 | 0 | 4 |
| Sam Moa | Catalans | 2017-19 | 60(4) | 6 | 0 | 0 | 24 |
|  | Hull | 2009-12 | 29(44) | 6 | 0 | 0 | 24 |
| Martin Moana | Salford | 2004 | 6(3) | 1 | 0 | 0 | 4 |
|  | Halifax | 1996-2001, 2003 | 126(22) | 62 | 0 | 1 | 249 |
|  | Wakefield | 2002 | 19(2) | 10 | 0 | 0 | 40 |
|  | Huddersfield | 2001 | 3(3) | 2 | 0 | 0 | 8 |
| Adam Mogg | Catalans | 2007-10 | 74 | 19 | 0 | 1 | 77 |
| Jon Molloy | Wakefield | 2013-16 | 25(18) | 5 | 0 | 0 | 20 |
|  | Huddersfield | 2011-12 | 2(1) | 0 | 0 | 0 | 0 |
| Steve Molloy | Huddersfield | 2000-01 | 26(20) | 3 | 0 | 0 | 12 |
|  | Sheffield | 1998-99 | 32(17) | 3 | 0 | 0 | 12 |
| Chris Molyneux | Huddersfield | 2000-01 | 1(18) | 0 | 0 | 0 | 0 |
|  | Sheffield | 1999 | 1(2) | 0 | 0 | 0 | 0 |
| Joel Monaghan | Castleford | 2016-17 | 29(3) | 13 | 0 | 0 | 52 |
|  | Warrington | 2011-15 | 127 | 125 | 2 | 0 | 504 |
| Michael Monaghan |  |  |  |  |  |  |  |
|  | Warrington | 2008-14 | 143(28) | 31 | 0 | 4 | 128 |
| Joel Moon | Leeds | 2013-18 | 136(1) | 61 | 0 | 0 | 244 |
|  | Salford | 2012 | 17 | 9 | 0 | 0 | 36 |
| Adrian Moore | Huddersfield | 1998-99 | 1(4) | 0 | 0 | 0 | 0 |
| Danny Moore | London | 2000 | 7 | 0 | 0 | 0 | 0 |
|  | Wigan | 1998-99 | 49(3) | 18 | 0 | 0 | 72 |
| Gareth Moore | Wakefield | 2011 | 5 | 1 | 14 | 1 | 33 |
| Jason Moore | Workington | 1996 | (5) | 0 | 0 | 0 | 0 |
| Richard Moore | Wakefield | 2007-10, 2014 | 52(57) | 10 | 0 | 0 | 40 |
|  | Leeds | 2012-13 | 3(27) | 1 | 0 | 0 | 4 |
|  | Crusaders | 2011 | 11(10) | 1 | 0 | 0 | 4 |
|  | Leigh | 2005 | 2(5) | 0 | 0 | 0 | 0 |
|  | Bradford | 2002-04 | 1(26) | 0 | 0 | 0 | 0 |
|  | London | 2002, 2004 | 5(9) | 2 | 0 | 0 | 8 |
| Scott Moore | Wakefield | 2015-16 | 12(2) | 0 | 0 | 0 | 0 |
|  | Castleford | 2008, 2015 | 24(6) | 2 | 0 | 0 | 8 |
|  | London | 2014 | 26 | 3 | 0 | 0 | 12 |
|  | Huddersfield | 2009, 2012 | 29(7) | 9 | 0 | 0 | 36 |
|  | Widnes | 2012 | 3(3) | 0 | 0 | 0 | 0 |
|  | St Helens | 2004-07, 2010-11 | 29(37) | 9 | 0 | 0 | 36 |
| Junior Moors | Castleford | 2015-19 | 44(59) | 18 | 0 | 0 | 72 |
| Dennis Moran | Wigan | 2005-06 | 39 | 17 | 1 | 1 | 71 |
|  | London | 2001-04 | 107(2) | 74 | 2 | 5 | 305 |
| Kieran Moran | Hull KR | 2016 | (5) | 0 | 0 | 0 | 0 |
| Pat Moran | Warrington | 2019 | (1) | 0 | 0 | 0 | 0 |
| Ryan Morgan | London | 2019 | 21 | 5 | 0 | 0 | 20 |
|  | St Helens | 2017-18 | 46 | 22 | 0 | 0 | 88 |
| Willie Morganson | Sheffield | 1997-98 | 18(12) | 5 | 3 | 0 | 26 |
| Paul Moriarty | Halifax | 1996 | 3(2) | 0 | 0 | 0 | 0 |
| Adrian Morley | Salford | 2014-15 | 31(14) | 2 | 0 | 0 | 8 |
|  | Warrington | 2007-13 | 135(21) | 8 | 0 | 0 | 32 |
|  | Bradford | 2005 | 2(4) | 0 | 0 | 0 | 0 |
|  | Leeds | 1996-2000 | 95(14) | 25 | 0 | 0 | 100 |
| Chris Morley | Salford | 1999 | 3(5) | 0 | 0 | 0 | 0 |
|  | Warrington | 1998 | 2(8) | 0 | 0 | 0 | 0 |
|  | St Helens | 1996-97 | 21(16) | 4 | 0 | 0 | 16 |
| Frazer Morris | Wakefield | 2016 | (1) | 0 | 0 | 0 | 0 |
| Glenn Morrison | Wakefield | 2010-11 | 43(1) | 9 | 0 | 0 | 36 |
|  | Bradford | 2007-09 | 48(2) | 19 | 0 | 0 | 76 |
| Iain Morrison | Hull KR | 2007 | 5(6) | 1 | 0 | 0 | 4 |
|  | Huddersfield | 2003-05 | 11(23) | 0 | 0 | 0 | 0 |
|  | London | 2001 | (1) | 0 | 0 | 0 | 0 |
| Daniel Mortimer | Leigh | 2017 | 3 | 0 | 0 | 0 | 0 |
| Dale Morton | Wakefield | 2009-11 | 22(3) | 8 | 5 | 0 | 42 |
| Gareth Morton | Hull KR | 2007 | 7(4) | 3 | 23 | 0 | 58 |
|  | Leeds | 2001-02 | 1(1) | 0 | 0 | 0 | 0 |
| Kieren Moss | Hull KR | 2018 | 2(1) | 4 | 0 | 0 | 16 |
| Lee Mossop | Salford | 2017-19 | 45(3) | 6 | 0 | 0 | 24 |
|  | Wigan | 2008-13, 2015-16 | 80(65) | 11 | 0 | 0 | 44 |
|  | Huddersfield | 2009 | 1(4) | 1 | 0 | 0 | 4 |
| Aaron Moule | Salford | 2006-07 | 45 | 17 | 0 | 0 | 68 |
|  | Widnes | 2004-05 | 29 | 12 | 0 | 0 | 48 |
| Bradley Moules | Wakefield | 2016 | (1) | 0 | 0 | 0 | 0 |
| Wilfried Moulinec | Paris | 1996 | 1 | 0 | 0 | 0 | 0 |
| Gregory Mounis | Catalans | 2006-16 | 149(105) | 27 | 19 | 0 | 146 |
| Arthur Mourgue | Catalans | 2018-19 | 2 | 1 | 0 | 0 | 4 |
| Mark Moxon | Huddersfield | 1998-2001 | 20(5) | 1 | 0 | 1 | 5 |
| Robbie Mulhern | Hull KR | 2016, 2018-19 | 38(20) | 3 | 0 | 0 | 12 |
|  | Leeds | 2014-15 | (5) | 0 | 0 | 0 | 0 |
| Anthony Mullally | Leeds | 2016-18 | 10(48) | 9 | 0 | 0 | 36 |
|  | Wakefield | 2015 | (2) | 0 | 0 | 0 | 0 |
|  | Huddersfield | 2013-15 | 12(24) | 5 | 0 | 0 | 20 |
|  | Bradford | 2014 | 1(5) | 0 | 0 | 0 | 0 |
|  | Widnes | 2012 | (9) | 0 | 0 | 0 | 0 |
| Jake Mullaney | Salford | 2014 | 12 | 2 | 24 | 0 | 56 |
| Craig Mullen | Wigan | 2018 | 1(1) | 0 | 0 | 0 | 0 |
| Brett Mullins | Leeds | 2001 | 5(3) | 1 | 0 | 0 | 4 |
| Damian Munro | Widnes | 2002 | 8(2) | 1 | 0 | 0 | 4 |
|  | Halifax | 1996-97 | 9(6) | 8 | 0 | 0 | 32 |
| Matt Munro | Oldham | 1996-97 | 26(5) | 8 | 0 | 0 | 32 |
| Ben Murdoch-Masila |  |  |  |  |  |  |  |
|  | Warrington | 2018-19 | 14(32) | 10 | 0 | 0 | 40 |
|  | Salford | 2016-17 | 46(1) | 15 | 0 | 0 | 60 |
| Craig Murdock | Salford | 2000 | (2) | 0 | 0 | 0 | 0 |
|  | Hull | 1998-99 | 21(6) | 8 | 0 | 2 | 34 |
|  | Wigan | 1996-98 | 18(17) | 14 | 0 | 0 | 56 |
| Aaron Murphy | Huddersfield | 2012-19 | 165(4) | 71 | 0 | 0 | 284 |
|  | Wakefield | 2008-11 | 57(2) | 12 | 0 | 0 | 48 |
| Jack Murphy | Wigan | 2012, 2014 | 3 | 1 | 0 | 0 | 4 |
|  | Salford | 2013 | 10 | 3 | 1 | 0 | 14 |
| Jamie Murphy | Crusaders | 2011 | (2) | 0 | 0 | 0 | 0 |
| Jobe Murphy | Bradford | 2013 | (4) | 0 | 0 | 0 | 0 |
| Justin Murphy | Catalans | 2006-08 | 59 | 49 | 0 | 0 | 196 |
|  | Widnes | 2004 | 5 | 1 | 0 | 0 | 4 |
| Daniel Murray | Hull KR | 2019 | 9(2) | 0 | 0 | 0 | 0 |
|  | Salford | 2017-19 | 14(14) | 2 | 0 | 0 | 8 |
| Doc Murray | Warrington | 1997 | (2) | 0 | 0 | 0 | 0 |
|  | Wigan | 1997 | 6(2) | 0 | 0 | 0 | 0 |
| Scott Murrell | Hull KR | 2007-12 | 114(24) | 24 | 26 | 1 | 149 |
|  | Leeds | 2005 | (1) | 0 | 0 | 0 | 0 |
|  | London | 2004 | 3(3) | 2 | 0 | 0 | 8 |
| David Mycoe | Sheffield | 1996-97 | 12(13) | 1 | 0 | 0 | 4 |
| Richie Myler | Leeds | 2018-19 | 47 | 11 | 6 | 1 | 57 |
|  | Catalans | 2016-17 | 40 | 21 | 2 | 0 | 88 |
|  | Warrington | 2010-15 | 127(4) | 69 | 1 | 1 | 279 |
|  | Salford | 2009 | 18 | 11 | 0 | 0 | 44 |
| Rob Myler | Oldham | 1996-97 | 19(2) | 6 | 0 | 0 | 24 |
| Stephen Myler | Salford | 2006 | 4(8) | 1 | 15 | 0 | 34 |
|  | Widnes | 2003-05 | 35(14) | 8 | 74 | 0 | 180 |
| Vinny Myler | Salford | 2004 | (4) | 0 | 0 | 0 | 0 |
|  | Bradford | 2003 | (1) | 0 | 0 | 0 | 0 |
| Matt Nable | London | 1997 | 2(2) | 1 | 0 | 0 | 4 |
| Kevin Naiqama | St Helens | 2019 | 27 | 18 | 0 | 0 | 72 |
| Brad Nairn | Workington | 1996 | 14 | 4 | 0 | 0 | 16 |
| Ben Nakubuwai | Salford | 2018-19 | 7(28) | 2 | 0 | 0 | 8 |
| Frank Napoli | London | 2000 | 14(6) | 2 | 0 | 0 | 8 |
| Carlo Napolitano | Salford | 2000 | (3) | 1 | 0 | 0 | 4 |
| Stephen Nash | Castleford | 2012 | 3(4) | 0 | 0 | 0 | 0 |
|  | Salford | 2007, 2009 | 2(18) | 1 | 0 | 0 | 4 |
|  | Widnes | 2005 | 4(1) | 0 | 0 | 0 | 0 |
| Curtis Naughton | Leigh | 2017 | 5 | 3 | 0 | 0 | 12 |
|  | Hull | 2015-16 | 26 | 13 | 1 | 0 | 54 |
|  | Bradford | 2013 | 1 | 0 | 0 | 0 | 0 |
| Ratu Naulago | Hull | 2019 | 20 | 13 | 0 | 0 | 52 |
| Romain Navarrete | Wigan | 2017-19 | 36(20) | 0 | 0 | 0 | 0 |
|  | Catalans | 2016-17 | 1(12) | 0 | 0 | 0 | 0 |
| Jim Naylor | Halifax | 2000 | 7(6) | 2 | 0 | 0 | 8 |
| Scott Naylor | Salford | 1997-98, 2004 | 30(1) | 9 | 0 | 0 | 36 |
|  | Bradford | 1999-2003 | 127(1) | 51 | 0 | 0 | 204 |
| Adam Neal | Salford | 2010-13 | 17(28) | 0 | 0 | 0 | 0 |
| Mike Neal | Salford | 1998 | (1) | 0 | 0 | 0 | 0 |
|  | Oldham | 1996-97 | 6(4) | 3 | 0 | 0 | 12 |
| Jonathan Neill | Huddersfield | 1998-99 | 20(11) | 0 | 0 | 0 | 0 |
|  | St Helens | 1996 | 1 | 0 | 0 | 0 | 0 |
| Chris Nero | Salford | 2011-13 | 31(16) | 7 | 0 | 0 | 28 |
|  | Bradford | 2008-10 | 65(5) | 24 | 0 | 0 | 96 |
|  | Huddersfield | 2004-07 | 97(8) | 38 | 0 | 0 | 152 |
| Jason Netherton | Hull KR | 2007-14 | 60(74) | 4 | 0 | 0 | 16 |
|  | London | 2003-04 | 6 | 0 | 0 | 0 | 0 |
|  | Halifax | 2002 | 2(3) | 0 | 0 | 0 | 0 |
|  | Leeds | 2001 | (3) | 0 | 0 | 0 | 0 |
| Kirk Netherton | Castleford | 2009-10 | 5(23) | 3 | 0 | 0 | 12 |
|  | Hull KR | 2007-08 | 9(15) | 2 | 0 | 0 | 8 |
| Paul Newlove | Castleford | 2004 | 5 | 1 | 0 | 0 | 4 |
|  | St Helens | 1996-2003 | 162 | 106 | 0 | 0 | 424 |
| Richard Newlove | Wakefield | 2003 | 17(5) | 8 | 0 | 0 | 32 |
| Harry Newman | Leeds | 2017-19 | 24 | 4 | 0 | 0 | 16 |
| Clint Newton | Hull KR | 2008-11 | 90(3) | 37 | 0 | 0 | 148 |
| Terry Newton | Wakefield | 2010 | (2) | 0 | 0 | 0 | 0 |
|  | Bradford | 2006-09 | 83(6) | 26 | 0 | 0 | 104 |
|  | Wigan | 2000-05 | 157(9) | 62 | 0 | 0 | 248 |
|  | Leeds | 1996-1999 | 55(14) | 4 | 0 | 0 | 16 |

| PLAYER | CLUB | YEAR | APP | TRIES | GOALS | FG | PTS |
|---|---|---|---|---|---|---|---|
| Gene Ngamu | Huddersfield | 1999-2000 | 29(2) | 9 | 67 | 0 | 170 |
| Danny Nicklas | Hull | 2010, 2012 | 2(8) | 0 | 0 | 0 | 0 |
| Sonny Nickle | St Helens | 1999-2002 | 86(18) | 14 | 0 | 0 | 56 |
| | Bradford | 1996-98 | 25(16) | 9 | 0 | 0 | 36 |
| Jason Nicol | Salford | 2000-02 | 52(7) | 11 | 0 | 0 | 44 |
| Tawera Nikau | Warrington | 2000-01 | 51 | 7 | 0 | 0 | 28 |
| Rob Nolan | Hull | 1998-99 | 20(11) | 6 | 0 | 0 | 24 |
| Paul Noone | Harlequins | 2006 | 5(2) | 0 | 0 | 0 | 0 |
| | Warrington | 2000-06 | 60(59) | 12 | 20 | 0 | 88 |
| Chris Norman | Halifax | 2003 | 13(3) | 2 | 0 | 0 | 8 |
| Dan Norman | Widnes | 2018 | (1) | 0 | 0 | 0 | 0 |
| Paul Norman | Oldham | 1996 | (1) | 0 | 0 | 0 | 0 |
| Andy Northey | St Helens | 1996-97 | 8(17) | 2 | 0 | 0 | 8 |
| Danny Nutley | Castleford | 2006 | 28 | 3 | 0 | 0 | 12 |
| | Warrington | 1998-2001 | 94(1) | 3 | 0 | 0 | 12 |
| Tony Nuttall | Oldham | 1996-97 | 1(7) | 0 | 0 | 0 | 0 |
| Frank-Paul Nuuausala | | | | | | | |
| | Wigan | 2016-18 | 34(8) | 2 | 0 | 0 | 8 |
| Levy Nzoungou | Hull | 2019 | (1) | 0 | 0 | 0 | 0 |
| | Salford | 2018 | (3) | 0 | 0 | 0 | 0 |
| Will Oakes | Hull KR | 2016, 2018-19 | 12 | 5 | 0 | 0 | 20 |
| Adam O'Brien | Huddersfield | 2017-19 | 40(31) | 12 | 0 | 0 | 48 |
| | Bradford | 2011-14 | 12(29) | 6 | 0 | 0 | 24 |
| Clinton O'Brien | Wakefield | 2003 | (2) | 0 | 0 | 0 | 0 |
| Gareth O'Brien | Salford | 2016-18 | 49(3) | 12 | 105 | 2 | 260 |
| | Warrington | 2011-15 | 48(3) | 16 | 69 | 3 | 205 |
| | St Helens | 2013 | 7 | 0 | 25 | 0 | 50 |
| | Castleford | 2013 | 2 | 0 | 0 | 1 | 1 |
| | Widnes | 2012 | 4 | 0 | 15 | 0 | 30 |
| Sam Obst | Hull | 2011 | 11(6) | 6 | 0 | 0 | 24 |
| | Wakefield | 2005-11 | 100(28) | 40 | 7 | 0 | 174 |
| Jamie O'Callaghan | London | 2012-14 | 44(2) | 4 | 0 | 0 | 16 |
| | Harlequins | 2008-11 | 54(3) | 12 | 0 | 0 | 48 |
| Eamon O'Carroll | Widnes | 2012-17 | 58(11) | 3 | 0 | 0 | 12 |
| | Hull | 2012 | 1(9) | 0 | 0 | 0 | 0 |
| | Wigan | 2006-11 | 2(59) | 3 | 0 | 0 | 12 |
| Matt O'Connor | Paris | 1997 | 11(4) | 1 | 26 | 2 | 58 |
| Terry O'Connor | Widnes | 2005 | 25 | 2 | 0 | 0 | 8 |
| | Wigan | 1996-2004 | 177(45) | 9 | 0 | 0 | 36 |
| Jarrod O'Doherty | Huddersfield | 2003 | 26 | 3 | 0 | 0 | 12 |
| David O'Donnell | Paris | 1997 | 21 | 3 | 0 | 0 | 12 |
| Luke O'Donnell | Huddersfield | 2011-13 | 22(2) | 2 | 0 | 0 | 8 |
| Martin Offiah | Salford | 2000-01 | 41 | 20 | 0 | 2 | 82 |
| | London | 1996-99 | 29(3) | 21 | 0 | 0 | 84 |
| | Wigan | 1996 | 8 | 7 | 0 | 0 | 28 |
| Jacob Ogden | London | 2019 | 2 | 0 | 0 | 0 | 0 |
| Mark O'Halloran | London | 2004-05 | 34(3) | 10 | 0 | 0 | 40 |
| Ryan O'Hara | Hull KR | 2012 | 8(7) | 1 | 0 | 0 | 4 |
| | Crusaders | 2010-11 | 41(8) | 3 | 0 | 0 | 12 |
| | Celtic | 2009 | 27 | 3 | 0 | 0 | 12 |
| Hefin O'Hare | Huddersfield | 2001, 2003-05 | 72(10) | 27 | 0 | 0 | 108 |
| Edwin Okanga-Ajwang | | | | | | | |
| | Salford | 2013 | 2 | 0 | 0 | 0 | 0 |
| Hitro Okesene | Hull | 1998 | 21(1) | 0 | 0 | 0 | 0 |
| Anderson Okiwe | Sheffield | 1997 | 1 | 0 | 0 | 0 | 0 |
| Tom Olbison | Widnes | 2017-18 | 17(22) | 4 | 0 | 0 | 16 |
| | Bradford | 2009-14 | 55(26) | 11 | 0 | 0 | 44 |
| Michael Oldfield | Catalans | 2014-15 | 41 | 28 | 0 | 0 | 112 |
| Mikolaj Oledzki | Leeds | 2017-19 | 15(24) | 3 | 0 | 0 | 12 |
| Jamie Olejnik | Paris | 1997 | 11 | 8 | 0 | 0 | 32 |
| Aaron Ollett | Hull KR | 2013-15 | 5(16) | 1 | 0 | 0 | 4 |
| Kevin O'Loughlin | Halifax | 1997-98 | 2(4) | 0 | 0 | 0 | 0 |
| | St Helens | 1997 | (3) | 0 | 0 | 0 | 0 |
| Sean O'Loughlin | Wigan | 2002-19 | 367(30) | 71 | 3 | 2 | 292 |
| Derrell Olpherts | Salford | 2018-19 | 35 | 11 | 0 | 0 | 44 |
| Mark O'Meley | Hull | 2010-12 | 70(13) | 13 | 0 | 0 | 52 |
| Jacques O'Neill | Castleford | 2019 | (11) | 1 | 0 | 0 | 4 |
| Jules O'Neill | Widnes | 2003-05 | 57(3) | 14 | 158 | 7 | 379 |
| | Wakefield | 2005 | 10(2) | 2 | 4 | 0 | 16 |
| | Wigan | 2002-03 | 29(1) | 12 | 72 | 0 | 192 |
| Julian O'Neill | Widnes | 2002-05 | 57(39) | 3 | 0 | 0 | 12 |
| | Wakefield | 2001 | 24(1) | 2 | 0 | 0 | 8 |
| | St Helens | 1997-2000 | 95(8) | 5 | 0 | 0 | 20 |
| Mark O'Neill | Hull KR | 2007 | 17 | 5 | 0 | 0 | 20 |
| | Leeds | 2006 | 1(8) | 0 | 0 | 0 | 0 |
| Steve O'Neill | Gateshead | 1999 | 1(1) | 0 | 0 | 0 | 0 |
| Tom O'Reilly | Warrington | 2001-02 | 8(6) | 1 | 0 | 0 | 4 |
| Matt Orford | Bradford | 2010 | 12 | 3 | 31 | 2 | 76 |
| Jack Ormondroyd | Leeds | 2017-18 | 3(9) | 0 | 0 | 0 | 0 |
| Gene Ormsby | Huddersfield | 2016-17 | 8 | 4 | 0 | 0 | 16 |
| | Warrington | 2014-16 | 37 | 26 | 0 | 0 | 104 |
| Chris Orr | Huddersfield | 1998 | 19(3) | 2 | 0 | 0 | 8 |
| Danny Orr | Castleford | 1997-2003, 2011-12 | 197(23) | 75 | 308 | 3 | 919 |
| | Harlequins | 2007-10 | 90(4) | 13 | 96 | 0 | 244 |
| | Wigan | 2004-06 | 66(2) | 18 | 12 | 0 | 96 |
| Gareth Owen | Salford | 2010, 2012-13 | 4(32) | 6 | 0 | 0 | 24 |
| Nick Owen | Leigh | 2005 | 8(1) | 1 | 11 | 0 | 26 |
| Richard Owen | Wakefield | 2014-15 | 29(1) | 9 | 0 | 0 | 36 |
| | Castleford | 2008-14 | 109(3) | 57 | 0 | 0 | 228 |
| Jack Owens | St Helens | 2016-17 | 31 | 8 | 14 | 0 | 60 |
| | Widnes | 2012-15 | 53(1) | 26 | 103 | 0 | 310 |
| Lopini Paea | Wakefield | 2015 | 1(3) | 0 | 0 | 0 | 0 |
| | Catalans | 2011-14 | 41(41) | 9 | 0 | 0 | 36 |
| Mickey Paea | Hull | 2014-15, | | | | | |
| | | 2018-19 | 78(18) | 9 | 0 | 0 | 36 |
| | Hull KR | 2012-13 | 34(17) | 5 | 0 | 0 | 20 |
| Liam Paisley | Wigan | 2018-19 | 6(2) | 2 | 0 | 0 | 8 |
| Mathias Pala | Catalans | 2011-15 | 28(1) | 4 | 0 | 0 | 16 |
| Iafeta Palea'aesina | Hull | 2014-16 | (47) | 1 | 0 | 0 | 4 |
| | Salford | 2011-12 | 4(37) | 3 | 0 | 0 | 12 |
| | Wigan | 2006-10 | 55(77) | 16 | 0 | 0 | 64 |
| Jason Palmada | Workington | 1996 | 12 | 2 | 0 | 0 | 8 |
| Junior Paramore | Castleford | 1996 | 5(5) | 3 | 0 | 0 | 12 |
| Matt Parcell | Hull KR | 2019 | 5 | 2 | 0 | 0 | 8 |
| | Leeds | 2017-19 | 50(16) | 27 | 0 | 0 | 108 |
| Paul Parker | Hull | 1999-2002 | 23(18) | 9 | 0 | 0 | 36 |
| Rob Parker | Castleford | 2011 | 4(2) | 2 | 0 | 0 | 8 |
| | Salford | 2009-11 | 23(14) | 4 | 0 | 0 | 16 |
| | Warrington | 2006-08 | 10(56) | 6 | 0 | 0 | 24 |
| | Bradford | 2000, 2002-05 | 19(76) | 14 | 0 | 0 | 56 |
| | London | 2001 | 9 | 1 | 0 | 0 | 4 |
| Wayne Parker | Halifax | 1996-97 | 12(1) | 0 | 0 | 0 | 0 |
| Ian Parry | Warrington | 2001 | (1) | 0 | 0 | 0 | 0 |
| Jules Parry | Paris | 1996 | 10(2) | 0 | 0 | 0 | 0 |
| Oliver Partington | Wigan | 2018-19 | 15(13) | 2 | 0 | 0 | 8 |
| Regis Pastre-Courtine | | | | | | | |
| | Paris | 1996 | 4(3) | 4 | 0 | 0 | 16 |
| Cory Paterson | Leigh | 2017 | 13 | 2 | 0 | 0 | 8 |
| | Salford | 2015 | 14(1) | 7 | 6 | 0 | 40 |
| | Hull KR | 2013 | 15 | 7 | 0 | 0 | 28 |
| Andrew Patmore | Oldham | 1996 | 8(5) | 3 | 0 | 0 | 12 |
| Larne Patrick | Castleford | 2016-17 | 14(7) | 1 | 0 | 0 | 4 |
| | Huddersfield | 2009-14, 2016 | 30(107) | 30 | 0 | 0 | 120 |
| | Wigan | 2015 | 7(20) | 4 | 0 | 0 | 16 |
| Luke Patten | Salford | 2011-12 | 53 | 16 | 0 | 0 | 64 |
| Declan Patton | Warrington | 2015-19 | 66(17) | 11 | 101 | 6 | 252 |
| Henry Paul | Harlequins | 2006-08 | 60(1) | 8 | 94 | 2 | 222 |
| | Bradford | 1999-2001 | 81(5) | 29 | 350 | 6 | 822 |
| | Wigan | 1996-98 | 60 | 37 | 23 | 0 | 194 |
| Junior Paul | London | 1996 | 3 | 1 | 0 | 0 | 4 |
| Robbie Paul | Salford | 2009 | 2(24) | 2 | 0 | 0 | 8 |
| | Huddersfield | 2006-07 | 44(8) | 7 | 0 | 0 | 28 |
| | Bradford | 1996-2005 | 198(31) | 121 | 3 | 0 | 490 |
| Pauli Pauli | Wakefield | 2018-19 | 14(30) | 10 | 0 | 0 | 40 |
| | Salford | 2019 | (3) | 3 | 0 | 0 | 12 |
| Joseph Paulo | St Helens | 2019 | 5(19) | 1 | 0 | 0 | 4 |
| Jason Payne | Castleford | 2006 | 1(1) | 0 | 0 | 0 | 0 |
| Lewis Peachey | Castleford | 2019 | 1 | 0 | 0 | 0 | 0 |
| Danny Peacock | Bradford | 1997-99 | 32(2) | 15 | 0 | 0 | 60 |
| Jamie Peacock | Leeds | 2006-15 | 234(16) | 24 | 0 | 0 | 96 |
| | Bradford | 1999-2005 | 163(25) | 38 | 0 | 0 | 152 |
| Martin Pearson | Wakefield | 2001 | 21(1) | 3 | 60 | 3 | 135 |
| | Halifax | 1997-98, 2000 | 55(6) | 24 | 181 | 0 | 458 |
| | Sheffield | 1999 | 17(6) | 9 | 36 | 2 | 110 |
| Jacques Pech | Paris | 1996 | 16 | 0 | 0 | 0 | 0 |
| Mike Pechey | Warrington | 1998 | 6(3) | 2 | 0 | 0 | 8 |
| Bill Peden | London | 2003 | 21(3) | 7 | 0 | 0 | 28 |
| Adam Peek | Crusaders | 2010-11 | 5(22) | 1 | 0 | 0 | 4 |
| | Celtic | 2009 | 5(12) | 3 | 0 | 0 | 12 |
| Eloi Pelissier | London | 2019 | 7(6) | 1 | 0 | 0 | 4 |
| | Leigh | 2017 | 4(16) | 1 | 0 | 0 | 0 |
| | Catalans | 2011-16 | 38(104) | 23 | 0 | 1 | 93 |
| Dimitri Pelo | Catalans | 2007-10 | 79 | 37 | 0 | 0 | 148 |
| Sean Penkywicz | Huddersfield | 2004-05 | 21(11) | 7 | 0 | 0 | 28 |
| | Halifax | 2000-03 | 29(27) | 8 | 0 | 0 | 32 |
| Julian Penni | Salford | 1998-99 | 4 | 0 | 0 | 0 | 0 |
| Kevin Penny | Warrington | 2006-09, 2014-17 | 83(1) | 52 | 0 | 0 | 208 |
| | Wakefield | 2011 | 5 | 1 | 0 | 0 | 4 |
| | Harlequins | 2010 | 5 | 3 | 0 | 0 | 12 |
| Lee Penny | Warrington | 1996-2003 | 140(5) | 54 | 0 | 0 | 216 |
| Paul Penrice | Workington | 1996 | 11(2) | 2 | 0 | 0 | 8 |
| Chris Percival | Widnes | 2002-03 | 26 | 6 | 0 | 0 | 24 |
| Mark Percival | St Helens | 2013-19 | 142(2) | 76 | 218 | 0 | 740 |
| Apollo Perelini | St Helens | 1996-2000 | 103(16) | 27 | 0 | 0 | 108 |
| Ugo Perez | Catalans | 2015, 2017-18 | 2(5) | 0 | 0 | 0 | 0 |
| Mark Perrett | Halifax | 1996-97 | 15(4) | 4 | 0 | 0 | 16 |
| Josh Perry | St Helens | 2011-13 | 32(9) | 2 | 0 | 0 | 8 |

## Super League Players 1996-2019

| PLAYER | CLUB | YEAR | APP | TRIES | GOALS | FG | PTS |
|---|---|---|---|---|---|---|---|
| Shane Perry | Catalans | 2009 | 8(8) | 1 | 0 | 0 | 4 |
| Adam Peters | Paris | 1997 | 16(3) | 0 | 0 | 0 | 0 |
| Dominic Peters | London | 1998-2003 | 58(11) | 12 | 0 | 0 | 48 |
| Mike Peters | Warrington | 2000 | 2(12) | 1 | 0 | 0 | 4 |
| | Halifax | 2000 | 1 | 0 | 0 | 0 | 0 |
| Willie Peters | Widnes | 2004 | 9 | 3 | 0 | 2 | 14 |
| | Wigan | 2000 | 29 | 15 | 5 | 6 | 76 |
| | Gateshead | 1999 | 27 | 11 | 1 | 6 | 52 |
| Dave Petersen | Hull KR | 2012 | 2(2) | 1 | 0 | 0 | 4 |
| Matt Petersen | Wakefield | 2008-09 | 14 | 3 | 0 | 0 | 12 |
| Nathaniel Peteru | Leeds | 2018-19 | 15(6) | 0 | 0 | 0 | 0 |
| Adrian Petrie | Workington | 1996 | (1) | 0 | 0 | 0 | 0 |
| Eddy Pettybourne | Wigan | 2014 | 1(15) | 0 | 0 | 0 | 0 |
| Dominique Peyroux | St Helens | 2016-19 | 81(17) | 15 | 0 | 0 | 60 |
| Cameron Phelps | Widnes | 2012-15 | 66(1) | 23 | 2 | 0 | 96 |
| | Hull | 2011 | 19 | 2 | 0 | 0 | 8 |
| | Wigan | 2008-10 | 43(1) | 14 | 4 | 0 | 64 |
| Joe Philbin | Warrington | 2014-19 | 18(82) | 10 | 0 | 0 | 40 |
| Rowland Phillips | Workington | 1996 | 22 | 1 | 0 | 0 | 4 |
| Nathan Picchi | Leeds | 1996 | (1) | 0 | 0 | 0 | 0 |
| Ian Pickavance | Hull | 1999 | 4(2) | 2 | 0 | 0 | 8 |
| | Huddersfield | 1999 | 3(14) | 0 | 0 | 0 | 0 |
| | St Helens | 1996-98 | 12(44) | 6 | 0 | 0 | 24 |
| James Pickering | Castleford | 1999 | 1(19) | 0 | 0 | 0 | 0 |
| Steve Pickersgill | Widnes | 2012-13 | 27(8) | 1 | 0 | 0 | 4 |
| | Warrington | 2005-09 | 1(36) | 0 | 0 | 0 | 0 |
| Nick Pinkney | Salford | 2000-02 | 64 | 29 | 0 | 0 | 116 |
| | Halifax | 1999 | 26(2) | 13 | 0 | 0 | 52 |
| | Sheffield | 1997-98 | 33 | 10 | 0 | 0 | 40 |
| Mikhail Piskunov | Paris | 1996 | 1(1) | 1 | 0 | 0 | 4 |
| Darryl Pitt | London | 1996 | 2(16) | 4 | 0 | 1 | 17 |
| Jay Pitts | London | 2019 | 27 | 7 | 0 | 0 | 28 |
| | Bradford | 2014 | 15(1) | 3 | 0 | 0 | 12 |
| | Hull | 2012-14 | 18(30) | 1 | 0 | 0 | 4 |
| | Leeds | 2009-12 | 10(15) | 2 | 0 | 0 | 8 |
| | Wakefield | 2008-09 | 9(8) | 2 | 0 | 0 | 8 |
| Andy Platt | Salford | 1997-98 | 20(3) | 1 | 0 | 0 | 4 |
| Michael Platt | Salford | 2001-02, 2014 | 4(1) | 1 | 0 | 0 | 4 |
| | Bradford | 2007-13 | 121(6) | 44 | 0 | 0 | 176 |
| | Castleford | 2006 | 26 | 7 | 0 | 0 | 28 |
| Willie Poching | Leeds | 2002-06 | 58(73) | 44 | 0 | 0 | 176 |
| | Wakefield | 1999-2001 | 65(4) | 20 | 0 | 0 | 80 |
| Ben Pomeroy | Warrington | 2017-18 | 3(7) | 1 | 0 | 0 | 4 |
| | Catalans | 2014-15 | 44 | 10 | 0 | 0 | 40 |
| Quentin Pongia | Wigan | 2003-04 | 15(10) | 0 | 0 | 0 | 0 |
| Justin Poore | Hull KR | 2014 | 7 | 0 | 0 | 0 | 0 |
| | Wakefield | 2013 | 23 | 1 | 0 | 0 | 4 |
| Dan Potter | Widnes | 2002-03 | 34(2) | 6 | 0 | 0 | 24 |
| | London | 2001 | 1(3) | 1 | 0 | 0 | 4 |
| Craig Poucher | Hull | 1999-2002 | 31(5) | 5 | 0 | 0 | 20 |
| Andy Powell | Wigan | 2013 | 2(3) | 1 | 0 | 0 | 4 |
| Bryn Powell | Salford | 2004 | 1(1) | 0 | 0 | 0 | 0 |
| Daio Powell | Sheffield | 1999 | 13(1) | 2 | 0 | 0 | 8 |
| | Halifax | 1997-98 | 30(3) | 17 | 0 | 0 | 68 |
| Daryl Powell | Leeds | 1998-2000 | 49(30) | 12 | 0 | 2 | 50 |
| Sam Powell | Wigan | 2012-19 | 124(49) | 21 | 4 | 4 | 96 |
| Karl Pratt | Bradford | 2003-05 | 35(19) | 18 | 0 | 0 | 72 |
| | Leeds | 1999-2002 | 62(12) | 33 | 0 | 0 | 132 |
| Paul Prescott | Wigan | 2004-13 | 49(75) | 4 | 0 | 0 | 16 |
| Steve Prescott | Hull | 1998-99, 2001-03 | 99 | 46 | 191 | 3 | 569 |
| | Wakefield | 2000 | 22(1) | 3 | 13 | 0 | 38 |
| | St Helens | 1996-97 | 32 | 15 | 17 | 0 | 94 |
| Lee Prest | Workington | 1996 | (1) | 0 | 0 | 0 | 0 |
| Gareth Price | Salford | 2002 | (2) | 0 | 0 | 0 | 0 |
| | London | 2002 | 2(2) | 3 | 0 | 0 | 12 |
| | St Helens | 1999 | (11) | 2 | 0 | 0 | 8 |
| Gary Price | Wakefield | 1999-2001 | 55(13) | 11 | 0 | 0 | 44 |
| Richard Price | Sheffield | 1996 | 1(2) | 0 | 0 | 0 | 0 |
| Tony Priddle | Paris | 1997 | 11(7) | 3 | 0 | 0 | 12 |
| Frank Pritchard | Hull | 2016 | 10(13) | 4 | 0 | 0 | 16 |
| Karl Pryce | Bradford | 2003-06, 2012 | 47(19) | 46 | 1 | 0 | 186 |
| | Harlequins | 2011 | 11(7) | 12 | 0 | 0 | 48 |
| | Wigan | 2009-10 | 11(2) | 12 | 0 | 0 | 48 |
| Leon Pryce | Hull | 2015-16 | 32(2) | 8 | 0 | 0 | 32 |
| | Catalans | 2012-14 | 72(2) | 15 | 0 | 0 | 60 |
| | St Helens | 2006-11 | 133(3) | 64 | 0 | 0 | 256 |
| | Bradford | 1998-2005 | 159(29) | 86 | 0 | 0 | 344 |
| Waine Pryce | Wakefield | 2007 | 10(2) | 4 | 0 | 0 | 16 |
| | Castleford | 2000-06 | 97(12) | 49 | 0 | 0 | 196 |
| Tony Puletua | Hull KR | 2015 | 7 | 0 | 0 | 0 | 0 |
| | Salford | 2014 | 16(9) | 3 | 0 | 0 | 12 |
| | St Helens | 2009-13 | 108(18) | 39 | 0 | 0 | 156 |
| Andrew Purcell | Castleford | 2000 | 15(5) | 3 | 0 | 0 | 12 |
| | Hull | 1999 | 27 | 4 | 0 | 0 | 16 |
| Rob Purdham | Harlequins | 2006-11 | 112(3) | 18 | 131 | 1 | 335 |
| | London | 2002-05 | 53(15) | 16 | 2 | 1 | 69 |
| Adrian Purtell | Bradford | 2012-14 | 45(1) | 16 | 0 | 0 | 64 |
| Luke Quigley | Catalans | 2007 | 16(1) | 1 | 0 | 0 | 4 |
| Adam Quinlan | Hull KR | 2018-19 | 31 | 16 | 0 | 0 | 64 |
| | St Helens | 2015 | 11 | 6 | 0 | 0 | 24 |
| Damien Quinn | Celtic | 2009 | 20(1) | 4 | 12 | 0 | 40 |
| Scott Quinnell | Wigan | 1996 | 6(3) | 1 | 0 | 0 | 4 |
| Florian Quintilla | Catalans | 2008-09 | 1(4) | 0 | 0 | 0 | 0 |
| Lee Radford | Hull | 1998, 2006-12 | 138(30) | 23 | 1 | 0 | 94 |
| | Bradford | 1999-2005 | 79(65) | 18 | 12 | 0 | 96 |
| Kris Radlinski | Wigan | 1996-2006 | 236(1) | 134 | 1 | 0 | 538 |
| Sebastien Raguin | Catalans | 2007-12 | 103(22) | 28 | 0 | 0 | 112 |
| Adrian Rainey | Castleford | 2002 | 4(7) | 1 | 0 | 0 | 4 |
| Andy Raleigh | Wakefield | 2012-14 | 42(21) | 9 | 0 | 0 | 36 |
| | Huddersfield | 2006-11 | 74(46) | 13 | 0 | 0 | 52 |
| Jean-Luc Ramondou | Paris | 1996 | 1(1) | 1 | 0 | 0 | 4 |
| Chad Randall | London | 2012-13 | 29(9) | 4 | 0 | 0 | 16 |
| | Harlequins | 2006-11 | 141(2) | 37 | 0 | 1 | 149 |
| Craig Randall | Halifax | 1999 | 8(11) | 4 | 0 | 0 | 16 |
| | Salford | 1997-98 | 12(18) | 4 | 0 | 0 | 16 |
| Tyler Randell | Wakefield | 2017-19 | 36(8) | 9 | 1 | 0 | 38 |
| Jordan Rankin | Castleford | 2019 | 22(2) | 10 | 19 | 0 | 78 |
| | Huddersfield | 2017-18 | 39 | 3 | 9 | 0 | 30 |
| | Hull | 2014-16 | 41(6) | 20 | 43 | 0 | 166 |
| Scott Ranson | Oldham | 1996-97 | 19(2) | 7 | 0 | 0 | 28 |
| Aaron Raper | Castleford | 1999-2001 | 48(4) | 4 | 2 | 1 | 21 |
| Sam Rapira | Huddersfield | 2016-17 | 29(19) | 3 | 0 | 0 | 12 |
| Steve Rapira | Salford | 2014 | 5(13) | 0 | 0 | 0 | 0 |
| Stefan Ratchford | Warrington | 2012-19 | 195(10) | 71 | 275 | 2 | 836 |
| | Salford | 2007, 2009-11 | 65(5) | 23 | 20 | 0 | 132 |
| Mike Ratu | Hull KR | 2010 | 5 | 1 | 0 | 0 | 4 |
| | Leeds | 2007, 2009 | 1(5) | 1 | 0 | 0 | 4 |
| Paul Rauhihi | Warrington | 2006-09 | 67(20) | 10 | 0 | 0 | 40 |
| Ben Rauter | Wakefield | 2001 | 15(6) | 4 | 0 | 0 | 16 |
| Nick Rawsthorne | Leigh | 2017 | 1 | 1 | 0 | 0 | 4 |
| | Hull | 2017 | 3 | 2 | 2 | 0 | 12 |
| Gareth Raynor | Bradford | 2011 | 18 | 4 | 0 | 0 | 16 |
| | Crusaders | 2010 | 7 | 4 | 0 | 0 | 16 |
| | Hull | 2001-09 | 186 | 102 | 0 | 0 | 408 |
| | Leeds | 2000 | (3) | 0 | 0 | 0 | 0 |
| Tony Rea | London | 1996 | 22 | 4 | 0 | 0 | 16 |
| Stuart Reardon | Crusaders | 2011 | 25 | 11 | 0 | 0 | 44 |
| | Bradford | 2003-05, 2010 | 78(11) | 37 | 0 | 0 | 148 |
| | Warrington | 2006-08 | 48 | 12 | 0 | 0 | 48 |
| | Salford | 2002 | 7(1) | 3 | 0 | 0 | 12 |
| Mark Reber | Wigan | 1999-2000 | 9(9) | 5 | 0 | 0 | 20 |
| Alan Reddicliffe | Warrington | 2001 | 1 | 0 | 0 | 0 | 0 |
| Tahi Reihana | Bradford | 1997-98 | 17(21) | 0 | 0 | 0 | 0 |
| Paul Reilly | Wakefield | 2008 | 5(2) | 1 | 0 | 0 | 4 |
| | Huddersfield | 1999-2001, 2003-07 | 150(8) | 35 | 1 | 0 | 142 |
| Robert Relf | Widnes | 2002-04 | 68(2) | 5 | 0 | 0 | 20 |
| Steve Renouf | Wigan | 2000-01 | 55 | 40 | 0 | 0 | 160 |
| Steele Retchless | London | 1998-2004 | 177(6) | 13 | 0 | 0 | 52 |
| Ben Reynolds | Wakefield | 2019 | 5 | 1 | 0 | 0 | 4 |
| | Leigh | 2017 | 16 | 6 | 48 | 0 | 120 |
| | Castleford | 2013-14 | 1(3) | 0 | 0 | 0 | 0 |
| Scott Rhodes | Hull | 2000 | 2 | 0 | 0 | 0 | 0 |
| Phillipe Ricard | Paris | 1996-97 | 2 | 0 | 0 | 0 | 0 |
| Andy Rice | Huddersfield | 2000-01 | 2(13) | 1 | 0 | 0 | 4 |
| Basil Richards | Huddersfield | 1998-99 | 28(17) | 1 | 0 | 0 | 4 |
| Craig Richards | Oldham | 1996 | 1 | 0 | 0 | 0 | 0 |
| Greg Richards | London | 2019 | 5(15) | 0 | 0 | 0 | 0 |
| | Leigh | 2017 | (1) | 0 | 0 | 0 | 0 |
| | St Helens | 2013-17 | 19(49) | 1 | 0 | 0 | 4 |
| Pat Richards | Catalans | 2016 | 19 | 9 | 69 | 0 | 174 |
| | Wigan | 2006-13 | 199 | 147 | 759 | 4 | 2110 |
| Andy Richardson | Hudds-Sheff | 2000 | (2) | 0 | 0 | 0 | 0 |
| Danny Richardson | St Helens | 2017-19 | 52(2) | 9 | 158 | 8 | 360 |
| Sean Richardson | Widnes | 2002 | 2(18) | 1 | 0 | 0 | 4 |
| | Wakefield | 1999 | 5(1) | 0 | 0 | 0 | 0 |
| | Castleford | 1996-97 | 3(8) | 1 | 0 | 0 | 4 |
| Mark Riddell | Wigan | 2009-10 | 45(11) | 5 | 2 | 0 | 24 |
| Martyn Ridyard | Huddersfield | 2017 | 7 | 1 | 26 | 0 | 56 |
| | Leigh | 2017 | 4 | 0 | 2 | 0 | 4 |
| Neil Rigby | St Helens | 2006 | (1) | 0 | 0 | 0 | 0 |
| Shane Rigon | Bradford | 2001 | 14(11) | 12 | 0 | 0 | 48 |
| Craig Rika | Halifax | 1996 | 2 | 0 | 0 | 0 | 0 |
| Chris Riley | Wakefield | 2014-15 | 44 | 16 | 0 | 0 | 64 |
| | Warrington | 2005-14 | 146(10) | 102 | 0 | 0 | 408 |
| | Harlequins | 2011 | 3 | 2 | 0 | 0 | 8 |

# Super League Players 1996-2019

| PLAYER | CLUB | YEAR | APP | TRIES | GOALS | FG | PTS |
|---|---|---|---|---|---|---|---|
| Glenn Riley | Warrington | 2013-14 | (15) | 0 | 0 | 0 | 0 |
| Peter Riley | Workington | 1996 | 7(5) | 0 | 0 | 0 | 0 |
| Julien Rinaldi | London | 2012 | 4(16) | 1 | 0 | 0 | 4 |
|  | Wakefield | 2002, 2010-11 | 27(9) | 6 | 0 | 0 | 24 |
|  | Bradford | 2009 | (7) | 1 | 0 | 0 | 4 |
|  | Harlequins | 2007-08 | 4(43) | 9 | 0 | 0 | 36 |
|  | Catalans | 2006 | 16(6) | 3 | 1 | 0 | 14 |
| Dean Ripley | Castleford | 2004 | 3(4) | 1 | 0 | 0 | 4 |
| Leroy Rivett | Warrington | 2002 | 9 | 1 | 0 | 0 | 4 |
|  | Hudds-Sheff | 2000 | 5(1) | 1 | 0 | 0 | 4 |
|  | Leeds | 1996-2000 | 39(15) | 21 | 0 | 0 | 84 |
| Jason Roach | Warrington | 1998-99 | 29(7) | 15 | 0 | 0 | 60 |
|  | Castleford | 1997 | 7 | 4 | 0 | 0 | 16 |
| Ben Roarty | Castleford | 1997 | 11(6) | 2 | 0 | 0 | 8 |
|  | Huddersfield | 2003-05 | 52 | 5 | 0 | 0 | 20 |
| Amos Roberts | Wigan | 2009-11 | 47(2) | 27 | 5 | 0 | 118 |
| Ben Roberts | Castleford | 2015-19 | 60(15) | 20 | 0 | 2 | 82 |
| Mark Roberts | Wigan | 2003 | (3) | 0 | 0 | 0 | 0 |
| Oliver Roberts | Huddersfield | 2016-19 | 40(43) | 13 | 0 | 0 | 52 |
|  | Bradford | 2013-14 | (5) | 0 | 0 | 0 | 0 |
| Robert Roberts | Huddersfield | 2001 | (1) | 0 | 0 | 0 | 0 |
|  | Halifax | 2000 | (3) | 0 | 0 | 0 | 0 |
|  | Hull | 1999 | 24(2) | 4 | 13 | 4 | 46 |
| Tyrone Roberts | Warrington | 2018 | 28 | 5 | 32 | 1 | 85 |
| Michael Robertson | London | 2012-13 | 35 | 17 | 0 | 0 | 68 |
| Stan Robin | Catalans | 2015-16 | 5(2) | 1 | 0 | 0 | 4 |
| Chad Robinson | Harlequins | 2009 | 13(1) | 2 | 0 | 0 | 8 |
| Connor Robinson | Hull KR | 2014-15 | (2) | 0 | 0 | 0 | 0 |
| Craig Robinson | Wakefield | 2005 | (1) | 0 | 0 | 0 | 0 |
| Jason Robinson | Wigan | 1996-2000 | 126(1) | 87 | 0 | 1 | 349 |
| Jeremy Robinson | Paris | 1997 | 10(3) | 1 | 21 | 0 | 46 |
| John Robinson | Widnes | 2003-04 | 7 | 1 | 0 | 0 | 4 |
| Luke Robinson | Huddersfield | 2008-15 | 191(18) | 45 | 4 | 0 | 188 |
|  | Salford | 2005-07 | 79 | 28 | 10 | 2 | 134 |
|  | Wigan | 2002-04 | 17(25) | 9 | 6 | 1 | 49 |
|  | Castleford | 2004 | 9 | 4 | 3 | 0 | 22 |
| Will Robinson | Hull | 2000 | 22 | 4 | 0 | 0 | 16 |
|  | Gateshead | 1999 | 28 | 9 | 0 | 0 | 36 |
| Ash Robson | Castleford | 2015 | 3 | 1 | 0 | 0 | 4 |
| James Roby | St Helens | 2004-19 | 282(123) | 98 | 1 | 1 | 395 |
| Mike Roby | St Helens | 2004 | (1) | 0 | 0 | 0 | 0 |
| Colton Roche | Huddersfield | 2018-19 | 1(7) | 0 | 0 | 0 | 0 |
| Carl Roden | Warrington | 1997 | 1 | 0 | 0 | 0 | 0 |
| Shane Rodney | London | 2012-13 | 28 | 3 | 12 | 0 | 36 |
| Matt Rodwell | Warrington | 2002 | 10 | 3 | 0 | 0 | 12 |
| Darren Rogers | Castleford | 1999-2004 | 162(1) | 81 | 0 | 0 | 324 |
|  | Salford | 1997-98 | 42 | 16 | 0 | 0 | 64 |
| Arthur Romano | Catalans | 2017, 2019 | 15 | 3 | 0 | 0 | 12 |
| Adam Rooks | Hull KR | 2019 | (4) | 0 | 0 | 0 | 0 |
| Jamie Rooney | Wakefield | 2003-09 | 113(7) | 60 | 321 | 21 | 903 |
|  | Castleford | 2001 | 2(1) | 0 | 6 | 0 | 12 |
| Jonathan Roper | Castleford | 2001 | 13 | 7 | 12 | 0 | 52 |
|  | Salford | 2000 | 1(4) | 1 | 3 | 0 | 10 |
|  | London | 2000 | 4 | 0 | 0 | 0 | 0 |
|  | Warrington | 1996-2000 | 75(8) | 33 | 71 | 0 | 274 |
| Scott Roskell | London | 1996-97 | 30(2) | 16 | 0 | 0 | 64 |
| Steve Rosolen | London | 1996-98 | 25(9) | 10 | 0 | 0 | 40 |
| Adam Ross | London | 1996 | (1) | 0 | 0 | 0 | 0 |
| Paul Round | Castleford | 1996 | (3) | 0 | 0 | 0 | 0 |
| Steve Rowlands | Widnes | 2004-05 | 18(3) | 2 | 15 | 0 | 38 |
|  | St Helens | 2003 | (1) | 0 | 0 | 0 | 0 |
| Paul Rowley | Leigh | 2005 | 15(7) | 3 | 0 | 0 | 12 |
|  | Huddersfield | 2001 | 24 | 3 | 0 | 0 | 12 |
|  | Halifax | 1996-2000 | 107(3) | 27 | 1 | 3 | 113 |
| Nigel Roy | London | 2001-04 | 100 | 39 | 0 | 0 | 156 |
| Nicky Royle | Widnes | 2004 | 13 | 7 | 0 | 0 | 28 |
| Shad Royston | Bradford | 2011 | 17(1) | 10 | 0 | 0 | 40 |
| Chris Rudd | Warrington | 1996-98 | 31(17) | 10 | 16 | 0 | 72 |
| Sean Rudder | Catalans | 2006 | 22(1) | 6 | 0 | 0 | 24 |
|  | Castleford | 2004 | 9(3) | 2 | 0 | 0 | 8 |
| Charly Runciman | Widnes | 2016-18 | 67 | 9 | 0 | 0 | 36 |
| James Rushforth | Halifax | 1997 | (4) | 0 | 0 | 0 | 0 |
| Danny Russell | Huddersfield | 1998-2000 | 50(13) | 8 | 0 | 0 | 32 |
| Ian Russell | Oldham | 1997 | 1(3) | 1 | 0 | 0 | 4 |
|  | Paris | 1996 | 3 | 0 | 0 | 0 | 0 |
| Matthew Russell | Warrington | 2014-18 | 77(4) | 22 | 0 | 0 | 88 |
|  | Hull | 2012 | 6 | 0 | 0 | 0 | 0 |
|  | Wigan | 2012 | 2 | 3 | 0 | 0 | 12 |
| Oliver Russell | Huddersfield | 2018-19 | 19 | 1 | 44 | 4 | 96 |
| Richard Russell | Castleford | 1996-98 | 37(4) | 2 | 0 | 0 | 8 |
| Robert Russell | Salford | 1998-99 | 2(1) | 0 | 1 | 0 | 2 |
| Sean Rutgerson | Salford | 2004-06 | 60(9) | 4 | 0 | 0 | 16 |
| Chris Ryan | London | 1998-99 | 44(3) | 17 | 10 | 0 | 88 |
| Matt Ryan | Wakefield | 2014-15 | 28(12) | 7 | 0 | 0 | 28 |
| Sean Ryan | Castleford | 2004 | 11(5) | 2 | 0 | 0 | 8 |
|  | Hull | 2002-03 | 53 | 8 | 0 | 0 | 32 |
| Justin Ryder | Wakefield | 2004 | 19(3) | 11 | 0 | 0 | 44 |
| Jason Ryles | Catalans | 2009 | 19(2) | 2 | 0 | 0 | 8 |
| Setaimata Sa | Widnes | 2016 | 7(5) | 3 | 0 | 0 | 12 |
|  | Hull | 2014-15 | 18(6) | 6 | 0 | 0 | 24 |
|  | Catalans | 2010-12 | 58(5) | 21 | 0 | 0 | 84 |
| Teddy Sadaoui | Catalans | 2006 | 7 | 0 | 0 | 0 | 0 |
| Liam Salter | Hull KR | 2012-16, 2018 | 83(3) | 17 | 0 | 0 | 68 |
| Matt Salter | London | 1997-99 | 14(34) | 0 | 0 | 0 | 0 |
| Ben Sammut | Hull | 2000 | 20 | 4 | 67 | 0 | 150 |
|  | Gateshead | 1999 | 26(2) | 6 | 17 | 0 | 58 |
| Jarrod Sammut | Wigan | 2019 | 6(6) | 2 | 0 | 0 | 8 |
|  | Wakefield | 2014-15 | 19(1) | 9 | 52 | 0 | 140 |
|  | Bradford | 2012-13 | 35(3) | 28 | 47 | 1 | 207 |
|  | Crusaders | 2010-11 | 17(16) | 17 | 0 | 0 | 68 |
| Dean Sampson | Castleford | 1996-2003 | 124(28) | 24 | 0 | 0 | 96 |
| Paul Sampson | London | 2004 | 1(2) | 1 | 0 | 0 | 4 |
|  | Wakefield | 2000 | 17 | 8 | 0 | 0 | 32 |
| Lee Sanderson | London | 2004 | 1(5) | 1 | 7 | 0 | 18 |
| Chris Sandow | Warrington | 2015-16 | 27(1) | 11 | 26 | 1 | 97 |
| Jason Sands | Paris | 1996-97 | 28 | 0 | 0 | 0 | 0 |
| Mitchell Sargent | Castleford | 2008-10 | 37(21) | 6 | 0 | 0 | 24 |
| Dan Sarginson | Wigan | 2014-16, 2018-19 | 112(2) | 30 | 0 | 0 | 120 |
|  | London | 2012-13 | 35(1) | 10 | 0 | 0 | 40 |
|  | Harlequins | 2011 | 8 | 5 | 0 | 0 | 20 |
| Matt Sarsfield | Salford | 2016 | 2(2) | 1 | 0 | 0 | 4 |
| Tevita Satae | Hull | 2019 | 1(3) | 0 | 0 | 0 | 0 |
| Junior Sa'u | Salford | 2014-19 | 115 | 46 | 0 | 0 | 184 |
|  | Wakefield | 2019 | 3 | 0 | 0 | 0 | 0 |
| Andre Savelio | Hull | 2019 | (6) | 2 | 0 | 0 | 8 |
|  | Warrington | 2017 | 3(14) | 4 | 0 | 0 | 16 |
|  | Castleford | 2016 | 6(1) | 1 | 0 | 0 | 4 |
|  | St Helens | 2014-16 | 12(25) | 2 | 0 | 0 | 8 |
| Lokeni Savelio | Halifax | 2000 | 2(11) | 0 | 0 | 0 | 0 |
|  | Salford | 1997-98 | 18(20) | 0 | 0 | 0 | 0 |
| Tom Saxton | Salford | 2007 | 5 | 0 | 0 | 0 | 0 |
|  | Wakefield | 2006 | 9(6) | 2 | 0 | 0 | 8 |
|  | Hull | 2005 | 19(8) | 3 | 0 | 0 | 12 |
|  | Castleford | 2002-04 | 37(12) | 11 | 0 | 0 | 44 |
| Jonathan Scales | Halifax | 2000 | 1 | 0 | 0 | 0 | 0 |
|  | Bradford | 1996-98 | 46(4) | 24 | 0 | 0 | 96 |
| Andrew Schick | Castleford | 1996-98 | 45(13) | 10 | 0 | 0 | 40 |
| Clinton Schifcofske | Crusaders | 2010-11 | 44 | 5 | 115 | 0 | 250 |
| Garry Schofield | Huddersfield | 1998 | (2) | 0 | 0 | 0 | 0 |
| Gary Schubert | Workington | 1996 | (1) | 0 | 0 | 0 | 0 |
| Matt Schultz | Hull | 1998-99 | 23(9) | 2 | 0 | 0 | 8 |
|  | Leeds | 1996 | 2(4) | 0 | 0 | 0 | 0 |
| John Schuster | Halifax | 1996-97 | 31 | 9 | 127 | 3 | 293 |
| Cameron Scott | Hull | 2018-19 | 7 | 0 | 0 | 0 | 0 |
| Nick Scruton | Hull KR | 2018 | 7(10) | 0 | 0 | 0 | 0 |
|  | Wakefield | 2014-16 | 62(3) | 9 | 0 | 0 | 36 |
|  | Bradford | 2009-14 | 70(27) | 5 | 0 | 0 | 20 |
|  | Leeds | 2002, 2004-08 | 11(53) | 3 | 0 | 0 | 12 |
|  | Hull | 2004 | 2(16) | 3 | 0 | 0 | 12 |
| Danny Sculthorpe | Huddersfield | 2009 | 5(8) | 0 | 0 | 0 | 0 |
|  | Wakefield | 2007-09 | 14(28) | 1 | 0 | 0 | 4 |
|  | Castleford | 2006 | 18(1) | 4 | 0 | 1 | 17 |
|  | Wigan | 2002-05 | 13(49) | 7 | 0 | 0 | 28 |
| Paul Sculthorpe | St Helens | 1998-2008 | 223(4) | 94 | 356 | 7 | 1095 |
|  | Warrington | 1996-97 | 40 | 6 | 0 | 0 | 24 |
| Mick Seaby | London | 1997 | 3(2) | 1 | 0 | 0 | 4 |
| Danny Seal | Halifax | 1996-99 | 8(17) | 3 | 0 | 0 | 12 |
| Matt Seers | Wakefield | 2003 | 11(1) | 2 | 0 | 0 | 8 |
| James Segeyaro | Leeds | 2016 | 3 | 1 | 0 | 0 | 4 |
| Paul Seguier | Catalans | 2016-17 | (7) | 0 | 0 | 0 | 0 |
| Anthony Seibold | London | 1999-2000 | 33(19) | 5 | 0 | 0 | 20 |
| Jesse Sene-Lefao | Castleford | 2017-19 | 57(20) | 15 | 0 | 0 | 60 |
| Innes Senior | Huddersfield | 2018-19 | 25 | 8 | 0 | 0 | 32 |
| Keith Senior | Leeds | 1999-2011 | 319(2) | 159 | 0 | 0 | 636 |
|  | Sheffield | 1996-99 | 90(2) | 40 | 0 | 0 | 160 |
| Louis Senior | Huddersfield | 2018-19 | 15 | 9 | 0 | 0 | 36 |
| Fili Seru | Hull | 1998-99 | 37(1) | 13 | 0 | 0 | 52 |
| Ava Seumanufagai | Leeds | 2019 | 12(2) | 1 | 0 | 0 | 4 |
| Anthony Seuseu | Halifax | 2003 | 1(11) | 1 | 0 | 0 | 4 |
| Jerry Seuseu | Wigan | 2005-06 | 29(9) | 1 | 0 | 0 | 4 |
| Brett Seymour | Hull | 2012-13 | 26(1) | 7 | 0 | 0 | 28 |
| Will Sharp | Hull | 2011-12 | 27(8) | 10 | 0 | 0 | 40 |
|  | Harlequins | 2010 | 6(5) | 19 | 0 | 0 | 76 |
| Jamie Shaul | Hull | 2013-19 | 150 | 79 | 0 | 0 | 316 |
| Darren Shaw | Salford | 2002 | 5(9) | 1 | 0 | 0 | 4 |
|  | London | 1996, 2002 | 22(8) | 3 | 0 | 0 | 12 |
|  | Castleford | 2000-01 | 50(6) | 1 | 0 | 0 | 4 |
|  | Sheffield | 1998-99 | 51(1) | 3 | 0 | 1 | 13 |
| Mick Shaw | Halifax | 1999 | 5 | 1 | 0 | 0 | 4 |
|  | Leeds | 1996 | 12(2) | 7 | 0 | 0 | 28 |

# Super League Players 1996-2019

| PLAYER | CLUB | YEAR | APP | TRIES | GOALS | FG | PTS |
|---|---|---|---|---|---|---|---|
| Ryan Shaw | Hull KR | 2016, 2018-19 | 44(1) | 19 | 125 | 0 | 326 |
|  | London | 2013 | 2 | 1 | 2 | 0 | 8 |
| Phil Shead | Paris | 1996 | 3(2) | 0 | 0 | 0 | 0 |
| Richard Sheil | St Helens | 1997 | (1) | 0 | 0 | 0 | 0 |
| Kelly Shelford | Warrington | 1996-97 | 25(3) | 4 | 0 | 2 | 18 |
| Kyle Shelford | Wigan | 2016 | (1) | 0 | 0 | 0 | 0 |
| Michael Shenton | Castleford | 2004, 2006, 2008-10, 2013-19 | 245(2) | 101 | 0 | 0 | 404 |
|  | St Helens | 2011-12 | 51 | 15 | 0 | 0 | 60 |
| Ryan Sheridan | Castleford | 2004 | 2 | 0 | 0 | 0 | 0 |
|  | Widnes | 2003 | 14(3) | 2 | 0 | 0 | 8 |
|  | Leeds | 1997-2002 | 123(7) | 46 | 0 | 1 | 185 |
|  | Sheffield | 1996 | 9(3) | 5 | 0 | 1 | 21 |
| Louis Sheriff | Hull KR | 2011-12 | 8 | 3 | 0 | 0 | 12 |
| Rikki Sheriffe | Bradford | 2009-10 | 51 | 14 | 0 | 0 | 56 |
|  | Harlequins | 2006-08 | 35(1) | 16 | 0 | 0 | 64 |
|  | Halifax | 2003 | 6(1) | 3 | 0 | 0 | 12 |
| Ian Sherratt | Oldham | 1996 | 5(3) | 1 | 0 | 0 | 4 |
| Brent Sherwin | Catalans | 2010 | 12 | 1 | 0 | 1 | 5 |
|  | Castleford | 2008-10 | 48(1) | 4 | 0 | 3 | 19 |
| Peter Shiels | St Helens | 2001-02 | 44(3) | 11 | 0 | 0 | 44 |
| Gary Shillabeer | Huddersfield | 1999 | (2) | 0 | 0 | 0 | 0 |
| Mark Shipway | Salford | 2004-05 | 30(12) | 3 | 0 | 0 | 12 |
| Jake Shorrocks | Wigan | 2016-17, 2019 | 8(18) | 2 | 8 | 0 | 24 |
|  | Salford | 2018 | 10 | 0 | 1 | 0 | 2 |
| Joe Shorrocks | Wigan | 2019 | (1) | 0 | 0 | 0 | 0 |
| Ian Sibbit | Bradford | 2011-12 | 11(7) | 0 | 0 | 0 | 0 |
|  | Salford | 2005-07, 2009-10 | 64(17) | 11 | 0 | 0 | 44 |
|  | Warrington | 1999-2001, 2003-04 | 63(18) | 24 | 0 | 0 | 96 |
| Mark Sibson | Huddersfield | 1999 | 2 | 2 | 0 | 0 | 8 |
| Adam Sidlow | Bradford | 2013-14 | 20(22) | 8 | 0 | 0 | 32 |
|  | Salford | 2009-12 | 34(44) | 14 | 0 | 0 | 56 |
| Harry Siejka | Wakefield | 2014 | 6(3) | 1 | 0 | 0 | 4 |
| Jordan Sigismeau | Catalans | 2015-16 | 11 | 3 | 0 | 0 | 12 |
| Josh Simm | St Helens | 2019 | 1 | 0 | 0 | 0 | 0 |
| Jon Simms | St Helens | 2002 | (1) | 0 | 0 | 0 | 0 |
| Craig Simon | Hull | 2000 | 23(2) | 8 | 0 | 0 | 32 |
|  | Gateshead | 1999 | 25(4) | 6 | 0 | 0 | 24 |
| Mickael Simon | Catalans | 2010-14, 2017-19 | 55(74) | 3 | 0 | 0 | 12 |
|  | Wakefield | 2015-16 | 15(22) | 3 | 0 | 0 | 12 |
| Darren Simpson | Huddersfield | 1998-99 | 17(1) | 5 | 0 | 0 | 20 |
| Jamie Simpson | Huddersfield | 2011 | 8(1) | 0 | 0 | 0 | 0 |
| Jared Simpson | Huddersfield | 2015-16 | 12 | 4 | 0 | 0 | 16 |
| Robbie Simpson | London | 1999 | 6(7) | 0 | 0 | 0 | 0 |
| Ashton Sims | Warrington | 2015-17 | 69(11) | 5 | 0 | 0 | 20 |
| Kevin Sinfield | Leeds | 1997-2015 | 425(29) | 70 | 1566 | 31 | 3443 |
| Matt Sing | Hull | 2007-08 | 41 | 14 | 0 | 0 | 56 |
| Wayne Sing | Paris | 1997 | 18(1) | 2 | 0 | 0 | 8 |
| Brad Singleton | Leeds | 2011-19 | 92(61) | 17 | 0 | 0 | 68 |
|  | Wakefield | 2013 | (1) | 0 | 0 | 0 | 0 |
| Fata Sini | Salford | 1997 | 22 | 7 | 0 | 0 | 28 |
| Ken Sio | Salford | 2019 | 20(1) | 13 | 13 | 0 | 78 |
|  | Hull KR | 2015-16 | 42 | 23 | 13 | 0 | 118 |
| Michael Sio | Wakefield | 2015-17 | 25(14) | 6 | 0 | 0 | 24 |
| John Skandalis | Huddersfield | 2007-08 | 37(5) | 4 | 0 | 0 | 16 |
| Dylan Skee | Harlequins | 2008-09 | (3) | 0 | 0 | 0 | 0 |
| Ben Skerrett | Castleford | 2003 | (1) | 0 | 0 | 0 | 0 |
| Kelvin Skerrett | Halifax | 1997-99 | 31(6) | 2 | 0 | 0 | 8 |
|  | Wigan | 1996 | 1(8) | 0 | 0 | 0 | 0 |
| Troy Slattery | Wakefield | 2002-03 | 33(5) | 4 | 0 | 0 | 16 |
|  | Huddersfield | 1999 | 3 | 1 | 0 | 0 | 4 |
| Mick Slicker | Huddersfield | 2001, 2003-05 | 17(48) | 2 | 0 | 0 | 8 |
|  | Sheffield | 1999 | (3) | 1 | 0 | 0 | 4 |
|  | Halifax | 1997 | 2(5) | 0 | 0 | 0 | 0 |
| Nick Slyney | London | 2014 | 20(4) | 3 | 0 | 0 | 12 |
| Ian Smales | Castleford | 1996-97 | 10(8) | 5 | 0 | 0 | 20 |
| Aaron Smith | St Helens | 2018-19 | 10(6) | 3 | 0 | 0 | 12 |
|  | Hull KR | 2018 | 3(1) | 0 | 0 | 0 | 0 |
| Aaron Smith | Castleford | 2006 | (2) | 0 | 0 | 0 | 0 |
|  | Bradford | 2003-04 | 12(1) | 3 | 0 | 0 | 12 |
| Andy Smith | Harlequins | 2007 | 6(3) | 3 | 0 | 0 | 12 |
|  | Bradford | 2004-06 | 9(9) | 4 | 0 | 0 | 16 |
|  | Salford | 2005 | 4 | 1 | 0 | 0 | 4 |
| Byron Smith | Castleford | 2004 | (9) | 0 | 0 | 0 | 0 |
|  | Halifax | 2003 | 6(1) | 0 | 0 | 0 | 0 |
| Cameron Smith | Leeds | 2016-19 | 12(24) | 2 | 1 | 0 | 10 |
| Chris Smith | Hull | 2001-02 | 12 | 3 | 0 | 0 | 12 |
|  | St Helens | 1998-2000 | 62(9) | 26 | 0 | 0 | 104 |
|  | Castleford | 1996-97 | 36(1) | 12 | 0 | 0 | 48 |
| Craig Smith | Wigan | 2002-04 | 77(3) | 10 | 0 | 0 | 40 |
| Damien Smith | St Helens | 1998 | 21(1) | 8 | 0 | 0 | 32 |
| Daniel Smith | Castleford | 2019 | 8(11) | 1 | 0 | 0 | 4 |
|  | Huddersfield | 2015-18 | 9(38) | 5 | 0 | 0 | 20 |
|  | Wakefield | 2014-15 | 21(15) | 6 | 0 | 0 | 24 |
| Danny Smith | Paris | 1996 | 10(2) | 1 | 15 | 0 | 34 |
|  | London | 1996 | 2(1) | 1 | 0 | 0 | 4 |
| Darren Smith | St Helens | 2003 | 25(1) | 14 | 0 | 0 | 56 |
| Gary Smith | Castleford | 2001 | (1) | 0 | 0 | 0 | 0 |
| Harry Smith | Wigan | 2019 | (1) | 1 | 1 | 0 | 6 |
| Hudson Smith | Bradford | 2000 | 8(22) | 2 | 0 | 0 | 8 |
|  | Salford | 1999 | 23(2) | 5 | 0 | 0 | 20 |
| James Smith | Salford | 2000 | 23(3) | 6 | 0 | 0 | 24 |
| Jamie Smith | Hull | 1998-99 | 24(6) | 6 | 12 | 0 | 48 |
|  | Workington | 1996 | 5(3) | 0 | 1 | 0 | 2 |
| Jason Smith | Hull | 2001-04 | 61(3) | 17 | 0 | 1 | 69 |
| Jeremy Smith | Wakefield | 2011 | 9(1) | 1 | 0 | 0 | 4 |
|  | Salford | 2009-10 | 27(17) | 2 | 0 | 0 | 8 |
| Kris Smith | London | 2001 | (1) | 0 | 0 | 0 | 0 |
|  | Halifax | 2001 | (1) | 0 | 0 | 0 | 0 |
| Lee Smith | Wakefield | 2012-13, 2015 | 30(4) | 16 | 54 | 2 | 174 |
|  | Leeds | 2005-12 | 125(10) | 60 | 34 | 1 | 309 |
| Leigh Smith | Workington | 1996 | 9 | 4 | 0 | 0 | 16 |
| Mark Smith | Widnes | 2005 | 12(15) | 4 | 0 | 0 | 16 |
|  | Wigan | 1999-2004 | 35(77) | 8 | 0 | 0 | 32 |
| Martyn Smith | Harlequins | 2010 | (2) | 0 | 0 | 0 | 0 |
| Matty Smith | Warrington | 2019 | 4(1) | 0 | 0 | 0 | 0 |
|  | Catalans | 2019 | 16 | 0 | 0 | 1 | 1 |
|  | St Helens | 2006-08, 2010, 2017-18 | 38(9) | 5 | 10 | 4 | 44 |
|  | Wigan | 2012-16 | 122(3) | 17 | 279 | 25 | 651 |
|  | Salford | 2010-12 | 67(4) | 13 | 6 | 1 | 65 |
|  | Celtic | 2009 | 15(1) | 3 | 2 | 1 | 17 |
| Michael Smith | Hull KR | 2007 | (3) | 1 | 0 | 0 | 4 |
|  | Castleford | 1998, 2001-04 | 86(33) | 32 | 0 | 0 | 128 |
|  | Hull | 1999 | 12(6) | 3 | 0 | 0 | 12 |
| Morgan Smith | London | 2019 | 15(1) | 1 | 1 | 2 | 8 |
|  | Warrington | 2016-18 | (18) | 1 | 1 | 0 | 6 |
| Paul Smith | Huddersfield | 2004-06 | 52(17) | 13 | 0 | 0 | 52 |
| Paul Smith | Warrington | 2001 | (1) | 0 | 0 | 0 | 0 |
|  | Castleford | 1997-2000 | 6(37) | 3 | 0 | 0 | 12 |
| Paul Smith | London | 1997 | 7(1) | 2 | 0 | 0 | 8 |
| Peter Smith | Oldham | 1996 | 2 | 0 | 0 | 0 | 0 |
| Richard Smith | Wakefield | 2001 | 8(1) | 1 | 0 | 0 | 4 |
|  | Salford | 1997 | (1) | 1 | 0 | 0 | 4 |
| Tim Smith | Wakefield | 2012-15 | 79 | 11 | 0 | 0 | 44 |
|  | Salford | 2014 | 12 | 2 | 7 | 0 | 22 |
|  | Wigan | 2008-09 | 13(8) | 2 | 0 | 0 | 8 |
| Tony Smith | Hull | 2001-03 | 43(5) | 26 | 0 | 0 | 104 |
|  | Wigan | 1997-2000 | 66(5) | 46 | 0 | 0 | 184 |
|  | Castleford | 1996-97 | 18(2) | 10 | 0 | 0 | 40 |
| Tony Smith | Workington | 1996 | 9 | 1 | 0 | 0 | 4 |
| Tyrone Smith | Harlequins | 2006-07 | 49(3) | 13 | 0 | 0 | 52 |
|  | London | 2005 | 20(4) | 11 | 0 | 0 | 44 |
| Morgan Smithies | Wigan | 2019 | 13(11) | 1 | 0 | 0 | 4 |
| Rob Smyth | Leigh | 2005 | 15(1) | 4 | 0 | 0 | 16 |
|  | Warrington | 2000-03 | 65 | 35 | 20 | 0 | 180 |
|  | London | 1998-2000 | 32(2) | 9 | 15 | 0 | 66 |
|  | Wigan | 1996 | 11(5) | 16 | 0 | 0 | 64 |
| Marc Sneyd | Hull | 2015-19 | 126 | 17 | 442 | 26 | 978 |
|  | Castleford | 2014 | 25(1) | 6 | 100 | 2 | 226 |
|  | Salford | 2010-13 | 33(12) | 4 | 61 | 3 | 141 |
| Steve Snitch | Castleford | 2010-12 | 38(18) | 10 | 0 | 0 | 40 |
|  | Wakefield | 2002-05, 2009 | 33(55) | 9 | 0 | 0 | 36 |
|  | Huddersfield | 2006-08 | 24(35) | 12 | 0 | 0 | 48 |
| Bright Sodje | Wakefield | 2000 | 15 | 4 | 0 | 0 | 16 |
|  | Sheffield | 1996-99 | 54 | 34 | 0 | 0 | 136 |
| Iosia Soliola | St Helens | 2010-14 | 83(24) | 27 | 0 | 0 | 108 |
| David Solomona | Warrington | 2010-12 | 8(49) | 16 | 1 | 0 | 66 |
|  | Bradford | 2007-09 | 44(9) | 19 | 0 | 0 | 76 |
|  | Wakefield | 2004-06 | 73(3) | 26 | 0 | 0 | 104 |
| Denny Solomona | Castleford | 2015-16 | 42 | 58 | 0 | 0 | 232 |
|  | London | 2014 | 19(1) | 8 | 0 | 0 | 32 |
| Alfred Songoro | Wakefield | 1999 | 8(5) | 4 | 0 | 0 | 16 |
| Romain Sort | Paris | 1997 | (1) | 0 | 0 | 0 | 0 |
| Paul Southern | Salford | 1997-2002 | 79(33) | 6 | 13 | 0 | 50 |
|  | St Helens | 2002 | 1(1) | 0 | 0 | 0 | 0 |
| Steve Southern | Wakefield | 2012 | 7(8) | 3 | 0 | 0 | 12 |
| Cain Southernwood | Bradford | 2010 | 2 | 0 | 0 | 0 | 0 |
| Roy Southernwood | Wakefield | 1999 | 1 | 0 | 0 | 0 | 0 |
|  | Halifax | 1996 | 2 | 0 | 0 | 0 | 0 |
| Jason Southwell | Huddersfield | 2004 | (1) | 0 | 0 | 0 | 0 |

## Super League Players 1996-2019

| PLAYER | CLUB | YEAR | APP | TRIES | GOALS | FG | PTS |
|---|---|---|---|---|---|---|---|
| Waisale Sovatabua | Wakefield | 2001-03 | 44(3) | 19 | 0 | 0 | 76 |
|  | Hudds-Sheff | 2000 | 23(1) | 8 | 0 | 0 | 32 |
|  | Sheffield | 1996-99 | 56(17) | 19 | 0 | 1 | 77 |
| Jamie Soward | London | 2013 | 6(1) | 4 | 21 | 0 | 58 |
| Yusef Sozi | London | 2000-01 | (5) | 0 | 0 | 0 | 0 |
| Scott Spaven | Hull KR | 2010 | (2) | 0 | 0 | 0 | 0 |
| Andy Speak | Castleford | 2001 | 4(4) | 0 | 0 | 0 | 0 |
|  | Wakefield | 2000 | 6(5) | 2 | 0 | 0 | 8 |
|  | Leeds | 1999 | 4 | 1 | 0 | 0 | 4 |
| Dom Speakman | St Helens | 2013 | (1) | 0 | 0 | 0 | 0 |
| Tim Spears | Castleford | 2003 | (3) | 0 | 0 | 0 | 0 |
| Jake Spedding | St Helens | 2016-18 | 3(1) | 0 | 0 | 0 | 0 |
| Ady Spencer | London | 1996-99 | 8(36) | 5 | 0 | 0 | 20 |
| Jack Spencer | Salford | 2009-11 | (7) | 0 | 0 | 0 | 0 |
| Tom Spencer | Wigan | 2012-13 | (7) | 0 | 0 | 0 | 0 |
| Rob Spicer | Wakefield | 2002-05 | 28(18) | 4 | 0 | 0 | 16 |
| Russ Spiers | Wakefield | 2011 | (2) | 0 | 0 | 0 | 0 |
| Gadwin Springer | Castleford | 2015-18 | 15(41) | 3 | 0 | 0 | 12 |
|  | Catalans | 2014-15 | (3) | 1 | 0 | 0 | 4 |
| Stuart Spruce | Widnes | 2002-03 | 45(4) | 19 | 0 | 0 | 76 |
|  | Bradford | 1996-2001 | 107(2) | 57 | 0 | 0 | 228 |
| Lee St Hilaire | Castleford | 1997 | 4(2) | 0 | 0 | 0 | 0 |
| Marcus St Hilaire | Bradford | 2006-07 | 34(1) | 12 | 0 | 0 | 48 |
|  | Huddersfield | 2003-05 | 72(2) | 30 | 0 | 0 | 120 |
|  | Leeds | 1996-2002 | 59(33) | 31 | 0 | 0 | 124 |
| Cyril Stacul | Catalans | 2007-12 | 61(1) | 18 | 0 | 0 | 72 |
| Dylan Stainton | Workington | 1996 | 2(3) | 0 | 0 | 0 | 0 |
| Mark Stamper | Workington | 1996 | (1) | 0 | 0 | 0 | 0 |
| John Stankevitch | Widnes | 2005 | 17(5) | 0 | 0 | 0 | 0 |
|  | St Helens | 2000-04 | 74(40) | 25 | 0 | 0 | 100 |
| Gareth Stanley | Bradford | 2000 | 1 | 1 | 0 | 0 | 4 |
| Craig Stapleton | Salford | 2009 | 24 | 2 | 0 | 0 | 8 |
|  | Leigh | 2005 | 27(1) | 4 | 0 | 0 | 16 |
| Graham Steadman | Castleford | 1996-97 | 11(17) | 5 | 0 | 0 | 20 |
| Jon Steel | Hull KR | 2007-08 | 18 | 6 | 0 | 0 | 24 |
| Jamie Stenhouse | Warrington | 2000-01 | 9(3) | 3 | 0 | 0 | 12 |
| Gareth Stephens | Sheffield | 1997-99 | 23(6) | 2 | 0 | 0 | 8 |
| David Stephenson | Hull | 1998 | 11(7) | 3 | 0 | 0 | 12 |
|  | Oldham | 1997 | 10(8) | 2 | 0 | 0 | 8 |
| Francis Stephenson |  |  |  |  |  |  |  |
|  | London | 2002-05 | 42(34) | 5 | 0 | 0 | 20 |
|  | Wigan | 2001 | 2(9) | 0 | 0 | 0 | 0 |
|  | Wakefield | 1999-2000 | 50(1) | 6 | 0 | 0 | 24 |
| Paul Sterling | Leeds | 1997-2000 | 79(12) | 50 | 0 | 0 | 200 |
| Paul Stevens | Oldham | 1996 | 2(1) | 0 | 0 | 0 | 0 |
|  | London | 1996 | (1) | 0 | 0 | 0 | 0 |
| Warren Stevens | Leigh | 2005 | 4(14) | 1 | 0 | 0 | 4 |
|  | Warrington | 1996-99, 2002-05 | 17(66) | 1 | 0 | 0 | 4 |
|  | Salford | 2001 | (8) | 0 | 0 | 0 | 0 |
| Anthony Stewart | Harlequins | 2006 | 4 | 0 | 0 | 0 | 0 |
|  | Salford | 2004-06 | 51(2) | 15 | 0 | 0 | 60 |
|  | St Helens | 1997-2003 | 93(23) | 44 | 0 | 0 | 176 |
| Glenn Stewart | Leigh | 2017 | 15 | 0 | 0 | 0 | 0 |
|  | Catalans | 2016 | 28 | 3 | 0 | 0 | 12 |
| Troy Stone | Widnes | 2002 | 18(6) | 1 | 0 | 0 | 4 |
|  | Huddersfield | 2001 | 12(1) | 1 | 0 | 0 | 4 |
| James Stosic | Wakefield | 2009 | 8(10) | 1 | 0 | 0 | 4 |
| Lynton Stott | Wakefield | 1999 | 21 | 4 | 6 | 1 | 29 |
|  | Sheffield | 1996-98 | 40(4) | 15 | 0 | 0 | 60 |
| Mitchell Stringer | Salford | 2005-06 | 12(4) | 0 | 0 | 0 | 0 |
|  | London | 2004-05 | 10(19) | 0 | 0 | 0 | 0 |
| Graham Strutton | London | 1996 | 9(1) | 2 | 0 | 0 | 8 |
| Matt Sturm | Leigh | 2005 | 8(19) | 3 | 0 | 0 | 12 |
|  | Warrington | 2002-04 | 1(18) | 0 | 0 | 0 | 0 |
|  | Huddersfield | 1998-99 | 46 | 8 | 0 | 0 | 32 |
| Anthony Sullivan | St Helens | 1996-2001 | 137(2) | 105 | 0 | 0 | 420 |
| Michael Sullivan | Warrington | 2006-07 | 21(16) | 8 | 1 | 0 | 34 |
| Phil Sumner | Warrington | 1996 | (5) | 0 | 0 | 0 | 0 |
| Alex Sutcliffe | Leeds | 2017, 2019 | 1(1) | 0 | 0 | 0 | 0 |
| Liam Sutcliffe | Leeds | 2013-19 | 111(31) | 44 | 167 | 2 | 512 |
|  | Bradford | 2014 | 3(1) | 1 | 0 | 0 | 4 |
| Ryan Sutton | Wigan | 2014-18 | 38(65) | 10 | 0 | 0 | 40 |
| Simon Svabic | Salford | 1998-2000 | 13(5) | 3 | 19 | 0 | 50 |
| Luke Swain | Salford | 2009-10 | 54 | 3 | 0 | 0 | 12 |
| Richard Swain | Hull | 2004-07 | 89 | 5 | 0 | 0 | 20 |
| Anthony Swann | Warrington | 2001 | 3 | 1 | 0 | 0 | 4 |
| Logan Swann | Warrington | 2005-06 | 49(1) | 17 | 0 | 0 | 68 |
|  | Bradford | 2004 | 25 | 6 | 0 | 0 | 24 |
| Willie Swann | Warrington | 1996-97 | 25(2) | 6 | 0 | 0 | 24 |
| Adam Swift | St Helens | 2012-19 | 120 | 80 | 0 | 0 | 320 |
| Nathan Sykes | Castleford | 1996-2004 | 158(52) | 3 | 0 | 0 | 12 |
| Paul Sykes | Wakefield | 2012-14 | 59(1) | 12 | 135 | 6 | 324 |
|  | Bradford | 1999-2002, 2008-12 | 99(4) | 35 | 64 | 2 | 270 |
|  | Harlequins | 2006-07 | 31(2) | 15 | 47 | 1 | 155 |
|  | London | 2001-05 | 95(1) | 26 | 219 | 3 | 545 |
| Wayne Sykes | London | 1999 | (2) | 0 | 0 | 0 | 0 |
| Tom Symonds | Huddersfield | 2016-18 | 6(1) | 3 | 0 | 0 | 12 |
| Ukuma Ta'ai | Huddersfield | 2013-19 | 115(57) | 42 | 0 | 0 | 168 |
| Semi Tadulala | Wakefield | 2004-07, 2011 | 92 | 37 | 0 | 0 | 148 |
|  | Bradford | 2008-09 | 49 | 30 | 0 | 0 | 120 |
| Whetu Taewa | Sheffield | 1997-98 | 33(7) | 8 | 0 | 0 | 32 |
| Zeb Taia | St Helens | 2017-19 | 80(1) | 19 | 0 | 0 | 76 |
|  | Catalans | 2013-15 | 75 | 35 | 0 | 0 | 140 |
| Alan Tait | Leeds | 1996 | 3(3) | 1 | 0 | 0 | 4 |
| Fetuli Talanoa | Hull | 2014-18 | 115(1) | 54 | 0 | 0 | 216 |
| Willie Talau | Salford | 2009-10 | 22 | 4 | 0 | 0 | 16 |
|  | St Helens | 2003-08 | 130(1) | 50 | 0 | 0 | 200 |
| Ian Talbot | Wakefield | 1999 | 9(5) | 2 | 31 | 0 | 70 |
|  | Wigan | 1997 | 3 | 1 | 0 | 0 | 4 |
| Albert Talipeau | Wakefield | 2004 | 2(3) | 0 | 0 | 0 | 0 |
| Gael Tallec | Halifax | 2000 | 5(19) | 3 | 0 | 0 | 12 |
|  | Castleford | 1998-99 | 19(21) | 3 | 0 | 0 | 12 |
|  | Wigan | 1996-97 | 8(12) | 3 | 0 | 0 | 12 |
| Joe Tamani | Bradford | 1996 | 11(3) | 4 | 0 | 0 | 16 |
| Ryan Tandy | Hull KR | 2007 | 8(4) | 2 | 0 | 0 | 8 |
| Adam Tangata | Wakefield | 2019 | 2(3) | 0 | 0 | 0 | 0 |
| Andrew Tangata-Toa |  |  |  |  |  |  |  |
|  | Huddersfield | 1999 | 15 | 2 | 0 | 0 | 8 |
| David Tangata-Toa | Celtic | 2009 | 1(18) | 4 | 0 | 0 | 16 |
|  | Hull KR | 2007 | (17) | 3 | 0 | 0 | 12 |
| Kelepi Tanginoa | Wakefield | 2019 | 12(2) | 1 | 0 | 0 | 4 |
| Jordan Tansey | Huddersfield | 2016 | 2 | 1 | 1 | 0 | 6 |
|  | Wakefield | 2015 | 4 | 1 | 0 | 0 | 4 |
|  | Castleford | 2013-15 | 44(1) | 15 | 0 | 0 | 60 |
|  | Crusaders | 2011 | 14(4) | 5 | 0 | 0 | 20 |
|  | Hull | 2009-10 | 30 | 9 | 0 | 0 | 36 |
|  | Leeds | 2006-08 | 18(32) | 19 | 3 | 0 | 82 |
| Lama Tasi | Warrington | 2019 | 9(8) | 0 | 0 | 0 | 0 |
|  | Salford | 2014-15, 2017-18 | 55(26) | 4 | 0 | 0 | 16 |
|  | St Helens | 2016 | 9(8) | 0 | 0 | 0 | 0 |
| Kris Tassell | Wakefield | 2002 | 24 | 10 | 0 | 0 | 40 |
|  | Salford | 2000-01 | 35(10) | 12 | 0 | 0 | 48 |
| Shem Tatupu | Wigan | 1996 | (3) | 0 | 0 | 0 | 0 |
| Tony Tatupu | Wakefield | 2000-01 | 20 | 2 | 0 | 0 | 8 |
|  | Warrington | 1997 | 21(1) | 6 | 0 | 0 | 24 |
| Taulima Tautai | Wigan | 2015-19 | 7(111) | 4 | 0 | 0 | 16 |
|  | Wakefield | 2013-14 | 6(19) | 2 | 0 | 0 | 8 |
| Dave Taylor | Catalans | 2016 | 20(4) | 8 | 0 | 0 | 32 |
| James Taylor | Leigh | 2005 | (4) | 0 | 0 | 0 | 0 |
| Joe Taylor | Paris | 1997 | 9(5) | 2 | 0 | 0 | 8 |
| Lawrence Taylor | Sheffield | 1996 | (1) | 0 | 0 | 0 | 0 |
| Scott Taylor | Hull | 2016-19 | 97(10) | 16 | 0 | 0 | 64 |
|  | Salford | 2015 | 23 | 5 | 0 | 0 | 20 |
|  | Wigan | 2013-14 | 18(29) | 6 | 0 | 0 | 24 |
|  | Hull KR | 2009-12 | 21(29) | 8 | 0 | 0 | 32 |
| Frederic Teixido | Sheffield | 1999 | (4) | 0 | 0 | 0 | 0 |
|  | Paris | 1996-97 | 2(3) | 1 | 0 | 0 | 4 |
| Lionel Teixido | Catalans | 2006-07 | 11(13) | 3 | 0 | 0 | 12 |
| Karl Temata | London | 2005, 2012 | 1(8) | 1 | 0 | 0 | 4 |
|  | Harlequins | 2006-11 | 94(22) | 7 | 0 | 0 | 28 |
| Jason Temu | Hull | 1998 | 13(2) | 1 | 0 | 0 | 4 |
|  | Oldham | 1996-97 | 25(3) | 1 | 0 | 0 | 4 |
| Paul Terry | London | 1997 | (1) | 0 | 0 | 0 | 0 |
| Anthony Thackeray |  |  |  |  |  |  |  |
|  | Castleford | 2008 | 3(6) | 0 | 0 | 0 | 0 |
|  | Hull | 2007 | 2 | 0 | 0 | 0 | 0 |
| Jamie Thackray | Crusaders | 2010 | 1(16) | 2 | 0 | 0 | 8 |
|  | Hull | 2005-06, 2008-09 | 37(45) | 6 | 0 | 0 | 24 |
|  | Leeds | 2006-07 | 5(27) | 7 | 0 | 0 | 28 |
|  | Castleford | 2003-04 | 7(11) | 3 | 0 | 0 | 12 |
|  | Halifax | 2000-02 | 10(38) | 3 | 0 | 0 | 12 |
| Adam Thaler | Castleford | 2002 | (1) | 0 | 0 | 0 | 0 |
| Josh Thewlis | Warrington | 2019 | 2 | 1 | 0 | 0 | 4 |
| Gareth Thomas | Crusaders | 2010-11 | 27(1) | 6 | 0 | 0 | 24 |
| Giles Thomas | London | 1997-99 | 1(2) | 0 | 0 | 0 | 0 |
| Oscar Thomas | London | 2014 | 4(2) | 0 | 1 | 0 | 2 |
| Rob Thomas | Harlequins | 2011 | (2) | 0 | 0 | 0 | 0 |
| Steve Thomas | London | 2004 | 4(2) | 0 | 0 | 0 | 0 |
|  | Warrington | 2001 | 2 | 0 | 0 | 0 | 0 |
| Alex Thompson | Warrington | 2009 | (1) | 1 | 0 | 0 | 4 |
| Alex Thompson | Sheffield | 1997 | 4(11) | 0 | 0 | 0 | 0 |
| Bobby Thompson | Salford | 1999 | 28 | 5 | 2 | 0 | 24 |
| Bodene Thompson | Warrington | 2018 | 7 | 0 | 0 | 0 | 0 |
| Corey Thompson | Widnes | 2016-17 | 48 | 36 | 9 | 0 | 162 |
| David Thompson | Leigh | 2017 | 1 | 0 | 0 | 0 | 0 |
|  | Hull KR | 2016 | 1 | 0 | 0 | 0 | 0 |
| Jordan Thompson | Hull | 2014-17, 2019 | 27(81) | 12 | 0 | 0 | 48 |
|  | Leeds | 2018 | 1 | 0 | 0 | 0 | 0 |
|  | Castleford | 2009-13 | 47(24) | 25 | 0 | 0 | 100 |

# Super League Players 1996-2019

| PLAYER | CLUB | YEAR | APP | TRIES | GOALS | FG | PTS |
|---|---|---|---|---|---|---|---|
| Luke Thompson | St Helens | 2013-19 | 94(54) | 25 | 0 | 0 | 100 |
| Sam Thompson | Harlequins | 2009 | (2) | 0 | 0 | 0 | 0 |
|  | St Helens | 2008 | (5) | 0 | 0 | 0 | 0 |
| Chris Thorman | Hull | 2009 | 19(2) | 1 | 0 | 0 | 4 |
|  | Huddersfield | 2000-01, |  |  |  |  |  |
|  |  | 2005-08 | 126(20) | 51 | 320 | 3 | 847 |
|  | London | 2003 | 26(1) | 7 | 81 | 1 | 191 |
|  | Sheffield | 1999 | 5(13) | 2 | 8 | 1 | 25 |
| Tony Thorniley | Warrington | 1997 | (5) | 0 | 0 | 0 | 0 |
| Andy Thornley | Salford | 2009 | (1) | 1 | 0 | 0 | 4 |
| Iain Thornley | Catalans | 2017-18 | 31(1) | 7 | 0 | 0 | 28 |
|  | Hull KR | 2016 | 21 | 10 | 0 | 0 | 40 |
|  | Wigan | 2012-14 | 40 | 25 | 0 | 0 | 100 |
| Danny Tickle | Hull KR | 2018 | 14(3) | 4 | 20 | 0 | 56 |
|  | Leigh | 2017 | 10(13) | 4 | 0 | 0 | 16 |
|  | Castleford | 2016 | 6(3) | 0 | 1 | 0 | 2 |
|  | Widnes | 2014-15 | 33(1) | 3 | 88 | 0 | 188 |
|  | Hull | 2007-13 | 159(5) | 45 | 528 | 1 | 1237 |
|  | Wigan | 2002-06 | 94(36) | 34 | 200 | 2 | 538 |
|  | Halifax | 2000-02 | 25(17) | 10 | 91 | 2 | 224 |
| Kris Tickle | Warrington | 2001 | (1) | 0 | 0 | 0 | 0 |
| Lewis Tierney | Catalans | 2017-19 | 48 | 14 | 0 | 0 | 56 |
|  | Wigan | 2013-17 | 35 | 17 | 0 | 0 | 68 |
| James Tilley | St Helens | 2013-14 | (3) | 0 | 0 | 0 | 0 |
| Dane Tilse | Hull KR | 2015-16 | 29(1) | 1 | 0 | 0 | 4 |
| John Timu | London | 1998-2000 | 57(3) | 11 | 0 | 0 | 44 |
| Kerrod Toby | London | 1997 | 2(2) | 0 | 0 | 0 | 0 |
| Tulsen Tollett | London | 1996-2001 | 105(5) | 38 | 49 | 1 | 251 |
| Joel Tomkins | Hull KR | 2018-19 | 27 | 6 | 0 | 0 | 24 |
|  | Wigan | 2005-11, |  |  |  |  |  |
|  |  | 2014-18 | 161(51) | 60 | 0 | 0 | 240 |
| Logan Tomkins | Salford | 2014-19 | 85(31) | 6 | 0 | 0 | 24 |
|  | Wigan | 2012-15 | 9(32) | 1 | 0 | 0 | 4 |
| Sam Tomkins | Catalans | 2019 | 24 | 9 | 76 | 1 | 189 |
|  | Wigan | 2009-13, |  |  |  |  |  |
|  |  | 2016-18 | 177(6) | 129 | 125 | 7 | 773 |
| Glen Tomlinson | Wakefield | 1999-2000 | 41(5) | 8 | 0 | 0 | 32 |
|  | Hull | 1998 | 5 | 1 | 0 | 0 | 4 |
|  | Bradford | 1996-97 | 27(13) | 12 | 0 | 0 | 48 |
| Willie Tonga | Leigh | 2017 | 3 | 0 | 0 | 0 | 0 |
|  | Catalans | 2015 | 18 | 6 | 0 | 0 | 24 |
| Ryan Tongia | Wakefield | 2011 | 4 | 2 | 0 | 0 | 8 |
| Ian Tonks | Castleford | 1996-2001 | 32(50) | 11 | 13 | 0 | 70 |
| Tony Tonks | Huddersfield | 2012 | (1) | 0 | 0 | 0 | 0 |
| Motu Tony | Wakefield | 2011-12 | 7(3) | 1 | 0 | 0 | 4 |
|  | Hull | 2005-09 | 76(20) | 25 | 0 | 0 | 100 |
|  | Castleford | 2004 | 8(1) | 1 | 0 | 0 | 4 |
| Mark Tookey | Harlequins | 2006 | 12(14) | 1 | 0 | 0 | 4 |
|  | London | 2005 | 13(14) | 5 | 0 | 0 | 20 |
|  | Castleford | 2004 | 2(8) | 1 | 0 | 0 | 4 |
| Clinton Toopi | Leeds | 2006-08 | 40(3) | 9 | 0 | 0 | 36 |
| David Tootill | Harlequins | 2008 | (4) | 0 | 0 | 0 | 0 |
| Paul Topping | Oldham | 1996-97 | 23(10) | 1 | 19 | 0 | 42 |
| Patrick Torreilles | Paris | 1996 | 9(1) | 1 | 25 | 0 | 54 |
| Albert Torrens | Huddersfield | 2006 | 7 | 5 | 0 | 0 | 20 |
| Mat Toshack | London | 1998-2004 | 120(21) | 24 | 0 | 0 | 96 |
| Julien Touxagas | Catalans | 2006-11 | 14(45) | 4 | 0 | 0 | 16 |
| Darren Treacy | Salford | 2002 | 24(1) | 6 | 1 | 0 | 26 |
| Dean Treister | Hull | 2003 | 16(1) | 3 | 0 | 0 | 12 |
| Rocky Trimarchi | Crusaders | 2010 | 16(8) | 0 | 0 | 0 | 0 |
| Steve Trindall | London | 2003-05 | 40(20) | 3 | 0 | 0 | 12 |
| Shane Tronc | Hull KR | 2010 | 8(3) | 2 | 0 | 0 | 8 |
| Kyle Trout | Hull KR | 2019 | 1(4) | 0 | 0 | 0 | 0 |
|  | Wakefield | 2012-15 | 6(17) | 3 | 0 | 0 | 12 |
| Owen Trout | Leeds | 2019 | 1(1) | 0 | 0 | 0 | 0 |
| George Truelove | Wakefield | 2002 | 2 | 1 | 0 | 0 | 4 |
|  | London | 2000 | 5 | 1 | 0 | 0 | 4 |
| Jake Trueman | Castleford | 2017-19 | 58(2) | 18 | 0 | 1 | 73 |
| Va'aiga Tuigamala | Wigan | 1996 | 21 | 10 | 3 | 0 | 46 |
| Fereti Tuilagi | St Helens | 1999-2000 | 43(15) | 21 | 0 | 0 | 84 |
|  | Halifax | 1996-98 | 55(3) | 27 | 0 | 0 | 108 |
| Carlos Tuimavave | Hull | 2016-19 | 88(5) | 29 | 0 | 0 | 116 |
| Evarn Tuimavave | Hull KR | 2013 | 11(12) | 2 | 0 | 0 | 8 |
| Sateki Tuipulotu | Leeds | 1996 | 6(3) | 1 | 2 | 0 | 8 |
| Anthony Tupou | Wakefield | 2016 | 12(9) | 4 | 0 | 0 | 16 |
| Bill Tupou | Wakefield | 2015-19 | 85(3) | 35 | 0 | 0 | 140 |
| Tame Tupou | Bradford | 2007-08 | 10(7) | 8 | 0 | 0 | 32 |
| Jansin Turgut | Salford | 2019 | 8(2) | 1 | 0 | 0 | 4 |
|  | Hull | 2015-18 | 10(18) | 3 | 0 | 0 | 12 |
| Neil Turley | Leigh | 2005 | 6(3) | 2 | 20 | 1 | 49 |
| Calum Turner | Castleford | 2018-19 | 5(5) | 3 | 10 | 0 | 32 |
| Darren Turner | Huddersfield | 2000-01, |  |  |  |  |  |
|  |  | 2003-04 | 42(13) | 13 | 0 | 0 | 52 |
|  | Sheffield | 1996-99 | 41(29) | 15 | 0 | 0 | 60 |
| Ian Turner | Paris | 1996 | 1(1) | 1 | 0 | 0 | 4 |

| PLAYER | CLUB | YEAR | APP | TRIES | GOALS | FG | PTS |
|---|---|---|---|---|---|---|---|
| Jordan Turner | Huddersfield | 2017-19 | 55 | 8 | 0 | 0 | 32 |
|  | St Helens | 2013-16 | 106(4) | 44 | 13 | 3 | 205 |
|  | Hull | 2010-12 | 62(5) | 28 | 0 | 0 | 112 |
|  | Salford | 2006-07, |  |  |  |  |  |
|  |  | 2009 | 22(10) | 4 | 1 | 0 | 18 |
| Chris Tuson | Hull | 2014 | 10(1) | 0 | 0 | 0 | 0 |
|  | Wigan | 2008, |  |  |  |  |  |
|  |  | 2010-13 | 24(49) | 13 | 0 | 0 | 52 |
|  | Castleford | 2010 | 3(5) | 0 | 0 | 0 | 0 |
| Gregory Tutard | Paris | 1996 | 1(1) | 0 | 0 | 0 | 0 |
| Brendon Tuuta | Warrington | 1998 | 18(2) | 4 | 0 | 0 | 16 |
|  | Castleford | 1996-97 | 41(1) | 3 | 0 | 0 | 12 |
| Steve Tyrer | Salford | 2010 | 20 | 6 | 9 | 0 | 42 |
|  | Celtic | 2009 | 8 | 2 | 5 | 0 | 18 |
|  | St Helens | 2006-08 | 17(3) | 12 | 42 | 0 | 132 |
| Bobby Tyson-Wilson | Hull | 2015 | (1) | 0 | 0 | 0 | 0 |
| Harry Tyson-Wilson | Hull | 2014 | (1) | 0 | 0 | 0 | 0 |
| Akuila Uate | Huddersfield | 2019 | 12 | 5 | 0 | 0 | 20 |
| Wayne Ulugia | Hull KR | 2014 | 3 | 1 | 0 | 0 | 4 |
| Mike Umaga | Halifax | 1996-97 | 38(1) | 16 | 5 | 0 | 74 |
| Kava Utoikamanu | Paris | 1996 | 6(3) | 0 | 0 | 0 | 0 |
| Frederic Vaccari | Catalans | 2010-11, |  |  |  |  |  |
|  |  | 2013-14 | 50 | 26 | 0 | 0 | 104 |
| David Vaealiki | Wigan | 2005-07 | 67(1) | 17 | 0 | 0 | 68 |
| Joe Vagana | Bradford | 2001-08 | 176(44) | 17 | 0 | 0 | 68 |
| Nigel Vagana | Warrington | 1997 | 20 | 17 | 0 | 0 | 68 |
| Tevita Vaikona | Bradford | 1998-2004 | 145(2) | 89 | 0 | 0 | 356 |
| Lesley Vainikolo | Bradford | 2002-07 | 132(4) | 136 | 1 | 0 | 546 |
| Junior Vaivai | Hull KR | 2018-19 | 22(1) | 8 | 0 | 0 | 32 |
| Eric Van Brussell | Paris | 1996 | 2 | 0 | 0 | 0 | 0 |
| Jace Van Dijk | Celtic | 2009 | 19 | 1 | 1 | 0 | 6 |
| Richard Varkulis | Warrington | 2004 | 4(1) | 3 | 0 | 0 | 12 |
| Marcus Vassilakopoulos | Sheffield | 1997-99 | 15(11) | 3 | 10 | 2 | 34 |
|  | Leeds | 1996-97 | 1(3) | 0 | 0 | 0 | 0 |
| Manu Vatuvei | Salford | 2017 | 7 | 5 | 0 | 0 | 20 |
| Atelea Vea | Leigh | 2017 | 19(1) | 5 | 0 | 0 | 20 |
|  | St Helens | 2015-16 | 19(17) | 10 | 0 | 0 | 40 |
|  | London | 2014 | 19(3) | 2 | 0 | 0 | 8 |
| Josh Veivers | Salford | 2012 | 5 | 2 | 0 | 0 | 8 |
|  | Wakefield | 2011 | 10(2) | 2 | 22 | 0 | 52 |
| Phil Veivers | Huddersfield | 1998 | 7(6) | 1 | 0 | 0 | 4 |
|  | St Helens | 1996 | (1) | 1 | 0 | 0 | 4 |
| Michael Vella | Hull KR | 2007-11 | 111(5) | 13 | 0 | 0 | 52 |
| Bruno Verges | Catalans | 2006 | 25 | 6 | 0 | 0 | 24 |
| Eric Vergniol | Paris | 1996 | 14(1) | 6 | 0 | 0 | 24 |
| Gray Viane | Salford | 2007 | 9 | 2 | 0 | 0 | 8 |
|  | Castleford | 2006 | 20(7) | 14 | 0 | 0 | 56 |
|  | Widnes | 2005 | 20 | 13 | 0 | 0 | 52 |
|  | St Helens | 2004 | 4 | 1 | 0 | 0 | 4 |
| Joe Vickery | Leeds | 2013 | 9 | 1 | 0 | 0 | 4 |
| Daniel Vidot | Salford | 2016 | 5(1) | 5 | 0 | 0 | 20 |
| Adrian Vowles | Castleford | 1997-2001, |  |  |  |  |  |
|  |  | 2003 | 125(1) | 29 | 1 | 1 | 119 |
|  | Wakefield | 2002-03 | 24(3) | 6 | 1 | 0 | 26 |
|  | Leeds | 2002 | 14(3) | 2 | 0 | 0 | 8 |
| Michael Wainwright | Castleford | 2008-10 | 70 | 22 | 0 | 0 | 88 |
|  | Wakefield | 2004-05 | 21(10) | 8 | 0 | 0 | 32 |
| Mike Wainwright | Salford | 2000-02, |  |  |  |  |  |
|  |  | 2007 | 75(3) | 9 | 0 | 0 | 36 |
|  | Warrington | 1996-99, |  |  |  |  |  |
|  |  | 2003-07 | 168(14) | 23 | 0 | 0 | 92 |
| Shannon Wakeman | Huddersfield | 2017-18 | 16(13) | 3 | 0 | 0 | 12 |
| Adam Walker | Salford | 2019 | 9(14) | 4 | 0 | 0 | 16 |
|  | Wakefield | 2017 | 5(1) | 0 | 0 | 0 | 0 |
|  | St Helens | 2017 | (9) | 1 | 0 | 0 | 4 |
|  | Hull KR | 2013-16 | 60(27) | 6 | 0 | 0 | 24 |
|  | Huddersfield | 2010-12 | 1(5) | 0 | 0 | 0 | 0 |
| Alex Walker | London | 2014, 2019 | 28 | 6 | 0 | 0 | 24 |
| Anthony Walker | Wakefield | 2015-17 | 1(11) | 1 | 0 | 0 | 4 |
|  | St Helens | 2013-14 | 9(7) | 2 | 0 | 0 | 8 |
| Ben Walker | Leeds | 2002 | 23(1) | 8 | 100 | 0 | 232 |
| Brad Walker | Widnes | 2016-18 | 3(5) | 0 | 0 | 0 | 0 |
| Chev Walker | Bradford | 2011-14 | 44(22) | 5 | 0 | 0 | 20 |
|  | Hull KR | 2008-09 | 24(7) | 5 | 0 | 0 | 20 |
|  | Leeds | 1999-2006 | 142(19) | 77 | 0 | 0 | 308 |
| Chris Walker | Catalans | 2010 | 11 | 6 | 2 | 0 | 28 |
| Danny Walker | Warrington | 2019 | 3(8) | 1 | 0 | 0 | 4 |
|  | Widnes | 2017-18 | 3(16) | 2 | 0 | 0 | 8 |
| Jack Walker | Leeds | 2017-19 | 42(4) | 13 | 0 | 0 | 52 |
| Jonathan Walker | Hull KR | 2014 | 2(6) | 0 | 0 | 0 | 0 |
|  | Castleford | 2010-13 | 17(31) | 4 | 0 | 0 | 16 |

| PLAYER | CLUB | YEAR | APP | TRIES | GOALS | FG | PTS |
|---|---|---|---|---|---|---|---|
| Jonny Walker | Wigan | 2010 | (1) | 0 | 0 | 0 | 0 |
| Matt Walker | Huddersfield | 2001 | 3(6) | 0 | 0 | 0 | 0 |
| Anthony Wall | Paris | 1997 | 9 | 3 | 3 | 0 | 18 |
| Jon Wallace | London | 2014 | 4(12) | 0 | 0 | 0 | 0 |
| Mark Wallace | Workington | 1996 | 14(1) | 3 | 0 | 0 | 12 |
| Elliot Wallis | Hull KR | 2018 | 4 | 2 | 0 | 0 | 8 |
| Alex Walmsley | St Helens | 2013-19 | 95(72) | 26 | 0 | 0 | 104 |
| Adam Walne | Huddersfield | 2018-19 | 4(8) | 0 | 0 | 0 | 0 |
|  | Salford | 2012-17 | 15(50) | 2 | 0 | 0 | 8 |
| Jordan Walne | Hull KR | 2018 | (6) | 0 | 0 | 0 | 0 |
|  | Salford | 2013-17 | 20(32) | 3 | 0 | 0 | 12 |
| Joe Walsh | Huddersfield | 2009 | 1(1) | 1 | 0 | 0 | 4 |
|  | Harlequins | 2007-08 | 1(4) | 0 | 0 | 0 | 0 |
| Liam Walsh | Widnes | 2017 | (1) | 0 | 0 | 0 | 0 |
| Luke Walsh | Catalans | 2017-18 | 23 | 2 | 71 | 4 | 154 |
|  | St Helens | 2014-16 | 56(2) | 14 | 188 | 9 | 441 |
| Lucas Walshaw | Wakefield | 2011-14 | 15(6) | 3 | 0 | 0 | 12 |
| Josh Walters | Leeds | 2014-18 | 15(36) | 9 | 0 | 0 | 36 |
| Kerrod Walters | Gateshead | 1999 | 10(12) | 2 | 1 | 0 | 10 |
| Kevin Walters | Warrington | 2001 | 1 | 0 | 0 | 0 | 0 |
| Jason Walton | Wakefield | 2016 | 7(8) | 0 | 0 | 0 | 0 |
|  | Salford | 2009, 2014-15 | 7(19) | 1 | 0 | 0 | 4 |
| Barry Ward | St Helens | 2002-03 | 20(30) | 4 | 0 | 0 | 16 |
| Danny Ward | Harlequins | 2008-11 | 89(7) | 4 | 0 | 0 | 16 |
|  | Hull KR | 2007 | 11(9) | 0 | 0 | 0 | 0 |
|  | Castleford | 2006 | 18(7) | 2 | 0 | 0 | 8 |
|  | Leeds | 1999-2005 | 70(48) | 9 | 0 | 1 | 37 |
| Robbie Ward | Leeds | 2014-15 | 5(3) | 1 | 0 | 0 | 4 |
| Stevie Ward | Leeds | 2012-19 | 85(29) | 19 | 0 | 0 | 76 |
| Joe Wardill | Hull KR | 2016, 2018 | 6(2) | 1 | 0 | 0 | 4 |
| Jake Wardle | Huddersfield | 2018-19 | 22 | 7 | 5 | 0 | 38 |
| Joe Wardle | Huddersfield | 2011-16, 2019 | 140 | 63 | 0 | 0 | 252 |
|  | Castleford | 2018 | 15(2) | 1 | 0 | 0 | 4 |
|  | Bradford | 2010 | 1(1) | 0 | 0 | 0 | 0 |
| Phil Waring | Salford | 1997-99 | 6(8) | 2 | 0 | 0 | 8 |
| Brett Warton | London | 1999-2001 | 49(7) | 14 | 133 | 0 | 322 |
| Kyle Warren | Castleford | 2002 | 13(14) | 3 | 0 | 0 | 12 |
| Danny Washbrook | Hull | 2005-11, 2016-19 | 136(71) | 19 | 0 | 0 | 76 |
|  | Wakefield | 2012-15 | 93(8) | 12 | 0 | 0 | 48 |
| Adam Watene | Wakefield | 2006-08 | 45(8) | 5 | 0 | 0 | 20 |
|  | Bradford | 2006 | (4) | 0 | 0 | 0 | 0 |
| Frank Watene | Wakefield | 1999-2001 | 24(37) | 6 | 0 | 0 | 24 |
| Trent Waterhouse | Warrington | 2012-14 | 65(5) | 15 | 0 | 0 | 60 |
| Luke Waterworth | Wigan | 2016 | 1 | 0 | 0 | 0 | 0 |
| Kallum Watkins | Leeds | 2008-19 | 215(7) | 110 | 85 | 0 | 610 |
| Dave Watson | Sheffield | 1998-99 | 41(4) | 4 | 0 | 0 | 16 |
| Ian Watson | Salford | 1997, 2002 | 24(17) | 8 | 3 | 5 | 43 |
|  | Workington | 1996 | 4(1) | 1 | 15 | 0 | 34 |
| Kris Watson | Warrington | 1996 | 11(2) | 2 | 0 | 0 | 8 |
| Anthony Watts | Widnes | 2012 | (1) | 0 | 0 | 0 | 0 |
| Brad Watts | Widnes | 2005 | 6 | 3 | 0 | 0 | 12 |
| Liam Watts | Castleford | 2018-19 | 50(1) | 4 | 0 | 0 | 16 |
|  | Hull | 2012-18 | 116(19) | 9 | 0 | 0 | 36 |
|  | Hull KR | 2008, 2010-12 | 31(26) | 6 | 0 | 0 | 24 |
| Michael Watts | Warrington | 2002 | 3 | 0 | 0 | 0 | 0 |
| Brent Webb | Catalans | 2013-14 | 10 | 2 | 0 | 0 | 8 |
|  | Leeds | 2007-12 | 137(1) | 73 | 0 | 0 | 292 |
| Jason Webber | Salford | 2000 | 25(1) | 10 | 0 | 0 | 40 |
| Ian Webster | St Helens | 2006 | 1 | 0 | 0 | 0 | 0 |
| Jake Webster | Castleford | 2013-18 | 103(12) | 45 | 0 | 0 | 180 |
|  | Hull KR | 2008-12 | 95(1) | 34 | 7 | 0 | 150 |
| James Webster | Hull | 2008 | 1 | 0 | 0 | 0 | 0 |
|  | Hull KR | 2007-08 | 36 | 2 | 0 | 2 | 10 |
| Pat Weisner | Hull KR | 2007 | (2) | 0 | 0 | 0 | 0 |
|  | Harlequins | 2006 | 10(6) | 3 | 0 | 0 | 12 |
| Taylor Welch | Warrington | 2008 | 1 | 0 | 0 | 0 | 0 |
| Kris Welham | Salford | 2017-19 | 72(1) | 26 | 0 | 0 | 104 |
|  | Hull KR | 2007-15 | 164(2) | 90 | 1 | 0 | 362 |
| Paul Wellens | St Helens | 1998-2015 | 399(40) | 199 | 34 | 1 | 865 |
| Calvin Wellington | St Helens | 2016 | 1 | 0 | 0 | 0 | 0 |
| Jack Wells | Wigan | 2016-17 | 4(11) | 1 | 0 | 0 | 4 |
| Jon Wells | Harlequins | 2006-09 | 66 | 10 | 0 | 0 | 40 |
|  | London | 2004-05 | 42(2) | 19 | 0 | 0 | 76 |
|  | Wakefield | 2003 | 22(1) | 1 | 0 | 0 | 4 |
|  | Castleford | 1996-2002 | 114(14) | 49 | 0 | 0 | 196 |
| Jack Welsby | St Helens | 2018-19 | 9(3) | 3 | 0 | 0 | 12 |
| Dwayne West | St Helens | 2000-02 | 8(16) | 6 | 0 | 0 | 24 |
|  | Wigan | 1999 | 1(1) | 0 | 0 | 0 | 0 |
| Joe Westerman | Hull | 2011-15, 2018-19 | 135(13) | 36 | 52 | 1 | 249 |
|  | Warrington | 2016-17 | 45(1) | 12 | 0 | 0 | 48 |
|  | Castleford | 2008-10 | 68(7) | 29 | 151 | 0 | 418 |
| Craig Weston | Widnes | 2002, 2004 | 23(9) | 2 | 1 | 2 | 12 |
|  | Huddersfield | 1998-99 | 46(1) | 15 | 15 | 0 | 90 |
| Dayne Weston | Leigh | 2017 | 6(5) | 1 | 0 | 0 | 4 |
| Ben Westwood | Warrington | 2002-19 | 363(29) | 112 | 64 | 0 | 576 |
|  | Wakefield | 1999-2002 | 31(7) | 8 | 1 | 0 | 34 |
| Michael Weyman | Hull KR | 2014 | 22(1) | 7 | 0 | 0 | 28 |
| Andrew Whalley | Workington | 1996 | (2) | 0 | 0 | 0 | 0 |
| Paul Whatuira | Huddersfield | 2008-10 | 59 | 23 | 0 | 0 | 92 |
| Scott Wheeldon | Castleford | 2014-15 | 14(23) | 5 | 0 | 0 | 20 |
|  | London | 2012-13 | 27(4) | 3 | 0 | 0 | 12 |
|  | Hull KR | 2009-12 | 30(42) | 4 | 0 | 0 | 16 |
|  | Hull | 2006-08 | 2(60) | 4 | 0 | 0 | 16 |
| Gary Wheeler | Warrington | 2015-16 | 6(4) | 4 | 0 | 0 | 16 |
|  | St Helens | 2008-14 | 48(10) | 17 | 13 | 0 | 94 |
| Matt Whitaker | Castleford | 2006 | 8(2) | 0 | 0 | 0 | 0 |
|  | Widnes | 2004-05 | 10(20) | 9 | 0 | 0 | 36 |
|  | Huddersfield | 2003-04 | 3(14) | 0 | 0 | 0 | 0 |
| Ben White | Leeds | 2014 | 1 | 0 | 0 | 0 | 0 |
| David White | Wakefield | 2000 | (1) | 0 | 0 | 0 | 0 |
| Josh White | Salford | 1998 | 18(3) | 5 | 5 | 1 | 31 |
|  | London | 1997 | 14(2) | 8 | 0 | 1 | 33 |
| Lloyd White | Widnes | 2012-18 | 72(43) | 27 | 24 | 1 | 157 |
|  | Crusaders | 2010-11 | 13(11) | 8 | 0 | 0 | 32 |
|  | Celtic | 2009 | 6 | 1 | 0 | 0 | 4 |
| Paul White | Salford | 2009 | 1 | 1 | 0 | 0 | 4 |
|  | Wakefield | 2006-07 | 24(12) | 12 | 0 | 0 | 48 |
|  | Huddersfield | 2003-05 | 11(32) | 17 | 16 | 0 | 100 |
| Elliott Whitehead | Catalans | 2013-15 | 64(1) | 30 | 0 | 0 | 120 |
|  | Bradford | 2009-13 | 90(10) | 30 | 0 | 0 | 120 |
| Harvey Whiteley | Leeds | 2017 | (1) | 0 | 0 | 0 | 0 |
| Richard Whiting | Hull | 2004-15 | 163(72) | 69 | 19 | 2 | 316 |
| Matt Whitley | Catalans | 2019 | 23(2) | 6 | 0 | 0 | 24 |
|  | Widnes | 2015-18 | 49(27) | 13 | 0 | 0 | 52 |
| Emmerson Whittel | Bradford | 2014 | (1) | 0 | 0 | 0 | 0 |
| Danny Whittle | Warrington | 1998 | (2) | 0 | 0 | 0 | 0 |
| David Whittle | St Helens | 2002 | 1(2) | 0 | 0 | 0 | 0 |
|  | Warrington | 2001 | 1(2) | 0 | 0 | 0 | 0 |
| Jon Whittle | Wakefield | 2006 | 8(2) | 3 | 0 | 0 | 12 |
|  | Widnes | 2005 | 13 | 2 | 0 | 0 | 8 |
|  | Wigan | 2003 | 1 | 0 | 0 | 0 | 0 |
| Joel Wicks | London | 2013-14 | 3(10) | 0 | 0 | 0 | 0 |
| Dean Widders | Castleford | 2009-11 | 25(32) | 23 | 0 | 0 | 92 |
| Stephen Wild | Salford | 2011-13 | 71 | 4 | 0 | 0 | 16 |
|  | Huddersfield | 2006-10 | 116(2) | 33 | 0 | 0 | 132 |
|  | Wigan | 2001-05 | 67(20) | 24 | 0 | 0 | 96 |
| Sam Wilde | Widnes | 2017-18 | 14(7) | 2 | 0 | 0 | 8 |
|  | Warrington | 2015-17 | 3(15) | 1 | 0 | 0 | 4 |
| Matty Wildie | Wakefield | 2010-14 | 13(26) | 3 | 0 | 0 | 12 |
| Brayden Wiliame | Catalans | 2017-19 | 64 | 25 | 0 | 0 | 100 |
| Oliver Wilkes | Wakefield | 2008-09, 2012-13 | 55(47) | 10 | 0 | 0 | 40 |
|  | Harlequins | 2010-11 | 39(15) | 4 | 0 | 0 | 16 |
|  | Wigan | 2006 | 1(5) | 0 | 0 | 0 | 0 |
|  | Leigh | 2005 | 13(1) | 1 | 0 | 0 | 4 |
|  | Huddersfield | 2000-01 | 1(6) | 0 | 0 | 0 | 0 |
|  | Sheffield | 1998 | (1) | 0 | 0 | 0 | 0 |
| Jon Wilkin | St Helens | 2003-18 | 350(30) | 78 | 0 | 2 | 314 |
| Alex Wilkinson | Hull | 2003-04 | 11(4) | 1 | 0 | 0 | 4 |
|  | Huddersfield | 2003 | 8 | 4 | 0 | 0 | 16 |
|  | London | 2002 | 5(1) | 0 | 0 | 0 | 0 |
|  | Bradford | 2000-01 | 3(3) | 1 | 0 | 0 | 4 |
| Bart Williams | London | 1998 | 5(3) | 1 | 0 | 0 | 4 |
| Connor Williams | Salford | 2016 | (1) | 0 | 0 | 0 | 0 |
| Daley Williams | Salford | 2006-07 | 9(2) | 4 | 0 | 0 | 16 |
| Danny Williams | Harlequins | 2006 | 9(13) | 4 | 0 | 0 | 16 |
|  | London | 2005 | 1(16) | 0 | 0 | 0 | 0 |
| Danny Williams | Bradford | 2014 | 7 | 2 | 0 | 0 | 8 |
|  | Salford | 2011-14 | 54 | 31 | 0 | 0 | 124 |
|  | Leeds | 2006, 2008 | 13(2) | 7 | 0 | 0 | 28 |
|  | Hull | 2008 | 3 | 0 | 0 | 0 | 0 |
| Dave Williams | Harlequins | 2008-11 | 1(17) | 0 | 0 | 0 | 0 |
| Desi Williams | Wigan | 2004 | 2 | 0 | 0 | 0 | 0 |
| George Williams | Wigan | 2013-19 | 149(13) | 55 | 56 | 1 | 333 |
| Jonny Williams | London | 2004 | (4) | 0 | 0 | 0 | 0 |
| Lee Williams | Crusaders | 2011 | 1(7) | 0 | 0 | 0 | 0 |
| Rhys Williams | London | 2019 | 29 | 13 | 0 | 0 | 52 |
|  | Warrington | 2010-13 | 23(1) | 15 | 0 | 0 | 60 |
|  | Salford | 2013 | 4 | 0 | 0 | 0 | 0 |
|  | Castleford | 2012 | 8 | 4 | 0 | 0 | 16 |
|  | Crusaders | 2011 | 6 | 3 | 0 | 0 | 12 |
| Sam Williams | Wakefield | 2017 | 17(5) | 4 | 26 | 0 | 68 |
|  | Catalans | 2014 | 11(1) | 4 | 21 | 0 | 58 |
| Luke Williamson | Harlequins | 2009-13 | 39 | 6 | 0 | 0 | 24 |
| John Wilshere | Salford | 2006-07, 2009 | 72(2) | 32 | 142 | 0 | 412 |
|  | Leigh | 2005 | 26 | 8 | 6 | 0 | 44 |
|  | Warrington | 2004 | 5 | 2 | 0 | 0 | 8 |

185

# Super League Players 1996-2019

| PLAYER | CLUB | YEAR | APP | TRIES | GOALS | FG | PTS |
|---|---|---|---|---|---|---|---|
| Craig Wilson | Hull | 2000 | 2(16) | 1 | 0 | 1 | 5 |
| | Gateshead | 1999 | 17(11) | 5 | 0 | 1 | 21 |
| George Wilson | Paris | 1996 | 7(2) | 3 | 0 | 0 | 12 |
| John Wilson | Catalans | 2006-08 | 69 | 23 | 0 | 0 | 92 |
| Oliver Wilson | Huddersfield | 2019 | (8) | 0 | 0 | 0 | 0 |
| Richard Wilson | Hull | 1998-99 | (13) | 0 | 0 | 0 | 0 |
| Scott Wilson | Warrington | 1998-99 | 23(2) | 6 | 0 | 0 | 24 |
| Johan Windley | Hull | 1999 | 2(2) | 1 | 0 | 0 | 4 |
| Paul Wingfield | Warrington | 1997 | 5(3) | 6 | 1 | 0 | 26 |
| Frank Winterstein | Widnes | 2012-13 | 37(9) | 16 | 0 | 0 | 64 |
| | Crusaders | 2010-11 | 26(19) | 4 | 0 | 0 | 16 |
| | Wakefield | 2009 | (5) | 0 | 0 | 0 | 0 |
| Lincoln Withers | Hull KR | 2012-13 | 18(22) | 10 | 0 | 0 | 40 |
| | Crusaders | 2010-11 | 47 | 4 | 0 | 0 | 16 |
| | Celtic | 2009 | 21 | 6 | 0 | 0 | 24 |
| Michael Withers | Wigan | 2007 | 6(1) | 1 | 0 | 0 | 4 |
| | Bradford | 1999-2006 | 156(6) | 94 | 15 | 4 | 410 |
| Michael Witt | London | 2012-13 | 37 | 10 | 89 | 1 | 219 |
| | Crusaders | 2010-11 | 39 | 13 | 47 | 4 | 150 |
| Jeff Wittenberg | Huddersfield | 1998 | 18(1) | 1 | 0 | 0 | 4 |
| | Bradford | 1997 | 8(9) | 4 | 0 | 0 | 16 |
| Josh Wood | Salford | 2015-19 | 19(17) | 2 | 0 | 0 | 8 |
| Kyle Wood | Wakefield | 2012-13, | | | | | |
| | | 2017-19 | 53(71) | 25 | 0 | 0 | 100 |
| | Huddersfield | 2011, 2013-16 | 39(33) | 7 | 0 | 0 | 28 |
| | Castleford | 2010 | 1(4) | 0 | 0 | 0 | 0 |
| Martin Wood | Sheffield | 1997-98 | 24(11) | 4 | 18 | 2 | 54 |
| Mikey Wood | Huddersfield | 2016-17 | 1(1) | 0 | 0 | 0 | 0 |
| Nathan Wood | Warrington | 2002-05 | 90 | 38 | 0 | 3 | 155 |
| | Wakefield | 2002 | 11 | 2 | 0 | 0 | 8 |
| Paul Wood | Warrington | 2000-14 | 138(171) | 40 | 0 | 0 | 160 |
| Phil Wood | Widnes | 2004 | 2(1) | 0 | 0 | 0 | 0 |
| Sam Wood | Bradford | 2013-14 | 7(1) | 0 | 0 | 0 | 0 |
| Sam Wood | Huddersfield | 2016-18 | 18 | 6 | 4 | 0 | 32 |
| James Woodburn-Hall | | | | | | | |
| | London | 2013-14 | 9(4) | 2 | 0 | 0 | 8 |
| Darren Woods | Widnes | 2005 | (1) | 0 | 0 | 0 | 0 |
| David Woods | Halifax | 2002 | 18(2) | 8 | 0 | 0 | 32 |
| Josh Woods | Wigan | 2017-18 | 10(1) | 1 | 4 | 1 | 13 |
| Simon Worrall | Leeds | 2008-09 | 5(16) | 1 | 0 | 0 | 4 |
| Michael Worrincy | Bradford | 2009-10 | 12(34) | 12 | 0 | 0 | 48 |
| | Harlequins | 2006-08 | 20(12) | 10 | 0 | 0 | 40 |
| Rob Worrincy | Castleford | 2004 | 1 | 0 | 0 | 0 | 0 |
| James Worthington | | | | | | | |
| | Wigan | 2017 | 1 | 2 | 0 | 0 | 8 |
| Troy Wozniak | Widnes | 2004 | 13(7) | 1 | 0 | 0 | 4 |
| Matthew Wray | Wakefield | 2002-03 | 13(3) | 2 | 0 | 0 | 8 |
| David Wrench | Wakefield | 2002-06 | 28(52) | 6 | 0 | 0 | 24 |
| | Leeds | 1999-2001 | 7(17) | 0 | 0 | 0 | 0 |
| Callum Wright | Wigan | 2014 | (2) | 0 | 0 | 0 | 0 |
| Craig Wright | Castleford | 2000 | 1(9) | 0 | 0 | 0 | 0 |
| Nigel Wright | Huddersfield | 1999 | 4(6) | 1 | 0 | 0 | 4 |
| | Wigan | 1996-97 | 5(5) | 2 | 0 | 1 | 9 |
| Ricky Wright | Sheffield | 1997-99 | 2(13) | 0 | 0 | 0 | 0 |
| Vincent Wulf | Paris | 1996 | 13(4) | 4 | 0 | 0 | 16 |
| Connor Wynne | Hull | 2019 | 5 | 3 | 0 | 0 | 12 |
| Andrew Wynyard | London | 1999-2000 | 34(6) | 4 | 0 | 0 | 16 |
| Bagdad Yaha | Paris | 1996 | 4(4) | 2 | 4 | 0 | 16 |
| Fouad Yaha | Catalans | 2015-19 | 72 | 43 | 0 | 0 | 172 |
| Malakai Yasa | Sheffield | 1996 | 1(3) | 0 | 0 | 0 | 0 |
| Andy Yates | Wakefield | 2016 | (7) | 0 | 0 | 0 | 0 |
| | Leeds | 2015 | (9) | 1 | 0 | 0 | 4 |
| Luke Yates | London | 2019 | 28 | 2 | 0 | 0 | 8 |
| Kirk Yeaman | Hull | 2001-16, 2018 | 322(18) | 159 | 0 | 0 | 636 |
| Dominic Young | Huddersfield | 2019 | 1 | 0 | 0 | 0 | 0 |
| Grant Young | London | 1998-99 | 22(2) | 2 | 0 | 0 | 8 |
| Nick Youngquest | Castleford | 2011-12 | 37 | 28 | 0 | 0 | 112 |
| | Crusaders | 2010 | 26(1) | 9 | 0 | 0 | 36 |
| Ronel Zenon | Paris | 1996 | (4) | 0 | 0 | 0 | 0 |
| Nick Zisti | Bradford | 1999 | 6(1) | 0 | 0 | 0 | 0 |
| Freddie Zitter | Catalans | 2006 | 1 | 0 | 0 | 0 | 0 |

*All totals in 'Super League Players 1996-2019' include play-off games & Super League Super 8s from 2015-2018. Super 8s (Qualifiers) not included.*

## OLD FACES - Players making their Super League debuts for new clubs in 2019

| PLAYER | CLUB | DEBUT vs | ROUND | DATE |
|---|---|---|---|---|
| Jordan Abdull | London | Wakefield (h) | 1 | 3/2/19 |
| Danny Addy | Hull KR | Hull FC (h) | 1 | 1/2/19 |
| | | *(club debut: Bradford (h), Ch1, 5/2/17)* | | |
| Wellington Albert | Leeds | Hull KR (a) | 9 | 4/4/19 |
| Ryan Atkins | Wakefield | London (h) (D2) | 29 | 13/9/19 |
| Danny Brough | Wakefield | London (a) (D2) | 1 | 3/2/19 |
| Mason Caton-Brown | | | | |
| | Wakefield | Castleford (a) (D2) | 11 | 18/4/19 |
| Chris Clarkson | Castleford | London (a) | 3 | 23/2/19 |
| James Cunningham | London | Wakefield (h) | 1 | 3/2/19 |
| | | *(club debut: Whitehaven (h) (D2), Ch20, 5/7/15)* | | |
| Matt Davis | Warrington | London (h) | 9 | 5/4/19 |
| Matty Dawson-Jones | | | | |
| | Hull FC | Hull KR (a) | 1 | 1/2/19 |
| Kieran Dixon | London | Wakefield (h) | 1 | 3/2/19 |
| | | *(club debut: Swinton (a) (D2), Ch1, 5/2/17)* | | |
| James Donaldson | Leeds | Warrington (a) | 1 | 2/2/19 |
| Josh Drinkwater | Hull KR | Hull FC (h) | 1 | 1/2/19 |
| Gil Dudson | Salford | Huddersfield (a) | 1 | 1/2/19 |
| Morgan Escare | Wakefield | Hull FC (h) | 25 | 11/8/19 |
| Matty Fleming | London | Wakefield (h) | 1 | 3/2/19 |
| | | *(club debut: Featherstone (h), Ch3, 18/2/18)* | | |
| Matty Fozard | London | Wakefield (h) | 1 | 3/2/19 |
| Mitch Garbutt | Hull KR | Hull FC (h) | 1 | 1/2/19 |
| Matty Gee | London | Wakefield (h) | 1 | 3/2/19 |
| | | *(club debut: Hull KR (h), Ch2, 12/2/17)* | | |
| Chris Green | Wakefield | Hull KR (a) | 26 | 18/8/19 |
| Scott Grix | Huddersfield | Salford (h) (D2) | 1 | 1/2/19 |
| Dean Hadley | Hull KR | Castleford (h) (D2) | 24 | 4/8/19 |
| Zak Hardaker | Wigan | St Helens (h) | 1 | 31/1/19 |
| Weller Hauraki | Hull KR | Hull FC (h) | 1 | 1/2/19 |
| Tom Holmes | Huddersfield | Salford (h) | 21 | 4/7/19 |
| Krisnan Inu | Salford | Wakefield (a) | 8 | 31/3/19 |
| Josh Johnson | Salford | Warrington (a) | 22 | 12/7/19 |
| Luis Johnson | Hull KR | London (a) | 19 | 20/6/19 |
| Elliot Kear | London | Wakefield (h) | 1 | 3/2/19 |
| | | *(club debut: Hunslet (a), Ch11, 3/5/15)* | | |
| Jimmy Keinhorst | Hull KR | Hull FC (h) | 1 | 1/2/19 |
| George King | Wakefield | London (h) | 1 | 3/2/19 |
| Craig Kopczak | Wakefield | London (a) | 1 | 3/2/19 |
| Olsi Krasniqi | London | St Helens (h) (D2) | 17 | 9/6/19 |
| Ryan Lannon | Hull KR | London (h) | 10 | 17/2/19 |
| Ryan Lannon | Salford | Castleford (h) (D2) | 19 | 21/6/19 |
| Adam Lawton | Salford | Catalans (a) | 5 | 9/3/19 |
| Jez Litten | Hull KR | Castleford (h) | 24 | 4/8/19 |
| Harvey Livett | Hull KR | London (a) | 19 | 20/6/19 |
| Tuimoala Lolohea | Salford | Wigan (a) | 20 | 28/6/19 |
| Robert Lui | Leeds | Catalans (h) | 20 | 30/6/19 |
| Shaun Lunt | Leeds | Hull KR (h) (D2) | 22 | 12/7/19 |
| Jake Mamo | Warrington | Huddersfield (a) | 3 | 22/2/19 |
| Antoni Maria | Hull KR | Leeds (a) | 13 | 28/4/19 |
| Nathan Mason | London | Wakefield (h) | 1 | 3/2/19 |
| Ryan Morgan | London | Salford (a) | 2 | 10/2/19 |
| Daniel Murray | Hull KR | London (a) | 19 | 20/6/19 |
| Levy Nzoungou | Hull FC | Catalans (a) | 10 | 13/4/19 |
| Matt Parcell | Hull KR | Hull FC (h) | 20 | 27/6/19 |
| Pauli Pauli | Salford | St Helens (a) | 15 | 17/5/19 |
| Eloi Pelissier | London | Wakefield (h) | 1 | 3/2/19 |
| | | *(club debut: Halifax (h), Ch21, 15/7/18)* | | |
| Jay Pitts | London | Wakefield (h) | 1 | 3/2/19 |
| | | *(club debut: Swinton (a), Ch1, 5/2/17)* | | |
| Jordan Rankin | Castleford | Catalans (h) | 1 | 1/2/19 |
| Ben Reynolds | Wakefield | Castleford (h) | 11 | 18/4/19 |
| Greg Richards | London | Wakefield (h) | 1 | 3/2/19 |
| Jarrod Sammut | Wigan | Hull FC (h) | 3 | 24/2/19 |
| Junior Sa'u | Wakefield | London (a) | 15 | 18/5/19 |
| Andre Savelio | Hull FC | Warrington (h) | 8 | 29/3/19 |
| Ken Sio | Salford | Huddersfield (a) | 1 | 1/2/19 |
| Daniel Smith | Castleford | Huddersfield (a) | 10 | 11/4/19 |
| Matty Smith | Catalans | Castleford (a) | 1 | 1/2/19 |
| Matty Smith | Warrington | St Helens (a) | 25 | 8/8/19 |
| Morgan Smith | London | Wigan (h) | 4 | 3/3/19 |
| Lama Tasi | Warrington | Hull KR (h) | 2 | 9/2/19 |
| Jordan Thompson | Hull FC | Hull KR (a) (D2) | 1 | 1/2/19 |
| Sam Tomkins | Catalans | Castleford (a) | 1 | 1/2/19 |
| Kyle Trout | Hull KR | Wigan (a) | 25 | 9/8/19 |
| Jansin Turgut | Salford | Huddersfield (a) | 1 | 1/2/19 |
| | | *(club debut: Leeds (a), S8Q5, 14/9/18)* | | |
| Adam Walker | Salford | Castleford (a) | 6 | 17/3/19 |
| Danny Walker | Warrington | Leeds (h) | 1 | 2/2/19 |
| Joe Wardle | Huddersfield | Salford (h) (D2) | 1 | 1/2/19 |
| Matt Whitley | Catalans | Castleford (a) | 1 | 1/2/19 |
| Rhys Williams | London | Wakefield (h) | 1 | 3/2/19 |
| | | *(club debut: Doncaster (h), Ch1, 15/2/15)* | | |
| Fouad Yaha | Catalans | Warrington (h) (D2) | 4 | 2/3/19 |

## NEW FACES - Players making their Super League debuts in 2019

| PLAYER | CLUB | DEBUT vs | ROUND | DATE |
|---|---|---|---|---|
| Sadiq Adebiyi | London | Castleford (h) | 3 | 23/2/19 |
| | | *(club debut: Hunslet (h), CS3, 23/8/15)* | | |
| Guy Armitage | London | Catalans (a) | 26 | 17/8/19 |
| Cory Aston | Castleford | Wakefield (h) | 11 | 18/4/19 |
| Blake Austin | Warrington | Leeds (h) | 1 | 2/2/19 |
| Harry Bardle | Hull KR | Huddersfield (a) | 7 | 22/3/19 |
| Joe Batchelor | St Helens | Hull FC (h) | 12 | 22/4/19 |
| Eddie Battye | London | Wakefield (h) | 1 | 3/2/19 |
| | | *(club debut: Oldham (a), Ch1, 7/2/16)* | | |
| Cheyse Blair | Castleford | Warrington (h) | 14 | 3/5/19 |
| Amir Bourouh | Wigan | Salford (a) | 12 | 22/4/19 |
| Jack Brown | Hull FC | Catalans (a) | 10 | 13/4/19 |
| Kieran Buchanan | Hull FC | Catalans (h) | 14 | 3/5/19 |
| Joe Bullock | Wigan | St Helens (a) | 1 | 31/1/19 |
| Luther Burrell | Warrington | London (a) | 21 | 6/7/19 |
| Chester Butler | Huddersfield | Catalans (h) | 29 | 13/9/19 |
| Rob Butler | London | Wigan (h) | 5 | 3/3/19 |
| | | *(club debut: Toronto (h), Ch4, 25/2/18)* | | |
| Liam Byrne | Wigan | Hull FC (h) | 3 | 24/2/19 |
| Jason Clark | Warrington | Leeds (h) | 1 | 2/2/19 |
| Lachlan Coote | St Helens | Wigan (h) | 1 | 31/1/19 |
| Jack Croft | Wakefield | Leeds (h) | 17 | 7/6/19 |
| | | *(club debut: St Helens (a), CCQF, 1/6/19)* | | |
| Matthew Davies | London | Warrington (a) | 9 | 5/4/19 |
| | | *(club debut: Dewsbury (h), Ch12, 28/4/18)* | | |
| Matt Davis | London | St Helens (a) (D2) | 5 | 8/3/19 |
| Sam Davis | London | Huddersfield (a) | 12 | 22/4/19 |
| | | *(club debut: Barrow (h), Ch1, 4/2/18)* | | |
| Riley Dean | Warrington | St Helens (h) | 25 | 8/8/19 |
| Josh Eaves | St Helens | London (a) | 23 | 21/7/19 |
| Izaac Farrell | Huddersfield | Salford (h) | 1 | 1/2/19 |
| | | *(club debut: Swinton (h), CC5, 23/4/17)* | | |
| Matt Frawley | Huddersfield | Salford (h) | 1 | 1/2/19 |
| Bevan French | Wigan | Hull KR (h) | 25 | 9/8/19 |
| Titus Gwaze | Wakefield | Warrington (a) | 19 | 21/6/19 |
| Owen Harrison | Hull KR | Hull FC (a) | 11 | 19/4/19 |
| | | *(club debut: Leigh (h), Ch1, 15/2/15)* | | |
| Ethan Havard | Wigan | Wakefield (h) | 23 | 18/7/19 |
| Callum Hazzard | St Helens | London (a) | 23 | 21/7/19 |
| Ben Hellewell | London | Warrington (h) | 21 | 6/7/19 |
| | | *(club debut: Doncaster (h), Ch1, 15/2/15)* | | |
| Daniel Hindmarsh | London | Salford (h) | 13 | 27/4/19 |
| | | *(club debut: Workington (a), CC4, 18/3/18)* | | |
| Konrad Hurrell | Leeds | Warrington (a) | 1 | 2/2/19 |
| Mark Ioane | London | Wakefield (h) | 1 | 3/2/19 |
| | | *(club debut: Oldham (a), Ch1, 7/2/16)* | | |

| PLAYER | CLUB | DEBUT vs | ROUND | DATE |
|---|---|---|---|---|
| Corey Johnson | Leeds | Warrington (h) | 29 | 13/9/19 |
| Sam Kasiano | Catalans | Leeds (h) | 7 | 23/3/19 |
| Lee Kershaw | Wakefield | Leeds (h) | 12 | 22/4/19 |
| Jon Luke Kirby | Huddersfield | Hull FC (a) | 27 | 30/8/19 |
| Brock Lamb | London | Salford (h) | 24 | 4/8/19 |
| Mikey Lewis | Hull KR | Wigan (a) | 25 | 9/8/19 |
| Kane Linnett | Hull KR | Hull FC (h) | 1 | 1/2/19 |
| Tuimoala Lolohea | Leeds | Warrington (a) | 1 | 2/2/19 |
| Joey Lussick | Salford | Huddersfield (a) | 1 | 1/2/19 |
| | | *(club debut: Hull KR (a), S8Q1, 10/8/18)* | | |
| Rhyse Martin | Leeds | Castleford (a) | 21 | 5/7/19 |
| Callum McLelland | Leeds | Castleford (h) | 15 | 16/5/19 |
| | | *(club debut: Workington (h), CC5, 12/4/19)* | | |
| James Meadows | London | Warrington (a) | 9 | 5/4/19 |
| | | *(club debut: Barrow (h), Ch1, 4/2/18)* | | |
| Trent Merrin | Leeds | Warrington (a) | 1 | 2/2/19 |
| Pat Moran | Warrington | Salford (h) | 22 | 12/7/19 |
| | | *(club debut: Bradford (h), CC5, 21/4/18)* | | |
| Kevin Naiqama | St Helens | Wigan (h) | 1 | 31/1/19 |
| Ratu Naulago | Hull FC | Wigan (a) | 3 | 24/2/19 |
| Jacob Ogden | London | St Helens (a) | 5 | 8/3/19 |
| | | *(club debut: Workington (a), CC4, 18/3/18)* | | |
| Jacques O'Neill | Castleford | Hull KR (h) | 4 | 1/3/19 |
| Joseph Paulo | St Helens | Wigan (h) | 1 | 31/1/19 |
| Lewis Peachey | Castleford | Catalans (a) | 12 | 22/4/19 |
| Adam Rooks | Hull KR | Catalans (h) | 6 | 17/3/19 |
| Tevita Satae | Hull FC | Salford (h) | 26 | 17/8/19 |
| Ava Seumanufagai | Leeds | Salford (a) | 14 | 3/5/19 |
| Joe Shorrocks | Wigan | Wakefield (a) | 10 | 12/4/19 |
| Josh Simm | St Helens | London (a) | 23 | 21/7/19 |
| Harry Smith | Wigan | Catalans (h) | 28 | 6/9/19 |
| Morgan Smithies | Wigan | Catalans (h) | 8 | 31/3/19 |
| Adam Tangata | Wakefield | Hull FC (h) | 25 | 11/8/19 |
| Kelepi Tanginoa | Wakefield | Catalans (MW) | 16 | 25/5/19 |
| Josh Thewlis | Warrington | Catalans (h) | 17 | 8/6/19 |
| Owen Trout | Leeds | Wakefield (a) | 12 | 22/4/19 |
| | | *(club debut: Workington (a), CC5, 12/4/19)* | | |
| Akuila Uate | Huddersfield | Salford (h) | 1 | 1/2/19 |
| Oliver Wilson | Huddersfield | Salford (a) | 21 | 4/7/19 |
| Connor Wynne | Hull FC | Salford (a) | 9 | 7/4/19 |
| Luke Yates | London | Wakefield (h) | 1 | 3/2/19 |
| Dominic Young | Huddersfield | St Helens (a) | 18 | 14/6/19 |

### Players making their club debuts in other competitions in 2019

| PLAYER | CLUB | DEBUT vs | ROUND | DATE |
|---|---|---|---|---|
| Muizz Mustapha | Leeds | Workington (h) | CC5 | 12/4/19 |

187

# SUPER LEAGUE RECORDS
# *1996-2019*

---

**COMPETITION**
*Includes play-off games & Super League Super 8s (2015-2018)*

**TRIES**
Danny McGuire (Hull Kingston Rovers/Leeds Rhinos)
(2001-2019) 247

**GOALS**
Kevin Sinfield (Leeds Rhinos) (1997-2015) 1,566

**FIELD GOALS**
Lee Briers (Warrington Wolves/St Helens) (1997-2013) 70

**POINTS**
Kevin Sinfield (Leeds Rhinos) (1997-2015) 3,443

**APPEARANCES**
Kevin Sinfield (Leeds Rhinos) (1997-2015) 454

**SEASON**
*Includes play-off games & Super League Super 8s (2015-2018)*
*(Play-offs in brackets)*

**TRIES**
Denny Solomona (Castleford Tigers) (2016) 40 (-)

**GOALS**
Henry Paul (Bradford Bulls) (2001) 178 (13)

**FIELD GOALS**
Lee Briers (Warrington Wolves) (2002) 11 (-)

**POINTS**
Pat Richards (Wigan Warriors) (2010) 434 (46)

*Includes play-off games & Super League Super 8s (2015-2018)*

**TRIES**
Lesley Vainikolo (Bradford Bulls) 6
(v Hull FC (h), 2/9/05)

**GOALS**
Henry Paul (Bradford Bulls) 14
(v Salford City Reds (h), 25/6/00)

**FIELD GOALS**
Lee Briers (Warrington Wolves) 5
(v Halifax Blue Sox (a), 25/5/02)

**POINTS**
Iestyn Harris (Leeds Rhinos) 42
(v Huddersfield Giants (h), 16/7/99)

*Includes play-off games & Super League Super 8s (2015-2018)*

**HIGHEST SCORE**
Bradford Bulls 96 Salford City Reds 16 (25/6/00)

**WIDEST MARGIN**
Leeds Rhinos 86 Huddersfield Giants 6 (16/7/99)
Bradford Bulls 96 Salford City Reds 16 (25/6/00)
Warrington Wolves 80 Wakefield Trinity Wildcats 0 (11/4/15)

**GRAND FINAL**
73,512 Leeds Rhinos v Wigan Warriors (10/10/15)

**PLAY-OFFS**
21,790 Wigan Warriors v St Helens (3/10/03)

**REGULAR SEASON** *(includes Super League Super 8s (2015-2018)*
31,555 Catalans Dragons v Wigan Warriors (18/5/19)
*(at Camp Nou, Barcelona)*

# SUPER LEAGUE XXIV
## *Club by Club*

---

**3rd November 2018 -** Jake Trueman signs new four-year deal to end of 2022 season.

**15th November 2018 -** Kieran Gill joins Newcastle Thunder on year-long loan.

**5th December 2018 -** Oliver Holmes, shoulder, and Will Maher, pectoral, to both miss pre-season.

**30th December 2018 -** 56-0 home win over Featherstone.

**6th January 2019 -** Luke Gale ruptures Achilles tendon in pre-season training.

**7th January 2019 -** former Leeds and Hull KR backrower Chris Clarkson given pre-season trial.

**11th January 2019 -** Joe Wardle leaves for Huddersfield with Jordan Rankin joining Tigers, both on initial loan deal.

**11th January 2019 -** Tigers given salary cap relief in light of Luke Gale injury. Jamie Ellis out for six months with knee injury.

**20th January 2019 -** 26-24 friendly win at Leeds.

**30th January 2019 -** Calum Turner joins Featherstone on loan.

**1st February 2019 -** Greg Eden scores two tries in 20-4 home, round-one win over Catalans.

**7th February 2019 -** two tries from Michael Shenton in 26-18 win at Hull FC. Mitch Clark damages knee ligaments. Mike McMeeken tears hamstring in training.

**14th February 2019 -** back rower Chris Clarkson signs contract for 2019 season.

**23rd February 2019 -** 40-6 win at London Broncos.

**28th February 2019 -** captain Michael Shenton signs new two-year contract extension to end of 2021.

**1st March 2019 -** hard-fought 32-16 home win over Hull KR maintains top-of-table position. Grant Millington takes two-match penalty notice for punching.

**7th March 2019 -** 24-10 round-five defeat at Warrington is first of season.

**15th March 2019 -** prop Nathan Massey agrees new two-year contract until end of 2021 season.

**17th March 2019 -** 24-20 home win over Salford.

**20th March 2019 -** Ben Roberts leaves club with immediate effect by mutual agreement.

**22nd March 2019 -** 42-12 home defeat by league leaders St Helens.

**28th March 2019 -** Brad Dwyer field goal means 21-20 defeat at Leeds.

**2nd April 2019 -** prop Daniel Smith joins from Huddersfield on contract to end of 2020.

**5th April 2019 -** 38-28 home win over Wigan after trailing 20-0 after 20 minutes.

**11th April 2019 -** Mike McMeeken returns after nine-game absence in 20-18 Thursday-night defeat at Huddersfield.

**12th April 2019 -** Melbourne Storm centre Cheyse Blair signs for the rest of 2019 season on three-and-a-half-year contract.

**18th April 2019 -** Jesse Sene-Lefao dislocates shoulder in nail-biting 28-26 Easter Thursday victory over Wakefield to retain Adam Watene Trophy.

# KEY DATES

**22nd April 2019 -** 37-16 defeat at Catalans despite two tries from Greg Eden.

**27th April 2019 -** two Peter Mata'utia penalties aren't enough to prevent 6-4 Saturday evening defeat at rain-soaked Wigan.

**3rd May 2019 -** prop Matt Cook signs one-year contract extension.

**3rd May 2019 -** 26-14 home defeat to second-placed Warrington.

**10th May 2019 -** Challenge Cup sixth-round exit after 28-12 defeat at Hull FC.

**16th May 2019 -** Jesse Sene-Lefao scores two tries in 30-8 win at Leeds.

**26th May 2019 -** 36-16 Magic Weekend defeat to St Helens at Anfield.

**6th June 2019 -** prop Mitch Clark to join Wigan at end of season.

**7th June 2019 -** Peter Mata'utia field goal earns golden-point 27-26, rain-swept home victory over Huddersfield.

**10th June 2019 -** Toulouse Olympique forward Tyla Hepi signs one-year contract for 2020 with further year option in club's favour.

**13th June 2019 -** 31-18 home defeat to Hull FC after leading 14-4 at half-time.

**27th June 2019 -** 26-16 defeat at Salford.

**30th June 2019 -** 42-10 home win over London Broncos moves Tigers from seventh into fourth spot.

**2nd July 2019 -** prop George Griffin signs from Salford on two-year contract from 2020 with option for further season.

**3rd July 2019 -** Cronulla winger Sosaia Feki and Salford winger Derrell Olpherts sign three-year contracts from 2020.

**4th July 2019 -** prop Liam Watts signs new contract until end of 2023

**5th July 2019 -** coach Daryl Powell signs new contract to end of 2022.

**5th July 2019 -** 18-10 home defeat by Leeds.

**12th July 2019 -** James Clare scores hat-trick in 36-16 win at Wakefield.

**18th July 2019 -** prop Mitch Clark leaves with immediate effect. Halfback Cory Aston signs for London Broncos for 2020.

**21st July 2019 -** 27-18 home win over Warrington.

**4th August 2019 -** Danny McGuire golden-point field goal means 27-26 defeat at Hull KR.

**5th August 2019 -** club releases statement confirming dropped winger Greg Eden is facing trial for ABH.

**8th August 2019 -** hooker/back row Jacques O'Neill signs one-year contract extension.

**10th August 2019 -** Jamie Ellis returns for first game of season in 20-6 win at London.

**13th August 2019 -** winger Tuoyo Egodo signs for London Broncos from 2020.

**18th August 2019 -** 24-0 away win at Huddersfield

**30th August 2019 -** 4-0 defeat at League Leaders St Helens.

**2nd September 2019 -** Kieran Gill signs for Newcastle Thunder.

**5th September 2019 -** Jake Trueman hat-trick inspires 44-12 home win over Hull FC to go into fifth spot.

**12th September 2019 -** 26-8 defeat to Wigan but Hull lose to St Helens ensuring Tigers' fifth-place finish. Jesse Sene-Lefao sent off and cops two-match ban for use of knees in tackle.

**19th September 2019 -** battling 14-12 win at Warrington in Elimination Play-off.

**26th September 2019 -** 22-0 elimination semi-final defeat at Salford.

**1st October 2019 -** Luke Gale signs for Leeds for undisclosed transfer fee.

**3rd October 2019 -** Jordan Rankin to remain on loan from Huddersfield for 2020 season.

**18th October 2019 -** halfback Danny Richardson transferred from St Helens for undisclosed fee to take up three-year contract.

### CLUB RECORDS

**Highest score:**
106-0 v Rochdale, 9/9/2007
**Highest score against:**
12-76 v Leeds, 14/8/2009
**Record attendance:**
25,449 v Hunslet, 9/3/35

### MATCH RECORDS

**Tries:**
5 Derek Foster v Hunslet, 10/11/72
John Joyner v Millom, 16/9/73
Steve Fenton v Dewsbury, 27/1/78
Ian French v Hunslet, 9/2/86
St John Ellis v Whitehaven, 10/12/89
Greg Eden v Warrington, 11/6/2017
**Goals:** 17 Sammy Lloyd v Millom, 16/9/73
**Points:** 43 Sammy Lloyd v Millom, 16/9/73

### SEASON RECORDS

**Tries:** 42 Denny Solomona 2016
**Goals:** 158 Sammy Lloyd 1976-77
**Points:** 355 Luke Gale 2017

### CAREER RECORDS

**Tries:** 206 Alan Hardisty 1958-71
**Goals:** 875 Albert Lunn 1951-63
**Points:** 1,870 Albert Lunn 1951-63
**Appearances:** 613 John Joyner 1973-92

# CASTLEFORD TIGERS

| DATE | FIXTURE | RESULT | SCORERS | LGE | ATT |
|------|---------|--------|---------|-----|-----|
| 1/2/19 | Catalans Dragons (h) | W20-4 | t:McShane,Eden(2) g:McShane(4) | 4th | 7,494 |
| 7/2/19 | Hull FC (a) | W18-26 | t:Shenton(2),Sene-Lefao,Clare,Moors g:McShane(2),Rankin | 3rd | 11,244 |
| 23/2/19 | London Broncos (a) | W6-40 | t:Mata'utia,Trueman,Moors,Sene-Lefao,Watts,Eden,Rankin | | |
| | | | g:McShane(5),Rankin | 1st | 2,053 |
| 1/3/19 | Hull KR (h) | W32-16 | t:Rankin,Watts,Eden(2),Clare,Clarkson g:McShane,Rankin(3) | 1st | 8,770 |
| 7/3/19 | Warrington (a) | L24-10 | t:Eden,Minikin g:Rankin | 2nd | 9,231 |
| 17/3/19 | Salford (h) | W24-20 | t:Massey,Rankin,Eden,Sene-Lefao g:Rankin(4) | 3rd | 7,750 |
| 22/3/19 | St Helens (h) | L12-42 | t:Shenton,Trueman g:Rankin(2) | 3rd | 8,042 |
| 28/3/19 | Leeds (a) | L21-20 | | 3rd | 12,295 |
| | | (aet) | t:Watts,Minikin,Clarkson,Foster g:Turner(2) | | |
| 5/4/19 | Wigan (h) | W38-28 | t:Holmes,Turner,Cook,Milner,Egodo,Mata'utia g:Mata'utia(5) | 3rd | 6,839 |
| 11/4/19 | Huddersfield (a) | L20-18 | t:Eden,Cook g:Mata'utia(5) | 3rd | 4,684 |
| 18/4/19 | Wakefield (h) | W28-26 | t:Clare(2),Sene-Lefao,Aston,Minikin g:Mata'utia(4) | 3rd | 9,316 |
| 22/4/19 | Catalans Dragons (a) | L37-16 | t:Eden(2),Aston g:Mata'utia(2) | 4th | 10,120 |
| 27/4/19 | Wigan (a) | L6-4 | g:Mata'utia(2) | 5th | 10,058 |
| 3/5/19 | Warrington (h) | L14-26 | t:Aston,Egodo,Minikin g:Mata'utia | 7th | 5,323 |
| 10/5/19 | Hull FC (a) (CCR6) | L28-12 | t:Clare,Aston g:Mata'utia(2) | N/A | 6,230 |
| 16/5/19 | Leeds (a) | W8-30 | t:Sene-Lefao(2),Eden,Clare,Trueman g:Mata'utia(5) | 5th | 13,286 |
| 26/5/19 | St Helens (MW) ● | L16-36 | t:Millington,Clarkson,Eden g:Mata'utia,Rankin | 5th | N/A |
| 7/6/19 | Huddersfield (h) | W27-26 | | 5th | 7,483 |
| | | (aet) | t:Minikin,Watts,Millington g:Mata'utia(7) fg:Mata'utia | | |
| 13/6/19 | Hull FC (h) | L18-31 | t:Minikin,Moors,Eden g:Mata'utia(3) | 5th | 6,344 |
| 21/6/19 | Salford (a) | L26-16 | t:Smith,Minikin,Rankin g:Mata'utia(2) | 7th | 2,829 |
| 30/6/19 | London Broncos (h) | W42-10 | t:Egodo(2),McMeeken(2),Rankin,Trueman,Clare,Clarkson g:Rankin(5) | 4th | 6,860 |
| 5/7/19 | Leeds (h) | L10-18 | t:Clare(2) g:Rankin | 6th | 8,147 |
| 12/7/19 | Wakefield (a) | W16-36 | t:Egodo,Holmes,Clare(3),Rankin(2) g:Mata'utia(4) | 6th | 6,244 |
| 21/7/19 | Warrington (h) | W27-18 | t:Clare,Minikin,Trueman,Egodo g:Mata'utia(5) fg:Trueman | 5th | 6,965 |
| 4/8/19 | Hull KR (a) | L27-26 | | 7th | 8,004 |
| | | (aet) | t:Mata'utia,Rankin,Clare,Minikin g:Mata'utia(5) | | |
| 10/8/19 | London Broncos (h) | W20-6 | t:Egodo(2),Holmes,O'Neill g:Ellis(2) | 6th | 5,497 |
| 18/8/19 | Huddersfield (a) | W0-24 | t:Clare,Milner,McMeeken,Sene-Lefao g:Ellis(4) | 6th | 4,636 |
| 30/8/19 | St Helens (a) | L4-0 | | 6th | 10,315 |
| 5/9/19 | Hull FC (h) | W44-12 | t:Blair,Trueman(3),Clare,Rankin,Cook g:Ellis(8) | 5th | 6,712 |
| 12/9/19 | Wigan (a) | L26-8 | t:Blair g:Ellis(2) | 5th | 11,001 |
| 19/9/19 | Warrington (a) (EPO) | W12-14 | t:Milner,Rankin g:Mata'utia(3) | N/A | 5,627 |
| 26/9/19 | Salford (a) (ESF) | L22-0 | | N/A | 4,800 |

● Played at Anfield, Liverpool

## APP    TRIES GOALS FG    PTS

| | D.O.B. | ALL | SL | ALL | SL | ALL | SL | ALL | SL | ALL | SL |
|---|--------|-----|-----|-----|-----|-----|-----|-----|-----|-----|-----|
| Cory Aston | 1/3/95 | 9 | 8 | 4 | 3 | 0 | 0 | 0 | 0 | 16 | 12 |
| Cheyse Blair | 18/1/92 | 18 | 17 | 2 | 2 | 0 | 0 | 0 | 0 | 8 | 8 |
| James Clare | 13/4/91 | 29(1) | 28(1) | 16 | 15 | 0 | 0 | 0 | 0 | 64 | 60 |
| Mitch Clark | 13/3/93 | (9) | (9) | 1 | 1 | 0 | 0 | 0 | 0 | 4 | 4 |
| Chris Clarkson | 7/4/90 | 12(8) | 11(8) | 4 | 4 | 0 | 0 | 0 | 0 | 16 | 16 |
| Matt Cook | 14/11/86 | (21) | (20) | 3 | 3 | 0 | 0 | 0 | 0 | 12 | 12 |
| Greg Eden | 14/11/90 | 21 | 21 | 13 | 13 | 0 | 0 | 0 | 0 | 52 | 52 |
| Tuoyo Egodo | 16/2/97 | 9(3) | 8(3) | 8 | 8 | 0 | 0 | 0 | 0 | 32 | 32 |
| Jamie Ellis | 4/10/89 | 5 | 5 | 0 | 0 | 16 | 16 | 0 | 0 | 32 | 32 |
| Alex Foster | 25/9/93 | 4(2) | 4(2) | 1 | 1 | 0 | 0 | 0 | 0 | 4 | 4 |
| Oliver Holmes | 7/8/92 | 12(3) | 12(3) | 3 | 3 | 0 | 0 | 0 | 0 | 12 | 12 |
| Will Maher | 4/11/95 | 4(5) | 3(5) | 0 | 0 | 0 | 0 | 0 | 0 | 0 | 0 |
| Nathan Massey | 11/7/89 | 26(1) | 25(1) | 1 | 1 | 0 | 0 | 0 | 0 | 4 | 4 |
| Peter Mata'utia | 2/11/90 | 31 | 30 | 3 | 3 | 56 | 54 | 1 | 1 | 125 | 121 |
| Mike McMeeken | 10/5/94 | 22 | 21 | 3 | 3 | 0 | 0 | 0 | 0 | 12 | 12 |
| Paul McShane | 19/11/89 | 26(2) | 25(2) | 1 | 1 | 12 | 12 | 0 | 0 | 28 | 28 |
| Grant Millington | 1/11/86 | 17(9) | 17(8) | 2 | 2 | 0 | 0 | 0 | 0 | 8 | 8 |
| Adam Milner | 19/12/91 | 11(17) | 11(16) | 3 | 3 | 0 | 0 | 0 | 0 | 12 | 12 |
| Greg Minikin | 29/3/95 | 30 | 29 | 9 | 9 | 0 | 0 | 0 | 0 | 36 | 36 |
| Junior Moors | 30/7/86 | 5(8) | 5(8) | 3 | 3 | 0 | 0 | 0 | 0 | 12 | 12 |
| Jacques O'Neill | 8/5/99 | (11) | (11) | 1 | 1 | 0 | 0 | 0 | 0 | 4 | 4 |
| Lewis Peachey | 25/3/01 | (1) | (1) | 0 | 0 | 0 | 0 | 0 | 0 | 0 | 0 |
| Jordan Rankin | 17/12/91 | 22(2) | 22(2) | 10 | 10 | 19 | 19 | 0 | 0 | 78 | 78 |
| Ben Roberts | 8/7/85 | (1) | (1) | 0 | 0 | 0 | 0 | 0 | 0 | 0 | 0 |
| Jesse Sene-Lefao | 8/12/89 | 20(5) | 20(4) | 7 | 7 | 0 | 0 | 0 | 0 | 28 | 28 |
| Michael Shenton | 22/7/86 | 12 | 12 | 3 | 3 | 0 | 0 | 0 | 0 | 12 | 12 |
| Daniel Smith | 20/3/93 | 8(11) | 8(11) | 1 | 1 | 0 | 0 | 0 | 0 | 4 | 4 |
| Jake Trueman | 16/2/99 | 31 | 30 | 8 | 8 | 0 | 0 | 1 | 1 | 33 | 33 |
| Calum Turner | 29/4/99 | 3(2) | 3(2) | 1 | 1 | 2 | 2 | 0 | 0 | 8 | 8 |
| Liam Watts | 8/7/90 | 29(1) | 28(1) | 4 | 4 | 0 | 0 | 0 | 0 | 16 | 16 |

*'SL' totals include regular season & play-offs; 'All' totals also include Challenge Cup*

Peter Mata'utia

**LEAGUE RECORD**
P29-W15-D0-L14
(5th/Elimination Semi-Final)
F646, A558, Diff+88
30 points.

**CHALLENGE CUP**
Round Six

**ATTENDANCES**
Best - v Wakefield (SL - 9,316)
Worst - v Warrington (SL - 5,323)
Total (SL only) - 101,542
Average (SL only) - 7,253
(Down by 351 on 2018)

**16th November 2018 -** former Widnes Vikings prop Eamon O'Carroll joins as assistant coach.

**4th January 2019 -** Dragons refuse RFL request to pay £500,000 deposit to enter Challenge Cup.

**15th January 2019 -** CEO Christophe Jouffret leaves the club.

**18th January 2019 -** Rémi Casty appointed club captain.

**18th January 2019 -** 38-14 home friendly win over President's XIII.

**21st January 2019 -** Dragons announce they will defend Challenge Cup in 2019.

**23rd January 2019 -** 22-18 home friendly win over Toulouse.

**1st February 2019 -** 20-4, round-one defeat at Castleford.

**9th February 2019 -** Brayden Wiliame scores two tries in 27-10 home win over Huddersfield.

**17th February 2019 -** winger Fouad Yaha returns from Agen rugby union on two-year contract.

**21st February 2019 -** David Mead out for two months with adductor injury suffered in 22-12 defeat at Wakefield.

**25th February 2019 -** Jodie Broughton suffers biceps tendon rupture in reserve game at Albi on return from ACL injury.

**2nd March 2019 -** Sam Tomkins kicks match-winning penalty from 45 metres to earn 23-22 home win over unbeaten Warrington.

**8th March 2019 -** prop Sam Kasiano signs from Melbourne Storm with immediate effect.

**9th March 2019 -** 46-0 home hammering by Salford. Michael McIlorum suffers pectoral injury.

**17th March 2019 -** 74th-minute Lewis Tierney try and Sam Tomkins conversion seals 18-16 comeback win at Hull KR.

**23rd March 2019 -** Sam Kasiano makes high-impact debut from bench as Fouad Yaha scores four tries in 26-22 home win over Leeds.

**31st March 2019 -** 42-0 hammering at Wigan.

**6th April 2019 -** late Tony Gigot try secures 18-10 home win over unbeaten St Helens.

**13th April 2019 -** Marc Sneyd golden-point field goal means 31-30 home defeat by Hull FC. Brayden Wiliame gets one-match penalty notice for shoulder charge

**18th April 2019 -** Matt Whitley scores two tries in 39-6 Easter Thursday win at London Broncos

**22nd April 2019 -** Julian Bousquet scores two tries in 37-16 home win over Castleford.

**25th April 2019 -** Antoni Maria joins Hull KR on one month loan.

**28th April 2019 -** 50-14 hammering at league leaders St Helens.

**3rd May 2019 -** 37-6 win at Hull FC.

**11th May 2019 -** Brayden Wiliame scores four tries in 62-6 Challenge Cup sixth round home win over League 1 Doncaster.

**18th May 2019 -** Super League regular-round record crowd of 31,555 see 33-16 Camp Nou win over Wigan. Greg Bird tears biceps.

# KEY DATES

**25th May 2019 -** Benjamin Garcia scores two tries in 25-18 Magic Weekend win over Wakefield at Anfield.

**29th May 2019 -** Michael McIlorum signs two-year contract to end of 2021.

**30th May 2019 -** Challenge Cup quarter-final exit after 51-8 defeat at Hull FC.

**7th June 2019 -** Greg Bird to retire at end of 2019 season.

**8th June 2019 -** 34-4 defeat at Warrington.

**15th June 2019 -** 30-12 home defeat to bottom side London Broncos. Jason Baitieri banned for two games for dangerous contact.

**19th June 2019 -** Jason Baitieri ban reduced to one game on appeal.

**22nd June 2019 -** 50-10 home defeat by Hull FC.

**26th June 2019 -** winger Lewis Tierney signs new two-year contract to end of 2021.

**30th June 2019 -** Sam Moa and Jason Baitieri suffer injuries in 31-12 defeat at bottom club Leeds.

**6th July 2019 -** Jodie Broughton scores hat-trick in 44-10 home hammering of Wakefield.

**12th July 2019 -** Sam Tomkins gets hat-trick as 32-28 win at Huddersfield moves Dragons into fourth spot. Kenny Edwards gets one-match for foul and abusive language to match official. Jodie Broughton suffers knee and neck injuries.

**18th July 2019 -** prop Paul Séguier joins Barrow on loan until end of season.

**21st July 2019 -** 40-14 defeat at Salford. Players given a week off.

**23rd July 2019 -** halfback Samisoni Langi signs new two-year contract to end of 2021.

**24th July 2019 -** halfback James Maloney signs from Penrith on three-year contract from 2020.

**26th July 2019 -** Benjamin Jullien signs new two-year contract to end of 2021.

**3rd August 2019 -** indisciplined 30-10 home win over Warrington amid televised crowd trouble.

**3rd August 2019 -** Brayden Wiliame, dangerous throw, Michael McIlorum and Mickael Simon, headbutt, get one-match; Sam Tomkins, punching, three matches, all on penalty notices. Kenny Edwards referred to tribunal for 'other contrary behaviour'.

**6th August 2019 -** Matty Smith joins Warrington on loan.

**7th August 2019 -** Sam Tomkins fails with disciplinary appeal. Michael McIlorum has ban increased to two games after appeal. Brayden Wiliame ban downgraded to no suspension, Mickael Simon found not guilty on appeal. Kenny Edwards found not guilty.

**9th August 2019 -** 48-8 defeat at Leeds.

**17th August 2019 -** 17-4 home defeat by London. Ben Garcia gets two-match penalty notice for dangerous throw on Brock Lamb.

**22nd August 2019 -** hooker Alrix Da Costa signs new two-year contract to end of 2021.

**31st August 2019 -** Michael McIlorum and Jason Baitieri back for 24-6 home defeat by Hull KR. David Mead suffers fractured cheek.

**6th September 2019 -** Sam Tomkins back as Rémi Casty breaks hand in third minute of 46-12 defeat at Wigan.

**12th September 2019 -** Jodie Broughton to join Halifax, Kenny Edwards Huddersfield and Tony Gigot St George Illawarra Dragons.

**13th September 2019 -** late 24-22 final-round defeat at Huddersfield.

**23rd September 2019 -** threequarter Arthur Romano signs new one-year contract.

**2nd October 2019 -** prop Lambert Belmas signs new one-year contract.

**14th October 2019 -** prop Antoni Maria signs new one-year contract.

**20th October 2019 -** backrower Joel Tomkins joins on two-year contract.

**22nd October 2019 -** coach Steve McNamara signs new three-year contract to end of 2022 season.

## CLUB RECORDS

**Highest score:** 92-8 v York, 12/5/2013
**Highest score against:**
0-62 v Hull FC, 12/5/2017
**Record attendance:** 31,555 v Wigan,
18/5/2019 *(Barcelona)*
11,856 v Wigan, 2/7/2016
*(Stade Gilbert Brutus)*

## MATCH RECORDS

**Tries:**
4 Justin Murphy v Warrington, 13/9/2008
Damien Cardace v Warrington, 31/3/2012
Kevin Larroyer v York, 12/5/2013
Jodie Broughton v St Helens, 14/4/2016
Fouad Yaha v Salford, 21/7/2018
David Mead v Huddersfield, 29/9/2018
Fouad Yaha v Leeds, 23/3/2019
Brayden Wiliame v Doncaster, 11/5/2019
**Goals:**
11 Thomas Bosc v Featherstone, 31/3/2007
Thomas Bosc v Batley, 29/5/2010
Scott Dureau v Widnes, 31/3/2012
**Points:**
26 Thomas Bosc v Featherstone, 31/3/2007

## SEASON RECORDS

**Tries:** 29 Morgan Escare 2014
**Goals:** 134 Scott Dureau 2012
**Points:** 319 Scott Dureau 2012

## CAREER RECORDS

**Tries:** 87 Vincent Duport
2007-2009; 2011-2018
**Goals:**
579 *(inc 14fg)* Thomas Bosc 2006-2017
**Points:** 1,380 Thomas Bosc 2006-2017
**Appearances:**
320 Remi Casty 2006-2013; 2015-2019

# CATALANS DRAGONS

| DATE | FIXTURE | RESULT | SCORERS | LGE | ATT |
|------|---------|--------|---------|-----|-----|
| 1/2/19 | Castleford (a) | L20-4 | t:Tierney | 8th | 7,494 |
| 9/2/19 | Huddersfield (h) | W27-10 | t:Wiliame(2),Tierney,Tomkins g:Tomkins(5) fg:Smith | 5th | 9,211 |
| 21/2/19 | Wakefield (a) | L22-12 | t:Langi(2) g:Tomkins(2) | 7th | 4,639 |
| 2/3/19 | Warrington (h) | W23-22 | t:Wiliame,Edwards,Casty g:Tomkins(5) fg:Gigot | 7th | 8,158 |
| 9/3/19 | Salford (h) | L0-46 | | 8th | 8,021 |
| 17/3/19 | Hull KR (a) | W16-18 | t:Wiliame,Albert,Tierney g:Tomkins(3) | 8th | 7,203 |
| 23/3/19 | Leeds (h) | W26-22 | t:Yaha(4),Albert g:Tomkins(3) | 6th | 8,220 |
| 31/3/19 | Wigan (a) | L42-0 | | 7th | 11,109 |
| 6/4/19 | St Helens (h) | W18-10 | t:Yaha,Tomkins,Gigot g:Tomkins(3) | 6th | 8,783 |
| 13/4/19 | Hull FC (h) | L30-31 | | 6th | 8,220 |
| | | *(aet)* | t:Gigot,Baitieri,Garcia,Yaha,Kasiano g:Tomkins(5) | | |
| 18/4/19 | London Broncos (a) | W6-39 | t:Whitley(2),Tierney,Bird,Romano,Tomkins g:Tomkins(7) fg:Tomkins | 6th | 2,153 |
| 22/4/19 | Castleford (h) | W37-16 | t:Bousquet(2),Gigot,Bird,Whitley,Tomkins g:Tomkins(6) fg:Gigot | 6th | 10,120 |
| 28/4/19 | St Helens (a) | L50-14 | t:Wiliame(2),Tierney g:Tomkins | 6th | 11,268 |
| 3/5/19 | Hull FC (a) | W6-37 | t:Yaha,Gigot,Wiliame,Romano,Whitley,Langi g:Tomkins(6) fg:Gigot | 4th | 9,830 |
| 11/5/19 | Doncaster (h) (CCR6) | W62-6 | t:Wiliame(4),Whitley(2),Baitieri,Mead(2),Yaha(2),Gigot g:Tomkins,Gigot(6) | N/A | 3,466 |
| 18/5/19 | Wigan (h) ● | W33-16 | t:McIlorum,Mead(2),Langi,Kasiano g:Gigot(6) fg:Gigot | 3rd | 31,555 |
| 25/5/19 | Wakefield (MW) ●● | W25-18 | t:Yaha,Gigot,Garcia(2) g:Gigot(4) fg:Gigot | 3rd | N/A |
| 30/5/19 | Hull FC (a) (CCQF) | L51-8 | t:Tierney(2) | N/A | 4,832 |
| 8/6/19 | Warrington (a) | L34-4 | t:Yaha | 3rd | 10,015 |
| 15/6/19 | London Broncos (h) | L12-30 | t:Yaha(3) | 4th | 8,137 |
| 22/6/19 | Hull FC (h) | L10-50 | t:Tomkins,Tierney g:Tomkins | 4th | 10,254 |
| 30/6/19 | Leeds (a) | L31-12 | t:Romano,Tomkins g:Tomkins(2) | 6th | 12,638 |
| 6/7/19 | Wakefield (h) | W44-10 | t:Broughton(3),Whitley,Langi,Edwards,Gigot(2) g:Tomkins(6) | 5th | 7,237 |
| 12/7/19 | Huddersfield (a) | W28-32 | t:Tomkins(3),Wiliame,Broughton(2) g:Tomkins(4) | 4th | 4,383 |
| 21/7/19 | Salford (a) | L40-14 | t:Kasiano,Wiliame g:Tomkins(3) | 6th | 2,785 |
| 3/8/19 | Warrington (h) | W30-10 | t:Yaha,Mead,Whitley,Gigot g:Tomkins(7) | 5th | 9,634 |
| 9/8/19 | Leeds (a) | L48-8 | t:Goudemand g:Gigot(2) | 7th | 11,336 |
| 17/8/19 | London Broncos (h) | L4-17 | t:Wiliame | 7th | 7,725 |
| 31/8/19 | Hull KR (h) | L6-24 | t:Mead g:Gigot | 7th | 8,315 |
| 6/9/19 | Wigan (a) | L46-12 | t:McIlorum,Tierney g:Tomkins(2) | 7th | 10,804 |
| 13/9/19 | Huddersfield (a) | L24-22 | t:Tierney(2),Mourgue g:Tomkins(5) | 7th | 5,242 |

● *Played at Camp Nou, Barcelona*
●● *Played at Anfield, Liverpool*

| | | APP | | TRIES | | GOALS | | FG | | PTS | |
|---|---|---|---|---|---|---|---|---|---|---|---|
| | D.O.B. | ALL | SL | ALL | SL | ALL | SL | ALL | SL | ALL | SL |
| Lucas Albert | 4/7/98 | 7(8) | 6(8) | 2 | 2 | 0 | 0 | 0 | 0 | 8 | 8 |
| Jason Baitieri | 2/7/89 | 4(17) | 3(16) | 2 | 1 | 0 | 0 | 0 | 0 | 8 | 4 |
| Lambert Belmas | 11/8/97 | (6) | (5) | 0 | 0 | 0 | 0 | 0 | 0 | 0 | 0 |
| Greg Bird | 10/2/84 | 12(3) | 12(3) | 2 | 2 | 0 | 0 | 0 | 0 | 8 | 8 |
| Julian Bousquet | 18/7/91 | 20(8) | 19(7) | 2 | 2 | 0 | 0 | 0 | 0 | 8 | 8 |
| Robin Brochon | 21/9/00 | 1 | 1 | 0 | 0 | 0 | 0 | 0 | 0 | 0 | 0 |
| Jodie Broughton | 9/1/88 | 3 | 3 | 5 | 5 | 0 | 0 | 0 | 0 | 20 | 20 |
| Remi Casty | 5/2/85 | 27 | 26 | 1 | 1 | 0 | 0 | 0 | 0 | 4 | 4 |
| Alrix Da Costa | 2/10/97 | 13(5) | 13(3) | 0 | 0 | 0 | 0 | 0 | 0 | 0 | 0 |
| Kenny Edwards | 13/9/89 | 12(9) | 11(8) | 2 | 2 | 0 | 0 | 0 | 0 | 8 | 8 |
| Benjamin Garcia | 5/4/93 | 13(3) | 12(3) | 3 | 3 | 0 | 0 | 0 | 0 | 12 | 12 |
| Tony Gigot | 27/12/90 | 26 | 24 | 9 | 8 | 19 | 13 | 5 | 5 | 79 | 63 |
| Mickael Goudemand | 9/3/96 | 5(15) | 5(15) | 1 | 1 | 0 | 0 | 0 | 0 | 4 | 4 |
| Benjamin Jullien | 1/3/95 | 13(3) | 12(3) | 0 | 0 | 0 | 0 | 0 | 0 | 0 | 0 |
| Sam Kasiano | 21/9/90 | 3(19) | 3(18) | 3 | 3 | 0 | 0 | 0 | 0 | 12 | 12 |
| Samisoni Langi | 11/6/93 | 28 | 27 | 5 | 5 | 0 | 0 | 0 | 0 | 20 | 20 |
| Antoni Maria | 21/3/87 | 3(12) | 3(12) | 0 | 0 | 0 | 0 | 0 | 0 | 0 | 0 |
| Michael McIlorum | 10/1/88 | 15 | 13 | 2 | 2 | 0 | 0 | 0 | 0 | 8 | 8 |
| David Mead | 4/11/88 | 19 | 17 | 6 | 4 | 0 | 0 | 0 | 0 | 24 | 16 |
| Sam Moa | 14/6/86 | 20 | 18 | 0 | 0 | 0 | 0 | 0 | 0 | 0 | 0 |
| Arthur Mourgue | 2/5/99 | 1 | 1 | 1 | 1 | 0 | 0 | 0 | 0 | 4 | 4 |
| Arthur Romano | 17/8/97 | 14 | 13 | 3 | 3 | 0 | 0 | 0 | 0 | 12 | 12 |
| Mickael Simon | 2/4/87 | 12(11) | 11(11) | 0 | 0 | 0 | 0 | 0 | 0 | 0 | 0 |
| Matty Smith | 23/7/87 | 16 | 16 | 0 | 0 | 0 | 0 | 1 | 1 | 1 | 1 |
| Lewis Tierney | 20/10/94 | 22 | 21 | 11 | 9 | 0 | 0 | 0 | 0 | 44 | 36 |
| Sam Tomkins | 23/3/89 | 26 | 24 | 9 | 9 | 77 | 76 | 1 | 1 | 191 | 189 |
| Matt Whitley | 20/1/96 | 24(3) | 23(2) | 8 | 6 | 0 | 0 | 0 | 0 | 32 | 24 |
| Brayden Wiliame | 17/12/92 | 27 | 25 | 14 | 10 | 0 | 0 | 0 | 0 | 56 | 40 |
| Fouad Yaha | 19/8/96 | 17 | 15 | 15 | 13 | 0 | 0 | 0 | 0 | 60 | 52 |

*'SL' totals include regular season only; 'All' totals also include Challenge Cup*

Sam Tomkins

**LEAGUE RECORD**
P29-W13-D0-L16
(7th)
F553, A745, Diff-192
26 points.

**CHALLENGE CUP**
Quarter Finalists

**ATTENDANCES**
Best - v Wigan (SL - 31,555)
Worst - v Doncaster (CC - 3,466)
Total (SL only) - 112,035
Average (SL only) - 8,618
(Up by 473 on 2018)

**1st November 2018 -** Fijian winger Akuila Uate signs from Manly Sea Eagles on three-year deal.

**3rd November 2018 -** Danny Brough leaves to join Wakefield. Scott Grix returns as assistant coach.

**14th November 2018 -** Jake Mamo leaves to join Warrington Wolves.

**11th December 2018 -** assistant coach Chris Thorman leaves the club.

**28th December 2018 -** 20-year-old half-back Oliver Russell joins Leigh on season-long loan deal.

**11th January 2019 -** Willie Poching joins as assistant coach.

**11th January 2019 -** Joe Wardle returns on loan from Castleford with view to permanent signing. Jordan Rankin heads other way.

**13th January 2019 -** 56-12 home win over Bradford in Michael Lawrence Testimonial.

**14th January 2019 -** hooker Adam O'Brien signs three-year contract extension until end of 2022 season.

**22nd January 2019 -** 28-24 defeat at Wakefield in final friendly.

**29th January 2019 -** prop Daniel Smith joins Featherstone on initial month's loan.

**1st February 2019 -** Ukuma Ta'ai misses 34-14 home round-one defeat to Salford due to visa problems. Halfback Izaac Farrell makes debut.

**9th February 2019 -** 27-10 defeat at Catalans.

**22nd February 2019 -** Jermaine McGillvary, Ukuma Ta'ai and Lee Gaskell return in 32-20 home defeat by Warrington.

**28th February 2019 -** halfback Tom Holmes joins former club Featherstone on loan as he recovers from pre-season knee surgery.

**3rd March 2019 -** 28-8 home defeat to Hull FC.

**8th March 2019 -** 14-6 round-five win at Wigan is first of season.

**14th March 2019 -** 40-12 home defeat to unbeaten St Helens.

**22nd March 2019 -** Kruise Leeming scores two tries in commanding 42-8 home win over Hull KR.

**27th March 2019 -** prop Daniel Smith leaves to join Castleford.

**31st March 2019 -** Akuila Uate scores try-double in 38-26 win at London Broncos.

**5th April 2019 -** Oliver Russell plays first game of season as late Danny Brough field goal means 17-16 defeat at Wakefield.

**11th April 2019 -** Izaac Farrell joins Workington on one-month's loan.

**11th April 2019 -** Alex Mellor scores hat-trick in 20-18 home win over Castleford.

**15th April 2019 -** Darnell McIntosh signs new two-year contract to end of 2021.

**19th April 2019 -** 38-18 Good Friday defeat at Leeds after trailing 30-0 at half-time.

**22nd April 2019 -** Jermaine McGillvary scores two tries in last-gasp 24-19 home, Easter Monday victory over London Broncos

**28th April 2019 -** 50-19 defeat at Warrington after leading 19-12 at half-time.

# KEY DATES

**2nd May 2019 -** Scott Grix joins Halifax on initial one-month loan.

**3rd May 2019 -** late penalty goal means 26-25 home defeat to Wakefield.

**12th May 2019 -** Challenge Cup sixth-round exit after 22-16 home defeat by St Helens.

**17th May 2019 -** 30-22 home win over Hull KR ends three-match losing run.

**20th May 2019 -** utility Chester Butler signs from Halifax on three-year deal from 2020

**25th May 2019 -** comprehensive 55-2 Magic Weekend win over Hull FC.

**30th May 2019 -** halfback Izaac Farrell released.

**7th June 2019 -** Peter Mata'utia field goal means golden point 27-26, rain-swept defeat at Castleford despite Lee Gaskell hat-trick.

**14th June 2019 -** Academy winger Dominic Young makes debut in rainy 38-2 defeat at St Helens.

**21st June 2019 -** 38-22 home defeat to Wigan.

**28th June 2019 -** captain Leroy Cudjoe returns after 10-month injury absence in 36-10 defeat at Wakefield.

**4th July 2019 -** Oliver Wilson makes Super League debut and Tom Holmes club debut in stunning Thursday night 36-18 TV win at Salford.

**12th July 2019 -** late comeback not enough in 32-28 home defeat to Catalans.

**19th July 2019 -** 18-12 win at Hull KR keeps Giants two points clear of relegation spot.

**2nd August 2019 -** Jermaine McGillvary makes 300th club appearance in 44-0 home hammering by Leeds.

**5th August 2019 -** Dale Ferguson leaves the club.

**11th August 2019 -** 32-12 defeat at Salford.

**18th August 2019 -** 24-0 home defeat by Castleford leaves Giants level bottom.

**30th August 2019 -** Louis Senior and Matt Frawley score late tries to gain 22-12 win at Hull FC.

**6th September 2019 -** 48-6 defeat at St Helens leaves Giants level bottom with one round to go.

**13th September 2019 -** Louis Senior scores four tries in 24-22 home win over Catalans that secures Super League status.

**20th September 2019 -** forward Kenny Edwards signs from Catalans on three-year deal.

**3rd October 2019 -** Joe Wardle agrees further one-year loan deal from Castleford.

**14th October 2019 -** Leeds fullback Ashton Golding signs on three-year deal.

**16th October 2019 -** Samoan International prop James Gavet signs from Newcastle Knights on two-year deal.

## CLUB RECORDS

**Highest score:**
142-4 v Blackpool, 26/11/94
**Highest score against:**
12-94 v Castleford, 18/9/88
**Record attendance:**
32,912 v Wigan, 4/3/50 *(Fartown)*
15,629 v Leeds, 10/2/2008
*(McAlpine/Galpharm/
John Smith's Stadium)*

## MATCH RECORDS

**Tries:**
10 Lionel Cooper v Keighley, 17/11/51
**Goals:** 18 Major Holland
v Swinton Park, 28/2/1914
**Points:** 39 Major Holland
v Swinton Park, 28/2/1914

## SEASON RECORDS

**Tries:** 80 Albert Rosenfeld 1913-14
**Goals:** 156 *(inc 2fg)* Danny Brough 2013
**Points:** 346 Danny Brough 2013

## CAREER RECORDS

**Tries:** 420 Lionel Cooper 1947-55
**Goals:** 958 Frank Dyson 1949-63
**Points:** 2,072 Frank Dyson 1949-63
**Appearances:** 485 Douglas Clark 1909-29

# HUDDERSFIELD GIANTS

| DATE | FIXTURE | RESULT | SCORERS | LGE | ATT |
|------|---------|--------|---------|-----|-----|
| 1/2/19 | Salford (h) | L14-34 | t:Uate,Leeming g:Farrell(3) | 10th | 5,387 |
| 9/2/19 | Catalans Dragons (a) | L27-10 | t:Frawley,Roberts g:Farrell | 11th | 9,211 |
| 22/2/19 | Warrington (h) | L20-32 | t:McGillvary,English,Turner,Uate g:Gaskell(2) | 12th | 6,076 |
| 3/3/19 | Hull FC (h) | L8-28 | t:McIntosh g:Russell(2) | 12th | 6,390 |
| 8/3/19 | Wigan (a) | W6-14 | t:Leeming,Joe Wardle g:Gaskell(3) | 12th | 10,114 |
| 14/3/19 | St Helens (h) | L12-40 | t:McGillvary,Turner g:Gaskell(2) | 12th | 4,495 |
| 22/3/19 | Hull KR (h) | W42-8 | t:Leeming(2),Roberts,McIntosh,McGillvary(2),Matagi g:Gaskell(7) | 11th | 5,289 |
| 31/3/19 | London Broncos (a) | W26-38 | t:Joe Wardle,Turner,Uate(2),McGillvary,Ikahihifo,Mellor g:Gaskell(5) | 9th | 1,419 |
| 5/4/19 | Wakefield (a) | L17-16 | t:McGillvary,McIntosh(2) g:Russell(2) | 10th | 4,730 |
| 11/4/19 | Castleford (h) | W20-18 | t:Mellor(3) g:McIntosh(4) | 8th | 4,684 |
| 19/4/19 | Leeds (a) | L38-18 | t:Uate,O'Brien,McIntosh g:Russell(3) | 8th | 13,743 |
| 22/4/19 | London Broncos (h) | W24-19 | t:Mellor,Grix,McGillvary(2) g:Russell(4) | 8th | 4,464 |
| 28/4/19 | Warrington (a) | L50-19 | t:L Senior,McIntosh,Mellor g:Russell(3) fg:Russell | 9th | 10,445 |
| 3/5/19 | Wakefield (h) | L25-26 | t:Frawley,McGillvary(2),O'Brien g:Russell(4) fg:Russell | 9th | 5,104 |
| 12/5/19 | St Helens (h) (CCR6) | L16-22 | t:Joe Wardle(2),Murphy g:Gaskell(2) | N/A | 3,533 |
| 17/5/19 | Hull KR (h) | W30-22 | t:McGillvary(2),I Senior,Joe Wardle,Jake Wardle,Leeming g:Russell(2),Gaskell | 9th | 4,621 |
| 25/5/19 | Hull FC (MW) ● | W55-2 | t:Joe Wardle,Jake Wardle,O'Brien(2),McIntosh(2),Mellor, McGillvary(2),Murphy g:Russell(7) fg:Russell | 8th | N/A |
| 7/6/19 | Castleford (a) | L27-26 (aet) | t:Gaskell(3),Joe Wardle g:Russell(5) | 9th | 7,483 |
| 14/6/19 | St Helens (a) | L38-2 | g:Russell | 9th | 9,527 |
| 21/6/19 | Wigan (h) | L22-38 | t:Hewitt,Frawley,L Senior,Turner g:Gaskell(3) | 9th | 5,578 |
| 28/6/19 | Wakefield (a) | L36-10 | t:Mellor,L Senior g:Gaskell | 10th | 4,846 |
| 4/7/19 | Salford (a) | W18-36 | t:English,I Senior,McIntosh(2),Leeming,Ta'ai,Jake Wardle g:Gaskell,McIntosh(3) | 10th | 2,368 |
| 12/7/19 | Catalans Dragons (h) | L28-32 | t:I Senior(2),Jake Wardle,McIntosh,Gaskell g:Jake Wardle(4) | 9th | 4,383 |
| 19/7/19 | Hull KR (a) | W12-18 | t:English,Mellor,McGillvary g:McIntosh(3) | 8th | 7,733 |
| 2/8/19 | Leeds (h) | L0-44 | | 10th | 6,809 |
| 11/8/19 | Salford (h) | L32-12 | t:McIntosh,Russell g:Russell(2) | 10th | 3,032 |
| 18/8/19 | Castleford (h) | L0-24 | | 10th | 4,636 |
| 30/8/19 | Hull FC (a) | W12-22 | t:McGillvary,Murphy,L Senior,Frawley g:Gaskell(3) | 10th | 10,114 |
| 6/9/19 | St Helens (a) | L48-6 | t:Lawrence g:Russell | 10th | 9,560 |
| 13/9/19 | Catalans Dragons (h) | W24-22 | t:L Senior(4),McGillvary g:Jake Wardle,Gaskell | 10th | 5,242 |

● *Played at Anfield, Liverpool*

| | | APP | | TRIES | | GOALS | | FG | | PTS | |
|---|---|---|---|---|---|---|---|---|---|---|---|
| | D.O.B. | ALL | SL | ALL | SL | ALL | SL | ALL | SL | ALL | SL |
| Chester Butler | 10/3/95 | (1) | (1) | 0 | 0 | 0 | 0 | 0 | 0 | 0 | 0 |
| Paul Clough | 27/9/87 | 10(6) | 9(6) | 0 | 0 | 0 | 0 | 0 | 0 | 0 | 0 |
| Leroy Cudjoe | 7/4/88 | 1 | 1 | 0 | 0 | 0 | 0 | 0 | 0 | 0 | 0 |
| Matty English | 14/11/97 | 14(6) | 13(6) | 3 | 3 | 0 | 0 | 0 | 0 | 12 | 12 |
| Izaac Farrell | 30/1/98 | 2 | 2 | 0 | 0 | 4 | 4 | 0 | 0 | 8 | 8 |
| Dale Ferguson | 13/4/88 | (1) | (1) | 0 | 0 | 0 | 0 | 0 | 0 | 0 | 0 |
| Matt Frawley | 24/12/94 | 20(2) | 19(2) | 4 | 4 | 0 | 0 | 0 | 0 | 16 | 16 |
| Lee Gaskell | 28/10/90 | 21 | 20 | 4 | 4 | 31 | 29 | 0 | 0 | 78 | 74 |
| Scott Grix | 1/5/84 | 4 | 4 | 1 | 1 | 0 | 0 | 0 | 0 | 4 | 4 |
| Sam Hewitt | 29/4/99 | 5(8) | 5(7) | 1 | 1 | 0 | 0 | 0 | 0 | 4 | 4 |
| Tom Holmes | 2/3/96 | 6 | 6 | 0 | 0 | 0 | 0 | 0 | 0 | 0 | 0 |
| Sebastine Ikahihifo | 27/1/91 | 8(10) | 8(10) | 1 | 1 | 0 | 0 | 0 | 0 | 4 | 4 |
| Jon Luke Kirby | 23/9/98 | (3) | (3) | 0 | 0 | 0 | 0 | 0 | 0 | 0 | 0 |
| Michael Lawrence | 12/4/90 | 18(8) | 18(8) | 1 | 1 | 0 | 0 | 0 | 0 | 4 | 4 |
| Kruise Leeming | 7/9/95 | 14(15) | 14(14) | 6 | 6 | 0 | 0 | 0 | 0 | 24 | 24 |
| Suaia Matagi | 23/3/88 | 22(7) | 21(7) | 1 | 1 | 0 | 0 | 0 | 0 | 4 | 4 |
| Jermaine McGillvary | 16/5/88 | 24 | 24 | 17 | 17 | 0 | 0 | 0 | 0 | 68 | 68 |
| Darnell McIntosh | 5/7/97 | 29 | 28 | 12 | 12 | 10 | 10 | 0 | 0 | 68 | 68 |
| Alex Mellor | 24/9/94 | 27 | 26 | 9 | 9 | 0 | 0 | 0 | 0 | 36 | 36 |
| Aaron Murphy | 26/11/88 | 18(4) | 17(4) | 3 | 2 | 0 | 0 | 0 | 0 | 12 | 8 |
| Adam O'Brien | 11/7/93 | 16(11) | 15(11) | 4 | 4 | 0 | 0 | 0 | 0 | 16 | 16 |
| Oliver Roberts | 24/12/94 | 2(12) | 2(11) | 2 | 2 | 0 | 0 | 0 | 0 | 8 | 8 |
| Colton Roche | 23/6/93 | (1) | (1) | 0 | 0 | 0 | 0 | 0 | 0 | 0 | 0 |
| Oliver Russell | 21/9/98 | 13 | 13 | 1 | 1 | 36 | 36 | 3 | 3 | 79 | 79 |
| Innes Senior | 30/5/00 | 18 | 17 | 4 | 4 | 0 | 0 | 0 | 0 | 16 | 16 |
| Louis Senior | 30/5/00 | 13 | 12 | 8 | 8 | 0 | 0 | 0 | 0 | 32 | 32 |
| Ukuma Ta'ai | 17/1/87 | 15(13) | 15(12) | 1 | 1 | 0 | 0 | 0 | 0 | 4 | 4 |
| Jordan Turner | 9/1/89 | 20 | 19 | 4 | 4 | 0 | 0 | 0 | 0 | 16 | 16 |
| Akuila Uate | 6/10/87 | 12 | 12 | 5 | 5 | 0 | 0 | 0 | 0 | 20 | 20 |
| Adam Walne | 3/10/90 | 3(4) | 3(4) | 0 | 0 | 0 | 0 | 0 | 0 | 0 | 0 |
| Jake Wardle | 18/11/98 | 18 | 18 | 4 | 4 | 5 | 5 | 0 | 0 | 26 | 26 |
| Joe Wardle | 22/9/91 | 16 | 15 | 7 | 5 | 0 | 0 | 0 | 0 | 28 | 20 |
| Oliver Wilson | 22/3/99 | (8) | (8) | 0 | 0 | 0 | 0 | 0 | 0 | 0 | 0 |
| Dominic Young | 9/8/01 | 1 | 1 | 0 | 0 | 0 | 0 | 0 | 0 | 0 | 0 |

Darnell McIntosh

**LEAGUE RECORD**
P29-W11-D0-L18
(10th)
F571, A776, Diff-205
22 points.

**CHALLENGE CUP**
Round Six

**ATTENDANCES**
Best - v Leeds (SL - 6,809)
Worst - v St Helens (CC - 3,533)
Total (SL only) - 73,158
Average (SL only) - 5,226
(Down by 245 on 2018)

*'SL' totals include regular season only; 'All' totals also include Challenge Cup*

# Super League XXIV - Club by Club

**HULL F.C.**
Est. 1865

## KEY DATES

**2nd November 2018 -** Jordan Abdull joins London Broncos for undisclosed fee.

**19th December 2018 -** 19-year-old winger Andrew Bulman granted permission to return home to Cumbria and join Whitehaven.

**6th January 2019 -** 18-year-old rugby union convert winger Charlie Graham scores hat-trick in 72-12 friendly win over Doncaster.

**19th January 2019 -** 28-18 friendly defeat at St Helens.

**30th January 2019 -** prop Lewis Bienek joins Batley on loan.

**1st February 2019 -** last-second 18-16 round-one defeat at Hull KR.

**7th February 2019 -** 26-18 home defeat to Castleford. Matty Dawson-Jones suffers season-ending ACL injury in training. Scott Taylor gets three games for two dangerous contact offences.

**22nd February 2019 -** Fijian winger Ratu Naulago signs one-year deal after gaining temporary release from British Army.

**24th February 2019 -** Marc Sneyd field goal seals 23-22 win at Wigan in first golden-point decider in Super League. Ratu Naulago scores two tries on professional debut as Gareth Ellis comes out of retirement.

**3rd March 2019 -** Albert Kelly returns in 28-8 win at Huddersfield. Jake Connor suffers knee injury.

**8th March 2019 -** 34-10 home win over Leeds is third on a row.

**10th March 2019 -** former St Helens and Warrington backrower Andre Savelio signs from Brisbane Broncos until end of 2021 season.

**15th March 2019 -** 32-12 home defeat by Wakefield ends winning run.

**24th March 2019 -** Jamie Shaul suffers concussion in 28-24 win at London Broncos.

**29th March 2019 -** 63-12 home humiliation by Warrington.

**4th April 2019 -** Hakim Miloudi joins Toronto Wolfpack on initial one-month loan, then signs permanently.

**7th April 2019 -** fullback Connor Wynne makes debut as Josh Griffin scores hat-trick in 23-16 win at Salford.

**9th April 2019 -** winger Fetuli Talanoa retires because of injuries.

**11th April 2019 -** Danny Langtree leaves the club.

**13th April 2019 -** second golden-point Marc Sneyd field goal of season seals 31-30 win at Catalans.

**16th April 2019 -** Marc Sneyd signs three-year contract extension to end of 2022 season.

**19th April 2019 -** Jack Logan scores hat-trick in record 56-12 home Good Friday win over Hull KR.

**22nd April 2019 -** 62-16 Easter Monday defeat at St Helens.

**28th April 2019 -** Joe Westerman scores two tries in 30-14 home win over Wakefield.

**3rd May 2019 -** halfbacks Albert Kelly and Marc Sneyd out for 37-6 home defeat by Catalans.

**11th May 2019 -** 28-12 home sixth round Challenge Cup win over Castleford.

**16th May 2019 -** halfback Liam Harris joins York on season-long loan.

**18th May 2019 -** Jamie Shaul returns after two months out with concussion in 19-12 win at Warrington.

**20th May 2019 -** Salford Red Devils second-rower Josh Jones signs on two-year deal from 2020.

**25th May 2019 -** Josh Bowden returns after a year out with ACL injury in 55-2 Magic Weekend defeat to Huddersfield at Anfield.

**29th May 2019 -** St Helens winger Adam Swift signs on two-year deal from 2020.

**30th May 2019 -** Ratu Naulago scores brace in 51-8 Challenge Cup quarter-final win over Catalans.

**7th June 2019 -** 35-32 home win over Salford. Josh Griffin sent off for spear tackle and gets one-match penalty notice.

**10th June 2019 -** Jordan Thompson rejoins Leigh Centurions with immediate effect.

**13th June 2019 -** Albert Kelly scores hat-trick in 31-18 comeback victory at Castleford.

**18th June 2019 -** young centre Cameron Scott joins York on loan.

**22nd June 2019 -** Josh Griffin stars in back row in 50-10 win at Catalans.

**24th June 2019 -** winger Bureta Faraimo signs two-year contract extension to end of 2021

**25th June 2019 -** Mahe Fonua returns from Wests Tigers on three-year deal from 2020.

**27th June 2019 -** Mark Minichiello makes 400th career appearance in 18-10 defeat at Hull KR. Joe Westerman dislocates knee and plays on.

**4th July 2019 -** winger Ratu Naulago signs to end of 2020 as club exercises one-year extension clause.

**5th July 2019 -** Gareth Ellis returns from ankle injury in 40-12 loss at St Helens.

**7th July 2019 -** Parramatta backrower Manu Ma'u signs for 2020 on two-year deal.

**21st July 2019 -** late Ratu Naulago try ensures 26-24 win at Leeds, the first for 12 years.

**27th July 2019 -** 22-14 Challenge Cup semi-final defeat to Warrington at Bolton.

**29th July 2019 -** Dean Hadley and Jez Litten join Hull KR with immediate effect.

**31st July 2019 -** Mark Minichiello to retire at end of season.

**1st August 2019 -** England Academy International outside back Joel Speed signs from City of Hull Academy.

**1st August 2019 -** late Zak Hardaker field goal means 15-14 home defeat to Wigan.

**6th August 2019 -** prop Chris Green goes to Wakefield on loan to end of season.

**7th August 2019 -** NZ Warriors forward Tevita Satae joins with immediate effect to end of 2021.

**9th August 2019 -** hooker Jordan Johnstone signs from Widnes Vikings on three-year deal from 2020.

**11th August 2019 -** Ratu Naulago scores try-double in 26-16 win at Wakefield.

**15th August 2019 -** NZ Warriors forward Ligi Sao signs two-year deal from 2020.

**17th August 2019 -** Tevita Satae makes debut in 44-22 home defeat to Salford.

**29th August 2019 -** Sika Manu to retire at end of season.

**30th August 2019 -** 22-12 home defeat to Huddersfield.

**5th September 2019 -** 44-12 defeat at Castleford sees Hull drop to sixth in table.

**14th September 2019 -** 22-6 home defeat by St Helens means sixth-place finish.

**14th September 2019 -** Mickey Paea, Mark Minichiello and Sika Manu retire and head back to Australia.

**20th September 2019 -** Danny Washbrook joins York.

**5th October 2019 -** Kieron Purtill joins as Attacking and Emerging Talent coach.

**12th October 2019 -** prop Chris Green signs permanently for Wakefield.

**18th October 2019 -** utility forward Joe Cator joins from Leigh on two-year deal. Gareth Ellis signs one-year playing contract.

## CLUB RECORDS

**Highest score:** 88-0 v Sheffield, 2/3/2003
**Highest score against:**
10-80 v Warrington, 30/8/2018
**Record attendance:**
28,798 v Leeds, 7/3/36 *(The Boulevard)*
23,004 v Hull KR, 2/9/2007 *(KC Stadium)*

## MATCH RECORDS

**Tries:** 7 Clive Sullivan v Doncaster, 15/4/68
**Goals:** 14 Jim Kennedy v Rochdale, 7/4/21
Sammy Lloyd v Oldham, 10/9/78
Matt Crowther v Sheffield, 2/3/2003
**Points:** 36 Jim Kennedy v Keighley, 29/1/21

## SEASON RECORDS

**Tries:** 52 Jack Harrison 1914-15
**Goals:** 170 Sammy Lloyd 1978-79
**Points:** 369 Sammy Lloyd 1978-79

## CAREER RECORDS

**Tries:** 250 Clive Sullivan 1961-74; 1981-85
**Goals:** 687 Joe Oliver 1928-37; 1943-45
**Points:** 1,842 Joe Oliver 1928-37; 1943-45
**Appearances:** 500 Edward Rogers 1906-25

**HULL F.C.**

**HULL F.C.**

| DATE | FIXTURE | RESULT | SCORERS | LGE | ATT |
|------|---------|--------|---------|-----|-----|
| 1/2/19 | Hull KR (a) | L18-16 | t:Manu,Dawson-Jones,Faraimo g:Sneyd(2) | 7th | 12,100 |
| 7/2/19 | Castleford (h) | L18-26 | t:Westerman,Connor,Lane g:Sneyd(3) | 9th | 11,244 |
| 24/2/19 | Wigan (a) | W22-23 *(aet)* | t:Tuimavave,Westerman,Naulago(2) g:Sneyd(3) fg:Sneyd | 6th | 10,971 |
| 3/3/19 | Huddersfield (a) | W8-28 | t:Westerman(2),Naulago,Griffin(2) g:Sneyd(4) | 5th | 6,390 |
| 8/3/19 | Leeds (h) | W34-10 | t:Naulago,Matongo,Sneyd,Shaul,Kelly,Hadley g:Sneyd(5) | 5th | 12,208 |
| 15/3/19 | Wakefield (h) | L12-32 | t:Houghton,Faraimo g:Sneyd(2) | 6th | 11,190 |
| 24/3/19 | London Broncos (a) | W24-28 | t:Griffin(2),Tuimavave,Thompson,Kelly,Faraimo g:Sneyd(2) | 5th | 2,257 |
| 29/3/19 | Warrington (h) | L12-63 | t:Kelly,Lane g:Sneyd(2) | 5th | 10,810 |
| 7/4/19 | Salford (a) | W16-23 | t:Griffin(3) g:Sneyd(5) fg:Sneyd | 6th | 3,609 |
| 13/4/19 | Catalans Dragons (a) | W30-31 *(aet)* | t:Brown,Wynne,Griffin(2),Faraimo g:Sneyd(5) fg:Sneyd | 5th | 8,220 |
| 19/4/19 | Hull KR (h) | W56-12 | t:Connor,Logan(3),Minichiello,Westerman,Kelly,Paea,Wynne g:Sneyd(10) | 4th | 20,044 |
| 22/4/19 | St Helens (a) | L62-16 | t:Westerman,Tuimavave,Litten g:Sneyd(2) | 5th | 11,268 |
| 28/4/19 | Wakefield (h) | W30-14 | t:Kelly,Wynne,Westerman(2) g:Sneyd(7) | 3rd | 10,254 |
| 3/5/19 | Catalans Dragons (h) | L6-37 | t:Paea g:Connor | 5th | 9,830 |
| 10/5/19 | Castleford (h) (CCR6) | W28-12 | t:Connor,Faraimo,Kelly,Minichiello g:Sneyd(6) | N/A | 6,230 |
| 18/5/19 | Warrington (a) | W12-19 | t:Paea,Taylor,Kelly g:Sneyd(3) fg:Sneyd | 4th | 10,600 |
| 25/5/19 | Huddersfield (MW) ● | L55-2 | g:Sneyd | 4th | N/A |
| 30/5/19 | Catalans Dragons (h) (CCQF) | W51-8 | t:Connor,Faraimo,Manu,Naulago(2),Kelly,Shaul,Houghton g:Sneyd(9) fg:Sneyd | N/A | 4,832 |
| 7/6/19 | Salford (h) | W35-32 | t:Kelly(2),Connor,Minichiello,Shaul,Naulago g:Sneyd(5) fg:Sneyd | 4th | 9,914 |
| 13/6/19 | Castleford (a) | W18-31 | t:Naulago(2),Kelly(3) g:Sneyd(5) fg:Sneyd | 3rd | 6,344 |
| 22/6/19 | Catalans Dragons (a) | W10-50 | t:Kelly,Westerman,Savelio,Griffin(2),Buchanan,Naulago,Shaul g:Sneyd(9) | 3rd | 10,254 |
| 27/6/19 | Hull KR (a) | L18-10 | t:Faraimo,Savelio g:Sneyd | 3rd | 10,221 |
| 5/7/19 | St Helens (h) | L12-40 | t:Shaul,Naulago g:Sneyd(2) | 3rd | 11,311 |
| 11/7/19 | London Broncos (h) | W35-22 | t:Tuimavave,Faraimo,Westerman,Connor,Griffin,Naulago g:Sneyd(5) fg:Sneyd | 3rd | 11,401 |
| 21/7/19 | Leeds (a) | W24-26 | t:Manu,Faraimo,Shaul,Naulago g:Sneyd(5) | 3rd | 13,351 |
| 27/7/19 | Warrington (CCSF) ●● | L14-22 | t:Faraimo,Taylor g:Sneyd(3) | N/A | 24,364 |
| 1/8/19 | Wigan (h) | L14-15 | t:Taylor g:Sneyd(5) | 3rd | 10,153 |
| 11/8/19 | Wakefield (a) | W16-26 | t:Faraimo,Tuimavave,Sneyd,Naulago(2) g:Sneyd(3) | 3rd | 5,600 |
| 17/8/19 | Salford (a) | L22-44 | t:Taylor,Paea,Faraimo,Lane g:Sneyd(3) | 4th | 11,217 |
| 30/8/19 | Huddersfield (h) | L12-22 | t:Shaul,Faraimo g:Sneyd(2) | 5th | 10,114 |
| 5/9/19 | Castleford (a) | L44-12 | t:Matongo,Logan g:Sneyd(2) | 6th | 6,712 |
| 13/9/19 | St Helens (h) | L6-22 | t:Taylor g:Sneyd | 6th | 11,004 |

● *Played at Anfield, Liverpool*  ●● *Played at University of Bolton Stadium*

| | | APP | | TRIES | | GOALS | | FG | | PTS | |
|---|---|---|---|---|---|---|---|---|---|---|---|
| | D.O.B. | ALL | SL | ALL | SL | ALL | SL | ALL | SL | ALL | SL |
| Josh Bowden | 14/1/92 | (14) | (12) | 0 | 0 | 0 | 0 | 0 | 0 | 0 | 0 |
| Jack Brown | 25/6/00 | (2) | (2) | 1 | 1 | 0 | 0 | 0 | 0 | 4 | 4 |
| Kieran Buchanan | 26/1/98 | 6(1) | 6(1) | 1 | 0 | 0 | 0 | 0 | 0 | 4 | 4 |
| Jake Connor | 18/10/94 | 23(3) | 21(2) | 6 | 4 | 1 | 1 | 0 | 0 | 26 | 18 |
| Matty Dawson-Jones | 2/10/90 | 1 | 1 | 1 | 1 | 0 | 0 | 0 | 0 | 4 | 4 |
| Gareth Ellis | 3/5/81 | 9(11) | 9(9) | 0 | 0 | 0 | 0 | 0 | 0 | 0 | 0 |
| Bureta Faraimo | 16/7/90 | 28 | 25 | 13 | 10 | 0 | 0 | 0 | 0 | 52 | 40 |
| Brad Fash | 24/1/96 | (19) | (17) | 0 | 0 | 0 | 0 | 0 | 0 | 0 | 0 |
| Chris Green | 3/1/90 | 6(7) | 5(6) | 0 | 0 | 0 | 0 | 0 | 0 | 0 | 0 |
| Josh Griffin | 9/5/90 | 29 | 26 | 12 | 12 | 0 | 0 | 0 | 0 | 48 | 48 |
| Dean Hadley | 5/8/92 | 8(8) | 8(6) | 1 | 1 | 0 | 0 | 0 | 0 | 4 | 4 |
| Danny Houghton | 25/9/88 | 29 | 26 | 1 | 1 | 0 | 0 | 0 | 0 | 4 | 4 |
| Albert Kelly | 21/3/91 | 20(2) | 17(2) | 14 | 12 | 0 | 0 | 0 | 0 | 56 | 48 |
| Jordan Lane | 20/10/97 | 7(9) | 6(9) | 3 | 3 | 0 | 0 | 0 | 0 | 12 | 12 |
| Jez Litten | 10/3/98 | (6) | (6) | 1 | 1 | 0 | 0 | 0 | 0 | 4 | 4 |
| Jack Logan | 8/9/95 | 8 | 7 | 4 | 4 | 0 | 0 | 0 | 0 | 16 | 16 |
| Sika Manu | 22/1/87 | 23(2) | 21(2) | 3 | 2 | 0 | 0 | 0 | 0 | 12 | 8 |
| Masi Matongo | 15/5/96 | 9(9) | 9(8) | 2 | 2 | 0 | 0 | 0 | 0 | 8 | 8 |
| Hakim Miloudi | 26/6/93 | 2 | 2 | 0 | 0 | 0 | 0 | 0 | 0 | 0 | 0 |
| Mark Minichiello | 30/1/82 | 26(1) | 23(1) | 3 | 2 | 0 | 0 | 0 | 0 | 12 | 8 |
| Ratu Naulago | 8/6/91 | 23 | 20 | 15 | 13 | 0 | 0 | 0 | 0 | 60 | 52 |
| Levy Nzoungou | 22/1/98 | (1) | (1) | 0 | 0 | 0 | 0 | 0 | 0 | 0 | 0 |
| Mickey Paea | 25/3/86 | 24(2) | 21(2) | 4 | 4 | 0 | 0 | 0 | 0 | 16 | 16 |
| Tevita Satae | 22/10/92 | 1(3) | 1(3) | 0 | 0 | 0 | 0 | 0 | 0 | 0 | 0 |
| Andre Savelio | 21/3/95 | (7) | (6) | 2 | 2 | 0 | 0 | 0 | 0 | 8 | 8 |
| Cameron Scott | 7/10/99 | 1 | 1 | 0 | 0 | 0 | 0 | 0 | 0 | 0 | 0 |
| Jamie Shaul | 1/7/92 | 23 | 21 | 7 | 6 | 0 | 0 | 0 | 0 | 28 | 24 |
| Marc Sneyd | 9/2/91 | 31 | 28 | 2 | 2 | 122 | 104 | 8 | 7 | 260 | 223 |
| Scott Taylor | 27/2/91 | 22(5) | 20(5) | 5 | 4 | 0 | 0 | 0 | 0 | 20 | 16 |
| Jordan Thompson | 4/9/91 | 2(10) | 2(10) | 1 | 1 | 0 | 0 | 0 | 0 | 4 | 4 |
| Carlos Tuimavave | 10/1/92 | 23(1) | 22(1) | 5 | 5 | 0 | 0 | 0 | 0 | 20 | 20 |
| Danny Washbrook | 18/9/85 | 3(3) | 3(3) | 0 | 0 | 0 | 0 | 0 | 0 | 0 | 0 |
| Joe Westerman | 15/11/89 | 24(2) | 21(2) | 10 | 10 | 0 | 0 | 0 | 0 | 40 | 40 |
| Connor Wynne | 15/1/01 | 5 | 5 | 3 | 3 | 0 | 0 | 0 | 0 | 12 | 12 |

*'SL' totals include regular season only; 'All' totals also include Challenge Cup*

Ratu Naulago

**LEAGUE RECORD**
P29-W15-D0-L14
(6th)
F645, A768, Diff-123
30 points.

**CHALLENGE CUP**
Semi-Finalists

**ATTENDANCES**
Best - v Hull KR (SL - 20,044)
Worst - v Catalans (CC - 4,832)
Total (SL only) - 160,694
Average (SL only) - 11,478
(Down by 376 on 2018)

**13th November 2018 -** prop Mitch Garbutt joins from Leeds Rhinos on three-year deal.

**15th November 2018 -** North Queensland Cowboys' Scotland international centre/backrower Kane Linnett joins on three-year deal,

**24th November 2018 -** Joel Tomkins signs three-year contract extension until end of 2021 season.

**28th December 2018 -** Australian halfback Josh Drinkwater joins on one-year deal.

**11th January 2019 -** Shaun Lunt steps down from captaincy as he recovers from viral illness. Joel Tomkins takes up role.

**25th January 2019 -** prop Josh Johnson released.

**1st February 2019 -** last-gasp Jimmy Keinhorst try secures 18-16 home opening round win over Hull FC.

**9th February 2019 -** 28-14 round-two defeat at Warrington.

**17th February 2019 -** Mitch Garbutt scores twice in hard-fought 22-12 home win over London Broncos.

**1st March 2019 -** Mose Masoe scores two tries in 32-16 defeat at Castleford as captain Joel Tomkins stands down awaiting hearing of disciplinary tribunal. Ryan Lannon damages ankle ligaments.

**6th March 2019 -** captain Joel Tomkins banned for two matches for questioning integrity of match official.

**11th March 2019 -** late Danny McGuire try seals 10-6 win at Wakefield. James Greenwood suffers ACL injury.

**22nd March 2019 -** Shaun Lunt returns from illness in 42-8 defeat at Huddersfield.

**29th March 2019 -** injury-hit side falls to 36-24 defeat at unbeaten league leaders St Helens.

**4th April 2019 -** Craig Hall stars as first-half blitz sets up 45-26 home win over Leeds.

**11th April 2019 -** two tries in final ten minutes secure 14-10 home Challenge Cup fifth-round win over Leigh.

**19th April 2019 -** record 56-12 Good Friday defeat at Hull FC.

**25th April 2019 -** Antoni Maria joins from Catalans on one month loan.

**11th May 2019 -** 32-18 sixth round Challenge Cup win at Salford.

**20th May 2019 -** props Nick Scruton and Lee Jewitt released.

**20th May 2019 -** Danny McGuire to become head of recruitment in 2020.

**22nd May 2019 -** centre Thomas Minns to return on expiration of doping ban on July 15th. Halfback Mikey Lewis joins Newcastle on loan.

**26th May 2019 -** late Ryan Shaw penalty goal secures 22-20 Magic Weekend win over Salford at Anfield. Joel Tomkins gets one game for crusher tackle.

**31st May 2019 -** Challenge Cup quarter-final exit after 28-22 home defeat by Warrington.

**5th June 2019 -** coach Tim Sheens leaves with immediate effect.

**6th June 2019 -** former Great Britain boss Tony Smith appointed head coach to end of season.

# KEY DATES

**15th June 2019 -** Adam Quinlan returns after nine-month injury absence and scores 76th minute winner in 16-14 home victory over Warrington.

**15th June 2019 -** Warrington backrower Luis Johnson joins on month's loan.

**16th June 2019 -** Craig Hall signs contract extension until end of 2020

**17th June 2019 -** Harvey Livett joins from Warrington on loan. Month-long loan swap deal sees Ryan Lannon returning to Salford with Daniel Murray joining Rovers.

**20th June 2019 -** 26-24 defeat at London Broncos after leading 18-8.

**25th June 2019 -** Junior Vaivai joins Toulouse.

**26th June 2019 -** Leeds hooker Matt Parcell joins on loan until end of 2019 with Shaun Lunt going the other way. Will Dagger joins Featherstone on loan.

**27th June 2019 -** late Matt Parcell try on debut seals 18-10 home win over Hull FC.

**12th July 2019 -** Danny McGuire inspires 32-16 victory at Leeds on 400th Super League appearance. Matt Parcell suffers shoulder injury.

**24th July 2019 -** Tommy Lee announces immediate retirement.

**28th July 2019 -** Hull FC duo Dean Hadley and Jez Litten sign three-year contracts to end of 2022 and arrive on loan until end of season

**4th August 2019 -** Danny McGuire golden-point field goal secures 27-26 home win over Castleford.

**5th August 2019 -** Dewsbury forward Kyle Trout arrives for rest of season.

**8th August 2019 -** centre Thomas Minns released from short-term contract by mutual consent after suffering foot injury in training.

**18th August 2019 -** 38-10 home defeat by Wakefield sinks Robins to equal bottom after London win at Catalans. Adam Quinlan suffers adductor injury.

**31st August 2019 -** head coach Tony Smith signs three-year contract to end of 2022.

**31st August 2019 -** Ryan Shaw kicks six goals in 24-6 win at Catalans.

**4th September 2019 -** Josh Drinkwater, Chris Atkin and James Greenwood to leave at end of season.

**6th September 2019 -** late Jay Pitts try means 20-16 home defeat to London as Robins go into last round level with three other teams at bottom of table.

**9th September 2019 -** captain Joel Tomkins banned for one game for punching, increased to two games on 'frivolous' appeal.

**13th September 2019 -** 17-16 last-round golden-point defeat at Salford, but London defeat at Wakefield secures Super League status.

**16th September 2019 -** Utility forward Danny Addy joins Leigh. Ryan Shaw leaves for Leeds rugby union club.

**18th September 2019 -** captain Joel Tomkins released on compassionate grounds and signs for Catalans.

**19th September 2019 -** threequarter Shaun Kenny-Dowall signs from Newcastle on two-year contract.

**23rd September 2019 -** stand-off Jason Abdull signs from London Broncos on two-year contract.

**26th September 2019 -** Bradford winger Ethan Ryan signs two-year deal.

**30th September 2019 -** utility Harvey Livett pens season-long loan from Warrington for 2020.

**4th October 2019 -** backrower Matty Gee signs from London on one-year deal.

**10th October 2019 -** Willie Poching joins as assistant coach as departure of James Webster announced.

**10th October 2019 -** centre Greg Minikin signs from Castleford on two-year contract.

**11th October 2019 -** Craig Hall joins Featherstone on season-long loan.

**11th October 2019 -** 18 year-old halfback Mikey Lewis signs until end of 2023 season.

**12th October 2019 -** prop Will Maher signs from Castleford on two-year contract.

**13th October 2019 -** winger Nick Rawsthorne signs from Toronto on two-year contract.

**14th October 2019 -** prop Kyle Trout signs one-year contract.

**30th October 2019 -** loanee Matt Parcell signs one-year contract.

## CLUB RECORDS

**Highest score:**
100-6 v Nottingham City, 19/8/90
**Highest score against:**
6-84 v Wigan, 1/4/2013
**Record attendance:**
27,670 v Hull FC, 3/4/53 *(Boothferry Park)*
12,100 v Hull FC, 1/2/2019 *(Craven Park)*

## MATCH RECORDS

**Tries:** 11 George West
v Brooklands Rovers, 4/3/1905
**Goals:**
14 Alf Carmichael v Merthyr, 8/10/1910
Mike Fletcher v Whitehaven, 18/3/90
Colin Armstrong v Nottingham City, 19/8/90
Damien Couturier v Halifax, 23/4/2006
**Points:** 53 George West
v Brooklands Rovers, 4/3/1905

## SEASON RECORDS

**Tries:** 45 Gary Prohm 1984-85
**Goals:** 199 Mike Fletcher 1989-90
**Points:** 450 Mike Fletcher 1989-90

## CAREER RECORDS

**Tries:** 207 Roger Millward 1966-80
**Goals:** 1,268 Mike Fletcher 1987-98
**Points:** 2,760 Mike Fletcher 1987-98
**Appearances:** 489 Mike Smith 1975-91

# HULL KINGSTON ROVERS

| DATE | FIXTURE | RESULT | SCORERS | LGE | ATT |
|---|---|---|---|---|---|
| 1/2/19 | Hull FC (h) | W18-16 | t:Tomkins,Garbutt,Keinhorst g:Drinkwater(3) | 6th | 12,100 |
| 9/2/19 | Warrington (a) | L28-14 | t:Crooks,Hall,Keinhorst g:Drinkwater | 7th | 10,515 |
| 17/2/19 | London Broncos (h) | W22-12 | t:Linnett,Garbutt(2),Hall g:Drinkwater,Hall(2) | 5th | 7,210 |
| 23/2/19 | Salford (h) | L22-24 | t:Hauraki,Hall,Lawler,Keinhorst g:Shaw(3) | 5th | 7,565 |
| 1/3/19 | Castleford (a) | L32-16 | t:Masoe(2),Atkin g:Shaw(2) | 8th | 8,770 |
| 10/3/19 | Wakefield (a) | W6-10 | t:McGuire g:Hall(3) | 6th | 5,559 |
| 17/3/19 | Catalans Dragons (h) | L16-18 | t:Hauraki,Tomkins,Hall g:Hall(2) | 7th | 7,203 |
| 22/3/19 | Huddersfield (a) | L42-8 | t:Hauraki g:Shaw(2) | 8th | 5,289 |
| 29/3/19 | St Helens (a) | L36-24 | t:Linnett(2),Oakes,Lunt g:Shaw(4) | 10th | 10,003 |
| 4/4/19 | Leeds (h) | W45-26 | t:Lee,McGuire,Oakes,Garbutt,Vaivai,Drinkwater,Crooks g:Hall(8) fg:McGuire | 8th | 8,292 |
| 11/4/19 | Leigh (h) (CCR5) | W14-10 | t:Keinhorst,Shaw,Hall g:Shaw | N/A | 2,188 |
| 19/4/19 | Hull FC (a) | L56-12 | t:Keinhorst,Hall g:Hall(2) | 9th | 20,044 |
| 22/4/19 | Warrington (h) | L6-54 | t:Crooks g:Hall | 10th | 7,111 |
| 28/4/19 | Leeds (a) | L28-24 | t:Crooks(2),Linnett,Hauraki g:Shaw(3),McGuire | 11th | 11,694 |
| 5/5/19 | St Helens (a) | L26-42 | t:Addy,Shaw,Keinhorst,Oakes g:Shaw(5) | 11th | 8,123 |
| 11/5/19 | Salford (a) (CCR6) | W18-32 | t:Linnett,Drinkwater,Vaivai,Addy,Hauraki g:Shaw(6) | N/A | 1,842 |
| 17/5/19 | Huddersfield (a) | L30-22 | t:Vaivai,Tomkins,Hall,Addy g:Shaw(3) | 11th | 4,621 |
| 26/5/19 | Salford (MW) ● | W22-20 | t:Linnett,Hall(2) g:Shaw(5) | 11th | N/A |
| 31/5/19 | Warrington (h) (CCQF) | L22-28 | t:Crooks,Drinkwater(2),Hall g:Shaw(3) | N/A | 3,311 |
| 9/6/19 | Wigan (h) | L18-19 | t:Keinhorst,Dagger,Lannon g:Shaw(3) | 11th | 8,010 |
| 15/6/19 | Warrington (h) | W16-14 | t:Masoe,Quinlan g:Shaw(4) | 11th | 7,390 |
| 20/6/19 | London Broncos (a) | L26-24 | t:Hauraki,Quinlan,Atkin,Drinkwater g:Shaw(4) | 12th | 1,503 |
| 27/6/19 | Hull FC (a) | W18-10 | t:Crooks,Tomkins,Parcell g:Shaw(3) | 11th | 10,221 |
| 5/7/19 | Wigan (a) | L52-10 | t:Quinlan(2) g:Shaw | 11th | 11,042 |
| 12/7/19 | Leeds (a) | W16-32 | t:Parcell,Linnett(2),Quinlan,Livett,Hall g:Hall(3),Drinkwater | 11th | 13,679 |
| 19/7/19 | Huddersfield (h) | L12-18 | t:Linnett,Hall g:Hall(2) | 11th | 7,733 |
| 4/8/19 | Castleford (h) | W27-26 (aet) | t:Hall,Quinlan,Crooks(2) g:Shaw(5) fg:McGuire | 11th | 8,004 |
| 9/8/19 | Wigan (a) | L36-18 | t:Shaw,Crooks,Drinkwater g:Shaw(3) | 11th | 10,702 |
| 18/8/19 | Wakefield (h) | L10-38 | t:Crooks,Garbutt g:Shaw | 11th | 8,095 |
| 31/8/19 | Catalans Dragons (a) | W6-24 | t:Shaw(2),McGuire g:Shaw(6) | 11th | 8,315 |
| 6/9/19 | London Broncos (h) | L16-20 | t:Dagger,Atkin,McGuire g:Shaw(2) | 11th | 8,020 |
| 13/9/19 | Salford (a) | L17-16 (aet) | t:Drinkwater,Linnett g:Shaw(4) | 11th | 5,393 |

● *Played at Anfield, Liverpool*

|  | | APP | | TRIES | | GOALS | | FG | | PTS | |
|---|---|---|---|---|---|---|---|---|---|---|---|
|  | D.O.B. | ALL | SL | ALL | SL | ALL | SL | ALL | SL | ALL | SL |
| Danny Addy | 15/1/91 | 11(11) | 9(10) | 3 | 2 | 0 | 0 | 0 | 0 | 12 | 8 |
| Chris Atkin | 7/2/93 | 11(18) | 11(15) | 3 | 3 | 0 | 0 | 0 | 0 | 12 | 12 |
| Harry Bardle | 18/6/00 | (1) | (1) | 0 | 0 | 0 | 0 | 0 | 0 | 0 | 0 |
| Ben Crooks | 15/6/93 | 27 | 24 | 11 | 10 | 0 | 0 | 0 | 0 | 44 | 40 |
| Will Dagger | 21/2/99 | 12 | 11 | 2 | 2 | 0 | 0 | 0 | 0 | 8 | 8 |
| Josh Drinkwater | 15/6/92 | 32 | 29 | 7 | 4 | 6 | 6 | 0 | 0 | 40 | 28 |
| Mitch Garbutt | 18/4/89 | 2(18) | 2(17) | 5 | 5 | 0 | 0 | 0 | 0 | 20 | 20 |
| James Greenwood | 17/6/91 | 1(4) | 1(4) | 0 | 0 | 0 | 0 | 0 | 0 | 0 | 0 |
| Dean Hadley | 5/8/92 | 5(1) | 5(1) | 0 | 0 | 0 | 0 | 0 | 0 | 0 | 0 |
| Craig Hall | 21/2/88 | 30 | 27 | 13 | 11 | 23 | 23 | 0 | 0 | 98 | 90 |
| Owen Harrison | 10/4/99 | 3(5) | 2(4) | 0 | 0 | 0 | 0 | 0 | 0 | 0 | 0 |
| Weller Hauraki | 18/2/85 | 27(5) | 25(4) | 6 | 5 | 0 | 0 | 0 | 0 | 24 | 20 |
| Lee Jewitt | 14/2/87 | 3 | 3 | 0 | 0 | 0 | 0 | 0 | 0 | 0 | 0 |
| Luis Johnson | 20/2/99 | 4 | 4 | 0 | 0 | 0 | 0 | 0 | 0 | 0 | 0 |
| Jimmy Keinhorst | 14/7/90 | 25(3) | 22(3) | 7 | 6 | 0 | 0 | 0 | 0 | 28 | 24 |
| Ryan Lannon | 11/1/96 | 1(7) | 1(5) | 1 | 1 | 0 | 0 | 0 | 0 | 4 | 4 |
| George Lawler | 1/9/95 | 25(1) | 22(1) | 1 | 1 | 0 | 0 | 0 | 0 | 4 | 4 |
| Tommy Lee | 1/2/88 | 10(4) | 9(4) | 1 | 1 | 0 | 0 | 0 | 0 | 4 | 4 |
| Mikey Lewis | 4/7/01 | 1 | 1 | 0 | 0 | 0 | 0 | 0 | 0 | 0 | 0 |
| Kane Linnett | 11/1/89 | 26(1) | 23(1) | 10 | 9 | 0 | 0 | 0 | 0 | 40 | 36 |
| Jez Litten | 10/3/98 | (4) | (4) | 0 | 0 | 0 | 0 | 0 | 0 | 0 | 0 |
| Harvey Livett | 4/1/97 | 1(3) | 1(3) | 1 | 1 | 0 | 0 | 0 | 0 | 4 | 4 |
| Shaun Lunt | 15/4/86 | 1(6) | 1(6) | 1 | 1 | 0 | 0 | 0 | 0 | 4 | 4 |
| Antoni Maria | 21/3/87 | 3(3) | 2(3) | 0 | 0 | 0 | 0 | 0 | 0 | 0 | 0 |
| Mose Masoe | 17/5/89 | 18(7) | 17(7) | 3 | 3 | 0 | 0 | 0 | 0 | 12 | 12 |
| Danny McGuire | 6/12/82 | 25 | 22 | 4 | 4 | 1 | 1 | 2 | 2 | 20 | 20 |
| Robbie Mulhern | 18/10/94 | 20(6) | 17(6) | 0 | 0 | 0 | 0 | 0 | 0 | 0 | 0 |
| Daniel Murray | 21/3/96 | 9(2) | 9(2) | 0 | 0 | 0 | 0 | 0 | 0 | 0 | 0 |
| Will Oakes | 27/2/99 | 7 | 7 | 3 | 3 | 0 | 0 | 0 | 0 | 12 | 12 |
| Matt Parcell | 30/10/92 | 5 | 5 | 2 | 2 | 0 | 0 | 0 | 0 | 8 | 8 |
| Adam Quinlan | 13/11/92 | 10 | 10 | 6 | 6 | 0 | 0 | 0 | 0 | 24 | 24 |
| Adam Rooks | 15/1/99 | (5) | (4) | 0 | 0 | 0 | 0 | 0 | 0 | 0 | 0 |
| Ryan Shaw | 27/2/92 | 22 | 19 | 5 | 4 | 73 | 63 | 0 | 0 | 166 | 142 |
| Joel Tomkins | 21/3/87 | 26 | 24 | 4 | 4 | 0 | 0 | 0 | 0 | 16 | 16 |
| Kyle Trout | 1/3/91 | 1(4) | 1(4) | 0 | 0 | 0 | 0 | 0 | 0 | 0 | 0 |
| Junior Vaivai | 18/1/90 | 12(2) | 11(1) | 3 | 2 | 0 | 0 | 0 | 0 | 12 | 8 |

Josh Drinkwater

*'SL' totals include regular season only; 'All' totals also include Challenge Cup*

**LEAGUE RECORD**
P29-W10-D0-L19
(11th)
F548, A768, Diff-220
20 points.

**CHALLENGE CUP**
Quarter Finalists

**ATTENDANCES**
Best - v Hull FC (SL - 12,100)
Worst - v Leigh (CC - 2,188)
Total (SL only) - 115,077
Average (SL only) - 8,220
(Up by 347 on 2018)

**28th September 2018 -** Joel Moon retires and returns to Australia.

**13th November 2018 -** Mitch Garbutt joins Hull KR.

**15th November 2018 -** prop Trent Merrin joins from Penrith Panthers as marquee signing on four-year contract.

**16th November 2018 -** Jamie Jones-Buchanan, one season, and Carl Ablett, two years, agree new deals. Winger Luke Briscoe, 24, commits to three-year contract.

**7th December 2018 -** James Donaldson, released by Hull KR, joins on pre-season trial.

**12th December 2018 -** prop Mikolaj Oledzki, 20, agrees new four-year contract to end of 2022 season.

**14th December 2018 -** Jamie Peacock returns to Headingley with commercial sales department.

**26th December 2018 -** Tui Lolohea stars in 10-4 Wetherby Whaler Challenge win over Wakefield.

**8th January 2019 -** James Donaldson signs one-year contract.

**9th January 2019 -** England Academy forward Muizz Mustapha signs new two-year contract.

**21st January 2019 -** Kallum Watkins returns from injury in 26-24 home friendly defeat to Castleford.

**2nd February 2019 -** 26-6 opening-round defeat at Warrington.

**7th February 2019 -** forwards Josh Walters and Jack Ormondroyd join Featherstone Rovers with immediate effect.

**8th February 2019 -** 34-16 defeat at Wigan.

**16th February 2019 -** prop Anthony Mullally joins former head coach Brian McDermott at Toronto Wolfpack.

**17th February 2019 -** Jack Walker scores hat-trick in 46-14 win at unbeaten Salford.

**22nd February 2019 -** 27-22 defeat at St Helens after leading 22-10 at half-time. Stevie Ward suffers knee injury which requires surgery.

**1st March 2019 -** Widnes Academy forwards Sam Walters and Jarrod O'Connor sign for undisclosed fees.

**23rd March 2019 -** Ash Handley scores hat-trick in 26-22 defeat at Catalans as Tui Lolohea is dropped. Brett Ferres sin-binned and banned for two games for use of knees.

**29th March 2019 -** PNG and former Widnes prop Wellington Albert arrives on month's trial.

**29th March 2019 -** golden-point Brad Dwyer field goal secures 21-20 home win over Castleford to end five-match losing run.

**4th April 2019 -** Konrad Hurrell scores four tries in 45-26 defeat at Hull KR.

**7th April 2019 -** assistant coach James Lowes leaves the club.

**10th April 2019 -** Cronulla Sharks prop Ava Seumanufagai joins on two-and-a-half-year contract.

**12th April 2019 -** Callum McLelland, Owen Trout and Muizz Mustapha make debuts in 78-6 home Challenge Cup fifth round win over League 1 Workington.

# KEY DATES

**19th April 2019 -** 38-18 home, sun-baked Good Friday win over Huddersfield lifts Rhinos off foot of table.

**22nd April 2019 -** Matt Parcell scores two tries in 26-24 Easter Monday defeat at Wakefield.

**3rd May 2019 -** Ava Seumanufagai makes debut in 28-16 defeat at Salford.

**7th May 2019 -** head coach David Furner leaves with immediate effect after 14 games in the post. Assistant coach Richard Agar takes charge on interim basis.

**11th May 2019 -** sixth-round Challenge Cup exit after 24-22 defeat at Championship Bradford.

**16th May 2019 -** 30-8 home defeat by Castleford as new North Stand opens.

**28th May 2019 -** 24-22 Magic Weekend win over London after leading 24-10.

**29th May 2019 -** halfback Jordan Lilley to join Bradford on permanent two-year deal from 2020 after 18-month loan spell.

**3rd June 2019 -** captain Kallum Watkins to leave Rhinos at end of season

**5th June 2019 -** 24-year-old Huddersfield backrower Alex Mellor signs for 2020 on three-year contract.

**6th June 2019 -** fullback Jack Walker signs new five-year contract to end of 2023.

**7th June 2019 -** hooker Brad Dwyer signs one-year contract extension for 2020.

**7th June 2019 -** 10-0 win at rain-soaked Wakefield.

**14th June 2019 -** Kallum Watkins to join Gold Coast Titans from 1st July.

**26th June 2019 -** hooker Shaun Lunt returns from Hull KR for remainder of 2019 season with Matt Parcell going the other way.

**26th June 2019 -** Salford halfback Robert Lui joins on loan for remainder of 2019 season and agrees two year contract from 2020. Tui Lolohea moves in opposite direction.

**30th June 2019 -** PNG second row Rhyse Martin signs from Canterbury-Bankstown Bulldogs on two-and-a-half year contract.

**30th June 2019 -** Trent Merrin captains side as 31-12 home victory over Catalans moves Rhinos off bottom of table.

**5th July 2019 -** Rhyse Martin makes debut in 18-10 win at Castleford.

**12th July 2019 -** Danny McGuire on his 400th Super League appearance inspires Hull KR to 32-16 win at Headingley. Shaun Lunt makes second debut.

**14th July 2019 -** 19-year-old centre Harry Newman signs new three-year deal to end of 2022.

**1st August 2019 -** Wellington Albert goes to Featherstone on loan.

**2nd August 2019 -** Konrad Hurrell and Ash Handley, in his 100th club game, each score twice in 44-0 win at Huddersfield. Tom Briscoe suffers knee injury.

**8th August 2019 -** Ash Handley signs new four-year contract to end of 2023 season.

**9th August 2019 -** 48-8 home hammering of Catalans despite 50th-minute send off of Brad Singleton. Singleton gets two-match ban.

**15th August 2019 -** Ash Handley scores two tries as winning run ends at three with 36-20 home defeat to St Helens.

**1st September 2019 -** Jack Walker scores two tries in 36-10 win at London Broncos.

**6th September 2019 -** 20-12 home defeat by Salford.

**9th September 2019 -** Richard Agar appointed permanent head coach for 2020 on rolling twelve-month contract.

**10th September 2019 -** Carl Ablett announces retirement.

**12th September 2019 -** forward James Donaldson agrees new two-year contract to end of 2021.

**13th September 2019 -** hooker Corey Johnson makes debut and Jamie Jones-Buchanan plays last game in 26-4 home final-round win over Warrington, meaning eighth-placed finish.

**1st October 2019 -** Castleford halfback Luke Gale signs three-year contract for undisclosed transfer fee.

**15th October 2019 -** Matt Parcell joins Hull KR on permanent deal.

**21st October 2019 -** Rhinos fined £20,000, half suspended for two years, for salary cap breaches in 2018.

## CLUB RECORDS

**Highest score:**
106-10 v Swinton, 11/2/2001
**Highest score against:**
6-74 v Wigan, 20/5/92
**Record attendance:**
40,175 v Bradford, 21/5/47

## MATCH RECORDS

**Tries:**
8 Fred Webster v Coventry, 12/4/1913
Eric Harris v Bradford, 14/9/31
**Goals:**
17 Iestyn Harris v Swinton, 11/2/2001
**Points:**
42 Iestyn Harris v Huddersfield, 16/7/99

## SEASON RECORDS

**Tries:** 63 Eric Harris 1935-36
**Goals:** 173 *(inc 5fg)* Kevin Sinfield 2012
**Points:** 431 Lewis Jones 1956-57

## CAREER RECORDS

**Tries:** 391 Eric Harris 1930-39
**Goals:**
1,831 *(inc 39fg)* Kevin Sinfield 1997-2015
**Points:** 3,967 Kevin Sinfield 1997-2015
**Appearances:** 625 John Holmes 1968-89

# *LEEDS RHINOS*

| DATE | FIXTURE | RESULT | SCORERS | LGE | ATT |
|------|---------|--------|---------|-----|-----|
| 2/2/19 | Warrington (a) | L26-6 | t:Ward g:Lolohea | 11th | 13,098 |
| 8/2/19 | Wigan (a) | L34-16 | t:Handley,Ferres,Watkins g:Lolohea(2) | 12th | 11,230 |
| 17/2/19 | Salford (a) | W14-46 | t:Cuthbertson,Walker(3),Hurrell(2),Parcell,Handley g:Lolohea(7) | 7th | 4,385 |
| 22/2/19 | St Helens (a) | L27-22 | t:Watkins,Hurrell,Handley,Oledzki g:Lolohea(3) | 8th | 11,318 |
| 1/3/19 | Wakefield (h) | L18-35 | t:Handley(2),T Briscoe(2) g:Lolohea | 10th | 13,148 |
| 8/3/19 | Hull FC (a) | L34-10 | t:Newman,T Briscoe g:Lolohea | 11th | 12,208 |
| 15/3/19 | London Broncos (h) | L16-18 | t:Myler,Merrin,T Briscoe g:Lolohea(2) | 11th | 11,229 |
| 23/3/19 | Catalans Dragons (a) | L26-22 | t:Handley(3),Hurrell g:L Sutcliffe(3) | 12th | 8,220 |
| 28/3/19 | Castleford (h) | W21-20 (aet) | t:Hurrell,Handley,L Sutcliffe,Merrin g:L Sutcliffe,Smith fg:Dwyer | 12th | 12,295 |
| 4/4/19 | Hull KR (a) | L45-26 | t:Hurrell(4),Singleton g:L Sutcliffe(3) | 12th | 8,292 |
| 12/4/19 | Workington (h) (CCR5) | W78-6 | t:L Briscoe,Golding(2),Newman(4),Albert,Myler(3),Ferres,Parcell g:L Sutcliffe(13) | N/A | 4,197 |
| 19/4/19 | Huddersfield (h) | W38-18 | t:Lolohea,Donaldson,Dwyer,Myler,T Briscoe,Handley g:L Sutcliffe(6),Lolohea | 11th | 13,743 |
| 22/4/19 | Wakefield (a) | L26-24 | t:L Sutcliffe,Ferres,Parcell(2) g:L Sutcliffe(4) | 11th | 6,785 |
| 28/4/19 | Hull KR (h) | W28-24 | t:Handley(2),T Briscoe,Walker,Parcell g:L Sutcliffe(4) | 10th | 11,694 |
| 3/5/19 | Salford (a) | L28-16 | t:Oledzki,Newman,Handley g:L Sutcliffe(2) | 10th | 3,368 |
| 11/5/19 | Bradford (a) (CCR6) | L24-22 | t:Lolohea,McLelland,Newman,T Briscoe g:L Sutcliffe(3) | N/A | 10,256 |
| 16/5/19 | Castleford (h) | L8-30 | t:Parcell g:L Sutcliffe(2) | 10th | 13,286 |
| 26/5/19 | London Broncos (MW) ● | W24-22 | t:L Sutcliffe,Handley,Walker,Newman,Myler g:L Sutcliffe(2) | 10th | N/A |
| 7/6/19 | Wakefield (a) | W0-10 | t:Lolohea g:L Sutcliffe(3) | 10th | 5,489 |
| 14/6/19 | Wigan (h) | L14-23 | t:Cuthbertson,Merrin g:L Sutcliffe(2),Lolohea | 10th | 13,105 |
| 21/6/19 | St Helens (a) | L36-10 | t:Dwyer,L Briscoe g:L Sutcliffe | 11th | 11,448 |
| 30/6/19 | Catalans Dragons (h) | W31-12 | t:Cuthbertson,T Briscoe,Singleton,Hurrell,Walker g:L Sutcliffe(5) fg:Myler | 9th | 12,638 |
| 5/7/19 | Castleford (a) | W10-18 | t:Merrin,Walker,Lui g:L Sutcliffe(3) | 9th | 8,147 |
| 12/7/19 | Hull KR (h) | L16-32 | t:Dwyer,L Sutcliffe,Hurrell,Martin | 10th | 13,679 |
| 21/7/19 | Hull FC (h) | L24-26 | t:Hurrell,T Briscoe(2),Handley g:Martin(4) | 10th | 13,351 |
| 2/8/19 | Huddersfield (a) | W0-44 | t:Cuthbertson,T Briscoe,Hurrell(2),Dwyer,Handley(2),L Sutcliffe g:Martin(6) | 8th | 6,809 |
| 9/8/19 | Catalans Dragons (h) | W48-8 | t:Handley(2),Martin,Myler(2),Lui,L Briscoe g:Martin(10) | 8th | 11,336 |
| 15/8/19 | St Helens (a) | L20-36 | t:Myler,Handley(2),Newman g:Martin(2) | 8th | 12,153 |
| 1/9/19 | London Broncos (a) | W10-36 | t:L Briscoe,Seumanufagai,Walker(2),Handley,Dwyer g:Martin(6) | 8th | 3,051 |
| 6/9/19 | Salford (h) | L12-20 | t:Myler,Jones-Buchanan g:Martin(2) | 8th | 12,436 |
| 13/9/19 | Warrington (h) | W26-4 | t:L Sutcliffe,Lui,Cuthbertson,L Briscoe g:Martin(4),Jones-Buchanan | 8th | 14,085 |

● *Played at Anfield, Liverpool*

|  |  | APP | | TRIES | | GOALS | | FG | | PTS | |
|--|----|-----|----|-------|----|-------|----|----|----|-----|----|
|  | D.O.B. | ALL | SL | ALL | SL | ALL | SL | ALL | SL | ALL | SL |
| Wellington Albert | 3/9/93 | 3(3) | 2(2) | 1 | 0 | 0 | 0 | 0 | 0 | 4 | 0 |
| Luke Briscoe | 11/3/94 | 7 | 6 | 5 | 4 | 0 | 0 | 0 | 0 | 20 | 16 |
| Tom Briscoe | 19/3/90 | 25 | 24 | 11 | 10 | 0 | 0 | 0 | 0 | 44 | 40 |
| Adam Cuthbertson | 24/2/85 | 10(13) | 10(12) | 5 | 5 | 0 | 0 | 0 | 0 | 20 | 20 |
| James Donaldson | 14/9/91 | 3(22) | 2(22) | 1 | 1 | 0 | 0 | 0 | 0 | 4 | 4 |
| Brad Dwyer | 28/4/93 | 21(8) | 20(8) | 5 | 5 | 0 | 0 | 1 | 1 | 21 | 21 |
| Brett Ferres | 17/4/86 | 20(2) | 19(2) | 3 | 2 | 0 | 0 | 0 | 0 | 12 | 8 |
| Ashton Golding | 4/9/96 | 1 | 0 | 2 | 0 | 0 | 0 | 0 | 0 | 8 | 0 |
| Ash Handley | 16/2/96 | 29 | 28 | 22 | 22 | 0 | 0 | 0 | 0 | 88 | 88 |
| Tom Holroyd | 9/2/01 | (3) | (3) | 0 | 0 | 0 | 0 | 0 | 0 | 0 | 0 |
| Konrad Hurrell | 5/8/91 | 25 | 24 | 14 | 14 | 0 | 0 | 0 | 0 | 56 | 56 |
| Corey Johnson | 16/11/00 | (1) | (1) | 0 | 0 | 0 | 0 | 0 | 0 | 0 | 0 |
| Jamie Jones-Buchanan | 1/8/81 | 4(5) | 4(4) | 1 | 1 | 1 | 1 | 0 | 0 | 6 | 6 |
| Tuimoala Lolohea | 23/1/95 | 17 | 15 | 3 | 2 | 19 | 19 | 0 | 0 | 50 | 46 |
| Robert Lui | 23/2/90 | 10 | 10 | 3 | 3 | 0 | 0 | 0 | 0 | 12 | 12 |
| Shaun Lunt | 15/4/86 | 5(1) | 5(1) | 0 | 0 | 0 | 0 | 0 | 0 | 0 | 0 |
| Rhyse Martin | 1/3/93 | 8(1) | 8(1) | 2 | 2 | 34 | 34 | 0 | 0 | 76 | 76 |
| Callum McLelland | 16/9/99 | 2(1) | 1 | 1 | 0 | 0 | 0 | 0 | 0 | 4 | 0 |
| Trent Merrin | 7/10/89 | 28 | 27 | 4 | 4 | 0 | 0 | 0 | 0 | 16 | 16 |
| Muizz Mustapha | 3/4/00 | (1) | 0 | 0 | 0 | 0 | 0 | 0 | 0 | 0 | 0 |
| Richie Myler | 21/5/90 | 28 | 27 | 10 | 7 | 0 | 0 | 1 | 1 | 41 | 29 |
| Harry Newman | 19/2/00 | 22 | 20 | 9 | 4 | 0 | 0 | 0 | 0 | 36 | 16 |
| Mikolaj Oledzki | 8/11/98 | 9(12) | 9(11) | 2 | 2 | 0 | 0 | 0 | 0 | 8 | 8 |
| Matt Parcell | 30/10/92 | 5(12) | 4(11) | 6 | 5 | 0 | 0 | 0 | 0 | 24 | 20 |
| Nathaniel Peteru | 1/1/92 | 15(4) | 14(3) | 0 | 0 | 0 | 0 | 0 | 0 | 0 | 0 |
| Ava Seumanufagai | 4/6/91 | 13(2) | 12(2) | 1 | 1 | 0 | 0 | 0 | 0 | 4 | 4 |
| Brad Singleton | 29/10/92 | 9(15) | 8(15) | 2 | 2 | 0 | 0 | 0 | 0 | 8 | 8 |
| Cameron Smith | 7/11/98 | 10(10) | 9(10) | 0 | 0 | 1 | 1 | 0 | 0 | 2 | 2 |
| Alex Sutcliffe | 21/1/99 | (1) | (1) | 0 | 0 | 0 | 0 | 0 | 0 | 0 | 0 |
| Liam Sutcliffe | 25/11/94 | 26(4) | 24(4) | 6 | 6 | 57 | 41 | 0 | 0 | 138 | 106 |
| Owen Trout | 15/10/99 | 2(1) | 1(1) | 0 | 0 | 0 | 0 | 0 | 0 | 0 | 0 |
| Jack Walker | 8/8/99 | 22 | 22 | 9 | 9 | 0 | 0 | 0 | 0 | 36 | 36 |
| Stevie Ward | 17/11/93 | 5(1) | 5(1) | 1 | 1 | 0 | 0 | 0 | 0 | 4 | 4 |
| Kallum Watkins | 12/3/91 | 19 | 17 | 2 | 2 | 0 | 0 | 0 | 0 | 8 | 8 |

*'SL' totals include regular season only; 'All' totals also include Challenge Cup*

Konrad Hurrell

**LEAGUE RECORD**
P29-W12-D0-L17
(8th)
F650, A644, Diff+6
24 points.

**CHALLENGE CUP**
Round Six

**ATTENDANCES**
Best - v Warrington (SL - 14,085)
Worst - v Workington (CC - 4,197)
Total (SL only) - 178,178
Average (SL only) - 12,727
(Up by 375 on 2018)

**30th September 2018** - 4-2 Million Pound Game win in Toronto secures return to Super League.

**26th October 2018** - 23-year-old halfback Matty Fozard joins on two-year deal from Sheffield Eagles. James Cunningham and Elliot Kear sign one-year deals.

**29th October 2018** - 25-year-old prop Nathan Mason joins from Huddersfield on two-year contract. Eloi Pelissier signs one-year deal.

**31st October 2018** - former St Helens prop Greg Richards joins on two-year contract. Young Academy hooker, Elmbridge Eagles product Matt Davies and 19-year-old threequarter Gideon Boafo, Croydon Hurricanes, sign one-year full-time contracts.

**2nd November 2018** - 22-year-old halfback Jordan Abdull signs from Hull FC on one-year deal.

**21st November 2018** - St Helens centre Ryan Morgan joins on loan for the 2019 season.

**5th December 2018** - prop Luke Yates joins from Newcastle Knights for 2019 season.

**4th January 2019** - 20-year-old halfback Morgan Smith signs from Warrington on one-year deal

**27th January 2019** - 20-0 win at Leigh in last pre-season friendly.

**3rd February 2019** - prop Eddie Battye and winger Rhys Williams score two tries each in shock 42-24 home win over Wakefield in round one.

**10th February 2019** - 24-0 round-two defeat at Salford.

**17th February 2019** - 22-12 defeat at Hull KR after leading 6-4 at half-time.

**24th February 2019** - 40-6 home defeat by Castleford.

**3 March 2019** - 18-16 comeback win from 10-0 down to stun champions Wigan at home.

**6th March 2019** - former second row Matt Davis re-joins from Warrington on one-month loan deal.

**8th March 2019** - centre Jacob Ogden makes Super League debut in 26-0 defeat at St Helens.

**15th March 2019** - Will Lovell scores in last minute to secure 18-16 win at Leeds.

**22nd March 2019** - dual registration agreement with Sheffield Eagles announced.

**24th March 2019** - 28-24 home defeat to Hull FC.

**31st March 2019** - 38-26 home defeat to Huddersfield.

**5th April 2019** - James Meadows and Matthew Davies make debuts in 48-12 defeat at Warrington.

**11th April 2019** - 24-16 fifth-round Challenge Cup exit at Championship Halifax.

**18th April 2019** - 39-6 home Easter Thursday defeat to Catalans.

**22nd April 2019** - Sam Davis makes Super League debut in 24-19 Easter Monday defeat at Huddersfield, thanks to late Jermaine McGillvary try.

**27th April 2019** - 30-10 home defeat to Salford after trailing 24-0 at half-time.

**2nd May 2019** - 18-8 defeat at Wigan after leading 8-6 at half-time.

**13th May 2019** - former prop Olsi Krasniqi signs for rest of 2019 season.

# KEY DATES

**18th May 2019** - Jordan Abdull scores four tries in 42-34 home win over Wakefield.

**26th May 2019** - 24-22 Magic Weekend defeat to Leeds at Anfield.

**9th June 2019** - golden-point field goal from Morgan Smith secures 23-22 home win over league leaders St Helens.

**16th June 2019** - Rhys Williams scores try-brace in 30-12 win at Catalans.

**20th June 2019** - Jordan Abdull stars as 26-24 home win over Hull KR makes it three in a row.

**26th June 2019** - assistant coach Jamie Langley signs two-year contract extension.

**30th June 2019** - winning run ends with 42-10 defeat at Castleford.

**6th July 2019** - 36-6 home defeat to Warrington after trailing 36-0 at half-time.

**11th July 2019** - 35-22 defeat at Hull after trailing 34-0 at half-time.

**15th July 2019** - halfback Morgan Smith signs new two-year contract

**16th July 2019** - Eloi Pelissier signs new two-year contract until 2021.

**18th July 2019** - halfback Cory Aston signs from Castleford on two-year deal.

**21st July 2019** - 32-12 home win over leaders St Helens to go equal on points with Hull KR and Leeds.

**28th July 2019** - Sydney Roosters halfback Brock Lamb signs for rest of season.

**1st August 2019** - prop Olsi Krasniqi signs new two-year deal from 2020.

**1st August 2019** - rugby union winger Guy Armitage signs with immediate effect until end of 2020.

**4th August 2019** - Brock Lamb makes debut in 58-28 home defeat to Salford after trailing 36-6 at half-time.

**10th August 2019** - 20-6 defeat at Castleford.

**13th August 2019** - former London Academy winger Tuoyo Egodo signs on two-year deal from Castleford.

**17th August 2019** - 17-4 win at Catalans moves Broncos to within two points of eleventh spot.

**30th August 2019** - London Academy product Daniel Hindmarsh signs for further two years until end of 2021.

**31st August 2019** - prop Eddie Battye signs two-year contract to end of 2021.

**1st September 2019** - 36-10 home defeat to Leeds leaves Broncos two points adrift.

**7th September 2019** - late Jay Pitts try secures 20-16 win at Hull KR to keep survival hopes alive.

**13th September 2019** - 19-10 last-round defeat at Wakefield means relegation from Super League.

**23rd September 2019** - Jordan Abdull signs for Hull KR.

**24th September 2019** - head coach Danny Ward re-signs on new two-year deal to end of 2021.

**24th September 2019** - prop forward Dan Norman signs from Widnes Vikings on two year deal.

**25th September 2019** - fullback Olly Ashall-Bott signs from Widnes Vikings on two-year deal.

**25th September 2019** - Alex Walker signs for Wakefield.

**11th October 2019** - Featherstone Rovers second rower Josh Walters joins on two-year deal.

**17th October 2019** - threequarters Elliot Kear and Rhys Williams and prop Luke Yates join Salford.

**24th October 2019** - back-rower Rhys Curran signs from Toulouse Olympique on two-year deal.

## CLUB RECORDS

**Highest score:** 82-0 v Highfield, 12/11/95
82-2 v Barrow, 20/5/2006
**Highest score against:**
6-82 v Warrington, 20/3/2011
10-82 v Warrington, 8/6/2013
**Record attendance:**
15,013 v Wakefield, 15/2/81
*(Craven Cottage)*
3,051 v Leeds, 1/9/2019
*(Trailfinders Sports Ground)*

## MATCH RECORDS

**Tries:**
5 Martin Offiah v Whitehaven, 14/3/99
Sean Morris v Batley, 13/9/2015
**Goals:**
13 Rob Purdham v Barrow, 20/5/2006
**Points:**
34 Rob Purdham v Barrow, 20/5/2006
Jarrod Sammut v Sheffield, 13/5/2018

## SEASON RECORDS

**Tries:** 43 Mark Johnson 1993-94
**Goals:** 159 John Gallagher 1993-94
**Points:** 384 John Gallagher 1993-94

## CAREER RECORDS

**Tries:**
109 Luke Dorn 2005-2006; 2009-2013
**Goals:** 309 Steve Diamond 1981-84
**Points:** 772 Paul Sykes 2001-2007
**Appearances:**
202 Steele Retchless 1998-2004

# LONDON BRONCOS

| DATE | FIXTURE | RESULT | SCORERS | LGE | ATT |
|---|---|---|---|---|---|
| 3/2/19 | Wakefield (h) | W42-24 | t:Fleming,Williams(2),Dixon,Battye(2),Fozard,Kear g:Abdull,Dixon(4) | 3rd | 2,149 |
| 10/2/19 | Salford (a) | L24-0 | | 6th | 3,246 |
| 17/2/19 | Hull KR (a) | L22-12 | t:Gee,Pitts g:Dixon(2) | 8th | 7,210 |
| 23/2/19 | Castleford (h) | L6-40 | t:Williams g:Dixon | 10th | 2,053 |
| 3/3/19 | Wigan (h) | W18-16 | t:Battye,Gee,Dixon g:Dixon(3) | 9th | 2,586 |
| 8/3/19 | St Helens (h) | L26-0 | | 9th | 9,090 |
| 15/3/19 | Leeds (a) | W16-18 | t:Pitts,Fozard,Lovell g:Dixon(3) | 9th | 11,229 |
| 24/3/19 | Hull FC (h) | L24-28 | t:Kear,Pelissier,Abdull,Williams g:Dixon(4) | 9th | 2,257 |
| 31/3/19 | Huddersfield (h) | L26-38 | t:Walker,Pitts,Williams,Dixon(2) g:Dixon(3) | 11th | 1,419 |
| 5/4/19 | Warrington (a) | L48-12 | t:Mason,Gee g:Dixon(2) | 11th | 11,718 |
| 11/4/19 | Halifax (a) (CCR5) | L24-16 | t:Ioane,Ogden(2) g:Smith(2) | N/A | 722 |
| 18/4/19 | Catalans Dragons (h) | L6-39 | t:Ioane g:Smith | 12th | 2,153 |
| 22/4/19 | Huddersfield (a) | L24-19 | t:Pitts,Williams,Morgan g:Dixon(3) fg:Smith | 12th | 4,464 |
| 27/4/19 | Salford (h) | L10-30 | t:Williams,Fleming g:Dixon | 12th | 1,133 |
| 2/5/19 | Wigan (a) | L18-8 | t:Pitts g:Dixon(2) | 12th | 9,907 |
| 18/5/19 | Wakefield (h) | W42-34 | t:Abdull(4),Williams(2),Dixon(2) g:Dixon(5) | 12th | 1,205 |
| 26/5/19 | Leeds (MW) ● | L24-22 | t:Morgan,Abdull(2),Walker g:Dixon(3) | 12th | N/A |
| 9/6/19 | St Helens (h) | W23-22 | | | |
| | | *(aet)* | t:Morgan(2),Cunningham,Pitts g:Dixon(3) fg:Smith | 12th | 2,801 |
| 15/6/19 | Catalans Dragons (a) | W12-30 | t:Abdull,Williams(2),Kear,Dixon g:Dixon(5) | 12th | 8,137 |
| 20/6/19 | Hull KR (h) | W26-24 | t:Smith,Walker,Abdull,Butler g:Dixon(5) | 10th | 1,503 |
| 30/6/19 | Castleford (a) | L42-10 | t:Dixon,Williams g:Dixon | 12th | 6,860 |
| 6/7/19 | Warrington (h) | L6-36 | t:Fozard g:Dixon | 12th | 2,357 |
| 11/7/19 | Hull FC (a) | L35-22 | t:Fleming,Abdull,Adebiyi(2) g:Dixon(3) | 12th | 11,401 |
| 21/7/19 | St Helens (h) | W32-12 | t:Fleming(2),Yates,Walker,Gee g:Dixon(6) | 12th | 2,087 |
| 4/8/19 | Salford (h) | L28-58 | t:Williams,Yates,Fleming,Adebiyi,Butler g:Dixon(4) | 12th | 1,445 |
| 10/8/19 | Castleford (a) | L20-6 | t:Lamb g:Dixon | 12th | 5,497 |
| 17/8/19 | Catalans Dragons (a) | W4-17 | t:Dixon,Walker g:Dixon(4) fg:Lamb | 12th | 7,725 |
| 1/9/19 | Leeds (h) | L10-36 | t:Dixon,Morgan g:Dixon | 12th | 3,051 |
| 6/9/19 | Hull KR (a) | W16-20 | t:Gee,Lamb,Pitts g:Dixon(4) | 12th | 8,020 |
| 13/9/19 | Wakefield (a) | L19-10 | t:Walker,Lamb g:Dixon | 12th | 6,230 |

● *Played at Anfield, Liverpool*

## APP TRIES GOALS FG PTS

| | D.O.B. | ALL | SL | ALL | SL | ALL | SL | ALL | SL | ALL | SL |
|---|---|---|---|---|---|---|---|---|---|---|---|
| Jordan Abdull | 5/2/96 | 25(3) | 25(2) | 10 | 10 | 1 | 1 | 0 | 0 | 42 | 42 |
| Sadiq Adebiyi | 8/1/97 | 6(7) | 6(7) | 3 | 3 | 0 | 0 | 0 | 0 | 12 | 12 |
| Guy Armitage | 29/11/91 | (2) | (2) | 0 | 0 | 0 | 0 | 0 | 0 | 0 | 0 |
| Eddie Battye | 24/7/91 | 19(11) | 19(10) | 3 | 3 | 0 | 0 | 0 | 0 | 12 | 12 |
| Rob Butler | 15/5/98 | 17(7) | 17(7) | 2 | 2 | 0 | 0 | 0 | 0 | 8 | 8 |
| James Cunningham | 3/4/94 | 24(2) | 24(1) | 1 | 1 | 0 | 0 | 0 | 0 | 4 | 4 |
| Matthew Davies | 9/4/98 | (1) | (1) | 0 | 0 | 0 | 0 | 0 | 0 | 0 | 0 |
| Matt Davis | 5/7/96 | 4 | 4 | 0 | 0 | 0 | 0 | 0 | 0 | 0 | 0 |
| Sam Davis | 11/11/98 | 2(1) | 2(1) | 0 | 0 | 0 | 0 | 0 | 0 | 0 | 0 |
| Kieran Dixon | 22/8/92 | 27 | 27 | 10 | 10 | 75 | 75 | 0 | 0 | 190 | 190 |
| Matty Fleming | 13/1/96 | 13(1) | 12(1) | 6 | 6 | 0 | 0 | 0 | 0 | 24 | 24 |
| Matty Fozard | 3/3/95 | 7(16) | 7(16) | 3 | 3 | 0 | 0 | 0 | 0 | 12 | 12 |
| Matty Gee | 12/12/94 | 15(8) | 14(8) | 5 | 5 | 0 | 0 | 0 | 0 | 20 | 20 |
| Ben Hellewell | 30/1/92 | 3 | 2 | 0 | 0 | 0 | 0 | 0 | 0 | 0 | 0 |
| Daniel Hindmarsh | 8/8/98 | (6) | (6) | 0 | 0 | 0 | 0 | 0 | 0 | 0 | 0 |
| Mark Ioane | 3/2/90 | 1(15) | 1(14) | 2 | 1 | 0 | 0 | 0 | 0 | 8 | 4 |
| Elliot Kear | 29/11/88 | 27 | 26 | 3 | 3 | 0 | 0 | 0 | 0 | 12 | 12 |
| Olsi Krasniqi | 26/6/92 | 8(1) | 8(1) | 0 | 0 | 0 | 0 | 0 | 0 | 0 | 0 |
| Brock Lamb | 29/1/97 | 6 | 6 | 3 | 3 | 0 | 0 | 1 | 1 | 13 | 13 |
| Will Lovell | 10/5/93 | 11(7) | 10(7) | 1 | 1 | 0 | 0 | 0 | 0 | 4 | 4 |
| Nathan Mason | 8/9/93 | 6(10) | 5(10) | 1 | 1 | 0 | 0 | 0 | 0 | 4 | 4 |
| James Meadows | 15/6/99 | 2 | 1 | 0 | 0 | 0 | 0 | 0 | 0 | 0 | 0 |
| Ryan Morgan | 4/5/90 | 22 | 21 | 5 | 5 | 0 | 0 | 0 | 0 | 20 | 20 |
| Jacob Ogden | 23/1/98 | 3 | 2 | 2 | 0 | 0 | 0 | 0 | 0 | 8 | 0 |
| Eloi Pelissier | 18/6/91 | 8(6) | 7(6) | 1 | 1 | 0 | 0 | 0 | 0 | 4 | 4 |
| Jay Pitts | 9/12/89 | 28 | 27 | 7 | 7 | 0 | 0 | 0 | 0 | 28 | 28 |
| Greg Richards | 12/7/95 | 6(15) | 5(15) | 0 | 0 | 0 | 0 | 0 | 0 | 0 | 0 |
| Morgan Smith | 30/4/98 | 16(1) | 15(1) | 1 | 1 | 3 | 1 | 2 | 2 | 12 | 8 |
| Alex Walker | 4/9/95 | 27 | 27 | 6 | 6 | 0 | 0 | 0 | 0 | 24 | 24 |
| Rhys Williams | 8/12/89 | 29 | 29 | 13 | 13 | 0 | 0 | 0 | 0 | 52 | 52 |
| Luke Yates | 6/3/95 | 28 | 28 | 2 | 2 | 0 | 0 | 0 | 0 | 8 | 8 |

*'SL' totals include regular season only; 'All' totals also include Challenge Cup*

Eddie Battye

**LEAGUE RECORD**
P29-W10-D0-L19
(12th)
F505, A787, Diff-282
20 points.

**CHALLENGE CUP**
Round Five

**ATTENDANCES**
Best - v Leeds (SL - 3,051)
Worst - v Salford (SL - 1,133)
Total (SL only) - 28,199
Average (SL only) - 2,014
(Up by 1,118 on 2018, Championship)

**5th November 2018 -** Kriss Brining released after missing 2018 season with injury, Gavin Bennion also released.

**7th November 2018 -** former Hull KR winger Ken Sio joins on three-year deal after two seasons with Newcastle Knights.

**12th November 2018 -** forwards Jansin Turgut and Adam Lawton sign for 2019 season.

**14th November 2018 -** former Widnes prop Gil Dudson joins on two-year deal.

**10th January 2019 -** prop Adam Walker signs for 2019 season at the end of ban for cocaine use.

**1st February 2019 -** Niall Evalds scores hat-trick in opening round, 34-14 win at Huddersfield.

**4th February 2019 -** Adam Lawton joins Rochdale on month's loan.

**10th February 2019 -** hard-fought 24-0 home victory over London Broncos.

**17th February 2019 -** 46-14 home defeat to Leeds.

**23rd February 2019 -** 24-22 win at Hull KR after trailing 22-8 at half-time.

**9th March 2019 -** Jake Bibby and George Griffin both score twice in commanding 46-0 win at Catalans.

**17th March 2019 -** Jake Bibby scores double in 24-20 defeat at Castleford.

**25th March 2019 -** 30-22 home defeat to Wigan.

**27th March 2019 -** Krisnan Inu signs on undisclosed contract.

**1st April 2019 -** Krisnan Inu makes debut in 33-22 defeat at Wakefield.

**8th April 2019 -** 23-16 home defeat to Hull FC.

**12th April 2019 -** Niall Evalds scores four of 13 tries in 76-6 win at Championship club Rochdale in fifth round of Challenge Cup.

**19th April 2019 -** stunning 36-12 Good Friday win at Warrington despite sin-binning of Kris Welham.

**22nd April 2019 -** Robert Lui misses 30-26 home, Easter Monday defeat to Wigan.

**27th April 2019 -** Niall Evalds becomes Salford's record Super League try-scorer in 30-10 win at London Broncos.

**28th April 2019 -** news emerges that Jansin Turgut is suspended by club for 'breach of off-field rules'.

**3rd May 2019 -** Adam Walker scores two tries in 28-16 home win over Leeds.

**10th May 2019 -** Jansin Turgut sacked.

**11th May 2019 -** Challenge Cup sixth round exit after 32-18 home defeat to Hull KR.

**14th May 2019 -** Wakefield prop Pauli Pauli joins on month's loan in swap deal with Junior Sa'u.

**17th May 2019 -** fightback from 16-0 down thwarted as Reds suffer late 32-30 defeat at St Helens.

**17th May 2019 -** Jansin Turgut suffers serious injuries in fall from car park in Ibiza.

**20th May 2019 -** second-rower Josh Jones to join Hull FC from 2020.

# KEY DATES

**26th May 2019 -** late penalty edges Salford to 22-20 Magic Weekend defeat by Hull KR at Anfield.

**6th June 2019 -** Jake Bibby signs for Wigan from 2020.

**7th June 2019 -** tries from Jake Bibby and Niall Evalds in last five minutes not enough in 35-32 defeat at Hull FC.

**10th June 2019 -** Junior Sa'u returns from loan at Wakefield.

**16th June 2019 -** Niall Evalds scores hat-trick in 44-20 home win over Wakefield.

**17th June 2019 -** prop Ryan Lannon returns from Hull KR on month's loan swap deal with Daniel Murray going in opposite direction.

**18th June 2019 -** assistant coach Martin Gleeson to leave for Wasps rugby union at end of June.

**21st June 2019 -** 26-16 home win over Castleford moves Red Devils into play-off spots.

**26th June 2019 -** Robert Lui joins Leeds for undisclosed fee. Tui Lolohea signs for Salford on two-year deal.

**28th June 2019 -** Tui Lolohea makes debut in 28-12 defeat at Wigan.

**2nd July 2019 -** Jackson Hastings to join Wigan for 2020. Prop George Griffin and winger Derrell Olpherts sign for Castleford for 2020.

**5th July 2019 -** Tyrone McCarthy try brace in 100th Super League appearance in 36-18 home defeat to Huddersfield.

**10th July 2019 -** prop Josh Johnson joins from Barrow Raiders.

**12th July 2019 -** Krisnan Inu try-brace in 22-12 win at second-placed Warrington.

**18th July 2019 -** centre Junior Sa'u signs for Leigh Centurions.

**21st July 2019 -** Kris Welham, in 300th career appearance, scores twice in 40-14 home win over Catalans.

**30th July 2019 -** Kris Welham signs contract extension for 2020.

**4th August 2019 -** Niall Evalds scores hat-trick in 58-28 win at London Broncos.

**11th August 2019 -** Krisnan Inu scores try and kicks eight goals in 32-12 home win over Huddersfield.

**16th August 2019 -** Paul Rowley appointed coaching consultant.

**17th August 2019 -** try-braces from Ken Sio, Lee Mossop and Krisnan Inu secure convincing 44-22 victory at Hull FC.

**19th August 2019 -** centre Dan Sarginson signs from Wigan Warriors for 2020.

**29th August 2019 -** 22-6 home win over Warrington marks first Super League winning run of six games. Ken Sio scores hat-trick.

**30th August 2019 -** forward Josh Johnson signs contract for 2020 season.

**4th September 2019 -** Hull KR halfback Chris Atkin signs for the 2020 season

**4th September 2019 -** Hull KR forward James Greenwood and Wakefield forward Pauli Pauli sign for 2020 season.

**6th September 2019 -** 20-12 win at Leeds is seventh consecutive top-flight victory, first time since 1976.

**13th September 2019 -** Australian hooker Connor Jones and prop Jack Ormondroyd unveiled as signings from Featherstone.

**13th September 2019 -** Krisnan Inu pots field goal in seventh minute of golden-point extra time to secure 17-16 last-round win over Hull KR and third spot on table.

**19th September 2019 -** Warrington stand-off Kevin Brown signs for 2020 season.

**21st September 2019 -** battling 18-12 defeat at Wigan in Qualifying Play-off.

**27th September 2019 -** 22-0 home win over Castleford in Elimination Semi-final.

**4th October 2019 -** 28-4 Final Eliminator win at Wigan secures first ever Grand Final berth.

**6th October 2019 -** Jackson Hastings wins Man of Steel.

**12th October 2019 -** 23-6 defeat to St Helens at Old Trafford.

**17th October 2019 -** threequarters Elliot Kear and Rhys Williams and prop Luke Yates join from London Broncos.

---

## CLUB RECORDS

**Highest score:**
100-12 v Gateshead, 23/3/2003
**Highest score against:**
16-96 v Bradford, 25/6/2000
**Record attendance:**
26,470 v Warrington, 13/2/37
*(The Willows)*
7,102 v Wakefield, 16/2/2014
*(AJ Bell Stadium)*

## MATCH RECORDS

**Tries:**
6 Frank Miles v Lees, 5/3/1898
Ernest Bone v Goole, 29/3/1902
Jack Hilton v Leigh, 7/10/39
**Goals:**
14 Steve Blakeley v Gateshead, 23/3/2003
**Points:**
39 Jim Lomas v Liverpool City, 2/2/1907

## SEASON RECORDS

**Tries:** 46 Keith Fielding 1973-74
**Goals:** 221 David Watkins 1972-73
**Points:** 493 David Watkins 1972-73

## CAREER RECORDS

**Tries:** 297 Maurice Richards 1969-83
**Goals:** 1,241 David Watkins 1967-79
**Points:** 2,907 David Watkins 1967-79
**Appearances:**
498 Maurice Richards 1969-83

# SALFORD RED DEVILS

| DATE | FIXTURE | RESULT | SCORERS | LGE | ATT |
|---|---|---|---|---|---|
| 1/2/19 | Huddersfield (a) | W14-34 | t:Sa'u,Sio(2),Evalds(3),Olpherts g:Lussick(2),Sio | 2nd | 5,387 |
| 10/2/19 | London Broncos (h) | W24-0 | t:Sio,Hastings,Evalds,Jones g:Hastings(4) | 1st | 3,246 |
| 17/2/19 | Leeds (h) | L14-46 | t:Lussick,Jones g:Sio(3) | 4th | 4,385 |
| 23/2/19 | Hull KR (a) | W22-24 | t:Lui,Jones,Olpherts,Sio,Lussick g:Sio(2) | 4th | 7,565 |
| 28/2/19 | St Helens (h) | L4-26 | t:Olpherts | 4th | 4,064 |
| 9/3/19 | Catalans Dragons (a) | W0-46 | t:Lussick,Griffin(2),Bibby(2),Hastings,Evalds,Sio g:Sio(7) | 4th | 8,021 |
| 17/3/19 | Castleford (a) | L24-20 | t:Bibby(2),Turgut,Lussick g:Lussick(2) | 4th | 7,750 |
| 24/3/19 | Wigan (h) | L22-30 | t:Jones,Olpherts,Evalds,Walker g:Chamberlain(3) | 4th | 4,470 |
| 31/3/19 | Wakefield (a) | L33-22 | t:Evalds,Welham,Olpherts,Hastings g:Chamberlain(3) | 5th | 4,356 |
| 7/4/19 | Hull FC (a) | L16-23 | t:Jones,Evalds,Hastings g:Chamberlain(2) | 7th | 3,609 |
| 12/4/19 | Rochdale (h) (CCR5) | W76-6 | t:Burke,Evalds(4),Dudson,Chamberlain,Tomkins,Bibby(2),Griffin,Lui,Inu g:Chamberlain(6),Inu(6) | N/A | 1,101 |
| 19/4/19 | Warrington (a) | W12-36 | t:Welham,Lussick,Murray,Lui,Bibby g:Inu(8) | 7th | 11,867 |
| 22/4/19 | Wigan (h) | L26-30 | t:Griffin,Evalds,Walker,Lussick g:Inu(5) | 7th | 4,017 |
| 27/4/19 | London Broncos (a) | W10-30 | t:Lussick,Evalds,Murray,Hastings,Mossop g:Inu(5) | 7th | 1,133 |
| 3/5/19 | Leeds (h) | W28-16 | t:Mossop,Walker(2),Lussick,Lui g:Inu(4) | 6th | 3,368 |
| 11/5/19 | Hull KR (h) (CCR6) | L18-32 | t:Inu,Evalds,Welham g:Inu(3) | N/A | 1,842 |
| 17/5/19 | St Helens (a) | L32-30 | t:Dudson,Evalds(2),Olpherts,Lui g:Inu(5) | 7th | 9,446 |
| 26/5/19 | Hull KR (MW) ● | W22-20 | t:Lussick,Pauli,Sio(2) g:Inu(2) | 7th | N/A |
| 7/6/19 | Hull FC (a) | L35-32 | t:Pauli(2),Bibby(2),Lui,Evalds g:Inu(4) | 7th | 9,914 |
| 16/6/19 | Wakefield (h) | W44-20 | t:Bibby(2),Evalds(3),Lussick,Lui,Welham g:Inu(6) | 6th | 2,950 |
| 21/6/19 | Castleford (h) | W26-16 | t:Evalds,Mossop,Hastings,Olpherts g:Inu(5) | 5th | 2,829 |
| 28/6/19 | Wigan (a) | L28-12 | t:Olpherts,Welham g:Inu(2) | 7th | 12,066 |
| 4/7/19 | Huddersfield (h) | L18-36 | t:McCarthy(2),Sio,Welham g:Inu | 7th | 2,368 |
| 12/7/19 | Warrington (h) | W12-22 | t:Lannon,Welham,Inu(2) g:Inu(3) | 7th | 9,509 |
| 21/7/19 | Catalans Dragons (h) | W40-14 | t:J Johnson,Olpherts,Welham(2),Lolohea,Evalds,Flanagan g:Inu(3),Lolohea(3) | 7th | 2,785 |
| 4/8/19 | London Broncos (a) | W28-58 | t:Inu(2),Flanagan,Jones,Evalds(3),Lolohea,Welham,Hastings g:Lolohea(8),Inu | 6th | 1,445 |
| 11/8/19 | Huddersfield (h) | W32-12 | t:Tomkins,Flanagan,Lolohea,Inu g:Inu(8) | 5th | 3,032 |
| 17/8/19 | Hull FC (a) | W22-44 | t:Sio(2),Mossop(2),Bibby,Inu(2),Hastings g:Inu(6) | 5th | 11,217 |
| 29/8/19 | Warrington (h) | W22-6 | t:Sio(3),Bibby g:Inu(3) | 4th | 4,879 |
| 6/9/19 | Leeds (a) | W12-20 | t:Evalds,Bibby,Lussick g:Inu(4) | 4th | 12,436 |
| 13/9/19 | Hull KR (h) | W17-16 (aet) | t:Bibby,Lolohea,Lussick g:Inu(2) fg:Inu | 3rd | 5,393 |
| 20/9/19 | Wigan (a) (QPO) | L18-12 | t:Griffin,Hastings g:Inu(2) | N/A | 9,247 |
| 26/9/19 | Castleford (h) (ESF) | W22-0 | t:McCarthy,Bibby,Hastings g:Inu(5) | N/A | 4,800 |
| 4/10/19 | Wigan (a) (FE) | W4-28 | t:Dudson,Lussick,Mossop g:Inu(8) | N/A | 9,858 |
| 12/10/19 | St Helens (GF) ●● | L6-23 | t:Bibby g:Inu | N/A | 64,102 |

● Played at Anfield, Liverpool
●● Played at Old Trafford, Manchester

| | | APP | | TRIES | | GOALS | | FG | | PTS | |
|---|---|---|---|---|---|---|---|---|---|---|---|
| | D.O.B. | ALL | SL | ALL | SL | ALL | SL | ALL | SL | ALL | SL |
| Jake Bibby | 17/6/96 | 27(1) | 25(1) | 17 | 15 | 0 | 0 | 0 | 0 | 68 | 60 |
| Greg Burke | 12/2/93 | 12(19) | 10(19) | 1 | 0 | 0 | 0 | 0 | 0 | 4 | 0 |
| Ed Chamberlain | 8/2/96 | 4 | 3 | 1 | 1 | 14 | 8 | 0 | 0 | 32 | 16 |
| Gil Dudson | 16/6/90 | 32 | 30 | 3 | 2 | 0 | 0 | 0 | 0 | 12 | 8 |
| Niall Evalds | 26/8/93 | 35 | 33 | 27 | 22 | 0 | 0 | 0 | 0 | 108 | 88 |
| Mark Flanagan | 4/12/87 | 12(12) | 12(12) | 3 | 3 | 0 | 0 | 0 | 0 | 12 | 12 |
| George Griffin | 26/6/92 | 19(6) | 17(6) | 5 | 4 | 0 | 0 | 0 | 0 | 20 | 16 |
| Jackson Hastings | 14/1/96 | 35 | 33 | 10 | 10 | 4 | 4 | 0 | 0 | 48 | 48 |
| Krisnan Inu | 17/3/87 | 26(1) | 24(1) | 9 | 7 | 102 | 93 | 1 | 1 | 241 | 215 |
| Greg Johnson | 20/2/90 | 1 | 1 | 0 | 0 | 0 | 0 | 0 | 0 | 0 | 0 |
| Josh Johnson | 25/7/94 | (7) | (7) | 1 | 1 | 0 | 0 | 0 | 0 | 4 | 4 |
| Josh Jones | 12/5/93 | 33 | 32 | 6 | 6 | 0 | 0 | 0 | 0 | 24 | 24 |
| Ryan Lannon | 11/1/96 | 7(2) | 7(2) | 1 | 1 | 0 | 0 | 0 | 0 | 4 | 4 |
| Adam Lawton | 13/6/93 | 1(1) | 1(1) | 0 | 0 | 0 | 0 | 0 | 0 | 0 | 0 |
| Tuimoala Lolohea | 23/1/95 | 14 | 14 | 4 | 4 | 11 | 11 | 0 | 0 | 38 | 38 |
| Robert Lui | 23/2/90 | 20 | 18 | 7 | 6 | 0 | 0 | 0 | 0 | 28 | 24 |
| Joey Lussick | 28/12/95 | 18(16) | 17(16) | 13 | 13 | 4 | 4 | 0 | 0 | 60 | 60 |
| Tyrone McCarthy | 21/4/88 | 13(12) | 13(10) | 3 | 3 | 0 | 0 | 0 | 0 | 12 | 12 |
| Lee Mossop | 17/1/89 | 20(2) | 19(2) | 6 | 6 | 0 | 0 | 0 | 0 | 24 | 24 |
| Daniel Murray | 21/3/96 | 5(7) | 5(6) | 2 | 2 | 0 | 0 | 0 | 0 | 8 | 8 |
| Ben Nakubuwai | 15/3/96 | 2(16) | 2(15) | 0 | 0 | 0 | 0 | 0 | 0 | 0 | 0 |
| Derrell Olpherts | 7/1/92 | 23 | 22 | 9 | 9 | 0 | 0 | 0 | 0 | 36 | 36 |
| Pauli Pauli | 4/8/94 | (3) | (3) | 3 | 3 | 0 | 0 | 0 | 0 | 12 | 12 |
| Junior Sa'u | 18/4/87 | 8 | 7 | 1 | 1 | 0 | 0 | 0 | 0 | 4 | 4 |
| Ken Sio | 29/10/90 | 21(1) | 20(1) | 13 | 13 | 13 | 13 | 0 | 0 | 78 | 78 |
| Logan Tomkins | 1/8/91 | 17(8) | 16(8) | 2 | 1 | 0 | 0 | 0 | 0 | 8 | 4 |
| Jansin Turgut | 8/3/96 | 8(2) | 8(2) | 1 | 1 | 0 | 0 | 0 | 0 | 4 | 4 |
| Adam Walker | 20/2/91 | 10(15) | 9(14) | 4 | 4 | 0 | 0 | 0 | 0 | 16 | 16 |
| Kris Welham | 12/5/87 | 31(2) | 30(1) | 10 | 9 | 0 | 0 | 0 | 0 | 40 | 36 |
| Josh Wood | 15/11/95 | 1(4) | 1(2) | 0 | 0 | 0 | 0 | 0 | 0 | 0 | 0 |

Jackson Hastings

**LEAGUE RECORD**
P29-W17-D0-L12
(3rd/Grand Final Runners-Up)
F783, A597, Diff+186
34 points.

**CHALLENGE CUP**
Round Six

**ATTENDANCES**
Best - v Hull KR (SL - 5,393)
Worst - v Rochdale (CC - 1,101)
Total (SL, inc play-offs) - 56,195
Average (SL, inc play-offs) - 3,746
(Up by 923 on 2018)

*'SL' totals include regular season & play-offs; 'All' totals also include Challenge Cup*

# KEY DATES

**31st October 2018 -** Ade Gardner leaves to join Warrington as Head of Performance.

**7th November 2018 -** Tommy Makinson wins Golden Boot after stellar performances for England.

**21st November 2018 -** Ryan Morgan joins London Broncos on loan for 2019. Liam Cooper re-joins Halifax on loan for season.

**8th January 2019 -** Louie McCarthy-Scarsbrook signs new contract to end of 2020.

**9th January 2019 -** prop Matty Lees signs new, improved three-year contract to end of 2021 season.

**19th January 2019 -** 28-18 home win over Hull FC in Jonny Lomax Testimonial.

**22nd January 2019 -** dual-registration partnership with Leigh announced.

**25th January 2019 -** prop Luke Douglas joins Leigh on month's loan.

**29th January 2019 -** club captain James Roby signs new contract to end of 2021 season.

**30th January 2019 -** Tommy Makinson signs new contract to end of 2022 season.

**31st January 2019 -** Kevin Naiqama scores in second minute of debut in 22-12 opening-round home win over Wigan.

**5th February 2019 -** Jonny Lomax signs new four-year contract until end of 2022 season.

**10th February 2019 -** last-gasp Louie McCarthy-Scarsbrook try secures 24-18 win at Wakefield.

**14th February 2019 -** Danny Richardson joins Leigh on loan.

**22nd February 2019 -** 27-22 home win over Leeds after trailing 22-10 at half-time.

**28th February 2019 -** James Roby scores try-brace in 26-4 win at Salford in rainy conditions.

**5th March 2019 -** Joe Batchelor month loan at York extended to week-to-week basis.

**8th March 2019 -** Theo Fages stars in 26-0 home victory over London Broncos.

**12th March 2019 -** winger Regan Grace signs contract extension to end of 2021 season.

**14th March 2019 -** 28-unanswered points secure 40-12 victory at Huddersfield.

**22nd March 2019 -** commanding 42-12 win at Castleford makes it seven wins from seven.

**6th April 2019 -** 18-10 defeat in rainy Perpignan ends opening winning run at eight matches.

**12th April 2019 -** 38-12 home win over Warrington puts Saints back at top of table.

**19th April 2019 -** Regan Grace hat-trick in 36-10 Good Friday win at Wigan. Mark Percival suffers early hamstring injury.

**22nd April 2019 -** Kevin Naiqama and Adam Swift both score hat-tricks in 62-16 Easter Monday home win over Hull FC. Morgan Knowles accepts one-match penalty notice for dangerous contact.

**28th April 2019 -** eight first teamers missing as Matty Costello grabs first career hat-trick in 50-14 home win over Catalans.

**5th May 2019 -** Kevin Naiqama and Tommy Makinson score hat-tricks in hard fought 42-26 win at Hull KR.

**5th May 2019 -** hooker Aaron Smith signs contract extension to end of 2022.

**12th May 2019 -** hard-fought 22-16, sixth round Challenge Cup victory at Huddersfield.

**17th May 2019 -** last-gasp James Bentley try, converted by hat-trick scorer Lachlan Coote, seals 32-30 home comeback win over Salford.

**26th May 2019 -** dominant 36-16 Magic Weekend win over Castleford at Anfield.

**29th May 2019 -** Adam Swift signs for Hull FC for 2020.

**31st May 2019 -** Zeb Taia signs contract extension to end of 2020 season.

**1st June 2019 -** 48-10 home win over Wakefield in Challenge Cup quarter-final

**3rd June 2019 -** Theo Fages signs contract extension to end of 2021 season.

**9th June 2019 -** Morgan Smith field goal means 23-22 golden-point defeat at bottom club London Broncos. James Roby to have groin surgery.

**10th June 2019 -** assistant coach Sean Long leaves to join Harlequins rugby union. Richard Marshall takes up role.

**14th June 2019 -** Tommy Makinson gets hat-trick in 38-2 home win over Huddersfield.

**21st June 2019 -** Louie McCarthy-Scarsbrook scores two tries in 36-10 home win over Leeds. Zeb Taia dislocates shoulder.

**28th June 2019 -** dramatic late comeback produces 21-10 win at Warrington to open up eight point gap at top of table. Club promises bans for fans using flares in away stand.

**5th July 2019 -** 40-12 home win over Hull FC.

**12th July 2019 -** 32-10 home win over Wigan in front of over 17,000 fans.

**21st July 2019 -** Josh Simm, Callum Hazzard and Josh Eaves make debuts in 32-12 defeat at London Broncos.

**27th July 2019 -** 26-2 Challenge Cup semi-final win over Halifax at University of Bolton Stadium.

**31st July 2019 -** head coach Justin Holbrook to leave at end of season to take charge at Gold Coast Titans.

**2nd August 2019 -** Zeb Taia returns from dislocated shoulder as three late first-half tries ensure 26-6 home win over Wakefield. Warrington's loss in Perpignan the day after means Saints win League Leaders Shield.

**8th August 2019 -** 30-12 win at Warrington in Wembley dress rehearsal.

**15th August 2019 -** 36-20 win at Leeds after being level at half-time. Kevin Naiqama scores hat-trick. Matty Lees out for season with abdominal injury.

**24th August 2019 -** 18-4 defeat to Warrington at Wembley.

**30th August 2019 -** Regan Grace scores only points on 32 minutes as 4-0 home win over Castleford extends lead at top of table to 16 points. Saints presented with League Leaders' Shield.

**6th September 2019 -** Luke Thompson scores two tries as 48-6 win over Huddersfield secures first unbeaten home season since 2002.

**10th September 2019 -** Newcastle Knights interim coach Kristian Woolf to take over as head coach on November 1st on two-year contract, having option to extend for further year.

**13th September 2019 -** Tommy Makinson scores first half hat-trick in hard 22-6 last-round win at Hull FC.

**27th September 2019 -** 40-10 home Qualifying Semi-final hammering of Wigan secures first Grand Final spot since 2014.

**6th October 2019 -** Justin Holbrook wins Super League coach of the year and Matt Lees young player of the year.

**12th October 2019 -** Luke Thompson wins Harry Sunderland Trophy in 23-6 Grand Final win over Salford.

**18th October 2019 -** scrum-half Danny Richardson signs for Castleford.

## CLUB RECORDS

**Highest score:**
112-0 v Carlisle, 14/9/86
**Highest score against:**
6-78 v Warrington, 12/4/1909
**Record attendance:**
35,695 v Wigan, 26/12/49 *(Knowsley Road)*
17,980 v Wigan, 6/4/2012
v Wigan, 18/4/2014
v South Sydney, 22/2/2015
v Wigan, 30/3/2018
*(Totally Wicked Stadium)*

## MATCH RECORDS

**Tries:** 6 Alf Ellaby v Barrow, 5/3/32
Steve Llewellyn v Castleford, 3/3/56
Steve Llewellyn v Liverpool, 20/8/56
Tom van Vollenhoven v Wakefield, 21/12/57
Tom van Vollenhoven v Blackpool, 23/4/62
Frank Myler v Maryport, 1/9/69
Shane Cooper v Hull, 17/2/88
**Goals:** 16 Paul Loughlin v Carlisle, 14/9/86
**Points:**
40 Paul Loughlin v Carlisle, 14/9/86

## SEASON RECORDS

**Tries:** 62 Tom van Vollenhoven 1958-59
**Goals:** 214 Kel Coslett 1971-72
**Points:** 452 Kel Coslett 1971-72

## CAREER RECORDS

**Tries:** 392 Tom van Vollenhoven 1957-68
**Goals:** 1,639 Kel Coslett 1962-76
**Points:** 3,413 Kel Coslett 1962-76
**Appearances:** 531 Kel Coslett 1962-76

# ST HELENS

| DATE | FIXTURE | RESULT | SCORERS | LGE | ATT |
|------|---------|--------|---------|-----|-----|
| 31/1/19 | Wigan (h) | W22-12 | t:Naiqama,Lomax,Grace,Roby g:Percival(3) | 5th | 16,508 |
| 10/2/19 | Wakefield (a) | W18-24 | t:Knowles,Makinson(2),Grace,McCarthy-Scarsbrook g:Percival(2) | 4th | 5,815 |
| 22/2/19 | Leeds (h) | W27-22 | t:Fages,Lomax,Walmsley(2),Thompson g:Percival(2),Coote fg:Roby | 3rd | 11,318 |
| 28/2/19 | Salford (a) | W4-26 | t:Percival,Lomax,Roby(2),Grace g:Coote(3) | 2nd | 4,064 |
| 8/3/19 | London Broncos (h) | W26-0 | t:Peyroux,Grace,Fages,Coote,Naiqama g:Coote(3) | 1st | 9,090 |
| 14/3/19 | Huddersfield (a) | W12-40 | t:Thompson,Knowles,Percival(2),Grace,Peyroux,Lomax g:Coote(6) | 1st | 4,495 |
| 22/3/19 | Castleford (a) | W12-42 | t:Coote,Grace,Peyroux(2),Taia,McCarthy-Scarsbrook,Percival,Lomax g:Coote(5) | 1st | 8,042 |
| 29/3/19 | Hull KR (h) | W36-24 | t:Coote,Welsby,Thompson,Amor,Smith,Grace g:Coote(6) | 1st | 10,003 |
| 6/4/19 | Catalans Dragons (a) | L18-10 | t:Peyroux,Makinson g:Coote | 2nd | 8,783 |
| 12/4/19 | Warrington (h) | W38-12 | t:Percival,McCarthy-Scarsbrook,Lomax,Lees,Grace,Makinson g:Coote(7) | 1st | 17,807 |
| 19/4/19 | Wigan (a) | W10-36 | t:Roby,Grace(3),Makinson,Coote g:Coote(6) | 1st | 22,050 |
| 22/4/19 | Hull FC (h) | W62-16 | t:Lomax(2),Naiqama(4),Swift(3),Coote,Welsby g:Coote(8),Richardson | 1st | 11,268 |
| 28/4/19 | Catalans Dragons (h) | W50-14 | t:Swift,Taia,Smith,Fages,Peyroux,Costello(3),Welsby g:Richardson(7) | 1st | 11,268 |
| 5/5/19 | Hull KR (a) | W26-42 | t:Naiqama(3),Makinson(3),Lomax,Grace g:Coote(5) | 1st | 8,123 |
| 12/5/19 | Huddersfield (a) (CCR6) | W16-22 | t:Grace,Fages,Coote,Naiqama g:Coote(3) | N/A | 3,533 |
| 17/5/19 | Salford (h) | W32-30 | t:Coote(3),Makinson(2),Bentley g:Coote(4) | 1st | 9,446 |
| 26/5/19 | Castleford (MW) ● | W16-36 | t:Makinson,Grace,Lomax,Fages,Ashworth,Coote,Naiqama g:Coote(4) | 1st | N/A |
| 1/6/19 | Wakefield (h) (CCQF) | W48-10 | t:Coote,Makinson,Knowles,Grace,Taia,Percival,Lomax,Naiqama g:Coote(8) | N/A | 6,453 |
| 9/6/19 | London Broncos (a) | L23-22 (aet) | t:Roby,Thompson,Percival,Grace g:Richardson(3) | 1st | 2,801 |
| 14/6/19 | Huddersfield (h) | W38-2 | t:Coote,Lomax(2),Makinson(3),Fages g:Coote(5) | 1st | 9,527 |
| 21/6/19 | Leeds (h) | W36-10 | t:Naiqama,McCarthy-Scarsbrook(2),Coote,Makinson,Bentley g:Coote(6) | 1st | 11,448 |
| 28/6/19 | Warrington (a) | W10-21 | t:Percival,Thompson,Walmsley g:Coote(4) fg:Coote | 1st | 14,211 |
| 5/7/19 | Hull FC (a) | W12-40 | t:Knowles,Fages,Coote(2),Grace,Ashworth,Lomax g:Coote(6) | 1st | 11,311 |
| 12/7/19 | Wigan (h) | W32-10 | t:Makinson(2),Coote,Naiqama,Lomax g:Coote(6) | 1st | 17,088 |
| 21/7/19 | London Broncos (a) | L32-12 | t:Smith,Richardson g:Richardson(2) | 1st | 2,087 |
| 27/7/19 | Halifax (CCSF) ●● | W2-26 | t:Roby,Peyroux,Lomax,Fages g:Richardson(5) | N/A | 24,364 |
| 2/8/19 | Wakefield (h) | W26-6 | t:Richardson,McCarthy-Scarsbrook,Makinson,Naiqama g:Richardson(5) | 1st | 9,494 |
| 8/8/19 | Warrington (a) | W12-30 | t:Naiqama,Lomax,Paulo,Costello,Makinson g:Richardson(5) | 1st | 10,987 |
| 15/8/19 | Leeds (a) | W20-36 | t:Grace(2),Naiqama(3),Taia g:Percival(6) | 1st | 12,153 |
| 24/8/19 | Warrington (CCF) ●●● | L4-18 | t:Fages | N/A | 62,717 |
| 30/8/19 | Castleford (h) | W4-0 | t:Grace | 1st | 10,315 |
| 6/9/19 | Huddersfield (h) | W48-6 | t:Thompson(2),Peyroux,Grace,Knowles,Amor,Lomax,Makinson g:Coote(8) | 1st | 9,560 |
| 13/9/19 | Hull FC (a) | W6-22 | t:Makinson(3),Percival,Grace g:Coote | 1st | 11,004 |
| 27/9/19 | Wigan (h) (QSF) | W40-10 | t:Fages,Naiqama,Thompson,Lomax,Taia,Percival(2) g:Coote(6) | N/A | 14,508 |
| 12/10/19 | Salford (GF) ●●●● | W6-23 | t:Knowles,Taia,Percival g:Coote(5) fg:Makinson | N/A | 64,102 |

● Played at Anfield, Liverpool  ●● Played at University of Bolton Stadium
●●● Played at Wembley Stadium  ●●●● Played at Old Trafford, Manchester

| | | APP | | TRIES | | GOALS | | FG | | PTS | |
|---|---|---|---|---|---|---|---|---|---|---|---|
| | D.O.B. | ALL | SL | ALL | SL | ALL | SL | ALL | SL | ALL | SL |
| Kyle Amor | 26/5/87 | 1(29) | 1(26) | 2 | 2 | 0 | 0 | 0 | 0 | 8 | 8 |
| Jack Ashworth | 3/7/95 | 1(27) | 1(23) | 2 | 2 | 0 | 0 | 0 | 0 | 8 | 8 |
| Joe Batchelor | 28/10/94 | 2(2) | 2(2) | 0 | 0 | 0 | 0 | 0 | 0 | 0 | 0 |
| James Bentley | 19/10/97 | 5(12) | 5(11) | 2 | 2 | 0 | 0 | 0 | 0 | 8 | 8 |
| Lachlan Coote | 6/4/90 | 27 | 24 | 16 | 14 | 117 | 106 | 1 | 1 | 299 | 269 |
| Matthew Costello | 9/4/98 | 10(1) | 9(1) | 4 | 4 | 0 | 0 | 0 | 0 | 16 | 16 |
| Josh Eaves | 20/10/97 | (2) | (2) | 0 | 0 | 0 | 0 | 0 | 0 | 0 | 0 |
| Theo Fages | 23/8/94 | 27 | 24 | 10 | 7 | 0 | 0 | 0 | 0 | 40 | 28 |
| Regan Grace | 12/12/96 | 33 | 29 | 22 | 20 | 0 | 0 | 0 | 0 | 88 | 80 |
| Callum Hazzard | 9/1/99 | (1) | (1) | 0 | 0 | 0 | 0 | 0 | 0 | 0 | 0 |
| Morgan Knowles | 5/11/96 | 29 | 26 | 6 | 5 | 0 | 0 | 0 | 0 | 24 | 20 |
| Matty Lees | 4/2/98 | 12(15) | 11(13) | 1 | 1 | 0 | 0 | 0 | 0 | 4 | 4 |
| Jonny Lomax | 4/9/90 | 30 | 26 | 19 | 17 | 0 | 0 | 0 | 0 | 76 | 68 |
| Tommy Makinson | 10/10/91 | 31 | 27 | 24 | 23 | 0 | 0 | 1 | 1 | 97 | 93 |
| Louie McCarthy-Scarsbrook | 14/1/86 | 8(19) | 7(17) | 6 | 6 | 0 | 0 | 0 | 0 | 24 | 24 |
| Kevin Naiqama | 4/2/89 | 31 | 27 | 20 | 18 | 0 | 0 | 0 | 0 | 80 | 72 |
| Joseph Paulo | 2/1/88 | 6(22) | 5(19) | 1 | 1 | 0 | 0 | 0 | 0 | 4 | 4 |
| Mark Percival | 29/5/94 | 26 | 23 | 12 | 11 | 13 | 13 | 0 | 0 | 74 | 70 |
| Dominique Peyroux | 21/1/89 | 31(1) | 27(1) | 8 | 7 | 0 | 0 | 0 | 0 | 32 | 28 |
| Danny Richardson | 2/9/96 | 12 | 10 | 2 | 2 | 28 | 23 | 0 | 0 | 64 | 54 |
| James Roby | 22/11/85 | 23 | 19 | 6 | 5 | 0 | 0 | 1 | 1 | 25 | 21 |
| Josh Simm | 27/2/01 | 1 | 1 | 0 | 0 | 0 | 0 | 0 | 0 | 0 | 0 |
| Aaron Smith | 12/10/96 | 10(6) | 10(5) | 3 | 3 | 0 | 0 | 0 | 0 | 12 | 12 |
| Adam Swift | 20/2/93 | 7 | 7 | 4 | 4 | 0 | 0 | 0 | 0 | 16 | 16 |
| Zeb Taia | 11/10/84 | 27 | 24 | 6 | 5 | 0 | 0 | 0 | 0 | 24 | 20 |
| Luke Thompson | 27/4/95 | 29 | 26 | 8 | 8 | 0 | 0 | 0 | 0 | 32 | 32 |
| Alex Walmsley | 10/4/90 | 27(1) | 23(1) | 3 | 3 | 0 | 0 | 0 | 0 | 12 | 12 |
| Jack Welsby | 17/3/01 | 9(2) | 9(2) | 3 | 3 | 0 | 0 | 0 | 0 | 12 | 12 |

'SL' totals include regular season & play-offs; 'All' totals also include Challenge Cup

Lachlan Coote

**LEAGUE RECORD**
P29-W26-D0-L3
(1st/Grand Final Winners,
Champions)
F916, A395, Diff+521
52 points.

**CHALLENGE CUP**
Runners-Up

**ATTENDANCES**
Best - v Warrington (SL - 17,807)
Worst - v Wakefield (CC - 6,453)
Total (SL, inc play-offs) - 178,648
Average (SL, inc play-offs) -11,910
(Up by 741 on 2018)

# Super League XXIV - Club by Club

**3rd November 2018 -** Danny Brough returns from Huddersfield on two-year deal. Scott Grix joins the Giants.

**5th November 2018 -** John Minards becomes non-executive Chairman. Michael Carter takes up chief executive role.

**20th November 2018 -** head coach Chris Chester signs new three-year deal.

**26th December 2018 -** 10-4 defeat at Headingley in Boxing Day challenge.

**13th January 2019 -** 30-24 home win over Hull FC in Danny Kirmond Testimonial to win David Topliss Trophy.

**22nd January 2019 -** 28-24 home win over Huddersfield in final friendly.

**23rd January 2019 -** Pauli Pauli sidelined for three months with knee injury suffered in friendly at Newcastle.

**3rd February 2019 -** shock 42-24 round-one defeat at London Broncos after leading 12-0. Tyler Randell aggravates shoulder injury.

**10th February 2019 -** last-gasp Louie McCarthy-Scarsbrook try means 24-18 home defeat by St Helens. Craig Huby out for four months with shoulder injury.

**21st February 2019 -** 22-12 home win over Catalans.

**28th February 2019 -** centre Joe Arundel signs new two-year deal to end of 2021.

**1st March 2019 -** Tom Johnstone scores first-half hat-trick in 35-18 win at Leeds.

**10th March 2019 -** late Danny McGuire try means 10-6 home defeat to Hull KR.

**15th March 2019 -** Tom Johnstone suffers season-ending ACL injury in 32-12 win at Hull FC.

**17th March 2019 -** prop Craig Kopczak signs new one-year contract to end of 2020 season.

**21st March 2019 -** club purchases Belle Vue Stadium with loan assistance from Wakefield council.

**21st March 2019 -** 34-32 home defeat to Warrington after trailing 34-12 on 63 minutes.

**1st April 2019 -** Danny Brough kicks five goals and a field goal in 33-22 home win over Salford. Centre Bill Tupou ruled out for three months with groin injury.

**5th April 2019 -** late Danny Brough field goal seals 17-16 home win over Huddersfield as David Fifita scores two tries.

**12th April 2019 -** Anthony England, Reece Lyne, Jacob Miller and Kyle Wood all withdrawn with injury in 30-20 home win over Wigan.

**16th April 2019 -** Mason Caton-Brown rejoins Trinity on contract to season end.

**16th April 2019 -** David Fifita extends contract to end of 2022.

**17th April 2019 -** Kyle Wood signs contract extension to end of 2021.

**18th April 2019 -** comeback from 26-4 down ends in 28-26 Good Friday defeat at Castleford.

**22nd April 2019 -** winger Lee Kershaw scores on debut in sun-baked 26-24 home win over Leeds.

**24th April 2019 -** youngster Connor Bailey signs three-year contract.

# KEY DATES

**29th April 2019 -** 30-14 defeat at Hull FC.

**5th May 2019 -** Tyler Randell returns for first time since round-one as late Ryan Hampshire penalty goal seals 26-25 win at Huddersfield.

**10th May 2019 -** three late tries seal 26-6 Challenge Cup sixth round win over Widnes

**14th May 2019 -** Junior Sa'u joins from Salford on one-month loan, with Pauli Pauli heading the other way.

**18th May 2019 -** Jacob Miller returns in 42-34 defeat at London.

**20th May 2019 -** Justin Horo leaves by mutual consent.

**21st May 2019 -** Manly forward Kelepi Tanginoa arrives on deal to end of 2021.

**26th May 2019 -** Kelepi Tanginoa makes debut in 25-18 Magic Weekend defeat to Catalans at Anfield.

**1st June 2019 -** centre Jack Croft makes impressive debut in 48-10 Challenge Cup quarter-final exit at St Helens.

**4th June 2019 -** winger Lee Kershaw signs new one-year deal to end of 2020.

**7th June 2019 -** 10-0 rain-soaked home defeat to Leeds.

**16th June 2019 -** Pauli Pauli back for 44-20 defeat at Salford.

**21st June 2019 -** David Fifita back for 30-6 defeat at Warrington.

**27th June 2019 -** Bill Tupou signs until end of 2022 and Reece Lyne until end of 2024.

**29th June 2019 -** Bill Tupou returns from three-month injury lay-off and Tyler Randell scores hat-trick as 36-10 home win over Huddersfield ends five-match losing league run.

**1st July 2019 -** Jordan Crowther signs two-year contract extension to end of 2021. Craig Huby, after shoulder injury curtails his season, leaves by mutual consent.

**1st July 2019 -** Tinirau Arona signs new three-year contract to end of 2022.

**6th July 2019 -** 44-10 hammering at Catalans.

**12th July 2019 -** 36-16 home defeat by Castleford.

**18th July 2019 -** 46-16 defeat at Wigan.

**2nd August 2019 -** 26-6 defeat at leaders St Helens.

**6th August 2019 -** Wigan fullback Morgan Escare and Hull prop Chris Green join on loan until end of season

**8th August 2019 -** Adam Tangata joins on loan from Halifax, with Keegan Hirst going in opposite direction.

**9th August 2019 -** Ryan Atkins rejoins from Warrington for remainder of season, with deal agreed for 2020.

**11th August 2019 -** Morgan Escare and Adam Tangata make debuts in 26-16 home defeat to Hull FC.

**14th August 2019 -** David Fifita succumbs to long-standing foot problem and has surgery.

**18th August 2019 -** 38-10 romp at Hull KR gives two point buffer with bottom three clubs. Chris Green makes debut.

**2nd September 2019 -** 24-16 home defeat to Wigan.

**6th September 2019 -** 23-16 defeat at Warrington leaves Trinity on 20 points with three other clubs going into last round.

**13th September 2019 -** 19-10 home win over London Broncos secures ninth-placed finish.

**20th September 2019 -** Danny Kirmond signs new contract for 2020. Ryan Hampshire, Anthony England, Tyler Randell, Keegan Hirst, Chris Annakin, Luke Hooley and Lewis Wray leave the club.

**24th September 2019 -** forward Joe Westerman signs from Hull FC on two-year deal.

**28th September 2019 -** London Broncos fullback Alex Walker joins on two-year deal.

**12th October 2019 -** prop Chris Green signs permanent two-year deal.

**16th October 2019 -** utility back Ryan Hampshire signs new two-year contract.

**21st October 2019 -** hooker Josh Wood signs on two-year deal from Salford.

## CLUB RECORDS

**Highest score:**
90-12 v Highfield, 27/10/92
**Highest score against:**
0-86 v Castleford, 17/4/95
**Record attendance:**
30,676 v Huddersfield, 26/2/21

## MATCH RECORDS

**Tries:**
7 Fred Smith v Keighley, 25/4/59
Keith Slater v Hunslet, 6/2/71
**Goals:**
13 Mark Conway v Highfield, 27/10/92
**Points:**
36 Jamie Rooney v Chorley, 27/2/2004

## SEASON RECORDS

**Tries:** 38 Fred Smith 1959-60
David Smith 1973-74
**Goals:** 163 Neil Fox 1961-62
**Points:** 407 Neil Fox 1961-62

## CAREER RECORDS

**Tries:** 272 Neil Fox 1956-74
**Goals:** 1,836 Neil Fox 1956-74
**Points:** 4,488 Neil Fox 1956-74
**Appearances:**
605 Harry Wilkinson 1930-49

# WAKEFIELD TRINITY

| DATE | FIXTURE | RESULT | SCORERS | LGE | ATT |
|------|---------|--------|---------|-----|-----|
| 3/2/19 | London Broncos (a) | L42-24 | t:Kopczak,Hampshire,Miller,Wood g:Brough(4) | 9th | 2,149 |
| 10/2/19 | St Helens (h) | L18-24 | t:Johnstone(2),Tupou g:Brough(3) | 10th | 5,815 |
| 21/2/19 | Catalans Dragons (h) | W22-12 | t:Johnstone,Fifita,Batchelor g:Brough(5) | 9th | 4,639 |
| 1/3/19 | Leeds (a) | W18-35 | t:Johnstone(3),Wood,Miller,Brough g:Brough(5) fg:Brough | 6th | 13,148 |
| 10/3/19 | Hull KR (h) | L6-10 | g:Brough(3) | 7th | 5,559 |
| 15/3/19 | Hull FC (a) | W12-32 | t:Hampshire,Tupou(2),Pauli,Lyne g:Brough(6) | 5th | 11,190 |
| 21/3/19 | Warrington (h) | L32-34 | t:Hampshire,Fifita,Wood(2),Jowitt,Arundel g:Brough(4) | 7th | 4,753 |
| 31/3/19 | Salford (h) | W33-22 | t:Fifita,Hampshire,Lyne,Pauli,Miller g:Brough(6) fg:Brough | 4th | 4,356 |
| 5/4/19 | Huddersfield (h) | W17-16 | t:Lyne,Fifita(2) g:Brough(2) fg:Brough | 4th | 4,730 |
| 12/4/19 | Wigan (h) | W30-20 | t:Kopczak,Arundel,Jowitt,Jones-Bishop(2) g:Brough(5) | 4th | 5,694 |
| 18/4/19 | Castleford (a) | L28-26 | t:Caton-Brown(2),Arundel,Reynolds,Arona g:Hampshire(3) | 5th | 9,316 |
| 22/4/19 | Leeds (h) | W26-24 | t:Kershaw,Lyne,Jones-Bishop,Jowitt g:Hampshire(5) | 3rd | 6,785 |
| 28/4/19 | Hull FC (a) | L30-14 | t:Jowitt(2),Horo g:Hampshire | 4th | 10,254 |
| 3/5/19 | Huddersfield (a) | W25-26 | t:Caton-Brown(2),Fifita,Jones-Bishop g:Hampshire(5) | 3rd | 5,104 |
| 10/5/19 | Widnes (h) (CCR6) | W26-6 | t:Jowitt,Fifita,Jones-Bishop,Kershaw,Horo g:Hampshire(3) | N/A | 3,055 |
| 18/5/19 | London Broncos (a) | L42-34 | t:Wood,Fifita(2),Caton-Brown(2),Hampshire g:Hampshire(5) | 6th | 1,205 |
| 25/5/19 | Catalans Dragons (MW) ● | L25-18 | t:Wood,Kirmond,Jones-Bishop g:Hampshire(3) | 6th | N/A |
| 1/6/19 | St Helens (a) (CCQF) | L48-10 | t:Croft,Randell g:Brough | N/A | 6,453 |
| 7/6/19 | Leeds (h) | L0-10 | | 6th | 5,489 |
| 16/6/19 | Salford (a) | L44-20 | t:Miller(2),Jones-Bishop(2) g:Brough(2) | 8th | 2,950 |
| 21/6/19 | Warrington (a) | L30-6 | t:Hampshire g:Brough | 8th | 8,635 |
| 28/6/19 | Huddersfield (h) | W36-10 | t:Randell(3),Crowther,Miller g:Brough(4),Hampshire(3) fg:Brough,Miller | 8th | 4,846 |
| 6/7/19 | Catalans Dragons (a) | L44-10 | t:Lyne,Tupou g:Brough | 8th | 7,237 |
| 12/7/19 | Castleford (h) | L16-36 | t:Wood,Brough g:Brough(4) | 8th | 6,244 |
| 18/7/19 | Wigan (a) | L46-16 | t:Hampshire(2),Jowitt g:Brough(2) | 9th | 10,203 |
| 2/8/19 | St Helens (a) | L26-6 | t:Tanginoa g:Brough | 9th | 9,494 |
| 11/8/19 | Hull FC (h) | L16-26 | t:Hampshire,Arundel,Miller g:Brough(2) | 9th | 5,600 |
| 18/8/19 | Hull KR (a) | W10-38 | t:Miller(2),Jones-Bishop,Wood,Tupou,Hampshire(2) g:Brough(5) | 9th | 8,095 |
| 1/9/19 | Wigan (h) | L16-24 | t:Batchelor,Miller,Jones-Bishop g:Brough(2) | 9th | 5,805 |
| 6/9/19 | Warrington (a) | L23-16 | t:Escare,Jones-Bishop,Hampshire g:Brough(2) | 9th | 10,158 |
| 13/9/19 | London Broncos (h) | W19-10 | t:Hampshire(2),Lyne g:Brough(3) fg:Brough | 9th | 6,230 |

● *Played at Anfield, Liverpool*

|  |  | APP | | TRIES | | GOALS | | FG | | PTS | |
|--|--|-----|--|-------|--|-------|--|----|--|-----|--|
|  | D.O.B. | ALL | SL | ALL | SL | ALL | SL | ALL | SL | ALL | SL |
| Chris Annakin | 30/1/91 | 1(7) | 1(6) | 0 | 0 | 0 | 0 | 0 | 0 | 0 | 0 |
| Tinirau Arona | 8/5/89 | 11(3) | 11(3) | 1 | 1 | 0 | 0 | 0 | 0 | 4 | 4 |
| Joe Arundel | 22/8/91 | 11(1) | 11(1) | 4 | 4 | 0 | 0 | 0 | 0 | 16 | 16 |
| Matty Ashurst | 1/11/89 | 12 | 11 | 0 | 0 | 0 | 0 | 0 | 0 | 0 | 0 |
| Ryan Atkins | 7/10/85 | 1 | 1 | 0 | 0 | 0 | 0 | 0 | 0 | 0 | 0 |
| James Batchelor | 9/4/98 | 11(2) | 11(1) | 2 | 2 | 0 | 0 | 0 | 0 | 8 | 8 |
| Danny Brough | 15/1/83 | 24 | 23 | 2 | 2 | 73 | 72 | 5 | 5 | 159 | 157 |
| Mason Caton-Brown | 24/5/93 | 10 | 9 | 6 | 6 | 0 | 0 | 0 | 0 | 24 | 24 |
| Jack Croft | 21/12/00 | 4 | 3 | 1 | 0 | 0 | 0 | 0 | 0 | 4 | 0 |
| Jordan Crowther | 19/2/97 | 15(5) | 14(4) | 1 | 1 | 0 | 0 | 0 | 0 | 4 | 4 |
| Anthony England | 19/10/86 | 16(2) | 15(2) | 0 | 0 | 0 | 0 | 0 | 0 | 0 | 0 |
| Morgan Escare | 18/10/91 | 5 | 5 | 1 | 1 | 0 | 0 | 0 | 0 | 4 | 4 |
| David Fifita | 28/6/89 | 17(6) | 16(6) | 9 | 8 | 0 | 0 | 0 | 0 | 36 | 32 |
| Chris Green | 3/1/90 | (4) | (4) | 0 | 0 | 0 | 0 | 0 | 0 | 0 | 0 |
| Titus Gwaze | 8/6/99 | (4) | (4) | 0 | 0 | 0 | 0 | 0 | 0 | 0 | 0 |
| Ryan Hampshire | 29/12/94 | 31 | 29 | 14 | 14 | 28 | 25 | 0 | 0 | 112 | 106 |
| Keegan Hirst | 13/12/88 | 3(15) | 2(14) | 0 | 0 | 0 | 0 | 0 | 0 | 0 | 0 |
| Justin Horo | 7/9/86 | 6(8) | 5(8) | 2 | 1 | 0 | 0 | 0 | 0 | 8 | 4 |
| Craig Huby | 21/5/86 | (1) | (1) | 0 | 0 | 0 | 0 | 0 | 0 | 0 | 0 |
| Tom Johnstone | 13/8/95 | 6 | 6 | 6 | 6 | 0 | 0 | 0 | 0 | 24 | 24 |
| Ben Jones-Bishop | 24/8/88 | 31 | 29 | 11 | 10 | 0 | 0 | 0 | 0 | 44 | 40 |
| Max Jowitt | 6/5/97 | 11 | 10 | 7 | 6 | 0 | 0 | 0 | 0 | 28 | 24 |
| Lee Kershaw | 2/5/99 | 6 | 4 | 2 | 1 | 0 | 0 | 0 | 0 | 8 | 4 |
| George King | 24/2/95 | 7(19) | 7(18) | 0 | 0 | 0 | 0 | 0 | 0 | 0 | 0 |
| Danny Kirmond | 11/11/85 | 17(1) | 15(1) | 1 | 1 | 0 | 0 | 0 | 0 | 4 | 4 |
| Craig Kopczak | 20/12/86 | 14(15) | 13(14) | 2 | 2 | 0 | 0 | 0 | 0 | 8 | 8 |
| Reece Lyne | 2/12/92 | 31 | 29 | 6 | 6 | 0 | 0 | 0 | 0 | 24 | 24 |
| Jacob Miller | 22/8/92 | 25 | 24 | 10 | 10 | 0 | 0 | 1 | 1 | 41 | 41 |
| Pauli Pauli | 4/8/94 | 9(9) | 9(8) | 2 | 2 | 0 | 0 | 0 | 0 | 8 | 8 |
| Tyler Randell | 31/8/92 | 11(5) | 10(5) | 4 | 3 | 0 | 0 | 0 | 0 | 16 | 12 |
| Ben Reynolds | 15/1/94 | 6 | 5 | 1 | 1 | 0 | 0 | 0 | 0 | 4 | 4 |
| Junior Sa'u | 18/4/87 | 3 | 3 | 0 | 0 | 0 | 0 | 0 | 0 | 0 | 0 |
| Adam Tangata | 17/3/91 | 2(3) | 2(3) | 0 | 0 | 0 | 0 | 0 | 0 | 0 | 0 |
| Kelepi Tanginoa | 1/3/94 | 13(2) | 12(2) | 1 | 1 | 0 | 0 | 0 | 0 | 4 | 4 |
| Bill Tupou | 2/7/90 | 15 | 15 | 5 | 5 | 0 | 0 | 0 | 0 | 20 | 20 |
| Kyle Wood | 18/6/89 | 18(12) | 17(11) | 8 | 8 | 0 | 0 | 0 | 0 | 32 | 32 |

Ryan Hampshire

**LEAGUE RECORD**
P29-W11-D0-L18
(9th)
F608, A723, Diff-115
22 points.

**CHALLENGE CUP**
Quarter Finalists

**ATTENDANCES**
Best - v Leeds (SL - 6,785)
Worst - v Widnes (CC - 3,055)
Total (SL only) - 76,545
Average (SL only) - 5,468
(Up by 412 on 2018)

*'SL' totals include regular season only; 'All' totals also include Challenge Cup*

**31st October 2018 -** Ade Gardner joins as Head of Performance.

**14th November 2018 -** utility back Jake Mamo signs from Huddersfield on one-year deal.

**20th November 2018 -** Ben Westwood signs new one-year contract for 2019.

**14th December 2018 -** second row Jack Hughes agrees three-year contract extension to end of 2022.

**24th December 2018 -** head coach Steve Price agrees two-year contract extension to November 2021.

**4th January 2019 -** Morgan Smith joins London Broncos.

**15th January 2019 -** England halfback Gareth Widdop to become marquee player on three-year contract from 2020.

**17th January 2019 -** Chris Hill and Jack Hughes named joint captains.

**27th January 2019 -** Kevin Brown ruled out for season with Achilles injury suffered in training.

**2nd February 2019 -** commanding 26-6 home round-one win over Leeds, despite sin-binnings of Jack Hughes and Toby King.

**4th February 2019 -** Ben Westwood banned for two games for dangerous contact on Konrad Hurrell. Toby King gets one game for dangerous throw on Stevie Ward.

**9th February 2019 -** 28-14 home win over Hull KR.

**19th February 2019 -** England rugby union centre Luther Burrell to join on July 1st on contract until November 2021.

**22nd February 2019 -** Ryan Atkins and Josh Charnley both score braces in 32-20 win at Huddersfield.

**2nd March 2019 -** late Sam Tomkins penalty means 23-22 defeat at Catalans.

**5th March 2019 -** young backrower Luis Johnson joins Widnes on loan.

**6th March 2019 -** second row Matt Davis re-joins London Broncos on one-month loan.

**7th March 2019 -** Ben Currie returns from 11-month absence in 24-10 home win over Castleford.

**16th March 2019 -** Ben Westwood gets four-match ban after being sent off for head butt in 25-12 win over Wigan.

**21st March 2019 -** Wolves hang on for 34-32 Thursday-night win at Wakefield after leading 34-12.

**29th March 2019 -** Blake Austin scores four tries in 63-12 win at Hull FC.

**2nd April 2019 -** Tom Lineham, Toby King and Joe Philbin sign new contracts to November 2021.

**6th April 2019 -** ex-Bronco Matt Davis makes debut in 48-12 home win over London.

**9th April 2019 -** Jake Mamo signs new contract to end of 2021.

**12th April 2019 -** 38-12 defeat at St Helens. Tom Lineham gets one-match penalty notice for late challenge on Regan Grace

**19th April 2019 -** shock 36-12 home defeat by Salford.

# KEY DATES

**22nd April 2019 -** Tom Lineham and Joe Philbin both score two tries in 54-6 Easter Monday win at Hull KR.

**24th April 2019 -** hooker Daryl Clark signs contract extension until November 2023.

**28th April 2019 -** 50-19 home win over Huddersfield after trailing 19-12 at half-time.

**12th May 2019 -** late Stefan Ratchford penalty goal secures 26-24 home Challenge Cup win over Wigan.

**18th May 2019 -** Stefan Ratchford ruptures pectoral in 19-12 home defeat to Hull FC.

**25th May 2019 -** 26-14 Magic Weekend win over Wigan at Anfield.

**31st May 2019 -** 28-22 win at Hull KR secures Challenge Cup semi-final spot.

**8th June 2019 -** 17-year-old fullback Josh Thewlis makes debut in 34-4 home win over Catalans.

**15th June 2019 -** late Adam Quinlan try means 16-14 defeat at Hull KR.

**15th June 2019 -** Luis Johnson and Harvey Livett go to Hull KR on loan.

**28th June 2019 -** 21-10 home defeat to St Helens opens up eight-point gap at top of table.

**1st July 2019 -** Bryson Goodwin to return to South Sydney at season end.

**6th July 2019 -** Luther Burrell makes debut in 36-6 win at London Broncos after leading 36-0 at half-time.

**9th July 2019 -** winger Josh Charnley signs new deal to end of 2022.

**12th July 2019 -** 22-12 home defeat to Salford.

**21st July 2019 -** 27-18 defeat at Castleford leaves Wolves ten points behind leaders St Helens.

**23rd July 2019 -** Jack Johnson transferred to Championship side Featherstone.

**27th July 2019 -** 22-14 Challenge Cup semi-final win over Hull FC at Bolton.

**31st July 2019 -** second-rower Ben Westwood to retire at end of season.

**3rd August 2019 -** 30-10 defeat at Catalans amid violence on field and in stand. Blake Austin suffers ankle sprain.

**6th August 2019 -** Matty Smith joins from Catalans on loan.

**8th August 2019 -** Matty Smith makes debut in 30-12 home defeat by St Helens.

**9th August 2019 -** Ryan Atkins rejoins Wakefield for remainder of season, with deal agreed for 2020.

**13th August 2019 -** halfback Kevin Brown joins Leigh on loan until end of season.

**13th August 2019 -** Matty Ashton signs from Swinton on two-year deal from 2020 for undisclosed transfer fee.

**15th August 2019 -** prop Sitaleki Akauola signs two-year contract extension to November 2021.

**16th August 2019 -** 20-6 defeat at Wigan.

**24th August 2019 -** Daryl Clark wins Lance Todd Trophy in 18-4 Challenge Cup Final win over St Helens.

**29th August 2019 -** Thursday-night 22-6 defeat at Salford.

**7th September 2019 -** Blake Austin returns as 23-16 win over Wakefield ends six-match losing run.

**10th September 2019 -** Wolves fined £2,000 by RFL for late change to squad for Challenge Cup semi-final against Hull FC.

**11th September 2019 -** young prop Samy Kibula signs from Wigan Warriors on one-year deal.

**13th September 2019 -** 26-4 last-round defeat at Leeds means fourth-placed finish.

**19th September 2019 -** 14-12 home defeat to Castleford in Elimination Play-off.

**29th September 2019 -** centres Anthony Gelling, two years, and Keanan Brand, three years, sign from Widnes Vikings.

**30th September 2019 -** Harvey Livett joins Hull KR on loan for 2020.

**24th October 2019 -** Wolves fined 15,000 pounds, five thousand suspended for two years, after RFL investigation into crowd violence in Perpignan on August 3. Dragons fined £27,500.

## CLUB RECORDS

**Highest score:**
112-0 v Swinton, 20/5/2011
**Highest score against:**
12-84 v Bradford, 9/9/2001
**Record attendance:**
34,404 v Wigan, 22/1/49 *(Wilderspool)*
15,008 v Widnes, 25/3/2016
*(Halliwell Jones Stadium)*

## MATCH RECORDS

**Tries:**
7 Brian Bevan v Leigh, 29/3/48
Brian Bevan v Bramley, 22/4/53
**Goals:**
16 Lee Briers v Swinton, 20/5/2011
**Points:**
44 Lee Briers v Swinton, 20/5/2011

## SEASON RECORDS

**Tries:** 66 Brian Bevan 1952-53
**Goals:** 170 Steve Hesford 1978-79
**Points:** 363 Harry Bath 1952-53

## CAREER RECORDS

**Tries:** 740 Brian Bevan 1945-62
**Goals:** 1,159 Steve Hesford 1975-85
**Points:** 2,586 Lee Briers 1997-2013
**Appearances:** 620 Brian Bevan 1945-62

# WARRINGTON WOLVES

| DATE | FIXTURE | RESULT | SCORERS | LGE | ATT |
|------|---------|--------|---------|-----|-----|
| 2/2/19 | Leeds (h) | W26-6 | t:Ratchford,Charnley,D Clark,Austin g:Ratchford(5) | 1st | 13,098 |
| 9/2/19 | Hull KR (h) | W28-14 | t:Livett(2),Lineham,Charnley,Cooper g:Ratchford(4) | 2nd | 10,515 |
| 22/2/19 | Huddersfield (a) | W20-32 | t:Atkins(2),Charnley(2),Austin,Murdoch-Masila g:Ratchford(4) | 2nd | 6,076 |
| 2/3/19 | Catalans Dragons (a) | L23-22 | t:Ratchford,D Clark,Atkins,Patton g:Ratchford(3) | 3rd | 8,158 |
| 7/3/19 | Castleford (h) | W24-10 | t:Mamo(2),Hughes,Murdoch-Masila g:Ratchford(4) | 3rd | 9,231 |
| 15/3/19 | Wigan (h) | W25-12 | t:Mamo,Ratchford,Charnley,Hughes g:Ratchford(4) fg:Patton | 2nd | 13,106 |
| 21/3/19 | Wakefield (a) | W32-34 | t:King,Charnley(2),Hill,Austin g:Ratchford(7) | 2nd | 4,753 |
| 29/3/19 | Hull FC (a) | W12-63 | t:Austin(4),D Clark,Charnley(3),Murdoch-Masila,Lineham(2) g:Ratchford(9) fg:Austin | 2nd | 10,810 |
| 5/4/19 | London Broncos (h) | W48-12 | t:Lineham(3),Charnley,Austin(2),J Clark,Ratchford,Atkins g:Ratchford(6) | 1st | 11,718 |
| 12/4/19 | St Helens (a) | L38-12 | t:Austin,D Clark g:Ratchford(2) | 2nd | 17,807 |
| 19/4/19 | Salford (h) | L12-36 | t:Austin,Goodwin g:Ratchford(2) | 2nd | 11,867 |
| 22/4/19 | Hull KR (a) | W6-54 | t:Austin,Lineham(2),Philbin(2),Charnley,Goodwin,King,Akauola g:Ratchford(9) | 2nd | 7,111 |
| 28/4/19 | Huddersfield (h) | W50-19 | t:Currie,Hill,Goodwin(2),Austin,D Clark,Murdoch-Masila g:Ratchford(9) | 2nd | 10,445 |
| 3/5/19 | Castleford (a) | W14-26 | t:Cooper,King(2),Currie g:Ratchford(5) | 2nd | 5,323 |
| 12/5/19 | Wigan (h) (CCR6) | W26-24 | t:Goodwin,Hughes,D Clark,Atkins g:Ratchford(5) | N/A | 7,086 |
| 18/5/19 | Hull FC (h) | L12-19 | t:King,Austin g:Ratchford(2) | 2nd | 10,600 |
| 25/5/19 | Wigan (MW) ● | W26-14 | t:Patton,Austin,King g:Patton(7) | 2nd | N/A |
| 31/5/19 | Hull KR (a) (CCQF) | W22-28 | t:Mamo,Austin,Lineham,Murdoch-Masila,Currie g:Patton(4) | N/A | 3,311 |
| 8/6/19 | Catalans Dragons (h) | W34-4 | t:D Clark,Austin,Goodwin,Akauola,Charnley g:Patton(7) | 2nd | 10,015 |
| 15/6/19 | Hull KR (a) | L16-14 | t:Goodwin,Charnley g:Patton(3) | 2nd | 7,390 |
| 21/6/19 | Wakefield (h) | W30-6 | t:Currie,Charnley,Cooper,Austin,J Johnson g:Patton(5) | 2nd | 8,635 |
| 28/6/19 | St Helens (h) | L10-21 | t:Mamo g:Patton(3) | 2nd | 14,211 |
| 6/7/19 | London Broncos (a) | W6-36 | t:Lineham,Cooper,Goodwin,Mamo,Hughes,King g:Patton(6) | 2nd | 2,357 |
| 12/7/19 | Salford (h) | L12-22 | t:J Clark,Davis g:Patton(2) | 2nd | 9,509 |
| 21/7/19 | Castleford (a) | L27-18 | t:Mamo,Lineham,King g:Patton(3) | 2nd | 6,965 |
| 27/7/19 | Hull FC (CCSF) ●● | W14-22 | t:Goodwin,Currie,King,Philbin g:Ratchford(3) | N/A | 24,364 |
| 3/8/19 | Catalans Dragons (a) | L30-10 | t:Mamo,Hill g:Ratchford | 2nd | 9,634 |
| 8/8/19 | St Helens (a) | L12-30 | t:Mamo,Thewlis g:Ratchford(2) | 2nd | 10,987 |
| 16/8/19 | Wigan (a) | L20-6 | t:Lineham g:Patton | 2nd | 12,555 |
| 24/8/19 | St Helens (CCF) ●●● | W4-18 | t:Philbin,Murdoch-Masila,D Clark g:Ratchford(2),Patton | N/A | 62,717 |
| 29/8/19 | Salford (a) | L22-6 | t:Walker g:Ratchford | 3rd | 4,879 |
| 6/9/19 | Wakefield (h) | W23-16 | t:D Clark,Currie,Charnley,Goodwin g:Ratchford(3) fg:Patton | 3rd | 10,158 |
| 13/9/19 | Leeds (a) | L26-4 | t:Charnley | 4th | 14,085 |
| 19/9/19 | Castleford (h) (EPO) | L12-14 | t:Mamo,Hill g:Ratchford(2) | N/A | 5,627 |

● Played at Anfield, Liverpool
●● Played at University of Bolton Stadium
●●● Played at Wembley Stadium

| | | APP | | TRIES | | GOALS | | FG | | PTS | |
|---|---|---|---|---|---|---|---|---|---|---|---|
| | D.O.B. | ALL | SL | ALL | SL | ALL | SL | ALL | SL | ALL | SL |
| Sitaleki Akauola | 7/4/92 | 4(15) | 4(12) | 2 | 2 | 0 | 0 | 0 | 0 | 8 | 8 |
| Ryan Atkins | 7/10/85 | 12 | 11 | 5 | 4 | 0 | 0 | 0 | 0 | 20 | 16 |
| Blake Austin | 1/2/91 | 30 | 27 | 19 | 18 | 0 | 0 | 1 | 1 | 77 | 73 |
| Luther Burrell | 6/12/87 | 2(1) | 2(1) | 0 | 0 | 0 | 0 | 0 | 0 | 0 | 0 |
| Josh Charnley | 26/6/91 | 29 | 26 | 17 | 17 | 0 | 0 | 0 | 0 | 68 | 68 |
| Daryl Clark | 10/2/93 | 31(1) | 27(1) | 9 | 7 | 0 | 0 | 0 | 0 | 36 | 28 |
| Jason Clark | 28/6/89 | 9(23) | 7(21) | 2 | 2 | 0 | 0 | 0 | 0 | 8 | 8 |
| Mike Cooper | 15/9/88 | 29 | 25 | 4 | 4 | 0 | 0 | 0 | 0 | 16 | 16 |
| Ben Currie | 15/7/94 | 28 | 24 | 6 | 4 | 0 | 0 | 0 | 0 | 24 | 16 |
| Matt Davis | 5/7/96 | 5(14) | 4(11) | 1 | 1 | 0 | 0 | 0 | 0 | 4 | 4 |
| Riley Dean | 10/8/01 | 1 | 1 | 0 | 0 | 0 | 0 | 0 | 0 | 0 | 0 |
| Bryson Goodwin | 30/12/85 | 28 | 24 | 10 | 8 | 0 | 0 | 0 | 0 | 40 | 32 |
| Chris Hill | 3/11/87 | 31 | 27 | 4 | 4 | 0 | 0 | 0 | 0 | 16 | 16 |
| Jack Hughes | 4/1/92 | 29(1) | 25(1) | 4 | 3 | 0 | 0 | 0 | 0 | 16 | 12 |
| Jack Johnson | 25/4/96 | 4 | 4 | 1 | 1 | 0 | 0 | 0 | 0 | 4 | 4 |
| Luis Johnson | 20/2/99 | (2) | (2) | 0 | 0 | 0 | 0 | 0 | 0 | 0 | 0 |
| Toby King | 9/7/96 | 30 | 26 | 9 | 8 | 0 | 0 | 0 | 0 | 36 | 32 |
| Tom Lineham | 21/9/91 | 23 | 20 | 12 | 11 | 0 | 0 | 0 | 0 | 48 | 44 |
| Harvey Livett | 4/1/97 | 6(5) | 6(5) | 2 | 2 | 0 | 0 | 0 | 0 | 8 | 8 |
| Jake Mamo | 6/6/94 | 17(5) | 15(4) | 10 | 9 | 0 | 0 | 0 | 0 | 40 | 36 |
| Pat Moran | 2/4/98 | (1) | (1) | 0 | 0 | 0 | 0 | 0 | 0 | 0 | 0 |
| Ben Murdoch-Masila | 7/2/91 | 7(21) | 6(18) | 6 | 4 | 0 | 0 | 0 | 0 | 24 | 16 |
| Declan Patton | 23/5/95 | 31 | 27 | 2 | 2 | 42 | 37 | 2 | 2 | 94 | 84 |
| Joe Philbin | 16/11/94 | 9(22) | 8(19) | 4 | 2 | 0 | 0 | 0 | 0 | 16 | 8 |
| Stefan Ratchford | 19/7/88 | 25 | 22 | 4 | 4 | 94 | 84 | 0 | 0 | 204 | 184 |
| Matty Smith | 23/7/87 | 4(1) | 4(1) | 0 | 0 | 0 | 0 | 0 | 0 | 0 | 0 |
| Lama Tasi | 3/5/90 | 9(8) | 9(8) | 0 | 0 | 0 | 0 | 0 | 0 | 0 | 0 |
| Josh Thewlis | 30/4/02 | 2 | 2 | 1 | 1 | 0 | 0 | 0 | 0 | 4 | 4 |
| Danny Walker | 29/6/99 | 3(8) | 3(8) | 1 | 1 | 0 | 0 | 0 | 0 | 4 | 4 |
| Ben Westwood | 25/7/81 | 4(6) | 4(6) | 0 | 0 | 0 | 0 | 0 | 0 | 0 | 0 |

*'SL' totals include regular season & play-offs; 'All' totals also include Challenge Cup*

Blake Austin

**LEAGUE RECORD**
P29-W16-D0-L13
(4th/Elimination Play-off)
F709, A533, Diff+176
32 points.

**CHALLENGE CUP**
Winners

**ATTENDANCES**
Best - v St Helens (SL - 14,211)
Worst - v Castleford (EPO - 5,627)
Total (SL, inc play-offs) - 159,722
Average (SL, inc play-offs) - 10,648
(Up by 866 on 2018)

**31st October 2018 -** captain Sean O'Loughlin signs new contract for 2019.

**21st November 2018 -** winger Dom Manfredi signs three-year contract extension to end of 2021.

**1st December 2018 -** halfback Jarrod Sammut joins on two-year contract following release from promoted London Broncos.

**14th December 2018 -** prop Caine Barnes goes back to Workington on one-year loan.

**17th December 2018 -** playmakers Sam Powell and Josh Woods and Academy scrum-half Harry Smith all sign three-year deals until 2022.

**30th January 2019 -** Wigan deducted two league points for minor breach of salary cap in 2017.

**31st January 2019 -** opening-round 22-12 defeat at St Helens.

**17th February 2019 -** 20-8 home defeat to Sydney Roosters in World Club Challenge. Liam Farrell suffers long-term pectoral injury.

**24th February 2019 -** Marc Sneyd field goal means 23-22 home defeat to Hull FC in first Super League game to go to golden point. Prop Liam Byrne scores try on debut.

**6th March 2019 -** Warriors' two-point deduction for salary cap breaches suspended until March 2020 following appeal.

**8th March 2019 -** 14-6 home defeat to previously win-less Huddersfield.

**15th March 2019 -** 25-12 defeat at Warrington.

**24th March 2019 -** George Williams scores hat-trick in 30-22 win at Salford as Joe Burgess comes back from ACL injury.

**31st March 2019 -** Joe Burgess scores hat-trick as loose forward Morgan Smithies makes debut in 42-0 home win over Catalans.

**2nd April 2019 -** Gabe Hamlin charged with anti-doping violation and provisionally suspended by RFL pending conclusion of case. He returns to Australia.

**5th April 2019 -** 38-28 defeat at Castleford after leading by 16 points at half-time. Dom Manfredi suffers season-ending ACL injury.

**12th April 2019 -** Joe Burgess scores hat-trick in 30-20 defeat at Wakefield. Sam Powell gets two-match ban for dangerous tackle.

**15th April 2019 -** Shaun Edwards confirms he will not become Wigan head coach for 2020.

**19th April 2019 -** 36-10 home Good Friday defeat to St Helens. Tom Davies suffers season-ending broken ankle.

**22nd April 2019 -** last-gasp Zak Hardaker try seals 30-26 Easter Monday win at Salford. 18-year-old hooker Amir Bourouh makes debut off bench.

**27th April 2019 -** Sam Powell returns and gets only try of rain-affected 6-4 home win over Castleford.

**8th May 2019 -** 21-year-old hooker Josh Ganson released from last season of three-year contract.

**12th May 2019 -** late Stefan Ratchford penalty goal means 26-24 Challenge Cup defeat at Warrington.

**18th May 2019 -** Super League regular-round record crowd of 31,555 sees 33-16 Camp Nou defeat by Catalans.

# KEY DATES

**25th May 2019 -** 26-14 defeat by Warrington in Anfield Magic Weekend.

**5th June 2019 -** Liam Forsyth joins Leigh Centurions with immediate effect.

**6th June 2019 -** Castleford forward Mitch Clark to join next season on three-year deal. Prop Tony Clubb signs contract extension to end of 2021.

**6th June 2019 -** Oliver Partington and Morgan Smithies, four years, and Jack Wells, two, sign new contracts.

**6th June 2019 -** 22-year-old Salford centre Jake Bibby signs on two-year deal. Joe Burgess signs new one-year contract.

**6th June 2019 -** one-year option on Chris Hankinson contract taken up by club.

**9th June 2019 -** Liam Farrell returns from injury as late Sam Powell field goal secures 19-18 win at Hull KR.

**14th June 2019 -** Oliver Partington scores first try in 23-14 win at Leeds.

**21st June 2019 -** Liam Paisley signs for Championship side Barrow Raiders

**21st June 2019 -** 38-22 win at Huddersfield moves Warriors to within two points of fourth place.

**25th June 2019 -** prop Taulima Tautai leaves by mutual consent in the wake of drink-driving conviction.

**28th June 2019 -** Liam Marshall scores either side of half-time in 28-12 home win over Salford as Warriors move into top-five.

**5th July 2019 -** Liam Marshall scores hat-trick in 52-10 home win over Hull KR.

**8th July 2019 -** head coach Adrian Lam signs contract to end of 2020 season.

**8th July 2019 -** centre Dan Sarginson to join Salford at end of season.

**8th July 2019 -** Jackson Hastings signs from Salford on two-year deal as marquee player. George Williams to join Canberra at end of season.

**12th July 2019 -** 32-10 defeat at St Helens ends five-match winning run. Joe Bullock injures knee.

**18th July 2019 -** Liam Farrell scores hat-trick in 46-16 home win over Wakefield. Forward Ethan Havard makes debut.

**27th July 2019 -** winger Bevan French signs with immediate effect on contract to end of 2021 after being granted release by Parramatta.

**28th July 2019 -** England and South Sydney Rabbitohs forward George Burgess signs for 2020 season on three-year deal.

**1st August 2019 -** Zak Hardaker kicks late field goal to secure 15-14 win at Hull FC. Liam Marshall scores tries either side of half-time to close the gap on third-placed Hull to two points. Sean O'Loughlin sustains pectoral injury.

**5th August 2019 -** Thomas Leuluai signs one-year contract extension for 2020 season.

**8th August 2019 -** fullback Morgan Escare joins Wakefield on loan to end of season.

**9th August 2019 -** two tries from Liam Farrell and Joe Burgess's 100th for the club help Warriors to 36-18 home victory over Hull KR. Bevan French makes debut off bench.

**16th August 2019 -** Bevan French scores first try for the club in 20-6 home victory over Warrington.

**1st September 2019 -** Liam Marshall scores hat-trick in tight 24-16 win at Wakefield.

**6th September 2019 -** Bevan French scores hat-trick in 46-12 home romp over Catalans. Debutant halfback Harry Smith scores try seven minutes after coming off bench.

**9th September 2019 -** Liam Farrell gets one-match penalty notice for dangerous throw.

**10th September 2019 -** Samy Kibula signs for Warrington and Caine Barnes joins Workington on permanent deal.

**12th September 2019 -** 26-8 home win over Castleford secures second-place finish.

**20th September 2019 -** 18-12 home Qualifying Play-off win over Salford.

**27th September 2019 -** 40-10 hammering at St Helens in Qualifying Semi-final.

**4th October 2019 -** 28-4 home defeat to Salford in Final Eliminator.

## CLUB RECORDS

**Highest score:**
116-0 v Flimby & Fothergill, 14/2/25
**Highest score against:**
0-75 v St Helens, 26/6/2005
**Record attendance:**
47,747 v St Helens, 27/3/59 *(Central Park)*
25,004 v St Helens, 25/3/2005
*(JJB/DW Stadium)*

## MATCH RECORDS

**Tries:** 10 Martin Offiah v Leeds, 10/5/92
Shaun Edwards v Swinton, 29/9/92
**Goals:** 22 Jim Sullivan
v Flimby & Fothergill, 14/2/25
**Points:** 44 Jim Sullivan
v Flimby & Fothergill, 14/2/25

## SEASON RECORDS

**Tries:** 62 Johnny Ring 1925-26
**Goals:** 186 Frano Botica 1994-95
**Points:** 462 Pat Richards 2010

## CAREER RECORDS

**Tries:** 478 Billy Boston 1953-68
**Goals:** 2,317 Jim Sullivan 1921-46
**Points:** 4,883 Jim Sullivan 1921-46
**Appearances:** 774 Jim Sullivan 1921-46

# WIGAN WARRIORS

| DATE | FIXTURE | RESULT | SCORERS | LGE | ATT |
|------|---------|--------|---------|-----|-----|
| 31/1/19 | St Helens (a) | L22-12 | t:Flower,Marshall g:Hardaker(2) | 12th | 16,508 |
| 8/2/19 | Leeds (h) | W34-16 | t:Sarginson,Flower,Greenwood,Bullock,Williams,Farrell g:Hardaker(5) | 8th | 11,230 |
| 17/2/19 | Sydney Roosters (h) (WCC) | L8-20 | t:Davies,Marshall | N/A | 21,331 |
| 24/2/19 | Hull FC (h) | L22-23 (aet) | t:Gildart(2),Byrne,Flower g:Hardaker(3) | 11th | 10,971 |
| 3/3/19 | London Broncos (a) | L18-16 | t:Paisley,Isa,Clubb g:Hardaker(2) | 11th | 2,586 |
| 8/3/19 | Huddersfield (h) | L6-14 | t:Escare g:Hardaker | 10th | 10,114 |
| 15/3/19 | Warrington (a) | L25-12 | t:Davies,Isa g:Hardaker(2) | 10th | 13,106 |
| 24/3/19 | Salford (a) | W22-30 | t:Williams(3),Leuluai,Greenwood g:Hardaker(5) | 10th | 4,470 |
| 31/3/19 | Catalans Dragons (h) | W42-0 | t:Burgess(3),Williams,Gildart,Hardaker,Sammut g:Hardaker(7) | 8th | 11,109 |
| 5/4/19 | Castleford (a) | L38-28 | t:Greenwood,Gildart(2),Williams,Burgess(2) g:Hardaker(2) | 9th | 6,839 |
| 12/4/19 | Wakefield (a) | L30-20 | t:Burgess(3),Williams g:Escare(2) | 10th | 5,694 |
| 19/4/19 | St Helens (h) | L10-36 | t:Hardaker,Williams g:Hardaker | 10th | 22,050 |
| 22/4/19 | Salford (h) | W26-30 | t:Burgess,Bullock,Greenwood(2),Hardaker g:Hardaker(5) | 9th | 4,017 |
| 27/4/19 | Castleford (h) | W6-4 | t:Powell g:Hardaker | 8th | 10,058 |
| 2/5/19 | London Broncos (h) | W18-8 | t:Jake Shorrocks,Hankinson,Escare g:Hardaker(3) | 8th | 9,907 |
| 12/5/19 | Warrington (a) (CCR6) | L26-24 | t:Powell,Leuluai,Sarginson,Hardaker g:Hardaker(4) | N/A | 7,086 |
| 18/5/19 | Catalans Dragons (a) ● | L33-16 | t:Marshall,Gildart,Hardaker g:Hardaker(2) | 8th | 31,555 |
| 25/5/19 | Warrington (MW) ●● | L26-14 | t:Burgess,Isa g:Hardaker(3) | 9th | N/A |
| 9/6/19 | Hull KR (a) | W18-19 | t:Williams,Sarginson,Burgess,Marshall g:Hardaker fg:Powell | 8th | 8,010 |
| 14/6/19 | Leeds (a) | W14-23 | t:Gildart,Partington,Clubb g:Hankinson(5) fg:Powell | 7th | 13,105 |
| 21/6/19 | Huddersfield (a) | W22-38 | t:Hankinson,O'Loughlin,Marshall,Burgess,Leuluai,Williams g:Hankinson(7) | 6th | 5,578 |
| 28/6/19 | Salford (h) | W28-12 | t:Marshall(2),Greenwood,Hardaker,Partington g:Hankinson(4) | 5th | 12,066 |
| 5/7/19 | Hull KR (h) | W52-10 | t:Farrell(2),Marshall(3),Hardaker,Williams,Gildart,Burgess g:Hardaker(8) | 4th | 11,042 |
| 12/7/19 | St Helens (a) | L32-10 | t:Hardaker g:Hardaker(3) | 5th | 17,088 |
| 18/7/19 | Wakefield (h) | W46-16 | t:Farrell(3),Hardaker,Isa,Jake Shorrocks,Sammut,Gildart g:Hardaker(7) | 4th | 10,203 |
| 1/8/19 | Hull FC (a) | W14-15 | t:Marshall(2) g:Hardaker(3) fg:Hardaker | 4th | 10,153 |
| 9/8/19 | Hull KR (h) | W36-18 | t:Williams,Marshall,Farrell(2),Burgess,Clubb g:Hardaker(6) | 4th | 10,702 |
| 16/8/19 | Warrington (h) | W20-6 | t:French,Williams,Hardaker g:Hardaker(4) | 3rd | 12,555 |
| 1/9/19 | Wakefield (a) | W16-24 | t:Marshall(3),Powell g:Hardaker(4) | 2nd | 5,805 |
| 6/9/19 | Catalans Dragons (a) | W46-12 | t:French(3),Hardaker,Leuluai,Smith,Sarginson,Gildart g:Hardaker(6),Smith | 2nd | 10,804 |
| 12/9/19 | Castleford (h) | W26-8 | t:Williams,Hardaker,Greenwood,Gildart,Smithies g:Hardaker(3) | 2nd | 11,001 |
| 20/9/19 | Salford (h) (QPO) | W18-12 | t:Gildart,Leuluai,Williams g:Hardaker(3) | N/A | 9,247 |
| 27/9/19 | St Helens (a) (QSF) | L40-10 | t:Marshall,French g:Hardaker | N/A | 14,508 |
| 4/10/19 | Salford (h) (FE) | L4-28 | t:French | N/A | 9,858 |

● *Played at Camp Nou, Barcelona* ●● *Played at Anfield, Liverpool*

| | | APP | | TRIES | | GOALS | | FG | | PTS | |
|---|---|---|---|---|---|---|---|---|---|---|---|
| | D.O.B. | ALL | SL | ALL | SL | ALL | SL | ALL | SL | ALL | SL |
| Amir Bourouh | 5/1/01 | (1) | (1) | 0 | 0 | 0 | 0 | 0 | 0 | 0 | 0 |
| Joe Bullock | 27/11/92 | 9(14) | 9(12) | 2 | 2 | 0 | 0 | 0 | 0 | 8 | 8 |
| Joe Burgess | 14/10/94 | 24 | 23 | 14 | 14 | 0 | 0 | 0 | 0 | 56 | 56 |
| Liam Byrne | 18/8/99 | 1(13) | 1(13) | 1 | 1 | 0 | 0 | 0 | 0 | 4 | 4 |
| Tony Clubb | 12/6/87 | 21(4) | 19(4) | 3 | 3 | 0 | 0 | 0 | 0 | 12 | 12 |
| Tom Davies | 11/1/97 | 8 | 7 | 2 | 1 | 0 | 0 | 0 | 0 | 8 | 4 |
| Morgan Escare | 18/10/91 | 5(1) | 5(1) | 2 | 2 | 2 | 2 | 0 | 0 | 12 | 12 |
| Liam Farrell | 2/7/90 | 17 | 16 | 8 | 8 | 0 | 0 | 0 | 0 | 32 | 32 |
| Ben Flower | 19/10/87 | 14(6) | 12(6) | 3 | 3 | 0 | 0 | 0 | 0 | 12 | 12 |
| Bevan French | 4/1/96 | 3(5) | 3(5) | 6 | 6 | 0 | 0 | 0 | 0 | 24 | 24 |
| Oliver Gildart | 6/8/96 | 34 | 32 | 12 | 12 | 0 | 0 | 0 | 0 | 48 | 48 |
| Joe Greenwood | 2/4/93 | 15(7) | 13(7) | 7 | 7 | 0 | 0 | 0 | 0 | 28 | 28 |
| Gabe Hamlin | 4/1/97 | (7) | (6) | 0 | 0 | 0 | 0 | 0 | 0 | 0 | 0 |
| Chris Hankinson | 30/11/93 | 13(5) | 13(4) | 2 | 2 | 16 | 16 | 0 | 0 | 40 | 40 |
| Zak Hardaker | 17/10/91 | 32 | 30 | 12 | 11 | 97 | 93 | 1 | 1 | 243 | 231 |
| Ethan Havard | 26/10/00 | (1) | (1) | 0 | 0 | 0 | 0 | 0 | 0 | 0 | 0 |
| Willie Isa | 1/1/89 | 31(3) | 30(2) | 4 | 4 | 0 | 0 | 0 | 0 | 16 | 16 |
| Thomas Leuluai | 22/6/85 | 31(1) | 29(1) | 5 | 4 | 0 | 0 | 0 | 0 | 20 | 16 |
| Dom Manfredi | 1/10/93 | 4 | 4 | 0 | 0 | 0 | 0 | 0 | 0 | 0 | 0 |
| Liam Marshall | 9/5/96 | 24 | 22 | 17 | 16 | 0 | 0 | 0 | 0 | 68 | 64 |
| Romain Navarrete | 30/6/94 | 17(7) | 16(6) | 0 | 0 | 0 | 0 | 0 | 0 | 0 | 0 |
| Sean O'Loughlin | 24/11/82 | 14(9) | 13(8) | 1 | 1 | 0 | 0 | 0 | 0 | 4 | 4 |
| Liam Paisley | 27/11/97 | 4 | 4 | 1 | 1 | 0 | 0 | 0 | 0 | 4 | 4 |
| Oliver Partington | 3/9/98 | 15(8) | 15(8) | 2 | 2 | 0 | 0 | 0 | 0 | 8 | 8 |
| Sam Powell | 3/7/92 | 24(3) | 22(3) | 3 | 2 | 0 | 0 | 2 | 2 | 14 | 10 |
| Jarrod Sammut | 15/2/87 | 6(6) | 6(6) | 2 | 2 | 0 | 0 | 0 | 0 | 8 | 8 |
| Dan Sarginson | 26/5/93 | 23 | 21 | 4 | 3 | 0 | 0 | 0 | 0 | 16 | 12 |
| Jake Shorrocks | 26/10/95 | 6(7) | 6(7) | 2 | 2 | 0 | 0 | 0 | 0 | 8 | 8 |
| Joe Shorrocks | 25/11/99 | (1) | (1) | 0 | 0 | 0 | 0 | 0 | 0 | 0 | 0 |
| Harry Smith | 25/1/00 | (1) | (1) | 1 | 1 | 1 | 1 | 0 | 0 | 6 | 6 |
| Morgan Smithies | 7/11/00 | 13(11) | 13(11) | 1 | 1 | 0 | 0 | 0 | 0 | 4 | 4 |
| Taulima Tautai | 3/4/88 | (13) | (12) | 0 | 0 | 0 | 0 | 0 | 0 | 0 | 0 |
| George Williams | 31/10/94 | 34 | 32 | 15 | 15 | 0 | 0 | 0 | 0 | 60 | 60 |

George Williams

**LEAGUE RECORD**
P29-W18-D0-L11
(2nd/Final Eliminator)
F699, A539, Diff+160
36 points.

**CHALLENGE CUP**
Round Six

**ATTENDANCES**
Best - v St Helens (SL - 22,050)
Worst - v Salford (QPO - 9,247)
Total (SL, inc play-offs) - 182,917
Average (SL, inc play-offs) - 11,432
(Down by 216 on 2018)

*'SL' totals include regular season & play-offs; 'All' totals also include Challenge Cup & World Club Challenge*

# SUPER LEAGUE XXIV
## *Round by Round*

## ROUND 1

*Thursday 31st January 2019*

**ST HELENS 22 WIGAN WARRIORS 12**

**SAINTS:** 23 Lachlan Coote (D); 2 Tommy Makinson; 3 Kevin Naiqama (D); 4 Mark Percival; 5 Regan Grace; 6 Theo Fages; 1 Jonny Lomax; 8 Alex Walmsley; 9 James Roby (C); 10 Luke Thompson; 11 Zeb Taia; 17 Dominique Peyroux; 15 Morgan Knowles. Subs (all used): 12 Joseph Paulo (D); 13 Louie McCarthy-Scarsbrook; 16 Kyle Amor; 19 Matty Lees.
**Tries:** Naiqama (2), Lomax (15), Grace (50), Roby (73);
**Goals:** Percival 3/4.
**WARRIORS:** 20 Zak Hardaker (D); 2 Tom Davies; 3 Dan Sarginson; 4 Oliver Gildart; 17 Liam Marshall; 6 George Williams; 7 Thomas Leuluai; 10 Ben Flower; 9 Sam Powell; 14 Romain Navarrete; 11 Joe Greenwood; 12 Liam Farrell; 13 Sean O'Loughlin (C). Subs (all used): 15 Willie Isa; 16 Gabe Hamlin; 8 Tony Clubb; 22 Joe Bullock (D).
**Tries:** Flower (28), Marshall (36); **Goals:** Hardaker 2/2.
**Rugby Leaguer & League Express Men of the Match:**
*Saints:* James Roby; *Warriors:* Joe Greenwood.
**Penalty count:** 7-7; **Half-time:** 12-12;
**Referee:** Robert Hicks; **Attendance:** 16,508.

*Friday 1st February 2019*

**CASTLEFORD TIGERS 20 CATALANS DRAGONS 4**

**TIGERS:** 1 Peter Mata'utia; 2 James Clare; 3 Greg Minikin; 4 Michael Shenton (C); 5 Greg Eden; 6 Jake Trueman; 32 Jordan Rankin (D); 8 Liam Watts; 9 Paul McShane; 10 Grant Millington; 15 Jesse Sene-Lefao; 12 Mike McMeeken; 14 Nathan Massey. Subs (all used): 13 Adam Milner; 16 Junior Moors; 17 Alex Foster; 18 Matt Cook.
**Tries:** McShane (12), Eden (34, 76); **Goals:** McShane 4/5.
**DRAGONS:** 29 Sam Tomkins (D); 3 David Mead; 6 Samisoni Langi; 4 Brayden Wiliame; 5 Lewis Tierney; 1 Tony Gigot; 7 Matty Smith (D); 15 Mickael Simon; 18 Alrix Da Costa; 10 Sam Moa; 11 Kenny Edwards; 12 Benjamin Garcia; 8 Remi Casty (C). Subs (all used): 14 Julian Bousquet; 17 Matt Whitley (D); 19 Mickael Goudemand; 24 Jason Baitieri.
**Try:** Tierney (65); **Goals:** Tomkins 0/1.
**Rugby Leaguer & League Express Men of the Match:**
*Tigers:* Paul McShane; *Dragons:* Tony Gigot.
**Penalty count:** 9-11; **Half-time:** 12-0;
**Referee:** James Child; **Attendance:** 7,494.

**HUDDERSFIELD GIANTS 14 SALFORD RED DEVILS 34**

**GIANTS:** 21 Scott Grix (D2); 1 Darnell McIntosh; 4 Jordan Turner; 35 Joe Wardle (D2); 5 Akuila Uate (D); 34 Izaac Farrell; 7 Matt Frawley (D); 19 Matty English; 14 Adam O'Brien; 10 Suaia Matagi; 15 Oliver Roberts; 12 Alex Mellor; 13 Michael Lawrence (C). Subs (all used): 9 Kruise Leeming; 26 Sebastine Ikahihifo; 27 Adam Walne; 29 Sam Hewitt.
**Tries:** Uate (44), Leeming (79); **Goals:** Farrell 3/3.
**RED DEVILS:** 1 Niall Evalds; 22 Derrell Olpherts; 3 Kris Welham; 4 Junior Sa'u; 23 Ken Sio (D); 6 Robert Lui; 31 Jackson Hastings; 8 Lee Mossop (C); 14 Joey Lussick; 10 Gil Dudson (D); 11 Josh Jones; 24 Jansin Turgut; 13 Mark Flanagan. Subs (all used): 12 George Griffin; 18 Ben Nakubuwai; 16 Greg Burke; 19 Logan Tomkins.
**Tries:** Sa'u (17), Sio (34, 70), Evalds (55, 58, 73), Olpherts (80); **Goals:** Lussick 2/5, Sio 1/3.
**Rugby Leaguer & League Express Men of the Match:**
*Giants:* Izaac Farrell; *Red Devils:* Niall Evalds.
**Penalty count:** 9-7; **Half-time:** 2-8;
**Referee:** Liam Moore; **Attendance:** 5,387.

**HULL KINGSTON ROVERS 18 HULL FC 16**

**HULL KR:** 17 Chris Atkin; 3 Ben Crooks; 4 Jimmy Keinhorst (D); 19 Junior Vaivai; 2 Craig Hall; 7 Danny McGuire; 24 Josh Drinkwater (D); 8 Robbie Mulhern; 21 George Lawler; 10 Mose Masoe; 11 Joel Tomkins (C); 23 Kane Linnett (D); 13 Weller Hauraki (D). Subs (all used): 12 James Greenwood; 14 Mitch Garbutt (D); 15 Tommy Lee; 20 Danny Addy.
**Tries:** Tomkins (32), Garbutt (35), Keinhorst (80);
**Goals:** Drinkwater 3/4.
**HULL FC:** 1 Jamie Shaul; 2 Bureta Faraimo; 3 Carlos Tuimavave; 4 Josh Griffin; 17 Matty Dawson-Jones (D); 30 Danny Washbrook; 7 Marc Sneyd; 8 Scott Taylor; 9 Danny Houghton (C); 19 Masi Matongo; 21 Sika Manu; 12 Mark Minichiello; 11 Dean Hadley. Subs (all used): 28 Jez Litten; 16 Jordan Thompson (D2); 22 Jordan Lane; 23 Mickey Paea.
**Tries:** Manu (15), Dawson-Jones (18), Faraimo (67);
**Goals:** Sneyd 2/4.
**Rugby Leaguer & League Express Men of the Match:**
*Hull KR:* Mitch Garbutt; *Hull FC:* Bureta Faraimo.
**Penalty count:** 8-7; **Half-time:** 14-12;
**Referee:** Ben Thaler; **Attendance:** 12,100.

*Saturday 2nd February 2019*

**WARRINGTON WOLVES 26 LEEDS RHINOS 6**

**WOLVES:** 1 Stefan Ratchford; 2 Tom Lineham; 3 Bryson Goodwin; 4 Ryan Atkins; 5 Josh Charnley; 15 Declan Patton; 6 Blake Austin (D); 8 Chris Hill (C); 9 Daryl Clark; 10 Mike Cooper; 18 Toby King; 12 Jack Hughes (C); 34 Ben Westwood. Subs (all used): 14 Jason Clark (D); 13 Ben Murdoch-Masila; 17 Joe Philbin; 21 Danny Walker (D).
**Tries:** Ratchford (15), Charnley (28), D Clark (31), Austin (58); **Goals:** Ratchford 5/5.
**Sin bin:** Hughes (12) - professional foul; King (73) - dangerous challenge.
**RHINOS:** 1 Jack Walker; 2 Tom Briscoe; 3 Kallum Watkins (C); 4 Konrad Hurrell (D); 5 Ash Handley; 6 Tuimoala Lolohea (D); 7 Richie Myler; 8 Adam Cuthbertson; 9 Matt Parcell; 11 Trent Merrin (D); 16 Brett Ferres; 15 Liam Sutcliffe; 13 Stevie Ward. Subs (all used): 14 Brad Dwyer; 25 James Donaldson (D); 19 Mikolaj Oledzki; 10 Brad Singleton.
**Try:** Ward (77); **Goals:** Lolohea 1/1.
**Rugby Leaguer & League Express Men of the Match:**
*Wolves:* Stefan Ratchford; *Rhinos:* James Donaldson.
**Penalty count:** 8-8; **Half-time:** 20-0;
**Referee:** Chris Kendall; **Attendance:** 13,098.

*Sunday 3rd February 2019*

**LONDON BRONCOS 42 WAKEFIELD TRINITY 24**

**BRONCOS:** 1 Alex Walker; 5 Kieran Dixon; 17 Matty Fleming; 4 Elliot Kear; 2 Rhys Williams; 6 Jordan Abdull (D); 7 James Cunningham; 15 Greg Richards (D); 14 Matty Fozard (D); 18 Nathan Mason (D); 12 Jay Pitts (C); 16 Matty Gee; 20 Luke Yates (D). Subs (all used): 8 Eddie Battye; 11 Will Lovell; 10 Mark Ioane; 9 Eloi Pelissier.
**Tries:** Fleming (18), Williams (25, 60), Dixon (32), Battye (35, 67), Fozard (38), Kear (77);
**Goals:** Abdull 1/3, Dixon 4/5.
**TRINITY:** 1 Ryan Hampshire; 5 Ben Jones-Bishop; 4 Reece Lyne; 3 Bill Tupou; 2 Tom Johnstone; 6 Jacob Miller (C); 7 Danny Brough (D2); 16 Tinirau Arona; 13 Tyler Randell; 15 Craig Kopczak (D); 11 Matty Ashurst; 19 James Batchelor; 22 George King (D). Subs (all used): 26 Jordan Crowther; 10 Anthony England; 9 Kyle Wood; 8 David Fifita.
**Tries:** Kopczak (3), Hampshire (10), Miller (21), Wood (53);
**Goals:** Brough 4/4.
**Sin bin:** Brough (75) - dissent.
**Rugby Leaguer & League Express Men of the Match:**
*Broncos:* Eddie Battye; *Trinity:* Craig Kopczak.
**Penalty count:** 6-8; **Half-time:** 26-18;
**Referee:** Tom Grant; **Attendance:** 2,149.

## ROUND 2

*Thursday 7th February 2019*

**HULL FC 18 CASTLEFORD TIGERS 26**

**HULL FC:** 1 Jamie Shaul; 2 Bureta Faraimo; 3 Carlos Tuimavave; 4 Josh Griffin; 27 Hakim Miloudi; 14 Jake Connor; 7 Marc Sneyd; 8 Scott Taylor; 9 Danny Houghton (C); 19 Masi Matongo; 12 Mark Minichiello; 21 Sika Manu; 13 Joe Westerman. Subs (all used): 16 Jordan Thompson; 22 Jordan Lane; 23 Mickey Paea; 28 Jez Litten.
**Tries:** Westerman (17), Connor (27), Lane (57);
**Goals:** Sneyd 3/3.
**TIGERS:** 1 Peter Mata'utia; 2 James Clare; 3 Greg Minikin; 4 Michael Shenton (C); 5 Greg Eden; 6 Jake Trueman; 32 Jordan Rankin; 8 Liam Watts; 9 Paul McShane; 10 Grant Millington; 15 Jesse Sene-Lefao; 17 Alex Foster; 14 Nathan Massey. Subs (all used): 16 Junior Moors; 13 Adam Milner; 19 Ben Roberts; 21 Mitch Clark.
**Tries:** Shenton (5, 40), Sene-Lefao (13), Clare (48), Moors (54); **Goals:** McShane 2/5, Rankin 1/1.
**Rugby Leaguer & League Express Men of the Match:**
*Hull FC:* Jake Connor; *Tigers:* Paul McShane.
**Penalty count:** 8-6; **Half-time:** 12-14;
**Referee:** Chris Kendall; **Attendance:** 11,244.

*Friday 8th February 2019*

**WIGAN WARRIORS 34 LEEDS RHINOS 16**

**WARRIORS:** 20 Zak Hardaker; 2 Tom Davies; 4 Oliver Gildart; 3 Dan Sarginson; 17 Liam Marshall; 6 George Williams; 7 Thomas Leuluai; 8 Tony Clubb; 9 Sam Powell; 10 Ben Flower; 11 Joe Greenwood; 12 Liam Farrell; 13 Sean O'Loughlin (C). Subs (all used): 14 Romain Navarrete; 15 Willie Isa; 16 Gabe Hamlin; 22 Joe Bullock.
**Tries:** Sarginson (7), Flower (21), Greenwood (27), Bullock (30), Williams (68), Farrell (77);
**Goals:** Hardaker 5/7.
**RHINOS:** 1 Jack Walker; 2 Tom Briscoe; 3 Kallum Watkins (C); 4 Konrad Hurrell; 5 Ash Handley; 6 Tuimoala Lolohea; 7 Richie Myler; 18 Nathaniel Peteru; 14 Brad Dwyer; 11 Trent Merrin; 16 Brett Ferres; 15 Liam Sutcliffe; 13 Stevie Ward. Subs (all used): 8 Adam Cuthbertson; 9 Matt Parcell; 19 Mikolaj Oledzki; 25 James Donaldson.
**Tries:** Handley (2), Ferres (15), Watkins (70);
**Goals:** Lolohea 2/3.
**On report:** Oledzki (37) - alleged bite on Powell.
**Rugby Leaguer & League Express Men of the Match:**
*Warriors:* Sean O'Loughlin; *Rhinos:* Nathaniel Peteru.
**Penalty count:** 7-5; **Half-time:** 22-12;
**Referee:** Ben Thaler; **Attendance:** 11,230.

*Saturday 9th February 2019*

**WARRINGTON WOLVES 28
HULL KINGSTON ROVERS 14**

**WOLVES:** 1 Stefan Ratchford; 2 Tom Lineham; 3 Bryson Goodwin; 4 Ryan Atkins; 5 Josh Charnley; 6 Blake Austin; 15 Declan Patton; 8 Chris Hill (C); 9 Daryl Clark; 10 Mike Cooper; 20 Harvey Livett; 12 Jack Hughes (C); 14 Jason Clark. Subs (all used): 13 Ben Murdoch-Masila; 16 Lama Tasi (D); 17 Joe Philbin; 21 Danny Walker.
**Tries:** Livett (21, 54), Lineham (40), Charnley (66), Cooper (79); **Goals:** Ratchford 4/5.
**Sin bin:** Austin (27) - late challenge on Tomkins.
**ROVERS:** 17 Chris Atkin; 3 Ben Crooks; 4 Jimmy Keinhorst; 23 Kane Linnett; 2 Craig Hall; 7 Danny McGuire; 24 Josh Drinkwater; 10 Mose Masoe; 15 Tommy Lee; 8 Robbie Mulhern; 11 Joel Tomkins (C); 13 Weller Hauraki; 21 George Lawler. Subs (all used): 14 Mitch Garbutt; 12 James Greenwood; 20 Danny Addy; 19 Junior Vaivai.
**Tries:** Crooks (8), Hall (28), Keinhorst (70);
**Goals:** Drinkwater 1/3.
**Rugby Leaguer & League Express Men of the Match:**
*Wolves:* Stefan Ratchford; *Rovers:* Mitch Garbutt.
**Penalty count:** 7-7; **Half-time:** 12-8;
**Referee:** Liam Moore; **Attendance:** 10,515.

**CATALANS DRAGONS 27 HUDDERSFIELD GIANTS 10**

**DRAGONS:** 29 Sam Tomkins; 4 Brayden Wiliame; 6 Samisoni Langi; 17 Matt Whitley; 5 Lewis Tierney; 1 Tony Gigot; 7 Matty Smith; 15 Mickael Simon; 9 Michael McIlorum; 10 Sam Moa; 11 Kenny Edwards; 16 Benjamin Jullien; 8 Remi Casty (C). Subs: 14 Julian Bousquet; 18 Alrix Da Costa (not used); 19 Mickael Goudemand; 24 Jason Baitieri.
**Tries:** Wiliame (16, 20), Tierney (37), Tomkins (67);
**Goals:** Tomkins 5/6; **Field goal:** Smith (80).
**GIANTS:** 21 Scott Grix; 1 Darnell McIntosh; 4 Jordan Turner; 35 Joe Wardle; 5 Akuila Uate; 34 Izaac Farrell; 7 Matt Frawley; 19 Matty English; 14 Adam O'Brien; 10 Suaia Matagi; 11 Aaron Murphy; 12 Alex Mellor; 13 Michael Lawrence (C). Subs (all used): 9 Kruise Leeming; 15 Oliver Roberts; 26 Sebastine Ikahihifo; 27 Adam Walne.
**Tries:** Frawley (6), Roberts (72);
**Goals:** Farrell 1/1, McIntosh 0/1.
**Rugby Leaguer & League Express Men of the Match:**
*Dragons:* Sam Tomkins; *Giants:* Matt Frawley.
**Penalty count:** 10-4; **Half-time:** 18-6;
**Referee:** Tom Grant; **Attendance:** 9,211.

*Sunday 10th February 2019*

**SALFORD RED DEVILS 24 LONDON BRONCOS 0**

**RED DEVILS:** 1 Niall Evalds; 22 Derrell Olpherts; 3 Kris Welham; 4 Junior Sa'u; 23 Ken Sio; 6 Robert Lui; 31 Jackson Hastings; 8 Lee Mossop (C); 14 Joey Lussick; 10 Gil Dudson; 11 Josh Jones; 24 Jansin Turgut; 13 Mark Flanagan. Subs (all used): 12 George Griffin; 18 Ben Nakubuwai; 16 Greg Burke; 19 Logan Tomkins.
**Tries:** Sio (20), Hastings (43), Evalds (70), Jones (79);
**Goals:** Hastings 4/5.
**Sin bin:** Mossop (76) - fighting.
**BRONCOS:** 1 Alex Walker; 5 Kieran Dixon; 19 Ryan Morgan (D); 4 Elliot Kear; 2 Rhys Williams; 6 Jordan Abdull; 7 James Cunningham; 15 Greg Richards; 14 Matty Fozard; 18 Nathan Mason; 12 Jay Pitts (C); 16 Matty Gee; 20 Luke Yates. Subs (all used): 8 Eddie Battye; 11 Will Lovell; 10 Mark Ioane; 9 Eloi Pelissier.
**Rugby Leaguer & League Express Men of the Match:**
*Red Devils:* Jackson Hastings; *Broncos:* Alex Walker.
**Penalty count:** 5-5; **Half-time:** 6-0;
**Referee:** James Child; **Attendance:** 3,246.

**WAKEFIELD TRINITY 18 ST HELENS 24**

**TRINITY:** 1 Ryan Hampshire; 2 Tom Johnstone; 3 Bill Tupou; 4 Reece Lyne; 5 Ben Jones-Bishop; 6 Jacob Miller (C); 7 Danny Brough; 8 David Fifita; 9 Kyle Wood; 10 Anthony England; 11 Matty Ashurst; 12 Danny Kirmond; 16 Tinirau Arona. Subs (all used): 15 Craig Kopczak; 17 Craig Huby; 22 George King; 14 Justin Horo.
**Tries:** Johnstone (20, 32), Tupou (71);
**Goals:** Brough 3/4, Hampshire 0/1.
**Sin bin:** Brough (17) - dissent.

**SAINTS:** 23 Lachlan Coote; 2 Tommy Makinson; 3 Kevin Naiqama; 4 Mark Percival; 5 Regan Grace; 6 Theo Fages; 1 Jonny Lomax; 8 Alex Walmsley; 9 James Roby (C); 10 Luke Thompson; 11 Zeb Taia; 17 Dominique Peyroux; 15 Morgan Knowles. Subs (all used): 12 Joseph Paulo; 13 Louie McCarthy-Scarsbrook; 19 Matty Lees; 16 Kyle Amor.
**Tries:** Knowles (9), Makinson (27, 66), Grace (48), McCarthy-Scarsbrook (78); **Goals:** Percival 2/5.
**Rugby Leaguer & League Express Men of the Match:** *Trinity:* David Fifita; *Saints:* Tommy Makinson.
**Penalty count:** 11-10; **Half-time:** 10-10;
**Referee:** Robert Hicks; **Attendance:** 5,815.

## ROUND 10

*Sunday 17th February 2019*

**HULL KINGSTON ROVERS 22 LONDON BRONCOS 12**

**ROVERS:** 26 Will Dagger; 3 Ben Crooks; 4 Jimmy Keinhorst; 19 Junior Vaivai; 2 Craig Hall; 7 Danny McGuire (C); 24 Josh Drinkwater; 8 Robbie Mulhern; 21 George Lawler; 10 Mose Masoe; 23 Kane Linnett; 13 Weller Hauraki; 12 James Greenwood. Subs (all used): 15 Tommy Lee; 14 Mitch Garbutt; 22 Ryan Lannon (D); 17 Chris Atkin.
**Tries:** Linnett (3), Garbutt (43, 56), Hall (48);
**Goals:** Drinkwater 1/2, Hall 2/2.
**BRONCOS:** 1 Alex Walker; 5 Kieran Dixon; 19 Ryan Morgan; 4 Elliot Kear; 2 Rhys Williams; 6 Jordan Abdull; 7 James Cunningham; 18 Nathan Mason; 14 Matty Fozard; 15 Greg Richards; 12 Jay Pitts (C); 16 Matty Gee; 20 Luke Yates. Subs (all used): 9 Eloi Pelissier; 10 Mark Ioane; 8 Eddie Battye; 11 Will Lovell.
**Tries:** Gee (9), Pitts (74); **Goals:** Dixon 2/2.
**Sin bin:** Pelissier (57) - high tackle on Dagger.
**Rugby Leaguer & League Express Men of the Match:** *Rovers:* Mitch Garbutt; *Broncos:* Jordan Abdull.
**Penalty count:** 9-8; **Half-time:** 4-6;
**Referee:** Scott Mikalauskas; **Attendance:** 7,210.

**SALFORD RED DEVILS 14 LEEDS RHINOS 46**

**RED DEVILS:** 1 Niall Evalds; 22 Derrell Olpherts; 3 Kris Welham; 4 Junior Sa'u; 23 Ken Sio; 6 Robert Lui; 31 Jackson Hastings; 8 Lee Mossop (C); 14 Joey Lussick; 10 Gil Dudson; 11 Josh Jones; 24 Jansin Turgut; 13 Mark Flanagan. Subs (all used): 12 George Griffin; 18 Ben Nakubuwai; 16 Greg Burke; 19 Logan Tomkins.
**Tries:** Lussick (7), Jones (44); **Goals:** Sio 3/3.
**Sin bin:** Turgut (51) - fighting.
**RHINOS:** 1 Jack Walker; 2 Tom Briscoe; 3 Kallum Watkins (C); 4 Konrad Hurrell; 5 Ash Handley; 6 Tuimoala Lolohea; 7 Richie Myler; 8 Adam Cuthbertson; 14 Brad Dwyer; 18 Nathaniel Peteru; 16 Brett Ferres; 13 Stevie Ward; 11 Trent Merrin. Subs (all used): 9 Matt Parcell; 10 Brad Singleton; 25 James Donaldson; 22 Cameron Smith.
**Tries:** Cuthbertson (17), Walker (20, 66, 68), Hurrell (23, 59), Parcell (63), Handley (71); **Goals:** Lolohea 7/9.
**Rugby Leaguer & League Express Men of the Match:** *Red Devils:* Josh Jones; *Rhinos:* Jack Walker.
**Penalty count:** 8-9; **Half-time:** 6-18;
**Referee:** James Child; **Attendance:** 4,385.

## ROUND 3

*Thursday 21st February 2019*

**WAKEFIELD TRINITY 22 CATALANS DRAGONS 12**

**TRINITY:** 1 Ryan Hampshire; 5 Ben Jones-Bishop; 4 Reece Lyne; 3 Bill Tupou; 2 Tom Johnstone; 6 Jacob Miller (C); 7 Danny Brough; 8 David Fifita; 9 Kyle Wood; 10 Anthony England; 19 James Batchelor; 11 Matty Ashurst; 16 Tinirau Arona. Subs (all used): 14 Justin Horo; 22 George King; 15 Craig Kopczak; 20 Keegan Hirst.
**Tries:** Johnstone (16), Fifita (31), Batchelor (36);
**Goals:** Brough 5/5.
**Sin bin:** Hirst (46) - high tackle on Baitieri;
Arona (72) - delaying restart.
**DRAGONS:** 29 Sam Tomkins; 3 David Mead; 6 Samisoni Langi; 4 Brayden Wiliame; 5 Lewis Tierney; 1 Tony Gigot; 7 Matty Smith; 15 Mickael Simon; 9 Michael McIlorum; 10 Sam Moa; 11 Kenny Edwards; 17 Matt Whitley; 8 Remi Casty (C). Subs (all used): 12 Benjamin Garcia; 19 Mickael Goudemand; 23 Antoni Maria; 24 Jason Baitieri.
**Tries:** Langi (19, 57); **Goals:** Tomkins 2/3.
**Sin bin:** Baitieri (69) - late challenge on Arona.
**On report:** Tomkins (36) - collision with referee.
**Rugby Leaguer & League Express Men of the Match:** *Trinity:* Danny Brough; *Dragons:* Michael McIlorum.
**Penalty count:** 8-7; **Half-time:** 20-8;
**Referee:** Chris Kendall; **Attendance:** 4,639.

*Friday 22nd February 2019*

**HUDDERSFIELD GIANTS 20**
**WARRINGTON WOLVES 32**

**GIANTS:** 1 Darnell McIntosh; 2 Jermaine McGillvary; 4 Jordan Turner; 35 Joe Wardle; 5 Akuila Uate; 6 Lee Gaskell; 7 Matt Frawley; 26 Sebastine Ikahihifo; 14 Adam O'Brien; 10 Suaia Matagi; 11 Aaron Murphy; 12 Alex Mellor; 13 Michael Lawrence (C). Subs (all used): 9 Kruise Leeming; 27 Adam Walne; 19 Matty English; 17 Ukuma Ta'ai.
**Tries:** McGillvary (37), English (47), Turner (74), Uate (79);
**Goals:** Gaskell 2/4.
**Sin bin:** Walne (49) - high tackle on Hill.
**On report:** Walne (19) - alleged late challenge on Patton.
**WOLVES:** 1 Stefan Ratchford; 2 Tom Lineham; 3 Bryson Goodwin; 4 Ryan Atkins; 5 Josh Charnley; 6 Blake Austin; 15 Declan Patton; 8 Chris Hill (C); 9 Daryl Clark; 10 Mike Cooper; 18 Toby King; 12 Jack Hughes (C); 16 Lama Tasi. Subs (all used): 13 Ben Murdoch-Masila; 17 Joe Philbin; 14 Jason Clark; 22 Jake Mamo (D).
**Tries:** Atkins (10, 51), Charnley (15, 34), Austin (60), Murdoch-Masila (65); **Goals:** Ratchford 4/7, Austin 0/1.
**Rugby Leaguer & League Express Men of the Match:** *Giants:* Alex Mellor; *Wolves:* Blake Austin.
**Penalty count:** 11-7; **Half-time:** 4-16;
**Referee:** James Child; **Attendance:** 6,076.

**ST HELENS 27 LEEDS RHINOS 22**

**SAINTS:** 23 Lachlan Coote; 2 Tommy Makinson; 3 Kevin Naiqama; 4 Mark Percival; 5 Regan Grace; 1 Jonny Lomax; 6 Theo Fages; 8 Alex Walmsley; 9 James Roby (C); 10 Luke Thompson; 11 Zeb Taia; 17 Dominique Peyroux; 15 Morgan Knowles. Subs (all used): 12 Joseph Paulo; 13 Louie McCarthy-Scarsbrook; 16 Kyle Amor; 19 Matty Lees.
**Tries:** Fages (5), Lomax (9), Walmsley (45, 50), Thompson (62); **Goals:** Percival 2/4, Coote 1/2;
**Field goal:** Roby (80).
**RHINOS:** 1 Jack Walker; 2 Tom Briscoe; 3 Kallum Watkins (C); 4 Konrad Hurrell; 5 Ash Handley; 6 Tuimoala Lolohea; 7 Richie Myler; 18 Nathaniel Peteru; 14 Brad Dwyer; 11 Trent Merrin; 16 Brett Ferres; 15 Liam Sutcliffe; 13 Stevie Ward. Subs (all used): 8 Adam Cuthbertson; 10 Brad Singleton; 19 Mikolaj Oledzki; 22 Cameron Smith.
**Tries:** Watkins (12), Hurrell (23), Handley (33), Oledzki (36);
**Goals:** Lolohea 3/4.
**Rugby Leaguer & League Express Men of the Match:** *Saints:* Alex Walmsley; *Rhinos:* Konrad Hurrell.
**Penalty count:** 3-3; **Half-time:** 10-22;
**Referee:** Robert Hicks; **Attendance:** 11,318.

*Saturday 23rd February 2019*

**HULL KINGSTON ROVERS 22**
**SALFORD RED DEVILS 24**

**ROVERS:** 26 Will Dagger; 5 Ryan Shaw; 4 Jimmy Keinhorst; 23 Kane Linnett; 2 Craig Hall; 7 Danny McGuire; 24 Josh Drinkwater; 8 Robbie Mulhern; 15 Tommy Lee; 10 Mose Masoe; 11 Joel Tomkins (C); 13 Weller Hauraki; 21 George Lawler. Subs (all used): 14 Mitch Garbutt; 22 Ryan Lannon; 17 Chris Atkin; 20 Danny Addy.
**Tries:** Hauraki (7), Hall (29), Lawler (33), Keinhorst (37);
**Goals:** Shaw 3/4.
**RED DEVILS:** 1 Niall Evalds; 22 Derrell Olpherts; 3 Kris Welham; 4 Junior Sa'u; 23 Ken Sio; 6 Robert Lui; 31 Jackson Hastings; 8 Lee Mossop (C); 14 Joey Lussick; 10 Gil Dudson; 11 Josh Jones; 24 Jansin Turgut; 12 George Griffin. Subs (all used): 17 Tyrone McCarthy; 20 Daniel Murray; 16 Greg Burke; 19 Logan Tomkins.
**Tries:** Lui (11), Jones (24), Olpherts (58), Sio (65), Lussick (71); **Goals:** Sio 2/5.
**Rugby Leaguer & League Express Men of the Match:** *Rovers:* George Lawler; *Red Devils:* Jackson Hastings.
**Penalty count:** 7-7; **Half-time:** 22-8;
**Referee:** Liam Moore; **Attendance:** 7,565.

**LONDON BRONCOS 6 CASTLEFORD TIGERS 40**

**BRONCOS:** 17 Matty Fleming; 5 Kieran Dixon; 19 Ryan Morgan; 4 Elliot Kear; 2 Rhys Williams; 6 Jordan Abdull; 7 James Cunningham; 13 Sadiq Adebiyi; 14 Matty Fozard; 10 Mark Ioane; 12 Jay Pitts (C); 11 Will Lovell; 20 Luke Yates. Subs (all used): 9 Eloi Pelissier; 18 Nathan Mason; 8 Eddie Battye; 15 Greg Richards.
**Try:** Williams (8); **Goals:** Dixon 1/1.
**TIGERS:** 1 Peter Mata'utia; 2 James Clare; 3 Greg Minikin; 4 Michael Shenton (C); 5 Greg Eden; 6 Jake Trueman; 32 Jordan Rankin; 8 Liam Watts; 9 Paul McShane; 10 Grant Millington; 15 Jesse Sene-Lefao; 33 Chris Clarkson (D); 14 Nathan Massey. Subs (all used): 13 Adam Milner; 16 Junior Moors; 18 Matt Cook; 25 Tuoyo Egodo.
**Tries:** Mata'utia (5), Trueman (16), Moors (26), Sene-Lefao (37), Watts (44), Eden (52), Rankin (71);
**Goals:** McShane 5/6, Rankin 1/1.
**Rugby Leaguer & League Express Men of the Match:** *Broncos:* Jordan Abdull; *Tigers:* Liam Watts.
**Penalty count:** 3-3; **Half-time:** 6-24;
**Referee:** Scott Mikalauskas; **Attendance:** 2,053.

*Sunday 24th February 2019*

**WIGAN WARRIORS 22 HULL FC 23**
*(after golden point extra-time)*

**WARRIORS:** 20 Zak Hardaker; 2 Tom Davies; 4 Oliver Gildart; 3 Dan Sarginson; 17 Liam Marshall; 6 George Williams; 7 Thomas Leuluai; 22 Joe Bullock; 9 Sam Powell; 10 Ben Flower; 11 Joe Greenwood; 15 Willie Isa; 13 Sean O'Loughlin (C). Subs (all used): 19 Taulima Tautai; 36 Liam Byrne (D); 16 Gabe Hamlin; 37 Jarrod Sammut (D).
**Tries:** Gildart (7, 78), Byrne (34), Flower (65);
**Goals:** Hardaker 3/4.
**Sin bin:** Tautai (38) - high tackle on Thompson.
**HULL FC:** 1 Jamie Shaul; 33 Ratu Naulago (D); 3 Carlos Tuimavave; 4 Josh Griffin; 2 Bureta Faraimo; 14 Jake Connor; 7 Marc Sneyd; 23 Mickey Paea; 9 Danny Houghton (C); 19 Masi Matongo; 21 Sika Manu; 12 Mark Minichiello; 13 Joe Westerman. Subs (all used): 34 Gareth Ellis; 16 Jordan Thompson; 22 Jordan Lane; 28 Jez Litten.
**Tries:** Tuimavave (14), Westerman (20), Naulago (29, 44);
**Goals:** Sneyd 3/4; **Field goal:** Sneyd (82).
**Rugby Leaguer & League Express Men of the Match:** *Warriors:* Ben Flower; *Hull FC:* Danny Houghton.
**Penalty count:** 6-6; **Half-time:** 12-16;
**Referee:** Ben Thaler; **Attendance:** 10,971.

## ROUND 4

*Thursday 28th February 2019*

**SALFORD RED DEVILS 4 ST HELENS 26**

**RED DEVILS:** 1 Niall Evalds; 22 Derrell Olpherts; 3 Kris Welham; 4 Junior Sa'u; 23 Ken Sio; 6 Robert Lui; 31 Jackson Hastings; 8 Lee Mossop (C); 14 Joey Lussick; 10 Gil Dudson; 11 Josh Jones; 24 Jansin Turgut; 20 Daniel Murray. Subs (all used): 17 Tyrone McCarthy; 18 Ben Nakubuwai; 16 Greg Burke; 19 Logan Tomkins.
**Try:** Olpherts (54); **Goals:** Sio 0/1.
**On report:** Turgut (43) - alleged dangerous contact.
**SAINTS:** 23 Lachlan Coote; 2 Tommy Makinson; 24 Matthew Costello; 4 Mark Percival; 5 Regan Grace; 1 Jonny Lomax; 6 Theo Fages; 8 Alex Walmsley; 9 James Roby (C); 10 Luke Thompson; 11 Zeb Taia; 17 Dominique Peyroux; 15 Morgan Knowles. Subs (all used): 19 Matty Lees; 13 Louie McCarthy-Scarsbrook; 12 Joseph Paulo; 16 Kyle Amor.
**Tries:** Percival (19), Lomax (32), Roby (39, 75), Grace (57);
**Goals:** Coote 3/5.
**Rugby Leaguer & League Express Men of the Match:** *Red Devils:* Jackson Hastings; *Saints:* James Roby.
**Penalty count:** 6-4; **Half-time:** 0-16;
**Referee:** Ben Thaler; **Attendance:** 4,064.

*Friday 1st March 2019*

**CASTLEFORD TIGERS 32 HULL KINGSTON ROVERS 16**

**TIGERS:** 1 Peter Mata'utia; 2 James Clare; 3 Greg Minikin; 4 Michael Shenton (C); 5 Greg Eden; 6 Jake Trueman; 32 Jordan Rankin; 8 Liam Watts; 9 Paul McShane; 10 Grant Millington; 15 Jesse Sene-Lefao; 33 Chris Clarkson; 14 Nathan Massey. Subs (all used): 16 Junior Moors; 18 Matt Cook; 25 Tuoyo Egodo; 29 Jacques O'Neill (D).
**Tries:** Rankin (16), Watts (22), Eden (38, 63), Clare (44), Clarkson (66); **Goals:** McShane 1/3, Rankin 3/3.
**Sin bin:** Millington (71) - fighting.
**On report:** Mata'utia (27) - alleged high tackle on Keinhorst.
**ROVERS:** 26 Will Dagger; 5 Ryan Shaw; 4 Jimmy Keinhorst; 19 Junior Vaivai; 2 Craig Hall; 7 Danny McGuire (C); 24 Josh Drinkwater; 16 Lee Jewitt; 15 Tommy Lee; 10 Mose Masoe; 23 Kane Linnett; 20 Danny Addy; 13 Weller Hauraki. Subs (all used): 8 Robbie Mulhern; 12 James Greenwood; 17 Chris Atkin; 22 Ryan Lannon.
**Tries:** Masoe (9, 49), Atkin (78); **Goals:** Shaw 2/3.
**Sin bin:** Greenwood (71) - fighting;
Hauraki (75) - repeated offences; McGuire (75) - dissent.
**Rugby Leaguer & League Express Men of the Match:** *Tigers:* Liam Watts; *Rovers:* Mose Masoe.
**Penalty count:** 12-8; **Half-time:** 14-6;
**Referee:** Gareth Hewer; **Attendance:** 8,770.

**LEEDS RHINOS 18 WAKEFIELD TRINITY 35**

**RHINOS:** 6 Tuimoala Lolohea; 2 Tom Briscoe; 3 Kallum Watkins (C); 4 Konrad Hurrell; 5 Ash Handley; 22 Cameron Smith; 7 Richie Myler; 18 Nathaniel Peteru; 14 Brad Dwyer; 11 Trent Merrin; 16 Brett Ferres; 15 Liam Sutcliffe; 8 Adam Cuthbertson. Subs (all used): 19 Mikolaj Oledzki; 9 Matt Parcell; 25 James Donaldson; 10 Brad Singleton.
**Tries:** Handley (3, 75), T Briscoe (24, 78); **Goals:** Lolohea 1/4.
**Sin bin:** Merrin (70) - dissent.

**TRINITY:** 1 Ryan Hampshire; 5 Ben Jones-Bishop; 4 Reece Lyne; 3 Bill Tupou; 2 Tom Johnstone; 6 Jacob Miller (C); 7 Danny Brough; 8 David Fifita; 9 Kyle Wood; 22 George King; 19 James Batchelor; 11 Matty Ashurst; 16 Tinirau Arona. Subs (all used): 15 Craig Kopczak; 24 Pauli Pauli; 20 Keegan Hirst; 14 Justin Horo.
**Tries:** Johnstone (11, 14, 22), Wood (32), Miller (60), Brough (67); **Goals:** Brough 5/7; **Field goal:** Brough (62).
**On report:**
Ashurst (5) - alleged dangerous contact on Merrin.
**Rugby Leaguer & League Express Men of the Match:**
*Rhinos:* Ash Handley; *Trinity:* Bill Tupou.
**Penalty count:** 8-9; **Half-time:** 10-22;
**Referee:** Chris Kendall; **Attendance:** 13,148.

*Saturday 2nd March 2019*

### CATALANS DRAGONS 23 WARRINGTON WOLVES 22

**DRAGONS:** 29 Sam Tomkins; 27 Fouad Yaha (D2); 6 Samisoni Langi; 4 Brayden Wiliame; 5 Lewis Tierney; 1 Tony Gigot; 7 Matty Smith; 15 Mickael Simon; 9 Michael McIlorum; 10 Sam Moa; 11 Kenny Edwards; 16 Benjamin Jullien; 8 Remi Casty (C). Subs (all used): 17 Matt Whitley; 19 Mickael Goudemand; 23 Antoni Maria; 24 Jason Baitieri.
**Tries:** Wiliame (2), Edwards (14), Casty (64);
**Goals:** Tomkins 5/5; **Field goal:** Gigot (38).
**WOLVES:** 1 Stefan Ratchford; 2 Tom Lineham; 3 Bryson Goodwin; 4 Ryan Atkins; 5 Josh Charnley; 6 Blake Austin; 15 Declan Patton; 8 Chris Hill (C); 9 Daryl Clark; 10 Mike Cooper; 18 Toby King; 12 Jack Hughes (C); 16 Lama Tasi. Subs (all used): 13 Ben Murdoch-Masila; 14 Jason Clark; 17 Joe Philbin; 22 Jake Mamo.
**Tries:** Ratchford (34), D Clark (45), Atkins (58), Patton (68); **Goals:** Ratchford 3/4.
**Rugby Leaguer & League Express Men of the Match:**
*Dragons:* Matty Smith; *Wolves:* Daryl Clark.
**Penalty count:** 8-3; **Half-time:** 15-6;
**Referee:** Robert Hicks; **Attendance:** 8,158.

*Sunday 3rd March 2019*

### HUDDERSFIELD GIANTS 8 HULL FC 28

**GIANTS:** 21 Scott Grix; 2 Jermaine McGillvary; 4 Jordan Turner; 20 Jake Wardle; 1 Darnell McIntosh; 23 Oliver Russell; 7 Matt Frawley; 17 Ukuma Ta'ai; 9 Kruise Leeming; 10 Suaia Matagi; 11 Aaron Murphy; 12 Alex Mellor; 13 Michael Lawrence (C). Subs (all used): 14 Adam O'Brien; 25 Colton Roche; 19 Matty English; 27 Adam Walne.
**Try:** McIntosh (30); **Goals:** Russell 2/2.
**HULL FC:** 14 Jake Connor; 2 Bureta Faraimo; 3 Carlos Tuimavave; 4 Josh Griffin; 33 Ratu Naulago; 6 Albert Kelly; 7 Marc Sneyd; 23 Mickey Paea; 9 Danny Houghton (C); 19 Masi Matongo; 12 Mark Minichiello; 21 Sika Manu; 13 Joe Westerman. Subs (all used): 16 Jordan Thompson; 22 Jordan Lane; 34 Gareth Ellis; 11 Dean Hadley.
**Tries:** Westerman (10, 44), Naulago (49), Griffin (64, 79);
**Goals:** Sneyd 4/5, Faraimo 0/1, Griffin 0/1.
**Rugby Leaguer & League Express Men of the Match:**
*Giants:* Oliver Russell; *Hull FC:* Joe Westerman.
**Penalty count:** 3-5; **Half-time:** 8-6;
**Referee:** Scott Mikalauskas; **Attendance:** 6,390.

### LONDON BRONCOS 18 WIGAN WARRIORS 16

**BRONCOS:** 1 Alex Walker; 5 Kieran Dixon; 19 Ryan Morgan; 4 Elliot Kear; 2 Rhys Williams; 6 Jordan Abdull; 7 James Cunningham; 8 Eddie Battye; 14 Matty Fozard; 18 Nathan Mason; 12 Jay Pitts (C); 11 Will Lovell; 20 Luke Yates. Subs (all used): 16 Matty Gee; 15 Greg Richards; 28 Morgan Smith (D); 23 Rob Butler.
**Tries:** Battye (31), Gee (36), Dixon (44); **Goals:** Dixon 3/4.
**WARRIORS:** 20 Zak Hardaker; 2 Tom Davies; 4 Oliver Gildart; 3 Dan Sarginson; 1 Morgan Escare; 6 George Williams; 37 Jarrod Sammut; 14 Romain Navarrete; 9 Sam Powell; 22 Joe Bullock; 29 Liam Paisley; 15 Willie Isa; 8 Tony Clubb. Subs (all used): 7 Thomas Leuluai; 24 Oliver Partington; 13 Sean O'Loughlin (C); 19 Taulima Tautai.
**Tries:** Paisley (9), Isa (28), Clubb (58); **Goals:** Hardaker 2/3.
**Rugby Leaguer & League Express Men of the Match:**
*Broncos:* Alex Walker; *Warriors:* Joe Bullock.
**Penalty count:** 10-7; **Half-time:** 12-10;
**Referee:** Tom Grant; **Attendance:** 2,586.

## ROUND 5

*Thursday 7th March 2019*

### WARRINGTON WOLVES 24 CASTLEFORD TIGERS 10

**WOLVES:** 1 Stefan Ratchford; 22 Jake Mamo; 3 Bryson Goodwin; 18 Toby King; 5 Josh Charnley; 6 Blake Austin; 15 Declan Patton; 8 Chris Hill (C); 9 Daryl Clark; 10 Mike Cooper; 11 Ben Currie; 12 Jack Hughes (C); 16 Lama Tasi. Subs (all used): 13 Ben Murdoch-Masila; 34 Ben Westwood; 17 Joe Philbin; 14 Jason Clark.
**Tries:** Mamo (21, 27), Hughes (36), Murdoch-Masila (49);
**Goals:** Ratchford 4/5.
**TIGERS:** 1 Peter Mata'utia; 2 James Clare; 3 Greg Minikin; 4 Michael Shenton (C); 5 Greg Eden; 6 Jake Trueman; 32 Jordan Rankin; 8 Liam Watts; 9 Paul McShane; 16 Junior Moors; 15 Jesse Sene-Lefao; 33 Chris Clarkson; 14 Nathan Massey. Subs (all used): 17 Alex Foster; 18 Matt Cook; 25 Tuoyo Egodo; 29 Jacques O'Neill.
**Tries:** Eden (8), Minikin (59); **Goals:** Rankin 1/2.
**Rugby Leaguer & League Express Men of the Match:**
*Wolves:* Daryl Clark; *Tigers:* Peter Mata'utia.
**Penalty count:** 6-9; **Half-time:** 16-4;
**Referee:** Chris Kendall; **Attendance:** 9,231.

*Friday 8th March 2019*

### HULL FC 34 LEEDS RHINOS 10

**HULL FC:** 1 Jamie Shaul; 33 Ratu Naulago; 3 Carlos Tuimavave; 4 Josh Griffin; 2 Bureta Faraimo; 6 Albert Kelly; 7 Marc Sneyd; 23 Mickey Paea; 9 Danny Houghton (C); 19 Masi Matongo; 12 Mark Minichiello; 21 Sika Manu; 13 Joe Westerman. Subs (all used): 8 Scott Taylor; 11 Dean Hadley; 16 Jordan Thompson; 34 Gareth Ellis.
**Tries:** Naulago (18), Matongo (24), Sneyd (27), Shaul (30), Kelly (34), Hadley (57); **Goals:** Sneyd 5/6.
**RHINOS:** 1 Jack Walker; 2 Tom Briscoe; 29 Harry Newman; 4 Konrad Hurrell; 5 Ash Handley; 6 Tuimoala Lolohea; 7 Richie Myler; 18 Nathaniel Peteru; 9 Matt Parcell; 19 Mikolaj Oledzki; 16 Brett Ferres (C); 15 Liam Sutcliffe; 11 Trent Merrin. Subs (all used): 8 Adam Cuthbertson; 10 Brad Singleton; 14 Brad Dwyer; 25 James Donaldson.
**Tries:** Newman (5), T Briscoe (8); **Goals:** Lolohea 1/2.
**Rugby Leaguer & League Express Men of the Match:**
*Hull FC:* Sika Manu; *Rhinos:* Jack Walker.
**Penalty count:** 10-8; **Half-time:** 30-10;
**Referee:** Ben Thaler; **Attendance:** 12,208.

### ST HELENS 26 LONDON BRONCOS 0

**SAINTS:** 23 Lachlan Coote; 2 Tommy Makinson; 3 Kevin Naiqama (C); 4 Mark Percival; 5 Regan Grace; 1 Jonny Lomax; 6 Theo Fages; 8 Alex Walmsley; 21 Aaron Smith; 10 Luke Thompson; 11 Zeb Taia; 17 Dominique Peyroux; 15 Morgan Knowles. Subs (all used): 12 Joseph Paulo; 13 Louie McCarthy-Scarsbrook; 16 Kyle Amor; 20 Jack Ashworth.
**Tries:** Peyroux (2), Grace (24), Fages (33), Coote (61), Naiqama (76); **Goals:** Coote 3/5.
**BRONCOS:** 1 Alex Walker; 4 Elliot Kear; 17 Matty Fleming; 24 Jacob Ogden; 2 Rhys Williams (C); 6 Jordan Abdull; 28 Morgan Smith; 8 Eddie Battye; 9 Eloi Pelissier; 23 Rob Butler; 20 Luke Yates; 11 Will Lovell; 29 Matt Davis (D2). Subs (all used): 10 Mark Ioane; 14 Matty Fozard; 16 Matty Gee; 13 Sadiq Adebiyi.
**Rugby Leaguer & League Express Men of the Match:**
*Saints:* Theo Fages; *Broncos:* Luke Yates.
**Penalty count:** 12-9; **Half-time:** 16-0;
**Referee:** Marcus Griffiths; **Attendance:** 9,090.

### WIGAN WARRIORS 6 HUDDERSFIELD GIANTS 14

**WARRIORS:** 20 Zak Hardaker; 21 Dom Manfredi; 23 Chris Hankinson; 4 Oliver Gildart; 17 Liam Marshall; 6 George Williams; 7 Thomas Leuluai; 8 Tony Clubb; 9 Sam Powell; 10 Ben Flower; 29 Liam Paisley; 15 Willie Isa; 13 Sean O'Loughlin (C). Subs (all used): 1 Morgan Escare; 16 Gabe Hamlin; 19 Taulima Tautai; 22 Joe Bullock.
**Try:** Escare (53); **Goals:** Hardaker 1/1.
**Sin bin:** Tautai (58) - kicking.
**GIANTS:** 1 Darnell McIntosh; 2 Jermaine McGillvary; 4 Jordan Turner; 20 Jake Wardle; 5 Akuila Uate; 6 Lee Gaskell; 7 Matt Frawley; 17 Ukuma Ta'ai; 9 Kruise Leeming; 26 Sebastine Ikahihifo; 35 Joe Wardle; 12 Alex Mellor; 11 Aaron Murphy. Subs (all used): 10 Suaia Matagi; 13 Michael Lawrence (C); 14 Adam O'Brien; 15 Oliver Roberts.
**Tries:** Leeming (12), Joe Wardle (65); **Goals:** Gaskell 3/3.
**Rugby Leaguer & League Express Men of the Match:**
*Warriors:* Gabe Hamlin; *Giants:* Kruise Leeming.
**Penalty count:** 5-6; **Half-time:** 0-6;
**Referee:** Robert Hicks; **Attendance:** 10,114.

*Saturday 9th March 2019*

### CATALANS DRAGONS 0 SALFORD RED DEVILS 46

**DRAGONS:** 29 Sam Tomkins; 27 Fouad Yaha; 17 Matt Whitley; 4 Brayden Wiliame; 5 Lewis Tierney; 6 Samisoni Langi; 7 Matty Smith; 8 Remi Casty (C); 9 Michael McIlorum; 10 Sam Moa; 11 Kenny Edwards; 16 Benjamin Jullien; 24 Jason Baitieri. Subs (all used): 13 Greg Bird; 14 Julian Bousquet; 19 Mickael Goudemand; 20 Lambert Belmas.
**RED DEVILS:** 1 Niall Evalds; 22 Derrell Olpherts; 3 Kris Welham; 5 Jake Bibby; 23 Ken Sio; 6 Robert Lui (C); 31 Jackson Hastings; 20 Daniel Murray; 14 Joey Lussick; 10 Gil Dudson; 11 Josh Jones; 24 Jansin Turgut; 13 Mark Flanagan. Subs (all used): 16 Greg Burke; 18 Ben Nakubuwai; 12 George Griffin; 25 Adam Lawton (D).
**Tries:** Lussick (8), Griffin (38, 46), Bibby (40, 41), Hastings (54), Evalds (58), Sio (79); **Goals:** Sio 7/9.
**Rugby Leaguer & League Express Men of the Match:**
*Dragons:* Benjamin Jullien; *Red Devils:* Jackson Hastings.
**Penalty count:** 10-6; **Half-time:** 0-18;
**Referee:** Scott Mikalauskas; **Attendance:** 8,021.

*Sunday 10th March 2019*

### WAKEFIELD TRINITY 6 HULL KINGSTON ROVERS 10

**TRINITY:** 1 Ryan Hampshire; 2 Tom Johnstone; 3 Bill Tupou; 4 Reece Lyne; 5 Ben Jones-Bishop; 6 Jacob Miller (C); 7 Danny Brough; 8 David Fifita; 9 Kyle Wood; 22 George King; 19 James Batchelor; 12 Danny Kirmond; 16 Tinirau Arona. Subs (all used): 14 Justin Horo; 24 Pauli Pauli; 15 Craig Kopczak; 20 Keegan Hirst.
**Goals:** Brough 3/3.
**ROVERS:** 26 Will Dagger; 25 Will Oakes; 4 Jimmy Keinhorst; 19 Junior Vaivai; 2 Craig Hall; 7 Danny McGuire (C); 24 Josh Drinkwater; 10 Mose Masoe; 15 Tommy Lee; 16 Lee Jewitt; 13 Weller Hauraki; 23 Kane Linnett; 21 George Lawler. Subs (all used): 14 Mitch Garbutt; 12 James Greenwood; 20 Danny Addy; 17 Chris Atkin.
**Try:** McGuire (73); **Goals:** Hall 3/4.
**Sin bin:** McGuire (33) - dissent.
**Rugby Leaguer & League Express Men of the Match:**
*Trinity:* Kyle Wood; *Rovers:* Mitch Garbutt.
**Penalty count:** 14-9; **Half-time:** 2-2;
**Referee:** Tom Grant; **Attendance:** 5,559.

## ROUND 6

*Thursday 14th March 2019*

### HUDDERSFIELD GIANTS 12 ST HELENS 40

**GIANTS:** 1 Darnell McIntosh; 2 Jermaine McGillvary; 4 Jordan Turner; 32 Innes Senior; 5 Akuila Uate; 6 Lee Gaskell; 7 Matt Frawley; 26 Sebastine Ikahihifo; 9 Kruise Leeming; 17 Ukuma Ta'ai; 35 Joe Wardle; 12 Alex Mellor; 13 Michael Lawrence (C). Subs (all used): 10 Suaia Matagi; 15 Oliver Roberts; 29 Sam Hewitt; 19 Matty English.
**Tries:** McGillvary (14), Turner (26); **Goals:** Gaskell 2/2.
**On report:** Lawrence (20) - alleged dangerous contact.
**SAINTS:** 23 Lachlan Coote; 2 Tommy Makinson; 3 Kevin Naiqama; 4 Mark Percival; 5 Regan Grace; 1 Jonny Lomax; 6 Theo Fages; 8 Alex Walmsley; 9 James Roby (C); 10 Luke Thompson; 11 Zeb Taia; 17 Dominique Peyroux; 15 Morgan Knowles. Subs (all used): 12 Joseph Paulo; 13 Louie McCarthy-Scarsbrook; 19 Matty Lees; 20 Jack Ashworth.
**Tries:** Thompson (3), Knowles (23), Percival (38, 55), Grace (63), Peyroux (68), Lomax (73); **Goals:** Coote 6/8.
**Rugby Leaguer & League Express Men of the Match:**
*Giants:* Lee Gaskell; *Saints:* Lachlan Coote.
**Penalty count:** 4-8; **Half-time:** 12-16;
**Referee:** Scott Mikalauskas; **Attendance:** 4,495.

*Friday 15th March 2019*

### HULL FC 12 WAKEFIELD TRINITY 32

**HULL FC:** 1 Jamie Shaul; 33 Ratu Naulago; 3 Carlos Tuimavave; 4 Josh Griffin; 2 Bureta Faraimo; 6 Albert Kelly; 7 Marc Sneyd; 8 Scott Taylor; 9 Danny Houghton (C); 19 Masi Matongo; 12 Mark Minichiello; 21 Sika Manu; 13 Joe Westerman. Subs (all used): 11 Dean Hadley; 16 Jordan Thompson; 28 Jez Litten; 34 Gareth Ellis.
**Tries:** Houghton (37), Faraimo (40); **Goals:** Sneyd 2/2.
**Sin bin:** Kelly (30) - high tackle on Wood;
Sneyd (63) - dissent.
**TRINITY:** 1 Ryan Hampshire; 5 Ben Jones-Bishop; 4 Reece Lyne; 3 Bill Tupou; 2 Tom Johnstone; 6 Jacob Miller (C); 7 Danny Brough; 10 Anthony England; 9 Kyle Wood; 8 David Fifita; 11 Matty Ashurst; 12 Danny Kirmond; 26 Jordan Crowther. Subs (all used): 14 Justin Horo; 15 Craig Kopczak; 16 Tinirau Arona; 24 Pauli Pauli.
**Tries:** Hampshire (28), Tupou (32, 51), Pauli (69), Lyne (76);
**Goals:** Brough 6/8.
**Sin bin:** Kirmond (49) - late challenge on Sneyd;
Pauli (80) - high tackle.
**Rugby Leaguer & League Express Men of the Match:**
*Hull FC:* Danny Houghton; *Trinity:* David Fifita.
**Penalty count:** 9-10; **Half-time:** 12-14;
**Referee:** Liam Moore; **Attendance:** 11,190.

### LEEDS RHINOS 16 LONDON BRONCOS 18

**RHINOS:** 1 Jack Walker; 2 Tom Briscoe; 29 Harry Newman; 4 Konrad Hurrell; 5 Ash Handley; 6 Tuimoala Lolohea; 7 Richie Myler; 18 Nathaniel Peteru; 9 Matt Parcell; 19 Mikolaj Oledzki; 16 Brett Ferres (C); 15 Liam Sutcliffe; 11 Trent Merrin. Subs (all used): 20 Jamie Jones-Buchanan; 8 Adam Cuthbertson; 32 Tom Holroyd; 25 James Donaldson.
**Tries:** Myler (43), Merrin (55), T Briscoe (60);
**Goals:** Lolohea 2/3.

**BRONCOS:** 1 Alex Walker; 5 Kieran Dixon; 19 Ryan Morgan; 4 Elliot Kear; 2 Rhys Williams; 6 Jordan Abdull; 7 James Cunningham; 8 Eddie Battye; 9 Eloi Pelissier; 23 Rob Butler; 12 Jay Pitts (C); 20 Luke Yates; 29 Matt Davis. Subs (all used): 18 Nathan Mason; 15 Greg Richards; 11 Will Lovell; 14 Matty Fozard.
**Tries:** Pitts (29), Fozard (76), Lovell (78); **Goals:** Dixon 3/4.
**Rugby Leaguer & League Express Men of the Match:** *Rhinos:* Nathaniel Peteru; *Broncos:* Eloi Pelissier.
**Penalty count:** 7-7; **Half-time:** 0-8;
**Referee:** Chris Kendall; **Attendance:** 11,229.

**WARRINGTON WOLVES 25 WIGAN WARRIORS 12**

**WOLVES:** 1 Stefan Ratchford; 22 Jake Mamo; 18 Toby King; 4 Ryan Atkins; 5 Josh Charnley; 6 Blake Austin; 15 Declan Patton; 8 Chris Hill (C); 9 Daryl Clark; 10 Mike Cooper; 11 Ben Currie; 12 Jack Hughes (C); 16 Lama Tasi. Subs (all used): 13 Ben Murdoch-Masila; 34 Ben Westwood; 17 Joe Philbin; 14 Jason Clark.
**Tries:** Mamo (7), Ratchford (31), Charnley (46), Hughes (78); **Goals:** Ratchford 4/5; **Field goal:** Patton (67).
**Dismissal:** Westwood (74) - head butt on Escare.
**Sin bin:** Patton (74) - fighting.
**WARRIORS:** 20 Zak Hardaker; 2 Tom Davies; 3 Dan Sarginson; 4 Oliver Gildart; 1 Morgan Escare; 6 George Williams; 37 Jarrod Sammut; 8 Tony Clubb; 7 Thomas Leuluai; 14 Romain Navarrete; 11 Joe Greenwood; 15 Willie Isa; 13 Sean O'Loughlin (C). Subs (all used): 24 Oliver Partington; 22 Joe Bullock; 16 Gabe Hamlin; 27 Jake Shorrocks.
**Tries:** Davies (60), Isa (63); **Goals:** Hardaker 2/2.
**Sin bin:** Sarginson (51) - high tackle on Atkins; Isa (74) - dangerous contact on King.
**On report:**
Greenwood (51) - alleged late challenge on Austin.
**Rugby Leaguer & League Express Men of the Match:** *Wolves:* Daryl Clark; *Warriors:* Sean O'Loughlin.
**Penalty count:** 12-5; **Half-time:** 12-0;
**Referee:** Ben Thaler; **Attendance:** 13,106.

*Sunday 17th March 2019*

**HULL KINGSTON ROVERS 16 CATALANS DRAGONS 18**

**ROVERS:** 26 Will Dagger; 2 Craig Hall; 4 Jimmy Keinhorst; 19 Junior Vaivai; 25 Will Oakes; 7 Danny McGuire; 24 Josh Drinkwater; 10 Mose Masoe; 20 Danny Addy; 21 George Lawler; 23 Kane Linnett; 11 Joel Tomkins (C); 13 Weller Hauraki. Subs: 14 Mitch Garbutt; 5 Ryan Shaw (not used); 17 Chris Atkin; 31 Adam Rooks (D).
**Tries:** Hauraki (44), Tomkins (49), Hall (64);
**Goals:** Hall 2/4.
**DRAGONS:** 29 Sam Tomkins; 27 Fouad Yaha; 6 Samisoni Langi; 4 Brayden Wiliame; 5 Lewis Tierney; 1 Tony Gigot; 7 Matty Smith; 8 Remi Casty (C); 22 Lucas Albert; 10 Sam Moa; 11 Kenny Edwards; 17 Matt Whitley; 13 Greg Bird. Subs (all used): 14 Julian Bousquet; 16 Benjamin Jullien; 19 Mickael Goudemand; 24 Jason Baitieri.
**Tries:** Wiliame (60), Albert (62), Tierney (75);
**Goals:** Tomkins 3/5.
**Rugby Leaguer & League Express Men of the Match:** *Rovers:* George Lawler; *Dragons:* Remi Casty.
**Penalty count:** 7-11; **Half-time:** 2-2;
**Referee:** James Child; **Attendance:** 7,203.

**CASTLEFORD TIGERS 24 SALFORD RED DEVILS 20**

**TIGERS:** 1 Peter Mata'utia; 3 Greg Minikin; 17 Alex Foster; 4 Michael Shenton (C); 5 Greg Eden; 6 Jake Trueman; 32 Jordan Rankin; 8 Liam Watts; 9 Paul McShane; 16 Junior Moors; 15 Jesse Sene-Lefao; 11 Oliver Holmes; 14 Nathan Massey. Subs: 13 Adam Milner; 18 Matt Cook; 25 Tuoyo Egodo (not used); 33 Chris Clarkson.
**Tries:** Massey (8), Rankin (16), Eden (47), Sene-Lefao (64);
**Goals:** Rankin 4/5.
**Sin bin:** McShane (31) - fighting.
**RED DEVILS:** 1 Niall Evalds; 22 Derrell Olpherts; 3 Kris Welham; 5 Jake Bibby; 23 Ken Sio; 6 Robert Lui; 31 Jackson Hastings; 20 Daniel Murray; 14 Joey Lussick; 10 Gil Dudson; 11 Josh Jones; 24 Jansin Turgut; 13 Mark Flanagan (C). Subs (all used): 15 Adam Walker (D); 18 Ben Nakubuwai; 19 Logan Tomkins; 12 George Griffin.
**Tries:** Bibby (27, 73), Turgut (52), Lussick (55);
**Goals:** Sio 0/1, Lussick 2/3.
**Rugby Leaguer & League Express Men of the Match:** *Tigers:* Peter Mata'utia; *Red Devils:* Jake Bibby.
**Penalty count:** 6-7; **Half-time:** 12-4;
**Referee:** Robert Hicks; **Attendance:** 7,750.

## ROUND 7

*Thursday 21st March 2019*

**WAKEFIELD TRINITY 32 WARRINGTON WOLVES 34**

**TRINITY:** 1 Ryan Hampshire; 5 Ben Jones-Bishop; 4 Reece Lyne; 18 Joe Arundel; 21 Max Jowitt; 6 Jacob Miller (C); 7 Danny Brough; 8 David Fifita; 9 Kyle Wood; 10 Anthony England; 24 Pauli Pauli; 14 Justin Horo; 26 Jordan Crowther. Subs (all used): 16 Tinirau Arona; 22 George King; 15 Craig Kopczak; 20 Keegan Hirst.
**Tries:** Hampshire (18), Fifita (56), Wood (64, 66), Jowitt (75), Arundel (77); **Goals:** Brough 4/6.
**WOLVES:** 1 Stefan Ratchford; 22 Jake Mamo; 18 Toby King; 4 Ryan Atkins; 5 Josh Charnley; 6 Blake Austin; 15 Declan Patton; 8 Chris Hill (C); 9 Daryl Clark; 10 Mike Cooper; 11 Ben Currie; 12 Jack Hughes (C); 17 Joe Philbin. Subs (all used): 13 Ben Murdoch-Masila; 21 Danny Walker; 16 Lama Tasi; 14 Jason Clark.
**Tries:** King (5), Charnley (9, 59), Hill (13), Austin (31);
**Goals:** Ratchford 7/7.
**Rugby Leaguer & League Express Men of the Match:** *Trinity:* David Fifita; *Wolves:* Blake Austin.
**Penalty count:** 13-7; **Half-time:** 6-26;
**Referee:** Ben Thaler; **Attendance:** 4,753.

*Friday 22nd March 2019*

**CASTLEFORD TIGERS 12 ST HELENS 42**

**TIGERS:** 1 Peter Mata'utia; 3 Greg Minikin; 17 Alex Foster; 4 Michael Shenton (C); 5 Greg Eden; 6 Jake Trueman; 32 Jordan Rankin; 8 Liam Watts; 9 Paul McShane; 10 Grant Millington; 11 Oliver Holmes; 16 Junior Moors; 14 Nathan Massey. Subs (all used): 2 James Clare; 13 Adam Milner; 15 Jesse Sene-Lefao; 18 Matt Cook.
**Tries:** Shenton (58), Trueman (79); **Goals:** Rankin 2/2.
**SAINTS:** 23 Lachlan Coote; 2 Tommy Makinson; 3 Kevin Naiqama; 4 Mark Percival; 5 Regan Grace; 1 Jonny Lomax; 6 Theo Fages; 8 Alex Walmsley; 9 James Roby (C); 10 Luke Thompson; 11 Zeb Taia; 17 Dominique Peyroux; 15 Morgan Knowles. Subs (all used): 12 Joseph Paulo; 13 Louie McCarthy-Scarsbrook; 19 Matty Lees; 20 Jack Ashworth.
**Tries:** Coote (4), Grace (22), Peyroux (33, 64), Taia (42), McCarthy-Scarsbrook (48), Percival (54), Lomax (71);
**Goals:** Coote 5/9.
**Rugby Leaguer & League Express Men of the Match:** *Tigers:* Peter Mata'utia; *Saints:* Lachlan Coote.
**Penalty count:** 6-7; **Half-time:** 0-18;
**Referee:** James Child; **Attendance:** 8,042.

**HUDDERSFIELD GIANTS 42**
**HULL KINGSTON ROVERS 8**

**GIANTS:** 1 Darnell McIntosh; 2 Jermaine McGillvary; 4 Jordan Turner; 32 Innes Senior; 5 Akuila Uate; 6 Lee Gaskell; 7 Matt Frawley; 19 Matty English; 9 Kruise Leeming; 10 Suaia Matagi; 35 Joe Wardle; 12 Alex Mellor; 13 Michael Lawrence (C). Subs (all used): 26 Sebastine Ikahihifo; 15 Oliver Roberts; 17 Ukuma Ta'ai; 29 Sam Hewitt.
**Tries:** Leeming (14, 42), Roberts (27), McIntosh (30), McGillvary (51, 55), Matagi (75); **Goals:** Gaskell 7/8.
**ROVERS:** 2 Craig Hall; 5 Ryan Shaw; 4 Jimmy Keinhorst; 19 Junior Vaivai; 25 Will Oakes; 24 Josh Drinkwater; 17 Chris Atkin; 10 Mose Masoe; 15 Tommy Lee; 21 George Lawler; 13 Weller Hauraki; 11 Joel Tomkins (C); 20 Danny Addy. Subs: 33 Harry Bardle (D); 28 Elliot Wallis (not used); 9 Shaun Lunt; 31 Adam Rooks.
**Try:** Hauraki (63); **Goals:** Shaw 2/2.
**Rugby Leaguer & League Express Men of the Match:** *Giants:* Kruise Leeming; *Rovers:* Weller Hauraki.
**Penalty count:** 6-11; **Half-time:** 20-2;
**Referee:** Greg Dolan; **Attendance:** 5,289.

*Saturday 23rd March 2019*

**CATALANS DRAGONS 26 LEEDS RHINOS 22**

**DRAGONS:** 29 Sam Tomkins; 27 Fouad Yaha; 6 Samisoni Langi; 4 Brayden Wiliame; 5 Lewis Tierney; 1 Tony Gigot; 7 Matty Smith; 8 Remi Casty (C); 22 Lucas Albert; 14 Julian Bousquet; 11 Kenny Edwards; 17 Matt Whitley; 19 Mickael Goudemand. Subs (all used): 18 Alrix Da Costa; 23 Antoni Maria; 24 Jason Baitieri; 28 Sam Kasiano (D).
**Tries:** Yaha (18, 31, 59, 72), Albert (36); **Goals:** Tomkins 3/5.
**RHINOS:** 1 Jack Walker; 2 Tom Briscoe; 3 Kallum Watkins (C); 4 Konrad Hurrell; 5 Ash Handley; 15 Liam Sutcliffe; 7 Richie Myler; 18 Nathaniel Peteru; 14 Brad Dwyer; 19 Mikolaj Oledzki; 22 Cameron Smith; 16 Brett Ferres; 11 Trent Merrin. Subs (all used): 9 Matt Parcell; 10 Brad Singleton; 20 Jamie Jones-Buchanan; 32 Tom Holroyd.
**Tries:** Handley (3, 12, 48), Hurrell (25); **Goals:** L Sutcliffe 3/5.
**Sin bin:** Ferres (35) - use of the knees on Whitley.
**Rugby Leaguer & League Express Men of the Match:** *Dragons:* Fouad Yaha; *Rhinos:* Ash Handley.
**Penalty count:** 8-8; **Half-time:** 16-16;
**Referee:** Robert Hicks; **Attendance:** 8,220.

*Sunday 24th March 2019*

**LONDON BRONCOS 24 HULL FC 28**

**BRONCOS:** 1 Alex Walker; 5 Kieran Dixon; 19 Ryan Morgan; 4 Elliot Kear; 2 Rhys Williams; 6 Jordan Abdull; 28 Morgan Smith; 8 Eddie Battye; 9 Eloi Pelissier; 23 Rob Butler; 12 Jay Pitts (C); 20 Luke Yates; 29 Matt Davis. Subs (all used): 11 Will Lovell; 14 Matty Fozard; 15 Greg Richards; 18 Nathan Mason.
**Tries:** Kear (12), Pelissier (30), Abdull (69), Williams (74);
**Goals:** Dixon 4/5.
**HULL FC:** 1 Jamie Shaul; 33 Ratu Naulago; 3 Carlos Tuimavave; 4 Josh Griffin; 2 Bureta Faraimo; 6 Albert Kelly; 7 Marc Sneyd; 23 Mickey Paea; 9 Danny Houghton (C); 19 Masi Matongo; 11 Dean Hadley; 21 Sika Manu; 34 Gareth Ellis. Subs (all used): 16 Jordan Thompson; 8 Scott Taylor; 22 Jordan Lane; 28 Jez Litten.
**Tries:** Griffin (10, 18), Tuimavave (41), Thompson (49), Kelly (54), Faraimo (63); **Goals:** Sneyd 2/6.
**Rugby Leaguer & League Express Men of the Match:** *Broncos:* Jordan Abdull; *Hull FC:* Danny Houghton.
**Penalty count:** 14-7; **Half-time:** 14-10;
**Referee:** Scott Mikalauskas; **Attendance:** 2,257.

**SALFORD RED DEVILS 22 WIGAN WARRIORS 30**

**RED DEVILS:** 1 Niall Evalds; 22 Derrell Olpherts; 2 Ed Chamberlain; 5 Jake Bibby; 23 Ken Sio; 6 Robert Lui; 31 Jackson Hastings; 20 Daniel Murray; 14 Joey Lussick; 10 Gil Dudson; 11 Josh Jones; 24 Jansin Turgut; 13 Mark Flanagan (C). Subs: 12 George Griffin; 18 Ben Nakubuwai; 15 Adam Walker; 25 Adam Lawton (not used).
**Tries:** Jones (4), Olpherts (37), Evalds (40), Walker (42);
**Goals:** Chamberlain 3/5.
**WARRIORS:** 20 Zak Hardaker; 21 Dom Manfredi; 3 Dan Sarginson; 4 Oliver Gildart; 5 Joe Burgess; 6 George Williams; 37 Jarrod Sammut; 8 Tony Clubb; 7 Thomas Leuluai; 14 Romain Navarrete; 15 Willie Isa; 11 Joe Greenwood; 13 Sean O'Loughlin (C). Subs (all used): 27 Jake Shorrocks; 16 Gabe Hamlin; 10 Ben Flower; 22 Joe Bullock.
**Tries:** Williams (25, 50, 62), Leuluai (29), Greenwood (33);
**Goals:** Hardaker 5/5.
**Rugby Leaguer & League Express Men of the Match:** *Red Devils:* Joey Lussick; *Warriors:* Joe Burgess.
**Penalty count:** 6-6; **Half-time:** 16-18;
**Referee:** Chris Kendall; **Attendance:** 4,470.

## ROUND 8

*Thursday 28th March 2019*

**LEEDS RHINOS 21 CASTLEFORD TIGERS 20**
*(after golden point extra-time)*

**RHINOS:** 1 Jack Walker; 2 Tom Briscoe; 3 Kallum Watkins (C); 4 Konrad Hurrell; 5 Ash Handley; 15 Liam Sutcliffe; 7 Richie Myler; 18 Nathaniel Peteru; 14 Brad Dwyer; 19 Mikolaj Oledzki; 20 Jamie Jones-Buchanan; 22 Cameron Smith; 11 Trent Merrin. Subs (all used): 10 Brad Singleton; 32 Tom Holroyd; 25 James Donaldson; 9 Matt Parcell.
**Tries:** Hurrell (3), Handley (31), L Sutcliffe (49), Merrin (53);
**Goals:** L Sutcliffe 1/3, Smith 1/2; **Field goal:** Dwyer (81).
**TIGERS:** 1 Peter Mata'utia; 2 James Clare; 3 Greg Minikin; 4 Michael Shenton (C); 5 Greg Eden; 6 Jake Trueman; 9 Paul McShane; 8 Liam Watts; 13 Adam Milner; 10 Grant Millington; 15 Jesse Sene-Lefao; 17 Alex Foster; 11 Oliver Holmes. Subs (all used): 16 Junior Moors; 18 Matt Cook; 27 Calum Turner; 33 Chris Clarkson.
**Tries:** Watts (21), Minikin (60), Clarkson (63), Foster (74);
**Goals:** Mata'utia 0/1, Turner 2/3.
**Rugby Leaguer & League Express Men of the Match:** *Rhinos:* Jack Walker; *Tigers:* Liam Watts.
**Penalty count:** 6-7; **Half time:** 10-4;
**Referee:** Ben Thaler; **Attendance:** 12,295.

*Friday 29th March 2019*

**HULL FC 12 WARRINGTON WOLVES 63**

**HULL FC:** 27 Hakim Miloudi; 4 Josh Griffin; 3 Carlos Tuimavave; 16 Jordan Thompson; 2 Bureta Faraimo; 6 Albert Kelly; 7 Marc Sneyd; 8 Scott Taylor; 9 Danny Houghton (C); 23 Mickey Paea; 12 Mark Minichiello; 21 Sika Manu; 13 Joe Westerman. Subs (all used): 11 Dean Hadley; 19 Masi Matongo; 22 Jordan Lane; 35 Andre Savelio (D).
**Tries:** Kelly (39), Lane (68); **Goals:** Sneyd 2/2.
**WOLVES:** 1 Stefan Ratchford; 2 Tom Lineham; 18 Toby King; 22 Jake Mamo; 5 Josh Charnley; 6 Blake Austin; 15 Declan Patton; 8 Chris Hill (C); 9 Daryl Clark; 10 Mike Cooper; 11 Ben Currie; 12 Jack Hughes (C); 17 Joe Philbin. Subs (all used): 13 Ben Murdoch-Masila; 14 Jason Clark; 16 Lama Tasi; 20 Harvey Livett.
**Tries:** Austin (7, 14, 32, 53), D Clark (11), Charnley (18, 21, 64), Murdoch-Masila (41), Lineham (59, 75);
**Goals:** Ratchford 9/11; **Field goal:** Austin (79).
**Rugby Leaguer & League Express Men of the Match:** *Hull FC:* Albert Kelly; *Wolves:* Blake Austin.
**Penalty count:** 9-4; **Half-time:** 6-34;
**Referee:** Robert Hicks; **Attendance:** 10,810.

Hull KR's Craig Hall makes a break against Leeds, with Danny McGuire in support

### ST HELENS 36 HULL KINGSTON ROVERS 24

**SAINTS:** 23 Lachlan Coote; 2 Tommy Makinson; 3 Kevin Naiqama (C); 29 Jack Welsby; 5 Regan Grace; 1 Jonny Lomax; 6 Theo Fages; 19 Matty Lees; 21 Aaron Smith; 10 Luke Thompson; 22 James Bentley; 17 Dominique Peyroux; 15 Morgan Knowles. Subs (all used): 12 Joseph Paulo; 13 Louie McCarthy-Scarsbrook; 16 Kyle Amor; 20 Jack Ashworth.
**Tries:** Coote (5), Welsby (14), Thompson (19), Amor (57), Smith (62), Grace (72); **Goals:** Coote 6/8.
**ROVERS:** 2 Craig Hall; 5 Ryan Shaw; 4 Jimmy Keinhorst; 3 Ben Crooks; 25 Will Oakes; 24 Josh Drinkwater; 17 Chris Atkin; 10 Mose Masoe; 15 Tommy Lee; 21 George Lawler; 11 Joel Tomkins (C); 23 Kane Linnett; 13 Weller Hauraki. Subs: 9 Shaun Lunt; 14 Mitch Garbutt; 19 Junior Vaivai (not used); 20 Danny Addy.
**Tries:** Linnett (23, 37), Oakes (27), Lunt (51);
**Goals:** Shaw 4/4.
**Rugby Leaguer & League Express Men of the Match:**
*Saints:* Lachlan Coote; *Rovers:* Kane Linnett.
**Penalty count:** 8-5; **Half-time:** 16-18;
**Referee:** Tom Grant; **Attendance:** 10,003.

*Sunday 31st March 2019*

### LONDON BRONCOS 26 HUDDERSFIELD GIANTS 38

**BRONCOS:** 1 Alex Walker; 5 Kieran Dixon; 17 Matty Fleming; 4 Elliot Kear; 2 Rhys Williams; 6 Jordan Abdull; 28 Morgan Smith; 20 Luke Yates; 9 Eloi Pelissier; 23 Rob Butler; 12 Jay Pitts (C); 16 Matty Gee; 29 Matt Davis. Subs (all used): 8 Eddie Battye; 14 Matty Fozard; 15 Greg Richards; 18 Nathan Mason.
**Tries:** Walker (6), Pitts (38), Williams (45), Dixon (59, 79).
**Goals:** Dixon 3/5.
**GIANTS:** 1 Darnell McIntosh; 2 Jermaine McGillvary; 4 Jordan Turner; 32 Innes Senior; 5 Akuila Uate; 6 Lee Gaskell; 7 Matt Frawley; 19 Matty English; 9 Kruise Leeming; 10 Suaia Matagi; 35 Joe Wardle; 12 Alex Mellor; 13 Michael Lawrence (C). Subs (all used): 14 Adam O'Brien; 15 Oliver Roberts; 26 Sebastine Ikahihifo; 17 Ukuma Ta'ai.
**Tries:** Joe Wardle (3), Turner (9), Uate (14, 54), McGillvary (30), Ikahihifo (36), Mellor (65);
**Goals:** Gaskell 5/7.

**Rugby Leaguer & League Express Men of the Match:**
*Broncos:* Alex Walker; *Giants:* Lee Gaskell.
**Penalty count:** 9-6; **Half-time:** 12-28;
**Referee:** Chris Kendall; **Attendance:** 1,419.

### WAKEFIELD TRINITY 33 SALFORD RED DEVILS 22

**TRINITY:** 1 Ryan Hampshire; 5 Ben Jones-Bishop; 4 Reece Lyne; 18 Joe Arundel; 3 Bill Tupou; 6 Jacob Miller (C); 7 Danny Brough; 8 David Fifita; 9 Kyle Wood; 10 Anthony England; 24 Pauli Pauli; 11 Matty Ashurst; 16 Tinirau Arona. Subs (all used): 26 Jordan Crowther; 22 George King; 15 Craig Kopczak; 14 Justin Horo.
**Tries:** Fifita (5), Hampshire (19), Lyne (25), Pauli (37), Miller (53); **Goals:** Brough 6/6; **Field goal:** Brough (68).
**RED DEVILS:** 1 Niall Evalds; 22 Derrell Olpherts; 5 Jake Bibby; 3 Kris Welham; 2 Ed Chamberlain; 6 Robert Lui; 31 Jackson Hastings; 25 Adam Lawton; 14 Joey Lussick; 10 Gil Dudson; 11 Josh Jones; 12 George Griffin; 13 Mark Flanagan (C). Subs (all used): 16 Greg Burke; 15 Adam Walker; 24 Jansin Turgut; 26 Krisnan Inu (D).
**Tries:** Evalds (9), Welham (32), Olpherts (58), Hastings (61); **Goals:** Chamberlain 3/4.
**Rugby Leaguer & League Express Men of the Match:**
*Trinity:* Pauli Pauli; *Red Devils:* Jackson Hastings.
**Penalty count:** 11-9; **Half-time:** 24-10;
**Referee:** Scott Mikalauskas; **Attendance:** 4,356.

### WIGAN WARRIORS 42 CATALANS DRAGONS 0

**WARRIORS:** 20 Zak Hardaker; 21 Dom Manfredi; 3 Dan Sarginson; 4 Oliver Gildart; 5 Joe Burgess; 6 George Williams; 37 Jarrod Sammut; 22 Joe Bullock; 7 Thomas Leuluai (C); 14 Romain Navarrete; 15 Willie Isa; 29 Liam Paisley; 24 Oliver Partington. Subs (all used): 27 Jake Shorrocks; 10 Ben Flower; 38 Morgan Smithies (D); 36 Liam Byrne.
**Tries:** Burgess (21, 50, 65), Williams (57), Gildart (62), Hardaker (68), Sammut (79); **Goals:** Hardaker 7/9.
**DRAGONS:** 29 Sam Tomkins; 27 Fouad Yaha; 6 Samisoni Langi; 4 Brayden Wiliame; 5 Lewis Tierney; 1 Tony Gigot; 7 Matty Smith; 8 Remi Casty (C); 22 Lucas Albert; 10 Sam Moa; 11 Kenny Edwards; 17 Matt Whitley; 13 Greg Bird. Subs (all used): 14 Julian Bousquet; 19 Mickael Goudemand; 24 Jason Baitieri; 28 Sam Kasiano.

**Rugby Leaguer & League Express Men of the Match:**
*Warriors:* Joe Burgess; *Dragons:* Matt Whitley.
**Penalty count:** 6-4; **Half-time:** 8-0;
**Referee:** James Child; **Attendance:** 11,109.

## ROUND 9

*Thursday 4th April 2019*

### HULL KINGSTON ROVERS 45 LEEDS RHINOS 26

**ROVERS:** 2 Craig Hall; 19 Junior Vaivai; 3 Ben Crooks; 23 Kane Linnett; 25 Will Oakes; 7 Danny McGuire; 24 Josh Drinkwater; 10 Mose Masoe; 15 Tommy Lee; 8 Robbie Mulhern; 11 Joel Tomkins (C); 13 Weller Hauraki; 21 George Lawler. Subs (all used): 9 Shaun Lunt; 4 Jimmy Keinhorst; 14 Mitch Garbutt; 20 Danny Addy.
**Tries:** Lee (4), McGuire (7), Oakes (15), Garbutt (26), Vaivai (33), Drinkwater (70), Crooks (80);
**Goals:** Hall 8/10; **Field goal:** McGuire (39).
**RHINOS:** 1 Jack Walker; 2 Tom Briscoe; 3 Kallum Watkins (C); 4 Konrad Hurrell; 5 Ash Handley; 15 Liam Sutcliffe; 6 Tuimoala Lolohea; 18 Nathaniel Peteru; 14 Brad Dwyer; 19 Mikolaj Oledzki; 22 Cameron Smith; 20 Jamie Jones-Buchanan; 11 Trent Merrin. Subs (all used): 36 Wellington Albert (D); 8 Adam Cuthbertson; 10 Brad Singleton; 25 James Donaldson.
**Tries:** Hurrell (21, 36, 61, 74), Singleton (50);
**Goals:** L Sutcliffe 3/5.
**Rugby Leaguer & League Express Men of the Match:**
*Rovers:* Craig Hall; *Rhinos:* Konrad Hurrell.
**Penalty count:** 10-8; **Half-time:** 31-10;
**Referee:** James Child; **Attendance:** 8,292.

*Friday 5th April 2019*

### CASTLEFORD TIGERS 38 WIGAN WARRIORS 28

**TIGERS:** 27 Calum Turner; 2 James Clare; 25 Tuoyo Egodo; 4 Michael Shenton (C); 5 Greg Eden; 1 Peter Mata'utia; 6 Jake Trueman; 8 Liam Watts; 13 Adam Milner; 10 Grant Millington; 11 Oliver Holmes; 15 Jesse Sene-Lefao; 14 Nathan Massey. Subs: 18 Matt Cook; 21 Mitch Clark; 29 Jacques O'Neill (not used); 23 Will Maher.

**Tries:** Holmes (27), Turner (40), Clark (46), Cook (49), Milner (52), Egodo (74), Mata'utia (80);
**Goals:** Turner 0/2, Mata'utia 5/5.
**WARRIORS:** 20 Zak Hardaker; 21 Dom Manfredi; 3 Dan Sarginson; 4 Oliver Gildart; 5 Joe Burgess; 6 George Williams; 37 Jarrod Sammut; 22 Joe Bullock; 7 Thomas Leuluai (C); 14 Romain Navarrete; 15 Willie Isa; 11 Joe Greenwood; 24 Oliver Partington. Subs (all used): 36 Liam Byrne; 19 Taulima Tautai; 38 Morgan Smithies; 27 Jake Shorrocks.
**Tries:** Greenwood (11), Gildart (14, 35), Williams (17), Burgess (22, 65); **Goals:** Hardaker 2/6.
**Rugby Leaguer & League Express Men of the Match:**
*Tigers:* Peter Mata'utia; *Warriors:* Oliver Gildart.
**Penalty count:** 3-4; **Half-time:** 8-24;
**Referee:** Chris Kendall; **Attendance:** 6,839.

**WAKEFIELD TRINITY 17 HUDDERSFIELD GIANTS 16**

**TRINITY:** 1 Ryan Hampshire; 5 Ben Jones-Bishop; 4 Reece Lyne; 18 Joe Arundel; 21 Max Jowitt; 6 Jacob Miller (C); 7 Danny Brough; 8 David Fifita; 9 Kyle Wood; 16 Tinirau Arona; 24 Pauli Pauli; 11 Matty Ashurst; 26 Jordan Crowther. Subs (all used): 14 Justin Horo; 15 Craig Kopczak; 20 Keegan Hirst; 22 George King.
**Tries:** Lyne (15), Fifita (65, 73); **Goals:** Brough 2/3;
**Field goal:** Brough (76).
**GIANTS:** 1 Darnell McIntosh; 2 Jermaine McGillvary; 4 Jordan Turner; 32 Innes Senior; 5 Akuila Uate; 23 Oliver Russell; 7 Matt Frawley; 19 Matty English; 9 Kruise Leeming; 10 Suaia Matagi; 29 Sam Hewitt; 12 Alex Mellor; 13 Michael Lawrence (C). Subs (all used): 14 Adam O'Brien; 15 Oliver Roberts; 26 Sebastine Ikahihifo; 17 Ukuma Ta'ai.
**Tries:** McGillvary (19), McIntosh (33, 68); **Goals:** Russell 2/4.
**Rugby Leaguer & League Express Men of the Match:**
*Trinity:* David Fifita; *Giants:* Darnell McIntosh.
**Penalty count:** 11-7; **Half-time:** 4-10;
**Referee:** Scott Mikalauskas; **Attendance:** 4,730.

**WARRINGTON WOLVES 48 LONDON BRONCOS 12**

**WOLVES:** 1 Stefan Ratchford; 2 Tom Lineham; 18 Toby King; 4 Ryan Atkins; 5 Josh Charnley; 6 Blake Austin; 15 Declan Patton; 8 Chris Hill (C); 9 Daryl Clark; 16 Lama Tasi; 11 Ben Currie; 20 Harvey Livett; 17 Joe Philbin. Subs (all used): 13 Ben Murdoch-Masila; 23 Matt Davis (D); 21 Danny Walker; 14 Jason Clark.
**Tries:** Lineham (16, 69, 77), Charnley (26), Austin (35, 61), J Clark (39), Ratchford (54), Atkins (57);
**Goals:** Ratchford 6/9.
**BRONCOS:** 1 Alex Walker; 5 Kieran Dixon; 19 Ryan Morgan; 17 Matty Fleming; 2 Rhys Williams; 28 Morgan Smith; 22 James Meadows; 15 Greg Richards; 9 Eloi Pelissier; 23 Rob Butler; 12 Jay Pitts (C); 16 Matty Gee; 11 Will Lovell. Subs (all used): 8 Eddie Battye; 10 Mark Ioane; 18 Nathan Mason; 25 Matthew Davies.
**Tries:** Mason (51), Gee (64); **Goals:** Dixon 2/2.
**Rugby Leaguer & League Express Men of the Match:**
*Wolves:* Blake Austin; *Broncos:* James Meadows.
**Penalty count:** 7-6; **Half-time:** 20-0;
**Referee:** Jack Smith; **Attendance:** 11,718.

*Saturday 6th April 2019*

**CATALANS DRAGONS 18 ST HELENS 10**

**DRAGONS:** 1 Tony Gigot; 27 Fouad Yaha; 6 Samisoni Langi; 4 Brayden Wiliame; 5 Lewis Tierney; 29 Sam Tomkins; 7 Matty Smith; 14 Julian Bousquet; 18 Alrix Da Costa; 10 Sam Moa; 16 Benjamin Jullien; 17 Matt Whitley; 8 Remi Casty (C). Subs (all used): 13 Greg Bird; 19 Mickael Goudemand; 22 Lucas Albert; 28 Sam Kasiano.
**Tries:** Yaha (7), Tomkins (33), Gigot (74);
**Goals:** Tomkins 3/5.
**SAINTS:** 23 Lachlan Coote; 2 Tommy Makinson; 3 Kevin Naiqama; 4 Mark Percival; 5 Regan Grace; 29 Jack Welsby; 7 Danny Richardson; 8 Alex Walmsley; 9 James Roby (C); 10 Luke Thompson; 11 Zeb Taia; 17 Dominique Peyroux; 15 Morgan Knowles. Subs (all used): 12 Joseph Paulo; 16 Kyle Amor; 19 Matty Lees; 20 Jack Ashworth.
**Tries:** Peyroux (3), Makinson (25); **Goals:** Coote 1/2.
**Rugby Leaguer & League Express Men of the Match:**
*Dragons:* Sam Tomkins; *Saints:* James Roby.
**Penalty count:** 5-6; **Half-time:** 10-10;
**Referee:** Robert Hicks; **Attendance:** 8,783.

*Sunday 7th April 2019*

**SALFORD RED DEVILS 16 HULL FC 23**

**RED DEVILS:** 1 Niall Evalds; 26 Krisnan Inu; 2 Ed Chamberlain; 5 Jake Bibby; 22 Derrell Olpherts; 6 Robert Lui; 31 Jackson Hastings; 15 Adam Walker; 14 Joey Lussick; 10 Gil Dudson; 11 Josh Jones; 12 George Griffin; 13 Mark Flanagan (C). Subs (all used): 16 Greg Burke; 3 Kris Welham; 18 Ben Nakubuwai; 24 Jansin Turgut.
**Tries:** Jones (18), Evalds (59), Hastings (70);
**Goals:** Chamberlain 2/3.
**HULL FC:** 36 Connor Wynne (D); 24 Jack Logan; 4 Josh Griffin; 3 Carlos Tuimavave; 2 Bureta Faraimo; 6 Albert Kelly; 7 Marc Sneyd; 8 Scott Taylor; 9 Danny Houghton (C); 23 Mickey Paea; 12 Mark Minichiello; 21 Sika Manu; 13 Joe Westerman. Subs (all used): 22 Jordan Lane; 35 Andre Savelio; 34 Gareth Ellis; 30 Danny Washbrook.
**Tries:** Griffin (5, 47, 51); **Goals:** Sneyd 5/6;
**Field goal:** Sneyd (73).
**Sin bin:** Logan (33) - professional foul.
**Rugby Leaguer & League Express Men of the Match:**
*Red Devils:* Niall Evalds; *Hull FC:* Marc Sneyd.
**Penalty count:** 7-9; **Half-time:** 6-10;
**Referee:** Gareth Hewer; **Attendance:** 3,609.

## ROUND 10

*Thursday 11th April 2019*

**HUDDERSFIELD GIANTS 20 CASTLEFORD TIGERS 18**

**GIANTS:** 1 Darnell McIntosh; 2 Jermaine McGillvary (C); 4 Jordan Turner; 20 Jake Wardle; 5 Akuila Uate; 6 Lee Gaskell; 7 Matt Frawley; 17 Ukuma Ta'ai; 9 Kruise Leeming; 10 Suaia Matagi; 35 Joe Wardle; 12 Alex Mellor; 11 Aaron Murphy. Subs (all used): 14 Adam O'Brien; 15 Oliver Roberts; 26 Sebastine Ikahihifo; 29 Sam Hewitt.
**Tries:** Mellor (13, 42, 70); **Goals:** McIntosh 4/5.
**TIGERS:** 27 Calum Turner; 2 James Clare; 3 Greg Minikin; 4 Michael Shenton (C); 5 Greg Eden; 1 Peter Mata'utia; 6 Jake Trueman; 8 Liam Watts; 13 Adam Milner; 10 Grant Millington; 15 Jesse Sene-Lefao; 12 Mike McMeeken; 16 Junior Moors. Subs (all used): 18 Matt Cook; 21 Mitch Clark; 29 Jacques O'Neill; 34 Daniel Smith (D).
**Tries:** Eden (2), Cook (47); **Goals:** Mata'utia 5/5.
**Sin bin:** Milner (78) - headbutt on O'Brien.
**Rugby Leaguer & League Express Men of the Match:**
*Giants:* Alex Mellor; *Tigers:* Matt Cook.
**Penalty count:** 11-13; **Half-time:** 6-8;
**Referee:** Ben Thaler; **Attendance:** 4,684.

*Friday 12th April 2019*

**ST HELENS 38 WARRINGTON WOLVES 12**

**SAINTS:** 23 Lachlan Coote; 2 Tommy Makinson; 3 Kevin Naiqama; 4 Mark Percival; 5 Regan Grace; 1 Jonny Lomax; 7 Danny Richardson; 8 Alex Walmsley; 9 James Roby (C); 10 Luke Thompson; 11 Zeb Taia; 17 Dominique Peyroux; 15 Morgan Knowles. Subs (all used): 12 Joseph Paulo; 13 Louie McCarthy-Scarsbrook; 16 Kyle Amor; 19 Matty Lees.
**Tries:** Percival (20), McCarthy-Scarsbrook (34), Lomax (36), Lees (50), Grace (60), Makinson (65); **Goals:** Coote 7/9.
**WOLVES:** 1 Stefan Ratchford; 2 Tom Lineham; 18 Toby King; 4 Ryan Atkins; 5 Josh Charnley; 6 Blake Austin; 15 Declan Patton; 8 Chris Hill (C); 9 Daryl Clark; 10 Mike Cooper; 11 Ben Currie; 12 Jack Hughes (C); 17 Joe Philbin. Subs (all used): 14 Jason Clark; 16 Lama Tasi; 13 Ben Murdoch-Masila; 23 Matt Davis.
**Tries:** Austin (14), D Clark (46); **Goals:** Ratchford 2/2.
**Sin bin:** Cooper (28) - high tackle on Richardson.
**On report:** Lineham (60) - alleged late challenge on Grace.
**Rugby Leaguer & League Express Men of the Match:**
*Saints:* Lachlan Coote; *Wolves:* Daryl Clark.
**Penalty count:** 8-6; **Half-time:** 20-6;
**Referee:** James Child; **Attendance:** 17,807.

**WAKEFIELD TRINITY 30 WIGAN WARRIORS 20**

**TRINITY:** 1 Ryan Hampshire; 5 Ben Jones-Bishop; 4 Reece Lyne; 18 Joe Arundel; 21 Max Jowitt; 6 Jacob Miller (C); 7 Danny Brough; 8 David Fifita; 9 Kyle Wood; 10 Anthony England; 24 Pauli Pauli; 11 Matty Ashurst; 16 Tinirau Arona. Subs (all used): 14 Justin Horo; 22 George King; 15 Craig Kopczak; 20 Keegan Hirst.
**Tries:** Kopczak (36), Arundel (38), Jowitt (40), Jones-Bishop (42, 60); **Goals:** Brough 5/6.
**Sin bin:** Pauli (80) - fighting.
**WARRIORS:** 1 Morgan Escare; 2 Tom Davies; 3 Dan Sarginson; 4 Oliver Gildart; 5 Joe Burgess; 6 George Williams; 27 Jake Shorrocks; 22 Joe Bullock; 7 Thomas Leuluai (C); 14 Romain Navarrete; 15 Willie Isa; 29 Liam Paisley; 38 Morgan Smithies. Subs (all used): 39 Joe Shorrocks (D); 9 Sam Powell; 19 Taulima Tautai; 24 Oliver Partington.
**Tries:** Burgess (23, 65, 78), Williams (53); **Goals:** Escare 2/4.
**Rugby Leaguer & League Express Men of the Match:**
*Trinity:* David Fifita; *Warriors:* Joe Burgess.
**Penalty count:** 10-5; **Half-time:** 16-4;
**Referee:** Robert Hicks; **Attendance:** 5,694.

*Saturday 13th April 2019*

**CATALANS DRAGONS 30 HULL FC 31**
*(after golden point extra-time)*

**DRAGONS:** 1 Tony Gigot; 5 Lewis Tierney; 6 Samisoni Langi; 4 Brayden Wiliame; 27 Fouad Yaha; 29 Sam Tomkins; 22 Lucas Albert; 14 Julian Bousquet; 18 Alrix Da Costa; 10 Sam Moa; 16 Benjamin Jullien; 17 Matt Whitley; 8 Remi Casty (C). Subs (all used): 12 Benjamin Garcia; 13 Greg Bird; 24 Jason Baitieri; 28 Sam Kasiano.
**Tries:** Gigot (6), Baitieri (44), Garcia (57), Yaha (68), Kasiano (79); **Goals:** Tomkins 5/6.
**Sin bin:** Wiliame (14) - shoulder charge.
**HULL FC:** 36 Connor Wynne; 24 Jack Logan; 4 Josh Griffin; 3 Carlos Tuimavave; 2 Bureta Faraimo; 14 Jake Connor; 7 Marc Sneyd; 34 Gareth Ellis; 9 Danny Houghton (C); 16 Jordan Thompson; 21 Sika Manu; 12 Mark Minichiello; 11 Dean Hadley. Subs (all used): 6 Albert Kelly; 22 Jordan Lane; 29 Levy Nzoungou (D); 37 Jack Brown (D).
**Tries:** Brown (27), Wynne (29), Griffin (37, 55), Faraimo (63); **Goals:** Sneyd 5/6; **Field goal:** Sneyd (82).
**Rugby Leaguer & League Express Men of the Match:**
*Dragons:* Remi Casty; *Hull FC:* Marc Sneyd.
**Penalty count:** 10-10; **Half-time:** 8-18;
**Referee:** Chris Kendall; **Attendance:** 8,220.

## ROUND 11

*Thursday 18th April 2019*

**CASTLEFORD TIGERS 28 WAKEFIELD TRINITY 26**

**TIGERS:** 1 Peter Mata'utia; 2 James Clare; 3 Greg Minikin; 4 Michael Shenton (C); 5 Greg Eden; 6 Jake Trueman; 24 Cory Aston (D); 8 Liam Watts; 13 Adam Milner; 15 Jesse Sene-Lefao; 11 Oliver Holmes; 12 Mike McMeeken; 14 Nathan Massey. Subs (all used): 16 Junior Moors; 21 Mitch Clark; 29 Jacques O'Neill; 34 Daniel Smith.
**Tries:** Clare (11, 18), Sene-Lefao (15), Aston (24), Minikin (46); **Goals:** Mata'utia 4/8.
**TRINITY:** 21 Max Jowitt; 34 Mason Caton-Brown (D2); 18 Joe Arundel; 4 Reece Lyne; 5 Ben Jones-Bishop; 1 Ryan Hampshire; 25 Ben Reynolds (D); 8 David Fifita; 9 Kyle Wood; 16 Tinirau Arona; 11 Matty Ashurst; 12 Danny Kirmond (C); 26 Jordan Crowther. Subs (all used): 24 Pauli Pauli; 15 Craig Kopczak; 22 George King; 20 Keegan Hirst.
**Tries:** Caton-Brown (32, 50), Arundel (62), Reynolds (67), Arona (71); **Goals:** Hampshire 3/5.
**Rugby Leaguer & League Express Men of the Match:**
*Tigers:* Liam Watts; *Trinity:* Pauli Pauli.
**Penalty count:** 7-6; **Half-time:** 22-4;
**Referee:** Chris Kendall; **Attendance:** 9,316.

**LONDON BRONCOS 6 CATALANS DRAGONS 39**

**BRONCOS:** 1 Alex Walker; 24 Jacob Ogden; 19 Ryan Morgan; 4 Elliot Kear; 2 Rhys Williams; 6 Jordan Abdull; 28 Morgan Smith; 8 Eddie Battye; 9 Eloi Pelissier; 23 Rob Butler; 12 Jay Pitts (C); 16 Matty Gee; 20 Luke Yates. Subs (all used): 10 Mark Ioane; 7 James Cunningham; 15 Greg Richards; 13 Sadiq Adebiyi.
**Try:** Ioane (64); **Goals:** Smith 1/1.
**Sin bin:** Pelissier (29) - retaliation.
**DRAGONS:** 1 Tony Gigot; 25 Arthur Romano; 6 Samisoni Langi; 17 Matt Whitley; 5 Lewis Tierney; 13 Greg Bird; 29 Sam Tomkins; 14 Julian Bousquet; 18 Alrix Da Costa; 10 Sam Moa; 19 Mickael Goudemand; 16 Benjamin Jullien; 8 Remi Casty (C). Subs (all used): 11 Kenny Edwards; 15 Mickael Simon; 24 Jason Baitieri; 28 Sam Kasiano.
**Tries:** Whitley (7, 60), Tierney (36), Bird (42), Romano (51), Tomkins (56); **Goals:** Tomkins 7/8;
**Field goal:** Tomkins (80).
**Sin bin:** Moa (29) - dangerous challenge on Abdull.
**Rugby Leaguer & League Express Men of the Match:**
*Broncos:* Rhys Williams; *Dragons:* Tony Gigot.
**Penalty count:** 9-8; **Half-time:** 0-14;
**Referee:** Tom Grant; **Attendance:** 2,153.

*Friday 19th April 2019*

**HULL FC 56 HULL KINGSTON ROVERS 12**

**HULL FC:** 36 Connor Wynne; 24 Jack Logan; 3 Carlos Tuimavave; 4 Josh Griffin; 2 Bureta Faraimo; 14 Jake Connor; 7 Marc Sneyd; 8 Scott Taylor; 9 Danny Houghton (C); 23 Mickey Paea; 12 Mark Minichiello; 22 Jordan Lane; 34 Gareth Ellis. Subs (all used): 6 Albert Kelly; 13 Joe Westerman; 19 Masi Matongo; 21 Sika Manu.
**Tries:** Connor (8), Logan (16, 19, 75), Minichiello (43), Westerman (63), Kelly (69), Paea (72), Wynne (76);
**Goals:** Sneyd 10/11.
**Sin bin:** Taylor (66) - high tackle on Crooks.
**HULL KR:** 2 Craig Hall; 3 Ben Crooks; 23 Kane Linnett; 4 Jimmy Keinhorst; 25 Will Oakes; 7 Danny McGuire; 24 Josh Drinkwater; 8 Robbie Mulhern; 15 Tommy Lee; 16 Lee Jewitt; 21 George Lawler; 11 Joel Tomkins (C); 13 Weller Hauraki. Subs (all used): 14 Mitch Garbutt; 9 Shaun Lunt; 20 Danny Addy; 30 Owen Harrison.
**Tries:** Keinhorst (12), Hall (38); **Goals:** Hall 2/2.
**Sin bin:** Crooks (66) - shoulder charge on Sneyd.
**Rugby Leaguer & League Express Men of the Match:**
*Hull FC:* Jake Connor; *Hull KR:* Joel Tomkins.
**Penalty count:** 10-2; **Half-time:** 18-12;
**Referee:** Ben Thaler; **Attendance:** 20,044.

**LEEDS RHINOS 38 HUDDERSFIELD GIANTS 18**

**RHINOS:** 6 Tuimoala Lolohea; 2 Tom Briscoe; 29 Harry Newman; 3 Kallum Watkins (C); 5 Ash Handley; 15 Liam Sutcliffe; 7 Richie Myler; 36 Wellington Albert; 14 Brad Dwyer; 18 Nathaniel Peteru; 16 Brett Ferres; 4 Konrad Hurrell; 25 James Donaldson. Subs (all used): 20 Jamie Jones-Buchanan; 10 Brad Singleton; 19 Mikolaj Oledzki; 9 Matt Parcell.
**Tries:** Lolohea (4), Donaldson (9), Dwyer (13), Myler (30), T Briscoe (35), Handley (70);
**Goals:** L Sutcliffe 6/7, Lolohea 1/1.
**Sin bin:** T Briscoe (16) - dangerous challenge on McIntosh; Peteru (66) - dangerous challenge on Russell.
**GIANTS:** 1 Darnell McIntosh; 2 Jermaine McGillvary; 4 Jordan Turner; 20 Jake Wardle; 5 Akuila Uate; 23 Oliver Russell; 7 Matt Frawley; 17 Ukuma Ta'ai; 9 Kruise Leeming; 10 Suaia Matagi; 35 Joe Wardle; 29 Sam Hewitt; 11 Aaron Murphy. Subs (all used): 8 Paul Clough; 13 Michael Lawrence (C); 26 Sebastine Ikahihifo; 14 Adam O'Brien.
**Tries:** Uate (44), O'Brien (56), McIntosh (61);
**Goals:** Russell 3/3.
**Rugby Leaguer & League Express Men of the Match:**
*Rhinos:* Brad Dwyer; *Giants:* Michael Lawrence.
**Penalty count:** 10-9; **Half-time:** 30-0;
**Referee:** Robert Hicks; **Attendance:** 13,743.

**WARRINGTON WOLVES 12 SALFORD RED DEVILS 36**

**WOLVES:** 1 Stefan Ratchford; 3 Bryson Goodwin; 12 Jack Hughes (C); 4 Ryan Atkins; 5 Josh Charnley; 6 Blake Austin; 15 Declan Patton; 8 Chris Hill (C); 9 Daryl Clark; 10 Mike Cooper; 11 Ben Currie; 20 Harvey Livett; 34 Ben Westwood. Subs (all used): 13 Ben Murdoch-Masila; 14 Jason Clark; 17 Joe Philbin; 23 Matt Davis.
**Tries:** Austin (22), Goodwin (64); **Goals:** Ratchford 2/2.
**RED DEVILS:** 1 Niall Evalds; 5 Jake Bibby; 26 Krisnan Inu; 3 Kris Welham; 22 Derrell Olpherts; 6 Robert Lui; 31 Jackson Hastings; 15 Adam Walker; 14 Joey Lussick; 10 Gil Dudson (C); 11 Josh Jones; 12 George Griffin; 16 Greg Burke. Subs (all used): 9 Josh Wood; 17 Tyrone McCarthy; 18 Ben Nakubuwai; 20 Daniel Murray.
**Tries:** Welham (9), Lussick (12), Murray (26), Lui (37), Bibby (48); **Goals:** Inu 8/9.
**Sin bin:** Welham (63) - repeated offences.
**Rugby Leaguer & League Express Men of the Match:**
*Wolves:* Blake Austin; *Red Devils:* Joey Lussick.
**Penalty count:** 10-10; **Half-time:** 6-28;
**Referee:** Gareth Hewer; **Attendance:** 11,867.

**WIGAN WARRIORS 10 ST HELENS 36**

**WARRIORS:** 20 Zak Hardaker; 2 Tom Davies; 23 Chris Hankinson; 4 Oliver Gildart; 5 Joe Burgess; 6 George Williams; 27 Jake Shorrocks; 10 Ben Flower; 7 Thomas Leuluai; 14 Romain Navarrete; 15 Willie Isa; 38 Morgan Smithies; 24 Oliver Partington. Subs (all used): 13 Sean O'Loughlin (C); 22 Joe Bullock; 19 Taulima Tautai; 11 Joe Greenwood.
**Tries:** Hardaker (11), Williams (39); **Goals:** Hardaker 1/2.
**SAINTS:** 23 Lachlan Coote; 2 Tommy Makinson; 3 Kevin Naiqama; 4 Mark Percival; 5 Regan Grace; 1 Jonny Lomax; 7 Danny Richardson; 8 Alex Walmsley; 9 James Roby (C); 10 Luke Thompson; 11 Zeb Taia; 17 Dominique Peyroux; 15 Morgan Knowles. Subs (all used): 12 Joseph Paulo; 13 Louie McCarthy-Scarsbrook; 21 Aaron Smith; 19 Matty Lees.
**Tries:** Roby (6), Grace (23, 33, 62), Makinson (47), Coote (70); **Goals:** Coote 6/8.
**Sin bin:**
Peyroux (79) - dangerous challenge on Jake Shorrocks.
**Rugby Leaguer & League Express Men of the Match:**
*Warriors:* Oliver Gildart; *Saints:* Luke Thompson.
**Penalty count:** 6-10; **Half-time:** 10-18;
**Referee:** James Child; **Attendance:** 22,050.

## ROUND 12

*Monday 22nd April 2019*

**HUDDERSFIELD GIANTS 24 LONDON BRONCOS 19**

**GIANTS:** 21 Scott Grix; 2 Jermaine McGillvary; 4 Jordan Turner; 20 Jake Wardle; 32 Innes Senior; 23 Oliver Russell; 7 Matt Frawley; 8 Paul Clough; 14 Adam O'Brien; 10 Suaia Matagi; 35 Joe Wardle; 12 Alex Mellor; 13 Michael Lawrence (C). Subs (all used): 9 Kruise Leeming; 11 Aaron Murphy; 19 Matty English; 17 Ukuma Ta'ai.
**Tries:** Mellor (27), Grix (28), McGillvary (52, 77);
**Goals:** Russell 4/4.
**BRONCOS:** 1 Alex Walker; 5 Kieran Dixon; 19 Ryan Morgan; 17 Matty Fleming; 2 Rhys Williams; 28 Morgan Smith; 7 James Cunningham; 23 Rob Butler; 9 Eloi Pelissier; 8 Eddie Battye; 12 Jay Pitts (C); 16 Matty Gee; 20 Luke Yates. Subs (all used): 10 Mark Ioane; 15 Greg Richards; 13 Sadiq Adebiyi; 26 Sam Davis.
**Tries:** Pitts (8), Williams (45), Morgan (62);
**Goals:** Dixon 3/4; **Field goal:** Smith (73).
**Rugby Leaguer & League Express Men of the Match:**
*Giants:* Jermaine McGillvary; *Broncos:* Jay Pitts.
**Penalty count:** 7-4; **Half-time:** 12-8;
**Referee:** Marcus Griffiths; **Attendance:** 4,464.

**HULL KINGSTON ROVERS 6**
**WARRINGTON WOLVES 54**

**ROVERS:** 26 Will Dagger; 2 Craig Hall; 4 Jimmy Keinhorst; 3 Ben Crooks; 19 Junior Vaivai; 24 Josh Drinkwater; 17 Chris Atkin; 8 Robbie Mulhern; 15 Tommy Lee; 30 Owen Harrison; 11 Joel Tomkins (C); 20 Danny Addy; 21 George Lawler. Subs (all used): 14 Mitch Garbutt; 23 Kane Linnett; 31 Adam Rooks; 13 Weller Hauraki.
**Try:** Crooks (9); **Goals:** Hall 1/1.
**WOLVES:** 1 Stefan Ratchford; 2 Tom Lineham; 3 Bryson Goodwin; 18 Toby King; 5 Josh Charnley; 6 Blake Austin; 15 Declan Patton; 8 Chris Hill (C); 9 Daryl Clark; 16 Lama Tasi; 13 Ben Murdoch-Masila; 12 Jack Hughes (C); 23 Matt Davis. Subs (all used): 14 Jason Clark; 17 Joe Philbin; 19 Sitaleki Akauola; 20 Harvey Livett.
**Tries:** Austin (19), Lineham (25, 72), Philbin (37, 65), Charnley (42), Goodwin (46), King (67), Akauola (75);
**Goals:** Ratchford 9/9.
**Rugby Leaguer & League Express Men of the Match:**
*Rovers:* Joel Tomkins; *Wolves:* Joe Philbin.
**Penalty count:** 7-7; **Half-time:** 6-18;
**Referee:** Jack Smith; **Attendance:** 7,111.

**SALFORD RED DEVILS 26 WIGAN WARRIORS 30**

**RED DEVILS:** 1 Niall Evalds; 5 Jake Bibby; 26 Krisnan Inu; 4 Junior Sa'u; 22 Derrell Olpherts; 9 Josh Wood; 31 Jackson Hastings; 15 Adam Walker; 19 Logan Tomkins; 10 Gil Dudson (C); 11 Josh Jones; 12 George Griffin; 16 Greg Burke. Subs (all used): 14 Joey Lussick; 20 Daniel Murray; 18 Ben Nakubuwai; 17 Tyrone McCarthy.
**Tries:** Griffin (27), Evalds (45), Walker (55), Lussick (66);
**Goals:** Inu 5/5.
**WARRIORS:** 1 Morgan Escare; 17 Liam Marshall; 20 Zak Hardaker; 4 Oliver Gildart; 5 Joe Burgess; 6 George Williams; 27 Jake Shorrocks; 10 Ben Flower; 7 Thomas Leuluai (C); 22 Joe Bullock; 15 Willie Isa; 11 Joe Greenwood; 24 Oliver Partington. Subs (all used): 19 Taulima Tautai; 38 Morgan Smithies; 23 Chris Hankinson; 41 Amir Bourouh (D).
**Tries:** Burgess (8), Bullock (15), Greenwood (49, 71), Hardaker (77); **Goals:** Hardaker 5/6.
**Rugby Leaguer & League Express Men of the Match:**
*Red Devils:* Jackson Hastings; *Warriors:* Joe Greenwood.
**Penalty count:** 12-13; **Half-time:** 6-14;
**Referee:** Ben Thaler; **Attendance:** 4,017.

**ST HELENS 62 HULL FC 16**

**SAINTS:** 23 Lachlan Coote; 18 Adam Swift; 3 Kevin Naiqama; 2 Tommy Makinson; 5 Regan Grace; 1 Jonny Lomax; 7 Danny Richardson; 19 Matty Lees; 9 James Roby (C); 10 Luke Thompson; 25 Joe Batchelor (D); 15 Morgan Knowles; 12 Joseph Paulo. Subs (all used): 16 Kyle Amor; 17 Dominique Peyroux; 20 Jack Ashworth; 29 Jack Welsby.
**Tries:** Lomax (18, 21), Naiqama (29, 64, 75, 78), Swift (32, 53, 59), Coote (39), Welsby (70);
**Goals:** Coote 8/9, Richardson 1/2.
**HULL FC:** 14 Jake Connor; 2 Bureta Faraimo; 32 Cameron Scott; 3 Carlos Tuimavave; 33 Ratu Naulago; 6 Albert Kelly; 7 Marc Sneyd; 8 Scott Taylor (C); 11 Dean Hadley; 19 Masi Matongo; 12 Mark Minichiello; 21 Sika Manu; 13 Joe Westerman. Subs (all used): 16 Jordan Thompson; 15 Chris Green; 28 Jez Litten; 20 Brad Fash.
**Tries:** Westerman (7), Tuimavave (11), Litten (48);
**Goals:** Sneyd 2/3.
**Rugby Leaguer & League Express Men of the Match:**
*Saints:* Jonny Lomax; *Hull FC:* Carlos Tuimavave.
**Penalty count:** 6-7; **Half-time:** 30-10;
**Referee:** Robert Hicks; **Attendance:** 11,268.

**WAKEFIELD TRINITY 26 LEEDS RHINOS 24**

**TRINITY:** 21 Max Jowitt; 5 Ben Jones-Bishop; 4 Reece Lyne; 34 Mason Caton-Brown; 29 Lee Kershaw (D); 25 Ben Reynolds; 1 Ryan Hampshire; 15 Craig Kopczak; 26 Jordan Crowther; 16 Tinirau Arona; 12 Danny Kirmond (C); 14 Justin Horo; 22 George King. Subs (all used): 20 Keegan Hirst; 24 Pauli Pauli; 8 David Fifita; 23 Chris Annakin.
**Tries:** Kershaw (10), Lyne (20), Jones-Bishop (55), Jowitt (60); **Goals:** Hampshire 5/6.
**RHINOS:** 6 Tuimoala Lolohea; 2 Tom Briscoe; 3 Kallum Watkins (C); 29 Harry Newman; 5 Ash Handley; 15 Liam Sutcliffe; 7 Richie Myler; 18 Nathaniel Peteru; 14 Brad Dwyer; 36 Wellington Albert; 16 Brett Ferres; 33 Owen Trout; 11 Trent Merrin. Subs (all used): 10 Brad Singleton; 25 James Donaldson; 19 Mikolaj Oledzki; 9 Matt Parcell.
**Tries:** L Sutcliffe (23), Ferres (32), Parcell (69, 79);
**Goals:** L Sutcliffe 4/4.
**Rugby Leaguer & League Express Men of the Match:**
*Trinity:* Max Jowitt; *Rhinos:* Matt Parcell.
**Penalty count:** 6-8; **Half-time:** 12-12;
**Referee:** Chris Kendall; **Attendance:** 6,785.

**CATALANS DRAGONS 37 CASTLEFORD TIGERS 16**

**DRAGONS:** 1 Tony Gigot; 3 David Mead; 6 Samisoni Langi; 4 Brayden Wiliame; 5 Lewis Tierney; 13 Greg Bird; 29 Sam Tomkins; 14 Julian Bousquet; 18 Alrix Da Costa; 10 Sam Moa; 19 Mickael Goudemand; 17 Matt Whitley; 8 Remi Casty (C). Subs (all used): 15 Mickael Simon; 11 Kenny Edwards; 24 Jason Baitieri; 28 Sam Kasiano.
**Tries:** Bousquet (11, 61), Gigot (24), Bird (49), Whitley (73), Tomkins (79); **Goals:** Tomkins 6/6;
**Field goal:** Gigot (58).
**TIGERS:** 1 Peter Mata'utia; 2 James Clare; 3 Greg Minikin; 4 Michael Shenton (C); 5 Greg Eden; 6 Jake Trueman; 24 Cory Aston; 8 Liam Watts; 9 Paul McShane; 34 Daniel Smith; 16 Junior Moors; 12 Mike McMeeken; 13 Adam Milner. Subs (all used): 21 Mitch Clark; 23 Will Maher; 28 Lewis Peachey (D); 33 Chris Clarkson.
**Tries:** Eden (38, 63), Aston (70); **Goals:** Mata'utia 2/3.
**Rugby Leaguer & League Express Men of the Match:**
*Dragons:* Matt Whitley; *Tigers:* Liam Watts.
**Penalty count:** 11-14; **Half-time:** 12-4;
**Referee:** James Child; **Attendance:** 10,120.

## ROUND 13

*Saturday 27th April 2019*

**LONDON BRONCOS 10 SALFORD RED DEVILS 30**

**BRONCOS:** 1 Alex Walker; 5 Kieran Dixon; 19 Ryan Morgan; 17 Matty Fleming; 2 Rhys Williams; 28 Morgan Smith; 7 James Cunningham; 8 Eddie Battye; 26 Sam Davis; 23 Rob Butler; 12 Jay Pitts (C); 20 Luke Yates; 11 Will Lovell. Subs (all used): 6 Jordan Abdull; 13 Sadiq Adebiyi; 16 Matty Gee; 21 Daniel Hindmarsh.
**Tries:** Williams (46), Fleming (71); **Goals:** Dixon 1/2.
**RED DEVILS:** 1 Niall Evalds; 5 Jake Bibby; 26 Krisnan Inu; 3 Kris Welham; 22 Derrell Olpherts; 6 Robert Lui; 31 Jackson Hastings; 13 Mark Flanagan (C); 14 Joey Lussick; 8 Lee Mossop; 11 Josh Jones; 12 George Griffin; 16 Greg Burke. Subs (all used): 9 Josh Wood; 17 Tyrone McCarthy; 18 Ben Nakubuwai; 20 Daniel Murray.
**Tries:** Lussick (5), Evalds (16), Murray (24), Hastings (29), Mossop (63); **Goals:** Inu 5/5.
**Rugby Leaguer & League Express Men of the Match:**
*Broncos:* Matty Fleming; *Red Devils:* Jackson Hastings.
**Penalty count:** 5-3; **Half-time:** 0-24;
**Referee:** Scott Mikalauskas; **Attendance:** 1,133.

**WIGAN WARRIORS 6 CASTLEFORD TIGERS 4**

**WARRIORS:** 20 Zak Hardaker; 17 Liam Marshall; 23 Chris Hankinson; 4 Oliver Gildart; 5 Joe Burgess; 6 George Williams; 27 Jake Shorrocks; 10 Ben Flower; 7 Thomas Leuluai; 22 Joe Bullock; 15 Willie Isa; 11 Joe Greenwood; 24 Oliver Partington. Subs (all used): 9 Sam Powell; 13 Sean O'Loughlin (C); 19 Taulima Tautai; 38 Morgan Smithies.
**Try:** Powell (53); **Goals:** Hardaker 1/1.
**TIGERS:** 1 Peter Mata'utia; 2 James Clare; 3 Greg Minikin; 25 Tuoyo Egodo; 5 Greg Eden; 6 Jake Trueman; 24 Cory Aston; 8 Liam Watts; 9 Paul McShane (C); 23 Will Maher; 33 Chris Clarkson; 12 Mike McMeeken; 14 Nathan Massey. Subs: 13 Adam Milner; 21 Mitch Clark; 28 Lewis Peachey (not used); 34 Daniel Smith.
**Goals:** Mata'utia 2/2.
**Rugby Leaguer & League Express Men of the Match:**
*Warriors:* Sam Powell; *Tigers:* Peter Mata'utia.
**Penalty count:** 5-5; **Half-time:** 0-4;
**Referee:** Chris Kendall; **Attendance:** 10,058.

*Sunday 28th April 2019*

**HULL FC 30 WAKEFIELD TRINITY 14**

**HULL FC:** 36 Connor Wynne; 24 Jack Logan; 3 Carlos Tuimavave; 14 Jake Connor; 4 Josh Griffin; 6 Albert Kelly; 7 Marc Sneyd; 8 Scott Taylor; 9 Danny Houghton (C); 23 Mickey Paea; 11 Dean Hadley; 21 Sika Manu; 34 Gareth Ellis. Subs (all used): 13 Joe Westerman; 15 Chris Green; 19 Masi Matongo; 20 Brad Fash.
**Tries:** Kelly (4), Wynne (23), Westerman (52, 58);
**Goals:** Sneyd 7/8.
**Sin bin:** Ellis (7) - high tackle on Caton-Brown.
**TRINITY:** 21 Max Jowitt; 5 Ben Jones-Bishop; 4 Reece Lyne; 34 Mason Caton-Brown; 29 Lee Kershaw; 1 Ryan Hampshire; 25 Ben Reynolds; 8 David Fifita; 9 Kyle Wood; 20 Keegan Hirst; 12 Danny Kirmond (C); 14 Justin Horo; 26 Jordan Crowther. Subs (all used): 16 Tinirau Arona; 22 George King; 23 Chris Annakin; 24 Pauli Pauli.
**Tries:** Jowitt (11, 74), Horo (33); **Goals:** Hampshire 1/3.
**Rugby Leaguer & League Express Men of the Match:**
*Hull FC:* Albert Kelly; *Trinity:* Kyle Wood.
**Penalty count:** 9-6; **Half-time:** 14-10;
**Referee:** Liam Moore; **Attendance:** 10,254.

Wakefield's Ben Jones-Bishop looks to escape from Huddersfield's Innes Senior

### LEEDS RHINOS 28 HULL KINGSTON ROVERS 24

**RHINOS:** 1 Jack Walker; 2 Tom Briscoe; 29 Harry Newman; 3 Kallum Watkins (C); 5 Ash Handley; 6 Tuimoala Lolohea; 7 Richie Myler, 19 Mikolaj Oledzki; 14 Brad Dwyer; 10 Brad Singleton; 22 Cameron Smith; 15 Liam Sutcliffe; 11 Trent Merrin. Subs (all used): 8 Adam Cuthbertson; 9 Matt Parcell; 25 James Donaldson; 33 Owen Trout.
**Tries:** Handley (2, 23), T Briscoe (38), Walker (40), Parcell (46); **Goals:** L Sutcliffe 4/6.
**ROVERS:** 2 Craig Hall; 5 Ryan Shaw; 4 Jimmy Keinhorst; 3 Ben Crooks; 19 Junior Vaivai; 7 Danny McGuire; 24 Josh Drinkwater; 8 Robbie Mulhern; 9 Shaun Lunt; 22 Ryan Lannon; 11 Joel Tomkins (C); 23 Kane Linnett; 21 George Lawler. Subs (all used): 13 Weller Hauraki; 17 Chris Atkin; 30 Owen Harrison; 34 Antoni Maria (D).
**Tries:** Crooks (50, 65), Linnett (74), Hauraki (78); **Goals:** Shaw 3/3, McGuire 1/1.
**Rugby Leaguer & League Express Men of the Match:** *Rhinos:* Jack Walker; *Rovers:* Ben Crooks.
**Penalty count:** 9-9; **Half-time:** 22-0;
**Referee:** James Child; **Attendance:** 11,694.

### ST HELENS 50 CATALANS DRAGONS 14

**SAINTS:** 29 Jack Welsby; 18 Adam Swift; 3 Kevin Naiqama; 24 Matthew Costello; 5 Regan Grace; 6 Theo Fages; 7 Danny Richardson; 19 Matty Lees; 21 Aaron Smith; 8 Alex Walmsley (C); 11 Zeb Taia; 17 Dominique Peyroux; 12 Joseph Paulo. Subs (all used): 16 Kyle Amor; 20 Jack Ashworth; 22 James Bentley; 25 Joe Batchelor.
**Tries:** Swift (10), Taia (22), Smith (30), Fages (44), Peyroux (50), Costello (53, 71, 75), Welsby (67);
**Goals:** Richardson 7/9.
**Sin bin:** Paulo (30) - fighting.
**DRAGONS:** 1 Tony Gigot; 3 David Mead; 6 Samisoni Langi; 4 Brayden Wiliame; 5 Lewis Tierney; 29 Sam Tomkins; 7 Matty Smith; 14 Julian Bousquet; 18 Alrix Da Costa; 10 Sam Moa; 16 Benjamin Jullien; 17 Matt Whitley; 8 Remi Casty (C). Subs (all used): 11 Kenny Edwards; 15 Mickael Simon; 19 Mickael Goudemand; 28 Sam Kasiano.
**Tries:** Wiliame (4, 36), Tierney (60); **Goals:** Tomkins 1/3.
**Rugby Leaguer & League Express Men of the Match:** *Saints:* Jack Welsby; *Dragons:* Sam Tomkins.
**Penalty count:** 5-6; **Half-time:** 16-10;
**Referee:** Robert Hicks; **Attendance:** 11,268.

### WARRINGTON WOLVES 50 HUDDERSFIELD GIANTS 19

**WOLVES:** 1 Stefan Ratchford; 2 Tom Lineham; 3 Bryson Goodwin; 18 Toby King; 5 Josh Charnley; 6 Blake Austin; 15 Declan Patton; 8 Chris Hill (C); 9 Daryl Clark; 10 Mike Cooper; 11 Ben Currie; 13 Ben Murdoch-Masila; 12 Jack Hughes (C). Subs (all used): 16 Lama Tasi; 17 Joe Philbin; 19 Sitaleki Akauola; 23 Matt Davis.
**Tries:** Currie (4), Hill (25), Goodwin (43, 72), Austin (53, 63), D Clark (56), Murdoch-Masila (77);
**Goals:** Ratchford 9/10.
**GIANTS:** 1 Darnell McIntosh; 2 Jermaine McGillvary; 31 Louis Senior; 32 Innes Senior; 5 Akuila Uate; 23 Oliver Russell; 7 Matt Frawley; 8 Paul Clough; 9 Kruise Leeming; 10 Suaia Matagi; 35 Joe Wardle; 12 Alex Mellor; 13 Michael Lawrence (C). Subs (all used): 16 Aaron Murphy; 14 Adam O'Brien; 17 Ukuma Ta'ai; 19 Matty English.
**Tries:** L Senior (30), McIntosh (33), Mellor (36);
**Goals:** Russell 3/3; **Field goal:** Russell (40).
**Rugby Leaguer & League Express Men of the Match:** *Wolves:* Chris Hill; *Giants:* Darnell McIntosh.
**Penalty count:** 11-4; **Half-time:** 12-19;
**Referee:** Tom Grant; **Attendance:** 10,445.

## ROUND 14

*Thursday 2nd May 2019*

### WIGAN WARRIORS 18 LONDON BRONCOS 8

**WARRIORS:** 20 Zak Hardaker; 17 Liam Marshall; 23 Chris Hankinson; 4 Oliver Gildart; 1 Morgan Escare; 6 George Williams; 27 Jake Shorrocks; 10 Ben Flower; 7 Thomas Leuluai; 22 Joe Bullock; 15 Willie Isa; 11 Joe Greenwood; 38 Morgan Smithies. Subs (all used): 9 Sam Powell; 13 Sean O'Loughlin (C); 14 Romain Navarrete; 19 Taulima Tautai.
**Tries:** Jake Shorrocks (16), Hankinson (49), Escare (57);
**Goals:** Hardaker 3/3.
**BRONCOS:** 1 Alex Walker; 5 Kieran Dixon; 19 Ryan Morgan; 4 Elliot Kear; 2 Rhys Williams; 28 Morgan Smith; 6 Jordan Abdull; 8 Eddie Battye; 7 James Cunningham; 23 Rob Butler; 12 Jay Pitts (C); 11 Will Lovell; 20 Luke Yates. Subs (all used): 9 Eloi Pelissier; 13 Sadiq Adebiyi; 15 Greg Richards; 21 Daniel Hindmarsh.
**Try:** Pitts (19); **Goals:** Dixon 2/2.

**Rugby Leaguer & League Express Men of the Match:** *Warriors:* Jake Shorrocks; *Broncos:* Jordan Abdull.
**Penalty count:** 7-7; **Half-time:** 6-8;
**Referee:** Robert Hicks; **Attendance:** 9,907.

*Friday 3rd May 2019*

### CASTLEFORD TIGERS 14 WARRINGTON WOLVES 26

**TIGERS:** 1 Peter Mata'utia; 25 Tuoyo Egodo; 3 Greg Minikin; 35 Cheyse Blair (D); 5 Greg Eden; 24 Cory Aston; 6 Jake Trueman; 8 Liam Watts; 9 Paul McShane (C); 23 Will Maher; 33 Chris Clarkson; 12 Mike McMeeken; 14 Nathan Massey. Subs (all used): 13 Adam Milner; 21 Mitch Clark; 27 Calum Turner; 34 Daniel Smith.
**Tries:** Aston (8), Egodo (59), Minikin (62);
**Goals:** Mata'utia 1/1, Turner 0/2.
**WOLVES:** 1 Stefan Ratchford; 24 Jack Johnson; 18 Toby King; 4 Ryan Atkins; 5 Josh Charnley; 6 Blake Austin; 15 Declan Patton; 8 Chris Hill (C); 9 Daryl Clark; 10 Mike Cooper; 11 Ben Currie; 12 Jack Hughes (C); 23 Matt Davis. Subs (all used): 16 Adam O'Brien; 19 Sitaleki Akauola; 14 Jason Clark; 20 Harvey Livett.
**Tries:** Cooper (13), King (32, 42), Currie (45);
**Goals:** Ratchford 5/6.
**Rugby Leaguer & League Express Men of the Match:** *Tigers:* Liam Watts; *Wolves:* Daryl Clark.
**Penalty count:** 6-6; **Half-time:** 6-14;
**Referee:** Chris Kendall; **Attendance:** 5,323.

### HUDDERSFIELD GIANTS 25 WAKEFIELD TRINITY 26

**GIANTS:** 1 Darnell McIntosh; 2 Jermaine McGillvary; 4 Jordan Turner; 32 Innes Senior; 5 Akuila Uate; 23 Oliver Russell; 7 Matt Frawley; 17 Ukuma Ta'ai; 9 Kruise Leeming; 10 Suaia Matagi; 11 Aaron Murphy; 12 Alex Mellor; 13 Michael Lawrence (C). Subs (all used): 14 Adam O'Brien; 15 Oliver Roberts; 29 Sam Hewitt; 8 Paul Clough.
**Tries:** Frawley (15), McGillvary (46, 50), O'Brien (54);
**Goals:** Russell 4/4; **Field goal:** Russell (71).
**Sin bin:** Ta'ai (68) - high tackle.
**TRINITY:** 21 Max Jowitt; 5 Ben Jones-Bishop; 4 Reece Lyne; 34 Mason Caton-Brown; 29 Lee Kershaw; 1 Ryan Hampshire; 25 Ben Reynolds; 8 David Fifita; 13 Tyler Randell; 16 Tinirau Arona; 12 Danny Kirmond (C); 14 Justin Horo; 26 Jordan Crowther. Subs (all used): 9 Kyle Wood; 15 Craig Kopczak; 22 George King; 24 Pauli Pauli.

**Tries:** Caton-Brown (6, 11), Fifita (23), Jones-Bishop (65); **Goals:** Hampshire 5/5.
**Rugby Leaguer & League Express Men of the Match:** *Giants:* Jermaine McGillvary; *Trinity:* Reece Lyne.
**Penalty count:** 5-7; **Half-time:** 6-18;
**Referee:** James Child; **Attendance:** 5,104.

**HULL FC 6 CATALANS DRAGONS 37**

**HULL FC:** 36 Connor Wynne; 2 Bureta Faraimo; 24 Jack Logan; 4 Josh Griffin; 38 Kieran Buchanan (D); 13 Joe Westerman; 14 Jake Connor; 8 Scott Taylor; 9 Danny Houghton (C); 23 Mickey Paea; 12 Mark Minichiello; 21 Sika Manu; 34 Gareth Ellis. Subs (all used): 15 Chris Green; 16 Jordan Thompson; 19 Masi Matongo; 20 Brad Fash.
**Try:** Paea (14); **Goals:** Connor 1/1.
**Sin bin:** Connor (36) - dissent.
**DRAGONS:** 1 Tony Gigot; 25 Arthur Romano; 6 Samisoni Langi; 4 Brayden Wiliame; 27 Fouad Yaha; 13 Greg Bird; 29 Sam Tomkins; 8 Remi Casty (C); 18 Alrix Da Costa; 10 Sam Moa; 17 Matt Whitley; 19 Mickael Goudemand; 24 Jason Baitieri. Subs (all used): 14 Julian Bousquet; 20 Lambert Belmas; 22 Lucas Albert; 28 Sam Kasiano.
**Tries:** Yaha (22), Gigot (26), Wiliame (31), Romano (43), Whitley (48), Langi (80); **Goals:** Tomkins 6/7;
**Field goal:** Gigot (73).
**Rugby Leaguer & League Express Men of the Match:** *Hull FC:* Mickey Paea; *Dragons:* Brayden Wiliame.
**Penalty count:** 5-12; **Half-time:** 6-18;
**Referee:** Ben Thaler; **Attendance:** 9,830.

**SALFORD RED DEVILS 28 LEEDS RHINOS 16**

**RED DEVILS:** 1 Niall Evalds; 5 Jake Bibby; 26 Krisnan Inu; 3 Kris Welham; 22 Derrell Olpherts; 6 Robert Lui; 31 Jackson Hastings; 8 Lee Mossop (C); 14 Joey Lussick; 10 Gil Dudson; 11 Josh Jones; 12 George Griffin; 16 Greg Burke. Subs (all used): 15 Adam Walker; 17 Tyrone McCarthy; 18 Ben Nakubuwai; 20 Daniel Murray.
**Tries:** Mossop (7), Walker (22, 54), Lussick (44), Lui (64); **Goals:** Inu 4/5.
**RHINOS:** 6 Tuimoala Lolohea; 2 Tom Briscoe; 3 Kallum Watkins (C); 29 Harry Newman; 5 Ash Handley; 15 Liam Sutcliffe; 7 Richie Myler; 18 Nathaniel Peteru; 9 Matt Parcell; 10 Brad Singleton; 20 Jamie Jones-Buchanan; 22 Cameron Smith; 11 Trent Merrin. Subs (all used): 8 Adam Cuthbertson; 14 Brad Dwyer; 19 Mikolaj Oledzki; 38 Ava Seumanufagai (D).
**Tries:** Oledzki (39), Newman (70), Handley (73);
**Goals:** L Sutcliffe 2/3.
**Rugby Leaguer & League Express Men of the Match:** *Red Devils:* Robert Lui; *Rhinos:* Brad Dwyer.
**Penalty count:** 4-6; **Half-time:** 12-6;
**Referee:** Scott Mikalauskas; **Attendance:** 3,368.

*Sunday 5th May 2019*

**HULL KINGSTON ROVERS 26 ST HELENS 42**

**ROVERS:** 2 Craig Hall; 5 Ryan Shaw; 19 Junior Vaivai; 3 Ben Crooks; 25 Will Oakes; 24 Josh Drinkwater; 7 Danny McGuire (C); 8 Robbie Mulhern; 20 Danny Addy; 34 Antoni Maria; 23 Kane Linnett; 4 Jimmy Keinhorst; 21 George Lawler. Subs: 9 Shaun Lunt; 17 Chris Atkin; 31 Adam Rooks (not used); 13 Weller Hauraki.
**Tries:** Addy (8), Shaw (11), Keinhorst (44), Oakes (60); **Goals:** Shaw 5/5.
**SAINTS:** 23 Lachlan Coote; 2 Tommy Makinson; 3 Kevin Naiqama; 24 Matthew Costello; 5 Regan Grace; 1 Jonny Lomax; 6 Theo Fages; 8 Alex Walmsley; 9 James Roby (C); 19 Matty Lees; 11 Zeb Taia; 17 Dominique Peyroux; 15 Morgan Knowles. Subs (all used): 12 Joseph Paulo; 16 Kyle Amor; 20 Jack Ashworth; 29 Jack Welsby.
**Tries:** Naiqama (18, 37, 64), Makinson (31, 49, 68), Lomax (47), Grace (79); **Goals:** Coote 5/8.
**Rugby Leaguer & League Express Men of the Match:** *Rovers:* Jimmy Keinhorst; *Saints:* Kevin Naiqama.
**Penalty count:** 5-5; **Half-time:** 14-18;
**Referee:** Liam Moore; **Attendance:** 8,123.

## ROUND 15

*Thursday 16th May 2019*

**LEEDS RHINOS 8 CASTLEFORD TIGERS 30**

**RHINOS:** 6 Tuimoala Lolohea; 2 Tom Briscoe; 29 Harry Newman; 3 Kallum Watkins (C); 5 Ash Handley; 23 Callum McLelland; 7 Richie Myler; 18 Nathaniel Peteru; 14 Brad Dwyer; 10 Brad Singleton; 22 Cameron Smith; 15 Liam Sutcliffe; 11 Trent Merrin. Subs (all used): 9 Matt Parcell; 19 Mikolaj Oledzki; 25 James Donaldson; 38 Ava Seumanufagai.
**Try:** Parcell (52); **Goals:** L Sutcliffe 2/2.
**Sin bin:** Watkins (25) - dangerous challenge on Eden.
**TIGERS:** 11 Peter Mata'utia; 2 James Clare; 3 Greg Minikin; 35 Cheyse Blair; 5 Greg Eden; 6 Jake Trueman; 24 Cory Aston; 8 Liam Watts; 9 Paul McShane (C); 10 Grant Millington; 15 Jesse Sene-Lefao; 12 Mike McMeeken; 14 Nathan Massey. Subs (all used): 13 Adam Milner; 18 Matt Cook; 21 Mitch Clark; 32 Jordan Rankin.
**Tries:** Sene-Lefao (17, 44), Eden (26), Clare (58), Trueman (65); **Goals:** Mata'utia 5/5.
**Rugby Leaguer & League Express Men of the Match:** *Rhinos:* Ash Handley; *Tigers:* Peter Mata'utia.
**Penalty count:** 9-8; **Half-time:** 2-12;
**Referee:** Chris Kendall; **Attendance:** 13,286.

*Friday 17th May 2019*

**HUDDERSFIELD GIANTS 30 HULL KINGSTON ROVERS 22**

**GIANTS:** 1 Darnell McIntosh; 2 Jermaine McGillvary; 4 Jordan Turner; 20 Jake Wardle; 32 Innes Senior; 6 Lee Gaskell; 23 Oliver Russell; 19 Matty English; 14 Adam O'Brien; 10 Suaia Matagi; 11 Aaron Murphy; 29 Sam Hewitt; 35 Joe Wardle. Subs (all used): 9 Kruise Leeming; 8 Paul Clough; 13 Michael Lawrence (C); 17 Ukuma Ta'ai.
**Tries:** McGillvary (5, 52), I Senior (13), Joe Wardle (60), Jake Wardle (63), Leeming (75);
**Goals:** Russell 2/5, Gaskell 1/2.
**Sin bin:** Joe Wardle (8) - dissent.
**ROVERS:** 2 Craig Hall; 5 Ryan Shaw; 4 Jimmy Keinhorst; 3 Ben Crooks; 19 Junior Vaivai; 7 Danny McGuire; 24 Josh Drinkwater; 34 Antoni Maria; 20 Danny Addy; 8 Robbie Mulhern; 23 Kane Linnett; 11 Joel Tomkins (C); 21 George Lawler. Subs (all used): 14 Mitch Garbutt; 13 Weller Hauraki; 22 Ryan Lannon; 17 Chris Atkin.
**Tries:** Vaivai (9), Tomkins (30), Hall (33), Addy (79);
**Goals:** Shaw 3/4.
**Sin bin:** Maria (69) - high tackle on Gaskell.
**Rugby Leaguer & League Express Men of the Match:** *Giants:* Kruise Leeming; *Rovers:* Danny Addy.
**Penalty count:** 8-8; **Half-time:** 8-16;
**Referee:** Robert Hicks; **Attendance:** 4,621.

**ST HELENS 32 SALFORD RED DEVILS 30**

**SAINTS:** 23 Lachlan Coote; 18 Adam Swift; 2 Tommy Makinson; 24 Matthew Costello; 5 Regan Grace; 1 Jonny Lomax (C); 6 Theo Fages; 8 Alex Walmsley; 21 Aaron Smith; 19 Matty Lees; 11 Zeb Taia; 17 Dominique Peyroux; 15 Morgan Knowles. Subs (all used): 12 Joseph Paulo; 16 Kyle Amor; 20 Jack Ashworth; 22 James Bentley.
**Tries:** Coote (5, 9, 65), Makinson (12, 67), Bentley (79); **Goals:** Coote 4/6.
**RED DEVILS:** 1 Niall Evalds; 22 Derrell Olpherts; 26 Krisnan Inu; 3 Kris Welham; 23 Ken Sio; 6 Robert Lui; 31 Jackson Hastings; 8 Lee Mossop (C); 14 Joey Lussick; 10 Gil Dudson; 11 Josh Jones; 12 George Griffin; 16 Greg Burke. Subs (all used): 15 Adam Walker; 20 Daniel Murray; 17 Tyrone McCarthy; 28 Pauli Pauli (D).
**Tries:** Dudson (16), Evalds (22, 54), Olpherts (29), Lui (60); **Goals:** Inu 5/5.
**Rugby Leaguer & League Express Men of the Match:** *Saints:* Lachlan Coote; *Red Devils:* Robert Lui.
**Penalty count:** 8-4; **Half-time:** 16-18;
**Referee:** Scott Mikalauskas; **Attendance:** 9,446.

*Saturday 18th May 2019*

**LONDON BRONCOS 42 WAKEFIELD TRINITY 34**

**BRONCOS:** 1 Alex Walker; 5 Kieran Dixon; 19 Ryan Morgan; 4 Elliot Kear; 2 Rhys Williams; 6 Jordan Abdull; 28 Morgan Smith; 8 Eddie Battye; 7 James Cunningham; 23 Rob Butler; 12 Jay Pitts (C); 11 Will Lovell; 20 Luke Yates. Subs (all used): 9 Eloi Pelissier; 15 Greg Richards; 16 Matty Gee; 13 Sadiq Adebiyi.
**Tries:** Abdull (10, 25, 33, 38), Williams (13, 63), Dixon (45, 59); **Goals:** Dixon 5/8.
**TRINITY:** 1 Ryan Hampshire; 5 Ben Jones-Bishop; 4 Reece Lyne; 35 Junior Sa'u (D); 34 Mason Caton-Brown; 25 Ben Reynolds; 6 Jacob Miller (C); 8 David Fifita; 13 Tyler Randell; 20 Keegan Hirst; 19 James Batchelor; 14 Justin Horo; 26 Jordan Crowther. Subs (all used): 22 George King; 12 Danny Kirmond; 15 Craig Kopczak; 9 Kyle Wood.
**Tries:** Wood (39), Fifita (64, 75), Caton-Brown (74, 77), Hampshire (78); **Goals:** Hampshire 5/6.
**Rugby Leaguer & League Express Men of the Match:** *Broncos:* Jordan Abdull; *Trinity:* Ryan Hampshire.
**Penalty count:** 7-5; **Half-time:** 26-6;
**Referee:** Liam Moore; **Attendance:** 1,205.

**WARRINGTON WOLVES 12 HULL FC 19**

**WOLVES:** 1 Stefan Ratchford; 3 Bryson Goodwin; 18 Toby King; 4 Ryan Atkins; 5 Josh Charnley; 6 Blake Austin; 15 Declan Patton; 8 Chris Hill (C); 9 Daryl Clark; 10 Mike Cooper; 11 Ben Currie; 12 Jack Hughes (C); 34 Ben Westwood. Subs (all used): 17 Joe Philbin; 13 Ben Murdoch-Masila; 14 Jason Clark; 19 Sitaleki Akauola.
**Tries:** King (10), Austin (54); **Goals:** Ratchford 2/2.
**Sin bin:** Murdoch-Masila (78) - fighting.
**On report:** Patton (50) - alleged bite on Connor.
**HULL FC:** 1 Jamie Shaul; 33 Ratu Naulago; 14 Jake Connor; 4 Josh Griffin; 38 Kieran Buchanan; 6 Albert Kelly; 7 Marc Sneyd; 8 Scott Taylor (C); 30 Danny Washbrook; 23 Mickey Paea; 11 Dean Hadley; 12 Mark Minichiello; 13 Joe Westerman. Subs (all used): 15 Chris Green; 16 Jordan Thompson; 19 Masi Matongo; 20 Brad Fash.
**Tries:** Paea (14), Taylor (17), Kelly (23); **Goals:** Sneyd 3/3;
**Field goal:** Sneyd (68).
**Sin bin:** Connor (56) - fighting.
**Rugby Leaguer & League Express Men of the Match:** *Wolves:* Sitaleki Akauola; *Hull FC:* Jamie Shaul.
**Penalty count:** 7-7; **Half-time:** 6-18;
**Referee:** James Child; **Attendance:** 10,600.

**CATALANS DRAGONS 33 WIGAN WARRIORS 16**

**DRAGONS:** 1 Tony Gigot; 27 Fouad Yaha; 3 David Mead; 4 Brayden Wiliame; 5 Lewis Tierney; 6 Samisoni Langi; 13 Greg Bird; 14 Julian Bousquet; 9 Michael Mcllorum; 10 Sam Moa; 11 Kenny Edwards; 17 Matt Whitley; 8 Remi Casty (C). Subs (all used): 12 Benjamin Garcia; 15 Mickael Simon; 24 Jason Baitieri; 28 Sam Kasiano.
**Tries:** Mcllorum (20), Mead (48, 68), Langi (52), Kasiano (54); **Goals:** Gigot 6/7; **Field goal:** Gigot (59).
**WARRIORS:** 20 Zak Hardaker; 17 Liam Marshall; 3 Dan Sarginson; 4 Oliver Gildart; 5 Joe Burgess; 6 George Williams; 7 Thomas Leuluai; 10 Ben Flower; 9 Sam Powell; 14 Romain Navarrete; 15 Willie Isa; 11 Joe Greenwood; 8 Tony Clubb. Subs (all used): 13 Sean O'Loughlin (C); 19 Taulima Tautai; 22 Joe Bullock; 23 Chris Hankinson.
**Tries:** Marshall (39), Gildart (73), Hardaker (80);
**Goals:** Hardaker 2/3.
**Rugby Leaguer & League Express Men of the Match:** *Dragons:* Samisoni Langi; *Warriors:* Zak Hardaker.
**Penalty count:** 8-8; **Half-time:** 8-6;
**Referee:** Ben Thaler; **Attendance:** 31,555
*(at Camp Nou, Barcelona).*

## ROUND 16 - MAGIC WEEKEND

*Saturday 25th May 2019*

**CATALANS DRAGONS 25 WAKEFIELD TRINITY 18**

**DRAGONS:** 1 Tony Gigot; 27 Fouad Yaha; 3 David Mead; 4 Brayden Wiliame; 5 Lewis Tierney; 6 Samisoni Langi; 7 Matty Smith; 14 Julian Bousquet; 18 Alrix Da Costa; 10 Sam Moa; 17 Matt Whitley; 12 Benjamin Garcia; 8 Remi Casty (C). Subs (all used): 11 Kenny Edwards; 15 Mickael Simon; 24 Jason Baitieri; 28 Sam Kasiano.
**Tries:** Yaha (15), Gigot (30), Garcia (55, 79);
**Goals:** Gigot 4/5; **Field goal:** Gigot (76).
**On report:** Moa (72) - alleged dangerous challenge.
**TRINITY:** 21 Max Jowitt; 5 Ben Jones-Bishop; 4 Reece Lyne; 35 Junior Sa'u; 34 Mason Caton-Brown; 6 Jacob Miller (C); 1 Ryan Hampshire; 8 David Fifita; 9 Kyle Wood; 15 Craig Kopczak; 11 Matty Ashurst; 12 Danny Kirmond; 22 George King. Subs (all used): 19 James Batchelor; 10 Anthony England; 13 Tyler Randell; 36 Kelepi Tanginoa (D).
**Tries:** Wood (41), Kirmond (44), Jones-Bishop (68);
**Goals:** Hampshire 3/4.
**Rugby Leaguer & League Express Men of the Match:** *Dragons:* Tony Gigot; *Trinity:* Kyle Wood.
**Penalty count:** 6-9; **Half-time:** 12-0;
**Referee:** Scott Mikalauskas.

**HUDDERSFIELD GIANTS 55 HULL FC 2**

**GIANTS:** 1 Darnell McIntosh; 2 Jermaine McGillvary; 4 Jordan Turner; 20 Jake Wardle; 32 Innes Senior; 6 Lee Gaskell; 23 Oliver Russell; 19 Matty English; 14 Adam O'Brien; 10 Suaia Matagi; 35 Joe Wardle; 12 Alex Mellor; 11 Aaron Murphy. Subs (all used): 9 Kruise Leeming; 8 Paul Clough; 13 Michael Lawrence (C); 17 Ukuma Ta'ai.
**Tries:** Joe Wardle (7), Jake Wardle (17), O'Brien (28, 44), McIntosh (32, 53), Mellor (58), McGillvary (62, 78), Murphy (71); **Goals:** Russell 7/10; **Field goal:** Russell (38).
**HULL FC:** 1 Jamie Shaul; 38 Kieran Buchanan; 4 Josh Griffin; 14 Jake Connor; 33 Ratu Naulago; 6 Albert Kelly; 7 Marc Sneyd; 8 Scott Taylor (C); 30 Danny Washbrook; 23 Mickey Paea; 11 Dean Hadley; 12 Mark Minichiello; 13 Joe Westerman. Subs (all used): 10 Josh Bowden; 15 Chris Green; 21 Sika Manu; 20 Brad Fash.
**Goals:** Sneyd 1/1.
**Rugby Leaguer & League Express Men of the Match:** *Giants:* Darnell McIntosh; *Hull FC:* Albert Kelly.
**Penalty count:** 5-6; **Half-time:** 21-2; **Referee:** Liam Moore.

**WARRINGTON WOLVES 26 WIGAN WARRIORS 14**

**WOLVES:** 22 Jake Mamo; 2 Tom Lineham; 3 Bryson Goodwin; 18 Toby King; 5 Josh Charnley; 6 Blake Austin; 15 Declan Patton; 8 Chris Hill (C); 9 Daryl Clark; 10 Mike Cooper; 11 Ben Currie; 12 Jack Hughes (C); 17 Joe Philbin. Subs (all used): 13 Ben Murdoch-Masila; 14 Jason Clark; 19 Sitaleki Akauola; 21 Danny Walker.
**Tries:** Patton (21), Austin (58), King (62); **Goals:** Patton 7/7.

**WARRIORS:** 20 Zak Hardaker; 23 Chris Hankinson; 3 Dan Sarginson; 4 Oliver Gildart; 5 Joe Burgess; 6 George Williams; 13 Sean O'Loughlin (C); 10 Ben Flower; 27 Jake Shorrocks; 22 Joe Bullock; 15 Willie Isa; 11 Joe Greenwood; 8 Tony Clubb. Subs (all used): 19 Taulima Tautai; 38 Morgan Smithies; 37 Jarrod Sammut; 24 Oliver Partington.
**Tries:** Burgess (46), Isa (74); **Goals:** Hardaker 3/4.
**Rugby Leaguer & League Express Men of the Match:** *Wolves:* Toby King; *Warriors:* Zak Hardaker.
**Penalty count:** 8-7; **Half-time:** 8-2; **Referee:** Chris Kendall.

**Attendance:** 30,057 *(at Anfield, Liverpool)*.

*Sunday 26th May 2019*

**HULL KINGSTON ROVERS 22 SALFORD RED DEVILS 20**

**ROVERS:** 2 Craig Hall; 3 Ben Crooks; 4 Jimmy Keinhorst; 23 Kane Linnett; 5 Ryan Shaw; 24 Josh Drinkwater; 7 Danny McGuire; 10 Mose Masoe; 20 Danny Addy; 8 Robbie Mulhern; 13 Weller Hauraki; 11 Joel Tomkins (C); 21 George Lawler. Subs: 17 Chris Atkin (not used); 9 Shaun Lunt; 14 Mitch Garbutt; 34 Antoni Maria.
**Tries:** Linnett (18), Hall (27, 44); **Goals:** Shaw 5/5.
**RED DEVILS:** 1 Niall Evalds; 23 Ken Sio; 3 Kris Welham; 26 Krisnan Inu; 22 Derrell Olpherts; 6 Robert Lui; 31 Jackson Hastings; 8 Lee Mossop (C); 14 Joey Lussick; 10 Gil Dudson; 11 Josh Jones; 12 George Griffin; 16 Greg Burke. Subs: 5 Jake Bibby (not used); 17 Tyrone McCarthy; 28 Pauli Pauli; 15 Adam Walker.
**Tries:** Lussick (39), Pauli (51), Sio (56, 70); **Goals:** Inu 2/4.
**Sin bin:** Pauli (30) - late challenge on Drinkwater.
**Rugby Leaguer & League Express Men of the Match:** *Rovers:* Craig Hall; *Red Devils:* Kris Welham.
**Penalty count:** 8-6; **Half-time:** 14-6; **Referee:** Ben Thaler.

**LEEDS RHINOS 24 LONDON BRONCOS 22**

**RHINOS:** 1 Jack Walker; 2 Tom Briscoe; 29 Harry Newman; 3 Kallum Watkins (C); 5 Ash Handley; 15 Liam Sutcliffe; 7 Richie Myler; 38 Ava Seumanufagai; 14 Brad Dwyer; 10 Brad Singleton; 25 James Donaldson; 22 Cameron Smith; 11 Trent Merrin. Subs (all used): 9 Matt Parcell; 18 Nathaniel Peteru; 19 Mikolaj Oledzki; 30 Alex Sutcliffe.
**Tries:** L Sutcliffe (5), Handley (10), Walker (43), Newman (65), Myler (68); **Goals:** L Sutcliffe 2/5.
**BRONCOS:** 1 Alex Walker; 5 Kieran Dixon; 19 Ryan Morgan; 4 Elliot Kear; 2 Rhys Williams; 6 Jordan Abdull; 28 Morgan Smith; 8 Eddie Battye; 7 James Cunningham; 23 Rob Butler; 12 Jay Pitts (C); 11 Will Lovell; 20 Luke Yates. Subs (all used): 15 Greg Richards; 14 Matty Fozard; 13 Sadiq Adebiyi; 16 Matty Gee.
**Tries:** Morgan (25), Abdull (49, 70), Walker (75); **Goals:** Dixon 3/4.
**Rugby Leaguer & League Express Men of the Match:** *Rhinos:* Richie Myler; *Broncos:* Alex Walker.
**Penalty count:** 3-9; **Half-time:** 10-6; **Referee:** James Child.

**CASTLEFORD TIGERS 16 ST HELENS 36**

**TIGERS:** 1 Peter Mata'utia; 2 James Clare; 3 Greg Minikin; 35 Cheyse Blair; 5 Greg Eden; 6 Jake Trueman; 24 Cory Aston; 8 Liam Watts; 9 Paul McShane (C); 34 Daniel Smith; 10 Grant Millington; 12 Mike McMeeken; 13 Adam Milner. Subs (all used): 18 Matt Cook; 23 Will Maher; 32 Jordan Rankin; 33 Chris Clarkson.
**Tries:** Millington (33), Clarkson (73), Eden (76); **Goals:** Mata'utia 1/1, Rankin 1/2.
**SAINTS:** 23 Lachlan Coote; 2 Tommy Makinson; 3 Kevin Naiqama; 24 Matthew Costello; 5 Regan Grace; 1 Jonny Lomax; 6 Theo Fages; 8 Alex Walmsley; 9 James Roby (C); 19 Matty Lees; 11 Zeb Taia; 17 Dominique Peyroux; 15 Morgan Knowles. Subs (all used): 12 Joseph Paulo; 20 Jack Ashworth; 21 Aaron Smith; 22 James Bentley.
**Tries:** Makinson (8), Grace (16), Lomax (19), Fages (23), Ashworth (47), Coote (60), Naiqama (67); **Goals:** Coote 4/7.
**Rugby Leaguer & League Express Men of the Match:** *Tigers:* Jake Trueman; *Saints:* Alex Walmsley.
**Penalty count:** 6-6; **Half-time:** 6-20; **Referee:** Robert Hicks.

**Attendance:** 26,812 *(at Anfield, Liverpool)*.

## ROUND 17

*Friday 7th June 2019*

**CASTLEFORD TIGERS 27 HUDDERSFIELD GIANTS 26**
*(after golden point extra-time)*

**TIGERS:** 1 Peter Mata'utia; 2 James Clare; 3 Greg Minikin; 35 Cheyse Blair; 5 Greg Eden; 6 Jake Trueman; 32 Jordan Rankin; 8 Liam Watts; 9 Paul McShane (C); 34 Daniel Smith; 33 Chris Clarkson; 12 Mike McMeeken; 14 Nathan Massey. Subs (all used): 10 Grant Millington; 13 Adam Milner; 18 Matt Cook; 21 Mitch Clark.
**Tries:** Minikin (38), Watts (63), Millington (77); **Goals:** Mata'utia 7/7; **Field goal:** Mata'utia (87).
**GIANTS:** 1 Darnell McIntosh; 2 Jermaine McGillvary; 4 Jordan Turner; 20 Jake Wardle; 32 Innes Senior; 6 Lee Gaskell; 23 Oliver Russell; 19 Matty English; 14 Adam O'Brien; 10 Suaia Matagi; 35 Joe Wardle; 12 Alex Mellor; 11 Aaron Murphy. Subs (all used): 9 Kruise Leeming; 8 Paul Clough; 13 Michael Lawrence (C); 17 Ukuma Ta'ai.
**Tries:** Gaskell (25, 32, 57), Joe Wardle (75); **Goals:** Russell 5/5.
**Rugby Leaguer & League Express Men of the Match:** *Tigers:* Peter Mata'utia; *Giants:* Lee Gaskell.
**Penalty count:** 9-9; **Half-time:** 10-12; **Referee:** Ben Thaler; **Attendance:** 7,483.

**HULL FC 35 SALFORD RED DEVILS 32**

**HULL FC:** 1 Jamie Shaul; 33 Ratu Naulago; 14 Jake Connor; 4 Josh Griffin; 2 Bureta Faraimo; 6 Albert Kelly; 7 Marc Sneyd; 15 Chris Green; 9 Danny Houghton (C); 23 Mickey Paea; 12 Mark Minichiello; 21 Sika Manu; 13 Joe Westerman. Subs (all used): 10 Josh Bowden; 11 Dean Hadley; 20 Brad Fash; 35 Andre Savelio.
**Tries:** Kelly (9, 25), Connor (11), Minichiello (14), Shaul (35), Naulago (66); **Goals:** Sneyd 5/7; **Field goal:** Sneyd (63).
**Dismissal:** Griffin (75) - dangerous challenge on Inu.
**Sin bin:** Green (75) - fighting.
**RED DEVILS:** 1 Niall Evalds; 23 Ken Sio; 3 Kris Welham; 26 Krisnan Inu; 5 Jake Bibby; 6 Robert Lui; 31 Jackson Hastings; 20 Daniel Murray; 14 Joey Lussick; 10 Gil Dudson (C); 11 Josh Jones; 12 George Griffin; 16 Greg Burke. Subs (all used): 15 Adam Walker; 17 Tyrone McCarthy; 19 Logan Tomkins; 28 Pauli Pauli.
**Tries:** Pauli (18, 71), Bibby (29, 77), Lui (43), Evalds (79); **Goals:** Inu 4/6.
**Sin bin:** Walker (75) - fighting.
**Rugby Leaguer & League Express Men of the Match:** *Hull FC:* Albert Kelly; *Red Devils:* Robert Lui.
**Penalty count:** 6-5; **Half-time:** 28-12; **Referee:** Liam Moore; **Attendance:** 9,914.

**WAKEFIELD TRINITY 0 LEEDS RHINOS 10**

**TRINITY:** 1 Ryan Hampshire; 5 Ben Jones-Bishop; 4 Reece Lyne; 32 Jack Croft; 35 Junior Sa'u; 6 Jacob Miller (C); 7 Danny Brough; 15 Craig Kopczak; 13 Tyler Randell; 10 Anthony England; 19 James Batchelor; 11 Matty Ashurst; 36 Kelepi Tanginoa. Subs (all used): 9 Kyle Wood; 22 George King; 26 Jordan Crowther; 20 Keegan Hirst.
**Goals:** Brough 0/1.
**RHINOS:** 6 Tuimoala Lolohea; 2 Tom Briscoe; 29 Harry Newman; 4 Konrad Hurrell; 5 Ash Handley; 15 Liam Sutcliffe; 7 Richie Myler; 38 Ava Seumanufagai; 14 Brad Dwyer; 10 Brad Singleton; 16 Brett Ferres; 3 Kallum Watkins (C); 11 Trent Merrin. Subs (all used): 22 Cameron Smith; 25 James Donaldson; 19 Mikolaj Oledzki; 8 Adam Cuthbertson.
**Try:** Lolohea (54); **Goals:** L Sutcliffe 3/5.
**Rugby Leaguer & League Express Men of the Match:** *Trinity:* Kelepi Tanginoa; *Rhinos:* Harry Newman.
**Penalty count:** 7-7; **Half-time:** 0-4; **Referee:** Robert Hicks; **Attendance:** 5,489.

*Saturday 8th June 2019*

**WARRINGTON WOLVES 34 CATALANS DRAGONS 4**

**WOLVES:** 31 Josh Thewlis (D); 24 Jack Johnson; 3 Bryson Goodwin; 18 Toby King; 5 Josh Charnley; 6 Blake Austin; 15 Declan Patton; 8 Chris Hill (C); 9 Daryl Clark; 10 Mike Cooper; 11 Ben Currie; 12 Jack Hughes (C); 17 Joe Philbin. Subs (all used): 14 Jason Clark; 13 Ben Murdoch-Masila; 19 Sitaleki Akauola; 23 Matt Davis.
**Tries:** D Clark (32), Austin (38), Goodwin (65), Akauola (70), Charnley (76); **Goals:** Patton 7/7.
**DRAGONS:** 1 Tony Gigot; 25 Arthur Romano; 3 David Mead; 6 Samisoni Langi; 27 Fouad Yaha; 29 Sam Tomkins; 7 Matty Smith; 15 Mickael Simon; 9 Michael McIlorum; 10 Sam Moa; 17 Matt Whitley; 12 Benjamin Garcia (C); 14 Julian Bousquet. Subs (all used): 16 Benjamin Jullien; 20 Lambert Belmas; 24 Jason Baitieri; 28 Sam Kasiano.
**Try:** Yaha (17); **Goals:** Tomkins 0/1.
**Rugby Leaguer & League Express Men of the Match:** *Wolves:* Bryson Goodwin; *Dragons:* Sam Moa.
**Penalty count:** 8-6; **Half-time:** 12-4; **Referee:** Chris Kendall; **Attendance:** 10,015.

*Sunday 9th June 2019*

**HULL KINGSTON ROVERS 18 WIGAN WARRIORS 19**

**ROVERS:** 2 Craig Hall; 3 Ben Crooks; 4 Jimmy Keinhorst; 23 Kane Linnett; 5 Ryan Shaw; 24 Josh Drinkwater; 26 Will Dagger; 30 Owen Harrison; 20 Danny Addy; 10 Mose Masoe; 11 Joel Tomkins (C); 13 Weller Hauraki; 21 George Lawler. Subs (all used): 17 Chris Atkin; 34 Antoni Maria; 22 Ryan Lannon; 8 Robbie Mulhern.
**Tries:** Keinhorst (18), Dagger (43), Lannon (54); **Goals:** Shaw 3/3.
**WARRIORS:** 20 Zak Hardaker; 17 Liam Marshall; 3 Dan Sarginson; 4 Oliver Gildart; 5 Joe Burgess; 6 George Williams; 7 Thomas Leuluai; 10 Ben Flower; 9 Sam Powell; 8 Tony Clubb; 15 Willie Isa; 12 Liam Farrell; 13 Sean O'Loughlin (C). Subs (all used): 22 Joe Bullock; 27 Jake Shorrocks; 38 Morgan Smithies; 19 Taulima Tautai.
**Tries:** Williams (11), Sarginson (36), Burgess (39), Marshall (66); **Goals:** Hardaker 1/1, Williams 0/3; **Field goal:** Powell (78).
**Rugby Leaguer & League Express Men of the Match:** *Rovers:* Craig Hall; *Warriors:* Dan Sarginson.
**Penalty count:** 4-5; **Half-time:** 6-14; **Referee:** Scott Mikalauskas; **Attendance:** 8,010.

**LONDON BRONCOS 23 ST HELENS 22**
*(after golden point extra-time)*

**BRONCOS:** 1 Alex Walker; 5 Kieran Dixon; 19 Ryan Morgan; 4 Elliot Kear; 2 Rhys Williams; 6 Jordan Abdull; 28 Morgan Smith; 8 Eddie Battye; 7 James Cunningham; 30 Olsi Krasniqi (D2); 12 Jay Pitts (C); 16 Matty Gee; 20 Luke Yates. Subs (all used): 14 Matty Fozard; 15 Greg Richards; 23 Rob Butler; 10 Mark Ioane.
**Tries:** Morgan (25, 54), Cunningham (40), Pitts (67); **Goals:** Dixon 3/4; **Field goal:** Smith (81).
**SAINTS:** 29 Jack Welsby; 18 Adam Swift; 3 Kevin Naiqama; 4 Mark Percival; 5 Regan Grace; 6 Theo Fages; 7 Danny Richardson; 19 Matty Lees; 9 James Roby (C); 10 Luke Thompson; 12 Joseph Paulo; 17 Dominique Peyroux; 15 Morgan Knowles. Subs (all used): 16 Kyle Amor; 20 Jack Ashworth; 13 Louie McCarthy-Scarsbrook; 24 Matthew Costello.
**Tries:** Roby (5), Thompson (10), Percival (49), Grace (79); **Goals:** Richardson 3/4.
**Rugby Leaguer & League Express Men of the Match:** *Broncos:* Ryan Morgan; *Saints:* James Roby.
**Penalty count:** 7-5; **Half-time:** 12-12; **Referee:** Marcus Griffiths; **Attendance:** 2,801.

## ROUND 18

*Thursday 13th June 2019*

**CASTLEFORD TIGERS 18 HULL FC 31**

**TIGERS:** 1 Peter Mata'utia; 2 James Clare; 3 Greg Minikin; 35 Cheyse Blair; 5 Greg Eden; 32 Jordan Rankin; 6 Jake Trueman; 8 Liam Watts; 9 Paul McShane (C); 34 Daniel Smith; 15 Jesse Sene-Lefao; 12 Mike McMeeken; 14 Nathan Massey. Subs (all used): 10 Grant Millington; 13 Adam Milner; 16 Junior Moors; 18 Matt Cook.
**Tries:** Minikin (11), Moors (37), Eden (61); **Goals:** Mata'utia 3/5.
**HULL FC:** 1 Jamie Shaul; 2 Bureta Faraimo; 38 Kieran Buchanan; 14 Jake Connor; 33 Ratu Naulago; 6 Albert Kelly; 7 Marc Sneyd; 15 Chris Green; 9 Danny Houghton (C); 23 Mickey Paea; 11 Dean Hadley; 12 Mark Minichiello; 13 Joe Westerman. Subs (all used): 8 Scott Taylor; 20 Brad Fash; 30 Danny Washbrook; 35 Andre Savelio.
**Tries:** Naulago (14, 47), Kelly (52, 65, 71); **Goals:** Sneyd 5/6; **Field goal:** Sneyd (75).
**Rugby Leaguer & League Express Men of the Match:** *Tigers:* Peter Mata'utia; *Hull FC:* Jake Connor.
**Penalty count:** 5-4; **Half-time:** 14-4; **Referee:** Robert Hicks; **Attendance:** 6,344.

*Friday 14th June 2019*

**LEEDS RHINOS 14 WIGAN WARRIORS 23**

**RHINOS:** 6 Tuimoala Lolohea; 2 Tom Briscoe; 29 Harry Newman; 4 Konrad Hurrell; 5 Ash Handley; 15 Liam Sutcliffe; 7 Richie Myler; 38 Ava Seumanufagai; 14 Brad Dwyer; 10 Brad Singleton; 3 Kallum Watkins (C); 16 Brett Ferres; 11 Trent Merrin. Subs: 8 Adam Cuthbertson; 25 James Donaldson; 22 Cameron Smith; 19 Mikolaj Oledzki (not used).
**Tries:** Cuthbertson (35), Merrin (50); **Goals:** L Sutcliffe 2/2, Lolohea 1/1.
**WARRIORS:** 3 Dan Sarginson; 17 Liam Marshall; 23 Chris Hankinson; 4 Oliver Gildart; 5 Joe Burgess; 6 George Williams; 7 Thomas Leuluai; 8 Tony Clubb; 9 Sam Powell; 14 Romain Navarrete; 15 Willie Isa; 12 Liam Farrell; 13 Sean O'Loughlin (C). Subs: 38 Morgan Smithies; 22 Joe Bullock; 24 Oliver Partington; 37 Jarrod Sammut (not used).
**Tries:** Gildart (20), Partington (59), Clubb (80); **Goals:** Hankinson 5/5; **Field goal:** Powell (39).
**Rugby Leaguer & League Express Men of the Match:** *Rhinos:* Trent Merrin; *Warriors:* Morgan Smithies.
**Penalty count:** 9-6; **Half-time:** 8-11; **Referee:** Chris Kendall; **Attendance:** 13,105.

**ST HELENS 38 HUDDERSFIELD GIANTS 2**

**SAINTS:** 23 Lachlan Coote; 2 Tommy Makinson; 3 Kevin Naiqama; 4 Mark Percival; 18 Adam Swift; 1 Jonny Lomax (C); 6 Theo Fages; 8 Alex Walmsley; 21 Aaron Smith; 10 Luke Thompson; 11 Zeb Taia; 15 Morgan Knowles; 12 Joseph Paulo. Subs (all used): 13 Louie McCarthy-Scarsbrook; 16 Kyle Amor; 20 Jack Ashworth; 22 James Bentley.
**Tries:** Coote (10), Lomax (13, 55), Makinson (18, 30, 52), Fages (27); **Goals:** Coote 5/7.
**GIANTS:** 1 Darnell McIntosh; 37 Dominic Young (D); 4 Jordan Turner; 20 Jake Wardle; 32 Innes Senior; 6 Lee Gaskell; 23 Oliver Russell; 10 Suaia Matagi; 14 Adam O'Brien; 19 Matty English; 29 Sam Hewitt; 12 Alex Mellor; 11 Aaron Murphy. Subs (all used): 7 Matt Frawley; 13 Michael Lawrence (C); 17 Ukuma Ta'ai; 8 Paul Clough.
**Goals:** Russell 1/1.
**Rugby Leaguer & League Express Men of the Match:**
*Saints:* Lachlan Coote; *Giants:* Dominic Young.
**Penalty count:** 3-8; **Half-time:** 26-2;
**Referee:** Scott Mikalauskas; **Attendance:** 9,527.

*Saturday 15th June 2019*

**HULL KINGSTON ROVERS 16 WARRINGTON WOLVES 14**

**ROVERS:** 1 Adam Quinlan; 5 Ryan Shaw; 2 Craig Hall; 3 Ben Crooks; 26 Will Dagger; 24 Josh Drinkwater; 17 Chris Atkin; 10 Mose Masoe; 21 George Lawler; 14 Mitch Garbutt; 13 Weller Hauraki; 11 Joel Tomkins (C); 8 Robbie Mulhern. Subs (all used): 4 Jimmy Keinhorst; 15 Tommy Lee; 30 Owen Harrison; 31 Adam Rooks.
**Tries:** Masoe (55), Quinlan (76); **Goals:** Shaw 4/4.
**WOLVES:** 22 Jake Mamo; 24 Jack Johnson; 3 Bryson Goodwin; 18 Toby King; 5 Josh Charnley; 6 Blake Austin; 15 Declan Patton; 8 Chris Hill (C); 21 Danny Walker; 10 Mike Cooper; 11 Ben Currie; 13 Ben Murdoch-Masila; 12 Jack Hughes (C). Subs (all used): 14 Jason Clark; 19 Sitaleki Akauola; 20 Harvey Livett; 23 Matt Davis.
**Tries:** Goodwin (24), Charnley (58); **Goals:** Patton 3/3.
**Rugby Leaguer & League Express Men of the Match:**
*Rovers:* Adam Quinlan; *Wolves:* Blake Austin.
**Penalty count:** 12-8; **Half-time:** 4-8;
**Referee:** James Child; **Attendance:** 7,390.

**CATALANS DRAGONS 12 LONDON BRONCOS 30**

**DRAGONS:** 1 Tony Gigot; 25 Arthur Romano; 3 David Mead; 6 Samisoni Langi; 27 Fouad Yaha; 29 Sam Tomkins; 7 Matty Smith; 14 Julian Bousquet; 18 Alrix Da Costa; 15 Mickael Simon; 16 Benjamin Jullien; 12 Benjamin Garcia; 8 Remi Casty (C). Subs (all used): 19 Mickael Goudemand; 23 Antoni Maria; 24 Jason Baitieri; 28 Sam Kasiano.
**Tries:** Yaha (16, 31, 76); **Goals:** Tomkins 0/2, Smith 0/1.
**BRONCOS:** 1 Alex Walker; 5 Kieran Dixon; 19 Ryan Morgan; 4 Elliot Kear; 2 Rhys Williams; 6 Jordan Abdull; 28 Morgan Smith; 8 Eddie Battye; 7 James Cunningham; 30 Olsi Krasniqi; 12 Jay Pitts (C); 17 Matty Fleming; 20 Luke Yates. Subs (all used): 10 Mark Ioane; 14 Matty Fozard; 15 Greg Richards; 23 Rob Butler.
**Tries:** Abdull (11), Williams (26, 72), Kear (59), Dixon (65);
**Goals:** Dixon 5/6.
**Rugby Leaguer & League Express Men of the Match:**
*Dragons:* Samisoni Langi; *Broncos:* Jordan Abdull.
**Penalty count:** 6-5; **Half-time:** 8-12;
**Referee:** Liam Moore; **Attendance:** 8,137.

*Sunday 16th June 2019*

**SALFORD RED DEVILS 44 WAKEFIELD TRINITY 20**

**RED DEVILS:** 1 Niall Evalds; 5 Jake Bibby; 26 Krisnan Inu; 3 Kris Welham; 22 Derrell Olpherts; 6 Robert Lui; 31 Jackson Hastings; 8 Lee Mossop (C); 19 Logan Tomkins; 10 Gil Dudson; 11 Josh Jones; 12 George Griffin; 17 Tyrone McCarthy. Subs (all used): 16 Greg Burke; 18 Ben Nakubuwai; 13 Mark Flanagan; 14 Joey Lussick.
**Tries:** Bibby (5, 28), Evalds (25, 74, 76), Lussick (36), Lui (49), Welham (63); **Goals:** Inu 6/9.
**TRINITY:** 1 Ryan Hampshire; 29 Lee Kershaw; 4 Reece Lyne; 32 Jack Croft; 5 Ben Jones-Bishop; 6 Jacob Miller (C); 7 Danny Brough; 10 Anthony England; 9 Kyle Wood; 15 Craig Kopczak; 12 Danny Kirmond; 24 Pauli Pauli; 26 Jordan Crowther. Subs (all used): 13 Tyler Randell; 20 Keegan Hirst; 22 George King; 36 Kelepi Tanginoa.
**Tries:** Miller (21, 56), Jones-Bishop (44, 69);
**Goals:** Brough 2/4.
**Rugby Leaguer & League Express Men of the Match:**
*Red Devils:* Robert Lui; *Trinity:* Jordan Crowther.
**Penalty count:** 7-9; **Half-time:** 20-6;
**Referee:** Marcus Griffiths; **Attendance:** 2,950.

## ROUND 19

*Thursday 20th June 2019*

**LONDON BRONCOS 26 HULL KINGSTON ROVERS 24**

**BRONCOS:** 1 Alex Walker; 5 Kieran Dixon; 19 Ryan Morgan; 4 Elliot Kear; 2 Rhys Williams; 6 Jordan Abdull; 28 Morgan Smith; 8 Eddie Battye; 7 James Cunningham; 30 Olsi Krasniqi; 12 Jay Pitts (C); 16 Matty Gee; 20 Luke Yates. Subs (all used): 10 Mark Ioane; 14 Matty Fozard; 18 Nathan Mason; 23 Rob Butler.
**Tries:** Smith (26), Walker (52), Abdull (60), Butler (75);
**Goals:** Dixon 5/6.
**ROVERS:** 1 Adam Quinlan; 5 Ryan Shaw; 23 Kane Linnett; 3 Ben Crooks; 2 Craig Hall; 24 Josh Drinkwater; 17 Chris Atkin; 8 Robbie Mulhern; 21 George Lawler; 10 Mose Masoe; 13 Weller Hauraki; 11 Joel Tomkins (C); 38 Luis Johnson (D). Subs (all used): 4 Jimmy Keinhorst; 15 Tommy Lee; 36 Daniel Murray (D); 37 Harvey Livett (D).
**Tries:** Hauraki (35), Quinlan (42), Atkin (45), Drinkwater (78); **Goals:** Shaw 4/4.
**Rugby Leaguer & League Express Men of the Match:**
*Broncos:* Jordan Abdull; *Rovers:* Josh Drinkwater.
**Penalty count:** 7-3; **Half-time:** 8-6;
**Referee:** Chris Kendall; **Attendance:** 1,503.

*Friday 21st June 2019*

**HUDDERSFIELD GIANTS 22 WIGAN WARRIORS 38**

**GIANTS:** 1 Darnell McIntosh; 32 Innes Senior; 4 Jordan Turner; 11 Aaron Murphy; 31 Louis Senior; 6 Lee Gaskell; 7 Matt Frawley; 8 Paul Clough; 14 Adam O'Brien (C); 10 Suaia Matagi; 15 Oliver Roberts; 12 Alex Mellor; 19 Matty English. Subs (all used): 9 Kruise Leeming; 17 Ukuma Ta'ai; 26 Sebastine Ikahihifo; 29 Sam Hewitt.
**Tries:** Hewitt (12), Frawley (33), L Senior (73), Turner (76);
**Goals:** Gaskell 3/4.
**Sin bin:** Ta'ai (79) - fighting.
**WARRIORS:** 20 Zak Hardaker; 17 Liam Marshall; 23 Chris Hankinson; 4 Oliver Gildart; 5 Joe Burgess; 6 George Williams; 7 Thomas Leuluai; 8 Tony Clubb; 9 Sam Powell; 14 Romain Navarrete; 15 Willie Isa; 12 Liam Farrell; 13 Sean O'Loughlin (C). Subs (all used): 11 Joe Greenwood; 24 Oliver Partington; 37 Jarrod Sammut; 38 Morgan Smithies.
**Tries:** Hankinson (7), O'Loughlin (18), Marshall (29), Burgess (45), Leuluai (55), Williams (66);
**Goals:** Hankinson 7/9.
**Sin bin:** Isa (79) - fighting.
**Rugby Leaguer & League Express Men of the Match:**
*Giants:* Ukuma Ta'ai; *Warriors:* George Williams.
**Penalty count:** 7-8; **Half-time:** 12-18;
**Referee:** Marcus Griffiths; **Attendance:** 5,578.

**SALFORD RED DEVILS 26 CASTLEFORD TIGERS 16**

**RED DEVILS:** 1 Niall Evalds; 5 Jake Bibby; 26 Krisnan Inu; 3 Kris Welham; 22 Derrell Olpherts; 6 Robert Lui; 31 Jackson Hastings; 8 Lee Mossop (C); 19 Logan Tomkins; 10 Gil Dudson; 11 Josh Jones; 29 Ryan Lannon (D2); 17 Tyrone McCarthy. Subs (all used): 13 Mark Flanagan; 14 Joey Lussick; 15 Adam Walker; 16 Greg Burke.
**Tries:** Evalds (18), Mossop (22), Hastings (30), Olpherts (61); **Goals:** Inu 5/6.
**On report:** Walker (42) - alleged dangerous contact; Hastings (56) - alleged dangerous challenge on Moors.
**TIGERS:** 1 Peter Mata'utia; 2 James Clare; 3 Greg Minikin; 35 Cheyse Blair; 25 Tuoyo Egodo; 6 Jake Trueman; 32 Jordan Rankin; 8 Liam Watts; 9 Paul McShane (C); 34 Daniel Smith; 15 Jesse Sene-Lefao; 12 Mike McMeeken; 14 Nathan Massey. Subs (all used): 10 Grant Millington; 13 Adam Milner; 16 Junior Moors; 18 Matt Cook.
**Tries:** Smith (25), Minikin (37), Rankin (40);
**Goals:** Mata'utia 2/3.
**Rugby Leaguer & League Express Men of the Match:**
*Red Devils:* Jackson Hastings; *Tigers:* Liam Watts.
**Penalty count:** 8-5; **Half-time:** 18-16;
**Referee:** Scott Mikalauskas; **Attendance:** 2,829.

**ST HELENS 36 LEEDS RHINOS 10**

**SAINTS:** 23 Lachlan Coote; 2 Tommy Makinson; 3 Kevin Naiqama; 4 Mark Percival; 5 Regan Grace; 1 Jonny Lomax (C); 6 Theo Fages; 8 Alex Walmsley; 21 Aaron Smith; 10 Luke Thompson; 11 Zeb Taia; 17 Dominique Peyroux; 13 Louie McCarthy-Scarsbrook. Subs (all used): 16 Kyle Amor; 19 Matty Lees; 20 Jack Ashworth; 22 James Bentley.
**Tries:** Naiqama (1), McCarthy-Scarsbrook (4, 75), Coote (19), Makinson (40), Bentley (78); **Goals:** Coote 6/6.
**RHINOS:** 1 Jack Walker; 2 Tom Briscoe; 29 Harry Newman; 4 Konrad Hurrell; 24 Luke Briscoe; 15 Liam Sutcliffe; 7 Richie Myler; 38 Ava Seumanufagai; 14 Brad Dwyer; 10 Brad Singleton; 16 Brett Ferres; 3 Kallum Watkins (C); 11 Trent Merrin. Subs (all used): 9 Matt Parcell; 8 Adam Cuthbertson; 25 James Donaldson; 19 Mikolaj Oledzki.
**Tries:** Dwyer (16), L Briscoe (45); **Goals:** L Sutcliffe 1/2.
**Sin bin:** Donaldson (75) - professional foul.
**Rugby Leaguer & League Express Men of the Match:**
*Saints:* Jonny Lomax; *Rhinos:* Trent Merrin.
**Penalty count:** 11-6; **Half-time:** 24-6;
**Referee:** Ben Thaler; **Attendance:** 11,448.

**WARRINGTON WOLVES 30 WAKEFIELD TRINITY 6**

**WOLVES:** 22 Jake Mamo; 24 Jack Johnson; 3 Bryson Goodwin; 18 Toby King; 5 Josh Charnley; 6 Blake Austin; 15 Declan Patton; 8 Chris Hill (C); 9 Daryl Clark; 10 Mike Cooper; 11 Ben Currie; 12 Jack Hughes (C); 17 Joe Philbin. Subs (all used): 13 Ben Murdoch-Masila; 14 Jason Clark; 19 Sitaleki Akauola; 23 Matt Davis.
**Tries:** Currie (18), Charnley (27), Cooper (35), Austin (43), J Johnson (80); **Goals:** Patton 5/6.
**TRINITY:** 1 Ryan Hampshire; 5 Ben Jones-Bishop; 4 Reece Lyne; 32 Jack Croft; 34 Mason Caton-Brown; 6 Jacob Miller (C); 7 Danny Brough; 10 Anthony England; 26 Jordan Crowther; 36 Kelepi Tanginoa; 24 Pauli Pauli; 8 David Fifita; 22 George King. Subs (all used): 9 Kyle Wood; 15 Craig Kopczak; 20 Keegan Hirst; 31 Titus Gwaze (D).
**Try:** Hampshire (1); **Goals:** Brough 1/1.
**Rugby Leaguer & League Express Men of the Match:**
*Wolves:* Declan Patton; *Trinity:* Jack Croft.
**Penalty count:** 6-3; **Half-time:** 16-6;
**Referee:** Liam Moore; **Attendance:** 8,635.

*Saturday 22nd June 2019*

**CATALANS DRAGONS 10 HULL FC 50**

**DRAGONS:** 29 Sam Tomkins; 27 Fouad Yaha; 3 David Mead; 4 Brayden Wiliame; 5 Lewis Tierney; 6 Samisoni Langi; 7 Matty Smith; 14 Julian Bousquet; 9 Michael Mcllorum; 10 Sam Moa; 16 Benjamin Jullien; 12 Benjamin Garcia; 8 Remi Casty (C). Subs (all used): 15 Mickael Simon; 19 Mickael Goudemand; 23 Antoni Maria; 28 Sam Kasiano.
**Tries:** Tomkins (8), Tierney (30); **Goals:** Tomkins 1/2.
**HULL FC:** 1 Jamie Shaul; 2 Bureta Faraimo; 38 Kieran Buchanan; 14 Jake Connor; 33 Ratu Naulago; 6 Albert Kelly; 7 Marc Sneyd; 15 Chris Green; 9 Danny Houghton (C); 23 Mickey Paea; 21 Sika Manu; 4 Josh Griffin; 13 Joe Westerman. Subs (all used): 8 Scott Taylor; 10 Josh Bowden; 20 Brad Fash; 35 Andre Savelio.
**Tries:** Kelly (13), Westerman (26), Savelio (35), Griffin (38, 60), Buchanan (44), Naulago (53), Shaul (67);
**Goals:** Sneyd 9/9.
**Rugby Leaguer & League Express Men of the Match:**
*Dragons:* Samisoni Langi; *Hull FC:* Josh Griffin.
**Penalty count:** 4-5; **Half-time:** 10-26;
**Referee:** Robert Hicks; **Attendance:** 10,254.

## ROUND 20

*Thursday 27th June 2019*

**HULL KINGSTON ROVERS 18 HULL FC 10**

**HULL KR:** 1 Adam Quinlan; 5 Ryan Shaw; 23 Kane Linnett; 3 Ben Crooks; 2 Craig Hall; 24 Josh Drinkwater; 7 Danny McGuire; 38 Luis Johnson; 39 Matt Parcell (D); 36 Daniel Murray; 11 Joel Tomkins (C); 13 Weller Hauraki; 21 George Lawler. Subs (all used): 10 Mose Masoe; 14 Mitch Garbutt; 17 Chris Atkin; 37 Harvey Livett.
**Tries:** Crooks (15), Tomkins (50), Parcell (79);
**Goals:** Shaw 3/3.
**HULL FC:** 1 Jamie Shaul; 2 Bureta Faraimo; 3 Carlos Tuimavave; 4 Josh Griffin; 33 Ratu Naulago; 14 Jake Connor; 7 Marc Sneyd; 15 Chris Green; 9 Danny Houghton (C); 23 Mickey Paea; 12 Mark Minichiello; 21 Sika Manu; 13 Joe Westerman. Subs (all used): 8 Scott Taylor; 10 Josh Bowden; 20 Brad Fash; 35 Andre Savelio.
**Tries:** Faraimo (9), Savelio (67); **Goals:** Sneyd 1/2.
**Rugby Leaguer & League Express Men of the Match:**
*Hull KR:* Matt Parcell; *Hull FC:* Bureta Faraimo.
**Penalty count:** 6-6; **Half-time:** 6-6;
**Referee:** Robert Hicks; **Attendance:** 10,221.

*Friday 28th June 2019*

**WAKEFIELD TRINITY 36 HUDDERSFIELD GIANTS 10**

**TRINITY:** 1 Ryan Hampshire; 5 Ben Jones-Bishop; 4 Reece Lyne; 3 Bill Tupou; 34 Mason Caton-Brown; 6 Jacob Miller (C); 7 Danny Brough; 10 Anthony England; 13 Tyler Randell; 15 Craig Kopczak; 24 Pauli Pauli; 36 Kelepi Tanginoa; 26 Jordan Crowther. Subs (all used): 8 David Fifita; 9 Kyle Wood; 22 George King; 31 Titus Gwaze.
**Tries:** Randell (10, 39, 72), Crowther (47), Miller (71);
**Goals:** Brough 4/5, Hampshire 3/3;
**Field goals:** Brough (44), Miller (75).

**GIANTS:** 1 Darnell McIntosh; 31 Louis Senior; 3 Leroy Cudjoe (C); 4 Jordan Turner; 32 Innes Senior; 6 Lee Gaskell; 7 Matt Frawley; 8 Paul Clough; 14 Adam O'Brien; 26 Sebastine Ikahihifo; 11 Aaron Murphy; 12 Alex Mellor; 13 Michael Lawrence. Subs (all used): 17 Ukuma Ta'ai; 16 Dale Ferguson; 10 Suaia Matagi; 9 Kruise Leeming.
**Tries:** Mellor (8), L Senior (27); **Goals:** Gaskell 1/2.
**Sin bin:** Murphy (34) - professional foul.
**Rugby Leaguer & League Express Men of the Match:** *Trinity:* Tyler Randell; *Giants:* Paul Clough.
**Penalty count:** 11-6; **Half-time:** 16-10;
**Referee:** Greg Dolan; **Attendance:** 4,846.

**WARRINGTON WOLVES 10 ST HELENS 21**

**WOLVES:** 22 Jake Mamo; 2 Tom Lineham; 3 Bryson Goodwin; 18 Toby King; 5 Josh Charnley; 6 Blake Austin; 15 Declan Patton; 8 Chris Hill (C); 9 Daryl Clark; 10 Mike Cooper; 11 Ben Currie; 12 Jack Hughes (C); 19 Sitaleki Akauola. Subs (all used): 14 Jason Clark; 16 Lama Tasi; 17 Joe Philbin; 23 Matt Davis.
**Try:** Mamo (75); **Goals:** Patton 3/4.
**Sin bin:** Hughes (54) - shoulder charge on Makinson.
**SAINTS:** 23 Lachlan Coote; 2 Tommy Makinson; 3 Kevin Naiqama; 4 Mark Percival; 5 Regan Grace; 1 Jonny Lomax (C); 6 Theo Fages; 8 Alex Walmsley; 21 Aaron Smith; 10 Luke Thompson; 15 Morgan Knowles; 17 Dominique Peyroux; 13 Louie McCarthy-Scarsbrook. Subs (all used): 12 Joseph Paulo; 16 Kyle Amor; 19 Matty Lees; 22 James Bentley.
**Tries:** Percival (61), Thompson (71), Walmsley (77); **Goals:** Coote 4/4; **Field goal:** Coote (75).
**Rugby Leaguer & League Express Men of the Match:** *Wolves:* Daryl Clark; *Saints:* Jonny Lomax.
**Penalty count:** 7-9; **Half-time:** 4-0;
**Referee:** Ben Thaler; **Attendance:** 14,211.

**WIGAN WARRIORS 28 SALFORD RED DEVILS 12**

**WARRIORS:** 20 Zak Hardaker; 17 Liam Marshall; 23 Chris Hankinson; 4 Oliver Gildart; 5 Joe Burgess; 6 George Williams; 7 Thomas Leuluai; 8 Tony Clubb; 9 Sam Powell; 14 Romain Navarrete; 15 Willie Isa; 11 Joe Greenwood; 13 Sean O'Loughlin (C). Subs (all used): 38 Morgan Smithies; 37 Jarrod Sammut; 24 Oliver Partington; 22 Joe Bullock.
**Tries:** Marshall (24, 50), Greenwood (32), Hardaker (43), Partington (79); **Goals:** Hankinson 4/5, Hardaker 0/1.
**Sin bin:** Navarrete (69) - fighting.
**RED DEVILS:** 1 Niall Evalds; 5 Jake Bibby; 26 Krisnan Inu; 3 Kris Welham; 22 Derrell Olpherts; 30 Tuimoala Lolohea (D); 31 Jackson Hastings; 18 Ben Nakubuwai; 19 Logan Tomkins; 10 Gil Dudson; 11 Josh Jones; 29 Ryan Lannon; 17 Tyrone McCarthy. Subs (all used): 14 Joey Lussick; 13 Mark Flanagan (C); 16 Greg Burke; 23 Ken Sio.
**Tries:** Olpherts (40), Welham (77); **Goals:** Inu 2/3.
**Sin bin:** Dudson (69) - fighting.
**Rugby Leaguer & League Express Men of the Match:** *Warriors:* George Williams; *Red Devils:* Krisnan Inu.
**Penalty count:** 5-6; **Half-time:** 10-6;
**Referee:** Chris Kendall; **Attendance:** 12,066.

*Sunday 30th June 2019*

**LEEDS RHINOS 31 CATALANS DRAGONS 12**

**RHINOS:** 1 Jack Walker; 2 Tom Briscoe; 29 Harry Newman; 4 Konrad Hurrell; 5 Ash Handley; 40 Robert Lui (D); 7 Richie Myler; 8 Adam Cuthbertson; 14 Brad Dwyer; 19 Mikolaj Oledzki; 15 Liam Sutcliffe; 16 Brett Ferres; 11 Trent Merrin (C). Subs (all used): 10 Brad Singleton; 22 Cameron Smith; 25 James Donaldson; 36 Wellington Albert.
**Tries:** Cuthbertson (8), T Briscoe (13), Singleton (18), Hurrell (67), Walker (76); **Goals:** L Sutcliffe 5/5;
**Field goal:** Myler (70).
**DRAGONS:** 29 Sam Tomkins; 2 Jodie Broughton; 3 David Mead; 4 Brayden Wiliame; 25 Arthur Romano; 6 Samisoni Langi; 7 Matty Smith; 28 Sam Kasiano; 18 Alrix Da Costa; 10 Sam Moa; 16 Benjamin Jullien; 12 Benjamin Garcia; 8 Remi Casty (C). Subs (all used): 14 Julian Bousquet; 15 Mickael Simon; 19 Mickael Goudemand; 23 Antoni Maria.
**Tries:** Romano (22), Tomkins (55); **Goals:** Tomkins 2/2.
**Rugby Leaguer & League Express Men of the Match:** *Rhinos:* Konrad Hurrell; *Dragons:* Sam Tomkins.
**Penalty count:** 10-7; **Half-time:** 18-6;
**Referee:** Scott Mikalauskas; **Attendance:** 12,638.

**CASTLEFORD TIGERS 42 LONDON BRONCOS 10**

**TIGERS:** 32 Jordan Rankin; 2 James Clare; 3 Greg Minikin; 35 Cheyse Blair; 25 Tuoyo Egodo; 6 Jake Trueman; 24 Cory Aston; 8 Liam Watts; 13 Adam Milner; 34 Daniel Smith; 15 Jesse Sene-Lefao; 12 Mike McMeeken; 14 Nathan Massey. Subs (all used): 9 Paul McShane (C); 10 Grant Millington; 18 Matt Cook; 33 Chris Clarkson.
**Tries:** Egodo (12, 47), McMeeken (27, 40), Rankin (41), Trueman (50), Clare (54), Clarkson (58);
**Goals:** Rankin 5/8.
**On report:** Milner (77) - alleged punching.
**BRONCOS:** 1 Alex Walker; 5 Kieran Dixon; 19 Ryan Morgan; 4 Elliot Kear; 2 Rhys Williams; 6 Jordan Abdull; 28 Morgan Smith; 8 Eddie Battye; 7 James Cunningham; 30 Olsi Krasniqi; 12 Jay Pitts (C); 16 Matty Gee; 20 Luke Yates. Subs (all used): 15 Greg Richards; 11 Will Lovell; 23 Rob Butler; 14 Matty Fozard.
**Tries:** Dixon (36), Williams (74); **Goals:** Dixon 1/2.
**On report:** Butler (77) - alleged punching.
**Rugby Leaguer & League Express Men of the Match:** *Tigers:* Mike McMeeken; *Broncos:* Rhys Williams.
**Penalty count:** 10-5; **Half-time:** 16-4;
**Referee:** Marcus Griffiths; **Attendance:** 6,860.

## ROUND 21

*Thursday 4th July 2019*

**SALFORD RED DEVILS 18 HUDDERSFIELD GIANTS 36**

**RED DEVILS:** 1 Niall Evalds; 21 Greg Johnson; 26 Krisnan Inu; 3 Kris Welham; 23 Ken Sio; 30 Tuimoala Lolohea; 31 Jackson Hastings; 18 Ben Nakubuwai; 14 Joey Lussick; 10 Gil Dudson; 11 Josh Jones; 29 Ryan Lannon; 17 Tyrone McCarthy. Subs (all used): 13 Mark Flanagan (C); 19 Logan Tomkins; 5 Jake Bibby; 16 Greg Burke.
**Tries:** McCarthy (3, 74), Sio (15), Welham (49);
**Goals:** Inu 1/4.
**GIANTS:** 31 Louis Senior; 2 Jermaine McGillvary; 1 Darnell McIntosh; 20 Jake Wardle; 32 Innes Senior; 6 Lee Gaskell; 24 Tom Holmes (D); 8 Paul Clough; 14 Adam O'Brien; 26 Sebastine Ikahihifo; 17 Ukuma Ta'ai; 12 Alex Mellor; 11 Aaron Murphy. Subs (all used): 9 Kruise Leeming; 19 Matty English; 36 Oliver Wilson (D); 13 Michael Lawrence (C).
**Tries:** English (29), I Senior (36), McIntosh (44, 78), Leeming (57), Ta'ai (60), Jake Wardle (70);
**Goals:** Gaskell 1/4, McIntosh 3/3.
**Rugby Leaguer & League Express Men of the Match:** *Red Devils:* Jackson Hastings; *Giants:* Kruise Leeming.
**Penalty count:** 5-6; **Half-time:** 8-10;
**Referee:** Robert Hicks; **Attendance:** 2,368.

*Friday 5th July 2019*

**CASTLEFORD TIGERS 10 LEEDS RHINOS 18**

**TIGERS:** 32 Jordan Rankin; 2 James Clare; 3 Greg Minikin; 35 Cheyse Blair; 5 Greg Eden; 1 Peter Mata'utia; 24 Cory Aston; 8 Liam Watts; 13 Adam Milner; 34 Daniel Smith; 15 Jesse Sene-Lefao; 12 Mike McMeeken; 14 Nathan Massey. Subs (all used): 9 Paul McShane (C); 10 Grant Millington; 18 Matt Cook; 33 Chris Clarkson.
**Tries:** Clare (61, 65); **Goals:** Mata'utia 0/1, Rankin 1/1.
**RHINOS:** 1 Jack Walker; 2 Tom Briscoe; 29 Harry Newman; 4 Konrad Hurrell; 5 Ash Handley; 40 Robert Lui; 7 Richie Myler; 38 Ava Seumanufagai; 14 Brad Dwyer; 8 Adam Cuthbertson; 16 Brett Ferres; 15 Liam Sutcliffe; 11 Trent Merrin (C). Subs (all used): 41 Rhyse Martin (D); 25 James Donaldson; 10 Brad Singleton; 22 Cameron Smith.
**Tries:** Merrin (19), Walker (44), Lui (73);
**Goals:** L Sutcliffe 3/4.
**Rugby Leaguer & League Express Men of the Match:** *Tigers:* Jesse Sene-Lefao; *Rhinos:* Robert Lui.
**Penalty count:** 13-6; **Half-time:** 0-6;
**Referee:** Ben Thaler; **Attendance:** 8,147.

**HULL FC 12 ST HELENS 40**

**HULL FC:** 1 Jamie Shaul; 33 Ratu Naulago; 14 Jake Connor; 4 Josh Griffin; 2 Bureta Faraimo; 6 Albert Kelly; 7 Marc Sneyd; 8 Scott Taylor; 9 Danny Houghton (C); 23 Mickey Paea; 12 Mark Minichiello; 21 Sika Manu; 13 Joe Westerman. Subs (all used): 3 Carlos Tuimavave; 10 Josh Bowden; 20 Brad Fash; 34 Gareth Ellis.
**Tries:** Shaul (67), Naulago (70); **Goals:** Sneyd 2/2.
**SAINTS:** 23 Lachlan Coote; 2 Tommy Makinson; 3 Kevin Naiqama; 4 Mark Percival; 5 Regan Grace; 1 Jonny Lomax (C); 6 Theo Fages; 8 Alex Walmsley; 22 James Bentley; 10 Luke Thompson; 15 Morgan Knowles; 17 Dominique Peyroux; 13 Louie McCarthy-Scarsbrook. Subs (all used): 12 Joseph Paulo; 16 Kyle Amor; 19 Matty Lees; 20 Jack Ashworth.
**Tries:** Knowles (6), Fages (8), Coote (20, 56), Grace (46), Ashworth (51), Lomax (54); **Goals:** Coote 6/7.
**Rugby Leaguer & League Express Men of the Match:** *Hull FC:* Albert Kelly; *Saints:* Lachlan Coote.
**Penalty count:** 6-7; **Half-time:** 0-18;
**Referee:** Chris Kendall; **Attendance:** 11,311.

**WIGAN WARRIORS 52 HULL KINGSTON ROVERS 10**

**WARRIORS:** 20 Zak Hardaker; 17 Liam Marshall; 3 Dan Sarginson; 4 Oliver Gildart; 5 Joe Burgess; 6 George Williams; 7 Thomas Leuluai (C); 8 Tony Clubb; 9 Sam Powell; 14 Romain Navarrete; 15 Willie Isa; 12 Liam Farrell; 38 Morgan Smithies. Subs (all used): 22 Joe Bullock; 23 Chris Hankinson; 24 Oliver Partington; 37 Jarrod Sammut.
**Tries:** Farrell (4, 61), Marshall (18, 21, 55), Hardaker (37), Williams (59), Gildart (63), Burgess (66);
**Goals:** Hardaker 8/10.
**Sin bin:** Navarrete (25) - late challenge on Hauraki.
**ROVERS:** 1 Adam Quinlan; 5 Ryan Shaw; 23 Kane Linnett; 3 Ben Crooks; 2 Craig Hall; 24 Josh Drinkwater; 7 Danny McGuire; 38 Luis Johnson; 39 Matt Parcell; 14 Mitch Garbutt; 11 Joel Tomkins (C); 37 Harvey Livett; 13 Weller Hauraki. Subs (all used): 8 Robbie Mulhern; 10 Mose Masoe; 17 Chris Atkin; 36 Daniel Murray.
**Tries:** Quinlan (13, 72); **Goals:** Shaw 1/2.
**Rugby Leaguer & League Express Men of the Match:** *Warriors:* Liam Farrell; *Rovers:* Danny McGuire.
**Penalty count:** 9-5; **Half-time:** 24-6;
**Referee:** Marcus Griffiths; **Attendance:** 11,042.

*Saturday 6th July 2019*

**LONDON BRONCOS 6 WARRINGTON WOLVES 36**

**BRONCOS:** 1 Alex Walker; 5 Kieran Dixon; 3 Ben Hellewell; 4 Elliot Kear; 2 Rhys Williams (C); 6 Jordan Abdull; 28 Morgan Smith; 15 Greg Richards; 7 James Cunningham; 23 Rob Butler; 13 Sadiq Adebiyi; 16 Matty Gee; 20 Luke Yates. Subs (all used): 14 Matty Fozard; 8 Eddie Battye; 17 Matty Fleming; 10 Mark Ioane.
**Try:** Fozard (42); **Goals:** Dixon 1/1.
**WOLVES:** 22 Jake Mamo; 2 Tom Lineham; 3 Bryson Goodwin; 18 Toby King; 5 Josh Charnley; 6 Blake Austin; 15 Declan Patton; 16 Lama Tasi; 9 Daryl Clark; 10 Mike Cooper; 11 Ben Currie; 12 Jack Hughes (C); 23 Matt Davis. Subs (all used): 14 Jason Clark; 17 Joe Philbin; 21 Danny Walker; 28 Luther Burrell (D).
**Tries:** Lineham (5), Cooper (13), Goodwin (17), Mamo (24), Hughes (35), King (37); **Goals:** Patton 6/6.
**Rugby Leaguer & League Express Men of the Match:** *Broncos:* Sadiq Adebiyi; *Wolves:* Ben Currie.
**Penalty count:** 5-5; **Half-time:** 0-36;
**Referee:** Greg Dolan; **Attendance:** 2,357.

**CATALANS DRAGONS 44 WAKEFIELD TRINITY 10**

**DRAGONS:** 29 Sam Tomkins; 2 Jodie Broughton; 3 David Mead; 4 Brayden Wiliame; 25 Arthur Romano; 6 Samisoni Langi; 1 Tony Gigot; 14 Julian Bousquet; 9 Michael McIlorum; 15 Mickael Simon; 17 Matt Whitley; 12 Benjamin Garcia; 8 Remi Casty (C). Subs (all used): 11 Kenny Edwards; 22 Lucas Albert; 23 Antoni Maria; 28 Sam Kasiano.
**Tries:** Broughton (10, 32, 43), Whitley (16), Langi (21), Edwards (54), Gigot (61, 69); **Goals:** Tomkins 6/8.
**TRINITY:** 1 Ryan Hampshire; 5 Ben Jones-Bishop; 4 Reece Lyne; 18 Joe Arundel; 3 Bill Tupou; 6 Jacob Miller (C); 7 Danny Brough; 8 David Fifita; 13 Tyler Randell; 15 Craig Kopczak; 24 Pauli Pauli; 36 Kelepi Tanginoa; 26 Jordan Crowther. Subs (all used): 9 Kyle Wood; 20 Keegan Hirst; 22 George King; 31 Titus Gwaze.
**Tries:** Lyne (26), Tupou (77); **Goals:** Brough 1/2.
**Rugby Leaguer & League Express Men of the Match:** *Dragons:* Michael McIlorum; *Trinity:* Pauli Pauli.
**Penalty count:** 8-7; **Half-time:** 20-6;
**Referee:** Liam Moore; **Attendance:** 7,237.

## ROUND 22

*Thursday 11th July 2019*

**HULL FC 35 LONDON BRONCOS 22**

**HULL FC:** 1 Jamie Shaul; 33 Ratu Naulago; 3 Carlos Tuimavave; 4 Josh Griffin; 2 Bureta Faraimo; 14 Jake Connor; 7 Marc Sneyd; 8 Scott Taylor; 9 Danny Houghton (C); 23 Mickey Paea; 21 Sika Manu; 12 Mark Minichiello; 13 Joe Westerman. Subs (all used): 10 Josh Bowden; 11 Dean Hadley; 15 Chris Green; 20 Brad Fash.
**Tries:** Tuimavave (5), Faraimo (8), Westerman (16), Connor (19), Griffin (22), Naulago (36); **Goals:** Sneyd 5/6;
**Field goal:** Sneyd (72).
**BRONCOS:** 5 Kieran Dixon; 4 Elliot Kear; 3 Ben Hellewell; 17 Matty Fleming; 2 Rhys Williams; 7 James Cunningham; 14 Matty Fozard; 8 Eddie Battye; 26 Sam Davis; 16 Matty Gee; 12 Jay Pitts (C); 13 Sadiq Adebiyi; 20 Luke Yates. Subs (all used): 10 Mark Ioane; 6 Jordan Abdull; 23 Rob Butler; 21 Daniel Hindmarsh.
**Tries:** Fleming (45), Abdull (55), Adebiyi (62, 80);
**Goals:** Dixon 3/4.
**Rugby Leaguer & League Express Men of the Match:** *Hull FC:* Josh Griffin; *Broncos:* Eddie Battye.
**Penalty count:** 6-4; **Half-time:** 34-0;
**Referee:** Liam Moore; **Attendance:** 11,401.

*Friday 12th July 2019*

**HUDDERSFIELD GIANTS 28 CATALANS DRAGONS 32**

**GIANTS:** 31 Louis Senior; 2 Jermaine McGillvary; 1 Darnell McIntosh; 20 Jake Wardle; 32 Innes Senior; 6 Lee Gaskell;

Salford's Krisnan Inu bursts past Warrington's Josh Charnley, Sitaleki Akauola and Blake Austin

24 Tom Holmes; 8 Paul Clough; 9 Kruise Leeming; 26 Sebastine Ikahihifo; 17 Ukuma Ta'ai; 12 Alex Mellor; 11 Aaron Murphy. Subs (all used): 7 Matt Frawley; 36 Oliver Wilson; 13 Michael Lawrence (C); 10 Suaia Matagi.
**Tries:** I Senior (23, 78), Jake Wardle (38), McIntosh (63), Gaskell (70); **Goals:** Jake Wardle 4/5.
**DRAGONS:** 29 Sam Tomkins; 2 Jodie Broughton; 3 David Mead; 4 Brayden Wiliame; 25 Arthur Romano; 6 Samisoni Langi; 1 Tony Gigot; 14 Julian Bousquet; 18 Alrix Da Costa; 15 Mickael Simon; 17 Matt Whitley; 12 Benjamin Garcia; 8 Remi Casty (C). Subs (all used): 11 Kenny Edwards; 22 Lucas Albert; 23 Antoni Maria; 28 Sam Kasiano.
**Tries:** Tomkins (9, 15, 34), Wiliame (27), Broughton (50, 59); **Goals:** Tomkins 4/6.
**Sin bin:** Edwards (74) - dissent.
**Rugby Leaguer & League Express Men of the Match:**
*Giants:* Innes Senior; *Dragons:* Sam Tomkins.
**Penalty count:** 8-2; **Half-time:** 12-22;
**Referee:** Greg Dolan; **Attendance:** 4,383.

### LEEDS RHINOS 16 HULL KINGSTON ROVERS 32

**RHINOS:** 1 Jack Walker; 2 Tom Briscoe; 29 Harry Newman; 4 Konrad Hurrell; 5 Ash Handley; 40 Robert Lui; 7 Richie Myler; 8 Adam Cuthbertson; 14 Brad Dwyer; 38 Ava Seumanufagai; 15 Liam Sutcliffe; 41 Rhyse Martin; 11 Trent Merrin (C). Subs (all used): 16 Brett Ferres; 25 James Donaldson; 39 Shaun Lunt (D2); 22 Cameron Smith.
**Tries:** Dwyer (24), L Sutcliffe (28). Hurrell (62), Martin (71); **Goals:** L Sutcliffe 0/2, Martin 0/2.
**ROVERS:** 1 Adam Quinlan; 2 Craig Hall; 4 Jimmy Keinhorst; 23 Kane Linnett; 3 Ben Crooks; 24 Josh Drinkwater; 7 Danny McGuire; 38 Luis Johnson; 39 Matt Parcell; 36 Daniel Murray; 13 Weller Hauraki; 11 Joel Tomkins (C); 21 George Lawler. Subs (all used): 14 Mitch Garbutt; 10 Mose Masoe; 37 Harvey Livett; 17 Chris Atkin.
**Tries:** Parcell (8), Linnett (17, 52), Quinlan (20), Livett (45), Hall (76); **Goals:** Hall 3/8, Drinkwater 1/2.
**Rugby Leaguer & League Express Men of the Match:**
*Rhinos:* Ava Seumanufagai; *Rovers:* Danny McGuire.
**Penalty count:** 10-10; **Half-time:** 8-14;
**Referee:** Robert Hicks; **Attendance:** 13,679.

### ST HELENS 32 WIGAN WARRIORS 10

**SAINTS:** 23 Lachlan Coote; 2 Tommy Makinson; 3 Kevin Naiqama; 4 Mark Percival; 5 Regan Grace; 1 Jonny Lomax (C); 6 Theo Fages; 8 Alex Walmsley; 22 James Bentley; 10 Luke Thompson; 15 Morgan Knowles; 17 Dominique Peyroux; 13 Louie McCarthy-Scarsbrook. Subs (all used): 16 Kyle Amor; 19 Matty Lees; 20 Jack Ashworth; 21 Aaron Smith.
**Tries:** Makinson (15, 35), Coote (43), Naiqama (50), Lomax (57); **Goals:** Coote 6/7.
**WARRIORS:** 20 Zak Hardaker; 17 Liam Marshall; 3 Dan Sarginson; 4 Oliver Gildart; 5 Joe Burgess; 6 George Williams; 7 Thomas Leuluai (C); 14 Romain Navarrete; 9 Sam Powell; 24 Oliver Partington; 15 Willie Isa; 12 Liam Farrell; 38 Morgan Smithies. Subs (all used): 22 Joe Bullock; 36 Liam Byrne; 23 Chris Hankinson; 27 Jake Shorrocks.
**Try:** Hardaker (63); **Goals:** Hardaker 3/3.
**Rugby Leaguer & League Express Men of the Match:**
*Saints:* Jonny Lomax; *Warriors:* Zak Hardaker.
**Penalty count:** 7-11; **Half-time:** 12-4;
**Referee:** Ben Thaler; **Attendance:** 17,088.

### WAKEFIELD TRINITY 16 CASTLEFORD TIGERS 36

**TRINITY:** 1 Ryan Hampshire; 5 Ben Jones-Bishop; 4 Reece Lyne; 3 Bill Tupou; 34 Mason Caton-Brown; 6 Jacob Miller (C); 7 Danny Brough; 10 Anthony England; 9 Kyle Wood; 36 Kelepi Tanginoa; 24 Pauli Pauli; 18 Joe Arundel; 19 James Batchelor. Subs (all used): 26 Jordan Crowther; 22 George King; 15 Craig Kopczak; 20 Keegan Hirst.
**Tries:** Wood (25), Brough (61); **Goals:** Brough 4/4.
**TIGERS:** 32 Jordan Rankin; 2 James Clare; 35 Cheyse Blair; 3 Greg Minikin; 25 Tuoyo Egodo; 6 Jake Trueman; 1 Peter Mata'utia; 8 Liam Watts; 9 Paul McShane (C); 33 Chris Clarkson; 15 Jesse Sene-Lefao; 12 Mike McMeeken; 13 Adam Milner. Subs (all used): 14 Nathan Massey; 24 Jacques O'Neill; 10 Grant Millington; 11 Oliver Holmes.
**Tries:** Egodo (31), Holmes (37), Clare (45, 70, 72), Rankin (56, 75); **Goals:** Mata'utia 4/7.
**Rugby Leaguer & League Express Men of the Match:**
*Trinity:* Danny Brough; *Tigers:* Jake Trueman.
**Penalty count:** 9-7; **Half-time:** 10-8;
**Referee:** Marcus Griffiths; **Attendance:** 6,244.

### WARRINGTON WOLVES 12 SALFORD RED DEVILS 22

**WOLVES:** 22 Jake Mamo; 2 Tom Lineham; 3 Bryson Goodwin; 18 Toby King; 5 Josh Charnley; 6 Blake Austin; 15 Declan Patton; 16 Lama Tasi; 9 Daryl Clark; 19 Sitaleki Akauola; 11 Ben Currie; 12 Jack Hughes (C); 23 Matt Davis. Subs (all used): 14 Jason Clark; 17 Joe Philbin; 21 Danny Walker; 26 Pat Moran.
**Tries:** J Clark (24), Davis (63); **Goals:** Patton 2/2.
**Sin bin:** Akauola (58) - dangerous contact on McCarthy.
**RED DEVILS:** 1 Niall Evalds; 26 Krisnan Inu; 3 Kris Welham; 4 Junior Sa'u; 5 Jake Bibby; 30 Tuimoala Lolohea; 31 Jackson Hastings; 15 Adam Walker; 19 Logan Tomkins; 10 Gil Dudson; 29 Ryan Lannon; 17 Tyrone McCarthy; 13 Mark Flanagan (C). Subs: 16 Greg Burke; 32 Josh Johnson (D); 14 Joey Lussick; 25 Adam Lawton (not used).
**Tries:** Lannon (4), Welham (44), Inu (47, 56);
**Goals:** Inu 3/5.
**Rugby Leaguer & League Express Men of the Match:**
*Wolves:* Daryl Clark; *Red Devils:* Jackson Hastings.
**Penalty count:** 5-4; **Half-time:** 6-8;
**Referee:** Chris Kendall; **Attendance:** 9,509.

## ROUND 23

*Thursday 18th July 2019*

### WIGAN WARRIORS 46 WAKEFIELD TRINITY 16

**WARRIORS:** 20 Zak Hardaker; 23 Chris Hankinson; 3 Dan Sarginson; 4 Oliver Gildart; 17 Liam Marshall; 6 George Williams; 37 Jarrod Sammut; 24 Oliver Partington; 9 Sam Powell; 14 Romain Navarrete; 15 Willie Isa; 12 Liam Farrell (C); 38 Morgan Smithies. Subs (all used): 21 Tony Clubb; 27 Jake Shorrocks; 36 Liam Byrne; 42 Ethan Havard (D).
**Tries:** Farrell (4, 31, 70), Hardaker (10), Isa (15), Jake Shorrocks (33), Sammut (40), Gildart (52);
**Goals:** Hardaker 7/8.
**TRINITY:** 21 Max Jowitt; 1 Ryan Hampshire; 3 Bill Tupou; 4 Reece Lyne; 5 Ben Jones-Bishop; 6 Jacob Miller (C); 7 Danny Brough; 10 Anthony England; 13 Tyler Randell; 36 Kelepi Tanginoa; 18 Joe Arundel; 19 James Batchelor;

227

George King. Subs (all used): 8 David Fifita; 9 Kyle Wood; 23 Chris Annakin; 24 Pauli Pauli.
**Tries:** Hampshire (45, 62), Jowitt (78); **Goals:** Brough 2/3.
**Rugby Leaguer & League Express Men of the Match:** *Warriors:* Liam Farrell; *Trinity:* Ryan Hampshire.
**Penalty count:** 6-5; **Half-time:** 34-0;
**Referee:** Robert Hicks; **Attendance:** 10,203.

*Friday 19th July 2019*

**HULL KINGSTON ROVERS 12 HUDDERSFIELD GIANTS 18**

**ROVERS:** 1 Adam Quinlan; 2 Craig Hall; 4 Jimmy Keinhorst; 23 Kane Linnett; 3 Ben Crooks; 24 Josh Drinkwater; 7 Danny McGuire; 36 Daniel Murray; 20 Danny Addy; 8 Robbie Mulhern; 13 Weller Hauraki; 11 Joel Tomkins (C); 21 George Lawler. Subs (all used): 10 Mose Masoe; 14 Mitch Garbutt; 17 Chris Atkin; 30 Owen Harrison.
**Tries:** Linnett (7), Hall (74); **Goals:** Hall 2/2.
**GIANTS:** 1 Darnell McIntosh; 2 Jermaine McGillvary; 31 Louis Senior; 20 Jake Wardle; 32 Innes Senior; 6 Lee Gaskell; 24 Tom Holmes; 19 Matty English; 14 Adam O'Brien; 27 Adam Walne; 12 Alex Mellor; 17 Ukuma Ta'ai; 13 Michael Lawrence (C). Subs (all used): 9 Kruise Leeming; 10 Suaia Matagi; 11 Aaron Murphy; 36 Oliver Wilson.
**Tries:** English (12), Mellor (46), McGillvary (78);
**Goals:** McIntosh 3/5.
**Rugby Leaguer & League Express Men of the Match:** *Rovers:* Weller Hauraki; *Giants:* Matty English.
**Penalty count:** 9-8; **Half-time:** 6-6;
**Referee:** Ben Thaler; **Attendance:** 7,733.

*Sunday 21st July 2019*

**LEEDS RHINOS 24 HULL FC 26**

**RHINOS:** 1 Jack Walker; 2 Tom Briscoe; 29 Harry Newman; 4 Konrad Hurrell; 5 Ash Handley; 40 Robert Lui; 15 Liam Sutcliffe; 38 Ava Seumanufagai; 39 Shaun Lunt; 10 Brad Singleton; 22 Cameron Smith; 41 Rhyse Martin; 11 Trent Merrin (C). Subs (all used): 16 Brett Ferres; 8 Adam Cuthbertson; 14 Brad Dwyer; 18 Nathaniel Peteru.
**Tries:** Hurrell (30), T Briscoe (55, 67), Handley (62);
**Goals:** Martin 4/4.
**HULL FC:** 1 Jamie Shaul; 2 Bureta Faraimo; 4 Josh Griffin; 3 Carlos Tuimavave; 33 Ratu Naulago; 14 Jake Connor; 7 Marc Sneyd; 8 Scott Taylor; 9 Danny Houghton (C); 23 Mickey Paea; 21 Sika Manu; 12 Mark Minichiello; 13 Joe Westerman. Subs (all used): 10 Josh Bowden; 20 Brad Fash; 22 Jordan Lane; 34 Gareth Ellis.
**Tries:** Manu (5), Faraimo (20), Shaul (44), Naulago (73);
**Goals:** Sneyd 5/5.
**Rugby Leaguer & League Express Men of the Match:** *Rhinos:* Jack Walker; *Hull FC:* Marc Sneyd.
**Penalty count:** 6-8; **Half-time:** 6-12;
**Referee:** Marcus Griffiths; **Attendance:** 13,351.

**LONDON BRONCOS 32 ST HELENS 12**

**BRONCOS:** 1 Alex Walker; 5 Kieran Dixon; 17 Matty Fleming; 4 Elliot Kear; 2 Rhys Williams; 6 Jordan Abdull; 14 Matty Fozard; 23 Rob Butler; 7 James Cunningham; 30 Olsi Krasniqi; 12 Jay Pitts (C); 13 Sadiq Adebiyi; 20 Luke Yates. Subs (all used): 8 Eddie Battye; 15 Greg Richards; 16 Matty Gee; 10 Mark Ioane.
**Tries:** Fleming (10, 74), Yates (25), Walker (63), Gee (70);
**Goals:** Dixon 6/6.
**SAINTS:** 29 Jack Welsby; 18 Adam Swift; 24 Matthew Costello; 30 Josh Simm (D); 5 Regan Grace; 12 Joseph Paulo; 7 Danny Richardson; 19 Matty Lees; 21 Aaron Smith; 13 Louie McCarthy-Scarsbrook; 22 James Bentley; 25 Joe Batchelor; 15 Morgan Knowles (C). Subs (all used): 16 Kyle Amor; 20 Jack Ashworth; 27 Josh Eaves (D); 28 Callum Hazzard (D).
**Tries:** Smith (22), Richardson (51); **Goals:** Richardson 2/2.
**Sin bin:** McCarthy-Scarsbrook (39) - obstruction.
**Rugby Leaguer & League Express Men of the Match:** *Broncos:* Jordan Abdull; *Saints:* Morgan Knowles.
**Penalty count:** 6-6; **Half-time:** 14-6;
**Referee:** Tom Grant; **Attendance:** 2,087.

**SALFORD RED DEVILS 40 CATALANS DRAGONS 14**

**RED DEVILS:** 1 Niall Evalds; 22 Derrell Olpherts; 3 Kris Welham; 5 Jake Bibby; 26 Krisnan Inu; 30 Tuimoala Lolohea; 31 Jackson Hastings; 15 Adam Walker; 19 Logan Tomkins; 10 Gil Dudson; 29 Ryan Lannon; 11 Josh Jones; 17 Tyrone McCarthy. Subs (all used): 16 Greg Burke; 32 Josh Johnson; 14 Joey Lussick; 13 Mark Flanagan (C).
**Tries:** J Johnson (27), Olpherts (37), Welham (40, 72), Lolohea (53), Evalds (63), Flanagan (74);
**Goals:** Inu 3/4, Lolohea 3/3.
**DRAGONS:** 29 Sam Tomkins; 25 Arthur Romano; 3 David Mead; 4 Brayden Wiliame; 27 Fouad Yaha; 1 Tony Gigot; 7 Matty Smith; 14 Julian Bousquet; 9 Michael McIlorum; 15 Mickael Simon; 17 Matt Whitley; 12 Benjamin Garcia; 8 Remi Casty (C). Subs (all used): 16 Benjamin Jullien; 22 Lucas Albert; 23 Antoni Maria; 28 Sam Kasiano.
**Tries:** Kasiano (33), Wiliame (43); **Goals:** Tomkins 3/3.
**Rugby Leaguer & League Express Men of the Match:** *Red Devils:* Kris Welham; *Dragons:* Sam Tomkins.
**Penalty count:** 3-6; **Half-time:** 16-8;
**Referee:** Chris Kendall; **Attendance:** 2,785.

**CASTLEFORD TIGERS 27 WARRINGTON WOLVES 18**

**TIGERS:** 32 Jordan Rankin; 2 James Clare; 3 Greg Minikin; 1 Peter Mata'utia; 25 Tuoyo Egodo; 6 Jake Trueman; 9 Paul McShane (C); 14 Nathan Massey; 13 Adam Milner; 33 Chris Clarkson; 11 Oliver Holmes; 12 Mike McMeeken; 15 Jesse Sene-Lefao. Subs: 8 Liam Watts; 10 Grant Millington; 24 Cory Aston (not used); 34 Daniel Smith.
**Tries:** Clare (11), Minikin (52), Trueman (59), Egodo (64);
**Goals:** Mata'utia 5/7; **Field goal:** Trueman (80).
**WOLVES:** 22 Jake Mamo; 2 Tom Lineham; 3 Bryson Goodwin; 18 Toby King; 5 Josh Charnley; 6 Blake Austin; 15 Declan Patton; 8 Chris Hill (C); 9 Daryl Clark; 10 Mike Cooper; 11 Ben Currie; 12 Jack Hughes (C); 14 Jason Clark. Subs (all used): 17 Joe Philbin; 23 Matt Davis; 16 Lama Tasi; 21 Danny Walker.
**Tries:** Mamo (35), Lineham (44), King (76);
**Goals:** Patton 3/4.
**Rugby Leaguer & League Express Men of the Match:** *Tigers:* Jake Trueman; *Wolves:* Daryl Clark.
**Penalty count:** 7-7; **Half-time:** 12-8;
**Referee:** Scott Mikalauskas; **Attendance:** 6,965.

## ROUND 24

*Thursday 1st August 2019*

**HULL FC 14 WIGAN WARRIORS 15**

**HULL FC:** 1 Jamie Shaul; 33 Ratu Naulago; 3 Carlos Tuimavave; 4 Josh Griffin; 2 Bureta Faraimo; 6 Albert Kelly; 7 Marc Sneyd; 8 Scott Taylor; 9 Danny Houghton (C); 15 Chris Green; 12 Mark Minichiello; 22 Jordan Lane; 13 Joe Westerman. Subs (all used): 14 Jake Connor; 19 Masi Matongo; 20 Brad Fash; 34 Gareth Ellis.
**Try:** Taylor (65); **Goals:** Sneyd 5/5.
**WARRIORS:** 20 Zak Hardaker; 17 Liam Marshall; 3 Dan Sarginson; 4 Oliver Gildart; 5 Joe Burgess; 6 George Williams; 7 Thomas Leuluai; 14 Romain Navarrete; 9 Sam Powell; 24 Oliver Partington; 15 Willie Isa; 12 Liam Farrell; 38 Morgan Smithies. Subs: 8 Tony Clubb; 13 Sean O'Loughlin (C); 16 Liam Byrne; 37 Jarrod Sammut (not used).
**Tries:** Marshall (25, 48); **Goals:** Hardaker 3/4;
**Field goal:** Hardaker (76).
**Rugby Leaguer & League Express Men of the Match:** *Hull FC:* Danny Houghton; *Warriors:* Zak Hardaker.
**Penalty count:** 10-8; **Half-time:** 6-10;
**Referee:** Ben Thaler; **Attendance:** 10,153.

*Friday 2nd August 2019*

**HUDDERSFIELD GIANTS 0 LEEDS RHINOS 44**

**GIANTS:** 1 Darnell McIntosh; 2 Jermaine McGillvary; 32 Innes Senior; 20 Jake Wardle; 31 Louis Senior; 6 Lee Gaskell; 7 Matt Frawley; 27 Adam Walne; 9 Kruise Leeming; 19 Matty English; 17 Ukuma Ta'ai; 12 Alex Mellor; 13 Michael Lawrence (C). Subs (all used): 14 Adam O'Brien; 15 Oliver Roberts; 10 Suaia Matagi; 11 Aaron Murphy.
**RHINOS:** 1 Jack Walker; 2 Tom Briscoe; 29 Harry Newman; 4 Konrad Hurrell; 5 Ash Handley; 40 Robert Lui; 7 Richie Myler; 8 Adam Cuthbertson; 39 Shaun Lunt; 38 Ava Seumanufagai; 41 Rhyse Martin; 16 Brett Ferres; 11 Trent Merrin (C). Subs (all used): 14 Brad Dwyer; 25 James Donaldson; 15 Liam Sutcliffe; 10 Brad Singleton.
**Tries:** Cuthbertson (18), T Briscoe (21), Hurrell (26, 58), Dwyer (36), Handley (47, 77), L Sutcliffe (73);
**Goals:** Martin 6/8.
**Rugby Leaguer & League Express Men of the Match:** *Giants:* Jermaine McGillvary; *Rhinos:* Konrad Hurrell.
**Penalty count:** 3-3; **Half-time:** 0-22;
**Referee:** Robert Hicks; **Attendance:** 6,809.

**ST HELENS 26 WAKEFIELD TRINITY 6**

**SAINTS:** 29 Jack Welsby; 2 Tommy Makinson; 3 Kevin Naiqama; 4 Mark Percival; 18 Adam Swift; 6 Theo Fages; 7 Danny Richardson; 19 Matty Lees; 9 James Roby (C); 10 Luke Thompson; 11 Zeb Taia; 17 Dominique Peyroux; 13 Louie McCarthy-Scarsbrook. Subs (all used): 12 Joseph Paulo; 16 Kyle Amor; 20 Jack Ashworth; 22 James Bentley.
**Tries:** Richardson (27), McCarthy-Scarsbrook (32), Makinson (35), Naiqama (70); **Goals:** Richardson 5/5.
**TRINITY:** 21 Max Jowitt; 5 Ben Jones-Bishop; 4 Reece Lyne; 18 Joe Arundel; 3 Bill Tupou; 1 Ryan Hampshire; 7 Danny Brough (C); 10 Anthony England; 13 Tyler Randell; 15 Craig Kopczak; 12 Danny Kirmond; 36 Kelepi Tanginoa; 23 Chris Annakin. Subs (all used): 16 David Fifita; 9 Kyle Wood; 20 Keegan Hirst; 22 George King.
**Try:** Tanginoa (78); **Goals:** Brough 1/2.
**Rugby Leaguer & League Express Men of the Match:** *Saints:* James Roby; *Trinity:* Chris Annakin.
**Penalty count:** 7-8; **Half-time:** 20-2;
**Referee:** Marcus Griffiths; **Attendance:** 9,494.

*Saturday 3rd August 2019*

**CATALANS DRAGONS 30 WARRINGTON WOLVES 10**

**DRAGONS:** 29 Sam Tomkins; 3 David Mead; 6 Samisoni Langi; 4 Brayden Wiliame; 27 Fouad Yaha; 13 Greg Bird; 1 Tony Gigot; 14 Julian Bousquet; 9 Michael McIlorum; 15 Mickael Simon; 17 Matt Whitley; 12 Benjamin Garcia; 8 Remi Casty (C). Subs: 11 Kenny Edwards; 18 Alrix Da Costa (not used); 23 Antoni Maria; 28 Sam Kasiano.
**Tries:** Yaha (35), Mead (54), Whitley (72), Gigot (76);
**Goals:** Tomkins 7/8.
**Dismissals:** Tomkins (80) - fighting;
McIlorum (80) - fighting.
**Sin bin:** McIlorum (15) - fighting.
**WOLVES:** 1 Stefan Ratchford; 2 Tom Lineham; 3 Bryson Goodwin; 18 Toby King; 22 Jake Mamo; 6 Blake Austin; 15 Declan Patton; 8 Chris Hill (C); 9 Daryl Clark; 10 Mike Cooper; 11 Ben Currie; 12 Jack Hughes (C); 14 Jason Clark. Subs (all used): 17 Joe Philbin; 19 Sitaleki Akauola; 20 Harvey Livett; 23 Matt Davis.
**Tries:** Mamo (26), Hill (43); **Goals:** Ratchford 1/2.
**Sin bin:** Hill (15) - fighting;
Mamo (65) - professional foul, (80) - fighting.
**Rugby Leaguer & League Express Men of the Match:** *Dragons:* Sam Tomkins; *Wolves:* Daryl Clark.
**Penalty count:** 8-7; **Half-time:** 8-4;
**Referee:** James Child; **Attendance:** 9,634.

*Sunday 4th August 2019*

**HULL KINGSTON ROVERS 27 CASTLEFORD TIGERS 26**
*(after golden point extra-time)*

**ROVERS:** 1 Adam Quinlan; 5 Ryan Shaw; 3 Ben Crooks; 4 Jimmy Keinhorst; 2 Craig Hall; 24 Josh Drinkwater; 7 Danny McGuire; 10 Mose Masoe; 17 Chris Atkin; 36 Daniel Murray; 11 Joel Tomkins (C); 13 Weller Hauraki; 21 George Lawler. Subs (all used): 40 Dean Hadley (D); 41 Jez Litten (D); 20 Danny Addy; 8 Robbie Mulhern.
**Tries:** Hall (9), Quinlan (12), Crooks (61, 64);
**Goals:** Shaw 5/5; **Field goal:** McGuire (81).
**TIGERS:** 32 Jordan Rankin; 2 James Clare; 3 Greg Minikin; 35 Cheyse Blair; 5 Greg Eden; 6 Jake Trueman; 1 Peter Mata'utia; 8 Liam Watts; 13 Adam Milner (C); 15 Jesse Sene-Lefao; 11 Oliver Holmes; 12 Mike McMeeken; 14 Nathan Massey. Subs (all used): 10 Grant Millington; 23 Will Maher; 29 Jacques O'Neill; 33 Chris Clarkson.
**Tries:** Mata'utia (16), Rankin (32), Clare (35), Minikin (48);
**Goals:** Mata'utia 5/6.
**Rugby Leaguer & League Express Men of the Match:** *Rovers:* Ben Crooks; *Tigers:* Liam Watts.
**Penalty count:** 4-6; **Half-time:** 14-20;
**Referee:** Chris Kendall; **Attendance:** 8,004.

**LONDON BRONCOS 28 SALFORD RED DEVILS 58**

**BRONCOS:** 1 Alex Walker; 5 Kieran Dixon; 4 Elliot Kear; 17 Matty Fleming; 2 Rhys Williams; 6 Jordan Abdull; 31 Brock Lamb (D); 30 Olsi Krasniqi; 7 James Cunningham; 23 Rob Butler; 12 Jay Pitts (C); 13 Sadiq Adebiyi; 20 Luke Yates. Subs (all used): 15 Greg Richards; 8 Eddie Battye; 14 Matty Fozard; 18 Nathan Mason.
**Tries:** Williams (19), Yates (56), Fleming (63), Adebiyi (71), Butler (78); **Goals:** Dixon 4/5.
**RED DEVILS:** 1 Niall Evalds; 22 Derrell Olpherts; 5 Jake Bibby; 3 Kris Welham; 26 Krisnan Inu; 30 Tuimoala Lolohea; 31 Jackson Hastings; 15 Adam Walker; 19 Logan Tomkins; 10 Gil Dudson; 11 Josh Jones; 17 Tyrone McCarthy; 13 Mark Flanagan. Subs (all used): 16 Greg Burke; 14 Joey Lussick; 8 Lee Mossop (C); 32 Josh Johnson.
**Tries:** Inu (7, 37), Flanagan (10), Jones (15), Evalds (23, 43, 75), Lolohea (30), Welham (53), Hastings (60); **Goals:** Lolohea 8/9, Inu 1/1.
**Sin bin:** Olpherts (77) - dangerous challenge.
**Rugby Leaguer & League Express Men of the Match:** *Broncos:* Luke Yates; *Red Devils:* Jackson Hastings.
**Penalty count:** 9-6; **Half-time:** 6-36;
**Referee:** Liam Moore; **Attendance:** 1,445.

## ROUND 25

*Thursday 8th August 2019*

**WARRINGTON WOLVES 12 ST HELENS 30**

**WOLVES:** 1 Stefan Ratchford; 31 Josh Thewlis; 3 Bryson Goodwin; 28 Luther Burrell; 22 Jake Mamo; 32 Riley Dean (D); 33 Matty Smith (D); 8 Chris Hill (C); 21 Danny Walker; 19 Sitaleki Akauola; 11 Ben Currie; 20 Harvey Livett; 34 Ben Westwood. Subs (all used): 13 Ben Murdoch-Masila; 23 Matt Davis; 16 Lama Tasi; 25 Luis Johnson.
**Tries:** Mamo (3), Thewlis (24); **Goals:** Ratchford 2/4.

**SAINTS:** 29 Jack Welsby; 2 Tommy Makinson; 3 Kevin Naiqama; 24 Matthew Costello; 5 Regan Grace; 1 Jonny Lomax (C); 7 Danny Richardson; 19 Matty Lees; 21 Aaron Smith; 10 Luke Thompson; 11 Zeb Taia; 17 Dominique Peyroux; 13 Louie McCarthy-Scarsbrook. Subs (all used): 12 Joseph Paulo; 16 Kyle Amor; 20 Jack Ashworth; 22 James Bentley.
**Tries:** Naiqama (11), Lomax (28), Paulo (45), Costello (63), Makinson (67); **Goals:** Richardson 5/5.
**Rugby Leaguer & League Express Men of the Match:** *Wolves:* Stefan Ratchford; *Saints:* Jack Welsby.
**Penalty count:** 9-8; **Half-time:** 10-12;
**Referee:** Ben Thaler; **Attendance:** 10,987.

*Friday 9th August 2019*

**LEEDS RHINOS 48 CATALANS DRAGONS 8**

**RHINOS:** 1 Jack Walker; 24 Luke Briscoe; 29 Harry Newman; 4 Konrad Hurrell; 5 Ash Handley; 40 Robert Lui; 7 Richie Myler; 38 Ava Seumanufagai; 39 Shaun Lunt; 8 Adam Cuthbertson; 16 Brett Ferres; 41 Rhyse Martin; 11 Trent Merrin (C). Subs (all used): 10 Brad Singleton; 25 James Donaldson; 14 Brad Dwyer; 15 Liam Sutcliffe.
**Tries:** Handley (9, 54), Martin (17), Myler (58, 71), Lui (64), L Briscoe (74); **Goals:** Martin 10/10.
**Dismissal:** Singleton (51) - high tackle on Kasiano.
**Sin bin:** Hurrell (39) - dangerous challenge on Bird.
**DRAGONS:** 1 Tony Gigot; 3 David Mead; 25 Arthur Romano; 4 Brayden Wiliame; 5 Lewis Tierney; 13 Greg Bird; 6 Samisoni Langi; 14 Julian Bousquet; 18 Alrix Da Costa; 15 Mickael Simon; 11 Kenny Edwards; 17 Matt Whitley; 8 Remi Casty (C). Subs (all used): 23 Antoni Maria; 28 Sam Kasiano; 19 Mickael Goudemand; 22 Lucas Albert.
**Try:** Goudemand (33); **Goals:** Gigot 2/2.
**Sin bin:** Mead (71) - late challenge on Walker.
**Rugby Leaguer & League Express Men of the Match:** *Rhinos:* Rhyse Martin; *Dragons:* Arthur Romano.
**Penalty count:** 11-8; **Half time:** 16-8;
**Referee:** Robert Hicks; **Attendance:** 11,336.

**WIGAN WARRIORS 36 HULL KINGSTON ROVERS 18**

**WARRIORS:** 20 Zak Hardaker; 17 Liam Marshall; 23 Chris Hankinson; 4 Oliver Gildart; 5 Joe Burgess; 6 George Williams; 7 Thomas Leuluai (C); 8 Tony Clubb; 9 Sam Powell; 24 Oliver Partington; 15 Willie Isa; 12 Liam Farrell; 38 Morgan Smithies. Subs (all used): 10 Ben Flower; 11 Joe Greenwood; 36 Liam Byrne; 43 Bevan French (D).
**Tries:** Williams (6), Marshall (16), Farrell (46, 74), Burgess (57), Clubb (68); **Goals:** Hardaker 6/6.
**ROVERS:** 1 Adam Quinlan; 5 Ryan Shaw; 3 Ben Crooks; 4 Jimmy Keinhorst; 26 Will Dagger; 32 Mikey Lewis (D); 24 Josh Drinkwater; 10 Mose Masoe; 17 Chris Atkin; 36 Daniel Murray; 11 Joel Tomkins (C); 13 Weller Hauraki; 40 Dean Hadley. Subs: 42 Kyle Trout (D); 8 Robbie Mulhern; 41 Jez Litten; 30 Owen Harrison (not used).
**Tries:** Shaw (11), Crooks (36), Drinkwater (49);
**Goals:** Shaw 3/3.
**Rugby Leaguer & League Express Men of the Match:** *Warriors:* Liam Farrell; *Rovers:* Dean Hadley.
**Penalty count:** 7-8; **Half-time:** 12-12;
**Referee:** Chris Kendall; **Attendance:** 10,702.

*Saturday 10th August 2019*

**CASTLEFORD TIGERS 20 LONDON BRONCOS 6**

**TIGERS:** 32 Jordan Rankin; 2 James Clare; 1 Peter Mata'utia; 35 Cheyse Blair; 25 Tuoyo Egodo; 20 Jamie Ellis; 6 Jake Trueman; 33 Chris Clarkson; 9 Paul McShane (C); 10 Grant Millington; 11 Oliver Holmes; 12 Mike McMeeken; 14 Nathan Massey. Subs (all used): 15 Jesse Sene-Lefao; 23 Will Maher; 29 Jacques O'Neill; 34 Daniel Smith.
**Tries:** Egodo (25, 63), Holmes (43), O'Neill (50);
**Goals:** Mata'utia 0/2, Ellis 2/2.
**BRONCOS:** 1 Alex Walker; 5 Kieran Dixon; 17 Matty Fleming; 4 Elliot Kear; 2 Rhys Williams; 6 Jordan Abdull; 31 Brock Lamb; 23 Rob Butler; 7 James Cunningham; 18 Nathan Mason; 12 Jay Pitts (C); 13 Sadiq Adebiyi; 20 Luke Yates. Subs (all used): 8 Eddie Battye; 10 Mark Ioane; 14 Matty Fozard; 30 Olsi Krasniqi.
**Try:** Lamb (21); **Goals:** Dixon 1/2.
**Rugby Leaguer & League Express Men of the Match:** *Tigers:* Jordan Rankin; *Broncos:* Luke Yates.
**Penalty count:** 11-6; **Half-time:** 4-6;
**Referee:** Scott Mikalauskas; **Attendance:** 5,497.

*Sunday 11th August 2019*

**SALFORD RED DEVILS 32 HUDDERSFIELD GIANTS 12**

**RED DEVILS:** 1 Niall Evalds; 22 Derrell Olpherts; 3 Kris Welham; 5 Jake Bibby; 26 Krisnan Inu; 30 Tuimoala Lolohea; 31 Jackson Hastings; 15 Adam Walker; 19 Logan Tomkins; 10 Gil Dudson; 11 Josh Jones; 29 Ryan Lannon; 13 Mark Flanagan. Subs (all used): 8 Lee Mossop (C); 14 Joey Lussick; 17 Tyrone McCarthy; 32 Josh Johnson.
**Tries:** Tomkins (15), Flanagan (66), Lolohea (78), Inu (80);
**Goals:** Inu 8/8.
**GIANTS:** 6 Lee Gaskell; 2 Jermaine McGillvary; 31 Louis Senior; 20 Jake Wardle; 1 Darnell McIntosh; 23 Oliver Russell; 24 Tom Holmes; 19 Matty English; 9 Kruise Leeming; 10 Suaia Matagi; 17 Ukuma Ta'ai; 35 Joe Wardle; 13 Michael Lawrence (C). Subs (all used): 14 Adam O'Brien; 15 Oliver Roberts; 26 Sebastine Ikahihifo; 36 Oliver Wilson.
**Tries:** McIntosh (33), Russell (50); **Goals:** Russell 2/3.
**Rugby Leaguer & League Express Men of the Match:** *Red Devils:* Krisnan Inu; *Giants:* Darnell McIntosh.
**Penalty count:** 9-6; **Half-time:** 10-6;
**Referee:** Marcus Griffiths; **Attendance:** 3,032.

**WAKEFIELD TRINITY 16 HULL FC 26**

**TRINITY:** 1 Ryan Hampshire; 5 Ben Jones-Bishop; 4 Reece Lyne; 3 Bill Tupou; 38 Morgan Escare (D); 6 Jacob Miller (C); 7 Danny Brough; 36 Kelepi Tanginoa; 9 Kyle Wood; 15 Craig Kopczak; 12 Danny Kirmond; 18 Joe Arundel; 19 James Batchelor. Subs (all used): 13 Tyler Randell; 8 David Fifita; 40 Adam Tangata (D); 23 Chris Annakin.
**Tries:** Hampshire (11), Arundel (54), Miller (74);
**Goals:** Brough 2/3.
**HULL FC:** 1 Jamie Shaul; 2 Bureta Faraimo; 4 Josh Griffin; 3 Carlos Tuimavave; 33 Ratu Naulago; 14 Jake Connor; 7 Marc Sneyd; 8 Scott Taylor; 9 Danny Houghton (C); 19 Masi Matongo; 22 Jordan Lane; 12 Mark Minichiello; 34 Gareth Ellis. Subs (all used): 10 Josh Bowden; 20 Brad Fash; 30 Danny Washbrook; 37 Jack Brown.
**Tries:** Faraimo (19), Tuimavave (24), Sneyd (27), Naulago (30, 51); **Goals:** Sneyd 3/6.
**Rugby Leaguer & League Express Men of the Match:** *Trinity:* Joe Arundel; *Hull FC:* Marc Sneyd.
**Penalty count:** 7-7; **Half-time:** 6-20;
**Referee:** Liam Moore; **Attendance:** 5,600.

## ROUND 26

*Thursday 15th August 2019*

**LEEDS RHINOS 20 ST HELENS 36**

**RHINOS:** 1 Jack Walker; 24 Luke Briscoe; 29 Harry Newman; 4 Konrad Hurrell; 5 Ash Handley; 40 Robert Lui; 7 Richie Myler; 8 Adam Cuthbertson; 39 Shaun Lunt; 38 Ava Seumanufagai; 41 Rhyse Martin; 16 Brett Ferres; 11 Trent Merrin (C). Subs (all used): 18 Nathaniel Peteru; 25 James Donaldson; 14 Brad Dwyer; 15 Liam Sutcliffe.
**Tries:** Myler (28), Handley (34, 70), Newman (74);
**Goals:** Martin 2/4.
**SAINTS:** 29 Jack Welsby; 24 Matthew Costello; 3 Kevin Naiqama; 4 Mark Percival; 5 Regan Grace; 1 Jonny Lomax (C); 6 Theo Fages; 10 Luke Thompson; 21 Aaron Smith; 19 Matty Lees; 11 Zeb Taia; 17 Dominique Peyroux; 22 James Bentley. Subs (all used): 20 Jack Ashworth; 16 Kyle Amor; 25 Joe Batchelor; 27 Josh Eaves.
**Tries:** Grace (19, 43), Naiqama (37, 60, 63), Taia (45);
**Goals:** Percival 6/7.
**Rugby Leaguer & League Express Men of the Match:** *Rhinos:* Ash Handley; *Saints:* Jonny Lomax.
**Penalty count:** 9-4; **Half-time:** 10-10;
**Referee:** Chris Kendall; **Attendance:** 12,153.

*Friday 16th August 2019*

**WIGAN WARRIORS 20 WARRINGTON WOLVES 6**

**WARRIORS:** 20 Zak Hardaker; 43 Bevan French; 3 Dan Sarginson; 4 Oliver Gildart; 17 Liam Marshall; 6 George Williams; 7 Thomas Leuluai (C); 8 Tony Clubb; 9 Sam Powell; 24 Oliver Partington; 15 Willie Isa; 12 Liam Farrell; 38 Morgan Smithies. Subs (all used): 11 Joe Greenwood; 14 Romain Navarrete; 36 Liam Byrne; 37 Jarrod Sammut.
**Tries:** French (15), Williams (17), Hardaker (25);
**Goals:** Hardaker 4/4.
**Sin bin:** Gildart (58) - high tackle on Mamo.
**WOLVES:** 1 Stefan Ratchford; 2 Tom Lineham; 3 Bryson Goodwin; 18 Toby King; 22 Jake Mamo; 15 Declan Patton; 33 Matty Smith; 8 Chris Hill (C); 9 Daryl Clark; 10 Mike Cooper; 11 Ben Currie; 20 Harvey Livett; 19 Sitaleki Akauola. Subs (all used): 13 Ben Murdoch-Masila; 14 Jason Clark; 17 Joe Philbin; 34 Ben Westwood.
**Try:** Lineham (72); **Goals:** Patton 1/1.
**Rugby Leaguer & League Express Men of the Match:** *Warriors:* Morgan Smithies; *Wolves:* Ben Murdoch-Masila.
**Penalty count:** 5-8; **Half-time:** 18-0;
**Referee:** Ben Thaler; **Attendance:** 12,555.

*Saturday 17th August 2019*

**CATALANS DRAGONS 4 LONDON BRONCOS 17**

**DRAGONS:** 1 Tony Gigot; 3 David Mead; 25 Arthur Romano; 4 Brayden Wiliame; 5 Lewis Tierney; 13 Greg Bird; 6 Samisoni Langi; 14 Julian Bousquet; 18 Alrix Da Costa; 28 Sam Kasiano; 17 Matt Whitley; 12 Benjamin Garcia; 8 Remi Casty (C). Subs (all used): 11 Kenny Edwards; 15 Mickael Simon; 22 Lucas Albert; 23 Antoni Maria.
**Try:** Wiliame (43); **Goals:** Gigot 0/1.
**Sin bin:** Bird (76) - dissent.
**BRONCOS:** 1 Alex Walker; 5 Kieran Dixon; 19 Ryan Morgan; 4 Elliot Kear; 2 Rhys Williams; 6 Jordan Abdull; 31 Brock Lamb; 8 Eddie Battye; 7 James Cunningham; 30 Olsi Krasniqi; 12 Jay Pitts (C); 11 Will Lovell; 20 Luke Yates. Subs (all used): 14 Matty Fozard; 16 Matty Gee; 21 Daniel Hindmarsh; 32 Guy Armitage (D).
**Tries:** Dixon (9), Walker (52); **Goals:** Dixon 4/4;
**Field goal:** Lamb (71).
**Sin bin:** Krasniqi (16) - dangerous challenge on Bird.
**Rugby Leaguer & League Express Men of the Match:** *Dragons:* Benjamin Garcia; *Broncos:* Jay Pitts.
**Penalty count:** 9-7; **Half-time:** 0-8;
**Referee:** Liam Moore; **Attendance:** 7,725.

**HULL FC 22 SALFORD RED DEVILS 44**

**HULL FC:** 1 Jamie Shaul; 2 Bureta Faraimo; 4 Josh Griffin; 3 Carlos Tuimavave; 33 Ratu Naulago; 14 Jake Connor; 7 Marc Sneyd; 8 Scott Taylor; 9 Danny Houghton (C); 23 Mickey Paea; 13 Joe Westerman; 22 Jordan Lane; 34 Gareth Ellis. Subs (all used): 10 Josh Bowden; 20 Brad Fash; 38 Kieran Buchanan; 39 Tevita Satae (D).
**Tries:** Taylor (8), Paea (17), Faraimo (22), Lane (60);
**Goals:** Sneyd 3/4.
**RED DEVILS:** 1 Niall Evalds; 23 Ken Sio; 3 Kris Welham; 5 Jake Bibby; 26 Krisnan Inu; 30 Tuimoala Lolohea; 31 Jackson Hastings; 8 Lee Mossop (C); 19 Logan Tomkins; 15 Adam Walker; 11 Josh Jones; 29 Ryan Lannon; 16 Greg Burke. Subs (all used): 13 Mark Flanagan; 14 Joey Lussick; 18 Ben Nakubuwai; 32 Josh Johnson.
**Tries:** Sio (4, 33), Mossop (26, 47), Bibby (43), Inu (65, 76), Hastings (72); **Goals:** Inu 6/8.
**Rugby Leaguer & League Express Men of the Match:** *Hull FC:* Marc Sneyd; *Red Devils:* Lee Mossop.
**Penalty count:** 6-3; **Half-time:** 16-16;
**Referee:** Scott Mikalauskas; **Attendance:** 11,217.

*Sunday 18th August 2019*

**HUDDERSFIELD GIANTS 0 CASTLEFORD TIGERS 24**

**GIANTS:** 6 Lee Gaskell; 2 Jermaine McGillvary; 1 Darnell McIntosh; 20 Jake Wardle; 31 Louis Senior; 23 Oliver Russell; 24 Tom Holmes; 26 Sebastine Ikahihifo; 9 Kruise Leeming; 27 Adam Walne; 17 Ukuma Ta'ai; 12 Alex Mellor; 13 Michael Lawrence (C). Subs (all used): 14 Adam O'Brien; 15 Oliver Roberts; 36 Oliver Wilson; 10 Suaia Matagi.
**Sin bin:** Wilson (56) - interference.
**TIGERS:** 32 Jordan Rankin; 2 James Clare; 1 Peter Mata'utia; 35 Cheyse Blair; 3 Greg Minikin; 6 Jake Trueman; 20 Jamie Ellis; 23 Will Maher; 9 Paul McShane (C); 10 Grant Millington; 11 Oliver Holmes; 12 Mike McMeeken; 14 Nathan Massey. Subs (all used): 13 Adam Milner; 15 Jesse Sene-Lefao; 29 Jacques O'Neill; 34 Daniel Smith.
**Tries:** Clare (7), Milner (49), McMeeken (59), Sene-Lefao (70); **Goals:** Ellis 4/5.
**Rugby Leaguer & League Express Men of the Match:** *Giants:* Lee Gaskell; *Tigers:* Jake Trueman.
**Penalty count:** 9-5; **Half-time:** 0-4;
**Referee:** James Child; **Attendance:** 4,636.

**HULL KINGSTON ROVERS 10 WAKEFIELD TRINITY 38**

**ROVERS:** 1 Adam Quinlan; 5 Ryan Shaw; 3 Ben Crooks; 23 Kane Linnett; 2 Craig Hall; 7 Danny McGuire; 24 Josh Drinkwater; 10 Mose Masoe; 17 Chris Atkin; 36 Daniel Murray; 11 Joel Tomkins (C); 13 Weller Hauraki; 40 Dean Hadley. Subs (all used): 14 Mitch Garbutt; 42 Kyle Trout; 41 Jez Litten; 8 Robbie Mulhern.
**Tries:** Crooks (33), Garbutt (36); **Goals:** Shaw 1/2.
**TRINITY:** 38 Morgan Escare; 5 Ben Jones-Bishop; 4 Reece Lyne; 3 Bill Tupou; 1 Ryan Hampshire; 6 Jacob Miller (C); 7 Danny Brough; 10 Anthony England; 9 Kyle Wood; 15 Craig Kopczak; 19 James Batchelor; 12 Danny Kirmond; 36 Kelepi Tanginoa. Subs (all used): 23 Chris Annakin; 39 Chris Green (D); 13 Tyler Randell; 40 Adam Tangata.
**Tries:** Miller (10, 69), Jones-Bishop (19), Wood (45), Tupou (64), Hampshire (73, 78); **Goals:** Brough 5/8.
**Rugby Leaguer & League Express Men of the Match:** *Rovers:* Mitch Garbutt; *Trinity:* Jacob Miller.
**Penalty count:** 11-5; **Half-time:** 10-14;
**Referee:** Robert Hicks; **Attendance:** 8,095.

St Helens' Danny Richardson leaves Castleford's Daniel Smith grounded as Jamie Ellis closes in

## ROUND 27

### Thursday 29th August 2019

#### SALFORD RED DEVILS 22 WARRINGTON WOLVES 6

**RED DEVILS:** 1 Niall Evalds; 23 Ken Sio; 3 Kris Welham; 5 Jake Bibby; 26 Krisnan Inu; 30 Tuimoala Lolohea; 31 Jackson Hastings; 8 Lee Mossop (C); 19 Logan Tomkins; 10 Gil Dudson; 11 Josh Jones; 17 Tyrone McCarthy; 16 Greg Burke. Subs (all used): 14 Joey Lussick; 32 Josh Johnson; 15 Adam Walker; 13 Mark Flanagan.
**Tries:** Sio (49, 57, 63), Bibby (59); **Goals:** Inu 3/5.
**WOLVES:** 1 Stefan Ratchford; 2 Tom Lineham; 3 Bryson Goodwin; 28 Luther Burrell; 22 Jake Mamo; 12 Jack Hughes (C); 33 Matty Smith; 17 Joe Philbin; 21 Danny Walker; 16 Lama Tasi; 20 Harvey Livett; 34 Ben Murdoch-Masila; 14 Jason Clark. Subs (all used): 9 Daryl Clark; 19 Sitaleki Akauola; 34 Ben Westwood; 25 Luis Johnson.
**Try:** Walker (79); **Goals:** Ratchford 1/1.
**Rugby Leaguer & League Express Men of the Match:** *Red Devils:* Ken Sio; *Wolves:* Danny Walker.
**Penalty count:** 7-10; **Half-time:** 2-0;
**Referee:** Chris Kendall; **Attendance:** 4,879.

### Friday 30th August 2019

#### HULL FC 12 HUDDERSFIELD GIANTS 22

**HULL FC:** 1 Jamie Shaul; 24 Jack Logan; 3 Carlos Tuimavave; 38 Kieran Buchanan; 2 Bureta Faraimo; 14 Jake Connor; 7 Marc Sneyd; 8 Scott Taylor; 9 Danny Houghton (C); 23 Mickey Paea; 21 Sika Manu; 22 Jordan Lane; 13 Joe Westerman. Subs (all used): 10 Josh Bowden; 20 Brad Fash; 34 Gareth Ellis; 39 Tevita Satae.
**Tries:** Shaul (14), Faraimo (30); **Goals:** Sneyd 2/2.
**GIANTS:** 1 Darnell McIntosh; 2 Jermaine McGillvary; 11 Aaron Murphy; 20 Jake Wardle; 31 Louis Senior; 6 Lee Gaskell; 7 Matt Frawley; 8 Paul Clough; 14 Adam O'Brien; 10 Suaia Matagi; 17 Ukuma Ta'ai; 12 Alex Mellor; 13 Michael Lawrence (C). Subs (all used): 9 Kruise Leeming; 29 Sam Hewitt; 30 Jon Luke Kirby (D); 36 Oliver Wilson.
**Tries:** McGillvary (19), Murphy (24), L Senior (67), Frawley (72); **Goals:** Gaskell 3/4.

**Rugby Leaguer & League Express Men of the Match:** *Hull FC:* Sika Manu; *Giants:* Lee Gaskell.
**Penalty count:** 8-7; **Half-time:** 12-10;
**Referee:** Liam Moore; **Attendance:** 10,114.

#### ST HELENS 4 CASTLEFORD TIGERS 0

**SAINTS:** 29 Jack Welsby; 2 Tommy Makinson; 24 Matthew Costello; 4 Mark Percival; 5 Regan Grace; 1 Jonny Lomax; 7 Danny Richardson; 10 Luke Thompson; 9 James Roby (C); 16 Kyle Amor; 11 Zeb Taia; 20 Jack Ashworth; 15 Morgan Knowles. Subs (all used): 8 Alex Walmsley; 13 Louie McCarthy-Scarsbrook; 12 Joseph Paulo; 22 James Bentley.
**Try:** Grace (32); **Goals:** Richardson 0/1.
**TIGERS:** 32 Jordan Rankin; 2 James Clare; 1 Peter Mata'utia; 35 Cheyse Blair; 3 Greg Minikin; 6 Jake Trueman; 20 Jamie Ellis; 8 Liam Watts; 9 Paul McShane (C); 10 Grant Millington; 11 Oliver Holmes; 12 Mike McMeeken; 14 Nathan Massey. Subs (all used): 13 Adam Milner; 15 Jesse Sene-Lefao; 29 Jacques O'Neill; 34 Daniel Smith.
**Rugby Leaguer & League Express Men of the Match:** *Saints:* Alex Walmsley; *Tigers:* Liam Watts.
**Penalty count:** 6-9; **Half-time:** 4-0;
**Referee:** James Child; **Attendance:** 10,315.

### Saturday 31st August 2019

#### CATALANS DRAGONS 6 HULL KINGSTON ROVERS 24

**DRAGONS:** 3 David Mead; 25 Arthur Romano; 17 Matt Whitley; 4 Brayden Wiliame; 5 Lewis Tierney; 6 Samisoni Langi; 1 Tony Gigot (C); 28 Sam Kasiano; 9 Michael McIlorum; 23 Antoni Maria; 11 Kenny Edwards; 13 Greg Bird; 19 Mickael Goudemand. Subs (all used): 15 Mickael Simon; 20 Lambert Belmas; 22 Lucas Albert; 24 Jason Baitieri.
**Try:** Mead (28); **Goals:** Gigot 1/1.
**ROVERS:** 26 Will Dagger; 5 Ryan Shaw; 23 Kane Linnett; 4 Jimmy Keinhorst; 3 Ben Crooks; 24 Josh Drinkwater; 7 Danny McGuire; 8 Robbie Mulhern; 17 Chris Atkin; 36 Daniel Murray; 11 Joel Tomkins (C); 13 Weller Hauraki; 40 Dean Hadley. Subs (all used): 10 Mose Masoe; 20 Danny Addy; 41 Jez Litten; 42 Kyle Trout.
**Tries:** Shaw (13, 20), McGuire (37); **Goals:** Shaw 6/7.
**Rugby Leaguer & League Express Men of the Match:** *Dragons:* David Mead; *Rovers:* Danny McGuire.
**Penalty count:** 10-11; **Half-time:** 6-16;
**Referee:** Ben Thaler; **Attendance:** 8,315.

### Sunday 1st September 2019

#### LONDON BRONCOS 10 LEEDS RHINOS 36

**BRONCOS:** 1 Alex Walker; 5 Kieran Dixon; 4 Elliot Kear; 19 Ryan Morgan; 2 Rhys Williams; 6 Jordan Abdull; 31 Brock Lamb; 30 Olsi Krasniqi; 7 James Cunningham; 8 Eddie Battye; 12 Jay Pitts (C); 11 Will Lovell; 20 Luke Yates. Subs (all used): 23 Rob Butler; 16 Matty Gee; 14 Matty Fozard; 18 Nathan Mason.
**Tries:** Dixon (42), Morgan (56); **Goals:** Dixon 1/2.
**Sin bin:** Dixon (71) - interference; Kear (78) - dissent.
**On report:** Kear (71) - alleged contact with referee.
**RHINOS:** 1 Jack Walker; 24 Luke Briscoe; 29 Harry Newman; 4 Konrad Hurrell; 5 Ash Handley; 40 Robert Lui; 7 Richie Myler; 19 Mikolaj Oledzki; 14 Brad Dwyer; 38 Ava Seumanufagai; 16 Brett Ferres; 41 Rhyse Martin; 11 Trent Merrin (C). Subs (all used): 8 Adam Cuthbertson; 25 James Donaldson; 22 Cameron Smith; 15 Liam Sutcliffe.
**Tries:** L Briscoe (7), Seumanufagai (18), Walker (37, 73), Handley (66), Dwyer (77); **Goals:** Martin 6/6.
**Rugby Leaguer & League Express Men of the Match:** *Broncos:* Nathan Mason; *Rhinos:* Jack Walker.
**Penalty count:** 5-8; **Half-time:** 0-18;
**Referee:** Robert Hicks; **Attendance:** 3,051.

#### WAKEFIELD TRINITY 16 WIGAN WARRIORS 24

**TRINITY:** 38 Morgan Escare; 5 Ben Jones-Bishop; 4 Reece Lyne; 3 Bill Tupou; 1 Ryan Hampshire; 6 Jacob Miller (C); 7 Danny Brough; 10 Anthony England; 9 Kyle Wood; 15 Craig Kopczak; 12 Danny Kirmond; 19 James Batchelor; 36 Kelepi Tanginoa. Subs (all used): 13 Tyler Randell; 23 Chris Annakin; 39 Chris Green; 40 Adam Tangata.
**Tries:** Batchelor (30), Miller (40), Jones-Bishop (69); **Goals:** Brough 2/3.
**WARRIORS:** 20 Zak Hardaker; 17 Liam Marshall; 3 Dan Sarginson; 4 Oliver Gildart; 5 Joe Burgess; 6 George Williams; 7 Thomas Leuluai (C); 8 Tony Clubb; 9 Sam Powell; 24 Oliver Partington; 15 Willie Isa; 12 Liam Farrell; 38 Morgan Smithies. Subs (all used): 11 Joe Greenwood; 14 Romain Navarrete; 36 Liam Byrne; 43 Bevan French.
**Tries:** Marshall (20, 28, 58), Powell (79); **Goals:** Hardaker 4/5.

**Rugby Leaguer & League Express Men of the Match:**
*Trinity:* Kelepi Tanginoa; *Warriors:* Liam Marshall.
**Penalty count:** 8-11; **Half-time:** 12-12;
**Referee:** Scott Mikalauskas; **Attendance:** 5,805.

## ROUND 28

*Thursday 5th September 2019*

### CASTLEFORD TIGERS 44 HULL FC 12

**TIGERS:** 32 Jordan Rankin; 2 James Clare; 1 Peter Mata'utia; 35 Cheyse Blair; 3 Greg Minikin; 6 Jake Trueman; 20 Jamie Ellis; 8 Liam Watts; 9 Paul McShane (C); 10 Grant Millington; 15 Jesse Sene-Lefao; 12 Mike McMeeken; 14 Nathan Massey. Subs (all used): 11 Oliver Holmes; 13 Adam Milner; 18 Matt Cook; 34 Daniel Smith.
**Tries:** Blair (8), Trueman (12, 18, 42), Clare (70), Rankin (76), Cook (78); **Goals:** Ellis 8/8.
**HULL FC:** 1 Jamie Shaul; 33 Ratu Naulago; 3 Carlos Tuimavave; 14 Jake Connor; 24 Jack Logan; 6 Albert Kelly; 7 Marc Sneyd; 8 Scott Taylor; 9 Danny Houghton (C); 23 Mickey Paea; 21 Sika Manu; 4 Josh Griffin; 34 Gareth Ellis. Subs (all used): 10 Josh Bowden; 19 Masi Matongo; 12 Mark Minichiello; 39 Tevita Satae.
**Tries:** Matongo (30), Logan (56); **Goals:** Sneyd 2/2.
**Sin bin:** Shaul (54) - professional foul; Connor (77) - dissent.
**Rugby Leaguer & League Express Men of the Match:**
*Tigers:* Jake Trueman; *Hull FC:* Tevita Satae.
**Penalty count:** 6-3; **Half-time:** 20-6;
**Referee:** Ben Thaler; **Attendance:** 6,712.

*Friday 6th September 2019*

### HULL KINGSTON ROVERS 16 LONDON BRONCOS 20

**ROVERS:** 2 Craig Hall; 26 Will Dagger; 3 Ben Crooks; 4 Jimmy Keinhorst; 5 Ryan Shaw; 24 Josh Drinkwater; 7 Danny McGuire; 8 Robbie Mulhern; 39 Matt Parcell; 36 Daniel Murray; 11 Joel Tomkins (C); 13 Weller Hauraki; 40 Dean Hadley. Subs (all used): 14 Mitch Garbutt; 42 Kyle Trout; 10 Mose Masoe; 17 Chris Atkin.
**Tries:** Dagger (21), Atkin (46), McGuire (51);
**Goals:** Shaw 2/3.
**BRONCOS:** 1 Alex Walker; 5 Kieran Dixon; 19 Ryan Morgan; 4 Elliot Kear; 2 Rhys Williams; 6 Jordan Abdull; 31 Brock Lamb; 8 Eddie Battye; 7 James Cunningham; 23 Rob Butler; 12 Jay Pitts (C); 16 Matty Gee; 20 Luke Yates. Subs (all used): 14 Matty Fozard; 18 Nathan Mason; 21 Daniel Hindmarsh; 32 Guy Armitage.
**Tries:** Gee (4), Lamb (10), Pitts (76); **Goals:** Dixon 4/5.
**On report:**
Cunningham (75) - alleged racial abuse of Masoe.
**Rugby Leaguer & League Express Men of the Match:**
*Rovers:* Matt Parcell; *Broncos:* Brock Lamb.
**Penalty count:** 8-5; **Half-time:** 6-14;
**Referee:** James Child; **Attendance:** 8,020.

### LEEDS RHINOS 12 SALFORD RED DEVILS 20

**RHINOS:** 1 Jack Walker; 24 Luke Briscoe; 29 Harry Newman; 4 Konrad Hurrell; 5 Ash Handley; 40 Robert Lui; 7 Richie Myler; 19 Mikolaj Oledzki; 39 Shaun Lunt; 38 Ava Seumanufagai; 41 Rhyse Martin; 15 Liam Sutcliffe; 11 Trent Merrin (C). Subs (all used): 13 Stevie Ward; 14 Brad Dwyer; 20 Jamie Jones-Buchanan; 22 Cameron Smith.
**Tries:** Myler (36), Jones-Buchanan (54); **Goals:** Martin 2/2.
**RED DEVILS:** 1 Niall Evalds; 23 Ken Sio; 3 Kris Welham; 5 Jake Bibby; 26 Krisnan Inu; 30 Tuimoala Lolohea; 31 Jackson Hastings; 8 Lee Mossop (C); 19 Logan Tomkins; 10 Gil Dudson; 11 Josh Jones; 12 George Griffin; 17 Tyrone McCarthy. Subs (all used): 14 Joey Lussick; 13 Mark Flanagan; 15 Adam Walker; 16 Greg Burke.
**Tries:** Evalds (22), Bibby (27), Lussick (72); **Goals:** Inu 4/4.
**Rugby Leaguer & League Express Men of the Match:**
*Rhinos:* Stevie Ward; *Red Devils:* Krisnan Inu.
**Penalty count:** 11-10; **Half-time:** 6-14;
**Referee:** Liam Moore; **Attendance:** 12,436.

### ST HELENS 48 HUDDERSFIELD GIANTS 6

**SAINTS:** 23 Lachlan Coote; 2 Tommy Makinson; 3 Kevin Naiqama; 4 Mark Percival; 5 Regan Grace; 1 Jonny Lomax; 6 Theo Fages; 8 Alex Walmsley; 9 James Roby (C); 10 Luke Thompson; 11 Zeb Taia; 17 Dominique Peyroux; 15 Morgan Knowles. Subs (all used): 13 Louie McCarthy-Scarsbrook; 16 Kyle Amor; 20 Jack Ashworth; 22 James Bentley.
**Tries:** Thompson (2, 62), Peyroux (16), Grace (22), Knowles (35), Amor (53), Lomax (69), Makinson (76);
**Goals:** Coote 8/8.
**GIANTS:** 1 Darnell McIntosh; 2 Jermaine McGillvary; 12 Alex Mellor; 20 Jake Wardle; 31 Louis Senior; 23 Oliver Russell; 24 Tom Holmes; 8 Paul Clough; 14 Adam O'Brien; 10 Suaia Matagi; 17 Ukuma Ta'ai; 29 Sam Hewitt; 13 Michael Lawrence (C). Subs (all used): 9 Kruise Leeming; 26 Sebastine Ikahihifo; 30 Jon Luke Kirby; 36 Oliver Wilson.
**Try:** Lawrence (42); **Goals:** Russell 1/1.
**Rugby Leaguer & League Express Men of the Match:**
*Saints:* Luke Thompson; *Giants:* Adam O'Brien.
**Penalty count:** 7-6; **Half-time:** 24-0;
**Referee:** Marcus Griffiths; **Attendance:** 9,560.

### WARRINGTON WOLVES 23 WAKEFIELD TRINITY 16

**WOLVES:** 1 Stefan Ratchford; 2 Tom Lineham; 3 Bryson Goodwin; 18 Toby King; 5 Josh Charnley; 6 Blake Austin; 15 Declan Patton; 8 Chris Hill (C); 9 Daryl Clark; 10 Mike Cooper; 11 Ben Currie; 13 Ben Murdoch-Masila; 14 Jason Clark. Subs (all used): 22 Jake Mamo; 33 Matty Smith; 19 Sitaleki Akauola; 17 Joe Philbin.
**Tries:** D Clark (19), Currie (21), Charnley (32), Goodwin (52);
**Goals:** Ratchford 3/5; **Field goal:** Patton (74).
**TRINITY:** 38 Morgan Escare; 5 Ben Jones-Bishop; 4 Reece Lyne; 18 Joe Arundel; 1 Ryan Hampshire; 6 Jacob Miller (C); 7 Danny Brough; 15 Craig Kopczak; 13 Tyler Randell; 40 Adam Tangata; 12 Danny Kirmond; 36 Kelepi Tanginoa; 26 Jordan Crowther. Subs (all used): 39 Chris Green; 31 Titus Gwaze; 22 George King; 9 Kyle Wood.
**Tries:** Escare (42), Jones-Bishop (48), Hampshire (62);
**Goals:** Brough 2/3.
**Rugby Leaguer & League Express Men of the Match:**
*Wolves:* Stefan Ratchford; *Trinity:* Jordan Crowther.
**Penalty count:** 9-10; **Half-time:** 16-0;
**Referee:** Chris Kendall; **Attendance:** 10,158.

### WIGAN WARRIORS 46 CATALANS DRAGONS 12

**WARRIORS:** 20 Zak Hardaker; 43 Bevan French; 3 Dan Sarginson; 4 Oliver Gildart; 5 Joe Burgess; 6 George Williams; 7 Thomas Leuluai (C); 8 Tony Clubb; 9 Sam Powell; 24 Oliver Partington; 15 Willie Isa; 12 Liam Farrell; 38 Morgan Smithies. Subs (all used): 11 Joe Greenwood; 14 Romain Navarrete; 36 Liam Byrne; 40 Harry Smith (D).
**Tries:** French (25, 36, 45), Hardaker (51), Leuluai (54), Smith (61), Sarginson (72), Gildart (80);
**Goals:** Hardaker 6/8, Smith 1/1.
**Sin bin:** Farrell (18) - dangerous challenge on Bird.
**DRAGONS:** 29 Sam Tomkins; 25 Arthur Romano; 6 Samisoni Langi; 4 Brayden Wiliame; 5 Lewis Tierney; 13 Greg Bird; 22 Lucas Albert; 14 Julian Bousquet; 9 Michael McIlorum; 23 Antoni Maria; 16 Benjamin Jullien; 17 Matt Whitley; 8 Remi Casty (C). Subs (all used): 15 Mickael Simon; 18 Alrix Da Costa; 19 Mickael Goudemand; 24 Jason Baitieri.
**Tries:** McIlorum (48), Tierney (76); **Goals:** Tomkins 2/2.
**Rugby Leaguer & League Express Men of the Match:**
*Warriors:* Bevan French; *Dragons:* Michael McIlorum.
**Penalty count:** 8-6; **Half-time:** 14-0;
**Referee:** Robert Hicks; **Attendance:** 10,804.

## ROUND 29

*Thursday 12th September 2019*

### WIGAN WARRIORS 26 CASTLEFORD TIGERS 8

**WARRIORS:** 20 Zak Hardaker; 43 Bevan French; 3 Dan Sarginson; 4 Oliver Gildart; 5 Joe Burgess; 6 George Williams; 7 Thomas Leuluai; 8 Tony Clubb; 9 Sam Powell; 24 Oliver Partington; 15 Willie Isa; 11 Joe Greenwood; 38 Morgan Smithies. Subs (all used): 10 Ben Flower; 13 Sean O'Loughlin (C); 14 Romain Navarrete; 36 Liam Byrne.
**Tries:** Williams (16), Hardaker (44), Greenwood (47), Gildart (63), Smithies (77); **Goals:** Hardaker 3/6.
**TIGERS:** 32 Jordan Rankin; 2 James Clare; 1 Peter Mata'utia; 35 Cheyse Blair; 3 Greg Minikin; 6 Jake Trueman; 20 Jamie Ellis; 8 Liam Watts; 9 Paul McShane (C); 10 Grant Millington; 15 Jesse Sene-Lefao; 12 Mike McMeeken; 14 Nathan Massey. Subs (all used): 11 Oliver Holmes; 18 Matt Cook; 33 Chris Clarkson; 34 Daniel Smith.
**Try:** Blair (80); **Goals:** Ellis 2/4.
**Dismissal:**
Sene-Lefao (66) - use of the knees on Partington.
**Rugby Leaguer & League Express Men of the Match:**
*Warriors:* Oliver Partington; *Tigers:* Paul McShane.
**Penalty count:** 10-6; **Half-time:** 4-2;
**Referee:** James Child; **Attendance:** 11,001.

*Friday 13th September 2019*

### HUDDERSFIELD GIANTS 24 CATALANS DRAGONS 22

**GIANTS:** 1 Darnell McIntosh; 2 Jermaine McGillvary; 11 Aaron Murphy; 20 Jake Wardle; 31 Louis Senior; 6 Lee Gaskell; 7 Matt Frawley; 8 Paul Clough; 14 Adam O'Brien (C); 10 Suaia Matagi; 17 Ukuma Ta'ai; 12 Alex Mellor; 26 Sebastine Ikahihifo. Subs (all used): 9 Kruise Leeming; 38 Chester Butler (D); 30 Jon Luke Kirby; 36 Oliver Wilson.
**Tries:** L Senior (4, 21, 54, 70), McGillvary (73);
**Goals:** Jake Wardle 1/3, Gaskell 1/2.
**DRAGONS:** 29 Sam Tomkins; 30 Robin Brochon; 25 Arthur Romano; 16 Benjamin Jullien; 5 Lewis Tierney; 22 Lucas Albert; 26 Arthur Mourgue; 14 Julian Bousquet; 9 Michael McIlorum; 23 Antoni Maria; 13 Greg Bird (C); 12 Benjamin Garcia; 24 Jason Baitieri. Subs (all used): 15 Mickael Simon; 18 Alrix Da Costa; 19 Mickael Goudemand; 20 Lambert Belmas.
**Tries:** Tierney (13, 27), Mourgue (46); **Goals:** Tomkins 5/5.
**Rugby Leaguer & League Express Men of the Match:**
*Giants:* Louis Senior; *Dragons:* Arthur Mourgue.
**Penalty count:** 7-4; **Half-time:** 10-14;
**Referee:** Ben Thaler; **Attendance:** 5,242.

### HULL FC 6 ST HELENS 22

**HULL FC:** 1 Jamie Shaul; 33 Ratu Naulago; 3 Carlos Tuimavave; 4 Josh Griffin; 2 Bureta Faraimo; 6 Albert Kelly; 7 Marc Sneyd; 8 Scott Taylor; 9 Danny Houghton (C); 39 Tevita Satae; 12 Mark Minichiello; 22 Jordan Lane; 34 Gareth Ellis. Subs (all used): 10 Josh Bowden; 14 Jake Connor; 19 Masi Matongo; 20 Brad Fash.
**Try:** Taylor (27); **Goals:** Sneyd 1/1.
**Sin bin:** Kelly (75) - dissent.
**SAINTS:** 23 Lachlan Coote; 2 Tommy Makinson; 3 Kevin Naiqama; 4 Mark Percival; 5 Regan Grace; 1 Jonny Lomax; 6 Theo Fages; 8 Alex Walmsley; 9 James Roby (C); 10 Luke Thompson; 11 Zeb Taia; 17 Dominique Peyroux; 15 Morgan Knowles. Subs (all used): 13 Louie McCarthy-Scarsbrook; 16 Kyle Amor; 20 Jack Ashworth; 22 James Bentley.
**Tries:** Makinson (9, 15, 34), Percival (63), Grace (76);
**Goals:** Coote 1/5.
**Rugby Leaguer & League Express Men of the Match:**
*Hull FC:* Tevita Satae; *Saints:* Lachlan Coote.
**Penalty count:** 11-8; **Half-time:** 6-14;
**Referee:** Liam Moore; **Attendance:** 11,004.

### LEEDS RHINOS 26 WARRINGTON WOLVES 4

**RHINOS:** 1 Jack Walker; 24 Luke Briscoe; 15 Liam Sutcliffe; 4 Konrad Hurrell; 5 Ash Handley; 40 Robert Lui; 7 Richie Myler; 8 Adam Cuthbertson; 14 Brad Dwyer; 18 Nathaniel Peteru; 13 Stevie Ward; 41 Rhyse Martin; 20 Jamie Jones-Buchanan (C). Subs (all used): 10 Brad Singleton; 25 James Donaldson; 22 Cameron Smith; 34 Corey Johnson (D).
**Tries:** L Sutcliffe (31), Lui (55), Cuthbertson (72), L Briscoe (78); **Goals:** Martin 4/4, Jones-Buchanan 1/1.
**WOLVES:** 1 Stefan Ratchford; 2 Tom Lineham; 3 Bryson Goodwin; 18 Toby King; 5 Josh Charnley; 6 Blake Austin; 33 Matty Smith; 8 Chris Hill (C); 9 Daryl Clark; 10 Mike Cooper; 11 Ben Currie; 13 Ben Murdoch-Masila; 14 Jason Clark. Subs: 12 Jack Hughes (C); 34 Ben Westwood; 19 Sitaleki Akauola; 22 Jake Mamo (not used).
**Try:** Charnley (69); **Goals:** Ratchford 0/1.
**Sin bin:** D Clark (9) - professional foul.
**Rugby Leaguer & League Express Men of the Match:**
*Rhinos:* Robert Lui; *Wolves:* Stefan Ratchford.
**Penalty count:** 8-5; **Half-time:** 8-0;
**Referee:** Marcus Griffiths; **Attendance:** 14,085.

### SALFORD RED DEVILS 17 HULL KINGSTON ROVERS 16
*(after golden point extra-time)*

**RED DEVILS:** 1 Niall Evalds; 23 Ken Sio; 3 Kris Welham; 5 Jake Bibby; 26 Krisnan Inu; 30 Tuimoala Lolohea; 31 Jackson Hastings; 15 Adam Walker; 19 Logan Tomkins; 8 Lee Mossop (C); 12 George Griffin; 11 Josh Jones; 16 Greg Burke. Subs (all used): 14 Joey Lussick; 18 Ben Nakubuwai; 32 Josh Johnson; 29 Ryan Lannon.
**Tries:** Bibby (33), Lolohea (44), Lussick (80);
**Goals:** Inu 2/4; **Field goal:** Inu (89).
**ROVERS:** 1 Adam Quinlan; 2 Craig Hall; 3 Ben Crooks; 23 Kane Linnett; 5 Ryan Shaw; 7 Danny McGuire (C); 24 Josh Drinkwater; 42 Kyle Trout; 39 Matt Parcell; 36 Daniel Murray; 40 Dean Hadley; 13 Weller Hauraki; 8 Robbie Mulhern. Subs (all used): 20 Danny Addy; 10 Mose Masoe; 17 Chris Atkin; 21 George Lawler.
**Tries:** Drinkwater (8), Linnett (57); **Goals:** Shaw 4/4.
**Sin bin:** McGuire (31) - professional foul.
**Rugby Leaguer & League Express Men of the Match:**
*Red Devils:* Jackson Hastings; *Rovers:* Ryan Shaw.
**Penalty count:** 10-6; **Half-time:** 4-8;
**Referee:** Chris Kendall; **Attendance:** 5,393.

### WAKEFIELD TRINITY 19 LONDON BRONCOS 10

**TRINITY:** 38 Morgan Escare; 5 Ben Jones-Bishop; 4 Reece Lyne; 41 Ryan Atkins (D2); 1 Ryan Hampshire; 6 Jacob Miller (C); 7 Danny Brough; 15 Craig Kopczak; 13 Tyler Randell; 40 Adam Tangata; 12 Danny Kirmond; 36 Kelepi Tanginoa; 26 Jordan Crowther. Subs (all used): 9 Kyle Wood; 39 Chris Green; 22 George King; 18 Joe Arundel.
**Tries:** Hampshire (24, 45), Lyne (54); **Goals:** Brough 3/4;
**Field goal:** Brough (68).
**Sin bin:** Hampshire (79) - professional foul.
**BRONCOS:** 1 Alex Walker; 5 Kieran Dixon; 19 Ryan Morgan; 4 Elliot Kear; 2 Rhys Williams; 6 Jordan Abdull; 31 Brock Lamb; 8 Eddie Battye; 7 James Cunningham; 23 Rob Butler; 16 Matty Gee; 12 Jay Pitts (C); 20 Luke Yates. Subs (all used): 14 Matty Fozard; 18 Nathan Mason; 21 Daniel Hindmarsh; 11 Will Lovell.
**Tries:** Walker (71), Lamb (80); **Goals:** Dixon 1/3.
**Rugby Leaguer & League Express Men of the Match:**
*Trinity:* Danny Brough; *Broncos:* Eddie Battye.
**Penalty count:** 6-7; **Half-time:** 8-0;
**Referee:** Robert Hicks; **Attendance:** 6,230.

Oliver Gildart dives past Ryan Lannon to score during Wigan's Qualifying Play-off win against Salford

## ELIMINATION PLAY-OFF

*Thursday 19th September 2019*

**WARRINGTON WOLVES 12 CASTLEFORD TIGERS 14**

**WOLVES:** 1 Stefan Ratchford; 2 Tom Lineham; 3 Bryson Goodwin; 18 Toby King; 5 Josh Charnley; 6 Blake Austin; 15 Declan Patton; 8 Chris Hill (C); 9 Daryl Clark; 10 Mike Cooper; 11 Ben Currie; 12 Jack Hughes (C); 14 Jason Clark. Subs (all used): 17 Joe Philbin; 34 Ben Westwood; 13 Ben Murdoch-Masila; 22 Jake Mamo.
**Tries:** Mamo (42), Hill (70); **Goals:** Ratchford 2/4.
**Sin bin:** Goodwin (79) - dissent.
**TIGERS:** 27 Calum Turner; 2 James Clare; 1 Peter Mata'utia; 35 Cheyse Blair; 3 Greg Minikin; 6 Jake Trueman; 32 Jordan Rankin; 8 Liam Watts; 9 Paul McShane (C); 10 Grant Millington; 11 Oliver Holmes; 33 Chris Clarkson; 34 Daniel Smith. Subs: 13 Adam Milner; 18 Matt Cook; 20 Jamie Ellis (not used); 29 Jacques O'Neill.
**Tries:** Milner (28), Rankin (49); **Goals:** Mata'utia 3/3.
**Rugby Leaguer & League Express Men of the Match:**
*Wolves:* Daryl Clark; *Tigers:* Jordan Rankin.
**Penalty count:** 5-7; **Half-time:** 0-6;
**Referee:** Chris Kendall; **Attendance:** 5,627.

## QUALIFYING PLAY-OFF

*Friday 20th September 2019*

**WIGAN WARRIORS 18 SALFORD RED DEVILS 12**

**WARRIORS:** 20 Zak Hardaker; 17 Liam Marshall; 23 Chris Hankinson; 4 Oliver Gildart; 5 Joe Burgess; 6 George Williams; 7 Thomas Leuluai; 8 Tony Clubb; 9 Sam Powell; 36 Liam Byrne; 15 Willie Isa; 12 Liam Farrell; 38 Morgan Smithies. Subs (all used): 11 Joe Greenwood; 13 Sean O'Loughlin (C); 43 Bevan French.
**Tries:** Gildart (24), Leuluai (53), Williams (56);
**Goals:** Hardaker 3/4.
**RED DEVILS:** 1 Niall Evalds; 23 Ken Sio; 3 Kris Welham; 5 Jake Bibby; 26 Krisnan Inu; 30 Tuimoala Lolohea; 31 Jackson Hastings; 8 Lee Mossop (C); 19 Logan Tomkins; 10 Gil Dudson; 12 George Griffin; 11 Josh Jones; 17 Tyrone McCarthy. Subs (all used): 13 Mark Flanagan; 14 Joey Lussick; 15 Adam Walker; 29 Ryan Lannon.
**Tries:** Griffin (38), Hastings (61); **Goals:** Inu 2/2.
**Rugby Leaguer & League Express Men of the Match:**
*Warriors:* Oliver Gildart; *Red Devils:* Jackson Hastings.
**Penalty count:** 5-7; **Half-time:** 6-6;
**Referee:** Robert Hicks; **Attendance:** 9,247.

## ELIMINATION SEMI-FINAL

*Thursday 26th September 2019*

**SALFORD RED DEVILS 22 CASTLEFORD TIGERS 0**

**RED DEVILS:** 1 Niall Evalds; 23 Ken Sio; 3 Kris Welham; 5 Jake Bibby; 26 Krisnan Inu; 30 Tuimoala Lolohea; 31 Jackson Hastings; 8 Lee Mossop (C); 19 Logan Tomkins; 10 Gil Dudson; 11 Josh Jones; 12 George Griffin; 17 Tyrone McCarthy. Subs (all used): 14 Joey Lussick; 13 Mark Flanagan; 15 Adam Walker; 16 Greg Burke.
**Tries:** McCarthy (11), Bibby (14), Hastings (72);
**Goals:** Inu 5/5.
**TIGERS:** 32 Jordan Rankin; 2 James Clare; 3 Greg Minikin; 35 Cheyse Blair; 5 Greg Eden; 6 Jake Trueman; 1 Peter Mata'utia; 8 Liam Watts; 9 Paul McShane (C); 10 Grant Millington; 11 Oliver Holmes; 33 Chris Clarkson; 34 Nathan Massey. Subs (all used): 13 Adam Milner; 18 Matt Cook; 29 Jacques O'Neill; 34 Daniel Smith.
**Rugby Leaguer & League Express Men of the Match:**
*Red Devils:* Josh Jones; *Tigers:* Oliver Holmes.
**Penalty count:** 8-4; **Half-time:** 14-0;
**Referee:** Ben Thaler; **Attendance:** 4,800.

## QUALIFYING SEMI-FINAL

*Friday 27th September 2019*

**ST HELENS 40 WIGAN WARRIORS 10**

**SAINTS:** 23 Lachlan Coote; 2 Tommy Makinson; 3 Kevin Naiqama; 4 Mark Percival; 5 Regan Grace; 1 Jonny Lomax; 6 Theo Fages; 8 Alex Walmsley; 9 James Roby (C); 10 Luke Thompson; 11 Zeb Taia; 17 Dominique Peyroux; 15 Morgan Knowles. Subs (all used): 13 Louie McCarthy-Scarsbrook; 16 Kyle Amor; 20 Jack Ashworth; 21 Aaron Smith.
**Tries:** Fages (4), Naiqama (10), Thompson (28), Lomax (34), Taia (46), Percival (60, 75); **Goals:** Coote 6/8.
**WARRIORS:** 20 Zak Hardaker; 17 Liam Marshall; 23 Chris Hankinson; 4 Oliver Gildart; 5 Joe Burgess; 6 George Williams; 7 Thomas Leuluai; 8 Tony Clubb; 9 Sam Powell; 24 Oliver Partington; 15 Willie Isa; 12 Liam Farrell; 13 Sean O'Loughlin (C). Subs (all used): 36 Liam Byrne; 10 Ben Flower; 41 Bevan French; 38 Morgan Smithies.
**Tries:** Marshall (19), French (79); **Goals:** Hardaker 1/2.
**Rugby Leaguer & League Express Men of the Match:**
*Saints:* Luke Thompson; *Warriors:* Zak Hardaker.
**Penalty count:** 4-4; **Half-time:** 26-6;
**Referee:** Chris Kendall; **Attendance:** 14,508.

## FINAL ELIMINATOR

*Friday 4th October 2019*

**WIGAN WARRIORS 4 SALFORD RED DEVILS 28**

**WARRIORS:** 20 Zak Hardaker; 17 Liam Marshall; 23 Chris Hankinson; 4 Oliver Gildart; 5 Joe Burgess; 6 George Williams; 7 Thomas Leuluai; 10 Ben Flower; 9 Sam Powell; 24 Oliver Partington; 15 Willie Isa; 12 Liam Farrell; 13 Sean O'Loughlin (C). Subs (all used): 8 Tony Clubb; 36 Liam Byrne; 38 Morgan Smithies; 43 Bevan French.
**Try:** French (72); **Goals:** Hardaker 0/1.
**RED DEVILS:** 1 Niall Evalds; 23 Ken Sio; 3 Kris Welham; 5 Jake Bibby; 26 Krisnan Inu; 30 Tuimoala Lolohea; 31 Jackson Hastings; 8 Lee Mossop (C); 19 Logan Tomkins; 10 Gil Dudson; 12 George Griffin; 11 Josh Jones; 17 Tyrone McCarthy. Subs (all used): 13 Mark Flanagan; 14 Joey Lussick; 15 Adam Walker; 16 Greg Burke.
**Tries:** Dudson (14), Lussick (45), Mossop (63);
**Goals:** Inu 8/8.
**Rugby Leaguer & League Express Men of the Match:**
*Warriors:* Bevan French; *Red Devils:* Gil Dudson.
**Penalty count:** 10-9; **Half-time:** 0-12;
**Referee:** Ben Thaler; **Attendance:** 9,858.

## GRAND FINAL

*Saturday 12th October 2019*

**SALFORD RED DEVILS 6 ST HELENS 23**

**RED DEVILS:** 1 Niall Evalds; 23 Ken Sio; 3 Kris Welham; 5 Jake Bibby; 26 Krisnan Inu; 30 Tuimoala Lolohea; 31 Jackson Hastings; 8 Lee Mossop (C); 19 Logan Tomkins; 10 Gil Dudson; 11 Josh Jones; 12 George Griffin; 17 Tyrone McCarthy. Subs (all used): 13 Mark Flanagan; 14 Joey Lussick; 15 Adam Walker; 16 Greg Burke.
**Try:** Bibby (32); **Goals:** Inu 1/1.
**SAINTS:** 23 Lachlan Coote; 2 Tommy Makinson; 3 Kevin Naiqama; 4 Mark Percival; 5 Regan Grace; 1 Jonny Lomax; 6 Theo Fages; 8 Alex Walmsley; 9 James Roby (C); 10 Luke Thompson; 11 Zeb Taia; 17 Dominique Peyroux; 15 Morgan Knowles. Subs (all used): 13 Louie McCarthy-Scarsbrook; 16 Kyle Amor; 20 Jack Ashworth; 21 Aaron Smith.
**Tries:** Knowles (16), Taia (24), Percival (50);
**Goals:** Coote 5/5; **Field goal:** Makinson (78).
**Rugby Leaguer & League Express Men of the Match:**
*Red Devils:* Josh Jones; *Saints:* Luke Thompson.
**Penalty count:** 5-6; **Half-time:** 6-12;
**Referee:** Chris Kendall; **Attendance:** 64,102
*(at Old Trafford, Manchester)*.

St Helens' Luke Thompson takes on Salford's Josh Jones during the Super League Grand Final

# SUPER LEAGUE XXIV
## *Opta Analysis*

### SUPER LEAGUE XXIV TOP PERFORMERS

#### TACKLES

| | | |
|---|---|---|
| Danny Houghton | Hull FC | 1259 |
| Luke Yates | London | 1211 |
| Willie Isa | Wigan | 971 |
| Sam Powell | Wigan | 948 |
| Alex Mellor | Huddersfield | 941 |
| Kyle Wood | Wakefield | 938 |
| Liam Watts | Castleford | 937 |
| Joey Lussick | Salford | 916 |
| Paul McShane | Castleford | 914 |
| Trent Merrin | Leeds | 902 |

#### DEFENDERS BEATEN

| | | |
|---|---|---|
| Josh Jones | Salford | 157 |
| Zak Hardaker | Wigan | 147 |
| David Fifita | Wakefield | 141 |
| Konrad Hurrell | Leeds | 138 |
| Mark Percival | St Helens | 137 |
| Jack Walker | Leeds | 130 |
| Daryl Clark | Warrington | 124 |
| Darnell McIntosh | Huddersfield | 122 |
| George Williams | Wigan | 122 |
| Jackson Hastings | Salford | 117 |

#### MISSED TACKLES

| | | |
|---|---|---|
| Robbie Mulhern | Hull KR | 113 |
| Matty Lees | St Helens | 106 |
| Jacob Miller | Wakefield | 106 |
| Brad Dwyer | Leeds | 101 |
| Weller Hauraki | Hull KR | 101 |
| Eddie Battye | London | 100 |
| Richie Myler | Leeds | 99 |
| Liam Watts | Castleford | 97 |
| Samisoni Langi | Catalans | 94 |
| Declan Patton | Warrington | 92 |

#### OFFLOADS

| | | |
|---|---|---|
| Liam Watts | Castleford | 62 |
| Trent Merrin | Leeds | 60 |
| Josh Jones | Salford | 58 |
| Adam Cuthbertson | Leeds | 52 |
| Mike Cooper | Warrington | 50 |
| Julian Bousquet | Catalans | 46 |
| George Williams | Wigan | 46 |
| Peter Mata'utia | Castleford | 41 |
| Krisnan Inu | Salford | 38 |
| Carlos Tuimavave | Hull FC | 38 |

#### TRY PASS

| | | |
|---|---|---|
| Jackson Hastings | Salford | 31 |
| Lachlan Coote | St Helens | 21 |
| Jonny Lomax | St Helens | 19 |
| Daryl Clark | Warrington | 18 |
| Theo Fages | St Helens | 18 |
| Sam Tomkins | Catalans | 16 |
| Lee Gaskell | Huddersfield | 15 |
| Paul McShane | Castleford | 15 |
| George Williams | Wigan | 15 |
| Marc Sneyd | Hull FC | 13 |

#### KICKS IN GENERAL PLAY

| | | |
|---|---|---|
| Jordan Abdull | London | 287 |
| Marc Sneyd | Hull FC | 278 |
| Josh Drinkwater | Hull KR | 250 |
| Jake Trueman | Castleford | 250 |
| Danny Brough | Wakefield | 248 |
| Blake Austin | Warrington | 207 |
| Jackson Hastings | Salford | 205 |
| Lee Gaskell | Huddersfield | 188 |
| Tony Gigot | Catalans | 172 |
| George Williams | Wigan | 170 |

#### CARRIES

| | | |
|---|---|---|
| Jackson Hastings | Salford | 563 |
| Rhys Williams | London | 467 |
| Josh Jones | Salford | 461 |
| Eddie Battye | London | 460 |
| Tommy Makinson | St Helens | 453 |
| Liam Watts | Castleford | 452 |
| Zak Hardaker | Wigan | 414 |
| Ryan Hampshire | Wakefield | 410 |
| Trent Merrin | Leeds | 408 |
| George Williams | Wigan | 408 |

#### ERRORS

| | | |
|---|---|---|
| Darnell McIntosh | Huddersfield | 49 |
| Konrad Hurrell | Leeds | 39 |
| George Williams | Wigan | 39 |
| Kris Welham | Salford | 38 |
| Blake Austin | Warrington | 37 |
| Joe Burgess | Wigan | 36 |
| Alex Walker | London | 36 |
| Lachlan Coote | St Helens | 35 |
| Jermaine McGillvary | Huddersfield | 35 |
| Kieran Dixon | London | 34 |

#### PENALTIES CONCEDED

| | | |
|---|---|---|
| Eddie Battye | London | 34 |
| Joey Lussick | Salford | 25 |
| Declan Patton | Warrington | 24 |
| Weller Hauraki | Hull KR | 23 |
| David Fifita | Wakefield | 22 |
| Jackson Hastings | Salford | 22 |
| Alex Mellor | Huddersfield | 22 |
| Trent Merrin | Leeds | 22 |
| Joel Tomkins | Hull KR | 22 |
| Liam Watts | Castleford | 22 |

#### CLEAN BREAKS

| | | |
|---|---|---|
| Tommy Makinson | St Helens | 36 |
| Josh Charnley | Warrington | 35 |
| Regan Grace | St Helens | 32 |
| James Clare | Castleford | 31 |
| Ash Handley | Leeds | 31 |
| Jermaine McGillvary | Huddersfield | 31 |
| Rhys Williams | London | 30 |
| Blake Austin | Warrington | 29 |
| Craig Hall | Hull KR | 29 |
| Joe Burgess | Wigan | 28 |

#### METRES

| | | |
|---|---|---|
| Tommy Makinson | St Helens | 3803 |
| Jackson Hastings | Salford | 3763 |
| Rhys Williams | London | 3616 |
| Josh Jones | Salford | 3383 |
| Oliver Gildart | Wigan | 3375 |
| Reece Lyne | Wakefield | 3274 |
| Ash Handley | Leeds | 3248 |
| Kieran Dixon | London | 3171 |
| Liam Watts | Castleford | 3160 |
| Jermaine McGillvary | Huddersfield | 3156 |

#### QUICK PLAY-THE-BALLS

| | | |
|---|---|---|
| Josh Jones | Salford | 77 |
| Elliot Kear | London | 76 |
| Carlos Tuimavave | Hull FC | 75 |
| James Clare | Castleford | 71 |
| Tom Briscoe | Leeds | 70 |
| Konrad Hurrell | Leeds | 67 |
| Peter Mata'utia | Castleford | 66 |
| Ben Crooks | Hull KR | 64 |
| Greg Minikin | Castleford | 61 |
| Reece Lyne | Wakefield | 59 |

*All statistics in Opta Analysis include Super League regular season only*

## SUPER LEAGUE XXIV TRIES SCORED/CONCEDED

### TOTAL TRIES SCORED

| | |
|---|---|
| St Helens | 150 |
| Salford Red Devils | 131 |
| Warrington Wolves | 112 |
| Leeds Rhinos | 108 |
| Wigan Warriors | 107 |
| Hull FC | 104 |
| Castleford Tigers | 103 |
| Wakefield Trinity | 96 |
| Huddersfield Giants | 94 |
| Catalans Dragons | 87 |
| Hull Kingston Rovers | 85 |
| London Broncos | 82 |

### TOTAL TRIES CONCEDED

| | |
|---|---|
| London Broncos | 141 |
| Hull FC | 135 |
| Hull Kingston Rovers | 135 |
| Huddersfield Giants | 128 |
| Wakefield Trinity | 127 |
| Catalans Dragons | 125 |
| Leeds Rhinos | 109 |
| Salford Red Devils | 102 |
| Castleford Tigers | 97 |
| Warrington Wolves | 87 |
| Wigan Warriors | 87 |
| St Helens | 67 |

Wigan's Liam Marshall dives past Hull Kingston Rovers' Matt Parcell to score. The Warriors scored more tries from their own half than any other team in Super League XXIV

### TRIES CONCEDED FROM OVER 50M

| | |
|---|---|
| Hull Kingston Rovers | 23 |
| London Broncos | 19 |
| Catalans Dragons | 18 |
| Wakefield Trinity | 17 |
| Hull FC | 15 |
| Salford Red Devils | 15 |
| Huddersfield Giants | 12 |
| Wigan Warriors | 11 |
| Castleford Tigers | 10 |
| Leeds Rhinos | 10 |
| Warrington Wolves | 9 |
| St Helens | 6 |

### TRIES SCORED FROM UNDER 10M

| | |
|---|---|
| Salford Red Devils | 67 |
| St Helens | 66 |
| Castleford Tigers | 57 |
| Warrington Wolves | 56 |
| Huddersfield Giants | 51 |
| Hull FC | 51 |
| Hull Kingston Rovers | 51 |
| Wigan Warriors | 48 |
| Wakefield Trinity | 46 |
| Leeds Rhinos | 45 |
| London Broncos | 44 |
| Catalans Dragons | 42 |

### SCORED FROM KICKS

| | |
|---|---|
| Hull Kingston Rovers | 19 |
| Salford Red Devils | 19 |
| Wigan Warriors | 16 |
| Wakefield Trinity | 14 |
| Castleford Tigers | 13 |
| Huddersfield Giants | 13 |
| London Broncos | 13 |
| Hull FC | 12 |
| St Helens | 12 |
| Catalans Dragons | 11 |
| Leeds Rhinos | 11 |
| Warrington Wolves | 9 |

### CONCEDED FROM KICKS

| | |
|---|---|
| Salford Red Devils | 21 |
| Catalans Dragons | 20 |
| Huddersfield Giants | 19 |
| Hull FC | 16 |
| Hull Kingston Rovers | 15 |
| Wakefield Trinity | 15 |
| London Broncos | 11 |
| Wigan Warriors | 11 |
| Leeds Rhinos | 10 |
| Castleford Tigers | 8 |
| St Helens | 8 |
| Warrington Wolves | 8 |

### TRIES SCORED FROM OWN HALF

| | |
|---|---|
| Wigan Warriors | 21 |
| Hull FC | 19 |
| Leeds Rhinos | 18 |
| Wakefield Trinity | 18 |
| Castleford Tigers | 13 |
| Catalans Dragons | 12 |
| St Helens | 12 |
| Salford Red Devils | 11 |
| Warrington Wolves | 11 |
| London Broncos | 10 |
| Huddersfield Giants | 5 |
| Hull Kingston Rovers | 8 |

### TRIES CONCEDED FROM UNDER 10M

| | |
|---|---|
| Hull FC | 74 |
| Huddersfield Giants | 71 |
| London Broncos | 69 |
| Leeds Rhinos | 61 |
| Wakefield Trinity | 61 |
| Hull Kingston Rovers | 59 |
| Salford Red Devils | 54 |
| Catalans Dragons | 47 |
| Warrington Wolves | 43 |
| Castleford Tigers | 42 |
| Wigan Warriors | 42 |
| St Helens | 39 |

## SUPER LEAGUE XXIV AVERAGES PER MATCH

### TACKLES

| | |
|---|---|
| Wigan Warriors | 342.4 |
| Huddersfield Giants | 341.1 |
| London Broncos | 340.2 |
| Leeds Rhinos | 335.4 |
| Catalans Dragons | 329.7 |
| Salford Red Devils | 322.1 |
| Hull Kingston Rovers | 319.1 |
| Hull FC | 319.0 |
| St Helens | 317.2 |
| Castleford Tigers | 316.1 |
| Wakefield Trinity | 307.9 |
| Warrington Wolves | 306.5 |

### CLEAN BREAKS

| | |
|---|---|
| St Helens | 9.0 |
| Leeds Rhinos | 7.3 |
| Warrington Wolves | 7.1 |
| Hull FC | 6.3 |
| Castleford Tigers | 6.2 |
| Catalans Dragons | 6.1 |
| Wigan Warriors | 6.1 |
| Salford Red Devils | 5.9 |
| Wakefield Trinity | 5.8 |
| Hull Kingston Rovers | 5.5 |
| Huddersfield Giants | 5.0 |
| London Broncos | 5.0 |

### OFFLOADS

| | |
|---|---|
| Leeds Rhinos | 13.3 |
| Warrington Wolves | 11.7 |
| Castleford Tigers | 11.6 |
| St Helens | 11.3 |
| Salford Red Devils | 11.1 |
| Catalans Dragons | 10.9 |
| Wakefield Trinity | 9.9 |
| Hull FC | 9.8 |
| Hull Kingston Rovers | 9.0 |
| Wigan Warriors | 8.1 |
| London Broncos | 7.7 |
| Huddersfield Giants | 6.8 |

### KICKS IN GENERAL PLAY

| | |
|---|---|
| Castleford Tigers | 19.8 |
| London Broncos | 19.3 |
| Salford Red Devils | 19.0 |
| Wigan Warriors | 18.9 |
| Huddersfield Giants | 18.6 |
| Hull Kingston Rovers | 18.6 |
| Wakefield Trinity | 17.6 |
| Catalans Dragons | 17.2 |
| Warrington Wolves | 16.9 |
| Hull FC | 16.4 |
| Leeds Rhinos | 16.3 |
| St Helens | 15.6 |

### MISSED TACKLES

| | |
|---|---|
| Hull Kingston Rovers | 41.4 |
| Catalans Dragons | 40.0 |
| London Broncos | 37.7 |
| Hull FC | 36.5 |
| Leeds Rhinos | 35.4 |
| St Helens | 35.2 |
| Wakefield Trinity | 34.9 |
| Castleford Tigers | 34.5 |
| Huddersfield Giants | 32.2 |
| Salford Red Devils | 32.1 |
| Warrington Wolves | 30.4 |
| Wigan Warriors | 28.8 |

### DEFENDERS BEATEN

| | |
|---|---|
| St Helens | 43.8 |
| Leeds Rhinos | 42.1 |
| Hull FC | 37.0 |
| Warrington Wolves | 36.6 |
| Salford Red Devils | 35.7 |
| Wakefield Trinity | 35.7 |
| Wigan Warriors | 34.8 |
| Castleford Tigers | 34.5 |
| London Broncos | 31.1 |
| Catalans Dragons | 30.0 |
| Huddersfield Giants | 29.9 |
| Hull Kingston Rovers | 28.1 |

### ERRORS

| | |
|---|---|
| St Helens | 12.4 |
| Warrington Wolves | 12.0 |
| Hull FC | 11.9 |
| Leeds Rhinos | 11.9 |
| Catalans Dragons | 11.3 |
| Wigan Warriors | 11.0 |
| Castleford Tigers | 10.9 |
| Huddersfield Giants | 10.7 |
| Hull Kingston Rovers | 10.6 |
| Wakefield Trinity | 10.4 |
| London Broncos | 10.1 |
| Salford Red Devils | 9.7 |

### PASSES

| | |
|---|---|
| St Helens | 227.2 |
| Castleford Tigers | 217.6 |
| Wigan Warriors | 217.3 |
| Wakefield Trinity | 214.5 |
| Salford Red Devils | 213.9 |
| Catalans Dragons | 211.2 |
| Huddersfield Giants | 203.5 |
| Hull Kingston Rovers | 202.0 |
| London Broncos | 200.8 |
| Leeds Rhinos | 199.5 |
| Warrington Wolves | 198.7 |
| Hull FC | 196.7 |

## SUPER LEAGUE XXIV PENALTIES

**TOTAL PENALTIES AWARDED**

| | |
|---|---|
| Wakefield Trinity | 234 |
| Castleford Tigers | 226 |
| Leeds Rhinos | 224 |
| Warrington Wolves | 224 |
| Hull FC | 223 |
| Hull Kingston Rovers | 222 |
| Catalans Dragons | 219 |
| St Helens | 211 |
| Wigan Warriors | 205 |
| Huddersfield Giants | 200 |
| London Broncos | 197 |
| Salford Red Devils | 195 |

**TOTAL PENALTIES CONCEDED**

| | |
|---|---|
| Catalans Dragons | 235 |
| Salford Red Devils | 229 |
| Hull Kingston Rovers | 228 |
| Warrington Wolves | 225 |
| Huddersfield Giants | 224 |
| Wakefield Trinity | 224 |
| Leeds Rhinos | 223 |
| Wigan Warriors | 213 |
| Castleford Tigers | 204 |
| St Helens | 198 |
| London Broncos | 193 |
| Hull FC | 184 |

**FOUL PLAY - AWARDED**

| | |
|---|---|
| Hull Kingston Rovers | 59 |
| Huddersfield Giants | 50 |
| Catalans Dragons | 49 |
| Warrington Wolves | 45 |
| London Broncos | 44 |
| Wakefield Trinity | 43 |
| Wigan Warriors | 43 |
| St Helens | 42 |
| Hull FC | 35 |
| Leeds Rhinos | 35 |
| Castleford Tigers | 34 |
| Salford Red Devils | 34 |

**FOUL PLAY - CONCEDED**

| | |
|---|---|
| Catalans Dragons | 53 |
| Warrington Wolves | 52 |
| Salford Red Devils | 50 |
| Wigan Warriors | 48 |
| Hull Kingston Rovers | 45 |
| Wakefield Trinity | 45 |
| Castleford Tigers | 41 |
| Huddersfield Giants | 41 |
| Hull FC | 38 |
| Leeds Rhinos | 37 |
| London Broncos | 33 |
| St Helens | 30 |

**OFFSIDE - AWARDED**

| | |
|---|---|
| Wakefield Trinity | 22 |
| Leeds Rhinos | 18 |
| Huddersfield Giants | 17 |
| Hull FC | 17 |
| Warrington Wolves | 14 |
| Hull Kingston Rovers | 12 |
| Salford Red Devils | 12 |
| St Helens | 12 |
| Castleford Tigers | 11 |
| Catalans Dragons | 11 |
| London Broncos | 11 |
| Wigan Warriors | 10 |

**OFFSIDE - CONCEDED**

| | |
|---|---|
| Salford Red Devils | 27 |
| Wigan Warriors | 22 |
| Hull Kingston Rovers | 19 |
| Huddersfield Giants | 17 |
| Warrington Wolves | 16 |
| Wakefield Trinity | 15 |
| Catalans Dragons | 12 |
| St Helens | 12 |
| London Broncos | 9 |
| Leeds Rhinos | 8 |
| Hull FC | 6 |
| Castleford Tigers | 4 |

**INTERFERENCE - AWARDED**

| | |
|---|---|
| Hull FC | 105 |
| St Helens | 102 |
| Leeds Rhinos | 100 |
| Warrington Wolves | 100 |
| Wigan Warriors | 98 |
| Wakefield Trinity | 95 |
| Catalans Dragons | 93 |
| Salford Red Devils | 90 |
| Castleford Tigers | 89 |
| Hull Kingston Rovers | 78 |
| London Broncos | 76 |
| Huddersfield Giants | 72 |

**INTERFERENCE - CONCEDED**

| | |
|---|---|
| Huddersfield Giants | 103 |
| Catalans Dragons | 102 |
| Hull Kingston Rovers | 99 |
| Wakefield Trinity | 98 |
| London Broncos | 95 |
| Wigan Warriors | 93 |
| St Helens | 91 |
| Leeds Rhinos | 89 |
| Castleford Tigers | 83 |
| Salford Red Devils | 83 |
| Hull FC | 82 |
| Warrington Wolves | 80 |

**OBSTRUCTION - AWARDED**

| | |
|---|---|
| Wakefield Trinity | 23 |
| Castleford Tigers | 21 |
| London Broncos | 19 |
| Hull FC | 16 |
| Salford Red Devils | 16 |
| Leeds Rhinos | 15 |
| Hull Kingston Rovers | 13 |
| Warrington Wolves | 13 |
| Catalans Dragons | 12 |
| Wigan Warriors | 10 |
| Huddersfield Giants | 9 |
| St Helens | 4 |

**OBSTRUCTION - CONCEDED**

| | |
|---|---|
| St Helens | 23 |
| Leeds Rhinos | 20 |
| Huddersfield Giants | 17 |
| Salford Red Devils | 16 |
| Hull FC | 15 |
| Catalans Dragons | 14 |
| Castleford Tigers | 12 |
| Wakefield Trinity | 12 |
| Warrington Wolves | 12 |
| Wigan Warriors | 12 |
| Hull Kingston Rovers | 9 |
| London Broncos | 9 |

**BALL STEALING - AWARDED**

| | |
|---|---|
| Castleford Tigers | 27 |
| Leeds Rhinos | 26 |
| Wakefield Trinity | 26 |
| St Helens | 22 |
| Hull Kingston Rovers | 21 |
| Salford Red Devils | 20 |
| Hull FC | 18 |
| Huddersfield Giants | 17 |
| Warrington Wolves | 17 |
| Catalans Dragons | 16 |
| London Broncos | 15 |
| Wigan Warriors | 11 |

**BALL STEALING - CONCEDED**

| | |
|---|---|
| Warrington Wolves | 37 |
| Castleford Tigers | 33 |
| Hull Kingston Rovers | 24 |
| Leeds Rhinos | 21 |
| London Broncos | 18 |
| Salford Red Devils | 18 |
| Wakefield Trinity | 18 |
| Huddersfield Giants | 16 |
| Catalans Dragons | 15 |
| Hull FC | 14 |
| Wigan Warriors | 13 |
| St Helens | 9 |

**OFFSIDE MARKERS - AWARDED**

| | |
|---|---|
| Huddersfield Giants | 14 |
| Warrington Wolves | 13 |
| Catalans Dragons | 11 |
| Castleford Tigers | 10 |
| Hull Kingston Rovers | 10 |
| London Broncos | 9 |
| St Helens | 9 |
| Wigan Warriors | 9 |
| Salford Red Devils | 7 |
| Hull FC | 6 |
| Leeds Rhinos | 6 |
| Wakefield Trinity | 3 |

**OFFSIDE MARKERS - CONCEDED**

| | |
|---|---|
| Catalans Dragons | 14 |
| Leeds Rhinos | 14 |
| Castleford Tigers | 11 |
| Hull Kingston Rovers | 11 |
| London Broncos | 10 |
| Warrington Wolves | 9 |
| Hull FC | 8 |
| Wigan Warriors | 8 |
| Huddersfield Giants | 7 |
| Wakefield Trinity | 6 |
| St Helens | 5 |
| Salford Red Devils | 4 |

**OFFSIDE FROM KICK - AWARDED**

| | |
|---|---|
| London Broncos | 12 |
| Salford Red Devils | 11 |
| Castleford Tigers | 10 |
| Huddersfield Giants | 10 |
| Leeds Rhinos | 9 |
| Wigan Warriors | 9 |
| Hull FC | 8 |
| Hull Kingston Rovers | 6 |
| St Helens | 5 |
| Wakefield Trinity | 5 |
| Catalans Dragons | 4 |
| Warrington Wolves | 4 |

**OFFSIDE FROM KICK - CONCEDED**

| | |
|---|---|
| Wakefield Trinity | 13 |
| Hull Kingston Rovers | 12 |
| Huddersfield Giants | 11 |
| Leeds Rhinos | 11 |
| Salford Red Devils | 11 |
| Hull FC | 6 |
| Wigan Warriors | 6 |
| Castleford Tigers | 5 |
| Catalans Dragons | 5 |
| London Broncos | 5 |
| St Helens | 5 |
| Warrington Wolves | 3 |

**DISSENT - AWARDED**

| | |
|---|---|
| Castleford Tigers | 7 |
| St Helens | 7 |
| Hull Kingston Rovers | 5 |
| Catalans Dragons | 4 |
| Wakefield Trinity | 4 |
| Warrington Wolves | 4 |
| Huddersfield Giants | 3 |
| Leeds Rhinos | 3 |
| Wigan Warriors | 3 |
| Hull FC | 1 |
| London Broncos | 1 |
| Salford Red Devils | 0 |

**DISSENT - CONCEDED**

| | |
|---|---|
| Catalans Dragons | 6 |
| Hull FC | 6 |
| Salford Red Devils | 5 |
| Wigan Warriors | 5 |
| Leeds Rhinos | 4 |
| Castleford Tigers | 3 |
| Hull Kingston Rovers | 3 |
| St Helens | 3 |
| Wakefield Trinity | 3 |
| Warrington Wolves | 3 |
| London Broncos | 1 |
| Huddersfield Giants | 0 |

## CASTLEFORD TIGERS
### *SUPER LEAGUE XXIV LEADERS*

**CARRIES**

| | |
|---|---|
| Liam Watts | 452 |
| Peter Mata'utia | 403 |
| James Clare | 385 |
| Greg Minikin | 321 |
| Jesse Sene-Lefao | 317 |

**OFFLOADS**

| | |
|---|---|
| Liam Watts | 62 |
| Peter Mata'utia | 41 |
| Jesse Sene-Lefao | 30 |
| Grant Millington | 27 |
| Mike McMeeken | 26 |

**METRES**

| | |
|---|---|
| Liam Watts | 3160 |
| James Clare | 2923 |
| Peter Mata'utia | 2758 |
| Greg Minikin | 2668 |
| Jesse Sene-Lefao | 2267 |

**TACKLES**

| | |
|---|---|
| Liam Watts | 937 |
| Paul McShane | 914 |
| Adam Milner | 656 |
| Mike McMeeken | 640 |
| Nathan Massey | 628 |

**CLEAN BREAKS**

| | |
|---|---|
| James Clare | 31 |
| Greg Eden | 22 |
| Greg Minikin | 19 |
| Jake Trueman | 16 |
| Jordan Rankin | 13 |

**DEFENDERS BEATEN**

| | |
|---|---|
| Peter Mata'utia | 94 |
| Jordan Rankin | 90 |
| Greg Minikin | 84 |
| Jake Trueman | 69 |
| Greg Eden | 64 |

**MARKER TACKLES**

| | |
|---|---|
| Paul McShane | 184 |
| Liam Watts | 183 |
| Nathan Massey | 119 |
| Mike McMeeken | 113 |
| Adam Milner | 111 |

**TRY ASSISTS**

| | |
|---|---|
| Paul McShane | 19 |
| Peter Mata'utia | 16 |
| Jake Trueman | 13 |
| Jordan Rankin | 12 |
| Michael Shenton | 5 |

**TOTAL OPTA INDEX**

| | |
|---|---|
| Liam Watts | 13584 |
| Jake Trueman | 13555 |
| Peter Mata'utia | 12968 |
| Jordan Rankin | 11590 |
| Paul McShane | 10878 |

## CATALANS DRAGONS
### *SUPER LEAGUE XXIV LEADERS*

**CARRIES**

| | |
|---|---|
| Samisoni Langi | 383 |
| Brayden Wiliame | 315 |
| Julian Bousquet | 302 |
| Tony Gigot | 262 |
| Lewis Tierney | 257 |

**OFFLOADS**

| | |
|---|---|
| Julian Bousquet | 46 |
| Tony Gigot | 33 |
| Sam Kasiano | 33 |
| Kenny Edwards | 21 |
| Matt Whitley | 20 |

**METRES**

| | |
|---|---|
| Samisoni Langi | 2769 |
| Brayden Wiliame | 2594 |
| Julian Bousquet | 2308 |
| Lewis Tierney | 1937 |
| Tony Gigot | 1698 |

**TACKLES**

| | |
|---|---|
| Remi Casty | 732 |
| Matt Whitley | 723 |
| Julian Bousquet | 673 |
| Alrix Da Costa | 618 |
| Jason Baitieri | 608 |

**CLEAN BREAKS**

| | |
|---|---|
| Brayden Wiliame | 24 |
| Lewis Tierney | 18 |
| Tony Gigot | 17 |
| David Mead | 16 |
| Arthur Romano | 14 |

**DEFENDERS BEATEN**

| | |
|---|---|
| Brayden Wiliame | 84 |
| Kenny Edwards | 81 |
| Sam Tomkins | 72 |
| Tony Gigot | 65 |
| Samisoni Langi | 55 |

**MARKER TACKLES**

| | |
|---|---|
| Matt Whitley | 144 |
| Jason Baitieri | 139 |
| Remi Casty | 138 |
| Alrix Da Costa | 124 |
| Mickael Goudemand | 110 |

**TRY ASSISTS**

| | |
|---|---|
| Sam Tomkins | 18 |
| Tony Gigot | 13 |
| Samisoni Langi | 9 |
| Brayden Wiliame | 7 |
| Michael McIlorum | 5 |

**TOTAL OPTA INDEX**

| | |
|---|---|
| Tony Gigot | 11232 |
| Matt Whitley | 10359 |
| Sam Tomkins | 10212 |
| Remi Casty | 10181 |
| Julian Bousquet | 9597 |

## HUDDERSFIELD GIANTS
### *SUPER LEAGUE XXIV LEADERS*

**CARRIES**

| | |
|---|---|
| Jermaine McGillvary | 383 |
| Darnell McIntosh | 380 |
| Michael Lawrence | 310 |
| Suaia Matagi | 307 |
| Ukuma Ta'ai | 298 |

**OFFLOADS**

| | |
|---|---|
| Darnell McIntosh | 26 |
| Jermaine McGillvary | 22 |
| Lee Gaskell | 18 |
| Sebastine Ikahihifo | 17 |
| Ukuma Ta'ai | 13 |

**METRES**

| | |
|---|---|
| Jermaine McGillvary | 3156 |
| Darnell McIntosh | 2834 |
| Ukuma Ta'ai | 2163 |
| Suaia Matagi | 2083 |
| Michael Lawrence | 2003 |

**TACKLES**

| | |
|---|---|
| Alex Mellor | 941 |
| Michael Lawrence | 865 |
| Kruise Leeming | 832 |
| Ukuma Ta'ai | 745 |
| Suaia Matagi | 687 |

**CLEAN BREAKS**

| | |
|---|---|
| Jermaine McGillvary | 31 |
| Darnell McIntosh | 22 |
| Lee Gaskell | 14 |
| Louis Senior | 10 |
| Jake Wardle | 8 |

**DEFENDERS BEATEN**

| | |
|---|---|
| Darnell McIntosh | 122 |
| Jermaine McGillvary | 114 |
| Ukuma Ta'ai | 67 |
| Sebastine Ikahihifo | 66 |
| Lee Gaskell | 63 |

**MARKER TACKLES**

| | |
|---|---|
| Alex Mellor | 176 |
| Kruise Leeming | 167 |
| Michael Lawrence | 166 |
| Adam O'Brien | 150 |
| Ukuma Ta'ai | 120 |

**TRY ASSISTS**

| | |
|---|---|
| Lee Gaskell | 18 |
| Darnell McIntosh | 13 |
| Kruise Leeming | 11 |
| Matt Frawley | 6 |
| Adam O'Brien | 6 |

**TOTAL OPTA INDEX**

| | |
|---|---|
| Darnell McIntosh | 13051 |
| Jermaine McGillvary | 12274 |
| Ukuma Ta'ai | 11861 |
| Alex Mellor | 11648 |
| Kruise Leeming | 11602 |

## HULL F.C.
### SUPER LEAGUE XXIV LEADERS

## HULL KINGSTON ROVERS
### SUPER LEAGUE XXIV LEADERS

## LEEDS RHINOS
### SUPER LEAGUE XXIV LEADERS

### CARRIES

| | HULL F.C. | | HULL KINGSTON ROVERS | | LEEDS RHINOS |
|---|---|---|---|---|---|
| Josh Griffin | 369 | Craig Hall | 321 | Trent Merrin | 408 |
| Bureta Faraimo | 350 | Mitch Garbutt | 317 | Ash Handley | 398 |
| Carlos Tuimavave | 302 | Robbie Mulhern | 311 | Konrad Hurrell | 337 |
| Mark Minichiello | 290 | Ben Crooks | 302 | Jack Walker | 321 |
| Scott Taylor | 280 | George Lawler | 302 | Tom Briscoe | 309 |

### OFFLOADS

| | HULL F.C. | | HULL KINGSTON ROVERS | | LEEDS RHINOS |
|---|---|---|---|---|---|
| Carlos Tuimavave | 38 | Danny McGuire | 27 | Trent Merrin | 60 |
| Joe Westerman | 32 | Joel Tomkins | 27 | Adam Cuthbertson | 52 |
| Bureta Faraimo | 30 | Kane Linnett | 26 | Brad Dwyer | 31 |
| Jake Connor | 26 | Craig Hall | 22 | Konrad Hurrell | 26 |
| Albert Kelly | 20 | Ben Crooks | 18 | Ash Handley | 22 |

### METRES

| | HULL F.C. | | HULL KINGSTON ROVERS | | LEEDS RHINOS |
|---|---|---|---|---|---|
| Josh Griffin | 3021 | Craig Hall | 2523 | Ash Handley | 3248 |
| Bureta Faraimo | 2778 | Mitch Garbutt | 2513 | Konrad Hurrell | 2925 |
| Scott Taylor | 2275 | Kane Linnett | 2197 | Trent Merrin | 2917 |
| Carlos Tuimavave | 2214 | Ben Crooks | 2147 | Jack Walker | 2654 |
| Mark Minichiello | 2011 | George Lawler | 2016 | Tom Briscoe | 2322 |

### TACKLES

| | HULL F.C. | | HULL KINGSTON ROVERS | | LEEDS RHINOS |
|---|---|---|---|---|---|
| Danny Houghton | 1259 | George Lawler | 833 | Trent Merrin | 902 |
| Joe Westerman | 669 | Robbie Mulhern | 816 | Brad Dwyer | 800 |
| Scott Taylor | 617 | Weller Hauraki | 735 | Liam Sutcliffe | 641 |
| Sika Manu | 536 | Joel Tomkins | 655 | Brad Singleton | 587 |
| Mark Minichiello | 529 | Mose Masoe | 547 | Adam Cuthbertson | 544 |

### CLEAN BREAKS

| | HULL F.C. | | HULL KINGSTON ROVERS | | LEEDS RHINOS |
|---|---|---|---|---|---|
| Ratu Naulago | 25 | Craig Hall | 29 | Ash Handley | 31 |
| Bureta Faraimo | 23 | Ryan Shaw | 15 | Tom Briscoe | 21 |
| Josh Griffin | 17 | Ben Crooks | 13 | Konrad Hurrell | 20 |
| Albert Kelly | 16 | Jimmy Keinhorst | 11 | Brad Dwyer | 16 |
| Carlos Tuimavave | 14 | Danny McGuire | 11 | Jack Walker | 16 |

### DEFENDERS BEATEN

| | HULL F.C. | | HULL KINGSTON ROVERS | | LEEDS RHINOS |
|---|---|---|---|---|---|
| Bureta Faraimo | 112 | Ben Crooks | 82 | Konrad Hurrell | 138 |
| Jamie Shaul | 95 | Craig Hall | 71 | Jack Walker | 130 |
| Carlos Tuimavave | 84 | Weller Hauraki | 60 | Tom Briscoe | 98 |
| Josh Griffin | 80 | Jimmy Keinhorst | 50 | Harry Newman | 93 |
| Albert Kelly | 72 | Danny McGuire | 49 | Ash Handley | 91 |

### MARKER TACKLES

| | HULL F.C. | | HULL KINGSTON ROVERS | | LEEDS RHINOS |
|---|---|---|---|---|---|
| Danny Houghton | 249 | Robbie Mulhern | 164 | Brad Dwyer | 148 |
| Joe Westerman | 102 | George Lawler | 119 | Trent Merrin | 142 |
| Sika Manu | 95 | Weller Hauraki | 104 | Brad Singleton | 115 |
| Scott Taylor | 95 | Joel Tomkins | 99 | Liam Sutcliffe | 109 |
| Dean Hadley | 72 | Mose Masoe | 98 | Adam Cuthbertson | 97 |

### TRY ASSISTS

| | HULL F.C. | | HULL KINGSTON ROVERS | | LEEDS RHINOS |
|---|---|---|---|---|---|
| Marc Sneyd | 21 | Josh Drinkwater | 18 | Brad Dwyer | 16 |
| Jake Connor | 15 | Danny McGuire | 13 | Tuimoala Lolohea | 11 |
| Danny Houghton | 12 | Craig Hall | 9 | Richie Myler | 11 |
| Albert Kelly | 11 | Chris Atkin | 6 | Konrad Hurrell | 7 |
| Carlos Tuimavave | 6 | Tommy Lee | 5 | Jack Walker | 7 |

### TOTAL OPTA INDEX

| | HULL F.C. | | HULL KINGSTON ROVERS | | LEEDS RHINOS |
|---|---|---|---|---|---|
| Danny Houghton | 14077 | George Lawler | 10394 | Trent Merrin | 14231 |
| Josh Griffin | 11095 | Weller Hauraki | 9579 | Ash Handley | 12992 |
| Bureta Faraimo | 10780 | Craig Hall | 9564 | Jack Walker | 11869 |
| Joe Westerman | 10711 | Mitch Garbutt | 9546 | Konrad Hurrell | 11628 |
| Scott Taylor | 10097 | Ben Crooks | 9525 | Brad Dwyer | 11083 |

| LONDON BRONCOS SUPER LEAGUE XXIV LEADERS | SALFORD RED DEVILS SUPER LEAGUE XXIV LEADERS | ST HELENS SUPER LEAGUE XXIV LEADERS |
|---|---|---|

### CARRIES

| LONDON BRONCOS | | SALFORD RED DEVILS | | ST HELENS | |
|---|---|---|---|---|---|
| Rhys Williams | 467 | Jackson Hastings | 563 | Tommy Makinson | 453 |
| Eddie Battye | 460 | Josh Jones | 461 | Alex Walmsley | 339 |
| Elliot Kear | 383 | Derrell Olpherts | 358 | Regan Grace | 332 |
| Alex Walker | 369 | Kris Welham | 335 | Luke Thompson | 327 |
| Kieran Dixon | 346 | Niall Evalds | 314 | Zeb Taia | 326 |

### OFFLOADS

| | | | | | |
|---|---|---|---|---|---|
| Eddie Battye | 35 | Josh Jones | 58 | Zeb Taia | 30 |
| Elliot Kear | 35 | Krisnan Inu | 38 | Alex Walmsley | 30 |
| Alex Walker | 25 | Jackson Hastings | 23 | Tommy Makinson | 29 |
| Jay Pitts | 22 | Derrell Olpherts | 20 | Kyle Amor | 25 |
| Rhys Williams | 15 | Adam Walker | 20 | Mark Percival | 22 |

### METRES

| | | | | | |
|---|---|---|---|---|---|
| Rhys Williams | 3616 | Jackson Hastings | 3763 | Tommy Makinson | 3803 |
| Kieran Dixon | 3171 | Josh Jones | 3383 | Alex Walmsley | 2728 |
| Elliot Kear | 2675 | Derrell Olpherts | 2583 | Regan Grace | 2646 |
| Eddie Battye | 2504 | Niall Evalds | 2513 | Luke Thompson | 2578 |
| Alex Walker | 1962 | Kris Welham | 2423 | Zeb Taia | 2349 |

### TACKLES

| | | | | | |
|---|---|---|---|---|---|
| Luke Yates | 1211 | Joey Lussick | 916 | Morgan Knowles | 813 |
| Eddie Battye | 851 | Gil Dudson | 725 | James Roby | 655 |
| Jay Pitts | 755 | Josh Jones | 702 | Dominique Peyroux | 645 |
| Matty Gee | 649 | Greg Burke | 681 | Matty Lees | 635 |
| James Cunningham | 628 | George Griffin | 681 | Luke Thompson | 586 |

### CLEAN BREAKS

| | | | | | |
|---|---|---|---|---|---|
| Rhys Williams | 30 | Niall Evalds | 22 | Tommy Makinson | 36 |
| Kieran Dixon | 26 | Jackson Hastings | 21 | Regan Grace | 32 |
| Ryan Morgan | 11 | Jake Bibby | 20 | Kevin Naiqama | 21 |
| Jordan Abdull | 10 | Krisnan Inu | 19 | Mark Percival | 18 |
| Elliot Kear | 10 | Ken Sio | 16 | Jonny Lomax | 17 |

### DEFENDERS BEATEN

| | | | | | |
|---|---|---|---|---|---|
| Kieran Dixon | 115 | Josh Jones | 157 | Mark Percival | 137 |
| Rhys Williams | 112 | Jackson Hastings | 117 | Tommy Makinson | 113 |
| Elliot Kear | 90 | Derrell Olpherts | 107 | Regan Grace | 101 |
| Alex Walker | 76 | Krisnan Inu | 101 | Jonny Lomax | 90 |
| Eddie Battye | 69 | Kris Welham | 75 | Alex Walmsley | 90 |

### MARKER TACKLES

| | | | | | |
|---|---|---|---|---|---|
| Luke Yates | 222 | Joey Lussick | 160 | Morgan Knowles | 177 |
| Eddie Battye | 149 | George Griffin | 148 | Matty Lees | 136 |
| Jay Pitts | 123 | Greg Burke | 127 | James Roby | 126 |
| Matty Gee | 110 | Gil Dudson | 119 | Dominique Peyroux | 119 |
| James Cunningham | 99 | Josh Jones | 105 | Luke Thompson | 115 |

### TRY ASSISTS

| | | | | | |
|---|---|---|---|---|---|
| Jordan Abdull | 14 | Jackson Hastings | 36 | Lachlan Coote | 22 |
| Alex Walker | 11 | Robert Lui | 15 | Theo Fages | 22 |
| Matty Fozard | 7 | Niall Evalds | 13 | Jonny Lomax | 21 |
| Jay Pitts | 6 | Joey Lussick | 13 | James Roby | 10 |
| Brock Lamb | 5 | Tuimoala Lolohea | 9 | Mark Percival | 9 |

### TOTAL OPTA INDEX

| | | | | | |
|---|---|---|---|---|---|
| Luke Yates | 14504 | Josh Jones | 17807 | Tommy Makinson | 14629 |
| Jay Pitts | 13001 | Jackson Hastings | 17133 | Lachlan Coote | 13190 |
| Rhys Williams | 12398 | Niall Evalds | 13366 | Luke Thompson | 11814 |
| Jordan Abdull | 11518 | Joey Lussick | 11040 | Jonny Lomax | 11662 |
| Alex Walker | 11408 | Derrell Olpherts | 10621 | Regan Grace | 10972 |

| WAKEFIELD TRINITY SUPER LEAGUE XXIV LEADERS | WARRINGTON WOLVES SUPER LEAGUE XXIV LEADERS | WIGAN WARRIORS SUPER LEAGUE XXIV LEADERS |
|---|---|---|

### CARRIES

| Wakefield | | Warrington | | Wigan | |
|---|---|---|---|---|---|
| Ryan Hampshire | 410 | Josh Charnley | 385 | Zak Hardaker | 334 |
| Reece Lyne | 407 | Chris Hill | 376 | George Williams | 324 |
| David Fifita | 311 | Blake Austin | 355 | Oliver Gildart | 281 |
| Ben Jones-Bishop | 309 | Daryl Clark | 279 | Dan Sarginson | 240 |
| Craig Kopczak | 273 | Tom Lineham | 275 | Willie Isa | 237 |

### OFFLOADS

| Wakefield | | Warrington | | Wigan | |
|---|---|---|---|---|---|
| David Fifita | 33 | Mike Cooper | 50 | George Williams | 46 |
| Reece Lyne | 32 | Jason Clark | 27 | Oliver Gildart | 25 |
| Ryan Hampshire | 30 | Daryl Clark | 26 | Zak Hardaker | 22 |
| Danny Brough | 18 | Bryson Goodwin | 23 | Sean O'Loughlin | 18 |
| Pauli Pauli | 14 | Chris Hill | 23 | Willie Isa | 15 |

### METRES

| Wakefield | | Warrington | | Wigan | |
|---|---|---|---|---|---|
| Reece Lyne | 3274 | Josh Charnley | 3070 | Oliver Gildart | 3375 |
| Ryan Hampshire | 2478 | Chris Hill | 2800 | Zak Hardaker | 3074 |
| David Fifita | 2221 | Daryl Clark | 2658 | George Williams | 2732 |
| Ben Jones-Bishop | 2126 | Blake Austin | 2414 | Dan Sarginson | 2245 |
| Craig Kopczak | 1977 | Bryson Goodwin | 2160 | Liam Marshall | 1871 |

### TACKLES

| Wakefield | | Warrington | | Wigan | |
|---|---|---|---|---|---|
| Kyle Wood | 938 | Daryl Clark | 882 | Willie Isa | 971 |
| Craig Kopczak | 592 | Chris Hill | 715 | Sam Powell | 948 |
| George King | 587 | Ben Currie | 707 | Morgan Smithies | 673 |
| David Fifita | 584 | Jason Clark | 704 | Oliver Partington | 564 |
| Jordan Crowther | 484 | Jack Hughes | 689 | Thomas Leuluai | 542 |

### CLEAN BREAKS

| Wakefield | | Warrington | | Wigan | |
|---|---|---|---|---|---|
| Ben Jones-Bishop | 23 | Josh Charnley | 35 | Joe Burgess | 28 |
| Ryan Hampshire | 20 | Blake Austin | 29 | Liam Marshall | 20 |
| Reece Lyne | 16 | Stefan Ratchford | 17 | George Williams | 18 |
| Max Jowitt | 10 | Bryson Goodwin | 16 | Oliver Gildart | 17 |
| Bill Tupou | 9 | Tom Lineham | 15 | Zak Hardaker | 12 |

### DEFENDERS BEATEN

| Wakefield | | Warrington | | Wigan | |
|---|---|---|---|---|---|
| David Fifita | 141 | Daryl Clark | 124 | Zak Hardaker | 147 |
| Reece Lyne | 111 | Blake Austin | 115 | George Williams | 122 |
| Ryan Hampshire | 88 | Bryson Goodwin | 95 | Oliver Gildart | 88 |
| Pauli Pauli | 78 | Josh Charnley | 67 | Dan Sarginson | 71 |
| Jacob Miller | 64 | Stefan Ratchford | 64 | Joe Burgess | 58 |

### MARKER TACKLES

| Wakefield | | Warrington | | Wigan | |
|---|---|---|---|---|---|
| Kyle Wood | 187 | Jason Clark | 142 | Willie Isa | 180 |
| George King | 117 | Daryl Clark | 133 | Sam Powell | 175 |
| David Fifita | 104 | Ben Currie | 130 | Morgan Smithies | 134 |
| Craig Kopczak | 102 | Jack Hughes | 117 | Oliver Partington | 107 |
| Danny Kirmond | 98 | Joe Philbin | 107 | Joe Bullock | 104 |

### TRY ASSISTS

| Wakefield | | Warrington | | Wigan | |
|---|---|---|---|---|---|
| Jacob Miller | 15 | Daryl Clark | 19 | George Williams | 21 |
| Ryan Hampshire | 14 | Declan Patton | 17 | Zak Hardaker | 12 |
| Danny Brough | 13 | Blake Austin | 12 | Sam Powell | 12 |
| Reece Lyne | 6 | Toby King | 10 | Oliver Gildart | 11 |
| Kyle Wood | 6 | Stefan Ratchford | 7 | Thomas Leuluai | 7 |

### TOTAL OPTA INDEX

| Wakefield | | Warrington | | Wigan | |
|---|---|---|---|---|---|
| Reece Lyne | 13950 | Daryl Clark | 15615 | Zak Hardaker | 16101 |
| David Fifita | 13211 | Blake Austin | 12679 | George Williams | 15930 |
| Ryan Hampshire | 12928 | Chris Hill | 12410 | Oliver Gildart | 12519 |
| Kyle Wood | 11132 | Josh Charnley | 12396 | Willie Isa | 11635 |
| Ben Jones-Bishop | 8882 | Toby King | 9903 | Sam Powell | 11212 |

# CHAMPIONSHIP 2019
## *Club by Club*

# BARROW RAIDERS

| DATE | FIXTURE | RESULT | SCORERS | LGE | ATT |
|------|---------|--------|---------|-----|-----|
| 3/2/19 | Batley (a) | W18-22 | t:Spedding(2),Smith,Charnock g:Dallimore(3) | 5th | 755 |
| 10/2/19 | Sheffield (h) | L22-24 | t:Puara,Amean(2),J Johnson g:Dallimore(3) | 6th | 1,514 |
| 17/2/19 | York (a) | L56-0 | | 11th | 1,575 |
| 24/2/19 | Dewsbury (h) | D20-20 | t:Stack(2),R Johnston g:Charnock(3),R Johnston | 11th | 1,321 |
| 3/3/19 | Rochdale (a) | L20-8 | t:Amean(2) | 10th | 514 |
| 10/3/19 | Widnes (h) | L4-20 | g:Dallimore(2) | 10th | 1,724 |
| 16/3/19 | Toulouse (a) | L50-0 | | 10th | 1,388 |
| 24/3/19 | Swinton (h) | L26-33 | t:Cross(2),Walne,Mossop g:Dallimore(5) | 10th | 1,357 |
| 31/3/19 | York (h) (CCR4) | L16-32 | t:Susino,J Johnson,Ritson g:Dallimore(2) | N/A | 898 |
| 7/4/19 | Leigh (a) | L46-30 | t:D Toal,Ritson,Stack,Cross,Riley g:Dallimore(3),Charnock(2) | 11th | 3,036 |
| 19/4/19 | Toronto (h) | L26-52 | t:J Johnson,Cross,Stack,Amean,Ritson g:Charnock(3) | 12th | 1,417 |
| 22/4/19 | Bradford (a) | L26-14 | t:S Toal,Susino,Charnock g:Charnock | 12th | 4,011 |
| 28/4/19 | Featherstone (h) | L12-26 | t:Smith,Stack g:Dallimore(2) | 12th | 1,277 |
| 5/5/19 | Halifax (h) | L46-10 | t:Spedding,Ritson g:Dallimore | 13th | 1,446 |
| 19/5/19 | Sheffield (SB) ● | L18-30 | t:Stack,Ritson,Smith g:Dallimore(3) | 13th | N/A |
| 26/5/19 | Rochdale (h) | W54-10 | t:Puara,Susino,Cross,Spedding,Amean(3),Ritson,D Toal g:Dallimore(9) | 12th | 1,114 |
| 5/6/19 | Bradford (h) (1895CR2) | W50-6 | t:Susino,Smith,B Carter,Stack,D Toal,Spedding,Dallimore(2),Cross g:Dallimore(7) | N/A | 1,161 |
| 9/6/19 | Widnes (a) | L38-14 | t:Cross,Ritson g:Dallimore(3) | 13th | 3,830 |
| 16/6/19 | Halifax (h) | W21-8 | t:Stack,Cross(2),Morrow g:Dallimore(2) fg:J Carter | 13th | 1,396 |
| 23/6/19 | Featherstone (a) | W16-38 | t:Amean(2),Dallimore,Morrow,Cresswell(3) g:Dallimore(5) | 13th | 1,928 |
| 26/6/19 | Leigh (a) (1895CQF) ●● | L19-18 | t:Walne,Cresswell,R Johnston g:R Johnston(3) | N/A | 1,012 |
| 30/6/19 | Toulouse (h) | L6-36 | t:Cresswell g:Dallimore | 13th | 1,422 |
| 7/7/19 | Dewsbury (a) | L40-26 | t:Puara,Cross,Ritson(2) g:Dallimore(5) | 13th | 856 |
| 14/7/19 | Leigh (h) | L8-24 | t:Cross,Ritson | 13th | 1,637 |
| 21/7/19 | Swinton (a) | L30-12 | t:Ritson,Cresswell g:Dallimore,White | 13th | 984 |
| 4/8/19 | York (h) | L16-24 | t:Ritson,Cresswell,Smith g:R Johnston,J Carter | 13th | 1,169 |
| 11/8/19 | Bradford (a) | L22-46 | t:Cross,Dallimore,Ford,Hulme g:Dallimore(3) | 13th | 1,470 |
| 18/8/19 | Sheffield (a) | L44-18 | t:Walker,Cross,Smith g:Dallimore(3) | 13th | 677 |
| 31/8/19 | Toronto (a) | L62-8 | t:Dallimore g:Dallimore(2) | 13th | 7,129 |
| 8/9/19 | Batley (h) | W24-16 | t:Cross,Puara,Amean,Susino g:Dallimore(4) | 13th | 1,214 |

● Played at Bloomfield Road, Blackpool
●● Played at Totally Wicked Stadium, St Helens

| | | APP | | TRIES | | GOALS | | FG | | PTS | |
|---|---|---|---|---|---|---|---|---|---|---|---|
| | D.O.B. | ALL | Ch | ALL | Ch | ALL | Ch | ALL | Ch | ALL | Ch |
| Stargroth Amean | 9/3/91 | 25 | 23 | 11 | 11 | 0 | 0 | 0 | 0 | 44 | 44 |
| Martin Aspinwall | 21/10/81 | 11(5) | 10(5) | 0 | 0 | 0 | 0 | 0 | 0 | 0 | 0 |
| Brett Carter | 9/7/88 | 6 | 3 | 1 | 0 | 0 | 0 | 0 | 0 | 4 | 0 |
| Jake Carter | 24/11/98 | 4(5) | 4(5) | 0 | 0 | 1 | 1 | 1 | 1 | 3 | 3 |
| Lewis Charnock | 2/9/94 | 17 | 16 | 2 | 2 | 9 | 9 | 0 | 0 | 26 | 26 |
| Bradd Crellin | 2/7/89 | 4(6) | 4(6) | 0 | 0 | 0 | 0 | 0 | 0 | 0 | 0 |
| Luke Cresswell | 5/5/95 | 17(3) | 15(3) | 7 | 6 | 0 | 0 | 0 | 0 | 28 | 24 |
| Deon Cross | 30/7/96 | 30 | 27 | 14 | 13 | 0 | 0 | 0 | 0 | 56 | 52 |
| Jamie Dallimore | 20/8/88 | 25 | 23 | 5 | 3 | 69 | 60 | 0 | 0 | 158 | 132 |
| Ryan Duffy | 13/5/93 | 3(5) | 3(5) | 0 | 0 | 0 | 0 | 0 | 0 | 0 | 0 |
| Adam Ford | 25/3/00 | 3 | 3 | 1 | 1 | 0 | 0 | 0 | 0 | 4 | 4 |
| Declan Hulme | 14/1/93 | 5(1) | 5(1) | 1 | 1 | 0 | 0 | 0 | 0 | 4 | 4 |
| Josh Johnson | 25/7/94 | 22 | 19 | 3 | 2 | 0 | 0 | 0 | 0 | 12 | 8 |
| Ryan Johnston | 16/3/98 | 8(4) | 7(4) | 2 | 1 | 5 | 2 | 0 | 0 | 18 | 8 |
| Tom Loxam | 27/1/92 | 7(1) | 7 | 0 | 0 | 0 | 0 | 0 | 0 | 0 | 0 |
| Willie Minoga | 17/9/87 | 4(7) | 3(7) | 0 | 0 | 0 | 0 | 0 | 0 | 0 | 0 |
| Danny Morrow | 30/4/90 | 13(1) | 11(1) | 2 | 2 | 0 | 0 | 0 | 0 | 8 | 8 |
| Nathan Mossop | 21/2/88 | 1(14) | (13) | 1 | 1 | 0 | 0 | 0 | 0 | 4 | 4 |
| Liam Paisley | 27/11/97 | 6 | 5 | 0 | 0 | 0 | 0 | 0 | 0 | 0 | 0 |
| Wartovo Puara | 24/6/90 | 30 | 27 | 4 | 4 | 0 | 0 | 0 | 0 | 16 | 16 |
| Glenn Riley | 29/1/92 | 2(16) | 2(14) | 1 | 1 | 0 | 0 | 0 | 0 | 4 | 4 |
| Theerapol Ritson | 7/1/96 | 21(2) | 20 | 12 | 11 | 0 | 0 | 0 | 0 | 48 | 44 |
| Paul Seguier | 8/9/97 | 1(5) | 1(5) | 0 | 0 | 0 | 0 | 0 | 0 | 0 | 0 |
| Jono Smith | 12/11/88 | 20(1) | 18(1) | 6 | 5 | 0 | 0 | 0 | 0 | 24 | 20 |
| Jake Spedding | 26/9/96 | 18(2) | 16(1) | 5 | 4 | 0 | 0 | 0 | 0 | 20 | 16 |
| Jarrad Stack | 13/2/88 | 21(2) | 20(2) | 8 | 7 | 0 | 0 | 0 | 0 | 32 | 28 |
| Alec Susino | 24/5/95 | 20(3) | 18(2) | 5 | 3 | 0 | 0 | 0 | 0 | 20 | 12 |
| Dan Toal | 22/9/89 | 3(11) | 1(10) | 3 | 2 | 0 | 0 | 0 | 0 | 12 | 8 |
| Shane Toal | 11/11/95 | 4 | 3 | 1 | 1 | 0 | 0 | 0 | 0 | 4 | 4 |
| Tom Walker | 25/12/94 | 11(16) | 11(13) | 1 | 1 | 0 | 0 | 0 | 0 | 4 | 4 |
| Jordan Walne | 28/12/92 | 21(3) | 19(3) | 2 | 1 | 0 | 0 | 0 | 0 | 8 | 4 |
| Ben White | 27/10/94 | 7(3) | 7(3) | 0 | 0 | 1 | 1 | 0 | 0 | 2 | 2 |

Deon Cross

**LEAGUE RECORD**
P27-W5-D1-L21 (13th)
F479, A861, Diff-382, 11 points.

**CHALLENGE CUP**
Round Four

**1895 CUP**
Quarter Finalists

**ATTENDANCES**
Best - v Widnes (Ch - 1,724)
Worst - v York (CC - 898)
Total (excluding Challenge Cup) - 19,193
Average (excluding Challenge Cup) - 1,371
(Up by 148 on 2018)

*'Ch' totals include Championship regular season only; 'All' totals also include Challenge Cup & 1895 Cup*

**CLUB RECORDS**
**MATCH RECORDS** — Highest score: 138-0 v Nottingham City, 27/11/94  **Highest score against:** 0-90 v Leeds, 11/2/90  **Record attendance:** 21,651 v Salford, 15/4/38
**Tries:** 6 Val Cumberbatch v Batley, 11/11/36; Jim Thornburrow v Maryport, 19/2/38; Steve Rowan v Nottingham City, 15/11/92
**Goals:** 17 Darren Carter v Nottingham City, 27/11/94  **Points:** 42 Darren Carter v Nottingham City, 27/11/94
**SEASON RECORDS** — **Tries:** 50 Jim Lewthwaite 1956-57  **Goals:** 135 Joe Ball 1956-57  **Points:** 323 Jamie Rooney 2010
**CAREER RECORDS** — **Tries:** 352 Jim Lewthwaite 1943-57  **Goals:** 1,099 *(inc 63fg)* Darren Holt 1998-2002; 2004-2009; 2012
**Points:** 2,403 Darren Holt 1998-2002; 2004-2009; 2012  **Appearances:** 500 Jim Lewthwaite 1943-57

# BATLEY BULLDOGS

| DATE | FIXTURE | RESULT | SCORERS | LGE | ATT |
|---|---|---|---|---|---|
| 3/2/19 | Barrow (h) | L18-22 | t:Wood,Leak,Brambani g:Scott(3) | 10th | 755 |
| 10/2/19 | Featherstone (a) | L42-14 | t:Campbell,Jouffret,Yates g:Scott | 12th | 2,145 |
| 17/2/19 | Halifax (a) | L20-18 | t:Brearley,Downs,Yates g:Scott(3) | 12th | 1,825 |
| 24/2/19 | Rochdale (h) | W18-12 | t:Galbraith(2),Reittie g:Scott(3) | 12th | 754 |
| 1/3/19 | Sheffield (a) | L44-16 | t:Wood,Downs,Smeaton g:Scott(2) | 11th | 791 |
| 10/3/19 | Bradford (h) | L6-16 | t:Yates g:Scott | 11th | 2,393 |
| 17/3/19 | Toronto (a) ● | L34-12 | t:Scott,Jouffret g:Scott(2) | 11th | N/A |
| 23/3/19 | Toulouse (h) | L12-38 | t:Jouffret,Leak g:Scott(2) | 12th | 857 |
| 31/3/19 | Lock Lane (h) (CCR4) | W62-6 | t:Yates,Dickinson,Reittie(3),Ward,Jouffret(2),Smeaton(2),Hemingway g:Scott(4),Jouffret(5) | N/A | 501 |
| 7/4/19 | Widnes (h) | W20-18 | t:Ward,Taira,Campbell g:Scott(4) | 10th | 1,420 |
| 14/4/19 | Doncaster (a) (CCR5) | L16-12 | t:Ward,Reittie g:Scott(2) | N/A | 539 |
| 19/4/19 | Dewsbury (a) | W8-20 | t:Leak,Taira,Brown g:Scott(4) | 9th | 1,276 |
| 22/4/19 | Swinton (h) | W32-18 | t:Wood(2),Jouffret(2),Bretherton,Smeaton g:Scott(4) | 9th | 817 |
| 28/4/19 | Leigh (h) | L16-36 | t:Leak,Campbell,Taira g:Scott(2) | 9th | 1,240 |
| 5/5/19 | York (a) | L28-24 | t:Campbell(2),Bienek(2),Bretherton g:Brambani,Scott | 9th | 1,978 |
| 19/5/19 | Dewsbury (SB) ●● | W30-14 | t:Tomlinson,Campbell,Brearley,Leak,Scott g:Jouffret(5) | 9th | N/A |
| 26/5/19 | Halifax (h) | W24-16 | t:Tomlinson(2),Galbraith,Gledhill g:Jouffret(4) | 9th | 1,368 |
| 2/6/19 | Rochdale (h) (1895CR2) | W38-18 | t:Brown,Galbraith,Downs,Leak,Brambani,Manning,Jouffret g:Jouffret(5) | N/A | 700 |
| 9/6/19 | Bradford (a) | L16-0 | | 9th | 3,414 |
| 16/6/19 | Sheffield (h) | L24-54 | t:Brearley,Tomlinson,Brown,Wood g:Jouffret(4) | 9th | 2,798 |
| 21/6/19 | Widnes (a) | L28-22 | t:Downs,Walker(2),Dickinson g:Jouffret(3) | 9th | 3,742 |
| 26/6/19 | York (a) (1895CQF) | W16-17 (aet) | t:Campbell,Wood,Brearley g:Jouffret(2) fg:Jouffret | N/A | 1,395 |
| 30/6/19 | Toronto (h) | L10-40 | t:Jouffret,Walker g:Jouffret | 9th | 894 |
| 7/7/19 | Swinton (a) | L20-18 | t:Brearley,Gledhill,Walker g:Jouffret(3) | 11th | 888 |
| 14/7/19 | York (h) | D14-14 | t:Broadbent,Jouffret g:Jouffret(3) | 10th | 1,009 |
| 21/7/19 | Leigh (a) | L48-12 | t:Walters,Jouffret g:Jouffret(2) | 10th | 3,125 |
| 28/7/19 | Sheffield (a) (1895CSF) | L18-2 | g:Jouffret | N/A | 727 |
| 4/8/19 | Rochdale (a) | W26-50 | t:Jouffret(2),Reittie(3),Brearley,Broadbent(2),Brown g:Jouffret(4),Wood(3) | 10th | 638 |
| 11/8/19 | Dewsbury (h) | W16-10 | t:Reittie(2),Smeaton g:Brambani(2) | 9th | 1,619 |
| 17/8/19 | Toulouse (a) | L46-0 | | 10th | 1,895 |
| 1/9/19 | Featherstone (h) | L0-64 | | 10th | 1,602 |
| 8/9/19 | Barrow (a) | L24-16 | t:Brambani,Leak,Brearley g:Brambani(2) | 10th | 1,214 |

● Played at KCOM Craven Park, Hull
●● Played at Bloomfield Road, Blackpool

| | | APP | | TRIES | | GOALS | | FG | | PTS | |
|---|---|---|---|---|---|---|---|---|---|---|---|
| | D.O.B. | ALL | Ch | ALL | Ch | ALL | Ch | ALL | Ch | ALL | Ch |
| Lewis Bienek | 11/4/98 | 3(13) | 3(10) | 2 | 2 | 0 | 0 | 0 | 0 | 8 | 8 |
| Dom Brambani | 10/5/85 | 22(1) | 20 | 3 | 2 | 5 | 5 | 0 | 0 | 22 | 18 |
| Paul Brearley | 5/2/92 | 19(6) | 15(5) | 6 | 6 | 0 | 0 | 0 | 0 | 24 | 24 |
| Alex Bretherton | 5/12/82 | 7(5) | 5(5) | 2 | 2 | 0 | 0 | 0 | 0 | 8 | 8 |
| Jack Broadbent | 1/11/01 | 11 | 9 | 3 | 3 | 0 | 0 | 0 | 0 | 12 | 12 |
| James Brown | 6/5/88 | 8(16) | 7(14) | 4 | 3 | 0 | 0 | 0 | 0 | 16 | 12 |
| Archie Bruce | 4/7/99 | (1) | (1) | 0 | 0 | 0 | 0 | 0 | 0 | 0 | 0 |
| Reiss Butterworth | 7/12/98 | 3(11) | 3(11) | 0 | 0 | 0 | 0 | 0 | 0 | 0 | 0 |
| Johnny Campbell | 17/7/87 | 24 | 19 | 7 | 6 | 0 | 0 | 0 | 0 | 28 | 24 |
| Tyler Dickinson | 18/8/96 | 14(1) | 11(1) | 2 | 1 | 0 | 0 | 0 | 0 | 8 | 4 |
| Jack Downs | 10/11/95 | 23 | 19 | 4 | 3 | 0 | 0 | 0 | 0 | 16 | 12 |
| Toby Everett | 22/12/95 | 16(9) | 14(7) | 0 | 0 | 0 | 0 | 0 | 0 | 0 | 0 |
| Lewis Galbraith | 1/2/95 | 16(2) | 15(1) | 4 | 3 | 0 | 0 | 0 | 0 | 16 | 12 |
| Adam Gledhill | 15/2/93 | 25(2) | 22(2) | 2 | 2 | 0 | 0 | 0 | 0 | 8 | 8 |
| Tom Hemingway | 6/12/86 | 2(3) | 1(3) | 1 | 0 | 0 | 0 | 0 | 0 | 4 | 0 |
| Louis Jouffret | 24/5/95 | 28 | 23 | 14 | 10 | 42 | 29 | 1 | 0 | 141 | 98 |
| Alistair Leak | 5/4/92 | 27(1) | 23(1) | 7 | 6 | 0 | 0 | 0 | 0 | 28 | 24 |
| Tom Lillycrop | 29/11/91 | 8(3) | 6(3) | 0 | 0 | 0 | 0 | 0 | 0 | 0 | 0 |
| Dane Manning | 15/4/89 | 27 | 22 | 1 | 0 | 0 | 0 | 0 | 0 | 4 | 0 |
| Wayne Reittie | 21/1/88 | 18 | 15 | 10 | 6 | 0 | 0 | 0 | 0 | 40 | 24 |
| Oliver Russell | 21/9/98 | 2 | 2 | 0 | 0 | 0 | 0 | 0 | 0 | 0 | 0 |
| Dave Scott | 8/6/93 | 28 | 23 | 2 | 2 | 38 | 32 | 0 | 0 | 84 | 72 |
| George Senior | 29/8/99 | (2) | (2) | 0 | 0 | 0 | 0 | 0 | 0 | 0 | 0 |
| Sam Smeaton | 26/10/88 | 25(1) | 21(1) | 5 | 3 | 0 | 0 | 0 | 0 | 20 | 12 |
| Jo Taira | 30/3/89 | 3(16) | 3(12) | 3 | 3 | 0 | 0 | 0 | 0 | 12 | 12 |
| Keenen Tomlinson | 22/5/97 | 12(6) | 10(6) | 4 | 4 | 0 | 0 | 0 | 0 | 16 | 16 |
| Niall Walker | 21/4/97 | 7 | 6 | 4 | 4 | 0 | 0 | 0 | 0 | 16 | 16 |
| Sam Walters | 25/12/00 | 1 | 1 | 1 | 1 | 0 | 0 | 0 | 0 | 4 | 4 |
| Michael Ward | 10/2/91 | (23) | (19) | 3 | 1 | 0 | 0 | 0 | 0 | 12 | 4 |
| Sam Wood | 11/6/97 | 21(5) | 20(3) | 6 | 5 | 3 | 3 | 0 | 0 | 30 | 26 |
| Danny Yates | 28/5/94 | 16(1) | 13(1) | 4 | 3 | 0 | 0 | 0 | 0 | 16 | 12 |

*'Ch' totals include Championship regular season only; 'All' totals also include Challenge Cup & 1895 Cup*

Louis Jouffret

**LEAGUE RECORD**
P27-W8-D1-L18 (10th)
F462, A756, Diff-294, 17 points.

**CHALLENGE CUP**
Round Five

**1895 CUP**
Semi-Finalists

**ATTENDANCES**
Best - v Sheffield (Ch - 2,798)
Worst - v Lock Lane (CC - 501)
Total (excluding Challenge Cup) - 18,226
Average (excluding Challenge Cup) - 1,302
(Up by 273 on 2018)

| | |
|---|---|
| **CLUB RECORDS** | |
| **MATCH RECORDS** | **Highest score:** 100-4 v Gateshead, 17/3/2010 **Highest score against:** 9-78 v Wakefield, 26/8/67 **Record attendance:** 23,989 v Leeds, 14/3/25 |
| | **Tries:** 5 Joe Oakland v Bramley, 19/12/1908; Tommy Brannan v Swinton, 17/1/20; Jim Wale v Bramley, 4/12/26; Jim Wale v Cottingham, 12/2/27; Tommy Oldroyd v Highfield, 6/3/94; Ben Feehan v Halifax, 10/8/2008; Jermaine McGillvary v Whitehaven, 24/5/2009 |
| | **Goals:** 16 Gareth Moore v Gateshead, 17/3/2010 **Points:** 40 Gareth Moore v Gateshead, 17/3/2010 |
| **SEASON RECORDS** | **Tries:** 30 Johnny Campbell 2010 **Goals:** 144 Barry Eaton 2004 **Points:** 308 Richard Price 1997 |
| **CAREER RECORDS** | **Tries:** 142 Craig Lingard 1998-2008 **Goals:** 463 Wharton 'Wattie' Davies 1897-1912 **Points:** 1,297 Wharton 'Wattie' Davies 1897-1912 |
| | **Appearances:** 421 Wharton 'Wattie' Davies 1897-1912 |

# BRADFORD BULLS

| DATE | FIXTURE | RESULT | SCORERS | LGE | ATT |
|------|---------|--------|---------|-----|-----|
| 3/2/19 | Featherstone (h) | W17-16 | t:Webster,Chisholm,Flanagan g:Chisholm(2) fg:Chisholm | 6th | 6,024 |
| 10/2/19 | Swinton (a) | W12-31 | t:Wildie,Hitchcox,Minchella,Crossley,Evans g:Chisholm(5) fg:Lilley | 4th | 1,498 |
| 15/2/19 | Sheffield (a) | L24-10 | t:Oakes,Ryan g:Lilley | 6th | 1,711 |
| 24/2/19 | York (h) | L14-24 | t:Ryan(2),Pickersgill g:Chisholm | 8th | 4,782 |
| 3/3/19 | Toulouse (h) | L0-14 | | 8th | 3,751 |
| 10/3/19 | Batley (a) | W6-16 | t:Ryan,Oakes,Kirk g:Lilley(2) | 8th | 2,393 |
| 17/3/19 | Widnes (a) | L25-20 | t:Foggin-Johnston,Farrell,J Green g:Minchella(4) | 8th | 5,335 |
| 24/3/19 | Leigh (h) | W26-12 | t:Webster,Storton,Ryan,Wildie,Evans g:Minchella(2),Milnes | 7th | 4,381 |
| 31/3/19 | Keighley (a) (CCR4) | W12-14 | t:Ryan,Flanagan g:Minchella(3) | N/A | 1,881 |
| 7/4/19 | Dewsbury (h) | W20-12 | t:Grant(2),Milnes,Minchella g:Minchella(2) | 6th | 4,068 |
| 14/4/19 | Featherstone (h) (CCR5) | W27-26 (aet) | t:Ryan,Grant,Lilley,Foggin-Johnston g:Minchella(5) fg:Lilley | N/A | 1,691 |
| 19/4/19 | Halifax (a) | W26-33 | t:Ryan,Minchella,Crossley,Webster g:Minchella(5),Milnes(3) fg:Lilley | 5th | 3,316 |
| 22/4/19 | Barrow (h) | W26-14 | t:Farrell,Grant,Minchella,Lilley,Webster g:Minchella(3) | 5th | 4,011 |
| 28/4/19 | Rochdale (h) | W52-16 | t:Crossley(2),Doyle(2),Oakes,Ryan(3),Webster g:Minchella(8) | 4th | 3,721 |
| 4/5/19 | Toronto (a) | L36-16 | t:Peltier,Milnes,Grant g:Minchella(2) | 6th | 8,363 |
| 11/5/19 | Leeds (h) (CCR6) | W24-22 | t:Grant,Webster,Hallas,Wood g:Milnes(4) | N/A | 10,256 |
| 18/5/19 | Halifax (SB) ● | L14-21 | t:Foggin-Johnston,Grant g:Minchella(3) | 7th | N/A |
| 26/5/19 | Featherstone (a) | L42-4 | t:Ryan | 7th | 2,903 |
| 2/6/19 | Halifax (h) (CCQF) | L16-20 | t:Milnes,Webster,Wildie g:Lilley(2) | N/A | 6,591 |
| 5/6/19 | Barrow (a) (1895CR2) | L50-6 | t:Pickersgill g:Stephenson | N/A | 1,161 |
| 9/6/19 | Batley (h) | W16-0 | t:Foggin-Johnston(2),Minchella g:Lilley(2) | 7th | 3,414 |
| 16/6/19 | Leigh (a) | L52-20 | t:Wildie,Flanagan,Storton g:Lilley(4) | 7th | 4,180 |
| 23/6/19 | Halifax (h) | W24-20 | t:Ryan,Minchella,Hitchcox g:Keyes(4) | 7th | 5,203 |
| 30/6/19 | Widnes (h) | W62-0 | t:Keyes(3),Minchella(3),Hitchcox,Pickersgill,Flanagan(2),Oakes g:Keyes(9) | 7th | 3,895 |
| 6/7/19 | Toulouse (a) | W24-26 | t:Keyes,Webster,Oakes,Pickersgill,Wildie g:Keyes(3) | 6th | 3,560 |
| 14/7/19 | Swinton (h) | D34-34 | t:Garside,Pickersgill,Webster,Lilley,Storton,Farrell g:Keyes(5) | 6th | 3,104 |
| 21/7/19 | York (a) | L25-24 | t:Ryan(3),Oakes,Hitchcox g:Keyes(2) | 6th | 4,007 |
| 4/8/19 | Toronto (a) | L20-25 | t:Hitchcox,Webster,Crossley g:Keyes(4) | 7th | 3,421 |
| 11/8/19 | Barrow (a) | W22-46 | t:Keyes,Garside,Ryan,Minchella(2),Flanagan,Oakes,Pickersgill g:Keyes(7) | 7th | 1,470 |
| 18/8/19 | Dewsbury (a) | W10-34 | t:Crossley,Wildie,Peltier,Minchella,Pickersgill,Oakes g:Keyes(5) | 7th | 2,285 |
| 1/9/19 | Sheffield (h) | W30-10 | t:Keyes,Webster,Peltier,Ryan,Pickersgill,Evans g:Keyes(3) | 6th | 7,541 |
| 8/9/19 | Rochdale (a) | W0-82 | t:Storton,Webster,Ryan,J Green,Oakes,Pickersgill,Lilley,Grant(3),Keyes(2),Peltier,Farrell,Wildie g:Keyes(10),Ryan | 6th | 1,328 |

● *Played at Bloomfield Road, Blackpool*

## APP   TRIES   GOALS   FG   PTS

Ethan Ryan

| | D.O.B. | ALL | Ch | ALL | Ch | ALL | Ch | ALL | Ch | ALL | Ch |
|---|--------|-----|-----|-----|-----|-----|-----|-----|-----|-----|-----|
| Cameron Berry | 7/8/01 | (1) | 0 | 0 | 0 | 0 | 0 | 0 | 0 | 0 | 0 |
| Joe Brown | 14/1/99 | 2 | 1 | 0 | 0 | 0 | 0 | 0 | 0 | 0 | 0 |
| Callum Bustin | 12/8/97 | 4(7) | 2(6) | 0 | 0 | 0 | 0 | 0 | 0 | 0 | 0 |
| Ryan Butterworth | 8/3/00 | 1 | 0 | 0 | 0 | 0 | 0 | 0 | 0 | 0 | 0 |
| Dane Chisholm | 4/7/90 | 3 | 3 | 1 | 1 | 8 | 8 | 1 | 1 | 21 | 21 |
| Steve Crossley | 28/11/89 | 27 | 23 | 6 | 6 | 0 | 0 | 0 | 0 | 24 | 24 |
| Elliott Culling | 30/8/99 | 1 | 0 | 0 | 0 | 0 | 0 | 0 | 0 | 0 | 0 |
| Thomas Doyle | 29/6/99 | 1(4) | (4) | 2 | 2 | 0 | 0 | 0 | 0 | 8 | 8 |
| Rhys Evans | 30/10/92 | 11(4) | 11(4) | 3 | 3 | 0 | 0 | 0 | 0 | 12 | 12 |
| Connor Farrell | 6/11/93 | 26(2) | 23(2) | 4 | 4 | 0 | 0 | 0 | 0 | 16 | 16 |
| George Flanagan | 8/10/86 | (20) | (17) | 6 | 5 | 0 | 0 | 0 | 0 | 24 | 20 |
| David Foggin-Johnston | 19/8/96 | 15 | 11 | 5 | 4 | 0 | 0 | 0 | 0 | 20 | 16 |
| Keelan Foster | 26/1/00 | (1) | 0 | 0 | 0 | 0 | 0 | 0 | 0 | 0 | 0 |
| Bradley Gallagher | 28/2/00 | 1 | 0 | 0 | 0 | 0 | 0 | 0 | 0 | 0 | 0 |
| Matt Garside | 1/10/90 | 13(1) | 11(1) | 2 | 2 | 0 | 0 | 0 | 0 | 8 | 8 |
| Ashley Gibson | 25/9/86 | 3(1) | 2(1) | 0 | 0 | 0 | 0 | 0 | 0 | 0 | 0 |
| Dalton Grant | 21/4/90 | 13 | 9 | 10 | 8 | 0 | 0 | 0 | 0 | 40 | 32 |
| Cobi Green | 4/3/99 | 1 | 0 | 0 | 0 | 0 | 0 | 0 | 0 | 0 | 0 |
| James Green | 29/11/90 | 3(15) | 3(13) | 2 | 2 | 0 | 0 | 0 | 0 | 8 | 8 |
| Sam Hallas | 18/10/96 | 23(4) | 20(4) | 1 | 0 | 0 | 0 | 0 | 0 | 4 | 0 |
| Jy Hitchcox | 18/8/89 | 13 | 13 | 6 | 6 | 0 | 0 | 0 | 0 | 24 | 24 |
| Evan Hodgson | 14/9/98 | (2) | (1) | 0 | 0 | 0 | 0 | 0 | 0 | 0 | 0 |
| Joe Keyes | 17/9/95 | 10 | 10 | 8 | 8 | 52 | 52 | 0 | 0 | 136 | 136 |
| Liam Kirk | 26/3/97 | 22(1) | 20(1) | 1 | 1 | 0 | 0 | 0 | 0 | 4 | 4 |
| Olsi Krasniqi | 26/6/92 | (2) | (2) | 0 | 0 | 0 | 0 | 0 | 0 | 0 | 0 |
| Jake Lightowler | 22/2/99 | (1) | 0 | 0 | 0 | 0 | 0 | 0 | 0 | 0 | 0 |
| Jordan Lilley | 4/9/96 | 27 | 24 | 4 | 3 | 11 | 9 | 3 | 2 | 41 | 32 |
| Jon Magrin | 8/10/94 | 6(2) | 5(1) | 0 | 0 | 0 | 0 | 0 | 0 | 0 | 0 |
| Rowan Milnes | 1/9/97 | 12 | 8 | 3 | 2 | 8 | 4 | 0 | 0 | 28 | 16 |
| Elliot Minchella | 28/1/96 | 30 | 26 | 12 | 12 | 37 | 29 | 0 | 0 | 122 | 106 |
| Ross Oakes | 12/10/96 | 25(3) | 21(3) | 9 | 9 | 0 | 0 | 0 | 0 | 36 | 36 |
| Ethan O'Hanlon | 19/5/01 | (1) | 0 | 0 | 0 | 0 | 0 | 0 | 0 | 0 | 0 |
| Ross Peltier | 24/4/92 | (16) | (13) | 4 | 4 | 0 | 0 | 0 | 0 | 16 | 16 |
| Brandon Pickersgill | 29/3/97 | 20(1) | 18(1) | 9 | 8 | 0 | 0 | 0 | 0 | 36 | 32 |
| Josh Rickett | 20/10/97 | 1 | 0 | 0 | 0 | 0 | 0 | 0 | 0 | 0 | 0 |
| Colton Roche | 23/6/93 | 1(5) | (5) | 0 | 0 | 0 | 0 | 0 | 0 | 0 | 0 |
| Ethan Ryan | 12/5/96 | 31 | 27 | 19 | 17 | 1 | 1 | 0 | 0 | 78 | 70 |
| Ebon Scurr | 11/5/00 | 1 | 0 | 0 | 0 | 0 | 0 | 0 | 0 | 0 | 0 |
| Alix Stephenson | 19/4/99 | 1(1) | (1) | 0 | 0 | 1 | 0 | 0 | 0 | 2 | 0 |
| Matthew Storton | 10/3/99 | 15(8) | 14(6) | 4 | 4 | 0 | 0 | 0 | 0 | 16 | 16 |
| Jake Webster | 29/10/83 | 22(3) | 20(2) | 12 | 10 | 0 | 0 | 0 | 0 | 48 | 40 |
| Matty Wildie | 25/10/90 | 22(6) | 19(5) | 7 | 6 | 0 | 0 | 0 | 0 | 28 | 24 |
| Oliver Wilson | 22/3/99 | 1 | 0 | 0 | 0 | 0 | 0 | 0 | 0 | 0 | 0 |
| Mikey Wood | 18/4/96 | 8(16) | 7(15) | 1 | 0 | 0 | 0 | 0 | 0 | 4 | 0 |

*'Ch' totals include Championship regular season only; 'All' totals also include Challenge Cup & 1895 Cup*

**LEAGUE RECORD**
P27-W16-D1-L10 (6th)
F717, A522, Diff+195, 33 points.

**CHALLENGE CUP**
Quarter Finalists

**1895 CUP**
Round Two

**ATTENDANCES**
Best - v Leeds (CC -10,256)
Worst - v Featherstone (CC - 1,691)
Total (excluding Challenge Cup) - 57,316
Average (excluding Challenge Cup) - 4,409
(Up by 725 on 2018, League 1)

| | |
|---|---|
| **CLUB RECORDS** **MATCH RECORDS** | **Highest score:** 124-0 v West Wales, 6/5/2018 **Highest score against:** 6-84 v Wigan, 21/4/2014 **Record attendance:** 69,429 v Huddersfield, 14/3/53 **Tries:** 6 Eric Batten v Leeds, 15/9/45; Trevor Foster v Wakefield, 10/4/48; Steve McGowan v Barrow, 8/11/92; Lesley Vainikolo v Hull, 2/9/2005 **Goals:** 20 Dane Chisholm v West Wales, 6/5/2018 **Points:** 48 Dane Chisholm v West Wales, 6/5/2018 |
| **SEASON RECORDS** **CAREER RECORDS** | **Tries:** 63 Jack McLean 1951-52 **Goals:** 213 *(inc 5fg)* Henry Paul 2001 **Points:** 457 Henry Paul 2001 **Tries:** 261 Jack McLean 1950-56 **Goals:** 1,165 *(inc 25fg)* Paul Deacon 1998-2009 **Points:** 2,605 Paul Deacon 1998-2009 **Appearances:** 588 Keith Mumby 1973-90; 1992-93 |

# DEWSBURY RAMS

| DATE | FIXTURE | RESULT | SCORERS | LGE | ATT |
|---|---|---|---|---|---|
| 10/2/19 | York (h) | L22-26 | t:Day(2),Garratt g:Sykes(5) | 10th | 1,275 |
| 17/2/19 | Swinton (h) | W38-24 | t:Garratt(2),Sykes,Ward,Worrincy,Harrison g:Sykes(7) | 9th | 993 |
| 24/2/19 | Barrow (a) | D20-20 | t:K Trout(2),Sykes g:Sykes(4) | 10th | 1,321 |
| 3/3/19 | Toronto (h) | L17-22 | t:Knowles g:Sykes(6) fg:Sykes | 9th | 1,251 |
| 10/3/19 | Halifax (a) | L26-0 | | 9th | 1,343 |
| 17/3/19 | Sheffield (h) | L13-16 | t:Sykes,Worrincy g:Sykes(2) fg:Sykes | 9th | 977 |
| 24/3/19 | Featherstone (a) | W22-32 | t:Finn,Morton(2),Kibula,Knowles,Day g:Sykes(3),Finn | 9th | 1,943 |
| 31/3/19 | West Hull (h) (CCR4) | W32-6 | t:Gabriel(2),Leeming(3),Morton g:Finn(4) | N/A | 366 |
| 7/4/19 | Bradford (a) | L20-12 | t:K Trout,Hooley g:Finn(2) | 9th | 4,068 |
| 14/4/19 | Thatto Heath (a) (CCR5) | W10-36 | t:Gabriel,Worrincy,Walshaw,Kibula,Ryder,Garratt,Ward g:Finn(4) | N/A | 1,000 |
| 19/4/19 | Batley (h) | L8-20 | t:Igbinedion g:Finn(2) | 10th | 1,276 |
| 22/4/19 | Leigh (a) | L34-12 | t:S Brown,K Trout g:Finn(2) | 10th | 3,043 |
| 28/4/19 | Widnes (a) | W24-25 | t:Hooley,Igbinedion,Gabriel(2),Finn g:Finn(2) fg:Finn | 10th | 3,851 |
| 4/5/19 | Toulouse (h) | L0-38 | | 10th | 786 |
| 10/5/19 | Halifax (h) (CCR6) | L6-34 | t:Walshaw g:Finn | N/A | 1,207 |
| 19/5/19 | Batley (SB) ● | L30-14 | t:Gabriel,Knowles,Day g:Finn | 10th | N/A |
| 26/5/19 | Swinton (a) | L22-17 | t:Gabriel,Morton,Worrincy g:Finn(2) fg:Knowles | 11th | 795 |
| 2/6/19 | Swinton (h) (1895CR2) | W44-26 | t:Walshaw,Worrincy(2),Day(2),Richardson,K Trout,Heckford g:Finn(6) | N/A | 453 |
| 9/6/19 | Rochdale (h) | W66-10 | t:K Trout,Morton,Walshaw,Day(2),Morris(2),Martin(2),Garratt,Annakin g:Finn(11) | 10th | 865 |
| 15/6/19 | Toronto (a) | L70-8 | t:Worrincy,Ryder | 11th | 6,745 |
| 23/6/19 | Leigh (h) | L0-40 | | 12th | 1,668 |
| 26/6/19 | Widnes (a) (1895CQF) | L54-6 | t:Waite-Pullan g:Sykes | N/A | 1,458 |
| 30/6/19 | York (a) | L24-21 | t:Finn,Worrincy(2),O Trout g:Sykes,Finn fg:Sykes | 12th | 1,338 |
| 7/7/19 | Barrow (a) | W40-26 | t:McGrath(2),Speakman,O Trout,Ryder,Sykes,Knowles g:Sykes(3),Finn(3) | 12th | 856 |
| 12/7/19 | Sheffield (a) | L28-22 | t:Speakman,K Trout,Knowles,Worrincy g:Sykes(3) | 12th | 691 |
| 21/7/19 | Halifax (h) | D28-28 | t:Day,Ryder,Gabriel,Worrincy(2) g:Sykes(4) | 12th | 1,136 |
| 28/7/19 | Rochdale (a) | W12-32 | t:Morris,Ryder,Garratt,Knowles(2),Worrincy g:Finn(4) | 10th | 574 |
| 4/8/19 | Featherstone (h) | L24-25 | t:Knowles,Morton,Flynn,Speakman g:Sykes(4) | 11th | 1,229 |
| 11/8/19 | Batley (a) | L16-10 | t:Walshaw,Morton g:Finn | 11th | 1,619 |
| 18/8/19 | Bradford (h) | L10-34 | t:Johnson,Ryder g:Finn | 11th | 2,285 |
| 31/8/19 | Toulouse (a) | L42-14 | t:Day(2),Reilly g:Finn | 12th | 2,055 |
| 8/9/19 | Widnes (h) | L8-22 | t:Worrincy(2) | 12th | 1,409 |

● *Played at Bloomfield Road, Blackpool*

## APP TRIES GOALS FG PTS

| | D.O.B. | ALL | Ch | ALL | Ch | ALL | Ch | ALL | Ch | ALL | Ch |
|---|---|---|---|---|---|---|---|---|---|---|---|
| Jordan Andrade | 24/1/92 | 2(6) | (6) | 0 | 0 | 0 | 0 | 0 | 0 | 0 | 0 |
| Chris Annakin | 30/1/91 | 10(2) | 9(2) | 1 | 1 | 0 | 0 | 0 | 0 | 4 | 4 |
| Alex Brown | 28/8/87 | 2 | 2 | 0 | 0 | 0 | 0 | 0 | 0 | 0 | 0 |
| Simon Brown | 23/6/89 | 11 | 9 | 1 | 1 | 0 | 0 | 0 | 0 | 4 | 4 |
| Sam Day | 12/6/94 | 14(13) | 13(12) | 11 | 9 | 0 | 0 | 0 | 0 | 44 | 36 |
| Callum Field | 7/10/97 | 5(8) | 5(5) | 0 | 0 | 0 | 0 | 0 | 0 | 0 | 0 |
| Liam Finn | 2/11/83 | 27 | 22 | 3 | 3 | 49 | 34 | 1 | 1 | 111 | 81 |
| Nyle Flynn | 27/7/97 | 1(4) | 1(4) | 1 | 1 | 0 | 0 | 0 | 0 | 4 | 4 |
| Andy Gabriel | 21/12/93 | 22 | 17 | 8 | 5 | 0 | 0 | 0 | 0 | 32 | 20 |
| Tom Garratt | 25/10/94 | 17(11) | 14(11) | 6 | 5 | 0 | 0 | 0 | 0 | 24 | 20 |
| Harvey Hallas | 14/11/97 | (4) | (4) | 0 | 0 | 0 | 0 | 0 | 0 | 0 | 0 |
| Owen Harrison | 10/4/99 | 3(2) | 3(2) | 1 | 1 | 0 | 0 | 0 | 0 | 4 | 4 |
| Lewis Heckford | 25/9/97 | 1 | 0 | 1 | 0 | 0 | 0 | 0 | 0 | 4 | 0 |
| Luke Hooley | 1/8/98 | 12(1) | 11(1) | 2 | 2 | 0 | 0 | 0 | 0 | 8 | 8 |
| Daniel Igbinedion | 26/1/95 | 22(5) | 18(5) | 2 | 2 | 0 | 0 | 0 | 0 | 8 | 8 |
| Liam Johnson | 12/5/97 | 1(2) | 1(2) | 1 | 1 | 0 | 0 | 0 | 0 | 4 | 4 |
| Samy Kibula | 7/8/99 | 10(2) | 8(1) | 2 | 1 | 0 | 0 | 0 | 0 | 8 | 4 |
| Ben Kilner | 11/5/99 | 2(2) | 2(1) | 0 | 0 | 0 | 0 | 0 | 0 | 0 | 0 |
| Danny King | 16/9/97 | 1(4) | (3) | 0 | 0 | 0 | 0 | 0 | 0 | 0 | 0 |
| Michael Knowles | 2/5/87 | 25(3) | 21(3) | 8 | 8 | 0 | 0 | 1 | 1 | 33 | 33 |
| Cameron Leeming | 3/7/95 | 3 | 1 | 3 | 0 | 0 | 0 | 0 | 0 | 12 | 0 |
| Liam Mackay | 26/10/90 | 2(6) | 2(3) | 0 | 0 | 0 | 0 | 0 | 0 | 0 | 0 |
| Joe Martin | 28/3/95 | 15 | 13 | 2 | 2 | 0 | 0 | 0 | 0 | 8 | 8 |
| Conor McGrath | 14/8/96 | 2 | 2 | 2 | 2 | 0 | 0 | 0 | 0 | 8 | 8 |
| Frazer Morris | 22/2/97 | 7(3) | 7(2) | 3 | 3 | 0 | 0 | 0 | 0 | 12 | 12 |
| Dale Morton | 31/10/90 | 21 | 18 | 7 | 6 | 0 | 0 | 0 | 0 | 28 | 24 |
| Muizz Mustapha | 3/4/00 | (2) | (2) | 0 | 0 | 0 | 0 | 0 | 0 | 0 | 0 |
| Luke Nelmes | 7/6/93 | (3) | (3) | 0 | 0 | 0 | 0 | 0 | 0 | 0 | 0 |
| Jack Ray | 8/10/98 | (2) | (1) | 0 | 0 | 0 | 0 | 0 | 0 | 0 | 0 |
| Martyn Reilly | 5/1/96 | 6(6) | 6(4) | 1 | 1 | 0 | 0 | 0 | 0 | 4 | 4 |
| Toby Richardson | 5/6/96 | 1(8) | 1(5) | 1 | 0 | 0 | 0 | 0 | 0 | 4 | 0 |
| Ellis Robson | 14/9/98 | 2(1) | 2(1) | 0 | 0 | 0 | 0 | 0 | 0 | 0 | 0 |
| Adam Ryder | 20/10/89 | 32 | 27 | 6 | 5 | 0 | 0 | 0 | 0 | 24 | 20 |
| Jode Sheriffe | 4/7/86 | 9(10) | 4(10) | 0 | 0 | 0 | 0 | 0 | 0 | 0 | 0 |
| Dom Speakman | 22/3/94 | 4 | 4 | 3 | 3 | 0 | 0 | 0 | 0 | 12 | 12 |
| Paul Sykes | 11/8/81 | 21 | 20 | 4 | 4 | 43 | 42 | 3 | 3 | 105 | 103 |
| Jacob Thomas | 9/10/93 | 1(1) | 1(1) | 0 | 0 | 0 | 0 | 0 | 0 | 0 | 0 |
| Kyle Trout | 1/3/91 | 24(1) | 22 | 7 | 6 | 0 | 0 | 0 | 0 | 28 | 24 |
| Owen Trout | 15/10/99 | 13(2) | 13(2) | 2 | 2 | 0 | 0 | 0 | 0 | 8 | 8 |
| Daniel Waite-Pullan | 14/11/98 | 5(2) | 5(1) | 1 | 0 | 0 | 0 | 0 | 0 | 4 | 0 |
| Lucas Walshaw | 4/8/92 | 22(3) | 17(3) | 5 | 2 | 0 | 0 | 0 | 0 | 20 | 8 |
| Robbie Ward | 27/10/95 | 11(7) | 7(7) | 2 | 1 | 0 | 0 | 0 | 0 | 8 | 4 |
| Harvey Whiteley | 26/9/98 | 1(2) | 1(1) | 0 | 0 | 0 | 0 | 0 | 0 | 0 | 0 |
| Rob Worrincy | 9/7/85 | 26 | 22 | 15 | 12 | 0 | 0 | 0 | 0 | 60 | 48 |

*'Ch' totals include Championship regular season only; 'All' totals also include Challenge Cup & 1895 Cup*

*Adam Ryder*

**LEAGUE RECORD**
P27-W6-D2-L19 (12th)
F513, A721, Diff-208, 14 points.

**CHALLENGE CUP**
Round Six

**1895 CUP**
Quarter Finalists

**ATTENDANCES**
Best - v Bradford (Ch - 2,285)
Worst - v West Hull (CC - 366)
Total (excluding Challenge Cup) - 16,459
Average (excluding Challenge Cup) - 1,176
(Up by 207 on 2018)

| CLUB RECORDS | **Highest score:** 90-5 v Blackpool, 4/4/93 **Highest score against:** 0-82 v Widnes, 30/11/86 |
|---|---|
| | **Record attendance:** 26,584 v Halifax, 30/10/20 *(Crown Flatt)*; 4,068 v Bradford, 6/4/2015 *(Tetley's Stadium)* |
| MATCH RECORDS | **Tries:** 8 Dai Thomas v Liverpool, 13/4/1907 |
| | **Goals:** 13 Greg Pearce v Blackpool Borough, 4/4/93; Francis Maloney v Hunslet, 25/3/2007 **Points:** 32 Les Holliday v Barrow, 11/9/94 |
| SEASON RECORDS | **Tries:** 40 Dai Thomas 1906-07 **Goals:** 169 Barry Eaton 2000 **Points:** 394 Barry Eaton 2000 |
| CAREER RECORDS | **Tries:** 144 Joe Lyman 1913-31 **Goals:** 863 Nigel Stephenson 1967-78; 1984-86 **Points:** 2,082 Nigel Stephenson 1967-78; 1984-86 |
| | **Appearances:** 454 Joe Lyman 1913-31 |

# FEATHERSTONE ROVERS

| DATE | FIXTURE | RESULT | SCORERS | LGE | ATT |
|------|---------|--------|---------|-----|-----|
| 3/2/19 | Bradford (a) | L17-16 | t:W Boas,Briscoe,King g:W Boas(2) | 9th | 6,024 |
| 10/2/19 | Batley (h) | W42-14 | t:W Boas,Teteh,King,Walters,Singleton,Day,C Smith,A Boas g:W Boas(5) | 5th | 2,145 |
| 17/2/19 | Leigh (a) | L29-20 | t:D Smith,Briscoe,Newman,W Boas g:W Boas(2) | 8th | 3,443 |
| 24/2/19 | Halifax (h) | W46-16 | t:King,Newman(2),Briscoe(2),Render,Cooper,Lockwood g:Turner(5),A Boas(2) | 4th | 2,534 |
| 3/3/19 | Widnes (a) | L44-22 | t:D Smith,Newman(2),King g:Turner(3) | 6th | 5,782 |
| 10/3/19 | Sheffield (h) | W32-14 | t:Lockwood,Turner(2),Golding,Bussey,Davies g:Turner(4) | 6th | 1,981 |
| 17/3/19 | Swinton (a) | W12-24 | t:Bussey(2),Golding,Ormondroyd g:Reynolds(4) | 6th | 923 |
| 24/3/19 | Dewsbury (h) | L22-32 | t:Briscoe,King,Golding,Reynolds g:Reynolds(3) | 6th | 1,943 |
| 30/3/19 | Swinton (h) (CCR4) | W38-14 | t:Teteh(3),Broadbent,Wheeldon,W Boas,Day,King g:King(3) | N/A | 691 |
| 6/4/19 | Toulouse (a) | L8-2 | g:Reynolds | 8th | 2,251 |
| 14/4/19 | Bradford (a) (CCR5) | L27-26 | | | |
| | | *(aet)* | t:Broadbent,Hardcastle,Harrison,Render g:W Boas(5) | N/A | 1,691 |
| 19/4/19 | York (h) | W42-12 | t:Sutcliffe(2),Walters,Davies,Hardcastle(2),Chisholm g:Chisholm(7) | 6th | 2,216 |
| 22/4/19 | Toronto (h) | L14-23 | t:Makatoa,Carey g:Chisholm(3) | 7th | 2,101 |
| 28/4/19 | Barrow (a) | W12-26 | t:Day,Sutcliffe,King,Chisholm(2) g:Chisholm(3) | 7th | 1,277 |
| 5/5/19 | Rochdale (a) | W10-56 | t:King,Harrison,Chisholm,Carey(2),Hardcastle,Cooper(2),Walters,Golding g:Chisholm(8) | 7th | 714 |
| 18/5/19 | York (SB) ● | W42-10 | t:Chisholm,Carey(2),Briscoe,Day,Sutcliffe,Hardcastle,Holmes g:Chisholm(5) | 6th | N/A |
| 26/5/19 | Bradford (h) | W42-4 | t:King,Chisholm(3),Davies,Briscoe,Carey,Walters g:Chisholm(5) | 4th | 2,903 |
| 5/6/19 | Widnes (a) (1895CR2) | L22-16 | t:Ormondroyd,Carey,Punchard g:Punchard(2) | N/A | 1,515 |
| 9/6/19 | Sheffield (a) | W18-38 | t:Ferguson,Holmes,King(2),Hardcastle,Harrison g:Chisholm(7) | 3rd | 1,321 |
| 16/6/19 | Widnes (h) | W22-4 | t:Sutcliffe(2),Carey,Holmes g:Chisholm(3) | 3rd | 2,380 |
| 23/6/19 | Barrow (h) | L16-38 | t:Chisholm,Sutcliffe(2) g:Chisholm(2) | 5th | 1,928 |
| 30/6/19 | Halifax (a) | W18-24 | t:Day,King,Briscoe,Hardcastle g:Chisholm(4) | 5th | 1,888 |
| 7/7/19 | Leigh (h) | W24-20 | t:Day,Briscoe,Chisholm,Walters g:Chisholm(3),Reynolds | 4th | 3,104 |
| 13/7/19 | Toronto (a) | L22-18 | t:Ormondroyd,Walters,Jones g:Dagger(3) | 5th | 7,891 |
| 21/7/19 | Rochdale (h) | W50-6 | t:Makatoa,King,Briscoe,Jones,Harrison,Golding,Day(2),Walters g:Chisholm(7) | 5th | 2,011 |
| 4/8/19 | Dewsbury (a) | W24-25 | t:Golding,Sutcliffe,McLelland,Albert,Carey g:Chisholm(2) fg:Chisholm | 5th | 1,229 |
| 11/8/19 | Swinton (h) | W66-16 | t:King(2),Albert,McLelland,Sutcliffe(2),Render,J Johnson,Carey,Day(2),Walters g:Chisholm(9) | 5th | 2,090 |
| 18/8/19 | York (a) | L22-18 | t:Render,McLelland,Sutcliffe g:Chisholm(3) | 5th | 3,115 |
| 1/9/19 | Batley (a) | W0-64 | t:Day,King,Chisholm(3),Hardcastle(2),Harrison,Lockwood,Jones(2) g:Chisholm(10) | 5th | 1,602 |
| 7/9/19 | Toulouse (h) | L24-26 | t:King(2),Chisholm,Sutcliffe g:Chisholm(4) | 5th | 2,334 |
| 15/9/19 | Leigh (a) (EPO) | W18-34 | t:Sutcliffe(2),Harrison,McLelland,Walters,Chisholm g:Chisholm(5) | N/A | 2,671 |
| 21/9/19 | York (a) (ESF) | W4-30 | t:Makatoa,Harrison,Day,J Johnson,Render g:Chisholm(5) | N/A | 3,222 |
| 29/9/19 | Toulouse (a) (FE) | W12-36 | t:Davies(2),Golding,Harrison,Chisholm,J Johnson,Render g:Chisholm(4) | N/A | 1,068 |
| 5/10/19 | Toronto (a) (GF) | L24-6 | t:Sutcliffe g:Chisholm | N/A | 9,974 |

● *Played at Bloomfield Road, Blackpool*

## APP  TRIES GOALS FG  PTS

| | | ALL | Ch | ALL | Ch | ALL | Ch | ALL | Ch | ALL | Ch |
|---|---|---|---|---|---|---|---|---|---|---|---|
| | D.O.B. | | | | | | | | | | |
| Wellington Albert | 3/9/93 | 5(7) | 5(6) | 2 | 2 | 0 | 0 | 0 | 0 | 8 | 8 |
| Jimmy Beckett | 29/8/99 | (2) | | 0 | 0 | 0 | 0 | 0 | 0 | 0 | 0 |
| Ase Boas | 26/12/88 | 5 | 5 | 1 | 1 | 2 | 2 | 0 | 0 | 8 | 8 |
| Watson Boas | 8/11/94 | 10 | 8 | 4 | 3 | 14 | 9 | 0 | 0 | 44 | 30 |
| Luke Briscoe | 11/3/94 | 17 | 17 | 10 | 10 | 0 | 0 | 0 | 0 | 40 | 40 |
| Jack Broadbent | 1/11/01 | 3 | 1 | 2 | 0 | 0 | 0 | 0 | 0 | 8 | 0 |
| Jack Bussey | 17/8/92 | 9(1) | 8(1) | 3 | 3 | 0 | 0 | 0 | 0 | 12 | 12 |
| Conor Carey | 7/4/95 | 24 | 23 | 10 | 9 | 0 | 0 | 0 | 0 | 40 | 36 |
| Dane Chisholm | 4/7/90 | 21 | 21 | 16 | 16 | 100 | 100 | 1 | 1 | 265 | 265 |
| Luke Cooper | 28/7/94 | 4(29) | 2(28) | 3 | 3 | 0 | 0 | 0 | 0 | 12 | 12 |
| Will Dagger | 21/2/99 | 4 | 4 | 0 | 0 | 3 | 3 | 0 | 0 | 6 | 6 |
| John Davies | 8/1/91 | 17(7) | 14(7) | 5 | 5 | 0 | 0 | 0 | 0 | 20 | 20 |
| Brad Day | 23/9/94 | 26(2) | 24(2) | 12 | 11 | 0 | 0 | 0 | 0 | 48 | 44 |
| Dale Ferguson | 13/4/88 | 3(1) | 2(1) | 1 | 1 | 0 | 0 | 0 | 0 | 4 | 4 |
| Ashton Golding | 4/9/96 | 22 | 22 | 7 | 7 | 0 | 0 | 0 | 0 | 28 | 28 |
| Josh Hardcastle | 28/8/92 | 26(3) | 23(3) | 9 | 8 | 0 | 0 | 0 | 0 | 36 | 32 |
| James Harrison | 15/6/96 | 14(15) | 12(14) | 8 | 7 | 0 | 0 | 0 | 0 | 32 | 28 |
| Tom Holmes | 2/3/96 | 6(1) | 6(1) | 3 | 3 | 0 | 0 | 0 | 0 | 12 | 12 |
| Corey Johnson | 16/11/00 | (2) | (1) | 0 | 0 | 0 | 0 | 0 | 0 | 0 | 0 |
| Jack Johnson | 25/4/96 | 9 | 9 | 3 | 3 | 0 | 0 | 0 | 0 | 12 | 12 |
| Connor Jones | 26/1/96 | 4(6) | 4(6) | 4 | 4 | 0 | 0 | 0 | 0 | 16 | 16 |
| Cameron King | 17/9/91 | 25(3) | 24(2) | 18 | 17 | 3 | 0 | 0 | 0 | 78 | 68 |
| James Lockwood | 21/3/86 | 31(2) | 30(1) | 3 | 3 | 0 | 0 | 0 | 0 | 12 | 12 |
| Makahesi Makatoa | 30/1/93 | 16(9) | 13(9) | 3 | 3 | 0 | 0 | 0 | 0 | 12 | 12 |
| Danny Maskill | 28/6/95 | 3(8) | 1(7) | 0 | 0 | 0 | 0 | 0 | 0 | 0 | 0 |
| Jimmy McDaniel | 25/9/96 | 2 | 1 | 0 | 0 | 0 | 0 | 0 | 0 | 0 | 0 |
| Callum McLelland | 16/9/99 | 12 | 11 | 4 | 4 | 0 | 0 | 0 | 0 | 16 | 16 |
| Harry Newman | 19/2/00 | 6 | 6 | 5 | 5 | 0 | 0 | 0 | 0 | 20 | 20 |
| Jack Ormondroyd | 7/11/91 | 8(20) | 7(18) | 2 | 2 | 0 | 0 | 0 | 0 | 12 | 8 |
| Morgan Punchard | 26/1/99 | 1 | 0 | 1 | 0 | 2 | 0 | 0 | 0 | 8 | 0 |
| Jack Render | 4/7/99 | 18(3) | 15(3) | 6 | 5 | 0 | 0 | 0 | 0 | 24 | 20 |
| Ben Reynolds | 15/1/94 | 6 | 6 | 1 | 1 | 9 | 0 | 0 | 0 | 22 | 22 |
| Jorge Richardson | 5/5/97 | 2 | 1 | 0 | 0 | 0 | 0 | 0 | 0 | 0 | 0 |
| Brad Singleton | 29/10/92 | 1 | 1 | 1 | 1 | 0 | 0 | 0 | 0 | 4 | 4 |
| Cameron Smith | 7/11/98 | 3 | 3 | 1 | 1 | 0 | 0 | 0 | 0 | 4 | 4 |
| Daniel Smith | 20/3/93 | 5(1) | 5(1) | 2 | 2 | 0 | 0 | 0 | 0 | 8 | 8 |
| Alex Sutcliffe | 21/1/99 | 19 | 18 | 16 | 16 | 0 | 0 | 0 | 0 | 64 | 64 |
| Thompson Teteh | 13/7/89 | 6 | 4 | 4 | 1 | 0 | 0 | 0 | 0 | 16 | 4 |
| Owen Trout | 15/10/99 | (1) | (1) | 0 | 0 | 0 | 0 | 0 | 0 | 0 | 0 |
| Calum Turner | 29/4/99 | 8 | 8 | 2 | 2 | 12 | 12 | 0 | 0 | 32 | 32 |
| Josh Walters | 23/12/94 | 26 | 25 | 9 | 9 | 0 | 0 | 0 | 0 | 36 | 36 |
| Scott Wheeldon | 23/2/86 | 15(4) | 14(4) | 1 | 0 | 0 | 0 | 0 | 0 | 4 | 0 |

*'Ch' totals include play-offs; 'All' totals also include Challenge Cup & 1895 Cup*

Dane Chisholm

**LEAGUE RECORD**
P27-W17-D0-L10
(5th/Grand Final Runners-Up)
F837, A471, Diff+366, 34 points.

**CHALLENGE CUP**
Round Five

**1895 CUP**
Round Two

**ATTENDANCES**
Best - v Leigh (Ch - 3,104)
Worst - v Swinton (CC - 691)
Total (excluding Challenge Cup) - 29,670
Average (excluding Challenge Cup) - 2,282
(Up by 198 on 2018)

| | |
|---|---|
| **CLUB RECORDS** | **Highest score:** 96-0 v Castleford Lock Lane, 8/2/2004 **Highest score against:** 14-80 v Bradford, 3/4/2005 **Record attendance:** 17,531 v St Helens, 21/3/59 |
| **MATCH RECORDS** | **Tries:** 6 Mike Smith v Doncaster, 13/4/68; Chris Bibb v Keighley, 17/9/89; Brad Dwyer v Rochdale, 1/7/2018 |
| | **Goals:** 13 Mark Knapper v Keighley, 17/9/89; Liam Finn v Hunslet Old Boys, 25/3/2012; Liam Finn v Swinton, 12/8/2012 |
| | **Points:** 40 Martin Pearson v Whitehaven, 26/11/95 |
| **SEASON RECORDS** | **Tries:** 48 Paul Newlove 1992-93 **Goals:** 183 *(inc 2fg)* Liam Finn 2012 **Points:** 436 Liam Finn 2012 |
| **CAREER RECORDS** | **Tries:** 162 Don Fox 1953-66 **Goals:** 1,210 Steve Quinn 1975-88 **Points:** 2,654 Steve Quinn 1975-88 **Appearances:** 440 Jim Denton 1921-34 |

# HALIFAX

| DATE | FIXTURE | RESULT | SCORERS | LGE | ATT |
|------|---------|--------|---------|-----|-----|
| 3/2/19 | Widnes (a) | L40-16 | t:Sharp,Tyrer,Kavanagh g:Tyrer(2) | 13th | 4,283 |
| 10/2/19 | Leigh (h) | W33-26 | t:Moore,Tyrer,White,Robinson(2),Barber g:Tyrer(4) fg:White | 9th | 2,245 |
| 17/2/19 | Batley (h) | W20-18 | t:Saltonstall,Tyrer,Robinson g:Tyrer(4) | 7th | 1,825 |
| 24/2/19 | Featherstone (a) | L46-16 | t:Sharp,Robinson,Laulu-Togaga'e g:Tyrer(2) | 9th | 2,534 |
| 3/3/19 | Swinton (h) | W18-16 | t:Saltonstall(2),Tyrer g:Tyrer(3) | 5th | 1,584 |
| 10/3/19 | Dewsbury (h) | W26-0 | t:Barber(3),Robinson g:Tyrer(5) | 5th | 1,343 |
| 17/3/19 | York (a) | L38-16 | t:Fleming,Robinson,Fairbank g:Tyrer(2) | 7th | 2,101 |
| 24/3/19 | Toronto (h) | L12-48 | t:Barber g:Tyrer(4) | 8th | 2,090 |
| 31/3/19 | Hunslet (h) (CCR4) | W24-28 | t:Woodburn-Hall,Barber,Laulu-Togaga'e,Morris,Cooper g:Tyrer(4) | N/A | 731 |
| 7/4/19 | Rochdale (a) | W24-48 | t:Tyrer(2),Woodburn-Hall(3),Sharp,Laulu-Togaga'e(2),Saltonstall g:Tyrer(6) | 7th | 827 |
| 11/4/19 | London Broncos (h) (CCR5) | W24-16 | t:Barber,Kaye,Chapman-Smith,Laulu-Togaga'e g:Tyrer(4) | N/A | 722 |
| 19/4/19 | Bradford (h) | L26-33 | t:Woodburn-Hall,Sharp,Robinson,Tyrer g:Tyrer(5) | 8th | 3,316 |
| 22/4/19 | Toulouse (a) | L56-4 | t:Robinson | 8th | 2,038 |
| 28/4/19 | Sheffield (a) | W24-32 | t:Barber,Murrell,Woodburn-Hall,Butler(2) g:Tyrer(6) | 8th | 966 |
| 5/5/19 | Barrow (h) | W46-10 | t:Butler,Larroyer(2),Barber,Moore,Connor Davies,Kavanagh,Woodburn-Hall g:Tyrer(7) | 8th | 1,446 |
| 10/5/19 | Dewsbury (a) (CCR6) | W6-34 | t:Butler(2),Woodburn-Hall,Saltonstall(2),Robinson g:Tyrer(4),White | N/A | 1,207 |
| 18/5/19 | Bradford (SB) ● | W14-21 | t:Kavanagh,Laulu-Togaga'e,Morris g:Tyrer(4) fg:Murrell | 8th | N/A |
| 26/5/19 | Batley (a) | L24-16 | t:Sharp(2),Scott Grix g:Tyrer(2) | 8th | 1,368 |
| 2/6/19 | Bradford (h) (CCQF) | W16-20 | t:Tyrer,Scott Grix,Woodburn-Hall g:Tyrer(4) | N/A | 6,591 |
| 5/6/19 | Sheffield (h) (1895CR2) ●● | L8-52 | t:Barker,Chapman-Smith | N/A | 312 |
| 9/6/19 | Leigh (a) | L31-8 | t:Butler,Woodburn-Hall | 8th | 3,361 |
| 16/6/19 | Barrow (a) | L21-8 | t:Robinson,Scott Grix | 8th | 1,396 |
| 23/6/19 | Bradford (h) | L24-20 | t:Robinson,Moore,Laulu-Togaga'e g:Tyrer(4) | 8th | 5,203 |
| 30/6/19 | Featherstone (h) | L18-24 | t:Saltonstall,Tyrer(2) g:Tyrer(3) | 8th | 1,888 |
| 6/7/19 | Toronto (a) | L34-12 | t:Cooper,Johnston g:Tyrer(2) | 8th | 6,749 |
| 14/7/19 | Widnes (h) | W40-10 | t:Tyrer(2),Tangata,Butler(3),Moore g:Tyrer(6) | 8th | 1,668 |
| 21/7/19 | Dewsbury (a) | D28-28 | t:Saltonstall,Laulu-Togaga'e(2),Larroyer,Fairbank g:Tyrer(4) | 8th | 1,136 |
| 27/7/19 | St Helens (CCSF) ●●● | L2-26 | g:Tyrer | N/A | 24,364 |
| 4/8/19 | Toulouse (a) | L22-30 | t:Kaye,Tangata,Tyrer,Robinson g:Tyrer(3) | 8th | 1,290 |
| 11/8/19 | Sheffield (a) | L18-20 | t:Robinson,Scott Grix,Tyrer g:Tyrer(3) | 8th | 1,205 |
| 18/8/19 | Swinton (a) | L32-12 | t:Saltonstall,Fairbank g:Tyrer,Woodburn-Hall | 8th | 909 |
| 1/9/19 | Rochdale (h) | W58-0 | t:Fairbank,Tyrer(2),Woodburn-Hall(2),Sharp(2),Cooper,McGrath(2),Fleming g:Tyrer(7) | 8th | 1,126 |
| 8/9/19 | York (h) | L8-14 | t:Sharp,Barber | 8th | 1,862 |

● *Played at Bloomfield Road, Blackpool* ●● *Played at Cougar Park, Keighley* ●●● *Played at University of Bolton Stadium*

| | D.O.B. | APP ALL | APP Ch | TRIES ALL | TRIES Ch | GOALS ALL | GOALS Ch | FG ALL | FG Ch | PTS ALL | PTS Ch |
|---|--------|---------|--------|-----------|----------|-----------|----------|--------|-------|---------|--------|
| Ed Barber | 26/4/90 | 23(3) | 18(3) | 10 | 8 | 0 | 0 | 0 | 0 | 40 | 32 |
| Calvin Barker | 22/8/98 | 1 | 0 | 1 | 0 | 0 | 0 | 0 | 0 | 4 | 0 |
| Dewi Billingham | 9/11/98 | 1 | 0 | 0 | 0 | 0 | 0 | 0 | 0 | 0 | 0 |
| Chester Butler | 10/3/95 | 11 | 8 | 9 | 7 | 0 | 0 | 0 | 0 | 36 | 28 |
| Will Calcott | 16/12/97 | 3(5) | 1(4) | 0 | 0 | 0 | 0 | 0 | 0 | 0 | 0 |
| Reece Chapman-Smith | 8/11/98 | 4(6) | 2(5) | 2 | 0 | 0 | 0 | 0 | 0 | 8 | 0 |
| Mitch Clark | 13/3/93 | (1) | (1) | 0 | 0 | 0 | 0 | 0 | 0 | 0 | 0 |
| Liam Cooper | 28/7/94 | 13(8) | 12(5) | 3 | 2 | 0 | 0 | 0 | 0 | 12 | 8 |
| Connor Davies | 17/1/97 | 2(9) | 1(8) | 1 | 1 | 0 | 0 | 0 | 0 | 4 | 4 |
| Curtis Davies | 17/1/97 | 1(6) | (5) | 0 | 0 | 0 | 0 | 0 | 0 | 0 | 0 |
| Henry Davies | 13/6/98 | (1) | 0 | 0 | 0 | 0 | 0 | 0 | 0 | 0 | 0 |
| Rhys Davies | 9/6/96 | (1) | 0 | 0 | 0 | 0 | 0 | 0 | 0 | 0 | 0 |
| Jacob Fairbank | 4/3/90 | 24(6) | 20(6) | 4 | 4 | 0 | 0 | 0 | 0 | 16 | 16 |
| Dan Fleming | 8/7/92 | 14(17) | 13(13) | 2 | 2 | 0 | 0 | 0 | 0 | 8 | 8 |
| Shane Grady | 13/12/89 | 7 | 6 | 0 | 0 | 0 | 0 | 0 | 0 | 0 | 0 |
| Scott Grix | 1/5/84 | 12 | 10 | 4 | 3 | 0 | 0 | 0 | 0 | 16 | 12 |
| Simon Grix | 28/9/85 | 6 | 6 | 0 | 0 | 0 | 0 | 0 | 0 | 0 | 0 |
| Tom Hall | 10/1/99 | (1) | 0 | 0 | 0 | 0 | 0 | 0 | 0 | 0 | 0 |
| Keegan Hirst | 13/12/88 | 4 | 4 | 0 | 0 | 0 | 0 | 0 | 0 | 0 | 0 |
| Ben Johnston | 8/3/92 | 10(3) | 9(3) | 1 | 1 | 0 | 0 | 0 | 0 | 4 | 4 |
| Dafydd Jones | 27/2/95 | 1 | 0 | 0 | 0 | 0 | 0 | 0 | 0 | 0 | 0 |
| Ben Kavanagh | 4/3/88 | 21(10) | 16(10) | 3 | 3 | 0 | 0 | 0 | 0 | 12 | 12 |
| Ben Kaye | 19/12/88 | 19(1) | 17 | 2 | 1 | 0 | 0 | 0 | 0 | 8 | 4 |
| Harry Kidd | 12/6/95 | (4) | (3) | 0 | 0 | 0 | 0 | 0 | 0 | 0 | 0 |
| Jon Luke Kirby | 23/9/98 | (2) | (2) | 0 | 0 | 0 | 0 | 0 | 0 | 0 | 0 |
| Kevin Larroyer | 19/6/89 | 22(8) | 20(6) | 3 | 3 | 0 | 0 | 0 | 0 | 12 | 12 |
| Quentin Laulu-Togaga'e | 1/12/84 | 21 | 18 | 9 | 7 | 0 | 0 | 0 | 0 | 36 | 28 |
| Will Maher | 4/11/95 | 1(1) | 1(1) | 0 | 0 | 0 | 0 | 0 | 0 | 0 | 0 |
| Conor McGrath | 14/8/96 | 4(1) | 3(1) | 2 | 2 | 0 | 0 | 0 | 0 | 8 | 8 |
| Brandon Moore | 27/7/96 | 13(17) | 10(16) | 4 | 4 | 0 | 0 | 0 | 0 | 16 | 16 |
| Elliot Morris | 4/1/96 | 10(15) | 8(12) | 2 | 1 | 0 | 0 | 0 | 0 | 8 | 4 |
| Scott Murrell | 5/9/85 | 27 | 23 | 1 | 1 | 0 | 0 | 1 | 1 | 5 | 5 |
| Jacques O'Neill | 8/5/99 | (1) | (1) | 0 | 0 | 0 | 0 | 0 | 0 | 0 | 0 |
| Shaun Robinson | 13/7/89 | 29 | 25 | 13 | 12 | 0 | 0 | 0 | 0 | 52 | 48 |
| James Saltonstall | 27/9/93 | 26(1) | 21(1) | 9 | 7 | 0 | 0 | 0 | 0 | 36 | 28 |
| Will Sharp | 12/5/86 | 25 | 22 | 9 | 9 | 0 | 0 | 0 | 0 | 36 | 36 |
| Jacob Smillie | 16/9/98 | 1 | 0 | 0 | 0 | 0 | 0 | 0 | 0 | 0 | 0 |
| Fraser Stroud | 12/4/99 | 1 | 0 | 0 | 0 | 0 | 0 | 0 | 0 | 0 | 0 |
| Jordan Syme | 14/11/96 | 1 | 0 | 0 | 0 | 0 | 0 | 0 | 0 | 0 | 0 |
| Adam Tangata | 17/3/91 | 9(1) | 7(1) | 2 | 2 | 0 | 0 | 0 | 0 | 8 | 8 |
| Steve Tyrer | 16/3/89 | 32 | 27 | 16 | 15 | 106 | 89 | 0 | 0 | 276 | 238 |
| Oliver Waite | 26/12/00 | 1 | 0 | 0 | 0 | 0 | 0 | 0 | 0 | 0 | 0 |
| Ben White | 27/10/94 | 12 | 9 | 1 | 1 | 1 | 0 | 1 | 1 | 7 | 5 |
| Elliott Windley | 9/7/99 | (1) | 0 | 0 | 0 | 0 | 0 | 0 | 0 | 0 | 0 |
| James Woodburn-Hall | 2/2/95 | 17(2) | 14(1) | 12 | 9 | 1 | 0 | 0 | 0 | 50 | 38 |

*'Ch' totals include Championship regular season only; 'All' totals also include Challenge Cup & 1895 Cup*

Steve Tyrer

**LEAGUE RECORD**
P27-W10-D1-L16 (8th)
F602, A685, Diff-83, 21 points.

**CHALLENGE CUP**
Semi-Finalists

**1895 CUP**
Round Two

**ATTENDANCES**
Best - v Bradford (Ch - 3,316)
Worst - v Sheffield (1895C - 312)
Total (excluding Challenge Cup - 23,200
Average (excluding Challenge Cup - 1,657
(Down by 351 on 2018)

| | |
|---|---|
| **CLUB RECORDS** | **Highest score:** 94-4 v Myton, 25/3/2012 **Highest score against:** 6-88 v Hull KR, 23/4/2006 |
| | **Record attendance:** 29,153 v Wigan, 21/3/59 *(Thrum Hall)*; 9,827 v Bradford, 12/3/2000 *(The Shay)* |
| **MATCH RECORDS** | **Tries:** 8 Keith Williams v Dewsbury, 9/11/57 **Goals:** 14 Bruce Burton v Hunslet, 27/8/72 |
| | **Points:** 32 John Schuster v Doncaster, 9/10/94; Steve Tyrer v Whitehaven, 7/2/2016 |
| **SEASON RECORDS** | **Tries:** 48 Johnny Freeman 1956-57 **Goals:** 156 Graham Holroyd 2008 **Points:** 362 John Schuster 1994-95 |
| **CAREER RECORDS** | **Tries:** 290 Johnny Freeman 1954-67 **Goals:** 1,028 Ronnie James 1961-71 **Points:** 2,191 Ronnie James 1961-71 **Appearances:** 482 Stan Kielty 1954-58 |

# LEIGH CENTURIONS

| DATE | FIXTURE | RESULT | SCORERS | LGE | ATT |
|------|---------|--------|---------|-----|-----|
| 3/2/19 | Toulouse (h) | W24-16 | t:Pownall,Marsh,Costello,Cator g:Ridyard(4) | 4th | 2,987 |
| 10/2/19 | Halifax (a) | L33-26 | t:A Thornley,Pownall,L Adamson,T Adamson g:Ridyard(5) | 7th | 2,245 |
| 17/2/19 | Featherstone (h) | W29-20 | t:McNally,Douglas,Spencer,Ridyard,Smith g:Ridyard(4) fg:Ridyard | 5th | 3,443 |
| 24/2/19 | Toronto (h) | L8-14 | t:Douglas g:Ridyard(2) | 7th | 2,020 |
| 3/3/19 | York (h) | L9-8 | t:A Thornley g:Ridyard(2) | 7th | 2,054 |
| 10/3/19 | Swinton (a) | W12-30 | t:Marsh(2),Hood,McNally,Costello,T Adamson g:Ridyard(3) | 7th | 366 |
| 17/3/19 | Rochdale (h) | W46-6 | t:I Thornley,T Adamson,Bentley(2),Pownall,McNally(2),Hood g:Richardson(7) | 5th | 2,666 |
| 24/3/19 | Bradford (a) | L26-12 | t:Brooks,Pownall g:Richardson(2) | 5th | 4,381 |
| 31/3/19 | Sheffield (a) (CCR4) | W12-34 | t:McNally,T Adamson,Cox,Gregson,Pownall,Brooks g:Ridyard(5) | N/A | 596 |
| 7/4/19 | Barrow (h) | W46-30 | t:McNally,Brooks,I Thornley(3),Swift(2),Woods g:Ridyard(7) | 5th | 3,036 |
| 11/4/19 | Hull KR (a) (CCR5) | L14-10 | t:Pownall,Cator g:Ridyard | N/A | 2,188 |
| 19/4/19 | Widnes (a) | L30-12 | t:Eaves,Pownall g:Ridyard(2) | 7th | 5,866 |
| 22/4/19 | Dewsbury (h) | W34-12 | t:I Thornley(3),Bentley(3),Costello g:Woods,Ridyard(2) | 6th | 3,043 |
| 28/4/19 | Batley (a) | W16-36 | t:I Thornley,Higginson(2),Marsh,Brierley,Eaves g:Brierley(6) | 5th | 1,240 |
| 5/5/19 | Sheffield (h) | W42-38 | t:A Thornley,McNally,Brierley,I Thornley,Laithwaite,Eaves,Hood g:Ridyard(7) | 4th | 3,031 |
| 19/5/19 | Widnes (SB) ● | W36-22 | t:T Adamson,McNally(2),Brierley(2),Laithwaite g:Ridyard(6) | 4th | N/A |
| 25/5/19 | Toulouse (a) | L44-16 | t:Simm,Brierley,McNally g:Ridyard,Brierley | 6th | 2,235 |
| 2/6/19 | Workington (h) (1895CR2) | W62-12 | t:Cox(2),McNally(3),Eaves,Bentley,Woods,Holroyd,Douglas,I Thornley g:Woods(9) | N/A | 1,660 |
| 9/6/19 | Halifax (h) | W31-8 | t:I Thornley,Cox(2),Hood,Brooks g:Ridyard(5) fg:Ridyard | 4th | 3,361 |
| 16/6/19 | Bradford (h) | W52-20 | t:I Thornley(2),Costello,McNally(2),A Thornley,Forsyth(2) g:Ridyard(10) | 4th | 4,180 |
| 23/6/19 | Dewsbury (a) | W0-40 | t:Forsyth(2),Douglas(2),Marsh(2),Cox g:Ridyard(6) | 3rd | 1,668 |
| 26/6/19 | Barrow (h) (1895CQF) ●● | W19-18 | t:McNally,Cator,Thompson g:Ridyard(3) fg:Ridyard | N/A | 1,012 |
| 30/6/19 | Sheffield (h) | W18-22 | t:Forsyth(2),Brierley,Ridyard g:Ridyard(3) | 3rd | 1,082 |
| 7/7/19 | Featherstone (a) | L24-20 | t:Paterson(2),Forsyth(2) g:Ridyard(2) | 5th | 3,104 |
| 14/7/19 | Barrow (h) | W8-24 | t:McNally,I Thornley,Ridyard,Thompson g:Ridyard(3),Paterson | 4th | 1,637 |
| 21/7/19 | Batley (h) | W48-12 | t:Brierley(2),Cator,Douglas,I Thornley(2),Woods,Higham,Marsh g:Brierley(6) | 4th | 3,125 |
| 28/7/19 | Widnes (h) (1895CSF) | L8-12 | t:Higson g:Brierley | N/A | 4,460 |
| 4/8/19 | Swinton (a) | W31-30 | t:A Thornley,Forsyth,Costello,Clark,Sa'u,Paterson g:Brierley(2),Ridyard fg:Brierley | 4th | 3,155 |
| 11/8/19 | Rochdale (h) | W18-50 | t:Reynolds,Higson,Cator,Brierley,Marsh,T Adamson(2),Thompson,Paterson g:Ridyard(7) | 3rd | 1,019 |
| 18/8/19 | Widnes (h) | W34-22 | t:Higson,A Thornley(2),Marsh(2),Hood g:Ridyard(5) | 3rd | 3,559 |
| 1/9/19 | York (h) | L23-24 | t:Brown,Hood,Brierley,Forsyth g:Brierley(3) fg:Woods | 4th | 3,408 |
| 7/9/19 | Toronto (a) | L46-12 | t:Brown,Brierley g:Ridyard(2) | 4th | 8,152 |
| 15/9/19 | Featherstone (h) (EPO) | L18-34 | t:Sa'u,Spencer,Marsh,T Adamson g:Brierley | N/A | 2,671 |

● Played at Bloomfield Road, Blackpool
●● Played at Totally Wicked Stadium, St Helens

## APP  TRIES  GOALS  FG  PTS

| | D.O.B. | ALL | Ch | ALL | Ch | ALL | Ch | ALL | Ch | ALL | Ch |
|---|--------|-----|-----|-----|-----|-----|-----|-----|-----|-----|-----|
| Luke Adamson | 17/11/87 | 15(7) | 13(5) | 1 | 1 | 0 | 0 | 0 | 0 | 4 | 4 |
| Toby Adamson | 28/5/90 | 30 | 25 | 8 | 7 | 0 | 0 | 0 | 0 | 32 | 28 |
| Jack Ashworth | 3/7/95 | 2(2) | 2(2) | 0 | 0 | 0 | 0 | 0 | 0 | 0 | 0 |
| Joe Batchelor | 28/10/94 | 5(1) | 3(1) | 0 | 0 | 0 | 0 | 0 | 0 | 0 | 0 |
| James Bentley | 19/10/97 | 6(1) | 5(1) | 6 | 5 | 0 | 0 | 0 | 0 | 24 | 20 |
| Ryan Brierley | 12/3/92 | 13 | 12 | 11 | 11 | 21 | 19 | 1 | 1 | 87 | 83 |
| Sam Brooks | 29/9/93 | 21(2) | 18(2) | 4 | 3 | 0 | 0 | 0 | 0 | 16 | 12 |
| Kevin Brown | 2/10/84 | 3 | 3 | 2 | 2 | 0 | 0 | 0 | 0 | 8 | 8 |
| Joe Cator | 15/6/98 | 20(13) | 15(13) | 5 | 3 | 0 | 0 | 0 | 0 | 20 | 12 |
| Mitch Clark | 13/3/93 | 1(6) | (6) | 1 | 1 | 0 | 0 | 0 | 0 | 4 | 4 |
| Matthew Costello | 9/4/98 | 9 | 9 | 5 | 5 | 0 | 0 | 0 | 0 | 20 | 20 |
| Mitch Cox | 15/11/93 | 11(2) | 7(2) | 6 | 3 | 0 | 0 | 0 | 0 | 24 | 12 |
| Luke Douglas | 12/5/86 | 27 | 24 | 6 | 5 | 0 | 0 | 0 | 0 | 24 | 20 |
| Josh Eaves | 20/10/97 | 1(7) | (6) | 4 | 3 | 0 | 0 | 0 | 0 | 16 | 12 |
| Jake Emmitt | 4/10/88 | 7(14) | 6(10) | 0 | 0 | 0 | 0 | 0 | 0 | 0 | 0 |
| Liam Forsyth | 17/12/95 | 10 | 10 | 10 | 10 | 0 | 0 | 0 | 0 | 40 | 40 |
| Nick Gregson | 4/4/97 | 3(4) | 1(3) | 1 | 0 | 0 | 0 | 0 | 0 | 4 | 0 |
| Jack Higginson | 4/4/97 | 4 | 4 | 2 | 2 | 0 | 0 | 0 | 0 | 8 | 8 |
| Micky Higham | 18/9/80 | 27(2) | 24(1) | 1 | 1 | 0 | 0 | 0 | 0 | 4 | 4 |
| Adam Higson | 19/5/87 | 5 | 4 | 3 | 2 | 0 | 0 | 0 | 0 | 12 | 8 |
| Gareth Hock | 5/9/83 | (6) | (5) | 0 | 0 | 0 | 0 | 0 | 0 | 0 | 0 |
| Brad Holroyd | 15/4/00 | 1 | 0 | 1 | 0 | 0 | 0 | 0 | 0 | 4 | 0 |
| Liam Hood | 6/1/92 | 5(20) | 4(18) | 6 | 6 | 0 | 0 | 0 | 0 | 24 | 24 |
| James Laithwaite | 23/9/91 | 6 | 6 | 2 | 2 | 0 | 0 | 0 | 0 | 8 | 8 |
| Stefan Marsh | 3/9/90 | 26 | 23 | 11 | 11 | 0 | 0 | 0 | 0 | 44 | 44 |
| Gregg McNally | 2/1/91 | 25 | 20 | 17 | 12 | 0 | 0 | 0 | 0 | 68 | 48 |
| Dec O'Donnell | 7/9/98 | (3) | (1) | 0 | 0 | 0 | 0 | 0 | 0 | 0 | 0 |
| Cory Paterson | 14/7/87 | 5(5) | 5(4) | 4 | 4 | 1 | 1 | 0 | 0 | 18 | 18 |
| Jonny Pownall | 22/8/91 | 12 | 10 | 7 | 5 | 0 | 0 | 0 | 0 | 28 | 20 |
| Ben Reynolds | 15/1/94 | 2 | 2 | 1 | 1 | 0 | 0 | 0 | 0 | 4 | 4 |
| Danny Richardson | 2/9/96 | 6 | 6 | 0 | 0 | 9 | 9 | 0 | 0 | 18 | 18 |
| Martyn Ridyard | 25/7/86 | 28 | 24 | 3 | 3 | 98 | 89 | 3 | 2 | 211 | 192 |
| Junior Sa'u | 18/4/87 | 6 | 5 | 2 | 2 | 0 | 0 | 0 | 0 | 8 | 8 |
| Josh Simm | 27/2/01 | 4 | 3 | 1 | 1 | 0 | 0 | 0 | 0 | 4 | 4 |
| Aaron Smith | 12/10/96 | (5) | (5) | 1 | 1 | 0 | 0 | 0 | 0 | 4 | 4 |
| Tom Spencer | 2/1/91 | 1(19) | 1(16) | 2 | 2 | 0 | 0 | 0 | 0 | 8 | 8 |
| Adam Swift | 20/2/93 | 1 | 1 | 2 | 2 | 0 | 0 | 0 | 0 | 8 | 8 |
| Jordan Thompson | 4/9/91 | 7(6) | 7(4) | 3 | 2 | 0 | 0 | 0 | 0 | 12 | 8 |
| Andy Thornley | 1/3/89 | 17(7) | 14(7) | 7 | 7 | 0 | 0 | 0 | 0 | 28 | 28 |
| Iain Thornley | 11/9/91 | 32 | 27 | 16 | 15 | 0 | 0 | 0 | 0 | 64 | 60 |
| Josh Woods | 13/12/97 | 25 | 23 | 3 | 2 | 10 | 1 | 1 | 1 | 33 | 11 |

Joe Cator

'Ch' totals include play-offs; 'All' totals also include Challenge Cup & 1895 Cup

**LEAGUE RECORD**
P27-W18-D0-L9
(4th/Elimination Play-off)
F792, A558, Diff+234, 36 points.

**CHALLENGE CUP**
Round Five

**1895 CUP**
Semi-Finalists

**ATTENDANCES**
Best - v Widnes (1895C - 4,460)
Worst - v Barrow (1895C - 1,012)
Total (all home games included) - 51,939
Average (all home games included) - 3,055
(Down by 192 on 2018)

| CLUB RECORDS | |
|---|---|
| | **Highest score:** 92-2 v Keighley, 30/4/86  **Highest score against:** 4-94 v Workington, 26/2/95 |
| | **Record attendance:** 31,326 v St Helens, 14/3/53 *(Hilton Park)*; 10,556 v Batley, 17/9/2016 *(Leigh Sports Village)* |
| **MATCH RECORDS** | **Tries:** 6 Jack Wood v York, 4/10/47; Neil Turley v Workington, 31/1/2001  **Goals:** 15 Mick Stacey v Doncaster, 28/3/76  **Points:** 42 Neil Turley v Chorley, 4/4/1999 |
| **SEASON RECORDS** | **Tries:** 55 Neil Turley 2001  **Goals:** 187 Neil Turley 2004  **Points:** 468 Neil Turley 2004 |
| **CAREER RECORDS** | **Tries:** 189 Mick Martyn 1954-67  **Goals:** 1,043 Jimmy Ledgard 1948-58  **Points:** 2,492 John Woods 1976-85; 1990-92  **Appearances:** 503 Albert Worrall 1920-38 |

# ROCHDALE HORNETS

| DATE | FIXTURE | RESULT | SCORERS | LGE | ATT |
|---|---|---|---|---|---|
| 10/2/19 | Toronto (h) | L6-58 | t:Lawton g:Abram | 13th | 694 |
| 16/2/19 | Toulouse (a) | L42-12 | t:B Wood,Akauola g:Abram(2) | 13th | 1,707 |
| 24/2/19 | Batley (a) | L18-12 | t:Lawton,Mitchell g:Abram(2) | 13th | 754 |
| 3/3/19 | Barrow (h) | W20-8 | t:Lawton,B Moores,Carberry g:Abram(4) | 12th | 514 |
| 17/3/19 | Leigh (a) | L46-6 | t:Millington g:Abram | 12th | 2,666 |
| 24/3/19 | Widnes (h) | L4-50 | t:Whittaker | 13th | 1,732 |
| 31/3/19 | Whitehaven (a) (CCR4) | W21-22 | t:Morris,Kay,Ainscough,Abram g:Abram(3) | N/A | 889 |
| 7/4/19 | Halifax (h) | L24-48 | t:Mitchell,Higginson,Robson,Forster g:Abram(4) | 13th | 827 |
| 12/4/19 | Salford (a) (CCR5) | L76-6 | t:Ainscough g:Abram | 13th | 1,101 |
| 19/4/19 | Swinton (a) | L36-22 | t:Abram,Kay(2),Forster g:Abram(3) | 14th | 826 |
| 22/4/19 | Sheffield (h) | L16-52 | t:Forster,B Wood,B Moores g:Abram(2) | 14th | 569 |
| 28/4/19 | Bradford (a) | L52-16 | t:B Moores,Gillam,B Wood g:Abram(2) | 14th | 3,721 |
| 5/5/19 | Featherstone (h) | L10-56 | t:Ainscough,Abram g:Abram | 14th | 714 |
| 12/5/19 | York (h) | L18-24 | t:Sheridan,Carberry,B Wood g:Abram(3) | 14th | 513 |
| 18/5/19 | Swinton (SB) ● | L30-40 | t:B Wood,Kay,Ainscough(2),Livett g:Abram(5) | 14th | N/A |
| 26/5/19 | Barrow (a) | L54-10 | t:J Johnson,B Wood g:Abram | 14th | 1,114 |
| 2/6/19 | Batley (a) (1895CR2) | L38-18 | t:Baker,B Wood,Ainscough g:Abram(3) | N/A | 700 |
| 9/6/19 | Dewsbury (h) | L66-10 | t:B Wood,S Moore g:Abram | 14th | 865 |
| 16/6/19 | York (a) | L60-0 | | 14th | 1,661 |
| 21/6/19 | Sheffield (a) | L46-24 | t:Abram,Marriott(2),B Wood g:Abram(4) | 14th | 543 |
| 30/6/19 | Swinton (h) ●● | L28-36 | t:Ainscough,Lawton,Bourrel(2),B Wood g:Abram(4) | 14th | 549 |
| 7/7/19 | Widnes (a) | L40-12 | t:Brown,Marriott g:Thomas(2) | 14th | 3,780 |
| 13/7/19 | Toulouse (h) | L0-68 | | 14th | 337 |
| 21/7/19 | Featherstone (a) | L50-6 | t:Ainscough gAbram | 14th | 2,011 |
| 28/7/19 | Dewsbury (h) | L12-32 | t:Williams(2) g:Abram(2) | 14th | 574 |
| 4/8/19 | Batley (h) | L26-50 | t:Shelford,Williams,Sheridan,Farrell,Abram g:Abram(3) | 14th | 638 |
| 11/8/19 | Leigh (h) | L18-50 | t:Abram,Gleeson,Ainscough g:Abram(3) | 14th | 1,019 |
| 17/8/19 | Toronto (a) | L46-0 | | 14th | 5,969 |
| 1/9/19 | Halifax (a) | L58-0 | | 14th | 1,126 |
| 8/9/19 | Bradford (h) | L0-82 | | 14th | 1,328 |

● Played at Bloomfield Road, Blackpool  ●● Played at Mayfield Sports Centre

| | | APP | | TRIES | | GOALS | | FG | | PTS | |
|---|---|---|---|---|---|---|---|---|---|---|---|
| | D.O.B. | ALL | Ch | ALL | Ch | ALL | Ch | ALL | Ch | ALL | Ch |
| Dan Abram | 11/11/95 | 29 | 26 | 6 | 5 | 56 | 49 | 0 | 0 | 136 | 118 |
| Shaun Ainscough | 27/11/89 | 26 | 23 | 9 | 6 | 0 | 0 | 0 | 0 | 36 | 24 |
| Sitaleki Akauola | 7/4/92 | 4 | 1 | 1 | 0 | 0 | 0 | 0 | 0 | 4 | 4 |
| Zac Baker | 1/3/92 | 12(1) | 11(1) | 1 | 0 | 0 | 0 | 0 | 0 | 4 | 0 |
| James Barran | 26/10/98 | 3 | 3 | 0 | 0 | 0 | 0 | 0 | 0 | 0 | 0 |
| Pierre-Louis Bourrel | 19/10/92 | 4(2) | 4(2) | 2 | 2 | 0 | 0 | 0 | 0 | 8 | 8 |
| Kevin Brown | 27/11/98 | 6 | 6 | 1 | 1 | 0 | 0 | 0 | 0 | 4 | 4 |
| Liam Carberry | 24/2/93 | 4(16) | 4(13) | 2 | 2 | 0 | 0 | 0 | 0 | 8 | 8 |
| Jordan Case | 10/4/93 | 14(1) | 14 | 0 | 0 | 0 | 0 | 0 | 0 | 0 | 0 |
| Mike Coleman | 24/7/96 | 2(3) | 2(2) | 0 | 0 | 0 | 0 | 0 | 0 | 0 | 0 |
| Jack Cottington | 7/4/98 | 5(1) | 5 | 0 | 0 | 0 | 0 | 0 | 0 | 0 | 0 |
| Matt Davis | 5/7/96 | 3(1) | 3(1) | 0 | 0 | 0 | 0 | 0 | 0 | 0 | 0 |
| Izaac Farrell | 30/1/98 | 12 | 12 | 1 | 1 | 0 | 0 | 0 | 0 | 4 | 4 |
| Paddy Flynn | 11/12/87 | 2 | 2 | 0 | 0 | 0 | 0 | 0 | 0 | 0 | 0 |
| Carl Forster | 4/6/92 | 5(3) | 4(3) | 3 | 3 | 0 | 0 | 0 | 0 | 12 | 12 |
| Ellis Gillam | 6/10/97 | 11(3) | 8(3) | 1 | 1 | 0 | 0 | 0 | 0 | 4 | 4 |
| Aidy Gleeson | 27/1/90 | 1(12) | 1(11) | 1 | 1 | 0 | 0 | 0 | 0 | 4 | 4 |
| Sam Grant | 24/3/99 | 2 | 2 | 0 | 0 | 0 | 0 | 0 | 0 | 0 | 0 |
| Declan Gregory | 18/1/97 | (7) | (6) | 0 | 0 | 0 | 0 | 0 | 0 | 0 | 0 |
| Reece Hamlett | 26/4/01 | 1 | 1 | 0 | 0 | 0 | 0 | 0 | 0 | 0 | 0 |
| Jack Higginson | 4/4/97 | 3 | 1 | 1 | 1 | 0 | 0 | 0 | 0 | 4 | 4 |
| Stuart Howarth | 25/1/90 | 6 | 5 | 0 | 0 | 0 | 0 | 0 | 0 | 0 | 0 |
| Elliott Jenkins | 6/2/99 | 2 | 2 | 0 | 0 | 0 | 0 | 0 | 0 | 0 | 0 |
| Jack Johnson | 25/4/96 | 5 | 5 | 1 | 1 | 0 | 0 | 0 | 0 | 4 | 4 |
| Luis Johnson | 20/2/99 | 8(2) | 7(2) | 0 | 0 | 0 | 0 | 0 | 0 | 0 | 0 |
| Dec Kay | 24/11/96 | 11(2) | 8(2) | 4 | 3 | 0 | 0 | 0 | 0 | 16 | 12 |
| Ben Kilner | 11/5/99 | 1(5) | 1(5) | 0 | 0 | 0 | 0 | 0 | 0 | 0 | 0 |
| Adam Lawton | 13/6/93 | 4(4) | 4(4) | 4 | 4 | 0 | 0 | 0 | 0 | 16 | 16 |
| Harvey Livett | 4/1/97 | 2 | 2 | 1 | 1 | 0 | 0 | 0 | 0 | 4 | 4 |
| Callum Marriott | 30/5/93 | 14(1) | 13(1) | 3 | 3 | 0 | 0 | 0 | 0 | 12 | 12 |
| Ryan Millington | 14/1/87 | 5(6) | 5(6) | 1 | 1 | 0 | 0 | 0 | 0 | 4 | 4 |
| Lee Mitchell | 8/9/88 | 24(4) | 22(4) | 2 | 2 | 0 | 0 | 0 | 0 | 8 | 8 |
| Scott Moore | 23/1/88 | 15 | 14 | 1 | 1 | 0 | 0 | 0 | 0 | 4 | 4 |
| Ben Moores | 6/12/93 | 11(5) | 10(4) | 3 | 3 | 0 | 0 | 0 | 0 | 12 | 12 |
| Pat Moran | 2/4/98 | 3(3) | 3(3) | 0 | 0 | 0 | 0 | 0 | 0 | 0 | 0 |
| Ben Morris | 1/8/97 | 9 | 6 | 1 | 0 | 0 | 0 | 0 | 0 | 4 | 0 |
| Nathan Reidy | 12/2/99 | 3(1) | 2(1) | 0 | 0 | 0 | 0 | 0 | 0 | 0 | 0 |
| Ellis Robson | 14/9/98 | 6(3) | 5(3) | 1 | 1 | 0 | 0 | 0 | 0 | 4 | 4 |
| Joe Ryan | 27/9/95 | 1(6) | (5) | 0 | 0 | 0 | 0 | 0 | 0 | 0 | 0 |
| Kyle Shelford | 13/9/96 | 11 | 11 | 1 | 1 | 0 | 0 | 0 | 0 | 4 | 4 |
| Lewis Sheridan | 14/1/94 | 4(7) | 4(7) | 2 | 2 | 0 | 0 | 0 | 0 | 8 | 8 |
| Jordan Syme | 14/11/96 | 3(3) | 3(3) | 0 | 0 | 0 | 0 | 0 | 0 | 0 | 0 |
| Seta Tala | 22/7/91 | 4(3) | 4(2) | 0 | 0 | 0 | 0 | 0 | 0 | 0 | 0 |
| Oscar Thomas | 3/1/94 | 12(2) | 11(2) | 0 | 0 | 2 | 2 | 0 | 0 | 4 | 4 |
| Danny Walker | 29/6/99 | (1) | (1) | 0 | 0 | 0 | 0 | 0 | 0 | 0 | 0 |
| Mike Weldon | 10/4/98 | 17(2) | 15(2) | 0 | 0 | 0 | 0 | 0 | 0 | 0 | 0 |
| Tyler Whittaker | 12/11/95 | 6 | 5 | 1 | 1 | 0 | 0 | 0 | 0 | 4 | 4 |
| Daley Williams | 15/5/86 | 7 | 7 | 3 | 3 | 0 | 0 | 0 | 0 | 12 | 12 |
| Brandon Wood | 31/7/00 | 30 | 27 | 10 | 9 | 0 | 0 | 0 | 0 | 40 | 36 |
| Callum Wood | 11/4/99 | 9(10) | 8(9) | 0 | 0 | 0 | 0 | 0 | 0 | 0 | 0 |
| James Worthington | 21/5/99 | 8 | 8 | 0 | 0 | 0 | 0 | 0 | 0 | 0 | 0 |

*Shaun Ainscough*

**LEAGUE RECORD**
P27-W1-D0-L26 (14th)
F342, A1268, Diff-926, 2 points.

**CHALLENGE CUP**
Round Five

**1895 CUP**
Round Two

**ATTENDANCES**
Best - v Widnes (Ch - 1,732)
Worst - v Toulouse (Ch - 337)
Total (all home games included) - 10,008
Average (all home games included) - 770
(Up by 197 on 2018)

*'Ch' totals include Championship
regular season only; 'All' totals also include
Challenge Cup & 1895 Cup*

| | |
|---|---|
| **CLUB RECORDS** | **Highest score:** 120-4 v Illingworth, 13/3/2005 **Highest score against:** 0-106 v Castleford, 9/9/2007 |
| | **Record attendance:** 26,664 v Oldham, 25/3/22 *(Athletic Grounds)*; 8,061 v Oldham, 26/12/89 *(Spotland)* |
| **MATCH RECORDS** | **Tries:** 5 Jack Corsi v Barrow, 31/12/21; Jack Corsi v Broughton Moor, 25/2/22; Jack Williams v St Helens, 4/4/33; Norman Brelsford v Whitehaven, 3/9/73; Marlon Billy v York, 8/4/2001 **Goals:** 18 Lee Birdseye v Illingworth, 13/3/2005 **Points:** 44 Lee Birdseye v Illingworth, 13/3/2005 |
| **SEASON RECORDS** | **Tries:** 31 Marlon Billy 2001 **Goals:** 150 Martin Strett 1994-95 **Points:** 350 Mick Nanyn 2003 |
| **CAREER RECORDS** | **Tries:** 103 Jack Williams 1931-37 **Goals:** 741 Walter Gowers 1922-36 |
| | **Points:** 1,497 Walter Gowers 1922-36; Paul Crook 2010-2016 **Appearances:** 456 Walter Gowers 1922-36 |

# SHEFFIELD EAGLES

| DATE | FIXTURE | RESULT | SCORERS | LGE | ATT |
|---|---|---|---|---|---|
| 3/2/19 | Swinton (h) | W64-10 | t:Davies,Millar(2),Glover,Guzdek,Makelim,Farrell,Thackeray(4),Blackmore g:Walker(8) | 1st | 1,259 |
| 10/2/19 | Barrow (a) | W22-24 | t:Farrell,Millar(2),Thackeray g:Walker(4) | 2nd | 1,514 |
| 15/2/19 | Bradford (h) | W24-10 | t:Guzdek,Glover,Knowles,Farrell g:Walker(4) | 2nd | 1,711 |
| 1/3/19 | Batley (h) | W44-16 | t:Glover,Thackeray,Broadbent,Farrell,Davies,Blackmore(2),P Burns g:Walker(6) | 2nd | 791 |
| 10/3/19 | Featherstone (a) | L32-14 | t:Millar(2),Farrell g:Walker | 2nd | 1,981 |
| 17/3/19 | Dewsbury (a) | W13-16 | t:Thackeray,Farrell,Blackmore g:Walker(2) | 3rd | 977 |
| 24/3/19 | York (a) | W16-24 | t:Millar,Glover,Hellewell(2) g:Walker(4) | 3rd | 1,822 |
| 31/3/19 | Leigh (h) (CCR4) | L12-34 | t:Millar,Davies g:Walker(2) | N/A | 596 |
| 6/4/19 | Toronto (a) ● | L40-10 | t:Davies,Millar g:Walker | 4th | 1,148 |
| 19/4/19 | Toulouse (h) | W44-16 | t:James(2),Thackeray(3),Esslemont,Millar g:Walker(8) | 3rd | 729 |
| 22/4/19 | Rochdale (a) | W16-52 | t:Hellewell(2),Glover(2),Blackmore(2),Walker,Moran,Esslemont g:Walker(8) | 3rd | 569 |
| 28/4/19 | Halifax (h) | L24-32 | t:Brown,Davey,Millar,Blackmore g:Walker(4) | 3rd | 966 |
| 5/5/19 | Leigh (a) | L42-38 | t:Brown,Blackmore,Millar,Glover,Thackeray(2),Meadows g:Glover(2),Walker(3) | 3rd | 3,031 |
| 19/5/19 | Barrow (SB) ●● | W18-30 | t:Farrell(2),Blackmore,Thackeray(2) g:Walker(5) | 3rd | N/A |
| 24/5/19 | Toronto (h) | L16-42 | t:Hellewell,Guzdek,Knowles g:Walker(2) | 5th | 932 |
| 31/5/19 | Widnes (a) | L36-6 | t:Blackmore g:Walker | 6th | 4,920 |
| 5/6/19 | Halifax (a) (1895CR2) ●●● | W8-52 | t:Crookes(2),P Burns,Thackeray,Guzdek,Blackmore(2),Taylor,Brown,Millar g:Walker(6) | N/A | 312 |
| 9/6/19 | Featherstone (h) | L18-38 | t:Moran,Hellewell,Mason g:Walker(3) | 6th | 1,321 |
| 16/6/19 | Batley (a) | W24-54 | t:Knowles(2),Crookes,Moran(2),Walker,Brown,Broadbent,Davies g:Walker(9) | 6th | 2,798 |
| 21/6/19 | Rochdale (h) | W46-24 | t:Millar(3),Davies,Meadows(2),Thackeray,Moran g:Walker(4),Guzdek(3) | 6th | 543 |
| 26/6/19 | Doncaster (a) (1895CQF) ●●●● | W28-32 | t:Ogden,Dixon,Millar,Guzdek,Crookes,Thackeray g:Walker(4) | N/A | 374 |
| 30/6/19 | Leigh (h) | L18-22 | t:Thackeray,Blackmore(2),Millar g:Walker | 6th | 1,082 |
| 5/7/19 | York (h) | L16-23 | t:Blackmore,Thackeray,Davies g:Walker(2) | 7th | 793 |
| 12/7/19 | Dewsbury (h) | W28-22 | t:Blackmore(2),Ogden,Farrell,Esslemont g:Walker(4) | 7th | 691 |
| 20/7/19 | Toulouse (a) | L56-18 | t:Thackeray,Farrell,Davies g:Walker(3) | 7th | 2,154 |
| 28/7/19 | Batley (h) (1895CSF) | W18-2 | t:Farrell,Ogden,Davies g:Walker(3) | N/A | 727 |
| 2/8/19 | Widnes (h) | W30-10 | t:Blackmore,Knowles,Thackeray,Yere g:Walker(5) | 6th | 772 |
| 11/8/19 | Halifax (a) | W18-20 | t:Davies,P Burns,Brown g:Walker(4) | 6th | 1,205 |
| 18/8/19 | Barrow (h) | W44-18 | t:Millar(2),Brown,Guzdek,Makelim(2),Yere(2) g:Walker(5),Guzdek | 6th | 677 |
| 24/8/19 | Widnes (1895CF) ●●●●● | W36-18 | t:Brown(3),Thackeray,Farrell,Makelim g:Walker(6) | N/A | N/A |
| 1/9/19 | Bradford (a) | L30-10 | t:Farrell,Meadows g:Walker | 7th | 7,541 |
| 8/9/19 | Swinton (a) | L48-16 | t:Brown,Hellewell,Makelim g:Walker(2) | 7th | 814 |

● *Played at New River Stadium, London* ●● *Played at Bloomfield Road, Blackpool* ●●● *Played at Cougar Park, Keighley*
●●●● *Played at LD Nutrition Stadium, Featherstone* ●●●●● *Played at Wembley Stadium*

| | | APP | | TRIES | | GOALS | | FG | | PTS | |
|---|---|---|---|---|---|---|---|---|---|---|---|
| | D.O.B. | ALL | Ch | ALL | Ch | ALL | Ch | ALL | Ch | ALL | Ch |
| Sadiq Adebiyi | 8/1/97 | (3) | (3) | 0 | 0 | 0 | 0 | 0 | 0 | 0 | 0 |
| Ben Blackmore | 19/2/93 | 31 | 26 | 18 | 16 | 0 | 0 | 0 | 0 | 72 | 64 |
| Blake Broadbent | 11/12/98 | 2(21) | 1(18) | 2 | 2 | 0 | 0 | 0 | 0 | 8 | 8 |
| Aaron Brown | 27/7/92 | 31(1) | 27 | 10 | 6 | 0 | 0 | 0 | 0 | 40 | 24 |
| Greg Burns | 25/3/95 | 14(2) | 11(1) | 0 | 0 | 0 | 0 | 0 | 0 | 0 | 0 |
| Paddy Burns | 15/3/98 | 3(16) | 1(14) | 3 | 2 | 0 | 0 | 0 | 0 | 12 | 8 |
| Jason Crookes | 21/4/90 | 13(2) | 11(2) | 4 | 1 | 0 | 0 | 0 | 0 | 16 | 4 |
| James Davey | 21/8/89 | 17(4) | 16(2) | 1 | 0 | 0 | 0 | 0 | 0 | 4 | 4 |
| Olly Davies | 30/11/95 | 28(2) | 24(1) | 10 | 8 | 0 | 0 | 0 | 0 | 40 | 32 |
| Rory Dixon | 17/10/97 | 6(6) | 5(5) | 1 | 0 | 0 | 0 | 0 | 0 | 4 | 0 |
| Sonny Esslemont | 29/12/93 | 7(11) | 4(11) | 3 | 3 | 0 | 0 | 0 | 0 | 12 | 12 |
| Joel Farrell | 15/3/94 | 31(1) | 27 | 13 | 11 | 0 | 0 | 0 | 0 | 52 | 44 |
| James Glover | 2/12/93 | 14 | 13 | 7 | 7 | 2 | 2 | 0 | 0 | 32 | 32 |
| Josh Guzdek | 22/4/95 | 32 | 27 | 6 | 4 | 4 | 4 | 0 | 0 | 32 | 24 |
| Ben Hellewell | 30/1/92 | 12(1) | 10(1) | 7 | 7 | 0 | 0 | 0 | 0 | 28 | 28 |
| Daniel Hindmarsh | 8/8/98 | (2) | (2) | 0 | 0 | 0 | 0 | 0 | 0 | 0 | 0 |
| Matt James | 26/3/87 | 13(1) | 12(1) | 2 | 2 | 0 | 0 | 0 | 0 | 8 | 8 |
| Brad Knowles | 31/7/93 | 20(6) | 17(6) | 5 | 5 | 0 | 0 | 0 | 0 | 20 | 20 |
| Corey Makelim | 6/1/94 | 3(20) | 1(18) | 5 | 4 | 0 | 0 | 0 | 0 | 20 | 16 |
| Nathan Mason | 8/9/93 | 2(6) | 2(4) | 1 | 1 | 0 | 0 | 0 | 0 | 4 | 4 |
| James Meadows | 15/6/99 | 2(5) | 2(5) | 4 | 4 | 0 | 0 | 0 | 0 | 16 | 16 |
| Ryan Millar | 12/5/94 | 32 | 27 | 20 | 17 | 0 | 0 | 0 | 0 | 80 | 68 |
| Pat Moran | 2/4/98 | 12 | 12 | 5 | 5 | 0 | 0 | 0 | 0 | 20 | 20 |
| Jacob Ogden | 23/1/98 | 15 | 13 | 3 | 1 | 0 | 0 | 0 | 0 | 12 | 4 |
| Shaun Pick | 21/9/93 | 9(8) | 5(7) | 0 | 0 | 0 | 0 | 0 | 0 | 0 | 0 |
| Lewis Taylor | 15/4/97 | (4) | (2) | 1 | 0 | 0 | 0 | 0 | 0 | 4 | 0 |
| Anthony Thackeray | 19/2/86 | 31(1) | 26(1) | 23 | 20 | 0 | 0 | 0 | 0 | 92 | 80 |
| James Thornton | 30/9/95 | (3) | (2) | 0 | 0 | 0 | 0 | 0 | 0 | 0 | 0 |
| Pat Walker | 24/3/86 | 31(1) | 26(1) | 2 | 2 | 125 | 104 | 0 | 0 | 258 | 216 |
| Menzie Yere | 24/10/83 | 5(1) | 5(1) | 3 | 3 | 0 | 0 | 0 | 0 | 12 | 12 |

Anthony Thackeray

**LEAGUE RECORD**
P27-W15-D0-L12 (7th)
F748, A694, Diff+54, 30 points.

**CHALLENGE CUP**
Round Four

**1895 CUP**
Winners

**ATTENDANCES**
Best - v Bradford (Ch - 1,711)
Worst - v Rochdale (Ch - 543)
Total (excluding Challenge Cup) - 12,994
Average (excluding Challenge Cup) - 928
(Up by 244 on 2018)

*'Ch' totals include Championship regular season only; 'All' totals also include Challenge Cup & 1895 Cup*

| CLUB RECORDS | |
|---|---|
| | **Highest score:** 112-6 v Leigh East, 7/4/2013  **Highest score against:** 0-88 v Hull, 2/3/2003 |
| | **Record attendance:** 10,603 v Bradford, 16/8/97 *(Don Valley Stadium)*; 1,711 v Bradford, 15/2/2019 *(Olympic Legacy Park)* |
| MATCH RECORDS | **Tries:** 5 Daryl Powell v Mansfield, 2/1/89; Menzie Yere v Leigh East, 7/4/2013; Quentin Laulu-Togaga'e v Rochdale, 7/9/2014; Garry Lo v Rochdale, 4/6/2017 |
| | **Goals:** 14 Dominic Brambani v Leigh East, 7/4/2013  **Points:** 32 Roy Rafferty v Fulham, 21/9/86 |
| SEASON RECORDS | **Tries:** 46 Menzie Yere 2013  **Goals:** 169 *(inc 1fg)* Dominic Brambani 2013  **Points:** 361 Dominic Brambani 2013 |
| CAREER RECORDS | **Tries:** 196 Menzie Yere 2009-2019  **Goals:** 986 Mark Aston 1986-2004  **Points:** 2,142 Mark Aston 1986-2004  **Appearances:** 389 Mark Aston 1986-2004 |

# SWINTON LIONS

| DATE | FIXTURE | RESULT | SCORERS | LGE | ATT |
|------|---------|--------|---------|-----|-----|
| 3/2/19 | Sheffield (a) | L64-10 | t:Gray,Brickhill g:Thomas | 14th | 1,259 |
| 10/2/19 | Bradford (h) | L12-31 | t:Butt,Forsyth g:Hankinson(2) | 14th | 1,498 |
| 17/2/19 | Dewsbury (a) | L38-24 | t:Fairclough,Shelford,Lloyd,Hatton,Butt g:Smith(2) | 14th | 993 |
| 24/2/19 | Toulouse (h) | L24-26 | t:Butt,Hansen,Fairclough,Forsyth g:Smith(4) | 14th | 601 |
| 3/3/19 | Halifax (a) | L18-16 | t:Ashton(2),Butt g:Smith(2) | 13th | 1,584 |
| 10/3/19 | Leigh (h) | L12-30 | t:Ashton(2) g:Smith(2) | 13th | 2,054 |
| 17/3/19 | Featherstone (h) | L12-24 | t:Bennion,Ashton g:Thomas(2) | 13th | 923 |
| 24/3/19 | Barrow (a) | W26-33 | t:Forsyth(2),Butt,Hansen,Bennion,Paisley g:Smith(2),Thomas(2) fg:Thomas | 11th | 1,357 |
| 30/3/19 | Featherstone (a) (CCR4) | L38-14 | t:Bennion,Butt,Aaronson g:Thomas | N/A | 691 |
| 7/4/19 | York (a) | L30-20 | t:Hansen,Smith,Forsyth,Waterworth g:Smith(2) | 12th | 1,606 |
| 19/4/19 | Rochdale (h) | W36-22 | t:Butt(4),Thomas,Forsyth,Bennion g:Thomas(4) | 11th | 826 |
| 22/4/19 | Batley (a) | L32-18 | t:Ashton(3) g:Thomas(3) | 11th | 817 |
| 28/4/19 | Toronto (a) | L52-10 | t:Ashton,Butt g:Smith | 11th | 9,562 |
| 5/5/19 | Widnes (h) | L10-32 | t:Butt,Ashton g:Smith | 12th | 1,469 |
| 18/5/19 | Rochdale (SB) ● | W30-40 | t:Butt,Halton,Ashton(2),Lloyd,Hansen,Fairclough,Paisley g:Smith(4) | 11th | N/A |
| 26/5/19 | Dewsbury (h) | W22-17 | t:Ashton,Paisley,Bennion(2) g:Fairclough(3) | 10th | 795 |
| 2/6/19 | Dewsbury (a) (1895CR2) | L44-26 | t:Byrne,Lloyd,Hansen,Brickhill,Wells g:Smith(3) | N/A | 453 |
| 9/6/19 | Toronto (h) | L14-34 | t:Butt(2),Fairclough g:Fairclough | 12th | 1,281 |
| 15/6/19 | Toulouse (h) | W18-20 | t:Lloyd,Paisley(3) g:Hansen(2) | 10th | 2,789 |
| 23/6/19 | York (h) | L12-26 | t:Ashton,Waterworth g:Hansen(2) | 11th | 976 |
| 30/6/19 | Rochdale (a) ●● | W28-36 | t:Moore,Wells,Ashton(2),Butt(2),Hansen g:Hansen(4) | 10th | 549 |
| 7/7/19 | Batley (h) | W20-18 | t:Lloyd,Bennion,Hatton g:Hansen(4) | 9th | 888 |
| 14/7/19 | Bradford (a) | D34-34 | t:Lepori,Bennion,Smith,Ashton(2),Kibula g:Hansen(5) | 9th | 3,104 |
| 21/7/19 | Barrow (h) | W30-12 | t:Ashton,Halton,Lloyd,Butt,Smith g:Hansen(5) | 9th | 984 |
| 4/8/19 | Leigh (a) | L31-30 | t:Ashton(4),Butt g:Hansen(5) | 9th | 3,155 |
| 11/8/19 | Featherstone (a) | L66-16 | t:Hansen,Fairclough,Waterworth g:Hansen(2) | 10th | 2,090 |
| 18/8/19 | Halifax (h) | W32-12 | t:Lepori(2),Mullen,Butt,Ashton,Hankinson g:Hansen(4) | 9th | 909 |
| 1/9/19 | Widnes (a) | L36-28 | t:Butt,Kibula,Hansen,Gregson,Ashton g:Hansen(4) | 9th | 3,928 |
| 8/9/19 | Sheffield (h) | W48-16 | t:Ashton(5),Bennion,Wells,Hansen,Morris g:Hansen(5),Ashton | 9th | 814 |

● *Played at Bloomfield Road, Blackpool*
●● *Played at Mayfield Sports Centre*

| | | APP | | TRIES | | GOALS | | FG | | PTS | |
|---|---|-----|-----|-------|-----|-------|-----|-----|-----|-----|-----|
| | D.O.B. | ALL | Ch | ALL | Ch | ALL | Ch | ALL | Ch | ALL | Ch |
| Harry Aaronson | 28/3/98 | 3(3) | 2(3) | 1 | 0 | 0 | 0 | 0 | 0 | 4 | 0 |
| Jamie Acton | 4/4/92 | 2(2) | 1(2) | 0 | 0 | 0 | 0 | 0 | 0 | 0 | 0 |
| Matty Ashton | 28/7/98 | 25 | 24 | 30 | 30 | 1 | 1 | 0 | 0 | 122 | 122 |
| Ben Austin | 3/5/95 | (2) | (2) | 0 | 0 | 0 | 0 | 0 | 0 | 0 | 0 |
| Gavin Bennion | 31/12/93 | 26 | 25 | 9 | 8 | 0 | 0 | 0 | 0 | 36 | 32 |
| Billy Brickhill | 30/4/97 | 3(24) | 3(22) | 2 | 1 | 0 | 0 | 0 | 0 | 8 | 4 |
| Mike Butt | 6/5/95 | 27 | 26 | 21 | 20 | 0 | 0 | 0 | 0 | 84 | 80 |
| Liam Byrne | 18/8/99 | 5(2) | 4(2) | 1 | 0 | 0 | 0 | 0 | 0 | 4 | 0 |
| Rob Fairclough | 10/9/97 | 25(2) | 23(2) | 5 | 5 | 4 | 4 | 0 | 0 | 28 | 28 |
| Liam Forsyth | 23/3/96 | 13 | 11 | 6 | 6 | 0 | 0 | 0 | 0 | 24 | 24 |
| Josh Ganson | 19/2/98 | (3) | (2) | 0 | 0 | 0 | 0 | 0 | 0 | 0 | 0 |
| Ryan Gray | 2/3/98 | 1 | 1 | 1 | 1 | 0 | 0 | 0 | 0 | 4 | 4 |
| Nick Gregson | 17/12/95 | 2(4) | 2(4) | 1 | 1 | 0 | 0 | 0 | 0 | 4 | 4 |
| Aaron Hall | 19/2/93 | 1(3) | (3) | 0 | 0 | 0 | 0 | 0 | 0 | 0 | 0 |
| Frankie Halton | 18/6/96 | 22(2) | 21(2) | 2 | 2 | 0 | 0 | 0 | 0 | 8 | 8 |
| Chris Hankinson | 30/11/93 | 8 | 8 | 1 | 1 | 2 | 2 | 0 | 0 | 8 | 8 |
| Jack Hansen | 12/1/97 | 29 | 27 | 9 | 8 | 42 | 42 | 0 | 0 | 120 | 116 |
| Lewis Hatton | 14/1/97 | 26(1) | 24(1) | 2 | 2 | 0 | 0 | 0 | 0 | 8 | 8 |
| Will Hope | 2/6/93 | 1 | 1 | 0 | 0 | 0 | 0 | 0 | 0 | 0 | 0 |
| Adam Jones | 13/4/97 | 4(10) | 4(9) | 0 | 0 | 0 | 0 | 0 | 0 | 0 | 0 |
| Paddy Jones | 7/2/97 | 16(10) | 16(9) | 0 | 0 | 0 | 0 | 0 | 0 | 0 | 0 |
| Jose Kenga | 3/5/95 | 1(15) | 1(13) | 0 | 0 | 0 | 0 | 0 | 0 | 0 | 0 |
| Samy Kibula | 7/8/99 | 2(9) | 2(9) | 2 | 2 | 0 | 0 | 0 | 0 | 8 | 8 |
| Adam Lawton | 13/6/93 | 1(3) | (3) | 0 | 0 | 0 | 0 | 0 | 0 | 0 | 0 |
| Richard Lepori | 22/10/91 | 9 | 9 | 3 | 3 | 0 | 0 | 0 | 0 | 12 | 12 |
| Rhodri Lloyd | 22/7/93 | 24 | 23 | 6 | 5 | 0 | 0 | 0 | 0 | 24 | 20 |
| Scott Taylor | 23/1/88 | (4) | (4) | 1 | 1 | 0 | 0 | 0 | 0 | 4 | 4 |
| Ben Morris | 1/8/97 | (4) | (4) | 1 | 1 | 0 | 0 | 0 | 0 | 4 | 4 |
| Craig Mullen | 15/1/98 | 10 | 10 | 1 | 1 | 0 | 0 | 0 | 0 | 4 | 4 |
| Liam Paisley | 27/11/97 | 11 | 11 | 6 | 6 | 0 | 0 | 0 | 0 | 24 | 24 |
| Oliver Partington | 3/9/98 | 2(1) | 2(1) | 0 | 0 | 0 | 0 | 0 | 0 | 0 | 0 |
| Mike Ratu | 16/10/87 | 1 | 0 | 0 | 0 | 0 | 0 | 0 | 0 | 0 | 0 |
| Kyle Shelford | 13/9/96 | 8(7) | 8(6) | 1 | 1 | 0 | 0 | 0 | 0 | 4 | 4 |
| Jake Shorrocks | 26/10/95 | 2(1) | 2(1) | 0 | 0 | 0 | 0 | 0 | 0 | 0 | 0 |
| Harry Smith | 25/1/00 | 15(1) | 13(1) | 3 | 3 | 23 | 20 | 0 | 0 | 58 | 52 |
| Oscar Thomas | 3/1/94 | 6(1) | 5(1) | 1 | 1 | 13 | 12 | 1 | 1 | 31 | 29 |
| Luke Waterworth | 20/6/96 | 27 | 25 | 3 | 3 | 0 | 0 | 0 | 0 | 12 | 12 |
| Jack Wells | 21/9/97 | 16 | 15 | 3 | 2 | 0 | 0 | 0 | 0 | 12 | 8 |
| Daley Williams | 15/5/86 | 3(1) | 2(1) | 0 | 0 | 0 | 0 | 0 | 0 | 0 | 0 |

Matty Ashton

**LEAGUE RECORD**
P27-W10-D1-L16 (9th)
F619, A803, Diff-184, 21 points.

**CHALLENGE CUP**
Round Four

**1895 CUP**
Round Two

**ATTENDANCES**
Best - v Leigh (Ch - 2,054)
Worst - v Toulouse (Ch - 601)
Total (all home games included) - 14,018
Average (all home games included) - 1,078
(Up by 310 on 2018)

*'Ch' totals include Championship regular season only; 'All' totals also include Challenge Cup & 1895 Cup*

| | |
|---|---|
| **CLUB RECORDS** | **Highest score:** 96-4 v Oxford, 12/7/2015 **Highest score against:** 0-112 v Warrington, 20/5/2011 |
| | **Record attendance:** 26,891 v Wigan, 12/2/64 *(Station Road)*; 2,155 v Toulouse, 28/4/2018 *(Heywood Road)* |
| **MATCH RECORDS** | **Tries:** 6 Mark Riley v Prescot, 11/8/96 **Goals:** 14 Ian Mort v Oxford, 12/7/2015 **Points:** 48 Ian Mort v Oxford, 12/7/2015 |
| **SEASON RECORDS** | **Tries:** 42 John Stopford 1963-64 **Goals:** 128 Albert Blan 1960-61 **Points:** 338 Ian Mort 2011 |
| **CAREER RECORDS** | **Tries:** 197 Frank Evans 1921-31 **Goals:** 970 Ken Gowers 1954-73 **Points:** 2,105 Ken Gowers 1954-73 **Appearances:** 601 Ken Gowers 1954-73 |

TORONTO
WOLFPACK

# TORONTO WOLFPACK

| DATE | FIXTURE | RESULT | SCORERS | LGE | ATT |
|------|---------|--------|---------|-----|-----|
| 3/2/19 | York (a) | W0-14 | t:Wheeler,Russell,Mellor g:O'Brien | 3rd | 2,518 |
| 10/2/19 | Rochdale (a) | W6-58 | t:Russell(4),Mellor,O'Brien,Lussick,Leutele,Stanley,Emmitt,Sidlow g:O'Brien(7) | 1st | 694 |
| 16/2/19 | Widnes (h) ● | W30-6 | t:Wallace,Ackers(2),Wheeler,Leutele g:O'Brien(5) | 1st | 1,817 |
| 24/2/19 | Leigh (a) | W8-14 | t:Wallace,Higson,Thompson g:O'Brien | 1st | 3,142 |
| 3/3/19 | Dewsbury (a) | W17-22 | t:Higson,Brierley,Wallace,O'Brien g:O'Brien(3) | 1st | 1,251 |
| 9/3/19 | Toulouse (a) ●● | L46-16 | t:Wallace,Beswick,Leutele g:O'Brien(2) | 1st | 6,103 |
| 17/3/19 | Batley (h) ●●● | W34-12 | t:Russell(2),Dixon,Logan,Leutele(2),Wilkin g:O'Brien(2),Brierley | 1st | N/A |
| 24/3/19 | Halifax (a) | W12-48 | t:Wilkin,Dixon(3),Wallace(2),Russell(2),Rawsthorne g:O'Brien(6) | 1st | 2,090 |
| 6/4/19 | Sheffield (h) ●●●● | W40-10 | t:Stanley,Russell(2),Olbison,Ackers,Wallace(2),Sidlow g:O'Brien,Wallace(3) | 1st | 1,148 |
| 19/4/19 | Barrow (a) | W26-52 | t:Wallace(3),O'Brien(3),Russell,Dixon,Ackers g:Wallace(8) | 1st | 1,417 |
| 22/4/19 | Featherstone (a) | W14-23 | t:O'Brien,Russell(3),Dixon g:Wallace fg:McCrone | 1st | 2,101 |
| 28/4/19 | Swinton (h) | W52-10 | t:O'Brien,Wallace(2),Thompson,Ackers,Dixon,Leutele,Olbison,Higson g:Wallace(8) | 1st | 9,562 |
| 4/5/19 | Bradford (h) | W36-16 | t:Rawsthorne(2),Sidlow,Leutele,Stanley,O'Brien,Kay g:O'Brien(4) | 1st | 8,363 |
| 18/5/19 | Toulouse (SB) ●●●●● | W42-14 | t:O'Brien,McCrone,Stanley(3),Lussick,Rawsthorne g:O'Brien(7) | 1st | N/A |
| 24/5/19 | Sheffield (a) | W16-42 | t:Wallace,Dixon(2),Kay,Stanley,Leutele,Rawsthorne,Ackers g:Wallace(5) | 1st | 932 |
| 9/6/19 | Swinton (a) | W14-34 | t:Dixon,Leutele(2),Stanley,Beswick,Sidlow g:Wallace(5) | 1st | 1,281 |
| 15/6/19 | Dewsbury (h) | W70-8 | t:O'Brien,Ackers,Russell(2),Mullally(2),Mellor,Kay(2),Sidlow,Wallace,Beswick g:O'Brien(11) | 1st | 6,745 |
| 22/6/19 | Toulouse (h) | W28-16 | t:Worthington(2),Russell,Ackers g:O'Brien(6) | 1st | 7,742 |
| 30/6/19 | Batley (a) | W10-40 | t:Russell(2),Leutele(2),O'Brien,Ackers(2) g:O'Brien(5),Wallace | 1st | 894 |
| 6/7/19 | Halifax (h) | W34-12 | t:Kay(2),Ackers,O'Brien(2),Olbison g:O'Brien(5) | 1st | 6,749 |
| 13/7/19 | Featherstone (h) | W22-18 | t:O'Brien,Stanley,Leutele,McCrone g:O'Brien(3) | 1st | 7,891 |
| 21/7/19 | Widnes (a) | W19-24 | t:Rawsthorne,Stanley,Thompson,Lussick,Mullally g:McCrone,Miloudi | 1st | 3,812 |
| 4/8/19 | Bradford (a) | W20-25 | t:Leutele(2),Rawsthorne(2),Kay g:Wallace,Miloudi fg:Miloudi | 1st | 3,421 |
| 10/8/19 | York (h) | W56-6 | t:O'Brien(3),Miloudi,McCrone(2),Dixon,Ackers(2),Rawsthorne,Russell g:O'Brien(5),Wallace | 1st | 7,262 |
| 17/8/19 | Rochdale (h) | W46-0 | t:O'Brien(2),Russell(3),Olbison,Stanley(2),Miloudi g:O'Brien(3),Miloudi(2) | 1st | 5,969 |
| 31/8/19 | Barrow (h) | W62-8 | t:McCrone,Dixon(2),Kay(3),Russell(2),Mellor,Mullally,Ackers g:O'Brien(9) | 1st | 7,129 |
| 7/9/19 | Leigh (h) | W46-12 | t:McCrone(2),Miloudi,O'Brien,Russell,Mellor,Kay,Beswick g:O'Brien(7) | 1st | 8,152 |
| 22/9/19 | Toulouse (h) (QSF) | W40-24 | t:Mellor(2),Leutele(3),McCrone,Kay,Stanley g:O'Brien(4) | N/A | 9,325 |
| 5/10/19 | Featherstone (h) (GF) | W24-6 | t:McCrone,Wallace,Thompson,Mellor g:O'Brien(2),Wallace(2) | N/A | 9,974 |

● *Played at Kingston Park, Newcastle* ●● *Played at Stade Ernest Wallon* ●●● *Played at KCOM Craven Park, Hull*
●●●● *Played at New River Stadium, London* ●●●●● *Played at Bloomfield Road, Blackpool*

| | | APP | | TRIES | | GOALS | | FG | | PTS | |
|---|---|---|---|---|---|---|---|---|---|---|---|
| | D.O.B. | ALL | Ch | ALL | Ch | ALL | Ch | ALL | Ch | ALL | Ch |
| Andy Ackers | 25/12/93 | 21(8) | 21(8) | 14 | 14 | 0 | 0 | 0 | 0 | 56 | 56 |
| Bob Beswick | 8/12/84 | 6(10) | 6(10) | 4 | 4 | 0 | 0 | 0 | 0 | 16 | 16 |
| Ryan Brierley | 12/3/92 | 1(4) | 1(4) | 1 | 1 | 1 | 1 | 0 | 0 | 6 | 6 |
| Andrew Dixon | 28/2/90 | 29 | 29 | 13 | 13 | 0 | 0 | 0 | 0 | 52 | 52 |
| Jake Emmitt | 4/10/88 | (2) | (2) | 1 | 1 | 0 | 0 | 0 | 0 | 4 | 4 |
| Brad Fash | 24/1/96 | (2) | (2) | 0 | 0 | 0 | 0 | 0 | 0 | 0 | 0 |
| Adam Higson | 19/5/87 | 7 | 7 | 3 | 3 | 0 | 0 | 0 | 0 | 12 | 12 |
| Liam Kay | 17/12/91 | 16 | 16 | 12 | 12 | 0 | 0 | 0 | 0 | 48 | 48 |
| Olsi Krasniqi | 26/6/92 | (1) | (1) | 0 | 0 | 0 | 0 | 0 | 0 | 0 | 0 |
| Ricky Leutele | 10/4/90 | 28 | 28 | 18 | 18 | 0 | 0 | 0 | 0 | 72 | 72 |
| Jack Logan | 8/9/95 | 3 | 3 | 1 | 1 | 0 | 0 | 0 | 0 | 4 | 4 |
| Darcy Lussick | 6/6/89 | 10(14) | 10(14) | 3 | 3 | 0 | 0 | 0 | 0 | 12 | 12 |
| Josh McCrone | 12/4/97 | 28 | 28 | 9 | 9 | 1 | 1 | 1 | 1 | 39 | 39 |
| Joe Mellor | 28/11/90 | 18(2) | 18(2) | 8 | 8 | 0 | 0 | 0 | 0 | 32 | 32 |
| Hakim Miloudi | 26/6/93 | 6(4) | 6(4) | 3 | 3 | 4 | 4 | 1 | 1 | 21 | 21 |
| Anthony Mullally | 28/6/91 | 10(14) | 10(14) | 4 | 4 | 0 | 0 | 0 | 0 | 16 | 16 |
| Gareth O'Brien | 31/10/91 | 26 | 26 | 20 | 20 | 99 | 99 | 0 | 0 | 278 | 278 |
| Tom Olbison | 20/3/91 | 17(12) | 17(12) | 4 | 4 | 0 | 0 | 0 | 0 | 16 | 16 |
| Nick Rawsthorne | 30/9/95 | 12(2) | 12(2) | 9 | 9 | 0 | 0 | 0 | 0 | 36 | 36 |
| Matty Russell | 6/6/93 | 21 | 21 | 27 | 27 | 0 | 0 | 0 | 0 | 108 | 108 |
| Adam Sidlow | 25/10/87 | 12(5) | 12(5) | 5 | 5 | 0 | 0 | 0 | 0 | 20 | 20 |
| Ashton Sims | 26/2/85 | 15(8) | 15(8) | 0 | 0 | 0 | 0 | 0 | 0 | 0 | 0 |
| Gadwin Springer | 4/4/93 | 5(12) | 5(12) | 0 | 0 | 0 | 0 | 0 | 0 | 0 | 0 |
| Chase Stanley | 31/5/89 | 16(1) | 16(1) | 13 | 13 | 0 | 0 | 0 | 0 | 52 | 52 |
| Bodene Thompson | 1/8/88 | 20(1) | 20(1) | 4 | 4 | 0 | 0 | 0 | 0 | 16 | 16 |
| Blake Wallace | 18/6/92 | 16(8) | 16(8) | 16 | 16 | 35 | 35 | 0 | 0 | 134 | 134 |
| Gary Wheeler | 30/9/89 | 2(1) | 2(1) | 2 | 2 | 0 | 0 | 0 | 0 | 8 | 8 |
| Jon Wilkin | 11/1/83 | 27 | 27 | 2 | 2 | 0 | 0 | 0 | 0 | 8 | 8 |
| Greg Worthington | 17/7/90 | 5(3) | 5(3) | 2 | 2 | 0 | 0 | 0 | 0 | 8 | 8 |

*'Ch' totals include play-offs*

Ricky Leutele

**LEAGUE RECORD**
P27-W26-D0-L1
(1st/Grand Final Winners, Champions)
F1010, A356, Diff+654, 52 points.

**CHALLENGE CUP**
Not entered

**1895 CUP**
Not entered

**ATTENDANCES**
Best - v Featherstone (GF - 9,974)
Worst - v Sheffield (Ch - 1,148)
Total (all home games included) - 97,828
Average (all home games included) - 6,988
(Up by 423 on 2018)

| | |
|---|---|
| CLUB RECORDS | Highest score: 82-6 v Doncaster, 9/4/2017 Highest score against: 10-66 v Warrington, 13/5/2018 Record attendance: 9,974 v Featherstone, 5/10/2019 |
| MATCH RECORDS | Tries: 5 Liam Kay v York, 1/7/2017 Goals: 13 Craig Hall v Doncaster, 9/4/2017 Points: 38 Craig Hall v Hemel, 15/7/2017 |
| SEASON RECORDS | Tries: 27 Liam Kay 2017; Matty Russell 2019 Goals: 171 Craig Hall 2017 Points: 442 Craig Hall 2017 |
| CAREER RECORDS | Tries: 65 Liam Kay 2017-2019 Goals: 171 Craig Hall 2017 Points: 466 Gareth O'Brien 2018-2019 Appearances: 73 Adam Sidlow 2017-2019 |

# TOULOUSE OLYMPIQUE

| DATE | FIXTURE | RESULT | SCORERS | LGE | ATT |
|---|---|---|---|---|---|
| 3/2/19 | Leigh (a) | L24-16 | t:Robin,Marcon(2) g:Kheirallah(2) | 11th | 2,987 |
| 9/2/19 | Widnes (h) | L24-36 | t:Parata,Robin(3) g:Kheirallah(4) | 11th | 2,189 |
| 16/2/19 | Rochdale (h) | W42-12 | t:Marguerite(2),Ford,Robin(2),Kheirallah,Bergal,Barthau g:Kheirallah(5) | 10th | 1,707 |
| 24/2/19 | Swinton (a) | W24-26 | t:Marguerite,Parata(2),Mika,Kheirallah g:Kheirallah(3) | 6th | 601 |
| 3/3/19 | Bradford (a) | W0-14 | t:Maurel,Robin g:Kheirallah(3) | 4th | 3,751 |
| 9/3/19 | Toronto (h) ● | W46-16 | t:Parata,Robin(2),Marguerite,Curran,Kheirallah(2) g:Kheirallah(9) | 4th | 6,103 |
| 16/3/19 | Barrow (h) | W50-0 | t:Marguerite,Ader(3),Maurel(2),Marion(2),Jussaume,Bretherton g:Kheirallah(4),Barthau | 2nd | 1,388 |
| 23/3/19 | Batley (a) | W12-38 | t:Bretherton,Mika,Sangare,Maurel(2),Barthau,Marcon g:Kheirallah(5) | 2nd | 857 |
| 6/4/19 | Featherstone (h) | W8-2 | t:Hepi g:Kheirallah(2) | 2nd | 2,251 |
| 19/4/19 | Sheffield (a) | L44-16 | t:Jussaume,Barthau,Marcon g:Kheirallah(2) | 2nd | 729 |
| 22/4/19 | Halifax (h) | W56-4 | t:Marion(3),Bretherton,Kheirallah(3),Jussaume,Ader,Bergal g:Kheirallah(8) | 2nd | 2,038 |
| 27/4/19 | York (h) | W30-26 | t:Ader,Curran,Kheirallah,Robin,Marion g:Marion(3),Maurel(2) | 2nd | 1,793 |
| 4/5/19 | Dewsbury (a) | W0-38 | t:Mika,Marion,Bretherton,Boyer,Ford,Kheirallah,Bell g:Marion(5) | 2nd | 786 |
| 18/5/19 | Toronto (SB) ●● | L42-14 | t:Bretherton,Curran g:Kheirallah(3) | 2nd | N/A |
| 25/5/19 | Leigh (h) | W44-16 | t:Marcon(2),Bell,Mika,Jussaume(2),P Vaivai,Robin g:Kheirallah(6) | 2nd | 2,235 |
| 8/6/19 | York (h) | W18-25 | t:Jussaume(2),Bell,Marcon g:Barthau(2) fg:Barthau | 2nd | 1,656 |
| 15/6/19 | Swinton (h) | L18-20 | t:Robin,Maurel,Marion,Marcon g:Barthau | 2nd | 2,789 |
| 22/6/19 | Toronto (a) | L28-16 | t:Boyer,Barthau,Santi g:Barthau(2) | 2nd | 7,742 |
| 30/6/19 | Barrow (a) | W6-36 | t:Maurel(2),Hepi,Bretherton,Mika,Bell,P Vaivai g:Barthau(4) | 2nd | 1,422 |
| 6/7/19 | Bradford (h) | L24-26 | t:Bretherton,Marion,Robin,Marguerite g:Kheirallah(4) | 3rd | 3,560 |
| 13/7/19 | Rochdale (a) | W0-68 | t:Bergal(3),J Vaivai,Mika,Marion,Robin(2),Kheirallah,P Vaivai g:Kheirallah(10) | 3rd | 337 |
| 20/7/19 | Sheffield (h) | W56-18 | t:Marcon(2),Bretherton,Mika,Kheirallah,Jussaume,Parata,Bergal(2),Robin g:Kheirallah(8) | 3rd | 2,154 |
| 4/8/19 | Halifax (a) | W22-30 | t:Bergal(2),Jussaume,Marion,P Vaivai g:Kheirallah(5) | 3rd | 1,290 |
| 10/8/19 | Widnes (a) | W12-28 | t:J Vaivai,Mika,Bergal,Bretherton,Dezaria g:Kheirallah(4) | 2nd | 3,643 |
| 17/8/19 | Batley (h) | W46-0 | t:P Vaivai,Curran,Ford,Bergal,Robin(2),Kheirallah,J Vaivai g:Kheirallah(7) | 2nd | 1,895 |
| 31/8/19 | Dewsbury (h) | W42-14 | t:Bell,Mika,J Vaivai,Robin(2),Marion,P Vaivai g:Marion(7) | 2nd | 2,055 |
| 7/9/19 | Featherstone (a) | W24-26 | t:Jussaume,Evans,Parata(2),Robin g:Kheirallah(3) | 2nd | 2,334 |
| 14/9/19 | York (h) (QPO) | W44-6 | t:Marcon,Kheirallah(2),Marguerite,Marion,Jussaume,Ford,Robin g:Kheirallah(6) | N/A | 1,132 |
| 22/9/19 | Toronto (a) (QSF) | L40-24 | t:Kheirallah(3),Barthau g:Kheirallah(4) | N/A | 9,325 |
| 29/9/19 | Featherstone (h) (FE) | L12-36 | t:Barthau,Marcon g:Kheirallah(2) | N/A | 1,068 |

● Played at Stade Ernest Wallon
●● Played at Bloomfield Road, Blackpool

|  |  | APP | | TRIES | | GOALS | | FG | | PTS | |
|---|---|---|---|---|---|---|---|---|---|---|---|
|  | D.O.B. | ALL | Ch | ALL | Ch | ALL | Ch | ALL | Ch | ALL | Ch |
| Bastien Ader | 6/6/91 | 18 | 18 | 5 | 5 | 0 | 0 | 0 | 0 | 20 | 20 |
| William Barthau | 30/1/90 | 10(6) | 10(6) | 6 | 6 | 12 | 12 | 1 | 1 | 49 | 49 |
| James Bell | 2/5/94 | 19(3) | 19(3) | 5 | 5 | 0 | 0 | 0 | 0 | 20 | 20 |
| Ilias Bergal | 6/4/96 | 9 | 9 | 14 | 14 | 0 | 0 | 0 | 0 | 56 | 56 |
| Justin Bouscayrol | 15/12/97 | (2) | (2) | 0 | 0 | 0 | 0 | 0 | 0 | 0 | 0 |
| Clement Boyer | 27/7/94 | 13(8) | 13(8) | 2 | 2 | 0 | 0 | 0 | 0 | 8 | 8 |
| Joe Bretherton | 5/10/95 | 18(5) | 18(5) | 9 | 9 | 0 | 0 | 0 | 0 | 36 | 36 |
| Jodie Broughton | 9/1/88 | 1 | 1 | 0 | 0 | 0 | 0 | 0 | 0 | 0 | 0 |
| Rhys Curran | 7/7/89 | 18 | 18 | 4 | 4 | 0 | 0 | 0 | 0 | 16 | 16 |
| Jordan Dezaria | 6/11/96 | 3(11) | 3(11) | 1 | 1 | 0 | 0 | 0 | 0 | 4 | 4 |
| Ben Evans | 30/10/92 | 5(14) | 5(14) | 1 | 1 | 0 | 0 | 0 | 0 | 4 | 4 |
| Johnathon Ford | 17/8/89 | 25 | 25 | 4 | 4 | 0 | 0 | 0 | 0 | 16 | 16 |
| Tyla Hepi | 15/6/93 | (27) | (27) | 2 | 2 | 0 | 0 | 0 | 0 | 8 | 8 |
| Mathieu Jussaume | 17/5/99 | 23 | 23 | 11 | 11 | 0 | 0 | 0 | 0 | 44 | 44 |
| Mark Kheirallah | 15/2/90 | 26 | 26 | 18 | 18 | 109 | 109 | 0 | 0 | 290 | 290 |
| Pierre-Jean Lima | 13/10/00 | (3) | (3) | 0 | 0 | 0 | 0 | 0 | 0 | 0 | 0 |
| Paul Marcon | 10/7/95 | 22 | 22 | 12 | 12 | 0 | 0 | 0 | 0 | 48 | 48 |
| Gavin Marguerite | 12/8/96 | 12 | 12 | 7 | 7 | 0 | 0 | 0 | 0 | 28 | 28 |
| Anthony Marion | 12/1/94 | 25(5) | 25(5) | 13 | 13 | 15 | 15 | 0 | 0 | 82 | 82 |
| Tony Maurel | 21/4/93 | 16 | 16 | 8 | 8 | 2 | 2 | 0 | 0 | 36 | 36 |
| Con Mika | 14/9/89 | 30 | 30 | 9 | 9 | 0 | 0 | 0 | 0 | 36 | 36 |
| Dean Parata | 4/10/91 | 14(13) | 14(13) | 7 | 7 | 0 | 0 | 0 | 0 | 28 | 28 |
| Maxime Puech | 16/3/94 | 14(4) | 14(4) | 0 | 0 | 0 | 0 | 0 | 0 | 0 | 0 |
| Stan Robin | 21/10/90 | 25 | 25 | 20 | 20 | 0 | 0 | 0 | 0 | 80 | 80 |
| Arthur Romano | 17/8/97 | 3 | 3 | 0 | 0 | 0 | 0 | 0 | 0 | 0 | 0 |
| Justin Sangare | 7/3/98 | (11) | (11) | 1 | 1 | 0 | 0 | 0 | 0 | 4 | 4 |
| Brenden Santi | 5/8/93 | 15(4) | 15(4) | 1 | 1 | 0 | 0 | 0 | 0 | 4 | 4 |
| Junior Vaivai | 18/1/90 | 8 | 8 | 4 | 4 | 0 | 0 | 0 | 0 | 16 | 16 |
| Paterika Vaivai | 14/2/92 | 18(4) | 18(4) | 6 | 6 | 0 | 0 | 0 | 0 | 24 | 24 |

'Ch' totals include play-offs

Anthony Marion

**LEAGUE RECORD**
P27-W20-D0-L7
(2nd/Final Eliminator)
F877, A446, Diff+431, 40 points.

**CHALLENGE CUP**
Not entered

**1895 CUP**
Not entered

**ATTENDANCES**
Best - v Toronto (Ch - 6,103)
Worst - v Featherstone (FE - 1,068)
Total (all home games included) - 34,357
Average (all home games included) - 2,290
(Down by 248 on 2018)

**CLUB RECORDS**
Highest score: 84-6 v Keighley, 18/6/2016  Highest score against: 10-90 v Featherstone, 3/7/2011
Record attendance: 6,103 v Toronto, 9/3/2019 *(Stade Ernest Wallon)*; 4,127 v Hull KR, 22/9/2018 *(Stade Ernest Argeles)*

**MATCH RECORDS**  Tries: 6 Ilias Bergal v Rochdale, 13/7/2019  Goals: 12 Mark Kheirallah v Keighley, 18/6/2016  Points: 40 Mark Kheirallah v Keighley, 18/6/2016
**SEASON RECORDS**  Tries: 36 Kuni Minga 2016  Goals: 171 Mark Kheirallah 2016  Points: 466 Mark Kheirallah 2016
**CAREER RECORDS**  Tries: 91 Mark Kheirallah 2016-2019  Goals: 549 Mark Kheirallah 2016-2019
Points: 1,463 Mark Kheirallah 2016-2019  Appearances: 128 Sebastien Planas 2009-2011; 2016-2018

● *Records only include seasons when the club competed in the British game (2009-2011 & 2016-2019)*

WIDNES VIKINGS

WIDNES VIKINGS

| DATE | FIXTURE | RESULT | SCORERS | LGE | ATT |
|---|---|---|---|---|---|
| 3/2/19 | Halifax (h) | W40-16 | t:Owens,Gelling(2),Ince(3),Craven g:Owens(6) | 2nd | 4,283 |
| 9/2/19 | Toulouse (a) | W24-36 | t:Hood,T Chapelhow,Gelling(2),Craven,Ince g:Owens(6) | 3rd | 2,189 |
| 16/2/19 | Toronto (a) ● | L30-6 | t:Walker g:Owens | 4th | 1,817 |
| 3/3/19 | Featherstone (h) | W44-22 | t:Hood,Gelling,Ince(2),Owens(2),Walker,Wilde g:Owens(6) | 14th | 5,782 |
| 10/3/19 | Barrow (a) | W4-20 | t:Craven,Walker,Ince,Cahill g:Gilmore(2) | 14th | 1,724 |
| 17/3/19 | Bradford (h) | W25-20 | t:Craven,Brand,Johnstone,Ince g:Owens(4) fg:Craven | 14th | 5,335 |
| 24/3/19 | Rochdale (a) | W4-50 | t:Ince(4),Hansen,Buckley,Brand,Wilde,Roby g:Owens(7) | 14th | 1,732 |
| 31/3/19 | Oldham (a) (CCR4) | W14-54 | t:Ince,Owens(3),Buckley(3),Brand,Roby,Johnstone g:Owens(7) | N/A | 1,247 |
| 7/4/19 | Batley (a) | L20-18 | t:Roby(2),Johnstone g:Owens(3) | 14th | 1,420 |
| 13/4/19 | York (h) (CCR5) | W44-12 | t:Freeman(4),Brand,Lyons,Ince,Owens g:Owens(6) | N/A | 2,229 |
| 19/4/19 | Leigh (h) | W30-12 | t:Walker,Lyons(2),Gelling,O'Neill g:Owens(5) | 13th | 5,866 |
| 22/4/19 | York (a) | L17-10 | t:Wilde,Ince g:Owens | 13th | 2,229 |
| 28/4/19 | Dewsbury (h) | L24-25 | t:Owens(3),Craven g:Owens(4) | 13th | 3,851 |
| 5/5/19 | Swinton (a) | W10-32 | t:T Chapelhow(2),Lyons,Wilde,Craven g:Owens(6) | 11th | 1,469 |
| 10/5/19 | Wakefield (a) (CCR6) | L26-6 | t:Roby g:Owens | N/A | 3,055 |
| 19/5/19 | Leigh (SB) ●● | L36-22 | t:Buckley,Craven(2),Roby g:Roby(3) | 12th | N/A |
| 26/5/19 | York (h) | L12-16 | t:Roby,Lyons g:Freeman(2) | 13th | 3,408 |
| 31/5/19 | Sheffield (h) | W36-6 | t:Cahill,Hatton,Owens,Dean,Ince,Brand(2) g:Owens(4) | 12th | 4,920 |
| 5/6/19 | Featherstone (h) (1895CR2) | W22-16 | t:Hatton(3),Lyons g:Owens(3) | N/A | 1,515 |
| 9/6/19 | Barrow (h) | W38-14 | t:J Chapelhow(2),Hatton(2),Craven,Roby,Lyons g:Owens(5) | 11th | 3,830 |
| 16/6/19 | Featherstone (a) | L22-4 | t:Ince | 12th | 2,380 |
| 21/6/19 | Batley (h) | W28-22 | t:Gelling,Norman,Hatton,Dean,J Chapelhow g:Edge(4) | 10th | 3,742 |
| 26/6/19 | Dewsbury (h) (1895CQF) | W54-6 | t:Gelling,Roby(3),Wilde(2),Dean,Walker g:Owens(7) | N/A | 1,458 |
| 30/6/19 | Bradford (a) | L62-0 | | 11th | 3,895 |
| 7/7/19 | Rochdale (h) | W40-12 | t:Roby,Ah Van(2),Owens(3),Craven,Ashall-Bott g:Owens(4) | 10th | 3,780 |
| 14/7/19 | Halifax (a) | L40-10 | t:Wilde,Hatton g:Owens | 11th | 1,668 |
| 21/7/19 | Toronto (h) | L19-24 | t:Roby,Craven,Ince g:Owens(3) fg:Craven | 11th | 3,812 |
| 28/7/19 | Leigh (a) (1895CSF) | W8-12 | t:Gelling,Owens g:Owens(2) | N/A | 4,460 |
| 2/8/19 | Sheffield (a) | L30-10 | t:Ince,Robson g:Owens | 12th | 772 |
| 10/8/19 | Toulouse (a) | L12-28 | t:Owens,Cahill g:Owens(2) | 12th | 3,643 |
| 18/8/19 | Leigh (a) | L34-22 | t:Hatton,Brand(2),Ashall-Bott g:Gilmore(3) | 12th | 3,559 |
| 24/8/19 | Sheffield (1895CF) ●●● | L36-18 | t:Hansen,Dean,Gilmore g:Owens(3) | N/A | N/A |
| 1/9/19 | Swinton (a) | W36-28 | t:Brand,Ah Van(2),Roby,Owens,Dean,Ganson g:Owens(3),Dean | 11th | 3,928 |
| 8/9/19 | Dewsbury (a) | W8-22 | t:Buckley(2),Owens,Dean g:Owens(3) | 11th | 1,409 |

● *Played at Kingston Park, Newcastle* ●● *Played at Bloomfield Road, Blackpool* ●●● *Played at Wembley Stadium*

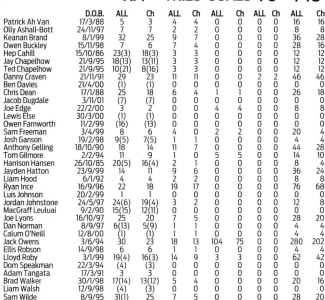

| | | APP | | TRIES | | GOALS | | FG | | PTS | |
|---|---|---|---|---|---|---|---|---|---|---|---|
| | D.O.B. | ALL | Ch | ALL | Ch | ALL | Ch | ALL | Ch | ALL | Ch |
| Patrick Ah Van | 17/3/88 | 5 | 3 | 4 | 4 | 0 | 0 | 0 | 0 | 16 | 16 |
| Olly Ashall-Bott | 24/11/97 | 7 | 7 | 2 | 2 | 0 | 0 | 0 | 0 | 8 | 8 |
| Keanan Brand | 8/1/99 | 32 | 25 | 9 | 7 | 0 | 0 | 0 | 0 | 36 | 28 |
| Owen Buckley | 15/11/98 | 7 | 6 | 7 | 4 | 0 | 0 | 0 | 0 | 28 | 16 |
| Hep Cahill | 15/10/86 | 23(3) | 18(3) | 3 | 3 | 0 | 0 | 0 | 0 | 12 | 12 |
| Jay Chapelhow | 21/9/95 | 18(13) | 13(11) | 3 | 3 | 0 | 0 | 0 | 0 | 12 | 12 |
| Ted Chapelhow | 21/9/95 | 10(21) | 8(16) | 3 | 3 | 0 | 0 | 0 | 0 | 12 | 12 |
| Danny Craven | 21/11/91 | 29 | 23 | 11 | 11 | 0 | 0 | 2 | 2 | 46 | 46 |
| Ben Davies | 21/4/00 | (1) | (1) | 0 | 0 | 0 | 0 | 0 | 0 | 0 | 0 |
| Chris Dean | 17/1/88 | 25 | 18 | 6 | 4 | 1 | 1 | 0 | 0 | 26 | 18 |
| Jacob Dugdale | 3/11/01 | (7) | (7) | 0 | 0 | 0 | 0 | 0 | 0 | 0 | 0 |
| Joe Edge | 22/2/00 | 3 | 2 | 0 | 0 | 4 | 4 | 0 | 0 | 8 | 8 |
| Lewis Else | 30/3/00 | (1) | (1) | 0 | 0 | 0 | 0 | 0 | 0 | 0 | 0 |
| Owen Farnworth | 11/2/99 | (16) | (13) | 0 | 0 | 0 | 0 | 0 | 0 | 0 | 0 |
| Sam Freeman | 3/4/99 | 8 | 6 | 4 | 0 | 2 | 2 | 0 | 0 | 20 | 4 |
| Josh Ganson | 19/2/98 | 9(5) | 7(5) | 1 | 1 | 0 | 0 | 0 | 0 | 4 | 4 |
| Anthony Gelling | 18/10/90 | 18 | 14 | 11 | 7 | 0 | 0 | 0 | 0 | 44 | 28 |
| Tom Gilmore | 2/2/94 | 11 | 9 | 1 | 0 | 5 | 5 | 0 | 0 | 14 | 10 |
| Harrison Hansen | 26/10/85 | 20(5) | 16(4) | 2 | 1 | 0 | 0 | 0 | 0 | 8 | 4 |
| Jayden Hatton | 23/9/99 | 14 | 11 | 9 | 6 | 0 | 0 | 0 | 0 | 36 | 24 |
| Liam Hood | 6/1/92 | 4 | 4 | 2 | 2 | 0 | 0 | 0 | 0 | 8 | 8 |
| Ryan Ince | 16/9/96 | 22 | 18 | 19 | 17 | 0 | 0 | 0 | 0 | 76 | 68 |
| Luis Johnson | 20/2/99 | 1 | 0 | 0 | 0 | 0 | 0 | 0 | 0 | 0 | 0 |
| Jordan Johnstone | 24/5/97 | 24(6) | 19(4) | 3 | 2 | 0 | 0 | 0 | 0 | 12 | 8 |
| MacGraff Leuluai | 9/2/90 | 15(15) | 12(11) | 0 | 0 | 0 | 0 | 0 | 0 | 0 | 0 |
| Joe Lyons | 16/10/97 | 25 | 20 | 7 | 5 | 0 | 0 | 0 | 0 | 28 | 20 |
| Dan Norman | 8/9/97 | 6(13) | 5(9) | 1 | 1 | 0 | 0 | 0 | 0 | 4 | 4 |
| Calum O'Neill | 12/8/00 | (1) | (1) | 1 | 1 | 0 | 0 | 0 | 0 | 4 | 4 |
| Jack Owens | 3/6/94 | 30 | 23 | 18 | 13 | 104 | 75 | 0 | 0 | 280 | 202 |
| Ellis Robson | 14/9/98 | 6 | 6 | 1 | 1 | 0 | 0 | 0 | 0 | 4 | 4 |
| Lloyd Roby | 3/1/99 | 19(4) | 16(3) | 14 | 9 | 3 | 3 | 0 | 0 | 62 | 42 |
| Dom Speakman | 22/3/94 | (4) | (3) | 0 | 0 | 0 | 0 | 0 | 0 | 0 | 0 |
| Adam Tangata | 17/3/91 | 3 | 3 | 0 | 0 | 0 | 0 | 0 | 0 | 0 | 0 |
| Brad Walker | 30/1/98 | 17(14) | 13(12) | 5 | 4 | 0 | 0 | 0 | 0 | 20 | 16 |
| Liam Walsh | 12/9/98 | (4) | (3) | 0 | 0 | 0 | 0 | 0 | 0 | 0 | 0 |
| Sam Wilde | 8/9/95 | 31(1) | 25 | 7 | 5 | 0 | 0 | 0 | 0 | 28 | 20 |

*'Ch' totals include Championship regular season only; 'All' totals also include Challenge Cup & 1895 Cup*

Jack Owens

**LEAGUE RECORD**
P27-W14-D0-L13 (11th)
F646, A586, Diff+60, 16 points.
*(12 points deducted for entering administration)*

**CHALLENGE CUP**
Round Six

**1895 CUP**
Runners-Up

**ATTENDANCES**
Best - v Leigh (Ch - 5,866)
Worst - v Dewsbury (1895C - 1,458)
Total (excluding Challenge Cup) - 59,153
Average (excluding Challenge Cup) - 3,943
*(Down by 681 on 2018, Super League)*

| CLUB RECORDS | **Highest score:** 90-4 v Doncaster, 10/6/2007; 90-0 v Coventry, 21/4/2018 **Highest score against:** 6-76 v Catalans Dragons, 31/3/2012 |
|---|---|
| | **Record attendance:** 24,205 v St Helens, 16/2/61 |
| MATCH RECORDS | **Tries:** 7 Phil Cantillon v York, 18/2/2001 **Goals:** 14 Mark Hewitt v Oldham, 25/7/99; Tim Hartley v Saddleworth, 7/3/2009 |
| | **Points:** 38 Gavin Dodd v Doncaster, 10/6/2007 |
| SEASON RECORDS | **Tries:** 58 Martin Offiah 1988-89 **Goals:** 161 Mick Nanyn 2007 **Points:** 434 Mick Nanyn 2007 |
| CAREER RECORDS | **Tries:** 234 Mal Aspey 1964-80 **Goals:** 1,083 Ray Dutton 1966-78 **Points:** 2,195 Ray Dutton 1966-78 **Appearances:** 591 Keith Elwell 1970-86 |

# YORK CITY KNIGHTS

| DATE | FIXTURE | RESULT | SCORERS | LGE | ATT |
|---|---|---|---|---|---|
| 3/2/19 | Toronto (h) | L0-14 | | 12th | 2,518 |
| 10/2/19 | Dewsbury (a) | W22-26 | t:Horne,Robson,Jordan-Roberts,Marsh g:Robinson(5) | 8th | 1,275 |
| 17/2/19 | Barrow (h) | W56-0 | t:Batchelor(2),Petersen,Salter,Robinson(2),Bass(3) g:Robinson(10) | 3rd | 1,575 |
| 24/2/19 | Bradford (a) | W14-24 | t:Robson,Mazive,Teanby,Marsh g:Robinson(4) | 3rd | 4,782 |
| 3/3/19 | Leigh (h) | W9-8 | t:Batchelor g:Robinson(2) fg:Robinson | 3rd | 2,020 |
| 17/3/19 | Halifax (h) | W38-16 | t:Mazive,S Scott,Cockayne(2),Marsh g:Robinson(9) | 4th | 2,101 |
| 24/3/19 | Sheffield (h) | L16-24 | t:Salter,Jubb,McGrath g:Robinson(2) | 4th | 1,822 |
| 31/3/19 | Barrow (a) (CCR4) | W16-32 | t:Stock,Whiteley,Teanby,Jordan-Roberts,Marsh g:Marsh(6) | N/A | 898 |
| 7/4/19 | Swinton (h) | W30-20 | t:Spears,Marsh(2),S Scott,Horne g:Robinson(4),Rawsthorne | 3rd | 1,606 |
| 13/4/19 | Widnes (a) (CCR5) | L44-12 | t:Hey,Baldwinson g:Rawsthorne,Heckford | N/A | 2,229 |
| 19/4/19 | Featherstone (a) | L42-12 | t:Spears,S Scott g:Robinson(2) | 4th | 2,216 |
| 22/4/19 | Widnes (h) | W17-10 | t:Bass,Rawsthorne,Robinson g:Robinson(2) fg:Robinson | 4th | 2,229 |
| 27/4/19 | Toulouse (a) | L30-26 | t:Mazive,Stock,Brining,Whiteley,S Scott g:Robinson(3) | 6th | 1,793 |
| 5/5/19 | Batley (h) | W28-24 | t:Marsh,Robinson,Stock,Dixon,Jubb g:Robinson(4) | 5th | 1,978 |
| 12/5/19 | Rochdale (a) | W18-24 | t:Marsh,Bass(2),Mazive,Blagbrough g:Robinson(2) | 3rd | 513 |
| 18/5/19 | Featherstone (SB) ● | L42-10 | t:Whiteley,Porter g:Robinson | 5th | N/A |
| 26/5/19 | Widnes (a) | W12-16 | t:Harris,Vaivai,Oakes g:Robinson(2) | 3rd | 3,408 |
| 2/6/19 | Newcastle (h) (1895CR2) | W30-16 | t:Oakes,Brining,Vaivai,Marsh,Stock g:Robinson(5) | N/A | 797 |
| 8/6/19 | Toulouse (h) | L18-25 | t:Teanby,Hey,Harris g:Robinson(3) | 5th | 1,656 |
| 16/6/19 | Rochdale (h) | W60-0 | t:Salter,Marsh(2),Whiteley(3),Stock,Harris,Vaivai,Teanby,S Scott g:Robinson(8) | 5th | 1,661 |
| 23/6/19 | Swinton (a) | W12-36 | t:C Scott,Stock,Horne,Salter g:Robinson(5) | 4th | 976 |
| 26/6/19 | Batley (h) (1895CQF) | L16-17 | | N/A | 1,395 |
| | | (aet) | t:Robinson,Jubb g:Robinson(4) | | |
| 30/6/19 | Dewsbury (h) | W24-21 | t:Brining,C Scott,Harris,Marsh g:Robinson(3),Harris | 4th | 1,338 |
| 5/7/19 | Sheffield (a) | W16-23 | t:Bass,C Scott,Stock,Oakes g:Robinson(2) fg:Robinson | 2nd | 793 |
| 14/7/19 | Batley (a) | D14-14 | t:C Scott,Jordan-Roberts g:Robinson(3) | 2nd | 1,009 |
| 21/7/19 | Bradford (h) | W25-24 | t:Oakes(2),Whiteley(2) g:Robinson(4) fg:Harris | 2nd | 4,007 |
| 4/8/19 | Barrow (a) | W16-24 | t:Marsh(3),Bass g:Robinson(4) | 2nd | 1,169 |
| 10/8/19 | Toronto (a) | L56-6 | t:Kelly g:Robinson | 4th | 7,262 |
| 18/8/19 | Featherstone (h) | W22-18 | t:Oakes,Brining,Horne,Porter g:Robinson(3) | 4th | 3,115 |
| 1/9/19 | Leigh (a) | W23-24 | t:Oakes(2),Marsh,Harris g:Robinson(4) | 3rd | 3,408 |
| 8/9/19 | Halifax (a) | W8-14 | t:Robinson,Chilton g:Robinson(3) | 3rd | 1,862 |
| 14/9/19 | Toulouse (a) (QPO) | L44-6 | t:Chilton g:Robinson | N/A | 1,132 |
| 21/9/19 | Featherstone (h) (ESF) | L4-30 | g:Robinson(2) | N/A | 3,222 |

● *Played at Bloomfield Road, Blackpool*

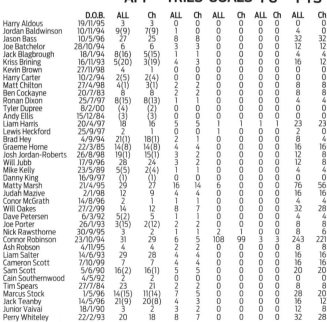

| | | APP | | TRIES | | GOALS | | FG | | PTS | |
|---|---|---|---|---|---|---|---|---|---|---|---|
| | D.O.B. | ALL | Ch | ALL | Ch | ALL | Ch | ALL | Ch | ALL | Ch |
| Harry Aldous | 19/11/95 | 3 | 3 | 0 | 0 | 0 | 0 | 0 | 0 | 0 | 0 |
| Jordan Baldwinson | 10/11/94 | 9(9) | 7(9) | 1 | 0 | 0 | 0 | 0 | 0 | 4 | 0 |
| Jason Bass | 10/5/96 | 27 | 25 | 8 | 8 | 0 | 0 | 0 | 0 | 32 | 32 |
| Joe Batchelor | 28/10/94 | 6 | 6 | 3 | 3 | 0 | 0 | 0 | 0 | 12 | 12 |
| Jack Blagbrough | 18/1/94 | 8(16) | 5(15) | 1 | 1 | 0 | 0 | 0 | 0 | 4 | 4 |
| Kriss Brining | 16/11/93 | 5(20) | 3(19) | 4 | 3 | 0 | 0 | 0 | 0 | 16 | 12 |
| Kevin Brown | 27/11/98 | 4 | 1 | 0 | 0 | 0 | 0 | 0 | 0 | 0 | 0 |
| Harry Carter | 10/2/94 | 2(5) | 2(4) | 0 | 0 | 0 | 0 | 0 | 0 | 0 | 0 |
| Matt Chilton | 27/4/98 | 4(1) | 3(1) | 2 | 2 | 0 | 0 | 0 | 0 | 8 | 8 |
| Ben Cockayne | 20/7/83 | 8 | 8 | 2 | 2 | 0 | 0 | 0 | 0 | 8 | 8 |
| Ronan Dixon | 25/7/97 | 8(15) | 8(13) | 1 | 1 | 0 | 0 | 0 | 0 | 4 | 4 |
| Tyler Dupree | 8/2/00 | (4) | (2) | 0 | 0 | 0 | 0 | 0 | 0 | 0 | 0 |
| Andy Ellis | 15/12/84 | (3) | (3) | 0 | 0 | 0 | 0 | 0 | 0 | 0 | 0 |
| Liam Harris | 20/4/97 | 18 | 16 | 5 | 5 | 1 | 1 | 1 | 1 | 23 | 23 |
| Lewis Heckford | 25/9/97 | 2 | 1 | 0 | 0 | 1 | 0 | 0 | 0 | 2 | 0 |
| Brad Hey | 4/9/94 | 21(1) | 18(1) | 2 | 1 | 0 | 0 | 0 | 0 | 8 | 4 |
| Graeme Horne | 22/3/85 | 14(8) | 14(8) | 4 | 4 | 0 | 0 | 0 | 0 | 16 | 16 |
| Josh Jordan-Roberts | 26/8/98 | 19(1) | 15(1) | 3 | 2 | 0 | 0 | 0 | 0 | 12 | 8 |
| Will Jubb | 17/9/96 | 28 | 24 | 3 | 2 | 0 | 0 | 0 | 0 | 12 | 8 |
| Mike Kelly | 23/5/89 | 5(5) | 2(4) | 1 | 1 | 0 | 0 | 0 | 0 | 4 | 4 |
| Danny King | 16/9/97 | (1) | (1) | 0 | 0 | 0 | 0 | 0 | 0 | 0 | 0 |
| Matty Marsh | 21/4/95 | 29 | 27 | 16 | 14 | 6 | 0 | 0 | 0 | 76 | 56 |
| Judah Mazive | 2/1/98 | 12 | 9 | 4 | 4 | 0 | 0 | 0 | 0 | 16 | 16 |
| Conor McGrath | 14/8/96 | 2 | 1 | 1 | 1 | 0 | 0 | 0 | 0 | 4 | 4 |
| Will Oakes | 27/2/99 | 14 | 12 | 8 | 7 | 0 | 0 | 0 | 0 | 32 | 28 |
| Dave Petersen | 6/3/92 | 5(2) | 5 | 1 | 1 | 0 | 0 | 0 | 0 | 4 | 4 |
| Joe Porter | 26/1/93 | 3(15) | 2(12) | 2 | 2 | 0 | 0 | 0 | 0 | 8 | 8 |
| Nick Rawsthorne | 30/9/95 | 3 | 2 | 1 | 1 | 2 | 1 | 0 | 0 | 8 | 6 |
| Connor Robinson | 23/10/94 | 31 | 29 | 6 | 5 | 108 | 99 | 3 | 3 | 243 | 221 |
| Ash Robson | 4/11/95 | 4 | 4 | 2 | 2 | 0 | 0 | 0 | 0 | 8 | 8 |
| Liam Salter | 14/6/93 | 29 | 28 | 4 | 4 | 0 | 0 | 0 | 0 | 16 | 16 |
| Cameron Scott | 7/10/99 | 7 | 7 | 4 | 4 | 0 | 0 | 0 | 0 | 16 | 16 |
| Sam Scott | 5/6/90 | 16(2) | 16(1) | 5 | 5 | 0 | 0 | 0 | 0 | 20 | 20 |
| Cain Southernwood | 4/5/92 | 2 | 2 | 0 | 0 | 0 | 0 | 0 | 0 | 0 | 0 |
| Tim Spears | 27/7/84 | 23 | 21 | 2 | 2 | 0 | 0 | 0 | 0 | 8 | 8 |
| Marcus Stock | 1/5/96 | 14(15) | 11(14) | 7 | 5 | 0 | 0 | 0 | 0 | 28 | 20 |
| Jack Teanby | 14/5/96 | 21(9) | 20(8) | 4 | 3 | 0 | 0 | 0 | 0 | 16 | 12 |
| Junior Vaivai | 18/1/90 | 3 | 2 | 3 | 2 | 0 | 0 | 0 | 0 | 12 | 8 |
| Perry Whiteley | 22/2/93 | 20 | 18 | 8 | 7 | 0 | 0 | 0 | 0 | 32 | 28 |

*'Ch' totals include play-offs; 'All' totals also include Challenge Cup & 1895 Cup*

Matty Marsh

**LEAGUE RECORD**
P27-W19-D1-L7
(3rd/Elimination Semi-Final)
F612, A529, Diff+83, 39 points.

**CHALLENGE CUP**
Round Five

**1895 CUP**
Quarter Finalists

**ATTENDANCES**
Best - v Bradford (Ch - 4,007)
Worst - v Newcastle (1895C - 797)
Total (all home games included) - 33,040
Average (all home games included) - 2,065
(Up by 441 on 2018, League 1)

| | |
|---|---|
| **CLUB RECORDS** | **Highest score:** 144-0 v West Wales, 29/4/2018  **Highest score against:** 0-98 v Rochdale, 8/4/2001 |
| **MATCH RECORDS** | **Record attendance:** 14,689 v Swinton, 10/2/34 *(Clarence Street)*; 4,221 v Bradford, 18/2/2018 *(Bootham Crescent)* <br> **Tries:** 7 Brad Davis v Highfield, 17/9/95; Kieren Moss v West Wales, 29/4/2018 |
| **SEASON RECORDS** | **Goals:** 21 Connor Robinson v West Wales, 11/8/2018  **Points:** 56 Chris Thorman v Northumbria University, 6/3/2011 <br> **Tries:** 35 John Crossley 1980-81  **Goals:** 186 *(inc 4fg)* Connor Robinson 2018  **Points:** 420 Connor Robinson 2018 |
| **CAREER RECORDS** | **Tries:** 167 Peter Foster 1955-67  **Goals:** 1,060 Vic Yorke 1954-67  **Points:** 2,159 Vic Yorke 1954-67  **Appearances:** 449 Willie Hargreaves 1952-65 |

# CHAMPIONSHIP 2019
## Round by Round

## ROUND 1

*Sunday 3rd February 2019*

**BATLEY BULLDOGS 18 BARROW RAIDERS 22**

**BULLDOGS:** 1 Dave Scott; 2 Wayne Reittie; 22 Sam Wood; 4 Lewis Galbraith; 5 Johnny Campbell; 6 Louis Jouffret; 7 Dom Brambani; 8 Adam Gledhill; 9 Alistair Leak; 15 Toby Everett; 11 Dane Manning; 12 Jack Downs; 17 Tyler Dickinson. Subs (all used): 13 James Brown; 21 Jo Taira; 16 Michael Ward; 23 Keenen Tomlinson.
**Tries:** Wood (6), Leak (27), Brambani (33); **Goals:** Scott 3/3.
**RAIDERS:** 1 Theerapol Ritson; 2 Stargroth Amean; 5 Deon Cross; 4 Jake Spedding; 21 Tom Loxam; 6 Jamie Dallimore; 7 Lewis Charnock; 8 Tom Walker; 14 Wartovo Puara; 28 Josh Johnson; 11 Jono Smith; 25 Jordan Walne; 13 Martin Aspinwall. Subs (all used): 22 Ryan Johnston; 12 Jarrad Stack; 26 Willie Minoga; 17 Ryan Duffy.
**Tries:** Spedding (11, 36), Smith (29), Charnock (53);
**Goals:** Dallimore 3/5.
**Sin bin:** Dallimore (17) - dissent.
**Rugby Leaguer & League Express Men of the Match:**
*Bulldogs:* James Brown; *Raiders:* Jake Spedding.
**Penalty count:** 11-5; **Half-time:** 18-14;
**Referee:** Michael Mannifield; **Attendance:** 755.

**BRADFORD BULLS 17 FEATHERSTONE ROVERS 16**

**BULLS:** 1 Brandon Pickersgill; 5 Jy Hitchcox; 31 Rhys Evans; 3 Jake Webster; 2 Ethan Ryan; 7 Dane Chisholm; 14 Jordan Lilley; 8 Liam Kirk; 9 Matty Wildie; 10 Steve Crossley; 25 Connor Farrell; 12 Elliot Minchella; 18 Sam Hallas. Subs (all used): 21 George Flanagan; 16 James Green; 26 Ross Oakes; 13 Mikey Wood.
**Tries:** Webster (29), Chisholm (43), Flanagan (51);
**Goals:** Chisholm 2/4; **Field goal:** Chisholm (69).
**ROVERS:** 1 Calum Turner; 2 Luke Briscoe; 3 Thompson Teteh; 27 Harry Newman; 5 Conor Carey; 6 Ase Boas; 7 Watson Boas; 8 Scott Wheeldon; 9 Cameron King; 29 Jack Ormondroyd; 12 Brad Day; 28 Josh Walters; 13 James Lockwood. Subs: 16 Danny Maskill (not used); 14 John Davies; 4 Josh Hardcastle; 15 Luke Cooper.
**Tries:** W Boas (12), Briscoe (58), King (63);
**Goals:** W Boas 2/3.
**Rugby Leaguer & League Express Men of the Match:**
*Bulls:* Dane Chisholm; *Rovers:* John Davies.
**Penalty count:** 10-5; **Half-time:** 4-6;
**Referee:** Jack Smith; **Attendance:** 6,024.

**LEIGH CENTURIONS 24 TOULOUSE OLYMPIQUE 16**

**CENTURIONS:** 1 Gregg McNally; 2 Jonny Pownall; 3 Iain Thornley; 24 Matthew Costello; 5 Stefan Marsh; 6 Martyn Ridyard; 7 Josh Woods; 23 Luke Douglas; 9 Micky Higham; 10 Sam Brooks; 11 Toby Adamson; 12 Andy Thornley; 13 Luke Adamson. Subs (all used): 25 Aaron Smith; 15 Joe Cator; 26 Jack Ashworth; 8 Tom Spencer.
**Tries:** Pownall (16), Marsh (22), Costello (24), Cator (44);
**Goals:** Ridyard 4/5.
**OLYMPIQUE:** 1 Mark Kheirallah; 5 Paul Marcon; 4 Gavin Marguerite; 3 Bastien Ader; 2 Tony Maurel; 6 Johnathon Ford; 7 Stan Robin; 8 Maxime Puech; 9 Anthony Marion; 10 Joe Bretherton; 11 Con Mika; 12 Rhys Curran; 22 Brenden Santi. Subs (all used): 14 Dean Parata; 18 Clement Boyer; 17 Paterika Vaivai; 15 Ben Evans.
**Tries:** Robin (5), Marcon (30, 71);
**Goals:** Kheirallah 2/2, Marion 0/1.
**Rugby Leaguer & League Express Men of the Match:**
*Centurions:* Joe Cator; *Olympique:* Rhys Curran.
**Penalty count:** 8-6; **Half-time:** 16-12;
**Referee:** Marcus Griffiths; **Attendance:** 2,987.

**SHEFFIELD EAGLES 64 SWINTON LIONS 10**

**EAGLES:** 1 Josh Guzdek; 2 Ryan Millar; 18 James Glover; 4 Jason Crookes; 5 Ben Blackmore; 6 Pat Walker; 7 Anthony Thackeray; 11 Brad Knowles; 9 James Davey; 10 Matt James; 12 Joel Farrell; 15 Olly Davies; 13 Aaron Brown. Subs (all used): 16 Corey Makelim; 17 Shaun Pick; 19 Sonny Esslemont; 22 Paddy Burns.
**Tries:** Davies (5), Millar (8, 80), Glover (21), Guzdek (27), Makelim (28), Farrell (31), Thackeray (50, 57, 63, 70), Blackmore (65); **Goals:** Walker 8/12.
**Sin bin:** Farrell (75) - fighting.
**LIONS:** 1 Jack Hansen; 2 Mike Butt; 3 Rhodri Lloyd; 25 Matty Ashton; 5 Ryan Gray; 6 Oscar Thomas; 7 Rob Fairclough; 8 Gavin Bennion; 9 Luke Waterworth; 10 Lewis Hatton; 11 Adam Jones; 22 Frankie Halton; 13 Will Hope. Subs (all used): 15 Ben Austin; 14 Billy Brickhill; 16 Paddy Jones; 19 Jose Kenga.
**Tries:** Gray (45), Brickhill (78); **Goals:** Thomas 1/2.
**Sin bin:** Fairclough (75) - fighting.
**Rugby Leaguer & League Express Men of the Match:**
*Eagles:* Anthony Thackeray; *Lions:* Billy Brickhill.
**Penalty count:** 6-10; **Half-time:** 30-0;
**Referee:** Matt Rossleigh; **Attendance:** 1,259.

**WIDNES VIKINGS 40 HALIFAX 16**

**VIKINGS:** 5 Jack Owens; 1 Olly Ashall-Bott; 24 Keanan Brand; 4 Anthony Gelling; 2 Ryan Ince; 6 Danny Craven; 21 Joe Lyons; 10 Adam Tangata; 9 Liam Hood; 11 Harrison Hansen; 17 Sam Wilde; 12 Chris Dean; 16 MacGraff Leuluai. Subs (all used): 18 Ted Chapelhow; 15 Jordan Johnstone; 20 Owen Farnworth; 19 Brad Walker.
**Tries:** Owens (3), Gelling (8, 51), Ince (12, 47, 70), Craven (39); **Goals:** Owens 6/7.
**HALIFAX:** 1 Quentin Laulu-Togaga'e; 5 Will Sharp; 3 Steve Tyrer; 23 James Woodburn-Hall; 2 Shaun Robinson; 6 Scott Murrell; 19 Ben White; 10 Jacob Fairbank; 9 Ben Kaye; 17 Ben Kavanagh; 16 Kevin Larroyer; 12 Ed Barber; 13 Simon Grix. Subs (all used): 8 Dan Fleming; 25 Liam Cooper; 14 Brandon Moore; 28 Will Calcott.
**Tries:** Sharp (18), Tyrer (28), Kavanagh (75);
**Goals:** Tyrer 2/3.
**Sin bin:** Moore (55) - high tackle;
Larroyer (69) - repeated offences.
**Rugby Leaguer & League Express Men of the Match:**
*Vikings:* Anthony Gelling; *Halifax:* Jacob Fairbank.
**Penalty count:** 14-7; **Half-time:** 22-10;
**Referee:** Scott Mikalauskas; **Attendance:** 4,283.

**YORK CITY KNIGHTS 0 TORONTO WOLFPACK 14**

**CITY KNIGHTS:** 1 Matty Marsh; 2 Ash Robson; 23 Jason Bass; 4 Brad Hey; 20 Perry Whiteley; 6 Ben Cockayne; 7 Connor Robinson; 15 Graeme Horne; 9 Will Jubb; 10 Jack Teanby; 11 Josh Jordan-Roberts; 3 Liam Salter; 25 Dave Petersen. Subs (all used): - Kriss Brining; 16 Jack Blagbrough; 8 Ronan Dixon; 17 Joe Porter.
**WOLFPACK:** 1 Gareth O'Brien; 2 Matty Russell; 3 Chase Stanley; 4 Ricky Leutele; 19 Gary Wheeler; 6 Joe Mellor; 7 Josh McCrone; 10 Ashton Sims; 14 Andy Ackers; 16 Tom Olbison; 11 Andrew Dixon; 12 Bodene Thompson; 13 Jon Wilkin. Subs: 17 Blake Wallace; 8 Adam Sidlow; 15 Darcy Lussick; 18 Gadwin Springer (not used).
**Tries:** Wheeler (24), Russell (68), Mellor (78);
**Goals:** O'Brien 1/3.
**Rugby Leaguer & League Express Men of the Match:**
*City Knights:* Jack Teanby; *Wolfpack:* Joe Mellor.
**Penalty count:** 6-10; **Half-time:** 0-4;
**Referee:** Gareth Hewer; **Attendance:** 2,518.

## ROUND 2

*Saturday 9th February 2019*

**TOULOUSE OLYMPIQUE 24 WIDNES VIKINGS 36**

**OLYMPIQUE:** 1 Mark Kheirallah; 2 Tony Maurel; 3 Bastien Ader; 4 Gavin Marguerite; 5 Paul Marcon; 6 Johnathon Ford; 7 Stan Robin; 17 Paterika Vaivai; 14 Dean Parata; 18 Clement Boyer; 11 Con Mika; 21 Jordan Dezaria; 22 Brenden Santi. Subs (all used): 9 Anthony Marion; 15 Ben Evans; 10 Joe Bretherton; 23 Justin Sangare.
**Tries:** Parata (14), Robin (18, 26, 75); **Goals:** Kheirallah 4/4.
**VIKINGS:** 1 Olly Ashall-Bott; 5 Jack Owens; 24 Keanan Brand; 4 Anthony Gelling; 2 Ryan Ince; 6 Danny Craven; 21 Joe Lyons; 10 Adam Tangata; 9 Liam Hood; 11 Harrison Hansen; 17 Sam Wilde; 12 Chris Dean; 16 MacGraff Leuluai. Subs (all used): 18 Ted Chapelhow; 15 Jordan Johnstone; 20 Owen Farnworth; 19 Brad Walker.
**Tries:** Hood (7), T Chapelhow (22), Gelling (35, 78), Craven (46), Ince (65); **Goals:** Owens 6/8.
**Rugby Leaguer & League Express Men of the Match:**
*Olympique:* Stan Robin; *Vikings:* Anthony Gelling.
**Penalty count:** 6-6; **Half-time:** 18-16;
**Referee:** Scott Mikalauskas; **Attendance:** 2,189.

*Sunday 10th February 2019*

**BARROW RAIDERS 22 SHEFFIELD EAGLES 24**

**RAIDERS:** 1 Theerapol Ritson; 2 Stargroth Amean; 5 Deon Cross; 4 Jake Spedding; 21 Tom Loxam; 6 Jamie Dallimore; 7 Lewis Charnock; 8 Tom Walker; 14 Wartovo Puara; 28 Josh Johnson; 11 Jono Smith; 25 Jordan Walne; 13 Martin Aspinwall. Subs (all used): 24 Jake Carter; 12 Jarrad Stack; 26 Willie Minoga; 17 Ryan Duffy.
**Tries:** Puara (10), Amean (41, 47), J Johnson (72);
**Goals:** Dallimore 3/4.
**EAGLES:** 1 Josh Guzdek; 2 Ryan Millar; 18 James Glover; 4 Jason Crookes; 5 Ben Blackmore; 6 Pat Walker; 7 Anthony Thackeray; 11 Brad Knowles; 9 James Davey; 10 Matt James; 15 Olly Davies; 12 Joel Farrell; 13 Aaron Brown. Subs (all used): 16 Corey Makelim; 22 Paddy Burns; 19 Sonny Esslemont; 17 Shaun Pick.
**Tries:** Farrell (23), Millar (39, 63), Thackeray (51);
**Goals:** Walker 4/5.
**Rugby Leaguer & League Express Men of the Match:**
*Raiders:* Wartovo Puara; *Eagles:* Pat Walker.
**Penalty count:** 13-12; **Half-time:** 6-10;
**Referee:** Matt Rossleigh; **Attendance:** 1,514.

**DEWSBURY RAMS 22 YORK CITY KNIGHTS 26**

**RAMS:** 1 Dale Morton; 23 Rob Worrincy; 19 Daniel Igbinedion; 4 Adam Ryder; 5 Alex Brown; 6 Paul Sykes; 7 Simon Brown; 30 Tom Garratt; 18 Sam Day; 36 Owen Harrison; 12 Michael Knowles; 11 Lucas Walshaw; 13 Kyle Trout. Subs (all used): 21 Jacob Thomas; 33 Callum Field; 34 Chris Annakin; 8 Jode Sheriffe.
**Tries:** Day (4, 14), Garratt (71); **Goals:** Sykes 5/5.
**Sin bin:** K Trout (64) - interference.
**CITY KNIGHTS:** 1 Matty Marsh; 2 Ash Robson; 23 Jason Bass; 4 Brad Hey; 20 Perry Whiteley; 6 Ben Cockayne; 7 Connor Robinson; 8 Ronan Dixon; 9 Will Jubb; 10 Jack Teanby; 11 Josh Jordan-Roberts; 3 Liam Salter; 15 Graeme Horne. Subs (all used): 26 Kriss Brining; 22 Marcus Stock; 16 Jack Blagbrough; 17 Joe Porter.
**Tries:** Horne (55), Robson (58), Jordan-Roberts (65), Marsh (77); **Goals:** Robinson 5/5.
**On report:** Cockayne (18) - alleged dangerous challenge.
**Rugby Leaguer & League Express Men of the Match:**
*Rams:* Sam Day; *City Knights:* Connor Robinson.
**Penalty count:** 11-15; **Half-time:** 14-0;
**Referee:** Michael Mannifield; **Attendance:** 1,275.

**FEATHERSTONE ROVERS 42 BATLEY BULLDOGS 14**

**ROVERS:** 1 Calum Turner; 2 Luke Briscoe; 3 Thompson Teteh; 28 Josh Walters; 5 Conor Carey; 6 Ase Boas; 7 Watson Boas; 30 Brad Singleton; 9 Cameron King; 29 Jack Ormondroyd; 12 Brad Day; 31 Cameron Smith; 13 James Lockwood. Subs (all used): 15 Luke Cooper; 14 John Davies; 26 Daniel Smith; 16 Danny Maskill.
**Tries:** W Boas (10), Teteh (31), King (35), Walters (44), Singleton (52), Day (54), C Smith (69), A Boas (76);
**Goals:** W Boas 5/8.
**BULLDOGS:** 1 Dave Scott; 2 Wayne Reittie; 22 Sam Wood; 3 Sam Smeaton; 5 Johnny Campbell; 6 Louis Jouffret; 7 Dom Brambani; 8 Adam Gledhill; 9 Alistair Leak; 15 Toby Everett; 11 Dane Manning; 12 Jack Downs; 17 Tyler Dickinson. Subs (all used): 13 James Brown; 16 Michael Ward; 14 Danny Yates; 24 Paul Brearley.
**Tries:** Campbell (14), Jouffret (25), Yates (79);
**Goals:** Scott 1/3.
**Rugby Leaguer & League Express Men of the Match:**
*Rovers:* Watson Boas; *Bulldogs:* Dane Manning.
**Penalty count:** 6-5; **Half-time:** 16-8;
**Referee:** Marcus Griffiths; **Attendance:** 2,145.

**HALIFAX 33 LEIGH CENTURIONS 26**

**HALIFAX:** 1 Quentin Laulu-Togaga'e; 5 Will Sharp; 3 Steve Tyrer; 20 James Saltonstall; 2 Shaun Robinson; 6 Scott Murrell; 19 Ben White; 8 Dan Fleming; 14 Brandon Moore; 17 Ben Kavanagh; 16 Kevin Larroyer; 12 Ed Barber; 13 Simon Grix. Subs (all used): 18 Elliot Morris; 10 Jacob Fairbank; 27 Reece Chapman-Smith; 28 Will Calcott.
**Tries:** Moore (4), Tyrer (19), White (29), Robinson (55, 58), Barber (63); **Goals:** Tyrer 4/6; **Field goal:** White (75).
**Sin bin:** Moore (67) - fighting.
**CENTURIONS:** 1 Gregg McNally; 2 Jonny Pownall; 3 Iain Thornley; 24 Matthew Costello; 5 Stefan Marsh; 6 Martyn Ridyard; 7 Josh Woods; 23 Luke Douglas; 9 Micky Higham; 10 Sam Brooks; 11 Toby Adamson; 12 Andy Thornley; 13 Luke Adamson. Subs (all used): 8 Tom Spencer; 15 Joe Cator; 25 Aaron Smith; 26 Jack Ashworth.
**Tries:** A Thornley (9), Pownall (12), L Adamson (69), T Adamson (79); **Goals:** Ridyard 5/6.
**Dismissal:** Pownall (67) - dissent.
**Sin bin:** Pownall (67) - fighting.
**Rugby Leaguer & League Express Men of the Match:**
*Halifax:* Jacob Fairbank; *Centurions:* Luke Douglas.
**Penalty count:** 8-11; **Half-time:** 18-14;
**Referee:** Gareth Hewer; **Attendance:** 2,245.

**ROCHDALE HORNETS 6 TORONTO WOLFPACK 58**

**HORNETS:** 7 Dan Abram; 2 Shaun Ainscough; 23 Jordan Case; 4 Ben Morris; 24 Brandon Wood; 13 Stuart Howarth; 14 Elliott Jenkins; 26 Pat Moran; 6 Scott Moore; 10 Carl Forster; 11 Lee Mitchell; 16 Mike Weldon; 18 Ryan Millington. Subs (all used): 30 Adam Lawton; 12 Ellis Gillam; 28 Matt Davis; 17 Liam Carberry.
**Try:** Lawton (20); **Goals:** Abram 1/1.
**WOLFPACK:** 1 Gareth O'Brien; 20 Adam Higson; 3 Chase Stanley; 4 Ricky Leutele; 2 Matty Russell; 6 Joe Mellor; 17 Blake Wallace; 10 Ashton Sims; 7 Josh McCrone; 16 Tom Olbison; 11 Andrew Dixon; 12 Bodene Thompson; 13 Jon Wilkin. Subs (all used): 14 Andy Ackers; 29 Jake Emmitt; 15 Darcy Lussick; 8 Adam Sidlow.
**Tries:** Russell (7, 47, 55, 74), Mellor (15), O'Brien (18), Lussick (26), Leutele (28), Stanley (53), Emmitt (58), Sidlow (78); **Goals:** O'Brien 7/11.
**Sin bin:** Wilkin (45) - dissent.
**Rugby Leaguer & League Express Men of the Match:**
*Hornets:* Scott Moore; *Wolfpack:* Matty Russell.
**Penalty count:** 9-7; **Half-time:** 6-26;
**Referee:** Jack Smith; **Attendance:** 694.

Championship 2019 - Round by Round

**SWINTON LIONS 12 BRADFORD BULLS 31**

**LIONS:** 1 Jack Hansen; 2 Mike Butt; 3 Rhodri Lloyd; 35 Chris Hankinson; 32 Liam Forsyth; 34 Harry Smith; 7 Rob Fairclough; 8 Gavin Bennion; 9 Luke Waterworth; 10 Lewis Hatton; 12 Kyle Shelford; 33 Liam Paisley; 31 Liam Byrne. Subs (all used): 14 Billy Brickhill; 15 Ben Austin; 16 Paddy Jones; 22 Frankie Halton.
**Tries:** Butt (12), Forsyth (16); **Goals:** Hankinson 2/3.
**BULLS:** 1 Brandon Pickersgill; 5 Jy Hitchcox; 31 Rhys Evans; 3 Jake Webster; 2 Ethan Ryan; 7 Dane Chisholm; 14 Jordan Lilley; 8 Liam Kirk; 9 Matty Wildie; 10 Steve Crossley; 25 Connor Farrell; 12 Elliot Minchella; 18 Sam Hallas. Subs (all used): 21 George Flanagan; 16 James Green; 26 Ross Oakes; 13 Mikey Wood.
**Tries:** Wildie (5), Hitchcox (35), Minchella (47), Crossley (70), Evans (73); **Goals:** Chisholm 5/6;
**Field goal:** Lilley (67).
**Rugby Leaguer & League Express Men of the Match:** *Lions:* Kyle Shelford; *Bulls:* Dane Chisholm.
**Penalty count:** 10-15; **Half-time:** 12-14;
**Referee:** John McMullen; **Attendance:** 1,498.

## ROUND 3

*Friday 15th February 2019*

**SHEFFIELD EAGLES 24 BRADFORD BULLS 10**

**EAGLES:** 1 Josh Guzdek; 2 Ryan Millar; 18 James Glover; 4 Jason Crookes; 5 Ben Blackmore; 6 Pat Walker; 7 Anthony Thackeray; 10 Matt James; 14 Greg Burns; 11 Brad Knowles; 12 Joel Farrell; 15 Olly Davies; 13 Aaron Brown. Subs (all used): 16 Corey Makelim; 21 Blake Broadbent; 19 Sonny Esslemont; 22 Paddy Burns.
**Tries:** Guzdek (26), Glover (66), Knowles (71), Farrell (77);
**Goals:** Walker 4/4.
**Sin bin:** Blackmore (49) - fighting.
**BULLS:** 1 Brandon Pickersgill; 5 Jy Hitchcox; 31 Rhys Evans; 26 Ross Oakes; 2 Ethan Ryan; 27 Rowan Milnes; 14 Jordan Lilley; 8 Liam Kirk; 9 Matty Wildie; 10 Steve Crossley; 25 Connor Farrell; 12 Elliot Minchella; 19 Jon Magrin. Subs (all used): 21 George Flanagan; 16 James Green; 11 Matt Garside; 33 Olsi Krasniqi.
**Tries:** Oakes (12), Ryan (15); **Goals:** Lilley 1/2.
**Dismissal:** J Green (49) - fighting.
**Sin bin:** Lilley (76) - dissent.
**Rugby Leaguer & League Express Men of the Match:** *Eagles:* Josh Guzdek; *Bulls:* Ethan Ryan.
**Penalty count:** 14-7; **Half-time:** 6-10;
**Referee:** Marcus Griffiths; **Attendance:** 1,711.

*Saturday 16th February 2019*

**TOULOUSE OLYMPIQUE 42 ROCHDALE HORNETS 12**

**OLYMPIQUE:** 1 Mark Kheirallah; 2 Tony Maurel; 3 Bastien Ader; 4 Gavin Marguerite; 20 Ilias Bergal; 6 Johnathon Ford; 7 Stan Robin; 10 Joe Bretherton; 14 Dean Parata; 18 Clement Boyer; 11 Con Mika; 12 Rhys Curran; 9 Anthony Marion. Subs (all used): 30 William Barthau; 15 Ben Evans; 16 Tyla Hepi; 23 Justin Sangare.
**Tries:** Marguerite (21, 41), Ford (24), Robin (32, 64), Kheirallah (40), Bergal (47), Barthau (71);
**Goals:** Kheirallah 5/8.
**HORNETS:** 7 Dan Abram; 2 Shaun Ainscough; 12 Ellis Gillam; 23 Jordan Case; 24 Brandon Wood; 29 Tyler Whittaker; 14 Elliott Jenkins; 26 Pat Moran; 8 Matt Davis; 28 Sitaleki Akauola; 16 Mike Weldon; 11 Lee Mitchell; 18 Ryan Millington. Subs (all used): 10 Carl Forster; 15 Declan Gregory; 22 Callum Wood; - Luis Johnson.
**Tries:** B Wood (16), Akauola (57); **Goals:** Abram 2/2.
**Rugby Leaguer & League Express Men of the Match:** *Olympique:* Stan Robin; *Hornets:* Sitaleki Akauola.
**Penalty count:** 9-10; **Half-time:** 22-6;
**Referee:** Michael Mannifield; **Attendance:** 1,707.

**TORONTO WOLFPACK 30 WIDNES VIKINGS 6**

**WOLFPACK:** 1 Gareth O'Brien; 20 Adam Higson; 19 Gary Wheeler; 4 Ricky Leutele; 2 Matty Russell; 6 Joe Mellor; 17 Blake Wallace; 10 Ashton Sims; 7 Josh McCrone; 18 Gadwin Springer; 11 Andrew Dixon; 12 Bodene Thompson; 13 Jon Wilkin. Subs (all used): 8 Adam Sidlow; 14 Andy Ackers; 15 Darcy Lussick; 16 Tom Olbison.
**Tries:** Wallace (14), Ackers (48, 70), Wheeler (54), Leutele (57); **Goals:** O'Brien 5/6.
**On report:** Lussick (26) - alleged dangerous challenge; Higson (32) - alleged dangerous challenge.
**VIKINGS:** 5 Jack Owens; 1 Olly Ashall-Bott; 24 Keanan Brand; 4 Anthony Gelling; 2 Ryan Ince; 6 Danny Craven; 21 Joe Lyons; 10 Adam Tangata; 9 Liam Hood; 11 Harrison Hansen; 17 Sam Wilde; 12 Chris Dean; 16 MacGraff Leuluai. Subs (all used): 8 Jay Chapelhow; 15 Jordan Johnstone; 18 Ted Chapelhow; 19 Brad Walker.
**Try:** Walker (75); **Goals:** Owens 1/1.
**Rugby Leaguer & League Express Men of the Match:** *Wolfpack:* Ricky Leutele; *Vikings:* Keanan Brand.
**Penalty count:** 7-7; **Half-time:** 8-0;
**Referee:** Liam Moore; **Attendance:** 1,817
*(at Kingston Park, Newcastle).*

*Sunday 17th February 2019*

**DEWSBURY RAMS 38 SWINTON LIONS 24**

**RAMS:** 35 Luke Hooley; 23 Rob Worrincy; 19 Daniel Igbinedion; 4 Adam Ryder; 1 Dale Morton; 6 Paul Sykes; 7 Simon Brown; 30 Tom Garratt; 18 Sam Day; 34 Chris Annakin; 11 Lucas Walshaw; 13 Kyle Trout; 33 Callum Field. Subs (all used): 8 Jode Sheriffe; 9 Robbie Ward; 12 Michael Knowles; 36 Owen Harrison.
**Tries:** Garratt (2, 30), Sykes (9), Ward (54), Worrincy (64), Harrison (70); **Goals:** Sykes 7/7.
**LIONS:** 1 Jack Hansen; 2 Mike Butt; 3 Rhodri Lloyd; 33 Liam Paisley; 32 Liam Forsyth; 34 Harry Smith; 7 Rob Fairclough; 8 Gavin Bennion; 9 Luke Waterworth; 10 Lewis Hatton; 12 Kyle Shelford; 22 Frankie Halton; 31 Liam Byrne. Subs (all used): 14 Billy Brickhill; 16 Paddy Jones; 35 Oliver Partington; 11 Adam Jones.
**Tries:** Fairclough (12), Shelford (34), Lloyd (46), Hatton (74), Butt (78); **Goals:** Smith 2/5.
**Sin bin:** Fairclough (56) - interference.
**Rugby Leaguer & League Express Men of the Match:** *Rams:* Paul Sykes; *Lions:* Jack Hansen.
**Penalty count:** 11-11; **Half-time:** 18-10;
**Referee:** Gareth Hewer; **Attendance:** 993.

**HALIFAX 20 BATLEY BULLDOGS 18**

**HALIFAX:** 1 Quentin Laulu-Togaga'e; 5 Will Sharp; 3 Steve Tyrer; 20 James Saltonstall; 2 Shaun Robinson; 19 Ben White; 6 Scott Murrell; 10 Jacob Fairbank; 14 Brandon Moore; 17 Ben Kavanagh; 16 Kevin Larroyer; 11 Shane Grady; 13 Simon Grix. Subs (all used): 8 Dan Fleming; 12 Ed Barber; 24 Curtis Davies; 28 Will Calcott.
**Tries:** Saltonstall (8), Tyrer (11), Robinson (39);
**Goals:** Tyrer 4/4.
**Sin bin:** Larroyer (67) - high tackle on Campbell.
**BULLDOGS:** 1 Dave Scott; 2 Wayne Reittie; 22 Sam Wood; 3 Sam Smeaton; 5 Johnny Campbell; 14 Danny Yates; 7 Dom Brambani; 8 Adam Gledhill; 9 Alistair Leak; 15 Toby Everett; 11 Dane Manning; 12 Jack Downs; 24 Paul Brearley. Subs (all used): 13 James Brown; 18 Tom Hemingway; 21 Jo Taira; 23 Keenen Tomlinson.
**Tries:** Brearley (41), Downs (46), Yates (75);
**Goals:** Scott 3/3.
**Rugby Leaguer & League Express Men of the Match:** *Halifax:* Will Sharp; *Bulldogs:* Alistair Leak.
**Penalty count:** 6-14; **Half-time:** 18-0;
**Referee:** Matt Rossleigh; **Attendance:** 1,825.

**LEIGH CENTURIONS 29 FEATHERSTONE ROVERS 20**

**CENTURIONS:** 1 Gregg McNally; 2 Jonny Pownall; 3 Iain Thornley; 24 Matthew Costello; 5 Stefan Marsh; 6 Martyn Ridyard; 27 Danny Richardson; 26 Jack Ashworth; 9 Micky Higham; 23 Luke Douglas; 11 Toby Adamson; 12 Andy Thornley; 10 Sam Brooks. Subs (all used): 25 Aaron Smith; 15 Joe Cator; 13 Luke Adamson; 8 Tom Spencer.
**Tries:** McNally (6), Douglas (17), Spencer (42), Ridyard (47), Smith (56); **Goals:** Ridyard 4/5;
**Field goal:** Ridyard (71).
**ROVERS:** 1 Calum Turner; 2 Luke Briscoe; 3 Thompson Teteh; 32 Alex Sutcliffe; 27 Harry Newman; 6 Ase Boas; 7 Watson Boas; 8 Scott Wheeldon; 9 Cameron King; 29 Jack Ormondroyd; 12 Brad Day; 28 Josh Walters; 26 Daniel Smith. Subs (all used): 13 James Lockwood; 15 Luke Cooper; 16 Danny Maskill; 25 Jack Render.
**Tries:** D Smith (23), Briscoe (31), Newman (37), W Boas (76); **Goals:** W Boas 2/3, King 0/1, Turner 0/1.
**Sin bin:** Day (15) - dangerous challenge.
**Rugby Leaguer & League Express Men of the Match:** *Centurions:* Luke Douglas; *Rovers:* Watson Boas.
**Penalty count:** 8-11; **Half-time:** 10-14;
**Referee:** Jack Smith; **Attendance:** 3,443.

**YORK CITY KNIGHTS 56 BARROW RAIDERS 0**

**CITY KNIGHTS:** 1 Matty Marsh; 2 Ash Robson; 23 Jason Bass; 3 Liam Salter; 21 Judah Mazive; 6 Ben Cockayne; 7 Connor Robinson; 8 Ronan Dixon; 26 Kriss Brining; 15 Graeme Horne; 11 Josh Jordan-Roberts; 33 Joe Batchelor; 25 Dave Petersen. Subs (all used): 14 Harry Carter; 10 Jack Teanby; 16 Jack Blagbrough; 17 Joe Porter.
**Tries:** Batchelor (3, 11), Petersen (35), Salter (39), Robinson (50, 61), Bass (56, 67, 76); **Goals:** Robinson 10/10.
**RAIDERS:** 1 Theerapol Ritson; 21 Tom Loxam; 5 Deon Cross; 4 Jake Spedding; 2 Stargroth Amean; 22 Ryan Johnston; 7 Lewis Charnock; 8 Tom Walker; 14 Wartovo Puara; 28 Josh Johnson; 11 Jono Smith; 12 Jarrad Stack; 25 Jordan Walne. Subs (all used): 9 Nathan Mossop; 13 Martin Aspinwall; 26 Willie Minoga; 20 Bradd Crellin.
**Sin bin:** Stack (49) - repeated offences; Mossop (65) - repeated offences.
**Rugby Leaguer & League Express Men of the Match:** *City Knights:* Ben Cockayne; *Raiders:* Jono Smith.
**Penalty count:** 14-9; **Half-time:** 26-0;
**Referee:** Liam Staveley; **Attendance:** 1,575.

## ROUND 4

*Sunday 24th February 2019*

**BARROW RAIDERS 20 DEWSBURY RAMS 20**

**RAIDERS:** 1 Theerapol Ritson; 2 Stargroth Amean; 12 Jarrad Stack; 4 Jake Spedding; 5 Deon Cross; 7 Lewis Charnock; 22 Ryan Johnston; 8 Tom Walker; 14 Wartovo Puara; 28 Josh Johnson; 11 Jono Smith; 25 Jordan Walne; 13 Martin Aspinwall. Subs (all used): 9 Nathan Mossop; 26 Willie Minoga; 20 Bradd Crellin; 16 Glenn Riley.
**Tries:** Stack (8, 27), R Johnston (73);
**Goals:** Charnock 3/4, R Johnston 1/1.
**RAMS:** 35 Luke Hooley; 23 Rob Worrincy; 3 Cameron Leeming; 4 Adam Ryder; 1 Dale Morton; 6 Paul Sykes; 7 Simon Brown; 30 Tom Garratt; 18 Sam Day; 33 Callum Field; 11 Lucas Walshaw; 19 Daniel Igbinedion; 13 Kyle Trout. Subs (all used): 16 Jordan Andrade; 9 Robbie Ward; 12 Michael Knowles; 10 Toby Richardson.
**Tries:** K Trout (17, 52), Sykes (62); **Goals:** Sykes 4/4.
**Rugby Leaguer & League Express Men of the Match:** *Raiders:* Jarrad Stack; *Rams:* Kyle Trout.
**Penalty count:** 9-8; **Half-time** 12-8;
**Referee:** Michael Mannifield; **Attendance:** 1,321.

**BATLEY BULLDOGS 18 ROCHDALE HORNETS 12**

**BULLDOGS:** 1 Dave Scott; 2 Wayne Reittie; 22 Sam Wood; 3 Sam Smeaton; 4 Lewis Galbraith; 14 Danny Yates; 7 Dom Brambani; 8 Adam Gledhill; 9 Alistair Leak; 15 Toby Everett; 11 Dane Manning; 12 Jack Downs; 13 James Brown. Subs (all used): 18 Tom Hemingway; 21 Jo Taira; 10 Tom Lillycrop; 25 Lewis Bienek.
**Tries:** Galbraith (8, 27), Reittie (70); **Goals:** Scott 3/4.
**HORNETS:** 7 Dan Abram; 2 Shaun Ainscough; 23 Jordan Case; 5 Paddy Flynn; 24 Brandon Wood; 29 Tyler Whittaker; 13 Stuart Howarth; 10 Carl Forster; 6 Scott Moore; 28 Sitaleki Akauola; 16 Mike Weldon; 11 Lee Mitchell; 8 Matt Davis. Subs (all used): 26 Pat Moran; 30 Adam Lawton; 17 Liam Carberry; 12 Ellis Gillam.
**Tries:** Lawton (32), Mitchell (75); **Goals:** Abram 2/2.
**Rugby Leaguer & League Express Men of the Match:** *Bulldogs:* Lewis Galbraith; *Hornets:* Shaun Ainscough.
**Penalty count:** 12-6; **Half-time:** 12-6;
**Referee:** Liam Staveley; **Attendance:** 754.

**BRADFORD BULLS 14 YORK CITY KNIGHTS 24**

**BULLS:** 1 Brandon Pickersgill; 5 Jy Hitchcox; 31 Rhys Evans; 3 Jake Webster; 2 Ethan Ryan; 14 Jordan Lilley; 7 Dane Chisholm; 8 Liam Kirk; 9 Matty Wildie; 10 Steve Crossley; 11 Matt Garside; 12 Elliot Minchella; 18 Sam Hallas. Subs (all used): 21 George Flanagan; 33 Olsi Krasniqi; 25 Connor Farrell; 29 Matthew Storton.
**Tries:** Ryan (39, 45), Pickersgill (54); **Goals:** Chisholm 1/3.
**CITY KNIGHTS:** 1 Matty Marsh; 2 Ash Robson; 23 Jason Bass; 3 Liam Salter; 21 Judah Mazive; 6 Ben Cockayne; 7 Connor Robinson; 8 Ronan Dixon; 26 Kriss Brining; 15 Graeme Horne; 33 Joe Batchelor; 4 Brad Hey; 25 Dave Petersen. Subs (all used): 14 Harry Carter; 22 Marcus Stock; 10 Jack Teanby; 17 Joe Porter.
**Tries:** Robson (8), Mazive (37), Teanby (60), Marsh (78);
**Goals:** Robinson 4/6.
**Sin bin:** Mazive (12) - delaying restart.
**Rugby Leaguer & League Express Men of the Match:** *Bulls:* Jake Webster; *City Knights:* Connor Robinson.
**Penalty count:** 8-7; **Half-time:** 4-12;
**Referee:** Greg Dolan; **Attendance:** 4,782.

**FEATHERSTONE ROVERS 46 HALIFAX 16**

**ROVERS:** 1 Calum Turner; 2 Luke Briscoe; 3 Thompson Teteh; 27 Harry Newman; 25 Jack Render; 6 Ase Boas; 7 Watson Boas; 8 Scott Wheeldon; 9 Cameron King; 30 Daniel Smith; 12 Brad Day; 28 Josh Walters; 13 James Lockwood. Subs (all used): 15 Luke Cooper; 14 John Davies; 16 Danny Maskill; 4 Josh Hardcastle.
**Tries:** King (9), Newman (14, 40), Briscoe (43, 63), Render (54), Cooper (68), Lockwood (79);
**Goals:** Turner 5/6, A Boas 2/2.
**HALIFAX:** 1 Quentin Laulu-Togaga'e; 5 Will Sharp; 3 Steve Tyrer; 20 James Saltonstall; 2 Shaun Robinson; 6 Scott Murrell; 19 Ben White; 8 Dan Fleming; 9 Ben Kaye; 10 Jacob Fairbank; 16 Kevin Larroyer; 11 Shane Grady; 13 Simon Grix. Subs (all used): 17 Ben Kavanagh; 15 Harry Kidd; 14 Brandon Moore; 12 Ed Barber.
**Tries:** Sharp (18), Robinson (60), Laulu-Togaga'e (72);
**Goals:** Tyrer 2/3.

**Rugby Leaguer & League Express Men of the Match:**
*Rovers:* Harry Newman; *Halifax:* Steve Tyrer.
**Penalty count:** 9-4; **Half-time:** 18-4;
**Referee:** Marcus Griffiths; **Attendance:** 2,534.

**LEIGH CENTURIONS 8 TORONTO WOLFPACK 14**

**CENTURIONS:** 6 Martyn Ridyard; 5 Stefan Marsh; 3 Iain Thornley; 24 James Bentley; 19 Mitch Cox; 7 Josh Woods; 27 Danny Richardson; 26 Jack Ashworth; 9 Micky Higham; 30 Luke Douglas; 11 Toby Adamson; 12 Andy Thornley; 10 Sam Brooks. Subs (all used): 18 Dec O'Donnell; 15 Joe Cator; 13 Luke Adamson; 8 Tom Spencer.
**Try:** Douglas (66); **Goals:** Ridyard 2/2.
**Sin bin:** Richardson (54) - professional foul.
**WOLFPACK:** 1 Gareth O'Brien; 20 Adam Higson; 3 Chase Stanley; 4 Ricky Leutele; 24 Nick Rawsthorne; 6 Joe Mellor; 17 Blake Wallace; 10 Ashton Sims; 7 Josh McCrone; 18 Gadwin Springer; 11 Andrew Dixon; 12 Bodene Thompson; 16 Tom Olbison. Subs (all used): 14 Andy Ackers; 15 Darcy Lussick; 21 Anthony Mullally; 8 Adam Sidlow.
**Tries:** Wallace (28), Higson (36), Thompson (55);
**Goals:** O'Brien 1/3.
**Rugby Leaguer & League Express Men of the Match:**
*Centurions:* Luke Douglas; *Wolfpack:* Adam Sidlow.
**Penalty count:** 8-6; **Half-time:** 2-10;
**Referee:** Tom Grant; **Attendance:** 3,142.

**SWINTON LIONS 24 TOULOUSE OLYMPIQUE 26**

**LIONS:** 1 Jack Hansen; 2 Mike Butt; 35 Chris Hankinson; 3 Rhodri Lloyd; 32 Liam Forsyth; 34 Harry Smith; 7 Rob Fairclough; 8 Gavin Bennion; 9 Luke Waterworth; 10 Lewis Hatton; 33 Liam Paisley; 22 Frankie Halton; 31 Oliver Partington. Subs (all used): 17 Aaron Hall; 12 Kyle Shelford; 11 Adam Jones; 16 Paddy Jones.
**Tries:** Butt (12), Hansen (25), Fairclough (59), Forsyth (73);
**Goals:** Smith 4/4.
**OLYMPIQUE:** 1 Mark Kheirallah; 4 Gavin Marguerite; 26 Arthur Romano; 25 Mathieu Jussaume; 3 Bastien Ader; 6 Johnathon Ford; 7 Stan Robin; 18 Clement Boyer; 14 Dean Parata; 10 Joe Bretherton; 11 Con Mika; 12 Rhys Curran; 22 Brenden Santi. Subs (all used): 21 Jordan Dezaria; 15 Ben Evans; 16 Tyla Hepi; 9 Anthony Marion.
**Tries:** Marguerite (3), Parata (6, 49), Mika (30), Kheirallah (35); **Goals:** Kheirallah 3/6.
**Rugby Leaguer & League Express Men of the Match:**
*Lions:* Harry Smith; *Olympique:* Stan Robin.
**Penalty count:** 7-9; **Half-time:** 12-18;
**Referee:** Jack Smith; **Attendance:** 601.

## ROUND 5

*Friday 1st March 2019*

**SHEFFIELD EAGLES 44 BATLEY BULLDOGS 16**

**EAGLES:** 1 Josh Guzdek; 2 Ryan Millar; 18 James Glover; 4 Jason Crookes; 5 Ben Blackmore; 6 Pat Walker; 7 Anthony Thackeray; 11 Brad Knowles; 9 James Davey; 10 Matt James; 12 Joel Farrell; 15 Olly Davies; 13 Aaron Brown. Subs (all used): 16 Corey Makelim; 21 Blake Broadbent; 19 Sonny Esslemont; 22 Paddy Burns.
**Tries:** Glover (32), Thackeray (39), Broadbent (47), Farrell (52), Davies (57), Blackmore (64, 68), P Burns (80);
**Goals:** Walker 6/8.
**Sin bin:** Knowles (18) - fighting.
**BULLDOGS:** 1 Dave Scott; 2 Wayne Reittie; 22 Sam Wood; 3 Sam Smeaton; 4 Lewis Galbraith; 6 Louis Jouffret; 7 Dom Brambani; 8 Adam Gledhill; 9 Alistair Leak; 10 Tom Lillycrop; 12 Jack Downs; 11 Dane Manning; 24 Paul Brearley. Subs (all used): 18 Tom Hemingway; 13 James Brown; 15 Toby Everett; 16 Michael Ward.
**Tries:** Wood (3), Downs (20), Smeaton (78);
**Goals:** Scott 2/4.
**Sin bin:** Manning (18) - fighting, (54) - high tackle on Farrell.
**Rugby Leaguer & League Express Men of the Match:**
*Eagles:* Joel Farrell; *Bulldogs:* Sam Wood.
**Penalty count:** 8-8; **Half-time:** 12-10;
**Referee:** Nick Bennett; **Attendance:** 791.

*Sunday 3rd March 2019*

**BRADFORD BULLS 0 TOULOUSE OLYMPIQUE 14**

**BULLS:** 1 Brandon Pickersgill; 31 Rhys Evans; 4 Ashley Gibson; 3 Jake Webster; 2 Ethan Ryan; 12 Elliot Minchella; 9 Matty Wildie; 8 Liam Kirk; 18 Sam Hallas; 10 Steve Crossley; 11 Matt Garside; 25 Connor Farrell; 13 Mikey Wood. Subs (all used): 21 George Flanagan; 15 Callum Bustin; 29 Matthew Storton; 26 Ross Oakes.
**OLYMPIQUE:** 1 Mark Kheirallah; 4 Gavin Marguerite; 26 Arthur Romano; 3 Bastien Ader; 2 Tony Maurel; 6 Johnathon Ford; 7 Stan Robin; 18 Clement Boyer; 14 Dean Parata; 10 Joe Bretherton; 11 Con Mika; 12 Rhys Curran; 22 Brenden Santi. Subs (all used): 9 Anthony Marion; 15 Ben Evans; 16 Tyla Hepi; 30 William Barthau.
**Tries:** Maurel (12), Robin (57); **Goals:** Kheirallah 3/3.
**Rugby Leaguer & League Express Men of the Match:**
*Bulls:* Callum Bustin; *Olympique:* Mark Kheirallah.
**Penalty count:** 8-5; **Half-time:** 0-6;
**Referee:** Jack Smith; **Attendance:** 3,751.

**DEWSBURY RAMS 17 TORONTO WOLFPACK 22**

**RAMS:** 35 Luke Hooley; 23 Rob Worrincy; 11 Lucas Walshaw; 4 Adam Ryder; 1 Dale Morton; 6 Paul Sykes; 12 Michael Knowles; 30 Tom Garratt; 18 Sam Day; 34 Chris Annakin; 32 Samy Kibula; 36 Owen Harrison; 13 Kyle Trout. Subs (all used): 9 Robbie Ward; 19 Daniel Igbinedion; 33 Callum Field; 16 Jordan Andrade.
**Try:** Knowles (21); **Goals:** Sykes 6/7; **Field goal:** Sykes (64).
**Dismissal:** Annakin (76) - spitting.
**Sin bin:** Igbinedion (74) - fighting.
**WOLFPACK:** 1 Gareth O'Brien; 20 Adam Higson; 24 Nick Rawsthorne; 4 Ricky Leutele; 2 Matty Russell; 17 Blake Wallace; 7 Josh McCrone; 8 Adam Sidlow; 14 Andy Ackers; 15 Darcy Lussick; 11 Andrew Dixon; 16 Tom Olbison; 13 Jon Wilkin. Subs (all used): 9 Bob Beswick; 21 Anthony Mullally; 18 Gadwin Springer; 23 Ryan Brierley.
**Tries:** Higson (34), Brierley (65), Wallace (67), O'Brien (70);
**Goals:** O'Brien 3/4.
**Sin bin:** Lussick (74) - fighting.
**Rugby Leaguer & League Express Men of the Match:**
*Rams:* Paul Sykes; *Wolfpack:* Gareth O'Brien.
**Penalty count:** 10-7; **Half-time:** 10-4;
**Referee:** Michael Mannifield; **Attendance:** 1,251.

**HALIFAX 18 SWINTON LIONS 16**

**HALIFAX:** 1 Quentin Laulu-Togaga'e; 5 Will Sharp; 3 Steve Tyrer; 20 James Saltonstall; 2 Shaun Robinson; 6 Scott Murrell; 7 Ben Johnston; 8 Dan Fleming; 9 Ben Kaye; 10 Jacob Fairbank; 16 Kevin Larroyer; 11 Shane Grady; 13 Simon Grix. Subs (all used): 17 Ben Kavanagh; 18 Elliot Morris; 14 Brandon Moore; 25 Liam Cooper.
**Tries:** Saltonstall (49, 73), Tyrer (69); **Goals:** Tyrer 3/3.
**LIONS:** 1 Jack Hansen; 2 Mike Butt; 32 Liam Forsyth; 31 Chris Hankinson; 25 Matty Ashton; 34 Harry Smith; 7 Rob Fairclough; 8 Gavin Bennion; 9 Luke Waterworth; 10 Lewis Hatton; 22 Frankie Halton; 12 Kyle Shelford; 19 Jose Kenga. Subs (all used): 35 Josh Ganson; 17 Aaron Hall; 11 Adam Jones; 4 Daley Williams.
**Tries:** Ashton (26, 31), Butt (61); **Goals:** Smith 2/3.
**Rugby Leaguer & League Express Men of the Match:**
*Halifax:* Simon Grix; *Lions:* Harry Smith.
**Penalty count:** 8-4; **Half-time:** 0-10;
**Referee:** Liam Staveley; **Attendance:** 1,584.

**ROCHDALE HORNETS 20 BARROW RAIDERS 8**

**HORNETS:** 7 Dan Abram; 2 Shaun Ainscough; 23 Jordan Case; 5 Paddy Flynn; 24 Brandon Wood; 13 Stuart Howarth; 29 Tyler Whittaker; 28 Sitaleki Akauola; 6 Scott Moore; 8 Matt Davis; 11 Lee Mitchell; 12 Ellis Gillam; 27 Harvey Livett. Subs (all used): 30 Adam Lawton; 26 Pat Moran; 9 Ben Moores; 17 Liam Carberry.
**Tries:** Lawton (26), B Moores (49), Carberry (67);
**Goals:** Abram 4/4.
**RAIDERS:** 18 Luke Cresswell; 5 Deon Cross; 12 Jarrad Stack; 4 Jake Spedding; 2 Stargroth Amean; 6 Jamie Dallimore; 7 Lewis Charnock; 8 Tom Walker; 14 Wartovo Puara; 28 Josh Johnson; 25 Jordan Walne; 11 Jono Smith; 13 Martin Aspinwall. Subs (all used): 9 Nathan Mossop; 20 Bradd Crellin; 26 Willie Minoga; 16 Glenn Riley.
**Tries:** Amean (3, 72); **Goals:** Dallimore 0/3.
**Rugby Leaguer & League Express Men of the Match:**
*Hornets:* Dan Abram; *Raiders:* Lewis Charnock.
**Penalty count:** 9-9; **Half-time:** 6-4;
**Referee:** Greg Dolan; **Attendance:** 514.

**WIDNES VIKINGS 44 FEATHERSTONE ROVERS 22**

**VIKINGS:** 5 Jack Owens; 22 Owen Buckley; 24 Keanan Brand; 4 Anthony Gelling; 2 Ryan Ince; 6 Danny Craven; 7 Tom Gilmore; 13 Hep Cahill; 9 Liam Hood; 11 Harrison Hansen; 17 Sam Wilde; 19 Brad Walker; 16 MacGraff Leuluai. Subs (all used): 18 Ted Chapelhow; 15 Jordan Johnstone; 8 Jay Chapelhow; 20 Owen Farnworth.
**Tries:** Hood (2), Gelling (8), Ince (12, 68), Owens (16, 56), Walker (37), Wilde (53); **Goals:** Owens 6/8.
**ROVERS:** 1 Calum Turner; 2 Luke Briscoe; 33 Ashton Golding; 27 Harry Newman; 25 Jack Render; 6 Ase Boas; 7 Watson Boas; 8 Scott Wheeldon; 9 Cameron King; 26 Daniel Smith; 14 John Davies; 17 James Harrison; 13 James Lockwood. Subs (all used): 4 Josh Hardcastle; 15 Luke Cooper; 16 Danny Maskill; 29 Jack Ormondroyd.
**Tries:** D Smith (48), Newman (62, 74), King (65);
**Goals:** Turner 3/4.
**Rugby Leaguer & League Express Men of the Match:**
*Vikings:* Danny Craven; *Rovers:* Cameron King.
**Penalty count:** 7-11; **Half-time:** 28-0;
**Referee:** Marcus Griffiths; **Attendance:** 5,782.

**YORK CITY KNIGHTS 9 LEIGH CENTURIONS 8**

**CITY KNIGHTS:** 1 Matty Marsh; 20 Perry Whiteley; 23 Jason Bass; 3 Liam Salter; 21 Judah Mazive; 6 Ben Cockayne; 7 Connor Robinson; 8 Ronan Dixon; 26 Kriss Brining; 16 Jack Blagbrough; 33 Joe Batchelor; 11 Josh Jordan-Roberts; 15 Graeme Horne. Subs (all used): 14 Harry Carter; 10 Jack Teanby; 22 Marcus Stock; 17 Joe Porter.
**Try:** Batchelor (5); **Goals:** Robinson 2/3;
**Field goal:** Robinson (69).
**CENTURIONS:** 6 Martyn Ridyard; 2 Jonny Pownall; 24 James Bentley; 3 Iain Thornley; 5 Stefan Marsh; 7 Josh Woods; 27 Danny Richardson; 30 Luke Douglas; 9 Micky Higham; 13 Luke Adamson; 11 Toby Adamson; 12 Andy Thornley; 15 Joe Cator. Subs (all used): 19 Mitch Cox; 25 Aaron Smith; 17 Nick Gregson; 8 Tom Spencer.
**Try:** A Thornley (35); **Goals:** Ridyard 2/3.
**Rugby Leaguer & League Express Men of the Match:**
*City Knights:* Connor Robinson; *Centurions:* Luke Douglas.
**Penalty count:** 7-7; **Half-time:** 6-6;
**Referee:** James Child; **Attendance:** 2,020.

## ROUND 6

*Saturday 9th March 2019*

**TOULOUSE OLYMPIQUE 46 TORONTO WOLFPACK 16**

**OLYMPIQUE:** 1 Mark Kheirallah; 2 Tony Maurel; 3 Bastien Ader; 26 Arthur Romano; 4 Gavin Marguerite; 6 Johnathon Ford; 7 Stan Robin; 10 Joe Bretherton; 14 Dean Parata; 18 Clement Boyer; 11 Con Mika; 12 Rhys Curran; 22 Brenden Santi. Subs (all used): 9 Anthony Marion; 15 Ben Evans; 16 Tyla Hepi; 30 William Barthau.
**Tries:** Parata (5), Robin (44, 49), Marguerite (56), Curran (69), Kheirallah (77, 79); **Goals:** Kheirallah 9/9.
**WOLFPACK:** 1 Gareth O'Brien; 20 Adam Higson; 25 Jack Logan; 4 Ricky Leutele; 2 Matty Russell; 17 Blake Wallace; 7 Josh McCrone; 16 Tom Olbison; 9 Bob Beswick; 18 Gadwin Springer; 11 Andrew Dixon; 12 Bodene Thompson; 13 Jon Wilkin. Subs (all used): 14 Andy Ackers; 29 Jake Emmitt; 15 Darcy Lussick; 21 Anthony Mullally.
**Tries:** Wallace (11), Beswick (14), Leutele (25);
**Goals:** O'Brien 2/3.
**Rugby Leaguer & League Express Men of the Match:**
*Olympique:* Stan Robin; *Wolfpack:* Ricky Leutele.
**Penalty count:** 10-5; **Half-time:** 6-16;
**Referee:** Gareth Hewer; **Attendance:** 6,103
*(at Stade Ernest Wallon).*

*Sunday 10th March 2019*

**BARROW RAIDERS 4 WIDNES VIKINGS 20**

**RAIDERS:** 18 Luke Cresswell; 2 Stargroth Amean; 12 Jarrad Stack; 4 Jake Spedding; 5 Deon Cross; 6 Jamie Dallimore; 7 Lewis Charnock; 16 Glenn Riley; 14 Wartovo Puara; 28 Josh Johnson; 11 Jono Smith; 19 Danny Morrow; 25 Jordan Walne. Subs (all used): 9 Nathan Mossop; 26 Willie Minoga; 8 Tom Walker; 13 Martin Aspinwall.
**Goals:** Dallimore 2/2.
**VIKINGS:** 5 Jack Owens; 2 Ryan Ince; 4 Anthony Gelling; 24 Keanan Brand; 22 Owen Buckley; 6 Danny Craven; 7 Tom Gilmore; 13 Hep Cahill; 15 Jordan Johnstone; 11 Harrison Hansen; 19 Brad Walker; 17 Sam Wilde; 16 MacGraff Leuluai. Subs (all used): 8 Jay Chapelhow; 18 Ted Chapelhow; 20 Owen Farnworth; 25 Lloyd Roby.
**Tries:** Craven (41), Walker (48), Ince (67), Cahill (74);
**Goals:** Gilmore 2/4.
**Rugby Leaguer & League Express Men of the Match:**
*Raiders:* Jono Smith; *Vikings:* Brad Walker.
**Penalty count:** 10-9; **Half-time:** 4-0;
**Referee:** James Child; **Attendance:** 1,724.

**BATLEY BULLDOGS 6 BRADFORD BULLS 16**

**BULLDOGS:** 1 Dave Scott; 23 Keenen Tomlinson; 3 Sam Smeaton; 4 Lewis Galbraith; 5 Johnny Campbell; 14 Danny Yates; 7 Dom Brambani; 15 Toby Everett; 18 Tom Hemingway; 10 Tom Lillycrop; 12 Jack Downs; 24 Paul Brearley; 17 Tyler Dickinson. Subs (all used): 13 James Brown; 9 Alistair Leak; 25 Lewis Bienek; 8 Adam Gledhill.
**Try:** Yates (68); **Goals:** Scott 1/1.
**Sin bin:** Lillycrop (75) - high tackle.
**BULLS:** 1 Brandon Pickersgill; 24 David Foggin-Johnston; 31 Rhys Evans; 26 Ross Oakes; 2 Ethan Ryan; 14 Jordan Lilley; 9 Matty Wildie; 15 Callum Bustin; 18 Sam Hallas; 10 Steve Crossley; 3 Jake Webster; 25 Connor Farrell; 13 Mikey Wood. Subs (all used): 16 James Green; 8 Liam Kirk; 29 Matthew Storton; 21 George Flanagan.
**Tries:** Ryan (22), Oakes (29), Kirk (36); **Goals:** Lilley 2/4.
**Rugby Leaguer & League Express Men of the Match:**
*Bulldogs:* Johnny Campbell; *Bulls:* Jordan Lilley.
**Penalty count:** 11-10; **Half-time:** 0-16;
**Referee:** Michael Mannifield; **Attendance:** 2,393.

*Championship 2019 - Round by Round*

**FEATHERSTONE ROVERS 32 SHEFFIELD EAGLES 14**

**ROVERS:** 33 Ashton Golding; 2 Luke Briscoe; 4 Josh Hardcastle; 17 James Harrison; 1 Calum Turner; 34 Ben Reynolds; 7 Watson Boas; 8 Scott Wheeldon; 9 Cameron King; 10 Jack Bussey; 14 John Davies; 31 Cameron Smith; 13 James Lockwood. Subs: 15 Luke Cooper; 29 Jack Ormondroyd; 16 Danny Maskill; 6 Ase Boas (not used).
**Tries:** Lockwood (8), Turner (16, 68), Golding (24), Bussey (59), Davies (75); **Goals:** Turner 4/6.
**Sin bin:** Bussey (46) - holding down.
**EAGLES:** 1 Josh Guzdek; 2 Ryan Millar; 18 James Glover; 4 Jason Crookes; 5 Ben Blackmore; 6 Pat Walker; 7 Anthony Thackeray; 11 Brad Knowles; 9 James Davey; 10 Matt James; 15 Olly Davies; 12 Joel Farrell; 13 Aaron Brown. Subs (all used): 14 Greg Burns; 21 Blake Broadbent; 22 Paddy Burns; 17 Shaun Pick.
**Tries:** Millar (20, 53), Farrell (40); **Goals:** Walker 1/3.
**Dismissal:**
Broadbent (37) - dangerous challenge on Hardcastle.
**Sin bin:** Davey (67) - high tackle on Briscoe.
**Rugby Leaguer & League Express Men of the Match:**
*Rovers:* James Lockwood; *Eagles:* Joel Farrell.
**Penalty count:** 8-5; **Half-time:** 16-10;
**Referee:** Liam Moore; **Attendance:** 1,981.

**HALIFAX 26 DEWSBURY RAMS 0**

**HALIFAX:** 27 Reece Chapman-Smith; 5 Will Sharp; 3 Steve Tyrer; 20 James Saltonstall; 2 Shaun Robinson; 6 Scott Murrell; 7 Ben Johnston; 8 Dan Fleming; 9 Ben Kaye; 10 Jacob Fairbank; 16 Kevin Larroyer; 11 Shane Grady; 12 Ed Barber. Subs (all used): 17 Ben Kavanagh; 18 Elliot Morris; 14 Brandon Moore; 25 Liam Cooper.
**Tries:** Barber (15, 47, 67), Robinson (40); **Goals:** Tyrer 5/5.
**Sin bin:** Barber (33) - fighting.
**RAMS:** 35 Luke Hooley; 23 Rob Worrincy; 11 Lucas Walshaw; 4 Adam Ryder; 1 Dale Morton; 6 Paul Sykes; 38 Liam Finn; 34 Chris Annakin; 18 Sam Day; 30 Tom Garratt; 36 Owen Trout; 32 Samy Kibula; 13 Kyle Trout. Subs (all used): 9 Robbie Ward; 12 Michael Knowles; 19 Daniel Igbinedion; 33 Muizz Mustapha.
**Rugby Leaguer & League Express Men of the Match:**
*Halifax:* Ed Barber; *Rams:* Adam Ryder.
**Penalty count:** 7-8; **Half-time:** 14-0;
**Referee:** Jack Smith; **Attendance:** 1,343.

**SWINTON LIONS 12 LEIGH CENTURIONS 30**

**LIONS:** 1 Jack Hansen; 2 Mike Butt; 32 Liam Forsyth; 4 Daley Williams; 25 Matty Ashton; 34 Harry Smith; 7 Rob Fairclough; 8 Gavin Bennion; 9 Luke Waterworth; 10 Lewis Hatton; 12 Kyle Shelford; 22 Frankie Halton; 35 Oliver Partington. Subs (all used): 14 Billy Brickhill; 11 Adam Jones; 19 Jose Kenga; 26 Jamie Acton.
**Tries:** Ashton (47, 70); **Goals:** Smith 2/2.
**Sin bin:** Partington (1) - fighting.
**CENTURIONS:** 1 Gregg McNally; 2 Jonny Pownall; 25 Matthew Costello; 3 Iain Thornley; 5 Stefan Marsh; 6 Martyn Ridyard; 29 Danny Richardson; 13 Luke Adamson; 9 Micky Higham; 10 Sam Brooks; 11 Toby Adamson; 24 James Bentley; 15 Joe Cator. Subs (all used): 27 Liam Hood; 8 Tom Spencer; 12 Andy Thornley; 17 Nick Gregson.
**Tries:** Marsh (3, 79), Hood (33), McNally (37), Costello (40), T Adamson (56); **Goals:** Ridyard 3/5, Richardson 0/1.
**Sin bin:** L Adamson (1) - fighting.
**Rugby Leaguer & League Express Men of the Match:**
*Lions:* Matty Ashton; *Centurions:* Martyn Ridyard.
**Penalty count:** 11-11; **Half-time:** 0-20;
**Referee:** Greg Dolan; **Attendance:** 2,054.

## ROUND 7

*Saturday 16th March 2019*

**TOULOUSE OLYMPIQUE 50 BARROW RAIDERS 0**

**OLYMPIQUE:** 1 Mark Kheirallah; 4 Gavin Marguerite; 3 Bastien Ader; 25 Mathieu Jussaume; 2 Tony Maurel; 6 Johnathon Ford; 7 Stan Robin; 15 Ben Evans; 14 Dean Parata; 18 Clement Boyer; 11 Con Mika; 10 Joe Bretherton; 22 Brenden Santi. Subs (all used): 8 Maxime Puech; 9 Anthony Marion; 16 Tyla Hepi; 30 William Barthau.
**Tries:** Marguerite (12), Ader (14, 35, 75), Maurel (42, 44), Marion (55, 69), Jussaume (58), Bretherton (77);
**Goals:** Kheirallah 4/7, Barthau 1/3.
**RAIDERS:** 18 Luke Cresswell; 2 Stargroth Amean; 12 Jarrad Stack; 4 Jake Spedding; 5 Deon Cross; 22 Ryan Johnston; 7 Lewis Charnock; 28 Josh Johnson; 14 Wartovo Puara; 25 Jordan Walne; 11 Jono Smith; 19 Danny Morrow; 20 Bradd Crellin. Subs (all used): 8 Tom Walker; 9 Nathan Mossop; 24 Jake Carter; 26 Willie Minoga.
**Sin bin:** Stack (54) - dissent.
**Rugby Leaguer & League Express Men of the Match:**
*Olympique:* Johnathon Ford; *Raiders:* Jarrad Stack.
**Penalty count:** 8-6; **Half-time:** 16-0;
**Referee:** Cameron Worsley; **Attendance:** 1,388.

*Sunday 17th March 2019*

**DEWSBURY RAMS 13 SHEFFIELD EAGLES 16**

**RAMS:** 2 Andy Gabriel; 23 Rob Worrincy; 35 Owen Trout; 4 Adam Ryder; 5 Alex Brown; 6 Paul Sykes; 38 Liam Finn; 34 Chris Annakin; 18 Sam Day; 36 Owen Harrison; 12 Michael Knowles; 32 Samy Kibula; 13 Kyle Trout. Subs (all used): 22 Danny King; 33 Muizz Mustapha; 37 Liam Mackay; 16 Jordan Andrade.
**Tries:** Sykes (46), Worrincy (51); **Goals:** Sykes 2/3;
**Field goal:** Sykes (63).
**Dismissal:** Kibula (28) - high tackle.
**Sin bin:** Annakin (22) - fighting;
Ryder (68) - high tackle on Farrell; Finn (75) - holding down.
**On report:** Knowles (24) - alleged dangerous challenge.
**EAGLES:** 1 Josh Guzdek; 2 Ryan Millar; 18 James Glover; 4 Jason Crookes; 5 Ben Blackmore; 6 Pat Walker; 7 Anthony Thackeray; 10 Matt James; 9 James Davey; 23 Rory Dixon; 12 Joel Farrell; 15 Olly Davies; 13 Aaron Brown. Subs (all used): 22 Paddy Burns; 21 Blake Broadbent; 16 Corey Makelim; 11 Brad Knowles.
**Tries:** Thackeray (57), Farrell (76), Blackmore (78);
**Goals:** Walker 2/4.
**Dismissal:** Knowles (22) - fighting.
**Sin bin:** Farrell (13) - high tackle.
**Rugby Leaguer & League Express Men of the Match:**
*Rams:* Owen Trout; *Eagles:* Joel Farrell.
**Penalty count:** 6-14; **Half-time:** 2-0;
**Referee:** Jack Smith; **Attendance:** 977.

**LEIGH CENTURIONS 46 ROCHDALE HORNETS 6**

**CENTURIONS:** 1 Gregg McNally; 2 Jonny Pownall; 3 Iain Thornley; 19 Mitch Cox; 5 Stefan Marsh; 6 Martyn Ridyard; 28 Danny Richardson; 30 Luke Douglas; 27 Liam Hood; 10 Sam Brooks; 11 Toby Adamson; 24 James Bentley; 15 Joe Cator. Subs (all used): 25 Aaron Smith; 12 Andy Thornley; 13 Luke Adamson; 8 Tom Spencer.
**Tries:** I Thornley (9), T Adamson (14), Bentley (17, 67), Pownall (27), McNally (33, 76), Hood (69);
**Goals:** Richardson 7/8.
**HORNETS:** 29 Tyler Whittaker; 2 Shaun Ainscough; 23 Jordan Case; 3 Seta Tala; 24 Brandon Wood; 7 Dan Abram; 6 Scott Moore; 26 Pat Moran; 22 Callum Wood; 27 Nathan Reidy; 11 Lee Mitchell; 16 Mike Weldon; 9 Ben Moores. Subs (all used): 17 Liam Carberry; 10 Carl Forster; 15 Declan Gregory; 18 Ryan Millington.
**Try:** Millington (78); **Goals:** Abram 1/1.
**Sin bin:** S Moore (27) - high tackle on Pownall.
**Rugby Leaguer & League Express Men of the Match:**
*Centurions:* Gregg McNally; *Hornets:* Lee Mitchell.
**Penalty count:** 12-9; **Half-time:** 30-0;
**Referee:** Marcus Griffiths; **Attendance:** 2,666.

**SWINTON LIONS 12 FEATHERSTONE ROVERS 24**

**LIONS:** 1 Jack Hansen; 2 Mike Butt; 35 Chris Hankinson; 32 Liam Forsyth; 25 Matty Ashton; 6 Oscar Thomas; 34 Harry Smith; 8 Gavin Bennion; 9 Luke Waterworth; 10 Lewis Hatton; 33 Liam Paisley; 22 Frankie Halton; 12 Kyle Shelford. Subs (all used): 14 Billy Brickhill; 16 Paddy Jones; 7 Rob Fairclough; 26 Jamie Acton.
**Tries:** Bennion (10), Ashton (51); **Goals:** Thomas 2/3.
**Sin bin:** Paisley (45) - fighting.
**On report:** Hatton (21) - alleged late challenge on W Boas.
**ROVERS:** 33 Ashton Golding; 2 Luke Briscoe; 17 James Harrison; 4 Josh Hardcastle; 25 Jack Render; 34 Ben Reynolds; 7 Watson Boas; 26 Daniel Smith; 9 Cameron King; 10 Jack Bussey; 14 John Davies; 31 Cameron Smith; 13 James Lockwood. Subs (all used): 12 Brad Day; 15 Luke Cooper; 8 Scott Wheeldon; 29 Jack Ormondroyd.
**Tries:** Bussey (19, 31), Golding (27), Ormondroyd (70);
**Goals:** Reynolds 4/4.
**Sin bin:** Briscoe (45) - fighting;
Hardcastle (50) - punching; King (79) - trip on Ashton.
**Rugby Leaguer & League Express Men of the Match:**
*Lions:* Matty Ashton; *Rovers:* Ben Reynolds.
**Penalty count:** 8-8; **Half-time:** 8-18;
**Referee:** Michael Mannifield; **Attendance:** 923.

**WIDNES VIKINGS 25 BRADFORD BULLS 20**

**VIKINGS:** 5 Jack Owens; 24 Keanan Brand; 12 Chris Dean; 4 Anthony Gelling; 2 Ryan Ince; 6 Danny Craven; 7 Tom Gilmore; 13 Hep Cahill; 15 Jordan Johnstone; 11 Harrison Hansen; 19 Brad Walker; 17 Sam Wilde; 16 MacGraff Leuluai. Subs (all used): 8 Jay Chapelhow; 18 Ted Chapelhow; 20 Owen Farnworth; 25 Lloyd Roby.
**Tries:** Craven (6), Brand (14), Johnstone (31), Ince (74);
**Goals:** Owens 4/5; **Field goal:** Craven (61).
**BULLS:** 1 Brandon Pickersgill; 24 David Foggin-Johnston; 31 Rhys Evans; 26 Ross Oakes; 2 Ethan Ryan; 12 Elliot Minchella; 9 Matty Wildie; 8 Liam Kirk; 18 Sam Hallas; 10 Steve Crossley; 11 Matt Garside; 25 Connor Farrell; 13 Mikey Wood. Subs (all used): 15 Callum Bustin; 16 James Green; 21 George Flanagan; 29 Matthew Storton.
**Tries:** Foggin-Johnston (20), Farrell (25), J Green (77);
**Goals:** Minchella 4/4.
**Rugby Leaguer & League Express Men of the Match:**
*Vikings:* Jordan Johnstone; *Bulls:* Matty Wildie.
**Penalty count:** 9-10; **Half-time:** 18-14;
**Referee:** Gareth Hewer; **Attendance:** 5,335.

**YORK CITY KNIGHTS 38 HALIFAX 16**

**CITY KNIGHTS:** 1 Matty Marsh; 23 Jason Bass; 3 Liam Salter; 11 Josh Jordan-Roberts; 21 Judah Mazive; 6 Ben Cockayne; 7 Connor Robinson; 16 Jack Blagbrough; 14 Harry Carter; 8 Ronan Dixon; 12 Sam Scott; 33 Joe Batchelor; 13 Tim Spears. Subs (all used): 26 Kriss Brining; 10 Jack Teanby; 15 Graeme Horne; 17 Joe Porter.
**Tries:** Mazive (2), S Scott (7), Cockayne (14, 56), Marsh (75);
**Goals:** Robinson 9/9.
**HALIFAX:** 27 Reece Chapman-Smith; 5 Will Sharp; 3 Steve Tyrer; 20 James Saltonstall; 2 Shaun Robinson; 6 Scott Murrell; 19 Ben White; 8 Dan Fleming; 9 Ben Kaye; 10 Jacob Fairbank; 16 Kevin Larroyer; 11 Shane Grady; 12 Ed Barber. Subs (all used): 17 Ben Kavanagh; 18 Elliot Morris; 14 Brandon Moore; 35 Will Maher.
**Tries:** Fleming (19), Robinson (28), Fairbank (69);
**Goals:** Tyrer 2/3.
**On report:**
Kaye (77) - alleged dangerous challenge on Batchelor.
**Rugby Leaguer & League Express Men of the Match:**
*City Knights:* Liam Salter; *Halifax:* Shane Grady.
**Penalty count:** 9-5; **Half-time:** 20-10;
**Referee:** Tom Grant; **Attendance:** 2,101.

**TORONTO WOLFPACK 34 BATLEY BULLDOGS 12**

**WOLFPACK:** 1 Gareth O'Brien; 25 Jack Logan; 3 Chase Stanley; 4 Ricky Leutele; 2 Matty Russell; 7 Josh McCrone; 17 Blake Wallace; 8 Adam Sidlow; 14 Andy Ackers; 18 Gadwin Springer; 11 Andrew Dixon; 16 Tom Olbison; 13 Jon Wilkin. Subs (all used): 23 Ryan Brierley; 15 Darcy Lussick; 21 Anthony Mullally; 26 Brad Fash.
**Tries:** Russell (5, 32), Dixon (11), Logan (26), Leutele (29, 38), Wilkin (55); **Goals:** O'Brien 2/6, Brierley 1/1.
**BULLDOGS:** 1 Dave Scott; 20 Niall Walker; 22 Sam Wood; 3 Sam Smeaton; 5 Johnny Campbell; 6 Louis Jouffret; 26 Oliver Russell; 8 Adam Gledhill; 9 Alistair Leak; 10 Tom Lillycrop; 11 Dane Manning; 4 Lewis Galbraith; 12 Jack Downs. Subs (all used): 13 James Brown; 17 Tyler Dickinson; 23 Keenen Tomlinson; 24 Paul Brearley.
**Tries:** Scott (15), Jouffret (59); **Goals:** Scott 2/2.
**Rugby Leaguer & League Express Men of the Match:**
*Wolfpack:* Jon Wilkin; *Bulldogs:* Dane Manning.
**Penalty count:** 6-6; **Half-time:** 28-6; **Referee:** Greg Dolan.
*(at KCOM Craven Park, Hull).*

## ROUND 8

*Saturday 23rd March 2019*

**BATLEY BULLDOGS 12 TOULOUSE OLYMPIQUE 38**

**BULLDOGS:** 1 Dave Scott; 20 Niall Walker; 22 Sam Wood; 4 Lewis Galbraith; 5 Johnny Campbell; 6 Louis Jouffret; 26 Oliver Russell; 8 Adam Gledhill; 9 Alistair Leak; 17 Tyler Dickinson; 12 Jack Downs; 23 Keenen Tomlinson; 11 Dane Manning. Subs (all used): 13 James Brown; 21 Jo Taira; 10 Tom Lillycrop; 3 Sam Smeaton.
**Tries:** Jouffret (23), Leak (39); **Goals:** Scott 2/2.
**Dismissal:** Galbraith (72) - dissent.
**Sin bin:** Lillycrop (51) - dissent.
**OLYMPIQUE:** 1 Mark Kheirallah; 5 Paul Marcon; 25 Mathieu Jussaume; 3 Bastien Ader; 2 Tony Maurel; 9 Anthony Marion; 30 William Barthau; 18 Clement Boyer; 14 Dean Parata; 10 Joe Bretherton; 11 Con Mika; 12 Rhys Curran; 22 Brenden Santi. Subs (all used): 24 Justin Bouscayrol; 8 Maxime Puech; 16 Tyla Hepi; 23 Justin Sangare.
**Tries:** Bretherton (14), Mika (32), Sangare (43), Maurel (51, 62), Barthau (66), Marcon (72);
**Goals:** Kheirallah 5/7.
**Rugby Leaguer & League Express Men of the Match:**
*Bulldogs:* James Brown; *Olympique:* William Barthau.
**Penalty count:** 10-7; **Half-time:** 12-10;
**Referee:** Tom Crashley; **Attendance:** 857.

*Sunday 24th March 2019*

**BARROW RAIDERS 26 SWINTON LIONS 33**

**RAIDERS:** 18 Luke Cresswell; 23 Shane Toal; 12 Jarrad Stack; 5 Deon Cross; 2 Stargroth Amean; 6 Jamie Dallimore; 7 Lewis Charnock; 28 Josh Johnson; 14 Wartovo Puara; 25 Jordan Walne; 26 Willie Minoga; 19 Danny Morrow; 20 Bradd Crellin. Subs (all used): 9 Nathan Mossop; 15 Dan Toal; 16 Glenn Riley; 30 Alec Susino.
**Tries:** Cross (7, 74), Walne (18), Mossop (37);
**Goals:** Dallimore 5/6.

**LIONS:** 1 Jack Hansen; 2 Mike Butt; 32 Chris Hankinson; 31 Liam Forsyth; 25 Matty Ashton; 34 Harry Smith; 7 Rob Fairclough; 8 Gavin Bennion; 9 Luke Waterworth; 10 Lewis Hatton; 35 Liam Paisley; 12 Kyle Shelford; 26 Jamie Acton. Subs (all used): 14 Billy Brickhill; 19 Jose Kenga; 16 Paddy Jones; 6 Oscar Thomas.
**Tries:** Forsyth (4, 34), Butt (45), Hansen (51), Bennion (68), Paisley (71); **Goals:** Smith 2/4, Thomas 2/2; **Field goal:** Thomas (78).
**Rugby Leaguer & League Express Men of the Match:** *Raiders:* Luke Cresswell; *Lions:* Harry Smith.
**Penalty count:** 8-11; **Half-time:** 18-12;
**Referee:** Marcus Griffiths; **Attendance:** 1,357.

**BRADFORD BULLS 26 LEIGH CENTURIONS 12**

**BULLS:** 2 Ethan Ryan; 24 David Foggin-Johnston; 3 Jake Webster; 26 Ross Oakes; 31 Rhys Evans; 27 Rowan Milnes; 9 Matty Wildie; 8 Liam Kirk; 18 Sam Hallas; 10 Steve Crossley; 25 Connor Farrell; 29 Matthew Storton; 12 Elliot Minchella. Subs (all used): 13 Mikey Wood; 16 James Green; 21 George Flanagan; 4 Ashley Gibson.
**Tries:** Webster (10), Storton (15), Ryan (51), Wildie (62), Evans (71); **Goals:** Minchella 2/5, Milnes 1/1.
**Sin bin:** Webster (49) - fighting.
**CENTURIONS:** 1 Gregg McNally; 2 Jonny Pownall; 4 Jack Higginson; 3 Iain Thornley; 5 Stefan Marsh; 28 Danny Richardson; 7 Josh Woods; 23 Luke Douglas; 9 Micky Higham; 10 Sam Brooks; 11 Toby Adamson; 24 James Bentley; 13 Luke Adamson. Subs (all used): 27 Liam Hood; 15 Joe Cator; 8 Tom Spencer; 29 Jake Emmitt.
**Tries:** Brooks (5), Pownall (19); **Goals:** Richardson 2/3.
**Sin bin:** Pownall (44) - dissent; Hood (49) - fighting.
**Rugby Leaguer & League Express Men of the Match:** *Bulls:* Matty Wildie; *Centurions:* Danny Richardson.
**Penalty count:** 15-13; **Half-time:** 12-12;
**Referee:** Tom Grant; **Attendance:** 4,381.

**FEATHERSTONE ROVERS 22 DEWSBURY RAMS 32**

**ROVERS:** 33 Ashton Golding; 2 Luke Briscoe; 4 Josh Hardcastle; 27 Harry Newman; 24 Jimmy McDaniel; 34 Ben Reynolds; 7 Watson Boas; 8 Scott Wheeldon; 9 Cameron King; 26 Daniel Smith; 14 John Davies; 17 James Harrison; 13 James Lockwood. Subs (all used): 15 Luke Cooper; 12 Brad Day; 29 Jack Ormondroyd; 23 Makahesi Makatoa.
**Tries:** Briscoe (14), King (18), Golding (51), Reynolds (54); **Goals:** Reynolds 3/4.
**RAMS:** 35 Luke Hooley; 23 Rob Worrincy; 11 Lucas Walshaw; 4 Adam Ryder; 1 Dale Morton; 6 Paul Sykes; 38 Liam Finn; 34 Chris Annakin; 9 Robbie Ward; 13 Kyle Trout; 15 Samy Kibula; 12 Michael Knowles; 19 Daniel Igbinedion. Subs (all used): 18 Sam Day; 36 Owen Harrison; 8 Jode Sheriffe; 16 Jordan Andrade.
**Tries:** Finn (6), Morton (22, 34), Kibula (43), Knowles (64), Day (68); **Goals:** Sykes 3/6, Finn 1/2.
**Sin bin:** Sykes (54) - dissent.
**Rugby Leaguer & League Express Men of the Match:** *Rovers:* Ben Reynolds; *Rams:* Liam Finn.
**Penalty count:** 10-6; **Half-time:** 10-14;
**Referee:** Gareth Hewer; **Attendance:** 1,943.

**HALIFAX 12 TORONTO WOLFPACK 48**

**HALIFAX:** 1 Quentin Laulu-Togaga'e; 5 Will Sharp; 3 Steve Tyrer; 20 James Saltonstall; 2 Shaun Robinson; 6 Scott Murrell; 7 Ben Johnston; 17 Ben Kavanagh; 9 Ben Kaye; 10 Jacob Fairbank; 16 Kevin Larroyer; 11 Shane Grady; 13 Simon Grix. Subs (all used): 8 Dan Fleming; 12 Ed Barber; 14 Brandon Moore; 18 Elliot Morris.
**Try:** Barber (76); **Goals:** Tyrer 4/4.
**WOLFPACK:** 1 Gareth O'Brien; 25 Jack Logan; 24 Nick Rawsthorne; 4 Ricky Leutele; 2 Matty Russell; 17 Blake Wallace; 7 Josh McCrone; 18 Gadwin Springer; 14 Andy Ackers; 8 Adam Sidlow; 11 Andrew Dixon; 16 Tom Olbison; 13 Jon Wilkin. Subs (all used): 10 Ashton Sims; 15 Darcy Lussick; 21 Anthony Mullally; 23 Ryan Brierley.
**Tries:** Wilkin (21), Dixon (25, 48, 61), Wallace (28, 51), Russell (36, 72), Rawsthorne (56); **Goals:** O'Brien 6/9.
**Rugby Leaguer & League Express Men of the Match:** *Halifax:* Will Sharp; *Wolfpack:* Jon Wilkin.
**Penalty count:** 4-5; **Half-time:** 6-22;
**Referee:** Liam Moore; **Attendance:** 2,090.

**ROCHDALE HORNETS 4 WIDNES VIKINGS 50**

**HORNETS:** 29 Tyler Whittaker; 2 Shaun Ainscough; 23 Jordan Case; 4 Ben Morris; 24 Brandon Wood; 6 Scott Moore; 7 Dan Abram; 28 Sitaleki Akauola; 9 Ben Moores; 27 Nathan Reidy; 11 Lee Mitchell; 16 Mike Weldon; 18 Ryan Millington. Subs (all used): 22 Callum Wood; 25 Ellis Robson; 26 Pat Moran; 17 Liam Carberry.
**Try:** Whittaker (10); **Goals:** Abram 0/1.
**VIKINGS:** 5 Jack Owens; 22 Owen Buckley; 24 Keanan Brand; 25 Lloyd Roby; 2 Ryan Ince; 6 Danny Craven; 21 Joe Lyons; 11 Harrison Hansen; 15 Jordan Johnstone; 13 Hep Cahill; 12 Chris Dean; 17 Sam Wilde; 32 Luis Johnson. Subs (all used): 8 Jay Chapelhow; 18 Ted Chapelhow; 16 MacGraff Leuluai; 19 Brad Walker.
**Tries:** Ince (5, 30, 35, 80), Hansen (23), Buckley (26), Brand (50), Wilde (63), Roby (67); **Goals:** Owens 7/9.
**Rugby Leaguer & League Express Men of the Match:** *Hornets:* Sitaleki Akauola; *Vikings:* Jack Owens.
**Penalty count:** 6-9; **Half-time:** 4-28;
**Referee:** Michael Mannifield; **Attendance:** 1,732.

**YORK CITY KNIGHTS 16 SHEFFIELD EAGLES 24**

**CITY KNIGHTS:** 1 Matty Marsh; - Conor McGrath; 3 Liam Salter; 4 Brad Hey; 20 Perry Whiteley; 6 Ben Cockayne; 7 Connor Robinson; 8 Ronan Dixon; 9 Will Jubb; 16 Jack Blagbrough; 12 Sam Scott; 33 Joe Batchelor; 13 Tim Spears. Subs (all used): 26 Kriss Brining; 10 Jack Teanby; 15 Graeme Horne; 17 Joe Porter.
**Tries:** Salter (35), Jubb (73), McGrath (76);
**Goals:** Robinson 2/3.
**EAGLES:** 1 Josh Guzdek; 2 Ryan Millar; 18 James Glover; 29 Ben Hellewell; 5 Ben Blackmore; 6 Pat Walker; 7 Anthony Thackeray; 10 Matt James; 9 James Davey; 11 Brad Knowles; 15 Olly Davies; 12 Joel Farrell; 13 Aaron Brown. Subs (all used): 30 Sadiq Adebiyi; 22 Paddy Burns; 23 Rory Dixon; 16 Corey Makelim.
**Tries:** Millar (26), Glover (59), Hellewell (64, 78);
**Goals:** Walker 4/5.
**Rugby Leaguer & League Express Men of the Match:** *City Knights:* Jack Teanby; *Eagles:* Anthony Thackeray.
**Penalty count:** 9-5; **Half-time:** 6-4;
**Referee:** Jack Smith; **Attendance:** 1,822.

## ROUND 9

*Saturday 6th April 2019*

**TOULOUSE OLYMPIQUE 8 FEATHERSTONE ROVERS 2**

**OLYMPIQUE:** 1 Mark Kheirallah; 2 Tony Maurel; 3 Bastien Ader; 25 Mathieu Jussaume; 5 Paul Marcon; 6 Johnathon Ford; 30 William Barthau; 22 Brenden Santi; 14 Dean Parata; 18 Clement Boyer; 11 Con Mika; 12 Rhys Curran; 9 Anthony Marion. Subs (all used): 19 James Bell; 8 Maxime Puech; 16 Tyla Hepi; 21 Jordan Dezaria.
**Try:** Hepi (43); **Goals:** Kheirallah 2/2.
**ROVERS:** 33 Ashton Golding; 2 Luke Briscoe; 28 Josh Walters; 4 Josh Hardcastle; 27 Harry Newman; 35 Jorge Richardson; 34 Ben Reynolds; 29 Jack Ormondroyd; 9 Cameron King; 23 Makahesi Makatoa; 14 John Davies; 12 Brad Day; 13 James Lockwood. Subs: 15 Luke Cooper; 8 Scott Wheeldon; 17 James Harrison; 25 Jack Render (not used).
**Goals:** Reynolds 1/1.
**Rugby Leaguer & League Express Men of the Match:** *Olympique:* Maxime Puech; *Rovers:* Ashton Golding.
**Penalty count:** 11-9; **Half-time:** 0-2;
**Referee:** Greg Dolan; **Attendance:** 2,251.

**TORONTO WOLFPACK 40 SHEFFIELD EAGLES 10**

**WOLFPACK:** 1 Gareth O'Brien; 27 Hakim Miloudi; 3 Chase Stanley; 4 Ricky Leutele; 2 Matty Russell; 17 Blake Wallace; 7 Josh McCrone; 8 Adam Sidlow; 14 Andy Ackers; 10 Ashton Sims; 11 Andrew Dixon; 16 Tom Olbison; 13 Jon Wilkin. Subs (all used): 18 Gadwin Springer; 15 Darcy Lussick; 21 Anthony Mullally; 26 Brad Fash.
**Tries:** Stanley (10), Russell (16, 62), Olbison (34), Ackers (40), Wallace (43, 77), Sidlow (79);
**Goals:** O'Brien 1/4, Wallace 3/4.
**EAGLES:** 1 Josh Guzdek; 2 Ryan Millar; 18 James Glover; 29 Ben Hellewell; 5 Ben Blackmore; 6 Pat Walker; 7 Anthony Thackeray; 8 Pat Moran; 9 James Davey; 10 Matt James; 15 Olly Davies; 12 Joel Farrell; 13 Aaron Brown. Subs (all used): 30 Sadiq Adebiyi; 31 Daniel Hindmarsh; 16 Corey Makelim; 11 Brad Knowles.
**Tries:** Davies (19), Millar (53); **Goals:** Walker 1/2.
**Rugby Leaguer & League Express Men of the Match:** *Wolfpack:* Gadwin Springer; *Eagles:* Josh Guzdek.
**Penalty count:** 10-12; **Half-time:** 18-4;
**Referee:** Matt Rossleigh; **Attendance:** 1,148
*(at New River Stadium, London).*

*Sunday 7th April 2019*

**BATLEY BULLDOGS 20 WIDNES VIKINGS 18**

**BULLDOGS:** 1 Dave Scott; 2 Wayne Reittie; 3 Sam Smeaton; 23 Keenen Tomlinson; 5 Johnny Campbell; 6 Louis Jouffret; 14 Danny Yates; 8 Adam Gledhill; 9 Alistair Leak; 10 Tom Lillycrop; 12 Jack Downs; 19 Alex Bretherton; 11 Dane Manning. Subs (all used): 15 Toby Everett; 21 Jo Taira; 16 Michael Ward; 24 Paul Brearley.
**Tries:** Ward (36), Taira (51), Campbell (71); **Goals:** Scott 4/4.
**Sin bin:** Everett (48) - dangerous contact.
**VIKINGS:** 25 Lloyd Roby; 2 Ryan Ince; 12 Chris Dean; 24 Keanan Brand; 27 Sam Freeman; 5 Jack Owens; 21 Joe Lyons; 8 Jay Chapelhow; 15 Jordan Johnstone; 13 Hep Cahill; 19 Brad Walker; 11 Harrison Hansen; 16 MacGraff Leuluai. Subs: 20 Owen Farnworth; 28 Dom Speakman; 23 Liam Walsh; 29 Jayden Hatton (not used).
**Tries:** Roby (30, 56), Johnstone (44); **Goals:** Owens 3/4.
**Rugby Leaguer & League Express Men of the Match:** *Bulldogs:* Louis Jouffret; *Vikings:* Hep Cahill.
**Penalty count:** 10-9; **Half-time:** 6-6;
**Referee:** Marcus Griffiths; **Attendance:** 1,420.

**BRADFORD BULLS 20 DEWSBURY RAMS 12**

**BULLS:** 2 Ethan Ryan; 22 Dalton Grant; 31 Rhys Evans; 3 Jake Webster; 24 David Foggin-Johnston; 14 Jordan Lilley; 27 Rowan Milnes; 8 Liam Kirk; 9 Matty Wildie; 10 Steve Crossley; 29 Matthew Storton; 25 Connor Farrell; 12 Elliot Minchella. Subs (all used): 15 Callum Bustin; 13 Mikey Wood; 21 George Flanagan; 18 Sam Hallas.
**Tries:** Grant (19, 39), Milnes (42), Minchella (65);
**Goals:** Lilley 0/2, Minchella 2/2.
**Sin bin:** Wood (33) - dangerous challenge.
**RAMS:** 35 Luke Hooley; 23 Rob Worrincy; 36 Owen Trout; 4 Adam Ryder; 1 Dale Morton; 12 Michael Knowles; 38 Liam Finn; 34 Chris Annakin; 18 Sam Day; 13 Kyle Trout; 11 Lucas Walshaw; 32 Samy Kibula; 19 Daniel Igbinedion. Subs (all used): 9 Robbie Ward; - Callum Field; 8 Jode Sheriffe; 30 Tom Garratt.
**Tries:** K Trout (20), Hooley (74); **Goals:** Finn 2/2.
**Rugby Leaguer & League Express Men of the Match:** *Bulls:* Elliot Minchella; *Rams:* Sam Day.
**Penalty count:** 9-10; **Half-time:** 8-6;
**Referee:** John McMullen; **Attendance:** 4,068.

**LEIGH CENTURIONS 46 BARROW RAIDERS 30**

**CENTURIONS:** 1 Gregg McNally; 2 Jonny Pownall; 25 Adam Swift; 3 Iain Thornley; 5 Stefan Marsh; 6 Martyn Ridyard; 7 Josh Woods; 30 Luke Douglas; 9 Micky Higham; 10 Sam Brooks; 11 Toby Adamson; 17 Nick Gregson; 13 Luke Adamson. Subs (all used): 27 Liam Hood; 15 Joe Cator; 8 Tom Spencer; 12 Andy Thornley.
**Tries:** McNally (12), Brooks (26), I Thornley (31, 34, 73), Swift (52, 67), Woods (62); **Goals:** Ridyard 7/8.
**Sin bin:** Marsh (47) - holding down;
Cator (47) - dangerous challenge.
**RAIDERS:** 1 Theerapol Ritson; 5 Deon Cross; 12 Jarrad Stack; 4 Jake Spedding; 21 Tom Loxam; 6 Jamie Dallimore; 22 Ryan Johnston; 28 Josh Johnson; 14 Wartovo Puara; 30 Alec Susino; 20 Bradd Crellin; 26 Willie Minoga; 7 Lewis Charnock. Subs (all used): 9 Nathan Mossop; 16 Glenn Riley; 8 Tom Walker; 15 Dan Toal.
**Tries:** D Toal (38), Ritson (41), Stack (57), Cross (78), Riley (79); **Goals:** Dallimore 3/4, Charnock 2/2.
**Sin bin:** Stack (29) - delaying restart.
**Rugby Leaguer & League Express Men of the Match:** *Centurions:* Iain Thornley; *Raiders:* Glenn Riley.
**Penalty count:** 17-11; **Half-time:** 22-8;
**Referee:** Ben Thaler; **Attendance:** 3,036.

**ROCHDALE HORNETS 24 HALIFAX 48**

**HORNETS:** 1 Dec Kay; 2 Shaun Ainscough; 25 Jack Higginson; 4 Ben Morris; 24 Brandon Wood; 13 Stuart Howarth; 7 Dan Abram; 11 Lee Mitchell; 6 Scott Moore; 10 Carl Forster; 23 Jordan Case; 16 Mike Weldon; 17 Liam Carberry. Subs (all used): 9 Ben Moores; 27 Ellis Robson; 20 Joe Ryan; 18 Ryan Millington.
**Tries:** Mitchell (2), Higginson (25), Robson (39), Forster (80); **Goals:** Abram 4/5.
**Sin bin:** Higginson (12) - professional foul.
**HALIFAX:** 1 Quentin Laulu-Togaga'e; 5 Will Sharp; 3 Steve Tyrer; 20 James Saltonstall; 2 Shaun Robinson; 6 Scott Murrell; 23 James Woodburn-Hall; 17 Ben Kavanagh; 9 Ben Kaye; 10 Jacob Fairbank; 12 Ed Barber; 25 Liam Cooper; 28 Will Calcott. Subs (all used): 27 Reece Chapman-Smith; 8 Dan Fleming; 14 Brandon Moore; 18 Elliot Morris.
**Tries:** Tyrer (16, 20), Woodburn-Hall (31, 34, 53), Sharp (46), Laulu-Togaga'e (60, 75), Saltonstall (71);
**Goals:** Tyrer 6/9.
**Rugby Leaguer & League Express Men of the Match:** *Hornets:* Jack Higginson; *Halifax:* James Woodburn-Hall.
**Penalty count:** 5-12; **Half-time:** 18-22;
**Referee:** Tom Crashley; **Attendance:** 827.

**YORK CITY KNIGHTS 30 SWINTON LIONS 20**

**CITY KNIGHTS:** 1 Matty Marsh; 21 Judah Mazive; 23 Jason Bass; 3 Liam Salter; 34 Nick Rawsthorne; 6 Ben Cockayne; 7 Connor Robinson; 10 Jack Teanby; 9 Will Jubb; 15 Graeme Horne; 33 Joe Batchelor; 12 Sam Scott; 13 Tim Spears. Subs (all used): 26 Kriss Brining; 8 Ronan Dixon; 22 Marcus Stock; 17 Joe Porter.
**Tries:** Spears (16), Marsh (36, 40), S Scott (52), Horne (67);
**Goals:** Robinson 4/4, Rawsthorne 1/1.

**LIONS:** 1 Jack Hansen; 2 Mike Butt; 3 Rhodri Lloyd; 32 Liam Forsyth; 25 Matty Ashton; 34 Harry Smith; 6 Oscar Thomas; 8 Gavin Bennion; 9 Luke Waterworth; 16 Paddy Jones; 31 Jack Wells; 12 Kyle Shelford; 14 Billy Brickhill. Subs (all used): 33 Josh Ganson; 17 Aaron Hall; 19 Jose Kenga; 20 Harry Aaronson.
**Tries:** Hansen (19), Smith (63), Forsyth (74), Waterworth (76); **Goals:** Thomas 0/1, Smith 2/3.
**Rugby Leaguer & League Express Men of the Match:** *City Knights:* Kriss Brining; *Lions:* Harry Smith.
**Penalty count:** 8-6; **Half-time:** 18-4;
**Referee:** Billy Pearson; **Attendance:** 1,606.

## ROUND 10

*Friday 19th April 2019*

### BARROW RAIDERS 26 TORONTO WOLFPACK 52

**RAIDERS:** 18 Luke Cresswell; 1 Theerapol Ritson; 5 Deon Cross; 4 Jake Spedding; 2 Stargroth Amean; 6 Jamie Dallimore; 22 Ryan Johnston; 28 Josh Johnson; 14 Wartovo Puara; 25 Jordan Walne; 19 Danny Morrow; 12 Jarrad Stack; 7 Lewis Charnock. Subs (all used): 9 Nathan Mossop; 30 Alec Susino; 16 Glenn Riley; 20 Bradd Crellin.
**Tries:** J Johnson (6), Cross (12), Stack (57), Amean (73), Ritson (78); **Goals:** Charnock 3/5.
**WOLFPACK:** 1 Gareth O'Brien; 23 Ryan Brierley; 27 Hakim Miloudi; 4 Ricky Leutele; 2 Matty Russell; 17 Blake Wallace; 7 Josh McCrone; 8 Adam Sidlow; 14 Andy Ackers; 10 Ashton Sims; 11 Andrew Dixon; 16 Tom Olbison; 13 Jon Wilkin. Subs (all used): 9 Bob Beswick; 15 Darcy Lussick; 21 Anthony Mullally; 33 Olsi Krasniqi.
**Tries:** Wallace (17, 24, 40), O'Brien (21, 28, 42), Russell (52), Dixon (61), Ackers (65); **Goals:** Wallace 8/9.
**Sin bin:** Krasniqi (73) - dangerous contact.
**Rugby Leaguer & League Express Men of the Match:** *Raiders:* Luke Cresswell; *Wolfpack:* Blake Wallace.
**Penalty count:** 7-9; **Half-time:** 12-28;
**Referee:** Billy Pearson; **Attendance:** 1,417.

### HALIFAX 26 BRADFORD BULLS 33

**HALIFAX:** 1 Quentin Laulu-Togaga'e; 5 Will Sharp; 3 Steve Tyrer; 20 James Saltonstall; 2 Shaun Robinson; 23 James Woodburn-Hall; 19 Ben White; 17 Ben Kavanagh; 14 Brandon Moore; 8 Dan Fleming; 16 Kevin Larroyer; 12 Ed Barber; 10 Jacob Fairbank. Subs (all used): 18 Elliot Morris; 24 Curtis Davies; 15 Harry Kidd; 28 Will Calcott.
**Tries:** Woodburn-Hall (3), Sharp (34), Robinson (39), Tyrer (51); **Goals:** Tyrer 5/6.
**BULLS:** 2 Ethan Ryan; 22 Dalton Grant; 3 Jake Webster; 26 Ross Oakes; 24 David Foggin-Johnston; 27 Rowan Milnes; 14 Jordan Lilley; 8 Liam Kirk; 9 Matty Wildie; 10 Steve Crossley; 29 Matthew Storton; 25 Connor Farrell; 12 Elliot Minchella. Subs (all used): 16 James Green; 15 Callum Bustin; 17 Ross Peltier; 18 Sam Hallas.
**Tries:** Ryan (15), Minchella (62), Crossley (70), Webster (76); **Goals:** Minchella 5/5, Milnes 3/3;
**Field goal:** Lilley (72).
**Rugby Leaguer & League Express Men of the Match:** *Halifax:* Ed Barber; *Bulls:* Ethan Ryan.
**Penalty count:** 12-7; **Half-time** 16-12;
**Referee:** Greg Dolan; **Attendance:** 3,316.

### SWINTON LIONS 36 ROCHDALE HORNETS 22

**LIONS:** 1 Jack Hansen; 2 Mike Butt; 32 Liam Forsyth; 3 Rhodri Lloyd; 25 Matty Ashton; 6 Oscar Thomas; 7 Rob Fairclough; 8 Gavin Bennion; 9 Luke Waterworth; 10 Lewis Hatton; 22 Frankie Halton; 31 Jack Wells; 16 Paddy Jones. Subs (all used): 14 Billy Brickhill; 12 Kyle Shelford; 11 Adam Jones; 20 Harry Aaronson.
**Tries:** Butt (4, 18, 25, 46), Thomas (20), Forsyth (37), Bennion (72); **Goals:** Thomas 4/7.
**On report:** A Jones (77) - alleged high tackle on Howarth.
**HORNETS:** 1 Dec Kay; 2 Shaun Ainscough; 3 Seta Tala; 24 Brandon Wood; 19 Jack Johnson; 13 Stuart Howarth; 7 Dan Abram; 11 Lee Mitchell; 6 Scott Moore; 21 Jack Cottington; 12 Ellis Gillam; 16 Mike Weldon; 17 Liam Carberry. Subs (all used): 10 Carl Forster; 27 Luis Johnson; 20 Joe Ryan; 18 Ryan Millington.
**Tries:** Abram (14), Kay (53, 55), Forster (70);
**Goals:** Abram 3/4.
**Sin bin:** S Moore (34) - late challenge on Fairclough.
**Rugby Leaguer & League Express Men of the Match:** *Lions:* Mike Butt; *Hornets:* Jack Johnson.
**Penalty count:** 11-12; **Half-time:** 26-4;
**Referee:** Matt Rossleigh; **Attendance:** 826.

### WIDNES VIKINGS 30 LEIGH CENTURIONS 12

**VIKINGS:** 5 Jack Owens; 27 Sam Freeman; 24 Keanan Brand; 4 Anthony Gelling; 2 Ryan Ince; 6 Danny Craven; 21 Joe Lyons; 13 Hep Cahill; 15 Jordan Johnstone; 18 Ted Chapelhow; 17 Sam Wilde; 19 Brad Walker; 16 MacGraff Leuluai. Subs (all used): 8 Jay Chapelhow; 25 Lloyd Roby; 23 Liam Walsh; 30 Calum O'Neill.
**Tries:** Walker (4), Lyons (14, 37), Gelling (19), O'Neill (63); **Goals:** Owens 5/6.
**CENTURIONS:** 1 Gregg McNally; 2 Jonny Pownall; 19 Mitch Cox; 3 Iain Thornley; 5 Stefan Marsh; 6 Martyn Ridyard; 7 Josh Woods; 30 Luke Douglas; 27 Liam Hood; 10 Sam Brooks; 11 Toby Adamson; 12 Andy Thornley; 15 Joe Cator. Subs (all used): 25 Josh Eaves; 8 Tom Spencer; 29 Jake Emmitt; 17 Nick Gregson.
**Tries:** Eaves (25), Pownall (35); **Goals:** Ridyard 2/2.
**Rugby Leaguer & League Express Men of the Match:** *Vikings:* Jack Owens; *Centurions:* Sam Brooks.
**Penalty count:** 7-9; **Half-time:** 22-12;
**Referee:** Scott Mikalauskas; **Attendance:** 5,866.

### FEATHERSTONE ROVERS 42 YORK CITY KNIGHTS 12

**ROVERS:** 25 Jack Render; 5 Conor Carey; 28 Josh Walters; 32 Alex Sutcliffe; 4 Josh Hardcastle; 10 Jack Bussey; 38 Dane Chisholm; 15 Luke Cooper; 9 Cameron King; 23 Makahesi Makatoa; 14 John Davies; 12 Brad Day; 13 James Lockwood. Subs: 29 Jack Ormondroyd; 8 Scott Wheeldon; 17 James Harrison; 7 Watson Boas (not used).
**Tries:** Sutcliffe (10, 42), Walters (15), Davies (48), Hardcastle (55, 60), Chisholm (62); **Goals:** Chisholm 7/9.
**CITY KNIGHTS:** 1 Matty Marsh; 20 Perry Whiteley; 3 Liam Salter; 4 Brad Hey; 23 Jason Bass; 35 Lewis Heckford; 7 Connor Robinson; 10 Jack Teanby; 9 Will Jubb; 15 Graeme Horne; 11 Josh Jordan-Roberts; 12 Sam Scott; 13 Tim Spears. Subs (all used): 26 Kriss Brining; 37 Jordan Baldwinson; 8 Ronan Dixon; 22 Marcus Stock.
**Tries:** Spears (34), S Scott (75); **Goals:** Robinson 2/2.
**Rugby Leaguer & League Express Men of the Match:** *Rovers:* Dane Chisholm; *City Knights:* Tim Spears.
**Penalty count:** 11-6; **Half-time:** 14-6;
**Referee:** John McMullen; **Attendance:** 2,216.

### SHEFFIELD EAGLES 44 TOULOUSE OLYMPIQUE 16

**EAGLES:** 1 Josh Guzdek; 2 Ryan Millar; 18 James Glover; 13 Aaron Brown; 5 Ben Blackmore; 6 Pat Walker; 7 Anthony Thackeray; 8 Pat Moran; 14 Greg Burns; 23 Rory Dixon; 12 Joel Farrell; 15 Olly Davies; 10 Matt James. Subs (all used): 19 Sonny Esslemont; 17 Shaun Pick; 16 Corey Makelim; 21 Blake Broadbent.
**Tries:** James (18, 79), Thackeray (23, 48, 65), Esslemont (37), Millar (62); **Goals:** Walker 8/8.
**OLYMPIQUE:** 1 Mark Kheirallah; 5 Paul Marcon; 25 Mathieu Jussaume; 3 Bastien Ader; 2 Tony Maurel; 30 William Barthau; 7 Stan Robin; 22 Brenden Santi; 14 Dean Parata; 18 Clement Boyer; 11 Con Mika; 12 Rhys Curran; 9 Anthony Marion. Subs (all used): 19 James Bell; 17 Paterika Vaivai; 16 Tyla Hepi; 21 Jordan Dezaria.
**Tries:** Jussaume (40), Barthau (52), Marcon (75);
**Goals:** Kheirallah 2/3.
**Rugby Leaguer & League Express Men of the Match:** *Eagles:* Anthony Thackeray; *Olympique:* Tyla Hepi.
**Penalty count:** 6-8; **Half-time:** 20-6;
**Referee:** Marcus Griffiths; **Attendance:** 729.

### DEWSBURY RAMS 8 BATLEY BULLDOGS 20

**RAMS:** 35 Luke Hooley; 23 Rob Worrincy; 1 Dale Morton; 4 Adam Ryder; 2 Andy Gabriel; 12 Michael Knowles; 38 Liam Finn; 30 Tom Garratt; 9 Robbie Ward; 32 Samy Kibula; 11 Lucas Walshaw; 19 Daniel Igbinedion; 13 Kyle Trout. Subs (all used): 18 Sam Day; 33 Callum Field; 36 Ellis Robson; 8 Jode Sheriffe.
**Try:** Igbinedion (35); **Goals:** Finn 2/2.
**BULLDOGS:** 1 Dave Scott; 2 Wayne Reittie; 3 Sam Smeaton; 22 Sam Wood; 5 Johnny Campbell; 6 Louis Jouffret; 7 Dom Brambani; 8 Adam Gledhill; 9 Alistair Leak; 10 Tom Lillycrop; 12 Jack Downs; 11 Dane Manning; 15 Toby Everett. Subs (all used): 13 James Brown; 27 Reiss Butterworth; 21 Jo Taira; 16 Michael Ward.
**Tries:** Leak (38), Taira (47), Brown (62); **Goals:** Scott 4/4.
**Dismissal:** Reittie (30) - high tackle.
**Sin bin:** Ward (33) - dangerous challenge.
**Rugby Leaguer & League Express Men of the Match:** *Rams:* Luke Hooley; *Bulldogs:* Alistair Leak.
**Penalty count:** 14-5; **Half-time:** 8-6;
**Referee:** Michael Mannifield; **Attendance:** 1,276.

## ROUND 11

*Monday 22nd April 2019*

### TOULOUSE OLYMPIQUE 56 HALIFAX 4

**OLYMPIQUE:** 1 Mark Kheirallah; 20 Ilias Bergal; 3 Bastien Ader; 25 Mathieu Jussaume; 5 Paul Marcon; 6 Johnathon Ford; 30 William Barthau; 8 Maxime Puech; 9 Anthony Marion; 10 Joe Bretherton; 11 Con Mika; 12 Rhys Curran; 19 James Bell. Subs (all used): 14 Dean Parata; 15 Ben Evans; 16 Tyla Hepi; 18 Clement Boyer.
**Tries:** Marion (1, 14, 65), Bretherton (9), Kheirallah (16, 32, 49), Jussaume (44), Ader (55), Bergal (69); **Goals:** Kheirallah 8/10.
**HALIFAX:** 1 Quentin Laulu-Togaga'e; 5 Will Sharp; 3 Steve Tyrer; 20 James Saltonstall; 2 Shaun Robinson; 23 James Woodburn-Hall; 19 Ben White; 17 Ben Kavanagh; 14 Brandon Moore; 8 Dan Fleming; 16 Kevin Larroyer; 12 Ed Barber; 10 Jacob Fairbank. Subs (all used): 18 Elliot Morris; 27 Reece Chapman-Smith; 15 Harry Kidd; 25 Liam Cooper.
**Try:** Robinson (35); **Goals:** Tyrer 0/1.
**Rugby Leaguer & League Express Men of the Match:** *Olympique:* Anthony Marion; *Halifax:* Steve Tyrer.
**Penalty count:** 8-4; **Half-time:** 28-4;
**Referee:** Scott Mikalauskas; **Attendance:** 2,038.

### BATLEY BULLDOGS 32 SWINTON LIONS 18

**BULLDOGS:** 1 Dave Scott; 2 Wayne Reittie; 3 Sam Smeaton; 22 Sam Wood; 5 Johnny Campbell; 6 Louis Jouffret; 7 Dom Brambani; 21 Jo Taira; 27 Reiss Butterworth; 15 Toby Everett; 12 Jack Downs; 24 Paul Brearley; 13 James Brown. Subs (all used): 25 Lewis Bienek; 19 Alex Bretherton; 16 Michael Ward; 4 Lewis Galbraith.
**Tries:** Wood (6, 54), Jouffret (12, 71), Bretherton (32), Smeaton (44); **Goals:** Scott 4/7.
**Sin bin:** Downs (37) - late challenge.
**LIONS:** 1 Jack Hansen; 2 Mike Butt; 4 Daley Williams; 3 Rhodri Lloyd; 25 Matty Ashton; 6 Oscar Thomas; 7 Rob Fairclough; 8 Gavin Bennion; 9 Luke Waterworth; 10 Lewis Hatton; 12 Kyle Shelford; 22 Frankie Halton; 16 Paddy Jones. Subs (all used): 11 Adam Jones; 14 Billy Brickhill; 19 Jose Kenga; 20 Harry Aaronson.
**Tries:** Ashton (48, 58, 62); **Goals:** Thomas 3/3.
**Rugby Leaguer & League Express Men of the Match:** *Bulldogs:* Johnny Campbell; *Lions:* Matty Ashton.
**Penalty count:** 6-9; **Half-time:** 16-0;
**Referee:** Liam Moore; **Attendance:** 817.

### BRADFORD BULLS 26 BARROW RAIDERS 14

**BULLS:** 1 Brandon Pickersgill; 22 Dalton Grant; 3 Jake Webster; 12 Elliot Minchella; 2 Ethan Ryan; 14 Jordan Lilley; 27 Rowan Milnes; 8 Liam Kirk; 18 Sam Hallas; 10 Steve Crossley; 29 Matthew Storton; 25 Connor Farrell; 13 Mikey Wood. Subs (all used): 17 Ross Peltier; 9 Matty Wildie; 28 Evan Hodgson; 32 Colton Roche.
**Tries:** Farrell (16), Grant (30), Minchella (50), Lilley (60), Webster (72); **Goals:** Minchella 3/5.
**Dismissal:** Farrell (79) - punching.
**RAIDERS:** 1 Theerapol Ritson; 23 Shane Toal; 5 Deon Cross; 4 Jake Spedding; 2 Stargroth Amean; 6 Jamie Dallimore; 7 Lewis Charnock; 28 Josh Johnson; 14 Wartovo Puara; 25 Jordan Walne; 26 Willie Minoga; 12 Jarrad Stack; 30 Alec Susino. Subs (all used): 9 Nathan Mossop; 16 Glenn Riley; 20 Bradd Crellin; 8 Tom Walker.
**Tries:** S Toal (45), Susino (66), Charnock (69);
**Goals:** Charnock 1/3.
**Rugby Leaguer & League Express Men of the Match:** *Bulls:* Jake Webster; *Raiders:* Shane Toal.
**Penalty count:** 10-7; **Half-time:** 10-0;
**Referee:** Nick Bennett; **Attendance:** 4,011.

### FEATHERSTONE ROVERS 14 TORONTO WOLFPACK 23

**ROVERS:** 25 Jack Render; 36 Jack Broadbent; 32 Alex Sutcliffe; 4 Josh Hardcastle; 5 Conor Carey; 10 Jack Bussey; 38 Dane Chisholm; 8 Scott Wheeldon; 16 Danny Maskill; 15 Luke Cooper; 12 Brad Day; 28 Josh Walters; 13 James Lockwood. Subs (all used): 9 Cameron King; 17 James Harrison; 23 Makahesi Makatoa; 29 Jack Ormondroyd.
**Tries:** Makatoa (26), Carey (43); **Goals:** Chisholm 3/3.
**WOLFPACK:** 1 Gareth O'Brien; 20 Adam Higson; 27 Hakim Miloudi; 4 Ricky Leutele; 2 Matty Russell; 17 Blake Wallace; 7 Josh McCrone; 8 Adam Sidlow; 9 Bob Beswick; 10 Ashton Sims; 11 Andrew Dixon; 16 Tom Olbison; 13 Jon Wilkin. Subs (all used): 14 Andy Ackers; 15 Darcy Lussick; 21 Anthony Mullally; 12 Bodene Thompson.
**Tries:** O'Brien (14), Russell (17, 30, 80), Dixon (75);
**Goals:** Wallace 1/5; **Field goal:** McCrone (39).
**Sin bin:** O'Brien (33) - high tackle.
**Rugby Leaguer & League Express Men of the Match:** *Rovers:* Dane Chisholm; *Wolfpack:* Matty Russell.
**Penalty count:** 7-6; **Half-time:** 6-13;
**Referee:** Gareth Hewer; **Attendance:** 2,101.

### LEIGH CENTURIONS 34 DEWSBURY RAMS 12

**CENTURIONS:** 1 Gregg McNally; 2 Jonny Pownall; 24 Matthew Costello; 3 Iain Thornley; 19 Mitch Cox; 6 Martyn Ridyard; 7 Josh Woods; 30 Luke Douglas; 9 Micky Higham; 29 Jake Emmitt; 11 Toby Adamson; 23 James Laithwaite; 15 Joe Cator. Subs (all used): 25 Josh Eaves; 27 Liam Hood; 10 Sam Brooks; 26 James Bentley.
**Tries:** I Thornley (6, 44, 80), Bentley (20, 52, 77), Costello (47); **Goals:** Woods 1/4, Ridyard 2/2, Costello 0/1.

Bradford's Connor Farrell looks for a way past Halifax's Brandon Moore and Elliot Morris

**RAMS:** 35 Luke Hooley; 23 Rob Worrincy; 1 Dale Morton; 4 Adam Ryder; 2 Andy Gabriel; 7 Simon Brown; 38 Liam Finn; 30 Tom Garratt; 37 Liam Mackay; 13 Kyle Trout; 32 Samy Kibula; 12 Michael Knowles; 19 Daniel Igbinedion. Subs (all used): 18 Sam Day; 11 Lucas Walshaw; 33 Callum Field; 24 Harvey Hallas.
**Tries:** S Brown (31), K Trout (55); **Goals:** Finn 2/2.
**Sin bin:** Knowles (69) - dissent.
**Rugby Leaguer & League Express Men of the Match:**
*Centurions:* James Bentley; *Rams:* Kyle Trout.
**Penalty count:** 8-9; **Half-time:** 8-6.
**Referee:** Billy Pearson; **Attendance:** 3,043.

### ROCHDALE HORNETS 16 SHEFFIELD EAGLES 52

**HORNETS:** 1 Dec Kay; 19 Jack Johnson; 4 Ben Morris; 12 Ellis Gillam; 24 Brandon Wood; 9 Ben Moores; 7 Dan Abram; 11 Lee Mitchell; 6 Scott Moore; 21 Jack Cottington; 16 Mike Weldon; 27 Luis Johnson; 10 Carl Forster. Subs (all used): 17 Liam Carberry; 3 Seta Tala; 22 Callum Wood; 18 Ryan Millington.
**Tries:** Forster (13), B Wood (70), B Moores (80); **Goals:** Abram 2/3.
**EAGLES:** 1 Josh Guzdek; 2 Ryan Millar; 18 James Glover; 29 Ben Hellewell; 5 Ben Blackmore; 6 Pat Walker; 7 Anthony Thackeray; 8 Pat Moran; 14 Greg Burns; 11 Brad Knowles; 15 Olly Davies; 12 Joel Farrell; 13 Aaron Brown. Subs (all used): 9 James Davey; 21 Blake Broadbent; 19 Sonny Esslemont; 10 Matt James.
**Tries:** Hellewell (16, 60), Glover (29, 64), Blackmore (36, 56), Walker (39), Moran (72), Esslemont (74); **Goals:** Walker 8/9.
**Rugby Leaguer & League Express Men of the Match:**
*Hornets:* Carl Forster; *Eagles:* Aaron Brown.
**Penalty count:** 10-8; **Half-time:** 6-22.
**Referee:** Matt Rossleigh; **Attendance:** 569.

### YORK CITY KNIGHTS 17 WIDNES VIKINGS 10

**CITY KNIGHTS:** 1 Matty Marsh; 21 Judah Mazive; 34 Nick Rawsthorne; 3 Liam Salter; 23 Jason Bass; 7 Connor Robinson; 9 Will Jubb; 15 Graeme Horne; 25 Dave Petersen; 10 Jack Teanby; 12 Sam Scott; 22 Marcus Stock; 13 Tim Spears. Subs (all used): 37 Jordan Baldwinson; 16 Jack Blagbrough; 26 Kriss Brining; 4 Brad Hey.
**Tries:** Bass (57), Rawsthorne (60), Robinson (73); **Goals:** Robinson 2/5; **Field goal:** Robinson (71).

**VIKINGS:** 5 Jack Owens; 2 Ryan Ince; 29 Jayden Hatton; 24 Keanan Brand; 27 Sam Freeman; 25 Lloyd Roby; 21 Joe Lyons; 18 Ted Chapelhow; 15 Jordan Johnstone; 13 Hep Cahill; 17 Sam Wilde; 19 Brad Walker; 16 MacGraff Leuluai. Subs (all used): 8 Jay Chapelhow; 28 Dom Speakman; 23 Liam Walsh; 33 Ben Davies.
**Tries:** Wilde (9), Ince (47); **Goals:** Owens 1/2.
**Rugby Leaguer & League Express Men of the Match:**
*City Knights:* Matty Marsh; *Vikings:* Sam Wilde.
**Penalty count:** 10-4; **Half-time:** 0-6.
**Referee:** Greg Dolan; **Attendance:** 2,229.

## ROUND 12

*Saturday 27th April 2019*

### TOULOUSE OLYMPIQUE 30 YORK CITY KNIGHTS 26

**OLYMPIQUE:** 1 Mark Kheirallah; 2 Tony Maurel; 3 Bastien Ader; 25 Mathieu Jussaume; 5 Paul Marcon; 6 Johnathon Ford; 7 Stan Robin; 8 Maxime Puech; 9 Anthony Marion; 10 Joe Bretherton; 11 Con Mika; 12 Rhys Curran; 19 James Bell. Subs (all used): 14 Dean Parata; 16 Tyla Hepi; 17 Paterika Vaivai; 18 Clement Boyer.
**Tries:** Ader (12), Curran (28), Kheirallah (41), Robin (52), Marion (73); **Goals:** Marion 3/3, Maurel 2/2.
**CITY KNIGHTS:** 1 Matty Marsh; 21 Judah Mazive; 23 Jason Bass; 3 Liam Salter; 20 Perry Whiteley; 35 Cain Southernwood; 7 Connor Robinson; 37 Jordan Baldwinson; 9 Will Jubb; 10 Jack Teanby; 22 Marcus Stock; 4 Brad Hey; 25 Dave Petersen. Subs (all used): 8 Ronan Dixon; 12 Sam Scott; 16 Jack Blagbrough; 26 Kriss Brining.
**Tries:** Mazive (9), Stock (22), Brining (32), Whiteley (63), S Scott (64); **Goals:** Robinson 3/5.
**Sin bin:** Marsh (29) - delaying restart.
**Rugby Leaguer & League Express Men of the Match:**
*Olympique:* Johnathon Ford; *City Knights:* Connor Robinson.
**Penalty count:** 2-6; **Half-time:** 12-16.
**Referee:** Marcus Griffiths; **Attendance:** 1,793.

*Sunday 28th April 2019*

### BARROW RAIDERS 12 FEATHERSTONE ROVERS 26

**RAIDERS:** 1 Theerapol Ritson; 23 Shane Toal; 5 Deon Cross; 2 Stargroth Amean; 4 Jake Spedding; 6 Jamie Dallimore; 22 Ryan Johnston; 30 Alec Susino; 14 Wartovo

Puara; 25 Jordan Walne; 11 Jono Smith; 12 Jarrad Stack; 7 Lewis Charnock. Subs (all used): 9 Nathan Mossop; 8 Tom Walker; 18 Luke Cresswell; 20 Bradd Crellin.
**Tries:** Smith (50), Stack (67); **Goals:** Dallimore 2/2.
**ROVERS:** 33 Ashton Golding; 25 Jack Render; 32 Alex Sutcliffe; 4 Josh Hardcastle; 5 Conor Carey; 38 Dane Chisholm; 23 Makahesi Makatoa; 8 Scott Wheeldon; 9 Cameron King; 10 Jack Bussey; 12 Brad Day; 28 Josh Walters; 13 James Lockwood. Subs (all used): 15 Luke Cooper; 29 Jack Ormondroyd; 17 James Harrison; 40 Tom Holmes.
**Tries:** Day (6), Sutcliffe (12), King (23), Chisholm (29, 80); **Goals:** Chisholm 3/5.
**Rugby Leaguer & League Express Men of the Match:**
*Raiders:* Alec Susino; *Rovers:* Dane Chisholm.
**Penalty count:** 8-8; **Half-time:** 0-22.
**Referee:** Jack Smith; **Attendance:** 1,277.

### BATLEY BULLDOGS 16 LEIGH CENTURIONS 36

**BULLDOGS:** 1 Dave Scott; 2 Wayne Reittie; 3 Sam Smeaton; 22 Sam Wood; 5 Johnny Campbell; 6 Louis Jouffret; 7 Dom Brambani; 25 Lewis Bienek; 9 Alistair Leak; 15 Toby Everett; 11 Dane Manning; 12 Jack Downs; 21 Jo Taira. Subs (all used): 24 Paul Brearley; 13 James Brown; 27 Reiss Butterworth; 16 Michael Ward.
**Tries:** Leak (7), Campbell (38), Taira (78); **Goals:** Scott 2/4.
**CENTURIONS:** 6 Martyn Ridyard; 4 Jack Higginson; 3 Iain Thornley; 12 Andy Thornley; 5 Stefan Marsh; 7 Josh Woods; 35 Ryan Brierley; 30 Luke Douglas; 9 Micky Higham; 10 Sam Brooks; 11 Toby Adamson; 23 James Laithwaite; 29 Jake Emmitt. Subs (all used): 27 Liam Hood; 15 Joe Cator; 8 Tom Spencer; 25 Josh Eaves.
**Tries:** I Thornley (23), Higginson (30, 79), Marsh (32), Brierley (51), Eaves (71); **Goals:** Brierley 6/7.
**Rugby Leaguer & League Express Men of the Match:**
*Bulldogs:* Alistair Leak; *Centurions:* Ryan Brierley.
**Penalty count:** 9-4; **Half-time:** 12-18.
**Referee:** John McMullen; **Attendance:** 1,240.

### BRADFORD BULLS 52 ROCHDALE HORNETS 16

**BULLS:** 2 Ethan Ryan; 22 Dalton Grant; 3 Jake Webster; 26 Ross Oakes; 24 David Foggin-Johnston; 14 Jordan Lilley; 27 Rowan Milnes; 8 Liam Kirk; 9 Matty Wildie; 10 Steve Crossley; 29 Matthew Storton; 25 Connor Farrell; 12 Elliot Minchella. Subs (all used): 33 Thomas Doyle; 16 James Green; 32 Colton Roche; 13 Mikey Wood.

**Tries:** Crossley (21, 66), Doyle (30, 56), Oakes (52), Ryan (62, 69, 72), Webster (75); **Goals:** Minchella 8/9.
**HORNETS:** 1 Dec Kay; 19 Jack Johnson; 4 Ben Morris; 3 Seta Tala; 24 Brandon Wood; 6 Scott Moore; 7 Dan Abram; 21 Jack Cottington; 9 Ben Moores; 17 Liam Carberry; 12 Ellis Gillam; 11 Lee Mitchell; 28 Luis Johnson. Subs (all used): 18 Ryan Millington; 27 Nathan Reidy; 25 Danny Walker; 20 Joe Ryan.
**Tries:** B Moores (6), Gillam (9), B Wood (37);
**Goals:** Abram 2/3.
**Rugby Leaguer & League Express Men of the Match:** *Bulls:* Thomas Doyle; *Hornets:* Dan Abram.
**Penalty count:** 11-6; **Half-time:** 12-16;
**Referee:** Gareth Hewer; **Attendance:** 3,721.

**SHEFFIELD EAGLES 24 HALIFAX 32**

**EAGLES:** 1 Josh Guzdek; 2 Ryan Millar; 18 James Glover; 13 Aaron Brown; 5 Ben Blackmore; 6 Pat Walker; 7 Anthony Thackeray; 8 Pat Moran; 14 Greg Burns; 23 Rory Dixon; 15 Olly Davies; 12 Joel Farrell; 10 Matt James. Subs (all used): 9 James Davey; 31 Nathan Mason; 11 Brad Knowles; 19 Sonny Esslemont.
**Tries:** Brown (14), Davey (26), Millar (38), Blackmore (59);
**Goals:** Walker 4/5.
**HALIFAX:** 1 Quentin Laulu-Togaga'e; 2 Shaun Robinson; 3 Steve Tyrer; 4 Chester Butler; 5 Will Sharp; 6 Scott Murrell; 23 James Woodburn-Hall; 18 Elliot Morris; 14 Brandon Moore; 17 Ben Kavanagh; 16 Kevin Larroyer; 12 Ed Barber; 10 Jacob Fairbank. Subs (all used): 8 Dan Fleming; 22 Connor Davies; 24 Curtis Davies; 27 Reece Chapman-Smith.
**Tries:** Barber (4), Murrell (32), Woodburn-Hall (34), Butler (44, 79); **Goals:** Tyrer 6/6.
**Rugby Leaguer & League Express Men of the Match:** *Eagles:* Ben Blackmore; *Halifax:* Chester Butler.
**Penalty count:** 9-7; **Half-time:** 20-18;
**Referee:** Billy Pearson; **Attendance:** 966.

**WIDNES VIKINGS 24 DEWSBURY RAMS 25**

**VIKINGS:** 5 Jack Owens; 27 Sam Freeman; 24 Keanan Brand; 25 Lloyd Roby; 2 Ryan Ince; 6 Danny Craven; 21 Joe Lyons; 13 Hep Cahill; 15 Jordan Johnstone; 18 Ted Chapelhow; 17 Sam Wilde; 11 Harrison Hansen; 16 MacGraff Leuluai. Subs (all used): 8 Jay Chapelhow; 28 Dom Speakman; 20 Owen Farnworth; 19 Brad Walker.
**Tries:** Owens (19, 37, 39), Craven (67); **Goals:** Owens 4/4.
**Sin bin:** Craven (8) - holding down.
**RAMS:** 35 Luke Hooley; 1 Dale Morton; 19 Daniel Igbinedion; 4 Adam Ryder; 2 Andy Gabriel; 38 Liam Finn; 7 Simon Brown; 33 Callum Field; 18 Sam Day; 30 Tom Garratt; 36 Ellis Robson; 12 Michael Knowles; 13 Kyle Trout. Subs (all used): 9 Robbie Ward; 37 Liam Mackay; 10 Toby Richardson; 24 Harvey Hallas.
**Tries:** Hooley (8), Igbinedion (17), Gabriel (33, 57), Finn (75);
**Goals:** Finn 2/5; **Field goal:** Finn (78).
**Rugby Leaguer & League Express Men of the Match:** *Vikings:* Jack Owens; *Rams:* Tom Garratt.
**Penalty count:** 6-7; **Half-time:** 18-14;
**Referee:** Matt Rossleigh; **Attendance:** 3,851.

**TORONTO WOLFPACK 52 SWINTON LIONS 10**

**WOLFPACK:** 1 Gareth O'Brien; 20 Adam Higson; 3 Chase Stanley; 4 Ricky Leutele; 24 Nick Rawsthorne; 17 Blake Wallace; 7 Josh McCrone; 15 Darcy Lussick; 14 Andy Ackers; 8 Adam Sidlow; 11 Andrew Dixon; 12 Bodene Thompson; 13 Jon Wilkin. Subs (all used): 9 Bob Beswick; 21 Anthony Mullally; 16 Tom Olbison; 10 Ashton Sims.
**Tries:** O'Brien (6), Wallace (11, 64), Thompson (34), Ackers (38), Dixon (46), Leutele (50), Olbison (55), Higson (68); **Goals:** Wallace 8/10.
**LIONS:** 25 Matty Ashton; 2 Mike Butt; 3 Rhodri Lloyd; 35 Liam Paisley; 20 Harry Aaronson; 1 Jack Hansen; 34 Harry Smith; 8 Gavin Bennion; 9 Luke Waterworth; 10 Lewis Hatton; 31 Jack Wells; 22 Frankie Halton; 16 Paddy Jones. Subs (all used): 14 Billy Brickhill; 11 Adam Jones; 19 Jose Kenga; 12 Kyle Shelford.
**Tries:** Ashton (23), Butt (73); **Goals:** Smith 1/2.
**Sin bin:** Bennion (40) - shoulder charge.
**Rugby Leaguer & League Express Men of the Match:** *Wolfpack:* Ricky Leutele; *Lions:* Gavin Bennion.
**Penalty count:** 7-8; **Half-time:** 24-6;
**Referee:** Greg Dolan; **Attendance:** 9,562.

## ROUND 13

*Saturday 4th May 2019*

**DEWSBURY RAMS 0 TOULOUSE OLYMPIQUE 38**

**RAMS:** 35 Luke Hooley; 1 Dale Morton; 19 Daniel Igbinedion; 4 Adam Ryder; 2 Andy Gabriel; 38 Liam Finn; 7 Simon Brown; 33 Callum Field; 9 Robbie Ward; 30 Tom Garratt; 36 Ellis Robson; 12 Michael Knowles; 13 Kyle Trout. Subs (all used): 18 Sam Day; 37 Liam Mackay; 10 Toby Richardson; 24 Harvey Hallas.
**OLYMPIQUE:** 1 Mark Kheirallah; 5 Paul Marcon; 21 Jordan Dezaria; 10 Joe Bretherton; 3 Bastien Ader; 6 Johnathon Ford; 9 Anthony Marion; 8 Maxime Puech; 14 Dean Parata; 17 Paterika Vaivai; 11 Con Mika; 12 Rhys Curran; 19 James Bell. Subs (all used): 15 Ben Evans; 18 Clement Boyer; 16 Tyla Hepi; 28 Pierre-Jean Lima.
**Tries:** Mika (12), Marion (26), Bretherton (42), Boyer (59), Ford (65), Kheirallah (70), Bell (75); **Goals:** Marion 5/7.
**Sin bin:** Dezaria (25) - professional foul.
**Rugby Leaguer & League Express Men of the Match:** *Rams:* Daniel Igbinedion; *Olympique:* Dean Parata.
**Penalty count:** 7-6; **Half-time:** 0-10;
**Referee:** Nick Bennett; **Attendance:** 786.

**TORONTO WOLFPACK 36 BRADFORD BULLS 16**

**WOLFPACK:** 1 Gareth O'Brien; 24 Nick Rawsthorne; 3 Chase Stanley; 4 Ricky Leutele; 5 Liam Kay; 6 Joe Mellor; 7 Josh McCrone; 15 Darcy Lussick; 9 Bob Beswick; 8 Adam Sidlow; 11 Andrew Dixon; 12 Bodene Thompson; 13 Jon Wilkin. Subs (all used): 14 Andy Ackers; 21 Anthony Mullally; 16 Tom Olbison; 10 Ashton Sims.
**Tries:** Rawsthorne (12, 20), Sidlow (27), Leutele (56), Stanley (63), O'Brien (66), Kay (80); **Goals:** O'Brien 4/7.
**BULLS:** 2 Ethan Ryan; 22 Dalton Grant; 12 Elliot Minchella; 26 Ross Oakes; 24 David Foggin-Johnston; 27 Rowan Milnes; 14 Jordan Lilley; 8 Liam Kirk; 18 Sam Hallas; 10 Steve Crossley; 29 Matthew Storton; 25 Connor Farrell; 13 Mikey Wood. Subs (all used): 33 Thomas Doyle; 1 Brandon Pickersgill; 16 James Green; 17 Ross Peltier.
**Tries:** Peltier (33), Milnes (36), Grant (71);
**Goals:** Minchella 2/3.
**Rugby Leaguer & League Express Men of the Match:** *Wolfpack:* Gareth O'Brien; *Bulls:* Rowan Milnes.
**Penalty count:** 2-2; **Half-time:** 14-12;
**Referee:** Marcus Griffiths; **Attendance:** 8,363.

*Sunday 5th May 2019*

**HALIFAX 46 BARROW RAIDERS 10**

**HALIFAX:** 23 James Woodburn-Hall; 5 Will Sharp; 3 Steve Tyrer; 4 Chester Butler; 2 Shaun Robinson; 6 Scott Murrell; 19 Ben White; 18 Elliot Morris; 14 Brandon Moore; 8 Dan Fleming; 12 Ed Barber; 16 Kevin Larroyer; 10 Jacob Fairbank. Subs (all used): 17 Ben Kavanagh; 22 Connor Davies; 24 Curtis Davies; 25 Liam Cooper.
**Tries:** Butler (4), Larroyer (9, 67), Barber (20), Moore (25), Connor Davies (37), Kavanagh (54), Woodburn-Hall (58); **Goals:** Tyrer 7/8.
**RAIDERS:** 1 Theerapol Ritson; 27 Brett Carter; 2 Stargroth Amean; 5 Deon Cross; 4 Jake Spedding; 6 Jamie Dallimore; 7 Lewis Charnock; 28 Josh Johnson; 14 Wartovo Puara; 8 Tom Walker; 11 Jono Smith; 20 Bradd Crellin; 30 Alec Susino. Subs (all used): 9 Nathan Mossop; 15 Dan Toal; 16 Glenn Riley; 18 Luke Cresswell.
**Tries:** Spedding (45), Ritson (73); **Goals:** Dallimore 1/2.
**Rugby Leaguer & League Express Men of the Match:** *Halifax:* Scott Murrell; *Raiders:* Stargroth Amean.
**Penalty count:** 7-6; **Half-time:** 28-0;
**Referee:** Gareth Hewer; **Attendance:** 1,446.

**LEIGH CENTURIONS 42 SHEFFIELD EAGLES 38**

**CENTURIONS:** 35 Ryan Brierley; 1 Gregg McNally; 3 Iain Thornley; 12 Andy Thornley; 4 Jack Higginson; 6 Martyn Ridyard; 7 Josh Woods; 30 Luke Douglas; 9 Micky Higham; 10 Sam Brooks; 11 Toby Adamson; 23 James Laithwaite; 15 Joe Cator. Subs (all used): 27 Liam Hood; 25 Josh Eaves; 29 Jake Emmitt; 8 Tom Spencer.
**Tries:** A Thornley (5), McNally (28), Brierley (43), I Thornley (45), Laithwaite (70), Eaves (75), Hood (79);
**Goals:** Ridyard 7/7.
**EAGLES:** 1 Josh Guzdek; 2 Ryan Millar; 18 James Glover; 27 Jacob Ogden; 5 Ben Blackmore; 32 James Meadows; 7 Anthony Thackeray; 8 Pat Moran; 9 James Davey; 10 Matt James; 15 Olly Davies; 12 Joel Farrell; 13 Aaron Brown. Subs (all used): 6 Pat Walker; 21 Blake Broadbent; 19 Sonny Esslemont; 11 Brad Knowles.
**Tries:** Brown (20), Blackmore (34), Millar (36), Glover (39), Thackeray (54, 64), Meadows (59);
**Goals:** Glover 2/4, Walker 3/3.
**Sin bin:** Davey (24) - dangerous challenge.
**Rugby Leaguer & League Express Men of the Match:** *Centurions:* Martyn Ridyard; *Eagles:* Anthony Thackeray.
**Penalty count:** 7-4; **Half-time:** 12-20;
**Referee:** Tom Grant; **Attendance:** 3,031.

**ROCHDALE HORNETS 10 FEATHERSTONE ROVERS 56**

**HORNETS:** 1 Dec Kay; 2 Shaun Ainscough; 4 Ben Morris; 3 Seta Tala; 24 Brandon Wood; 6 Scott Moore; 7 Dan Abram; 17 Liam Carberry; 9 Ben Moores; 21 Jack Cottington; 27 Luis Johnson; 12 Ellis Gillam; 11 Lee Mitchell. Subs (all used): 20 Joe Ryan; 18 Ryan Millington; 15 Declan Gregory; 22 Callum Wood.
**Tries:** Ainscough (15), Abram (68); **Goals:** Abram 1/2.
**ROVERS:** 33 Ashton Golding; 25 Jack Render; 32 Alex Sutcliffe; 4 Josh Hardcastle; 5 Conor Carey; 38 Dane Chisholm; 40 Tom Holmes; 23 Makahesi Makatoa; 9 Cameron King; 17 James Harrison; 14 John Davies; 28 Josh Walters; 13 James Lockwood. Subs: 15 Luke Cooper; 29 Jack Ormondroyd; 12 Brad Day (not used); 16 Danny Maskill.
**Tries:** King (2), Harrison (8), Chisholm (12), Carey (25, 57), Hardcastle (46), Cooper (49, 65), Walters (70), Golding (76); **Goals:** Chisholm 8/10.
**Rugby Leaguer & League Express Men of the Match:** *Hornets:* Lee Mitchell; *Rovers:* Cameron King.
**Penalty count:** 5-5; **Half-time:** 4-22;
**Referee:** Billy Pearson; **Attendance:** 714.

**SWINTON LIONS 10 WIDNES VIKINGS 32**

**LIONS:** 25 Matty Ashton; 2 Mike Butt; 3 Rhodri Lloyd; 32 Liam Paisley; 20 Harry Aaronson; 34 Harry Smith; 1 Jack Hansen; 8 Gavin Bennion; 9 Luke Waterworth; 16 Paddy Jones; 22 Frankie Halton; 11 Adam Jones; 31 Jack Wells. Subs (all used): 14 Billy Brickhill; 12 Kyle Shelford; 33 Adam Lawton; 7 Rob Fairclough.
**Tries:** Butt (21), Ashton (50); **Goals:** Smith 1/3.
**Sin bin:** Butt (74) - dissent.
**On report:** Lloyd (78) - alleged use of the knees.
**VIKINGS:** 5 Jack Owens; 29 Jayden Hatton; 25 Lloyd Roby; 24 Keanan Brand; 27 Sam Freeman; 6 Danny Craven; 21 Joe Lyons; 18 Ted Chapelhow; 15 Jordan Johnstone; 8 Jay Chapelhow; 17 Sam Wilde; 12 Chris Dean; 13 Hep Cahill. Subs (all used): 26 Dan Norman; 16 MacGraff Leuluai; 20 Owen Farnworth; 19 Brad Walker.
**Tries:** T Chapelhow (4, 74), Lyons (11), Wilde (27), Craven (69); **Goals:** Owens 6/6.
**Rugby Leaguer & League Express Men of the Match:** *Lions:* Gavin Bennion; *Vikings:* Danny Craven.
**Penalty count:** 7-7; **Half-time:** 4-18;
**Referee:** Michael Mannifield; **Attendance:** 1,469.

**YORK CITY KNIGHTS 28 BATLEY BULLDOGS 24**

**CITY KNIGHTS:** 1 Matty Marsh; 21 Judah Mazive; 23 Jason Bass; 3 Liam Salter; 20 Perry Whiteley; 35 Cain Southernwood; 7 Connor Robinson; 37 Jordan Baldwinson; 9 Will Jubb; 10 Jack Teanby; 11 Josh Jordan-Roberts; 22 Marcus Stock; 13 Tim Spears. Subs (all used): 26 Kriss Brining; 15 Graeme Horne; 16 Jack Blagbrough; 8 Ronan Dixon.
**Tries:** Marsh (8), Robinson (17), Stock (24), Dixon (40), Jubb (62); **Goals:** Robinson 4/5.
**BULLDOGS:** 1 Dave Scott; 4 Lewis Galbraith; 3 Sam Smeaton; 22 Sam Wood; 5 Johnny Campbell; 6 Louis Jouffret; 7 Dom Brambani; 8 Adam Gledhill; 9 Alistair Leak; 15 Toby Everett; 24 Paul Brearley; 19 Alex Bretherton; 11 Dane Manning. Subs (all used): 25 Lewis Bienek; 13 James Brown; 27 Reiss Butterworth; 16 Michael Ward.
**Tries:** Campbell (14, 58), Bienek (35, 64), Bretherton (72);
**Goals:** Brambani 1/2, Scott 1/3.
**Rugby Leaguer & League Express Men of the Match:** *City Knights:* Connor Robinson; *Bulldogs:* Lewis Bienek.
**Penalty count:** 7-9; **Half-time:** 22-10;
**Referee:** Greg Dolan; **Attendance:** 1,978.

## ROUND 6

*Sunday 12th May 2019*

**ROCHDALE HORNETS 18 YORK CITY KNIGHTS 24**

**HORNETS:** 19 Jack Johnson; 18 Reece Hamlett; 23 Jordan Case; 5 James Worthington; 24 Brandon Wood; 29 Lewis Sheridan; 7 Dan Abram; 11 Lee Mitchell; 6 Scott Moore; 21 Jack Cottington; 25 Luis Johnson; 12 Ellis Gillam; 9 Ben Moores. Subs (all used): 20 Joe Ryan; 27 Mike Coleman; 15 Declan Gregory; 17 Liam Carberry.
**Tries:** Sheridan (27), Carberry (53), B Wood (70);
**Goals:** Abram 3/3.
**CITY KNIGHTS:** 23 Jason Bass; 21 Judah Mazive; 3 Liam Salter; 4 Brad Hey; 20 Perry Whiteley; 1 Matty Marsh; 7 Connor Robinson; 37 Jordan Baldwinson; 9 Will Jubb; 10 Jack Teanby; 11 Josh Jordan-Roberts; 22 Marcus Stock; 13 Tim Spears. Subs (all used): 26 Kriss Brining; 19 Mike Kelly; 16 Jack Blagbrough; 17 Joe Porter.
**Tries:** Marsh (6), Bass (18, 38), Mazive (24), Blagbrough (55); **Goals:** Robinson 2/5.
**Rugby Leaguer & League Express Men of the Match:** *Hornets:* Dan Abram; *City Knights:* Jason Bass.
**Penalty count:** 8-4; **Half-time:** 6-18;
**Referee:** John McMullen; **Attendance:** 513.

## ROUND 14 - SUMMER BASH

*Saturday 18th May 2019*

**TORONTO WOLFPACK 42 TOULOUSE OLYMPIQUE 14**

**WOLFPACK:** 1 Gareth O'Brien; 24 Nick Rawsthorne; 3 Chase Stanley; 4 Ricky Leutele; 5 Liam Kay; 6 Joe Mellor;

7 Josh McCrone; 8 Adam Sidlow; 14 Andy Ackers; 15 Darcy Lussick; 11 Andrew Dixon; 12 Bodene Thompson; 13 Jon Wilkin. Subs (all used): 9 Bob Beswick; 10 Ashton Sims; 16 Tom Olbison; 21 Anthony Mullally.
**Tries:** O'Brien (14), McCrone (23), Stanley (27, 31, 64), Lussick (61), Rawsthorne (71); **Goals:** O'Brien 7/8.
**OLYMPIQUE:** 1 Mark Kheirallah; 5 Paul Marcon; 25 Mathieu Jussaume; 10 Joe Bretherton; 30 William Barthau; 6 Johnathon Ford; 7 Stan Robin; 8 Maxime Puech; 9 Anthony Marion; 18 Clement Boyer; 11 Con Mika; 12 Rhys Curran; 22 Brenden Santi. Subs (all used): 14 Dean Parata; 19 James Bell; 16 Tyla Hepi; 17 Paterika Vaivai.
**Tries:** Bretherton (47), Curran (79); **Goals:** Kheirallah 3/3.
**Rugby Leaguer & League Express Men of the Match:** *Wolfpack:* Darcy Lussick; *Olympique:* Rhys Curran.
**Penalty count:** 6-4; **Half-time:** 22-2; **Referee:** Jack Smith.

### ROCHDALE HORNETS 30 SWINTON LIONS 40

**HORNETS:** 1 Dec Kay; 24 Brandon Wood; 23 Jordan Case; 26 James Worthington; 2 Shaun Ainscough; 9 Ben Moores; 7 Dan Abram; 11 Lee Mitchell; 6 Scott Moore; 8 Callum Marriott; 27 Mike Coleman; 30 Luis Johnson; 12 Harvey Livett. Subs (all used): 10 Aidy Gleeson; 17 Liam Carberry; 13 Ellis Robson; 15 Declan Gregory.
**Tries:** B Wood (13), Kay (22), Ainscough (30, 45), Livett (40); **Goals:** Abram 5/5.
**LIONS:** 1 Jack Hansen; 2 Mike Butt; 3 Rhodri Lloyd; 31 Liam Forsyth; 25 Matty Ashton; 34 Harry Smith; 7 Rob Fairclough; 8 Gavin Bennion; 9 Luke Waterworth; 10 Lewis Hatton; 32 Liam Paisley; 22 Frankie Halton; 35 Jack Wells. Subs (all used): 14 Billy Brickhill; 11 Adam Jones; 16 Paddy Jones; 36 Adam Lawton.
**Tries:** Butt (6), Halton (25), Ashton (41, 75), Lloyd (53), Hansen (55), Fairclough (58), Paisley (66);
**Goals:** Smith 4/8.
**Rugby Leaguer & League Express Men of the Match:** *Hornets:* Dan Abram; *Lions:* Frankie Halton.
**Penalty count:** 9-7; **Half-time:** 24-10;
**Referee:** Gareth Hewer.

### FEATHERSTONE ROVERS 42 YORK CITY KNIGHTS 10

**ROVERS:** 33 Ashton Golding; 5 Conor Carey; 32 Alex Sutcliffe; 4 Josh Hardcastle; 2 Luke Briscoe; 38 Dane Chisholm; 40 Tom Holmes; 8 Scott Wheeldon; 9 Cameron King; 23 Makahesi Makatoa; 12 Brad Day; 28 Josh Walters; 13 James Lockwood. Subs (all used): 14 John Davies; 15 Luke Cooper; 17 James Harrison; 29 Jack Ormondroyd.
**Tries:** Chisholm (21), Carey (37, 51), Briscoe (39), Day (54), Sutcliffe (58), Hardcastle (64), Holmes (66);
**Goals:** Chisholm 5/8.
**Sin bin:** Wheeldon (7) - dissent.
**CITY KNIGHTS:** 38 Liam Harris; 20 Perry Whiteley; 3 Liam Salter; 23 Jason Bass; 24 Kevin Brown; 1 Matty Marsh; 7 Connor Robinson; 10 Jack Teanby; 9 Will Jubb; 39 Harry Aldous; 22 Marcus Stock; 4 Brad Hey; 13 Tim Spears. Subs (all used): 14 Harry Carter; 17 Joe Porter; 16 Jack Blagbrough; 36 Tyler Dupree.
**Tries:** Whiteley (70), Porter (73); **Goals:** Robinson 1/2.
**Rugby Leaguer & League Express Men of the Match:** *Rovers:* Dane Chisholm; *City Knights:* Joe Porter.
**Penalty count:** 8-5; **Half-time:** 14-0;
**Referee:** Billy Pearson.

### BRADFORD BULLS 14 HALIFAX 21

**BULLS:** 2 Ethan Ryan; 22 Dalton Grant; 3 Jake Webster; 26 Ross Oakes; 24 David Foggin-Johnston; 27 Rowan Milnes; 14 Jordan Lilley; 8 Liam Kirk; 18 Sam Hallas; 10 Steve Crossley; 29 Matthew Storton; 12 Elliot Minchella; 13 Mikey Wood. Subs (all used): 25 Connor Farrell; 9 Matty Wildie; 16 James Green; 33 Colton Roche.
**Tries:** Foggin-Johnston (5), Grant (15); **Goals:** Minchella 3/4.
**HALIFAX:** 1 Quentin Laulu-Togaga'e; 5 Will Sharp; 4 Chester Butler; 3 Steve Tyrer; 2 Shaun Robinson; 6 Scott Murrell; 30 Scott Grix; 17 Ben Kavanagh; 9 Ben Kaye; 18 Elliot Morris; 12 Ed Barber; 25 Liam Cooper; 10 Jacob Fairbank. Subs (all used): 14 Brandon Moore; 8 Dan Fleming; 16 Kevin Larroyer; 22 Connor Davies.
**Tries:** Kavanagh (8), Laulu-Togaga'e (25), Morris (65);
**Goals:** Tyrer 4/4; **Field goal:** Murrell (77).
**Rugby Leaguer & League Express Men of the Match:** *Bulls:* Ethan Ryan; *Halifax:* Scott Murrell.
**Penalty count:** 7-7; **Half-time:** 14-12; **Referee:** Tom Grant.

**Attendance:** 7,912 *(at Bloomfield Road, Blackpool)*.

*Sunday 19th May 2019*

### BARROW RAIDERS 18 SHEFFIELD EAGLES 30

**RAIDERS:** 1 Theerapol Ritson; 5 Deon Cross; 12 Jarrad Stack; 2 Stargroth Amean; 4 Jake Spedding; 6 Jamie Dallimore; 7 Lewis Charnock; 28 Josh Johnson; 14 Wartovo Puara; 29 Alec Susino; 25 Jordan Walne; 11 Jono Smith; 13 Martin Aspinwall. Subs (all used): 8 Tom Walker; 9 Nathan Mossop; 15 Dan Toal; 16 Glenn Riley.
**Tries:** Stack (13), Ritson (75), Smith (78);
**Goals:** Dallimore 3/4.
**EAGLES:** 1 Josh Guzdek; 2 Ryan Millar; 18 James Glover; 29 Ben Hellewell; 5 Ben Blackmore; 6 Pat Walker; 7 Anthony Thackeray; 8 Pat Moran; 14 Greg Burns; 10 Matt James; 15 Olly Davies; 12 Joel Farrell; 13 Aaron Brown. Subs (all used): 16 Corey Makelim; 31 Nathan Mason; 19 Sonny Esslemont; 11 Brad Knowles.
**Tries:** Farrell (25, 47), Blackmore (55), Thackeray (58, 61);
**Goals:** Walker 5/5.
**Sin bin:** Thackeray (70) - dissent.
**Rugby Leaguer & League Express Men of the Match:** *Raiders:* Theerapol Ritson; *Eagles:* Joel Farrell.
**Penalty count:** 6-4; **Half-time:** 8-6;
**Referee:** Michael Mannifield.

### BATLEY BULLDOGS 30 DEWSBURY RAMS 14

**BULLDOGS:** 1 Dave Scott; 23 Keenen Tomlinson; 3 Sam Smeaton; 22 Sam Wood; 5 Johnny Campbell; 6 Louis Jouffret; 7 Dom Brambani; 8 Adam Gledhill; 9 Alistair Leak; 15 Toby Everett; 24 Paul Brearley; 11 Dane Manning; 13 James Brown. Subs (all used): 25 Lewis Bienek; 27 Reiss Butterworth; 21 Jo Taira; 16 Michael Ward.
**Tries:** Tomlinson (6), Campbell (12), Brearley (63), Leak (75), Scott (77); **Goals:** Jouffret 5/6.
**RAMS:** 35 Luke Hooley; 23 Rob Worrincy; 1 Dale Morton; 4 Adam Ryder; 2 Andy Gabriel; 7 Simon Brown; 38 Liam Finn; 32 Samy Kibula; 37 Liam Mackay; 36 Ben Kilner; 11 Lucas Walshaw; 12 Michael Knowles; 33 Callum Field. Subs (all used): 18 Sam Day; 19 Daniel Igbinedion; 30 Tom Garratt; 16 Jordan Andrade.
**Tries:** Gabriel (20), Knowles (78), Day (79); **Goals:** Finn 1/3.
**Rugby Leaguer & League Express Men of the Match:** *Bulldogs:* Paul Brearley; *Rams:* Sam Day.
**Penalty count:** 4-4; **Half-time:** 10-4;
**Referee:** Matt Rossleigh.

### LEIGH CENTURIONS 36 WIDNES VIKINGS 22

**CENTURIONS:** 6 Martyn Ridyard; 1 Gregg McNally; 3 Iain Thornley; 25 Josh Simm; 5 Stefan Marsh; 35 Ryan Brierley; 7 Josh Woods; 30 Luke Douglas; 9 Micky Higham; 29 Jake Emmitt; 11 Toby Adamson; 23 James Laithwaite; 15 Joe Cator. Subs (all used): 27 Liam Hood; 8 Tom Spencer; 12 Andy Thornley; 24 Joe Batchelor.
**Tries:** T Adamson (25), McNally (27, 75), Brierley (35, 45), Laithwaite (47); **Goals:** Ridyard 6/8.
**VIKINGS:** 25 Lloyd Roby; 29 Jayden Hatton; 12 Chris Dean; 24 Keanan Brand; 22 Owen Buckley; 6 Danny Craven; 7 Tom Gilmore; 18 Ted Chapelhow; 15 Jordan Johnstone; 8 Jay Chapelhow; 17 Sam Wilde; 19 Brad Walker; 13 Hep Cahill. Subs (all used): 11 Harrison Hansen; 34 Josh Ganson; 20 Owen Farnworth; 16 MacGraff Leuluai.
**Tries:** Buckley (14), Craven (55, 65), Roby (61);
**Goals:** Roby 3/5.
**Rugby Leaguer & League Express Men of the Match:** *Centurions:* Ryan Brierley; *Vikings:* Danny Craven.
**Penalty count:** 4-5; **Half-time:** 18-6; **Referee:** Greg Dolan.

**Attendance:** 7,158 *(at Bloomfield Road, Blackpool)*.

## ROUND 15

*Friday 24th May 2019*

### SHEFFIELD EAGLES 16 TORONTO WOLFPACK 42

**EAGLES:** 1 Josh Guzdek; 2 Ryan Millar; 27 Jacob Ogden; 29 Ben Hellewell; 5 Ben Blackmore; 6 Pat Walker; 7 Anthony Thackeray; 8 Pat Moran; 9 James Davey; 11 Brad Knowles; 12 Joel Farrell; 15 Olly Davies; 13 Aaron Brown. Subs (all used): 4 Jason Crookes; 31 Daniel Hindmarsh; 16 Corey Makelim; 21 Blake Broadbent.
**Tries:** Hellewell (39), Guzdek (56), Knowles (78);
**Goals:** Walker 2/3.
**WOLFPACK:** 1 Gareth O'Brien; 5 Liam Kay; 3 Chase Stanley; 4 Ricky Leutele; 2 Matty Russell; 17 Blake Wallace; 7 Josh McCrone; 8 Adam Sidlow; 14 Andy Ackers; 15 Darcy Lussick; 11 Andrew Dixon; 12 Bodene Thompson; 13 Jon Wilkin. Subs (all used): 24 Nick Rawsthorne; 10 Ashton Sims; 21 Anthony Mullally; 16 Tom Olbison.
**Tries:** Wallace (6), Dixon (13, 18), Kay (27), Stanley (30), Leutele (47), Rawsthorne (52), Ackers (64);
**Goals:** Wallace 5/8.
**Rugby Leaguer & League Express Men of the Match:** *Eagles:* Anthony Thackeray; *Wolfpack:* Andy Ackers.
**Penalty count:** 7-6; **Half-time:** 4-28;
**Referee:** Billy Pearson; **Attendance:** 932.

*Saturday 25th May 2019*

### TOULOUSE OLYMPIQUE 44 LEIGH CENTURIONS 16

**OLYMPIQUE:** 1 Mark Kheirallah; 5 Paul Marcon; 25 Mathieu Jussaume; 4 Gavin Marguerite; 28 Jodie Broughton; 6 Johnathon Ford; 7 Stan Robin; 8 Maxime Puech; 14 Dean Parata; 17 Paterika Vaivai; 11 Con Mika; 19 James Bell; 9 Anthony Marion. Subs (all used): 22 Brenden Santi; 16 Tyla Hepi; 15 Ben Evans; 21 Jordan Dezaria.
**Tries:** Marcon (7, 61), Bell (29), Mika (45), Jussaume (49, 64), P Vaivai (66), Robin (76);
**Goals:** Kheirallah 6/8.
**CENTURIONS:** 6 Martyn Ridyard; 1 Gregg McNally; 24 Josh Simm; 3 Iain Thornley; 4 Jack Higginson; 35 Ryan Brierley; 7 Josh Woods; 30 Luke Douglas; 27 Liam Hood; 10 Sam Brooks; 11 Toby Adamson; 23 James Laithwaite; 29 Jake Emmitt. Subs (all used): 9 Micky Higham; 8 Tom Spencer; 12 Andy Thornley; 15 Joe Cator.
**Tries:** Simm (54), Brierley (70), McNally (80);
**Goals:** Ridyard 1/1, Brierley 1/3.
**Rugby Leaguer & League Express Men of the Match:** *Olympique:* Johnathon Ford; *Centurions:* Luke Douglas.
**Penalty count:** 5-8; **Half-time:** 12-2;
**Referee:** Marcus Griffiths; **Attendance:** 2,235.

*Sunday 26th May 2019*

### BARROW RAIDERS 54 ROCHDALE HORNETS 10

**RAIDERS:** 1 Theerapol Ritson; 5 Deon Cross; 12 Jarrad Stack; 2 Stargroth Amean; 4 Jake Spedding; 6 Jamie Dallimore; 7 Lewis Charnock; 28 Josh Johnson; 14 Wartovo Puara; 29 Alec Susino; 25 Jordan Walne; 11 Jono Smith; 13 Martin Aspinwall. Subs (all used): 9 Nathan Mossop; 8 Tom Walker; 15 Dan Toal; 16 Glenn Riley.
**Tries:** Puara (9), Susino (14), Cross (17), Spedding (27), Amean (30, 36, 40), Ritson (64), D Toal (67);
**Goals:** Dallimore 9/9.
**HORNETS:** 19 Jack Johnson; 2 Shaun Ainscough; 23 Jordan Case; 26 James Worthington; 24 Brandon Wood; 29 Zac Baker; 7 Dan Abram; 11 Lee Mitchell; 9 Ben Moores; 8 Callum Marriott; 12 Ellis Gillam; 25 Luis Johnson; 27 Ellis Robson. Subs (all used): 18 Mike Coleman; 15 Declan Gregory; 28 Aidy Gleeson; 17 Liam Carberry.
**Tries:** J Johnson (4), B Wood (32); **Goals:** Abram 1/2.
**Rugby Leaguer & League Express Men of the Match:** *Raiders:* Jamie Dallimore; *Hornets:* Jack Johnson.
**Penalty count:** 6-7; **Half-time:** 42-10;
**Referee:** Matt Rossleigh; **Attendance:** 1,114.

### BATLEY BULLDOGS 24 HALIFAX 16

**BULLDOGS:** 1 Dave Scott; 23 Keenen Tomlinson; 4 Lewis Galbraith; 22 Sam Wood; 5 Johnny Campbell; 6 Louis Jouffret; 7 Dom Brambani; 8 Adam Gledhill; 9 Alistair Leak; 15 Toby Everett; 11 Dane Manning; 19 Alex Bretherton; 13 James Brown. Subs (all used): 16 Michael Ward; 21 Jo Taira; 27 Reiss Butterworth; 25 Lewis Bienek.
**Tries:** Tomlinson (9, 56), Galbraith (47), Gledhill (65);
**Goals:** Jouffret 4/6.
**HALIFAX:** 30 Scott Grix; 5 Will Sharp; 4 Chester Butler; 3 Steve Tyrer; 2 Shaun Robinson; 6 Scott Murrell; 19 Ben White; 8 Dan Fleming; 14 Brandon Moore; 35 Adam Tangata; 16 Kevin Larroyer; 25 Liam Cooper; 22 Connor Davies. Subs (all used): 24 Curtis Davies; 10 Jacob Fairbank; 34 Jon Luke Kirby; 18 Elliot Morris.
**Tries:** Sharp (25, 76), Scott Grix (60); **Goals:** Tyrer 2/3.
**Rugby Leaguer & League Express Men of the Match:** *Bulldogs:* Dane Manning; *Halifax:* Steve Tyrer.
**Penalty count:** 6-6; **Half-time:** 6-6;
**Referee:** Nick Bennett; **Attendance:** 1,368.

### FEATHERSTONE ROVERS 42 BRADFORD BULLS 4

**ROVERS:** 25 Jack Render; 5 Conor Carey; 28 Josh Walters; 4 Josh Hardcastle; 2 Luke Briscoe; 38 Dane Chisholm; 40 Tom Holmes; 8 Scott Wheeldon; 9 Cameron King; 17 James Harrison; 14 John Davies; 12 Brad Day; 13 James Lockwood. Subs (all used): 23 Makahesi Makatoa; 29 Jack Ormondroyd; 15 Luke Cooper; 39 Dale Ferguson.
**Tries:** King (8), Chisholm (16, 66, 80), Davies (60), Briscoe (63), Carey (73), Walters (75); **Goals:** Chisholm 5/10.
**BULLS:** 2 Ethan Ryan; 1 Brandon Pickersgill; 12 Elliot Minchella; 26 Ross Oakes; 24 David Foggin-Johnston; 9 Matty Wildie; 14 Jordan Lilley; 8 Liam Kirk; 18 Sam Hallas; 10 Steve Crossley; 29 Matthew Storton; 25 Connor Farrell; 13 Mikey Wood. Subs (all used): 21 George Flanagan; 16 James Green; 33 Colton Roche; 20 Alix Stephenson.
**Try:** Ryan (47); **Goals:** Minchella 0/1.
**Rugby Leaguer & League Express Men of the Match:** *Rovers:* Dane Chisholm; *Bulls:* Ethan Ryan.
**Penalty count:** 7-3; **Half-time:** 10-0;
**Referee:** Gareth Hewer; **Attendance:** 2,903.

### SWINTON LIONS 22 DEWSBURY RAMS 17

**LIONS:** 25 Matty Ashton; 2 Mike Butt; 3 Rhodri Lloyd; 35 Liam Paisley; 32 Liam Forsyth; 1 Jack Hansen; 7 Rob Fairclough; 8 Gavin Bennion; 9 Luke Waterworth; 10 Lewis Hatton; 22 Frankie Halton; 33 Jack Wells; 36 Liam Byrne. Subs (all used): 14 Billy Brickhill; 11 Adam Jones; 16 Paddy Jones; 31 Adam Lawton.

**Tries:** Ashton (28), Paisley (63), Bennion (75, 79);
**Goals:** Fairclough 3/4.
**Sin bin:** Hatton (16) - fighting.
**RAMS:** 1 Dale Morton; 23 Rob Worrincy; 19 Daniel Igbinedion; 4 Adam Ryder; 2 Andy Gabriel; 7 Simon Brown; 38 Liam Finn; 30 Tom Garratt; 9 Robbie Ward; 34 Chris Annakin; 11 Lucas Walshaw; 12 Michael Knowles; 13 Kyle Trout. Subs (all used): 18 Sam Day; 16 Jordan Andrade; 32 Samy Kibula; 36 Ben Kilner.
**Tries:** Gabriel (17), Morton (21), Worrincy (53);
**Goals:** Finn 2/3; **Field goal:** Knowles (77).
**Dismissal:** Kibula (79) - dissent.
**Sin bin:** Knowles (60) - dissent.
**Rugby Leaguer & League Express Men of the Match:**
*Lions:* Gavin Bennion; *Rams:* Simon Brown.
**Penalty count:** 15-10; **Half-time:** 4-10;
**Referee:** Michael Mannifield; **Attendance:** 795.

**WIDNES VIKINGS 12 YORK CITY KNIGHTS 16**

**VIKINGS:** 27 Sam Freeman; 22 Owen Buckley; 25 Lloyd Roby; 24 Keanan Brand; 2 Ryan Ince; 6 Danny Craven; 21 Joe Lyons; 13 Hep Cahill; 34 Josh Ganson; 11 Harrison Hansen; 17 Sam Wilde; 12 Chris Dean; 15 Jordan Johnstone. Subs (all used): 18 Ted Chapelhow; 19 Brad Walker; 20 Owen Farnworth; 26 Dan Norman.
**Tries:** Roby (5), Lyons (32); **Goals:** Freeman 2/3.
**CITY KNIGHTS:** 1 Matty Marsh; 20 Perry Whiteley; 3 Liam Salter; 39 Junior Vaivai; 37 Will Oakes; 38 Liam Harris; 7 Connor Robinson; 10 Jack Teanby; 9 Will Jubb; 35 Harry Aldous; 11 Josh Jordan-Roberts; 12 Sam Scott; 13 Tim Spears. Subs (all used): 26 Kriss Brining; 15 Graeme Horne; 22 Marcus Stock; 17 Joe Porter.
**Tries:** Harris (17), Vaivai (36), Oakes (66);
**Goals:** Robinson 2/3.
**Rugby Leaguer & League Express Men of the Match:**
*Vikings:* Jordan Johnstone; *City Knights:* Liam Harris.
**Penalty count:** 7-10; **Half-time:** 10-10;
**Referee:** John McMullen; **Attendance:** 3,408.

## ROUND 4

*Friday 31st May 2019*

**WIDNES VIKINGS 36 SHEFFIELD EAGLES 6**

**VIKINGS:** 5 Jack Owens; 29 Jayden Hatton; 12 Chris Dean; 24 Keanan Brand; 2 Ryan Ince; 6 Danny Craven; 21 Joe Lyons; 13 Hep Cahill; 34 Josh Ganson; 8 Jay Chapelhow; 11 Harrison Hansen; 17 Sam Wilde; 15 Jordan Johnstone. Subs (all used): 18 Ted Chapelhow; 19 Brad Walker; 26 Dan Norman; 16 MacGraff Leuluai.
**Tries:** Cahill (3), Hatton (14), Owens (19), Dean (26), Ince (34), Brand (43, 55); **Goals:** Owens 4/7.
**EAGLES:** 1 Josh Guzdek; 2 Ryan Millar; 27 Jacob Ogden; 29 Ben Hellewell; 5 Ben Blackmore; 6 Pat Walker; 7 Anthony Thackeray; 8 Pat Moran; 9 James Davey; 31 Nathan Mason; 15 Olly Davies; 12 Joel Farrell; 13 Aaron Brown. Subs (all used): 4 Jason Crookes; 21 Blake Broadbent; 16 Corey Makelim; 17 Shaun Pick.
**Try:** Blackmore (65); **Goals:** Walker 1/1.
**Rugby Leaguer & League Express Men of the Match:**
*Vikings:* Joe Lyons; *Eagles:* Pat Moran.
**Penalty count:** 6-4; **Half-time:** 26-0;
**Referee:** Gareth Hewer; **Attendance:** 4,920.

## ROUND 16

*Saturday 8th June 2019*

**YORK CITY KNIGHTS 18 TOULOUSE OLYMPIQUE 25**

**CITY KNIGHTS:** 1 Matty Marsh; 23 Jason Bass; 3 Liam Salter; 4 Brad Hey; 37 Will Oakes; 38 Liam Harris; 7 Connor Robinson; 10 Jack Teanby; 9 Will Jubb; 16 Jack Blagbrough; 35 Harry Aldous; 12 Sam Scott; 13 Tim Spears. Subs (all used): 26 Kriss Brining; 15 Graeme Horne; 22 Marcus Stock; 17 Joe Porter.
**Tries:** Teanby (12), Hey (24), Harris (55);
**Goals:** Robinson 3/3.
**Sin bin:** Marsh (78) - obstruction.
**OLYMPIQUE:** 1 Mark Kheirallah; 5 Paul Marcon; 25 Mathieu Jussaume; 4 Gavin Marguerite; 2 Tony Maurel; 30 William Barthau; 7 Stan Robin; 8 Maxime Puech; 14 Dean Parata; 17 Paterika Vaivai; 11 Con Mika; 19 James Bell; 9 Anthony Marion. Subs (all used): 18 Clement Boyer; 15 Ben Evans; 16 Tyla Hepi; 22 Brenden Santi.
**Tries:** Jussaume (15, 73), Bell (29), Marcon (59);
**Goals:** Barthau 4/5; **Field goal:** Barthau (80).
**Rugby Leaguer & League Express Men of the Match:**
*City Knights:* Will Jubb; *Olympique:* William Barthau.
**Penalty count:** 4-9; **Half-time:** 12-12;
**Referee:** James Child; **Attendance:** 1,656.

*Sunday 9th June 2019*

**BRADFORD BULLS 16 BATLEY BULLDOGS 0**

**BULLS:** 2 Ethan Ryan; 22 Dalton Grant; 3 Jake Webster; 26 Ross Oakes; 24 David Foggin-Johnston; 14 Jordan Lilley; 9 Matty Wildie; 8 Liam Kirk; 18 Sam Hallas; 15 Callum Bustin; 29 Matthew Storton; 25 Connor Farrell; 12 Elliot Minchella. Subs (all used): 21 George Flanagan; 34 Colton Roche; 13 Mikey Wood; 17 Ross Peltier.
**Tries:** Foggin-Johnston (9, 51), Minchella (61);
**Goals:** Lilley 2/3.
**BULLDOGS:** 1 Dave Scott; 23 Keenen Tomlinson; 3 Sam Smeaton; 22 Sam Wood; 5 Johnny Campbell; 6 Louis Jouffret; 7 Dom Brambani; 8 Adam Gledhill; 9 Alistair Leak; 25 Lewis Bienek; 12 Jack Downs; 11 Dane Manning; 13 James Brown. Subs (all used): 24 Paul Brearley; 27 Reiss Butterworth; 21 Jo Taira; 16 Michael Ward.
**Sin bin:** Gledhill (77) - fighting.
**Rugby Leaguer & League Express Men of the Match:**
*Bulls:* David Foggin-Johnston; *Bulldogs:* Dave Scott.
**Penalty count:** 8-5; **Half-time:** 4-0;
**Referee:** Matt Rossleigh; **Attendance:** 3,414.

**DEWSBURY RAMS 66 ROCHDALE HORNETS 10**

**RAMS:** 42 Joe Martin; 23 Rob Worrincy; 1 Dale Morton; 4 Adam Ryder; 2 Andy Gabriel; 6 Paul Sykes; 38 Liam Finn; 34 Chris Annakin; 18 Sam Day; 8 Jode Sheriffe; 11 Lucas Walshaw; 12 Michael Knowles; 13 Kyle Trout. Subs (all used): 19 Daniel Igbinedion; 10 Toby Richardson; 33 Frazer Morris; 30 Tom Garratt.
**Tries:** K Trout (7), Morton (26), Walshaw (31), Day (39, 64), Morris (46, 48), Martin (51, 73), Garratt (54), Annakin (77); **Goals:** Finn 11/11.
**HORNETS:** 7 Dan Abram; 2 Shaun Ainscough; 23 Jordan Case; 26 Daley Williams; 24 Brandon Wood; 29 Izaac Farrell; 19 Oscar Thomas; 11 Lee Mitchell; 6 Scott Moore; 30 Adam Lawton; 18 Mike Coleman; 25 Luis Johnson; 27 Ellis Robson. Subs (all used): 17 Liam Carberry; 28 Aidy Gleeson; 1 Dec Kay; 22 Callum Wood.
**Tries:** B Wood (2), S Moore (42); **Goals:** Abram 1/2.
**Rugby Leaguer & League Express Men of the Match:**
*Rams:* Sam Day; *Hornets:* Luis Johnson.
**Penalty count:** 13-7; **Half-time:** 24-4;
**Referee:** Gareth Hewer; **Attendance:** 865.

**LEIGH CENTURIONS 31 HALIFAX 8**

**CENTURIONS:** 1 Gregg McNally; 19 Mitch Cox; 3 Iain Thornley; 25 Liam Forsyth; 5 Stefan Marsh; 6 Martyn Ridyard; 7 Josh Woods; 26 Luke Douglas; 9 Micky Higham; 10 Sam Brooks; 11 Toby Adamson; 30 Joe Batchelor; 15 Joe Cator. Subs (all used): 8 Tom Spencer; 12 Andy Thornley; 24 Gareth Hock; 27 Liam Hood.
**Tries:** I Thornley (12), Cox (17, 21), Hood (52), Brooks (76);
**Goals:** Ridyard 5/7; **Field goal:** Ridyard (71).
**Sin bin:** I Thornley (68) - fighting.
**HALIFAX:** 30 Scott Grix; 20 James Saltonstall; 3 Steve Tyrer; 4 Chester Butler; 5 Will Sharp; 6 Scott Murrell; 1 Quentin Laulu-Togaga'e; 17 Ben Kavanagh; 9 Ben Kaye; 35 Adam Tangata; 25 Liam Cooper; 16 Kevin Larroyer; 10 Jacob Fairbank. Subs (all used): 8 Dan Fleming; 14 Brandon Moore; 18 Elliot Morris; 23 James Woodburn-Hall.
**Tries:** Butler (64), Woodburn-Hall (80); **Goals:** Tyrer 0/2.
**Dismissal:** Fleming (68) - fighting.
**Sin bin:** Fairbank (40) - fighting.
**Rugby Leaguer & League Express Men of the Match:**
*Centurions:* Gregg McNally; *Halifax:* Chester Butler.
**Penalty count:** 8-9; **Half-time:** 16-0;
**Referee:** Jack Smith; **Attendance:** 3,361.

**SHEFFIELD EAGLES 18 FEATHERSTONE ROVERS 38**

**EAGLES:** 1 Josh Guzdek; 2 Ryan Millar; 27 Jacob Ogden; 29 Ben Hellewell; 4 Jason Crookes; 6 Pat Walker; 7 Anthony Thackeray; 8 Pat Moran; 9 James Davey; 31 Nathan Mason; 12 Joel Farrell; 15 Olly Davies; 13 Aaron Brown. Subs (all used): 11 Brad Knowles; 16 Corey Makelim; 17 Shaun Pick; 21 Blake Broadbent.
**Tries:** Moran (20), Hellewell (51), Mason (64);
**Goals:** Walker 3/3.
**ROVERS:** 33 Ashton Golding; 2 Luke Briscoe; 32 Alex Sutcliffe; 4 Josh Hardcastle; 5 Conor Carey; 38 Dane Chisholm; 40 Tom Holmes; 17 James Harrison; 9 Cameron King; 39 Dale Ferguson; 12 Brad Day; 28 Josh Walters; 13 James Lockwood. Subs (all used): 8 Scott Wheeldon; 15 Luke Cooper; 25 Jack Render; 29 Jack Ormondroyd.
**Tries:** Ferguson (7), Holmes (13), King (16, 42), Hardcastle (46), Harrison (76); **Goals:** Chisholm 7/7.
**Rugby Leaguer & League Express Men of the Match:**
*Eagles:* Josh Guzdek; *Rovers:* Brad Day.
**Penalty count:** 7-6; **Half-time:** 6-18;
**Referee:** Billy Pearson; **Attendance:** 1,321.

**WIDNES VIKINGS 38 BARROW RAIDERS 14**

**VIKINGS:** 5 Jack Owens; 25 Lloyd Roby; 24 Keanan Brand; 4 Anthony Gelling; 29 Jayden Hatton; 6 Danny Craven; 21 Joe Lyons; 13 Hep Cahill; 15 Jordan Johnstone; 8 Jay Chapelhow; 17 Sam Wilde; 12 Chris Dean; 19 Brad Walker. Subs (all used): 18 Ted Chapelhow; 34 Josh Ganson; 16 MacGraff Leuluai; 26 Dan Norman.
**Tries:** J Chapelhow (11, 26), Hatton (33, 60), Craven (43), Roby (47), Lyons (50); **Goals:** Owens 5/7.
**RAIDERS:** 1 Theerapol Ritson; 27 Brett Carter; 2 Stargroth Amean; 4 Jake Spedding; 5 Deon Cross; 6 Jamie Dallimore; 24 Jake Carter; 28 Josh Johnson; 14 Wartovo Puara; 8 Tom Walker; 11 Jono Smith; 19 Danny Morrow; 29 Alec Susino. Subs (all used): 18 Luke Cresswell; 15 Dan Toal; 13 Martin Aspinwall; 25 Jordan Walne.
**Tries:** Cross (64), Ritson (75); **Goals:** Dallimore 3/3.
**Rugby Leaguer & League Express Men of the Match:**
*Vikings:* Danny Craven; *Raiders:* Deon Cross.
**Penalty count:** 9-5; **Half-time:** 16-2;
**Referee:** Tom Grant; **Attendance:** 3,830.

**SWINTON LIONS 14 TORONTO WOLFPACK 34**

**LIONS:** 25 Matty Ashton; 2 Mike Butt; 3 Rhodri Lloyd; 35 Liam Paisley; 28 Richard Lepori; 1 Jack Hansen; 7 Rob Fairclough; 8 Gavin Bennion; 9 Luke Waterworth; 10 Lewis Hatton; 33 Jack Wells; 11 Adam Jones; 16 Paddy Jones. Subs (all used): 14 Billy Brickhill; 31 Samy Kibula; 19 Jose Kenga; 12 Kyle Shelford.
**Tries:** Butt (57, 80), Fairclough (69); **Goals:** Fairclough 1/3.
**WOLFPACK:** 17 Blake Wallace; 5 Liam Kay; 3 Chase Stanley; 4 Ricky Leutele; 24 Nick Rawsthorne; 6 Joe Mellor; 7 Josh McCrone; 16 Tom Olbison; 9 Bob Beswick; 21 Anthony Mullally; 11 Andrew Dixon; 12 Bodene Thompson; 13 Jon Wilkin. Subs (all used): 14 Andy Ackers; 8 Adam Sidlow; 22 Greg Worthington; 23 Ryan Brierley.
**Tries:** Dixon (12), Leutele (19, 60), Stanley (28), Beswick (63), Sidlow (76); **Goals:** Wallace 5/6.
**Rugby Leaguer & League Express Men of the Match:**
*Lions:* Rob Fairclough; *Wolfpack:* Anthony Mullally.
**Penalty count:** 4-3; **Half-time:** 0-16;
**Referee:** Greg Dolan; **Attendance:** 1,281.

## ROUND 17

*Saturday 15th June 2019*

**TOULOUSE OLYMPIQUE 18 SWINTON LIONS 20**

**OLYMPIQUE:** 30 William Barthau; 5 Paul Marcon; 25 Mathieu Jussaume; 21 Jordan Dezaria; 2 Tony Maurel; 9 Anthony Marion; 7 Stan Robin; 8 Maxime Puech; 14 Dean Parata; 17 Paterika Vaivai; 11 Con Mika; 19 James Bell; 22 Brenden Santi. Subs (all used): 15 Ben Evans; 16 Tyla Hepi; 18 Clement Boyer; 23 Justin Sangare.
**Tries:** Robin (7), Maurel (24), Marion (33), Marcon (65);
**Goals:** Barthau 1/4.
**Sin bin:** Robin (55) - fighting.
**LIONS:** 25 Matty Ashton; 2 Mike Butt; 3 Rhodri Lloyd; 32 Liam Paisley; 28 Richard Lepori; 1 Jack Hansen; 7 Rob Fairclough; 8 Gavin Bennion; 9 Luke Waterworth; 10 Lewis Hatton; 11 Adam Jones; 33 Jack Wells; 16 Paddy Jones. Subs (all used): 14 Billy Brickhill; 12 Kyle Shelford; 22 Frankie Halton; 35 Samy Kibula.
**Tries:** Lloyd (20), Paisley (47, 52, 75);
**Goals:** Fairclough 0/2, Hansen 2/2.
**Sin bin:** Butt (55) - fighting.
**Rugby Leaguer & League Express Men of the Match:**
*Olympique:* Anthony Marion; *Lions:* Liam Paisley.
**Penalty count:** 8-11; **Half-time:** 14-4;
**Referee:** Greg Dolan; **Attendance:** 2,789.

**TORONTO WOLFPACK 70 DEWSBURY RAMS 8**

**WOLFPACK:** 1 Gareth O'Brien; 5 Liam Kay; 22 Greg Worthington; 4 Ricky Leutele; 2 Matty Russell; 6 Joe Mellor; 7 Josh McCrone; 16 Tom Olbison; 14 Andy Ackers; 8 Adam Sidlow; 11 Andrew Dixon; 12 Bodene Thompson; 13 Jon Wilkin. Subs (all used): 9 Bob Beswick; 21 Anthony Mullally; 17 Blake Wallace; 24 Nick Rawsthorne.
**Tries:** O'Brien (7), Ackers (9), Russell (14, 16), Mullally (24, 36), Mellor (39), Kay (45, 60), Sidlow (62), Wallace (72), Beswick (75); **Goals:** O'Brien 11/12.
**RAMS:** 42 Joe Martin; 23 Rob Worrincy; 39 Owen Trout; 4 Adam Ryder; 2 Andy Gabriel; 6 Paul Sykes; 7 Simon Brown; 30 Tom Garratt; 41 Harvey Whiteley; 36 Ben Kilner; 10 Toby Richardson; 13 Kyle Trout; 33 Frazer Morris. Subs (all used): 35 Luke Hooley; 22 Danny King; 17 Martyn Reilly; 24 Harvey Hallas.
**Tries:** Worrincy (32), Ryder (67); **Goals:** Sykes 0/2.
**Rugby Leaguer & League Express Men of the Match:**
*Wolfpack:* Gareth O'Brien; *Rams:* Rob Worrincy.
**Penalty count:** 5-3; **Half-time:** 40-4;
**Referee:** Tom Grant; **Attendance:** 6,745.

*Sunday 16th June 2019*

**BARROW RAIDERS 21 HALIFAX 8**

**RAIDERS:** 1 Theerapol Ritson; 27 Brett Carter; 12 Jarrad Stack; 2 Stargroth Amean; 5 Deon Cross; 6 Jamie Dallimore; 24 Jake Carter; 28 Josh Johnson; 14 Wartovo Puara; 29 Alec Susino; 25 Jordan Walne; 11 Jono Smith; 13 Martin Aspinwall. Subs (all used): 4 Jake Spedding; 8 Tom Walker; 16 Glenn Riley; 19 Danny Morrow.
**Tries:** Stack (7), Cross (23, 65), Morrow (67);
**Goals:** Dallimore 2/4; **Field goal:** J Carter (70).
**Sin bin:** Dallimore (50) - fighting.
**HALIFAX:** 30 Scott Grix; 2 Shaun Robinson; 3 Steve Tyrer; 23 James Woodburn-Hall; 20 James Saltonstall; 6 Scott Murrell; 1 Quentin Laulu-Togaga'e; 34 Will Maher; 9 Ben Kaye; 8 Dan Fleming; 16 Kevin Larroyer; 17 Ben Kavanagh; 10 Jacob Fairbank. Subs (all used): 14 Brandon Moore; 35 Adam Tangata; 39 Jon Luke Kirby; 18 Elliot Morris.
**Tries:** Robinson (35), Scott Grix (42); **Goals:** Tyrer 0/2.
**Rugby Leaguer & League Express Men of the Match:**
*Raiders:* Danny Morrow; *Halifax:* Scott Grix.
**Penalty count:** 8-8; **Half-time:** 10-4;
**Referee:** Gareth Hewer; **Attendance:** 1,396.

**BATLEY BULLDOGS 24 SHEFFIELD EAGLES 54**

**BULLDOGS:** 1 Dave Scott; 23 Keenen Tomlinson; 3 Sam Smeaton; 22 Sam Wood; 5 Johnny Campbell; 6 Louis Jouffret; 7 Dom Brambani; 8 Adam Gledhill; 9 Alistair Leak; 15 Toby Everett; 12 Jack Downs; 11 Dane Manning; 24 Paul Brearley. Subs (all used): 16 Michael Ward; 13 James Brown; 27 Reiss Butterworth; 25 Lewis Bienek.
**Tries:** Brearley (26), Tomlinson (32), Brown (63), Wood (75); **Goals:** Jouffret 4/4.
**EAGLES:** 1 Josh Guzdek; 2 Ryan Millar; 27 Jacob Ogden; 4 Jason Crookes; 5 Ben Blackmore; 6 Pat Walker; 7 Anthony Thackeray; 8 Pat Moran; 9 James Davey; 11 Brad Knowles; 29 Ben Hellewell; 12 Joel Farrell; 13 Aaron Brown. Subs (all used): 32 James Meadows; 15 Olly Davies; 21 Blake Broadbent; 22 Paddy Burns.
**Tries:** Knowles (5, 71), Crookes (15), Moran (19, 73), Walker (44), Brown (51), Broadbent (54), Davies (69);
**Goals:** Walker 9/9.
**Rugby Leaguer & League Express Men of the Match:**
*Bulldogs:* James Brown; *Eagles:* James Meadows.
**Penalty count:** 2-6; **Half-time:** 12-18;
**Referee:** Jack Smith; **Attendance:** 2,798.

**FEATHERSTONE ROVERS 22 WIDNES VIKINGS 4**

**ROVERS:** 33 Ashton Golding; 5 Conor Carey; 4 Josh Hardcastle; 32 Alex Sutcliffe; 2 Luke Briscoe; 38 Dane Chisholm; 40 Tom Holmes; 8 Scott Wheeldon; 9 Cameron King; 39 Dale Ferguson; 12 Brad Day; 28 Josh Walters; 13 James Lockwood. Subs (all used): 23 Makahesi Makatoa; 29 Jack Ormondroyd; 15 Luke Cooper; 17 James Harrison.
**Tries:** Sutcliffe (8, 80), Carey (46), Holmes (71);
**Goals:** Chisholm 3/5.
**VIKINGS:** 5 Jack Owens; 29 Jayden Hatton; 4 Anthony Gelling; 24 Keanan Brand; 2 Ryan Ince; 6 Danny Craven; 21 Joe Lyons; 13 Hep Cahill; 15 Jordan Johnstone; 8 Jay Chapelhow; 17 Sam Wilde; 12 Chris Dean; 16 MacGraff Leuluai. Subs (all used): 18 Ted Chapelhow; 34 Josh Ganson; 26 Dan Norman; 19 Brad Walker.
**Try:** Ince (60); **Goals:** Owens 0/1.
**Rugby Leaguer & League Express Men of the Match:**
*Rovers:* Ashton Golding; *Vikings:* Jack Owens.
**Penalty count:** 8-9; **Half-time:** 8-0;
**Referee:** Michael Mannifield; **Attendance:** 2,380.

**LEIGH CENTURIONS 52 BRADFORD BULLS 20**

**CENTURIONS:** 1 Gregg McNally; 31 Matthew Costello; 3 Iain Thornley; 25 Liam Forsyth; 5 Stefan Marsh; 6 Martyn Ridyard; 7 Josh Woods; 26 Luke Douglas; 9 Micky Higham; 10 Sam Brooks; 30 Joe Batchelor; 12 Andy Thornley; 15 Joe Cator. Subs (all used): 27 Liam Hood; 22 Jordan Thompson; 24 Gareth Hock; 13 Luke Adamson.
**Tries:** I Thornley (10, 80), Costello (20), McNally (39, 68), A Thornley (58), Forsyth (70, 77); **Goals:** Ridyard 10/12.
**Sin bin:** Brooks (13) - dissent;
McNally (44) - professional foul.
**BULLS:** 2 Ethan Ryan; 22 Dalton Grant; 4 Ashley Gibson; 26 Ross Oakes; 24 David Foggin-Johnston; 9 Matty Wildie; 14 Jordan Lilley; 8 Liam Kirk; 18 Sam Hallas; 10 Steve Crossley; 11 Matt Garside; 29 Matthew Storton; 12 Elliot Minchella. Subs (all used): 21 George Flanagan; 19 Jon Magrin; 13 Mikey Wood; 17 Ross Peltier.
**Tries:** Wildie (29), Flanagan (52), Storton (79);
**Goals:** Lilley 4/4.
**Rugby Leaguer & League Express Men of the Match:**
*Centurions:* Luke Douglas; *Bulls:* Matty Wildie.
**Penalty count:** 9-12; **Half-time:** 22-8;
**Referee:** Ben Thaler; **Attendance:** 4,180.

**YORK CITY KNIGHTS 60 ROCHDALE HORNETS 0**

**CITY KNIGHTS:** 1 Matty Marsh; 23 Jason Bass; 3 Liam Salter; 30 Junior Vaivai; 20 Perry Whiteley; 38 Liam Harris; 7 Connor Robinson; 15 Graeme Horne; 9 Will Jubb; 10 Jack Teanby; 11 Josh Jordan-Roberts; 12 Sam Scott; 13 Tim Spears. Subs (all used): 40 Andy Ellis; 8 Ronan Dixon; 36 Tyler Dupree; 22 Marcus Stock.
**Tries:** Salter (7), Marsh (17, 29), Whiteley (32, 73, 79), Stock (39), Harris (42), Vaivai (56), Teanby (61), S Scott (75); **Goals:** Robinson 8/11.
**HORNETS:** 7 Dan Abram; 2 Shaun Ainscough; 26 Daley Williams; 5 James Worthington; 24 Brandon Wood; 19 Oscar Thomas; 29 Izaac Farrell; 30 Adam Lawton; 6 Scott Moore; 8 Callum Marriott; 18 Zac Baker; 16 Mike Weldon; 27 Ellis Robson. Subs (all used): 9 Ben Moores; 11 Lee Mitchell; 3 Seta Tala; 28 Aidy Gleeson.
**Rugby Leaguer & League Express Men of the Match:**
*City Knights:* Junior Vaivai; *Hornets:* Dan Abram.
**Penalty count:** 7-6; **Half-time:** 26-0;
**Referee:** Aaron Moore; **Attendance:** 1,661.

## ROUND 18

*Friday 21st June 2019*

**SHEFFIELD EAGLES 46 ROCHDALE HORNETS 24**

**EAGLES:** 1 Josh Guzdek; 2 Ryan Millar; 27 Jacob Ogden; 4 Jason Crookes; 5 Ben Blackmore; 32 James Meadows; 6 Pat Walker; 8 Pat Moran; 9 James Davey; 11 Brad Knowles; 12 Joel Farrell; 15 Olly Davies; 13 Aaron Brown. Subs (all used): 17 Shaun Pick; 22 Paddy Burns; 7 Anthony Thackeray; 21 Blake Broadbent.
**Tries:** Millar (15, 51, 79), Davies (30), Meadows (39, 60), Thackeray (45), Moran (75); **Goals:** Walker 4/5, Guzdek 3/3.
**Sin bin:** Meadows (6) - interference.
**HORNETS:** 7 Dan Abram; 1 Dec Kay; 26 Daley Williams; 5 James Worthington; 24 Brandon Wood; 19 Oscar Thomas; 29 Izaac Farrell; 8 Callum Marriott; 22 Callum Wood; 11 Lee Mitchell; 18 Zac Baker; 25 Kyle Shelford; 27 Ellis Robson. Subs (all used): 12 Ellis Gillam; 28 Aidy Gleeson; 30 Adam Lawton; 14 Lewis Sheridan.
**Tries:** Abram (3), Marriott (34, 77), B Wood (53);
**Goals:** Abram 4/4.
**Rugby Leaguer & League Express Men of the Match:**
*Eagles:* Ryan Millar; *Hornets:* Callum Marriott.
**Penalty count:** 12-6; **Half-time:** 16-12;
**Referee:** Cameron Worsley; **Attendance:** 543.

**WIDNES VIKINGS 28 BATLEY BULLDOGS 22**

**VIKINGS:** 25 Lloyd Roby; 35 Joe Edge; 24 Keanan Brand; 4 Anthony Gelling; 29 Jayden Hatton; 7 Tom Gilmore; 21 Joe Lyons; 11 Harrison Hansen; 34 Josh Ganson; 8 Jay Chapelhow; 17 Sam Wilde; 12 Chris Dean; 19 Brad Walker. Subs (all used): 26 Dan Norman; 31 Jacob Dugdale; 16 MacGraff Leuluai; 18 Ted Chapelhow.
**Tries:** Gelling (15), Norman (40), Hatton (42), Dean (52), J Chapelhow (70); **Goals:** Edge 4/5.
**BULLDOGS:** 1 Dave Scott; 20 Niall Walker; 3 Sam Smeaton; 28 Jack Broadbent; 5 Johnny Campbell; 6 Louis Jouffret; 7 Dom Brambani; 17 Tyler Dickinson; 27 Reiss Butterworth; 10 Tom Lillycrop; 12 Jack Downs; 24 Paul Brearley; 11 Dane Manning. Subs (all used): 19 Alex Bretherton; 25 Lewis Bienek; 16 Michael Ward; 22 Sam Wood.
**Tries:** Downs (30), Walker (34, 78), Dickinson (65);
**Goals:** Jouffret 3/4.
**Rugby Leaguer & League Express Men of the Match:**
*Vikings:* Jacob Dugdale; *Bulldogs:* Niall Walker.
**Penalty count:** 9-3; **Half-time:** 10-12;
**Referee:** Gareth Hewer; **Attendance:** 3,742.

*Saturday 22nd June 2019*

**TORONTO WOLFPACK 28 TOULOUSE OLYMPIQUE 16**

**WOLFPACK:** 1 Gareth O'Brien; 5 Liam Kay; 22 Greg Worthington; 4 Ricky Leutele; 2 Matty Russell; 6 Joe Mellor; 7 Josh McCrone; 21 Anthony Mullally; 14 Andy Ackers; 8 Adam Sidlow; 11 Andrew Dixon; 12 Bodene Thompson; 13 Jon Wilkin. Subs (all used): 17 Blake Wallace; 15 Darcy Lussick; 16 Tom Olbison; 27 Hakim Miloudi.
**Tries:** Worthington (5, 34), Russell (27), Ackers (77);
**Goals:** O'Brien 6/7.
**OLYMPIQUE:** 30 William Barthau; 5 Paul Marcon; 11 Con Mika; 19 James Bell; 2 Tony Maurel; 9 Anthony Marion; 7 Stan Robin; 15 Ben Evans; 14 Dean Parata; 17 Paterika Vaivai; 22 Brenden Santi; 10 Joe Bretherton; 18 Clement Boyer. Subs (all used): 24 Justin Bouscayrol; 21 Jordan Dezaria; 16 Tyla Hepi; 23 Justin Sangare.
**Tries:** Boyer (17), Barthau (47), Santi (65);
**Goals:** Barthau 2/3.
**Rugby Leaguer & League Express Men of the Match:**
*Wolfpack:* Greg Worthington; *Olympique:* William Barthau.
**Penalty count:** 16-10; **Half-time:** 18-6;
**Referee:** Greg Dolan; **Attendance:** 7,742.

*Sunday 23rd June 2019*

**BRADFORD BULLS 24 HALIFAX 20**

**BULLS:** 1 Brandon Pickersgill; 2 Ethan Ryan; 3 Jake Webster; 26 Ross Oakes; 5 Jy Hitchcox; 6 Joe Keyes; 14 Jordan Lilley; 19 Jon Magrin; 18 Sam Hallas; 10 Steve Crossley; 11 Matt Garside; 25 Connor Farrell; 12 Elliot Minchella. Subs (all used): 21 George Flanagan; 13 Mikey Wood; 17 Ross Peltier; 29 Matthew Storton.
**Tries:** Ryan (3), Minchella (27), Hitchcox (33, 42);
**Goals:** Keyes 4/6.
**Sin bin:** Flanagan (59) - tripping.
**HALIFAX:** 30 Scott Grix; 2 Shaun Robinson; 3 Steve Tyrer; 20 James Saltonstall; 5 Will Sharp; 6 Scott Murrell; 1 Quentin Laulu-Togaga'e; 17 Ben Kavanagh; 14 Brandon Moore; 18 Elliot Morris; 25 Liam Cooper; 4 Chester Butler; 35 Adam Tangata. Subs (all used): 7 Ben Johnston; 34 Mitch Clark; 10 Jacob Fairbank; 16 Kevin Larroyer.
**Tries:** Robinson (19), Moore (64), Laulu-Togaga'e (66);
**Goals:** Tyrer 4/4.
**Rugby Leaguer & League Express Men of the Match:**
*Bulls:* Joe Keyes; *Halifax:* Jacob Fairbank.
**Penalty count:** 8-6; **Half-time:** 20-8;
**Referee:** Jack Smith; **Attendance:** 5,203.

**DEWSBURY RAMS 0 LEIGH CENTURIONS 40**

**RAMS:** 42 Joe Martin; 23 Rob Worrincy; 32 Owen Trout; 4 Adam Ryder; 2 Andy Gabriel; 6 Paul Sykes; 38 Liam Finn; 34 Chris Annakin; 9 Robbie Ward; 8 Jode Sheriffe; 11 Lucas Walshaw; 12 Michael Knowles; 13 Kyle Trout. Subs (all used): 18 Sam Day; 10 Toby Richardson; 19 Daniel Igbinedion; 30 Tom Garratt.
**Sin bin:** Gabriel (70) - dissent.
**CENTURIONS:** 1 Gregg McNally; 19 Mitch Cox; 3 Iain Thornley; 25 Liam Forsyth; 5 Stefan Marsh; 6 Martyn Ridyard; 7 Josh Woods; 26 Luke Douglas; 9 Micky Higham; 13 Luke Adamson; 30 Cory Paterson; 12 Andy Thornley; 22 Jordan Thompson. Subs (all used): 27 Liam Hood; 15 Joe Cator; 24 Gareth Hock; 29 Jake Emmitt.
**Tries:** Forsyth (3, 60), Douglas (8, 76), Marsh (23, 35), Cox (72); **Goals:** Ridyard 6/8.
**Rugby Leaguer & League Express Men of the Match:**
*Rams:* Adam Ryder; *Centurions:* Josh Woods.
**Penalty count:** 7-11; **Half-time:** 0-24;
**Referee:** Billy Pearson; **Attendance:** 1,668.

**FEATHERSTONE ROVERS 16 BARROW RAIDERS 38**

**ROVERS:** 1 Calum Turner; 5 Conor Carey; 4 Josh Hardcastle; 32 Alex Sutcliffe; 25 Jack Render; 38 Dane Chisholm; 40 Tom Holmes; 8 Scott Wheeldon; 9 Cameron King; 23 Makahesi Makatoa; 12 Brad Day; 28 Josh Walters; 13 James Lockwood. Subs (all used): 41 Corey Johnson; 29 Jack Ormondroyd; 15 Luke Cooper; 17 James Harrison.
**Tries:** Chisholm (10), Sutcliffe (33, 49); **Goals:** Chisholm 2/3.
**RAIDERS:** 18 Luke Cresswell; 1 Theerapol Ritson; 4 Jake Spedding; 2 Stargroth Amean; 5 Deon Cross; 6 Jamie Dallimore; 24 Jake Carter; 28 Josh Johnson; 14 Wartovo Puara; 29 Alec Susino; 19 Danny Morrow; 25 Jordan Walne; 15 Dan Toal. Subs (all used): - Ben White; 8 Tom Walker; 16 Glenn Riley; 11 Jono Smith.
**Tries:** Amean (4, 63), Dallimore (18), Morrow (21), Cresswell (67, 72, 77); **Goals:** Dallimore 5/7.
**Rugby Leaguer & League Express Men of the Match:**
*Rovers:* Alex Sutcliffe; *Raiders:* Wartovo Puara.
**Penalty count:** 8-7; **Half-time:** 10-16;
**Referee:** Aaron Moore; **Attendance:** 1,928.

**SWINTON LIONS 12 YORK CITY KNIGHTS 26**

**LIONS:** 25 Matty Ashton; 2 Mike Butt; 3 Rhodri Lloyd; 32 Craig Mullen; 28 Richard Lepori; 1 Jack Hansen; 7 Rob Fairclough; 8 Gavin Bennion; 9 Luke Waterworth; 10 Lewis Hatton; 22 Frankie Halton; 33 Jack Wells; 16 Paddy Jones. Subs (all used): 14 Billy Brickhill; 35 Scott Moore; 36 Liam Byrne; 31 Samy Kibula.
**Tries:** Ashton (71), Waterworth (77); **Goals:** Hansen 2/2.
**CITY KNIGHTS:** 1 Matty Marsh; 23 Jason Bass; 3 Liam Salter; 41 Cameron Scott; 20 Perry Whiteley; 38 Liam Harris; 7 Connor Robinson; 10 Jack Teanby; 9 Will Jubb; 15 Graeme Horne; 11 Josh Jordan-Roberts; 12 Sam Scott; 13 Tim Spears. Subs (all used): 40 Andy Ellis; 8 Ronan Dixon; 22 Marcus Stock; 37 Jordan Baldwinson.
**Tries:** C Scott (14), Stock (58), Horne (63), Salter (69);
**Goals:** Robinson 5/6.
**Rugby Leaguer & League Express Men of the Match:**
*Lions:* Samy Kibula; *City Knights:* Connor Robinson.
**Penalty count:** 12-8; **Half-time:** 0-8;
**Referee:** Michael Mannifield; **Attendance:** 976.

*Championship 2019 - Round by Round*

## ROUND 19

*Sunday 30th June 2019*

### BARROW RAIDERS 6 TOULOUSE OLYMPIQUE 36

**RAIDERS:** 18 Luke Cresswell; 1 Theerapol Ritson; 2 Stargroth Amean; 35 Liam Paisley; 5 Deon Cross; 6 Jamie Dallimore; 34 Ben White; 28 Josh Johnson; 14 Wartovo Puara; 29 Alec Susino; 11 Jono Smith; 19 Danny Morrow; 13 Martin Aspinwall. Subs (all used): 25 Jordan Walne; 8 Tom Walker; 24 Jake Carter; 15 Dan Toal.
**Try:** Cresswell (24); **Goals:** Dallimore 1/1.
**Sin bin:** D Toal (37) - fighting.
**OLYMPIQUE:** 30 William Barthau; 5 Paul Marcon; 25 Mathieu Jussaume; 19 James Bell; 2 Tony Maurel; 6 Johnathon Ford; 7 Stan Robin; 8 Maxime Puech; 9 Anthony Marion; 17 Paterika Vaivai; 11 Con Mika; 10 Joe Bretherton; 22 Brenden Santi. Subs (all used): 14 Dean Parata; 18 Clement Boyer; 16 Tyla Hepi; 23 Justine Sangare.
**Tries:** Maurel (8, 10), Hepi (28), Bretherton (35), Mika (39), Bell (43), P Vaivai (66); **Goals:** Barthau 4/7.
**Sin bin:** Hepi (37) - fighting.
**Rugby Leaguer & League Express Men of the Match:** *Raiders:* Josh Johnson; *Olympique:* Stan Robin.
**Penalty count:** 7-9; **Half-time:** 6-24;
**Referee:** Tom Grant; **Attendance:** 1,422.

### BATLEY BULLDOGS 10 TORONTO WOLFPACK 40

**BULLDOGS:** 1 Dave Scott; 20 Niall Walker; 22 Sam Wood; 28 Jack Broadbent; 23 Keenen Tomlinson; 6 Louis Jouffret; 14 Danny Yates; 8 Adam Gledhill; 9 Alistair Leak; 17 Tyler Dickinson; 12 Jack Downs; 24 Paul Brearley; 11 Dane Manning. Subs (all used): 13 James Brown; 19 Alex Bretherton; 21 Jo Taira; 27 Reiss Butterworth.
**Tries:** Jouffret (29), Walker (50); **Goals:** Jouffret 1/2.
**WOLFPACK:** 1 Gareth O'Brien; 5 Liam Kay; 22 Greg Worthington; 4 Ricky Leutele; 2 Matty Russell; 17 Blake Wallace; 7 Josh McCrone; 16 Tom Olbison; 14 Andy Ackers; 21 Anthony Mullally; 11 Andrew Dixon; 12 Bodene Thompson; 13 Jon Wilkin. Subs (all used): 6 Joe Mellor; 10 Ashton Sims; 18 Gadwin Springer; 27 Hakim Miloudi.
**Tries:** Russell (4, 25), Leutele (9, 75), O'Brien (34), Ackers (42, 60); **Goals:** O'Brien 5/5, Wallace 1/1, Miloudi 0/1.
**Rugby Leaguer & League Express Men of the Match:** *Bulldogs:* Louis Jouffret; *Wolfpack:* Andy Ackers.
**Penalty count:** 7-7; **Half-time:** 6-24;
**Referee:** Cameron Worsley; **Attendance:** 894.

### BRADFORD BULLS 62 WIDNES VIKINGS 0

**BULLS:** 1 Brandon Pickersgill; 2 Ethan Ryan; 26 Ross Oakes; 3 Jake Webster; 5 Jy Hitchcox; 6 Joe Keyes; 14 Jordan Lilley; 19 Jon Magrin; 18 Sam Hallas; 8 Liam Kirk; 11 Matt Garside; 25 Connor Farrell; 12 Elliot Minchella. Subs (all used): 21 George Flanagan; 13 Mikey Wood; 15 Callum Bustin; 17 Ross Peltier.
**Tries:** Keyes (6, 23, 54), Minchella (9, 66, 70), Hitchcox (27), Pickersgill (31), Flanagan (35, 61), Oakes (42);
**Goals:** Keyes 9/11.
**VIKINGS:** 5 Jack Owens; 25 Lloyd Roby; 24 Keanan Brand; 4 Anthony Gelling; 35 Joe Edge; 6 Danny Craven; 21 Joe Lyons; 11 Harrison Hansen; 34 Josh Ganson; 18 Ted Chapelhow; 17 Sam Wilde; 19 Brad Walker; 15 Jordan Johnstone. Subs (all used): 26 Dan Norman; 31 Jacob Dugdale; 20 Owen Farnworth; 16 MacGraff Leuluai.
**Sin bin:** Craven (26) - delaying restart.
**Rugby Leaguer & League Express Men of the Match:** *Bulls:* Joe Keyes; *Vikings:* Harrison Hansen.
**Penalty count:** 8-3; **Half-time:** 34-0;
**Referee:** Billy Pearson; **Attendance:** 3,895.

### HALIFAX 18 FEATHERSTONE ROVERS 24

**HALIFAX:** 30 Scott Grix; 2 Shaun Robinson; 3 Steve Tyrer; 20 James Saltonstall; 5 Will Sharp; 1 Quentin Laulu-Togaga'e; 7 Ben Johnston; 17 Ben Kavanagh; 9 Ben Kaye; 18 Elliot Morris; 12 Ed Barber; 25 Liam Cooper; 35 Adam Tangata. Subs (all used): 8 Dan Fleming; 10 Jacob Fairbank; 16 Kevin Larroyer; 32 Jacques O'Neill.
**Tries:** Saltonstall (25), Tyrer (60, 62); **Goals:** Tyrer 3/3.
**ROVERS:** 1 Calum Turner; 44 Will Dagger; 4 Josh Hardcastle; 5 Conor Carey; 2 Luke Briscoe; 38 Dane Chisholm; 37 Callum McLelland; 8 Scott Wheeldon; 9 Cameron King; 29 Jack Ormondroyd; 12 Brad Day; 28 Josh Walters; 13 James Lockwood. Subs: 3 Thompson Teteh (not used); 15 Luke Cooper; 16 Danny Maskill (not used); 23 Makahesi Makatoa.
**Tries:** Day (4), King (34), Briscoe (56), Hardcastle (74);
**Goals:** Chisholm 4/5.
**Rugby Leaguer & League Express Men of the Match:** *Halifax:* Jacques O'Neill; *Rovers:* Brad Day.
**Penalty count:** 5-11; **Half-time:** 6-14;
**Referee:** Gareth Hewer; **Attendance:** 1,888.

### ROCHDALE HORNETS 28 SWINTON LIONS 36

**HORNETS:** 7 Dan Abram; 2 Shaun Ainscough; 23 Jordan Case; 5 James Worthington; 24 Brandon Wood; 19 Oscar Thomas; 29 Izaac Farrell; 8 Callum Marriott; 22 Callum Wood; 30 Adam Lawton; 18 Zac Baker; 16 Mike Weldon; 25 Kyle Shelford. Subs (all used): 28 Aidy Gleeson; 14 Lewis Sheridan; 11 Lee Mitchell; 6 Pierre-Louis Bourrel.
**Tries:** Ainscough (13), Lawton (17), Bourrel (51, 63), B Wood (77); **Goals:** Abram 4/5.
**LIONS:** 25 Matty Ashton; 2 Mike Butt; 32 Craig Mullen; 3 Rhodri Lloyd; 28 Richard Lepori; 1 Jack Hansen; 7 Rob Fairclough; 8 Gavin Bennion; 9 Luke Waterworth; 16 Paddy Jones; 33 Jack Wells; 22 Frankie Halton; 31 Liam Byrne. Subs (all used): 14 Billy Brickhill; 35 Samy Kibula; 10 Lewis Hatton; 29 Scott Moore.
**Tries:** Moore (29), Wells (36), Ashton (39, 41), Butt (58, 79), Hansen (72); **Goals:** Hansen 4/7.
**Sin bin:** Butt (3) - trip; Moore (61) - high tackle.
**Rugby Leaguer & League Express Men of the Match:** *Hornets:* Callum Marriott; *Lions:* Matty Ashton.
**Penalty count:** 6-4; **Half-time:** 10-14;
**Referee:** Liam Moore; **Attendance:** 549 *(at Mayfield Sports Centre).*

### SHEFFIELD EAGLES 18 LEIGH CENTURIONS 22

**EAGLES:** 1 Josh Guzdek; 2 Ryan Millar; 27 Jacob Ogden; 4 Jason Crookes; 5 Ben Blackmore; 6 Pat Walker; 7 Anthony Thackeray; 8 Pat Moran; 9 James Davey; 11 Brad Knowles; 12 Joel Farrell; 15 Olly Davies; 13 Aaron Brown. Subs (all used): 32 James Meadows; 22 Paddy Burns; 31 Nathan Mason; 30 Sadiq Adebiyi.
**Tries:** Thackeray (30), Blackmore (57, 75), Millar (68);
**Goals:** Walker 1/2, Meadows 0/2.
**Dismissal:** Meadows (80) - dissent.
**CENTURIONS:** 35 Ryan Brierley; 40 Matthew Costello; 3 Iain Thornley; 41 Josh Simm; 25 Liam Forsyth; 6 Martyn Ridyard; 7 Josh Woods; 8 Tom Spencer; 9 Micky Higham; 13 Luke Adamson; 11 Toby Adamson; 12 Andy Thornley; 15 Joe Cator. Subs (all used): 27 Liam Hood; 30 Cory Paterson; 22 Jordan Thompson; 24 Gareth Hock.
**Tries:** Forsyth (26, 51), Brierley (34), Ridyard (63);
**Goals:** Ridyard 3/4.
**Rugby Leaguer & League Express Men of the Match:** *Eagles:* Ryan Millar; *Centurions:* Liam Forsyth.
**Penalty count:** 10-4; **Half-time:** 6-10;
**Referee:** Michael Mannifield; **Attendance:** 1,082.

### YORK CITY KNIGHTS 24 DEWSBURY RAMS 21

**CITY KNIGHTS:** 1 Matty Marsh; 39 Will Oakes; 3 Liam Salter; 41 Cameron Scott; 20 Perry Whiteley; 38 Liam Harris; 7 Connor Robinson; 10 Jack Teanby; 14 Harry Carter; 15 Graeme Horne; 4 Brad Hey; 12 Sam Scott; 13 Tim Spears. Subs (all used): 26 Kriss Brining; 8 Ronan Dixon; 16 Jack Blagbrough; 22 Marcus Stock.
**Tries:** Brining (35), C Scott (38), Harris (45), Marsh (79);
**Goals:** Robinson 3/3, Harris 1/1, Oakes 0/1.
**Dismissal:** Dixon (48) - high tackle on Gabriel.
**Sin bin:** Spears (15) - trip;
S Scott (20) - dangerous challenge on O Trout.
**RAMS:** 42 Joe Martin; 23 Rob Worrincy; 32 Owen Trout; 4 Adam Ryder; 2 Andy Gabriel; 6 Paul Sykes; 38 Liam Finn; 19 Daniel Igbinedion; 9 Robbie Ward; 30 Tom Garratt; 34 Daniel Waite-Pullan; 12 Michael Knowles; 13 Kyle Trout. Subs (all used): 22 Danny King; 36 Nyle Flynn; 33 Frazer Morris; 17 Martyn Reilly.
**Tries:** Finn (4), Worrincy (13, 66), O Trout (22);
**Goals:** Sykes 1/3, Finn 1/1; **Field goal:** Sykes (73).
**Rugby Leaguer & League Express Men of the Match:** *City Knights:* Liam Harris; *Rams:* Rob Worrincy.
**Penalty count:** 9-4; **Half-time:** 14-14;
**Referee:** Matt Rossleigh; **Attendance:** 1,338.

## ROUND 20

*Friday 5th July 2019*

### SHEFFIELD EAGLES 16 YORK CITY KNIGHTS 23

**EAGLES:** 1 Josh Guzdek; 2 Ryan Millar; 27 Jacob Ogden; 4 Jason Crookes; 5 Ben Blackmore; 6 Pat Walker; 7 Anthony Thackeray; 11 Brad Knowles; 9 James Davey; 22 Paddy Burns; 12 Joel Farrell; 15 Olly Davies; 13 Aaron Brown. Subs (all used): 32 James Meadows; 21 Blake Broadbent; 31 Nathan Mason; 19 Sonny Esslemont.
**Tries:** Blackmore (40), Thackeray (54), Davies (70);
**Goals:** Walker 2/3.
**CITY KNIGHTS:** 23 Jason Bass; 39 Will Oakes; 4 Brad Hey; 41 Cameron Scott; 20 Perry Whiteley; 38 Liam Harris; 7 Connor Robinson; 10 Jack Teanby; 9 Will Jubb; 15 Graeme Horne; 11 Josh Jordan-Roberts; 3 Liam Salter; 13 Tim Spears. Subs (all used): 26 Kriss Brining; 37 Jordan Baldwinson; 16 Jack Blagbrough; 22 Marcus Stock.
**Tries:** Bass (32), C Scott (43), Stock (48), Oakes (67);
**Goals:** Robinson 3/4; **Field goal:** Robinson (77).
**Rugby Leaguer & League Express Men of the Match:** *Eagles:* Olly Davies; *City Knights:* Jason Bass.
**Penalty count:** 5-6; **Half-time:** 6-6;
**Referee:** Aaron Moore; **Attendance:** 793.

*Saturday 6th July 2019*

### TORONTO WOLFPACK 34 HALIFAX 12

**WOLFPACK:** 1 Gareth O'Brien; 5 Liam Kay; 24 Nick Rawsthorne; 4 Ricky Leutele; 2 Matty Russell; 6 Joe Mellor; 7 Josh McCrone; 10 Ashton Sims; 9 Bob Beswick; 21 Anthony Mullally; 11 Andrew Dixon; 12 Bodene Thompson; 13 Jon Wilkin. Subs (all used): 14 Andy Ackers; 15 Darcy Lussick; 18 Gadwin Springer; 16 Tom Olbison.
**Tries:** Kay (13, 28), Ackers (44), O'Brien (53, 57), Olbison (77); **Goals:** O'Brien 5/6.
**Sin bin:** Leutele (30) - dangerous challenge.
**HALIFAX:** 30 Scott Grix; 5 Will Sharp; 20 James Saltonstall; 3 Steve Tyrer; 2 Shaun Robinson; 1 Quentin Laulu-Togaga'e; 7 Ben Johnston; 8 Dan Fleming; 9 Ben Kaye; 18 Elliot Morris; 12 Ed Barber; 25 Liam Cooper; 16 Kevin Larroyer. Subs (all used): 14 Brandon Moore; 17 Ben Kavanagh; 22 Connor Davies; 27 Reece Chapman-Smith.
**Tries:** Cooper (63), Johnston (66); **Goals:** Tyrer 2/2.
**Rugby Leaguer & League Express Men of the Match:** *Wolfpack:* Gareth O'Brien; *Halifax:* Liam Cooper.
**Penalty count:** 11-9; **Half-time:** 10-0;
**Referee:** Michael Mannifield; **Attendance:** 6,749.

### TOULOUSE OLYMPIQUE 24 BRADFORD BULLS 26

**OLYMPIQUE:** 1 Mark Kheirallah; 2 Tony Maurel; 19 James Bell; 25 Mathieu Jussaume; 4 Gavin Marguerite; 7 Stan Robin; 6 Johnathon Ford; 8 Maxime Puech; 9 Anthony Marion; 17 Paterika Vaivai; 11 Con Mika; 10 Joe Bretherton; 22 Brenden Santi. Subs (all used): 14 Dean Parata; 23 Justin Sangare; 18 Clement Boyer; 16 Tyla Hepi.
**Tries:** Bretherton (23), Marion (26), Robin (29), Marguerite (61); **Goals:** Kheirallah 4/5.
**BULLS:** 1 Brandon Pickersgill; 2 Ethan Ryan; 26 Ross Oakes; 3 Jake Webster; 5 Jy Hitchcox; 6 Joe Keyes; 14 Jordan Lilley; 8 Liam Kirk; 18 Sam Hallas; 19 Jon Magrin; 11 Matt Garside; 25 Connor Farrell; 12 Elliot Minchella. Subs (all used): 15 Callum Bustin; 9 Matty Wildie; 13 Mikey Wood; 17 Ross Peltier.
**Tries:** Keyes (8), Webster (14), Oakes (46), Pickersgill (56), Wildie (70); **Goals:** Keyes 3/5.
**Rugby Leaguer & League Express Men of the Match:** *Olympique:* Mark Kheirallah; *Bulls:* Jordan Lilley.
**Penalty count:** 5-6; **Half-time:** 18-8;
**Referee:** Cameron Worsley; **Attendance:** 3,560.

*Sunday 7th July 2019*

### DEWSBURY RAMS 40 BARROW RAIDERS 26

**RAMS:** 42 Joe Martin; 23 Rob Worrincy; 32 Owen Trout; 4 Adam Ryder; 36 Conor McGrath; 6 Paul Sykes; 38 Liam Finn; 8 Jode Sheriffe; 43 Dom Speakman; 19 Daniel Igbinedion; 34 Daniel Waite-Pullan; 12 Michael Knowles; 13 Kyle Trout. Subs (all used): 18 Sam Day; 11 Lucas Walshaw; 17 Martyn Reilly; 30 Tom Garratt.
**Tries:** McGrath (19, 76), Speakman (23), O Trout (51), Ryder (54), Sykes (63), Knowles (68);
**Goals:** Sykes 3/5, Finn 3/3.
**RAIDERS:** 18 Luke Cresswell; 1 Theerapol Ritson; 12 Jarrad Stack; 2 Stargroth Amean; 5 Deon Cross; 6 Jamie Dallimore; 34 Ben White; 28 Josh Johnson; 14 Wartovo Puara; 29 Alec Susino; 11 Jono Smith; 19 Danny Morrow; 25 Jordan Walne. Subs (all used): 22 Ryan Johnston; 13 Martin Aspinwall; 8 Tom Walker; 15 Dan Toal.
**Tries:** Puara (4), Cross (9), Ritson (42, 73);
**Goals:** Dallimore 5/6.
**Rugby Leaguer & League Express Men of the Match:** *Rams:* Paul Sykes; *Raiders:* Theerapol Ritson.
**Penalty count:** 6-7; **Half-time:** 10-12;
**Referee:** Jack Smith; **Attendance:** 856.

### FEATHERSTONE ROVERS 24 LEIGH CENTURIONS 20

**ROVERS:** 33 Ashton Golding; 44 Will Dagger; 5 Conor Carey; 4 Josh Hardcastle; 2 Luke Briscoe; 34 Ben Reynolds; 38 Dane Chisholm; 23 Makahesi Makatoa; 10 Jack Bussey; 42 Wellington Albert; 12 Brad Day; 28 Josh Walters; 13 James Lockwood. Subs (all used): 16 Danny Maskill; 29 Jack Ormondroyd; 15 Luke Cooper; 17 James Harrison.
**Tries:** Day (8), Briscoe (29), Chisholm (42), Walters (57);
**Goals:** Chisholm 3/3, Reynolds 1/1.
**CENTURIONS:** 1 Gregg McNally; 25 Liam Forsyth; 3 Iain Thornley; 40 Matthew Costello; 5 Stefan Marsh; 6 Martyn Ridyard; 7 Josh Woods; 26 Luke Douglas; 9 Micky Higham; 22 Jordan Thompson; 11 Toby Adamson; 30 Cory Paterson; 13 Luke Adamson. Subs (all used): 15 Joe Cator; 29 Jake Emmitt; 24 Gareth Hock; 27 Liam Hood.
**Tries:** Paterson (3, 38), Forsyth (19, 78); **Goals:** Ridyard 2/4.

Barrow's Liam Paisley wrapped up by the Leigh defence

**Rugby Leaguer & League Express Men of the Match:**
*Rovers:* Brad Day; *Centurions:* Cory Paterson.
**Penalty count:** 6-8; **Half-time:** 12-14;
**Referee:** Scott Mikalauskas; **Attendance:** 3,104.

### SWINTON LIONS 20 BATLEY BULLDOGS 18

**LIONS:** 1 Jack Hansen; 2 Mike Butt; 3 Rhodri Lloyd; 32 Craig Mullen; 25 Matty Ashton; - Jake Shorrocks; 7 Rob Fairclough; 8 Gavin Bennion; 9 Luke Waterworth; 10 Lewis Hatton; 33 Jack Wells; 22 Frankie Halton; 16 Paddy Jones. Subs (all used): 14 Billy Brickhill; 36 Liam Byrne; 31 Samy Kibula; 35 Scott Moore.
**Tries:** Lloyd (22), Bennion (62), Hatton (70);
**Goals:** Hansen 4/4.
**Sin bin:** Moore (45) - dangerous contact on Taira.
**BULLDOGS:** 1 Dave Scott; 20 Niall Walker; 3 Sam Smeaton; 28 Jack Broadbent; 4 Lewis Galbraith; 6 Louis Jouffret; 14 Danny Yates; 17 Tyler Dickinson; 9 Alistair Leak; 13 James Brown; 24 Paul Brearley; 19 Alex Bretherton; 11 Dane Manning. Subs (all used): 8 Adam Gledhill; 21 Jo Taira; 23 Keenen Tomlinson; 16 Michael Ward.
**Tries:** Brearley (35), Gledhill (39), Walker (51);
**Goals:** Jouffret 3/4.
**Sin bin:** Manning (4) - dangerous challenge on P Jones.
**Rugby Leaguer & League Express Men of the Match:**
*Lions:* Gavin Bennion; *Bulldogs:* Louis Jouffret.
**Penalty count:** 7-8; **Half-time:** 8-12;
**Referee:** Tom Grant; **Attendance:** 888.

### WIDNES VIKINGS 40 ROCHDALE HORNETS 12

**VIKINGS:** 5 Jack Owens; 1 Olly Ashall-Bott; 25 Lloyd Roby; 12 Chris Dean; 36 Patrick Ah Van; 6 Danny Craven; 7 Tom Gilmore; 8 Jay Chapelhow; 15 Jordan Johnstone; 18 Ted Chapelhow; 17 Sam Wilde; 11 Harrison Hansen; 13 Hep Cahill. Subs (all used): 26 Dan Norman; 31 Jacob Dugdale; 16 MacGraff Leuluai; 20 Owen Farnworth.
**Tries:** Roby (2), Ah Van (7, 60), Owens (35, 57, 66), Craven (50), Ashall-Bott (63); **Goals:** Owens 4/8.
**Sin bin:** Cahill (63) - fighting.
**HORNETS:** 19 Oscar Thomas; 2 Shaun Ainscough; 23 Jordan Case; 24 Brandon Wood; 18 Kevin Brown; 6 Pierre-Louis Bourrel; 29 Izaac Farrell; 8 Callum Marriott; 22 Callum Wood; 30 Adam Lawton; 16 Mike Weldon; 25 Kyle Shelford; 5 Ellis Robson. Subs (all used): 28 Zac Baker; 15 Lewis Sheridan; 10 Ben Kilner; 11 Lee Mitchell.
**Tries:** Brown (27), Marriott (79); **Goals:** Thomas 2/2.
**Sin bin:** C Wood (63) - fighting.

**Rugby Leaguer & League Express Men of the Match:**
*Vikings:* Patrick Ah Van; *Hornets:* Oscar Thomas.
**Penalty count:** 6-8; **Half-time:** 12-6;
**Referee:** Gareth Hewer; **Attendance:** 3,780.

## ROUND 21

*Friday 12th July 2019*

### SHEFFIELD EAGLES 28 DEWSBURY RAMS 22

**EAGLES:** 1 Josh Guzdek; 2 Ryan Millar; 3 Menzie Yere; 27 Jacob Ogden; 5 Ben Blackmore; 6 Pat Walker; 7 Anthony Thackeray; 17 Shaun Pick; 9 James Davey; 11 Brad Knowles; 15 Olly Davies; 12 Joel Farrell; 13 Aaron Brown. Subs (all used): 16 Corey Makelim; 19 Sonny Esslemont; 22 Paddy Burns; 21 Blake Broadbent.
**Tries:** Blackmore (4, 38), Ogden (12), Farrell (63), Esslemont (68); **Goals:** Walker 4/5.
**RAMS:** 42 Joe Martin; 23 Rob Worrincy; 32 Owen Trout; 4 Adam Ryder; - Conor McGrath; 6 Paul Sykes; 38 Liam Finn; 8 Jode Sheriffe; 43 Dom Speakman; 19 Daniel Igbinedion; 34 Daniel Waite-Pullan; 12 Michael Knowles; 13 Kyle Trout. Subs (all used): 18 Sam Day; 11 Lucas Walshaw; 39 Chris Annakin; 30 Tom Garratt.
**Tries:** Speakman (25), K Trout (29), Knowles (51), Worrincy (70); **Goals:** Sykes 3/4.
**Rugby Leaguer & League Express Men of the Match:**
*Eagles:* Sonny Esslemont; *Rams:* Kyle Trout.
**Penalty count:** 5-4; **Half-time:** 16-10;
**Referee:** Gareth Hewer; **Attendance:** 691.

*Saturday 13th July 2019*

### ROCHDALE HORNETS 0 TOULOUSE OLYMPIQUE 68

**HORNETS:** 7 Dan Abram; 18 Kevin Brown; 23 Jordan Case; 24 Brandon Wood; 2 Shaun Ainscough; 6 Pierre-Louis Bourrel; 29 Izaac Farrell; 8 Callum Marriott; 22 Callum Wood; 11 Lee Mitchell; 16 Mike Weldon; 25 Kyle Shelford; 5 Zac Baker. Subs (all used): 10 Ben Kilner; 15 Lewis Sheridan; 19 Oscar Thomas; 28 Aidy Gleeson.
**OLYMPIQUE:** 1 Mark Kheirallah; 5 Paul Marcon; 25 Mathieu Jussaume; 26 Junior Vaivai; 20 Ilias Bergal; 6 Johnathon Ford; 7 Stan Robin; 22 Brenden Santi; 9 Anthony Marion; 17 Paterika Vaivai; 11 Con Mika; 10 Joe Bretherton; 19 James Bell. Subs (all used): 16 Tyla Hepi; 21 Jordan Dezaria; 23 Justin Sangare; 28 Pierre-Jean Lima.

**Tries:** Bergal (11, 16, 27, 31, 55, 79), J Vaivai (13), Mika (36), Marion (49), Kheirallah (61, 70), P Vaivai (77);
**Goals:** Kheirallah 10/12.
**On report:** Bretherton (10) - alleged shoulder charge.
**Rugby Leaguer & League Express Men of the Match:**
*Hornets:* Lee Mitchell; *Olympique:* Junior Vaivai.
**Penalty count:** 4-3; **Half-time:** 0-32;
**Referee:** Matt Rossleigh; **Attendance:** 337.

### TORONTO WOLFPACK 22 FEATHERSTONE ROVERS 18

**WOLFPACK:** 1 Gareth O'Brien; 24 Nick Rawsthorne; 3 Chase Stanley; 4 Ricky Leutele; 5 Liam Kay; 6 Joe Mellor; 7 Josh McCrone; 15 Darcy Lussick; 14 Andy Ackers; 21 Anthony Mullally; 11 Andrew Dixon; 16 Tom Olbison; 13 Jon Wilkin. Subs (all used): 9 Bob Beswick; 10 Ashton Sims; 18 Gadwin Springer; 22 Greg Worthington.
**Tries:** O'Brien (2), Stanley (36), Leutele (48), McCrone (65); **Goals:** O'Brien 3/4, Rawsthorne 0/1.
**Sin bin:** Lussick (16) - punching Bussey.
**ROVERS:** 33 Ashton Golding; 25 Jack Render; 4 Josh Hardcastle; 5 Conor Carey; 2 Luke Briscoe; 44 Will Dagger; 37 Callum McLelland; 42 Wellington Albert; 10 Jack Bussey; 17 James Harrison; 12 Brad Day; 28 Josh Walters; 13 James Lockwood. Subs (all used): 45 Connor Jones; 23 Makahesi Makatoa; 29 Jack Ormondroyd; 15 Luke Cooper.
**Tries:** Ormondroyd (43), Walters (55), Jones (72);
**Goals:** Dagger 3/3.
**Rugby Leaguer & League Express Men of the Match:**
*Wolfpack:* Ricky Leutele; *Rovers:* Connor Jones.
**Penalty count:** 10-8; **Half-time:** 14-0;
**Referee:** Jack Smith; **Attendance:** 7,891.

*Sunday 14th July 2019*

### BARROW RAIDERS 8 LEIGH CENTURIONS 24

**RAIDERS:** 18 Luke Cresswell; 1 Theearapol Ritson; 3 Declan Hulme; 2 Stargroth Amean; 5 Deon Cross; 6 Jamie Dallimore; 24 Jake Carter; 25 Jordan Walne; 14 Wartovo Puara; 32 Alec Susino; 35 Liam Paisley; 12 Jarrad Stack; 13 Martin Aspinwall. Subs: 16 Glenn Riley; 8 Tom Walker; 34 Ben White; 27 Brett Carter (not used).
**Tries:** Cross (8), Ritson (54); **Goals:** Dallimore 0/2.
**Sin bin:** Dallimore (70) - fighting.
**CENTURIONS:** 1 Gregg McNally; 25 Liam Forsyth; 3 Iain Thornley; 12 Andy Thornley; 5 Stefan Marsh; 6 Martyn Ridyard; 7 Josh Woods; 10 Sam Brooks; 9 Micky Higham;

13 Luke Adamson; 11 Toby Adamson; 40 Joe Batchelor; 15 Joe Cator. Subs (all used): 27 Liam Hood; 30 Cory Paterson; 22 Jordan Thompson; 29 Jake Emmitt.
**Tries:** McNally (38), I Thornley (42), Ridyard (47), Thompson (71); **Goals:** Ridyard 3/3, Paterson 1/2.
**Sin bin:** Woods (70) - fighting.
**Rugby Leaguer & League Express Men of the Match:** *Raiders:* Luke Cresswell; *Centurions:* Martyn Ridyard.
**Penalty count:** 5-6; **Half-time:** 4-6;
**Referee:** Tom Grant; **Attendance:** 1,637.

**BATLEY BULLDOGS 14 YORK CITY KNIGHTS 14**

**BULLDOGS:** 1 Dave Scott; 4 Lewis Galbraith; 3 Sam Smeaton; 28 Jack Broadbent; 5 Johnny Campbell; 6 Louis Jouffret; 14 Danny Yates; 8 Adam Gledhill; 9 Alistair Leak; 17 Tyler Dickinson; 22 Sam Wood; 11 Dane Manning; 13 James Brown. Subs (all used): 25 Lewis Bienek; 15 Toby Everett; 27 Reiss Butterworth; 16 Michael Ward.
**Tries:** Broadbent (15), Jouffret (59); **Goals:** Jouffret 3/3.
**Sin bin:** Yates (43) - fighting.
**CITY KNIGHTS:** 1 Matty Marsh; 23 Jason Bass; 4 Brad Hey; 41 Cameron Scott; 20 Perry Whiteley; 38 Liam Harris; 7 Connor Robinson; 8 Ronan Dixon; 9 Will Jubb; 10 Jack Teanby; 11 Josh Jordan-Roberts; 3 Liam Salter; 22 Marcus Stock. Subs (all used): 26 Kriss Brining; 15 Graeme Horne; 16 Jack Blagbrough; 37 Jordan Baldwinson.
**Tries:** C Scott (54), Jordan-Roberts (67);
**Goals:** Robinson 3/5.
**Sin bin:** Robinson (43) - fighting.
**Rugby Leaguer & League Express Men of the Match:** *Bulldogs:* Dane Manning; *City Knights:* Jack Teanby.
**Penalty count:** 3-6; **Half-time:** 6-2;
**Referee:** Scott Mikalauskas; **Attendance:** 1,009.

**BRADFORD BULLS 34 SWINTON LIONS 34**

**BULLS:** 1 Brandon Pickersgill; 2 Ethan Ryan; 26 Ross Oakes; 3 Jake Webster; 5 Jy Hitchcox; 6 Joe Keyes; 14 Jordan Lilley; 19 Jon Magrin; 9 Matty Wildie; 8 Liam Kirk; 11 Matt Garside; 25 Connor Farrell; 12 Elliot Minchella. Subs (all used): 18 Sam Hallas; 29 Matthew Storton; 33 Thomas Doyle; 17 Ross Peltier.
**Tries:** Garside (30), Pickersgill (36), Webster (40), Lilley (60), Storton (67), Farrell (80); **Goals:** Keyes 5/6.
**Sin bin:** Kirk (21) - professional foul; Webster (70) - fighting.
**LIONS:** 1 Jack Hansen; 25 Matty Ashton; 3 Rhodri Lloyd; 32 Craig Mullen; 28 Richard Lepori; 34 Harry Smith; 7 Rob Fairclough; 8 Gavin Bennion; 9 Luke Waterworth; 10 Lewis Hatton; 22 Frankie Halton; 35 Samy Kibula; 16 Paddy Jones. Subs (all used): 14 Billy Brickhill; 29 Scott Moore; 33 Ben Morris; 19 Jose Kenga.
**Tries:** Lepori (2), Bennion (12), Smith (14), Ashton (33, 73), Kibula (51); **Goals:** Hansen 5/6.
**Dismissal:** Lepori (70) - fighting.
**Sin bin:** Hatton (48) - high tackle; P Jones (70) - fighting.
**Rugby Leaguer & League Express Men of the Match:** *Bulls:* Joe Keyes; *Lions:* Samy Kibula.
**Penalty count:** 14-7; **Half-time:** 18-22;
**Referee:** Cameron Worsley; **Attendance:** 3,104.

**HALIFAX 40 WIDNES VIKINGS 10**

**HALIFAX:** 1 Quentin Laulu-Togaga'e; 20 James Saltonstall; 23 James Woodburn-Hall; 3 Steve Tyrer; 2 Shaun Robinson; 6 Scott Murrell; 7 Ben Johnston; 18 Elliot Morris; 9 Ben Kaye; 8 Dan Fleming; 4 Chester Butler; 12 Ed Barber; 35 Adam Tangata. Subs (all used): 14 Brandon Moore; 17 Ben Kavanagh; 16 Kevin Larroyer; 10 Jacob Fairbank.
**Tries:** Tyrer (11, 55), Tangata (18), Butler (26, 72, 80), Moore (44); **Goals:** Tyrer 6/7.
**VIKINGS:** 5 Jack Owens; 1 Olly Ashall-Bott; 36 Patrick Ah Van; 24 Keanan Brand; 29 Jayden Hatton; 6 Danny Craven; 7 Tom Gilmore; 13 Hep Cahill; 15 Jordan Johnstone; 11 Harrison Hansen; 17 Sam Wilde; 12 Chris Dean; 16 MacGraff Leuluai. Subs (all used): 26 Dan Norman; 31 Jacob Dugdale; 8 Jay Chapelhow; 19 Brad Walker.
**Tries:** Wilde (29), Hatton (34); **Goals:** Owens 1/2.
**Rugby Leaguer & League Express Men of the Match:** *Halifax:* Steve Tyrer; *Vikings:* Brad Walker.
**Penalty count:** 7-5; **Half-time:** 18-10;
**Referee:** James Child; **Attendance:** 1,668.

## ROUND 22

*Saturday 20th July 2019*

**TOULOUSE OLYMPIQUE 56 SHEFFIELD EAGLES 18**

**OLYMPIQUE:** 1 Mark Kheirallah; 20 Ilias Bergal; 26 Junior Vaivai; 25 Mathieu Jussaume; 5 Paul Marcon; 7 Stan Robin; 6 Johnathon Ford; 18 Clement Boyer; 9 Anthony Marion; 17 Paterika Vaivai; 11 Con Mika; 10 Joe Bretherton; 19 James Bell. Subs (all used): 14 Dean Parata; 23 Justin Sangare; 16 Tyla Hepi; 21 Jordan Dezaria.
**Tries:** Marcon (3, 51), Bretherton (10), Mika (31), Kheirallah (34), Jussaume (39), Parata (41), Bergal (44, 79), Robin (71); **Goals:** Kheirallah 8/10.
**EAGLES:** 1 Josh Guzdek; 2 Ryan Millar; 19 Sonny Esslemont; 27 Jacob Ogden; 5 Ben Blackmore; 6 Pat Walker; 7 Anthony Thackeray; 17 Shaun Pick; 14 Greg Burns; 11 Brad Knowles; 15 Olly Davies; 12 Joel Farrell; 13 Aaron Brown. Subs (all used): 23 Rory Dixon; 16 Corey Makelim; 21 Blake Broadbent; 22 Paddy Burns.
**Tries:** Thackeray (18), Farrell (59), Davies (73);
**Goals:** Walker 3/3.
**Rugby Leaguer & League Express Men of the Match:** *Olympique:* Mark Kheirallah; *Eagles:* Anthony Thackeray.
**Penalty count:** 3-3; **Half-time:** 28-6;
**Referee:** James Child; **Attendance:** 2,154.

*Sunday 21st July 2019*

**DEWSBURY RAMS 28 HALIFAX 28**

**RAMS:** 42 Joe Martin; 23 Rob Worrincy; 11 Lucas Walshaw; 4 Adam Ryder; 2 Andy Gabriel; 6 Paul Sykes; 38 Liam Finn; 17 Martyn Reilly; 18 Sam Day; 33 Frazer Morris; 19 Daniel Igbinedion; 12 Michael Knowles; 13 Kyle Trout. Subs (all used): 34 Daniel Waite-Pullan; 32 Owen Trout; 8 Jode Sheriffe; 30 Tom Garratt.
**Tries:** Day (31), Ryder (52), Gabriel (63), Worrincy (74, 77);
**Goals:** Sykes 4/6.
**HALIFAX:** 1 Quentin Laulu-Togaga'e; 20 James Saltonstall; 3 Steve Tyrer; 23 James Woodburn-Hall; 2 Shaun Robinson; 6 Scott Murrell; 7 Ben Johnston; 18 Elliot Morris; 9 Ben Kaye; 8 Dan Fleming; 12 Ed Barber; 4 Chester Butler; 35 Adam Tangata. Subs (all used): 10 Jacob Fairbank; 16 Kevin Larroyer; 17 Ben Kavanagh; 14 Brandon Moore.
**Tries:** Saltonstall (26), Laulu-Togaga'e (35, 48), Larroyer (56), Fairbank (71); **Goals:** Tyrer 4/5.
**Rugby Leaguer & League Express Men of the Match:** *Rams:* Rob Worrincy; *Halifax:* Quentin Laulu-Togaga'e.
**Penalty count:** 8-5; **Half-time:** 6-12;
**Referee:** Matt Rossleigh; **Attendance:** 1,136.

**FEATHERSTONE ROVERS 50 ROCHDALE HORNETS 6**

**ROVERS:** 33 Ashton Golding; 2 Luke Briscoe; 5 Conor Carey; 4 Josh Hardcastle; 44 Will Dagger; 34 Ben Reynolds; 38 Dane Chisholm; 23 Makahesi Makatoa; 9 Cameron King; 29 Jack Ormondroyd; 12 Brad Day; 28 Josh Walters; 13 James Lockwood. Subs (all used): 15 Luke Cooper; 17 James Harrison; 42 Wellington Albert; 45 Connor Jones.
**Tries:** Makatoa (15), King (20), Briscoe (28), Jones (37), Harrison (47), Golding (51), Day (68, 78), Walters (76);
**Goals:** Chisholm 7/10.
**HORNETS:** 7 Dan Abram; 18 Kevin Brown; 5 James Worthington; 24 Brandon Wood; 2 Shaun Ainscough; 6 Pierre-Louis Bourrel; 23 Izaac Farrell; 8 Callum Marriott; 22 Callum Wood; 28 Ben Kilner; 16 Mike Weldon; 29 Kyle Shelford; 19 Oscar Thomas. Subs (all used): 17 Liam Carberry; 15 Lewis Sheridan; 1 Dec Kay; 10 Aidy Gleeson.
**Try:** Ainscough (11); **Goals:** Abram 1/1.
**Rugby Leaguer & League Express Men of the Match:** *Rovers:* Dane Chisholm; *Hornets:* Shaun Ainscough.
**Penalty count:** 14-4; **Half-time:** 20-6;
**Referee:** Aaron Moore; **Attendance:** 2,011.

**LEIGH CENTURIONS 48 BATLEY BULLDOGS 12**

**CENTURIONS:** 1 Gregg McNally; 32 Adam Higson; 3 Iain Thornley; 44 Junior Sa'u; 5 Stefan Marsh; 35 Ryan Brierley; 7 Josh Woods; 26 Luke Douglas; 9 Micky Higham; 13 Luke Adamson; 11 Toby Adamson; 30 Cory Paterson; 15 Joe Cator. Subs (all used): 27 Liam Hood; 28 Mitch Clark; 29 Jake Emmitt; 22 Jordan Thompson.
**Tries:** Brierley (2, 80), Cator (10), Douglas (19), I Thornley (22, 64), Woods (40), Higham (69), Marsh (77);
**Goals:** Brierley 6/9.
**BULLDOGS:** 1 Dave Scott; 2 Wayne Reittie; 3 Sam Smeaton; 28 Jack Broadbent; 23 Keenen Tomlinson; 6 Louis Jouffret; 14 Danny Yates; 8 Adam Gledhill; 9 Alistair Leak; 17 Tyler Dickinson; 29 Sam Walters; 22 Sam Wood; 25 Lewis Bienek. Subs (all used): 27 Reiss Butterworth; 15 Toby Everett; 10 Tom Lillycrop; 16 Michael Ward.
**Tries:** Walters (32), Jouffret (36); **Goals:** Jouffret 2/2.
**Rugby Leaguer & League Express Men of the Match:** *Centurions:* Luke Douglas; *Bulldogs:* Sam Walters.
**Penalty count:** 8-7; **Half-time:** 30-12;
**Referee:** Billy Pearson; **Attendance:** 3,125.

**SWINTON LIONS 30 BARROW RAIDERS 12**

**LIONS:** 25 Matty Ashton; 2 Mike Butt; 3 Rhodri Lloyd; 32 Craig Mullen; 28 Richard Lepori; 1 Jack Hansen; 7 Rob Fairclough; 8 Gavin Bennion; 9 Luke Waterworth; 10 Lewis Hatton; 33 Jack Wells; 22 Frankie Halton; 16 Paddy Jones. Subs (all used): 14 Billy Brickhill; 35 Nick Gregson; 34 Harry Smith; 31 Samy Kibula.
**Tries:** Ashton (25), Halton (29), Lloyd (50), Butt (74), Smith (78); **Goals:** Hansen 5/8.
**On report:**
Bennion (71) - alleged dangerous contact on Amean.
**RAIDERS:** 18 Luke Cresswell; 1 Theerapol Ritson; 2 Stargroth Amean; 3 Declan Hulme; 5 Deon Cross; 6 Jamie Dallimore; 7 Lewis Charnock; 36 Paul Seguier; 14 Wartovo Puara; 29 Alec Susino; 35 Liam Paisley; 12 Jarrad Stack; 13 Martin Aspinwall. Subs (all used): 34 Ben White; 25 Jordan Walne; 8 Tom Walker; 17 Ryan Duffy.
**Tries:** Ritson (45), Cresswell (56);
**Goals:** Dallimore 1/2, White 1/1.
**Sin bin:** Dallimore (49) - dissent.
**Rugby Leaguer & League Express Men of the Match:** *Lions:* Samy Kibula; *Raiders:* Stargroth Amean.
**Penalty count:** 9-5; **Half-time:** 14-2;
**Referee:** Gareth Hewer; **Attendance:** 984.

**YORK CITY KNIGHTS 25 BRADFORD BULLS 24**

**CITY KNIGHTS:** 23 Jason Bass; 39 Will Oakes; 3 Liam Salter; 41 Cameron Scott; 20 Perry Whiteley; 38 Liam Harris; 7 Connor Robinson; 10 Jack Teanby; 9 Will Jubb; 22 Marcus Stock; 12 Sam Scott; 11 Josh Jordan-Roberts; 13 Tim Spears. Subs (all used): 26 Kriss Brining; 8 Ronan Dixon; 16 Jack Blagbrough; 27 Jordan Baldwinson.
**Tries:** Oakes (29, 34), Whiteley (59, 64);
**Goals:** Robinson 4/5; **Field goal:** Harris (80).
**Sin bin:** Dixon (32) - holding down.
**BULLS:** 34 Joe Brown; 5 Jy Hitchcox; 3 Jake Webster; 26 Ross Oakes; 2 Ethan Ryan; 6 Joe Keyes; 14 Jordan Lilley; 10 Steve Crossley; 9 Matty Wildie; 18 Sam Hallas; 29 Matthew Storton; 25 Connor Farrell; 12 Elliot Minchella. Subs (all used): 31 Rhys Evans; 21 George Flanagan; 13 Mikey Wood; 17 Ross Peltier.
**Tries:** Ryan (3, 38, 55), Oakes (72), Hitchcox (75);
**Goals:** Keyes 2/4, Lilley 0/1.
**Rugby Leaguer & League Express Men of the Match:** *City Knights:* Sam Scott; *Bulls:* Ethan Ryan.
**Penalty count:** 7-6; **Half-time:** 14-8;
**Referee:** Greg Dolan; **Attendance:** 4,007.

**WIDNES VIKINGS 19 TORONTO WOLFPACK 24**

**VIKINGS:** 5 Jack Owens; 2 Ryan Ince; 12 Chris Dean; 25 Lloyd Roby; 29 Jayden Hatton; 6 Danny Craven; 21 Joe Lyons; 8 Jay Chapelhow; 15 Jordan Johnstone; 26 Dan Norman; 17 Sam Wilde; 37 Ellis Robson; 19 Brad Walker. Subs (all used): 13 Hep Cahill; 34 Josh Ganson; 18 Ted Chapelhow; 11 Harrison Hansen.
**Tries:** Roby (26), Craven (30), Ince (58);
**Goals:** Owens 3/3; **Field goal:** Craven (73).
**WOLFPACK:** 6 Joe Mellor; 5 Liam Kay; 3 Chase Stanley; 22 Greg Worthington; 24 Nick Rawsthorne; 13 Jon Wilkin; 7 Josh McCrone; 11 Andrew Dixon; 9 Bob Beswick; 12 Bodene Thompson; 15 Darcy Lussick; 21 Anthony Mullally; 14 Andy Ackers. Subs (all used): 10 Ashton Sims; 16 Tom Olbison; 19 Gary Wheeler; 27 Hakim Miloudi.
**Tries:** Rawsthorne (8), Stanley (39), Thompson (46), Lussick (51), Mullally (74);
**Goals:** Rawsthorne 0/2, McCrone 1/2, Miloudi 1/1.
**Rugby Leaguer & League Express Men of the Match:** *Vikings:* Danny Craven; *Wolfpack:* Andy Ackers.
**Penalty count:** 4-5; **Half-time:** 12-8;
**Referee:** Liam Moore; **Attendance:** 3,812.

## ROUND 1

*Sunday 28th July 2019*

**ROCHDALE HORNETS 12 DEWSBURY RAMS 32**

**HORNETS:** 1 Dec Kay; 2 Shaun Ainscough; 24 Brandon Wood; 26 Daley Williams; 7 Dan Abram; 6 Pierre-Louis Bourrel; 29 Izaac Farrell; 11 Lee Mitchell; 15 Lewis Sheridan; 16 Mike Weldon; 25 Zac Baker; 14 Kyle Shelford; 19 Oscar Thomas. Subs (all used): 10 Ben Kilner; 8 Callum Marriott; 12 Jordan Syme; 22 Callum Wood.
**Tries:** Williams (18, 39); **Goals:** Abram 2/2.
**RAMS:** 42 Joe Martin; 23 Rob Worrincy; 11 Lucas Walshaw; 4 Adam Ryder; 2 Andy Gabriel; 6 Paul Sykes; 38 Liam Finn; 17 Martyn Reilly; 43 Dom Speakman; 33 Frazer Morris; 32 Owen Trout; 12 Michael Knowles; 13 Kyle Trout. Subs (all used): 18 Sam Day; 8 Jode Sheriffe; 36 Nyle Flynn; 30 Tom Garratt.
**Tries:** Morris (8), Ryder (31), Garratt (43), Knowles (48, 60), Worrincy (51); **Goals:** Sykes 0/3, Finn 4/4.
**Rugby Leaguer & League Express Men of the Match:** *Hornets:* Izaac Farrell; *Rams:* Michael Knowles.
**Penalty count:** 7-7; **Half-time:** 12-8;
**Referee:** James Child; **Attendance:** 574.

## ROUND 23

*Friday 2nd August 2019*

### SHEFFIELD EAGLES 30 WIDNES VIKINGS 10

**EAGLES:** 1 Josh Guzdek; 2 Ryan Millar; 3 Menzie Yere; 27 Jacob Ogden; 5 Ben Blackmore; 6 Pat Walker; 7 Anthony Thackeray; 17 Shaun Pick; 14 Greg Burns; 11 Brad Knowles; 12 Joel Farrell; 15 Olly Davies; 13 Aaron Brown. Subs (all used): 16 Corey Makelim; 22 Paddy Burns; 23 Rory Dixon; 21 Blake Broadbent.
**Tries:** Blackmore (4), Knowles (21), Thackeray (46, 57), Yere (63); **Goals:** Walker 5/5.
**VIKINGS:** 5 Jack Owens; 2 Ryan Ince; 25 Lloyd Roby; 24 Keanan Brand; 1 Olly Ashall-Bott; 6 Danny Craven; 21 Joe Lyons; 26 Dan Norman; 15 Jordan Johnstone; 8 Jay Chapelhow; 17 Sam Wilde; 37 Ellis Robson; 19 Brad Walker. Subs (all used): 18 Ted Chapelhow; 34 Josh Ganson; 11 Harrison Hansen; 16 MacGraff Leuluai.
**Tries:** Ince (30), Robson (50); **Goals:** Owens 1/2.
**Rugby Leaguer & League Express Men of the Match:** *Eagles:* Anthony Thackeray; *Vikings:* MacGraff Leuluai.
**Penalty count:** 4-4; **Half-time:** 12-4;
**Referee:** Greg Dolan; **Attendance:** 772.

*Sunday 4th August 2019*

### BARROW RAIDERS 16 YORK CITY KNIGHTS 24

**RAIDERS:** 18 Luke Cresswell; 5 Deon Cross; 3 Declan Hulme; 12 Jarrad Stack; 1 Theerapol Ritson; 34 Ben White; 22 Ryan Johnston; 8 Tom Walker; 14 Wartovo Puara; 29 Alec Susino; 11 Jono Smith; 35 Liam Paisley; 25 Jordan Walne. Subs (all used): 24 Jake Carter; 17 Ryan Duffy; 13 Martin Aspinwall; 36 Paul Seguier.
**Tries:** Ritson (13), Cresswell (60), Smith (72);
**Goals:** R Johnston 1/2, J Carter 1/1.
**CITY KNIGHTS:** 1 Matty Marsh; 23 Jason Bass; 41 Cameron Scott; 4 Brad Hey; 39 Will Oakes; 38 Liam Harris; 7 Connor Robinson; 16 Jack Blagbrough; 9 Will Jubb; 10 Jack Teanby; 19 Mike Kelly; 3 Liam Salter; 13 Tim Spears. Subs (all used): 8 Ronan Dixon; 22 Marcus Stock; 26 Kriss Brining; 37 Jordan Baldwinson.
**Tries:** Marsh (5, 24, 33), Bass (58); **Goals:** Robinson 4/4.
**Rugby Leaguer & League Express Men of the Match:** *Raiders:* Ben White; *City Knights:* Matty Marsh.
**Penalty count:** 6-5; **Half-time:** 4-18;
**Referee:** Jack Smith; **Attendance:** 1,169.

### BRADFORD BULLS 20 TORONTO WOLFPACK 25

**BULLS:** 1 Brandon Pickersgill; 5 Jy Hitchcox; 3 Jake Webster; 26 Ross Oakes; 2 Ethan Ryan; 6 Joe Keyes; 14 Jordan Lilley; 8 Liam Kirk; 9 Matty Wildie; 10 Steve Crossley; 11 Matt Garside; 29 Matthew Storton; 12 Elliot Minchella. Subs (all used): 16 James Green; 31 Rhys Evans; 21 George Flanagan; 13 Mikey Wood.
**Tries:** Hitchcox (17), Webster (25), Crossley (29);
**Goals:** Keyes 4/4.
**WOLFPACK:** 27 Hakim Miloudi; 5 Liam Kay; 22 Greg Worthington; 4 Ricky Leutele; 24 Nick Rawsthorne; 6 Joe Mellor; 17 Blake Wallace; 21 Anthony Mullally; 14 Andy Ackers; 10 Ashton Sims; 11 Andrew Dixon; 12 Bodene Thompson; 13 Jon Wilkin. Subs: 1 Gareth O'Brien (not used); 9 Bob Beswick; 16 Tom Olbison; 18 Gadwin Springer.
**Tries:** Leutele (6, 42), Rawsthorne (44, 76), Kay (51);
**Goals:** Wallace 1/3, Miloudi 1/2; **Field goal:** Miloudi (60).
**Rugby Leaguer & League Express Men of the Match:** *Bulls:* Elliot Minchella; *Wolfpack:* Hakim Miloudi.
**Penalty count:** 9-4; **Half time:** 18-4;
**Referee:** Scott Mikalauskas; **Attendance:** 3,421.

### DEWSBURY RAMS 24 FEATHERSTONE ROVERS 25

**RAMS:** 42 Joe Martin; 1 Dale Morton; 11 Lucas Walshaw; 4 Adam Ryder; 2 Andy Gabriel; 6 Paul Sykes; 38 Liam Finn; 17 Martyn Reilly; 43 Dom Speakman; 33 Frazer Morris; 32 Owen Trout; 12 Michael Knowles; 13 Kyle Trout. Subs (all used): 18 Sam Day; 8 Jode Sheriffe; 36 Nyle Flynn; 30 Tom Garratt.
**Tries:** Knowles (18), Morton (58), Flynn (66), Speakman (76); **Goals:** Sykes 4/5.
**ROVERS:** 33 Ashton Golding; 46 Jack Johnson; 5 Conor Carey; 32 Alex Sutcliffe; 25 Jack Render; 38 Dane Chisholm; 37 Callum McLelland; 8 Scott Wheeldon; 9 Cameron King; 42 Wellington Albert; 12 Brad Day; 28 Josh Walters; 13 James Lockwood. Subs: 14 John Davies; 45 Connor Jones (not used); 23 Makahesi Makatoa; 17 James Harrison.
**Tries:** Golding (26), Sutcliffe (34), McLelland (38), Albert (62), Carey (70); **Goals:** Chisholm 2/6;
**Field goal:** Chisholm (78).
**On report:** Makatoa (48) - alleged bite.
**Rugby Leaguer & League Express Men of the Match:** *Rams:* Joe Martin; *Rovers:* Dane Chisholm.
**Penalty count:** 6-7; **Half-time:** 8-12;
**Referee:** Billy Pearson; **Attendance:** 1,229.

### HALIFAX 22 TOULOUSE OLYMPIQUE 30

**HALIFAX:** 30 Scott Grix; 2 Shaun Robinson; 3 Steve Tyrer; 20 James Saltonstall; 5 Will Sharp; 6 Scott Murrell; 23 James Woodburn-Hall; 35 Adam Tangata; 9 Ben Kaye; 17 Ben Kavanagh; 12 Ed Barber; 25 Liam Cooper; 10 Jacob Fairbank. Subs (all used): 8 Dan Fleming; 14 Brandon Moore; 16 Kevin Larroyer; 22 Connor Davies.
**Tries:** Kaye (17), Tangata (20), Tyrer (32), Robinson (41);
**Goals:** Tyrer 3/4.
**OLYMPIQUE:** 1 Mark Kheirallah; 5 Paul Marcon; 25 Mathieu Jussaume; 26 Junior Vaivai; 20 Ilias Bergal; 6 Johnathon Ford; 7 Stan Robin; 18 Clement Boyer; 9 Anthony Marion; 17 Paterika Vaivai; 11 Con Mika; 10 Joe Bretherton; 19 James Bell. Subs (all used): 14 Dean Parata; 16 Tyla Hepi; 21 Jordan Dezaria; 23 Justin Sangare.
**Tries:** Bergal (3, 28), Jussaume (38), Marion (51), P Vaivai (65); **Goals:** Kheirallah 5/7.
**Sin bin:** Bretherton (35) - late challenge on Murrell.
**Rugby Leaguer & League Express Men of the Match:** *Halifax:* Jacob Fairbank; *Olympique:* Justin Sangare.
**Penalty count:** 10-6; **Half-time:** 16-14;
**Referee:** Cameron Worsley; **Attendance:** 1,290.

### LEIGH CENTURIONS 31 SWINTON LIONS 30

**CENTURIONS:** 1 Gregg McNally; 33 Matthew Costello; 3 Iain Thornley; 44 Junior Sa'u; 25 Liam Forsyth; 6 Martyn Ridyard; 35 Ryan Brierley; 26 Luke Douglas; 27 Liam Hood; 10 Sam Brooks; 23 James Laithwaite; 12 Andy Thornley; 30 Cory Paterson. Subs (all used): 41 Josh Eaves; 15 Joe Cator; 28 Mitch Clark; 29 Jake Emmitt.
**Tries:** A Thornley (5), Forsyth (35), Costello (39), Clark (46), Sa'u (60), Paterson (67);
**Goals:** Brierley 2/5, Ridyard 1/1; **Field goal:** Brierley (78).
**Sin bin:** Brierley (21) - holding down; Cator (56) - fighting.
**LIONS:** 1 Jack Hansen; 2 Mike Butt; 31 Chris Hankinson; 32 Craig Mullen; 25 Matty Ashton; - Jake Shorrocks; 7 Rob Fairclough; 16 Paddy Jones; 9 Luke Waterworth; 10 Lewis Hatton; 3 Rhodri Lloyd; 22 Frakie Halton; 30 Nick Gregson. Subs: 14 Billy Brickhill; 19 Jose Kenga; 35 Samy Kibula; 37 Ben Morris (not used).
**Tries:** Ashton (13, 19, 30, 80), Butt (38); **Goals:** Hansen 5/6.
**Sin bin:** Lloyd (56) - fighting; Kibula (56) - fighting.
**Rugby Leaguer & League Express Men of the Match:** *Centurions:* Jake Emmitt; *Lions:* Matty Ashton.
**Penalty count:** 5-7; **Half-time:** 14-24;
**Referee:** Gareth Hewer; **Attendance:** 3,155.

### ROCHDALE HORNETS 26 BATLEY BULLDOGS 50

**HORNETS:** 7 Dan Abram; 2 Shaun Ainscough; 26 Daley Williams; 24 Brandon Wood; 18 Kevin Brown; 14 James Barran; 29 Izaac Farrell; 8 Callum Marriott; 22 Callum Wood; 11 Lee Mitchell; 25 Zac Baker; 23 Kyle Shelford; 19 Oscar Thomas. Subs (all used): 16 Mike Weldon; 15 Lewis Sheridan; 10 Ben Kilner; 12 Jordan Syme.
**Tries:** Shelford (9), Williams (18), Sheridan (28), Farrell (55), Abram (71); **Goals:** Abram 3/5.
**BULLDOGS:** 6 Louis Jouffret; 2 Wayne Reittie; 3 Sam Smeaton; 4 Lewis Galbraith; 28 Jack Broadbent; 14 Danny Yates; 7 Dom Brambani; 8 Adam Gledhill; 9 Alistair Leak; 17 Tyler Dickinson; 12 Jack Downs; 24 Paul Brearley; 11 Dane Manning. Subs (all used): 19 Alex Bretherton; 13 James Brown; 15 Toby Everett; 22 Sam Wood.
**Tries:** Jouffret (15, 46), Reittie (25, 61, 80), Brearley (31), Broadbent (44, 57), Brown (64);
**Goals:** Jouffret 4/5, Wood 3/3, Brambani 0/1.
**Rugby Leaguer & League Express Men of the Match:** *Hornets:* Dan Abram; *Bulldogs:* Louis Jouffret.
**Penalty count:** 7-8; **Half-time:** 14-18;
**Referee:** Michael Mannifield; **Attendance:** 638.

## ROUND 24

*Saturday 10th August 2019*

### WIDNES VIKINGS 12 TOULOUSE OLYMPIQUE 28

**VIKINGS:** 5 Jack Owens; 2 Ryan Ince; 4 Anthony Gelling; 24 Keanan Brand; 29 Jayden Hatton; 6 Danny Craven; 7 Tom Gilmore; 8 Jay Chapelhow; 15 Jordan Johnstone; 26 Dan Norman; 17 Sam Wilde; 37 Ellis Robson; 13 Hep Cahill. Subs (all used): 16 MacGraff Leuluai; 31 Jacob Dugdale; 18 Ted Chapelhow; 11 Harrison Hansen.
**Tries:** Owens (52), Cahill (76); **Goals:** Owens 2/2.
**OLYMPIQUE:** 1 Mark Kheirallah; 4 Gavin Marguerite; 25 Matthieu Jussaume; 26 Junior Vaivai; 20 Ilias Bergal; 6 Johnathon Ford; 7 Stan Robin; 17 Paterika Vaivai; 9 Anthony Marion; 15 Ben Evans; 11 Con Mika; 10 Joe Bretherton; 19 James Bell. Subs (all used): 14 Dean Parata; 21 Jordan Dezaria; 16 Tyla Hepi; 23 Justin Sangare.
**Tries:** J Vaivai (3), Mika (49), Bergal (59), Bretherton (61), Dezaria (72); **Goals:** Kheirallah 4/6.
**Rugby Leaguer & League Express Men of the Match:** *Vikings:* Jordan Johnstone; *Olympique:* Tyla Hepi.
**Penalty count:** 7-8; **Half-time:** 0-8;
**Referee:** James Child; **Attendance:** 3,643.

### TORONTO WOLFPACK 56 YORK CITY KNIGHTS 6

**WOLFPACK:** 1 Gareth O'Brien; 24 Nick Rawsthorne; 27 Hakim Miloudi; 4 Ricky Leutele; 2 Matty Russell; 6 Joe Mellor; 7 Josh McCrone; 15 Darcy Lussick; 14 Andy Ackers; 10 Ashton Sims; 11 Andrew Dixon; 16 Tom Olbison; 13 Jon Wilkin. Subs (all used): 9 Bob Beswick; 18 Gadwin Springer; 3 Chase Stanley; 17 Blake Wallace.
**Tries:** O'Brien (5, 19, 22), Miloudi (24), McCrone (27, 44), Dixon (38), Ackers (41, 79), Rawsthorne (54), Russell (61);
**Goals:** O'Brien 5/10, Wallace 1/1.
**CITY KNIGHTS:** 1 Matty Marsh; 23 Jason Bass; 4 Brad Hey; 41 Cameron Scott; 39 Will Oakes; 38 Liam Harris; 7 Connor Robinson; 37 Jordan Baldwinson; 9 Will Jubb; 10 Jack Teanby; 11 Josh Jordan-Roberts; 3 Liam Salter; 22 Marcus Stock. Subs (all used): 5 Matt Chilton; 19 Mike Kelly; 16 Jack Blagbrough; - Danny King.
**Try:** Kelly (51); **Goals:** Robinson 1/1.
**Rugby Leaguer & League Express Men of the Match:** *Wolfpack:* Gareth O'Brien; *City Knights:* Mike Kelly.
**Penalty count:** 9-7; **Half-time:** 32-0;
**Referee:** Tom Grant; **Attendance:** 7,262.

*Sunday 11th August 2019*

### BARROW RAIDERS 22 BRADFORD BULLS 46

**RAIDERS:** 18 Luke Cresswell; 33 Adam Ford; 35 Liam Paisley; 3 Declan Hulme; 5 Deon Cross; 6 Jamie Dallimore; 34 Ben White; 8 Tom Walker; 14 Wartovo Puara; 16 Glenn Riley; 11 Jono Smith; 25 Jordan Walne; 29 Alec Susino. Subs (all used): 22 Ryan Johnston; 15 Dan Toal; 17 Ryan Duffy; 36 Paul Seguier.
**Tries:** Cross (10), Dallimore (42), Ford (50), Hulme (72);
**Goals** Dallimore 3/4.
**BULLS:** 1 Brandon Pickersgill; 5 Jy Hitchcox; 31 Rhys Evans; 26 Ross Oakes; 2 Ethan Ryan; 6 Joe Keyes; 14 Jordan Lilley; 10 Steve Crossley; 9 Matty Wildie; 18 Sam Hallas; 11 Matt Garside; 25 Connor Farrell; 12 Elliot Minchella. Subs (all used): 13 Mikey Wood; 21 George Flanagan; 3 Jake Webster; 16 James Green.
**Tries:** Keyes (5), Garside (13), Ryan (18), Minchella (31, 54), Flanagan (35), Oakes (44), Pickersgill (78);
**Goals:** Keyes 7/9.
**Rugby Leaguer & League Express Men of the Match:** *Raiders:* Luke Cresswell; *Bulls:* Joe Keyes.
**Penalty count:** 6-9; **Half-time:** 6-32;
**Referee:** Jack Smith; **Attendance:** 1,470.

### BATLEY BULLDOGS 16 DEWSBURY RAMS 10

**BULLDOGS:** 6 Louis Jouffret; 2 Wayne Reittie; 3 Sam Smeaton; 4 Lewis Galbraith; 28 Jack Broadbent; 14 Danny Yates; 7 Dom Brambani; 8 Adam Gledhill; 9 Alistair Leak; 17 Tyler Dickinson; 12 Jack Downs; 11 Dane Manning; 24 Paul Brearley. Subs (all used): 19 Alex Bretherton; 15 Toby Everett; 22 Sam Wood; 13 James Brown.
**Tries:** Reittie (12, 59), Smeaton (51); **Goals:** Brambani 2/4.
**Sin bin:** Manning (33) - dangerous challenge on Sheriffe.
**RAMS:** 42 Joe Martin; 23 Rob Worrincy; 1 Dale Morton; 4 Adam Ryder; 2 Andy Gabriel; 6 Paul Sykes; 38 Liam Finn; 33 Frazer Morris; 18 Sam Day; 17 Martyn Reilly; 11 Lucas Walshaw; 12 Michael Knowles; 19 Daniel Igbinedion. Subs (all used): 32 Owen Trout; 36 Nyle Flynn; 8 Jode Sheriffe; 30 Tom Garratt.
**Tries:** Walshaw (62), Morton (70);
**Goals:** Sykes 0/1, Finn 1/1.
**Sin bin:** Martin (75) - delaying restart; Finn (77) - dissent.
**Rugby Leaguer & League Express Men of the Match:** *Bulldogs:* Sam Smeaton; *Rams:* Joe Martin.
**Penalty count:** 9-5; **Half-time:** 6-0;
**Referee:** Cameron Worsley; **Attendance:** 1,619.

### FEATHERSTONE ROVERS 66 SWINTON LIONS 16

**ROVERS:** 33 Ashton Golding; 25 Jack Render; 5 Conor Carey; 32 Alex Sutcliffe; 46 Jack Johnson; 37 Callum McLelland; 38 Dane Chisholm; 23 Makahesi Makatoa; 9 Cameron King; 17 James Harrison; 12 Brad Day; 28 Josh Walters; 13 James Lockwood. Subs (all used): 14 John Davies; 15 Luke Cooper; 42 Wellington Albert; 45 Connor Jones.
**Tries:** King (14, 45), Albert (20), McLelland (22), Sutcliffe (27, 75), Render (37), J Johnson (49), Carey (55), Day (58, 63), Walters (73); **Goals:** Chisholm 9/12.
**LIONS:** 1 Jack Hansen; 2 Mike Butt; 3 Rhodri Lloyd; 32 Craig Mullen; 25 Matty Ashton; 34 Harry Smith; 7 Rob Fairclough; 16 Paddy Jones; 9 Luke Waterworth; 10 Lewis Hatton; 35 Samy Kibula; 22 Frankie Halton; 30 Nick Gregson. Subs (all used): 14 Billy Brickhill; 19 Jose Kenga; 37 Ben Morris; 31 Jake Shorrocks.
**Tries:** Hansen (33), Fairclough (64), Waterworth (69);
**Goals:** Hansen 2/3.
**Rugby Leaguer & League Express Men of the Match:** *Rovers:* Cameron King; *Lions:* Luke Waterworth.
**Penalty count:** 10-6; **Half-time:** 28-6;
**Referee:** Greg Dolan; **Attendance:** 2,090.

**HALIFAX 18 SHEFFIELD EAGLES 20**

**HALIFAX:** 30 Scott Grix; 2 Shaun Robinson; 3 Steve Tyrer; 20 James Saltonstall; 21 Conor McGrath; 6 Scott Murrell; 23 James Woodburn-Hall; 33 Keegan Hirst; 14 Brandon Moore; 10 Jacob Fairbank; 25 Liam Cooper; 12 Ed Barber; 16 Kevin Larroyer. Subs (all used): 7 Ben Johnston; 8 Dan Fleming; 22 Connor Davies; 17 Ben Kavanagh.
**Tries:** Robinson (10), Scott Grix (63), Tyrer (72);
**Goals:** Tyrer 3/3.
**EAGLES:** 1 Josh Guzdek; 2 Ryan Millar; 3 Menzie Yere; 27 Jacob Ogden; 5 Ben Blackmore; 6 Pat Walker; 7 Anthony Thackeray; 17 Shaun Pick; 14 Greg Burns; 11 Brad Knowles; 15 Olly Davies; 12 Joel Farrell; 13 Aaron Brown. Subs (all used): 16 Corey Makelim; 21 Blake Broadbent; 22 Paddy Burns; 23 Rory Dixon.
**Tries:** Davies (18), P Burns (23), Brown (34);
**Goals:** Walker 4/4.
**Rugby Leaguer & League Express Men of the Match:**
*Halifax:* Keegan Hirst; *Eagles:* Olly Davies.
**Penalty count:** 5-2; **Half-time:** 6-18;
**Referee:** Gareth Hewer; **Attendance:** 1,205.

**ROCHDALE HORNETS 18 LEIGH CENTURIONS 50**

**HORNETS:** 7 Dan Abram; 2 Shaun Ainscough; 26 Daley Williams; 24 Brandon Wood; 18 Kevin Brown; 14 James Barran; 29 Izaac Farrell; 10 Aidy Gleeson; 15 Lewis Sheridan; 8 Callum Marriott; 12 Jordan Syme; 25 Zac Baker; 23 Kyle Shelford. Subs (all used): 22 Callum Wood; 19 Oscar Thomas; 11 Lee Mitchell; 6 Pierre-Louis Bourrel.
**Tries:** Abram (35), Gleeson (75), Ainscough (79);
**Goals:** Abram 3/3.
**Sin bin:** Ainscough (17) - fighting.
**CENTURIONS:** 35 Ryan Brierley; 32 Adam Higson; 25 Liam Forsyth; 44 Junior Sa'u; 5 Stefan Marsh; 6 Martyn Ridyard; 34 Ben Reynolds; 30 Cory Paterson; 9 Micky Higham; 22 Jordan Thompson; 11 Toby Adamson; 10 Sam Brooks; 15 Joe Cator. Subs (all used): 40 Josh Eaves; 19 Mitch Cox; 28 Mitch Clark; 29 Jake Emmitt.
**Tries:** Reynolds (4), Higson (7), Cator (10), Brierley (16), Marsh (19), T Adamson (25, 61), Thompson (28), Paterson (67); **Goals:** Ridyard 7/9.
**Sin bin:** Higham (17) - fighting.
**Rugby Leaguer & League Express Men of the Match:**
*Hornets:* Shaun Ainscough; *Centurions:* Martyn Ridyard.
**Penalty count:** 4-7; **Half-time:** 6-40;
**Referee:** Billy Pearson; **Attendance:** 1,019.

## ROUND 25

*Saturday 17th August 2019*

**TORONTO WOLFPACK 46 ROCHDALE HORNETS 0**

**WOLFPACK:** 1 Gareth O'Brien; 5 Liam Kay; 3 Chase Stanley; 4 Ricky Leutele; 2 Matty Russell; 17 Blake Wallace; 7 Josh McCrone; 15 Darcy Lussick; 14 Andy Ackers; 10 Ashton Sims; 11 Andrew Dixon; 12 Bodene Thompson; 16 Tom Olbison. Subs (all used): 6 Joe Mellor; 9 Bob Beswick; 18 Gadwin Springer; 27 Hakim Miloudi.
**Tries:** O'Brien (24, 69), Russell (34, 49, 66), Olbison (44), Stanley (59, 73), Miloudi (63);
**Goals:** O'Brien 3/7, Miloudi 2/2.
**Sin bin:** Lussick (58) - fighting.
**HORNETS:** 7 Dan Abram; 2 Shaun Ainscough; 26 Daley Williams; 24 Brandon Wood; 18 Kevin Brown; 19 Oscar Thomas; 14 James Barran; 11 Lee Mitchell; 22 Callum Wood; 8 Callum Marriott; 12 Jordan Syme; 23 Kyle Shelford; 25 Zac Baker. Subs (all used): 9 Ben Moores; 17 Liam Carberry; 21 Aidy Gleeson; 28 Ben Kilner.
**Sin bin:** Barran (58) - fighting.
**Rugby Leaguer & League Express Men of the Match:**
*Wolfpack:* Matty Russell; *Hornets:* James Barran.
**Penalty count:** 8-5; **Half-time:** 12-0;
**Referee:** Matt Rossleigh; **Attendance:** 5,969.

**TOULOUSE OLYMPIQUE 46 BATLEY BULLDOGS 0**

**OLYMPIQUE:** 1 Mark Kheirallah; 3 Bastien Ader; 25 Mathieu Jussaume; 26 Junior Vaivai; 20 Ilias Bergal; 6 Johnathon Ford; 7 Stan Robin; 17 Paterika Vaivai; 9 Anthony Marion; 15 Ben Evans; 11 Con Mika; 12 Rhys Curran; 19 James Bell. Subs (all used): 14 Dean Parata; 16 Tyla Hepi; 21 Jordan Dezaria; 28 Pierre-Jean Lima.
**Tries:** P Vaivai (6), Curran (17), Ford (26), Bergal (31), Robin (46, 70), Kheirallah (58), J Vaivai (76);
**Goals:** Kheirallah 7/8.
**Sin bin:** Mika (43) - fighting; P Vaivai (67) - punching Reittie.
**BULLDOGS:** 6 Louis Jouffret; 2 Wayne Reittie; 3 Sam Smeaton; 4 Lewis Galbraith; 28 Jack Broadbent; 14 Danny Yates; 7 Dom Brambani; 8 Adam Gledhill; 27 Reiss Butterworth; 15 Toby Everett; 22 Sam Wood; 11 Dane Manning; 24 Paul Brearley. Subs (all used): 16 Michael Ward; 23 Keenen Tomlinson; 30 Archie Bruce; 31 George Senior.
**Sin bin:** Galbraith (43) - fighting.
**Rugby Leaguer & League Express Men of the Match:**
*Olympique:* Mark Kheirallah; *Bulldogs:* Dom Brambani.
**Penalty count:** 8-6; **Half-time:** 22-0;
**Referee:** Billy Pearson; **Attendance:** 1,895.

*Sunday 18th August 2019*

**DEWSBURY RAMS 10 BRADFORD BULLS 34**

**RAMS:** 42 Joe Martin; 1 Dale Morton; 4 Adam Ryder; 32 Owen Trout; 2 Andy Gabriel; 38 Liam Finn; 6 Paul Sykes; 33 Frazer Morris; 9 Robbie Ward; 17 Martyn Reilly; 34 Daniel Waite-Pullan; 12 Michael Knowles; 19 Daniel Igbinedion. Subs (all used): 18 Sam Day; 15 Liam Johnson; 40 Luke Nelmes; 30 Tom Garratt.
**Tries:** Johnson (50), Ryder (76); **Goals:** Finn 1/2.
**Dismissal:** Knowles (55) - use of the elbow on Lilley.
**Sin bin:** Sykes (34) - dissent;
O Trout (66) - professional foul.
**BULLS:** 1 Brandon Pickersgill; 5 Jy Hitchcox; 31 Rhys Evans; 26 Ross Oakes; 2 Ethan Ryan; 6 Joe Keyes; 14 Jordan Lilley; 10 Steve Crossley; 9 Matty Wildie; 16 James Green; 11 Matt Garside; 25 Connor Farrell; 12 Elliot Minchella. Subs (all used): 33 Thomas Doyle; 18 Sam Hallas; 3 Jake Webster; 17 Ross Peltier.
**Tries:** Crossley (17), Wildie (23), Peltier (32), Minchella (47), Pickersgill (57), Oakes (62); **Goals:** Keyes 5/6.
**Sin bin:** Hitchcox (55) - fighting.
**Rugby Leaguer & League Express Men of the Match:**
*Rams:* Dale Morton; *Bulls:* Brandon Pickersgill.
**Penalty count:** 11-13; **Half-time:** 0-18;
**Referee:** Jack Smith; **Attendance:** 2,285.

**LEIGH CENTURIONS 34 WIDNES VIKINGS 22**

**CENTURIONS:** 35 Ryan Brierley; 32 Adam Higson; 3 Iain Thornley; 44 Junior Sa'u; 5 Stefan Marsh; 6 Martyn Ridyard; 34 Ben Reynolds; 26 Luke Douglas; 9 Micky Higham; 22 Jordan Thompson; 11 Toby Adamson; 12 Andy Thornley; 15 Joe Cator. Subs (all used): 27 Liam Hood; 28 Mitch Clark; 29 Jake Emmitt; 30 Cory Paterson.
**Tries:** Higson (7), A Thornley (18, 32), Marsh (39, 67), Hood (52); **Goals:** Ridyard 5/6.
**VIKINGS:** 1 Olly Ashall-Bott; 2 Ryan Ince; 25 Lloyd Roby; 24 Keanan Brand; 29 Jayden Hatton; 7 Tom Gilmore; 21 Joe Lyons; 18 Ted Chapelhow; 34 Josh Ganson; 13 Hep Cahill; 11 Harrison Hansen; 37 Ellis Robson; 19 Brad Walker. Subs (all used): 8 Jay Chapelhow; 31 Jacob Dugdale; 20 Owen Farnworth; 16 MacGraff Leuluai.
**Tries:** Hatton (10), Brand (48, 75), Ashall-Bott (58);
**Goals:** Gilmore 3/4.
**Rugby Leaguer & League Express Men of the Match:**
*Centurions:* Luke Douglas; *Vikings:* Jayden Hatton.
**Penalty count:** 10-6; **Half-time:** 22-6;
**Referee:** Greg Dolan; **Attendance:** 3,559.

**SHEFFIELD EAGLES 44 BARROW RAIDERS 18**

**EAGLES:** 1 Josh Guzdek; 2 Ryan Millar; 3 Menzie Yere; 27 Jacob Ogden; 5 Ben Blackmore; 6 Pat Walker; 7 Anthony Thackeray; 17 Shaun Pick; 14 Greg Burns; 11 Brad Knowles; 19 Sonny Esslemont; 12 Joel Farrell; 13 Aaron Brown. Subs (all used): 16 Corey Makelim; 23 Rory Dixon; 32 James Meadows; 29 Ben Hellewell.
**Tries:** Millar (3, 21), Brown (23), Guzdek (58), Makelim (62, 73), Yere (67, 80);
**Goals:** Walker 5/6, Guzdek 1/1, Yere 0/1.
**Sin bin:** Knowles (50) - fighting.
**RAIDERS:** 18 Luke Cresswell; 5 Deon Cross; 3 Declan Hulme; 12 Jarrad Stack; 21 Tom Loxam; 6 Jamie Dallimore; 34 Ben White; 8 Tom Walker; 14 Wartovo Puara; 17 Ryan Duffy; 11 Jono Smith; 19 Danny Morrow; 29 Alec Susino. Subs (all used): 22 Ryan Johnston; 15 Dan Toal; 16 Glenn Riley; 36 Paul Seguier.
**Tries:** Walker (26), Cross (33), Smith (43);
**Goals:** Dallimore 3/3.
**Sin bin:** Morrow (75) - dissent.
**Rugby Leaguer & League Express Men of the Match:**
*Eagles:* Corey Makelim; *Raiders:* Jono Smith.
**Penalty count:** 12-4; **Half-time:** 16-12;
**Referee:** Gareth Hewer; **Attendance:** 677.

**SWINTON LIONS 32 HALIFAX 12**

**LIONS:** 25 Matty Ashton; 2 Mike Butt; 32 Chris Hankinson; - Craig Mullen; 28 Richard Lepori; 1 Jack Hansen; 7 Rob Fairclough; 8 Gavin Bennion; 9 Luke Waterworth; 10 Lewis Hatton; 3 Rhodri Lloyd; 33 Jack Wells; 16 Paddy Jones. Subs (all used): 14 Billy Brickhill; 35 Nick Gregson; 31 Samy Kibula; 19 Jose Kenga.
**Tries:** Lepori (8, 44), Mullen (12), Butt (26), Ashton (30), Hankinson (61); **Goals:** Hansen 4/7.
**Dismissal:** Lloyd (77) - fighting.
**Sin bin:** Fairclough (20) - fighting; Butt (33) - fighting.
**HALIFAX:** 30 Scott Grix; 2 Shaun Robinson; 3 Steve Tyrer; 20 James Saltonstall; 21 Conor McGrath; 6 Scott Murrell; 23 James Woodburn-Hall; 29 Keegan Hirst; 14 Brandon Moore; 10 Jacob Fairbank; 25 Liam Cooper; 12 Ed Barber; 16 Kevin Larroyer. Subs (all used): 7 Ben Johnston; 8 Dan Fleming; 22 Connor Davies; 17 Ben Kavanagh.
**Tries:** Saltonstall (35), Fairbank (80);
**Goals:** Tyrer 1/1, Woodburn-Hall 1/1.
**Dismissal:** Barber (33) - dangerous challenge;
Tyrer (77) - fighting.
**Sin bin:** Barber (20) - fighting.
**Rugby Leaguer & League Express Men of the Match:**
*Lions:* Rob Fairclough; *Halifax:* Brandon Moore.
**Penalty count:** 9-10; **Half-time:** 20-6;
**Referee:** Steve Race; **Attendance:** 909.

**YORK CITY KNIGHTS 22 FEATHERSTONE ROVERS 18**

**CITY KNIGHTS:** 1 Matty Marsh; 39 Will Oakes; 3 Liam Salter; 23 Jason Bass; 20 Perry Whiteley; 38 Liam Harris; 7 Connor Robinson; 8 Ronan Dixon; 9 Will Jubb; 15 Graeme Horne; 17 Joe Porter; 12 Sam Scott; 13 Tim Spears. Subs (all used): 26 Kriss Brining; 37 Jordan Baldwinson; 22 Marcus Stock; 10 Jack Teanby.
**Tries:** Oakes (25), Brining (39), Horne (66), Porter (73);
**Goals:** Robinson 3/4.
**ROVERS:** 33 Ashton Golding; 25 Jack Render; 32 Alex Sutcliffe; 5 Conor Carey; 46 Jack Johnson; 38 Dane Chisholm; 37 Callum McLelland; 42 Wellington Albert; 9 Cameron King; 17 James Harrison; 12 Brad Day; 28 Josh Walters; 13 James Lockwood. Subs (all used): 15 Luke Cooper; 14 John Davies; 45 Connor Jones; 23 Makahesi Makatoa.
**Tries:** Render (1), McLelland (20), Sutcliffe (79);
**Goals:** Chisholm 3/4.
**Sin bin:** Chisholm (38) - holding down.
**Rugby Leaguer & League Express Men of the Match:**
*City Knights:* Graeme Horne; *Rovers:* Brad Day.
**Penalty count:** 6-5; **Half-time:** 10-12;
**Referee:** Tom Grant; **Attendance:** 3,115.

## ROUND 26

*Saturday 31st August 2019*

**TOULOUSE OLYMPIQUE 42 DEWSBURY RAMS 14**

**OLYMPIQUE:** 2 Tony Maurel; 5 Paul Marcon; 25 Mathieu Jussaume; 26 Junior Vaivai; 20 Ilias Bergal; 6 Johnathon Ford; 7 Stan Robin; 17 Paterika Vaivai; 9 Anthony Marion; 15 Ben Evans; 11 Con Mika; 12 Rhys Curran; 19 James Bell. Subs (all used): 14 Dean Parata; 8 Maxime Puech; 16 Tyla Hepi; 22 Brenden Santi.
**Tries:** Bell (6), Mika (10), J Vaivai (19), Robin (42, 55), Marion (62), P Vaivai (65); **Goals:** Marion 7/7.
**RAMS:** 42 Joe Martin; 21 Jacob Thomas; 19 Daniel Igbinedion; 32 Owen Trout; 4 Adam Ryder; 38 Liam Finn; 6 Paul Sykes; 33 Frazer Morris; 18 Sam Day; 30 Tom Garratt; 15 Liam Johnson; 34 Daniel Waite-Pullan; 36 Nyle Flynn. Subs (all used): 41 Harvey Whiteley; 27 Jack Ray; 17 Martyn Reilly; 40 Luke Nelmes.
**Tries:** Day (50, 75), Reilly (57); **Goals:** Finn 1/3.
**Sin bin:** Igbinedion (54) - punching Jussaume.
**Rugby Leaguer & League Express Men of the Match:**
*Olympique:* Stan Robin; *Rams:* Sam Day.
**Penalty count:** 4-5; **Half-time:** 18-0;
**Referee:** Jack Smith; **Attendance:** 2,055.

**TORONTO WOLFPACK 62 BARROW RAIDERS 8**

**WOLFPACK:** 1 Gareth O'Brien; 5 Liam Kay; 3 Chase Stanley; 4 Ricky Leutele; 2 Matty Russell; 6 Joe Mellor; 7 Josh McCrone; 15 Darcy Lussick; 14 Andy Ackers; 10 Ashton Sims; 11 Andrew Dixon; 12 Bodene Thompson; 13 Jon Wilkin. Subs (all used): 17 Blake Wallace; 18 Gadwin Springer; 21 Anthony Mullally; 16 Tom Olbison.
**Tries:** McCrone (2), Dixon (15, 56), Kay (26, 40, 72), Russell (28, 66), Mellor (34), Mullally (38), Ackers (43);
**Goals:** O'Brien 9/11.
**RAIDERS:** 18 Luke Cresswell; 21 Tom Loxam; 5 Deon Cross; 2 Stargroth Amean; 33 Adam Ford; 6 Jamie Dallimore; 34 Ben White; 8 Tom Walker; 14 Wartovo Puara; 17 Ryan Duffy; 19 Danny Morrow; 12 Jarrad Stack; 29 Alec Susino. Subs (only two named): 36 Paul Seguier; 25 Jordan Walne (not used).
**Try:** Dallimore (47); **Goals:** Dallimore 2/2.
**Sin bin:** Amean (65) - professional foul.
**Rugby Leaguer & League Express Men of the Match:**
*Wolfpack:* Liam Kay; *Raiders:* Jamie Dallimore.
**Penalty count:** 5-4; **Half-time:** 40-2;
**Referee:** Aaron Moore; **Attendance:** 7,129.

*Sunday 1st September 2019*

**BATLEY BULLDOGS 0 FEATHERSTONE ROVERS 64**

**BULLDOGS:** 1 Dave Scott; 2 Wayne Reittie; 28 Jack Broadbent; 4 Lewis Galbraith; 5 Johnny Campbell; 14 Danny Yates; 7 Dom Brambani; 8 Adam Gledhill; 9 Alistair Leak; 15 Toby Everett; 12 Jack Downs; 19 Alex Bretherton; 24 Paul Brearley. Subs (all used): 21 Jo Taira; 23 Keenen Tomlinson; 31 George Senior; 16 Michael Ward.
**ROVERS:** 33 Ashton Golding; 46 Jack Johnson; 4 Josh Hardcastle; 32 Alex Sutcliffe; 5 Conor Carey; 38 Dane Chisholm; 37 Callum McLelland; 23 Makahesi Makatoa; 9 Cameron King; 14 John Davies; 12 Brad Day; 28 Josh Walters; 13 James Lockwood. Subs (all used): 15 Luke Cooper; 17 James Harrison; 45 Connor Jones; 29 Jack Ormondroyd.
**Tries:** Day (15), King (21), Chisholm (24, 51, 64), Hardcastle (28, 68), Harrison (30), Lockwood (44), Jones (61, 75); **Goals:** Chisholm 10/11.
**Rugby Leaguer & League Express Men of the Match:**
*Bulldogs:* Wayne Reittie; *Rovers:* Dane Chisholm.
**Penalty count:** 3-7; **Half-time:** 0-30;
**Referee:** Gareth Hewer; **Attendance:** 1,602.

**BRADFORD BULLS 30 SHEFFIELD EAGLES 10**

**BULLS:** 1 Brandon Pickersgill; 5 Jy Hitchcox; 3 Jake Webster; 26 Ross Oakes; 2 Ethan Ryan; 6 Joe Keyes; 14 Jordan Lilley; 16 James Green; 18 Sam Hallas; 10 Steve Crossley; 29 Matthew Storton; 25 Connor Farrell; 12 Elliot Minchella. Subs (all used): 13 Mikey Wood; 31 Rhys Evans; 9 Matty Wildie; 17 Ross Peltier.
**Tries:** Keyes (4), Webster (26), Peltier (55), Ryan (60), Pickersgill (64), Evans (74); **Goals:** Keyes 3/6.
**EAGLES:** 16 Corey Makelim; 2 Ryan Millar; 29 Ben Hellewell; 1 Josh Guzdek; 5 Ben Blackmore; 6 Pat Walker; 7 Anthony Thackeray; 23 Rory Dixon; 14 Greg Burns; 21 Blake Broadbent; 19 Sonny Esslemont; 12 Joel Farrell; 13 Aaron Brown. Subs (all used): 32 James Meadows; 31 James Thornton; 3 Menzie Yere; 25 Lewis Taylor.
**Tries:** Farrell (19), Meadows (49); **Goals:** Walker 1/2.
**Sin bin:** Farrell (62) - dissent.
**Rugby Leaguer & League Express Men of the Match:**
*Bulls:* Joe Keyes; *Eagles:* Anthony Thackeray.
**Penalty count:** 12-9; **Half-time:** 12-4;
**Referee:** Billy Pearson; **Attendance:** 7,541.

**HALIFAX 58 ROCHDALE HORNETS 0**

**HALIFAX:** 23 James Woodburn-Hall; 2 Shaun Robinson; 3 Steve Tyrer; 20 James Saltonstall; 5 Will Sharp; 6 Scott Murrell; 7 Ben Johnston; 10 Jacob Fairbank; 9 Ben Kaye; 33 Keegan Hirst; 25 Liam Cooper; 17 Ben Kavanagh; 16 Kevin Larroyer. Subs (all used): 14 Brandon Moore; 8 Dan Fleming; 18 Elliot Morris; 21 Conor McGrath.
**Tries:** Fairbank (3), Tyrer (18, 28), Woodburn-Hall (21, 47), Sharp (42), Cooper (45), McGrath (59, 71), Fleming (76); **Goals:** Tyrer 7/11.
**HORNETS:** 7 Dan Abram; 2 Shaun Ainscough; 5 James Worthington; 18 Sam Grant; 24 Brandon Wood; 19 Oscar Thomas; 29 Izaac Farrell; 8 Callum Marriott; 9 Ben Moores; 10 Mike Weldon; 11 Lee Mitchell; 14 Kyle Shelford; 25 Zac Baker. Subs (all used): 12 Jordan Syme; 15 Lewis Sheridan; 21 Aidy Gleeson; 22 Callum Wood.
**Sin bin:** Baker (42) - late challenge on Murrell, (62) - high tackle on Murrell; B Wood (75) - dissent.
**Rugby Leaguer & League Express Men of the Match:**
*Halifax:* James Woodburn-Hall; *Hornets:* Kyle Shelford.
**Penalty count:** 9-5; **Half-time:** 20-0;
**Referee:** Cameron Worsley; **Attendance:** 1,126.

**LEIGH CENTURIONS 23 YORK CITY KNIGHTS 24**

**CENTURIONS:** 35 Ryan Brierley; 19 Mitch Cox; 3 Iain Thornley; 25 Liam Forsyth; 5 Stefan Marsh; 36 Kevin Brown; 7 Josh Woods; 26 Luke Douglas; 9 Micky Higham; 29 Jake Emmitt; 11 Toby Adamson; 22 Jordan Thompson; 15 Joe Cator. Subs (all used): 13 Luke Adamson; 27 Liam Hood; 28 Mitch Clark; 30 Cory Paterson.
**Tries:** Brown (30), Hood (39), Brierley (45), Forsyth (75); **Goals:** Brierley 3/4; **Field goal:** Woods (65).
**CITY KNIGHTS:** 1 Matty Marsh; 39 Will Oakes; 23 Jason Bass; 4 Brad Hey; 5 Matt Chilton; 38 Liam Harris; 7 Connor Robinson; 37 Jordan Baldwinson; 9 Will Jubb; 15 Graeme Horne; 17 Joe Porter; 12 Sam Scott; 13 Tim Spears. Subs (all used): 26 Kriss Brining; 22 Marcus Stock; 16 Jack Blagbrough; 19 Mike Kelly.
**Tries:** Oakes (19, 58), Marsh (48), Harris (68); **Goals:** Robinson 4/5.
**Rugby Leaguer & League Express Men of the Match:**
*Centurions:* Liam Hood; *City Knights:* Graeme Horne.
**Penalty count:** 7-4; **Half-time:** 12-8;
**Referee:** Marcus Griffiths; **Attendance:** 3,408.

**WIDNES VIKINGS 36 SWINTON LIONS 28**

**VIKINGS:** 5 Jack Owens; 25 Lloyd Roby; 4 Anthony Gelling; 24 Keanan Brand; 36 Patrick Ah Van; 6 Danny Craven; 21 Joe Lyons; 8 Jay Chapelhow; 34 Josh Ganson; 26 Dan Norman; 17 Sam Wilde; 12 Chris Dean; 37 Ellis Robson. Subs (all used): 18 Ted Chapelhow; 31 Jacob Dugdale; 13 Hep Cahill; 19 Brad Walker.
**Tries:** Brand (20), Ah Van (23, 49), Roby (43), Owens (53), Dean (67), Ganson (70); **Goals:** Owens 3/6, Dean 1/1.
**LIONS:** 25 Matty Ashton; 2 Mike Butt; 3 Rhodri Lloyd; 34 Craig Mullen; 28 Richard Lepori; 1 Jack Hansen; 7 Rob Fairclough; 8 Gavin Bennion; 14 Billy Brickhill; 10 Lewis Hatton; 22 Frankie Halton; 33 Jack Wells; 16 Paddy Jones. Subs (all used): 36 Ben Morris; 35 Nick Gregson; 19 Jose Kenga; 31 Samy Kibula.
**Tries:** Butt (32), Kibula (35), Hansen (56), Gregson (74), Ashton (78); **Goals:** Hansen 4/5.
**Rugby Leaguer & League Express Men of the Match:**
*Vikings:* Chris Dean; *Lions:* Jack Hansen.
**Penalty count:** 9-5; **Half-time:** 8-10;
**Referee:** Greg Dolan; **Attendance:** 3,928.

## ROUND 27

*Saturday 7th September 2019*

**FEATHERSTONE ROVERS 24
TOULOUSE OLYMPIQUE 26**

**ROVERS:** 33 Ashton Golding; 5 Conor Carey; 32 Alex Sutcliffe; 4 Josh Hardcastle; 46 Jack Johnson; 37 Callum McLelland; 38 Dane Chisholm; 42 Wellington Albert; 9 Cameron King; 14 John Davies; 12 Brad Day; 28 Josh Walters; 13 James Lockwood. Subs (all used): 15 Luke Cooper; 17 James Harrison; 29 Jack Ormondroyd; 45 Connor Jones.
**Tries:** King (10, 17), Chisholm (23), Sutcliffe (77);
**Goals:** Chisholm 4/4.
**OLYMPIQUE:** 1 Mark Kheirallah; 5 Paul Marcon; 25 Mathieu Jussaume; 3 Bastien Ader; 20 Ilias Bergal; 6 Johnathon Ford; 7 Stan Robin; 8 Maxime Puech; 9 Anthony Marion; 17 Paterika Vaivai; 11 Con Mika; 12 Rhys Curran; 19 James Bell. Subs (all used): 14 Dean Parata; 15 Ben Evans; 16 Tyla Hepi; 10 Joe Bretherton.
**Tries:** Jussaume (31), Evans (34), Parata (52, 72), Robin (66); **Goals:** Kheirallah 3/5.
**Rugby Leaguer & League Express Men of the Match:**
*Rovers:* James Lockwood; *Olympique:* Dean Parata.
**Penalty count:** 6-5; **Half-time:** 18-8;
**Referee:** Greg Dolan; **Attendance:** 2,334.

*Sunday 8th September 2019*

**BARROW RAIDERS 24 BATLEY BULLDOGS 16**

**RAIDERS:** 18 Luke Cresswell; 33 Adam Ford; 2 Stargroth Amean; 9 Deon Cross; 1 Theerapol Ritson; 6 Jamie Dallimore; 34 Ben White; 29 Alec Susino; 14 Wartovo Puara; 17 Ryan Duffy; 19 Danny Morrow; 12 Jarrad Stack; 21 Tom Loxam. Subs (all used): 24 Jake Carter; 36 Paul Seguier; 16 Glenn Riley; 3 Declan Hulme.
**Tries:** Cross (1), Puara (25), Amean (29), Susino (52);
**Goals:** Dallimore 4/5.
**Sin bin:** Stack (16) - fighting.
**BULLDOGS:** 6 Louis Jouffret; 2 Wayne Reittie; 20 Niall Walker; 4 Lewis Galbraith; 5 Johnny Campbell; 14 Danny Yates; 7 Dom Brambani; 8 Adam Gledhill; 9 Alistair Leak; 21 Jo Taira; 23 Keenen Tomlinson; 24 Paul Brearley; 22 Sam Wood. Subs (all used): 25 Lewis Bienek; 27 Reiss Butterworth; 15 Toby Everett; 16 Michael Ward.

**Tries:** Brambani (10), Leak (20), Brearley (35);
**Goals:** Brambani 2/3.
**Sin bin:** Galbraith (16) - fighting.
**Rugby Leaguer & League Express Men of the Match:**
*Raiders:* Luke Cresswell; *Bulldogs:* Danny Yates.
**Penalty count:** 10-7; **Half-time:** 18-16;
**Referee:** Tom Crashley; **Attendance:** 1,214.

**DEWSBURY RAMS 8 WIDNES VIKINGS 22**

**RAMS:** 42 Joe Martin; 23 Rob Worrincy; 1 Dale Morton; 4 Adam Ryder; 2 Andy Gabriel; 6 Paul Sykes; 38 Liam Finn; 30 Tom Garratt; 18 Sam Day; 17 Martyn Reilly; 11 Lucas Walshaw; 32 Owen Trout; 19 Daniel Igbinedion. Subs (all used): 9 Robbie Ward; 15 Liam Johnson; 8 Jode Sheriffe; 40 Luke Nelmes.
**Tries:** Worrincy (30, 62); **Goals:** Finn 0/2.
**Sin bin:** Morton (54) - trip on Buckley.
**VIKINGS:** 5 Jack Owens; 25 Lloyd Roby; 4 Anthony Gelling; 24 Keanan Brand; 22 Owen Buckley; 6 Danny Craven; 21 Joe Lyons; 8 Jay Chapelhow; 34 Josh Ganson; 26 Dan Norman; 17 Sam Wilde; 12 Chris Dean; 37 Ellis Robson. Subs (all used): 18 Ted Chapelhow; 38 Lewis Else; 13 Hep Cahill; 19 Brad Walker.
**Tries:** Buckley (19, 50), Owens (37), Dean (44);
**Goals:** Owens 3/5.
**Rugby Leaguer & League Express Men of the Match:**
*Rams:* Daniel Igbinedion; *Vikings:* Jack Owens.
**Penalty count:** 11-8; **Half-time:** 4-10;
**Referee:** Cameron Worsley; **Attendance:** 1,409.

**HALIFAX 8 YORK CITY KNIGHTS 14**

**HALIFAX:** 23 James Woodburn-Hall; 21 Conor McGrath; 3 Steve Tyrer; 12 Ed Barber; 5 Will Sharp; 6 Scott Murrell; 7 Ben Johnston; 10 Jacob Fairbank; 9 Ben Kaye; 33 Keegan Hirst; 25 Liam Cooper; 17 Ben Kavanagh; 16 Kevin Larroyer. Subs (all used): 8 Dan Fleming; 20 James Saltonstall; 14 Brandon Moore; 22 Connor Davies.
**Tries:** Sharp (8), Barber (39); **Goals:** Tyrer 0/2.
**Dismissal:** Moore (73) - dissent.
**CITY KNIGHTS:** 1 Matty Marsh; 39 Will Oakes; 23 Jason Bass; 4 Brad Hey; 5 Matt Chilton; 38 Liam Harris; 7 Connor Robinson; 37 Jordan Baldwinson; 9 Will Jubb; 22 Marcus Stock; 3 Liam Salter; 12 Sam Scott; 13 Tim Spears. Subs (all used): 8 Ronan Dixon; 15 Graeme Horne; 10 Jack Teanby; 19 Mike Kelly.
**Tries:** Robinson (51), Chilton (58); **Goals:** Robinson 3/3.
**Rugby Leaguer & League Express Men of the Match:**
*Halifax:* James Woodburn-Hall; *City Knights:* Will Jubb.
**Penalty count:** 7-10; **Half-time:** 8-0;
**Referee:** Tom Grant; **Attendance:** 1,862.

**ROCHDALE HORNETS 0 BRADFORD BULLS 82**

**HORNETS:** 7 Dan Abram; 2 Shaun Ainscough; 15 Lewis Sheridan; 14 Sam Grant; 24 Brandon Wood; 19 Oscar Thomas; 29 Izaac Farrell; 8 Callum Marriott; 9 Ben Moores; 11 Lee Mitchell; 23 Kyle Shelford; 12 Jordan Syme; 25 Zac Baker. Subs (all used): 22 Callum Wood; 16 Mike Weldon; 21 Aidy Gleeson; 17 Liam Carberry.
**BULLS:** 1 Brandon Pickersgill; 22 Dalton Grant; 3 Jake Webster; 26 Ross Oakes; 2 Ethan Ryan; 6 Joe Keyes; 14 Jordan Lilley; 10 Steve Crossley; 18 Sam Hallas; 16 James Green; 29 Matthew Storton; 25 Connor Farrell; 12 Elliot Minchella. Subs (all used): 9 Matty Wildie; 31 Rhys Evans; 13 Mikey Wood; 17 Ross Peltier.
**Tries:** Storton (2), Webster (12), Ryan (14), J Green (19), Oakes (24), Pickersgill (29), Lilley (32), Grant (36, 54, 60), Keyes (43, 74), Peltier (47), Farrell (64), Wildie (76);
**Goals:** Keyes 10/14, Ryan 1/1.
**Rugby Leaguer & League Express Men of the Match:**
*Hornets:* Izaac Farrell; *Bulls:* Joe Keyes.
**Penalty count:** 5-10; **Half-time:** 0-46;
**Referee:** Jack Smith; **Attendance:** 1,328.

**SWINTON LIONS 48 SHEFFIELD EAGLES 16**

**LIONS:** 25 Matty Ashton; 2 Mike Butt; 32 Chris Hankinson; 34 Craig Mullen; 28 Richard Lepori; 1 Jack Hansen; 7 Rob Fairclough; 8 Gavin Bennion; 14 Billy Brickhill; 10 Lewis Hatton; 3 Rhodri Lloyd; 33 Jack Wells; 22 Frankie Halton. Subs (all used): 36 Ben Morris; 35 Nick Gregson; 16 Paddy Jones; 19 Jose Kenga.
**Tries:** Ashton (9, 17, 44, 58, 77), Bennion (11), Wells (21), Hansen (63), Morris (80); **Goals:** Hansen 5/8, Ashton 1/1.
**EAGLES:** 1 Josh Guzdek; 2 Ryan Millar; 3 Menzie Yere; 29 Ben Hellewell; 5 Ben Blackmore; 6 Pat Walker; 7 Anthony Thackeray; 23 Rory Dixon; 14 Greg Burns; 19 Sonny Esslemont; 15 Olly Davies; 12 Joel Farrell; 13 Aaron Brown. Subs (all used): 16 Corey Makelim; 31 James Thornton; 21 Blake Broadbent; 25 Lewis Taylor.
**Tries:** Brown (36), Hellewell (52), Makelim (67);
**Goals:** Walker 2/3.

**Rugby Leaguer & League Express Men of the Match:**
*Lions:* Matty Ashton; *Eagles:* Ryan Millar.
**Penalty count:** 6-6; **Half-time:** 20-6.
**Referee:** Billy Pearson; **Attendance:** 814.

## QUALIFYING PLAY-OFF

*Saturday 14th September 2019*

### TOULOUSE OLYMPIQUE 44 YORK CITY KNIGHTS 6

**OLYMPIQUE:** 1 Mark Kheirallah; 5 Paul Marcon; 25 Mathieu Jussaume; 3 Bastien Ader; 4 Gavin Marguerite; 7 Stan Robin; 6 Johnathon Ford; 17 Paterika Vaivai; 9 Anthony Marion; 8 Maxime Puech; 11 Con Mika; 12 Rhys Curran; 19 James Bell. Subs (all used): 30 William Barthau; 15 Ben Evans; 16 Tyla Hepi; 10 Joe Bretherton.
**Tries:** Marcon (13), Kheirallah (21, 24), Marguerite (40), Marion (53), Jussaume (63), Ford (73), Robin (79);
**Goals:** Kheirallah 6/9.
**CITY KNIGHTS:** 1 Matty Marsh; 39 Will Oakes; 3 Liam Salter; 4 Brad Hey; 5 Matt Chilton; 38 Liam Harris; 7 Connor Robinson; 37 Jordan Baldwinson; 9 Will Jubb; 22 Marcus Stock; 12 Sam Scott; 19 Mike Kelly; 13 Tim Spears. Subs (all used): 16 Jack Blagbrough; 11 Josh Jordan-Roberts; 10 Jack Teanby; 8 Ronan Dixon.
**Try:** Chilton (27); **Goals:** Robinson 1/1.
**Rugby Leaguer & League Express Men of the Match:**
*Olympique:* Mark Kheirallah; *City Knights:* Connor Robinson.
**Penalty count:** 3-4; **Half-time:** 22-6;
**Referee:** Greg Dolan; **Attendance:** 1,132.

## ELIMINATION PLAY-OFF

*Sunday 15th September 2019*

### LEIGH CENTURIONS 18 FEATHERSTONE ROVERS 34

**CENTURIONS:** 35 Ryan Brierley; 32 Adam Higson; 3 Iain Thornley; 44 Junior Sa'u; 5 Stefan Marsh; 36 Kevin Brown; 7 Josh Woods; 26 Luke Douglas; 9 Micky Higham; 10 Sam Brooks; 11 Toby Adamson; 22 Jordan Thompson; 13 Luke Adamson. Subs (all used): 27 Liam Hood; 15 Joe Cator; 28 Mitch Clark; 8 Tom Spencer.
**Tries:** Sa'u (29), Spencer (43), Marsh (57), T Adamson (73);
**Goals:** Brierley 1/4.
**ROVERS:** 33 Ashton Golding; 46 Jack Johnson; 4 Josh Hardcastle; 32 Alex Sutcliffe; 5 Conor Carey; 37 Callum McLelland; 38 Dane Chisholm; 14 John Davies; 45 Connor Jones; 23 Makahesi Makatoa; 12 Brad Day; 28 Josh Walters; 13 James Lockwood. Subs: 15 Luke Cooper; 17 James Harrison; 25 Jack Render (not used); 42 Wellington Albert.
**Tries:** Sutcliffe (8, 25), Harrison (21), McLelland (50), Walters (63), Chisholm (66); **Goals:** Chisholm 5/7.
**Rugby Leaguer & League Express Men of the Match:**
*Centurions:* Liam Hood; *Rovers:* Callum McLelland.
**Penalty count:** 5-6; **Half-time:** 4-14;
**Referee:** Gareth Hewer; **Attendance:** 2,671.

## ELIMINATION SEMI-FINAL

*Saturday 21st September 2019*

### YORK CITY KNIGHTS 4 FEATHERSTONE ROVERS 30

**CITY KNIGHTS:** 1 Matty Marsh; 39 Will Oakes; 23 Jason Bass; 4 Brad Hey; 20 Perry Whiteley; 38 Liam Harris; 7 Connor Robinson; 22 Marcus Stock; 9 Will Jubb; 10 Jack Teanby; 3 Liam Salter; 12 Sam Scott; 13 Tim Spears. Subs (all used): 8 Ronan Dixon; 15 Graeme Horne; 37 Jordan Baldwinson; 40 Andy Ellis.
**Goals:** Robinson 2/2.
**ROVERS:** 33 Ashton Golding; 46 Jack Johnson; 4 Josh Hardcastle; 32 Alex Sutcliffe; 5 Conor Carey; 37 Callum McLelland; 38 Dane Chisholm; 23 Makahesi Makatoa; 45 Connor Jones; 14 John Davies; 12 Brad Day; 28 Josh Walters; 13 James Lockwood. Subs (all used): 15 Luke Cooper; 17 James Harrison; 25 Jack Render; 42 Wellington Albert.
**Tries:** Makatoa (27), Harrison (47), Day (50), J Johnson (73), Render (78); **Goals:** Chisholm 5/6.
**Rugby Leaguer & League Express Men of the Match:**
*City Knights:* Matty Marsh; *Rovers:* Callum McLelland.
**Penalty count:** 8-7; **Half-time:** 4-8;
**Referee:** Ben Thaler; **Attendance:** 3,222.

## QUALIFYING SEMI-FINAL

*Sunday 22nd September 2019*

### TORONTO WOLFPACK 40 TOULOUSE OLYMPIQUE 24

**WOLFPACK:** 1 Gareth O'Brien; 5 Liam Kay; 3 Chase Stanley; 4 Ricky Leutele; 2 Matty Russell; 6 Joe Mellor; 7 Josh McCrone; 21 Anthony Mullally; 14 Andy Ackers; 10 Ashton Sims; 11 Andrew Dixon; 12 Bodene Thompson; 13 Jon Wilkin. Subs (all used): 17 Blake Wallace; 15 Darcy Lussick; 18 Gadwin Springer; 16 Tom Olbison.

Featherstone's Brad Day tackled by York's Will Jubb during the play-offs

**Tries:** Mellor (10, 34), Leutele (16, 28, 67), McCrone (31), Kay (47), Stanley (60); **Goals:** O'Brien 4/8.
**OLYMPIQUE:** 1 Mark Kheirallah; 5 Paul Marcon; 25 Mathieu Jussaume; 26 Junior Vaivai; 3 Bastien Ader; 6 Johnathon Ford; 7 Stan Robin; 8 Maxime Puech; 9 Anthony Marion; 17 Paterika Vaivai; 11 Con Mika; 12 Rhys Curran; 19 James Bell. Subs (all used): 30 William Barthau; 15 Ben Evans; 16 Tyla Hepi; 10 Joe Bretherton.
**Tries:** Kheirallah (19, 73, 75), Barthau (54);
**Goals:** Kheirallah 4/4.
**Rugby Leaguer & League Express Men of the Match:**
*Wolfpack:* Ricky Leutele; *Olympique:* Paterika Vaivai.
**Penalty count:** 2-2; **Half-time:** 26-6;
**Referee:** Gareth Hewer; **Attendance:** 9,325.

## FINAL ELIMINATOR

*Sunday 29th September 2019*

### TOULOUSE OLYMPIQUE 12 FEATHERSTONE ROVERS 36

**OLYMPIQUE:** 1 Mark Kheirallah; 5 Paul Marcon; 25 Mathieu Jussaume; 26 Junior Vaivai; 3 Bastien Ader; 6 Johnathon Ford; 30 William Barthau; 8 Maxime Puech; 9 Anthony Marion; 17 Paterika Vaivai; 11 Con Mika; 12 Rhys Curran; 19 James Bell. Subs (all used): 14 Dean Parata; 10 Joe Bretherton; 21 Jordan Dezaria; 22 Brenden Santi.
**Tries:** Barthau (8), Marcon (49); **Goals:** Kheirallah 2/2.
**ROVERS:** 33 Ashton Golding; 46 Jack Johnson; 5 Conor Carey; 32 Alex Sutcliffe; 25 Jack Render; 37 Callum McLelland; 38 Dane Chisholm; 23 Makahesi Makatoa; 45 Connor Jones; 14 John Davies; 4 Josh Hardcastle; 17 James Harrison; 13 James Lockwood. Subs (all used): 15 Luke Cooper; 42 Wellington Albert; 10 Jack Bussey; 29 Jack Ormondroyd.

**Tries:** Davies (5, 17), Golding (28), Harrison (45), Chisholm (54), J Johnson (62), Render (68);
**Goals:** Chisholm 4/7.
**Rugby Leaguer & League Express Men of the Match:**
*Olympique:* Paul Marcon; *Rovers:* John Davies.
**Penalty count:** 6-6; **Half-time:** 6-18;
**Referee:** Robert Hicks; **Attendance:** 1,068.

## GRAND FINAL

*Saturday 5th October 2019*

### TORONTO WOLFPACK 24 FEATHERSTONE ROVERS 6

**WOLFPACK:** 1 Gareth O'Brien; 5 Liam Kay; 3 Chase Stanley; 4 Ricky Leutele; 2 Matty Russell; 6 Joe Mellor; 7 Josh McCrone; 21 Anthony Mullally; 14 Andy Ackers; 10 Ashton Sims; 11 Andrew Dixon; 12 Bodene Thompson; 13 Jon Wilkin. Subs (all used): 17 Blake Wallace; 15 Darcy Lussick; 16 Tom Olbison; 18 Gadwin Springer.
**Tries:** McCrone (32), Wallace (57), Thompson (62), Mellor (70); **Goals:** O'Brien 2/3, Wallace 2/2.
**ROVERS:** 33 Ashton Golding; 25 Jack Render; 4 Josh Hardcastle; 32 Alex Sutcliffe; 46 Jack Johnson; 38 Dane Chisholm; 37 Callum McLelland; 14 John Davies; 45 Connor Jones; 29 Jack Ormondroyd; 10 Jack Bussey; 17 James Harrison; 13 James Lockwood. Subs (all used): 42 Wellington Albert; 15 Luke Cooper; 23 Makahesi Makatoa; 9 Cameron King.
**Try:** Sutcliffe (28); **Goals:** Chisholm 1/1.
**Rugby Leaguer & League Express Men of the Match:**
*Wolfpack:* Jon Wilkin; *Rovers:* Ashton Golding.
**Penalty count:** 10-7; **Half-time:** 4-6;
**Referee:** Chris Kendall; **Attendance:** 9,974.

Toronto's Bodene Thompson fends off Featherstone's James Harrison during the Championship Grand Final

# LEAGUE 1 2019
## *Club by Club*

---

# COVENTRY BEARS

| DATE | FIXTURE | RESULT | SCORERS | LGE | ATT |
|---|---|---|---|---|---|
| 17/2/19 | West Wales (h) | W28-4 | t:Freeman(2),Hall,Jones,Morley-Samuels g:Newman(4) | 1st | 526 |
| 24/2/19 | Newcastle (h) | W32-28 | t:Jones,Hall(2),Butler,Freeman,Newman g:Newman(4) | 2nd | 360 |
| 3/3/19 | Keighley (a) | L40-8 | t:Barratt g:Newman(2) | 5th | 915 |
| 8/3/19 | Doncaster (a) (CCR3) | L38-16 | t:K Williams(2),Hall,Gover | N/A | 381 |
| 24/3/19 | Hunslet (a) | L44-10 | t:Sherratt,Petersen g:Thomas | 7th | 542 |
| 7/4/19 | Doncaster (a) | L44-18 | t:Jones,Ryan,Carter g:Newman(3) | 8th | 562 |
| 19/4/19 | London Skolars (h) | L28-30 | t:Richardson,S Davis,Hall(2),Freeman g:Newman(4) | 8th | 353 |
| 11/5/19 | Workington (h) ● | W41-30 | t:Jones(2),Newman(2),Pearce-Paul,Rance,Hall g:Newman(6) fg:Newman | 8th | 303 |
| 19/5/19 | Oldham (h) | L34-18 | t:Pearce-Paul,Hall,S Davis g:Newman(3) | 8th | 451 |
| 26/5/19 | North Wales (h) ● | L18-34 | t:Rance,Taylor,Hall g:Newman(3) | 9th | 395 |
| 9/6/19 | Whitehaven (a) | L32-18 | t:Newman,S Davis,Hall g:Newman(3) | 9th | 915 |
| 16/6/19 | Workington (a) ●● | L54-16 | t:S Davis,Jones,Fellows g:Hall(2) | 9th | 895 |
| 29/6/19 | Doncaster (h) ● | L10-54 | t:Hall,Rance g:Sanderson | 9th | 386 |
| 6/7/19 | London Skolars (a) | W20-36 | t:S Davis,Hall(2),Freeman,Sherratt(2) g:Sanderson(6) | 9th | 216 |
| 14/7/19 | Hunslet (h) ●●● | L20-48 | t:Taylor,Rance,Hall g:Hall(4) | 9th | 420 |
| 20/7/19 | West Wales (a) | L44-16 | t:Rance,Carter,Green g:Sanderson(2) | 9th | 352 |
| 4/8/19 | Keighley (h) ●●● | L20-46 | t:S Davis,Hall(2),Rance g:Hall(2) | 9th | 345 |
| 11/8/19 | North Wales (a) | L33-16 | t:Rance,Whiteley,Hall g:Hall(2) | 9th | 256 |
| 18/8/19 | Newcastle (a) | L88-6 | t:Ray g:Hall | 9th | 711 |
| 1/9/19 | Oldham (h) ●●● | L6-50 | t:Jones g:Hall | 9th | 280 |
| 7/9/19 | Whitehaven (h) ●●● | L0-72 | | 9th | 652 |

● Played at Ivor Preece Field, Broadstreet  ●● Played at Borough Park  ●●● Played at Webb Ellis Road, Rugby

| | D.O.B. | APP ALL | APP L1 | TRIES ALL | TRIES L1 | GOALS ALL | GOALS L1 | FG ALL | FG L1 | PTS ALL | PTS L1 |
|---|---|---|---|---|---|---|---|---|---|---|---|
| Chris Barratt | 7/2/93 | 17(2) | 16(2) | 1 | 1 | 0 | 0 | 0 | 0 | 4 | 4 |
| Dewi Billingham | 9/11/98 | (2) | (2) | 0 | 0 | 0 | 0 | 0 | 0 | 0 | 0 |
| Rob Butler | 15/5/98 | 1 | 1 | 1 | 1 | 0 | 0 | 0 | 0 | 4 | 4 |
| Errol Carter | 22/1/96 | 12(1) | 12(1) | 2 | 2 | 0 | 0 | 0 | 0 | 8 | 8 |
| Nathan Conroy | 6/3/95 | 19(1) | 18(1) | 0 | 0 | 0 | 0 | 0 | 0 | 0 | 0 |
| Matthew Davies | 9/4/98 | 3 | 3 | 0 | 0 | 0 | 0 | 0 | 0 | 0 | 0 |
| Sam Davis | 11/11/98 | 6(6) | 6(6) | 6 | 6 | 0 | 0 | 0 | 0 | 24 | 24 |
| Jack Daynes | 12/6/98 | (1) | (1) | 0 | 0 | 0 | 0 | 0 | 0 | 0 | 0 |
| Zak Fellows | 14/12/99 | 1(4) | 1(4) | 1 | 1 | 0 | 0 | 0 | 0 | 4 | 4 |
| Nyle Flynn | 27/7/97 | 1 | 1 | 0 | 0 | 0 | 0 | 0 | 0 | 0 | 0 |
| Hayden Freeman | 20/8/97 | 21 | 20 | 5 | 5 | 0 | 0 | 0 | 0 | 20 | 20 |
| Dan Gover | 23/9/93 | 1(3) | (3) | 1 | 0 | 0 | 0 | 0 | 0 | 4 | 0 |
| Ben Gray | 12/11/95 | 1(2) | 1(2) | 0 | 0 | 0 | 0 | 0 | 0 | 0 | 0 |
| Cobi Green | 4/3/99 | 2 | 2 | 1 | 1 | 0 | 0 | 0 | 0 | 4 | 4 |
| Elliot Hall | 6/7/97 | 20 | 19 | 17 | 16 | 12 | 12 | 0 | 0 | 92 | 88 |
| Harvey Hallas | 14/11/97 | (1) | (1) | 0 | 0 | 0 | 0 | 0 | 0 | 0 | 0 |
| Lawrence Haywood | 30/9/95 | (3) | (3) | 0 | 0 | 0 | 0 | 0 | 0 | 0 | 0 |
| Daniel Hindmarsh | 8/8/98 | 1 | 1 | 0 | 0 | 0 | 0 | 0 | 0 | 0 | 0 |
| Jacob Jones | 15/2/99 | 19(1) | 18(1) | 7 | 7 | 0 | 0 | 0 | 0 | 28 | 28 |
| Harry Kaufman | 20/12/91 | 6(7) | 6(7) | 0 | 0 | 0 | 0 | 0 | 0 | 0 | 0 |
| Mike Kelly | 23/5/89 | 1 | 1 | 0 | 0 | 0 | 0 | 0 | 0 | 0 | 0 |
| Joslin Landu | 11/6/99 | 1(1) | 1(1) | 0 | 0 | 0 | 0 | 0 | 0 | 0 | 0 |
| James Mason | 27/1/95 | 4 | 4 | 0 | 0 | 0 | 0 | 0 | 0 | 0 | 0 |
| James Meadows | 15/6/99 | 1 | 1 | 0 | 0 | 0 | 0 | 0 | 0 | 0 | 0 |
| Callum Merrett | 27/9/97 | (1) | 0 | 0 | 0 | 0 | 0 | 0 | 0 | 0 | 0 |
| Dante Morley-Samuels | 22/11/98 | 1(1) | (1) | 1 | 1 | 0 | 0 | 0 | 0 | 4 | 4 |
| Nick Newman | 15/12/96 | 10 | 9 | 4 | 4 | 32 | 32 | 1 | 1 | 81 | 81 |
| Kameron Pearce-Paul | 28/2/97 | 17 | 16 | 2 | 2 | 0 | 0 | 0 | 0 | 8 | 8 |
| Dave Petersen | 6/3/92 | 1 | 1 | 1 | 1 | 0 | 0 | 0 | 0 | 4 | 4 |
| Ollie Purslow | 17/9/87 | 5(5) | 5(4) | 0 | 0 | 0 | 0 | 0 | 0 | 0 | 0 |
| Reece Rance | 17/7/93 | 14(1) | 14(1) | 7 | 7 | 0 | 0 | 0 | 0 | 28 | 28 |
| Jack Ray | 8/10/98 | 5(4) | 5(4) | 1 | 1 | 0 | 0 | 0 | 0 | 4 | 4 |
| Martyn Reilly | 5/1/96 | (1) | (1) | 0 | 0 | 0 | 0 | 0 | 0 | 0 | 0 |
| Toby Richardson | 5/6/96 | 2(3) | 2(3) | 1 | 1 | 0 | 0 | 0 | 0 | 4 | 4 |
| Peter Ryan | 25/2/95 | 11(1) | 11 | 1 | 1 | 0 | 0 | 0 | 0 | 4 | 4 |
| Joe Sanderson | 17/3/97 | 3 | 3 | 0 | 0 | 9 | 9 | 0 | 0 | 18 | 18 |
| Sam Scott | 5/6/90 | 1 | 1 | 0 | 0 | 0 | 0 | 0 | 0 | 0 | 0 |
| Mitch Shaw | 25/8/98 | 5(1) | 4(1) | 0 | 0 | 0 | 0 | 0 | 0 | 0 | 0 |
| Brad Sheridan | 24/3/94 | 9(3) | 9(3) | 0 | 0 | 0 | 0 | 0 | 0 | 0 | 0 |
| Kieran Sherratt | 15/11/95 | 17(1) | 16(1) | 3 | 3 | 0 | 0 | 0 | 0 | 12 | 12 |
| Cameron Stewart | 1/3/99 | (9) | (9) | 0 | 0 | 0 | 0 | 0 | 0 | 0 | 0 |
| Marcus Stock | 1/5/96 | (1) | (1) | 0 | 0 | 0 | 0 | 0 | 0 | 0 | 0 |
| Lewis Taylor | 15/4/97 | 8(1) | 8(1) | 2 | 2 | 0 | 0 | 0 | 0 | 8 | 8 |
| Jacob Thomas | 9/10/93 | 1(1) | 1(1) | 0 | 0 | 1 | 1 | 0 | 0 | 2 | 2 |
| Euan Tiernan | 13/5/98 | 2(3) | 1(3) | 0 | 0 | 0 | 0 | 0 | 0 | 0 | 0 |
| Will Tully | 8/11/99 | 1(7) | 1(6) | 0 | 0 | 0 | 0 | 0 | 0 | 0 | 0 |
| Harvey Whiteley | 26/9/98 | 3(3) | 3(3) | 1 | 1 | 0 | 0 | 0 | 0 | 4 | 4 |
| Kadeem Williams | 23/3/95 | 17 | 16 | 2 | 0 | 0 | 0 | 0 | 0 | 8 | 0 |
| Reece Williams | 28/2/95 | 2(1) | 2(1) | 0 | 0 | 0 | 0 | 0 | 0 | 0 | 0 |
| Zak Williams | 17/9/96 | (1) | (1) | 0 | 0 | 0 | 0 | 0 | 0 | 0 | 0 |

Elliot Hall

**LEAGUE RECORD**
P20-W4-D0-L16 (9th)
F365, A829, Diff-464, 8 points.

**CHALLENGE CUP**
Round Three

**1895 CUP**
Not entered

**ATTENDANCES**
Best - v Whitehaven (L1 - 652)
Worst - v Oldham (L1 - 280)
Total (all home games included) - 4,020
Average (all home games included) - 402
(Up by 15 on 2018)

*'L1' totals include League 1 regular season only; 'All' totals also include Challenge Cup*

| | |
|---|---|
| **CLUB RECORDS** | **Highest score:** 64-6 v West Wales, 25/7/2018  **Highest score against:** 6-98 v Keighley, 6/5/2018  **Record attendance:** 1,465 v Bradford, 30/6/2018 |
| **MATCH RECORDS** | **Tries:** 3 *(10 players)*  **Goals:** 8 Connor Robinson v Hemel, 19/4/2015; Ben Stead v West Wales, 25/7/2018  **Points:** 22 Dan Parker v London Skolars, 7/6/2015 |
| **SEASON RECORDS** | **Tries:** 17 Elliot Hall 2019  **Goals:** 61 Ben Stead 2018  **Points:** 138 Brad Delaney 2017 |
| **CAREER RECORDS** | **Tries:** 36 Hayden Freeman 2016-2019  **Goals:** 61 Ben Stead 2018  **Points:** 144 Hayden Freeman 2016-2019  **Appearances:** 106 Chris Barratt 2015-2019 |

# DONCASTER

| DATE | FIXTURE | RESULT | SCORERS | LGE | ATT |
|------|---------|--------|---------|-----|-----|
| 16/2/19 | Newcastle (a) | W26-32 | t:Bower,Hedges,Tali,Chrimes,Howden,Kesik g:Beharrell(4) | 3rd | 1,817 |
| 24/2/19 | Hunslet (h) | L18-20 | t:Douglas(2),Bower g:Beharrell(3) | 5th | 734 |
| 3/3/19 | Workington (h) | W20-10 | t:Miloudi(2),Cross g:Beharrell(4) | 4th | 640 |
| 8/3/19 | Coventry (h) (CCR3) | W38-16 | t:Doherty,Douglas(2),Cox,Bower,Beharrell(2) g:Beharrell(5) | N/A | 381 |
| 17/3/19 | Whitehaven (a) | L26-8 | t:Chrimes,Tali | 6th | 702 |
| 31/3/19 | Featherstone Lions (a) (CCR4) ● | W6-46 | t:Chrimes(2),Doherty,Owen,Bastas,Cross(3),Bower g:Howden(5) | N/A | N/A |
| 7/4/19 | Coventry (h) | W44-18 | t:Bower(2),Spiers,Brown,Ogden,Hedges,Douglas,Buchanan g:Howden(4),Hedges(2) | 6th | 562 |
| 14/4/19 | Batley (h) (CCR5) | W16-12 | t:Bower,Yere,Doherty g:Hedges(2) | N/A | 539 |
| 19/4/19 | Keighley (a) | L26-18 | t:Yere,Tali(2),Townsend g:Harris | 6th | 1,040 |
| 28/4/19 | North Wales (h) | L10-12 | t:Tali,Howden g:Beharrell | 6th | 658 |
| 5/5/19 | West Wales (h) (1895CR1) | W70-6 | t:Halliday(5),Yere,Nzoungou,Howden,Boas(2),Tali(2) g:Beharrell(11) | N/A | 248 |
| 11/5/19 | Catalans Dragons (a) (CCR6) | L62-6 | t:Bower g:Beharrell | N/A | 3,466 |
| 18/5/19 | London Skolars (a) | L22-6 | t:England g:Beharrell | 7th | 608 |
| 26/5/19 | West Wales (h) | W54-0 | t:Tali(2),Chrimes,Beharrell,Yere(2),Bower,Boas,Howden,Doherty g:Beharrell(7) | 6th | 525 |
| 2/6/19 | Oldham (a) (1895CR2) | W12-24 | t:Chrimes,Boas,Ogden,Doherty g:Beharrell(4) | N/A | 283 |
| 9/6/19 | Oldham (h) | W31-0 | t:Hedges(2),Boas,Doherty,Howden g:Beharrell(5) fg:Beharrell | 6th | 678 |
| 14/6/19 | Hunslet (a) | W20-22 | t:Howden,Boas,Beharrell,Cameron Scott g:Beharrell(3) | 7th | 664 |
| 22/6/19 | Newcastle (h) ● | L18-19 | t:Doherty(3) g:Beharrell(3) | 6th | 549 |
| 26/6/19 | Sheffield (h) (1895CQF) ● | L28-32 | t:Doherty,Litten(2),Beharrell g:Beharrell(6) | N/A | 374 |
| 29/6/19 | Coventry (a) ●● | W10-54 | t:Tali(3),Buchanan(2),Hedges(2),Connor Scott,Boas,Lawton g:Buchanan(7) | 6th | 386 |
| 6/7/19 | West Wales (a) | W0-72 | t:Doherty(4),Kesik,Foster,Boas,Connor Scott,Bastas,Bower(3),Owen,Tali g:Hedges(8) | 4th | 198 |
| 14/7/19 | Whitehaven (h) ● | L12-22 | t:Doherty,Chase g:Beharrell(2) | 5th | 780 |
| 21/7/19 | North Wales (a) | W0-30 | t:Chrimes,Kesik,Tali,Bower,Connor Scott g:Beharrell(4),Litten | 4th | 372 |
| 11/8/19 | London Skolars (h) | W23-22 | t:Beharrell,Doherty,Spiers,Chase g:Beharrell(3) fg:Beharrell | 5th | 585 |
| 18/8/19 | Oldham (a) | L40-14 | t:Doherty(2),Spiers g:Howden | 5th | 745 |
| 1/9/19 | Keighley (h) | W48-12 | t:Halliday(3),Foster,Tali,Boas,Boyle,Doherty,Bower g:Beharrell(4),Howden(2) | 5th | 892 |
| 8/9/19 | Workington (a) | W4-30 | t:Halliday(2),Tali,Beharrell,Mariano g:Beharrell(5) | 4th | 1,201 |
| 15/9/19 | Newcastle (a) (QPO) | W6-20 | t:Doherty,Tali,Mariano,Chrimes g:Beharrell(2) | N/A | 668 |
| 22/9/19 | Oldham (a) (QSF) | L22-12 | t:Beharrell,Kesik g:Beharrell(2) | N/A | 529 |
| 29/9/19 | Newcastle (a) (FE) | L34-4 | t:Chase | N/A | 480 |

● *Played at LD Nutrition Stadium, Featherstone*  ●● *Played at Ivor Preece Field, Broadstreet*

|  | | APP | | TRIES | | GOALS | | FG | | PTS | |
|--|----|-----|----|-------|----|-------|----|----|----|-----|----|
|  | D.O.B. | ALL | L1 | ALL | L1 | ALL | L1 | ALL | L1 | ALL | L1 |
| Guy Armitage | 29/11/91 | 1 | 1 | 0 | 0 | 0 | 0 | 0 | 0 | 0 | 0 |
| Stefanos Bastas | 22/12/93 | (9) | (3) | 2 | 1 | 0 | 0 | 0 | 0 | 8 | 4 |
| Matty Beharrell | 29/3/94 | 24 | 19 | 8 | 5 | 80 | 53 | 2 | 2 | 194 | 128 |
| Watson Boas | 8/11/94 | 10(7) | 8(7) | 9 | 6 | 0 | 0 | 0 | 0 | 36 | 24 |
| Connor Bower | 18/1/97 | 26(2) | 20(2) | 14 | 10 | 0 | 0 | 0 | 0 | 56 | 40 |
| Ryan Boyle | 17/10/87 | 19(10) | 14(8) | 1 | 1 | 0 | 0 | 0 | 0 | 4 | 4 |
| Jack Brown | 25/6/00 | 2(8) | 2(8) | 1 | 1 | 0 | 0 | 0 | 0 | 4 | 4 |
| Kieran Buchanan | 26/1/98 | 6 | 4 | 3 | 3 | 7 | 7 | 0 | 0 | 26 | 26 |
| Rangi Chase | 11/4/86 | 9 | 9 | 3 | 3 | 0 | 0 | 0 | 0 | 12 | 12 |
| Matty Chrimes | 2/11/97 | 23(2) | 18(1) | 8 | 5 | 0 | 0 | 0 | 0 | 32 | 20 |
| Jordan Cox | 27/5/92 | 3 | 1 | 1 | 0 | 0 | 0 | 0 | 0 | 4 | 0 |
| Kieran Cross | 18/2/95 | 2(6) | 2(4) | 4 | 1 | 0 | 0 | 0 | 0 | 16 | 4 |
| Ryan Dixon | 11/8/93 | 3(1) | 2(1) | 0 | 0 | 0 | 0 | 0 | 0 | 0 | 0 |
| Sam Doherty | 14/11/93 | 27 | 21 | 20 | 15 | 0 | 0 | 0 | 0 | 80 | 60 |
| Brandon Douglas | 17/8/97 | 6(12) | 6(7) | 5 | 3 | 0 | 0 | 0 | 0 | 20 | 12 |
| Brad England | 20/11/94 | 2(1) | 2(1) | 1 | 1 | 0 | 0 | 0 | 0 | 4 | 4 |
| Brad Fash | 24/1/96 | 1 | | 0 | 0 | 0 | 0 | 0 | 0 | 0 | 0 |
| Brad Foster | 28/8/95 | 20(1) | 16(1) | 2 | 2 | 0 | 0 | 0 | 0 | 8 | 8 |
| Dean Hadley | 5/8/92 | 1 | 1 | 0 | 0 | 0 | 0 | 0 | 0 | 0 | 0 |
| Tom Halliday | 2/2/97 | 6(1) | 4(1) | 10 | 5 | 0 | 0 | 0 | 0 | 40 | 20 |
| Liam Harris | 20/4/97 | 1 | 1 | 0 | 0 | 1 | 1 | 0 | 0 | 2 | 2 |
| Jordie Hedges | 4/8/95 | 17(9) | 12(8) | 6 | 6 | 12 | 10 | 0 | 0 | 48 | 44 |
| Evan Hodgson | 14/9/98 | 9 | 8 | 0 | 0 | 0 | 0 | 0 | 0 | 0 | 0 |
| Jordan Howden | 6/5/96 | 23 | 17 | 6 | 5 | 12 | 7 | 0 | 0 | 48 | 34 |
| Kyle Kesik | 3/6/89 | 29(1) | 22(1) | 4 | 4 | 0 | 0 | 0 | 0 | 16 | 16 |
| Jordan Lane | 20/10/97 | 1 | | 0 | 0 | 0 | 0 | 0 | 0 | 0 | 0 |
| Danny Langtree | 18/2/91 | 3 | 3 | 0 | 0 | 0 | 0 | 0 | 0 | 0 | 0 |
| Kieron Lawton | 7/5/02 | 2(1) | 1 | 1 | 1 | 0 | 0 | 0 | 0 | 4 | 4 |
| Jez Litten | 10/3/98 | (6) | (5) | 2 | 0 | 1 | 1 | 0 | 0 | 10 | 2 |
| Frankie Mariano | 10/5/87 | 5(2) | 5(2) | 2 | 2 | 0 | 0 | 0 | 0 | 8 | 8 |
| Hakim Miloudi | 26/6/93 | 3 | 3 | 2 | 2 | 0 | 0 | 0 | 0 | 8 | 8 |
| Levy Nzoungou | 22/1/98 | 12(1) | 9(1) | 1 | 0 | 0 | 0 | 0 | 0 | 4 | 0 |
| Callum Ogden | 26/4/97 | 5(5) | 3(2) | 2 | 1 | 0 | 0 | 0 | 0 | 8 | 4 |
| Richard Owen | 25/4/90 | 5(2) | 3(2) | 2 | 1 | 0 | 0 | 0 | 0 | 8 | 4 |
| Charlie Patterson-Lund | 27/4/00 | 1 | | 0 | 0 | 0 | 0 | 0 | 0 | 0 | 0 |
| Lee Registe | 17/3/98 | 1 | | 0 | 0 | 0 | 0 | 0 | 0 | 0 | 0 |
| Cameron Scott | 7/10/99 | 3 | 2 | 1 | 1 | 0 | 0 | 0 | 0 | 4 | 4 |
| Connor Scott | 27/5/93 | 10(13) | 8(10) | 3 | 3 | 0 | 0 | 0 | 0 | 12 | 12 |
| Russ Spiers | 28/4/91 | 18(9) | 12(8) | 3 | 3 | 0 | 0 | 0 | 0 | 12 | 12 |
| Jason Tali | 7/7/89 | 29 | 23 | 17 | 15 | 0 | 0 | 0 | 0 | 68 | 60 |
| Elliott Townsend | 21/1/96 | 1(3) | (2) | 1 | 1 | 0 | 0 | 0 | 0 | 4 | 4 |
| Danny Washbrook | 18/9/85 | 5 | 4 | 0 | 0 | 0 | 0 | 0 | 0 | 0 | 0 |
| Brandan Wilkinson | 7/9/97 | 4(4) | 3(3) | 0 | 0 | 0 | 0 | 0 | 0 | 0 | 0 |
| Connor Wynne | 15/1/01 | 3(1) | 3(1) | 0 | 0 | 0 | 0 | 0 | 0 | 0 | 0 |
| Menzie Yere | 24/10/83 | 9(2) | 6(2) | 5 | 3 | 0 | 0 | 0 | 0 | 20 | 12 |

*'L1' totals include play-offs; 'All' totals also include Challenge Cup & 1895 Cup*

Sam Doherty

**LEAGUE RECORD**
P20-W12-D0-L8 (4th/Final Eliminator)
F564, A309, Diff+255, 24 points.

**CHALLENGE CUP**
Round Six

**1895 CUP**
Quarter Finalists

**ATTENDANCES**
Best - v Keighley (L1 - 892)
Worst - v West Wales (1895C - 248)
Total (excluding Challenge Cup) - 7,225
Average (excluding Challenge Cup) - 602
(Down by 205 on 2018)

| CLUB RECORDS | |
|---|---|
| | **Highest score:** 102-6 v West Wales, 15/7/2018 **Highest score against:** 4-90 v Widnes, 10/6/2007 |
| | **Record attendance:** 10,000 v Bradford, 16/2/52 *(York Road)*; 6,528 v Castleford, 12/4/2007 *(Keepmoat Stadium)* |
| MATCH RECORDS | **Tries:** 6 Kane Epati v Oldham, 30/7/2006; Lee Waterman v Sharlston, 24/3/2012 |
| | **Goals:** 15 Liam Harris v West Wales, 15/7/2018 **Points:** 38 Liam Harris v West Wales, 15/7/2018 |
| SEASON RECORDS | **Tries:** 36 Lee Waterman 2012 **Goals:** 129 Jonny Woodcock 2002 **Points:** 306 Jonny Woodcock 2002 |
| CAREER RECORDS | **Tries:** 112 Mark Roache 1985-97 **Goals:** 850 David Noble 1976-77; 1980-89; 1992 **Points:** 1,751 David Noble 1976-77; 1980-89; 1992 |
| | **Appearances:** 327 Audley Pennant 1980-83; 1985-97 |

# HUNSLET

| DATE | FIXTURE | RESULT | SCORERS | LGE | ATT |
|------|---------|--------|---------|-----|-----|
| 24/2/19 | Doncaster (a) | W18-20 | t:Heaton,Potts,Robinson g:Dean(4) | 6th | 734 |
| 3/3/19 | West Wales (h) | W58-4 | t:Potts(3),Haley,Heaton,Dean,Bloomfield(2),Kidd,Ashton,Flynn g:Dean(6),Nicklas | 1st | 560 |
| 9/3/19 | West Bowling (h) (CCR3) | W56-10 | t:Chappell,Lee,Webb(3),Tonks(2),Ashton(2),Southernwood(2) g:Dean(6) | N/A | 399 |
| 17/3/19 | North Wales (a) | W12-22 | t:Tonks,Potts,Lee g:Dean(5) | 1st | 317 |
| 24/3/19 | Coventry (h) | W44-10 | t:Tonks,Chappell,Robinson(2),Heaton(2),Potts,Bloomfield g:Sanderson(6) | 1st | 542 |
| 31/3/19 | Halifax (h) (CCR4) | L24-28 | t:Lee,Dean,Potts,Chappell g:Dean(4) | N/A | 731 |
| 7/4/19 | Whitehaven (a) | L16-12 | t:Lee,Watson g:Dean(2) | 1st | 724 |
| 19/4/19 | Oldham (a) | W28-36 | t:Potts(2),Dean,Robinson,Heaton(2) g:Dean(6) | 1st | 652 |
| 28/4/19 | London Skolars (h) | L26-42 | t:Tonks,Heaton,Watson,Webb,Robinson g:Dean(2),Chappell | 2nd | 661 |
| 4/5/19 | Workington (h) (1895CR1) | L28-31 | t:Lee,Ashton(2),Flynn,Watson g:Dean(4) | N/A | 296 |
| 19/5/19 | Workington (a) | L12-4 | t:Potts | 4th | 610 |
| 26/5/19 | Newcastle (a) | W18-32 | t:Saltonstall(2),Woodburn-Hall,Chappell(2),Potts g:Dean(4) | 4th | 624 |
| 7/6/19 | Keighley (h) | W34-0 | t:Heaton(2),Chappell,Potts,Emmett,Straugheir,Braham g:Dean(2),Nicklas | 2nd | 668 |
| 14/6/19 | Doncaster (h) | L20-22 | t:Potts(2),Straugheir,Chappell g:Dean(2) | 4th | 664 |
| 22/6/19 | West Wales (a) | W10-72 | t:Potts(3),Lee(2),Watson,Dean,Halafihi(2),Robinson,Heaton(2),Chappell g:Dean(10) | 2nd | 283 |
| 7/7/19 | Newcastle (h) | L12-26 | t:Woodburn-Hall,Tonks g:Dean(2) | 5th | 746 |
| 14/7/19 | Coventry (a) ● | W20-48 | t:Ashton,Tonks,Potts(2),Chappell,Watson,Dean(2),Bloomfield g:Dean(6) | 4th | 420 |
| 27/7/19 | Whitehaven (h) | L12-19 | t:Chappell g:Dean(4) | 5th | 540 |
| 4/8/19 | North Wales (h) | W42-18 | t:Tonks,Straugheir,Kirby,Martin,Watson(2),Andrade g:Sanderson(7) | 4th | 488 |
| 10/8/19 | Keighley (a) | W10-32 | t:Braham,Andrade,Straugheir,Ashton,Bloomfield g:Sanderson(6) | 4th | 522 |
| 23/8/19 | London Skolars (a) | W30-34 | t:Halafihi,Ashton,Robinson,Emmett,Lancaster,Potts g:Sanderson(4),Brown | 4th | 1,035 |
| 1/9/19 | Workington (h) | L16-30 | t:Straugheir,Martin,Halafihi g:Sanderson(2) | 4th | 521 |
| 8/9/19 | Oldham (h) | L20-34 | t:Braham,Watson,Chappell g:Sanderson(4) | 5th | 688 |
| 15/9/19 | Workington (h) (EPO) | L24-32 | t:Ashton(2),Wright,Watson g:Sanderson(4) | N/A | 332 |

● *Played at Webb Ellis Road, Rugby*

## APP   TRIES  GOALS  FG    PTS

| | D.O.B. | ALL | L1 | ALL | L1 | ALL | L1 | ALL | L1 | ALL | L1 |
|---|--------|-----|-----|-----|-----|-----|-----|-----|-----|-----|-----|
| Jordan Andrade | 24/1/92 | 1(3) | 1(3) | 2 | 2 | 0 | 0 | 0 | 0 | 8 | 8 |
| Tom Ashton | 20/6/92 | 18(1) | 15(1) | 10 | 6 | 0 | 0 | 0 | 0 | 40 | 24 |
| Dale Bloomfield | 24/10/87 | 14 | 12 | 5 | 5 | 0 | 0 | 0 | 0 | 20 | 20 |
| Zach Braham | 14/1/95 | 10(11) | 10(8) | 3 | 3 | 0 | 0 | 0 | 0 | 12 | 12 |
| Tommy Brierley | 8/9/96 | 1(1) | (1) | 0 | 0 | 0 | 0 | 0 | 0 | 0 | 0 |
| Simon Brown | 23/6/89 | 6 | 6 | 0 | 0 | 1 | 1 | 0 | 0 | 2 | 2 |
| Will Calcott | 16/12/97 | (1) | (1) | 0 | 0 | 0 | 0 | 0 | 0 | 0 | 0 |
| Reece Chapman-Smith | 8/11/98 | 6 | 6 | 0 | 0 | 0 | 0 | 0 | 0 | 0 | 0 |
| Nathan Chappell | 4/12/89 | 15 | 13 | 9 | 11 | 1 | 1 | 0 | 0 | 46 | 38 |
| Reece Dean | 30/11/96 | 16 | 13 | 6 | 5 | 69 | 55 | 0 | 0 | 162 | 130 |
| Rory Dixon | 17/10/97 | (3) | (3) | 0 | 0 | 0 | 0 | 0 | 0 | 0 | 0 |
| Mike Emmett | 13/5/87 | 19(4) | 16(4) | 2 | 2 | 0 | 0 | 0 | 0 | 8 | 8 |
| Nyle Flynn | 27/7/97 | 1(4) | 1(1) | 2 | 1 | 0 | 0 | 0 | 0 | 8 | 4 |
| Vila Halafihi | 24/1/94 | 12(12) | 11(10) | 4 | 4 | 0 | 0 | 0 | 0 | 16 | 16 |
| Michael Haley | 19/9/87 | 1(16) | 1(16) | 1 | 1 | 0 | 0 | 0 | 0 | 4 | 4 |
| Dan Hawksworth | 30/3/93 | 8(9) | 6(8) | 0 | 0 | 0 | 0 | 0 | 0 | 0 | 0 |
| Ben Heaton | 12/3/90 | 13 | 11 | 11 | 11 | 0 | 0 | 0 | 0 | 44 | 44 |
| Lewis Heckford | 25/9/97 | 1(2) | 1(2) | 0 | 0 | 0 | 0 | 0 | 0 | 0 | 0 |
| Aiden Hema | 27/10/95 | (6) | (5) | 0 | 0 | 0 | 0 | 0 | 0 | 0 | 0 |
| Harry Kidd | 12/6/95 | (2) | (2) | 1 | 1 | 0 | 0 | 0 | 0 | 4 | 4 |
| Jon Luke Kirby | 23/9/98 | 10(2) | 8(1) | 1 | 1 | 0 | 0 | 0 | 0 | 4 | 4 |
| Callum Lancaster | 13/10/96 | 3 | 3 | 1 | 1 | 0 | 0 | 0 | 0 | 4 | 4 |
| Jack Lee | 1/11/88 | 16 | 13 | 7 | 4 | 0 | 0 | 0 | 0 | 28 | 16 |
| Charlie Martin | 2/12/92 | 11(5) | 9(5) | 2 | 2 | 0 | 0 | 0 | 0 | 8 | 8 |
| Richard Moore | 2/2/81 | 1 | 1 | 0 | 0 | 0 | 0 | 0 | 0 | 0 | 0 |
| Danny Nicklas | 29/6/91 | 13 | 13 | 0 | 0 | 2 | 2 | 0 | 0 | 4 | 4 |
| Romain Pallares | 7/5/98 | (2) | (2) | 0 | 0 | 0 | 0 | 0 | 0 | 0 | 0 |
| Gareth Potts | 25/7/90 | 20 | 19 | 20 | 19 | 0 | 0 | 0 | 0 | 80 | 76 |
| Adam Robinson | 8/4/87 | 19 | 17 | 7 | 7 | 0 | 0 | 0 | 0 | 28 | 28 |
| James Saltonstall | 27/9/93 | 1 | 1 | 2 | 2 | 0 | 0 | 0 | 0 | 8 | 8 |
| Joe Sanderson | 17/3/97 | 10 | 8 | 0 | 0 | 33 | 33 | 0 | 0 | 66 | 66 |
| Cain Southernwood | 4/5/92 | 4 | 3 | 2 | 0 | 0 | 0 | 0 | 0 | 8 | 0 |
| Duane Straugheir | 29/9/89 | 16 | 15 | 5 | 5 | 0 | 0 | 0 | 0 | 20 | 20 |
| Josh Tonks | 14/8/91 | 19 | 17 | 8 | 6 | 0 | 0 | 0 | 0 | 32 | 24 |
| Jimmy Watson | 9/9/91 | 22 | 19 | 9 | 8 | 0 | 0 | 0 | 0 | 36 | 32 |
| Marcus Webb | 11/1/97 | 2 | 1 | 4 | 1 | 0 | 0 | 0 | 0 | 16 | 4 |
| James Woodburn-Hall | 2/2/95 | 2 | 2 | 2 | 2 | 0 | 0 | 0 | 0 | 8 | 8 |
| Ryan Wright | 28/10/91 | 1(12) | 1(11) | 1 | 1 | 0 | 0 | 0 | 0 | 4 | 4 |

*'L1' totals include play-offs; 'All' totals also include Challenge Cup & 1895 Cup*

Gareth Potts

**LEAGUE RECORD**
P20-W12-D0-L8
(5th/Elimination Play-off)
F596, A379, Diff+217, 24 points.

**CHALLENGE CUP**
Round Four

**1895 CUP**
Round One

**ATTENDANCES**
Best - v Newcastle (L1 - 746)
Worst - v Workington (1895C - 296)
Total (excluding Challenge Cup) - 6,706
Average (excluding Challenge Cup) - 559
(Down by 57 on 2018)

| CLUB RECORDS | Highest score: 86-0 v West Wales, 27/5/2018; 86-6 v West Wales, 4/8/2018  Highest score against: 0-82 v Bradford, 2/3/2003 |
|---|---|
| | Record attendance: 24,700 v Wigan, 15/3/24 *(Parkside)*; 2,454 v Wakefield, 13/4/98 *(South Leeds Stadium)* |
| MATCH RECORDS | Tries: 7 George Dennis v Bradford, 20/1/34  Goals: 13 Joe Sanderson v West Wales, 27/5/2018; Joe Sanderson v West Wales, 4/8/2018 |
| | Points: 30 Simon Wilson v Highfield, 21/1/96; Joe Sanderson v West Wales, 27/5/2018 |
| SEASON RECORDS | Tries: 34 Alan Snowden 1956-57  Goals: 181 Billy Langton 1958-59  Points: 380 Billy Langton 1958-59 |
| CAREER RECORDS | Tries: 154 Fred Williamson 1943-55  Goals: 1,044 Billy Langton 1955-66  Points: 2,202 Billy Langton 1955-66  Appearances: 579 Geoff Gunney 1951-73 |

# KEIGHLEY COUGARS

| DATE | FIXTURE | RESULT | SCORERS | LGE | ATT |
|------|---------|--------|---------|-----|-----|
| 17/2/19 | Whitehaven (a) | L28-16 | t:Welham,Miller,Dixon g:Hardcastle(2) | 11th | 897 |
| 3/3/19 | Coventry (h) | W40-8 | t:Hallett(2),Cooke,Dixon,Miller,Coventry,Feather g:Hardcastle(6) | 11th | 915 |
| 10/3/19 | Distington (h) (CCR3) | W28-14 | t:Coventry,Hallas,Seeley(2),Muranka,Dixon g:Hardcastle(2) | N/A | 508 |
| 16/3/19 | London Skolars (a) | D18-18 | t:Hardcastle,Miller,Levy g:Hardcastle(3) | 11th | 262 |
| 24/3/19 | North Wales (h) | W24-22 | t:Hallas,Lynam(2),Parker g:Hardcastle(4) | 11th | 859 |
| 31/3/19 | Bradford (h) (CCR4) | L12-14 | t:Feather,Seeley g:Hardcastle(2) | N/A | 1,881 |
| 6/4/19 | West Wales (a) | W12-56 | t:Lynam,Cooke,Miller(3),Levy,Wray,Hardcastle(2),Coventry g:Hardcastle(8) | 11th | 238 |
| 19/4/19 | Doncaster (h) | W26-18 | t:Hallett,Hardcastle,Prell,Parker g:Hardcastle(5) | 11th | 1,040 |
| 28/4/19 | Workington (h) | W32-26 | t:Hardcastle,Prell,Parker,Feather(2) g:Hardcastle(6) | 11th | 948 |
| 4/5/19 | Newcastle (a) (1895CR1) | L38-12 | t:Welham,Cullimore g:Miller(2) | N/A | 340 |
| 19/5/19 | Newcastle (a) | L40-12 | t:Miller,Dixon g:Miller(2) | 11th | 1,423 |
| 25/5/19 | Oldham (h) | L12-52 | t:Sheriff,Miller g:Miller(2) | 11th | 836 |
| 7/6/19 | Hunslet (a) | L34-0 | | 11th | 668 |
| 16/6/19 | Oldham (a) | L28-4 | t:Muranka | 11th | 591 |
| 22/6/19 | London Skolars (h) | W38-26 | t:Fitzpatrick-Parry,Muranka,Aitchison,Miller,Wright,Feather g:Hardcastle(7) | 10th | 686 |
| 30/6/19 | North Wales (a) | L14-6 | t:Prell g:Hardcastle | 10th | 315 |
| 14/7/19 | West Wales (h) | W50-18 | t:Hallett,Cooke,Miller(3),Hardcastle(2),Thackray,Muranka g:Hardcastle(7) | 10th | 702 |
| 21/7/19 | Workington (a) | L52-4 | t:Muranka | 10th | 947 |
| 4/8/19 | Coventry (a) ● | W20-46 | t:Hallett,Miller,Levy,Welham(2),Dixon,Muranka(2) g:Miller(7) | 10th | 345 |
| 10/8/19 | Hunslet (h) | L10-32 | t:Dixon,Muranka g:Hardcastle | 10th | 522 |
| 18/8/19 | Whitehaven (h) | L19-48 | t:Sheriff,Miller,Hallett g:Hardcastle(3) fg:Hardcastle | 10th | 782 |
| 1/9/19 | Doncaster (a) | L48-12 | t:Gaylor,Muranka g:Hardcastle(2) | 10th | 892 |
| 8/9/19 | Newcastle (h) | L22-32 | t:Prell(2),Moran,Dixon g:Miller(3) | 10th | 825 |

● *Played at Webb Ellis Road, Rugby*

| | | APP | | TRIES | | GOALS | | FG | | PTS | |
|---|---|---|---|---|---|---|---|---|---|---|---|
| | D.O.B. | ALL | L1 | ALL | L1 | ALL | L1 | ALL | L1 | ALL | L1 |
| Jordan Aitchison | 6/8/93 | 2 | 2 | 1 | 1 | 0 | 0 | 0 | 0 | 4 | 4 |
| Adam Allerton | 31/3/96 | 1 | 1 | 0 | 0 | 0 | 0 | 0 | 0 | 0 | 0 |
| Jack Arnold | 23/9/97 | 3(6) | 2(5) | 0 | 0 | 0 | 0 | 0 | 0 | 0 | 0 |
| Matthew Bailey | 1/12/91 | 17(5) | 15(5) | 0 | 0 | 0 | 0 | 0 | 0 | 0 | 0 |
| Mark Barlow | 16/2/84 | (2) | (2) | 0 | 0 | 0 | 0 | 0 | 0 | 0 | 0 |
| Jimmy Beckett | 29/8/99 | 5 | 5 | 0 | 0 | 0 | 0 | 0 | 0 | 0 | 0 |
| Will Cooke | 22/12/96 | 18 | 16 | 3 | 3 | 0 | 0 | 0 | 0 | 12 | 12 |
| Jack Coventry | 5/3/94 | 9(12) | 8(10) | 3 | 2 | 0 | 0 | 0 | 0 | 12 | 8 |
| Chris Cullimore | 13/2/93 | 4(7) | 4(6) | 1 | 0 | 0 | 0 | 0 | 0 | 4 | 0 |
| Spencer Darley | 25/9/98 | 3(3) | 3(3) | 0 | 0 | 0 | 0 | 0 | 0 | 0 | 0 |
| Davey Dixon | 31/5/97 | 19 | 16 | 7 | 6 | 0 | 0 | 0 | 0 | 28 | 24 |
| James Feather | 15/4/84 | 21 | 19 | 5 | 4 | 0 | 0 | 0 | 0 | 20 | 16 |
| Jordan Fitzpatrick-Parry | 26/7/92 | 3 | 3 | 1 | 1 | 0 | 0 | 0 | 0 | 4 | 4 |
| Darren Forde | 8/1/96 | 1 | 1 | 0 | 0 | 0 | 0 | 0 | 0 | 0 | 0 |
| Billy Gaylor | 30/4/97 | 2(10) | 1(9) | 1 | 1 | 0 | 0 | 0 | 0 | 4 | 4 |
| Harvey Hallas | 14/11/97 | 4(7) | 3(6) | 2 | 1 | 0 | 0 | 0 | 0 | 8 | 4 |
| Macauley Hallett | 27/11/95 | 23 | 20 | 6 | 6 | 0 | 0 | 0 | 0 | 24 | 24 |
| Benn Hardcastle | 4/1/90 | 17 | 15 | 7 | 7 | 59 | 55 | 1 | 1 | 147 | 139 |
| Dom Horn | 13/3/95 | 3(1) | 3(1) | 0 | 0 | 0 | 0 | 0 | 0 | 0 | 0 |
| Aaron Levy | 19/12/95 | 13(2) | 11(1) | 3 | 3 | 0 | 0 | 0 | 0 | 12 | 12 |
| Josh Lynam | 16/2/93 | 10(1) | 8(1) | 3 | 3 | 0 | 0 | 0 | 0 | 12 | 12 |
| Jack Miller | 28/11/94 | 23 | 20 | 14 | 14 | 16 | 14 | 0 | 0 | 88 | 84 |
| Luke Million | 28/12/97 | 4(2) | 2(1) | 0 | 0 | 0 | 0 | 0 | 0 | 0 | 0 |
| Kieran Moran | 2/11/96 | 1(7) | 1(6) | 1 | 1 | 0 | 0 | 0 | 0 | 4 | 4 |
| Jason Muranka | 4/8/89 | 20 | 17 | 9 | 8 | 0 | 0 | 0 | 0 | 36 | 32 |
| Matt Nicholson | 11/9/91 | 1 | 1 | 0 | 0 | 0 | 0 | 0 | 0 | 0 | 0 |
| Dan Parker | 11/3/93 | 11(5) | 10(4) | 3 | 3 | 0 | 0 | 0 | 0 | 12 | 12 |
| Taylor Prell | 3/7/96 | 11 | 11 | 5 | 5 | 0 | 0 | 0 | 0 | 20 | 20 |
| Alfie Seeley | 30/12/96 | 15 | 12 | 3 | 0 | 0 | 0 | 0 | 0 | 12 | 0 |
| Louis Sheriff | 6/9/92 | 6(2) | 6(2) | 2 | 2 | 0 | 0 | 0 | 0 | 8 | 8 |
| Jamie Thackray | 30/9/79 | 4(9) | 3(8) | 1 | 1 | 0 | 0 | 0 | 0 | 4 | 4 |
| Matt Welham | 1/2/93 | 17 | 14 | 4 | 3 | 0 | 0 | 0 | 0 | 16 | 12 |
| Alex Williams | 8/8/93 | 1 | 0 | 0 | 0 | 0 | 0 | 0 | 0 | 0 | 0 |
| Reece Williams | 28/2/95 | (1) | (1) | 0 | 0 | 0 | 0 | 0 | 0 | 0 | 0 |
| Lewis Wray | 6/5/98 | 7(7) | 7(6) | 1 | 1 | 0 | 0 | 0 | 0 | 4 | 4 |
| Ryan Wright | 28/10/91 | (3) | (3) | 1 | 1 | 0 | 0 | 0 | 0 | 4 | 4 |

*'L1' totals include League 1 regular season only; 'All' totals also include Challenge Cup & 1895 Cup*

Jack Miller

**LEAGUE RECORD**
P20-W8-D1-L11 (10th)
F447, A576, Diff-129, 5 points.
*(12 points deducted for transfer of club membership)*

**CHALLENGE CUP**
Round Four

**1895 CUP**
Round One

**ATTENDANCES**
Best - v Bradford (CC - 1,881)
Worst - v Distington (CC - 508)
Total (excluding Challenge Cup) - 8,115
Average (excluding Challenge Cup) - 812
(Up by 31 on 2018)

| | |
|---|---|
| **CLUB RECORDS** **MATCH RECORDS** | **Highest score:** 112-6 v West Wales, 15/9/2018  **Highest score against:** 2-92 v Leigh, 30/4/86  **Record attendance:** 14,500 v Halifax, 3/3/51  **Tries:** 6 Jason Critchley v Widnes, 18/8/96 |
| | **Goals:** 15 John Wasyliw v Nottingham City, 1/11/92; Martyn Wood v Lancashire Lynx, 1/5/2000  **Points:** 36 John Wasyliw v Nottingham City, 1/11/92 |
| **SEASON RECORDS** | **Tries:** 45 Nick Pinkney 1994-95  **Goals:** 187 John Wasyliw 1992-93  **Points:** 490 John Wasyliw 1992-93 |
| **CAREER RECORDS** | **Tries:** 155 Sam Stacey 1904-20  **Goals:** 967 Brian Jefferson 1965-77  **Points:** 2,116 Brian Jefferson 1965-77 |
| | **Appearances:** 372 Hartley Tempest 1902-15; David McGoun 1925-38 |

# LONDON SKOLARS

| DATE | FIXTURE | RESULT | SCORERS | LGE | ATT |
|---|---|---|---|---|---|
| 23/2/19 | West Wales (a) | W18-28 | t:Grant(3),Caro,Williams g:Thorman,Barran(3) | 4th | 250 |
| 2/3/19 | Newcastle (h) | L12-48 | t:Meadows,M Greenhalgh g:Thorman(2) | 8th | 302 |
| 10/3/19 | North Wales (h) (CCR3) | L18-31 | t:Bryan,Mbaraga,Macani g:Thorman(3) | N/A | 170 |
| 16/3/19 | Keighley (h) | D18-18 | t:Mullen,Brown,Williams g:Thorman(3) | 8th | 262 |
| 24/3/19 | Oldham (a) | L34-4 | t:Brown | 8th | 709 |
| 6/4/19 | Workington (h) | W34-32 | t:Brown,Bishay,Macani(2),Caro,Wilkinson g:Thorman(5) | 7th | 629 |
| 19/4/19 | Coventry (a) | W28-30 | t:Brown,Williams(2),Macani,Juma g:Thorman(5) | 3rd | 353 |
| 28/4/19 | Hunslet (a) | W26-42 | t:Wilkinson,Barran,Brown(2),Thorman,Macani,Juma g:Thorman(7) | 3rd | 661 |
| 11/5/19 | North Wales (h) | W19-18 | t:Brown,Macani,Bryan g:Thorman(2),Barran fg:Mullen | 2nd | 248 |
| 18/5/19 | Doncaster (h) | W22-6 | t:Macani,Ogden,Palumbo g:Thorman(4),Barran | 2nd | 608 |
| 25/5/19 | Whitehaven (a) | L32-6 | t:Scott g:Thorman | 2nd | 811 |
| 15/6/19 | West Wales (h) | W51-6 | t:M Greenhalgh,Williams(3),Mullen,Jennings,Jy-mel Coleman,Scott,Juma g:Thorman(7) fg:Thorman | 2nd | 290 |
| 22/6/19 | Keighley (a) | L38-26 | t:Macani(2),Scott,Bishay g:Thorman(3),Barran(2) | 5th | 686 |
| 29/6/19 | Whitehaven (h) | L6-28 | t:Juma g:Smith | 5th | 442 |
| 6/7/19 | Coventry (h) | L20-36 | t:Juma(2),Agoro(2) g:Thorman(2) | 6th | 216 |
| 14/7/19 | Workington (a) ● | L32-22 | t:J Greenhalgh,Barran,Macani g:Thorman(5) | 6th | 810 |
| 20/7/19 | Newcastle (a) | L34-16 | t:Caro,Yates,Williams g:Thorman(2) | 7th | 1,098 |
| 3/8/19 | Oldham (h) | L14-15 | t:Macani,Caro g:Thorman(3) | 7th | 355 |
| 11/8/19 | Doncaster (a) | L23-22 | t:Wilkinson,Armitage g:Thorman(3) | 7th | 585 |
| 23/8/19 | Hunslet (h) | L30-34 | t:Scott,Yates,Williams(2),Wilkinson g:Thorman(3),Bishay(2) | 8th | 1,035 |
| 7/9/19 | North Wales (a) | L36-18 | t:Scott,Williams,Caro g:Thorman(3) | 8th | 421 |

● *Played at Borough Park*

| | D.O.B. | APP ALL | APP L1 | TRIES ALL | TRIES L1 | GOALS ALL | GOALS L1 | FG ALL | FG L1 | PTS ALL | PTS L1 |
|---|---|---|---|---|---|---|---|---|---|---|---|
| Mo Agoro | 29/1/93 | 4 | 4 | 2 | 2 | 0 | 0 | 0 | 0 | 8 | 8 |
| Isaac Ah Kuoi-Atmore | 5/10/97 | (6) | (5) | 0 | 0 | 0 | 0 | 0 | 0 | 0 | 0 |
| Guy Armitage | 29/11/91 | 1 | 1 | 3 | 3 | 0 | 0 | 0 | 0 | 12 | 12 |
| James Barran | 26/10/98 | 14 | 13 | 2 | 2 | 7 | 7 | 0 | 0 | 22 | 22 |
| Mike Bishay | 8/2/93 | 11(7) | 10(7) | 2 | 2 | 2 | 2 | 0 | 0 | 12 | 12 |
| Gideon Boafo | 10/2/99 | 2 | 2 | 0 | 0 | 0 | 0 | 0 | 0 | 0 | 0 |
| Joe Brown | 14/1/99 | 7 | 7 | 7 | 7 | 0 | 0 | 0 | 0 | 28 | 28 |
| Lamont Bryan | 12/4/88 | 11(8) | 10(8) | 2 | 1 | 0 | 0 | 0 | 0 | 8 | 4 |
| Omari Caro | 7/3/91 | 14(1) | 13(1) | 5 | 5 | 0 | 0 | 0 | 0 | 20 | 20 |
| Kayne Chan-Kitchener | 18/11/01 | 1 | 1 | 0 | 0 | 0 | 0 | 0 | 0 | 0 | 0 |
| Tommy Chipchase | 25/8/98 | (1) | (1) | 0 | 0 | 0 | 0 | 0 | 0 | 0 | 0 |
| Jermaine Coleman | 17/6/82 | 3 | 3 | 0 | 0 | 0 | 0 | 0 | 0 | 0 | 0 |
| Jy-mel Coleman | 13/10/88 | 6(2) | 6(2) | 1 | 1 | 0 | 0 | 0 | 0 | 4 | 4 |
| Matthew Davies | 9/4/98 | (7) | (7) | 0 | 0 | 0 | 0 | 0 | 0 | 0 | 0 |
| Sam Grant | 24/3/99 | 4 | 3 | 3 | 3 | 0 | 0 | 0 | 0 | 12 | 12 |
| Judd Greenhalgh | 16/1/93 | 12(2) | 11(2) | 1 | 1 | 0 | 0 | 0 | 0 | 4 | 4 |
| Mike Greenhalgh | 8/6/94 | 12(1) | 11(1) | 2 | 2 | 0 | 0 | 0 | 0 | 8 | 8 |
| Daniel Hindmarsh | 8/8/98 | 10 | 10 | 0 | 0 | 0 | 0 | 0 | 0 | 0 | 0 |
| Elliot Jennings | 28/4/95 | 8 | 8 | 1 | 1 | 0 | 0 | 0 | 0 | 4 | 4 |
| Lameck Juma | 6/12/90 | 13 | 12 | 6 | 6 | 0 | 0 | 0 | 0 | 24 | 24 |
| Malikhi Lloyd-Jones | 29/8/94 | 5(4) | 5(3) | 0 | 0 | 0 | 0 | 0 | 0 | 0 | 0 |
| Iliess Macani | 6/12/93 | 21 | 20 | 11 | 10 | 0 | 0 | 0 | 0 | 44 | 40 |
| Jon Magrin | 8/10/94 | 1(7) | 1(7) | 0 | 0 | 0 | 0 | 0 | 0 | 0 | 0 |
| Will Martin | 28/12/93 | 4(1) | 4 | 0 | 0 | 0 | 0 | 0 | 0 | 0 | 0 |
| Eddie Mbaraga | 9/9/87 | 1(4) | 1(3) | 1 | 0 | 0 | 0 | 0 | 0 | 4 | 0 |
| James Meadows | 15/6/99 | 3 | 3 | 1 | 1 | 0 | 0 | 0 | 0 | 4 | 4 |
| Craig Mullen | 15/1/98 | 7 | 7 | 2 | 2 | 0 | 0 | 1 | 1 | 9 | 9 |
| Jacob Ogden | 23/1/98 | 5 | 5 | 1 | 1 | 0 | 0 | 0 | 0 | 4 | 4 |
| Ronny Palumbo | 22/4/91 | 7(3) | 7(3) | 1 | 1 | 0 | 0 | 0 | 0 | 4 | 4 |
| Xavier Rice | 27/9/96 | 1(1) | (1) | 0 | 0 | 0 | 0 | 0 | 0 | 0 | 0 |
| Matt Ross | 2/9/92 | 4(8) | 4(8) | 0 | 0 | 0 | 0 | 0 | 0 | 0 | 0 |
| Liam Scott | 24/9/94 | 7(11) | 7(11) | 5 | 5 | 0 | 0 | 0 | 0 | 20 | 20 |
| Joe Shorrocks | 25/11/99 | 1 | 1 | 0 | 0 | 0 | 0 | 0 | 0 | 0 | 0 |
| Harry Smith | 25/1/00 | 1 | 1 | 0 | 0 | 1 | 1 | 0 | 0 | 2 | 2 |
| Michael Sykes | 10/12/86 | 2(3) | 2(3) | 0 | 0 | 0 | 0 | 0 | 0 | 0 | 0 |
| Neil Thorman | 4/6/84 | 20 | 19 | 1 | 1 | 64 | 61 | 1 | 1 | 133 | 127 |
| Robert Tuliatu | 11/10/95 | 6(6) | 6(6) | 0 | 0 | 0 | 0 | 0 | 0 | 0 | 0 |
| Richard Wilkinson | 26/10/93 | 15 | 15 | 4 | 4 | 0 | 0 | 0 | 0 | 16 | 16 |
| Jordan Williams | 4/6/97 | 21 | 20 | 11 | 11 | 0 | 0 | 0 | 0 | 44 | 44 |
| Jerome Yates | 31/10/97 | 8 | 7 | 2 | 2 | 0 | 0 | 0 | 0 | 8 | 8 |

*'L1' totals include League 1 regular season only; 'All' totals also include Challenge Cup*

Iliess Macani

**LEAGUE RECORD**
P20-W7-D1-L12 (8th)
F440, A542, Diff-102, 15 points.

**CHALLENGE CUP**
Round Three

**1895 CUP**
Not entered

**ATTENDANCES**
Best - v Hunslet (L1 - 1,035)
Worst - v North Wales (CC - 170)
Total (excluding Challenge Cup) - 4,387
Average (excluding Challenge Cup) - 439
(Up by 38 on 2018)

**CLUB RECORDS** Highest score: 76-8 v West Wales, 7/4/2018; 76-6 v Hemel, 8/9/2018 Highest score against: 4-98 v Sheffield, 3/8/2003 Record attendance: 1,524 v Toronto, 4/3/2017

**MATCH RECORDS** Tries: 5 Mark Cantoni v Gateshead, 27/6/2004 Goals: 12 Neil Thorman v West Wales, 7/4/2018 Points: 28 Dylan Skee v South Wales, 29/7/2012
**SEASON RECORDS** Tries: 20 Mark Cantoni 2004; James Anthony 2013 Goals: 100 Dylan Skee 2013 Points: 248 Dylan Skee 2013
**CAREER RECORDS** Tries: 57 Austen Aggrey 2004-2012 Goals: 230 (inc 1fg) Dylan Skee 2011-2013 Points: 579 Dylan Skee 2011-2013 Appearances: 198 Gareth Honor 2003-2013

# NEWCASTLE THUNDER

| DATE | FIXTURE | RESULT | SCORERS | LGE | ATT |
|---|---|---|---|---|---|
| 16/2/19 | Doncaster (h) | L26-32 | t:Clegg(2),Taulapapa,Young,Agoro g:Finn(3) | 9th | 1,817 |
| 24/2/19 | Coventry (a) | L32-28 | t:Clegg,Agoro,Simons,Finn,McAvoy g:Finn(4) | 8th | 360 |
| 2/3/19 | London Skolars (a) | W12-48 | t:Agoro,Carlile,J Aldous,Jowitt(2),Taulapapa,Luckley,Ollett,Arundel g:Finn(6) | 6th | 302 |
| 9/3/19 | West Wales (h) (CCR3) | W48-0 | t:Carlile(2),Taulapapa,Young,Ollett,Doyle-Manga,Agoro(2),Sidney g:Marginet(6) | N/A | 329 |
| 16/3/19 | West Wales (h) | W56-6 | t:Young(2),Taulapapa,Carlile,Agoro(3),Aston(2),Fitzsimmons(2),Rowe g:Aston(4) | 2nd | 678 |
| 24/3/19 | Workington (a) | L32-30 | t:Ollett,McAvoy,Young,Aston,Brown g:Coleman(5) | 5th | 859 |
| 31/3/19 | Workington (a) (CCR4) | L21-20 | t:Taulapapa(2),Carlile(2) g:Coleman(2) | N/A | N/A |
| 7/4/19 | Oldham (h) | W28-22 | t:Clegg(3),Gill,Craig g:Coleman(4) | 3rd | 889 |
| 28/4/19 | Whitehaven (a) | D12-12 | t:Gill g:Coleman(4) | 5th | 852 |
| 4/5/19 | Keighley (h) (1895CR1) | W38-12 | t:Agoro(2),Clegg(2),Marginet,Gill(2) g:Marginet(5) | N/A | 340 |
| 19/5/19 | Keighley (h) | W40-12 | t:Agoro(2),Gill(2),Marginet,Doyle-Manga(2) g:Marginet(6) | 5th | 1,423 |
| 26/5/19 | Hunslet (h) | L18-32 | t:Gill,Clegg,Young g:Coates(3) | 5th | 624 |
| 2/6/19 | York (a) (1895CR2) | L30-16 | t:Simons,Fitzsimmons,Young g:Lewis(2) | N/A | 797 |
| 9/6/19 | North Wales (a) | W12-48 | t:Blanke,Lewis,Young(3),Carlile,Brown,Gill(2) g:Lewis(6) | 5th | 302 |
| 16/6/19 | Whitehaven (h) | W26-20 | t:Clarke,Clegg,Young(2),Lewis g:Lewis(3) | 5th | 1,079 |
| 22/6/19 | Doncaster (a) ● | W18-19 | t:Edwards,McAvoy,Lewis g:Lewis(3) fg:Newman | 4th | 549 |
| 30/6/19 | Workington (a) | W48-10 | t:Brown,Wright(2),Lewis(3),Taulapapa(3),Clarke g:Lewis,Wright(3) | 3rd | 1,077 |
| 7/7/19 | Hunslet (a) | W12-26 | t:Brown,Clarke,Simons,Gill,Carlile g:Wright(3) | 2nd | 746 |
| 20/7/19 | London Skolars (h) | W34-16 | t:Lewis,Wright(3),Newman,Mustapha g:Wright(5) | 2nd | 1,098 |
| 3/8/19 | West Wales (a) | W6-68 | t:Edwards(2),Clegg,Laulu-Togaga'e,Gill(4),Young,Taulapapa,Clarke, Mustapha,Simons g:Clarke(8) | 2nd | 302 |
| 11/8/19 | Oldham (a) | L28-20 | t:Laulu-Togaga'e,Fitzsimmons,Gill,Clegg g:Clarke(2) | 3rd | 702 |
| 18/8/19 | Coventry (h) | W88-6 | t:Fitzsimmons(2),Young(4),Ollett,Edwards,Carlile,Clegg,Laulu-Togaga'e, Gill(3),Taulapapa,Newman g:Clarke(12) | 3rd | 711 |
| 1/9/19 | North Wales (h) | W46-22 | t:Gill(2),Laulu-Togaga'e(2),Wright(3),Mustapha,Newman,Simons g:Clarke(3) | 3rd | 883 |
| 8/9/19 | Keighley (a) | W22-32 | t:Clegg(2),Newman(2),Gill(2) g:Clarke(3),Wright | 3rd | 825 |
| 15/9/19 | Doncaster (h) (QPO) | L6-20 | t:Clegg g:Clarke | N/A | 668 |
| 22/9/19 | Workington (h) (ESF) | W38-18 | t:Gill(3),Newman(2),Laulu-Togaga'e,Clegg g:Clarke(5) | N/A | 678 |
| 29/9/19 | Doncaster (h) (FE) | W34-4 | t:Gill(3),Carlile,Young,Clegg g:Clarke(5) | N/A | 480 |
| 6/10/19 | Oldham (a) (POF) | L18-14 | t:Taulapapa(2),Edwards g:Clarke | N/A | 1,209 |

● *Played at LD Nutrition Stadium, Featherstone*

Kieran Gill

| | | APP | | TRIES | | GOALS | | FG | | PTS | |
|---|---|---|---|---|---|---|---|---|---|---|---|
| | D.O.B. | ALL | L1 | ALL | L1 | ALL | L1 | ALL | L1 | ALL | L1 |
| Mo Agoro | 29/1/93 | 11(1) | 8 | 12 | 8 | 0 | 0 | 0 | 0 | 48 | 32 |
| Harry Aldous | 19/11/95 | 10(7) | 9(7) | 0 | 0 | 0 | 0 | 0 | 0 | 0 | 0 |
| Jack Aldous | 3/4/91 | 10(12) | 8(12) | 1 | 1 | 0 | 0 | 0 | 0 | 4 | 4 |
| Joe Arundel | 22/8/91 | 1 | 1 | 1 | 1 | 0 | 0 | 0 | 0 | 4 | 4 |
| Cory Aston | 1/3/95 | 3 | 3 | 3 | 3 | 4 | 4 | 0 | 0 | 20 | 20 |
| Jared Blanke | 14/3/89 | 8(13) | 7(10) | 1 | 1 | 0 | 0 | 0 | 0 | 4 | 4 |
| Joe Brown | 24/4/87 | 15(1) | 12 | 4 | 4 | 0 | 0 | 0 | 0 | 16 | 16 |
| Keal Carlile | 20/3/90 | 20(3) | 17(3) | 10 | 6 | 0 | 0 | 0 | 0 | 40 | 24 |
| Jed Charlton | 14/1/99 | (1) | 0 | 0 | 0 | 0 | 0 | 0 | 0 | 0 | 0 |
| Rhys Clarke | 12/3/91 | 23 | 20 | 4 | 4 | 40 | 40 | 0 | 0 | 96 | 96 |
| Connor Clayton | 31/1/94 | (2) | (1) | 0 | 0 | 0 | 0 | 0 | 0 | 0 | 0 |
| Alex Clegg | 9/7/99 | 25 | 22 | 18 | 16 | 0 | 0 | 0 | 0 | 72 | 64 |
| Dan Coates | 30/8/99 | 5 | 3 | 0 | 0 | 3 | 3 | 0 | 0 | 6 | 6 |
| Jy-mel Coleman | 13/10/88 | 5 | 3 | 0 | 0 | 15 | 13 | 0 | 0 | 30 | 26 |
| Tyler Craig | 4/7/93 | 9 | 7 | 1 | 1 | 0 | 0 | 0 | 0 | 4 | 4 |
| Jordan Crowther | 19/2/97 | (1) | (1) | 0 | 0 | 0 | 0 | 0 | 0 | 0 | 0 |
| Carne Doyle-Manga | 6/7/94 | 3(9) | 1(7) | 3 | 2 | 0 | 0 | 0 | 0 | 12 | 8 |
| Joel Edwards | 17/7/88 | 16 | 15 | 5 | 5 | 0 | 0 | 0 | 0 | 20 | 20 |
| Liam Finn | 2/11/83 | 3 | 3 | 1 | 1 | 13 | 13 | 0 | 0 | 30 | 30 |
| Conor Fitzsimmons | 7/5/98 | 19(4) | 16(4) | 6 | 5 | 0 | 0 | 0 | 0 | 24 | 20 |
| Kieran Gill | 4/12/95 | 23 | 21 | 28 | 26 | 0 | 0 | 0 | 0 | 112 | 104 |
| Ollie Gowing | 24/7/00 | (1) | (1) | 0 | 0 | 0 | 0 | 0 | 0 | 0 | 0 |
| Max Jowitt | 6/5/97 | 1 | 1 | 2 | 2 | 0 | 0 | 0 | 0 | 8 | 8 |
| Quentin Laulu-Togaga'e | 1/12/84 | 9 | 9 | 6 | 6 | 0 | 0 | 0 | 0 | 24 | 24 |
| Mikey Lewis | 4/7/01 | 7 | 6 | 7 | 7 | 15 | 13 | 0 | 0 | 58 | 54 |
| Sam Luckley | 29/11/95 | 13(10) | 12(10) | 1 | 1 | 0 | 0 | 0 | 0 | 4 | 4 |
| Remy Marginet | 27/5/89 | 9 | 7 | 2 | 1 | 17 | 6 | 0 | 0 | 42 | 16 |
| Liam McAvoy | 24/9/93 | 21(4) | 19(4) | 3 | 3 | 0 | 0 | 0 | 0 | 12 | 12 |
| Muizz Mustapha | 3/4/00 | 2(5) | 2(5) | 3 | 3 | 0 | 0 | 0 | 0 | 12 | 12 |
| Nick Newman | 15/12/96 | 14 | 14 | 7 | 7 | 0 | 0 | 1 | 1 | 29 | 29 |
| Aaron Ollett | 19/11/92 | 13(7) | 10(6) | 4 | 3 | 0 | 0 | 0 | 0 | 16 | 12 |
| Alex Rowe | 11/3/85 | (13) | (10) | 1 | 1 | 0 | 0 | 0 | 0 | 4 | 4 |
| Niall Sidney | 3/8/98 | 1(1) | 0 | 1 | 0 | 0 | 0 | 0 | 0 | 4 | 0 |
| Evan Simons | 11/10/91 | 10(16) | 8(15) | 5 | 4 | 0 | 0 | 0 | 0 | 20 | 16 |
| Misi Taulapapa | 25/1/82 | 24 | 21 | 13 | 10 | 0 | 0 | 0 | 0 | 52 | 40 |
| David Weetman | 24/5/98 | (1) | 0 | 0 | 0 | 0 | 0 | 0 | 0 | 0 | 0 |
| Matthew Wright | 30/1/91 | 6 | 6 | 8 | 8 | 12 | 12 | 0 | 0 | 56 | 56 |
| Lewis Young | 1/7/95 | 25 | 21 | 18 | 16 | 0 | 0 | 0 | 0 | 72 | 64 |

*'L1' totals include play-offs; 'All' totals also include Challenge Cup & 1895 Cup*

**LEAGUE RECORD**
P20-W14-D1-L5
(3rd/Play-off Final Runners-Up)
F741, A364, Diff+377, 29 points.

**CHALLENGE CUP**
Round Four

**1895 CUP**
Round Two

**ATTENDANCES**
Best - v Doncaster (L1 - 1,817)
Worst - v West Wales (CC - 329)
Total (excluding Challenge Cup) - 12,445
Average (excluding Challenge Cup) - 889
(Down by 134 on 2018)

| CLUB RECORDS | |
|---|---|
| MATCH RECORDS | **Highest score:** 98-6 v West Wales, 23/9/2018 **Highest score against:** 0-132 v Blackpool Panthers, 16/5/2010 **Record attendance:** 6,631 v Bradford, 16/5/99 *(Gateshead International Stadium)*; 4,137 v Bradford, 18/5/2018 *(Kingston Park)* **Tries:** 5 Andy Walker v London Skolars, 22/6/2003 **Goals:** 12 Rhys Clarke v Coventry, 18/8/2019 **Points:** 28 Benn Hardcastle v Oxford, 18/6/2017 |
| SEASON RECORDS | **Tries:** 28 Kieran Gill 2019 **Goals:** 129 *(inc 1fg)* Dan Russell 2008 **Points:** 293 Dan Russell 2008 |
| CAREER RECORDS | **Tries:** 74 Kevin Neighbour 2001-2006; 2008-2010 **Goals:** 283 *(inc 8fg)* Benn Hardcastle 2013-2017 **Points:** 682 Benn Hardcastle 2013-2017 **Appearances:** 228 Joe Brown 2005-2006; 2010-2019 |

# NORTH WALES CRUSADERS

| DATE | FIXTURE | RESULT | SCORERS | LGE | ATT |
|------|---------|--------|---------|-----|-----|
| 24/2/19 | Workington (a) | L48-18 | t:Houghton,Price,Connor g:Baker(3) | 9th | 901 |
| 3/3/19 | Oldham (h) | L14-16 | t:Hurst,Brennan g:Baker,Stead(2) | 9th | 426 |
| 10/3/19 | London Skolars (a) (CCR3) | W18-31 | t:Baker(2),Ashall,Hazzard,Atherton g:Baker(5) fg:Roper | N/A | 170 |
| 17/3/19 | Hunslet (h) | L12-22 | t:Freeman,Jenkins g:Freeman(2) | 9th | 317 |
| 24/3/19 | Keighley (a) | L24-22 | t:Conroy,Stead,Hazzard g:Stead(5) | 9th | 859 |
| 30/3/19 | Thatto Heath (a) (CCR4) | L16-14 | t:Massam(2),Worrall g:Stead | N/A | 737 |
| 19/4/19 | West Wales (h) | W70-8 | t:Massam(4),Hurst,Roper(2),Morley-Samuels(2),Eccleston,Hazzard(2) g:Stead(11) | 9th | 282 |
| 28/4/19 | Doncaster (a) | W10-12 | t:Hurst,Baker g:Stead(2) | 8th | 658 |
| 11/5/19 | London Skolars (a) | L19-18 | t:Hazzard,Fairhurst g:Stead(5) | 9th | 248 |
| 19/5/19 | Whitehaven (h) | L14-28 | t:Baker,Massam g:Stead,Baker(2) | 9th | 342 |
| 26/5/19 | Coventry (a) ● | W18-34 | t:Eccleston,Baker,Massam(2),W Thompson,Ashall g:Baker(2),Fairhurst(3) | 8th | 395 |
| 9/6/19 | Newcastle (h) | L12-48 | t:Hurst,Smith g:Fairhurst(2) | 8th | 302 |
| 23/6/19 | Whitehaven (a) | W22-24 | t:Hurst,Baker,Massam(2),Ashall g:Fairhurst(2) | 8th | 781 |
| 30/6/19 | Keighley (h) | W14-6 | t:Hurst,Ashall g:Stead(3) | 8th | 315 |
| 7/7/19 | Workington (a) | W30-18 | t:Stead,Roper,Morley-Samuels(2),Baker g:Stead(5) | 8th | 363 |
| 14/7/19 | Oldham (a) | L46-30 | t:Stead,Atherton,Massam(2),Gregory g:Stead(5) | 8th | 616 |
| 21/7/19 | Doncaster (h) | L0-30 | | 8th | 372 |
| 4/8/19 | Hunslet (a) | L42-18 | t:Gregory,Atherton,Walker g:Stead(3) | 8th | 488 |
| 11/8/19 | Coventry (h) | W33-16 | t:A Thompson,Massam,Gregory,Brennan,Eccleston,Ryan g:Stead(4) fg:Roper | 8th | 256 |
| 17/8/19 | West Wales (a) | W16-56 | t:Stead,Eccleston(2),W Thompson,Roper,Eckley,Ryan,Morley-Samuels, Massam(2),Fairhurst g:Stead(3),Roper,Fairhurst(2) | 7th | 272 |
| 1/9/19 | Newcastle (a) | L46-22 | t:Reid,Massam(2),Wild g:Stead(3) | 7th | 883 |
| 7/9/19 | London Skolars (h) | W36-18 | t:Massam(2),Wild(2),Atherton,Walker,Eckley g:Stead(3),Wild | 7th | 421 |

● *Played at Ivor Preece Field, Broadstreet*

| | | APP | | TRIES | | GOALS | | FG | | PTS | |
|---|---|---|---|---|---|---|---|---|---|---|---|
| | D.O.B. | ALL | L1 | ALL | L1 | ALL | L1 | ALL | L1 | ALL | L1 |
| Karl Ashall | 3/11/89 | 17(1) | 15(1) | 4 | 3 | 0 | 0 | 0 | 0 | 16 | 12 |
| Simon Atherton | 8/11/90 | 16(1) | 14(1) | 4 | 3 | 0 | 0 | 0 | 0 | 16 | 12 |
| Kenny Baker | 1/3/92 | 16 | 14 | 7 | 5 | 13 | 8 | 0 | 0 | 54 | 36 |
| Brad Brennan | 18/1/93 | 8(13) | 8(11) | 2 | 2 | 0 | 0 | 0 | 0 | 8 | 8 |
| Joe Connor | 17/12/90 | 1 | 1 | 1 | 1 | 0 | 0 | 0 | 0 | 4 | 4 |
| Gavin Conroy | 6/3/95 | 3 | 2 | 1 | 1 | 0 | 0 | 0 | 0 | 4 | 4 |
| Dave Eccleston | 12/9/96 | 17 | 16 | 5 | 5 | 0 | 0 | 0 | 0 | 20 | 20 |
| Alex Eckley | 25/8/99 | 5(4) | 5(2) | 2 | 2 | 0 | 0 | 0 | 0 | 8 | 8 |
| Lewis Fairhurst | 24/12/96 | 13 | 13 | 2 | 2 | 9 | 9 | 0 | 0 | 26 | 26 |
| Sam Freeman | 3/4/99 | 1 | 1 | 1 | 1 | 2 | 2 | 0 | 0 | 8 | 8 |
| Declan Gregory | 18/1/97 | 2(8) | 2(8) | 3 | 3 | 0 | 0 | 0 | 0 | 12 | 12 |
| Callum Hazzard | 9/1/99 | 12(6) | 10(6) | 5 | 4 | 0 | 0 | 0 | 0 | 20 | 16 |
| Jack Houghton | 10/1/97 | 10(1) | 8(1) | 1 | 1 | 0 | 0 | 0 | 0 | 4 | 4 |
| Kenny Hughes | 30/3/90 | 4(9) | 4(8) | 0 | 0 | 0 | 0 | 0 | 0 | 0 | 0 |
| Earl Hurst | 21/4/89 | 19 | 17 | 6 | 6 | 0 | 0 | 0 | 0 | 24 | 24 |
| Elliott Jenkins | 6/2/99 | 4 | 4 | 1 | 1 | 0 | 0 | 0 | 0 | 4 | 4 |
| Rob Massam | 29/11/87 | 19 | 17 | 20 | 18 | 0 | 0 | 0 | 0 | 80 | 72 |
| Dante Morley-Samuels | 22/11/98 | 12 | 12 | 5 | 5 | 0 | 0 | 0 | 0 | 20 | 20 |
| Jordan Penny | 26/4/98 | 2(1) | 2(1) | 0 | 0 | 0 | 0 | 0 | 0 | 0 | 0 |
| Dan Price | 5/10/92 | 3 | 2 | 1 | 1 | 0 | 0 | 0 | 0 | 4 | 4 |
| Matt Reid | 16/9/92 | 15 | 14 | 1 | 1 | 0 | 0 | 0 | 0 | 4 | 4 |
| Steve Roper | 10/11/86 | 21 | 19 | 4 | 4 | 1 | 1 | 2 | 1 | 20 | 19 |
| Joe Ryan | 27/9/95 | 1(7) | 1(7) | 2 | 2 | 0 | 0 | 0 | 0 | 8 | 8 |
| Ryan Smith | 25/9/89 | 8(2) | 6(2) | 1 | 1 | 0 | 0 | 0 | 0 | 4 | 4 |
| Ben Stead | 13/10/92 | 16(2) | 15(1) | 4 | 4 | 56 | 55 | 0 | 0 | 128 | 126 |
| Jacob Thomas | 9/10/93 | (1) | (1) | 0 | 0 | 0 | 0 | 0 | 0 | 0 | 0 |
| Alex Thompson | 11/2/90 | 4(6) | 4(6) | 1 | 1 | 0 | 0 | 0 | 0 | 4 | 4 |
| Warren Thompson | 24/2/90 | 15(7) | 13(7) | 2 | 2 | 0 | 0 | 0 | 0 | 8 | 8 |
| James Tilley | 11/11/93 | 1(2) | 1(2) | 0 | 0 | 0 | 0 | 0 | 0 | 0 | 0 |
| Jonny Walker | 26/9/86 | 7(12) | 7(10) | 2 | 2 | 0 | 0 | 0 | 0 | 8 | 8 |
| Liam Walsh | 12/9/98 | (2) | (2) | 0 | 0 | 0 | 0 | 0 | 0 | 0 | 0 |
| Stephen Wild | 26/4/81 | 13 | 13 | 3 | 3 | 1 | 1 | 0 | 0 | 14 | 14 |
| Chris Worrall | 11/10/96 | 1(3) | (3) | 1 | 0 | 0 | 0 | 0 | 0 | 4 | 0 |

*'L1' totals include League 1 regular season only; 'All' totals also include Challenge Cup*

Rob Massam

**LEAGUE RECORD**
P20-W9-D0-L11 (7th)
F489, A501, Diff-12, 18 points.

**CHALLENGE CUP**
Round Four

**1895 CUP**
Not entered

**ATTENDANCES**
Best - v Oldham (L1 - 426)
Worst - v Coventry (L1 - 256)
Total (all home games included) - 3,396
Average (all home games included) - 340
(Down by 34 on 2018)

**CLUB RECORDS**
Highest score: 82-6 v West Hull, 6/4/2013 Highest score against: 4-98 v Wigan, 15/4/2012
Record attendance: 1,562 v South Wales, 1/9/2013 *(Racecourse Ground)*; 886 v Bradford, 12/8/2018 *(Queensway Stadium)*

**MATCH RECORDS**
Tries: 5 Rob Massam v Rochdale, 30/6/2013; Jono Smith v Hemel, 16/5/2015
Goals: 11 Tommy Johnson v West Hull, 6/4/2013; Ian Mort v Hemel, 16/5/2015; Ben Stead v West Wales, 19/4/2019
Points: 30 Tommy Johnson v West Hull, 6/4/2013

**SEASON RECORDS**
Tries: 29 Rob Massam 2015 Goals: 109 Tommy Johnson 2015 Points: 266 Tommy Johnson 2015

**CAREER RECORDS**
Tries: 118 Rob Massam 2012-2016; 2019 Goals: 542 Tommy Johnson 2012-2018 Points: 1,308 Tommy Johnson 2012-2018
Appearances: 168 Jonny Walker 2012-2019

# OLDHAM

| DATE | FIXTURE | RESULT | SCORERS | LGE | ATT |
|---|---|---|---|---|---|
| 17/2/19 | Workington (h) | L28-32 | t:Joy,Hawkyard,Jones-Bishop(2) g:Hewitt(6) | 8th | 765 |
| 24/2/19 | Whitehaven (h) | W36-12 | t:McComb(3),Hawkyard(2),Hewitt g:Hewitt(6) | 3rd | 546 |
| 3/3/19 | North Wales (a) | W14-16 | t:Kershaw(2),Hewitt g:Hewitt(2) | 3rd | 426 |
| 10/3/19 | Haydock (h) (CCR3) | W80-10 | t:Maders(3),Bowman,Wilkinson(3),Whittel,McComb(3),Brook,Johnson(2) g:Brook(12) | N/A | 508 |
| 24/3/19 | London Skolars (h) | W34-4 | t:Joy(2),McComb,Spencer,Johnson,Kershaw g:Hewitt(5) | 2nd | 709 |
| 31/3/19 | Widnes (h) (CCR4) | L14-54 | t:McComb,Owen,Hawkyard g:Hewitt | N/A | 1,247 |
| 7/4/19 | Newcastle (a) | L28-22 | t:Law,Jones-Bishop,Kershaw,Bowman g:Hewitt(3) | 4th | 889 |
| 19/4/19 | Hunslet (h) | L28-36 | t:Bowman,Johnson,McComb(2) g:Hewitt(6) | 5th | 652 |
| 27/4/19 | West Wales (a) | W8-72 | t:Bent(2),Maders(2),Bridge,McComb(2),Hawkyard(2),Crook,Gwaze,Holmes(2),Langtree g:Crook(8) | 4th | 197 |
| 5/5/19 | Whitehaven (h) (1895CR1) | W48-12 | t:Langtree,Hawkyard,Wilkinson(2),Johnson,Holmes(2),Crook g:Crook(8) | N/A | 369 |
| 19/5/19 | Coventry (h) | W34-18 | t:Hewitt,Langtree(2),Wilkinson,Bridge,Hawkyard g:Crook(5) | 3rd | 451 |
| 25/5/19 | Keighley (a) | W12-52 | t:Bent,Owen,Crook,Langtree,Hewitt,McComb,Holmes,Whittel(2) g:Crook(8) | 3rd | 836 |
| 2/6/19 | Doncaster (h) (1895CR2) | L12-24 | t:Brook,Maders g:Crook(2) | N/A | 283 |
| 9/6/19 | Doncaster (h) | L31-0 | | 4th | 678 |
| 16/6/19 | Keighley (h) | W28-4 | t:Langtree,Bowman(2),Aaronson(2) g:Crook(4) | 3rd | 591 |
| 23/6/19 | Workington (a) ● | W16-26 | t:Hewitt,Langtree(2),Hawkyard g:Hewitt(5) | 3rd | 1,013 |
| 30/6/19 | West Wales (h) | W56-6 | t:Langtree(3),Leeming(2),Greenwood,Owen,Maders,McComb,Wilkinson(2) g:Hewitt(6) | 2nd | 552 |
| 7/7/19 | Whitehaven (a) | L16-10 | t:Law,McComb g:Hewitt | 3rd | 1,102 |
| 14/7/19 | North Wales (h) | W46-30 | t:Hawkyard(2),Bridge,Kershaw,Wilkinson,Joy,Aaronson(2) g:Hewitt(7) | 2nd | 616 |
| 3/8/19 | London Skolars (a) | W14-15 | t:Leeming,Hewitt g:Hewitt(3) fg:Hewitt | 3rd | 355 |
| 11/8/19 | Newcastle (h) | W28-20 | t:Johnson,Bridge(2),Leeming,Owen g:Crook(4) | 2nd | 702 |
| 18/8/19 | Doncaster (h) | W40-14 | t:Bent,Hawkyard,Langtree,Crook,Leeming,Wilkinson,Owen g:Crook(6) | 2nd | 745 |
| 1/9/19 | Coventry (a) ●● | W6-50 | t:Bent,Langtree(2),Brook,Holmes,Johnson,Kay,Joy,Davies g:Crook(7) | 2nd | 280 |
| 8/9/19 | Hunslet (h) | W20-34 | t:Bridge,Langtree(3),Crook g:Crook(7) | 2nd | 688 |
| 22/9/19 | Doncaster (h) (QSF) | W22-12 | t:Hewitt,Whittel,Crook g:Crook(5) | N/A | 529 |
| 6/10/19 | Newcastle (h) (POF) | W18-14 | t:Langtree,McComb,Beckett g:Crook(3) | N/A | 1,209 |

● *Played at Borough Park*
●● *Played at Webb Ellis Road, Rugby*

Zack McComb

|  | D.O.B. | APP ALL | L1 | TRIES ALL | L1 | GOALS ALL | L1 | FG ALL | L1 | PTS ALL | L1 |
|---|---|---|---|---|---|---|---|---|---|---|---|
| Harry Aaronson | 28/3/98 | 9 | 8 | 4 | 4 | 0 | 0 | 0 | 0 | 16 | 16 |
| Jimmy Beckett | 29/8/99 | (6) | (6) | 1 | 1 | 0 | 0 | 0 | 0 | 4 | 4 |
| Liam Bent | 11/10/97 | 22(2) | 18(2) | 5 | 5 | 0 | 0 | 0 | 0 | 20 | 20 |
| Anthony Bowman | 18/3/92 | 9 | 7 | 5 | 4 | 0 | 0 | 0 | 0 | 20 | 16 |
| Danny Bridge | 4/1/93 | 16 | 15 | 6 | 6 | 0 | 0 | 0 | 0 | 24 | 24 |
| Adam Brook | 29/9/94 | 11 | 9 | 3 | 1 | 12 | 0 | 0 | 0 | 36 | 4 |
| Ben Calland | 24/9/96 | 7(2) | 4(2) | 0 | 0 | 0 | 0 | 0 | 0 | 0 | 0 |
| Paul Crook | 28/8/86 | 13 | 10 | 6 | 5 | 67 | 57 | 0 | 0 | 158 | 134 |
| Ben Davies | 2/11/89 | (13) | (10) | 1 | 1 | 0 | 0 | 0 | 0 | 4 | 4 |
| Jamie Greenwood | 27/10/98 | (11) | (8) | 1 | 1 | 0 | 0 | 0 | 0 | 4 | 4 |
| Nick Gregson | 17/12/95 | 1(1) | 1(1) | 0 | 0 | 0 | 0 | 0 | 0 | 0 | 0 |
| Danny Grimshaw | 25/2/82 | 2 | 2 | 0 | 0 | 0 | 0 | 0 | 0 | 0 | 0 |
| Titus Gwaze | 8/6/99 | 3(11) | 2(8) | 1 | 1 | 0 | 0 | 0 | 0 | 4 | 4 |
| Ritchie Hawkyard | 21/1/86 | 22 | 19 | 12 | 10 | 0 | 0 | 0 | 0 | 48 | 40 |
| Dave Hewitt | 4/11/95 | 23 | 21 | 7 | 7 | 51 | 50 | 1 | 1 | 131 | 129 |
| Jack Holmes | 5/1/94 | 16 | 12 | 6 | 4 | 0 | 0 | 0 | 0 | 24 | 16 |
| Luke Hooley | 1/8/98 | 1 | 1 | 0 | 0 | 0 | 0 | 0 | 0 | 0 | 0 |
| Kyran Johnson | 23/3/94 | 15 | 12 | 7 | 4 | 0 | 0 | 0 | 0 | 28 | 16 |
| Aaron Jones-Bishop | 18/1/90 | 6 | 5 | 3 | 3 | 0 | 0 | 0 | 0 | 12 | 12 |
| Phil Joy | 4/9/91 | 21 | 17 | 5 | 5 | 0 | 0 | 0 | 0 | 20 | 20 |
| Dec Kay | 24/11/96 | 5 | 5 | 1 | 1 | 0 | 0 | 0 | 0 | 4 | 4 |
| Lee Kershaw | 2/5/99 | 7 | 7 | 5 | 5 | 0 | 0 | 0 | 0 | 20 | 20 |
| Danny Langtree | 18/2/91 | 18 | 17 | 18 | 17 | 0 | 0 | 0 | 0 | 72 | 68 |
| Scott Law | 19/2/85 | 20(6) | 18(4) | 2 | 2 | 0 | 0 | 0 | 0 | 8 | 8 |
| Cameron Leeming | 3/7/95 | 10 | 10 | 5 | 5 | 0 | 0 | 0 | 0 | 20 | 20 |
| Harry Maders | 15/3/99 | 10 | 6 | 7 | 3 | 0 | 0 | 0 | 0 | 28 | 12 |
| Zack McComb | 9/9/95 | 24 | 21 | 16 | 12 | 0 | 0 | 0 | 0 | 64 | 48 |
| Frazer Morris | 22/2/97 | (2) | (2) | 0 | 0 | 0 | 0 | 0 | 0 | 0 | 0 |
| Luke Nelmes | 7/6/93 | (1) | (1) | 0 | 0 | 0 | 0 | 0 | 0 | 0 | 0 |
| Gareth Owen | 3/7/92 | 24(1) | 21(1) | 5 | 4 | 0 | 0 | 0 | 0 | 20 | 16 |
| Ed Smith | 12/11/92 | (3) | (3) | 0 | 0 | 0 | 0 | 0 | 0 | 0 | 0 |
| Jack Spencer | 21/12/90 | 12(11) | 10(9) | 1 | 1 | 0 | 0 | 0 | 0 | 4 | 4 |
| Emmerson Whittel | 13/9/94 | 9(15) | 7(14) | 4 | 3 | 0 | 0 | 0 | 0 | 16 | 12 |
| Matty Wilkinson | 13/6/96 | 2(18) | 1(16) | 10 | 5 | 0 | 0 | 0 | 0 | 40 | 20 |

*'L1' totals include play-offs; 'All' totals also include Challenge Cup & 1895 Cup*

**LEAGUE RECORD**
P20-W15-D0-L5
(2nd/Play-off Final Winners)
F655, A341, Diff+314, 30 points.

**CHALLENGE CUP**
Round Four

**1895 CUP**
Round Two

**ATTENDANCES**
Best - v Widnes (CC - 1,247)
Worst - v Doncaster (1895C - 283)
Total (excluding Challenge Cup) - 8,719
Average (excluding Challenge Cup) - 623
(Up by 118 on 2018)

| CLUB RECORDS | **Highest score:** 102-6 v West Wales, 8/7/2018  **Highest score against:** 0-84 v Widnes, 25/7/99 |
|---|---|
|  | **Record attendance:** 28,000 v Huddersfield, 24/2/1912 *(Watersheddings)*; 1,405 v Keighley, 20/9/2015 *(Vestacare Stadium)* |
| MATCH RECORDS | **Tries:** 7 James Miller v Barry, 31/10/1908 **Goals:** 14 Bernard Ganley v Liverpool City, 4/4/59 |
|  | **Points:** 34 Andy Ballard v London Skolars, 2/5/2009; Chris Baines v Hunslet, 20/9/2009; Lewis Palfrey v Hemel, 9/8/2015 |
| SEASON RECORDS | **Tries:** 49 Reg Farrar 1921-22 **Goals:** 200 Bernard Ganley 1957-58 **Points:** 412 Bernard Ganley 1957-58 |
| CAREER RECORDS | **Tries:** 174 Alan Davies 1950-61 **Goals:** 1,358 Bernard Ganley 1951-61 **Points:** 2,761 Bernard Ganley 1951-61 **Appearances:** 627 Joe Ferguson 1899-1923 |

# WEST WALES RAIDERS

| DATE | FIXTURE | RESULT | SCORERS | LGE | ATT |
|------|---------|--------|---------|-----|-----|
| 17/2/19 | Coventry (a) | L28-4 | t:Kaye | 10th | 526 |
| 23/2/19 | London Skolars (h) | L18-28 | t:Maiden,Desmond-Walker,Palumbo g:Hunt(3) | 10th | 250 |
| 3/3/19 | Hunslet (a) | L58-4 | t:Sabour | 10th | 560 |
| 9/3/19 | Newcastle (a) (CCR3) | L48-0 | | N/A | 329 |
| 16/3/19 | Newcastle (a) | L56-6 | t:Herron g:Hunt | 10th | 678 |
| 24/3/19 | Whitehaven (h) | L16-30 | t:Tuliatu,Shallish,Connor g:Hunt(2) | 10th | 173 |
| 6/4/19 | Keighley (h) | L12-56 | t:Sabour(2),Jefferies | 10th | 238 |
| 19/4/19 | North Wales (a) | L70-8 | t:Jennings(2) | 10th | 282 |
| 27/4/19 | Oldham (h) | L8-72 | t:Kaye,Jennings | 10th | 197 |
| 5/5/19 | Doncaster (a) (1895CR1) | L70-6 | t:Kaye g:Cowburn | N/A | 248 |
| 26/5/19 | Doncaster (a) | L54-0 | | 10th | 525 |
| 8/6/19 | Workington (h) | L12-58 | t:Cowburn,M Evans g:Cowburn(2) | 10th | 321 |
| 15/6/19 | London Skolars (a) | L51-6 | t:Bateman g:Cowburn | 10th | 290 |
| 22/6/19 | Hunslet (a) | L10-72 | t:Matamosi(2) g:Cowburn | 11th | 283 |
| 30/6/19 | Oldham (a) | L56-6 | t:Parry g:Cowburn | 11th | 552 |
| 6/7/19 | Doncaster (h) | L0-72 | | 11th | 198 |
| 14/7/19 | Keighley (a) | L50-18 | t:Shaw,Baker,M Evans g:Cowburn(3) | 11th | 702 |
| 20/7/19 | Coventry (h) | W44-16 | t:Desmond-Walker,Bateman(2),M Evans,Snook(2),Shaw,Parry g:Cowburn(6) | 11th | 352 |
| 3/8/19 | Newcastle (h) | L6-68 | t:Parry g:Cowburn | 11th | 302 |
| 11/8/19 | Workington (a) | L66-22 | t:Cowburn,Jennings,Baker,Sabour g:Cowburn(3) | 11th | 908 |
| 17/8/19 | North Wales (h) | L16-56 | t:Shaw,Parry,Snook g:Cowburn(2) | 11th | 272 |
| 1/9/19 | Whitehaven (a) | L74-6 | t:Parry g:Cowburn | 11th | 972 |

| | | APP | | TRIES | | GOALS | | FG | | PTS | |
|---|---|---|---|---|---|---|---|---|---|---|---|
| | D.O.B. | ALL | L1 | ALL | L1 | ALL | L1 | ALL | L1 | ALL | L1 |
| Sam Baker | 8/10/92 | 10(2) | 9(2) | 2 | 2 | 0 | 0 | 0 | 0 | 8 | 8 |
| Ashley Bateman | 11/2/90 | 16 | 15 | 3 | 3 | 0 | 0 | 0 | 0 | 12 | 12 |
| Nicolas Bertolas | 25/5/96 | (1) | (1) | 0 | 0 | 0 | 0 | 0 | 0 | 0 | 0 |
| Gioele Celerino | 4/10/93 | 9(1) | 9(1) | 0 | 0 | 0 | 0 | 0 | 0 | 0 | 0 |
| Liam Clark | 10/2/95 | 4 | 3 | 0 | 0 | 0 | 0 | 0 | 0 | 0 | 0 |
| Mike Connor | 27/3/94 | 13 | 12 | 1 | 1 | 0 | 0 | 0 | 0 | 4 | 4 |
| Phil Cowburn | 15/10/90 | 19 | 18 | 2 | 2 | 22 | 21 | 0 | 0 | 52 | 50 |
| Dalton Desmond-Walker | 25/4/93 | 12(8) | 12(6) | 2 | 2 | 0 | 0 | 0 | 0 | 8 | 8 |
| Dai Evans | 30/7/92 | 6 | 5 | 0 | 0 | 0 | 0 | 0 | 0 | 0 | 0 |
| Morgan Evans | 23/3/92 | 12(1) | 11(1) | 3 | 3 | 0 | 0 | 0 | 0 | 12 | 12 |
| Kurtis Haile | 11/10/90 | 1(1) | 1(1) | 0 | 0 | 0 | 0 | 0 | 0 | 0 | 0 |
| Macauley Harris | 27/2/99 | (2) | (2) | 0 | 0 | 0 | 0 | 0 | 0 | 0 | 0 |
| Sam Herron | 13/12/93 | 20(1) | 18(1) | 1 | 1 | 0 | 0 | 0 | 0 | 4 | 4 |
| Tyler Hunt | 1/3/00 | 20 | 18 | 0 | 0 | 6 | 6 | 0 | 0 | 12 | 12 |
| Morgan Jefferies | 6/9/96 | 6 | 5 | 1 | 1 | 0 | 0 | 0 | 0 | 4 | 4 |
| Paddy Jennings | 7/12/97 | 8(2) | 7(1) | 4 | 4 | 0 | 0 | 0 | 0 | 16 | 16 |
| Matt Jones | 12/12/00 | (1) | (1) | 0 | 0 | 0 | 0 | 0 | 0 | 0 | 0 |
| Dimosthenis Kartsonakis | 11/9/95 | (1) | (1) | 0 | 0 | 0 | 0 | 0 | 0 | 0 | 0 |
| Rowland Kaye | 27/8/99 | 15 | 13 | 3 | 2 | 0 | 0 | 0 | 0 | 12 | 8 |
| Alex King | 14/11/96 | 3(1) | 1(1) | 0 | 0 | 0 | 0 | 0 | 0 | 0 | 0 |
| Brad Kislingbury | 2/2/96 | 6 | 5 | 0 | 0 | 0 | 0 | 0 | 0 | 0 | 0 |
| Dan Maiden | 11/1/97 | 10(7) | 10(6) | 1 | 1 | 0 | 0 | 0 | 0 | 4 | 4 |
| Robert Matamosi | 23/2/97 | 3 | 3 | 2 | 2 | 0 | 0 | 0 | 0 | 8 | 8 |
| Joe McClean | 10/8/89 | (2) | (2) | 0 | 0 | 0 | 0 | 0 | 0 | 0 | 0 |
| Matthew Morgan | 17/1/01 | 2(2) | 2(2) | 0 | 0 | 0 | 0 | 0 | 0 | 0 | 0 |
| Callum Mulkeen | 10/12/90 | 3(10) | 2(10) | 0 | 0 | 0 | 0 | 0 | 0 | 0 | 0 |
| Emosi Nadaubale | 6/11/92 | 2 | 2 | 0 | 0 | 0 | 0 | 0 | 0 | 0 | 0 |
| Ronny Palumbo | 22/4/91 | 7 | 6 | 1 | 1 | 0 | 0 | 0 | 0 | 4 | 4 |
| Connor Parker | 23/10/97 | 3(2) | 3(2) | 0 | 0 | 0 | 0 | 0 | 0 | 0 | 0 |
| Steve Parry | 19/10/88 | 11 | 11 | 5 | 5 | 0 | 0 | 0 | 0 | 20 | 20 |
| Alan Pope | 1/4/85 | (4) | (4) | 0 | 0 | 0 | 0 | 0 | 0 | 0 | 0 |
| Ross Price | 14/12/92 | (1) | (1) | 0 | 0 | 0 | 0 | 0 | 0 | 0 | 0 |
| Liam Rice-Wilson | 16/3/96 | 15(2) | 13(2) | 0 | 0 | 0 | 0 | 0 | 0 | 0 | 0 |
| Morgan Rowlands | 30/3/99 | 1(5) | 1(4) | 0 | 0 | 0 | 0 | 0 | 0 | 0 | 0 |
| Mickael Sabour | 24/6/94 | 11(1) | 9(1) | 4 | 4 | 0 | 0 | 0 | 0 | 16 | 16 |
| Ryan Shallish | 25/2/93 | 1(8) | 1(8) | 1 | 1 | 0 | 0 | 0 | 0 | 4 | 4 |
| Mitch Shaw | 25/8/98 | 7(1) | 7(1) | 3 | 3 | 0 | 0 | 0 | 0 | 12 | 12 |
| Liam Silver | 9/12/97 | 1(1) | 1 | 0 | 0 | 0 | 0 | 0 | 0 | 0 | 0 |
| James Smith | 18/7/00 | 2 | 2 | 0 | 0 | 0 | 0 | 0 | 0 | 0 | 0 |
| Archie Snook | 26/3/99 | 19(2) | 18(1) | 3 | 3 | 0 | 0 | 0 | 0 | 12 | 12 |
| Robert Tuliatu | 11/10/95 | 4(1) | 3(1) | 1 | 1 | 0 | 0 | 0 | 0 | 4 | 4 |
| Chris Vitalini | 5/5/87 | 2(6) | 2(6) | 0 | 0 | 0 | 0 | 0 | 0 | 0 | 0 |
| Nye Walker | 16/1/00 | 2(8) | 2(8) | 0 | 0 | 0 | 0 | 0 | 0 | 0 | 0 |

Dalton Desmond-Walker

'L1' totals include League 1 regular season only; 'All' totals also include Challenge Cup & 1895 Cup

**LEAGUE RECORD**
P20-W1-D0-L19 (11th)
F222, A1091, Diff-869, 2 points.

**CHALLENGE CUP**
Round Three

**1895 CUP**
Round One

**ATTENDANCES**
Best - v Coventry (L1 - 352)
Worst - v Whitehaven (L1 - 173)
Total (all home games included) - 2,586
Average (all home games included) - 259
(Down by 63 on 2018)

| | |
|---|---|
| CLUB RECORDS | **Highest score:** 44-16 v Coventry, 20/7/2019 **Highest score against:** 0-144 v York, 29/4/2018 **Record attendance:** 826 v Bradford, 9/9/2018 |
| MATCH RECORDS | **Tries:** 2 *(6 players)* **Goals:** 6 Phil Cowburn v Coventry, 20/7/2019 **Points:** 12 Phil Cowburn v Coventry, 20/7/2019 |
| SEASON RECORDS | **Tries:** 8 Steve Parry 2018 **Goals:** 22 Phil Cowburn 2019 **Points:** 52 Phil Cowburn 2019 |
| CAREER RECORDS | **Tries:** 13 Steve Parry 2018-2019 **Goals:** 22 Phil Cowburn 2018-2019 **Points:** 68 Phil Cowburn 2018-2019 **Appearances:** 42 Archie Snook 2018-2019 |

# WHITEHAVEN

| DATE | FIXTURE | RESULT | SCORERS | LGE | ATT |
|---|---|---|---|---|---|
| 17/2/19 | Keighley (h) | W28-16 | t:Taylor,Moore(2),Bulman(2) g:Moore(3),Holliday | 2nd | 897 |
| 24/2/19 | Oldham (a) | L36-12 | t:C Phillips,Bulman g:Moore(2) | 7th | 546 |
| 10/3/19 | Wigan St Patricks (h) (CCR3) | W74-4 | t:C Phillips(2),Bulman(6),D Thompson(4),Forrester,Taylor g:Holliday(9) | N/A | 464 |
| 17/3/19 | Doncaster (h) | W26-8 | t:Mossop,Moore,Parker,Aiye g:Moore(3),Holliday(2) | 5th | 702 |
| 24/3/19 | West Wales (a) | W16-30 | t:Moore,C Phillips(3),Shackley,Taylor g:Moore(3) | 4th | 173 |
| 31/3/19 | Rochdale (h) (CCR4) | L21-22 | t:C Phillips,Moore g:Moore(2),Holliday(4) fg:Forrester | N/A | 889 |
| 7/4/19 | Hunslet (h) | W16-12 | t:Wilkinson,Parker,Aiye g:Moore,Holliday | 2nd | 724 |
| 19/4/19 | Workington (a) | W18-33 | t:Forrester,Burns(2),Moore,B Phillips g:Holliday(4),Moore(2) fg:Carter | 2nd | 1,981 |
| 28/4/19 | Newcastle (h) | D12-12 | t:D Thompson,Burns g:Holliday(2) | 1st | 852 |
| 5/5/19 | Oldham (a) (1895CR1) | L48-12 | t:Carter,Holliday g:Moore(2) | N/A | 369 |
| 19/5/19 | North Wales (a) | W14-28 | t:Forrester,Dowsett,Taylor,C Phillips,Bulman g:Moore(4) | 1st | 342 |
| 25/5/19 | London Skolars (h) | W32-6 | t:Aiye(2),Forster,Newton,B Phillips g:Moore(6) | 1st | 811 |
| 9/6/19 | Coventry (h) | W32-18 | t:Bulman(2),Forrester(2),Mossop,Moore(2) g:Holliday(2) | 1st | 915 |
| 16/6/19 | Newcastle (a) | L26-20 | t:Parker,Moore,B Phillips g:Moore(4) | 1st | 1,079 |
| 23/6/19 | North Wales (h) | L22-24 | t:Shackley,McAvoy(2),C Phillips g:Moore(3) | 1st | 781 |
| 29/6/19 | London Skolars (a) | W6-28 | t:Coward,Forrester,D Thompson,Holliday,C Phillips g:Holliday(4) | 1st | 442 |
| 7/7/19 | Oldham (h) | W16-10 | t:D Thompson,Burns g:Holliday(2),Burns(2) | 1st | 1,102 |
| 14/7/19 | Doncaster (a) ● | W12-22 | t:Forster(2),Bulman g:Holliday(5) | 1st | 780 |
| 27/7/19 | Hunslet (h) | W12-19 | t:Kelly,D Thompson g:Burns(3),Holliday(2) fg:Holliday | 1st | 540 |
| 4/8/19 | Workington (h) | D12-12 | t:Shackley g:Burns(3),Moore | 1st | 2,360 |
| 18/8/19 | Keighley (a) | W19-48 | t:Aiye(2),Forrester(3),C Phillips(2),Bulman g:Burns,Holliday(7) | 1st | 782 |
| 1/9/19 | West Wales (h) | W74-6 | t:Forrester(3),Burns(2),Newton,C Phillips,D Thompson(2),Bulman(2),Moore,Coward g:Moore(10),Holliday | 1st | 972 |
| 7/9/19 | Coventry (a) ●● | W0-72 | t:Burns(4),Moore,Shackley,Taylor,Forster,D Thompson(2),B Phillips,C Phillips,Bulman g:Moore(6),Holliday(4) | 1st | 652 |

● *Played at LD Nutrition Stadium, Featherstone*
●● *Played at Webb Ellis Road, Rugby*

| | D.O.B. | APP | | TRIES | | GOALS | | FG | | PTS | |
|---|---|---|---|---|---|---|---|---|---|---|---|
| | | ALL | L1 | ALL | L1 | ALL | L1 | ALL | L1 | ALL | L1 |
| Dion Aiye | 6/11/87 | 6(14) | 5(12) | 6 | 6 | 0 | 0 | 0 | 0 | 24 | 24 |
| Jake Bradley | 29/4/01 | 1(4) | (3) | 0 | 0 | 0 | 0 | 0 | 0 | 0 | 0 |
| Lewis Brown | 29/11/98 | (1) | 0 | 0 | 0 | 0 | 0 | 0 | 0 | 0 | 0 |
| Andrew Bulman | 4/10/99 | 17 | 16 | 17 | 11 | 0 | 0 | 0 | 0 | 68 | 44 |
| Jordan Burns | 2/9/95 | 18 | 15 | 10 | 10 | 9 | 9 | 0 | 0 | 58 | 58 |
| Jake Carter | 24/11/98 | 2(1) | 1(1) | 1 | 0 | 0 | 0 | 1 | 1 | 5 | 1 |
| Kris Coward | 1/10/81 | 20(1) | 19 | 2 | 2 | 0 | 0 | 0 | 0 | 8 | 8 |
| Sam Dowsett | 2/11/92 | 18(1) | 15(1) | 1 | 1 | 0 | 0 | 0 | 0 | 4 | 4 |
| Sam Forrester | 28/6/93 | 21 | 19 | 12 | 11 | 0 | 0 | 1 | 0 | 49 | 44 |
| Carl Forster | 4/6/92 | 1(10) | 1(10) | 4 | 4 | 0 | 0 | 0 | 0 | 16 | 16 |
| Ellis Gillam | 6/10/97 | 5 | 5 | 0 | 0 | 0 | 0 | 0 | 0 | 0 | 0 |
| Connor Holliday | 9/6/95 | 10(12) | 7(12) | 2 | 1 | 50 | 37 | 1 | 1 | 109 | 79 |
| Ethan Kelly | 31/12/94 | (12) | (12) | 1 | 1 | 0 | 0 | 0 | 0 | 4 | 4 |
| Kurt Maudling | 5/2/89 | 5(5) | 2(5) | 0 | 0 | 0 | 0 | 0 | 0 | 0 | 0 |
| Scott McAvoy | 9/4/86 | 1(1) | 1 | 2 | 2 | 0 | 0 | 0 | 0 | 8 | 8 |
| Ruairi McGoff | 5/1/85 | 2(2) | (1) | 0 | 0 | 0 | 0 | 0 | 0 | 0 | 0 |
| Jake Moore | 6/9/96 | 16(1) | 14(1) | 11 | 10 | 52 | 48 | 0 | 0 | 148 | 136 |
| Jason Mossop | 12/9/85 | 21 | 19 | 2 | 2 | 0 | 0 | 0 | 0 | 8 | 8 |
| James Newton | 20/12/91 | 5(13) | 5(11) | 2 | 2 | 0 | 0 | 0 | 0 | 8 | 8 |
| Jessie Joe Parker | 22/8/85 | 13(2) | 10(2) | 3 | 3 | 0 | 0 | 0 | 0 | 12 | 12 |
| Brett Phillips | 25/10/88 | 17 | 16 | 4 | 4 | 0 | 0 | 0 | 0 | 16 | 16 |
| Callum Phillips | 19/2/92 | 21 | 19 | 14 | 11 | 0 | 0 | 0 | 0 | 56 | 44 |
| Marc Shackley | 14/1/89 | 21(1) | 20 | 4 | 4 | 0 | 0 | 0 | 0 | 16 | 16 |
| Chris Taylor | 25/10/93 | 23 | 20 | 5 | 4 | 0 | 0 | 0 | 0 | 20 | 16 |
| Dave Thompson | 13/9/95 | 17 | 15 | 12 | 8 | 0 | 0 | 0 | 0 | 48 | 32 |
| Jordan Thomson | 23/1/93 | (7) | (6) | 0 | 0 | 0 | 0 | 0 | 0 | 0 | 0 |
| Matty While | 25/11/96 | 1 | 0 | 0 | 0 | 0 | 0 | 0 | 0 | 0 | 0 |
| Tom Wilkinson | 19/4/96 | 17(4) | 16(3) | 1 | 1 | 0 | 0 | 0 | 0 | 4 | 4 |

*'L1' totals include League 1 regular season only; 'All' totals also include Challenge Cup & 1895 Cup*

Andrew Bulman

**LEAGUE RECORD**
P20-W15-D2-L3 (1st/Champions)
F582, A283, Diff+299, 32 points.

**CHALLENGE CUP**
Round Four

**1895 CUP**
Round One

**ATTENDANCES**
Best - v Workington (L1 - 2,360)
Worst - v Wigan St Patricks (CC - 464)
Total (excluding Challenge Cup) - 10,116
Average (excluding Challenge Cup) - 1,012
(Up by 260 on 2018)

| | |
|---|---|
| CLUB RECORDS | |
| MATCH RECORDS | Highest score: 86-6 v Highfield, 25/1/95 **Highest score against:** 8-106 v Wigan, 12/5/2008 **Record attendance:** 18,500 v Wakefield, 19/3/60 |
| | **Tries:** 6 Vince Gribbin v Doncaster, 18/11/84; Andrew Bulman v Wigan St Patricks, 10/3/2019 |
| | **Goals:** 13 Lee Anderson v Highfield, 25/1/95 **Points:** 32 Mick Nanyn v Batley, 22/8/2004 |
| SEASON RECORDS | **Tries:** 34 Mike Pechey 1994-95 **Goals:** 141 John McKeown 1956-57 **Points:** 398 Mick Nanyn 2004 |
| CAREER RECORDS | **Tries:** 239 Craig Calvert 2004-2017 **Goals:** 1,050 John McKeown 1948-61 **Points:** 2,133 John McKeown 1948-61 **Appearances:** 417 John McKeown 1948-61 |

# WORKINGTON TOWN

| DATE | FIXTURE | RESULT | SCORERS | LGE | ATT |
|---|---|---|---|---|---|
| 17/2/19 | Oldham (a) | W28-32 | t:Miller(2),Mellor,Singleton,Maudling,Penkywicz g:Forber(4) | 4th | 765 |
| 24/2/19 | North Wales (h) | W48-18 | t:Maudling,Wilkes,Singleton,Doran,Barnes,Penkywicz,Tickle,Mellor g:Forber(8) | 1st | 901 |
| 3/3/19 | Doncaster (a) | L20-10 | t:Miller,Mellor g:Forber | 2nd | 640 |
| 17/3/19 | Siddal (h) (CCR3) | W22-0 | t:Rooke,Penkywicz,Scholey,Wilkes g:Forber(3) | N/A | 355 |
| 24/3/19 | Newcastle (h) | W32-30 | t:Hopkins,Rooke,Miller,Singleton,Doran g:Forber(6) | 3rd | 859 |
| 31/3/19 | Newcastle (h) (CCR4) | W21-20 | t:Rooke,Mellor,Hopkins g:Forber(4) fg:Doran | N/A | N/A |
| 6/4/19 | London Skolars (a) | L34-32 | t:Walsh,Scholey,Rooke,Olstrom,Singleton,Moimoi g:Forber(4) | 5th | 629 |
| 12/4/19 | Leeds (a) (CCR5) | L78-6 | t:Barnes g:Forber | N/A | 4,197 |
| 19/4/19 | Whitehaven (h) | L18-33 | t:Doran(2),Tickle g:Forber(3) | 7th | 1,981 |
| 28/4/19 | Keighley (a) | L32-26 | t:Hewitt(2),Worthington,Wilkes g:Forber(3),Farrell(2) | 7th | 948 |
| 4/5/19 | Hunslet (a) (1895CR1) | W28-31 | t:Wilkes(3),O'Donnell,Rooke g:Forber(5) fg:Doran | N/A | 296 |
| 11/5/19 | Coventry (a) ● | L41-30 | t:Rooke(2),Walsh,Fieldhouse,Doran g:Farrell(5) | 7th | 303 |
| 19/5/19 | Hunslet (h) | W12-4 | t:Curwen,Maudling g:Forber(2) | 6th | 610 |
| 2/6/19 | Leigh (a) (1895CR2) | L62-12 | t:Tickle,Forber g:Forber(2) | N/A | 1,660 |
| 8/6/19 | West Wales (a) | W12-58 | t:Maudling,Moimoi,Penkywicz,Singleton,Scholey,Fieldhouse,O'Donnell, Hopkins,Wilkes,Marwood g:Forber(9) | 7th | 321 |
| 16/6/19 | Coventry (h) ●● | W54-16 | t:Mellor(2),Doran,Scholey,Singleton,Wellington,Fieldhouse(2),Bolton,Curwen g:Forber(6),Moimoi | 6th | 895 |
| 23/6/19 | Oldham (h) ●● | L16-26 | t:Maudling,Singleton,Penkywicz g:Doran(2) | 7th | 1,013 |
| 30/6/19 | Newcastle (a) | L48-10 | t:Penkywicz,Doran g:Doran | 7th | 1,077 |
| 7/7/19 | North Wales (a) | L30-18 | t:Forber,Singleton,O'Donnell g:Forber(3) | 7th | 363 |
| 14/7/19 | London Skolars (h) ●● | W32-22 | t:Singleton,Doran(2),O'Donnell,Mellor,Scholey g:Forber(4) | 7th | 810 |
| 21/7/19 | Keighley (h) | W52-4 | t:O'Donnell,Walsh,Moimoi,Singleton,Forber,Curwen,Maudling,Hewitt,Rooke g:Forber(6),Doran(2) | 6th | 947 |
| 4/8/19 | Whitehaven (a) | D12-12 | t:Wellington,Doran g:Forber(2) | 6th | 2,360 |
| 11/8/19 | West Wales (h) | W66-22 | t:Walsh(2),Tickle,Bolton,Maudling(2),Barnes,Penkywicz,Marwood(2),Hopkins g:Forber(11) | 6th | 908 |
| 1/9/19 | Hunslet (a) | W16-30 | t:O'Donnell,Moimoi(2),Curwen,Singleton g:Forber(5) | 6th | 521 |
| 8/9/19 | Doncaster (h) | L4-30 | t:Barnes | 6th | 1,201 |
| 15/9/19 | Hunslet (a) (EPO) | W24-32 | t:Maudling,Scholey,Penkywicz(2),Moimoi g:Forber(6) | N/A | 332 |
| 22/9/19 | Newcastle (a) (ESF) | L38-18 | t:Marwood,Singleton,Dawson g:Forber(3) | N/A | 678 |

● *Played at Ivor Preece Field, Broadstreet*
●● *Played at Borough Park*

## APP TRIES GOALS FG PTS

| | D.O.B. | ALL | L1 | ALL | L1 | ALL | L1 | ALL | L1 | ALL | L1 |
|---|---|---|---|---|---|---|---|---|---|---|---|
| Caine Barnes | 22/2/99 | 15(5) | 11(4) | 4 | 3 | 0 | 0 | 0 | 0 | 16 | 12 |
| Russ Bolton | 1/3/92 | 10 | 9 | 2 | 2 | 0 | 0 | 0 | 0 | 8 | 8 |
| Reiss Butterworth | 7/12/98 | 1(1) | 1(1) | 0 | 0 | 0 | 0 | 0 | 0 | 0 | 0 |
| Tom Curwen | 15/8/89 | 1(22) | (19) | 4 | 4 | 0 | 0 | 0 | 0 | 16 | 16 |
| Andrew Dawson | 12/3/89 | 10(12) | 10(9) | 1 | 1 | 0 | 0 | 0 | 0 | 4 | 4 |
| Jamie Doran | 8/12/94 | 27 | 22 | 10 | 10 | 5 | 5 | 2 | 0 | 52 | 50 |
| Izaac Farrell | 30/1/98 | 4(1) | 3 | 0 | 0 | 7 | 7 | 0 | 0 | 14 | 14 |
| Ryan Fieldhouse | 10/4/88 | 7 | 6 | 4 | 4 | 0 | 0 | 0 | 0 | 16 | 16 |
| Carl Forber | 17/3/85 | 24 | 19 | 3 | 2 | 101 | 86 | 0 | 0 | 214 | 180 |
| Sam Hewitt | 29/4/99 | 5(1) | 4(1) | 3 | 3 | 0 | 0 | 0 | 0 | 12 | 12 |
| Sam Hopkins | 17/2/90 | 11(12) | 7(12) | 4 | 3 | 0 | 0 | 0 | 0 | 16 | 12 |
| Tyler Lancaster | 10/9/99 | 4(2) | 3(2) | 0 | 0 | 0 | 0 | 0 | 0 | 0 | 0 |
| Blain Marwood | 23/1/98 | 1(5) | 1(5) | 4 | 4 | 0 | 0 | 0 | 0 | 16 | 16 |
| Gordon Maudling | 9/2/91 | 23(1) | 19(1) | 9 | 9 | 0 | 0 | 0 | 0 | 36 | 36 |
| Tyllar Mellor | 21/4/99 | 17 | 14 | 7 | 6 | 0 | 0 | 0 | 0 | 28 | 24 |
| Elliott Miller | 14/9/90 | 5 | 4 | 4 | 4 | 0 | 0 | 0 | 0 | 16 | 16 |
| Fuifui Moimoi | 26/9/79 | 13(8) | 12(6) | 6 | 6 | 1 | 1 | 0 | 0 | 26 | 26 |
| Dec O'Donnell | 7/9/98 | 9(7) | 9(5) | 6 | 5 | 0 | 0 | 0 | 0 | 24 | 20 |
| Karl Olstrom | 21/9/91 | 6(2) | 3(1) | 1 | 1 | 0 | 0 | 0 | 0 | 4 | 4 |
| Sean Penkywicz | 18/5/82 | 22(1) | 19(1) | 9 | 8 | 0 | 0 | 0 | 0 | 36 | 32 |
| Colton Roche | 23/6/93 | (3) | (3) | 0 | 0 | 0 | 0 | 0 | 0 | 0 | 0 |
| Scott Rooke | 3/11/94 | 13 | 9 | 8 | 5 | 0 | 0 | 0 | 0 | 32 | 20 |
| Oliver Russell | 21/9/98 | 1 | 1 | 0 | 0 | 0 | 0 | 0 | 0 | 0 | 0 |
| Stevie Scholey | 7/1/96 | 26(1) | 21(1) | 6 | 5 | 0 | 0 | 0 | 0 | 24 | 20 |
| Innes Senior | 30/5/00 | 1 | 1 | 0 | 0 | 0 | 0 | 0 | 0 | 0 | 0 |
| Perry Singleton | 5/1/94 | 23(1) | 20 | 12 | 12 | 0 | 0 | 0 | 0 | 48 | 48 |
| Dominic Smallwood | 8/12/97 | (2) | (1) | 0 | 0 | 0 | 0 | 0 | 0 | 0 | 0 |
| Clayton Sutton | 11/11/89 | (1) | (1) | 0 | 0 | 0 | 0 | 0 | 0 | 0 | 0 |
| Danny Tickle | 10/3/83 | 24 | 19 | 4 | 3 | 0 | 0 | 0 | 0 | 16 | 12 |
| Jonathan Walsh | 16/11/89 | 21(2) | 18(2) | 5 | 5 | 0 | 0 | 0 | 0 | 20 | 20 |
| Calvin Wellington | 10/12/95 | 8 | 7 | 2 | 2 | 0 | 0 | 0 | 0 | 8 | 8 |
| Oliver Wilkes | 2/5/80 | 13(2) | 10(2) | 7 | 3 | 0 | 0 | 0 | 0 | 28 | 12 |
| James Worthington | 21/5/99 | 6 | 4 | 1 | 1 | 0 | 0 | 0 | 0 | 4 | 4 |

*'L1' totals include play-offs; 'All' totals also include Challenge Cup & 1895 Cup*

Carl Forber

**LEAGUE RECORD**
P20-W10-D1-L9
(6th/Elimination Semi-Final)
F592, A478, Diff+114, 21 points.

**CHALLENGE CUP**
Round Five

**1895 CUP**
Round Two

**ATTENDANCES**
Best - v Whitehaven (L1 - 1,981)
Worst - v Siddal (CC - 355)
Total (excluding Challenge Cup) - 10,125
Average (excluding Challenge Cup) - 1,013
(Up by 231 on 2018)

| CLUB RECORDS | |
|---|---|
| MATCH RECORDS | **Highest score:** 94-4 v Leigh, 26/2/95 **Highest score against:** 0-92 v Bradford, 14/2/99 **Record attendance:** 17,741 v Wigan, 3/3/65 |
| | **Tries:** 7 Ike Southward v Blackpool, 17/9/55 **Goals:** 14 Darren Holt v Gateshead, 12/6/2011 |
| | **Points:** 42 Dean Marwood v Highfield, 1/11/92; Dean Marwood v Leigh, 26/2/95 |
| SEASON RECORDS | **Tries:** 49 Johnny Lawrenson 1951-52 **Goals:** 186 Lyn Hopkins 1981-82 **Points:** 438 Lyn Hopkins 1981-82 |
| CAREER RECORDS | **Tries:** 274 Ike Southward 1952-68 **Goals:** 809 Iain MacCorquodale 1972-80 **Points:** 1,813 Carl Forber 2007-2009; 2012-2019 |
| | **Appearances:** 419 Paul Charlton 1961-69; 1975-80 |

# LEAGUE 1 2019
## *Round by Round*

## ROUND 1

*Saturday 16th February 2019*

### NEWCASTLE THUNDER 26 DONCASTER 32

**THUNDER:** 1 Lewis Young; 2 Mo Agoro; 3 Misi Taulapapa; 4 Joe Brown; 5 Alex Clegg; 6 Remy Marginet; 7 Liam Finn; 10 Jack Aldous; 9 Evan Simons; 8 Liam McAvoy; 18 Rhys Clarke; 11 Aaron Ollett; 13 Sam Luckley. Subs (all used): 15 Jared Blanke; 19 Harry Aldous; 14 Keal Carlile; 16 Alex Rowe.
**Tries:** Clegg (5, 79), Taulapapa (24), Young (32), Agoro (37); **Goals:** Finn 3/5.
**DONCASTER:** 1 Connor Wynne; 5 Sam Doherty; 3 Connor Bower; 4 Jason Tali; 19 Matty Chrimes; 6 Jordan Howden; 7 Matty Beharrell; 10 Ryan Boyle; 9 Kyle Kesik; 17 Brandon Douglas; 22 Brad Foster; 28 Danny Langtree; 13 Jordie Hedges. Subs (all used): 14 Connor Scott; 8 Russ Spiers; 21 Ryan Dixon; 15 Kieran Cross.
**Tries:** Bower (12), Hedges (42), Tali (52), Chrimes (56), Howden (63), Kesik (75); **Goals:** Beharrell 4/6.
**Sin bin:** Kesik (76) - professional foul.
**Rugby Leaguer & League Express Men of the Match:** *Thunder:* Misi Taulapapa; *Doncaster:* Kyle Kesik.
**Penalty count:** 8-8; **Half-time:** 22-4;
**Referee:** Nick Bennett; **Attendance:** 1,817.

*Sunday 17th February 2019*

### COVENTRY BEARS 28 WEST WALES RAIDERS 4

**BEARS:** 1 Elliot Hall; 2 Hayden Freeman; 3 Kadeem Williams; 4 Kameron Pearce-Paul; 5 Reece Rance; 6 Brad Sheridan; 7 Nick Newman; 8 Ollie Purslow; 9 Nathan Conroy; 10 Peter Ryan; 11 Jacob Jones; 12 Chris Barratt; 13 Ben Gray. Subs (all used): 14 Dante Morley-Samuels; 15 Dan Gover; 16 Will Tully; 17 Kieran Sherratt.
**Tries:** Freeman (8, 13), Hall (34), Jones (50), Morley-Samuels (62); **Goals:** Newman 4/6.
**RAIDERS:** 1 Phil Cowburn; 2 Dai Evans; 3 Ronny Palumbo; 24 Morgan Jefferies; 23 Rowland Kaye; 6 Ashley Bateman; 7 Tyler Hunt; 8 Connor Parker; 26 Alex King; 10 Sam Herron; 20 Mike Connor; 13 Dan Maiden; 17 Chris Vitalini. Subs (all used): 14 Dalton Desmond-Walker; 15 Archie Snook; 18 Ross Price; 25 Mickael Sabour.
**Try:** Kaye (72); **Goals:** Hunt 0/2.
**Rugby Leaguer & League Express Men of the Match:** *Bears:* Hayden Freeman; *Raiders:* Rowland Kaye.
**Penalty count:** 14-13; **Half-time:** 18-0;
**Referee:** Cameron Worsley; **Attendance:** 526.

### OLDHAM 28 WORKINGTON TOWN 32

**OLDHAM:** 5 Ritchie Hawkyard; 2 Aaron Jones-Bishop; 3 Zack McComb; 4 Jack Holmes; 21 Lee Kershaw; 15 Adam Brook; 7 Dave Hewitt; 8 Phil Joy; 9 Gareth Owen; 10 Scott Law; 26 Anthony Bowman; 12 Emmerson Whittel; 13 Jack Spencer. Subs (all used): 23 Luke Nelmes; 24 Liam Bent; 20 Matty Wilkinson; 29 Titus Gwaze.
**Tries:** Joy (10), Hawkyard (17), Jones-Bishop (51, 60); **Goals:** Hewitt 6/7.
**TOWN:** 2 Tyllar Mellor; 20 Jonathan Walsh; 3 Elliott Miller; 4 Perry Singleton; 21 James Worthington; 6 Jamie Doran; 7 Carl Forber; 8 Oliver Wilkes; 9 Sean Penkywicz; 10 Stevie Scholey; 19 Caine Barnes; 12 Gordon Maudling; 11 Danny Tickle. Subs (all used): 14 Andrew Dawson; 15 Tom Curwen; 23 Reiss Butterworth; 22 Colton Roche.
**Tries:** Miller (3, 34), Mellor (6), Singleton (44), Maudling (72), Penkywicz (76); **Goals:** Forber 4/6.
**Rugby Leaguer & League Express Men of the Match:** *Oldham:* Aaron Jones-Bishop; *Town:* Carl Forber.
**Penalty count:** 10-10; **Half-time:** 14-16;
**Referee:** John McMullen; **Attendance:** 765.

### WHITEHAVEN 28 KEIGHLEY COUGARS 16

**WHITEHAVEN:** 1 Sam Forrester; 19 Andrew Bulman; 23 Jason Mossop; 3 Chris Taylor; 5 Dave Thompson; 6 Dion Aiye; 7 Callum Phillips; 8 Marc Shackley; 9 James Newton; 10 Kris Coward; 12 Jake Moore; 11 Brett Phillips; 13 Tom Wilkinson. Subs (all used): 14 Sam Dowsett; 4 Jessie Joe Parker; 15 Connor Holliday; 18 Jordan Thomson.
**Tries:** Taylor (26), Moore (34, 61), Bulman (55, 68); **Goals:** Moore 3/5, Holliday 1/1.
**Sin bin:** Coward (78) - fighting.
**COUGARS:** 21 Matt Welham; 5 Davey Dixon; 4 Will Cooke; 23 Macauley Hallett; 1 Alfie Seeley; 15 Jack Miller; 7 Benn Hardcastle; 19 Matthew Bailey; 9 James Feather; 10 Jamie Thackray; 11 Josh Lynam; 13 Jason Muranka; 29 Jimmy Beckett. Subs (all used): 8 Jack Coventry; 14 Luke Million; 26 Reece Williams; 27 Lewis Wray.
**Tries:** Welham (11), Miller (21), Dixon (51); **Goals:** Hardcastle 2/3.
**Sin bin:** Feather (78) - fighting.
**Rugby Leaguer & League Express Men of the Match:** *Whitehaven:* Jake Moore; *Cougars:* Benn Hardcastle.
**Penalty count:** 9-5; **Half-time:** 12-12;
**Referee:** Steve Race; **Attendance:** 897.

## ROUND 2

*Saturday 23rd February 2019*

### WEST WALES RAIDERS 18 LONDON SKOLARS 28

**RAIDERS:** 5 Liam Clark; 2 Dai Evans; 19 Brad Kislingbury; 24 Morgan Jefferies; 23 Rowland Kaye; 6 Ashley Bateman; 7 Tyler Hunt; 20 Mike Connor; 9 Liam Rice-Wilson; 10 Sam Herron; 15 Archie Snook; 3 Ronny Palumbo; 13 Dan Maiden. Subs (all used): 14 Dalton Desmond-Walker; 26 Alex King; 11 Robert Tuliatu; 18 Ryan Shallish.
**Tries:** Maiden (5), Desmond-Walker (50), Palumbo (80); **Goals:** Hunt 3/3.
**SKOLARS:** 14 Richard Wilkinson; 5 Omari Caro; 1 Iliess Macani; 3 Sam Grant; 2 Gideon Boafo; 6 James Barran; 7 Mike Bishay; 20 Lamont Bryan; 9 Neil Thorman; 10 Judd Greenhalgh; 11 Jordan Williams; 12 Mike Greenhalgh; 13 Daniel Hindmarsh. Subs (all used): 15 Xavier Rice; 16 Liam Scott; 17 Isaac Ah Kuoi-Atmore; 19 Matt Ross.
**Tries:** Grant (2, 33, 57), Caro (62), Williams (72); **Goals:** Thorman 1/1, Barran 3/4.
**Rugby Leaguer & League Express Men of the Match:** *Raiders:* Ronny Palumbo; *Skolars:* Sam Grant.
**Penalty count:** 6-6; **Half-time:** 6-12;
**Referee:** Craig Smith; **Attendance:** 250.

*Sunday 24th February 2019*

### COVENTRY BEARS 32 NEWCASTLE THUNDER 28

**BEARS:** 1 Elliot Hall; 19 Hayden Freeman; 3 Kadeem Williams; 4 Kameron Pearce-Paul; 5 Reece Rance; 6 James Meadows; 7 Nick Newman; 8 Rob Butler; 9 Nathan Conroy; 10 Peter Ryan; 11 Jacob Jones; 12 Chris Barratt; 13 Kieran Sherratt. Subs (all used): 17 Sam Davis; 21 Ollie Purslow; 15 Will Tully; 20 Ben Gray.
**Tries:** Jones (4), Hall (12, 15), Butler (36), Freeman (54), Newman (61); **Goals:** Newman 4/6.
**Sin bin:** Butler (66) - fighting.
**THUNDER:** 1 Lewis Young; 2 Mo Agoro; 3 Misi Taulapapa; 4 Joe Brown; 5 Alex Clegg; 6 Remy Marginet; 7 Liam Finn; 8 Liam McAvoy; 9 Evan Simons; 10 Jack Aldous; 18 Rhys Clarke; 11 Aaron Ollett; 12 Sam Luckley. Subs (all used): 19 Harry Aldous; 21 Jared Blanke; 15 Connor Clayton; 16 Alex Rowe.
**Tries:** Clegg (21), Agoro (26), Simons (31), Finn (43), McAvoy (64); **Goals:** Finn 4/5.
**Rugby Leaguer & League Express Men of the Match:** *Bears:* James Meadows; *Thunder:* Remy Marginet.
**Penalty count:** 6-3; **Half-time:** 22-16;
**Referee:** Tom Crashley; **Attendance:** 360.

### DONCASTER 18 HUNSLET 20

**DONCASTER:** 1 Hakim Miloudi; 5 Sam Doherty; 3 Connor Bower; 4 Jason Tali; 19 Matty Chrimes; 6 Jordan Howden; 7 Matty Beharrell; 10 Ryan Boyle; 9 Kyle Kesik; 17 Brandon Douglas; - Brad Fash; 21 Ryan Dixon; 25 Danny Washbrook. Subs (all used): 14 Connor Scott; 15 Kieran Cross; 8 Russ Spiers; 13 Jordie Hedges.
**Tries:** Douglas (4, 53), Bower (13); **Goals:** Beharrell 3/3.
**HUNSLET:** 1 Jimmy Watson; 2 Gareth Potts; 4 Ben Heaton; 3 Tom Ashton; 5 Dale Bloomfield; 21 Reece Dean; 22 Danny Nicklas; 10 Adam Robinson; 14 Ryan Wright; 8 Richard Moore; 12 Duane Straugheir; 11 Josh Tonks; 13 Mike Emmett. Subs (all used): 20 Vila Halafihi; 16 Zach Braham; 15 Michael Haley; 17 Dan Hawksworth.
**Tries:** Heaton (35), Potts (40), Robinson (65); **Goals:** Dean 4/5.
**Sin bin:** Tonks (57) - fighting; Nicklas (59) - high tackle.
**Rugby Leaguer & League Express Men of the Match:** *Doncaster:* Brad Fash; *Hunslet:* Reece Dean.
**Penalty count:** 10-14; **Half-time:** 12-10;
**Referee:** Steve Race; **Attendance:** 734.

### OLDHAM 36 WHITEHAVEN 12

**OLDHAM:** 5 Ritchie Hawkyard; 2 Aaron Jones-Bishop; 16 Zack McComb; 22 Danny Grimshaw; 21 Lee Kershaw; 15 Adam Brook; 7 Dave Hewitt; 8 Phil Joy; 9 Gareth Owen; 10 Scott Law; 26 Anthony Bowman; 12 Emmerson Whittel; 24 Liam Bent. Subs (all used): 13 Jack Spencer; 29 Titus Gwaze; 19 Jamie Greenwood; 18 Ben Davies.
**Tries:** McComb (10, 15, 27), Hawkyard (33, 75), Hewitt (62); **Goals:** Hewitt 6/7.
**Sin bin:** Bowman (48) - shoulder charge.
**WHITEHAVEN:** 2 Jordan Burns; 5 Dave Thompson; 3 Chris Taylor; 23 Jason Mossop; 19 Andrew Bulman; 1 Sam Forrester; 7 Callum Phillips; 8 Marc Shackley; 9 James Newton; 10 Kris Coward; 12 Jake Moore; 11 Brett Phillips; 6 Dion Aiye. Subs (all used): 4 Jessie Joe Parker; 15 Connor Holliday; 13 Tom Wilkinson; - Ethan Kelly.
**Tries:** C Phillips (36), Bulman (43); **Goals:** Moore 2/2.
**Rugby Leaguer & League Express Men of the Match:** *Oldham:* Zack McComb; *Whitehaven:* Ethan Kelly.
**Penalty count:** 9-8; **Half-time:** 22-6;
**Referee:** Cameron Worsley; **Attendance:** 546.

### WORKINGTON TOWN 48 NORTH WALES CRUSADERS 18

**TOWN:** 2 Tyllar Mellor; 21 Innes Senior; 3 Elliott Miller; 4 Perry Singleton; 20 Jonathan Walsh; 6 Jamie Doran; 7 Carl Forber; 8 Oliver Wilkes; 9 Sean Penkywicz; 10 Stevie Scholey; 12 Gordon Maudling; 19 Caine Barnes; 11 Danny Tickle. Subs (all used): 14 Andrew Dawson; 15 Tom Curwen; - Sam Hopkins; 22 Colton Roche.
**Tries:** Maudling (3), Wilkes (6), Singleton (36), Doran (38), Barnes (49), Penkywicz (65), Tickle (71), Mellor (78); **Goals:** Forber 8/8.
**CRUSADERS:** 1 Dan Price; 2 Gavin Conroy; 3 Dave Eccleston; 4 Earl Hurst; 5 Rob Massam; 6 Ben Stead; 7 Steve Roper; 25 Callum Hazzard; 15 Kenny Hughes; 10 Warren Thompson; 11 Joe Connor; 12 Jack Houghton; 13 Kenny Baker. Subs (all used): 14 Karl Ashall; 8 Brad Brennan; 16 Simon Atherton; 17 Jonny Walker.
**Tries:** Houghton (17), Price (23), Connor (58); **Goals:** Baker 3/4.
**Rugby Leaguer & League Express Men of the Match:** *Town:* Perry Singleton; *Crusaders:* Kenny Baker.
**Penalty count:** 8-6; **Half-time:** 24-14;
**Referee:** Andrew Sweet; **Attendance:** 901.

## ROUND 3

*Saturday 2nd March 2019*

### LONDON SKOLARS 12 NEWCASTLE THUNDER 48

**SKOLARS:** 14 Richard Wilkinson; 2 Gideon Boafo; 1 Iliess Macani; 3 Sam Grant; 5 Lameck Juma; 6 James Barran; 7 James Meadows; 8 Judd Greenhalgh; 9 Neil Thorman; 10 Liam Scott; 12 Mike Greenhalgh; 11 Jordan Williams; 13 Daniel Hindmarsh. Subs (all used): 15 Isaac Ah Kuoi-Atmore; 20 Mike Bishay; 16 Matt Ross; 17 Lamont Bryan.
**Tries:** Meadows (15), M Greenhalgh (18); **Goals:** Thorman 2/2.
**Sin bin:** Bryan (23) - fighting.
**THUNDER:** 11 Max Jowitt; 2 Mo Agoro; 3 Misi Taulapapa; 4 Joe Arundel; 5 Alex Clegg; 6 Remy Marginet; 7 Liam Finn; 8 Liam McAvoy; 9 Evan Simons; 27 Jared Blanke; 15 Conor Fitzsimmons; 12 Aaron Ollett; 13 Jack Aldous. Subs (all used): 14 Keal Carlile; 19 Harry Aldous; 20 Sam Luckley; 10 Jordan Crowther.
**Tries:** Agoro (10), Carlile (36), J Aldous (42), Jowitt (47, 79), Taulapapa (55), Luckley (60), Ollett (68), Arundel (75); **Goals:** Finn 6/9.
**Sin bin:** Luckley (23) - fighting.
**Rugby Leaguer & League Express Men of the Match:** *Skolars:* Mike Greenhalgh; *Thunder:* Keal Carlile.
**Penalty count:** 5-8; **Half-time:** 12-10;
**Referee:** Andrew Sweet; **Attendance:** 302.

*Sunday 3rd March 2019*

### DONCASTER 20 WORKINGTON TOWN 10

**DONCASTER:** 1 Hakim Miloudi; 19 Matty Chrimes; 3 Connor Bower; 4 Jason Tali; 5 Sam Doherty; 15 Kieran Cross; 7 Matty Beharrell; 10 Ryan Boyle; 9 Kyle Kesik; 17 Brandon Douglas; 30 Danny Langtree; 21 Ryan Dixon; 26 Levy Nzoungou. Subs (all used): 14 Connor Scott; 13 Jordie Hedges; 8 Russ Spiers; 20 Callum Ogden.
**Tries:** Miloudi (17, 23), Cross (50); **Goals:** Beharrell 4/4.
**Sin bin:** Dixon (48) - high tackle on Dawson.
**TOWN:** 2 Tyllar Mellor; 21 James Worthington; 3 Elliott Miller; 4 Perry Singleton; 20 Jonathan Walsh; 6 Jamie Doran; 7 Carl Forber; 8 Oliver Wilkes; 9 Sean Penkywicz; 10 Stevie Scholey; 13 Karl Olstrom; 12 Gordon Maudling; 11 Danny Tickle. Subs (all used): 14 Andrew Dawson; 15 Tom Curwen; 23 Sam Hewitt; 25 Sam Hopkins.
**Tries:** Miller (37), Mellor (60); **Goals:** Forber 1/2.
**Rugby Leaguer & League Express Men of the Match:** *Doncaster:* Hakim Miloudi; *Town:* Tyllar Mellor.
**Penalty count:** 8-8; **Half-time:** 12-6;
**Referee:** Tom Crashley; **Attendance:** 640.

### HUNSLET 58 WEST WALES RAIDERS 4

**HUNSLET:** 1 Jimmy Watson; 2 Gareth Potts; 4 Ben Heaton; 3 Tom Ashton; 5 Dale Bloomfield; 21 Reece Dean; 22 Danny Nicklas; 15 Michael Haley; 20 Vila Halafihi; 17 Dan Hawksworth; 11 Josh Tonks; 12 Duane Straugheir; 13 Mike Emmett. Subs (all used): 16 Zach Braham; 18 Nyle Flynn; 14 Ryan Wright; 31 Harry Kidd.
**Tries:** Potts (14, 22, 52), Haley (24), Heaton (30), Dean (32), Bloomfield (36, 43), Kidd (38), Ashton (48), Flynn (55); **Goals:** Dean 6/9, Nicklas 1/2.
**Dismissal:** Dean (50) - fighting.
**Sin bin:** Tonks (50) - fighting.
**RAIDERS:** 5 Liam Clark; 25 Mickael Sabour; 19 Brad Kislingbury; 24 Morgan Jefferies; 22 Kurtis Haile; 6 Ashley Bateman; 7 Tyler Hunt; 20 Mike Connor; 9 Liam Rice-Wilson; 10 Sam Herron; 15 Archie Snook; 3 Ronny Palumbo; 11 Robert Tuliatu. Subs (all used): 14 Dalton Desmond-Walker; 23 Ryan Shallish; 8 Connor Parker; 21 Morgan Rowlands.
**Try:** Sabour (72); **Goals:** Hunt 0/1.

**Dismissal:** Desmond-Walker (50) - fighting.
**Sin bin:** Tuliatu (50) - fighting.
**Rugby Leaguer & League Express Men of the Match:**
*Hunslet:* Reece Dean; *Raiders:* Sam Herron.
**Penalty count:** 8-4; **Half-time:** 38-0;
**Referee:** Paul Marklove; **Attendance:** 560.

**KEIGHLEY COUGARS 40 COVENTRY BEARS 8**

**COUGARS:** 21 Matt Welham; 5 Davey Dixon; 4 Will Cooke; 23 Macauley Hallett; 2 Darren Forde; 15 Jack Miller; 7 Benn Hardcastle; 19 Matthew Bailey; 9 James Feather; 25 Jack Arnold; 11 Josh Lynam; 13 Jason Muranka; 29 Jimmy Beckett. Subs (all used): 8 Jack Coventry; 10 Jamie Thackray; 17 Billy Gaylor; 27 Lewis Wray.
**Tries:** Hallett (24, 44), Cooke (35), Dixon (42), Miller (52), Coventry (67), Feather (77); **Goals:** Hardcastle 6/8.
**BEARS:** 1 Elliot Hall; 2 Hayden Freeman; 3 Kadeem Williams; 4 Kameron Pearce-Paul; 5 Reece Rance; 6 Matthew Davies; 7 Nick Newman; 10 Peter Ryan; 9 Nathan Conroy; 8 Ollie Purslow; 11 Jacob Jones; 12 Chris Barratt; 13 Kieran Sherratt. Subs (all used): 14 Sam Davis; 17 Mitch Shaw; 18 Ben Gray; 20 Dan Gover.
**Try:** Barratt (21); **Goals:** Newman 2/2.
**Rugby Leaguer & League Express Men of the Match:**
*Cougars:* Macauley Hallett; *Bears:* Chris Barratt.
**Penalty count:** 4-6; **Half-time:** 10-8;
**Referee:** Jon Roberts; **Attendance:** 915.

**NORTH WALES CRUSADERS 14 OLDHAM 16**

**CRUSADERS:** 1 Elliott Jenkins; 5 Rob Massam; 4 Earl Hurst; 3 Simon Atherton; 2 Dave Eccleston; 6 Steve Roper; 7 Ben Stead; 8 Warren Thompson; 15 Karl Ashall; 10 Callum Hazzard; 11 Jack Houghton; 12 Stephen Wild; 13 Kenny Baker. Subs (all used): 14 Kenny Hughes; 17 Brad Brennan; 20 Joe Ryan; 18 Jonny Walker.
**Tries:** Hurst (14), Brennan (48); **Goals:** Baker 1/1, Stead 2/2.
**Sin bin:** Eccleston (80) - dangerous challenge.
**OLDHAM:** 5 Ritchie Hawkyard; 21 Lee Kershaw; 3 Zack McComb; 22 Danny Grimshaw; 2 Aaron Jones-Bishop; 26 Anthony Bowman; 7 Dave Hewitt; 8 Phil Joy; 9 Gareth Owen; 10 Scott Law; 11 Ben Calland; 12 Emmerson Whittel; 24 Liam Bent. Subs (all used): 13 Jack Spencer; 18 Ben Davies; 20 Matty Wilkinson; 29 Titus Gwaze.
**Tries:** Kershaw (60, 68), Hewitt (74); **Goals:** Hewitt 2/4.
**Sin bin:** Jones-Bishop (29) - dangerous challenge.
**Rugby Leaguer & League Express Men of the Match:**
*Crusaders:* Steve Roper; *Oldham:* Lee Kershaw.
**Penalty count:** 6-4; **Half-time:** 6-0;
**Referee:** Matt Rossleigh; **Attendance:** 426.

## ROUND 4

*Saturday 16th March 2019*

**LONDON SKOLARS 18 KEIGHLEY COUGARS 18**

**SKOLARS:** 1 Craig Mullen; 2 Iliess Macani; 4 Omari Caro; 3 Jacob Ogden; 20 Joe Brown; 14 Richard Wilkinson; 7 James Meadows; 16 Will Martin; 9 Neil Thorman; 10 Malikhi Lloyd-Jones; 12 Mike Greenhalgh; 11 Jordan Williams; 13 Daniel Hindmarsh. Subs (all used): 15 Isaac Ah Kuoi-Atmore; 18 Eddie Mbaraga; 8 Michael Sykes; 22 Lamont Bryan.
**Tries:** Mullen (12), Brown (30), Williams (34);
**Goals:** Thorman 3/3.
**Sin bin:** M Greenhalgh (32) - fighting.
**COUGARS:** 21 Matt Welham; 5 Davey Dixon; 4 Will Cooke; 23 Macauley Hallett; 1 Alfie Seeley; 15 Jack Miller; 7 Benn Hardcastle; 19 Matthew Bailey; 9 James Feather; 30 Harvey Hallas; 11 Josh Lynam; 13 Jason Muranka; 29 Jimmy Beckett. Subs (all used): 8 Jack Coventry; 12 Aaron Levy; 17 Billy Gaylor; 27 Lewis Wray.
**Tries:** Hardcastle (2), Miller (48), Levy (75);
**Goals:** Hardcastle 3/3.
**Sin bin:** Lynam (32) - fighting.
**Rugby Leaguer & League Express Men of the Match:**
*Skolars:* James Meadows; *Cougars:* James Feather.
**Penalty count:** 2-7; **Half-time:** 18-6;
**Referee:** Matt Rossleigh; **Attendance:** 262.

**NEWCASTLE THUNDER 56 WEST WALES RAIDERS 6**

**THUNDER:** 1 Lewis Young; 2 Mo Agoro; 4 Misi Taulapapa; 3 Kieran Gill; 20 Tyler Craig; 6 Remy Marginet; - Cory Aston; 10 Jack Aldous; 9 Keal Carlile; 8 Sam Luckley; 12 Conor Fitzsimmons; 11 Aaron Ollett; 13 Liam McAvoy. Subs (all used): 14 Evan Simons; 17 Carne Doyle-Manga; 16 Alex Rowe; 19 Harry Aldous.
**Tries:** Young (1, 43), Taulapapa (5), Carlile (8), Agoro (11, 17, 55), Aston (19, 78), Fitzsimmons (22, 63), Rowe (74); **Goals:** Marginet 0/1, Aston 4/11.
**Sin bin:** J Aldous (80) - fighting.
**RAIDERS:** 1 Phil Cowburn; 2 Dai Evans; 25 Callum Mulkeen; 3 Ronny Palumbo; 5 Liam Clark; 9 Liam Rice-Wilson; 7 Tyler Hunt; 17 Chris Vitalini; 21 Morgan Rowlands; 10 Sam Herron; 15 Archie Snook; 20 Mike Connor; 6 Ashley Bateman. Subs (all used): 13 Dan Maiden; 23 Ryan Shallish; 29 Dimosthenis Kartsonakis; 22 Kurtis Haile.
**Try:** Herron (34); **Goals:** Hunt 1/1.
**Sin bin:** Vitalini (50) - dissent; Shallish (80) - fighting.
**Rugby Leaguer & League Express Men of the Match:**
*Thunder:* Misi Taulapapa; *Raiders:* Sam Herron.
**Penalty count:** 5-8; **Half-time:** 34-6;
**Referee:** Liam Staveley; **Attendance:** 678.

*Sunday 17th March 2019*

**NORTH WALES CRUSADERS 12 HUNSLET 22**

**CRUSADERS:** 1 Ryan Smith; 2 Sam Freeman; 3 Matt Reid; 4 Earl Hurst; 5 Rob Massam; 6 Steve Roper; 7 Elliott Jenkins; 10 Warren Thompson; 9 Karl Ashall; 8 Callum Hazzard; 11 Jack Houghton; 12 Simon Atherton; 13 Kenny Baker. Subs (all used): 14 Kenny Hughes; 17 Brad Brennan; 21 Joe Ryan; 18 Jonny Walker.
**Tries:** Freeman (31), Jenkins (74); **Goals:** Freeman 2/3.
**HUNSLET:** 1 Jimmy Watson; 2 Gareth Potts; 30 Charlie Martin; 3 Tom Ashton; 5 Dale Bloomfield; 21 Reece Dean; 22 Danny Nicklas; 32 Jon Luke Kirby; 9 Jack Lee; 10 Adam Robinson; 11 Josh Tonks; 12 Duane Straugheir; 13 Mike Emmett. Subs (all used): 20 Vila Halafihi; 16 Zach Braham; 17 Dan Hawksworth; 31 Harry Kidd.
**Tries:** Tonks (10), Potts (23), Lee (66); **Goals:** Dean 5/6.
**Rugby Leaguer & League Express Men of the Match:**
*Crusaders:* Matt Reid; *Hunslet:* Zach Braham.
**Penalty count:** 9-8; **Half-time:** 6-14;
**Referee:** John McMullen; **Attendance:** 317.

**WHITEHAVEN 26 DONCASTER 8**

**WHITEHAVEN:** 3 Chris Taylor; 19 Andrew Bulman; 23 Jason Mossop; 4 Jessie Joe Parker; 5 Dave Thompson; 1 Sam Forrester; 7 Callum Phillips; 8 Marc Shackley; 14 Sam Dowsett; 10 Kris Coward; 12 Jake Moore; 11 Brett Phillips; 13 Tom Wilkinson. Subs (all used): 9 James Newton; 6 Dion Aiye; 15 Connor Holliday; 25 Kurt Maudling.
**Tries:** Mossop (42), Moore (48), Parker (58), Aiye (75);
**Goals:** Moore 3/3, Holliday 2/2.
**DONCASTER:** 1 Hakim Miloudi; 5 Sam Doherty; 3 Connor Bower; 4 Jason Tali; 19 Matty Chrimes; 6 Jordan Howden; 7 Matty Beharrell; 10 Ryan Boyle; 9 Kyle Kesik; 17 Brandon Douglas; 28 Jordan Cox; - Danny Langtree; - Levy Nzoungou. Subs (all used): 15 Kieran Cross; 14 Connor Scott; 8 Russ Spiers; 13 Jordie Hedges.
**Tries:** Chrimes (24), Tali (52); **Goals:** Beharrell 0/2.
**Sin bin:** Bower (37) - late challenge.
**Rugby Leaguer & League Express Men of the Match:**
*Whitehaven:* Jake Moore; *Doncaster:* Kyle Kesik.
**Penalty count:** 16-5; **Half-time:** 0-4;
**Referee:** Tom Crashley; **Attendance:** 702.

## ROUND 5

*Sunday 24th March 2019*

**WEST WALES RAIDERS 16 WHITEHAVEN 30**

**RAIDERS:** 1 Phil Cowburn; 25 Liam Silver; 19 Brad Kislingbury; 24 Morgan Jefferies; 23 Rowland Kaye; 6 Ashley Bateman; 7 Tyler Hunt; 11 Robert Tuliatu; 9 Liam Rice-Wilson; 10 Sam Herron; 15 Archie Snook; 20 Mike Connor; 3 Ronny Palumbo. Subs (all used): 8 Connor Parker; 17 Chris Vitalini; 18 Ryan Shallish; 21 Sam Baker.
**Tries:** Tuliatu (7), Shallish (50), Connor (59);
**Goals:** Hunt 2/3.
**WHITEHAVEN:** 3 Chris Taylor; 5 Dave Thompson; 4 Jessie Joe Parker; 23 Jason Mossop; 19 Andrew Bulman; 1 Sam Forrester; 7 Callum Phillips; 8 Marc Shackley; 9 James Newton; 10 Kris Coward; 11 Brett Phillips; 12 Jake Moore; 6 Dion Aiye. Subs (all used): 21 Jake Bradley; 15 Connor Holliday; 24 Ethan Kelly; 13 Tom Wilkinson.
**Tries:** Moore (2), C Phillips (11, 26, 29), Shackley (19), Taylor (65); **Goals:** Moore 3/5, Holliday 0/1.
**Rugby Leaguer & League Express Men of the Match:**
*Raiders:* Ryan Shallish; *Whitehaven:* Callum Phillips.
**Penalty count:** 5-8; **Half-time:** 6-26;
**Referee:** Billy Pearson; **Attendance:** 173.

**HUNSLET 44 COVENTRY BEARS 10**

**HUNSLET:** 1 Jimmy Watson; 2 Gareth Potts; 4 Ben Heaton; 23 Nathan Chappell; 5 Dale Bloomfield; 22 Danny Nicklas; 6 Joe Sanderson; 32 Jon Luke Kirby; 9 Jack Lee; 10 Adam Robinson; 11 Josh Tonks; 12 Duane Straugheir; 13 Mike Emmett. Subs (all used): 20 Vila Halafihi; 31 Will Calcott; 17 Dan Hawksworth; 30 Charlie Martin.
**Tries:** Tonks (8), Chappell (15), Robinson (25, 61), Heaton (29, 65), Potts (32), Bloomfield (74);
**Goals:** Sanderson 6/8.
**BEARS:** 1 Kameron Pearce-Paul; 4 Hayden Freeman; 5 Errol Carter; 3 Kadeem Williams; 2 Reece Rance; 6 Mitch Shaw; 7 Jacob Thomas; 10 Peter Ryan; 9 Nathan Conroy; 8 Toby Richardson; 11 Kieran Sherratt; 12 Chris Barratt; 19 Dave Petersen. Subs (all used): 20 Dan Gover; 15 Will Tully; 16 Marcus Stock; 17 Jacob Jones.
**Tries:** Sherratt (43), Petersen (80); **Goals:** Thomas 1/2.
**Rugby Leaguer & League Express Men of the Match:**
*Hunslet:* Vila Halafihi; *Bears:* Nathan Conroy.
**Penalty count:** 7-10; **Half-time:** 28-0;
**Referee:** Jon Roberts; **Attendance:** 542.

**KEIGHLEY COUGARS 24
NORTH WALES CRUSADERS 22**

**COUGARS:** 21 Matt Welham; 5 Davey Dixon; 4 Will Cooke; 23 Macauley Hallett; 1 Alfie Seeley; 15 Jack Miller; 7 Benn Hardcastle; 19 Matthew Bailey; 9 James Feather; 30 Harvey Hallas; 11 Josh Lynam; 12 Aaron Levy; 29 Jimmy Beckett. Subs (all used): 8 Jack Coventry; 17 Billy Gaylor; 22 Dan Parker; 27 Lewis Wray.
**Tries:** Hallas (16), Lynam (29, 77), Parker (47);
**Goals:** Hardcastle 4/6.
**CRUSADERS:** 1 Dan Price; 2 Gavin Conroy; 3 Simon Atherton; 4 Earl Hurst; 5 Rob Massam; 6 Steve Roper; 7 Ben Stead; - Callum Hazzard; - Karl Ashall; 10 Warren Thompson; 11 Jack Houghton; 12 Stephen Wild; 13 Kenny Baker. Subs (all used): 15 Alex Thompson; 16 Brad Brennan; 17 Alex Eckley; 20 Chris Worrall.
**Tries:** Conroy (12), Stead (24), Hazzard (65);
**Goals:** Stead 5/5.
**Sin bin:** Roper (74) - shoulder charge on Seeley.
**On report:**
Brennan (45) - alleged dangerous contact on Wray.
**Rugby Leaguer & League Express Men of the Match:**
*Cougars:* James Feather; *Crusaders:* Ben Stead.
**Penalty count:** 10-9; **Half-time:** 10-16;
**Referee:** Andrew Sweet; **Attendance:** 859.

**OLDHAM 34 LONDON SKOLARS 4**

**OLDHAM:** 5 Ritchie Hawkyard; 1 Kyran Johnson; 3 Zack McComb; 28 Jack Holmes; 21 Lee Kershaw; 15 Adam Brook; 7 Dave Hewitt; 8 Phil Joy; 9 Gareth Owen; 26 Scott Law; 17 Ben Calland; 12 Emmerson Whittel; 13 Jack Spencer. Subs (all used): 24 Liam Bent; 30 Titus Gwaze; 18 Ben Davies; 20 Matty Wilkinson.
**Tries:** Joy (15, 52), McComb (20), Spencer (67), Johnson (71), Kershaw (78); **Goals:** Hewitt 5/7.
**SKOLARS:** 1 Craig Mullen; 2 Iliess Macani; 4 Omari Caro; 3 Jacob Ogden; 5 Joe Brown; 14 Richard Wilkinson; 6 James Meadows; 23 Will Martin; 9 Mike Bishay; 10 Malikhi Lloyd-Jones; 11 Jordan Williams; 12 Lamont Bryan; 13 Daniel Hindmarsh. Subs (all used): 22 Liam Scott; 17 Isaac Ah Kuoi-Atmore; 16 Matt Ross; 8 Michael Sykes.
**Try:** Brown (63); **Goals:** Brown 0/1.
**Rugby Leaguer & League Express Men of the Match:**
*Oldham:* Lee Kershaw; *Skolars:* James Meadows.
**Penalty count:** 8-3; **Half-time:** 12-0;
**Referee:** Nick Bennett; **Attendance:** 709.

**WORKINGTON TOWN 32 NEWCASTLE THUNDER 30**

**TOWN:** 2 Tyllar Mellor; 20 Jonathan Walsh; 3 Elliott Miller; 4 Perry Singleton; 16 Scott Rooke; 6 Jamie Doran; 7 Carl Forber; 8 Oliver Wilkes; 9 Sean Penkywicz; 10 Stevie Scholey; 13 Karl Olstrom; 12 Gordon Maudling; 11 Danny Tickle. Subs (all used): - Fuifui Moimoi; 18 Clayton Sutton; 19 Caine Barnes; 25 Sam Hopkins.
**Tries:** Hopkins (25), Rooke (30), Miller (38), Singleton (53), Doran (65); **Goals:** Forber 6/6.
**THUNDER:** 1 Lewis Young; 2 Mo Agoro; 4 Misi Taulapapa; 3 Kieran Gill; 5 Joe Brown; 17 Jy-mel Coleman; 6 Cory Aston; 10 Jack Aldous; 9 Keal Carlile; 8 Liam McAvoy; 11 Conor Fitzsimmons; 12 Aaron Ollett; 13 Sam Luckley. Subs (all used): 14 Evan Simons; 15 Carne Doyle-Manga; 16 Alex Rowe; 19 Harry Aldous.
**Tries:** Ollett (7), McAvoy (13), Young (21), Aston (70), Brown (74); **Goals:** Coleman 5/5.
**Rugby Leaguer & League Express Men of the Match:**
*Town:* Jamie Doran; *Thunder:* Cory Aston.
**Penalty count:** 8-9; **Half-time:** 18-18;
**Referee:** Cameron Worsley; **Attendance:** 859.

## ROUND 6

*Saturday 6th April 2019*

**LONDON SKOLARS 34 WORKINGTON TOWN 32**

**SKOLARS:** 1 Joe Brown; 20 Jerome Yates; 3 Sam Grant; 4 Omari Caro; 2 Iliess Macani; 6 James Barran; 14 Richard Wilkinson; 10 Matt Ross; 9 Neil Thorman; 8 Michael Sykes; 11 Jordan Williams; 12 Lamont Bryan; 7 Mike Bishay. Subs (all used): 15 Isaac Ah Kuoi-Atmore; - Malikhi Lloyd-Jones; 13 Liam Scott; 18 Judd Greenhalgh.

**Tries:** Brown (14), Bishay (23), Macani (42, 57), Caro (45), Wilkinson (72); **Goals:** Thorman 5/6.
**TOWN:** 2 Tyllar Mellor; 20 Jonathan Walsh; 19 Caine Barnes; 4 Perry Singleton; 16 Scott Rooke; 6 Jamie Doran; 7 Carl Forber; 8 Oliver Wilkes; 5 Reiss Butterworth; 10 Stevie Scholey; 12 Gordon Maudling; 13 Karl Olstrom; 26 Sam Hopkins. Subs (all used): 14 Andrew Dawson; 25 Fuifui Moimoi; 17 Colton Roche; 23 Dominic Smallwood.
**Tries:** Walsh (6), Scholey (11), Rooke (26), Olstrom (32), Singleton (36), Moimoi (80); **Goals:** Forber 4/7.
**Rugby Leaguer & League Express Men of the Match:** *Skolars:* Neil Thorman; *Town:* Karl Olstrom.
**Penalty count:** 4-7; **Half-time:** 10-26;
**Referee:** Nick Bennett; **Attendance:** 629.

**WEST WALES RAIDERS 12 KEIGHLEY COUGARS 56**

**RAIDERS:** 1 Phil Cowburn; 22 Paddy Jennings; 19 Brad Kislingbury; 24 Morgan Jefferies; 25 Mickael Sabour; 3 Ronny Palumbo; 7 Tyler Hunt; 11 Robert Tuliatu; 9 Liam Rice-Wilson; 10 Sam Herron; 15 Archie Snook; 20 Mike Connor; 8 Connor Parker. Subs (all used): 6 Morgan Rowlands; 13 Dan Maiden; 14 Dalton Desmond-Walker; 18 Ryan Shallish.
**Tries:** Sabour (26, 66), Jefferies (36); **Goals:** Hunt 0/3.
**COUGARS:** 21 Matt Welham; 5 Davey Dixon; 4 Will Cooke; 23 Macauley Hallett; 1 Alfie Seeley; 15 Jack Miller; 7 Benn Hardcastle; 19 Matthew Bailey; 14 Luke Million; 27 Lewis Wray; 11 Josh Lynam; 12 Aaron Levy; 32 Matt Nicholson. Subs (all used): 8 Jack Coventry; 17 Billy Gaylor; 22 Dan Parker; 25 Jack Arnold.
**Tries:** Lynam (12), Cooke (15), Miller (18, 54, 75), Levy (29), Wray (39), Hardcastle (44, 77), Coventry (49); **Goals:** Hardcastle 8/10.
**Rugby Leaguer & League Express Men of the Match:** *Raiders:* Mickael Sabour; *Cougars:* Jack Miller.
**Penalty count:** 6-7; **Half-time:** 8-26;
**Referee:** Aaron Moore; **Attendance:** 238.

*Sunday 7th April 2019*

**DONCASTER 44 COVENTRY BEARS 18**

**DONCASTER:** 1 Kieran Buchanan; 5 Sam Doherty; 3 Connor Bower; 4 Jason Tali; 19 Matty Chrimes; 6 Jordan Howden; 15 Kieran Cross; 10 Ryan Boyle; 20 Callum Ogden; 17 Brandon Douglas; 26 Jack Brown; 22 Brad Foster; 9 Kyle Kesik. Subs (all used): 13 Jordie Hedges; 14 Connor Scott; 8 Russ Spiers; 30 Elliott Townsend.
**Tries:** Bower (3, 49), Spiers (27), Brown (35), Ogden (42), Hedges (52), Douglas (55), Buchanan (62); **Goals:** Howden 4/6, Hedges 2/2.
**BEARS:** 1 Elliot Hall; 2 Hayden Freeman; 3 Kadeem Williams; 4 Kameron Pearce-Paul; 5 Errol Carter; 6 Mitch Shaw; 7 Nick Newman; 8 Peter Ryan; 9 Nathan Conroy; 10 Euan Tiernan; 11 Jacob Jones; 12 Mike Kelly; 13 Kieran Sherratt. Subs (all used): 14 Jacob Thomas; 15 Ollie Purslow; 16 Toby Richardson; 17 Harry Kaufman.
**Tries:** Jones (5), Ryan (21), Carter (72); **Goals:** Newman 3/3.
**Sin bin:** Purslow (34) - dissent;
Freeman (42) - dangerous challenge on Doherty;
Sherratt (62) - high tackle on Hedges.
**Rugby Leaguer & League Express Men of the Match:** *Doncaster:* Jack Brown; *Bears:* Mike Kelly.
**Penalty count:** 13-6; **Half-time:** 16-12;
**Referee:** Cameron Worsley; **Attendance:** 562.

**NEWCASTLE THUNDER 28 OLDHAM 22**

**THUNDER:** 1 Lewis Young; 2 Mo Agoro; 4 Tyler Craig; 3 Kieran Gill; 5 Alex Clegg; 7 Cory Aston; 6 Jy-mel Coleman; 8 Jack Aldous; 9 Keal Carlile; 10 Carne Doyle-Manga; 18 Rhys Clarke; 11 Aaron Ollett; 13 Evan Simons. Subs (all used): 14 Liam McAvoy; 12 Conor Fitzsimmons; 16 Alex Rowe; 17 Jared Blanke.
**Tries:** Clegg (24, 50, 66), Gill (39), Craig (42);
**Goals:** Coleman 4/6.
**OLDHAM:** 1 Kyran Johnson; 2 Aaron Jones-Bishop; 28 Jack Holmes; 3 Zack McComb; 21 Lee Kershaw; 26 Anthony Bowman; 7 Dave Hewitt; 13 Jack Spencer; 9 Gareth Owen; 25 Scott Law; 17 Ben Calland; 12 Emmerson Whittel; 24 Liam Bent. Subs (all used): 19 Jamie Greenwood; 30 Titus Gwaze; 18 Frazer Morris; 20 Matty Wilkinson.
**Tries:** Law (2), Jones-Bishop (6), Kershaw (17), Bowman (32); **Goals:** Hewitt 3/4.
**Sin bin:** Spencer (62) - high tackle.
**Rugby Leaguer & League Express Men of the Match:** *Thunder:* Evan Simons; *Oldham:* Dave Hewitt.
**Penalty count:** 4-7; **Half-time:** 10-22;
**Referee:** Michael Mannifield; **Attendance:** 889.

**WHITEHAVEN 16 HUNSLET 12**

**WHITEHAVEN:** 3 Chris Taylor; 15 Connor Holliday; 23 Jason Mossop; 4 Jessie Joe Parker; 2 Jordan Burns; 1 Sam Forrester; 7 Callum Phillips; 8 Marc Shackley; 14 Sam Dowsett; 10 Kris Coward; 12 Jake Moore; 11 Brett Phillips; 6 Dion Aiye. Subs (all used): 25 Kurt Maudling; 13 Tom Wilkinson; 18 Jordan Thomson; 22 Ruairi McGoff.
**Tries:** Wilkinson (14), Parker (20), Aiye (53);
**Goals:** Moore 1/2, Holliday 1/1.
**HUNSLET:** 1 Jimmy Watson; 2 Gareth Potts; 30 Charlie Martin; 3 Tom Ashton; 5 Dale Bloomfield; 21 Reece Dean; 22 Danny Nicklas; 31 Jon Luke Kirby; 9 Jack Lee; 10 Adam Robinson; 11 Josh Tonks; 18 Nyle Flynn; 13 Mike Emmett. Subs (all used): 20 Vila Halafihi; 16 Zach Braham; 19 Aiden Hema; 15 Michael Haley.
**Tries:** Lee (5), Watson (62); **Goals:** Dean 2/2.
**Sin bin:** Braham (50) - kicking Shackley.
**Rugby Leaguer & League Express Men of the Match:** *Whitehaven:* Dion Aiye; *Hunslet:* Reece Dean.
**Penalty count:** 10-6; **Half-time:** 10-6;
**Referee:** Liam Staveley; **Attendance:** 724.

## ROUND 7

*Friday 19th April 2019*

**NORTH WALES CRUSADERS 70 WEST WALES RAIDERS 8**

**CRUSADERS:** 1 Lewis Fairhurst; 2 Dave Eccleston; 3 Dante Morley-Samuels; 4 Earl Hurst; 5 Rob Massam; 6 Steve Roper; 7 Ben Stead; 10 Warren Thompson; 9 Karl Ashall; 8 Callum Hazzard; 11 Jack Houghton; 12 Stephen Wild; 13 Kenny Baker. Subs (all used): 14 Kenny Hughes; 18 Brad Brennan; 21 Alex Thompson; 17 Jonny Walker.
**Tries:** Massam (8, 34, 59, 69), Hurst (12), Roper (24, 71), Morley-Samuels (28, 38), Eccleston (30), Hazzard (64, 80);
**Goals:** Stead 11/12.
**RAIDERS:** 1 Phil Cowburn; 22 Paddy Jennings; 19 Brad Kislingbury; 23 Rowland Kaye; 25 Mickael Sabour; 9 Liam Rice-Wilson; 7 Tyler Hunt; 8 Connor Parker; 6 Ashley Bateman; 10 Sam Herron; 15 Archie Snook; 20 Mike Connor; 14 Dalton Desmond-Walker. Subs (all used): 13 Dan Maiden; 26 Morgan Rowlands; 21 Sam Baker; 17 Callum Mulkeen.
**Tries:** Jennings (2, 76); **Goals:** Hunt 0/2.
**Rugby Leaguer & League Express Men of the Match:** *Crusaders:* Rob Massam; *Raiders:* Ashley Bateman.
**Penalty count:** 5-4; **Half-time:** 42-4;
**Referee:** Michael Smaill; **Attendance:** 282.

**COVENTRY BEARS 28 LONDON SKOLARS 30**

**BEARS:** 1 Elliot Hall; 2 Hayden Freeman; 3 Kadeem Williams; 4 Kameron Pearce-Paul; 5 Errol Carter; 6 Mitch Shaw; 7 Nick Newman; 8 Peter Ryan; 9 Nathan Conroy; 10 Lewis Taylor; 11 Jacob Jones; 12 Chris Barratt; 13 Kieran Sherratt. Subs (all used): 14 Sam Davis; 15 Toby Richardson; 16 Harry Kaufman; 17 Cameron Stewart.
**Tries:** Richardson (21), S Davis (38), Hall (69, 75), Freeman (78); **Goals:** Newman 4/5.
**SKOLARS:** 1 Joe Brown; 2 Iliess Macani; 4 Omari Caro; 3 Craig Mullen; 5 Lameck Juma; 6 James Barran; 14 Richard Wilkinson; 10 Malikhi Lloyd-Jones; 9 Neil Thorman; 20 Matt Ross; 11 Jordan Williams; 12 Lamont Bryan; 7 Mike Bishay. Subs (all used): 13 Liam Scott; 16 Jon Magrin; 15 Ronny Palumbo; 22 Robert Tuliatu.
**Tries:** Brown (2), Williams (18, 61), Macani (53), Juma (79);
**Goals:** Thorman 5/6.
**Rugby Leaguer & League Express Men of the Match:** *Bears:* Elliot Hall; *Skolars:* Neil Thorman.
**Penalty count:** 15-8; **Half-time:** 12-12;
**Referee:** Tom Crashley; **Attendance:** 353.

**KEIGHLEY COUGARS 26 DONCASTER 18**

**COUGARS:** 21 Matt Welham; 1 Alfie Seeley; 4 Will Cooke; 23 Macauley Hallett; 31 Taylor Prell; 15 Jack Miller; 7 Benn Hardcastle; 19 Matthew Bailey; 14 Luke Million; 8 Jack Coventry; 12 Aaron Levy; 13 Jason Muranka; 9 James Feather. Subs (all used): 10 Jamie Thackray; 17 Billy Gaylor; 22 Dan Parker; 25 Jack Arnold.
**Tries:** Hallett (4), Hardcastle (15), Prell (43), Parker (49);
**Goals:** Hardcastle 5/5.
**DONCASTER:** 1 Kieran Buchanan; 5 Sam Doherty; 4 Jason Tali; 26 Menzie Yere; 19 Matty Chrimes; 6 Jordan Howden; 30 Liam Harris; 17 Brandon Douglas; 20 Callum Ogden; 10 Ryan Boyle; 22 Brad Foster; 3 Connor Bower; 9 Kyle Kesik. Subs (all used): 8 Russ Spiers; 14 Connor Scott; 13 Jordie Hedges; 31 Elliott Townsend.
**Tries:** Yere (2), Tali (12, 19), Townsend (29);
**Goals:** Harris 1/3, Howden 0/1.
**Rugby Leaguer & League Express Men of the Match:** *Cougars:* Jack Miller; *Doncaster:* Jason Tali.
**Penalty count:** 7-10; **Half-time:** 12-18;
**Referee:** Cameron Worsley; **Attendance:** 1,040.

**OLDHAM 28 HUNSLET 36**

**OLDHAM:** 5 Ritchie Hawkyard; 1 Kyran Johnson; 3 Zack McComb; 28 Jack Holmes; 2 Aaron Jones-Bishop; 26 Anthony Bowman; 7 Dave Hewitt; 8 Phil Joy; 9 Gareth Owen; 17 Scott Law; 12 Emmerson Whittel; 16 Danny Langtree; 24 Liam Bent. Subs (all used): 13 Jack Spencer; 30 Titus Gwaze; 18 Ben Davies; 20 Jamie Greenwood.
**Tries:** Bowman (20), Johnson (23), McComb (44, 64);
**Goals:** Hewitt 6/6.
**Sin bin:** Owen (66) - fighting; Langtree (67) - retaliation.
**HUNSLET:** 1 Jimmy Watson; 2 Gareth Potts; 4 Ben Heaton; 3 Tom Ashton; 5 Dale Bloomfield; 21 Reece Dean; 22 Danny Nicklas; 17 Dan Hawksworth; 9 Jack Lee; 10 Adam Robinson; 11 Josh Tonks; 30 Charlie Martin; 13 Mike Emmett. Subs (all used): 20 Vila Halafihi; 16 Zach Braham; 14 Ryan Wright; 15 Michael Haley.
**Tries:** Potts (3, 60), Dean (8), Robinson (72), Heaton (74, 79); **Goals:** Dean 6/8.
**Dismissal:** Hawksworth (67) - high tackle on Langtree.
**Sin bin:** Emmett (66) - fighting.
**Rugby Leaguer & League Express Men of the Match:** *Oldham:* Zack McComb; *Hunslet:* Adam Robinson.
**Penalty count:** 11-8; **Half-time:** 14-14;
**Referee:** Jon Roberts; **Attendance:** 652.

**WORKINGTON TOWN 18 WHITEHAVEN 33**

**TOWN:** 6 Jamie Doran; 16 Scott Rooke; 5 James Worthington; 4 Perry Singleton; 2 Tyllar Mellor; 23 Izaac Farrell; 7 Carl Forber; 10 Stevie Scholey; 9 Sean Penkywicz; 22 Sam Hopkins; 12 Gordon Maudling; 19 Caine Barnes; 11 Danny Tickle. Subs (all used): 15 Tom Curwen; 14 Andrew Dawson; 25 Fuifui Moimoi; 17 Tyler Lancaster.
**Tries:** Doran (26, 30), Tickle (70); **Goals:** Forber 3/3.
**WHITEHAVEN:** 3 Chris Taylor; 15 Connor Holliday; 23 Jason Mossop; 4 Jessie Joe Parker; 2 Jordan Burns; 1 Sam Forrester; 7 Callum Phillips; 8 Marc Shackley; 14 Sam Dowsett; 10 Kris Coward; 11 Brett Phillips; 12 Jake Moore; 13 Tom Wilkinson. Subs (all used): 6 Dion Aiye; - Jake Carter; 25 Kurt Maudling; 9 James Newton.
**Tries:** Forrester (5), Burns (36, 65), Moore (44), B Phillips (50); **Goals:** Holliday 4/4, Moore 2/3;
**Field goal:** Carter (75).
**Rugby Leaguer & League Express Men of the Match:** *Town:* Stevie Scholey; *Whitehaven:* Marc Shackley.
**Penalty count:** 8-6; **Half-time:** 12-12;
**Referee:** Nick Bennett; **Attendance:** 1,981.

## ROUND 8

*Saturday 27th April 2019*

**WEST WALES RAIDERS 8 OLDHAM 72**

**RAIDERS:** 1 Phil Cowburn; 21 Sam Baker; 22 Paddy Jennings; 23 Rowland Kaye; 25 Mickael Sabour; 9 Liam Rice-Wilson; 7 Tyler Hunt; 14 Dalton Desmond-Walker; 6 Ashley Bateman; 10 Sam Herron; 15 Archie Snook; 20 Mike Connor; 13 Dan Maiden. Subs (all used): 12 Morgan Evans; 18 Ryan Shallish; 2 Morgan Rowlands; 17 Callum Mulkeen.
**Tries:** Kaye (29), Jennings (79); **Goals:** Rice-Wilson 0/2.
**OLDHAM:** 5 Ritchie Hawkyard; 1 Kyran Johnson; 3 Zack McComb; 4 Jack Holmes; 27 Harry Maders; 6 Paul Crook; 7 Dave Hewitt; 13 Jack Spencer; 9 Gareth Owen; 10 Scott Law; 25 Danny Bridge; 16 Danny Langtree; 24 Liam Bent. Subs (all used): 12 Emmerson Whittel; 29 Titus Gwaze; 19 Jamie Greenwood; 17 Frazer Morris.
**Tries:** Bent (2, 11), Maders (6, 55), Bridge (18), McComb (21, 35), Hawkyard (25, 47), Crook (32), Gwaze (39), Holmes (65, 76), Langtree (71);
**Goals:** Crook 8/14.
**Rugby Leaguer & League Express Men of the Match:** *Raiders:* Phil Cowburn; *Oldham:* Ritchie Hawkyard.
**Penalty count:** 2-6; **Half-time:** 4-44;
**Referee:** Brandon Robinson; **Attendance:** 197.

*Sunday 28th April 2019*

**DONCASTER 10 NORTH WALES CRUSADERS 12**

**DONCASTER:** 31 Watson Boas; 2 Richard Owen; 4 Jason Tali; 1 Kieran Buchanan; 19 Matty Chrimes; 6 Jordan Howden; 7 Matty Beharrell; 10 Ryan Boyle; 20 Callum Ogden; 8 Russ Spiers; 26 Menzie Yere; 22 Brad Foster; 13 Jordie Hedges. Subs (all used): 14 Connor Scott; 17 Brandon Douglas; 16 Brandan Wilkinson; 9 Kyle Kesik.
**Tries:** Tali (33), Howden (53); **Goals:** Beharrell 1/2.
**CRUSADERS:** 1 Lewis Fairhurst; 2 Dave Eccleston; 3 Dante Morley-Samuels; 4 Earl Hurst; 5 Rob Massam; 6 Steve Roper; 7 Ben Stead; 8 Callum Hazzard; 9 Karl Ashall; 10 Warren Thompson; 11 Jack Houghton; 12 Stephen Wild; 13 Kenny Baker. Subs (all used): 14 Kenny Hughes; 18 Brad Brennan; 21 Alex Thompson; 17 Jonny Walker.
**Tries:** Hurst (11), Baker (49); **Goals:** Stead 2/3.
**Rugby Leaguer & League Express Men of the Match:** *Doncaster:* Watson Boas; *Crusaders:* Kenny Baker.
**Penalty count:** 6-8; **Half-time:** 4-4;
**Referee:** Joe Stearne; **Attendance:** 658.

**HUNSLET 26 LONDON SKOLARS 42**

**HUNSLET:** 1 Jimmy Watson; 2 Gareth Potts; 4 Ben Heaton; 3 Tom Ashton; 25 Marcus Webb; 21 Reece Dean;

22 Danny Nicklas; 31 Jon Luke Kirby; 9 Jack Lee; 10 Adam Robinson; 11 Josh Tonks; 23 Nathan Chappell; 13 Mike Emmett. Subs (all used): 14 Ryan Wright; 15 Michael Haley; 16 Zach Braham; 20 Vila Halafihi.
**Tries:** Tonks (3), Heaton (21), Watson (37), Webb (71), Robinson (74); **Goals:** Dean 2/3, Nicklas 0/1, Chappell 1/1.
**SKOLARS:** 1 Joe Brown; 2 Iliess Macani; 3 Craig Mullen; 15 Jacob Ogden; 5 Lameck Juma; 6 James Barran; 14 Richard Wilkinson; 13 Liam Scott; 9 Neil Thorman; 10 Malikhi Lloyd-Jones; 11 Jordan Williams; 12 Ronny Palumbo; 7 Mike Bishay. Subs (all used): 20 Lamont Bryan; 16 Jon Magrin; 17 Robert Tuliatu; 4 Omari Caro.
**Tries:** Wilkinson (9), Barran (14), Brown (25, 48), Thorman (42), Macani (55), Juma (67);
**Goals:** Thorman 7/8.
**Rugby Leaguer & League Express Men of the Match:**
*Hunslet:* Josh Tonks; *Skolars:* Ronny Palumbo.
**Penalty count:** 7-5; **Half-time:** 16-18;
**Referee:** Aaron Moore; **Attendance:** 661.

#### KEIGHLEY COUGARS 32 WORKINGTON TOWN 26

**COUGARS:** 1 Alfie Seeley; 21 Matt Welham; 4 Will Cooke; 23 Macauley Hallett; 31 Taylor Prell; 15 Jack Miller; 7 Benn Hardcastle; 19 Matthew Bailey; 9 James Feather; 8 Jack Coventry; 12 Aaron Levy; 13 Jason Muranka; 27 Lewis Wray. Subs (all used): 10 Jamie Thackray; 17 Billy Gaylor; 22 Dan Parker; 25 Jack Arnold.
**Tries:** Hardcastle (12), Prell (22), Parker (27), Feather (73, 77); **Goals:** Hardcastle 6/8.
**TOWN:** 23 Izaac Farrell; 5 James Worthington; 17 Sam Hewitt; 4 Perry Singleton; 20 Jonathan Walsh; 6 Jamie Doran; 7 Carl Forber; 8 Oliver Wilkes; 9 Sean Penkywicz; 25 Fuifui Moimoi; 12 Gordon Maudling; 19 Caine Barnes; 11 Danny Tickle. Subs (all used): 10 Stevie Scholey; 14 Andrew Dawson; 15 Tom Curwen; 24 Sam Hopkins.
**Tries:** Hewitt (36, 53), Worthington (56), Wilkes (67);
**Goals:** Forber 3/3, Farrell 2/2.
**Sin bin:** Barnes (40) - dangerous challenge on Parker; Forber (52) - dissent.
**Rugby Leaguer & League Express Men of the Match:**
*Cougars:* James Feather; *Town:* Sam Hewitt.
**Penalty count:** 12-7; **Half-time:** 18-6;
**Referee:** Steve Race; **Attendance:** 948.

#### WHITEHAVEN 12 NEWCASTLE THUNDER 12

**WHITEHAVEN:** 3 Chris Taylor; 5 Dave Thompson; 23 Jason Mossop; 4 Jessie Joe Parker; 2 Jordan Burns; 1 Sam Forrester; - Jake Carter; 8 Marc Shackley; 14 Sam Dowsett; 10 Kris Coward; 12 Jake Moore; 11 Brett Phillips; 13 Tom Wilkinson. Subs (all used): 6 Dion Aiye; 9 James Newton; 15 Connor Holliday; 18 Jordan Thomson.
**Tries:** D Thompson (26), Burns (58);
**Goals:** Moore 0/1, Holliday 2/2.
**THUNDER:** 1 Lewis Young; 2 Mo Agoro; 3 Tyler Craig; 4 Kieran Gill; 5 Alex Clegg; 7 Jy-mel Coleman; 6 Remy Marginet; 8 Liam McAvoy; 9 Keal Carlile; 10 Jared Blanke; 12 Conor Fitzsimmons; 18 Rhys Clarke; 13 Evan Simons. Subs (all used): 11 Aaron Ollett; 20 Sam Luckley; 16 Alex Rowe; 14 Jack Aldous.
**Try:** Gill (78); **Goals:** Coleman 4/4.
**Rugby Leaguer & League Express Men of the Match:**
*Whitehaven:* Marc Shackley; *Thunder:* Lewis Young.
**Penalty count:** 6-5; **Half-time:** 4-2;
**Referee:** Michael Mannifield; **Attendance:** 852.

## ROUND 1

*Saturday 11th May 2019*

#### LONDON SKOLARS 19 NORTH WALES CRUSADERS 18

**SKOLARS:** 1 Joe Brown; 2 Iliess Macani; 4 Omari Caro; 3 Jacob Ogden; 5 Lameck Juma; 6 James Barran; 7 Craig Mullen; 8 Liam Scott; 9 Neil Thorman; 10 Malikhi Lloyd-Jones; 11 Jordan Williams; 12 Ronny Palumbo; 14 Mike Bishay. Subs (all used): 22 Jon Magrin; 15 Robert Tuliatu; 16 Matt Ross; 20 Lamont Bryan.
**Tries:** Brown (40), Macani (52), Bryan (74);
**Goals:** Thorman 2/2, Barran 1/1; **Field goal:** Mullen (77).
**CRUSADERS:** 1 Lewis Fairhurst; 2 Dave Eccleston; 3 Matt Reid; 4 Earl Hurst; 5 Rob Massam; 6 Steve Roper; 7 Ben Stead; 8 Callum Hazzard; 9 Karl Ashall; 10 Warren Thompson; 11 Alex Thompson; 12 Simon Atherton; 13 Kenny Baker. Subs (all used): 14 Kenny Hughes; 15 Brad Brennan; 16 Jonny Walker; 17 Chris Worrall.
**Tries:** Hazzard (10), Fairhurst (62); **Goals:** Stead 5/5.
**Rugby Leaguer & League Express Men of the Match:**
*Skolars:* Joe Brown; *Crusaders:* Ben Stead.
**Penalty count:** 6-7; **Half-time:** 6-12;
**Referee:** Tom Crashley; **Attendance:** 248.

## ROUND 4

*Saturday 11th May 2019*

#### COVENTRY BEARS 41 WORKINGTON TOWN 30

**BEARS:** 1 Elliot Hall; 2 Hayden Freeman; 3 Kadeem Williams; 4 Kameron Pearce-Paul; 5 Reece Rance; 6 Brad Sheridan; 7 Nick Newman; 8 Peter Ryan; 9 Mitch Shaw; 10 Lewis Taylor; 11 Jacob Jones; 12 Kieran Sherratt; 13 Chris Barratt. Subs (all used): 14 Nathan Conroy; 15 Will Tully; 16 Harvey Hallas; 17 Harry Kaufman.
**Tries:** Jones (14, 68), Newman (17, 34), Pearce-Paul (30), Rance (38), Hall (64); **Goals:** Newman 6/7;
**Field goal:** Newman (75).
**TOWN:** 1 Ryan Fieldhouse; 16 Scott Rooke; 19 Caine Barnes; 21 Tyler Lancaster; 20 Jonathan Walsh; 6 Jamie Doran; 23 Izaac Farrell; 8 Oliver Wilkes; 9 Sean Penkywicz; - Fuifui Moimoi; 12 Gordon Maudling; 10 Stevie Scholey; 11 Danny Tickle. Subs: 15 Tom Curwen; 17 Dec O'Donnell; 14 Andrew Dawson (not used); 22 Sam Hopkins.
**Tries:** Rooke (7, 80), Walsh (46), Fieldhouse (51), Doran (72); **Goals:** Farrell 5/5.
**Rugby Leaguer & League Express Men of the Match:**
*Bears:* Nick Newman; *Town:* Scott Rooke.
**Penalty count:** 8-10; **Half-time:** 28-6;
**Referee:** Steve Race; **Attendance:** 303
*(at Ivor Preece Field, Broadstreet).*

## ROUND 9

*Saturday 18th May 2019*

#### LONDON SKOLARS 22 DONCASTER 6

**SKOLARS:** 1 Joe Brown; 2 Iliess Macani; 3 Jacob Ogden; 4 Lameck Juma; 5 Jerome Yates; 6 James Barran; 14 Richard Wilkinson; 15 Matt Ross; 9 Neil Thorman; 10 Liam Scott; 11 Jordan Williams; 12 Ronny Palumbo; 13 Daniel Hindmarsh. Subs (all used): 7 Mike Bishay; 17 Malikhi Lloyd-Jones; 16 Jon Magrin; 20 Lamont Bryan.
**Tries:** Macani (5), Ogden (58), Palumbo (70);
**Goals:** Thorman 4/4, Barran 1/1.
**DONCASTER:** 1 Watson Boas; 5 Sam Doherty; 3 Connor Bower; 4 Jason Tali; 19 Matty Chrimes; 13 Jordie Hedges; 7 Matty Beharrell; 8 Russ Spiers; 9 Kyle Kesik; 10 Ryan Boyle; 22 Brad Foster; 11 Brad England; 31 Levy Nzoungou. Subs (all used): 27 Jack Brown; 17 Brandon Douglas; 20 Callum Ogden; 26 Menzie Yere.
**Try:** England (19); **Goals:** Beharrell 1/1.
**Rugby Leaguer & League Express Men of the Match:**
*Skolars:* Iliess Macani; *Doncaster:* Jack Brown.
**Penalty count:** 4-7; **Half-time:** 10-6;
**Referee:** Tom Crashley; **Attendance:** 608.

*Sunday 19th May 2019*

#### NORTH WALES CRUSADERS 14 WHITEHAVEN 28

**CRUSADERS:** 1 Lewis Fairhurst; 2 Dave Eccleston; 3 Dante Morley-Samuels; 4 Earl Hurst; 5 Rob Massam; 6 Steve Roper; 7 Ben Stead; 8 Callum Hazzard; 9 Karl Ashall; 10 Warren Thompson; 11 Simon Atherton; 12 Matt Reid; 13 Kenny Baker. Subs (all used): 14 Kenny Hughes; 15 Jacob Thomas; 17 Brad Brennan; 21 Chris Worrall.
**Tries:** Baker (55), Massam (58); **Goals:** Stead 1/1, Baker 2/2.
**WHITEHAVEN:** 3 Chris Taylor; 2 Jordan Burns; 23 Jason Mossop; 4 Jessie Joe Parker; 19 Andrew Bulman; 1 Sam Forrester; 7 Callum Phillips; 8 Marc Shackley; 14 Sam Dowsett; 10 Kris Coward; 11 Brett Phillips; 12 Jake Moore; 13 Tom Wilkinson. Subs (all used): 6 Dion Aiye; - Carl Forster; 15 Connor Holliday; 9 James Newton.
**Tries:** Forrester (16), Dowsett (18), Taylor (38), C Phillips (48), Bulman (78); **Goals:** Moore 4/6, Holliday 0/1.
**Rugby Leaguer & League Express Men of the Match:**
*Crusaders:* Kenny Baker; *Whitehaven:* Sam Dowsett.
**Penalty count:** 8-11; **Half-time:** 2-16;
**Referee:** Joe Stearne; **Attendance:** 342.

#### NEWCASTLE THUNDER 40 KEIGHLEY COUGARS 12

**THUNDER:** 1 Lewis Young; 2 Mo Agoro; 3 Joe Brown; 4 Kieran Gill; 5 Alex Clegg; 6 Dan Coates; 7 Remy Marginet; 8 Liam McAvoy; 9 Keal Carlile; 10 Jared Blanke; 11 Conor Fitzsimmons; 18 Rhys Clarke; 13 Sam Luckley. Subs (all used): 14 Evan Simons; 15 Carne Doyle-Manga; 16 Alex Rowe; 17 Jack Aldous.
**Tries:** Agoro (9, 79), Gill (16, 72), Marginet (19), Doyle-Manga (48, 76); **Goals:** Marginet 6/8.
**Sin bin:** Clarke (22) - fighting.
**COUGARS:** 1 Alfie Seeley; 5 Davey Dixon; 4 Will Cooke; 23 Macauley Hallett; 21 Matt Welham; 22 Dan Parker; 15 Jack Miller; 19 Matthew Bailey; 9 James Feather; 10 Jamie Thackray; 11 Josh Lynam; 13 Jason Muranka; 29 Jimmy Beckett. Subs (all used): 8 Jack Coventry; 18 Chris Cullimore; 25 Jack Arnold; 30 Harvey Hallas.
**Tries:** Miller (27), Dixon (32); **Goals:** Miller 2/2.
**Sin bin:** Beckett (22) - fighting.
**Rugby Leaguer & League Express Men of the Match:**
*Thunder:* Remy Marginet; *Cougars:* James Feather.
**Penalty count:** 13-7; **Half-time:** 16-12;
**Referee:** Andrew Sweet; **Attendance:** 1,423.

#### OLDHAM 34 COVENTRY BEARS 18

**OLDHAM:** 5 Ritchie Hawkyard; 1 Kyran Johnson; 3 Zack McComb; 28 Jack Holmes; 27 Harry Maders; 6 Paul Crook; 7 Dave Hewitt; 10 Scott Law; 9 Gareth Owen; 13 Jack Spencer; 25 Danny Bridge; 16 Danny Langtree; 29 Titus Gwaze. Subs (all used): 12 Emmerson Whittel; 11 Ben Calland; 20 Matty Wilkinson; 18 Ben Davies.
**Tries:** Hewitt (21), Langtree (26, 37), Wilkinson (39), Bridge (54), Hawkyard (70); **Goals:** Crook 5/6.
**BEARS:** 1 Elliott Hall; 2 Hayden Freeman; 3 Kadeem Williams; 4 Kameron Pearce-Paul; 5 Reece Rance; 6 Brad Sheridan; 7 Nick Newman; 8 Peter Ryan; 9 Nathan Conroy; 10 Lewis Taylor; 11 Jacob Jones; 12 Kieran Sherratt; 13 Chris Barratt. Subs (all used): 14 Sam Davis; 15 Toby Richardson; 16 Harry Kaufman; 17 Euan Tiernan.
**Tries:** Pearce-Paul (49), Hall (64), S Davis (74);
**Goals:** Newman 3/3.
**Rugby Leaguer & League Express Men of the Match:**
*Oldham:* Danny Langtree; *Bears:* Sam Davis.
**Penalty count:** 4-7; **Half-time:** 22-0;
**Referee:** Brad Milligan; **Attendance:** 451.

#### WORKINGTON TOWN 12 HUNSLET 4

**TOWN:** 1 Ryan Fieldhouse; 20 Jonathan Walsh; 19 Caine Barnes; 21 Tyler Lancaster; - Russ Bolton; 6 Jamie Doran; 7 Carl Forber; 25 Fuifui Moimoi; 9 Sean Penkywicz; 22 Sam Hopkins; 12 Gordon Maudling; 10 Stevie Scholey; 11 Danny Tickle. Subs (all used): 14 Andrew Dawson; 15 Tom Curwen; 16 Scott Rooke (not used); 17 Dec O'Donnell.
**Tries:** Curwen (34), Maudling (78); **Goals:** Forber 2/4.
**HUNSLET:** 1 Jimmy Watson; 2 Gareth Potts; 23 Nathan Chappell; 4 Ben Heaton; 5 Dale Bloomfield; 6 Joe Sanderson; 22 Danny Nicklas; 10 Adam Robinson; 9 Jack Lee; 31 Jon Luke Kirby; 11 Josh Tonks; 12 Duane Straugheir; 13 Mike Emmett. Subs (all used): 20 Vila Halafihi; 16 Zach Braham; 32 Rory Dixon; 30 Charlie Martin.
**Try:** Potts (71); **Goals:** Sanderson 0/1.
**Rugby Leaguer & League Express Men of the Match:**
*Town:* Stevie Scholey; *Hunslet:* Jimmy Watson.
**Penalty count:** 6-5; **Half-time:** 6-0;
**Referee:** Nick Bennett; **Attendance:** 610.

## ROUND 10

*Saturday 25th May 2019*

#### WHITEHAVEN 32 LONDON SKOLARS 6

**WHITEHAVEN:** 3 Chris Taylor; 2 Jordan Burns; 23 Jason Mossop; 15 Connor Holliday; 19 Andrew Bulman; 1 Sam Forrester; 7 Callum Phillips; 8 Marc Shackley; 14 Sam Dowsett; 10 Kris Coward; 11 Brett Phillips; 12 Jake Moore; 13 Tom Wilkinson. Subs (all used): 6 Dion Aiye; - Carl Forster; 9 James Newton; 18 Jordan Thomson.
**Tries:** Aiye (39, 70), Forster (50), Newton (66), B Phillips (78); **Goals:** Moore 6/6.
**Sin bin:** Taylor (75) - fighting.
**SKOLARS:** 14 Richard Wilkinson; 2 Iliess Macani; 12 Ronny Palumbo; 3 Craig Mullen; 5 Elliot Jennings; 6 James Barran; 7 Jermaine Coleman; 19 Will Martin; 9 Neil Thorman; 21 Liam Scott; 11 Jordan Williams; 20 Lamont Bryan; 13 Robert Tuliatu. Subs (all used): 17 Jy-mel Coleman; 15 Malikhi Lloyd-Jones; 16 Jon Magrin; 22 Matt Ross.
**Try:** Scott (8); **Goals:** Thorman 1/1.
**Sin bin:** Tuliatu (75) - fighting.
**Rugby Leaguer & League Express Men of the Match:**
*Whitehaven:* Dion Aiye; *Skolars:* Neil Thorman.
**Penalty count:** 10-4; **Half-time:** 6-6;
**Referee:** John McMullen; **Attendance:** 811.

#### KEIGHLEY COUGARS 12 OLDHAM 52

**COUGARS:** 33 Louis Sheriff; 5 Davey Dixon; 4 Will Cooke; 23 Macauley Hallett; 31 Taylor Prell; 22 Dan Parker; 15 Jack Miller; 19 Matthew Bailey; 9 James Feather; 8 Jack Coventry; 11 Josh Lynam; 13 Jason Muranka; 27 Lewis Wray. Subs (all used): 10 Jamie Thackray; 16 Kieran Moran; 18 Chris Cullimore; 30 Harvey Hallas.
**Tries:** Sheriff (19), Miller (58); **Goals:** Miller 2/2.
**OLDHAM:** 5 Ritchie Hawkyard; 1 Kyran Johnson; 3 Zack McComb; 11 Ben Calland; 4 Jack Holmes; 6 Paul Crook; 7 Dave Hewitt; 8 Phil Joy; 9 Gareth Owen; 13 Jack Spencer; 25 Danny Bridge; 16 Danny Langtree; 24 Liam Bent. Subs (all used): 10 Scott Law; 12 Emmerson Whittel; 20 Matty Wilkinson; 29 Titus Gwaze.
**Tries:** Bent (3), Owen (13), Crook (30), Langtree (47), Hewitt (51), McComb (53), Holmes (64), Whittel (71, 78);
**Goals:** Crook 8/10.

**Rugby Leaguer & League Express Men of the Match:**
*Cougars:* Taylor Prell; *Oldham:* Danny Langtree.
**Penalty count:** 9-6; **Half-time:** 6-18;
**Referee:** Andrew Sweet; **Attendance:** 836.

*Sunday 26th May 2019*

**COVENTRY BEARS 18 NORTH WALES CRUSADERS 34**

**BEARS:** 1 Elliot Hall; 2 Hayden Freeman; 3 Kadeem Williams; 4 Kameron Pearce-Paul; 5 Reece Rance; 6 Brad Sheridan; 7 Nick Newman; 8 Peter Ryan; 9 Nathan Conroy; 10 Lewis Taylor; 11 Jacob Jones; 12 Kieran Sherratt; 13 Chris Barratt. Subs (all used): 14 Sam Davis; 15 Harry Kauffman; 16 Will Tully; 21 Martyn Reilly.
**Tries:** Rance (7), Taylor (48), Hall (58); **Goals:** Newman 3/3.
**Sin bin:** Rance (14) - trip.
**CRUSADERS:** 1 Lewis Fairhurst; 2 Dave Eccleston; 3 Simon Atherton; 4 Earl Hurst; 5 Rob Massam; 6 Steve Roper; 7 Ryan Smith; 8 Callum Hazzard; 9 Karl Ashall; 10 Warren Thompson; 11 Matt Reid; 12 Stephen Wild; 13 Kenny Baker. Subs (all used): 14 Kenny Hughes; 17 Brad Brennan; 18 Jonny Walker; 21 Liam Walsh.
**Tries:** Eccleston (12), Baker (25), Massam (41, 53), W Thompson (75), Ashall (77);
**Goals:** Baker 2/3, Fairhurst 3/3.
**Sin bin:** Hughes (40) - late challenge.
**Rugby Leaguer & League Express Men of the Match:**
*Bears:* Elliot Hall; *Crusaders:* Rob Massam.
**Penalty count:** 7-9; **Half-time:** 6-12;
**Referee:** Liam Staveley; **Attendance:** 395
*(at Ivor Preece Field, Broadstreet).*

**DONCASTER 54 WEST WALES RAIDERS 0**

**DONCASTER:** 6 Jordan Howden; 5 Sam Doherty; 3 Connor Bower; 4 Jason Tali; 19 Matty Chrimes; 30 Watson Boas; 7 Matty Beharrell; 10 Ryan Boyle; 9 Kyle Kesik; 8 Russ Spiers; 26 Menzie Yere; 11 Brad England; 22 Brad Foster. Subs (all used): 15 Kieran Cross; 17 Brandon Douglas; 14 Connor Scott; 24 Levy Nzoungou.
**Tries:** Tali (4, 12), Chrimes (7), Beharrell (19), Yere (37, 63), Bower (43), Boas (50), Howden (56), Doherty (79);
**Goals:** Beharrell 7/10.
**RAIDERS:** 1 Phil Cowburn; 2 Dai Evans; 23 Rowland Kaye; 20 Mike Connor; 5 Sam Baker; 22 Steve Parry; 7 Tyler Hunt; 16 Ryan Shallish; 9 Liam Rice-Wilson; 10 Sam Herron; 24 Gioele Celerino; 15 Archie Snook; 12 Morgan Evans. Subs (all used): 17 Callum Mulkeen; 26 Matthew Morgan; 14 Dalton Desmond-Walker; - Nye Walker.
**Rugby Leaguer & League Express Men of the Match:**
*Doncaster:* Menzie Yere; *Raiders:* Gioele Celerino.
**Penalty count:** 6-6; **Half-time:** 30-0;
**Referee:** Kevin Moore; **Attendance:** 525.

**NEWCASTLE THUNDER 18 HUNSLET 32**

**THUNDER:** 1 Lewis Young; 19 Misi Taulapapa; 3 Joe Brown; 4 Kieran Gill; 5 Alex Clegg; 6 Dan Coates; 7 Remy Marginet; 8 Liam McAvoy; 9 Keal Carlile; 10 Jared Blanke; 11 Conor Fitzsimmons; 12 Tyler Craig; 13 Joel Edwards. Subs (all used): 14 Evan Simons; 17 Jack Aldous; 15 Carne Doyle-Manga; 20 Aaron Ollett.
**Tries:** Gill (58), Clegg (63), Young (71); **Goals:** Coates 3/3.
**Sin bin:** McAvoy (17) - late challenge.
**HUNSLET:** 24 James Woodburn-Hall; 2 Gareth Potts; 4 Ben Heaton; 23 Nathan Chappell; 25 James Saltonstall; 21 Reece Dean; 7 Cain Southernwood; 16 Zach Braham; 9 Jack Lee; 10 Adam Robinson; 11 Josh Tonks; 12 Duane Straugheir; 13 Mike Emmett. Subs (all used): 20 Vila Halafihi; 31 Rory Dixon; 15 Michael Haley; 30 Charlie Martin.
**Tries:** Saltonstall (13, 65), Woodburn-Hall (27), Chappell (39, 55), Potts (79); **Goals:** Dean 4/7.
**Rugby Leaguer & League Express Men of the Match:**
*Thunder:* Alex Clegg; *Hunslet:* Nathan Chappell.
**Penalty count:** 3-12; **Half-time:** 0-16;
**Referee:** Tom Crashley; **Attendance:** 624.

## ROUND 11

*Friday 7th June 2019*

**HUNSLET 34 KEIGHLEY COUGARS 0**

**HUNSLET:** 21 Reece Dean; 2 Gareth Potts; 4 Ben Heaton; 23 Nathan Chappell; 5 Dale Bloomfield; 22 Danny Nicklas; 7 Cain Southernwood; 16 Zach Braham; 9 Jack Lee; 10 Adam Robinson; 11 Josh Tonks; 12 Duane Straugheir; 13 Mike Emmett. Subs (all used): 31 Rory Dixon; 20 Vila Halafihi; 19 Aiden Hema; 30 Charlie Martin.
**Tries:** Heaton (2, 42), Chappell (12), Potts (28), Emmett (38), Straugheir (40), Braham (80);
**Goals:** Dean 2/6, Nicklas 1/1.
**On report:**
Martin (60) - alleged dangerous contact on Hardcastle.
**COUGARS:** 33 Louis Sheriff; 5 Davey Dixon; 4 Will Cooke; 23 Macauley Hallett; 31 Taylor Prell; 15 Jack Miller; 7 Benn Hardcastle; 19 Matthew Bailey; 9 James Feather; 10 Jamie Thackray; 11 Josh Lynam; 22 Dan Parker; 16 Kieran Moran. Subs (all used): 8 Jack Coventry; 18 Chris Cullimore; 30 Harvey Hallas; - Dom Horn.
**Sin bin:** Lynam (57) - delaying restart.
**Rugby Leaguer & League Express Men of the Match:**
*Hunslet:* Duane Straugheir; *Cougars:* Josh Lynam.
**Penalty count:** 8-5; **Half-time:** 24-0;
**Referee:** Andrew Sweet; **Attendance:** 668.

*Saturday 8th June 2019*

**WEST WALES RAIDERS 12 WORKINGTON TOWN 58**

**RAIDERS:** 1 Phil Cowburn; 21 Sam Baker; 20 Mike Connor; 2 Dai Evans; 5 James Smith; 22 Steve Parry; 7 Tyler Hunt; 12 Morgan Evans; 9 Liam Rice-Wilson; 10 Sam Herron; 15 Archie Snook; 23 Rowland Kaye; 6 Ashley Bateman. Subs (all used): 14 Dalton Desmond-Walker; 24 Gioele Celerino; 16 Nye Walker; 13 Dan Maiden.
**Tries:** Cowburn (51), M Evans (70); **Goals:** Cowburn 2/2.
**TOWN:** 1 Ryan Fieldhouse; 20 Jonathan Walsh; 26 Calvin Wellington; 4 Perry Singleton; 2 Russ Bolton; 6 Jamie Doran; 7 Carl Forber; 25 Fuifui Moimoi; 9 Sean Penkywicz; 8 Oliver Wilkes; 12 Gordon Maudling; 10 Stevie Scholey; 11 Danny Tickle. Subs (all used): 22 Sam Hopkins; 17 Dec O'Donnell; 15 Tom Curwen; 27 Blain Marwood.
**Tries:** Maudling (9), Moimoi (12), Penkywicz (26), Singleton (30), Scholey (38), Fieldhouse (46), O'Donnell (60), Hopkins (63), Wilkes (66), Marwood (72);
**Goals:** Forber 9/10.
**Rugby Leaguer & League Express Men of the Match:**
*Raiders:* Phil Cowburn; *Town:* Carl Forber.
**Penalty count:** 8-11; **Half-time:** 0-28;
**Referee:** Paul Marklove; **Attendance:** 321.

*Sunday 9th June 2019*

**NORTH WALES CRUSADERS 12 NEWCASTLE THUNDER 48**

**CRUSADERS:** 1 Lewis Fairhurst; 4 Dante Morley-Samuels; 3 Simon Atherton; 2 Earl Hurst; 5 Rob Massam; 6 Steve Roper; 7 Ryan Smith; 8 Warren Thompson; 15 Kenny Hughes; 10 Callum Hazzard; 11 Matt Reid; 12 Stephen Wild; 13 Kenny Baker. Subs (all used): 14 Declan Gregory; 17 Brad Brennan; 21 Liam Walsh; 18 Jonny Walker.
**Tries:** Hurst (5), Smith (72); **Goals:** Fairhurst 2/2.
**THUNDER:** 1 Lewis Young; 19 Misi Taulapapa; 3 Joe Brown; 4 Kieran Gill; 5 Alex Clegg; 6 Dan Coates; 7 Mikey Lewis; 8 Joel Edwards; 9 Keal Carlile; 10 Jared Blanke; 11 Conor Fitzsimmons; 18 Rhys Clarke; 13 Evan Simons. Subs (all used): 20 Liam McAvoy; 2 Sam Luckley; 16 Jack Aldous; 12 Aaron Ollett.
**Tries:** Blanke (12), Lewis (22), Young (36, 40, 41), Carlile (46), Brown (48), Gill (76, 80); **Goals:** Lewis 6/9.
**Rugby Leaguer & League Express Men of the Match:**
*Crusaders:* Stephen Wild; *Thunder:* Lewis Young.
**Penalty count:** 4-5; **Half-time:** 6-22;
**Referee:** Michael Mannifield; **Attendance:** 302.

**WHITEHAVEN 32 COVENTRY BEARS 18**

**WHITEHAVEN:** 3 Chris Taylor; 19 Andrew Bulman; 23 Jason Mossop; 15 Connor Holliday; 5 Dave Thompson; 1 Sam Forrester; 7 Callum Phillips; 8 Marc Shackley; 14 Sam Dowsett; 10 Kris Coward; 11 Brett Phillips; 12 Jake Moore; 13 Tom Wilkinson. Subs (all used): 6 Dion Aiye; - Carl Forster; 24 Ethan Kelly; 25 Kurt Maudling.
**Tries:** Bulman (1, 16), Forrester (45, 49), Mossop (58), Moore (62, 69); **Goals:** Holliday 2/7.
**BEARS:** 1 Elliot Hall; 2 Hayden Freeman; 3 Jacob Jones; 4 Kadeem Williams; 5 Errol Carter; 6 Matthew Davies; 7 Nick Newman; 8 Daniel Hindmarsh; 9 Nathan Conroy; 10 Lewis Taylor; 11 Harry Kaufman; 12 Kieran Sherratt; 13 Chris Barratt. Subs (all used): 14 Sam Davis; 15 Jack Ray; 16 Will Tully; 18 Cameron Stewart.
**Tries:** Newman (19), S Davis (36), Hall (76);
**Goals:** Newman 3/4.
**Rugby Leaguer & League Express Men of the Match:**
*Whitehaven:* Jake Moore; *Bears:* Nick Newman.
**Penalty count:** 7-5; **Half-time:** 8-14;
**Referee:** Aaron Moore; **Attendance:** 915.

**DONCASTER 31 OLDHAM 0**

**DONCASTER:** 6 Jordan Howden; 5 Sam Doherty; 1 Cameron Scott; 4 Jason Tali; 19 Matty Chrimes; 30 Watson Boas; 7 Matty Beharrell; 14 Connor Scott; 9 Kyle Kesik; 8 Russ Spiers; 26 Menzie Yere; 22 Brad Foster; 13 Jordie Hedges. Subs (all used): 10 Ryan Boyle; 3 Connor Bower; 24 Jack Brown; 25 Jez Litten.
**Tries:** Hedges (3, 48), Boas (18), Doherty (68), Howden (74); **Goals:** Beharrell 5/8;
**Field goal:** Beharrell (80).
**Sin bin:** Brown (53) - dangerous challenge; Litten (66) - fighting.
**OLDHAM:** 5 Ritchie Hawkyard; 27 Harry Maders; 3 Zack McComb; 4 Jack Holmes; 28 Harry Aaronson; 26 Anthony Bowman; 7 Dave Hewitt; 29 Titus Gwaze; 9 Gareth Owen; 13 Jack Spencer; 25 Danny Bridge; 16 Danny Langtree; 24 Liam Bent. Subs (all used): 10 Scott Law; 17 Ben Davies; 12 Emmerson Whittel; 20 Matty Wilkinson.
**Sin bin:** Owen (66) - fighting; Hawkyard (66) - fighting.
**Rugby Leaguer & League Express Men of the Match:**
*Doncaster:* Jordie Hedges; *Oldham:* Anthony Bowman.
**Penalty count:** 6-6; **Half-time:** 16-0;
**Referee:** Tom Crashley; **Attendance:** 678.

## ROUND 12

*Friday 14th June 2019*

**HUNSLET 20 DONCASTER 22**

**HUNSLET:** 21 Reece Dean; 2 Gareth Potts; 4 Ben Heaton; 23 Nathan Chappell; 1 Jimmy Watson; 22 Danny Nicklas; 7 Cain Southernwood; 16 Zach Braham; 9 Jack Lee; 10 Adam Robinson; 11 Josh Tonks; 12 Duane Straugheir; 13 Mike Emmett. Subs (all used): 15 Michael Haley; 17 Dan Hawksworth; 20 Vila Halafihi; 30 Charlie Martin.
**Tries:** Potts (13, 24), Straugheir (22), Chappell (63);
**Goals:** Dean 2/4.
**DONCASTER:** 6 Jordan Howden; 5 Sam Doherty; 1 Cameron Scott; 4 Jason Tali; 19 Matty Chrimes; 30 Watson Boas; 7 Matty Beharrell; 14 Connor Scott; 9 Kyle Kesik; 8 Russ Spiers; 22 Brad Foster; 26 Menzie Yere; 13 Jordie Hedges. Subs (all used): 10 Ryan Boyle; 28 Jack Brown; - Jez Litten; 3 Connor Bower.
**Tries:** Howden (7), Boas (37), Beharrell (60), Cameron Scott (70); **Goals:** Beharrell 3/4.
**Rugby Leaguer & League Express Men of the Match:**
*Hunslet:* Zach Braham; *Doncaster:* Matty Beharrell.
**Penalty count:** 4-5; **Half-time:** 14-12;
**Referee:** Steve Race; **Attendance:** 664.

*Saturday 15th June 2019*

**LONDON SKOLARS 51 WEST WALES RAIDERS 6**

**SKOLARS:** 1 James Barran; 2 Iliess Macani; 3 Craig Mullen; 4 Lameck Juma; 5 Elliot Jennings; 6 Jy-mel Coleman; 14 Richard Wilkinson; 10 Daniel Hindmarsh; 9 Neil Thorman; 16 Will Martin; 11 Jordan Williams; 12 Mike Greenhalgh; 13 Lamont Bryan. Subs (all used): 7 Mike Bishay; 19 Judd Greenhalgh; - Liam Scott; 8 Michael Sykes.
**Tries:** M Greenhalgh (9), Williams (13, 49, 69), Mullen (22), Jennings (44), Jy-mel Coleman (53), Scott (57), Juma (62); **Goals:** Thorman 7/9;
**Field goal:** Thorman (80).
**RAIDERS:** 1 Phil Cowburn; 25 Mickael Sabour; 20 Mike Connor; 4 Paddy Jennings; 5 James Smith; 22 Steve Parry; 7 Tyler Hunt; 14 Dalton Desmond-Walker; 9 Liam Rice-Wilson; 10 Sam Herron; 15 Archie Snook; 12 Morgan Evans; 6 Ashley Bateman. Subs (all used): 24 Callum Mulkeen; 3 Mitch Shaw; 16 Nye Walker; 17 Chris Vitalini.
**Try:** Bateman (2); **Goals:** Cowburn 1/1.
**Rugby Leaguer & League Express Men of the Match:**
*Skolars:* Jordan Williams; *Raiders:* Steve Parry.
**Penalty count:** 9-7; **Half-time:** 18-6;
**Referee:** Brandon Robinson; **Attendance:** 290.

*Sunday 16th June 2019*

**NEWCASTLE THUNDER 26 WHITEHAVEN 20**

**THUNDER:** 1 Lewis Young; 19 Misi Taulapapa; 3 Joe Brown; 4 Kieran Gill; 5 Alex Clegg; 6 Nick Newman; 7 Mikey Lewis; 10 Jared Blanke; 9 Keal Carlile; 8 Joel Edwards; 11 Conor Fitzsimmons; 18 Rhys Clarke; 13 Harry Aldous. Subs (all used): 14 Evan Simons; 12 Liam McAvoy; 15 Jack Aldous; 20 Sam Luckley.
**Tries:** Clarke (19), Clegg (55), Young (60, 79), Lewis (68);
**Goals:** Lewis 3/5.
**WHITEHAVEN:** 3 Chris Taylor; 2 Jordan Burns; 4 Jessie Joe Parker; 23 Jason Mossop; 5 Dave Thompson; 1 Sam Forrester; 7 Callum Phillips; 8 Marc Shackley; 9 James Newton; 10 Kris Coward; 11 Brett Phillips; 12 Jake Moore; 13 Tom Wilkinson. Subs (all used): 6 Dion Aiye; 26 Carl Forster; 15 Connor Holliday; 18 Jordan Thomson.
**Tries:** Parker (9), Moore (45), B Phillips (70);
**Goals:** Moore 4/5.
**Rugby Leaguer & League Express Men of the Match:**
*Thunder:* Harry Aldous; *Whitehaven:* Carl Forster.
**Penalty count:** 9-11; **Half-time:** 6-8;
**Referee:** Cameron Worsley; **Attendance:** 1,079.

**OLDHAM 28 KEIGHLEY COUGARS 4**

**OLDHAM:** 5 Ritchie Hawkyard; 28 Harry Aaronson; 3 Zack McComb; 26 Anthony Bowman; 27 Harry Maders; 6 Paul

Crook; 7 Dave Hewitt; 13 Jack Spencer; 9 Gareth Owen; 10 Scott Law; 16 Danny Langtree; 25 Danny Bridge; 24 Liam Bent. Subs (all used): 12 Emmerson Whittel; 19 Jamie Greenwood; 18 Ben Davies; 15 Nick Gregson.
**Tries:** Langtree (16), Bowman (20, 50), Aaronson (26, 67);
**Goals:** Crook 4/5.
**COUGARS:** 21 Matt Welham; 5 Davey Dixon; 33 Louis Sheriff; 23 Macauley Hallett; 1 Alfie Seeley; 38 Jordan Aitchison; 15 Jack Miller; 19 Matthew Bailey; 18 Chris Cullimore; 13 Jason Muranka; 35 Dom Horn; 22 Dan Parker; 9 James Feather. Subs (all used): 8 Jack Coventry; 10 Jamie Thackray; 27 Lewis Wray; 36 Ryan Wright.
**Try:** Muranka (80); **Goals:** Miller 0/1.
**Rugby Leaguer & League Express Men of the Match:**
*Oldham:* Danny Langtree; *Cougars:* Macauley Hallett.
**Penalty count:** 8-8; **Half-time:** 16-0;
**Referee:** Kevin Moore; **Attendance:** 591.

**WORKINGTON TOWN 54 COVENTRY BEARS 16**

**TOWN:** 1 Ryan Fieldhouse; 2 Tyllar Mellor; 26 Calvin Wellington; 4 Perry Singleton; - Russ Bolton; 6 Jamie Doran; 7 Carl Forber; 8 Oliver Wilkes; 9 Sean Penkywicz; 25 Fuifui Moimoi; 10 Stevie Scholey; 12 Gordon Maudling; 11 Danny Tickle. Subs (all used): 14 Andrew Dawson; 15 Tom Curwen; 13 Karl Olstrom; 17 Dec O'Donnell.
**Tries:** Mellor (4, 42), Doran (6), Scholey (18), Singleton (38), Wellington (39), Fieldhouse (46, 80), Bolton (56), Curwen (61); **Goals:** Forber 6/9, Moimoi 1/1.
**BEARS:** 1 Elliot Hall; 5 Errol Carter; 3 Hayden Freeman; 4 Kameron Pearce-Paul; 2 Reece Rance; 6 Matthew Davies; 7 Nathan Conroy; 8 Peter Ryan; 9 Sam Davis; 10 Will Tully; 11 Jacob Jones; 12 Kieran Sherratt; 13 Chris Barratt. Subs (all used): 14 Brad Sheridan; 15 Harry Kaufman; 20 Cameron Stewart; 16 Zak Fellows.
**Tries:** S Davis (9), Jones (29), Fellows (68); **Goals:** Hall 2/3.
**Rugby Leaguer & League Express Men of the Match:**
*Town:* Ryan Fieldhouse; *Bears:* Sam Davis.
**Penalty count:** 7-7; **Half-time:** 26-12;
**Referee:** Brad Milligan; **Attendance:** 895
*(at Borough Park).*

## ROUND 13

*Saturday 22nd June 2019*

**DONCASTER 18 NEWCASTLE THUNDER 19**

**DONCASTER:** 6 Jordan Howden; 16 Guy Armitage; 3 Connor Bower; 4 Jason Tali; 5 Sam Doherty; 30 Watson Boas; 7 Matty Beharrell; 31 Levy Nzoungou; 9 Kyle Kesik; 14 Connor Scott; 26 Menzie Yere; 22 Brad Foster; 13 Jordie Hedges. Subs (all used): 10 Ryan Boyle; 24 Jack Brown; 8 Russ Spiers; 25 Jez Litten.
**Tries:** Doherty (19, 56, 64); **Goals:** Beharrell 3/3.
**THUNDER:** 1 Lewis Young; 19 Misi Taulapapa; 3 Joe Brown; 4 Kieran Gill; 5 Alex Clegg; 6 Nick Newman; 7 Mikey Lewis; 8 Liam McAvoy; 9 Keal Carlile; 10 Jared Blanke; 13 Harry Aldous; 18 Rhys Clarke; 11 Joel Edwards. Subs (all used): 14 Evan Simons; 15 Sam Luckley; 16 Jack Aldous; 17 Aaron Ollett.
**Tries:** Edwards (5), McAvoy (10), Lewis (36);
**Goals:** Lewis 3/3; **Field goal:** Newman (79).
**Rugby Leaguer & League Express Men of the Match:**
*Doncaster:* Sam Doherty; *Thunder:* Mikey Lewis.
**Penalty count:** 3-2; **Half-time:** 6-18;
**Referee:** Matt Rossleigh; **Attendance:** 549
*(at LD Nutrition Stadium, Featherstone).*

**KEIGHLEY COUGARS 38 LONDON SKOLARS 26**

**COUGARS:** 38 Jordan Aitchison; 20 Jordan Fitzpatrick-Parry; 4 Will Cooke; 23 Macauley Hallett; 21 Matt Welham; 15 Jack Miller; 7 Benn Hardcastle; 19 Matthew Bailey; 18 Chris Cullimore; 27 Lewis Wray; 35 Dom Horn; 13 Jason Muranka; 9 James Feather. Subs (all used): 8 Jack Coventry; 10 Jamie Thackray; 11 Josh Lynam; 36 Ryan Wright.
**Tries:** Fitzpatrick-Parry (10), Muranka (19), Aitchison (25), Miller (36), Wright (51), Feather (56);
**Goals:** Hardcastle 7/7.
**SKOLARS:** 1 James Barran; 2 Iliess Macani; 3 Omari Caro; 4 Lameck Juma; 5 Elliot Jennings; 6 Jy-mel Coleman; 7 Jermaine Coleman; 10 Judd Greenhalgh; 9 Neil Thorman; 22 Mike Greenhalgh; 11 Jordan Williams; 13 Daniel Hindmarsh; 12 Lamont Bryan. Subs (all used): 14 Mike Bishay; 15 Matthew Davies; 16 Robert Tuliatu; 17 Liam Scott.
**Tries:** Macani (40, 42), Scott (60), Bishay (76);
**Goals:** Thorman 3/3, Barran 2/2.
**Sin bin:** Tuliatu (19) - dangerous challenge.
**Rugby Leaguer & League Express Men of the Match:**
*Cougars:* Jason Muranka; *Skolars:* Iliess Macani.
**Penalty count:** 7-5; **Half-time:** 24-8;
**Referee:** Michael Smaill; **Attendance:** 686.

**WEST WALES RAIDERS 10 HUNSLET 72**

**RAIDERS:** 1 Phil Cowburn; 2 Robert Matamosi; 3 Emosi Nadaubale; 4 Paddy Jennings; 23 Mickael Sabour; 9 Liam Rice-Wilson; 7 Tyler Hunt; 10 Sam Herron; 19 Mitch Shaw; 14 Dalton Desmond-Walker; 15 Archie Snook; 20 Mike Connor; 12 Morgan Evans. Subs (all used): 13 Dan Maiden; 17 Chris Vitalini; 18 Ryan Shallish; 24 Callum Mulkeen.
**Tries:** Matamosi (43, 80); **Goals:** Cowburn 1/2.
**HUNSLET:** 1 Jimmy Watson; 2 Gareth Potts; 23 Nathan Chappell; 3 Tom Ashton; 5 Dale Bloomfield; 21 Reece Dean; 22 Danny Nicklas; 16 Zach Braham; 9 Jack Lee; 10 Adam Robinson; 4 Ben Heaton; 20 Vila Halafihi; 13 Mike Emmett. Subs (all used): - Romain Pallares; 15 Michael Haley; 17 Dan Hawksworth; 24 Tommy Brierley.
**Tries:** Potts (3, 16, 20), Lee (7, 25), Watson (34), Dean (37), Halafihi (49, 63), Robinson (53), Heaton (56, 69), Chappell (75); **Goals:** Dean 10/13.
**Rugby Leaguer & League Express Men of the Match:**
*Raiders:* Robert Matamosi; *Hunslet:* Jack Lee.
**Penalty count:** 6-6; **Half-time:** 0-40;
**Referee:** Craig Smith; **Attendance:** 283.

*Sunday 23rd June 2019*

**WHITEHAVEN 22 NORTH WALES CRUSADERS 24**

**WHITEHAVEN:** 3 Chris Taylor; 19 Andrew Bulman; 23 Jason Mossop; 4 Jessie Joe Parker; 5 Dave Thompson; 1 Sam Forrester; 7 Callum Phillips; 8 Marc Shackley; 14 Sam Dowsett; 26 Carl Forster; 20 Scott McAvoy; 12 Jake Moore; 13 Tom Wilkinson. Subs (all used): 6 Dion Aiye; 15 Connor Holliday; 24 Ethan Kelly; 9 James Newton.
**Tries:** Shackley (15), McAvoy (30, 35), C Phillips (70);
**Goals:** Moore 3/3, Holliday 0/1.
**CRUSADERS:** 1 Lewis Fairhurst; 4 Dante Morley-Samuels; 3 Matt Reid; 2 Earl Hurst; 5 Rob Massam; 6 Steve Roper; 7 Ryan Smith; 8 Jonny Walker; 9 Karl Ashall; 17 Brad Brennan; 11 Jack Houghton; 12 Stephen Wild; 13 Kenny Baker. Subs (all used): 14 Kenny Hughes; 21 Callum Hazzard; 10 Warren Thompson; 18 Joe Ryan.
**Tries:** Hurst (21), Baker (25), Massam (38, 77), Ashall (79);
**Goals:** Fairhurst 2/5.
**Rugby Leaguer & League Express Men of the Match:**
*Whitehaven:* Jake Moore; *Crusaders:* Rob Massam.
**Penalty count:** 5-5; **Half-time:** 18-16;
**Referee:** Nick Bennett; **Attendance:** 781.

**WORKINGTON TOWN 16 OLDHAM 26**

**TOWN:** 1 Ryan Fieldhouse; 2 Tyllar Mellor; 26 Calvin Wellington; 4 Perry Singleton; 23 Russ Bolton; 6 Jamie Doran; 9 Sean Penkywicz; 8 Oliver Wilkes; 17 Dec O'Donnell; 25 Fuifui Moimoi; 10 Stevie Scholey; 12 Gordon Maudling; 14 Andrew Dawson. Subs (all used): 20 Jonathan Walsh; 15 Tom Curwen; 22 Sam Hopkins; 27 Blain Marwood.
**Tries:** Maudling (7), Singleton (9), Penkywicz (67);
**Goals:** Doran 2/3.
**Sin bin:** Maudling (43) - dangerous contact.
**OLDHAM:** 5 Ritchie Hawkyard; 27 Harry Maders; 3 Zack McComb; 23 Cameron Leeming; 28 Harry Aaronson; 15 Adam Brook; 7 Dave Hewitt; 8 Phil Joy; 9 Gareth Owen; 10 Scott Law; 25 Danny Bridge; 16 Danny Langtree; 24 Liam Bent. Subs (all used): 20 Matty Wilkinson; 13 Jack Spencer; 12 Emmerson Whittel; 18 Ben Davies.
**Tries:** Hewitt (3), Langtree (16, 51), Hawkyard (72);
**Goals:** Hewitt 5/5.
**Sin bin:** Bridge (46) - interference.
**Rugby Leaguer & League Express Men of the Match:**
*Town:* Sean Penkywicz; *Oldham:* Danny Langtree.
**Penalty count:** 7-7; **Half-time:** 10-14;
**Referee:** Steve Race; **Attendance:** 1,013 *(at Borough Park).*

## ROUND 14

*Saturday 29th June 2019*

**COVENTRY BEARS 10 DONCASTER 54**

**BEARS:** 1 Elliot Hall; 2 Hayden Freeman; 3 Kadeem Williams; 4 Kameron Pearce-Paul; 5 Reece Rance; 6 Joe Sanderson; 7 Nathan Conroy; 8 Lewis Taylor; 9 Sam Davis; 10 Ollie Purslow; 11 Kieran Sherratt; 12 Harry Kaufman; 13 Chris Barratt. Subs (all used): 14 Cameron Stewart; 15 Jack Ray; 16 Jack Daynes; 17 Lawrence Haywood.
**Tries:** Hall (25), Rance (80); **Goals:** Sanderson 1/2.
**Dismissal:** Ray (51) - fighting.
**DONCASTER:** 1 Kieran Buchanan; 29 Kieron Lawton; 3 Connor Bower; 4 Jason Tali; 5 Sam Doherty; 30 Watson Boas; 7 Matty Beharrell; 28 Jack Brown; 9 Kyle Kesik; 10 Ryan Boyle; 22 Brad Foster; - Evan Hodgson; - Dean Hadley. Subs (all used): 13 Jordie Hedges; 14 Connor Scott; 8 Russ Spiers; 2 Richard Owen.
**Tries:** Tali (5, 20, 43), Buchanan (30, 70), Hedges (36, 66), Connor Scott (56), Boas (60), Lawton (75);
**Goals:** Buchanan 7/9, Beharrell 0/1.
**Dismissal:** Spiers (51) - fighting.

**Rugby Leaguer & League Express Men of the Match:**
*Bears:* Jack Ray; *Doncaster:* Jason Tali.
**Penalty count:** 7-10; **Half-time:** 6-20;
**Referee:** Aaron Moore; **Attendance:** 386
*(at Ivor Preece Field, Broadstreet).*

**LONDON SKOLARS 6 WHITEHAVEN 28**

**SKOLARS:** 2 Iliess Macani; 20 Mo Agoro; 3 Jordan Williams; 4 Lameck Juma; 5 Omari Caro; 6 Mike Bishay; 7 Harry Smith; 10 Judd Greenhalgh; 9 Neil Thorman; 22 Mike Greenhalgh; 1 Joe Shorrocks; 12 Ronny Palumbo; 13 Daniel Hindmarsh. Subs (all used): 14 Matthew Davies; 15 Lamont Bryan; 16 Robert Tuliatu; 17 Liam Scott.
**Try:** Juma (42); **Goals:** Smith 1/1.
**WHITEHAVEN:** 2 Jordan Burns; 5 Dave Thompson; 3 Chris Taylor; 23 Jason Mossop; 19 Andrew Bulman; 1 Sam Forrester; 7 Callum Phillips; 8 Marc Shackley; 14 Sam Dowsett; 10 Kris Coward; 25 Kurt Maudling; 15 Connor Holliday; 13 Tom Wilkinson. Subs (all used): 6 Dion Aiye; 24 Ethan Kelly; 9 James Newton; 18 Jordan Thomson.
**Tries:** Coward (15), Forrester (33), D Thompson (37), Holliday (47), C Phillips (70); **Goals:** Holliday 4/6.
**Sin bin:** D Thompson (78) - trip.
**Rugby Leaguer & League Express Men of the Match:**
*Skolars:* Lamont Bryan; *Whitehaven:* Callum Phillips.
**Penalty count:** 8-7; **Half-time:** 0-18;
**Referee:** John McMullen; **Attendance:** 442.

*Sunday 30th June 2019*

**NORTH WALES CRUSADERS 14**
**KEIGHLEY COUGARS 6**

**CRUSADERS:** 1 Lewis Fairhurst; 2 Dave Eccleston; 3 Matt Reid; 4 Earl Hurst; 5 Dante Morley-Samuels; 6 Steve Roper; 7 Ryan Smith; 18 Jonny Walker; 15 Kenny Hughes; 17 Joe Ryan; 11 Kenny Baker; 12 Simon Atherton; 13 Karl Ashall. Subs (all used): 14 Declan Gregory; 9 Ben Stead; - Callum Hazzard; 10 Warren Thompson.
**Tries:** Hurst (31), Ashall (42); **Goals:** Stead 3/3.
**COUGARS:** 31 Taylor Prell; 20 Jordan Fitzpatrick-Parry; 4 Will Cooke; 23 Macauley Hallett; 21 Matt Welham; 15 Jack Miller; 7 Benn Hardcastle; 19 Matthew Bailey; 18 Chris Cullimore; 27 Lewis Wray; 22 Dan Parker; 13 Jason Muranka; 9 James Feather. Subs (all used): 8 Jack Coventry; 10 Jamie Thackray; 36 Ryan Wright; 39 Spencer Darley.
**Try:** Prell (21); **Goals:** Hardcastle 1/1.
**Rugby Leaguer & League Express Men of the Match:**
*Crusaders:* Earl Hurst; *Cougars:* Taylor Prell.
**Penalty count:** 5-3; **Half-time:** 8-6;
**Referee:** Kevin Moore; **Attendance:** 315.

**NEWCASTLE THUNDER 48 WORKINGTON TOWN 10**

**THUNDER:** 5 Alex Clegg; 19 Misi Taulapapa; 3 Joe Brown; 4 Kieran Gill; 11 Matthew Wright; 6 Nick Newman; 7 Mikey Lewis; 8 Liam McAvoy; 9 Keal Carlile; 10 Joel Edwards; 18 Rhys Clarke; 17 Conor Fitzsimmons; 13 Harry Aldous. Subs (all used): 12 Sam Luckley; 15 Jared Blanke; 14 Evan Simons; 20 Jack Aldous.
**Tries:** Brown (11), Wright (13, 64), Lewis (16, 67, 74), Taulapapa (19, 25, 57), Clarke (80);
**Goals:** Lewis 1/5, Newman 0/1, Wright 3/4.
**TOWN:** 1 Ryan Fieldhouse; 2 Tyllar Mellor; 18 Calvin Wellington; 4 Perry Singleton; 20 Jonathan Walsh; 6 Jamie Doran; 21 Oliver Russell; 10 Stevie Scholey; 17 Dec O'Donnell; 25 Fuifui Moimoi; 5 Sam Hewitt; 12 Gordon Maudling; 11 Danny Tickle. Subs (all used): 8 Oliver Wilkes; 14 Andrew Dawson; 15 Tom Curwen; 9 Sean Penkywicz.
**Tries:** Penkywicz (48), Doran (59); **Goals:** Doran 1/2.
**Rugby Leaguer & League Express Men of the Match:**
*Thunder:* Nick Newman; *Town:* Jamie Doran.
**Penalty count:** 5-5; **Half-time:** 22-0;
**Referee:** Tom Crashley; **Attendance:** 1,077.

**OLDHAM 56 WEST WALES RAIDERS 6**

**OLDHAM:** 4 Jack Holmes; 28 Harry Aaronson; 3 Zack McComb; 29 Cameron Leeming; 27 Harry Maders; 15 Adam Brook; 7 Dave Hewitt; 8 Phil Joy; 20 Matty Wilkinson; 10 Scott Law; 16 Danny Langtree; 25 Danny Bridge; 17 Nick Gregson. Subs: 12 Emmerson Whittel; 19 Jamie Greenwood; 9 Gareth Owen; 6 Paul Crook (not used).
**Tries:** Langtree (10, 13, 20), Leeming (26, 52), Greenwood (40), Owen (42), Maders (47), McComb (60), Wilkinson (74, 78); **Goals:** Hewitt 6/11.
**RAIDERS:** 1 Phil Cowburn; 4 Paddy Jennings; 3 Emosi Nadaubale; 15 Archie Snook; 25 Mickael Sabour; 22 Steve Parry; 7 Tyler Hunt; 10 Sam Herron; 19 Mitch Shaw; 14 Dalton Desmond-Walker; 18 Gioele Celerino; 12 Morgan Evans; 6 Ashley Bateman. Subs (all used): 13 Dan Maiden; 9 Liam Rice-Wilson; 16 Nye Walker; 24 Callum Mulkeen.
**Try:** Parry (69); **Goals:** Cowburn 1/1.
**Rugby Leaguer & League Express Men of the Match:**
*Oldham:* Danny Langtree; *Raiders:* Steve Parry.
**Penalty count:** 5-3; **Half-time:** 28-0;
**Referee:** Liam Staveley; **Attendance:** 552.

## ROUND 15

*Saturday 6th July 2019*

**LONDON SKOLARS 20 COVENTRY BEARS 36**

**SKOLARS:** 1 Mike Bishay; 5 Mo Agoro; 3 Ronny Palumbo; 4 Lameck Juma; 2 Iliess Macani; 14 Richard Wilkinson; 6 James Barran; 10 Judd Greenhalgh; 9 Neil Thorman; 22 Mike Greenhalgh; 11 Jordan Williams; 12 Lamont Bryan; 13 Daniel Hindmarsh. Subs (all used): 20 Matthew Davies; 17 Liam Scott; 15 Robert Tuliatu; 16 Jy-mel Coleman.
**Tries:** Juma (4, 47), Agoro (7, 26); **Goals:** Thorman 2/4.
**BEARS:** 1 Elliot Hall; 2 Zak Fellows; 3 Hayden Freeman; 4 Jacob Jones; 5 Reece Rance; 6 Nathan Conroy; 7 Joe Sanderson; 8 Peter Ryan; 9 Sam Davis; 10 Ollie Purslow; 11 Kieran Sherratt; 12 Harry Kaufman; 15 Nyle Flynn. Subs (all used): 14 Errol Carter; 13 Chris Barratt; 16 Jack Ray; 20 Lewis Taylor.
**Tries:** S Davis (23), Hall (36, 59), Freeman (54), Sherratt (72, 77); **Goals:** Sanderson 6/6.
**Rugby Leaguer & League Express Men of the Match:** *Skolars:* Robert Tuliatu; *Bears:* Kieran Sherratt.
**Penalty count:** 5-6; **Half-time:** 16-12;
**Referee:** Craig Smith; **Attendance:** 216.

**WEST WALES RAIDERS 0 DONCASTER 72**

**RAIDERS:** 1 Phil Cowburn; 4 Paddy Jennings; 6 Ashley Bateman; 24 Callum Mulkeen; 25 Mickael Sabour; 22 Steve Parry; 19 Mitch Shaw; 14 Dalton Desmond-Walker; 9 Liam Rice-Wilson; 10 Sam Herron; 18 Gioele Celerino; 12 Morgan Evans; 13 Dan Maiden. Subs (all used): 16 Nye Walker; 17 Chris Vitalini; 20 Ryan Shallish; 26 Matt Jones.
**Sin bin:** Desmond-Walker (70) - dangerous contact.
**DONCASTER:** 2 Richard Owen; 5 Sam Doherty; 3 Connor Bower; 4 Jason Tali; 19 Matty Chrimes; 13 Jordie Hedges; 24 Watson Boas; 14 Connor Scott; 9 Kyle Kesik; 8 Russ Spiers; 22 Brad Foster; 28 Evan Hodgson; 27 Levy Nzoungou. Subs (all used): 25 Stefanos Bastas; 10 Ryan Boyle; 1 Connor Wynne; 26 Menzie Yere.
**Tries:** Doherty (2, 64, 71, 78), Kesik (8), Foster (12), Boas (19), Connor Scott (22), Bastas (36), Bower (42, 46, 58), Owen (51), Tali (74);
**Goals:** Hedges 8/14.
**Rugby Leaguer & League Express Men of the Match:** *Raiders:* Ashley Bateman; *Doncaster:* Connor Bower.
**Penalty count:** 5-10; **Half-time:** 0-36;
**Referee:** Andrew Sweet; **Attendance:** 198.

*Sunday 7th July 2019*

**NORTH WALES CRUSADERS 30 WORKINGTON TOWN 18**

**CRUSADERS:** 1 Lewis Fairhurst; 2 Dave Eccleston; 3 Matt Reid; 4 Earl Hurst; 5 Dante Morley-Samuels; 6 Steve Roper; 7 Ben Stead; 8 Brad Brennan; 14 Kenny Hughes; 17 Jonny Walker; 11 Kenny Baker; 12 Simon Atherton; 13 Stephen Wild. Subs (all used): 15 Declan Gregory; 18 Jack Houghton; 21 Callum Hazzard; 10 Warren Thompson.
**Tries:** Stead (17), Roper (25), Morley-Samuels (30, 63), Baker (70); **Goals:** Stead 5/7.
**TOWN:** 2 Tyllar Mellor; 16 Scott Rooke; 21 Tyler Lancaster; 4 Perry Singleton; - Russ Bolton; 6 Jamie Doran; 7 Carl Forber; 25 Fuifui Moimoi; 9 Sean Penkywicz; 14 Andrew Dawson; 10 Stevie Scholey; 11 Danny Tickle; 22 Sam Hopkins. Subs (all used): 17 Dec O'Donnell; 20 Jonathan Walsh; 15 Tom Curwen; 8 Oliver Wilkes.
**Tries:** Forber (9), Singleton (35), O'Donnell (80);
**Goals:** Forber 3/3.
**Rugby Leaguer & League Express Men of the Match:** *Crusaders:* Simon Atherton; *Town:* Fuifui Moimoi.
**Penalty count:** 8-5; **Half-time:** 18-12;
**Referee:** John McMullen; **Attendance:** 363.

**HUNSLET 12 NEWCASTLE THUNDER 26**

**HUNSLET:** 25 James Woodburn-Hall; 2 Gareth Potts; 4 Ben Heaton; 23 Nathan Chappell; 1 Jimmy Watson; 21 Reece Dean; 22 Danny Nicklas; 31 Jon Luke Kirby; 20 Vila Halafihi; 10 Adam Robinson; 11 Josh Tonks; 30 Charlie Martin; 13 Mike Emmett. Subs (all used): 3 Tom Ashton; 15 Michael Haley; 17 Dan Hawksworth; - Romain Pallares.
**Tries:** Woodburn-Hall (2), Tonks (22); **Goals:** Dean 2/3.
**Sin bin:** Heaton (36) - fighting;
Dean (76) - high tackle on Gill.
**THUNDER:** 5 Alex Clegg; 19 Misi Taulapapa; 11 Matthew Wright; 4 Kieran Gill; 3 Joe Brown; 6 Nick Newman; 7 Mikey Lewis; 8 Liam McAvoy; 9 Keal Carlile; 10 Joel Edwards; 17 Conor Fitzsimmons; 18 Rhys Clarke; 13 Harry Aldous. Subs (all used): 14 Evan Simons; 15 Jared Blanke; 20 Jack Aldous; 12 Sam Luckley.
**Tries:** Brown (10), Clarke (45), Simons (53), Gill (65), Carlile (80); **Goals:** Wright 3/5.
**Sin bin:** Brown (36) - fighting.
**Rugby Leaguer & League Express Men of the Match:** *Hunslet:* Josh Tonks; *Thunder:* Evan Simons.
**Penalty count:** 5-5; **Half-time:** 12-4;
**Referee:** Matt Rossleigh; **Attendance:** 746.

**WHITEHAVEN 16 OLDHAM 10**

**WHITEHAVEN:** 2 Jordan Burns; 19 Andrew Bulman; 23 Jason Mossop; 3 Chris Taylor; 5 Dave Thompson; 1 Sam Forrester; 7 Callum Phillips; 8 Marc Shackley; 14 Sam Dowsett; 10 Kris Coward; - Ellis Gillam; 15 Connor Holliday; 13 Tom Wilkinson. Subs (all used): 6 Dion Aiye; 26 Carl Forster; 24 Ethan Kelly; 9 James Newton.
**Tries:** D Thompson (41), Burns (71);
**Goals:** Holliday 2/3, Burns 2/4.
**OLDHAM:** 5 Ritchie Hawkyard; 28 Harry Aaronson; 3 Zack McComb; 29 Cameron Leeming; 4 Jack Holmes; 15 Adam Brook; 7 Dave Hewitt; 8 Phil Joy; 9 Gareth Owen; 10 Scott Law; 25 Danny Bridge; 16 Danny Langtree; 24 Liam Bent. Subs (all used): 13 Jack Spencer; 12 Emmerson Whittel; 20 Matty Wilkinson; 19 Jamie Greenwood.
**Tries:** Law (15), McComb (60); **Goals:** Hewitt 1/2.
**Rugby Leaguer & League Express Men of the Match:** *Whitehaven:* Jordan Burns; *Oldham:* Scott Law.
**Penalty count:** 9-5; **Half-time:** 0-6;
**Referee:** Tom Crashley; **Attendance:** 1,102.

## ROUND 16

*Sunday 14th July 2019*

**COVENTRY BEARS 20 HUNSLET 48**

**BEARS:** 1 Elliot Hall; 5 Errol Carter; 3 Hayden Freeman; 4 Jacob Jones; 2 Reece Rance; 6 Cobi Green; 7 Nathan Conroy; 8 Lewis Taylor; 9 Harvey Whiteley; 10 Jack Ray; 11 Kieran Sherratt; 12 Sam Scott; 13 Harry Kaufman. Subs (all used): 14 Brad Sheridan; 15 Ollie Purslow; 16 Cameron Stewart; 17 Chris Barratt.
**Tries:** Taylor (7), Rance (32), Hall (50); **Goals:** Hall 4/4.
**HUNSLET:** 1 Jimmy Watson; 2 Gareth Potts; 23 Nathan Chappell; 3 Tom Ashton; 5 Dale Bloomfield; 21 Reece Dean; 7 Simon Brown; 16 Zach Braham; 20 Vila Halafihi; 10 Adam Robinson; 11 Josh Tonks; 30 Charlie Martin; 13 Mike Emmett. Subs (all used): 15 Michael Haley; 17 Dan Hawksworth; 31 Jon Luke Kirby; 14 Ryan Wright.
**Tries:** Ashton (20), Tonks (30), Potts (35, 63), Chappell (36), Watson (57), Dean (59, 73), Bloomfield (65);
**Goals:** Dean 6/9.
**Rugby Leaguer & League Express Men of the Match:** *Bears:* Elliot Hall; *Hunslet:* Reece Dean.
**Penalty count:** 8-7; **Half-time:** 14-22;
**Referee:** Tom Crashley; **Attendance:** 420
*(at Webb Ellis Road, Rugby).*

**DONCASTER 12 WHITEHAVEN 22**

**DONCASTER:** 1 Connor Wynne; 5 Sam Doherty; 3 Connor Bower; 4 Jason Tali; 19 Matty Chrimes; 33 Rangi Chase; 7 Matty Beharrell; 10 Ryan Boyle; 9 Kyle Kesik; 14 Connor Scott; 26 Evan Hodgson; 30 Danny Washbrook; 13 Jordie Hedges. Subs: 2 Richard Owen (not used); 31 Jack Brown; 25 Stefanos Bastas; 24 Jez Litten.
**Tries:** Doherty (7), Chase (27); **Goals:** Beharrell 2/2.
**Sin bin:** Beharrell (78) - dissent.
**WHITEHAVEN:** 2 Jordan Burns; 15 Connor Holliday; 4 Jessie Joe Parker; 23 Jason Mossop; 19 Andrew Bulman; 3 Chris Taylor; 7 Callum Phillips; 8 Marc Shackley; 14 Sam Dowsett; 10 Kris Coward; 27 Ellis Gillam; 25 Kurt Maudling; 13 Tom Wilkinson. Subs (all used): 21 Jake Bradley; 26 Carl Forster; 24 Ethan Kelly; 9 James Newton.
**Tries:** Forster (34, 41), Bulman (71); **Goals:** Holliday 5/5.
**Dismissal:** Burns (78) - punching.
**Rugby Leaguer & League Express Men of the Match:** *Doncaster:* Rangi Chase; *Whitehaven:* Jessie Joe Parker.
**Penalty count:** 5-3; **Half-time:** 12-8;
**Referee:** Billy Pearson; **Attendance:** 780
*(at LD Nutrition Stadium, Featherstone).*

**KEIGHLEY COUGARS 50 WEST WALES RAIDERS 18**

**COUGARS:** 31 Taylor Prell; 5 Davey Dixon; 4 Will Cooke; 23 Macauley Hallett; 1 Alfie Seeley; 15 Jack Miller; 7 Benn Hardcastle; 19 Matthew Bailey; 9 James Feather; 27 Lewis Wray; 12 Aaron Levy; 13 Jason Muranka; 22 Dan Parker. Subs (all used): 10 Jamie Thackray; 18 Chris Cullimore; 33 Louis Sheriff; 39 Spencer Darley.
**Tries:** Hallett (9), Cooke (35), Miller (38, 59, 72), Hardcastle (44, 63), Thackray (55), Muranka (78);
**Goals:** Hardcastle 7/9.
**Sin bin:** Hallett (45) - fighting.
**RAIDERS:** 1 Phil Cowburn; 21 Sam Baker; 15 Archie Snook; 6 Ashley Bateman; 23 Rowland Kaye; 22 Steve Parry; 7 Tyler Hunt; 14 Dalton Desmond-Walker; 19 Mitch Shaw; 10 Sam Herron; 13 Dan Maiden; 18 Gioele Celerino; 12 Morgan Evans. Subs (all used): 16 Nye Walker; 20 Alan Pope; 24 Callum Mulkeen; 25 Macauley Harris.
**Tries:** Shaw (19), Baker (50), M Evans (67);
**Goals:** Cowburn 3/3.
**Sin bin:** Pope (45) - fighting;
Hunt (53) - dangerous challenge on Seeley.
**Rugby Leaguer & League Express Men of the Match:** *Cougars:* Jack Miller; *Raiders:* Morgan Evans.
**Penalty count:** 9-8; **Half-time:** 16-6;
**Referee:** Joe Stearne; **Attendance:** 702.

**OLDHAM 46 NORTH WALES CRUSADERS 30**

**OLDHAM:** 5 Ritchie Hawkyard; 28 Harry Aaronson; 3 Zack McComb; 29 Cameron Leeming; 21 Lee Kershaw; 15 Adam Brook; 7 Dave Hewitt; 8 Phil Joy; 9 Gareth Owen; 13 Jack Spencer; 16 Danny Langtree; 25 Danny Bridge; 24 Liam Bent. Subs (all used): 12 Emmerson Whittel; 11 Ben Calland; 20 Matty Wilkinson; 10 Scott Law.
**Tries:** Hawkyard (7, 34), Bridge (25), Kershaw (28), Wilkinson (42), Joy (52), Aaronson (69, 77);
**Goals:** Hewitt 7/8.
**CRUSADERS:** 1 Dante Morley-Samuels; 2 Dave Eccleston; 3 Matt Reid; 4 Earl Hurst; 5 Rob Massam; 6 Steve Roper; 7 Ben Stead; 16 Brad Brennan; 9 Karl Ashall; 15 Jonny Walker; 11 Jack Houghton; 12 Simon Atherton; 13 Alex Eckley. Subs (all used): 14 Declan Gregory; 8 Callum Hazzard; 10 Warren Thompson; 17 Alex Thompson.
**Tries:** Stead (4), Atherton (48), Massam (60, 79), Gregory (63); **Goals:** Stead 5/7.
**Rugby Leaguer & League Express Men of the Match:** *Oldham:* Ritchie Hawkyard; *Crusaders:* Simon Atherton.
**Penalty count:** 4-6; **Half-time:** 22-10;
**Referee:** Liam Staveley; **Attendance:** 616.

**WORKINGTON TOWN 32 LONDON SKOLARS 22**

**TOWN:** 2 Tyllar Mellor; 20 Jonathan Walsh; 3 Sam Hewitt; 4 Perry Singleton; 16 Scott Rooke; 6 Jamie Doran; 7 Carl Forber; 25 Fuifui Moimoi; 17 Dec O'Donnell; 10 Stevie Scholey; 12 Gordon Maudling; 11 Danny Tickle; 14 Andrew Dawson. Subs: 13 Karl Olstrom (not used); 22 Sam Hopkins; 15 Tom Curwen; 19 Caine Barnes (not used).
**Tries:** Singleton (3), Doran (26, 79), O'Donnell (53), Mellor (58), Scholey (75); **Goals:** Forber 4/6.
**Dismissal:** O'Donnell (56) - punching.
**SKOLARS:** 2 Iliess Macani; 1 Elliot Jennings; 3 Omari Caro; 4 Lameck Juma; 5 Mo Agoro; 6 James Barran; 7 Mike Bishay; 18 Judd Greenhalgh; 9 Neil Thorman; 22 Mike Greenhalgh; 12 Robert Tuliatu; 11 Jordan Williams; 13 Lamont Bryan. Subs: 16 Liam Scott; 10 Matt Ross; 15 Ronny Palumbo; 14 Jermaine Coleman (not used).
**Tries:** J Greenhalgh (7), Barran (31), Macani (70);
**Goals:** Thorman 5/5.
**Sin bin:** Barran (55) - high tackle.
**Rugby Leaguer & League Express Men of the Match:** *Town:* Tyllar Mellor; *Skolars:* Iliess Macani.
**Penalty count:** 10-3; **Half-time:** 10-14;
**Referee:** Aaron Moore; **Attendance:** 810
*(at Borough Park).*

## ROUND 17

*Saturday 20th July 2019*

**NEWCASTLE THUNDER 34 LONDON SKOLARS 16**

**THUNDER:** 1 Lewis Young; 19 Misi Taulapapa; 11 Matthew Wright; 4 Kieran Gill; 5 Alex Clegg; 7 Nick Newman; 6 Mikey Lewis; 10 Joel Edwards; 9 Keal Carlile; 8 Liam McAvoy; 18 Rhys Clarke; 17 Conor Fitzsimmons; 13 Jack Aldous. Subs (all used): 27 Jared Blanke; 14 Evan Simons; 12 Sam Luckley; 20 Muizz Mustapha.
**Tries:** Lewis (17), Wright (29, 42, 68), Newman (63), Mustapha (75); **Goals:** Wright 5/6.
**SKOLARS:** 2 Iliess Macani; 5 Elliot Jennings; 3 Omari Caro; 4 Lameck Juma; 1 Jerome Yates; 6 James Barran; 23 Jy-mel Coleman; 18 Judd Greenhalgh; 9 Neil Thorman; 22 Mike Greenhalgh; 12 Robert Tuliatu; 11 Jordan Williams; 13 Mike Bishay. Subs (all used): 17 Liam Scott; 15 Matt Ross; 20 Ronny Palumbo; 8 Eddie Mbaraga.
**Tries:** Caro (48), Yates (52), Williams (60);
**Goals:** Thorman 2/3.
**Rugby Leaguer & League Express Men of the Match:** *Thunder:* Matthew Wright; *Skolars:* Jordan Williams.
**Penalty count:** 7-6; **Half-time:** 12-0;
**Referee:** Cameron Worsley; **Attendance:** 1,098.

**WEST WALES RAIDERS 44 COVENTRY BEARS 16**

**RAIDERS:** 1 Phil Cowburn; 21 Sam Baker; 6 Ashley Bateman; 15 Archie Snook; 23 Rowland Kaye; 22 Steve Parry; 7 Tyler Hunt; 14 Dalton Desmond-Walker; 19 Mitch Shaw; 10 Sam Herron; 13 Dan Maiden; 18 Gioele Celerino; 12 Morgan Evans. Subs (all used): 3 Nicolas Bertolas; 16 Nye Walker; 17 Chris Vitalini; 20 Alan Pope.
**Tries:** Desmond-Walker (6), Bateman (10, 51), M Evans (19), Snook (39, 60), Shaw (47), Parry (69);
**Goals:** Cowburn 6/8.

**BEARS:** 1 Elliot Hall; 5 Errol Carter; 3 Hayden Freeman; 4 Jacob Jones; 2 Reece Rance; 6 Cobi Green; 7 Joe Sanderson; 20 Ollie Purslow; 9 Harvey Whiteley; 8 Jack Ray; 11 Kieran Sherratt; 12 Harry Kaufman; 13 Chris Barratt. Subs (all used): 14 Brad Sheridan; 15 Cameron Stewart; 16 Dewi Billingham; 17 Zak Williams.
**Tries:** Rance (44), Carter (73), Green (75);
**Goals:** Sanderson 2/3.
**Rugby Leaguer & League Express Men of the Match:** *Raiders:* Morgan Evans; *Bears:* Jack Ray.
**Penalty count:** 7-7; **Half-time:** 20-0;
**Referee:** Michael Smaill; **Attendance:** 352.

*Sunday 21st July 2019*

**NORTH WALES CRUSADERS 0 DONCASTER 30**

**CRUSADERS:** 1 Lewis Fairhurst; 2 Dave Eccleston; 3 Matt Reid; 4 Simon Atherton; 5 Dante Morley-Samuels; 6 Steve Roper; 7 Ben Stead; 10 Warren Thompson; 9 Karl Ashall; 8 Brad Brennan; 11 Alex Eckley; 12 Kenny Baker; 13 Stephen Wild. Subs (all used): 14 Declan Gregory; 15 Ryan Smith; 20 Alex Thompson; 17 Jonny Walker.
**DONCASTER:** 1 Connor Wynne; 5 Sam Doherty; 3 Connor Bower; 4 Jason Tali; 19 Matty Chrimes; 33 Rangi Chase; 7 Matty Beharrell; 10 Ryan Boyle; 9 Kyle Kesik; 14 Connor Scott; 26 Evan Hodgson; 24 Danny Washbrook; 13 Jordie Hedges. Subs (all used): 27 Jack Brown; 2 Richard Owen; 22 Brad Foster; 29 Jez Litten.
**Tries:** Chrimes (14), Kesik (20), Tali (60), Bower (73), Connor Scott (79); **Goals:** Beharrell 4/5, Litten 1/1.
**Rugby Leaguer & League Express Men of the Match:** *Crusaders:* Ben Stead; *Doncaster:* Danny Washbrook.
**Penalty count:** 9-5; **Half-time:** 0-14;
**Referee:** Michael Mannifield; **Attendance:** 372.

**WORKINGTON TOWN 52 KEIGHLEY COUGARS 4**

**TOWN:** 2 Tyllar Mellor; 16 Scott Rooke; 23 Sam Hewitt; 4 Perry Singleton; 20 Jonathan Walsh; 6 Jamie Doran; 7 Carl Forber; 14 Andrew Dawson; 9 Sean Penkywicz; 10 Stevie Scholey; 11 Danny Tickle; 12 Gordon Maudling; 17 Dec O'Donnell. Subs (all used): 15 Tom Curwen; 19 Caine Barnes; 22 Sam Hopkins; 25 Fuifui Moimoi.
**Tries:** O'Donnell (7), Walsh (15), Moimoi (33), Singleton (38), Forber (42), Curwen (48), Maudling (68), Hewitt (74), Rooke (80); **Goals:** Forber 6/7, Doran 2/3.
**Sin bin:** Hewitt (77) - trip on Miller.
**COUGARS:** 31 Taylor Prell; 5 Davey Dixon; 4 Will Cooke; 23 Macauley Hallett; 1 Alfie Seeley; 15 Jack Miller; 7 Benn Hardcastle; 19 Matthew Bailey; 9 James Feather; 27 Lewis Wray; 12 Aaron Levy; 13 Jason Muranka; 22 Dan Parker. Subs (all used): 18 Chris Cullimore; 30 Harvey Hallas; 33 Louis Sheriff; 39 Spencer Darley.
**Try:** Muranka (19); **Goals:** Hardcastle 0/1.
**Rugby Leaguer & League Express Men of the Match:** *Town:* Perry Singleton; *Cougars:* Alfie Seeley.
**Penalty count:** 5-7; **Half-time:** 24-4;
**Referee:** Kevin Moore; **Attendance:** 947.

*Saturday 27th July 2019*

**HUNSLET 12 WHITEHAVEN 19**

**HUNSLET:** 1 Jimmy Watson; 2 Gareth Potts; 23 Nathan Chappell; 3 Tom Ashton; 24 Reece Chapman-Smith; 7 Simon Brown; 21 Reece Dean; 31 Jon Luke Kirby; 9 Jack Lee; 10 Adam Robinson; 11 Josh Tonks; 12 Duane Straugheir; 20 Vila Halafihi. Subs (all used): 13 Mike Emmett; 15 Michael Haley; 16 Zach Braham; 14 Ryan Wright.
**Try:** Chappell (46); **Goals:** Dean 4/4.
**Sin bin:** Brown (59) - dissent.
**On report:**
Robinson (61) - alleged late challenge on C Phillips.
**WHITEHAVEN:** 2 Jordan Burns; 5 Dave Thompson; 3 Chris Taylor; 23 Jason Mossop; 19 Andrew Bulman; 1 Sam Forrester; 7 Callum Phillips; 8 Marc Shackley; 14 Sam Dowsett; 10 Kris Coward; 11 Brett Phillips; 27 Ellis Gillam; 13 Tom Wilkinson. Subs (all used): 26 Carl Forster; 15 Connor Holliday; 9 James Newton; 24 Ethan Kelly.
**Tries:** Kelly (56), D Thompson (67);
**Goals:** Burns 3/3, Holliday 2/3; **Field goal:** Holliday (75).
**Rugby Leaguer & League Express Men of the Match:** *Hunslet:* Adam Robinson; *Whitehaven:* Callum Phillips.
**Penalty count:** 5-13; **Half-time:** 4-2;
**Referee:** Michael Mannifield; **Attendance:** 540.

## ROUND 18

*Saturday 3rd August 2019*

**LONDON SKOLARS 14 OLDHAM 15**

**SKOLARS:** 2 Iliess Macani; 5 Mo Agoro; 3 Omari Caro; 4 Elliot Jennings; 1 Jerome Yates; 14 Richard Wilkinson; 21 Jy-mel Coleman; 10 Judd Greenhalgh; 9 Neil Thorman; 22 Mike Greenhalgh; 12 Robert Tuliatu; 11 Jordan Williams; 18 Eddie Mbaraga. Subs (all used): 20 Matthew Davies; 15 Matt Ross; 17 Liam Scott; 16 Lamont Bryan.
**Tries:** Macani (20), Caro (79); **Goals:** Thorman 3/3.
**OLDHAM:** 5 Ritchie Hawkyard; 21 Lee Kershaw; 3 Zack McComb; 29 Cameron Leeming; 28 Harry Aaronson; 15 Adam Brook; 7 Dave Hewitt; 8 Phil Joy; 9 Gareth Owen; 13 Jack Spencer; 25 Danny Bridge; 16 Danny Langtree; 24 Liam Bent. Subs (all used): 10 Scott Law; 20 Matty Wilkinson; 30 Ed Smith; 17 Jimmy Beckett.
**Tries:** Leeming (3), Hewitt (14); **Goals:** Hewitt 3/3;
**Field goal:** Hewitt (45).
**Rugby Leaguer & League Express Men of the Match:** *Skolars:* Iliess Macani; *Oldham:* Dave Hewitt.
**Penalty count:** 6-5; **Half-time:** 6-14;
**Referee:** Liam Staveley; **Attendance:** 355.

**WEST WALES RAIDERS 6 NEWCASTLE THUNDER 68**

**RAIDERS:** 1 Phil Cowburn; 2 Robert Matamosi; 15 Archie Snook; 23 Rowland Kaye; 21 Sam Baker; 22 Steve Parry; 7 Tyler Hunt; 14 Dalton Desmond-Walker; 19 Mitch Shaw; 10 Sam Herron; 18 Gioele Celerino; 12 Morgan Evans; 13 Dan Maiden. Subs (all used): 4 Joe McClean; 16 Nye Walker; 17 Chris Vitalini; 20 Alan Pope.
**Try:** Parry (53); **Goals:** Cowburn 1/1.
**THUNDER:** 1 Lewis Young; 19 Misi Taulapapa; 17 Harry Aldous; 4 Kieran Gill; 5 Alex Clegg; 2 Quentin Laulu-Togaga'e; 6 Nick Newman; 8 Liam McAvoy; 9 Keal Carlile; 10 Joel Edwards; 12 Muizz Mustapha; 18 Rhys Clarke; 14 Evan Simons. Subs (all used): 20 Sam Luckley; 15 Jared Blanke; 11 Carne Doyle-Manga; 13 Aaron Ollett.
**Tries:** Edwards (3, 64), Clegg (9), Laulu-Togaga'e (25), Gill (28, 39, 45, 78), Young (36), Taulapapa (42), Clarke (58), Mustapha (72), Simons (80); **Goals:** Clarke 8/13.
**Rugby Leaguer & League Express Men of the Match:** *Raiders:* Phil Cowburn; *Thunder:* Kieran Gill.
**Penalty count:** 5-7; **Half-time:** 0-32;
**Referee:** John McMullen; **Attendance:** 302.

*Sunday 4th August 2019*

**COVENTRY BEARS 20 KEIGHLEY COUGARS 46**

**BEARS:** 1 Elliot Hall; 5 Errol Carter; 3 Hayden Freeman; 4 Kameron Pearce-Paul; 2 Reece Rance; 6 Brad Sheridan; 7 Nathan Conroy; 8 Lewis Taylor; 9 Sam Davis; 10 Jack Ray; 11 Kadeem Williams; 12 Jacob Jones; 13 Harry Kaufman. Subs (all used): 14 Harvey Whiteley; 20 Ollie Purslow; 16 Dewi Billingham; 21 Cameron Stewart.
**Tries:** S Davis (13), Hall (22, 80), Rance (78); **Goals:** Hall 2/4.
**COUGARS:** 1 Alfie Seeley; 5 Davey Dixon; 21 Matt Welham; 23 Macauley Hallett; 2 Adam Allerton; 15 Jack Miller; 9 James Feather; 8 Jack Coventry; 18 Chris Cullimore; 29 Spencer Darley; 22 Dan Parker; 13 Jason Muranka; 12 Aaron Levy. Subs (all used): 16 Kieran Moran; 25 Harvey Hallas; 19 Matthew Bailey; 24 Mark Barlow.
**Tries:** Hallett (2), Miller (6), Levy (26), Welham (33, 66), Dixon (43), Muranka (55, 61); **Goals:** Miller 7/8.
**Rugby Leaguer & League Express Men of the Match:** *Bears:* Sam Davis; *Cougars:* Jack Miller.
**Penalty count:** 9-5; **Half-time:** 10-22;
**Referee:** Aaron Moore; **Attendance:** 345
*(at Webb Ellis Road, Rugby).*

**HUNSLET 42 NORTH WALES CRUSADERS 18**

**HUNSLET:** 1 Jimmy Watson; 5 Dale Bloomfield; 23 Nathan Chappell; 30 Charlie Martin; 3 Tom Ashton; 6 Joe Sanderson; 7 Simon Brown; 16 Zach Braham; 9 Jack Lee; 31 Jon Luke Kirby; 11 Josh Tonks; 12 Duane Straugheir; 20 Vila Halafihi. Subs (all used): 32 Jordan Andrade; 15 Michael Haley; 17 Dan Hawksworth; 14 Ryan Wright.
**Tries:** Tonks (8), Straugheir (13), Kirby (23), Martin (40), Watson (50, 63), Andrade (75); **Goals:** Sanderson 7/7.
**Sin bin:** Watson (78) - delaying restart.
**CRUSADERS:** 1 Lewis Fairhurst; 2 Dave Eccleston; 3 Simon Atherton; 4 Jordan Penny; 5 Rob Massam; 6 Steve Roper; 7 Ben Stead; 17 Jonny Walker; 9 Karl Ashall; 18 Brad Brennan; 11 Matt Reid; 12 Stephen Wild; 13 Alex Eckley. Subs (all used): 14 Declan Gregory; 8 Callum Hazzard; 10 Warren Thompson; 20 Joe Ryan.
**Tries:** Gregory (30), Atherton (32), Walker (79);
**Goals:** Stead 3/3.
**Rugby Leaguer & League Express Men of the Match:** *Hunslet:* Joe Sanderson; *Crusaders:* Declan Gregory.
**Penalty count:** 7-8; **Half-time:** 24-12;
**Referee:** Kevin Moore; **Attendance:** 488.

**WHITEHAVEN 12 WORKINGTON TOWN 12**

**WHITEHAVEN:** 2 Jordan Burns; 19 Andrew Bulman; 23 Jason Mossop; 3 Chris Taylor; 5 Dave Thompson; 1 Sam Forrester; 7 Callum Phillips; 8 Marc Shackley; 14 Sam Dowsett; 10 Kris Coward; 27 Ellis Gillam; 11 Brett Phillips; 13 Tom Wilkinson. Subs (all used): 12 Jake Moore; 26 Carl Forster; 24 Ethan Kelly; 9 James Newton.
**Try:** Shackley (56); **Goals:** Burns 3/3, Moore 1/2.
**TOWN:** 2 Tyllar Mellor; 21 Russ Bolton; 18 Calvin Wellington; 4 Perry Singleton; 20 Jonathan Walsh; 6 Jamie Doran; 7 Carl Forber; 14 Andrew Dawson; 9 Sean Penkywicz; 10 Stevie Scholey; 11 Danny Tickle; 12 Gordon Maudling; 17 Dec O'Donnell. Subs (all used): 25 Fuifui Moimoi; 15 Tom Curwen; 19 Caine Barnes; 22 Sam Hopkins.
**Tries:** Wellington (37), Doran (46); **Goals:** Forber 2/2.
**Rugby Leaguer & League Express Men of the Match:** *Whitehaven:* Marc Shackley; *Town:* Jamie Doran.
**Penalty count:** 12-9; **Half-time:** 6-6;
**Referee:** Matt Rossleigh; **Attendance:** 2,360.

## ROUND 19

*Saturday 10th August 2019*

**KEIGHLEY COUGARS 10 HUNSLET 32**

**COUGARS:** 33 Louis Sheriff; 5 Davey Dixon; 21 Matt Welham; 23 Macauley Hallett; 31 Taylor Prell; 15 Jack Miller; 7 Benn Hardcastle; 8 Jack Coventry; 9 James Feather; 39 Spencer Darley; 22 Dan Parker; 13 Jason Muranka; 12 Aaron Levy. Subs (all used): 16 Kieran Moran; 17 Billy Gaylor; 19 Matthew Bailey; 25 Jack Arnold.
**Tries:** Dixon (33), Muranka (49); **Goals:** Hardcastle 1/2.
**Dismissal:** Parker (80) - headbutt.
**Sin bin:** Moran (39) - dangerous challenge;
Prell (78) - fighting.
**HUNSLET:** 1 Jimmy Watson; 25 Callum Lancaster; 3 Tom Ashton; 24 Reece Chapman-Smith; 5 Dale Bloomfield; 6 Joe Sanderson; 22 Danny Nicklas; 16 Zach Braham; 9 Jack Lee; 17 Dan Hawksworth; 11 Josh Tonks; 12 Duane Straugheir; 20 Vila Halafihi. Subs (all used): 13 Mike Emmett; 14 Ryan Wright; 15 Michael Haley; 32 Jordan Andrade.
**Tries:** Braham (11), Andrade (54), Straugheir (65), Ashton (69), Bloomfield (72); **Goals:** Sanderson 6/8.
**Dismissals:** Tonks (80) - fighting;
Bloomfield (80) - fighting.
**Sin bin:** Straugheir (78) - fighting.
**Rugby Leaguer & League Express Men of the Match:** *Cougars:* Dan Parker; *Hunslet:* Zach Braham.
**Penalty count:** 6-6; **Half-time:** 4-12;
**Referee:** Nick Bennett; **Attendance:** 522.

*Sunday 11th August 2019*

**NORTH WALES CRUSADERS 33 COVENTRY BEARS 16**

**CRUSADERS:** 1 Lewis Fairhurst; 2 Dave Eccleston; 3 Alex Thompson; 4 Jordan Penny; 5 Rob Massam; 6 Steve Roper; 7 Ryan Smith; 17 Jonny Walker; 9 Ben Stead; 18 Brad Brennan; 11 Alex Eckley; 12 Stephen Wild; 13 Karl Ashall. Subs (all used): 15 Declan Gregory; 20 Joe Ryan; 8 Callum Hazzard; 10 Warren Thompson.
**Tries:** A Thompson (38), Massam (50), Gregory (52), Brennan (64), Eccleston (71), Ryan (76);
**Goals:** Fairhurst 0/1, Stead 4/5; **Field goal:** Roper (80).
**BEARS:** 1 Elliot Hall; 2 Reece Rance; 3 Kadeem Williams; 4 Kameron Pearce-Paul; 5 Errol Carter; 6 Brad Sheridan; 7 Nathan Conroy; 8 Jack Ray; 9 Sam Davis; 10 Chris Barratt; 11 Jacob Jones; 12 James Mason; 13 Hayden Freeman. Subs (all used): 14 Harvey Whiteley; 15 Lawrence Haywood; 16 Euan Tiernan; 17 Zak Fellows.
**Tries:** Rance (21), Whiteley (28), Hall (30); **Goals:** Hall 2/3.
**Rugby Leaguer & League Express Men of the Match:** *Crusaders:* Alex Thompson; *Bears:* Reece Rance.
**Penalty count:** 6-3; **Half-time:** 4-16;
**Referee:** Craig Smith; **Attendance:** 256.

**DONCASTER 23 LONDON SKOLARS 22**

**DONCASTER:** 6 Jordan Howden; 5 Sam Doherty; 3 Connor Bower; 4 Jason Tali; 19 Matty Chrimes; 33 Rangi Chase; 7 Matty Beharrell; 14 Connor Scott; 9 Kyle Kesik; 8 Russ Spiers; 26 Evan Hodgson; 22 Brad Foster; 13 Jordie Hedges. Subs (all used): 24 Watson Boas; 17 Brandon Douglas; 25 Stefanos Bastas; 12 Frankie Mariano.
**Tries:** Beharrell (9), Doherty (12), Spiers (21), Chase (51);
**Goals:** Beharrell 3/4; **Field goal:** Beharrell (77).
**SKOLARS:** 2 Iliess Macani; 5 Elliot Jennings; 3 Guy Armitage; 4 Lameck Juma; 1 Jerome Yates; 14 Richard Wilkinson; 17 Jy-mel Coleman; 21 Daniel Hindmarsh; 9 Neil Thorman; 10 Judd Greenhalgh; 12 Ronny Palumbo; 11 Jordan Williams; 13 Robert Tuliatu. Subs (all used): 16 Lamont Bryan; 15 Jon Magrin; 7 Mike Bishay; 20 Matthew Davies.
**Tries:** Wilkinson (24), Armitage (28, 61, 71);
**Goals:** Thorman 3/4.
**Rugby Leaguer & League Express Men of the Match:** *Doncaster:* Matty Beharrell; *Skolars:* Guy Armitage.
**Penalty count:** 3-7; **Half-time:** 16-12;
**Referee:** Steve Race; **Attendance:** 585.

**OLDHAM 28 NEWCASTLE THUNDER 20**

**OLDHAM:** 5 Ritchie Hawkyard; 28 Harry Aaronson; 3 Zack McComb; 29 Cameron Leeming; 1 Kyran Johnson; 6 Paul

Crook; 7 Dave Hewitt; 8 Phil Joy; 9 Gareth Owen; 10 Scott Law; 16 Danny Langtree; 25 Danny Bridge; 24 Liam Bent. Subs (all used): 12 Emmerson Whittel; 30 Ed Smith; 17 Jimmy Beckett; 20 Matty Wilkinson.
**Tries:** Johnson (18), Bridge (38, 59), Leeming (45), Owen (77); **Goals:** Crook 4/5.
**THUNDER:** 1 Lewis Young; 19 Misi Taulapapa; 3 Joe Brown; 4 Kieran Gill; 5 Alex Clegg; 6 Quentin Laulu-Togaga'e; 7 Nick Newman; 8 Liam McAvoy; 9 Aaron Ollett; 10 Joel Edwards; 17 Conor Fitzsimmons; 18 Rhys Clarke; 13 Harry Aldous. Subs (all used): 12 Sam Luckley; 15 Jared Blanke; 11 Muizz Mustapha; 14 Evan Simons.
**Tries:** Laulu-Togaga'e (9), Fitzsimmons (15), Gill (23), Clegg (33); **Goals:** Clarke 2/4.
**Rugby Leaguer & League Express Men of the Match:** *Oldham:* Matty Wilkinson; *Thunder:* Quentin Laulu-Togaga'e.
**Penalty count:** 8-5; **Half-time:** 12-20;
**Referee:** Matt Rossleigh; **Attendance:** 702.

**WORKINGTON TOWN 66 WEST WALES RAIDERS 22**

**TOWN:** 2 Tyllar Mellor; 21 Russ Bolton; 18 Calvin Wellington; 4 Perry Singleton; 20 Jonathan Walsh; 6 Jamie Doran; 7 Carl Forber; 14 Andrew Dawson; 9 Sean Penkywicz; 10 Stevie Scholey; 11 Danny Tickle; 12 Gordon Maudling; 17 Dec O'Donnell. Subs (all used): - Blain Marwood; 15 Tom Curwen; 19 Caine Barnes; 22 Sam Hopkins.
**Tries:** Walsh (2, 49), Tickle (20), Bolton (22), Maudling (30, 60), Barnes (37), Penkywicz (53), Marwood (62, 75), Hopkins (73); **Goals:** Forber 11/11.
**Sin bin:** Barnes (59) - fighting.
**RAIDERS:** 1 Phil Cowburn; 21 Sam Baker; 23 Rowland Kaye; 15 Archie Snook; 25 Mickael Sabour; 22 Steve Parry; 7 Tyler Hunt; 14 Dalton Desmond-Walker; 9 Liam Rice-Wilson; 10 Sam Herron; 13 Dan Maiden; 18 Gioele Celerino; 16 Nye Walker. Subs (all used): 24 Callum Mulkeen; 2 Matthew Morgan; 4 Paddy Jennings; 3 Macauley Harris.
**Tries:** Cowburn (10), Jennings (42), Baker (46), Sabour (67); **Goals:** Cowburn 3/4.
**Sin bin:** Celerino (59) - fighting.
**Rugby Leaguer & League Express Men of the Match:** *Town:* Jamie Doran; *Raiders:* Tyler Hunt.
**Penalty count:** 7-7; **Half-time:** 30-6;
**Referee:** Brad Milligan; **Attendance:** 908.

## ROUND 20

*Saturday 17th August 2019*

**WEST WALES RAIDERS 16
NORTH WALES CRUSADERS 56**

**RAIDERS:** 1 Phil Cowburn; 21 Sam Baker; 6 Ashley Bateman; 15 Archie Snook; 23 Rowland Kaye; 22 Steve Parry; 7 Matthew Morgan; 16 Nye Walker; 19 Mitch Shaw; 14 Dalton Desmond-Walker; 13 Dan Maiden; 18 Gioele Celerino; 12 Morgan Evans. Subs (all used): 20 Alan Pope; 4 Joe McClean; 24 Callum Mulkeen; 9 Liam Rice-Wilson.
**Tries:** Shaw (28), Parry (70), Snook (72);
**Goals:** Cowburn 2/3.
**CRUSADERS:** 1 Lewis Fairhurst; 2 Dave Eccleston; 3 Dante Morley-Samuels; 4 Earl Hurst; 5 Rob Massam; 6 Steve Roper; 7 Elliott Jenkins; 16 Brad Brennan; 9 Ben Stead; 10 Warren Thompson; 11 Alex Eckley; 12 Matt Reid; 13 Alex Thompson. Subs (all used): 14 Declan Gregory; 15 Jonny Walker; 8 James Tilley; 17 Joe Ryan.
**Tries:** Stead (11), Eccleston (14, 37), W Thompson (23), Roper (33), Eckley (40), Ryan (47), Morley-Samuels (61), Massam (68, 75), Fairhurst (78);
**Goals:** Stead 3/5, Roper 1/3, Fairhurst 2/3.
**Rugby Leaguer & League Express Men of the Match:** *Raiders:* Archie Snook; *Crusaders:* Warren Thompson.
**Penalty count:** 3-5; **Half-time:** 6-30;
**Referee:** Brad Milligan; **Attendance:** 272.

*Sunday 18th August 2019*

**KEIGHLEY COUGARS 19 WHITEHAVEN 48**

**COUGARS:** 33 Louis Sheriff; 5 Davey Dixon; 21 Matt Welham; 23 Macauley Hallett; 31 Taylor Prell; 15 Jack Miller; 7 Benn Hardcastle; 8 Jack Coventry; 9 James Feather; 25 Jack Arnold; 22 Dan Parker; 13 Jason Muranka; 12 Aaron Levy. Subs (all used): 16 Kieran Moran; 17 Billy Gaylor; 19 Matthew Bailey; 27 Lewis Wray.
**Tries:** Sheriff (4), Miller (11), Hallett (80);
**Goals:** Hardcastle 3/4; **Field goal:** Hardcastle (40).
**Sin bin:** Dixon (57) - professional foul.
**On report:**
Parker (20) - alleged dangerous contact on Mossop.
**WHITEHAVEN:** 2 Jordan Burns; 19 Andrew Bulman; 23 Jason Mossop; 3 Chris Taylor; 5 Dave Thompson; 1 Sam Forrester; 7 Callum Phillips; 8 Marc Shackley; 14 Sam Dowsett; 10 Kris Coward; 11 Brett Phillips; 27 Ellis Gillam; 13 Tom Wilkinson. Subs (all used): 6 Dion Aiye; 15 Connor Holliday; 24 Ethan Kelly; 26 Carl Forster.
**Tries:** Aiye (30, 49), Forrester (41, 62, 71), C Phillips (54, 78), Bulman (66); **Goals:** Burns 1/1, Holliday 7/7.
**Rugby Leaguer & League Express Men of the Match:** *Cougars:* James Feather; *Whitehaven:* Dion Aiye.
**Penalty count:** 4-15; **Half-time:** 15-6;
**Referee:** Michael Mannifield; **Attendance:** 782.

**NEWCASTLE THUNDER 88 COVENTRY BEARS 6**

**THUNDER:** 1 Lewis Young; 19 Misi Taulapapa; 2 Tyler Craig; 4 Kieran Gill; 5 Alex Clegg; 6 Quentin Laulu-Togaga'e; 7 Nick Newman; 10 Joel Edwards; 9 Aaron Ollett; 8 Liam McAvoy; 18 Rhys Clarke; 17 Conor Fitzsimmons; 13 Sam Luckley. Subs (all used): 11 Jack Aldous; 12 Muizz Mustapha; 3 Keal Carlile; 15 Carne Doyle-Manga.
**Tries:** Fitzsimmons (18, 77), Young (20, 31, 54, 77), Ollett (23), Edwards (27), Carlile (34), Clegg (37), Laulu-Togaga'e (39), Gill (60, 64, 66), Taulapapa (67), Newman (78); **Goals:** Clarke 12/16.
**BEARS:** 1 Elliot Hall; 2 Hayden Freeman; 3 Kadeem Williams; 4 Kameron Pearce-Paul; 5 Errol Carter; 6 Brad Sheridan; 7 Nathan Conroy; 8 Jack Ray; 9 Harvey Whiteley; 10 Joslin Landu; 11 Jacob Jones; 12 James Mason; 13 Chris Barratt. Subs (all used): 14 Lawrence Haywood; 15 Reece Williams; 17 Zak Fellows; 16 Euan Tiernan.
**Try:** Ray (11); **Goals:** Hall 1/1.
**Rugby Leaguer & League Express Men of the Match:** *Thunder:* Lewis Young; *Bears:* Jack Ray.
**Penalty count:** 6-9; **Half-time:** 46-6;
**Referee:** Andrew Sweet; **Attendance:** 711.

**OLDHAM 40 DONCASTER 14**

**OLDHAM:** 5 Ritchie Hawkyard; 28 Dec Kay; 3 Zack McComb; 29 Cameron Leeming; 1 Kyran Johnson; 6 Paul Crook; 7 Dave Hewitt; 8 Phil Joy; 9 Gareth Owen; 10 Scott Law; 16 Danny Langtree; 25 Danny Bridge; 24 Liam Bent. Subs (all used): 12 Emmerson Whittel; 15 Ed Smith; 17 Jimmy Beckett; 20 Matty Wilkinson.
**Tries:** Bent (15), Hawkyard (20), Langtree (28), Crook (55), Leeming (58), Wilkinson (67), Owen (78);
**Goals:** Crook 6/7.
**DONCASTER:** 2 Richard Owen; 5 Sam Doherty; 3 Connor Bower; 4 Jason Tali; 19 Matty Chrimes; 6 Jordan Howden; 33 Rangi Chase; 8 Russ Spiers; 9 Kyle Kesik; 14 Connor Scott; 30 Evan Hodgson; 22 Brad Foster; 13 Jordie Hedges. Subs (all used): 27 Jack Brown; 10 Ryan Boyle; 24 Watson Boas; 12 Frankie Mariano.
**Tries:** Doherty (10, 39), Spiers (72);
**Goals:** Hedges 0/1, Howden 1/2.
**Rugby Leaguer & League Express Men of the Match:** *Oldham:* Gareth Owen; *Doncaster:* Evan Hodgson.
**Penalty count:** 8-5; **Half-time:** 18-8;
**Referee:** John McMullen; **Attendance:** 745.

*Friday 23rd August 2019*

**LONDON SKOLARS 30 HUNSLET 34**

**SKOLARS:** 2 Iliess Macani; 5 Elliot Jennings; 3 Omari Caro; 4 Jordan Williams; 1 Jerome Yates; 14 Richard Wilkinson; 6 Jermaine Coleman; 10 Judd Greenhalgh; 9 Neil Thorman; 13 Liam Scott; 12 Lamont Bryan; 11 Robert Tuliatu; 20 Matt Ross. Subs (all used): 15 Matthew Davies; 16 Jon Magrin; 17 Mike Greenhalgh; 7 Mike Bishay.
**Tries:** Scott (15), Yates (17), Williams (21, 50), Wilkinson (60); **Goals:** Thorman 3/5, Bishay 2/2.
**Sin bin:** J Greenhalgh (32) - fighting.
**HUNSLET:** 1 Jimmy Watson; 2 Gareth Potts; 24 Reece Chapman-Smith; 3 Tom Ashton; 26 Callum Lancaster; 6 Joe Sanderson; 7 Simon Brown; 16 Zach Braham; 20 Vila Halafihi; 10 Adam Robinson; 30 Charlie Martin; 12 Duane Straugheir; 17 Dan Hawksworth. Subs (all used): 14 Ryan Wright; 13 Mike Emmett; 15 Michael Haley; 25 Lewis Heckford.
**Tries:** Halafihi (10), Ashton (26), Robinson (38), Emmett (43), Lancaster (72), Potts (80);
**Goals:** Sanderson 4/4, Brown 1/2.
**Sin bin:** Wright (32) - fighting.
**Rugby Leaguer & League Express Men of the Match:** *Skolars:* Jordan Williams; *Hunslet:* Callum Lancaster.
**Penalty count:** 7-8; **Half-time:** 18-18;
**Referee:** Matt Rossleigh; **Attendance:** 1,035.

## ROUND 21

*Sunday 1st September 2019*

**COVENTRY BEARS 6 OLDHAM 50**

**BEARS:** 1 Elliot Hall; 2 Hayden Freeman; 3 Kadeem Williams; 4 Kameron Pearce-Paul; 5 Errol Carter; 6 Brad Sheridan; 7 Nathan Conroy; 8 Toby Richardson; 9 Kieran Sherratt; 20 Reece Williams; 11 Jacob Jones; 12 James Mason; 13 Chris Barratt. Subs (all used): 10 Joslin Landu; 15 Cameron Stewart; 16 Harry Kaufman; 17 Zak Fellows.
**Try:** Jones (73); **Goals:** Hall 1/1.
**OLDHAM:** 22 Luke Hooley; 28 Dec Kay; 4 Jack Holmes; 29 Cameron Leeming; 1 Kyran Johnson; 6 Paul Crook; 15 Adam Brook; 30 Phil Joy; 9 Gareth Owen; 10 Scott Law; 12 Emmerson Whittel; 16 Danny Langtree; 24 Liam Bent. Subs (all used): 17 Jimmy Beckett; 19 Jamie Greenwood; 13 Jack Spencer; 18 Ben Davies.
**Tries:** Bent (14), Langtree (22, 70), Brook (25), Holmes (35), Johnson (45), Kay (60), Joy (65), Davies (75);
**Goals:** Crook 7/9.
**Rugby Leaguer & League Express Men of the Match:** *Bears:* Toby Richardson; *Oldham:* Dec Kay.
**Penalty count:** 8-6; **Half-time:** 0-24;
**Referee:** Liam Staveley; **Attendance:** 280
*(at Webb Ellis Road, Rugby).*

**DONCASTER 48 KEIGHLEY COUGARS 12**

**DONCASTER:** 6 Jordan Howden; 5 Sam Doherty; 3 Connor Bower; 4 Jason Tali; 25 Tom Halliday; 33 Rangi Chase; 7 Matty Beharrell; 27 Levy Nzoungou; 9 Kyle Kesik; 8 Russ Spiers; 30 Evan Hodgson; 12 Frankie Mariano; 22 Brad Foster. Subs (all used): 24 Watson Boas; 16 Brandan Wilkinson; 17 Brandon Douglas; 10 Ryan Boyle.
**Tries:** Halliday (8, 33, 59), Foster (17), Tali (21), Boas (42), Boyle (71), Doherty (76), Bower (78);
**Goals:** Beharrell 4/6, Howden 2/3.
**COUGARS:** 33 Louis Sheriff; 5 Davey Dixon; 4 Will Cooke; 23 Macauley Hallett; 31 Taylor Prell; 15 Jack Miller; 7 Benn Hardcastle; 8 Jack Coventry; 9 James Feather; 39 Spencer Darley; 35 Dom Horn; 13 Jason Muranka; 12 Aaron Levy. Subs (all used): 16 Kieran Moran; 17 Billy Gaylor; 19 Matthew Bailey; 30 Harvey Hallas.
**Tries:** Gaylor (48), Muranka (69); **Goals:** Hardcastle 2/2.
**Rugby Leaguer & League Express Men of the Match:** *Doncaster:* Rangi Chase; *Cougars:* Jason Muranka.
**Penalty count:** 5-7; **Half-time:** 20-0;
**Referee:** Joe Stearne; **Attendance:** 892.

**HUNSLET 16 WORKINGTON TOWN 30**

**HUNSLET:** 1 Jimmy Watson; 2 Gareth Potts; 23 Nathan Chappell; 3 Tom Ashton; 24 Reece Chapman-Smith; 6 Joe Sanderson; 7 Simon Brown; 17 Dan Hawksworth; 20 Vila Halafihi; 10 Adam Robinson; 30 Charlie Martin; 12 Duane Straugheir; 13 Mike Emmett. Subs (all used): 25 Lewis Heckford; 14 Ryan Wright; 15 Michael Haley; 19 Aiden Hema.
**Tries:** Straugheir (30), Martin (40), Halafihi (42);
**Goals:** Sanderson 2/3.
**Sin bin:** Chappell (60) - dissent.
**TOWN:** 6 Jamie Doran; 20 Jonathan Walsh; 19 Caine Barnes; 4 Perry Singleton; 16 Scott Rooke; 7 Carl Forber; 17 Dec O'Donnell; 25 Fuifui Moimoi; 9 Sean Penkywicz; 14 Andrew Dawson; 11 Danny Tickle; 10 Stevie Scholey; 22 Sam Hopkins. Subs: 27 Blain Marwood; 15 Tom Curwen; 18 Calvin Wellington (not used); 21 Russ Bolton (not used).
**Tries:** O'Donnell (9), Moimoi (25, 41), Curwen (67), Singleton (72); **Goals:** Forber 5/5.
**Rugby Leaguer & League Express Men of the Match:** *Hunslet:* Vila Halafihi; *Town:* Jamie Doran.
**Penalty count:** 5-9; **Half-time:** 12-12;
**Referee:** Tom Crashley; **Attendance:** 521.

**NEWCASTLE THUNDER 46
NORTH WALES CRUSADERS 22**

**THUNDER:** 1 Lewis Young; 5 Alex Clegg; 4 Kieran Gill; 2 Matthew Wright; 19 Misi Taulapapa; 6 Quentin Laulu-Togaga'e; 7 Nick Newman; 8 Sam Luckley; 9 Aaron Ollett; 10 Jack Aldous; 12 Conor Fitzsimmons; 18 Rhys Clarke; 13 Joel Edwards. Subs (all used): 14 Evan Simons; 20 Muizz Mustapha; 3 Ollie Gowing; 16 Alex Rowe.
**Tries:** Gill (6, 50), Laulu-Togaga'e (14, 33), Wright (25, 47, 66), Mustapha (57), Newman (71), Simons (75); **Goals:** Clarke 3/6, Wright 0/2, Newman 0/2.
**CRUSADERS:** 1 Elliott Jenkins; 2 Dave Eccleston; 3 Dante Morley-Samuels; 4 Earl Hurst; 5 Rob Massam; 6 Steve Roper; 7 Ben Stead; 8 Brad Brennan; 9 Declan Gregory; 21 James Tilley; 11 Matt Reid; 12 Simon Atherton; 13 Stephen Wild. Subs (all used): 14 Ryan Smith; 10 Warren Thompson; 18 Alex Thompson; 15 Jordan Penny.
**Tries:** Reid (18), Massam (37, 80), Wild (78);
**Goals:** Stead 3/4.
**Rugby Leaguer & League Express Men of the Match:** *Thunder:* Lewis Young; *Crusaders:* Declan Gregory.
**Penalty count:** 3-5; **Half-time:** 20-10;
**Referee:** John McMullen; **Attendance:** 883.

**WHITEHAVEN 74 WEST WALES RAIDERS 6**

**WHITEHAVEN:** 2 Jordan Burns; 19 Andrew Bulman; 4 Jessie Joe Parker; 3 Chris Taylor; 5 Dave Thompson; 1 Sam Forrester; 7 Callum Phillips; 8 Marc Shackley; 9 James Newton; 10 Kris Coward; 12 Jake Moore; 11 Brett Phillips; 6 Dion Aiye. Subs (all used): 21 Jake Bradley; 15 Connor Holliday; 24 Ethan Kelly; 25 Kurt Maudling.
**Tries:** Forrester (10, 16, 52), Burns (20, 63), Newton (27), C Phillips (29), D Thompson (37, 79), Bulman (43, 67), Moore (72), Coward (77); **Goals:** Moore 10/12, Holliday 1/1.

**RAIDERS:** 1 Phil Cowburn; 2 Robert Matamosi; 6 Ashley Bateman; 15 Archie Snook; 21 Sam Baker; 25 Matthew Morgan; 7 Tyler Hunt; 14 Dalton Desmond-Walker; 22 Steve Parry; 12 Morgan Evans; 13 Dan Maiden; 23 Rowland Kaye; 18 Gioele Celerino. Subs (both used, only two named): 24 Callum Mulkeen; 10 Sam Herron.
**Try:** Parry (39); **Goals:** Cowburn 1/1.
**Rugby Leaguer & League Express Men of the Match:**
*Whitehaven:* Sam Forrester; *Raiders:* Steve Parry.
**Penalty count:** 6-4; **Half-time:** 34-6;
**Referee:** Craig Smith; **Attendance:** 972.

## ROUND 22

*Saturday 7th September 2019*

**COVENTRY BEARS 0 WHITEHAVEN 72**

**BEARS:** 1 Elliot Hall; 2 Hayden Freeman; 3 Kadeem Williams; 4 Kameron Pearce-Paul; 5 Errol Carter; 6 Brad Sheridan; 7 Nathan Conroy; 8 Chris Barratt; 9 Sam Davis; 10 Reece Williams; 11 Jacob Jones; 12 James Mason; 13 Kieran Sherratt. Subs (all used): 14 Harvey Whiteley; 15 Jack Ray; 16 Cameron Stewart; 17 Reece Rance.
**WHITEHAVEN:** 2 Jordan Burns; 5 Dave Thompson; 3 Chris Taylor; 23 Jason Mossop; 19 Andrew Bulman; 1 Sam Forrester; 7 Callum Phillips; 8 Marc Shackley; 14 Sam Dowsett; 10 Kris Coward; 11 Brett Phillips; 12 Jake Moore; 13 Tom Wilkinson. Subs (all used): 6 Dion Aiye; 15 Connor Holliday; 24 Ethan Kelly; 26 Carl Forster.
**Tries:** Burns (6, 19, 63, 80), Moore (12), Shackley (23), Taylor (25), Forster (35), D Thompson (38, 73), B Phillips (49), C Phillips (57), Bulman (60);
**Goals:** Moore 6/8, Holliday 4/5.
**Rugby Leaguer & League Express Men of the Match:**
*Bears:* Nathan Conroy; *Whitehaven:* Jordan Burns.
**Penalty count:** 3-10; **Half-time:** 0-36;
**Referee:** Andrew Sweet; **Attendance:** 652
*(at Webb Ellis Road, Rugby).*

**NORTH WALES CRUSADERS 36 LONDON SKOLARS 18**

**CRUSADERS:** 1 Dave Eccleston; 3 Dante Morley-Samuels; 2 Earl Hurst; 4 Alex Thompson; 5 Rob Massam; 6 Karl Ashall; 7 Ben Stead; 17 Jonny Walker; 9 Declan Gregory; 10 Warren Thompson; 11 Matt Reid; 12 Simon Atherton; 13 Stephen Wild. Subs (all used): 21 Alex Eckley; 8 James Tilley; 18 Joe Ryan; 16 Brad Brennan.
**Tries:** Massam (31, 44), Wild (37, 69), Atherton (66), Walker (79), Eckley (80);
**Goals:** Stead 3/6, Walker 0/1, Wild 1/1.
**SKOLARS:** 2 Iliess Macani; 1 Kayne Chan-Kitchener; 3 Omari Caro; 4 Jordan Williams; 5 Jerome Yates; 14 Richard Wilkinson; 19 Jy-mel Coleman; 10 Judd Greenhalgh; 9 Neil Thorman; 8 Michael Sykes; 11 Jon Magrin; 12 Mike Greenhalgh; 13 Liam Scott. Subs (all used): 15 Matthew Davies; 7 Mike Bishay; 18 Eddie Mbaraga; 17 Tommy Chipchase.
**Tries:** Scott (12), Williams (25), Caro (51);
**Goals:** Thorman 3/3.
**Rugby Leaguer & League Express Men of the Match:**
*Crusaders:* Stephen Wild; *Skolars:* Jerome Yates.
**Penalty count:** 4-3; **Half-time:** 12-12;
**Referee:** Kevin Moore; **Attendance:** 421.

*Sunday 8th September 2019*

**HUNSLET 20 OLDHAM 34**

**HUNSLET:** 1 Jimmy Watson; 2 Gareth Potts; 24 Reece Chapman-Smith; 3 Tom Ashton; 26 Callum Lancaster; 6 Joe Sanderson; 25 Lewis Heckford; 16 Zach Braham; 20 Vila Halafihi; 17 Dan Hawksworth; 23 Nathan Chappell; 12 Duane Straugheir; 13 Mike Emmett. Subs (all used): 32 Jordan Andrade; 14 Ryan Wright; 15 Michael Haley; 19 Aiden Hema.
**Tries:** Braham (2), Watson (20), Chappell (30);
**Goals:** Sanderson 4/4.
**OLDHAM:** 5 Ritchie Hawkyard; 28 Dec Kay; 3 Zack McComb; 4 Jack Holmes; 1 Kyran Johnson; 6 Paul Crook; 7 Dave Hewitt; 30 Phil Joy; 9 Gareth Owen; 10 Scott Law; 25 Danny Bridge; 16 Danny Langtree; 24 Liam Bent. Subs (all used): 20 Matthew Wilkinson; 12 Emmerson Whittel; 13 Jack Spencer; 18 Ben Davies.
**Tries:** Bridge (13), Langtree (25, 35, 76), Crook (65);
**Goals:** Crook 7/8.
**Rugby Leaguer & League Express Men of the Match:**
*Hunslet:* Duane Straugheir; *Oldham:* Paul Crook.
**Penalty count:** 6-12; **Half-time:** 20-18;
**Referee:** John McMullen; **Attendance:** 688.

**KEIGHLEY COUGARS 22 NEWCASTLE THUNDER 32**

**COUGARS:** 1 Alfie Seeley; 5 Davey Dixon; 31 Taylor Prell; 23 Macauley Hallett; 20 Jordan Fitzpatrick-Parry; 17 Billy Gaylor; 15 Jack Miller; 8 Jack Coventry; 9 James Feather; 30 Harvey Hallas; 4 Will Cooke; 13 Jason Muranka; 12 Aaron Levy. Subs (all used): 16 Kieran Moran; 18 Chris Cullimore; 19 Matthew Bailey; 24 Mark Barlow.
**Tries:** Prell (22, 51), Moran (39), Dixon (48);
**Goals:** Miller 3/4.

Fuifui Moimoi on the charge during Workington's play-off win at Hunslet

**THUNDER:** 1 Lewis Young; 19 Misi Taulapapa; 11 Matthew Wright; 4 Kieran Gill; 5 Alex Clegg; 6 Quentin Laulu-Togaga'e; 7 Nick Newman; 10 Joel Edwards; 9 Aaron Ollett; 13 Sam Luckley; 17 Conor Fitzsimmons; 18 Rhys Clarke; 12 Muizz Mustapha. Subs (all used): 8 Liam McAvoy; 14 Evan Simons; 15 Jared Blanke; 20 Harry Aldous.
**Tries:** Clegg (4, 60), Newman (19, 74), Gill (26, 71);
**Goals:** Clarke 3/5, Wright 1/1.
**Rugby Leaguer & League Express Men of the Match:**
*Cougars:* Will Cooke; *Thunder:* Kieran Gill.
**Penalty count:** 8-6; **Half-time:** 12-16;
**Referee:** Liam Staveley; **Attendance:** 825.

**WORKINGTON TOWN 4 DONCASTER 30**

**TOWN:** 6 Jamie Doran; 16 Scott Rooke; 18 Calvin Wellington; 4 Perry Singleton; 20 Jonathan Walsh; 17 Dec O'Donnell; 7 Carl Forber; 14 Andrew Dawson; 9 Sean Penkywicz; 10 Stevie Scholey; 22 Sam Hopkins; 19 Caine Barnes; 11 Danny Tickle. Subs (all used): 27 Blain Marwood; 15 Tom Curwen; 12 Gordon Maudling; 25 Fuifui Moimoi.
**Try:** Barnes (76); **Goals:** Forber 0/1.
**DONCASTER:** 6 Jordan Howden; 1 Tom Halliday; 3 Connor Bower; 4 Jason Tali; 19 Matty Chrimes; 33 Rangi Chase; 7 Matty Beharrell; 8 Russ Spiers; 9 Kyle Kesik; 10 Ryan Boyle; 26 Evan Hodgson; 12 Frankie Mariano; 22 Brad Foster. Subs (all used): 17 Brandon Douglas; 24 Watson Boas; 16 Brandan Wilkinson; 13 Jordie Hedges.
**Tries:** Halliday (5, 61), Tali (23), Beharrell (28), Mariano (71);
**Goals:** Beharrell 5/6.
**Rugby Leaguer & League Express Men of the Match:**
*Town:* Tom Curwen; *Doncaster:* Matty Beharrell.
**Penalty count:** 7-4; **Half-time:** 0-18;
**Referee:** Gareth Hewer; **Attendance:** 1,201.

## QUALIFYING PLAY-OFF

*Sunday 15th September 2019*

**NEWCASTLE THUNDER 6 DONCASTER 20**

**THUNDER:** 1 Lewis Young; 19 Misi Taulapapa; 11 Matthew Wright; 4 Kieran Gill; 5 Alex Clegg; 6 Quentin Laulu-Togaga'e; 7 Nick Newman; 8 Liam McAvoy; 9 Keal Carlile; 10 Sam Luckley; 18 Rhys Clarke; 17 Conor Fitzsimmons; 14 Evan Simons. Subs (all used): 20 Muizz Mustapha; 15 Jared Blanke; 13 Harry Aldous; 12 Aaron Ollett.
**Try:** Clegg (78); **Goals:** Clarke 1/1.
**Sin bin:** Wright (30) - high tackle on Halliday.
**DONCASTER:** 6 Jordan Howden; 5 Sam Doherty; 3 Connor Bower; 4 Jason Tali; 1 Tom Halliday; 33 Rangi Chase; 7 Matty Beharrell; 31 Levy Nzoungou; 9 Kyle Kesik; 8 Russ Spiers; 12 Frankie Mariano; 13 Jordie Hedges; 16 Brandan Wilkinson. Subs (all used): 24 Watson Boas; 10 Ryan Boyle; 17 Brandon Douglas; 19 Matty Chrimes.
**Tries:** Doherty (2), Tali (35), Mariano (47), Chrimes (62);
**Goals:** Beharrell 2/5.
**Rugby Leaguer & League Express Men of the Match:**
*Thunder:* Muizz Mustapha; *Doncaster:* Frankie Mariano.
**Penalty count:** 6-11; **Half-time:** 0-8;
**Referee:** Billy Pearson; **Attendance:** 668.

## ELIMINATION PLAY-OFF

*Sunday 15th September 2019*

**HUNSLET 24 WORKINGTON TOWN 32**

**HUNSLET:** 1 Jimmy Watson; 2 Gareth Potts; 30 Charlie Martin; 3 Tom Ashton; 24 Reece Chapman-Smith; 6 Joe Sanderson; 7 Simon Brown; 32 Jordan Andrade; 20 Vila Halafihi; 10 Adam Robinson; 11 Josh Tonks; 12 Duane Straugheir; 16 Zach Braham. Subs (all used): 14 Ryan Wright; 13 Mike Emmett; 15 Michael Haley; 19 Aiden Hema.
**Tries:** Ashton (9, 25), Wright (19), Watson (37);
**Goals:** Sanderson 4/5.
**TOWN:** 21 Russ Bolton; 20 Jonathan Walsh; 19 Caine Barnes; 4 Perry Singleton; 12 Gordon Maudling; 6 Jamie Doran; 7 Carl Forber; 14 Andrew Dawson; 9 Sean Penkywicz; 25 Fuifui Moimoi; 10 Stevie Scholey; 11 Danny Tickle; 17 Dec O'Donnell. Subs: 15 Tom Curwen; 22 Sam Hopkins; - Tyler Lancaster (not used); 27 Blain Marwood (not used).
**Tries:** Maudling (1), Scholey (12), Penkywicz (29, 71), Moimoi (53); **Goals:** Forber 6/6.
**Rugby Leaguer & League Express Men of the Match:**
*Hunslet:* Tom Ashton; *Town:* Sean Penkywicz.
**Penalty count:** 6-7; **Half-time:** 24-18;
**Referee:** Tom Grant; **Attendance:** 332.

Oldham's Jimmy Beckett races towards the Newcastle line during the League 1 Play-off Final

## QUALIFYING SEMI-FINAL

*Sunday 22nd September 2019*

### OLDHAM 22 DONCASTER 12

**OLDHAM:** 5 Ritchie Hawkyard; 28 Dec Kay; 3 Zack McComb; 29 Cameron Leeming; 1 Kyran Johnson; 6 Paul Crook; 7 Dave Hewitt; 8 Phil Joy; 9 Gareth Owen; 10 Scott Law; 16 Danny Langtree; 25 Danny Bridge; 24 Liam Bent. Subs (all used): 12 Emmerson Whittel; 17 Jimmy Beckett; 13 Jack Spencer; 20 Matty Wilkinson.
**Tries:** Hewitt (17), Whittel (47), Crook (56);
**Goals:** Crook 5/5.
**DONCASTER:** 6 Jordan Howden; 5 Sam Doherty; 3 Connor Bower; 4 Jason Tali; 1 Tom Halliday; 33 Rangi Chase; 7 Matty Beharrell; 27 Levy Nzoungou; 9 Kyle Kesik; 8 Russ Spiers; 12 Frankie Mariano; 31 Danny Washbrook; 16 Brandan Wilkinson. Subs (all used): 24 Watson Boas; 10 Ryan Boyle; 26 Jack Brown; 13 Jordie Hedges.
**Tries:** Beharrell (26), Kesik (79); **Goals:** Beharrell 2/2.
**Rugby Leaguer & League Express Men of the Match:**
*Oldham:* Dave Hewitt; *Doncaster:* Brandan Wilkinson.
**Penalty count:** 10-10; **Half-time:** 8-6;
**Referee:** Liam Moore; **Attendance:** 529.

## ELIMINATION SEMI-FINAL

*Sunday 22nd September 2019*

### NEWCASTLE THUNDER 38 WORKINGTON TOWN 18

**THUNDER:** 1 Lewis Young; 5 Alex Clegg; 3 Joe Brown; 4 Kieran Gill; 19 Misi Taulapapa; 6 Quentin Laulu-Togaga'e; 7 Nick Newman; 8 Liam McAvoy; 9 Keal Carlile; 13 Harry

Aldous; 10 Joel Edwards; 18 Rhys Clarke; 15 Sam Luckley. Subs (all used): 14 Evan Simons; 17 Conor Fitzsimmons; 20 Jack Aldous; 16 Alex Rowe.
**Tries:** Gill (1, 33, 76), Newman (14, 21), Laulu-Togaga'e (29), Clegg (58); **Goals:** Clarke 5/7.
**Sin bin:** Luckley (79) - late challenge on Forber.
**TOWN:** 21 Russ Bolton; 27 Blain Marwood; 19 Caine Barnes; 4 Perry Singleton; 20 Jonathan Walsh; 6 Jamie Doran; 7 Carl Forber; 14 Andrew Dawson; 9 Sean Penkywicz; 25 Fuifui Moimoi; 10 Stevie Scholey; 12 Gordon Maudling; 22 Sam Hopkins. Sub (used, only one named): - Tyler Lancaster.
**Tries:** Marwood (7), Singleton (36), Dawson (72);
**Goals:** Forber 3/3.
**Rugby Leaguer & League Express Men of the Match:**
*Thunder:* Nick Newman; *Town:* Perry Singleton.
**Penalty count:** 9-8; **Half-time:** 28-12;
**Referee:** James Child; **Attendance:** 678.

## FINAL ELIMINATOR

*Sunday 29th September 2019*

### NEWCASTLE THUNDER 34 DONCASTER 4

**THUNDER:** 1 Lewis Young; 19 Misi Taulapapa; 2 Tyler Craig; 4 Kieran Gill; 5 Alex Clegg; 6 Quentin Laulu-Togaga'e; 7 Nick Newman; 8 Liam McAvoy; 9 Keal Carlile; 13 Harry Aldous; 10 Joel Edwards; 18 Rhys Clarke; 15 Sam Luckley. Subs (all used): 14 Evan Simons; 17 Conor Fitzsimmons; 20 Jack Aldous; 16 Alex Rowe.
**Tries:** Gill (6, 59, 75), Carlile (12), Young (27), Clegg (68); **Goals:** Clarke 5/7.
**DONCASTER:** 6 Jordan Howden; 5 Sam Doherty; 3 Connor Bower; 4 Jason Tali; 19 Matty Chrimes; 33 Rangi

Chase; 7 Matty Beharrell; 27 Levy Nzoungou; 9 Kyle Kesik; 10 Ryan Boyle; 22 Brad Foster; 12 Frankie Mariano; 16 Brandan Wilkinson. Subs (all used): 11 Brad England; 24 Watson Boas; 1 Tom Halliday; 14 Connor Scott.
**Try:** Chase (42); **Goals:** Beharrell 0/1.
**Rugby Leaguer & League Express Men of the Match:**
*Thunder:* Lewis Young; *Doncaster:* Brad Foster.
**Penalty count:** 12-5; **Half-time:** 18-0;
**Referee:** Jack Smith; **Attendance:** 480.

## PLAY-OFF FINAL

*Sunday 6th October 2019*

### OLDHAM 18 NEWCASTLE THUNDER 14

**OLDHAM:** 5 Ritchie Hawkyard; 55 Dec Kay; 3 Zack McComb; 29 Cameron Leeming; 1 Kyran Johnson; 6 Paul Crook; 7 Dave Hewitt; 8 Phil Joy; 9 Gareth Owen; 10 Scott Law; 25 Danny Bridge; 16 Danny Langtree; 24 Liam Bent. Subs (all used): 17 Jimmy Beckett; 12 Emmerson Whittel; 13 Jack Spencer; 20 Matty Wilkinson.
**Tries:** Langtree (14), McComb (52), Beckett (64);
**Goals:** Crook 3/3.
**THUNDER:** 1 Lewis Young; 19 Misi Taulapapa; 2 Tyler Craig; 4 Kieran Gill; 5 Alex Clegg; 6 Quentin Laulu-Togaga'e; 7 Nick Newman; 8 Liam McAvoy; 9 Keal Carlile; 15 Sam Luckley; 18 Rhys Clarke; 10 Joel Edwards; 13 Harry Aldous. Subs (all used): 14 Evan Simons; 20 Jack Aldous; 16 Carne Doyle-Manga; 17 Conor Fitzsimmons.
**Tries:** Taulapapa (9, 56), Edwards (47); **Goals:** Clarke 1/3.
**Rugby Leaguer & League Express Men of the Match:**
*Oldham:* Dave Hewitt; *Thunder:* Sam Luckley.
**Penalty count:** 2-5; **Half-time:** 6-4;
**Referee:** Gareth Hewer; **Attendance:** 1,209.

# CHALLENGE CUP 2019
## *Round by Round*

## ROUND 3

*Friday 8th March 2019*

### DONCASTER 38 COVENTRY BEARS 16

**DONCASTER:** 2 Richard Owen; 5 Sam Doherty; 3 Connor Bower; 19 Matty Chrimes; 1 Lee Registe; 6 Jordan Howden; 7 Matty Beharrell; 14 Connor Scott; 9 Kyle Kesik; 8 Russ Spiers; 28 Jordan Cox; 21 Ryan Dixon; 13 Jordie Hedges. Subs (all used): 26 Stefanos Bastas; 17 Brandon Douglas; 10 Ryan Boyle; 15 Kieran Cross.
**Tries:** Doherty (22), Douglas (31, 60), Cox (56), Bower (65), Beharrell (66, 75); **Goals:** Beharrell 5/7.
**BEARS:** 1 Dante Morley-Samuels; 2 Hayden Freeman; 3 Kadeem Williams; 4 Kameron Pearce-Paul; 5 Elliot Hall; 6 Mitch Shaw; 7 Nick Newman; 10 Euan Tiernan; 9 Nathan Conroy; 22 Dan Gover; 11 Jacob Jones; 12 Chris Barratt; 13 Kieran Sherratt. Subs (all used): 14 Callum Merrett; 20 Ollie Purslow; 8 Peter Ryan; 16 Will Tully.
**Tries:** K Williams (5, 45), Hall (19), Gover (62); **Goals:** Newman 0/3, Merrett 0/1.
**Rugby Leaguer & League Express Men of the Match:** *Doncaster:* Matty Beharrell; *Bears:* Dan Gover.
**Penalty count:** 5-5; **Half-time:** 12-8;
**Referee:** Nick Bennett; **Attendance:** 381.

*Saturday 9th March 2019*

### THATTO HEATH CRUSADERS 30 ROCHDALE MAYFIELD 24

**CRUSADERS:** 1 Ben Heyes; 2 Adam Saunders; 3 Corey Lee; 4 Matty Norton; 5 Niall Allen; 6 Josh Crehan; 7 Bobbie Goulding; 8 Adam Hesketh; 9 Lewis Foster; 10 Mike Stark; 11 Adam Prendergast; 12 Jamie Tracey; 13 Andy Lea. Subs (all used): 14 Sean Kenny; 15 Luke Bradshaw; 16 Max Dudley; 21 Brad Ashurst.
**Tries:** Stark (10), Allen (13), Saunders (40, 49, 53), Heyes (51); **Goals:** Goulding 3/6.
**Dismissal:** Tracey (30) - high tackle.
**MAYFIELD:** 1 Wayne English; 2 Jack McConachie; 3 Liam Whalley; 4 Lewis Butterworth; 5 Munya Samanyanga; 6 Zac Hartley; 7 Cole Connolly; 8 Jimmy Connaughton; 9 Lewis Sheridan; 10 Mark Biggins; 11 Zac Baker; 12 Callum Marriott; 13 Aidie Gleeson. Subs (all used): 14 Declan Sheridan; 15 Nicholas Hargreaves; 16 Shaun Hurley; 17 Cameron Connolly.
**Tries:** Baker (30), McConachie (38, 78), Hargreaves (62), Cameron Connolly (75); **Goals:** Hartley 2/5.
**Sin bin:** English (40) - delaying restart.
**Rugby Leaguer & League Express Men of the Match:** *Crusaders:* Adam Saunders; *Mayfield:* Declan Sheridan.
**Penalty count:** 7-7; **Half-time:** 16-8;
**Referee:** Paul Marklove; **Attendance:** 350.

### WIGAN ST JUDES 4 LOCK LANE 24

**ST JUDES:** 1 Paul Pendlebury; 2 Barry Rothwell; 3 Connor Parkinson; 16 Corey Bennie; 5 Joey Brady; 17 Danny Fallon; 6 Rob Fenney; 8 Tom Owen; 9 Danny Clayton; 10 Brett Taberner; 11 Connor Ratcliffe; 12 Gavin Rodden; 13 Joshua Hill. Subs (all used): 14 Jason Holland; 15 Aaron Smith; 18 Daniel Munt; - Nathan Moore.
**Try:** Rodden (19); **Goals:** Fallon 0/1.
**LOCK LANE:** 1 Lewis Price; 2 Connor Turner; 3 Cory Southern; 4 Jordan Bull; 5 Tom Sowerby; 6 Connor Land; 7 Danny Sowerby; 8 Sean Hesketh; 9 Craig Savage; 10 Rob Firth; 11 Alex Palmer; 12 Danny Holmes; 13 Chris Siddons. Subs (all used): 14 Jack Lee; 15 Dale Cogan; 16 Ryan Kelsey; 17 Craig Jones.
**Tries:** Savage (16), Siddons (35), Price (40), Cogan (54); **Goals:** Turner 4/4.
**Rugby Leaguer & League Express Men of the Match:** *St Judes:* Connor Ratcliffe; *Lock Lane:* Chris Siddons.
**Penalty count:** 4-5; **Half-time:** 4-18;
**Referee:** Craig Smith; **Attendance:** 300.

### YORK ACORN 10 FEATHERSTONE LIONS 20

**ACORN:** 1 Callum Worthington; 2 Jake Calam; 3 Jordan Potter; 4 Ryan Gallacher; 5 Martin Pedersen-Scott; 6 Antony Chilton; 7 Lewis Brown; 8 Nathan Welsh; 9 Lewis Lord; 10 Tom Hill; 11 Matthew Woods; 12 Jordan Hyde; 13 Reece Rushworth. Subs (all used): 14 Jimmy Mountford; 15 Adam Endersby; 20 Jack Byrnes; 17 Josh Thompson.
**Tries:** Gallacher (1), Calam (36); **Goals:** Chilton 1/2.
**Dismissal:** Hill (65) - fighting.
**Sin bin:** Thompson (70) - fighting.
**LIONS:** 1 Ian Jackson; 2 Connor Paver; 3 Gaz Gale; 4 Danny Glassell; 5 Jack Ellam; 6 Jake Perkins; 7 Josh Maden; 8 Brendon Gibbins; 9 Scott Glassell; 10 Ben Mawson; 11 Gareth Williamson; 12 Harry McAllister; 13 Dean Gamble. Subs (all used): 14 Davi Garahan; 15 Evan Morris; 16 Jack Lloyd; 17 Richard Frankland.
**Tries:** D Glassell (14, 55), Paver (25), S Glassell (65), Mawson (72); **Goals:** Jackson 0/5.
**Dismissal:** Frankland (65) - fighting.
**Sin bin:** D Glassell (70) - fighting.
**Rugby Leaguer & League Express Men of the Match:** *Acorn:* Reece Rushworth; *Lions:* Ben Mawson.
**Penalty count:** 9-11; **Half-time:** 10-8;
**Referee:** Joe Stearne; **Attendance:** 385.

### NEWCASTLE THUNDER 48 WEST WALES RAIDERS 0

**THUNDER:** 1 Lewis Young; 2 Mo Agoro; 3 Joe Brown; 4 Misi Taulapapa; 5 Niall Sidney; 6 Remy Marginet; 7 Jy-mel Coleman; 10 Jack Aldous; 9 Keal Carlile; 8 Liam McAvoy; 12 Conor Fitzsimmons; 11 Aaron Ollett; 19 Harry Aldous. Subs (all used): 14 Connor Clayton; 15 Jared Blanke; 16 Alex Rowe; 18 Carne Doyle-Manga.
**Tries:** Carlile (15, 28), Taulapapa (18), Young (31), Ollett (35), Doyle-Manga (55), Agoro (70, 74), Sidney (76);
**Goals:** Marginet 6/9.
**Sin bin:** Doyle-Manga (38) - late challenge.
**RAIDERS:** 5 Liam Clark; 2 Dai Evans; 23 Rowland Kaye; 24 Morgan Jefferies; 25 Mickael Sabour; 26 Alex King; 7 Tyler Hunt; 11 Robert Tuliatu; 9 Liam Rice-Wilson; 10 Sam Herron; 20 Mike Connor; 3 Ronny Palumbo; 6 Ashley Bateman. Subs (all used): 15 Archie Snook; 14 Dalton Desmond-Walker; 21 Morgan Rowlands; 22 Paddy Jennings.
**Rugby Leaguer & League Express Men of the Match:** *Thunder:* Remy Marginet; *Raiders:* Dai Evans.
**Penalty count:** 7-7; **Half-time:** 24-0;
**Referee:** Liam Staveley; **Attendance:** 329.

### HUNSLET 56 WEST BOWLING 10

**HUNSLET:** 1 Jimmy Watson; 25 Marcus Webb; 23 Nathan Chappell; 4 Ben Heaton; 3 Tom Ashton; 21 Reece Dean; 7 Cain Southernwood; 17 Dan Hawksworth; 9 Jack Lee; 10 Adam Robinson; 11 Josh Tonks; 12 Duane Straugheir; 13 Mike Emmett. Subs (all used): 20 Vila Halafihi; 31 Jon Luke Kirby; 16 Zach Braham; 18 Nyle Flynn.
**Tries:** Chappell (8), Lee (12), Webb (26, 72, 79), Tonks (31, 65), Ashton (45, 47), Southernwood (49, 68);
**Goals:** Dean 6/11.
**Sin bin:** Webb (37) - fighting.
**WEST BOWLING:** 1 Jay Panter; 2 Kyle Moore; 3 Daniel Gregory; 4 Jack Milburn; 5 Joe Hammond; 6 Harry Williams; 7 Ben Heald; 8 Christopher Watson; 9 Daniel Halmshaw; 10 Nathaniel Light; 11 Richard Lumb; 12 Chris Anderson; 13 Oliver Bartle. Subs (all used): 14 Kieron Baker; 15 Lewis Galtress; 16 Ryan Patchett; 17 Gavin Wilkinson.
**Tries:** Lumb (4), Hammond (39); **Goals:** Williams 1/2.
**Rugby Leaguer & League Express Men of the Match:** *Hunslet:* Adam Robinson; *West Bowling:* Harry Williams.
**Penalty count:** 8-4; **Half-time:** 20-10;
**Referee:** Michael Smaill; **Attendance:** 399.

*Sunday 10th March 2019*

### LONDON SKOLARS 18 NORTH WALES CRUSADERS 31

**SKOLARS:** 1 Iliess Macani; 2 Jerome Yates; 4 Omari Caro; 3 Sam Grant; 5 Lameck Juma; 6 James Barran; 7 Neil Thorman; 8 Judd Greenhalgh; 9 Mike Bishay; 10 Lamont Bryan; 12 Mike Greenhalgh; 11 Jordan Williams; 14 Xavier Rice. Subs (all used): 13 Isaac Ah Kuoi-Atmore; 17 Eddie Mbaraga; 15 Malikhi Lloyd-Jones; 16 Will Martin.
**Tries:** Bryan (30), Mbaraga (52), Macani (72);
**Goals:** Thorman 3/3.
**Sin bin:** J Greenhalgh (14) - dangerous contact on Hurst.
**CRUSADERS:** 1 Ryan Smith; 22 Dave Eccleston; 3 Matt Reid; 4 Earl Hurst; 5 Rob Massam; 6 Steve Roper; 7 Ben Stead; 10 Warren Thompson; 15 Karl Ashall; 23 Callum Hazzard; 11 Jack Houghton; 12 Simon Atherton; 13 Kenny Baker. Subs (all used): 17 Brad Brennan; 14 Kenny Hughes; 18 Jonny Walker; 21 Alex Eckley.
**Tries:** Baker (10, 39), Ashall (17), Hazzard (45), Atherton (79); **Goals:** Baker 5/5; **Field goal:** Roper (77).
**Rugby Leaguer & League Express Men of the Match:** *Skolars:* Iliess Macani; *Crusaders:* Kenny Baker.
**Penalty count:** 10-9; **Half-time:** 6-18;
**Referee:** Billy Pearson; **Attendance:** 170.

### WEST HULL 26 DEWSBURY MOOR 10

**WEST HULL:** 1 Luke Moss; 2 Jamie Leigh; 3 Jack Lazenby; 4 Ryan Langton; 5 Reece Gooch; 6 Josh Wood; 7 Scott Spaven; 8 Calvin Parker; 9 Nathan Powley; 10 Will Gardiner; 11 Benn Arbon; 12 Jacob Moore; 13 Ryan Steen. Subs (all used): 18 Alex Holdstock; 20 Ryan Wilson; 15 Sam Cator; 19 Bobby Tyson-Wilson.
**Tries:** Wood (30), Gooch (37, 78), Moss (64), Langton (79);
**Goals:** Wilson 2/3, Holdstock 1/2.
**DEWSBURY MOOR:** 1 Jordan Foster; 2 Sam Thornton; 3 George Croisdale; 4 Anthony Boardman; 5 Jermaine Davies; 6 Bradley Foster; 7 Aiden Ineson; 8 James Samme; 9 Jack Richardson; 10 Ashley Boddy; 11 Oliver Davidson; 12 Peter Robinson; 13 Dominic Horne. Subs (all used): 14 Archie Bruce; 15 Bartley O'Brien; 16 Bradley Adams; 17 Oliver Agers.
**Tries:** Thornton (7, 44); **Goals:** J Foster 1/2.
**Rugby Leaguer & League Express Men of the Match:** *West Hull:* Ryan Steen; *Dewsbury Moor:* James Samme.
**Penalty count:** 7-7; **Half-time:** 12-4;
**Referee:** Andrew Sweet; **Attendance:** 92.

### KEIGHLEY COUGARS 28 DISTINGTON 14

**COUGARS:** 21 Matt Welham; 5 Davey Dixon; 4 Will Cooke; 23 Macauley Hallett; 1 Alfie Seeley; 15 Jack Miller; 7 Benn Hardcastle; 19 Matthew Bailey; 9 James Feather; 25 Jack Arnold; 12 Aaron Levy; 13 Jason Muranka; 22 Dan Parker. Subs (all used): 8 Jack Coventry; 10 Jamie Thackray; 14 Luke Million; 30 Harvey Hallas.
**Tries:** Coventry (36), Hallas (52), Seeley (57, 63), Muranka (59), Dixon (80); **Goals:** Hardcastle 2/5, Miller 0/1.
**Sin bin:** Feather (30) - fighting.
**DISTINGTON:** 1 Steven Conway; 19 Greg Bedford; 3 Clayton Sutton; 4 Gavin Martin; 18 Phil Lister; 6 Scott George; 7 Matt Hewer; 8 Bryan Ritchie; 9 Jamie Friel; 20 Carl Stephenson; 11 Grant Dryden; 12 Liam McNicholas; 13 Sean Sutton. Subs (all used): 14 Ryan Hodgson; 15 Shaun Adams; 16 Adam Conway; 17 Stephen Clarke.
**Tries:** Lister (47), McNicholas (69); **Goals:** C Sutton 3/4.
**Sin bin:** George (30) - fighting; Adams (77) - dissent.
**Rugby Leaguer & League Express Men of the Match:** *Cougars:* Matt Welham; *Distington:* Gavin Martin.
**Penalty count:** 12-7; **Half-time:** 6-4;
**Referee:** Steve Race; **Attendance:** 508.

### OLDHAM 80 HAYDOCK 10

**OLDHAM:** 1 Kyran Johnson; 2 Aaron Jones-Bishop; 4 Jack Holmes; 16 Zack McComb; 27 Harry Maders; 15 Adam Brook; 26 Anthony Bowman; 8 Phil Joy; 20 Matty Wilkinson; 13 Jack Spencer; 12 Emmerson Whittel; 11 Ben Calland; 24 Liam Bent. Subs (all used): 29 Titus Gwaze; 19 Jamie Greenwood; 10 Scott Law; 18 Ben Davies.
**Tries:** Maders (7, 52, 57), Bowman (9), Wilkinson (15, 22, 68), Whittel (25), McComb (35, 39, 79), Brook (42), Johnson (45, 66); **Goals:** Brook 12/14.
**HAYDOCK:** 1 Steve Jones; 5 Karl Dinsdale; 3 Danny Lee; 4 Dean Dollin; 2 Danny Davies; 6 Jordan Gibson; 7 Andy Bacon; 8 Adam Brown; 9 Mike Sexton; 10 Scott Johnson; 11 Danny Gee; 12 David Frodsham; 17 Rob Sexton. Subs (all used): 15 Gary Anderton; 20 Carl Cheetham; 14 Johnny Travena; 16 Kyle Braithwaite.
**Tries:** Johnson (61), Gibson (76); **Goals:** Jones 1/2.
**Rugby Leaguer & League Express Men of the Match:** *Oldham:* Adam Brook; *Haydock:* Jordan Gibson.
**Penalty count:** 8-7; **Half-time:** 42-0;
**Referee:** Aaron Moore; **Attendance:** 508.

### WHITEHAVEN 74 WIGAN ST PATRICKS 4

**WHITEHAVEN:** 2 Jordan Burns; 5 Dave Thompson; 3 Chris Taylor; 4 Jessie Joe Parker; 19 Andrew Bulman; 1 Sam Forrester; 7 Callum Phillips; 22 Ruairi McGoff; 14 Sam Dowsett; 17 Matty While; 15 Connor Holliday; 25 Kurt Maudling; 21 Jake Bradley. Subs (all used): 6 Dion Aiye; 16 Lewis Brown; 8 Marc Shackley; 13 Tom Wilkinson.
**Tries:** C Phillips (2, 39), Bulman (6, 12, 30, 53, 70, 72), D Thompson (35, 67, 73, 80), Forrester (47), Taylor (77);
**Goals:** Holliday 9/13, Shackley 0/1.
**ST PATRICKS:** 1 Curtis Hampson; 2 Matthew Velvin; 3 Luke Warburton; 4 Sam Arrowsmith; 5 Connor McGaughey; 6 Joe Prior; 7 Josh Yates; 8 Jamie Bristo; 9 Joe Higham; 10 Joe Turton; 11 Andrew Higham; 12 Daniel Ryding; 13 Jonathan Brown. Subs (all used): 14 Adam Rosser; 15 Ryan Braddock; 16 Daniel McGoldrick; 17 Connor Webb.
**Try:** Ryding (17); **Goals:** Hampson 0/1.
**Sin bin:** Brown (66) - use of the elbow.
**Rugby Leaguer & League Express Men of the Match:** *Whitehaven:* Andrew Bulman; *St Patricks:* Daniel Ryding.
**Penalty count:** 10-8; **Half-time:** 30-4;
**Referee:** Cameron Worsley; **Attendance:** 464.

*Sunday 17th March 2019*

### WORKINGTON TOWN 22 SIDDAL 0

**TOWN:** 2 Tyllar Mellor; 20 Jonathan Walsh; 21 James Worthington; 3 Elliott Miller; 16 Scott Rooke; 6 Jamie Doran; 7 Carl Forber; 8 Oliver Wilkes; 9 Sean Penkywicz; 10 Stevie Scholey; 13 Karl Olstrom; 11 Danny Tickle; 25 Sam Hopkins. Subs (only three named): 4 Perry Singleton; 15 Tom Curwen (not used); 19 Caine Barnes.
**Tries:** Rooke (6), Penkywicz (9), Scholey (13), Wilkes (64);
**Goals:** Forber 3/4.
**SIDDAL:** 1 Gareth Blackburn; 2 Sam Walsh; 3 Lewis Hosty; 4 Fred Walker; 5 Dom Booth; 6 Chris Brooke; 7 Christian Ackroyd; 8 George Ambler; 9 Danny Rushworth; 10 Jack Georgiou; 11 Danny Williams; 12 Ben Hinsley; 13 Canaan Smithies. Subs (all used): 14 Eddie Ainley; 15 Sean McCormack; 16 Gareth English; 17 Jake Turner.
**Rugby Leaguer & League Express Men of the Match:** *Town:* Sam Hopkins; *Siddal:* Ben Hinsley.
**Penalty count:** 11-6; **Half-time:** 16-0;
**Referee:** Billy Pearson; **Attendance:** 355.

## ROUND 4

*Saturday 30th March 2019*

### FEATHERSTONE ROVERS 38 SWINTON LIONS 14

**ROVERS:** 25 Jack Render; 36 Jack Broadbent; 3 Thompson Teteh; 17 James Harrison; 4 Josh Hardcastle; 35 Jorge Richardson; 7 Watson Boas; 8 Scott Wheeldon; 9 Cameron King; 23 Makahesi Makatoa; 14 John Davies; 12 Brad Day; 13 James Lockwood. Subs (all used): 15 Luke Cooper; 29 Jack Ormondroyd; 16 Danny Maskill; 19 Jimmy Beckett.
**Tries:** Teteh (6, 9, 25), Broadbent (19), Wheeldon (30), W Boas (38), Day (46), King (54);
**Goals:** W Boas 0/1, King 3/7.
**Sin bin:** Wheeldon (63) - high tackle on Acton.
**LIONS:** 1 Jack Hansen; 2 Mike Butt; 31 Liam Forsyth; 6 Oscar Thomas; 20 Harry Aaronson; 34 Harry Smith; 7 Rob Fairclough; 8 Gavin Bennion; 9 Luke Waterworth; 17 Aaron Hall; 4 Daley Williams; 10 Lewis Hatton; 26 Jamie Acton. Subs (all used): 14 Billy Brickhill; 36 Josh Ganson; 16 Paddy Jones; 19 Jose Kenga.
**Tries:** Bennion (15), Butt (22), Aaronson (68);
**Goals:** Thomas 1/3.
**Sin bin:** Hatton (31) - dissent.
**Rugby Leaguer & League Express Men of the Match:** *Rovers:* Thompson Teteh; *Lions:* Jamie Acton.
**Penalty count:** 10-12; **Half-time:** 30-10;
**Referee:** Liam Moore; **Attendance:** 691.

### THATTO HEATH CRUSADERS 16 NORTH WALES CRUSADERS 14

**THATTO HEATH:** 1 Ben Heyes; 2 Adam Saunders; 3 Corey Lee; 4 Matty Norton; 5 Niall Allen; 6 Josh Crehan; 7 Bobbie Goulding; 8 Mike Stark; 9 Lewis Foster; 10 Andy Lea; 11 Adam Prendergast; 12 Connor Dwyer; 13 Jamie Tracey. Subs (all used): 14 Luke Bradshaw; 15 Adam Hesketh; 16 Max Dudley; 17 Brad Ashurst.
**Tries:** Foster (12), Dwyer (28), Norton (51);
**Goals:** Goulding 2/4.
**NORTH WALES:** 1 Dan Price; 2 Gavin Conroy; 3 Simon Atherton; 4 Earl Hurst; 5 Rob Massam; 6 Steve Roper; 7 Ryan Smith; 8 Callum Hazzard; 9 Karl Ashall; 10 Warren Thompson; 11 Jack Houghton; 12 Chris Worrall; 13 Kenny Baker. Subs (all used): 14 Ben Stead; 15 Brad Brennan; 16 Alex Eckley; 17 Jonny Walker.
**Tries:** Massam (32, 79), Worrall (68);
**Goals:** Baker 0/1, Stead 1/2.
**Rugby Leaguer & League Express Men of the Match:** *Thatto Heath:* Lewis Foster; *North Wales:* Rob Massam.
**Penalty count:** 3-12; **Half-time:** 10-4;
**Referee:** John McMullen; **Attendance:** 737.

*Sunday 31st March 2019*

### FEATHERSTONE LIONS 6 DONCASTER 46

**LIONS:** 1 Ian Jackson; 2 Connor Paver; 21 Danny Thompson; 4 Davi Garahan; 5 Jack Ellam; 6 Tom Wandless; 7 Josh Maden; 8 Evan Morris; 9 Scott Glassell; 10 Ben Mawson; 11 Gareth Williamson; 12 Joe Fox; 13 Dean Gamble. Subs (all used): 15 Jake Wood; 16 Harry McAllister; 17 George Nuttall; 18 Danny Gilbert.
**Try:** Nuttall (21); **Goals:** Jackson 1/1.
**Sin bin:** Fox (34) - professional foul.
**DONCASTER:** 2 Richard Owen; 5 Sam Doherty; 3 Connor Bower; 4 Jason Tali; 19 Matty Chrimes; 6 Jordan Howden; 13 Jordie Hedges; 10 Ryan Boyle; 20 Callum Ogden; 14 Connor Scott; 28 Jordan Cox; 26 Elliott Townsend; 9 Kyle Kesik. Subs (all used): 15 Kieran Cross; 17 Brandon Douglas; 8 Russ Spiers; 25 Stefanos Bastas.
**Tries:** Chrimes (7, 60), Doherty (15), Owen (35), Bastas (37), Cross (47, 74, 78), Bower (56);
**Goals:** Hedges 0/2, Howden 5/7.
**Sin bin:** Douglas (44) - holding down.
**Rugby Leaguer & League Express Men of the Match:** *Lions:* Scott Glassell; *Doncaster:* Kieran Cross.
**Penalty count:** 6-7; **Half-time:** 6-20;
**Referee:** Andrew Sweet; **Attendance:** N/A *(at LD Nutrition Stadium).*

### KEIGHLEY COUGARS 12 BRADFORD BULLS 14

**COUGARS:** 21 Matt Welham; 5 Davey Dixon; 4 Will Cooke; 23 Macauley Hallett; 1 Alfie Seeley; 15 Jack Miller; 7 Benn Hardcastle; 19 Matthew Bailey; 14 Luke Million; 30 Harvey Hallas; 11 Josh Lynam; 13 Jason Muranka; 9 James Feather. Subs (all used): 8 Jack Coventry; 12 Aaron Levy; 17 Billy Gaylor; 22 Dan Parker.
**Tries:** Feather (24), Seeley (60); **Goals:** Hardcastle 2/2.
**Sin bin:** Lynam (74) - dissent.
**BULLS:** 2 Ethan Ryan; 22 Dalton Grant; 4 Ashley Gibson; 26 Ross Oakes; 24 David Foggin-Johnston; 1 Brandon Pickersgill; 27 Rowan Milnes; 30 Oliver Wilson; 9 Matty Wildie; 10 Steve Crossley; 11 Matt Garside; 29 Matthew Storton; 12 Elliot Minchella. Subs (all used): 15 Callum Bustin; 21 George Flanagan; 19 Jon Magrin; 28 Evan Hodgson.
**Tries:** Ryan (38), Flanagan (43); **Goals:** Minchella 3/4.
**Rugby Leaguer & League Express Men of the Match:** *Cougars:* James Feather; *Bulls:* Steve Crossley.
**Penalty count:** 2-11; **Half-time:** 6-4;
**Referee:** Marcus Griffiths; **Attendance:** 1,881.

### BARROW RAIDERS 16 YORK CITY KNIGHTS 32

**RAIDERS:** 18 Luke Cresswell; 27 Brett Carter; 4 Jake Spedding; 5 Deon Cross; 23 Shane Toal; 6 Jamie Dallimore; 7 Lewis Charnock; 28 Josh Johnson; 14 Wartovo Puara; 30 Alec Susino; 26 Willie Minoga; 19 Danny Morrow; 15 Dan Toal. Subs (all used): 9 Nathan Mossop; 1 Theerapol Ritson; 16 Glenn Riley; 8 Tom Walker.
**Tries:** Susino (25), J Johnson (45), Ritson (47);
**Goals:** Dallimore 2/3.
**Dismissal:** D Toal (79) - fighting.
**CITY KNIGHTS:** 24 Kevin Brown; 21 Judah Mazive; 4 Brad Hey; 20 Perry Whiteley; - Conor McGrath; 1 Matty Marsh; 9 Will Jubb; 16 Jack Blagbrough; 26 Kriss Brining; 22 Marcus Stock; 11 Josh Jordan-Roberts; 19 Mike Kelly; 13 Tim Spears. Subs (all used): 25 Dave Petersen; 17 Joe Porter; 12 Sam Scott; 10 Jack Teanby.
**Tries:** Stock (12), Whiteley (14), Teanby (29), Jordan-Roberts (72), Marsh (78); **Goals:** Marsh 6/8.
**Rugby Leaguer & League Express Men of the Match:** *Raiders:* Alec Susino; *City Knights:* Matty Marsh.
**Penalty count:** 6-10; **Half-time:** 6-18;
**Referee:** Gareth Hewer; **Attendance:** 898.

### BATLEY BULLDOGS 62 LOCK LANE 6

**BULLDOGS:** 1 Dave Scott; 2 Wayne Reittie; 3 Sam Smeaton; 23 Keenen Tomlinson; 5 Johnny Campbell; 6 Louis Jouffret; 14 Danny Yates; 15 Toby Everett; 18 Tom Hemingway; 17 Tyler Dickinson; 24 Paul Brearley; 19 Alex Bretherton; 11 Dane Manning. Subs (all used): 7 Dom Brambani; 16 Michael Ward; 21 Jo Taira; 25 Lewis Bienek.
**Tries:** Yates (4), Dickinson (16), Reittie (28, 42, 79), Ward (36), Jouffret (49, 53), Smeaton (55, 75), Hemingway (65); **Goals:** Scott 4/4, Jouffret 5/7.
**LOCK LANE:** 1 Lewis Price; 2 Adam Rothwell; 3 Nick Saxton; 4 Tommy Newbould; 5 Tom Sowerby; 6 Danny Sowerby; 7 Connor Land; 8 Sean Hesketh; 9 Craig Savage; 10 Rob Firth; 11 Cory Southern; 17 Steve Scott; 13 Chris Siddons. Subs (all used): 14 Craig Duncan; 15 Jack Lee; 16 Mitchell Platt; 18 Craig Jones.
**Try:** Land (33); **Goals:** Land 1/1.
**Rugby Leaguer & League Express Men of the Match:** *Bulldogs:* Jo Taira; *Lock Lane:* Craig Savage.
**Penalty count:** 8-6; **Half-time:** 24-6;
**Referee:** Nick Bennett; **Attendance:** 501.

### DEWSBURY RAMS 32 WEST HULL 6

**RAMS:** 1 Dale Morton; 23 Rob Worrincy; 3 Cameron Leeming; 4 Adam Ryder; 2 Andy Gabriel; 7 Simon Brown; 38 Liam Finn; 8 Jode Sheriffe; 9 Robbie Ward; 16 Jordan Andrade; 11 Lucas Walshaw; 32 Samy Kibula; 19 Daniel Igbinedion. Subs (all used): 22 Danny King; 27 Jack Ray; 37 Liam Mackay; 33 Callum Field.
**Tries:** Gabriel (12, 53), Leeming (23, 60, 77), Morton (33);
**Goals:** Finn 4/6.
**WEST HULL:** 1 Harry Tyson-Wilson; 2 Nev Morrison; 14 Jack Watts; 4 Jack Lazenby; 5 Ryan Langton; 7 Ian Kerman; 6 Scott Spaven; 20 Ryan Wilson; 9 Nathan Powley; 8 Lee Cator; 12 Louis Crowther; 11 Benn Arbon; 13 Ryan Steen. Subs (all used): 16 Josh Wood; 15 Sam Cator; 10 Oscar Ellerington; 19 Bobby Tyson-Wilson.
**Try:** Lazenby (73); **Goals:** R Wilson 1/1.
**Rugby Leaguer & League Express Men of the Match:** *Rams:* Cameron Leeming; *West Hull:* Jack Lazenby.
**Penalty count:** 6-7; **Half-time:** 18-0;
**Referee:** Cameron Worsley; **Attendance:** 366.

### HUNSLET 24 HALIFAX 28

**HUNSLET:** 1 Jimmy Watson; 2 Gareth Potts; 23 Nathan Chappell; 3 Tom Ashton; 5 Dale Bloomfield; 6 Joe Sanderson; 21 Reece Dean; 31 Jon Luke Kirby; 9 Jack Lee; 10 Adam Robinson; 11 Josh Tonks; 30 Charlie Martin; 13 Mike Emmett. Subs (all used): 16 Zach Braham; 17 Dan Hawksworth; 18 Nyle Flynn; 20 Vila Halafihi.
**Tries:** Lee (24), Dean (28), Potts (35), Chappell (79);
**Goals:** Dean 4/6.
**Sin bin:** Chappell (56) - dangerous challenge.
**HALIFAX:** 1 Quentin Laulu-Togaga'e; 2 Shaun Robinson; 3 Steve Tyrer; 20 James Saltonstall; 5 Will Sharp; 6 Scott Murrell; 23 James Woodburn-Hall; 17 Ben Kavanagh; 14 Brandon Moore; 18 Elliot Morris; 12 Ed Barber; 11 Shane Grady; 10 Jacob Fairbank. Subs (all used): 8 Dan Fleming; 25 Liam Cooper; 27 Reece Chapman-Smith; 28 Will Calcott.
**Tries:** Woodburn-Hall (12), Barber (51), Laulu-Togaga'e (57), Morris (74), Cooper (76); **Goals:** Tyrer 4/5.
**Rugby Leaguer & League Express Men of the Match:** *Hunslet:* Adam Robinson; *Halifax:* James Woodburn-Hall.
**Penalty count:** 6-11; **Half-time:** 16-6;
**Referee:** Billy Pearson; **Attendance:** 731.

### OLDHAM 14 WIDNES VIKINGS 54

**OLDHAM:** 5 Ritchie Hawkyard; 1 Kyran Johnson; 3 Zack McComb; 28 Jack Holmes; 27 Harry Maders; 6 Paul Crook; 7 Dave Hewitt; 8 Phil Joy; 9 Gareth Owen; 26 Scott Law; 17 Ben Calland; 12 Emmerson Whittel; 24 Liam Bent. Subs (all used): 13 Jack Spencer; 30 Titus Gwaze; 18 Ben Davies; 19 Jamie Greenwood.
**Tries:** McComb (57), Owen (62), Hawkyard (68);
**Goals:** Hewitt 1/3.
**Sin bin:** Law (77) - fighting; Joy (80) - high tackle.
**VIKINGS:** 25 Lloyd Roby; 2 Ryan Ince; 12 Chris Dean; 24 Keanan Brand; 22 Owen Buckley; 5 Jack Owens; 21 Joe Lyons; 11 Harrison Hansen; 15 Jordan Johnstone; 13 Hep Cahill; 19 Brad Walker; 17 Sam Wilde; 16 MacGraff Leuluai. Subs (all used): 8 Jay Chapelhow; 18 Ted Chapelhow; 20 Owen Farnworth; 28 Dom Speakman.
**Tries:** Ince (7), Owens (11, 35, 39), Buckley (17, 26, 46), Brand (23), Roby (42), Johnstone (78); **Goals:** Owens 7/10.
**Sin bin:** Cahill (77) - fighting.
**Rugby Leaguer & League Express Men of the Match:** *Oldham:* Gareth Owen; *Vikings:* Jack Owens.
**Penalty count:** 4-9; **Half-time:** 0-38;
**Referee:** Jack Smith; **Attendance:** 1,247.

### SHEFFIELD EAGLES 12 LEIGH CENTURIONS 34

**EAGLES:** 1 Josh Guzdek; 2 Ryan Millar; 18 James Glover; 19 Sonny Esslemont; 5 Ben Blackmore; 6 Pat Walker; 7 Anthony Thackeray; 11 Brad Knowles; 14 Greg Burns; 10 Matt James; 12 Joel Farrell; 15 Olly Davies; 13 Aaron Brown. Subs (all used): 9 James Davey; 17 Shaun Pick; 23 Rory Dixon; 25 Lewis Taylor.
**Tries:** Millar (25), Davies (51); **Goals:** Walker 2/2.
**CENTURIONS:** 1 Gregg McNally; 2 Jonny Pownall; 3 Iain Thornley; 19 Mitch Cox; 12 Andy Thornley; 7 Josh Woods; 6 Martyn Ridyard; 29 Jake Emmitt; 27 Liam Hood; 10 Sam Brooks; 11 Toby Adamson; 17 Nick Gregson; 15 Joe Cator. Subs (all used): 9 Micky Higham; 8 Tom Spencer; 13 Luke Adamson; 18 Dec O'Donnell.
**Tries:** McNally (3), T Adamson (30), Cox (39), Gregson (58), Pownall (64), Brooks (66); **Goals:** Ridyard 5/6.
**Rugby Leaguer & League Express Men of the Match:** *Eagles:* Josh Guzdek; *Centurions:* Martyn Ridyard.
**Penalty count:** 11-4; **Half-time:** 6-18;
**Referee:** Greg Dolan; **Attendance:** 596.

### WHITEHAVEN 21 ROCHDALE HORNETS 22

**WHITEHAVEN:** 3 Chris Taylor; 15 Connor Holliday; 23 Jason Mossop; 4 Jessie Joe Parker; 2 Jordan Burns; 1 Sam Forrester; 7 Callum Phillips; 8 Marc Shackley; 14 Sam Dowsett; 10 Kris Coward; 12 Jake Moore; 25 Kurt Maudling; 13 Tom Wilkinson. Subs (all used): 6 Dion Aiye; 9 James Newton; 18 Jordan Thomson; 22 Ruairi McGoff.
**Tries:** C Phillips (6), Moore (29);
**Goals:** Moore 2/2, Holliday 4/4; **Field goal:** Forrester (70).
**HORNETS:** 1 Dec Kay; 2 Shaun Ainscough; 25 Jack Higginson; 4 Ben Morris; 24 Brandon Wood; 13 Stuart Howarth; 7 Dan Abram; 11 Lee Mitchell; 6 Scott Moore; 10 Carl Forster; 12 Ellis Gillam; 16 Mike Weldon; 18 Ryan Millington. Subs (all used): 17 Liam Carberry; 23 Jordan Case; 9 Ben Moores; 20 Joe Ryan.
**Tries:** Morris (15), Kay (39), Ainscough (77), Abram (79);
**Goals:** Abram 3/4.
**Sin bin:** Abram (23) - delaying restart.
**Rugby Leaguer & League Express Men of the Match:** *Whitehaven:* Marc Shackley; *Hornets:* Ben Moores.
**Penalty count:** 8-8; **Half-time:** 14-12;
**Referee:** Matt Rossleigh; **Attendance:** 889.

### WORKINGTON TOWN 21 NEWCASTLE THUNDER 20

**TOWN:** 2 Tyllar Mellor; 20 Jonathan Walsh; 19 Caine Barnes; 4 Perry Singleton; 16 Scott Rooke; 6 Jamie Doran; 7 Carl Forber; 8 Oliver Wilkes; 13 Karl Olstrom; 10 Stevie Scholey; 11 Danny Tickle; 12 Gordon Maudling; 25 Sam Hopkins. Subs (all used): 14 Andrew Dawson; 15 Tom Curwen; 23 Dominic Smallwood; - Fuifui Moimoi.
**Tries:** Rooke (5), Mellor (34), Hopkins (42);
**Goals:** Forber 4/4; **Field goal:** Doran (77).
**THUNDER:** 1 Alex Clegg; 2 Mo Agoro; 3 Tyler Craig; 4 Kieran Gill; 5 Misi Taulapapa; 6 Lewis Young; 7 Jy-mel Coleman; 8 Jack Aldous; 9 Keal Carlile; 10 Carne Doyle-Manga; 11 Rhys Clarke; 12 Aaron Ollett; 13 Evan Simons. Subs (all used): 14 David Weetman; 15 Alex Rowe; 16 Jared Blanke; 17 Joe Brown.
**Tries:** Taulapapa (13, 61), Carlile (24, 56);
**Goals:** Coleman 2/4.
**Rugby Leaguer & League Express Men of the Match:** *Town:* Perry Singleton; *Thunder:* Keal Carlile.
**Penalty count:** 7-7; **Half-time:** 12-10;
**Referee:** Tom Crashley; **Attendance:** N/A.

## ROUND 5

*Thursday 11th April 2019*

**HALIFAX 24 LONDON BRONCOS 16**

**HALIFAX:** 1 Quentin Laulu-Togaga'e; 27 Reece Chapman-Smith; 3 Steve Tyrer; 20 James Saltonstall; 2 Shaun Robinson; 23 James Woodburn-Hall; 19 Ben White; 17 Ben Kavanagh; 9 Ben Kaye; 8 Dan Fleming; 16 Kevin Larroyer; 12 Ed Barber; 28 Will Calcott. Subs (all used): 15 Harry Kidd; 18 Elliot Morris; 24 Curtis Davies; 25 Liam Cooper.
**Tries:** Barber (16), Kaye (37), Chapman-Smith (54), Laulu-Togaga'e (63); **Goals:** Tyrer 4/4.
**BRONCOS:** 17 Matty Fleming; 24 Jacob Ogden; 19 Ryan Morgan; 4 Elliot Kear; 3 Ben Hellewell; 28 Morgan Smith; 22 James Meadows; 15 Greg Richards; 9 Eloi Pelissier; 18 Nathan Mason; 12 Jay Pitts (C); 16 Matty Gee; 11 Will Lovell. Subs (all used): 6 Jordan Abdull; 7 James Cunningham; 8 Eddie Battye; 10 Mark Ioane.
**Tries:** Ioane (26), Ogden (47, 71); **Goals:** Smith 2/3.
**Rugby Leaguer & League Express Men of the Match:** *Halifax:* Ed Barber; *Broncos:* Jay Pitts.
**Penalty count:** 7-10; **Half-time:** 12-6;
**Referee:** Tom Grant; **Attendance:** 722.

**HULL KINGSTON ROVERS 14 LEIGH CENTURIONS 10**

**ROVERS:** 26 Will Dagger; 5 Ryan Shaw; 4 Jimmy Keinhorst; 3 Ben Crooks; 2 Craig Hall; 24 Josh Drinkwater; 7 Danny McGuire; 8 Robbie Mulhern; 15 Tommy Lee; 21 George Lawler; 23 Kane Linnett; 11 Joel Tomkins (C); 13 Weller Hauraki. Subs (all used): 17 Chris Atkin; 20 Danny Addy; 19 Junior Vaivai; 30 Owen Harrison (D).
**Tries:** Keinhorst (37), Shaw (72), Hall (74);
**Goals:** Hall 0/2, Shaw 1/1.
**Sin bin:** Shaw (79) - dangerous challenge.
**CENTURIONS:** 1 Gregg McNally; 2 Jonny Pownall; 3 Iain Thornley; 19 Mitch Cox; 5 Stefan Marsh; 6 Martyn Ridyard; 7 Josh Woods; 10 Sam Brooks; 9 Micky Higham; 13 Luke Adamson; 11 Toby Adamson; 12 Andy Thornley; 15 Joe Cator. Subs (all used): 18 Dec O'Donnell; 29 Jake Emmitt; 8 Tom Spencer; 17 Nick Gregson.
**Tries:** Pownall (6), Cator (23); **Goals:** Ridyard 1/2.
**Rugby Leaguer & League Express Men of the Match:** *Rovers:* Craig Hall; *Centurions:* Luke Adamson.
**Penalty count:** 14-10; **Half-time:** 4-10;
**Referee:** Liam Moore; **Attendance:** 2,188.

*Friday 12th April 2019*

**LEEDS RHINOS 78 WORKINGTON TOWN 6**

**RHINOS:** 6 Tuimoala Lolohea; 24 Luke Briscoe; 3 Kallum Watkins (C); 29 Harry Newman; 21 Ashton Golding; 15 Liam Sutcliffe; 7 Richie Myler; 36 Wellington Albert; 9 Matt Parcell; 10 Brad Singleton; 16 Brett Ferres; 33 Owen Trout (D); 25 James Donaldson. Subs (all used): 18 Nathaniel Peteru; 20 Jamie Jones-Buchanan; 37 Muizz Mustapha (D); 23 Callum McLelland (D).
**Tries:** L Briscoe (2), Golding (4, 79), Newman (7, 18, 30, 64), Albert (9), Myler (38, 43, 54), Ferres (51), Parcell (70);
**Goals:** L Sutcliffe 13/13.
**TOWN:** 2 Tyllar Mellor; 20 Jonathan Walsh; 21 James Worthington; 4 Perry Singleton; 16 Scott Rooke; 6 Jamie Doran; 7 Carl Forber; - Sam Hopkins; 13 Karl Olstrom; 10 Stevie Scholey; 19 Caine Barnes; 12 Gordon Maudling; 11 Danny Tickle. Subs (all used): 14 Andrew Dawson; 25 Fuifui Moimoi; 26 Izaac Farrell; 15 Tom Curwen.
**Try:** Barnes (33); **Goals:** Forber 1/1.
**Rugby Leaguer & League Express Men of the Match:** *Rhinos:* Harry Newman; *Town:* Perry Singleton.
**Penalty count:** 4-3; **Half time:** 42-6;
**Referee:** Marcus Griffiths; **Attendance:** 4,197.

**SALFORD RED DEVILS 76 ROCHDALE HORNETS 6**

**RED DEVILS:** 1 Niall Evalds; 2 Ed Chamberlain; 26 Krisnan Inu; 4 Junior Sa'u; 5 Jake Bibby; 6 Robert Lui; 31 Jackson Hastings; 15 Adam Walker; 19 Logan Tomkins; 10 Gil Dudson (C); 11 Josh Jones; 12 George Griffin; 16 Greg Burke. Subs (all used): 18 Ben Nakubuwai; 9 Josh Wood; 17 Tyrone McCarthy; 3 Kris Welham.
**Tries:** Burke (3), Evalds (6, 26, 49, 54), Dudson (11), Chamberlain (14), Tomkins (24), Bibby (36, 46), Griffin (58), Lui (61), Inu (71); **Goals:** Chamberlain 6/7, Inu 6/6.
**HORNETS:** 1 Dec Kay; 2 Shaun Ainscough; 25 Jack Higginson; 4 Ben Morris; 24 Brandon Wood; 29 Tyler Whittaker; 7 Dan Abram; 20 Joe Ryan; 9 Ben Moores; 27 Nathan Reidy; 12 Ellis Gillam; 16 Mike Weldon; 18 Ryan Millington. Subs (all used): 21 Jack Cottington; 3 Seta Tala; 22 Callum Wood; 17 Liam Carberry.
**Try:** Ainscough (32); **Goals:** Abram 1/1.
**Rugby Leaguer & League Express Men of the Match:** *Red Devils:* Niall Evalds; *Hornets:* Callum Wood.
**Penalty count:** 6-5; **Half-time:** 40-6;
**Referee:** Greg Dolan; **Attendance:** 1,101.

*Saturday 13th April 2019*

**WIDNES VIKINGS 44 YORK CITY KNIGHTS 12**

**VIKINGS:** 5 Jack Owens; 27 Sam Freeman; 24 Keanan Brand; 4 Anthony Gelling; 2 Ryan Ince; 6 Danny Craven; 21 Joe Lyons; 8 Jay Chapelhow; 15 Jordan Johnstone; 13 Hep Cahill; 17 Sam Wilde; 12 Chris Dean; 16 MacGraff Leuluai. Subs (all used): 18 Ted Chapelhow; 20 Owen Farnworth; 23 Liam Walsh; 25 Lloyd Roby.
**Tries:** Freeman (5, 32, 51, 63), Brand (39), Lyons (70), Ince (76), Owens (78); **Goals:** Owens 6/8.
**CITY KNIGHTS:** 24 Kevin Brown; 21 Judah Mazive; 23 Jason Bass; 34 Nick Rawsthorne; 20 Perry Whiteley; - Lewis Heckford; 26 Kriss Brining; - Jordan Baldwinson; 9 Will Jubb; 16 Jack Blagbrough; 4 Brad Hey; 11 Josh Jordan-Roberts; 17 Joe Porter. Subs (all used): 25 Dave Petersen; 8 Ronan Dixon; 22 Marcus Stock; 19 Mike Kelly.
**Tries:** Hey (2), Baldwinson (54);
**Goals:** Rawsthorne 1/1, Heckford 1/1.
**Rugby Leaguer & League Express Men of the Match:** *Vikings:* Sam Freeman; *City Knights:* Lewis Heckford.
**Penalty count:** 5-7; **Half-time:** 18-6;
**Referee:** Jack Smith; **Attendance:** 2,229.

*Sunday 14th April 2019*

**BRADFORD BULLS 27 FEATHERSTONE ROVERS 26**
*(after golden point extra-time)*

**BULLS:** 2 Ethan Ryan; 22 Dalton Grant; 12 Elliot Minchella; 26 Ross Oakes; 24 David Foggin-Johnston; 14 Jordan Lilley; 27 Rowan Milnes; 15 Callum Bustin; 9 Matty Wildie; 10 Steve Crossley; 11 Matt Garside; 25 Connor Farrell; 18 Sam Hallas. Subs (all used): 16 James Green; 3 Jake Webster; 21 George Flanagan; 17 Ross Peltier.
**Tries:** Ryan (13), Grant (71), Lilley (76), Foggin-Johnston (79); **Goals:** Minchella 5/5;
**Field goal:** Lilley (85).
**ROVERS:** 25 Jack Render; 36 Jack Broadbent; 4 Josh Hardcastle; 28 Josh Walters; 32 Alex Sutcliffe; 10 Jack Bussey; 7 Watson Boas; 29 Jack Ormondroyd; 16 Danny Maskill; 15 Luke Cooper; 12 Brad Day; 14 John Davies; 23 Makahesi Makatoa. Subs (all used): 13 James Lockwood; 9 Cameron King; 17 James Harrison; 19 Jimmy Beckett.
**Tries:** Broadbent (3), Hardcastle (39), Harrison (62), Render (65); **Goals:** W Boas 5/7.
**Rugby Leaguer & League Express Men of the Match:** *Bulls:* Elliot Minchella; *Rovers:* Jack Bussey.
**Penalty count:** 9-10; **Half-time:** 8-14;
**Referee:** Matt Rossleigh; **Attendance:** 1,691.

**DONCASTER 16 BATLEY BULLDOGS 12**

**DONCASTER:** 1 Kieran Buchanan; 5 Sam Doherty; 4 Jason Tali; 26 Menzie Yere; 19 Matty Chrimes; 9 Kyle Kesik; 13 Jordie Hedges; 10 Ryan Boyle; 20 Callum Ogden; 8 Russ Spiers; 3 Connor Bower; 30 Charlie Patterson-Lund; 22 Brad Foster. Subs (all used): 14 Connor Scott; 25 Stefanos Bastas; 31 Elliott Townsend; 29 Kieron Lawton.
**Tries:** Bower (37), Yere (58), Doherty (65);
**Goals:** Hedges 2/3.
**BULLDOGS:** 1 Dave Scott; 2 Wayne Reittie; 3 Sam Smeaton; 24 Paul Brearley; 5 Johnny Campbell; 6 Louis Jouffret; 14 Danny Yates; 8 Adam Gledhill; 9 Alistair Leak; 10 Tom Lillycrop; 12 Jack Downs; 19 Alex Bretherton; 11 Dane Manning. Subs (all used): 15 Toby Everett; 4 Lewis Galbraith; 21 Jo Taira; 16 Michael Ward.
**Tries:** Ward (48), Reittie (53); **Goals:** Scott 2/2.
**Sin bin:** Taira (57) - high tackle on Kesik.
**Rugby Leaguer & League Express Men of the Match:** *Doncaster:* Kyle Kesik; *Bulldogs:* Michael Ward.
**Penalty count:** 9-9; **Half-time:** 6-0;
**Referee:** Billy Pearson; **Attendance:** 539.

**THATTO HEATH CRUSADERS 10 DEWSBURY RAMS 36**

**CRUSADERS:** 1 Ben Heyes; 2 Adam Saunders; 3 Corey Lee; 4 Matty Norton; 5 Niall Allen; 6 Josh Crehan; 7 Bobbie Goulding; 8 Andy Lea; 9 Lewis Foster; 10 Mike Stark; 11 Adam Prendergast; 12 Connor Dwyer; 13 Jamie Tracey. Subs (all used): 14 Connor Dutton; 15 Adam Hesketh; 16 Max Dudley; 21 Brad Ashurst.
**Tries:** Norton (15), Stark (27); **Goals:** Goulding 1/2.
**RAMS:** 2 Andy Gabriel; 23 Rob Worrincy; 11 Lucas Walshaw; 4 Adam Ryder; 3 Cameron Leeming; 12 Michael Knowles; 38 Liam Finn; 8 Jode Sheriffe; 9 Robbie Ward; 16 Jordan Andrade; 22 Danny King; 32 Samy Kibula; 30 Tom Garratt. Subs (all used): 39 Harvey Whiteley; 37 Liam Mackay; 33 Callum Field; 10 Toby Richardson.
**Tries:** Gabriel (3), Worrincy (22), Walshaw (41), Kibula (53), Ryder (66), Garratt (70), Ward (79); **Goals:** Finn 4/7.
**Rugby Leaguer & League Express Men of the Match:** *Crusaders:* Ben Heyes; *Rams:* Michael Knowles.
**Penalty count:** 6-3; **Half-time:** 10-10;
**Referee:** Cameron Worsley; **Attendance:** 1,000.

## ROUND 6

*Friday 10th May 2019*

**HULL FC 28 CASTLEFORD TIGERS 12**

**HULL FC:** 6 Albert Kelly; 33 Ratu Naulago; 24 Jack Logan; 4 Josh Griffin; 2 Bureta Faraimo; 14 Jake Connor; 7 Marc Sneyd; 8 Scott Taylor; 9 Danny Houghton (C); 23 Mickey Paea; 12 Mark Minichiello; 21 Sika Manu; 13 Joe Westerman. Subs (all used): 11 Dean Hadley; 15 Chris Green; 19 Masi Matongo; 34 Gareth Ellis.
**Tries:** Connor (10), Faraimo (16), Kelly (19), Minichiello (70);
**Goals:** Sneyd 6/6.
**TIGERS:** 1 Peter Mata'utia; 25 Tuoyo Egodo; 3 Greg Minikin; 35 Cheyse Blair; 2 James Clare; 6 Jake Trueman; 24 Cory Aston; 8 Liam Watts; 9 Paul McShane (C); 23 Will Maher; 12 Mike McMeeken; 33 Chris Clarkson; 14 Nathan Massey. Subs (all used): 10 Grant Millington; 13 Adam Milner; 15 Jesse Sene-Lefao; 18 Matt Cook.
**Tries:** Clare (30), Aston (75); **Goals:** Mata'utia 2/3.
**Rugby Leaguer & League Express Men of the Match:** *Hull FC:* Jake Connor; *Tigers:* Liam Watts.
**Penalty count:** 6-8; **Half-time:** 20-8;
**Referee:** Robert Hicks; **Attendance:** 6,230.

**WAKEFIELD TRINITY 26 WIDNES VIKINGS 6**

**TRINITY:** 21 Max Jowitt; 5 Ben Jones-Bishop; 4 Reece Lyne; 34 Mason Caton-Brown; 29 Lee Kershaw; 25 Ben Reynolds; 1 Ryan Hampshire; 8 David Fifita; 9 Kyle Wood; 20 Keegan Hirst; 12 Danny Kirmond (C); 14 Justin Horo; 26 Jordan Crowther. Subs (all used): 19 James Batchelor; 24 Pauli Pauli; 15 Craig Kopczak; 23 Chris Annakin.
**Tries:** Jowitt (33), Fifita (43), Jones-Bishop (74), Kershaw (76), Horo (80); **Goals:** Hampshire 3/5.
**VIKINGS:** 5 Jack Owens; 29 Jayden Hatton; 25 Lloyd Roby; 24 Keanan Brand; 27 Sam Freeman; 6 Danny Craven; 21 Joe Lyons; 18 Ted Chapelhow; 15 Jordan Johnstone; 8 Jay Chapelhow; 17 Sam Wilde; 12 Chris Dean; 13 Hep Cahill. Subs (all used): 26 Dan Norman; 16 MacGraff Leuluai; 20 Owen Farnworth; 19 Brad Walker.
**Try:** Roby (20); **Goals:** Owens 1/1.
**Dismissal:** Owens (64) - dissent.
**Rugby Leaguer & League Express Men of the Match:** *Trinity:* Max Jowitt; *Vikings:* Danny Craven.
**Penalty count:** 6-4; **Half-time:** 6-6;
**Referee:** Gareth Hewer; **Attendance:** 3,055.

**DEWSBURY RAMS 6 HALIFAX 34**

**RAMS:** 2 Andy Gabriel; 23 Rob Worrincy; 11 Lucas Walshaw; 4 Adam Ryder; 1 Dale Morton; 7 Simon Brown; 38 Liam Finn; 30 Tom Garratt; 9 Robbie Ward; 8 Jode Sheriffe; 13 Kyle Trout; 12 Michael Knowles; 19 Daniel Igbinedion. Subs (all used): 37 Liam Mackay; 33 Callum Field; 32 Samy Kibula; 36 Ben Kilner.
**Try:** Walshaw (30); **Goals:** Finn 1/1.
**Sin bin:** Finn (9) - professional foul.
**HALIFAX:** 23 James Woodburn-Hall; 20 James Saltonstall; 3 Steve Tyrer; 4 Chester Butler; 2 Shaun Robinson; 6 Scott Murrell; 19 Ben White; 17 Ben Kavanagh; 9 Ben Kaye; 18 Elliot Morris; 12 Ed Barber; 16 Kevin Larroyer; 10 Jacob Fairbank. Subs (all used): 14 Brandon Moore; 8 Dan Fleming; 25 Liam Cooper; 22 Connor Davies.
**Tries:** Butler (6, 45), Woodburn-Hall (10), Saltonstall (22, 75), Robinson (51);
**Goals:** Tyrer 4/5, White 1/2.
**Rugby Leaguer & League Express Men of the Match:** *Rams:* Lucas Walshaw; *Halifax:* Ben White.
**Penalty count:** 6-5; **Half-time:** 6-18;
**Referee:** Marcus Griffiths; **Attendance:** 1,207.

*Saturday 11th May 2019*

**CATALANS DRAGONS 62 DONCASTER 6**

**DRAGONS:** 1 Tony Gigot; 25 Arthur Romano; 3 David Mead; 4 Brayden Wiliame; 27 Fouad Yaha; 22 Lucas Albert; 29 Sam Tomkins; 15 Mickael Simon; 9 Michael McIlorum; 10 Sam Moa; 11 Kenny Edwards; 16 Benjamin Jullien; 24 Jason Baitieri (C). Subs (all used): 14 Julian Bousquet; 17 Matt Whitley; 18 Alrix Da Costa; 20 Lambert Belmas.
**Tries:** Wiliame (8, 55, 66, 69), Whitley (29, 43), Baitieri (35), Mead (46, 50), Yaha (56, 73), Gigot (59);
**Goals:** Tomkins 1/1, Gigot 6/11.
**DONCASTER:** 1 Kieran Buchanan; 5 Sam Doherty; 3 Connor Bower; 4 Jason Tali; 30 Tom Halliday; 6 Jordan Howden; 7 Matty Beharrell; 8 Russ Spiers; 9 Kyle Kesik; 10 Ryan Boyle; 22 Brad Foster; 13 Jordie Hedges; 16 Brandan Wilkinson. Subs (all used): 14 Connor Scott; 17 Brandon Douglas; 19 Matty Chrimes; 20 Callum Ogden.
**Try:** Bower (14); **Goals:** Beharrell 1/1.
**Rugby Leaguer & League Express Men of the Match:** *Dragons:* Jason Baitieri; *Doncaster:* Matty Beharrell.
**Penalty count:** 6-3; **Half-time:** 18-6;
**Referee:** Liam Moore; **Attendance:** 3,466.

**SALFORD RED DEVILS 18**
**HULL KINGSTON ROVERS 32**

**RED DEVILS:** 1 Niall Evalds; 22 Derrell Olpherts; 26 Krisnan Inu; 3 Kris Welham; 23 Ken Sio; 6 Robert Lui; 31 Jackson Hastings; 8 Lee Mossop (C); 14 Joey Lussick; 10 Gil Dudson; 5 Jake Bibby; 12 George Griffin; 16 Greg Burke. Subs (all used): 15 Adam Walker; 20 Daniel Murray; 9 Josh Wood; 17 Tyrone McCarthy.
**Tries:** Inu (15), Evalds (21), Welham (35); **Goals:** Inu 3/5.
**ROVERS:** 2 Craig Hall; 5 Ryan Shaw; 4 Jimmy Keinhorst; 3 Ben Crooks; 19 Junior Vaivai; 7 Danny McGuire; 24 Josh Drinkwater; 30 Owen Harrison; 20 Danny Addy; 8 Robbie Mulhern; 23 Kane Linnett; 11 Joel Tomkins (C); 21 George Lawler. Subs (all used): 31 Adam Rooks; 17 Chris Atkin; 13 Weller Hauraki; 22 Ryan Lannon.
**Tries:** Linnett (6), Drinkwater (51), Vaivai (58), Addy (63), Hauraki (80); **Goals:** Shaw 6/6.
**Rugby Leaguer & League Express Men of the Match:**
*Red Devils:* Lee Mossop; *Rovers:* Robbie Mulhern.
**Penalty count:** 6-5; **Half-time:** 14-6;
**Referee:** Chris Kendall; **Attendance:** 1,842.

**BRADFORD BULLS 24 LEEDS RHINOS 22**

**BULLS:** 2 Ethan Ryan; 22 Dalton Grant; 3 Jake Webster; 26 Ross Oakes; 24 David Foggin-Johnston; 14 Jordan Lilley; 27 Rowan Milnes; 8 Liam Kirk; 18 Sam Hallas; 10 Steve Crossley; 12 Elliot Minchella; 25 Connor Farrell; 13 Mikey Wood. Subs (all used): 9 Matty Wildie; 16 James Green; 17 Ross Peltier; 29 Matthew Storton.
**Tries:** Grant (7), Webster (24), Hallas (27), Wood (32); **Goals:** Minchella 0/2, Milnes 4/4.
**RHINOS:** 6 Tuimoala Lolohea; 2 Tom Briscoe; 29 Harry Newman; 4 Konrad Hurrell; 5 Ash Handley; 15 Liam Sutcliffe; 23 Callum McLelland; 38 Ava Seumanufagai; 14 Brad Dwyer; 18 Nathaniel Peteru; 22 Cameron Smith; 3 Kallum Watkins (C); 11 Trent Merrin. Subs (all used): 8 Adam Cuthbertson; 9 Matt Parcell; 19 Mikolaj Oledzki; 36 Wellington Albert.
**Tries:** Lolohea (4), McLelland (14), Newman (49), T Briscoe (74); **Goals:** L Sutcliffe 3/5.
**Rugby Leaguer & League Express Men of the Match:**
*Bulls:* Jordan Lilley; *Rhinos:* Mikolaj Oledzki.
**Penalty count:** 9-4; **Half-time:** 22-14;
**Referee:** Ben Thaler; **Attendance:** 10,256.

*Sunday 12th May 2019*

**WARRINGTON WOLVES 26 WIGAN WARRIORS 24**

**WOLVES:** 1 Stefan Ratchford; 5 Josh Charnley; 18 Toby King; 4 Ryan Atkins; 3 Bryson Goodwin; 6 Blake Austin; 15 Declan Patton; 8 Chris Hill (C); 9 Daryl Clark; 10 Mike Cooper; 11 Ben Currie; 12 Jack Hughes (C); 23 Matt Davis. Subs (all used): 14 Jason Clark; 13 Ben Murdoch-Masila; 17 Joe Philbin; 19 Sitaleki Akauola.
**Tries:** Goodwin (7), Hughes (28), D Clark (37), Atkins (47); **Goals:** Ratchford 5/5.
**WARRIORS:** 20 Zak Hardaker; 17 Liam Marshall; 3 Dan Sarginson; 4 Oliver Gildart; 5 Joe Burgess; 6 George Williams; 7 Thomas Leuluai; 10 Ben Flower; 9 Sam Powell; 14 Romain Navarrete; 15 Willie Isa; 11 Joe Greenwood; 8 Tony Clubb. Subs (all used): 22 Joe Bullock; 23 Chris Hankinson; 13 Sean O'Loughlin (C); 19 Taulima Tautai.
**Tries:** Powell (25), Leuluai (34), Sarginson (52), Hardaker (56); **Goals:** Hardaker 4/5.
**Rugby Leaguer & League Express Men of the Match:**
*Wolves:* Daryl Clark; *Warriors:* Thomas Leuluai.
**Penalty count:** 3-8; **Half-time:** 18-12;
**Referee:** James Child; **Attendance:** 7,086.

**HUDDERSFIELD GIANTS 16 ST HELENS 22**

**GIANTS:** 1 Darnell McIntosh; 31 Louis Senior; 4 Jordan Turner; 11 Aaron Murphy; 32 Innes Senior; 6 Lee Gaskell; 7 Matt Frawley; 19 Matty English; 14 Adam O'Brien; 10 Suaia Matagi; 35 Joe Wardle; 12 Alex Mellor; 8 Paul Clough (C). Subs (all used): 9 Kruise Leeming; 15 Oliver Roberts; 29 Sam Hewitt; 17 Ukuma Ta'ai.
**Tries:** Joe Wardle (18, 53), Murphy (30); **Goals:** Gaskell 2/3.
**SAINTS:** 23 Lachlan Coote; 2 Tommy Makinson; 3 Kevin Naiqama; 24 Matthew Costello; 5 Regan Grace; 1 Jonny Lomax; 6 Theo Fages; 8 Alex Walmsley; 9 James Roby (C); 19 Matty Lees; 11 Zeb Taia; 17 Dominique Peyroux; 15 Morgan Knowles. Subs (all used): 12 Joseph Paulo; 20 Jack Ashworth; 16 Kyle Amor; 21 Aaron Smith.
**Tries:** Grace (12), Fages (35), Coote (51), Naiqama (61); **Goals:** Coote 3/6.
**Rugby Leaguer & League Express Men of the Match:**
*Giants:* Joe Wardle; *Saints:* Regan Grace.
**Penalty count:** 5-4; **Half-time:** 10-12;
**Referee:** Scott Mikalauskas; **Attendance:** 3,533.

No way through the St Helens defence for Halifax's James Saltonstall

## QUARTER FINALS

*Thursday 30th May 2019*

**HULL FC 51 CATALANS DRAGONS 8**

**HULL FC:** 1 Jamie Shaul; 33 Ratu Naulago; 14 Jake Connor; 4 Josh Griffin; 2 Bureta Faraimo; 6 Albert Kelly; 7 Marc Sneyd; 15 Chris Green; 9 Danny Houghton (C); 23 Mickey Paea; 12 Mark Minichiello; 21 Sika Manu; 13 Joe Westerman. Subs (all used): 10 Josh Bowden; 11 Dean Hadley; 20 Brad Fash; 35 Andre Savelio.
**Tries:** Connor (5), Faraimo (7), Manu (47), Naulago (52, 68), Kelly (61), Shaul (70), Houghton (78); **Goals:** Sneyd 9/10; **Field goal:** Sneyd (66).
**DRAGONS:** 1 Tony Gigot; 27 Fouad Yaha; 3 David Mead; 4 Brayden Wiliame; 5 Lewis Tierney; 6 Samisoni Langi; 29 Sam Tomkins; 14 Julian Bousquet; 9 Michael McIlorum; 10 Sam Moa; 17 Matt Whitley; 12 Benjamin Garcia; 8 Remi Casty (C). Subs (all used): 11 Kenny Edwards; 18 Alrix Da Costa; 24 Jason Baitieri; 28 Sam Kasiano.
**Tries:** Tierney (16, 21); **Goals:** Tomkins 0/2.
**Rugby Leaguer & League Express Men of the Match:**
*Hull FC:* Marc Sneyd; *Dragons:* Michael McIlorum.
**Penalty count:** 7-5; **Half-time:** 12-8;
**Referee:** Ben Thaler; **Attendance:** 4,832.

*Friday 31st May 2019*

**HULL KINGSTON ROVERS 22**
**WARRINGTON WOLVES 28**

**ROVERS:** 2 Craig Hall; 5 Ryan Shaw; 23 Kane Linnett; 4 Jimmy Keinhorst; 3 Ben Crooks; 24 Josh Drinkwater; 7 Danny McGuire (C); 34 Antoni Maria; 20 Danny Addy; 10 Mose Masoe; 21 George Lawler; 13 Weller Hauraki; 8 Robbie Mulhern. Subs (all used): 17 Chris Atkin; 14 Mitch Garbutt; 22 Ryan Lannon; 30 Owen Harrison (not used).
**Tries:** Crooks (55), Drinkwater (62, 71), Hall (77); **Goals:** Shaw 3/4.

**WOLVES:** 22 Jake Mamo; 2 Tom Lineham; 3 Bryson Goodwin; 18 Toby King; 5 Josh Charnley; 6 Blake Austin; 15 Declan Patton; 8 Chris Hill (C); 9 Daryl Clark; 10 Mike Cooper; 11 Ben Currie; 12 Jack Hughes (C); 17 Joe Philbin. Subs (all used): 14 Jason Clark; 13 Ben Murdoch-Masila; 19 Sitaleki Akauola; 23 Matt Davis.
**Tries:** Mamo (12), Austin (39), Lineham (42), Murdoch-Masila (52), Currie (74); **Goals:** Patton 4/6.
**Sin bin:** Lineham (18) - late challenge on Keinhorst; Patton (21) - persistent team offences.
**Rugby Leaguer & League Express Men of the Match:**
*Rovers:* Craig Hall; *Wolves:* Blake Austin.
**Penalty count:** 10-6; **Half-time:** 0-12;
**Referee:** Robert Hicks; **Attendance:** 3,311.

*Saturday 1st June 2019*

**ST HELENS 48 WAKEFIELD TRINITY 10**

**SAINTS:** 23 Lachlan Coote; 2 Tommy Makinson; 3 Kevin Naiqama; 4 Mark Percival; 5 Regan Grace; 1 Jonny Lomax; 7 Danny Richardson; 8 Alex Walmsley; 9 James Roby (C); 10 Luke Thompson; 11 Zeb Taia; 17 Dominique Peyroux; 15 Morgan Knowles. Subs (all used): 12 Joseph Paulo; 13 Louie McCarthy-Scarsbrook; 19 Matty Lees; 20 Jack Ashworth.
**Tries:** Coote (3), Makinson (21), Knowles (25), Grace (33), Taia (61), Percival (65), Lomax (71), Naiqama (76); **Goals:** Coote 8/11.
**TRINITY:** 1 Ryan Hampshire; 29 Lee Kershaw; 4 Reece Lyne; 32 Jack Croft (D); 5 Ben Jones-Bishop; 6 Jacob Miller (C); 7 Danny Brough; 10 Anthony England; 13 Tyler Randell; 15 Craig Kopczak; 12 Danny Kirmond; 11 Matty Ashurst; 36 Kelepi Tanginoa. Subs (all used): 9 Kyle Wood; 20 Keegan Hirst; 22 George King; 26 Jordan Crowther.
**Tries:** Croft (6), Randell (50); **Goals:** Brough 1/2.
**Sin bin:** Hampshire (27) - professional foul.
**Rugby Leaguer & League Express Men of the Match:**
*Saints:* Zeb Taia; *Trinity:* Jack Croft.
**Penalty count:** 8-7; **Half-time:** 26-6;
**Referee:** Chris Kendall; **Attendance:** 6,453.

Warrington's Stefan Ratchford kicks ahead during the Wolves' Challenge Cup Final win against St Helens

*Sunday 2nd June 2019*

**BRADFORD BULLS 16 HALIFAX 20**

**BULLS:** 2 Ethan Ryan; 22 Dalton Grant; 3 Jake Webster; 26 Ross Oakes; 24 David Foggin-Johnston; 14 Jordan Lilley; 27 Rowan Milnes; 8 Liam Kirk; 9 Matty Wildie; 10 Steve Crossley; 12 Elliot Minchella; 25 Connor Farrell; 18 Sam Hallas. Subs (all used): 17 Ross Peltier; 13 Mikey Wood; 21 George Flanagan; 29 Matthew Storton.
**Tries:** Milnes (8), Webster (54), Wildie (69);
**Goals:** Minchella 0/2, Lilley 2/3.
**On report:** Wood (49) - alleged bite.
**HALIFAX:** 1 Quentin Laulu-Togaga'e; 20 James Saltonstall; 3 Steve Tyrer; 4 Chester Butler; 5 Will Sharp; 6 Scott Murrell; 30 Scott Grix; 17 Ben Kavanagh; 14 Brandon Moore; 35 Adam Tangata; 25 Liam Cooper; 12 Ed Barber; 10 Jacob Fairbank. Subs (all used): 23 James Woodburn-Hall; 16 Kevin Larroyer; 8 Dan Fleming; 18 Elliot Morris.
**Tries:** Tyrer (46), Scott Grix (65), Woodburn-Hall (74);
**Goals:** Tyrer 4/4.
**Sin bin:** Tangata (14) - dangerous challenge on Lilley.
**Rugby Leaguer & League Express Men of the Match:**
*Bulls:* Matty Wildie; *Halifax:* Brandon Moore.
**Penalty count:** 7-7; **Half-time:** 6-0;
**Referee:** Scott Mikalauskas; **Attendance:** 6,591.

## SEMI-FINALS

*Saturday 27th July 2019*

**HULL FC 14 WARRINGTON WOLVES 22**

**HULL FC:** 1 Jamie Shaul; 2 Bureta Faraimo; 4 Josh Griffin;

3 Carlos Tuimavave; 33 Ratu Naulago; 6 Albert Kelly; 7 Marc Sneyd; 8 Scott Taylor; 9 Danny Houghton (C); 23 Mickey Paea; 22 Jordan Lane; 12 Mark Minichiello; 13 Joe Westerman. Subs (all used): 34 Gareth Ellis; 10 Josh Bowden; 20 Brad Fash; 14 Jake Connor.
**Tries:** Faraimo (24), Taylor (66); **Goals:** Sneyd 3/5.
**WOLVES:** 1 Stefan Ratchford; 2 Tom Lineham; 3 Bryson Goodwin; 18 Toby King; 22 Jake Mamo; 6 Blake Austin; 15 Declan Patton; 8 Chris Hill (C); 9 Daryl Clark; 10 Mike Cooper; 11 Ben Currie; 12 Jack Hughes (C); 14 Jason Clark. Subs: 17 Joe Philbin; 13 Ben Murdoch-Masila; 23 Matt Davis; 16 Lama Tasi (not used).
**Tries:** Goodwin (7), Currie (34), King (49), Philbin (79);
**Goals:** Ratchford 3/4.
**Rugby Leaguer & League Express Men of the Match:**
*Hull FC:* Danny Houghton; *Wolves:* Blake Austin.
**Penalty count:** 5-4; **Half-time:** 8-10;
**Referee:** Robert Hicks.

**HALIFAX 2 ST HELENS 26**

**HALIFAX:** 30 Scott Grix; 2 Shaun Robinson; 3 Steve Tyrer; 20 James Saltonstall; 5 Will Sharp; 6 Scott Murrell; 7 Ben Johnston; 35 Adam Tangata; 14 Brandon Moore; 17 Ben Kavanagh; 4 Chester Butler; 12 Ed Barber; 10 Jacob Fairbank. Subs (all used): 9 Ben Kaye; 18 Elliot Morris; 8 Dan Fleming; 16 Kevin Larroyer.
**Goals:** Tyrer 1/1.
**SAINTS:** 1 Jonny Lomax; 2 Tommy Makinson; 3 Kevin Naiqama; 4 Mark Percival; 5 Regan Grace; 6 Theo Fages; 7 Danny Richardson; 8 Alex Walmsley; 9 James Roby (C); 10 Luke Thompson; 13 Louie McCarthy-Scarsbrook; 17 Dominique Peyroux; 12 Joseph Paulo. Subs (all used): 16 Kyle Amor; 19 Matty Lees; 20 Jack Ashworth; 22 James Bentley.

**Tries:** Roby (35), Peyroux (48), Lomax (61), Fages (70);
**Goals:** Richardson 5/5.
**Rugby Leaguer & League Express Men of the Match:**
*Halifax:* Scott Grix; *Saints:* James Roby.
**Penalty count:** 3-4; **Half-time:** 2-8; **Referee:** Chris Kendall.

**Attendance:** 24,364 (both at University of Bolton Stadium).

## FINAL

*Saturday 24th August 2019*

**ST HELENS 4 WARRINGTON WOLVES 18**

**SAINTS:** 23 Lachlan Coote; 2 Tommy Makinson; 3 Kevin Naiqama; 4 Mark Percival; 5 Regan Grace; 1 Jonny Lomax; 6 Theo Fages; 8 Alex Walmsley; 9 James Roby (C); 10 Luke Thompson; 11 Zeb Taia; 17 Dominique Peyroux; 15 Morgan Knowles. Subs (all used): 13 Louie McCarthy-Scarsbrook; 16 Kyle Amor; 20 Jack Ashworth; 12 Joseph Paulo.
**Try:** Fages (56); **Goals:** Coote 0/1.
**WOLVES:** 1 Stefan Ratchford; 2 Tom Lineham; 3 Bryson Goodwin; 18 Toby King; 5 Josh Charnley; 11 Ben Currie; 15 Declan Patton; 8 Chris Hill (C); 9 Daryl Clark; 10 Mike Cooper; 13 Ben Murdoch-Masila; 12 Jack Hughes (C); 14 Jason Clark. Subs (all used): 19 Sitaleki Akauola; 17 Joe Philbin; 23 Matt Davis; 22 Jake Mamo.
**Tries:** Philbin (26), Murdoch-Masila (33), D Clark (72);
**Goals:** Ratchford 2/2, Patton 1/1.
**Rugby Leaguer & League Express Men of the Match:**
*Saints:* Tommy Makinson; *Wolves:* Daryl Clark.
**Penalty count:** 4-2; **Half-time:** 0-12;
**Referee:** Robert Hicks; **Attendance:** 62,717 (at Wembley Stadium).

305

# 1895 CUP 2019
## Round by Round

306

## ROUND 1

*Saturday 4th May 2019*

### NEWCASTLE THUNDER 38 KEIGHLEY COUGARS 12

**THUNDER:** 1 Lewis Young; 2 Mo Agoro; 3 Joe Brown; 4 Kieran Gill; 5 Alex Clegg; 7 Remy Marginet; 6 Dan Coates; 10 Jared Blanke; 12 Aaron Ollett; 8 Liam McAvoy; 18 Rhys Clarke; 11 Conor Fitzsimmons; 13 Sam Luckley. Subs (all used): 9 Evan Simons; 14 Niall Sidney; 15 Carne Doyle-Manga; 16 Alex Rowe.
**Tries:** Agoro (11, 51), Clegg (18, 53), Marginet (35), Gill (49, 61); **Goals:** Coates 0/2, Marginet 5/5.
**Sin bin:** Marginet (9) - kicking Seeley.
**COUGARS:** 1 Alfie Seeley; 5 Davey Dixon; 3 Alex Williams; 23 Macauley Hallett; 21 Matt Welham; 17 Billy Gaylor; 15 Jack Miller; 8 Jack Coventry; 14 Luke Million; 10 Jamie Thackray; 12 Aaron Levy; 13 Jason Muranka; 11 Josh Lynam. Subs (all used): 16 Kieran Moran; 18 Chris Cullimore; 25 Jack Arnold; 27 Lewis Wray.
**Tries:** Welham (25), Cullimore (76); **Goals:** Miller 2/2.
**Rugby Leaguer & League Express Men of the Match:** *Thunder:* Remy Marginet; *Cougars:* Jason Muranka.
**Penalty count:** 8-7; **Half-time:** 14-6;
**Referee:** Tom Crashley; **Attendance:** 340.

### HUNSLET 28 WORKINGTON TOWN 31

**HUNSLET:** 1 Jimmy Watson; 24 Tommy Brierley; 4 Ben Heaton; 3 Tom Ashton; 5 Dale Bloomfield; 6 Joe Sanderson; 21 Reece Dean; 17 Dan Hawksworth; 9 Jack Lee; 31 Jon Luke Kirby; 20 Vila Halafihi; 30 Charlie Martin; 13 Mike Emmett. Subs (all used): 14 Ryan Wright; 16 Zach Braham; 18 Nyle Flynn; 19 Aiden Hema.
**Tries:** Lee (26), Ashton (38, 77), Flynn (47), Watson (68); **Goals:** Dean 4/6.
**TOWN:** 23 Izaac Farrell; 16 Scott Rooke; 19 Caine Barnes; 4 Perry Singleton; 12 Gordon Maudling; 6 Jamie Doran; 7 Carl Forber; 8 Oliver Wilkes; 9 Sean Penkywicz; 15 Tom Curwen; 10 Stevie Scholey; 11 Danny Tickle; 25 Fuifui Moimoi. Subs: 17 Dec O'Donnell; 5 Tyler Lancaster (not used); 20 Jonathan Walsh (not used); 14 Andrew Dawson (not used).
**Tries:** Wilkes (10, 19, 63), O'Donnell (52), Rooke (55); **Goals:** Forber 5/5; **Field goal:** Doran (73).
**Rugby Leaguer & League Express Men of the Match:** *Hunslet:* Tom Ashton; *Town:* Oliver Wilkes.
**Penalty count:** 6-5; **Half-time:** 12-12;
**Referee:** Craig Smith; **Attendance:** 296.

*Sunday 5th May 2019*

### DONCASTER 70 WEST WALES RAIDERS 6

**DONCASTER:** 6 Jordan Howden; 1 Tom Halliday; 4 Jason Tali; 26 Menzie Yere; 19 Matty Chrimes; 30 Watson Boas; 7 Matty Beharrell; 8 Russ Spiers; 9 Kyle Kesik; 10 Ryan Boyle; 3 Connor Bower; 22 Brad Foster; 31 Levy Nzoungou. Subs (all used): 17 Brandon Douglas; 16 Brandan Wilkinson; 25 Stefanos Bastas; 20 Callum Ogden.
**Tries:** Halliday (9, 40, 57, 60, 62), Yere (18), Nzoungou (23), Howden (41), Boas (45, 47), Tali (66, 74);
**Goals:** Beharrell 11/12.
**RAIDERS:** 1 Phil Cowburn; 21 Sam Baker; 19 Brad Kislingbury; 22 Paddy Jennings; 25 Mickael Sabour; 9 Liam Rice-Wilson; 7 Tyler Hunt; 17 Callum Mulkeen; 26 Alex King; 10 Sam Herron; 15 Archie Snook; 23 Rowland Kaye; 12 Morgan Evans. Subs (all used, only three named): 13 Dan Maiden; 14 Dalton Desmond-Walker; 5 Liam Silver.
**Try:** Kaye (5); **Goals:** Cowburn 1/1.
**Rugby Leaguer & League Express Men of the Match:** *Doncaster:* Tom Halliday; *Raiders:* Rowland Kaye.
**Penalty count:** 7-6; **Half-time:** 24-6;
**Referee:** Cameron Worsley; **Attendance:** 248.

### OLDHAM 48 WHITEHAVEN 12

**OLDHAM:** 5 Ritchie Hawkyard; 1 Kyran Johnson; 3 Zack McComb; 28 Jack Holmes; 27 Harry Maders; 6 Paul Crook; 7 Dave Hewitt; 8 Phil Joy; 9 Gareth Owen; 13 Jack Spencer; 25 Danny Bridge; 16 Danny Langtree; 24 Liam Bent. Subs (all used): 12 Emmerson Whittel; 30 Titus Gwaze; 20 Matty Wilkinson; 17 Scott Law.
**Tries:** Langtree (3), Hawkyard (8), Wilkinson (30, 50), Johnson (39), Holmes (68, 76), Crook (72);
**Goals:** Crook 8/8.
**WHITEHAVEN:** 3 Chris Taylor; 5 Dave Thompson; 23 Jason Mossop; 4 Jessie Joe Parker; 2 Jordan Burns; 6 Dion Aiye; - Jake Carter; 22 Ruairi McGoff; 14 Sam Dowsett; 25 Kurt Maudling; 11 Brett Phillips; 15 Connor Holliday; 12 Jake Moore. Subs (all used): 10 Kris Coward; 21 Jake Bradley; 9 James Newton; 20 Scott McAvoy.
**Tries:** Carter (17), Holliday (35); **Goals:** Moore 2/2.
**Sin bin:** D Thompson (57) - dangerous challenge.
**Rugby Leaguer & League Express Men of the Match:** *Oldham:* Paul Crook; *Whitehaven:* Jake Carter.
**Penalty count:** 10-9; **Half-time:** 24-12;
**Referee:** Jon Roberts; **Attendance:** 369.

## ROUND 2

*Sunday 2nd June 2019*

### BATLEY BULLDOGS 38 ROCHDALE HORNETS 18

**BULLDOGS:** 1 Dave Scott; 23 Keenen Tomlinson; 4 Lewis Galbraith; 22 Sam Wood; 5 Johnny Campbell; 6 Louis Jouffret; 7 Dom Brambani; 8 Adam Gledhill; 9 Alistair Leak; 15 Toby Everett; 12 Jack Downs; 11 Dane Manning; 13 James Brown. Subs (all used): 16 Michael Ward; 21 Jo Taira; 24 Paul Brearley; 25 Lewis Bienek.
**Tries:** Brown (4), Galbraith (23), Downs (39), Leak (45), Brambani (49), Manning (54), Jouffret (58);
**Goals:** Jouffret 5/7.
**HORNETS:** 7 Dan Abram; 2 Shaun Ainscough; 4 Ben Morris; 24 Brandon Wood; 1 Dec Kay; 29 Zac Baker; 19 Oscar Thomas; 8 Callum Marriott; 22 Callum Wood; 11 Lee Mitchell; 25 Luis Johnson; 12 Ellis Gilliam; 27 Ellis Robson. Subs (all used): 17 Liam Carberry; 18 Mike Coleman; 15 Declan Gregory; 28 Aidy Gleeson.
**Tries:** Baker (17), B Wood (29), Ainscough (62);
**Goals:** Abram 3/3.
**Rugby Leaguer & League Express Men of the Match:** *Bulldogs:* Dom Brambani; *Hornets:* Shaun Ainscough.
**Penalty count:** 9-6; **Half-time:** 16-12;
**Referee:** Billy Pearson; **Attendance:** 700.

### DEWSBURY RAMS 44 SWINTON LIONS 26

**RAMS:** 42 Joe Martin; 23 Rob Worrincy; 1 Dale Morton; 4 Adam Ryder; 2 Andy Gabriel; 14 Lewis Heckford; 38 Liam Finn; 8 Jode Sheriffe; 18 Sam Day; 34 Chris Annakin; 11 Lucas Walshaw; 12 Michael Knowles; 19 Daniel Igbinedion. Subs (all used): 13 Kyle Trout; 10 Toby Richardson; 33 Frazer Morris; 17 Martyn Reilly.
**Tries:** Walshaw (1), Worrincy (17, 75), Day (24, 44), Richardson (53), K Trout (60), Heckford (67);
**Goals:** Finn 6/8.
**LIONS:** 1 Jack Hansen; 25 Matty Ashton; 3 Rhodri Lloyd; 21 Mike Ratu; 32 Liam Forsyth; 34 Harry Smith; 7 Rob Fairclough; 31 Adam Lawton; 9 Luke Waterworth; 10 Lewis Hatton; 33 Jack Wells; 22 Frankie Halton; 36 Liam Byrne. Subs (all used): 14 Billy Brickhill; 11 Adam Jones; 19 Jose Kenga; 12 Kyle Shelford.
**Tries:** Byrne (8), Lloyd (38), Hansen (41), Brickhill (47), Wells (70); **Goals:** Smith 3/5.
**Rugby Leaguer & League Express Men of the Match:** *Rams:* Sam Day; *Lions:* Adam Lawton.
**Penalty count:** 8-9; **Half-time:** 18-10;
**Referee:** Jack Smith; **Attendance:** 453.

### LEIGH CENTURIONS 62 WORKINGTON TOWN 12

**CENTURIONS:** 1 Gregg McNally; 21 Brad Holroyd; 3 Iain Thornley; 25 James Bentley; 19 Mitch Cox; 17 Nick Gregson; 7 Josh Woods; 30 Luke Douglas; 9 Micky Higham; 10 Sam Brooks; 11 Toby Adamson; 12 Andy Thornley; 15 Joe Cator. Subs (all used): 31 Josh Eaves; 29 Jake Emmitt; 24 Gareth Hock; 8 Tom Spencer.
**Tries:** Cox (3, 17), McNally (8, 57, 70), Eaves (39), Bentley (42), Woods (47), Holroyd (51), Douglas (74), I Thornley (80); **Goals:** Woods 9/11.
**TOWN:** 1 Ryan Fieldhouse; 26 Calvin Wellington; 19 Caine Barnes; 21 Tyler Lancaster; 2 Russ Bolton; 6 Jamie Doran; 7 Carl Forber; 10 Stevie Scholey; 9 Sean Penkywicz; 22 Sam Hopkins; 5 Sam Hewitt; 12 Gordon Maudling; 11 Danny Tickle. Subs (all used): 14 Andrew Dawson; 17 Dec O'Donnell; 15 Tom Curwen; 13 Karl Olstrom.
**Tries:** Tickle (34), Forber (64); **Goals:** Forber 2/2.
**Sin bin:** O'Donnell (67) - holding down.
**Rugby Leaguer & League Express Men of the Match:** *Centurions:* Josh Woods; *Town:* Stevie Scholey.
**Penalty count:** 8-5; **Half-time:** 24-6;
**Referee:** Andrew Sweet; **Attendance:** 1,660.

### OLDHAM 12 DONCASTER 24

**OLDHAM:** 5 Ritchie Hawkyard; 28 Harry Aaronson; 26 Anthony Bowman; 4 Jack Holmes; 27 Harry Maders; 6 Paul Crook; 15 Adam Brook; 8 Phil Joy; 9 Gareth Owen; 10 Scott Law; 11 Ben Calland; 24 Liam Bent; 29 Titus Gwaze. Subs (all used): 13 Jack Spencer; 20 Matty Wilkinson; 19 Jamie Greenwood; 18 Ben Davies.
**Tries:** Brook (35), Maders (75); **Goals:** Crook 2/2.
**DONCASTER:** 6 Jordan Howden; 5 Sam Doherty; 1 Cameron Scott; 4 Jason Tali; 19 Matty Chrimes; 30 Watson Boas; 7 Matty Beharrell; 10 Ryan Boyle; 9 Kyle Kesik; 8 Russ Spiers; 26 Menzie Yere; 22 Brad Foster; 24 Levy Nzoungou. Subs (all used): 20 Callum Ogden; 17 Brandon Douglas; 13 Jordie Hedges; 25 Stefanos Bastas.
**Tries:** Chrimes (26), Boas (56), Ogden (59), Doherty (62);
**Goals:** Beharrell 4/4.
**Sin bin:** Boyle (74) - repeated team offences; Nzoungou (78) - fighting.
**Rugby Leaguer & League Express Men of the Match:** *Oldham:* Ritchie Hawkyard; *Doncaster:* Matty Beharrell.
**Penalty count:** 9-8; **Half-time:** 6-6;
**Referee:** Matt Rossleigh; **Attendance:** 283.

### YORK CITY KNIGHTS 30 NEWCASTLE THUNDER 16

**CITY KNIGHTS:** 1 Matty Marsh; 24 Kevin Brown; 23 Jason Bass; 30 Junior Vaivai; 37 Will Oakes; 38 Liam Harris; 7 Connor Robinson; 10 Jack Teanby; 9 Will Jubb; 22 Marcus Stock; 11 Josh Jordan-Roberts; 19 Mike Kelly; 13 Tim Spears. Subs (all used): 26 Kriss Brining; 16 Jack Blagbrough; 17 Joe Porter; 36 Tyler Dupree.
**Tries:** Oakes (15), Brining (35), Vaivai (40), Marsh (45), Stock (75); **Goals:** Robinson 5/6.
**THUNDER:** 1 Lewis Young; 5 Alex Clegg; 4 Tyler Craig; 3 Joe Brown; 2 Misi Taulapapa; 6 Dan Coates; 19 Mikey Lewis; 8 Joel Edwards; 9 Keal Carlile; 15 Carne Doyle-Manga; 11 Conor Fitzsimmons; 18 Rhys Clarke; 14 Evan Simons. Subs (all used): 13 Aaron Ollett; 12 Mo Agoro; 10 Jared Blanke; - Jed Charlton.
**Tries:** Simons (12), Fitzsimmons (31), Young (79);
**Goals:** Coates 0/1, Lewis 2/2.
**Rugby Leaguer & League Express Men of the Match:** *City Knights:* Matty Marsh; *Thunder:* Joel Edwards.
**Penalty count:** 8-7; **Half-time:** 16-10;
**Referee:** Nick Bennett; **Attendance:** 797.

*Wednesday 5th June 2019*

### BARROW RAIDERS 50 BRADFORD BULLS 6

**RAIDERS:** 1 Theerapol Ritson; 27 Brett Carter; 12 Jarrad Stack; 2 Stargroth Amean; 5 Deon Cross; 6 Jamie Dallimore; 14 Wartovo Puara; 28 Josh Johnson; 9 Nathan Mossop; 25 Jordan Walne; 11 Jono Smith; 19 Danny Morrow; 13 Martin Aspinwall. Subs (all used): 4 Jake Spedding; 8 Tom Walker; 15 Dan Toal; 29 Alec Susino.
**Tries:** Susino (32), Smith (42), B Carter (45), Stack (50), D Toal (59), Spedding (69), Dallimore (75, 80), Cross (78);
**Goals:** Dallimore 7/9.
**BULLS:** 6 Joe Brown; 20 Alix Stephenson; 3 Elliott Culling; 4 Ryan Butterworth; 5 Josh Rickett; 1 Brandon Pickersgill; 7 Cobi Green; 15 Callum Bustin; 33 Thomas Doyle; 19 Jon Magrin; 32 Colton Roche; 12 Bradley Gallagher; 13 Ebon Scurr. Subs (all used): 10 Keelan Foster; 17 Jake Lightowler; 9 Cameron Berry; 16 Ethan O'Hanlon.
**Try:** Pickersgill (22); **Goals:** Stephenson 1/1.
**Rugby Leaguer & League Express Men of the Match:** *Raiders:* Jono Smith; *Bulls:* Jon Magrin.
**Penalty count:** 8-6; **Half-time:** 4-6;
**Referee:** James Child; **Attendance:** 1,161.

### HALIFAX 8 SHEFFIELD EAGLES 52

**HALIFAX:** 27 Reece Chapman-Smith; 32 Dafydd Jones; 21 Conor McGrath; 33 Calvin Barker; 36 Jacob Smillie; 19 Ben White; 37 Fraser Stroud; 28 Will Calcott; 24 Curtis Davies; 34 Dewi Billingham; 31 Jordan Syme; 38 Oliver Waite; 22 Connor Davies. Subs (all used): 39 Rhys Davies; 40 Tom Hall; 41 Elliott Windley; 42 Henry Davies.
**Tries:** Barker (24), Chapman-Smith (64); **Goals:** White 0/2.
**EAGLES:** 1 Josh Guzdek; 2 Ryan Millar; 13 Aaron Brown; 4 Jason Crookes; 5 Ben Blackmore; 6 Pat Walker; 7 Anthony Thackeray; 17 Shaun Pick; 9 James Davey; 21 Blake Broadbent; 19 Sonny Esslemont; 15 Olly Davies; 22 Paddy Burns. Subs (all used): 12 Joel Farrell; 14 Greg Burns; 16 Corey Makelim; 25 Lewis Taylor.
**Tries:** Crookes (4, 76), P Burns (9), Thackeray (15), Guzdek (18), Blackmore (32, 71), Taylor (38), Brown (59), Millar (68); **Goals:** Walker 6/10.
**Rugby Leaguer & League Express Men of the Match:** *Halifax:* Reece Chapman-Smith; *Eagles:* Ryan Millar.
**Penalty count:** 3-4; **Half-time:** 4-30;
**Referee:** Tom Grant; **Attendance:** 312
*(at Cougar Park, Keighley).*

### WIDNES VIKINGS 22 FEATHERSTONE ROVERS 16

**VIKINGS:** 5 Jack Owens; 29 Jayden Hatton; 12 Chris Dean; 24 Keanan Brand; 2 Ryan Ince; 6 Danny Craven; 21 Joe Lyons; 13 Hep Cahill; 34 Josh Ganson; 8 Jay Chapelhow; 17 Sam Wilde; 11 Harrison Hansen; 16 MacGraff Leuluai. Subs (all used): 18 Ted Chapelhow; 19 Brad Walker; 15 Jordan Johnstone; 26 Dan Norman.
**Tries:** Hatton (3, 20, 55), Lyons (15); **Goals:** Owens 3/4.
**ROVERS:** 25 Jack Render; 24 Jimmy McDaniel; 3 Thompson Teteh; 5 Conor Carey; 4 Josh Hardcastle; 37 Callum McLelland; 21 Morgan Punchard; 23 Makahesi Makatoa; 16 Danny Maskill; 15 Luke Cooper; 14 John Davies; 17 James Harrison; 39 Dale Ferguson. Subs (all used): 41 Corey Johnson; 29 Jack Ormondroyd; 43 Owen Trout; 42 Wellington Albert.
**Tries:** Ormondroyd (38), Carey (67), Punchard (79);
**Goals:** Punchard 2/3.
**Rugby Leaguer & League Express Men of the Match:** *Vikings:* Jayden Hatton; *Rovers:* Wellington Albert.
**Penalty count:** 6-6; **Half-time:** 16-6;
**Referee:** Greg Dolan; **Attendance:** 1,515.

Sheffield's Aaron Brown dives over for a try against Widnes during the 1895 Cup Final

## QUARTER FINALS

*Wednesday 26th June 2019*

### DONCASTER 28 SHEFFIELD EAGLES 32

**DONCASTER:** 6 Jordan Howden; 5 Sam Doherty; 3 Connor Bower; 4 Jason Tali; 29 Kieron Lawton; 30 Danny Washbrook; 7 Matty Beharrell; 24 Levy Nzoungou; 9 Kyle Kesik; 8 Russ Spiers; 26 Evan Hodgson; 31 Jordan Lane; 13 Jordie Hedges. Subs (all used): 1 Jez Litten; 10 Ryan Boyle; 14 Connor Scott; 25 Stefanos Bastas.
**Tries:** Doherty (4), Litten (22, 54), Beharrell (58);
**Goals:** Beharrell 6/7.
**EAGLES:** 1 Josh Guzdek; 2 Ryan Millar; 27 Jacob Ogden; 4 Jason Crookes; 5 Ben Blackmore; 6 Pat Walker; 7 Anthony Thackeray; 23 Rory Dixon; 16 Corey Makelim; 17 Shaun Pick; 19 Sonny Esslemont; 12 Joel Farrell; 22 Paddy Burns. Subs (all used): 13 Aaron Brown; 15 Olly Davies; 21 Blake Broadbent; 29 James Thornton.
**Tries:** Ogden (11), Dixon (14), Millar (65), Guzdek (69), Crookes (72), Thackeray (79); **Goals:** Walker 4/6.
**Rugby Leaguer & League Express Men of the Match:** *Doncaster:* Jez Litten; *Eagles:* Anthony Thackeray.
**Penalty count:** 6-6; **Half-time:** 16-12;
**Referee:** Cameron Worsley; **Attendance:** 374
*(at LD Nutrition Stadium, Featherstone).*

### LEIGH CENTURIONS 19 BARROW RAIDERS 18

**CENTURIONS:** 1 Gregg McNally; 19 Mitch Cox; 3 Iain Thornley; 33 Josh Simm; 5 Stefan Marsh; 6 Martyn Ridyard; 7 Josh Woods; 26 Luke Douglas; 31 Josh Eaves; 13 Luke Adamson; 11 Toby Adamson; 40 Joe Batchelor; 15 Joe Cator. Subs (all used): 27 Liam Hood; 22 Jordan Thompson; 29 Jake Emmitt; 30 Cory Paterson.
**Tries:** McNally (10), Cator (24), Thompson (64);
**Goals:** Ridyard 3/5. **Field goal:** Ridyard (77).
**On report:**
Batchelor (61) - alleged dangerous challenge on D Toal.
**RAIDERS:** 18 Luke Cresswell; 27 Brett Carter; 2 Stargroth Amean; 4 Jake Spedding; 5 Deon Cross; 22 Ryan Johnston; 14 Wartovo Puara; 28 Josh Johnson; 11 Jono Smith; 29 Alec Susino; 25 Jordan Walne; 35 Liam Paisley; 15 Dan Toal. Subs (all used): 1 Theerapol Ritson; 8 Tom Walker; 16 Glenn Riley; 21 Tom Loxam.
**Tries:** Walne (29), Cresswell (45), R Johnston (48);
**Goals:** R Johnston 3/4.
**Rugby Leaguer & League Express Men of the Match:** *Centurions:* Josh Simm; *Raiders:* Ryan Johnston.
**Penalty count:** 8-7; **Half-time:** 10-6;
**Referee:** Gareth Hewer; **Attendance:** 1,012
*(at Totally Wicked Stadium, St Helens).*

### YORK CITY KNIGHTS 16 BATLEY BULLDOGS 17
*(after golden point extra-time)*

**CITY KNIGHTS:** 5 Matt Chilton; 21 Judah Mazive; 3 Liam Salter; 4 Brad Hey; 39 Will Oakes; 38 Liam Harris; 7

Connor Robinson; 37 Jordan Baldwinson; 9 Will Jubb; 16 Jack Blagbrough; 11 Josh Jordan-Roberts; 19 Mike Kelly; 22 Marcus Stock. Subs (all used): 8 Ronan Dixon; 14 Harry Carter; 17 Joe Porter; 36 Tyler Dupree.
**Tries:** Robinson (3), Jubb (74); **Goals:** Robinson 4/4.
**BULLDOGS:** 1 Dave Scott; 20 Niall Walker; 3 Sam Smeaton; 28 Jack Broadbent; 5 Johnny Campbell; 6 Louis Jouffret; 14 Danny Yates; 17 Tyler Dickinson; 9 Alistair Leak; 10 Tom Lillycrop; 12 Jack Downs; 24 Paul Brearley; 11 Dane Manning. Subs (all used): 13 James Brown; 16 Michael Ward; 21 Jo Taira; 22 Sam Wood.
**Tries:** Campbell (23), Wood (63), Jouffret (69);
**Goals:** Jouffret 2/3. **Field goal:** Jouffret (82).
**Rugby Leaguer & League Express Men of the Match:** *City Knights:* Marcus Stock; *Bulldogs:* Louis Jouffret.
**Penalty count:** 7-7; **Half-time:** 6-6;
**Referee:** Tom Grant; **Attendance:** 1,395.

### WIDNES VIKINGS 54 DEWSBURY RAMS 6

**VIKINGS:** 5 Jack Owens; 25 Lloyd Roby; 24 Keanan Brand; 4 Anthony Gelling; 35 Joe Edge; 6 Danny Craven; 7 Tom Gilmore; 11 Harrison Hansen; 34 Josh Ganson; 8 Jay Chapelhow; 17 Sam Wilde; 12 Chris Dean; 19 Brad Walker. Subs (all used): 18 Ted Chapelhow; 15 Jordan Johnstone; 16 MacGraff Leuluai; 26 Dan Norman.
**Tries:** Gelling (7, 25, 40), Roby (10, 53, 57), Wilde (31, 34), Dean (38), Walker (51); **Goals:** Owens 7/10.
**RAMS:** 42 Joe Martin; 35 Luke Hooley; 19 Daniel Igbinedion; 4 Adam Ryder; 2 Andy Gabriel; 6 Paul Sykes; 38 Liam Finn; 8 Jode Sheriffe; 9 Robbie Ward; 30 Tom Garratt; 11 Lucas Walshaw; 12 Michael Knowles; 13 Kyle Trout. Subs (all used): 18 Sam Day; 10 Toby Richardson; 34 Daniel Waite-Pullan; 17 Martyn Reilly.
**Try:** Waite-Pullan (75); **Goals:** Sykes 1/1, Finn 0/1.
**Sin bin:** Sykes (66) - dissent.
**Rugby Leaguer & League Express Men of the Match:** *Vikings:* Harrison Hansen; *Rams:* Adam Ryder.
**Penalty count:** 8-7; **Half-time:** 38-2;
**Referee:** Michael Mannifield; **Attendance:** 1,458.

## SEMI-FINALS

*Sunday 28th July 2019*

### SHEFFIELD EAGLES 18 BATLEY BULLDOGS 2

**EAGLES:** 1 Josh Guzdek; 2 Ryan Millar; 27 Jacob Ogden; 29 Ben Hellewell; 4 Jake Spedding; 6 Pat Walker; 7 Anthony Thackeray; 17 Shaun Pick; 14 Greg Burns; 11 Brad Knowles; 12 Joel Farrell; 15 Olly Davies; 13 Aaron Brown. Subs (all used): 16 Corey Makelim; 21 Blake Broadbent; 31 Nathan Mason; 22 Paddy Burns.
**Tries:** Farrell (27), Ogden (65), Davies (79);
**Goals:** Walker 3/3.
**BULLDOGS:** 1 Dave Scott; 2 Wayne Reittie; 3 Sam Smeaton; 28 Jack Broadbent; 5 Johnny Campbell; 6 Louis Jouffret; 7 Dom Brambani; 8 Adam Gledhill; 9 Alistair Leak; 17 Tyler Dickinson; 12 Jack Downs; 11 Dane Manning;

24 Paul Brearley. Subs (all used): 25 Lewis Bienek; 13 James Brown; 15 Toby Everett; 22 Sam Wood.
**Goals:** Jouffret 1/1.
**Rugby Leaguer & League Express Men of the Match:** *Eagles:* Josh Guzdek; *Bulldogs:* Adam Gledhill.
**Penalty count:** 7-6; **Half-time:** 6-2;
**Referee:** Gareth Hewer; **Attendance:** 727.

### LEIGH CENTURIONS 8 WIDNES VIKINGS 12

**CENTURIONS:** 1 Gregg McNally; 32 Adam Higson; 3 Iain Thornley; 44 Junior Sa'u; 5 Stefan Marsh; 6 Martyn Ridyard; 35 Ryan Brierley; 26 Luke Douglas; 9 Micky Higham; 28 Mitch Clark; 11 Toby Adamson; 41 Joe Batchelor; 15 Joe Cator. Subs (all used): 27 Liam Hood; 22 Jordan Thompson; 29 Jake Emmitt; 13 Luke Adamson.
**Try:** Higson (75); **Goals:** Brierley 2/3.
**Sin bin:** Clark (3) - fighting.
**VIKINGS:** 5 Jack Owens; 2 Ryan Ince; 4 Anthony Gelling; 24 Keanan Brand; 36 Patrick Ah Van; 6 Danny Craven; 21 Joe Lyons; 8 Jay Chapelhow; 15 Jordan Johnstone; 26 Dan Norman; 17 Sam Wilde; 12 Chris Dean; 19 Brad Walker. Subs: 18 Ted Chapelhow; 16 MacGraff Leuluai; 11 Harrison Hansen; 1 Olly Ashall-Bott (not used).
**Tries:** Gelling (54), Owens (65); **Goals:** Owens 2/3.
**Sin bin:** Johnstone (3) - fighting.
**Rugby Leaguer & League Express Men of the Match:** *Centurions:* Joe Cator; *Vikings:* Danny Craven.
**Penalty count:** 14-7; **Half-time:** 2-2;
**Referee:** Ben Thaler; **Attendance:** 4,460.

## FINAL

*Saturday 24th August 2019*

### SHEFFIELD EAGLES 36 WIDNES VIKINGS 18

**EAGLES:** 1 Josh Guzdek; 2 Ryan Millar; 29 Ben Hellewell; 13 Aaron Brown; 5 Ben Blackmore; 6 Pat Walker; 7 Anthony Thackeray; 17 Shaun Pick; 14 Greg Burns; 11 Brad Knowles; 15 Olly Davies; 12 Joel Farrell; 16 Corey Makelim. Subs (all used): 9 James Davey; 21 Blake Broadbent; 22 Paddy Burns; 31 Nathan Mason.
**Tries:** Brown (22, 49, 76), Thackeray (26), Farrell (42), Makelim (55); **Goals:** Walker 6/9.
**VIKINGS:** 5 Jack Owens; 29 Jayden Hatton; 4 Anthony Gelling; 24 Keanan Brand; 36 Patrick Ah Van; 6 Danny Craven; 7 Tom Gilmore; 18 Ted Chapelhow; 15 Jordan Johnstone; 13 Hep Cahill; 11 Harrison Hansen; 12 Chris Dean; 19 Brad Walker. Subs (all used): 8 Jay Chapelhow; 16 MacGraff Leuluai; 26 Dan Norman; 17 Sam Wilde.
**Tries:** Hansen (14), Dean (16), Gilmore (36);
**Goals:** Owens 3/3.
**Rugby Leaguer & League Express Men of the Match:** *Eagles:* Aaron Brown; *Vikings:* Harrison Hansen.
**Penalty count:** 7-6; **Half-time:** 12-18;
**Referee:** Chris Kendall. *(at Wembley Stadium).*

# GRAND FINALS
## *1998-2018*

## 1998

**DIVISION ONE GRAND FINAL**

*Saturday 26th September 1998*

**FEATHERSTONE ROVERS 22 WAKEFIELD TRINITY 24**

**ROVERS:** 1 Steve Collins; 2 Carl Hall; 3 Shaun Irwin; 4 Danny Baker; 5 Karl Pratt; 6 Jamie Coventry; 7 Ty Fallins; 8 Chico Jackson; 9 Richard Chapman; 10 Stuart Dickens; 11 Gary Price; 12 Neil Lowe; 13 Richard Slater. Subs: 14 Paddy Handley for Coventry (70); 15 Asa Amone for Lowe (50); 16 Micky Clarkson for Jackson (50); 17 Steve Dooler (not used). **Tries:** Baker (15), Jackson (45), Collins (49), Hall (69); **Goals:** Chapman 3.
**TRINITY:** 1 Martyn Holland; 2 Josh Bostock; 3 Adam Hughes; 4 Martin Law; 5 Kevin Gray; 6 Garen Casey; 7 Roger Kenworthy; 8 Francis Stephenson; 9 Roy Southernwood; 10 Gary Lord; 11 Ian Hughes; 12 Sonny Whakarau; 13 Matt Fuller. Subs: 14 Sean Richardson for I Hughes (32); 15 Andy Fisher for Lord (26); 16 David Mycoe (not used); 17 Wayne McDonald for Whakarau (70); Lord for Stephenson (40); Stephenson for Lord (70).
**Tries:** Southernwood (2), Bostock (7, 25), Casey (58), Stephenson (76); **Goals:** Casey 2.
**League Express Men of the Match:**
*Rovers:* Richard Chapman; *Trinity:* Garen Casey.
**Penalty count:** 8-3; **Half time:** 6-12.
**Referee:** Nick Oddy (Halifax); **Attendance:** 8,224 *(at McAlpine Stadium, Huddersfield).*

**SUPER LEAGUE GRAND FINAL**

*Saturday 24th October 1998*

**LEEDS RHINOS 4 WIGAN WARRIORS 10**

**RHINOS:** 1 Iestyn Harris (C); 22 Leroy Rivett; 3 Richie Blackmore; 4 Brad Godden; 5 Francis Cummins; 13 Daryl Powell; 7 Ryan Sheridan; 8 Martin Masella; 21 Terry Newton; 25 Darren Fleary; 11 Adrian Morley; 17 Anthony Farrell; 12 Marc Glanville. Subs: 20 Jamie Mathiou for Masella (25); 24 Marcus St Hilaire for Powell (40); 14 Graham Holroyd for Newton (49); 27 Andy Hay for Fleary (54); Powell for Godden (58); Masella for Mathiou (71).
**Try:** Blackmore (20).
**WARRIORS:** 1 Kris Radlinski; 2 Jason Robinson; 3 Danny Moore; 4 Gary Connolly; 5 Mark Bell; 6 Henry Paul; 7 Tony Smith; 16 Terry O'Connor; 9 Robbie McCormack; 10 Tony Mestrov; 20 Lee Gilmour; 17 Stephen Holgate; 13 Andy Farrell (C). Subs: 8 Neil Cowie for O'Connor (18BB, rev 48); 14 Mick Cassidy for McCormack (19BB, rev 27); 25 Paul Johnson for Moore (37); 12 Simon Haughton for Gilmour (27BB, rev 33); Haughton for Holgate (33); Cowie for Mestrov (54); Cassidy for Haughton (64); Holgate for Cowie (68); Haughton for Gilmour (71BB, rev 75); Mestrov for O'Connor (75BB).
**Try:** Robinson (37); **Goals:** Farrell 3.
**League Express Men of the Match:**
*Rhinos:* Iestyn Harris; *Warriors:* Jason Robinson.
**Penalty count:** 7-13; **Half-time:** 4-6.
**Referee:** Russell Smith (Castleford); **Attendance:** 43,553 *(at Old Trafford, Manchester).*

## 1999

**NORTHERN FORD PREMIERSHIP GRAND FINAL**

*Saturday 25th September 1999*

**DEWSBURY RAMS 11 HUNSLET HAWKS 12**

**RAMS:** 1 Nathan Graham; 2 Alex Godfrey; 3 Paul Evans; 4 Brendan O'Meara; 5 Adrian Flynn; 6 Richard Agar; 7 Barry Eaton; 8 Alan Boothroyd; 9 Paul Delaney; 10 Matthew Long; 11 Andy Spink; 12 Mark Haigh; 13 Damian Ball. Subs: 14 Brendan Williams for Eaton (5BB, rev 15); 15 Sean Richardson for Haigh (50); 16 Simon Hicks for Long (25); 17 Paul Medley for Spink (50); Williams for Evans (61); Long for Boothroyd (71); Spink for Long (78).
**Tries:** Flynn (27), Ball (54); **Goal:** Eaton; **Field goal:** Agar.
**HAWKS:** 1 Abraham Fatnowna; 2 Chris Ross; 3 Shaun Irwin; 4 Paul Cook; 5 Iain Higgins; 6 Marcus Vassilakopoulos; 7 Latham Tawhai; 8 Richard Hayes; 9 Richard Pachniuk; 10 Steve Pryce; 11 Rob Wilson; 12 Jamie Leighton; 13 Lee St Hilaire. Subs: 14 Mick Coyle for Wilson (57); 15 Phil Kennedy for Pryce (35); 16 Jamie Thackray for St Hilaire (25); 17 Richard Baker for Higgins (55); Higgins for Fatnowna (62); Pryce for Kennedy (65).
**Tries:** Cook (31), Higgins (46); **Goal:** Ross;
**Field goals:** Tawhai, Leighton.
**League Express Men of the Match:**
*Rams:* Barry Eaton; *Hawks:* Latham Tawhai.
**Penalty count:** 8-5; **Half-time:** 7-7.
**Referee:** Steve Ganson (St Helens); **Attendance:** 5,783 *(at Headingley Stadium, Leeds).*

**SUPER LEAGUE GRAND FINAL**

*Saturday 9th October 1999*

**BRADFORD BULLS 6 ST HELENS 8**

**BULLS:** 28 Stuart Spruce; 2 Tevita Vaikona; 20 Scott Naylor; 5 Michael Withers; 17 Leon Pryce; 6 Henry Paul; 1 Robbie Paul (C); 10 Paul Anderson; 9 James Lowes; 29 Stuart Fielden; 15 David Boyle; 23 Bernard Dwyer; 13 Steve McNamara. Subs: 14 Paul Deacon for R Paul (53); 4 Nathan McAvoy (not used); 12 Mike Forshaw for McNamara (18); 22 Brian McDermott for Anderson (18); Anderson for Fielden (61); Fielden for Dwyer (65); R Paul for Deacon (72).
**Try:** H Paul (18); **Goal:** H Paul.
**SAINTS:** 1 Paul Atcheson; 14 Chris Smith; 3 Kevin Iro; 4 Paul Newlove; 5 Anthony Sullivan; 13 Paul Sculthorpe; 20 Tommy Martyn; 8 Apollo Perelini; 9 Keiron Cunningham; 10 Julian O'Neill; 2 Fereti Tuilagi; 21 Sonny Nickle; 11 Chris Joynt (C). Subs: 26 Paul Wellens for Martyn (52); 6 Sean Hoppe for Newlove (43); 16 Vila Matautia for O'Neill (20); 7 Sean Long for Perelini (24); Perelini for Matautia (46); O'Neill for Perelini (69).
**Tries:** Iro (65); **Goals:** Long 2.
**League Express Men of the Match:**
*Bulls:* Henry Paul; *Saints:* Kevin Iro.
**Penalty count:** 4-7; **Half-time:** 6-2.
**Referee:** Stuart Cummings (Widnes).
**Attendance:** 50,717 *(at Old Trafford, Manchester).*

## 2000

**NORTHERN FORD PREMIERSHIP GRAND FINAL**

*Saturday 29th July 2000*

**DEWSBURY RAMS 13 LEIGH CENTURIONS 12**

**RAMS:** 1 Nathan Graham; 2 Richard Baker; 4 Dan Potter; 3 Brendan O'Meara; 5 Adrian Flynn; 6 Richard Agar; 7 Barry Eaton; 8 Shayne Williams; 9 David Mycoe; 10 Mark Haigh; 11 Sean Richardson; 12 Daniel Frame; 13 Damian Ball. Subs: 14 Gavin Wood (not used); 15 Paul Delaney for Mycoe (53); 16 Ryan McDonald for Haigh (30); 17 Matthew Long for Williams (23); Haigh for McDonald (64).
**Tries:** Eaton (2), Long (23); **Goals:** Eaton 2;
**Field goal:** Agar.
**Sin bin:** Williams (66) - use of the elbow.
**On report:** Richardson (20) - high tackle on Donlan.
**CENTURIONS:** 1 Stuart Donlan; 5 David Ingram; 3 Paul Anderson; 4 Andy Fairclough; 2 Alan Cross; 6 Liam Bretherton; 7 Kieron Purtill; 8 Tim Street; 9 Mick Higham; 10 Andy Leatham; 11 Simon Baldwin; 12 Heath Cruckshank; 13 Adam Bristow. Subs: 14 James Arkwright for Cross (68); 15 Paul Norman for Street (36); 16 Radney Bowker (not used); 17 David Whittle for Leathem (24); Street for Norman (62).
**Tries:** Higham (29, 69); **Goals:** Bretherton 2.
**Sin bin:** Whittle (66) - retaliation.
**League Express Men of the Match:**
*Rams:* Richard Agar; *Centurions:* Mick Higham.
**Penalty count:** 4-4; **Half-time:** 10-6;
**Referee:** Robert Connolly (Wigan); **Attendance:** 8,487 *(at Gigg Lane, Bury).*

**SUPER LEAGUE GRAND FINAL**

*Saturday 14th October 2000*

**ST HELENS 29 WIGAN WARRIORS 16**

**SAINTS:** 17 Paul Wellens; 24 Steve Hall; 3 Kevin Iro; 15 Sean Hoppe; 5 Anthony Sullivan; 20 Tommy Martyn; 7 Sean Long; 8 Apollo Perelini; 9 Keiron Cunningham; 10 Julian O'Neill; 11 Chris Joynt (C); 22 Tim Jonkers; 13 Paul Sculthorpe. Subs: 14 Fereti Tuilagi for O'Neill (20); 12 Sonny Nickle for Perelini (28); 26 John Stankevitch for Jonkers (50); 23 Scott Barrow (not used); Perelini for Nickle (52); Jonkers for Stankevitch (66); Stankevitch for Perelini (67BB); O'Neill for Hall (74).
**Tries:** Hoppe (7), Joynt (28, 50), Tuilagi (69), Jonkers (80); **Goals:** Long 4; **Field goal:** Sculthorpe.
**WARRIORS:** 5 Jason Robinson; 2 Brett Dallas; 1 Kris Radlinski; 3 Steve Renouf; 26 David Hodgson; 6 Tony Smith; 7 Willie Peters; 8 Terry O'Connor; 9 Terry Newton; 10 Neil Cowie; 11 Mick Cassidy; 12 Denis Betts; 13 Andy Farrell (C). Subs: 23 Brady Malam for Cowie (30); 17 Tony Mestrov for O'Connor (43); 19 Chris Chester for Cassidy (47BB, rev 69); 14 Lee Gilmour for Betts (51); O'Connor for Mestrov (61); Cowie for Malam (67); Chester for Newton (75).
**Tries:** Farrell (13), Hodgson (58), Smith (61);
**Goals:** Farrell 2.
**League Express Men of the Match:**
*Saints:* Chris Joynt; *Warriors:* Andy Farrell.
**Penalty count:** 10-6; **Half-time:** 11-4;
**Referee:** Russell Smith (Castleford); **Attendance:** 58,132 *(at Old Trafford, Manchester).*

## 2001

**NORTHERN FORD PREMIERSHIP GRAND FINAL**

*Saturday 28th July 2001*

**OLDHAM 14 WIDNES VIKINGS 24**

**OLDHAM:** 1 Mark Sibson; 2 Joey Hayes; 3 Anthony Gibbons; 4 Pat Rich; 5 Joe McNicholas; 6 David Gibbons; 7 Neil Roden; 8 Leo Casey; 9 Keith Brennan; 10 Paul Norton; 11 Phil Farrell; 12 Bryan Henare; 13 Kevin Mannion. Subs: 14 Mike Ford for Mannion (27); 15 Jason Clegg for Casey (18); 16 John Hough for Brennan (44); 17 Danny Guest for Norton (40BB, rev 54); Mannion for Henare (66); Guest for Clegg (73).
**Tries:** Brennan (9), Ford (74), Mannion (80); **Goal:** Rich.
**VIKINGS:** 1 Paul Atcheson; 2 Damian Munro; 3 Craig Weston; 4 Jason Demetriou; 5 Chris Percival; 6 Richard Agar; 7 Martin Crompton; 8 Simon Knox; 9 Phil Cantillon; 10 Stephen Holgate; 11 Steve Gee; 12 Sean Richardson; 13 Tommy Hodgkinson. Subs: 14 Andy Craig for Percival (65); 15 Chris McKinney for Gee (41); 16 Joe Faimalo for Knox (32); 17 Matthew Long for Holgate (23); Knox for Long (49BB, rev 61); Holgate for Long (74).
**Tries:** Gee (17), Demetriou (38, 60), Cantillon (50), Munro (69); **Goals:** Weston 2.
**League Express Men of the Match:**
*Oldham:* Jason Clegg; *Vikings:* Phil Cantillon.
**Penalty count:** 8-5; **Half-time:** 4-10.
**Referee:** Steve Ganson (St Helens); **Attendance:** 8,974 *(at Spotland, Rochdale).*

*Grand Finals 1998-2018*

**SUPER LEAGUE GRAND FINAL**

*Saturday 13th October 2001*

**BRADFORD BULLS 37 WIGAN WARRIORS 6**

**BULLS:** 5 Michael Withers; 2 Tevita Vaikona; 20 Scott Naylor; 23 Graham Mackay; 3 Leon Pryce; 6 Henry Paul; 1 Robbie Paul (C); 8 Joe Vagana; 9 James Lowes; 22 Brian McDermott; 11 Daniel Gartner; 19 Jamie Peacock; 12 Mike Forshaw. Subs: 29 Stuart Fielden for McDermott (21BB, rev 65); 10 Paul Anderson for Vagana (22); 15 Shane Rigon for Pryce (40); 7 Paul Deacon for R Paul (69); Vagana for Anderson (53); Fielden for Gartner (72); Anderson for Vagana (74).
**Tries:** Lowes (9), Withers (11, 27, 31), Fielden (65), Mackay (72); **Goals:** H Paul 5, Mackay; **Field goal:** H Paul.
**WARRIORS:** 1 Kris Radlinski; 2 Brett Dallas; 4 Gary Connolly; 3 Steve Renouf; 5 Brian Carney; 6 Matthew Johns; 7 Adrian Lam; 8 Terry O'Connor; 9 Terry Newton; 20 Harvey Howard; 11 Mick Cassidy; 14 David Furner; 13 Andy Farrell (C). Subs: 15 Paul Johnson for Carney (12BB); 10 Neil Cowie for Howard (17); 12 Denis Betts for O'Connor (32); 19 Chris Chester for Farrell (59); O'Connor for Cowie (55); Howard for Newton (64); Cowie for Cassidy (72).
**Try:** Lam (63); **Goal:** Furner.
**League Express Men of the Match:**
*Bulls:* Michael Withers; *Warriors:* Adrian Lam.
**Penalty count:** 6-7; **Half-time:** 26-0;
**Referee:** Stuart Cummings (Widnes);
**Attendance:** 60,164 *(at Old Trafford, Manchester)*.

## 2002

**NORTHERN FORD PREMIERSHIP GRAND FINAL**

*Saturday 12th October 2002*

**HUDDERSFIELD GIANTS 38 LEIGH CENTURIONS 16**

**GIANTS:** 1 Ben Cooper; 2 Hefin O'Hare; 3 Eorl Crabtree; 4 Graeme Hallas; 5 Marcus St Hilaire; 6 Stanley Gene; 7 Chris Thorman; 8 Michael Slicker; 9 Paul March; 10 Jeff Wittenberg; 11 David Atkins; 12 Robert Roberts; 13 Steve McNamara. Subs: 14 Heath Cruckshank for Roberts (24BB); 15 Chris Molyneux for Slicker (53); 16 Darren Turner for March (21); 17 Andy Rice for Cruckshank (57); Roberts for Wittenberg (34); Wittenberg for Roberts (74).
**Tries:** O'Hare (12, 78), St Hilaire (34, 53), Thorman (46), Gene (57); **Goals:** McNamara 7.
**Sin bin:** Roberts (47) - fighting.
**CENTURIONS:** 1 Neil Turley; 2 Leon Felton; 4 Jon Roper; 3 Dale Cardoza; 5 Oliver Marns; 6 Willie Swann; 7 Bobbie Goulding; 8 Vila Matautia; 9 Paul Rowley; 10 David Bradbury; 11 Simon Baldwin; 12 Andrew Isherwood; 13 Adam Bristow. Subs: 14 Gareth Price for Bradbury (24BB, rev 35); 15 John Duffy for Swann (32); 16 John Hamilton for Bristow (46BB, rev 57); 17 David Whittle for Matautia (22); Matautia for Bradbury (53BB); Swann for Goulding (58); Hamilton for Whittle (67); Bradbury for Turley (72); Goulding for Swann (75).
**Tries:** Cardoza (9), Marns (18), Hamilton (70);
**Goals:** Turley 2.
**Sin bin:** Whittle (47) - fighting; Bristow (74) - interference.
**On report:** Isherwood (66) - high tackle on Roberts.
**Rugby Leaguer & League Express Men of the Match:**
*Giants:* Chris Thorman; *Centurions:* Adam Bristow.
**Penalty count:** 11-11; **Half-time:** 14-10;
**Referee:** Karl Kirkpatrick (Warrington);
**Attendance:** 9,051 *(at Halton Stadium, Widnes)*.

**SUPER LEAGUE GRAND FINAL**

*Saturday 19th October 2002*

**BRADFORD BULLS 18 ST HELENS 19**

**BULLS:** 6 Michael Withers; 2 Tevita Vaikona; 20 Scott Naylor; 15 Brandon Costin; 5 Lesley Vainikolo; 1 Robbie Paul (C); 7 Paul Deacon; 8 Joe Vagana; 9 James Lowes; 29 Stuart Fielden; 11 Daniel Gartner; 12 Jamie Peacock; 13 Mike Forshaw. Subs: 14 Lee Gilmour for Gartner (21); 10 Paul Anderson for Vagana (25); 22 Brian McDermott for Fielden (34); 3 Leon Pryce for Vainikolo (53); Fielden for Anderson (55); Vainikolo for Paul (77).
**Tries:** Naylor (3), Paul (44), Withers (47); **Goals:** Deacon 3.
**SAINTS:** 1 Paul Wellens; 5 Darren Albert; 3 Martin Gleeson; 4 Paul Newlove; 19 Anthony Stewart; 13 Paul Sculthorpe; 7 Sean Long; 8 Darren Britt; 9 Keiron Cunningham; 10 Barry Ward; 23 Mike Bennett; 15 Tim Jonkers; 11 Chris Joynt (C). Subs: 2 Sean Hoppe for Wellens (3); 12 Peter Shiels for Ward (27); 14 John Stankevitch for Britt (31BB, rev 58); 17 Mick Higham for Joynt (54); Stankevitch for Shiels (58); Joynt for Britt (75); Shiels for Jonkers (77).
**Tries:** Bennett (24), Long (32), Gleeson (56);
**Goals:** Long 3; **Field goal:** Long.
**Rugby Leaguer & League Express Men of the Match:**
*Bulls:* Paul Deacon; *Saints:* Mike Bennett.
**Penalty count:** 5-4; **Half-time:** 12-8;
**Referee:** Russell Smith (Castleford); **Attendance:** 61,138 *(at Old Trafford, Manchester)*.

## 2003

**NATIONAL LEAGUE TWO GRAND FINAL**

*Sunday 5th October 2003*

**KEIGHLEY COUGARS 13 SHEFFIELD EAGLES 11**

**COUGARS:** 1 Matt Foster; 2 Max Tomlinson; 3 David Foster; 4 James Rushforth; 5 Andy Robinson; 6 Paul Ashton; 7 Matt Firth; 8 Phil Stephenson; 9 Simeon Hoyle; 10 Danny Ekis; 11 Oliver Wilkes; 12 Ian Sinfield; 13 Lee Patterson. Subs (all used): 14 Chris Wainwright; 15 Richard Mervill; 16 Mick Durham; 17 Jason Ramshaw.
**Tries:** M Foster (7), Robinson (74); **Goals:** Ashton 2;
**Field goal:** Firth.
**EAGLES:** 1 Andy Poynter; 2 Tony Weller; 3 Richard Goddard; 4 Tom O'Reilly; 5 Greg Hurst; 6 Gavin Brown; 7 Mark Aston; 8 Jack Howieson; 9 Gareth Stanley; 10 Dale Laughton; 11 Andy Raleigh; 12 Craig Brown; 13 Wayne Flynn. Subs (all used): 14 Peter Reilly; 15 Simon Tillyer; 16 Nick Turnbull; 17 Mitchell Stringer.
**Try:** O'Reilly (51); **Goals:** G Brown 3; **Field goal:** Reilly.
**Rugby Leaguer & League Express Men of the Match:**
*Cougars:* Simeon Hoyle; *Eagles:* Andy Raleigh.
**Penalty count:** 6-8; **Half-time:** 9-4;
**Referee:** Peter Taberner (Wigan).
*(at Halton Stadium, Widnes)*.

**NATIONAL LEAGUE ONE GRAND FINAL**

*Sunday 5th October 2003*

**LEIGH CENTURIONS 14 SALFORD CITY REDS 31**

**CENTURIONS:** 1 Neil Turley; 2 Damian Munro; 3 Alan Hadcroft; 4 Danny Halliwell; 5 Leroy Rivett; 6 John Duffy; 7 Tommy Martyn; 8 Sonny Nickle; 9 Patrick Weisner; 10 Paul Norman; 11 Sean Richardson; 12 Willie Swann; 13 Adam Bristow. Subs (all used): 14 David Bradbury; 15 Lee Sanderson; 16 Bryan Henare; 17 Ricky Bibey.
**Tries:** Richardson (33), Halliwell (38), Swann (65);
**Goal:** Turley.
**On report:** Nickle (60) - late tackle on Clinch.
**CITY REDS:** 1 Jason Flowers; 2 Danny Arnold; 3 Stuart Littler; 4 Alan Hunte; 5 Andy Kirk; 6 Cliff Beverley; 7 Gavin Clinch; 8 Neil Baynes; 9 Malcolm Alker; 10 Andy Coley; 11 Simon Baldwin; 12 Paul Highton; 13 Chris Charles. Subs (all used): 14 Steve Blakeley; 15 David Highton; 16 Martin Moana; 17 Gareth Haggerty.
**Tries:** Hunte (3, 52), Beverley (23), Littler (73);
**Goals:** Charles 6, Blakeley; **Field goal:** Blakeley.
**Rugby Leaguer & League Express Men of the Match:**
*Centurions:* Willie Swann; *City Reds:* Gavin Clinch.
**Penalty count:** 10-10; **Half-time:** 10-16;
**Referee:** Richard Silverwood (Dewsbury);
**Attendance:** 9,186 *(at Halton Stadium, Widnes)*.

**SUPER LEAGUE GRAND FINAL**

*Saturday 18th October 2003*

**BRADFORD BULLS 25 WIGAN WARRIORS 12**

**BULLS:** 17 Stuart Reardon; 2 Tevita Vaikona; 6 Michael Withers; 4 Shontayne Hape; 5 Lesley Vainikolo; 15 Karl Pratt; 7 Paul Deacon; 8 Joe Vagana; 9 James Lowes; 29 Stuart Fielden; 11 Daniel Gartner; 12 Jamie Peacock; 13 Mike Forshaw. Subs (all used): 10 Paul Anderson; 18 Lee Radford; 3 Leon Pryce; 1 Robbie Paul (C).
**Tries:** Reardon (51), Hape (59), Lowes (75);
**Goals:** Deacon 6/6; **Field goal:** Deacon.
**WARRIORS:** 1 Kris Radlinski; 5 Brian Carney; 18 Martin Aspinwall; 14 David Hodgson; 2 Brett Dallas; 15 Sean O'Loughlin; 20 Luke Robinson; 30 Quentin Pongia; 9 Terry Newton; 10 Craig Smith; 11 Mick Cassidy; 12 Danny Tickle; 13 Andy Farrell (C). Subs (all used): 4 Paul Johnson; 8 Terry O'Connor; 23 Gareth Hock; 17 Mark Smith.
**Tries:** Tickle (17), Radlinski (72); **Goals:** Farrell 2/3.
**Rugby Leaguer & League Express Men of the Match:**
*Bulls:* Stuart Reardon; *Warriors:* Kris Radlinski.
**Penalty count:** 7-6; **Half-time:** 4-6;
**Referee:** Karl Kirkpatrick (Warrington);
**Attendance:** 65,537 *(at Old Trafford, Manchester)*.

## 2004

**NATIONAL LEAGUE ONE GRAND FINAL**

*Sunday 10th October 2004*

**LEIGH CENTURIONS 32 WHITEHAVEN 16**
*(after extra-time)*

**CENTURIONS:** 1 Neil Turley; 2 Rob Smyth; 3 Danny Halliwell; 4 Ben Cooper; 5 David Alstead; 6 John Duffy; 7 Tommy Martyn; 8 Simon Knox; 9 Paul Rowley; 10 Matt Sturm; 11 David Larder; 12 Oliver Wilkes; 13 Ian Knott. Subs (all used): 14 Dave McConnell; 15 Heath Cruckshank; 16 Richard Marshall; 17 Willie Swann.
**Tries:** Cooper (27, 83), Martyn (61), Turley (87);
**Goals:** Turley 6/8; **Field goals:** Turley 2, Rowley, Martyn.
**WHITEHAVEN:** 1 Gary Broadbent; 2 Craig Calvert; 3 David Seeds; 4 Mick Nanyn; 5 Wesley Wilson; 6 Leroy Joe; 7 Sam Obst; 8 Marc Jackson; 9 Aaron Lester; 10 David Fatialofa; 11 Paul Davidson; 12 Howard Hill; 13 Craig Walsh. Subs (all used): 14 Spencer Miller; 15 Carl Sice; 16 Chris McKinney; 17 Ryan Tandy.
**Tries:** Wilson (2, 71), Calvert (45); **Goals:** Nanyn 2/6.
**Rugby Leaguer & League Express Men of the Match:**
*Centurions:* Neil Turley; *Whitehaven:* Aaron Lester.
**Penalty count:** 5-9; **Half-time:** 7-6; **Full-time:** 16-16;
**Referee:** Ronnie Laughton (Barnsley);
**Attendance:** 11,005 *(at Halton Stadium, Widnes)*.

**SUPER LEAGUE GRAND FINAL**

*Saturday 16th October 2004*

**BRADFORD BULLS 8 LEEDS RHINOS 16**

**BULLS:** 6 Michael Withers; 17 Stuart Reardon; 16 Paul Johnson; 4 Shontayne Hape; 5 Lesley Vainikolo; 18 Iestyn Harris; 7 Paul Deacon; 8 Joe Vagana; 1 Robbie Paul (C); 29 Stuart Fielden; 12 Jamie Peacock; 13 Logan Swann; 11 Lee Radford. Subs: 10 Paul Anderson for Vagana (14); 15 Karl Pratt for Paul (23); 27 Rob Parker for Anderson (24); 19 Jamie Langley for Peacock (32); Paul for Withers (ht); Peacock for Radford (48); Radford for Swann (54); Vagana for Parker (56); Parker for Fielden (63); Fielden for Vagana (67); Swann for Langley (68).
**Tries:** Vainikolo (7), Hape (43); **Goals:** Deacon 0/2.
**RHINOS:** 21 Richard Mathers; 18 Mark Calderwood; 5 Chev Walker; 4 Keith Senior; 22 Marcus Bai; 13 Kevin Sinfield (C); 6 Danny McGuire; 19 Danny Ward; 9 Matt Diskin; 8 Ryan Bailey; 3 Chris McKenna; 29 Ali Lauitiiti; 11 David Furner. Subs: 16 Willie Poching for Furner (19); 10 Barrie McDermott for Ward (22); Ward for Bailey (29); 7 Rob Burrow for Lauitiiti (30); Bailey for McDermott (41); 20 Jamie Jones-Buchanan for McKenna (48); Lauitiiti for Ward (50); Furner for Sinfield (60); McKenna for Poching (63); Sinfield for Diskin (67); Poching for McKenna (72); Ward for Bailey (73).
**Tries:** Diskin (15), McGuire (75); **Goals:** Sinfield 4/4.
**Rugby Leaguer & League Express Men of the Match:**
*Bulls:* Lesley Vainikolo; *Rhinos:* Richard Mathers.
**Penalty count:** 5-5; **Half-time:** 4-10;
**Referee:** Steve Ganson (St Helens);
**Attendance:** 65,547 *(at Old Trafford, Manchester)*.

## 2005

**NATIONAL LEAGUE ONE GRAND FINAL**

*Sunday 9th October 2005*

**CASTLEFORD TIGERS 36 WHITEHAVEN 8**

**TIGERS:** 1 Michael Platt; 2 Waine Pryce; 3 Michael Shenton; 4 Jon Hepworth; 5 Damien Blanch; 6 Brad Davis; 7 Andrew Henderson; 8 Adam Watene; 9 Aaron Smith; 10 Richard Fletcher; 11 Tom Haughey; 12 Steve Crouch; 13 Deon Bird. Subs (all used): 14 Paul Handforth; 15 Craig Huby; 16 Adrian Vowles; 17 Frank Watene.
**Tries:** Huby (22), Crouch (24), Blanch (26), Davis (33, 45), Haughey (52); **Goals:** Fletcher 2/3, Huby 3/4, Hepworth 1/1.
**WHITEHAVEN:** 1 Gary Broadbent; 2 Craig Calvert; 3 David Seeds; 4 Mick Nanyn; 5 Wesley Wilson; 6 Leroy Joe; 7 Joel Penny; 8 Ryan Tandy; 9 Carl Sice; 10 David Fatialofa; 11 Spencer Miller; 12 Howard Hill; 13 Aaron Lester. Subs (all used): 14 Carl Rudd; 15 Aaron Summers; 16 Craig Chambers; 17 Marc Jackson.
**Tries:** Seeds (56), Calvert (78); **Goals:** Nanyn 0/2.
**Sin bin:** Joe (16) - late tackle on Davis.
**On report:** Joe (16) - late tackle on Davis;
Sice (40) - alleged biting.
**Rugby Leaguer & League Express Men of the Match:**
*Tigers:* Brad Davis; *Whitehaven:* Wesley Wilson.
**Penalty count:** 4-9; **Half-time:** 26-0;
**Referee:** Steve Ganson (St Helens);
**Attendance:** 13,300 *(at Halton Stadium, Widnes)*.

**SUPER LEAGUE GRAND FINAL**

*Saturday 15th October 2005*

**BRADFORD BULLS 15 LEEDS RHINOS 6**

**BULLS:** 6 Michael Withers; 3 Leon Pryce; 13 Ben Harris; 4 Shontayne Hape; 5 Lesley Vainikolo; 18 Iestyn Harris; 7 Paul Deacon; 12 Jamie Peacock (C); 9 Ian Henderson; 29 Stuart Fielden; 16 Paul Johnson; 10 Brad Meyers; 11 Lee Radford. Subs (all used): 24 Adrian Morley for Johnson (5); 19 Jamie Langley for Peacock (24); 8 Joe Vagana for Fielden (24); Johnson for Radford (24); 1 Robbie Paul for Henderson (31); Peacock for Vagana (45); Fielden for Morley (49); Henderson for Paul (54); Radford for Meyers (60); Morley for Peacock (62); Meyers for Langley (73); Peacock for Johnson (74).

**Tries:** L Pryce (29), Vainikolo (53); **Goals:** Deacon 3/5; **Field goal:** I Harris.
**RHINOS:** 1 Richard Mathers; 2 Mark Calderwood; 3 Chev Walker; 12 Chris McKenna; 5 Marcus Bai; 6 Danny McGuire; 7 Rob Burrow; 8 Ryan Bailey; 14 Andrew Dunemann; 15 Danny Ward; 20 Gareth Ellis; 16 Willie Poching; 13 Kevin Sinfield (C). Subs (all used): 10 Barrie McDermott for Ward (17); 11 Ali Lauitiiti for Poching (21); 18 Jamie Jones-Buchanan for Bailey (31); Ward for McDermott (34); 9 Matt Diskin for Ellis (48); Poching for Lauitiiti (48); McDermott for Ward (54); Ellis for Poching (61); Lauitiiti for McDermott (61); Poching for Dunemann (65); Ward for Jones-Buchanan (68); Dunemann for Ellis (71).
**Try:** McGuire (22); **Goals:** Sinfield 1/2.
**Rugby Leaguer & League Express Men of the Match:**
*Bulls:* Leon Pryce; *Rhinos:* Danny McGuire.
**Penalty count:** 6-8; **Half-time:** 8-6;
**Referee:** Ashley Klein (Keighley); **Attendance:** 65,537
*(at Old Trafford, Manchester).*

## 2006

### NATIONAL LEAGUE TWO GRAND FINAL

*Sunday 8th October 2006*

#### SHEFFIELD EAGLES 35 SWINTON LIONS 10

**EAGLES:** 1 Johnny Woodcock; 5 Greg Hurst; 4 Jimmy Walker; 3 James Ford; 2 Rob Worrincy; 6 Brendon Lindsay; 7 Gavin Brown; 8 Jack Howieson; 9 Paul Pickering; 10 Mitchell Stringer; 11 Andy Hay; 12 Dale Holdstock; 13 Andy Smith. Subs (all used): 14 Craig Poucher; 15 Martin Ostler; 16 Sean Dickinson; 17 Waisale Sovatabua.
**Tries:** Worrincy (21, 43), Lindsay (38), Woodcock (39), Walker (51), Hay (60); **Goals:** Woodcock 5/6;
**Field goal:** G Brown.
**LIONS:** 1 Wayne English; 2 Andy Saywell; 3 Darren Woods; 4 David Alstead; 5 Marlon Billy; 6 Martin Moana; 7 Chris Hough; 8 Bruce Johnson; 9 Phil Wood; 10 Dave Newton; 11 Kris Smith; 12 Ian Sinfield; 13 Lee Marsh. Subs (all used): 14 Liam McGovern; 15 Chris Morley; 16 Danny Aboushakra; 17 Ian Parry.
**Tries:** Saywell (35), Alstead (74); **Goals:** McGovern 1/2.
**Rugby Leaguer & League Express Men of the Match:**
*Eagles:* Johnny Woodcock; *Lions:* Wayne English.
**Penalty count:** 3-4; **Half-time:** 16-4;
**Referee:** Peter Taberner (Wigan).
*(at Halliwell Jones Stadium, Warrington).*

*Dewsbury Rams were National League Two Champions in 2006. This game was to determine who took the second promotion place.*

### NATIONAL LEAGUE ONE GRAND FINAL

*Sunday 8th October 2006*

#### HULL KINGSTON ROVERS 29 WIDNES VIKINGS 16

**ROVERS:** 1 Ben Cockayne; 2 Leroy Rivett; 3 Gareth Morton; 4 Jon Goddard; 5 Byron Ford; 6 Scott Murrell; 7 James Webster; 8 Makali Aizue; 9 Ben Fisher; 10 David Tangata-Toa; 11 Iain Morrison; 12 Michael Smith; 13 Tommy Gallagher. Subs (all used): 14 Pat Weisner; 15 Dwayne Barker; 16 Jason Netherton; 17 Dave Wilson.
**Tries:** Ford (6), Goddard (18, 36), Murrell (24), Weisner (43); **Goals:** Morton 4/6; **Field goal:** Murrell.
**VIKINGS:** 1 Gavin Dodd; 2 Damien Blanch; 3 Sean Gleeson; 4 Daryl Cardiss; 5 John Kirkpatrick; 6 Dennis Moran; 7 Ian Watson; 8 Terry O'Connor; 9 Mark Smith; 10 Barrie McDermott; 11 Mick Cassidy; 12 David Allen; 13 Bob Beswick. Subs (all used): 14 Aaron Summers; 15 Oliver Wilkes; 16 Jordan James; 17 Ryan Tandy.
**Tries:** Dodd (32), Tandy (57), Blanch (70); **Goals:** Dodd 2/3.
**Rugby Leaguer & League Express Men of the Match:**
*Rovers:* James Webster; *Vikings:* Mark Smith.
**Penalty count:** 8-5; **Half-time:** 22-4;
**Referee:** Phil Bentham (Warrington); **Attendance:** 13,024
*(at Halliwell Jones Stadium, Warrington).*

#### SUPER LEAGUE GRAND FINAL

*Saturday 14th October 2006*

#### HULL FC 4 ST HELENS 26

**HULL:** 1 Shaun Briscoe; 14 Motu Tony; 4 Sid Domic; 3 Kirk Yeaman; 5 Gareth Raynor; 13 Paul Cooke; 7 Richard Horne; 8 Ewan Dowes; 9 Richard Swain (C); 10 Garreth Carvell; 11 Lee Radford; 12 Shayne McMenemy; 24 Danny Washbrook. Subs: 15 Paul King for Carvell (17); 19 Graeme Horne for Radford (23); 26 Scott Wheeldon for Dowes (27); 6 Richard Whiting for McMenemy (29); Dowes for Wheeldon (49); Carvell for King (49); Radford for G Horne (51); McMenemy for Whiting (55); King for Carvell (68); Wheeldon for Dowes (73); Whiting for Tony (76); G Horne for Radford (77).
**Try:** Domic (24); **Goals:** Cooke 0/1.

Jamie Lyon chaired from the field after St Helens' 2006 win against Hull FC

**SAINTS:** 1 Paul Wellens; 2 Ade Gardner; 3 Jamie Lyon; 4 Willie Talau; 5 Francis Meli; 6 Leon Pryce; 7 Sean Long (C); 17 Paul Anderson; 9 Keiron Cunningham; 10 Jason Cayless; 11 Lee Gilmour; 12 Jon Wilkin; 16 Jason Hooper. Subs: 23 Maurie Fa'asavalu for Cayless (25); 19 James Graham for Cayless (25!); 15 Mike Bennett for Fa'asavalu (28); 14 James Roby for Cunningham (31); P Anderson for Wilkin (33); Cunningham for Gilmour (49); Cayless for P Anderson (52); Wilkin for Hooper (56); Fa'asavalu for Cayless (58); Gilmour for Graham (66); Cayless for Fa'asavalu (72); P Anderson for Wilkin (75).
**Tries:** Meli (17), Pryce (29), Talau (49), Gardner (52), Cunningham (62); **Goals:** Lyon 3/5.
**Rugby Leaguer & League Express Men of the Match:**
*Hull:* Shaun Briscoe; *Saints:* Paul Wellens.
**Penalty count:** 4-2; **Half-time:** 4-10;
**Referee:** Karl Kirkpatrick (Warrington);
**Attendance:** 72,582 *(at Old Trafford, Manchester).*

## 2007

### NATIONAL LEAGUE TWO GRAND FINAL

*Sunday 7th October 2007*

#### FEATHERSTONE ROVERS 24 OLDHAM 6

**ROVERS:** 1 Loz Wildbore; 2 Danny Kirmond; 3 Jon Whittle; 4 Wayne McHugh; 5 Ade Adebisi; 6 Andy Kain; 7 Paul Handforth; 8 Gareth Handford; 9 Joe McLocklan; 10 Stuart Dickens; 11 Jamie Field; 12 Richard Blakeway; 13 Tom Haughey. Subs (all used): 14 Jamie Benn; 15 Ian Tonks; 16 James Houston; 17 Gavin Swinson.
**Tries:** McHugh (39, 49), Handforth (46);
**Goals:** Dickens 5/6; **Field goals:** Wildbore (66, 70).
**Dismissal:** Blakeway (64) – head butt on Roberts.
**OLDHAM:** 1 Gareth Langley; 2 Byron Ford; 3 Craig Littler; 4 Adam Hughes; 5 Lucas Onyango; 6 Neil Roden; 7 James Coyle; 8 Anthony Tonks; 9 Simeon Hoyle; 10 Richard Mervill; 11 Ian Sinfield; 12 Robert Roberts; 13 Geno Costin. Subs (all used): 14 Ian Hodson; 15 Alex Wilkinson; 16 Said Tamghart; 17 Matty Brooks.
**Try:** Hughes (31); **Goals:** Langley 1/2.
**Rugby Leaguer & League Express Men of the Match:**
*Rovers:* Paul Handforth; *Oldham:* Robert Roberts.
**Penalty count:** 9-5; **Half-time:** 10-6;
**Referee:** Gareth Hewer. *(at Headingley Carnegie, Leeds).*

*Celtic Crusaders were National League Two Champions in 2007. This game was to determine who took the second promotion place.*

### NATIONAL LEAGUE ONE GRAND FINAL

*Sunday 7th October 2007*

#### CASTLEFORD TIGERS 42 WIDNES VIKINGS 10

**TIGERS:** 1 Stuart Donlan; 2 Danny Williams; 3 Michael Shenton; 4 Ryan McGoldrick; 5 Kirk Dixon; 6 Anthony Thackeray; 7 Danny Brough; 8 Liam Higgins; 9 Andrew Henderson; 10 Awen Guttenbeil; 11 Joe Westerman; 12 Ryan Clayton; 13 Peter Lupton. Subs (all used): 14 Mark Leafa; 15 Chris Charles; 16 Michael Wainwright; 17 Ryan Boyle.
**Tries:** Wainwright (20), McGoldrick (29), Guttenbeil (44, 76), M Shenton (52), Westerman (62), Clayton (66);
**Goals:** Brough 6/9; **Field goals:** Brough (25, 55).
**VIKINGS:** 1 Scott Grix; 2 Damien Blanch; 3 Toa Kohe-Love; 4 Mick Nanyn; 5 Gavin Dodd; 6 Dennis Moran; 7 Joel Penny; 8 Mick Cassidy; 9 Mark Smith; 10 Oliver Wilkes; 11 Joel Tomkins; 12 Paul Noone; 13 Bob Beswick. Subs (all used): 14 Aaron Summers; 15 Jordan James; 16 Ian Webster; 17 Lee Doran.
**Tries:** Nanyn (35), Wilkes (69); **Goals:** Nanyn 1/2.
**Rugby Leaguer & League Express Men of the Match:**
*Tigers:* Danny Brough; *Vikings:* Scott Grix.
**Penalty count:** 7-2; **Half-time:** 13-4;
**Referee:** Phil Bentham; **Attendance:** 20,814
*(at Headingley Carnegie, Leeds).*

#### SUPER LEAGUE GRAND FINAL

*Saturday 13th October 2007*

#### LEEDS RHINOS 33 ST HELENS 6

**RHINOS:** 1 Brent Webb; 5 Lee Smith; 3 Clinton Toopi; 4 Keith Senior; 2 Scott Donald; 6 Danny McGuire; 7 Rob Burrow; 8 Kylie Leuluai; 9 Matt Diskin; 10 Jamie Peacock; 11 Jamie Jones-Buchanan; 12 Gareth Ellis; 13 Kevin Sinfield (C). Subs (all used): 14 Ali Lauitiiti for Diskin (23); 16 Ryan Bailey for Leuluai (18); 18 Ian Kirke for Jones-Buchanan (33); 22 Carl Ablett for Kirke (57); Leuluai for Bailey (55); Jones-Buchanan for Lauitiiti (60); Diskin for Ablett (63); Kirke for Leuluai (65); Bailey for Kirke (76).
**Tries:** Webb (19), Lauitiiti (50), Donald (52), Smith (69), Jones-Buchanan (80); **Goals:** Sinfield 6/7;
**Field goal:** Burrow (55).
**SAINTS:** 1 Paul Wellens; 2 Ade Gardner; 3 Matt Gidley; 4 Willie Talau; 5 Francis Meli; 6 Leon Pryce; 7 Sean Long; 8 Nick Fozzard; 9 Keiron Cunningham (C); 10 Jason Cayless; 11 Lee Gilmour; 30 Chris Flannery; 12 Jon Wilkin. Subs (all used): 17 James Graham for Cayless (15); 14 James Roby for Cunningham (23); 23 Maurie Fa'asavalu for Fozzard

(23); 15 Mike Bennett for Wilkin (31); Cayless for Fa'asavalu (34); Cunningham for Flannery (51); Wilkin for Bennett (55); Fa'asavalu for Cayless (55); Fozzard for Graham (57); Cayless for Fozzard (68); Graham for Fa'asavalu (68); Bennett for Gilmour (72).
**Try:** Roby (27); **Goals:** Long 1/2.
**Rugby Leaguer & League Express Men of the Match:** *Rhinos:* Rob Burrow; *Saints:* Sean Long.
**Penalty count:** 4-5; **Half-time:** 8-6; **Referee:** Ashley Klein; **Attendance:** 71,352 *(at Old Trafford, Manchester).*

## 2008

### NATIONAL LEAGUE TWO GRAND FINAL

*Sunday 28th September 2008*

### DONCASTER 18 OLDHAM 10

**DONCASTER:** 1 Zebastian Luisi; 2 Dean Colton; 3 Andreas Bauer; 4 Shaun Leaf; 5 Wayne Reittie; 6 Kyle Wood; 7 Kyle Gale; 8 Nathan Freer; 9 Corey Lawrie; 10 Alex Benson; 11 Peter Green; 12 Craig Lawton; 13 Josh Weeden. Subs (all used): 14 Kyle Briggs; 15 Chris Buttery; 16 Michael Haley; 17 Mark Castle.
**Tries:** Buttery (44), Gale (49), Briggs (73); **Goals:** Gale 3/4.
**OLDHAM:** 1 Paul O'Connor; 2 Gareth Langley; 3 Marcus St Hilaire; 4 Mick Nanyn; 5 Daryl Cardiss; 6 Phil Joseph; 7 James Coyle; 8 Adam Robinson; 9 Matty Brooks; 10 Richard Mervill; 11 Tommy Goulden; 12 Danny Halliwell; 13 Robert Roberts. Subs (all used): 14 Ian Hodson; 15 Luke Menzies; 16 Chris Baines; 17 Said Tamghart.
**Tries:** Hodson (34), Nanyn (62); **Goals:** Nanyn 1/4.
**Rugby Leaguer & League Express Men of the Match:** *Doncaster:* Luke Gale; *Oldham:* Adam Robinson.
**Penalty count:** 7-8; **Half-time:** 2-6;
**Referee:** Ronnie Laughton.
*(at Halliwell Jones Stadium, Warrington).*

*Gateshead Thunder were National League Two Champions in 2008. This game was to determine who took the second promotion place.*

### NATIONAL LEAGUE ONE GRAND FINAL

*Sunday 28th September 2008*

### CELTIC CRUSADERS 18 SALFORD CITY REDS 36
*(after extra-time)*

**CRUSADERS:** 1 Tony Duggan; 2 Luke Dyer; 3 Josh Hannay; 4 Mark Dalle Cort; 5 Anthony Blackwood; 6 Damien Quinn; 7 Jace Van Dijk; 8 Jordan James; 9 Neil Budworth; 10 David Tangata-Toa; 11 Chris Beasley; 12 Darren Mapp; 13 Terry Martin. Subs (all used): 14 Aaron Summers; 15 Ian Webster; 16 Mark Lennon; 17 Neale Wyatt.
**Tries:** Blackwood (38), Dyer (50), J James (54), Tangata-Toa (66); **Goals:** Hannay 0/1, Lennon 1/3.
**CITY REDS:** 1 Karl Fitzpatrick; 2 Matt Gardner; 3 Stuart Littler; 4 John Wilshere; 5 Paul White; 6 Robbie Paul; 7 Richard Myler; 8 Paul Highton; 9 Malcolm Alker; 10 Craig Stapleton; 11 Ian Sibbit; 12 Luke Adamson; 13 Jordan Turner. Subs (all used): 14 Stefan Ratchford; 15 Steve Bannister; 16 Lee Jewitt; 17 Phil Leuluai.
**Tries:** White (5, 86), Gardner (26), Fitzpatrick (63), Sibbit (83), Myler (99); **Goals:** Wilshere 6/7.
**Rugby Leaguer & League Express Men of the Match:** *Crusaders:* Tony Duggan; *City Reds:* John Wilshere.
**Penalty count:** 5-5; **Half-time:** 4-10; **Full-time:** 18-18.
**Referee:** Ben Thaler; **Attendance:** 7,104
*(at Halliwell Jones Stadium, Warrington).*

### SUPER LEAGUE GRAND FINAL

*Saturday 4th October 2008*

### LEEDS RHINOS 24 ST HELENS 16

**RHINOS:** 5 Lee Smith; 22 Ryan Hall; 19 Carl Ablett; 4 Keith Senior; 2 Scott Donald; 6 Danny McGuire; 7 Rob Burrow; 8 Kylie Leuluai; 9 Matt Diskin; 10 Jamie Peacock; 11 Jamie Jones-Buchanan; 12 Gareth Ellis; 13 Kevin Sinfield (C). Subs (all used): 17 Nick Scruton; 14 Ali Lauitiiti; 18 Ian Kirke; 16 Ryan Bailey.
**Tries:** Smith (23), Hall (37), McGuire (49, 63);
**Goals:** Sinfield 4/4.
**SAINTS:** 1 Paul Wellens; 2 Ade Gardner; 3 Matt Gidley; 4 Willie Talau; 5 Francis Meli; 6 Leon Pryce; 7 Sean Long; 18 Bryn Hargreaves; 9 Keiron Cunningham (C); 17 James Graham; 11 Lee Gilmour; 12 Jon Wilkin; 16 Chris Flannery. Subs (all used): 8 Nick Fozzard; 21 Paul Clough; 14 James Roby; 23 Maurie Fa'asavalu.
**Tries:** Graham (6), Gidley (43), Gardner (59);
**Goals:** Long 2/3.
**Rugby Leaguer & League Express Men of the Match:** *Rhinos:* Jamie Peacock; *Saints:* Sean Long.
**Penalty count:** 6-8; **Half-time:** 12-6;
**Referee:** Ashley Klein; **Attendance:** 68,810
*(at Old Trafford, Manchester).*

## 2009

### CHAMPIONSHIP ONE GRAND FINAL

*Sunday 4th October 2009*

### KEIGHLEY COUGARS 28 OLDHAM 26

**COUGARS:** 1 George Rayner; 2 Sam Gardner; 3 Dan Potter; 4 Oliver Pursglove; 5 Gavin Duffy; 6 Jon Presley; 7 Danny Jones; 17 Scott Law; 14 Jamaine Wray; 8 Andy Shickell; 11 Will Cartledge; 18 Greg Nicholson; 13 Carl Hughes. Subs (all used): 21 Ryan Smith; 28 Ryan Benjafield; 9 James Feather; 16 Brendan Rawlins.
**Tries:** Gardner (24), Jones (42, 50), Presley (63), Pursglove (67); **Goals:** Jones 4/5.
**OLDHAM:** 4 Paul Reilly; 21 Lucas Onyango; 24 Marcus St Hilaire; 22 Phil Joseph; 1 Paul O'Connor; 18 Neil Roden; 7 Thomas Coyle; 15 Jason Boults; 30 Martin Roden; 16 Wayne Kerr; 23 Chris Baines; 12 Tommy Goulden; 28 Craig Lawton. Subs (all used): 10 Jamie I'Anson; 25 Luke Menzies; 27 Matt Ashe; 29 Ben Heaton.
**Tries:** Menzies (35, 76), N Roden (54), St Hilaire (70), Kerr (78); **Goals:** Baines 3/4, Ashe 0/1.
**Rugby Leaguer & League Express Men of the Match:** *Cougars:* Danny Jones; *Oldham:* Luke Menzies.
**Penalty count:** 9-2; **Half-time:** 4-6;
**Referee:** Ronnie Laughton.
*(at Halliwell Jones Stadium, Warrington).*

*Dewsbury Rams were Championship One Champions in 2009. This game was to determine who took the second promotion place.*

### CHAMPIONSHIP GRAND FINAL

*Sunday 4th October 2009*

### BARROW RAIDERS 26 HALIFAX 18

**RAIDERS:** 1 Gary Broadbent; 36 Andy Ballard; 32 Andreas Bauer; 4 Liam Harrison; 5 James Nixon; 24 Jamie Rooney; 31 James Coyle; 34 Rob Roberts; 9 Andy Ellis; 8 Brett McDermott; 33 Dave Allen; 22 Ned Catic; 26 Zebastian Luisi. Subs (all used): 15 Chris Young; 13 Andy Bracek; 35 Danny Halliwell; 14 Paul Noone.
**Tries:** Harrison (33), Ballard (37), Allen (61), Bauer (66, 78); **Goals:** Rooney 3/5.
**HALIFAX:** 4 Shad Royston; 5 James Haley; 15 Mark Roberts; 2 Lee Paterson; 23 Rob Worrincy; 19 Mick Govin; 7 Ben Black; 21 Neil Cherryholme; 9 Sean Penkywicz; 22 David Wrench; 11 David Larder; 27 Steve Bannister; 12 Paul Smith. Subs (all used): 13 Bob Beswick; 14 Mark Gleeson; 16 Said Tamghart; 26 Dominic Maloney.
**Tries:** Haley (12), Royston (31), Black (45), Govin (70); **Goals:** Paterson 1/5.
**Rugby Leaguer & League Express Men of the Match:** *Raiders:* Gary Broadbent; *Halifax:* Mick Govin.
**Penalty count:** 8-5; **Half-time:** 10-10;
**Referee:** Phil Bentham; **Attendance:** 11,398
*(at Halliwell Jones Stadium, Warrington).*

### SUPER LEAGUE GRAND FINAL

*Saturday 10th October 2009*

### LEEDS RHINOS 18 ST HELENS 10

**RHINOS:** 1 Brent Webb; 2 Scott Donald; 3 Lee Smith; 4 Keith Senior; 5 Ryan Hall; 6 Danny McGuire; 7 Rob Burrow; 8 Kylie Leuluai; 14 Matt Diskin; 10 Jamie Peacock; 11 Jamie Jones-Buchanan; 18 Carl Ablett; 13 Kevin Sinfield (C). Subs (all used): 16 Ryan Bailey for Leuluai (19); 19 Luke Burgess for Peacock (29); 17 Ian Kirke for Jones-Buchanan (29); 12 Ali Lauitiiti for Ablett (29); Jones-Buchanan for Lauitiiti (36); Peacock for Burgess (46); Leuluai for Bailey (53); Ablett for Kirke (57); Burgess for Diskin (62); Bailey for Leuluai (67); Diskin for Burgess (69); Kirke for Jones-Buchanan (76).
**Tries:** Diskin (30), Smith (37, 72); **Goals:** Sinfield 2/4;
**Field goals:** Sinfield (42), Burrow (78).
**SAINTS:** 1 Paul Wellens; 2 Ade Gardner; 3 Matt Gidley; 18 Kyle Eastmond; 5 Francis Meli; 6 Leon Pryce; 7 Sean Long; 10 James Graham; 9 Keiron Cunningham (C); 16 Tony Puletua; 12 Jon Wilkin; 11 Lee Gilmour; 13 Chris Flannery. Subs (all used): 14 James Roby for Cunningham (25); 15 Bryn Hargreaves for Puletua (24); 17 Paul Clough for Gilmour (31); 23 Maurie Fa'asavalu for Graham (31); Graham for Fa'asavalu (48); Puletua for Hargreaves (50); Gilmour for Clough (61); Wilkin for Roby (65); Roby for Flannery (73).
**Try:** Eastmond (13); **Goals:** Eastmond 3/3.
**Rugby Leaguer & League Express Men of the Match:** *Rhinos:* Kevin Sinfield; *Saints:* James Graham.
**Penalty count:** 8-7; **Half-time:** 8-8;
**Referee:** Steve Ganson; **Attendance:** 63,259
*(at Old Trafford, Manchester).*

## 2010

### CHAMPIONSHIP ONE GRAND FINAL

*Sunday 26th September 2010*

### OLDHAM 4 YORK CITY KNIGHTS 25

**OLDHAM:** 1 Paul O'Connor; 2 Lucas Onyango; 24 Marcus St Hilaire; 4 Mick Fogerty; 5 John Gillam; 6 Neil Roden; 28 Gregg McNally; 8 Jason Boults; 9 Martin Roden; 16 Wayne Kerr; 18 Chris Clarke; 13 Joe Chandler; 21 Valu Bentley. Subs (all used): 10 Dave Ellison; 19 Ben Heaton; 17 Danny Whitmore; 7 Matt Ashe.
**Try:** Fogerty (20); **Goals:** McNally 0/1.
**CITY KNIGHTS:** 31 James Haynes; 2 Wayne Reittie; 3 Mike Mitchell; 4 Lee Waterman; 28 Danny Wilson; 6 Chris Thorman; 1 Danny Ratcliffe; 17 Nathan Freer; 33 Jack Lee; 10 Alex Benson; 11 Jordan Ross; 29 Ryan Esders; 15 Luke Dinsdale; 26 Steve Lewis; 30 Jack Stearman.
**Tries:** Reittie (7), Haynes (26), Thorman (64), Lewis (74);
**Goals:** Waterman 2/3, Thorman 2/2;
**Field goal:** Thorman (69).
**Rugby Leaguer & League Express Men of the Match:** *Oldham:* Neil Roden; *City Knights:* Chris Thorman.
**Penalty count:** 2-7; **Half-time:** 4-10;
**Referee:** Gareth Hewer.
*(at Halliwell Jones Stadium, Warrington).*

*Hunslet Hawks were Championship One Champions in 2010. This game was to determine who took the second promotion place.*

### CHAMPIONSHIP GRAND FINAL

*Sunday 26th September 2010*

### FEATHERSTONE ROVERS 22 HALIFAX 23
*(after golden point extra-time)*

**ROVERS:** 1 Ian Hardman; 26 Zak Hardaker; 3 Sam Smeaton; 4 Liam Welham; 2 Tom Saxton; 6 Kyle Briggs; 9 Liam Finn; 17 Tony Tonks; 31 Ben Kaye; 10 Stuart Dickens; 18 Tim Spears; 13 Jamie Field; 11 Matty Dale. Subs (all used): 19 Ross Divorty; 16 Dane Manning; 12 Jon Grayshon; 7 Andy Kain.
**Tries:** Briggs (28), Hardaker (30, 52), Dale (45);
**Goals:** Briggs 3/4.
**HALIFAX:** 4 Shad Royston; 2 Lee Paterson; 6 Luke Branighan; 18 Dylan Nash; 23 Rob Worrincy; 26 Graham Holroyd; 7 Ben Black; 10 Neil Cherryholme; 13 Bob Beswick; 8 Makali Aizue; 11 David Larder; 22 David Wrench; 27 Sam Barlow. Subs (all used): 9 Sean Penkywicz; 17 Frank Watene; 19 Dominic Maloney; 24 Steve Bannister.
**Tries:** Worrincy (20), Black (58), Branighan (60), Bannister (75); **Goals:** Paterson 3/4; **Field goal:** Black (82).
**On report:** Barlow (35) - alleged high tackle on Divorty.
**Rugby Leaguer & League Express Men of the Match:** *Rovers:* Tom Saxton; *Halifax:* Ben Black.
**Penalty count:** 2-6; **Half-time:** 12-4; **Full-time:** 22-22;
**Referee:** Robert Hicks; **Attendance:** 9,443
*(at Halliwell Jones Stadium, Warrington).*

### SUPER LEAGUE GRAND FINAL

*Saturday 2nd October 2010*

### ST HELENS 10 WIGAN WARRIORS 22

**SAINTS:** 1 Paul Wellens; 30 Jamie Foster; 3 Matt Gidley; 5 Francis Meli; 24 Jonny Lomax; 12 Jon Wilkin; 34 Matty Smith; 10 James Graham; 9 Keiron Cunningham (C); 15 Bryn Hargreaves; 4 Iosia Soliola; 13 Chris Flannery; 11 Tony Puletua. Subs (all used): 17 Paul Clough; 14 James Roby; 22 Andrew Dixon; 25 Jacob Emmitt.
**Tries:** Dixon (28), Meli (74); **Goals:** Foster 1/2.
**WARRIORS:** 6 Sam Tomkins; 24 Darrell Goulding; 3 Martin Gleeson; 4 George Carmont; 5 Pat Richards; 19 Paul Deacon; 7 Thomas Leuluai; 8 Stuart Fielden; 15 Michael McIlorum; 10 Andy Coley; 11 Harrison Hansen; 12 Joel Tomkins; 13 Sean O'Loughlin (C). Subs (all used): 9 Mark Riddell; 17 Iafeta Palea'aesina; 25 Liam Farrell; 14 Paul Prescott.
**Tries:** Gleeson (4, 16), Goulding (20), S Tomkins (53);
**Goals:** Richards 2/3, Riddell 1/3, S Tomkins 0/1.
**Rugby Leaguer & League Express Men of the Match:** *Saints:* Tony Puletua; *Warriors:* Thomas Leuluai.
**Penalty count:** 6-11; **Half-time:** 6-16;
**Referee:** Richard Silverwood; **Attendance:** 71,526
*(at Old Trafford, Manchester).*

## 2011

### CHAMPIONSHIP ONE GRAND FINAL

*Sunday 2nd October 2011*

### KEIGHLEY COUGARS 32 WORKINGTON TOWN 12

**COUGARS:** 18 James Haythornthwaite; 4 Danny Lawton;

22 Ben Sagar; 33 Jake Normington; 5 Gavin Duffy; 6 Jason Demetriou; 36 Jy-Mel Coleman; 17 Ryan Benjafield; 9 James Feather; 10 Scott Law; 11 Will Cartledge; 12 Oliver Pursglove; 21 Richard Jones. Subs (all used): 14 Jamaine Wray; 8 Andy Shickell; 16 Brendan Rawlins; 7 Ryan Smith.
**Tries:** Lawton (5), Feather (20), Rawlins (25), Pursglove (32), Normington (69, 77); **Goals:** Lawton 4/6.
**TOWN:** 1 Brett Carter; 2 Elliott Miller; 3 Jason Mossop; 4 Aaron Low; 5 Neil Frazer; 24 Darren Holt; 7 Scott Kaighan; 10 Kris Coward; 13 Karl Olstrum; 29 Dave Armitstead; 11 Mike Whitehead; 18 Joe McKenna; 12 Jarrad Stack. Subs (all used): 23 Marc Bainbridge; 15 Ruairi McGoff; 32 Chris Clough; 17 James Robinson.
**Tries:** Kaighan (65), Frazer (74); **Goals:** Holt 2/2.
**Rugby Leaguer & League Express Men of the Match:** *Cougars:* Jason Demetriou; *Town:* Jarrad Stack.
**Penalty count:** 7-5; **Half-time:** 22-0; **Referee:** Tim Roby. *(at Halliwell Jones Stadium, Warrington).*

*Swinton Lions were Championship One Champions in 2011. This game was to determine who took the second promotion place.*

#### CHAMPIONSHIP GRAND FINAL

*Sunday 2nd October 2011*

#### FEATHERSTONE ROVERS 40 SHEFFIELD EAGLES 4

**ROVERS:** 1 Ian Hardman; 33 Ben Cockayne; 3 Sam Smeaton; 17 Greg Worthington; 5 Tom Saxton; 6 Andy Kain; 7 Liam Finn; 8 Tony Tonks; 9 Ben Kaye; 10 Stuart Dickens; 11 Jon Grayshon; 12 Tim Spears; 28 Jon Hepworth. Subs (all used): 18 Ross Divorty; 13 Matty Dale; 4 Andrew Bostock; 30 Kirk Netherton.
**Tries:** Spears (4), Finn (7, 39), Hardman (42), Cockayne (56), Hepworth (59), Saxton (79); **Goals:** Finn 6/7.
**Sin bin:** Netherton (54) - fighting.
**EAGLES:** 6 Quentin Laulu-Togagae; 5 Tim Bergin; 26 Corey Hanson; 1 Misi Taulapapa; 16 Vinny Finigan; 13 Dane McDonald; 7 Simon Brown; 8 Jack Howieson; 9 Andrew Henderson; 10 Mitchell Stringer; 11 Alex Szostak; 12 Peter Green; 19 Joe Hirst. Subs (all used): 22 Ryan Hepworth; 30 Sam Scott; 20 Pat Smith; 14 Jonny Woodcock.
**Try:** McDonald (12); **Goals:** Brown 0/1.
**Sin bin:** Hirst (54) - fighting.
**Rugby Leaguer & League Express Men of the Match:** *Rovers:* Liam Finn; *Eagles:* Joe Hirst.
**Penalty count:** 7-11; **Half-time:** 18-4;
**Referee:** Matthew Thomason; **Attendance:** 7,263 *(at Halliwell Jones Stadium, Warrington).*

#### SUPER LEAGUE GRAND FINAL

*Saturday 8th October 2011*

#### LEEDS RHINOS 32 ST HELENS 16

**RHINOS:** 1 Brent Webb; 23 Ben Jones-Bishop; 27 Zak Hardaker; 12 Carl Ablett; 5 Ryan Hall; 13 Kevin Sinfield (C); 6 Danny McGuire; 8 Kylie Leuluai; 9 Danny Buderus; 10 Jamie Peacock; 11 Jamie Jones-Buchanan; 3 Brett Delaney; 21 Chris Clarkson. Subs (all used): 7 Rob Burrow; 16 Ryan Bailey; 17 Ian Kirke; 14 Ali Lauititi.
**Tries:** Burrow (34), Webb (65), Hall (70), Ablett (74), Hardaker (80); **Goals:** Sinfield 6/7.
**SAINTS:** 1 Paul Wellens (C); 28 Tom Makinson; 3 Michael Shenton; 5 Francis Meli; 22 Jamie Foster; 25 Lee Gaskell; 20 Jonny Lomax; 10 James Graham (C); 9 James Roby; 11 Tony Puletua; 12 Jon Wilkin; 4 Iosia Soliola; 16 Paul Clough. Subs (all used): 19 Andrew Dixon; 14 Scott Moore; 15 Louie McCarthy-Scarsbrook; 17 Gary Wheeler.
**Tries:** Makinson (50), Shenton (55); **Goals:** Foster 4/5.
**Rugby Leaguer & League Express Men of the Match:** *Rhinos:* Rob Burrow; *Saints:* Lee Gaskell.
**Penalty count:** 5-7; **Half-time:** 8-2;
**Referee:** Phil Bentham; **Attendance:** 69,107 *(at Old Trafford, Manchester).*

#### 2012

#### CHAMPIONSHIP ONE GRAND FINAL

*Sunday 30th September 2012*

#### BARROW RAIDERS 13 DONCASTER 16

**RAIDERS:** 1 Andy Ballard; 2 Lee Haney; 3 Chris Larkin; 4 Aaron Low; 5 James Nixon; 6 Scott Kaighan; 7 Liam Campbell; 8 Jamie Butler; 9 James Dandy; 10 Ryan Duffy; 11 Liam Harrison; 12 James Gordon; 13 Daniel Toal. Subs (all used): 14 Liam Finch; 15 Martin Ostler; 16 Ruairi McGoff; 17 Andrew Dawson.
**Tries:** Larkin (4), Low (77); **Goals:** Ballard 2/3;
**Field goal:** Kaighan (39).
**DONCASTER:** 1 Lee Waterman; 2 Tom Hodson; 3 Chris Spurr; 4 Danny Cowling; 5 Stewart Sanderson; 6 Kyle Kesik; 7 Craig Fawcett; 8 Mark Castle; 9 Mike Emmett; 10 Russ Spiers; 11 Lucas Walshaw; 12 Michael Kelly; 13 Carl Hughes.

**Danny Buderus takes on James Roby and Louie McCarthy-Scarsbrook during Leeds' victory against St Helens in 2011**

Subs (all used): 14 Nathan Powley; 15 Craig Robinson; 16 Grant Edwards; 17 Liam Cunningham.
**Tries:** Sanderson (11), Waterman (46), Fawcett (57); **Goals:** Hodson 2/3.
**Rugby Leaguer & League Express Men of the Match:** *Raiders:* Liam Harrison; *Doncaster:* Craig Fawcett.
**Penalty count:** 4-5; **Half-time:** 7-4; **Referee:** Jamie Leahy. *(at Halliwell Jones Stadium, Warrington).*

#### CHAMPIONSHIP GRAND FINAL

*Sunday 30th September 2012*

#### FEATHERSTONE ROVERS 16 SHEFFIELD EAGLES 20

**ROVERS:** 1 Ian Hardman; 2 Tangi Ropati; 3 Nathan Chappell; 4 Greg Worthington; 5 Tom Saxton; 6 Andy Kain; 7 Liam Finn; 8 Anthony England; 9 Ben Kaye; 10 James Lockwood; 11 Matty Dale; 12 Tim Spears; 13 Kyle Briggs. Subs (all used): 14 Dominic Maloney; 15 Stuart Dickens; 16 Andrew Bostock; 17 Jon Hepworth.
**Tries:** Hardman (17), Hepworth (51); **Goals:** Finn 4/4.
**On report:**
Maloney (57) - alleged use of the elbow on Turner.
**EAGLES:** 1 Quentin Laulu-Togagae; 2 Misi Taulapapa; 3 Duane Straugheir; 4 Menzie Yere; 5 Scott Turner; 6 Simon Brown; 7 Dominic Brambani; 8 Jack Howieson; 9 Andrew Henderson; 10 Mitchell Stringer; 11 Michael Knowles; 12 Sam Scott; 13 Alex Szostak. Subs (all used): 14 James Davey; 15 Peter Green; 16 Dane McDonald; 17 Liam Higgins.
**Tries:** Turner (9), Laulu-Togagae (32), McDonald (46), Taulapapa (57); **Goals:** Brown 2/5.
**Rugby Leaguer & League Express Men of the Match:** *Rovers:* Ian Hardman; *Eagles:* Michael Knowles.
**Penalty count:** 4-6; **Half-time:** 8-10; **Referee:** Tim Roby; **Attendance:** 6,409 *(at Halliwell Jones Stadium, Warrington).*

#### SUPER LEAGUE GRAND FINAL

*Saturday 6th October 2012*

#### LEEDS RHINOS 26 WARRINGTON WOLVES 18

**RHINOS:** 4 Zak Hardaker; 2 Ben Jones-Bishop; 3 Kallum Watkins; 12 Carl Ablett; 5 Ryan Hall; 13 Kevin Sinfield (C); 6 Danny McGuire; 8 Kylie Leuluai; 9 Danny Buderus; 10 Jamie Peacock; 11 Jamie Jones-Buchanan; 15 Brett Delaney; 16 Ryan Bailey. Subs (all used): 17 Ian Kirke; 20 Darrell Griffin; 25 Stevie Ward; 31 Shaun Lunt.

**Tries:** Sinfield (19), Jones-Bishop (28), Ablett (59), Hall (72); **Goals:** Sinfield 5/5.
**WOLVES:** 1 Brett Hodgson; 5 Joel Monaghan; 19 Stefan Ratchford; 4 Ryan Atkins; 2 Chris Riley; 6 Lee Briers; 7 Richard Myler; 20 Chris Hill; 14 Mick Higham; 13 Ben Harrison; 12 Ben Westwood; 11 Trent Waterhouse; 15 Simon Grix. Subs (all used): 8 Adrian Morley (C); 9 Michael Monaghan; 16 Paul Wood; 17 Michael Cooper.
**Tries:** Myler (4), J Monaghan (38), Atkins (45);
**Goals:** Hodgson 3/4.
**Rugby Leaguer & League Express Men of the Match:** *Rhinos:* Kevin Sinfield; *Wolves:* Richard Myler.
**Penalty count:** 6-5; **Half-time:** 14-14;
**Referee:** Richard Silverwood; **Attendance:** 70,676 *(at Old Trafford, Manchester).*

#### 2013

#### CHAMPIONSHIP ONE GRAND FINAL

*Sunday 29th September 2013*

#### OLDHAM 18 ROCHDALE HORNETS 32

**OLDHAM:** 1 Richard Lepori; 2 Mo Agoro; 21 David Cookson; 25 Jonathan Ford; 5 Dale Bloomfield; 23 Lewis Palfrey; 16 Kenny Hughes; 18 Phil Joy; 9 Sam Gee; 10 Jason Boults; 11 Josh Crowley; 12 Danny Langtree; 13 Mark Hobson. Subs (all used): 14 Adam Files; 19 Michael Ward; 22 Liam Thompson; 28 Matthew Haggarty.
**Tries:** Ford (12), Hughes (38), Cookson (44);
**Goals:** Palfrey 3/3.
**HORNETS:** 1 Wayne English; 2 Gareth Langley; 20 Daniel Davies; 23 Dave Hull; 17 Martin Waring; 6 Paul Crook; 7 Steve Roper; 29 Carl Forster; 31 Chris Hough; 10 Warren Thompson; 26 Dave Llewellyn; 14 Alex Trumper; 18 Joe Greenwood. Subs (all used): 8 John Cookson; 9 Alex McClurg; 11 Chris Baines; 13 Jordan Case.
**Tries:** Llewellyn (5), Davies (20), Hull (58), Cookson (71), English (78); **Goals:** Crook 6/6.
**Rugby Leaguer & League Express Men of the Match:** *Oldham:* Lewis Palfrey; *Hornets:* Paul Crook.
**Penalty count:** 1-2; **Half-time:** 12-12;
**Referee:** Chris Leatherbarrow. *(at Leigh Sports Village).*

*North Wales Crusaders were Championship One Champions in 2013. This game was to determine who took the second promotion place.*

# *Grand Finals 1998-2018*

### CHAMPIONSHIP GRAND FINAL

*Sunday 29th September 2013*

**BATLEY BULLDOGS 12 SHEFFIELD EAGLES 19**

**BULLDOGS:** 1 Miles Greenwood; 5 Johnny Campbell; 3 Jason Walton; 4 Danny Maun; 21 Greg Johnson; 26 Ben Black; 7 Gareth Moore; 8 Byron Smith; 9 Paul Mennell; 28 Anthony Mullally, 11 Alex Bretherton; 16 John Davies; 13 Ashley Lindsay. Subs (all used): 14 George Flanagan; 15 Keegan Hirst; 19 Alex Rowe; 17 Liam Walmsley.
**Try:** Campbell (13); **Goals:** Moore 4/5.
**EAGLES:** 1 Quentin Laulu-Togagae; 5 Misi Taulapapa; 4 Tom Armstrong; 3 Menzie Yere; 2 Scott Turner; 6 Pat Walker; 7 Dominic Brambani; 25 Eddie Battye; 9 Andrew Henderson; 10 Mitchell Stringer; 11 Michael Knowles; 15 Alex Szostak; 13 Joe Hirst. Subs (all used): 14 James Davey; 12 Peter Green; 16 Duane Straugheir; 21 Matt Garside.
**Tries:** Turner (56, 67), Yere (61), Laulu-Togagae (70);
**Goals:** Brambani 1/5; **Field goal:** Walker (74).
**Rugby Leaguer & League Express Men of the Match:**
*Bulldogs:* Keegan Hirst; *Eagles:* Dominic Brambani.
**Penalty count:** 6-7; **Half-time:** 12-0;
**Referee:** Matthew Thomason; **Attendance:** 6,374
*(at Leigh Sports Village).*

### SUPER LEAGUE GRAND FINAL

*Saturday 5th October 2013*

**WARRINGTON WOLVES 16 WIGAN WARRIORS 30**

**WOLVES:** 19 Stefan Ratchford; 5 Joel Monaghan; 3 Chris Bridge; 4 Ryan Atkins; 2 Chris Riley; 6 Lee Briers; 7 Richard Myler; 16 Paul Wood; 14 Mick Higham; 18 Chris Hill; 13 Ben Harrison; 12 Ben Westwood; 15 Simon Grix. Subs (all used): 9 Michael Monaghan; 8 Adrian Morley (C); 17 Michael Cooper; 10 Garreth Carvell.
**Tries:** J Monaghan (20), Grix (24), Westwood (27);
**Goals:** Ratchford 2/3.
**On report:** Westwood (2) - alleged punch on Green.
**WARRIORS:** 1 Sam Tomkins; 2 Josh Charnley; 3 Darrell Goulding; 17 Iain Thornley; 5 Pat Richards; 6 Blake Green; 7 Matty Smith; 10 Lee Mossop; 9 Michael McIlorum; 20 Gil Dudson; 11 Harrison Hansen; 12 Liam Farrell; 13 Sean O'Loughlin (C). Subs (all used): 15 Ben Flower; 4 Jack Hughes; 26 Dominic Crosby; 21 Scott Taylor.
**Tries:** Goulding (37), McIlorum (47), Charnley (53), Green (65), Richards (74); **Goals:** Richards 5/6.
**Rugby Leaguer & League Express Men of the Match:**
*Wolves:* Chris Hill; *Warriors:* Michael McIlorum.
**Penalty count:** 7-10; **Half-time:** 16-6;
**Referee:** Richard Silverwood; **Attendance:** 66,281
*(at Old Trafford, Manchester).*

## 2014

### CHAMPIONSHIP ONE GRAND FINAL

*Sunday 5th October 2014*

**HUNSLET HAWKS 17 OLDHAM 16**

*(after golden point extra-time)*

**HAWKS:** 2 Jimmy Watson; 36 Gavin Duffy; 4 Danny Maun; 3 Lee Brickwood; 37 James Duckworth; 6 Thomas Coyle; 20 Danny Ansell; 38 Richard Moore; 9 David March; 10 James Houston; 11 John Oakes; 12 Aaron Lyons; 31 Luke Briscoe. Subs (all used): 27 Liam Hood; 8 Michael Haley; 1 Stuart Kain; 40 Luke Hardbottle.
**Tries:** Watson (22), Duckworth (45), T Coyle (53);
**Goals:** March 2/3; **Field goal:** T Coyle (85).
**OLDHAM:** 4 Steven Nield; 29 Adam Clay; 21 David Cookson; 25 Jonathan Ford; 5 Dale Bloomfield; 6 Lewis Palfrey; 26 Steve Roper; 8 Phil Joy; 30 Gareth Owen; 10 Jason Boults; 11 Josh Crowley; 12 Danny Langtree; 22 Liam Thompson. Subs (all used): 19 Michael Ward; 28 Nathan Mason; 16 Kenny Hughes; 20 George Tyson.
**Tries:** Roper (5), Bloomfield (31), Langtree (74);
**Goals:** Roper 2/3.
**Rugby Leaguer & League Express Men of the Match:**
*Hawks:* Liam Hood; *Oldham:* Jonathan Ford.
**Penalty count:** 4-3; **Half-time:** 6-10; **Referee:** Joe Cobb.
*(at Headingley Carnegie, Leeds).*

### CHAMPIONSHIP GRAND FINAL

*Sunday 5th October 2014*

**FEATHERSTONE ROVERS 12 LEIGH CENTURIONS 36**

**ROVERS:** 2 Will Sharp; 35 Jason Crookes; 1 Ian Hardman; 18 Jamie Cording; 36 Ben Blackmore; 23 Andy Kain; 7 Gareth Moore; 8 Steve Crossley; 9 Andy Ellis; 13 Matt James; 31 Shaun Pick; 11 James Lockwood; 12 Tim Spears. Subs (all used): 30 Luke Teasdale; 6 Jack Bussey; 42 Chris Annakin; 10 Keegan Hirst.
**Tries:** Sharp (27, 51); **Goals:** Moore 2/2.
**Sin bin:** Crookes (68) - high tackle on Armstrong.
**CENTURIONS:** 1 Gregg McNally; 22 Adam Higson; 34 Michael Platt; 4 Tom Armstrong; 15 Liam Kay; 6 Martyn Ridyard; 7 Ryan Brierley; 29 Jake Emmitt; 14 Sean Penkywicz; 10 Oliver Wilkes; 11 Matt Sarsfield; 30 Kurt Haggerty; 13 Sam Barlow. Subs (all used): 9 Bob Beswick; 18 Jamie Acton; 16 Martin Aspinwall; 33 Jonathan Walker.
**Tries:** Sarsfield (5), McNally (17), Armstrong (22), Higson (65), Barlow (70), Brierley (80);
**Goals:** Ridyard 6/8.
**Sin bin:** Penkywicz (68) - retaliation.
**Rugby Leaguer & League Express Men of the Match:**
*Rovers:* Jack Bussey; *Centurions:* Tom Armstrong.
**Penalty count:** 6-8; **Half-time:** 6-20;
**Referee:** Matthew Thomason; **Attendance:** 9,164
*(at Headingley Carnegie, Leeds).*

### SUPER LEAGUE GRAND FINAL

*Saturday 11th October 2014*

**ST HELENS 14 WIGAN WARRIORS 6**

**SAINTS:** 17 Paul Wellens (C); 2 Tom Makinson; 22 Mark Percival; 4 Josh Jones; 5 Adam Swift; 15 Mark Flanagan; 6 Lance Hohaia; 16 Kyle Amor; 9 James Roby; 8 Mose Masoe; 10 Louie McCarthy-Scarsbrook; 11 Iosia Soliola; 3 Jordan Turner. Subs (all used): 28 Luke Thompson; 13 Willie Manu; 18 Alex Walmsley; 27 Greg Richards.
**Tries:** Soliola (54), Makinson (69); **Goals:** Percival 3/3.
**WARRIORS:** 1 Matt Bowen; 2 Josh Charnley; 5 Anthony Gelling; 23 Dan Sarginson; 32 Joe Burgess; 6 Blake Green; 7 Matty Smith; 10 Ben Flower; 9 Sam Powell; 17 Dominic Crosby; 11 Joel Tomkins; 12 Liam Farrell; 13 Sean O'Loughlin (C). Subs (all used): 22 Eddy Pettybourne; 24 Tony Clubb; 25 John Bateman; 27 George Williams.
**Try:** Burgess (40); **Goals:** Smith 1/3.
**Dismissal:** Flower (2) - punching Hohaia.
**Rugby Leaguer & League Express Men of the Match:**
*Saints:* James Roby; *Warriors:* Liam Farrell.
**Penalty count:** 9-7; **Half-time:** 2-6;
**Referee:** Phil Bentham; **Attendance:** 70,102
*(at Old Trafford, Manchester).*

## 2015

### SUPER LEAGUE GRAND FINAL

*Saturday 10th October 2015*

**LEEDS RHINOS 22 WIGAN WARRIORS 20**

**RHINOS:** 1 Zak Hardaker; 2 Tom Briscoe; 3 Kallum Watkins; 4 Joel Moon; 5 Ryan Hall; 13 Kevin Sinfield (C); 6 Danny McGuire; 30 Mitch Garbutt; 7 Rob Burrow; 10 Jamie Peacock; 12 Carl Ablett; 15 Brett Delaney; 19 Brad Singleton. Subs (all used): 8 Kylie Leuluai; 17 Adam Cuthbertson; 20 Jimmy Keinhorst; 21 Josh Walters.
**Tries:** McGuire (7, 35), Moon (27), Walters (64);
**Goals:** Sinfield 3/4.
**WARRIORS:** 1 Matt Bowen; 22 Dominic Manfredi; 14 John Bateman; 34 Oliver Gildart; 5 Joe Burgess; 6 George Williams; 7 Matty Smith; 8 Dominic Crosby; 9 Michael McIlorum; 10 Ben Flower; 11 Joel Tomkins; 12 Liam Farrell; 13 Sean O'Loughlin (C). Subs (all used): 16 Sam Powell; 17 Tony Clubb; 23 Lee Mossop; 25 Larne Patrick.
**Tries:** Burgess (4), Manfredi (46), Bowen (49);
**Goals:** Bowen 4/4.
**Rugby Leaguer & League Express Men of the Match:**
*Rhinos:* Danny McGuire; *Warriors:* Matt Bowen.
**Penalty count:** 5-4; **Half-time:** 16-6;
**Referee:** Ben Thaler; **Attendance:** 73,512
*(at Old Trafford, Manchester).*

## 2016

### SUPER LEAGUE GRAND FINAL

*Saturday 8th October 2016*

**WARRINGTON WOLVES 6 WIGAN WARRIORS 12**

**WOLVES:** 6 Stefan Ratchford; 2 Tom Lineham; 3 Rhys Evans; 4 Ryan Atkins; 5 Matthew Russell; 1 Kurt Gidley; 26 Declan Patton; 8 Chris Hill (C); 9 Daryl Clark; 10 Ashton Sims; 27 Sam Wilde; 12 Jack Hughes; 14 Joe Westerman. Subs (all used): 24 Toby King; 18 George King; 7 Chris Sandow; 33 Ryan Bailey.
**Try:** Patton (21); **Goals:** Patton 1/1.
**WARRIORS:** 4 Dan Sarginson; 2 Josh Charnley; 3 Anthony Gelling; 20 Oliver Gildart; 22 Lewis Tierney; 6 George Williams; 7 Matty Smith; 24 Frank-Paul Nuuausala; 16 Sam Powell; 10 Ben Flower; 14 John Bateman; 25 Willie Isa. Subs (all used): 8 Dominic Crosby; 19 Taulima Tautai; 21 Ryan Sutton; 13 Sean O'Loughlin (C).
**Tries:** Gildart (55), Charnley (63); **Goals:** Smith 2/4.

**Rugby Leaguer & League Express Men of the Match:**
*Wolves:* Kurt Gidley; *Warriors:* Liam Farrell.
**Penalty count:** 4-6; **Half-time:** 6-2;
**Referee:** Robert Hicks; **Attendance:** 70,202
*(at Old Trafford, Manchester).*

## 2017

### SUPER LEAGUE GRAND FINAL

*Saturday 7th October 2017*

**CASTLEFORD TIGERS 6 LEEDS RHINOS 24**

**TIGERS:** 5 Greg Eden; 2 Greg Minikin; 3 Jake Webster; 4 Michael Shenton (C); 25 Jy Hitchcox; 16 Ben Roberts; 7 Luke Gale; 14 Nathan Massey; 9 Paul McShane; 15 Jesse Sene-Lefao; 11 Oliver Holmes; 12 Mike McMeeken; 13 Adam Milner. Subs (all used): 10 Grant Millington; 17 Junior Moors; 18 Matt Cook; 34 Alex Foster.
**Try:** Foster (79); **Goals:** Gale 1/1.
**RHINOS:** 31 Jack Walker; 2 Tom Briscoe; 3 Kallum Watkins; 14 Liam Sutcliffe; 5 Ryan Hall; 4 Joel Moon; 6 Danny McGuire (C); 16 Brad Singleton; 9 Matt Parcell; 17 Mitch Garbutt; 13 Stevie Ward; 11 Jamie Jones-Buchanan; 10 Adam Cuthbertson. Subs (all used): 20 Anthony Mullally; 12 Carl Ablett; 7 Rob Burrow; 19 Brett Ferres.
**Tries:** Briscoe (11, 59), McGuire (51, 70); **Goals:** Watkins 3/4;
**Field goal:** McGuire.
**Rugby Leaguer & League Express Men of the Match:**
*Tigers:* Matt Cook; *Rhinos:* Danny McGuire.
**Penalty count:** 5-1; **Half-time:** 0-7;
**Referee:** James Child; **Attendance:** 72,827
*(at Old Trafford, Manchester).*

## 2018

### SUPER LEAGUE GRAND FINAL

*Saturday 13th October 2018*

**WARRINGTON WOLVES 4 WIGAN WARRIORS 12**

**WOLVES:** 1 Stefan Ratchford; 2 Tom Lineham; 3 Bryson Goodwin; 18 Toby King; 27 Josh Charnley; 4 Kevin Brown; 7 Tyrone Roberts; 8 Chris Hill (C); 9 Daryl Clark; 10 Mike Cooper; 30 Bodene Thompson; 12 Jack Hughes; 34 Ben Westwood. Subs (all used): 17 Joe Philbin; 13 Ben Murdoch-Masila; 19 George King; 15 Declan Patton.
**Try:** Charnley (12); **Goals:** Roberts 0/1.
**WARRIORS:** 1 Sam Tomkins; 21 Dom Manfredi; 4 Oliver Gildart; 3 Dan Sarginson; 2 Tom Davies; 6 George Williams; 9 Thomas Leuluai; 25 Romain Navarrete; 7 Sam Powell; 10 Ben Flower; 40 Joe Greenwood; 14 John Bateman; 13 Sean O'Loughlin (C). Subs (all used): 20 Morgan Escare; 15 Ryan Sutton; 12 Liam Farrell; 8 Tony Clubb.
**Tries:** Manfredi (25, 77), Davies (31); **Goals:** S Tomkins 0/4.
**Rugby Leaguer & League Express Men of the Match:**
*Wolves:* Stefan Ratchford; *Warriors:* Dom Manfredi.
**Penalty count:** 7-4; **Half-time:** 4-8;
**Referee:** Robert Hicks; **Attendance:** 64,892
*(at Old Trafford, Manchester).*

# 2019 SEASON
## Stats round-up

### SUPER LEAGUE CLUBS - AVERAGES

| | 2019 Avg | 2018 Avg | Diff |
|---|---|---|---|
| Leeds Rhinos | 12,727 | 12,352 | +375 |
| St Helens | 11,910 | 11,169 | +741 |
| Hull FC | 11,478 | 11,854 | -376 |
| Wigan Warriors | 11,432 | 11,648 | -216 |
| Warrington Wolves | 10,648 | 9,782 | +866 |
| Catalans Dragons | 8,618 | 8,145 | +473 |
| Hull Kingston Rovers | 8,220 | 7,873 | +347 |
| Castleford Tigers | 7,253 | 7,604 | -351 |
| Wakefield Trinity | 5,468 | 5,056 | +412 |
| Huddersfield Giants | 5,226 | 5,471 | -245 |
| Salford Red Devils | 3,746 | 2,823 | +923 |
| London Broncos | 2,014 | 896 | +1,118 |
| | | *(Championship)* | |
| | | | |
| **2019 Average** | 8,228 | | |
| **2018 Average** | 8,200 | | |
| **Difference** | +28 | | |

### CHAMPIONSHIP CLUBS - AVERAGES

| | 2019 Avg | 2018 Avg | Diff |
|---|---|---|---|
| Toronto Wolfpack | 6,988 | 6,565 | +423 |
| Bradford Bulls | 4,409 | 3,684 | +725 |
| | | *(League 1)* | |
| Widnes Vikings | 3,943 | 4,624 | -681 |
| | | *(Super League)* | |
| Leigh Centurions | 3,055 | 3,247 | -192 |
| Toulouse Olympique | 2,290 | 2,538 | -248 |
| Featherstone Rovers | 2,282 | 2,084 | +198 |
| York City Knights | 2,065 | 1,624 | +441 |
| | | *(League 1)* | |
| Halifax | 1,657 | 2,008 | -351 |
| Barrow Raiders | 1,371 | 1,223 | +148 |
| Batley Bulldogs | 1,302 | 1,029 | +273 |
| Dewsbury Rams | 1,176 | 969 | +207 |
| Swinton Lions | 1,078 | 768 | +310 |
| Sheffield Eagles | 928 | 684 | +244 |
| Rochdale Hornets | 770 | 573 | +197 |
| | | | |
| **2019 Average** | 2,380 | | |
| **2018 Average** | 1,882 | | |
| **Difference** | +498 | | |

### LEAGUE 1 CLUBS - AVERAGES

| | 2019 Avg | 2018 Avg | Diff |
|---|---|---|---|
| Workington Town | 1,013 | 782 | +231 |
| Whitehaven | 1,012 | 752 | +260 |
| Newcastle Thunder | 889 | 1,023 | -134 |
| Keighley Cougars | 812 | 781 | +31 |
| Oldham | 623 | 505 | +118 |
| Doncaster | 602 | 807 | -205 |
| Hunslet | 559 | 616 | -57 |
| London Skolars | 439 | 401 | +38 |
| Coventry Bears | 402 | 387 | +15 |
| North Wales Crusaders | 340 | 374 | -34 |
| West Wales Raiders | 259 | 322 | -63 |
| | | | |
| **2019 Average** | 632 | | |
| **2018 Average** | 874 | | |
| **Difference** | -242 | | |

### BEST ATTENDANCES

| | | Round | Date |
|---|---|---|---|
| 64,102 | Salford v St Helens | SLGF | 12/10/19 |
| | *(at Old Trafford, Manchester)* | | |
| 62,717 | St Helens v Warrington | CCF | 24/8/19 |
| | *(at Wembley Stadium)* | | |
| 31,555 | Catalans Dragons v Wigan | SLR15 | 18/5/19 |
| | *(at Camp Nou, Barcelona)* | | |
| 24,364 | Hull FC v Warrington | CCSF | 27/7/19 |
| | Halifax v St Helens | CCSF | 27/7/19 |
| | *(at University of Bolton Stadium)* | | |
| 22,050 | Wigan v St Helens | SLR11 | 19/4/19 |
| 21,331 | Wigan v Sydney Roosters | WCC | 17/2/19 |
| 20,044 | Hull FC v Hull KR | SLR11 | 19/4/19 |
| 17,807 | St Helens v Warrington | SLR10 | 12/4/19 |
| 17,088 | St Helens v Wigan | SLR22 | 12/7/19 |
| 16,508 | St Helens v Wigan | SLR1 | 31/1/19 |
| 14,508 | St Helens v Wigan | SLQSF | 27/9/19 |
| 14,211 | Warrington v St Helens | SLR20 | 28/6/19 |
| 14,085 | Leeds v Warrington | SLR29 | 13/9/19 |
| 13,743 | Leeds v Huddersfield | SLR11 | 19/4/19 |
| 13,679 | Leeds v Hull KR | SLR22 | 12/7/19 |
| 13,351 | Leeds v Hull FC | SLR23 | 21/7/19 |
| 13,286 | Leeds v Castleford | SLR15 | 16/5/19 |
| 13,148 | Leeds v Wakefield | SLR4 | 1/3/19 |
| 13,106 | Warrington v Wigan | SLR6 | 15/3/19 |
| 13,105 | Leeds v Wigan | SLR18 | 14/6/19 |

## LEADING SCORERS

Matty Ashton

Kieran Gill

### CHAMPIONSHIP *(Regular season & play-offs)*

#### TRIES

| | | | |
|---|---|---|---|
| 1 | Matty Ashton | Swinton Lions | 30 |
| 2 | Matty Russell | Toronto Wolfpack | 27 |
| 3 | Anthony Thackeray | Sheffield Eagles | 20 |
| | Mike Butt | Swinton Lions | 20 |
| | Gareth O'Brien | Toronto Wolfpack | 20 |
| | Stan Robin | Toulouse Olympique | 20 |
| 7 | Ricky Leutele | Toronto Wolfpack | 18 |
| | Mark Kheirallah | Toulouse Olympique | 18 |
| 9 | Ethan Ryan | Bradford Bulls | 17 |
| | Dane Chisholm | Featherstone Rovers/Bradford Bulls | 17 |
| | Cameron King | Featherstone Rovers | 17 |
| | Ryan Millar | Sheffield Eagles | 17 |
| | Ryan Ince | Widnes Vikings | 17 |

#### GOALS

| | | | |
|---|---|---|---|
| 1 | Mark Kheirallah | Toulouse Olympique | 109 |
| 2 | Dane Chisholm | Featherstone Rovers/Bradford Bulls | 108 |
| 3 | Pat Walker | Sheffield Eagles | 104 |
| 4 | Gareth O'Brien | Toronto Wolfpack | 99 |
| | Connor Robinson | York City Knights | 99 |
| 6 | Martyn Ridyard | Leigh Centurions | 89 |
| | Steve Tyrer | Halifax | 89 |
| 8 | Jack Owens | Widnes Vikings | 75 |
| 9 | Jamie Dallimore | Barrow Raiders | 60 |
| 10 | Joe Keyes | Bradford Bulls | 52 |

#### POINTS

| | | | T | G | FG | Pts |
|---|---|---|---|---|---|---|
| 1 | Mark Kheirallah | Toulouse Olympique | 18 | 109 | 0 | 290 |
| 2 | Dane Chisholm | Featherstone Rovers/ Bradford Bulls | 17 | 108 | 2 | 286 |
| 3 | Gareth O'Brien | Toronto Wolfpack | 20 | 99 | 0 | 278 |
| 4 | Steve Tyrer | Halifax | 15 | 89 | 0 | 238 |
| 5 | Connor Robinson | York City Knights | 5 | 99 | 3 | 221 |
| 6 | Pat Walker | Sheffield Eagles | 2 | 104 | 0 | 216 |
| 7 | Jack Owens | Widnes Vikings | 13 | 75 | 0 | 202 |
| 8 | Martyn Ridyard | Leigh Centurions | 3 | 89 | 2 | 192 |
| 9 | Joe Keyes | Bradford Bulls | 8 | 52 | 0 | 136 |
| 10 | Blake Wallace | Toronto Wolfpack | 16 | 35 | 0 | 134 |

### LEAGUE 1 *(Regular season & play-offs)*

#### TRIES

| | | | |
|---|---|---|---|
| 1 | Kieran Gill | Newcastle Thunder | 26 |
| 2 | Gareth Potts | Hunslet | 19 |
| 3 | Rob Massam | North Wales Crusaders | 18 |
| 4 | Danny Langtree | Oldham | 17 |
| 5 | Elliot Hall | Coventry Bears | 16 |
| | Alex Clegg | Newcastle Thunder | 16 |
| | Lewis Young | Newcastle Thunder | 16 |
| 8 | Sam Doherty | Doncaster | 15 |
| | Jason Tali | Doncaster | 15 |
| 10 | Jack Miller | Keighley Cougars | 14 |

#### GOALS

| | | | |
|---|---|---|---|
| 1 | Carl Forber | Workington Town | 86 |
| 2 | Neil Thorman | London Skolars | 61 |
| 3 | Paul Crook | Oldham | 57 |
| 4 | Reece Dean | Hunslet | 55 |
| | Benn Hardcastle | Keighley Cougars | 55 |
| | Ben Stead | North Wales Crusaders | 55 |
| 7 | Matty Beharrell | Doncaster | 53 |
| 8 | Dave Hewitt | Oldham | 50 |
| 9 | Jake Moore | Whitehaven | 48 |
| 10 | Joe Sanderson | Hunslet/Coventry Bears | 42 |

#### POINTS

| | | | T | G | FG | Pts |
|---|---|---|---|---|---|---|
| 1 | Carl Forber | Workington Town | 2 | 86 | 0 | 180 |
| 2 | Benn Hardcastle | Keighley Cougars | 7 | 55 | 1 | 139 |
| 3 | Jake Moore | Whitehaven | 10 | 48 | 0 | 136 |
| 4 | Paul Crook | Oldham | 5 | 57 | 0 | 134 |
| 5 | Reece Dean | Hunslet | 5 | 55 | 0 | 130 |
| 6 | Dave Hewitt | Oldham | 7 | 50 | 1 | 129 |
| 7 | Matty Beharrell | Doncaster | 5 | 53 | 2 | 128 |
| 8 | Neil Thorman | London Skolars | 1 | 61 | 1 | 127 |
| 9 | Ben Stead | North Wales Crusaders | 4 | 55 | 0 | 126 |
| 10 | Nick Newman | Newcastle Thunder/ Coventry Bears | 11 | 32 | 2 | 110 |

## LEADING SCORERS

Tommy
Makinson

### SUPER LEAGUE *(Regular season & play-offs)*

#### TRIES

| | | | |
|---|---|---|---|
| 1 | Tommy Makinson | St Helens | 23 |
| 2 | Ash Handley | Leeds Rhinos | 22 |
| | Niall Evalds | Salford Red Devils | 22 |
| 4 | Regan Grace | St Helens | 20 |
| 5 | Kevin Naiqama | St Helens | 18 |
| | Blake Austin | Warrington Wolves | 18 |
| 7 | Jermaine McGillvary | Huddersfield Giants | 17 |
| | Jonny Lomax | St Helens | 17 |
| | Josh Charnley | Warrington Wolves | 17 |
| 10 | Liam Marshall | Wigan Warriors | 16 |

#### GOALS

| | | | |
|---|---|---|---|
| 1 | Lachlan Coote | St Helens | 106 |
| 2 | Marc Sneyd | Hull FC | 104 |
| 3 | Zak Hardaker | Wigan Warriors | 93 |
| | Krisnan Inu | Salford Red Devils | 93 |
| 5 | Stefan Ratchford | Warrington Wolves | 84 |
| 6 | Sam Tomkins | Catalans Dragons | 76 |
| 7 | Kieran Dixon | London Broncos | 75 |
| 8 | Danny Brough | Wakefield Trinity | 72 |
| 9 | Ryan Shaw | Hull Kingston Rovers | 63 |
| 10 | Peter Mata'utia | Castleford Tigers | 54 |

#### GOALS PERCENTAGE

| | | | G | Att | % |
|---|---|---|---|---|---|
| 1 | Declan Patton | Warrington Wolves | 37 | 40 | 92.50 |
| 2 | Ryan Shaw | Hull Kingston Rovers | 63 | 70 | 90.00 |
| 3 | Rhyse Martin | Leeds Rhinos | 34 | 40 | 85.00 |
| 4 | Jamie Ellis | Castleford Tigers | 16 | 19 | 84.21 |
| | Chris Hankinson | Wigan Warriors | 16 | 19 | 84.21 |
| 6 | Danny Richardson | St Helens | 23 | 28 | 82.14 |
| 7 | Marc Sneyd | Hull FC | 104 | 127 | 81.88 |
| 8 | Tony Gigot | Catalans Dragons | 13 | 16 | 81.25 |
| 9 | Krisnan Inu | Salford Red Devils | 93 | 116 | 80.17 |
| 10 | Oliver Russell | Huddersfield Giants | 36 | 45 | 80.00 |

*(10 minimum attempts to qualify)*

#### POINTS

| | | | T | G | FG | Pts |
|---|---|---|---|---|---|---|
| 1 | Lachlan Coote | St Helens | 14 | 106 | 1 | 269 |
| 2 | Zak Hardaker | Wigan Warriors | 11 | 93 | 1 | 231 |
| 3 | Marc Sneyd | Hull FC | 2 | 104 | 7 | 223 |
| 4 | Krisnan Inu | Salford Red Devils | 7 | 93 | 1 | 215 |
| 5 | Kieran Dixon | London Broncos | 10 | 75 | 0 | 190 |
| 6 | Sam Tomkins | Catalans Dragons | 9 | 76 | 1 | 189 |
| 7 | Stefan Ratchford | Warrington Wolves | 4 | 84 | 0 | 184 |
| 8 | Danny Brough | Wakefield Trinity | 2 | 72 | 5 | 157 |
| 9 | Ryan Shaw | Hull Kingston Rovers | 4 | 63 | 0 | 142 |
| 10 | Peter Mata'utia | Castleford Tigers | 3 | 54 | 1 | 121 |

#### CONSECUTIVE APPEARANCES *(all club games included)*

| | | | |
|---|---|---|---|
| 1 | Eddie Battye | London Broncos | 58 |
| 2 | Ryan Hampshire | Wakefield Trinity | 49 |
| 3 | Reece Lyne | Wakefield Trinity | 48 |
| 4 | Niall Evalds | Salford Red Devils | 44 |
| 5 | George Williams | Wigan Warriors | 43 |
| 6 | Oliver Gildart | Wigan Warriors | 41 |
| 7 | Josh Drinkwater | Hull Kingston Rovers/ Catalans Dragons | 39 |
| 8 | Jackson Hastings | Salford Red Devils | 36 |
| 9 | Willie Isa | Wigan Warriors | 34 |
| 10 | Ben Jones-Bishop | Wakefield Trinity | 33 |

Declan
Patton

# LEADING SCORERS

## CHALLENGE CUP

### TRIES

| | | | |
|---|---|---|---|
| 1 | Andrew Bulman | Whitehaven | 6 |
| 2 | Harry Newman | Leeds Rhinos | 5 |
| | Niall Evalds | Salford Red Devils | 5 |
| 4 | Brayden Wiliame | Catalans Dragons | 4 |
| | Wayne Reittie | Batley Bulldogs | 4 |
| | Sam Freeman | Widnes Vikings | 4 |
| | Jack Owens | Widnes Vikings | 4 |
| | Connor Bower | Doncaster | 4 |
| | Keal Carlile | Newcastle Thunder | 4 |
| | Zack McComb | Oldham | 4 |
| | Dave Thompson | Whitehaven | 4 |

### GOALS

| | | | |
|---|---|---|---|
| 1 | Marc Sneyd | Hull FC | 18 |
| 2 | Steve Tyrer | Halifax | 17 |
| 3 | Liam Sutcliffe | Leeds Rhinos | 16 |
| 4 | Jack Owens | Widnes Vikings | 14 |
| 5 | Connor Holliday | Whitehaven | 13 |

### POINTS

| | | | T | G | FG | Pts |
|---|---|---|---|---|---|---|
| 1 | Jack Owens | Widnes Vikings | 4 | 14 | 0 | 44 |
| 2 | Steve Tyrer | Halifax | 1 | 17 | 0 | 38 |
| 3 | Marc Sneyd | Hull FC | 0 | 18 | 1 | 37 |
| 4 | Liam Sutcliffe | Leeds Rhinos | 0 | 16 | 0 | 32 |
| 5 | Lachlan Coote | St Helens | 2 | 11 | 0 | 30 |

## 1895 CUP

### TRIES

| | | | |
|---|---|---|---|
| 1 | Tom Halliday | Doncaster | 5 |
| 2 | Gregg McNally | Leigh Centurions | 4 |
| | Aaron Brown | Sheffield Eagles | 4 |
| | Anthony Gelling | Widnes Vikings | 4 |
| 5 | Jason Crookes | Sheffield Eagles | 3 |
| | Anthony Thackeray | Sheffield Eagles | 3 |
| | Jayden Hatton | Widnes Vikings | 3 |
| | Lloyd Roby | Widnes Vikings | 3 |
| | Watson Boas | Doncaster | 3 |
| | Oliver Wilkes | Workington Town | 3 |

### GOALS

| | | | |
|---|---|---|---|
| 1 | Matty Beharrell | Doncaster | 21 |
| 2 | Pat Walker | Sheffield Eagles | 19 |
| 3 | Jack Owens | Widnes Vikings | 15 |
| 4 | Paul Crook | Oldham | 10 |
| 5 | Connor Robinson | York City Knights | 9 |
| | Josh Woods | Leigh Centurions | 9 |

### POINTS

| | | | T | G | FG | Pts |
|---|---|---|---|---|---|---|
| 1 | Matty Beharrell | Doncaster | 1 | 21 | 0 | 46 |
| 2 | Pat Walker | Sheffield Eagles | 0 | 19 | 0 | 38 |
| 3 | Jack Owens | Widnes Vikings | 1 | 15 | 0 | 34 |
| 4 | Louis Jouffret | Batley Bulldogs | 2 | 8 | 1 | 25 |
| 5 | Paul Crook | Oldham | 1 | 10 | 0 | 24 |

## ALL COMPETITIONS

### TRIES

| | | | |
|---|---|---|---|
| 1 | Matty Ashton | Swinton Lions | 30 |
| 2 | Kieran Gill | Newcastle Thunder | 28 |
| 3 | Niall Evalds | Salford Red Devils | 27 |
| | Matty Russell | Toronto Wolfpack | 27 |
| 5 | Tommy Makinson | St Helens | 24 |
| 6 | Anthony Thackeray | Sheffield Eagles | 23 |
| 7 | Ash Handley | Leeds Rhinos | 22 |
| | Regan Grace | St Helens | 22 |
| 9 | Mike Butt | Swinton Lions | 21 |
| 10 | Kevin Naiqama | St Helens | 20 |
| | Ryan Millar | Sheffield Eagles | 20 |
| | Gareth O'Brien | Toronto Wolfpack | 20 |
| | Stan Robin | Toulouse Olympique | 20 |
| | Sam Doherty | Doncaster | 20 |
| | Gareth Potts | Hunslet | 20 |
| | Rob Massam | North Wales Crusaders | 20 |

### GOALS

| | | | |
|---|---|---|---|
| 1 | Pat Walker | Sheffield Eagles | 125 |
| 2 | Marc Sneyd | Hull FC | 122 |
| 3 | Lachlan Coote | St Helens | 117 |
| 4 | Mark Kheirallah | Toulouse Olympique | 109 |
| 5 | Dane Chisholm | Featherstone Rovers/Bradford Bulls | 108 |
| | Connor Robinson | York City Knights | 108 |
| 7 | Steve Tyrer | Halifax | 106 |
| 8 | Jack Owens | Widnes Vikings | 104 |
| 9 | Krisnan Inu | Salford Red Devils | 102 |
| 10 | Carl Forber | Workington Town | 101 |

### POINTS

| | | | T | G | FG | Pts |
|---|---|---|---|---|---|---|
| 1 | Lachlan Coote | St Helens | 16 | 117 | 1 | 299 |
| 2 | Mark Kheirallah | Toulouse Olympique | 18 | 109 | 0 | 290 |
| 3 | Dane Chisholm | Featherstone Rovers/ Bradford Bulls | 17 | 108 | 2 | 286 |
| 4 | Jack Owens | Widnes Vikings | 18 | 104 | 0 | 280 |
| 5 | Gareth O'Brien | Toronto Wolfpack | 20 | 99 | 0 | 278 |
| 6 | Steve Tyrer | Halifax | 16 | 106 | 0 | 276 |
| 7 | Marc Sneyd | Hull FC | 2 | 122 | 8 | 260 |
| 8 | Pat Walker | Sheffield Eagles | 2 | 125 | 0 | 258 |
| 9 | Zak Hardaker | Wigan Warriors | 12 | 97 | 1 | 243 |
| | Connor Robinson | York City Knights | 6 | 108 | 3 | 243 |

### FIELD GOALS

| | | | |
|---|---|---|---|
| 1 | Marc Sneyd | Hull FC | 8 |
| 2 | Danny Brough | Wakefield Trinity | 5 |
| | Tony Gigot | Catalans Dragons | 5 |
| 4 | Oliver Russell | Huddersfield Giants | 3 |
| | Jordan Lilley | Bradford Bulls | 3 |
| | Martyn Ridyard | Leigh Centurions | 3 |
| | Connor Robinson | York City Knights | 3 |
| | Paul Sykes | Dewsbury Rams | 3 |

## LEADING SCORERS

Matty Ashton

Pat Walker

Lachlan Coote

## FINAL TABLES

### SUPER LEAGUE

| | P | W | D | L | F | A | D | Pts |
|---|---|---|---|---|---|---|---|---|
| St Helens | 29 | 26 | 0 | 3 | 916 | 395 | 521 | 52 |
| Wigan Warriors | 29 | 18 | 0 | 11 | 699 | 539 | 160 | 36 |
| Salford Red Devils | 29 | 17 | 0 | 12 | 783 | 597 | 186 | 34 |
| Warrington Wolves | 29 | 16 | 0 | 13 | 709 | 533 | 176 | 32 |
| Castleford Tigers | 29 | 15 | 0 | 14 | 646 | 558 | 88 | 30 |
| Hull FC | 29 | 15 | 0 | 14 | 645 | 768 | -123 | 30 |
| Catalans Dragons | 29 | 13 | 0 | 16 | 553 | 745 | -192 | 26 |
| Leeds Rhinos | 29 | 12 | 0 | 17 | 650 | 644 | 6 | 24 |
| Wakefield Trinity | 29 | 11 | 0 | 18 | 608 | 723 | -115 | 22 |
| Huddersfield Giants | 29 | 11 | 0 | 18 | 571 | 776 | -205 | 22 |
| Hull Kingston Rovers | 29 | 10 | 0 | 19 | 548 | 768 | -220 | 20 |
| London Broncos | 29 | 10 | 0 | 19 | 505 | 787 | -282 | 20 |

### CHAMPIONSHIP

| | P | W | D | L | F | A | D | Pts |
|---|---|---|---|---|---|---|---|---|
| Toronto Wolfpack | 27 | 26 | 0 | 1 | 1010 | 356 | 654 | 52 |
| Toulouse Olympique | 27 | 20 | 0 | 7 | 877 | 446 | 431 | 40 |
| York City Knights | 27 | 19 | 1 | 7 | 612 | 529 | 83 | 39 |
| Leigh Centurions | 27 | 18 | 0 | 9 | 792 | 558 | 234 | 36 |
| Featherstone Rovers | 27 | 17 | 0 | 10 | 837 | 471 | 366 | 34 |
| Bradford Bulls | 27 | 16 | 1 | 10 | 717 | 522 | 195 | 33 |
| Sheffield Eagles | 27 | 15 | 0 | 12 | 748 | 694 | 54 | 30 |
| Halifax | 27 | 10 | 1 | 16 | 602 | 685 | -83 | 21 |
| Swinton Lions | 27 | 10 | 1 | 16 | 619 | 803 | -184 | 21 |
| Batley Bulldogs | 27 | 8 | 1 | 18 | 462 | 756 | -294 | 17 |
| Widnes Vikings * | 27 | 14 | 0 | 13 | 646 | 586 | 60 | 16 |
| Dewsbury Rams | 27 | 6 | 2 | 19 | 513 | 721 | -208 | 14 |
| Barrow Raiders | 27 | 5 | 1 | 21 | 479 | 861 | -382 | 11 |
| Rochdale Hornets | 27 | 1 | 0 | 26 | 342 | 1268 | -926 | 2 |

*\* Denotes twelve points deducted for entering administration*

### LEAGUE 1

| | P | W | D | L | F | A | D | Pts |
|---|---|---|---|---|---|---|---|---|
| Whitehaven | 20 | 15 | 2 | 3 | 582 | 283 | 299 | 32 |
| Oldham | 20 | 15 | 0 | 5 | 655 | 341 | 314 | 30 |
| Newcastle Thunder | 20 | 14 | 1 | 5 | 741 | 364 | 377 | 29 |
| Doncaster | 20 | 12 | 0 | 8 | 564 | 309 | 255 | 24 |
| Hunslet | 20 | 12 | 0 | 8 | 596 | 379 | 217 | 24 |
| Workington Town | 20 | 10 | 1 | 9 | 592 | 478 | 114 | 21 |
| North Wales Crusaders | 20 | 9 | 0 | 11 | 489 | 501 | -12 | 18 |
| London Skolars | 20 | 7 | 1 | 12 | 440 | 542 | -102 | 15 |
| Coventry Bears | 20 | 4 | 0 | 16 | 365 | 829 | -464 | 8 |
| Keighley Cougars * | 20 | 8 | 1 | 11 | 447 | 576 | -129 | 5 |
| West Wales Raiders | 20 | 1 | 0 | 19 | 222 | 1091 | -869 | 2 |

*\* Denotes twelve points deducted for transfer of club membership*